MEDICAL MALPRACTICE SERIES

MEDICAL MALPRACTICE

Handling Orthopedic Cases

Volume 1
Chapters 1 through 32

William N. Harsha, M.D., M.S., J.D.

SHEPARD'S/McGRAW-HILL, INC.
P.O. Box 35300
Colorado Springs, Colorado 80935-3530

McGRAW-HILL, INC.

New York • St Louis • San Francisco • Auckland • Bogotá
Caracas • Colorado Springs • Hamburg • Lisbon • London
Madrid • Mexico • Milan • Montreal • New Delhi
Panama • Paris • San Juan • São Paulo
Singapore • Sydney • Tokyo • Toronto

Information has been obtained by Shepard's/McGraw-Hill, Inc. from sources believed to be reliable. However, because of the possibility of human or mechanical error by our sources, Shepard's/McGraw-Hill, Inc., or others, Shepard's/McGraw-Hill, Inc. does not guarantee the accuracy, adequacy, or completeness of any information and is not responsible for any errors or omissions or for the results obtained from use of such information.

1 2 3 4 5 6 7 8 9 10 SHHI 9 9 8 7 6 5 4 3 2 1 0

Library of Congress Cataloging-in-Publication Data

Harsha, William N.

Medical malpractice—handling orthopedic cases / William N. Harsha.

p. cm. — (Medical malpractice series)

Includes bibliographical references and index.

ISBN 0-07-172208-4 (hard cover)

1. Orthopedists—Malpractice—United States. 2. Actions and defenses—United States. I. Title. II. Title: Handling orthopedic cases. III. Series.

[DNLM: 1. Malpractice—legislation. 2. Orthopedics—legislation. WE 33.1 H324m]

KF2910.0783H37 1990

346.7303'32—dc20

[347.306332]

DNLM/DLC

for Library of Congress

90-9168

CIP

ISBN 0-07-172208-4

MMHOC2/3

The sponsoring editor for this book was Bradley Abramson. The editor was Dale R. Agthe, assisted by Laurel Cohn and Frear Simons.

Shepard's Medical Malpractice Series

Medical Malpractice: Bases of Liability
Medical Malpractice: Handling Dental Cases
Medical Malpractice: Handling General Surgery Cases
Medical Malpractice: Handling Plastic Surgery Cases
Medical Malpractice: Handling Urology Cases
Medical Malpractice: Pharmacy Law
Medical Malpractice: Psychiatric Care

I want to dedicate this book to my wife, Jean, and to my children whose indulgence, cooperation, and support provided time and stimulus to the work.

Acknowledgment

Without the great contribution to medical and legal, particularly orthopedic and negligence writings, this book would not have been possible. It has been my pleasure and privilege to review hundreds of pieces of medical, legal, social, and lay literature as part of the research for this work, and for this I am deeply thankful to hundreds of authors. I have tried to acknowledge all in the references in this book or otherwise credit directly. It seems inevitable that omissions may have been made—this being unintentional—and for this I apologize in advance. There is, in fact, very little new news revealed, but this book is designed to collate information at the medicolegal interface to those interested, and to focus attention on issues of medical—or more specifically orthopedic—negligence in a manner that is helpful to the reader.

Many have cooperated in this writing endeavor and I thank them. Singular credit is due to Mrs. Renee Pierce, whose secretarial, typing, and editing skills were essential to the completion of this book.

Acknowledgment

Contents

Detailed

Volume 1

2 Patient Understanding

3 Patients' Bill of Rights

4 Physician Behavior

5 Physician Education

6 Physician-Patient Relationship

7 Contributory Negligence

8 Pleadings, Theories, and Defenses of Negligence Liability

9 Res Ipsa Loquitur

15 Patient Behavioral Considerations: Somatization

18 Physical Medicine

29 Autogenous Bone Graft

30 Muscle Injuries

31 Skin Injuries

32 Tendon and Ligament Injuries

Volume 2

38 Bone and Soft Tissue Fixation Devices

39 Injuries to the Vascular System

40 Nerve and Head Injuries

47 Acute Hand Injuries

48 Pelvis, Hip, and Femur

51 Ankle and Foot Injuries

1

General Considerations

§1.01 Introduction

The purpose of this book is to review current thinking in America concerning tortious behavior as it relates to orthopedic medicine and surgery. The book is intended to assist attorneys, paralegals, and physicians at the medical-legal interface to be knowledgeable and skillful in these areas.

The quality of medical care is determined by two main factors: the quality of the decisions that determine what actions are taken, and the quality with which those actions are carried out. If wrong actions are chosen, no matter how well executed, the quality of care suffers. Similarly, if the correct actions are chosen, but poorly carried out, the quality of care suffers. The importance of ensuring the quality of execution is well understood. In contrast, the medical profession has done far less to develop and evaluate the decisionmaking process.

In general, the goal of health practice decisionmaking is to choose the action most likely to deliver the results that the patient feels desirable. This identifies the two main steps of a decision: (1) identifying the outcome of alternate treatments, and (2) comparing the desirability of the outcome of each option. The first step involves collecting and analyzing whatever evidence exists regarding the benefit, the injury potential, and the cost of each option. Because the available evidence is never perfect or complete, this step involves some subjective judgment. The results of this analysis form the basis for the second step.

Three types of comparisons are required in the second step: (1) the benefits of a practice must be compared with the injury potential (such as danger to life or limb, side effects, inconvenience, and anxiety), (2) the health outcomes must be compared with whatever costs will have to be paid, and (3) if resources are limited and it is not possible to do everything desired, the amount of benefit gained and the resource consumed by a medical practice must be compared with either practice to give priority to the practice giving the highest total yield.

Explicitly or implicitly, consciously or unconsciously, correctly or incorrectly, each of these steps is performed every time a decision is made. The validity of this process is seen if we were to imagine trying to advise a patient without considering any result of that advice. To do so would well describe negligent physician behavior. Imagine not having any idea of the magnitude of the benefits or harms of the practice and imagine not caring whether the benefits outweigh the potential harm.

Any health care professional who makes a responsible decision must have some idea of the evidence that justifies its use, consequences, and desirability.[1]

§1.02 What is Orthopedics?

The term *orthopedics* is derived from a combined Greek word. It seems to be defined in at least two ways. In the first, *ortho* means straight, and *pedics* means child—orthopedics being interpreted as "straightening of the child." In other literature, sometimes described in more pure Greek, it is interpreted as "free from deformity."

The orthopedist dealt largely with children's deformities and fractures of bones and dislocations of joints in America in the 19th century, and until about 1930. From that time, a wide and rapid advance in the types of patients and types of treatments has occurred in the specialty of orthopedic medicine and surgery.

Orthopedic medicine and surgery refers to the diagnosis and treatment of diseases of the bones, joints, and spine, including deformities, infections, arthritis, fractures, and dislocations, as well as diseases and injuries of the spine.

The name "orthopedics" was originated by Nicolas Andre in Paris in 1741 while working with spinal curvature (scoliosis) cases. Soon afterward, treatment of club feet and congenitally dislocated feet came within the orthopedic purview. After World War II, orthopedic surgery became a distinct specialty. Today, orthopedic surgery/medicine makes up the largest part of traumatic surgery and is absorbing an increasing share from the general surgeon.

Sports medicine, hand and foot problems, total joint replacement for painful arthritis or injury residuals of the back and neck, and treatment of fractures or dislocations remain the principal interest of this specialty. The

---

[1] Eddy, *Anatomy of a Decision,* 263 JAMA 441 (1990).

growth in orthopedics is directly related to the increase in motorized traffic, industrial activity, and the fast pace of society with its emphasis and interest in athletic performance. Sports medicine alone is a $40 billion business annually.

§1.03 Orthopedic Malpractice

Orthopedic malpractice refers to deviations, violations, or departures from the accepted standard of quality of care, verified by the professional opinion of the same type of specialist, based on a reasonable degree of medical certainty and probability.

Orthopedic malpractice is the fastest growing area of medical negligence litigation. Prosthetic replacements of joints (total joint replacement) is now the "bread and butter" of the general orthopedic practice, with fractures being second in many centers. Major fracture trauma is down from its high level in the 1960s, in part due to the price of fuel, lower speed limits, and increasing (generally mandated by law) use of seat belts. Improved motor vehicle equipment, thought by some to have resulted from greater design and manufacture care stemming from strict liability litigation, plays a part in the decreased severity of road trauma. Low back surgery results in more malpractice claims than any other single area of the body.

Orthopedic malpractice is unique, with informed consent and surgical indications being very important issues. The reason for this is that orthopedic scientific literature is full of studies regarding the percentage of serious complications. It is, therefore, fair to say that the orthopedist knows the relative likelihood of success of any particular operation and the frequency of complications before the operation is indicated. The orthopedic surgeon must inform the patient beforehand, fully knowing the potential outcome of the surgery for each particular problem.

Orthopedic problems such as congenital dislocation of the hip and club feet must be diagnosed as early as possible. Any delay in diagnosis and treatment lessens the chance of a satisfactory treatment outcome. Good communications and referrals from a pediatrician or family practitioner are essential to good care, each doctor knowing and doing the simple diagnostic tests for these birth-related, potentially crippling orthopedic problems.

Perthes' disease and slipped capital femoral epiphysis are two other childhood problems which are easy to miss and give poor results if treated late. In all of these birth-related problems, failure to avail the patient of specific diagnostic testing will occur when the orthopedist (or other physician) is less than diligent. Standard x-rays, CT scanning, MRI studies, and ultrasound studies are helpful in early diagnosis. Failure to diagnose hip disease in the patient who presents with knee pain continues to be a common, but preventable, occurrence.

Scoliosis (spinal curvature) should be diagnosed early for best results. School monitoring and referral to a spine specialist are an important step in arresting the progress of this problem. It is much better to diagnose and treat a scoliotic patient early (five to six years of age) than late (12 years or older).

Long-range planning is part of any proposed operation during the preoperative period. Checking all instrumentation and implants before surgery, much like airplane pilots check out their equipment before a flight, is as important as talking with the patient and fully understanding each other. Conservative (noninvasive) treatment takes precedence over surgical procedures if the track record of the patient is good.

Errors in preoperative planning and/or patient evaluation account for many orthopedic negligence claims. Equally incomplete intrasurgical and postsurgical care leads to patient injury and negligence claims. The very busy surgeon, the orthopedist who has a repetitive practice, and the orthopedist who delegates much patient care to others are the types of orthopedists most often involved in negligence litigation.

Intraoperatively, the surgeon shows his or her skill in rapid, sharp dissection with minimal soft tissue damage, yet the surgeon must also show anatomic acumen in avoiding injury to remote (or in operative field) nerves, vessels, and other vital structures. Many risks of surgery are known to the surgeon and to the patient once he or she has afforded the patient a careful informed consent discussion, but all injuries to tissues at risk are not "to be expected" if they result from negligent or unskillful surgical technique.

§1.04 The Team

The orthopedist is a member of the health care team and is within the chain of command of the hospital. Good communication skills are vital among orthopedists, radiologists, laboratories, and nurses. Accurate, current recordkeeping is an essential part of this care. Since the first duty of the orthopedic nurse is to the patient and not to the doctor, it is the nurse's responsibility to alert the orthopedist (and others) to any adverse progress of the patient. If the nurse does not act, the chain of command should be implemented through supervisors, administrators, service chiefs, and others to protect the patient. The treating doctor incurs liability if he or she knows or should have known of inadequate and/or incompetent nursing care and does not correct the situation.[2]

§1.05 Certification

Board certification by the American Board of Orthopedic Surgery seems the preferable way of credentialing a physician who practices orthopedic medicine and surgery, but it is not the only way. Physicians who have taken similar training as orthopedic residents, but for one reason or another have

---

[2] Gardner, *Negligent Disability and Orthopedic Malpractice,* 1 Expert Witness J 1 (1989).

not completed the board, are called *board eligible* and are capable of competent practice in orthopedic medicine and surgery.

At this time in the United States, there is a general rule that any physician who undertakes the care of an orthopedic problem will be held to that same degree of care that the patient would have received had he or she been cared for by a board-certified orthopedic surgeon.

Medical negligence (malpractice) litigation is designed to determine the presence or absence of liability in a dispute between a patient and a physician, hospital, or other paramedical personnel—nurses, physical therapists, x-ray technicians, pharmacists, etc. It is essential that the attorneys representing each litigant understand the basic legal tenets, as well as the basic medical facts, that pertain to the case at hand. Understanding the relationship between legal and medical knowledge is essential to an appropriate resolution of these problems.

Orthopedic medicine and surgery practitioners have all of the usual problems that other medical practitioners must face in the daily practice of medicine for their patients, plus other problems. In recent years, the advent of implants, bone cement, organ (bone) donations and transplants, and the use of a number of externally applied devices and machines to facilitate healing have all presented additional risks to the patient and additional potential liabilities to the orthopedist.

§1.06 Text Organization

This book is set out in chapter form, first as an overview of the body as a whole, and then with special attention being given to each of the orthopedic-related areas. Attention will be given to the special problems which the orthopedist encounters in daily practice, as well as to the unusual relationships an orthopedist may have with hospitals and patients, as a diagnostician, therapist, disability evaluator, and patient advocate. Cross references from one section of the book to another and to reference resources will be used to expand specific subject matter.

As the orthopedist practices his or her specialty in a hospital environment, the potential liabilities that may affect him or her present themselves in the emergency room, in the operating room, in patient care—both preoperative and postoperative, in evaluation and recordkeeping, and in patient care orders and the orthopedist's responsibility when those orders may or may not be fulfilled by nursing staff or other medical personnel.

The orthopedist is frequently faced with vicarious liability arising from his or her relationship with other physicians and other medical personnel, referring physicians, consulting physicians, intern and resident staff, volunteer hospital personnel, and Diagnostic Related Group and other government mandated patient-control entities.

Considerable attention will be given to the physician-patient relationships, including initial history taking, initial physical examination, recordkeeping, and the accuracy and completeness of records. Communication between a patient and a physician is a most crucial area, from the initial visit to the last, and good communication with the patient's family is essential. An increasing number of malpractice actions are filed against physicians based on lack of informed consent or incomplete consent.

The standard of care for the practice of orthopedics will be discussed at length. In addition to the standard of care as accepted by the community in which the physician is practicing, the concept of criticism of orthopedic care will be introduced as a prominent vehicle for settling alleged negligence claims prior to the court decision.

Physician competency is an ongoing problem in the practice of medicine. Orthopedic medicine, in particular, is a rapidly expanding field with many innovative ideas being introduced. Some of these ideas are still considered experimental, and this must be understood by the practitioner as well as by patients. Some techniques carrying inherent risks include the various new joint implants, devices used to facilitate and assure spinal fusions, rehabilitative devices and machines, the use of chemical substances—both diagnostic and therapeutic drugs as well as implant stabilizers—cements, etc., and the use of blood and blood products.

The concepts of respondeat superior, res ipsa loquitur, and related doctrines are outlined.

Pertinent topics relating to the office management of patients and its attendant recordkeeping will be discussed, including patient accommodation in such matters as completing insurance forms and disability evaluation summaries, and preserving and furnishing patient records, x-rays, etc.

All chapters will include a discussion of diagnosis and treatment, if indicated, and usual and unusual orthopedic problems and their possible complications. Each chapter also deals with injuries or diseases involving more specific locations of an area of the body.

Informative and pertinent cases of law, with comments and annotations, are interjected in the discussion of each chapter. These cases will reflect opinions germane to the orthopedic problem under discussion as they pertain to medical negligence. However, as often happens in case law reviews of this sort, the judgments of triers of fact are not always based on one factual situation, but on a combination of several. An attempt will be made to identify those facts that are pertinent to the practice of orthopedic medicine, although mention of other faults in the trial will be made for completeness.

Law review articles have been written about a number of orthopedic malpractice case problems. These will be reviewed and cited where appropriate.

Where blatant or obvious medical malpractice has occurred, there will be little discussion, but where there is a difference of opinion as to treatment of choice, as to current treatments, and as to safe treatments, or where valid criticism of a practitioner's acts can be made or difficulty in supporting such acts exists, those points will be highlighted.

A review of the methods for determining awards against physicians will be discussed. Discussion will include present trends in the amounts awarded plaintiffs for various types of damages. Patient compliance and contributory negligence by the patient or by others are considered. Medical malpractice arbitration panels or boards are discussed. An attempt is made to correlate damages and awards and payment techniques on a state-by-state basis, as well as in the federal sector.

Each chapter contains a list of pertinent references to both periodicals and textbooks. Some of these have been reviewed in preparing this text, but are not specifically referred to. They are resources for expanding the medical and/or legal information offered in each chapter.

2

Patient Understanding

§2.01 Unrealistic Patient Expectations

Consumers of medical care may, in many instances, have unrealistic expectations concerning the outcome of medical interventions. Patients may expect a particular medical result and be disappointed when that result is not achieved, through no fault of the treating physician or health care system. This sense of disappointment may contribute to the filing of malpractice claims against physicians.

The development of patient expectations regarding medical care is not well understood. Psychological and social factors are involved in determining what patients expect from medical treatment. An important social factor is that the momentum of technological accomplishments in the field of medicine creates the belief that medicine can literally work miracles in every case. The electronic and print media contribute to unrealistic expectations by emphasizing dramatic scientific breakthroughs without any mention of the normal delay in bringing new technologies to the bedside, or of the inherent risks and adverse effects involved in their use. The result is that many health care consumers remain unaware of the limitations of medical science. Unless consumer perceptions are corrected, medical treatment will continue to be viewed as a risk-free activity.

Ideally, effective communication between patient and physician through the informed consent process should make patients aware of all of the ramifications of treatment options and develop a realistic view of the probabilities of success. However, in practice, this communication may not fulfill these goals. First, physicians need to communicate fully with their patients regarding the inherent risks of a particular medical intervention. However, there are profound psychological factors in the physician-patient relationship which make this communication difficult. Since most patients are usually unaware of the basic complexities of medical science, statements of the risks and benefits of a proposed treatment which presume broad medical knowledge may not succeed in informing the patient. The process for patient decisionmaking may not always take into account the psychological factors influencing patient understanding. The patient's need to know the capabilities of medical science and the patient's need to know the risks and benefits associated with specific treatments must be respected.

Regardless of the exact genesis of high expectations by the patient or unrealistic perceptions about medical capabilities, anything less than a perfect medical result can lead to a malpractice claim, attempting to fix blame on the physician or health care institution even though the results may represent an appropriate outcome under the circumstances.

§2.02 Unrealistic Physician Expectations

Analogous problems exist with regard to the physician's expectations about the professional liability system. Health care providers may not fully appreciate the nature of the legal system as a mechanism of social dispute resolution, with the limitations inherent in any human decisionmaking system. Just as patients should understand the capabilities and limitations of medical intervention, physicians should understand the legal system. Physicians are often confused by the operation of the legal system, and their contacts with the professional liability system are usually unpleasant. Providers are typically defendants, subjected to deposition, cross-examination, and professional embarrassment during the course of a malpractice lawsuit. Often, physician expectations about the professional liability system are as unrealistic as patient expectations about medicine.[1]

Just as health care users need to be educated about the complexities and limitations of medical care, health care professionals need to be educated about malpractice risks and the changing health care environment. Such education is aimed at increasing the awareness of health professionals about liability risks within their particular practice and how to reduce them in a responsible and patient-sensitive manner.

§2.03 Adverse Medical Outcomes

The issue of medical malpractice is a recurring one for everyone—patients, physicians and other health care providers, insurance and liability systems, and society in general. To understand the issue of medical malpractice and to manage the problem, we must understand the professional and governmental activities that influence how medical care is delivered, how its

[1] J. Katz, The Silent World of Doctor and Patient (1984).

quality is maintained, and how the medical care system works to prevent adverse medical outcomes that give rise to malpractice litigation.

It is important to define and understand the terms commonly used to describe results of physician-patient encounters ("outcomes" of medical intervention) and to distinguish them conceptually from similar terms.

When patients receive medical care, the results are not always favorable. Some patients do not improve, some experience transient ill effects, some are permanently harmed, and some die. These undesirable results, or adverse medical outcomes, may be divided into two categories.

The *avoidable adverse outcomes* are situations in which a health care provider does not adhere to accepted standards of medical care and the patient is harmed as a result. Some of these instances result from an act or omission by a health care provider. Others result from failure of some aspect of the health care system but are not related to the performance of any one health care provider. *Unavoidable adverse outcomes* are instances in which a health care provider treats the patient using currently accepted standard of care methods, but the natural course of the patient's prior condition or the side effects of proper treatment result in an adverse outcome.

In either case, the patient who is harmed may choose to file a malpractice claim against the health care provider. Only then can a determination of malpractice be made through the professional liability system.

§2.04 The Nature of Medical Malpractice

Malpractice refers to a judicial determination that there has been a negligent (or willful) failure to adhere to the current standards of medical care, resulting in injury to the patient. In its technical meaning, the term malpractice is a narrow one, describing a judicial determination of a patient's claim concerning the outcome of a medical intervention, although it is commonly used more generally to refer to any health care provider behavior that fails to meet current medical standards of care, whether a legal determination has been made or not.

Malpractice claims can be resolved prior to a judicial determination, by agreement of the parties. These settlements between patients (claimants) and health care providers (defendants) are influenced by the assessment of what a potential judicial determination would be. Factors other than the potential judicial determination, such as the cost of protracted litigation compared to an early settlement, also influence such settlements—in which the interests of the insurer play a significant role. As a result, settlements cannot be equated directly with a determination of malpractice.

An understanding and analysis of the issue of medical liability and malpractice necessarily depends on knowing how many avoidable adverse outcomes there are. It is difficult to determine this accurately, and attempts to measure the actual frequency of such events have serious limitations that must be taken into account in drawing wider conclusions. The few studies in this area, however, tend to suggest that relatively few of the avoidable adverse outcomes give rise to malpractice claims.

Also elusive is the identification of the characteristics of the physicians responsible for the malpractice claims, judgments, and settlements. It is often said that a small percentage of physicians are responsible for most of the paid claims and that the problem of harm to patients could be solved by identifying those few physicians and rehabilitating them or eliminating them from practice. It is not clear that this is the case, and there is little data on which to base a comprehensive judgment. A study in Pennsylvania found that while one per cent of physicians were indeed responsible for 25 per cent of paid claims, as many as 20 per cent had three or more paid claims over a 10-year period. Another study found that 42 per cent of physicians with claims against them in a given year (1984) had previous claims against them. Certain specialties are subject to a disproportionate number of claims.

3

Patients' Rights

§3.01 Generally

A great change has occurred in physician-patient relations in the last two decades. A positive move from the doctors' paternalist order, "It's right because I say so" to "Patients have rights, too," has taken place.

The congressional mandate for peer review was an early reflection of this move. The stated purpose of Peer Review Organizations (PROs) is to "ensure" that "patients receive quality care." (Federal Register July 7, 1984: Part V. Wash Rep on Med and H Perspectives No. 19 1984 and HHHS News Mar. 12, 1986) (*See* Appendix 3-1, Cases 1 and 2.)

The need perceived by the American people for protection of their rights is now a major public issue. Financially-secure, peer-reviewed health for all is discussed daily in the media. The monetary aspect of patient care is a focal point in patient care and directly impinges on the concept of patients' rights. Patients' rights, especially for such select groups as the handicapped and the mentally impaired, have been espoused by the federal government for years.

§3.02 Consent

Consent is simply permission to touch the patient and avoids an implication of battery. *Informed consent* is the informing of the patient—a patient capable of understanding—of what is to be done, the risks, and the alternatives. Informed consent is usually written. *Implied consent* is most often used in physician-patient relationships. In other words, every touch, every manipulation, and every treatment that a physician does to and for the patient does not require a written consent. A typical example is a patient about to have a blood test. When asked by the physician to roll up his or her sleeves, the patient will do so; the tourniquet is applied, the needle is inserted into a vein, and blood is withdrawn. The patient knows what will be done and the purpose, and gives consent by allowing it. Yet, there is no written document.

Although the line can be difficult to draw, the more risky diagnostic tests or procedures more appropriately require a written informed consent.

§3.03 Patients' Bill of Rights

The following Bill of Rights is a direct expansion of the physicians' Hippocratic Oath:

> Whereas everyone has the fundamental human right to enjoyment of the highest reasonable standard of health;
>
> Whereas everyone has the right to receive such health care through a common standard of achievement for all health care providers;
>
> Whereas everyone has the right to protection and to personal dignity as a health care consumer;
>
> Whereas the federal government and various states have enacted bills of rights for patients;
>
> Whereas the American Hospital Association has adopted a Patients' Bill of Rights and whereas the American Medical Association has stated that under certain circumstances, it is not unethical to permit a patient to die;
>
> Therefore; a Patients' Bill of Rights provides for universal recognition and implementation of:
>
> 1. The right to appropriate any necessary high-quality health care based on individual need at a reasonable cost;

2. The right to full freedom of choice of class or kind of health care provider, without obligation on any particular provider to treat a particular patient except in an emergency or pursuant to Title 9;
3. The right to personal service from the doctor or under the doctor's supervision and responsibility;
4. The right to personal dignity, privacy and respectful treatment, with disclosure of diagnosis, risks and prognosis;
5. The right to participate in self-determination in planning treatment and to second and third opinions;
6. The right to protection against both over utilization (including unnecessary test and x-rays) or under utilization of services arising out of financial considerations rather than the individual patient's needs;
7. The right to safeguards against experimental research without free informed consent;
8. The right to show medical records and x-rays to other health care providers, in order to avoid unnecessary repetition;
9. The right to appeal, before an independent and impartial tribunal, from an institution or third party payers, denial of service, refusal of reimbursement, or discharge or transfer from a health facility;
10. The right to decline treatment or to choose to die, if the patient's condition is beyond doubt irreversible even where death is not imminent.

Other rights could well be added to this list as needed. (*See* Appendix 3-1, Case 3.)

§3.04 Confidentiality

The orthopedist occasionally is faced with questions of confidentiality as a patient is examined and treated. Some areas are covered by law, such as knowledge that the patient is a wanted criminal; appropriate reporting of this person is necessary. Suspicion of child abuse is legally reportable. Some infectious diseases must be reported by law.

If the patient has an infectious venereal disease, confidential reporting is in order, but conveying that information to a third party without the patient's consent breaches the patient's privilege. If a person with syphilis or AIDS knowingly proposes to potentially infect another, the question of privilege is weighed against the public good.[1]

---

[1] L. Gastin & W.J. Currin, AIDS Screening, Confidentiality, and the Duty to the Patient; Rosenfield, *Legal Aspects of Medical Practice,* Amer Coll of Leg Med J.

In this category of problems, with various states having different laws, counsel with another physician with an informed attorney would dilute the physician's liability.[2] (*See* Appendix 3-1, Case 4.)

§3.05 Need for Patient Advocate

The intrusion of third parties into the practice of medicine confuses physicians and their patients. For major diseases, patients need more formal guidance at the outset than is generally provided by medical caretakers. Some suggest an advocate plan to fill this need. It could strengthen the physician-patient relationship and promote an enlightened free choice of physicians. The plan should be insulated against the large institutional dominance of the health care system because it would be initiated by the patient under physician control. It would use valuable medical talent now being lost by forced retirement.

At this time, there is a pervasive concern on the physician's part about the waste of his or her talent by patient care restrictions, and time wasted by the tremendous paperwork required by third-party carriers and agencies that dominate patient care. Expressions commonly heard among physicians include "Medicine is no fun any more." "Every patient represents a lawsuit infringing upon the very real 'good rapport' of the therapeutic value of the physician-patient relationship," and "It's just not worth the risk to practice medicine in the present environment."[3] (*See* Appendix 3-1, Case 5.)

§3.06 Death and Dying

> It is not a question of dying earlier or later, but of dying well or ill. And dying well means escape from the danger of living ill.
>
> —Seneca, 4 B.C. to 65 A.D.

The definition of death and dealing with death by doctors as it occurs in their patients have always been difficult. These days, the doctor can easily use technology to fight death and to ignore the "natural course" of death that occurred in years past.

Generally, patients view death in one of two ways. One group follows Emily Dickinson, the well-known poet, who wrote about her being in and at death all of her adult life. Her well-known phrase, "ample make this bed, allow me to die in a bed of flowers with friends about" supports a substantial number of patients who wish to terminate their life in a natural way.

The other group of patients seems to follow Dylan Thomas, who wrote poetry to his father as his terminus came. His famous phrase is "Do not go gentle into that good night; rage, rage against the dying of the light." Rather

---

[2] S. Bok Secrets, On the Ethics of Concealment and Revelation (1982); J.C. Bruce, Privacy and Confidentiality of Health Care Information (1984).

[3] Moore, *Need for a Patient Advocate,* 262 JAMA 259 (1989).

than allow the natural course, he would recommend still another consultation to see what else could be done to prolong life in a patient who otherwise is dead socially, physically, and probably mentally.

Since the mid-1950s, when cardiopulmonary resuscitation (CPR) became known and popular, the road to death has taken a conspicuous detour. Thus, there are old and new images of death.

The rights and duties have been advanced by many thoughtful persons, including:

1. Right to life
2. Right to die
3. Duty to live
4. Duty to die

There is a spectrum of attitudes toward life. One such attitude, "Thou shall not kill," sanctifies life and is commonly called *vitalism,* a strong attitude in many religions, perhaps being the strongest in Buddhism. The philosophy here is that life is an end in itself. The second of these spectra, "custodianship of the body," states that there is a duty to respect life and work against suicide; there is no referee in death and life is not worshiped as an end in itself. This philosophy is embraced by God-fearing theologies—strongly by the Catholic spectra, but close by are the thoughts of other Christians and those of the Jewish faith. The third attitude is set forth as "quality of life," in contrast to the sanctity of life. This attitude regards life as having a good purpose, as existing primarily to serve other goods: when life has lost its purpose, it ceases to do good or to be good, and in fact is detrimental to the concept of good.

The issue of accepting, abetting, or at least not hindering the natural course of death when it is imminent without meddling or intervention, has been the subject of numerous law review articles, medical ethics articles and books, as well as a topic of debate in hospital physician conference rooms, law school classrooms, law offices, courtrooms, and jury deliberation rooms.

In many respects, the patient is in a position of needing to negotiate how and when he or she wants to die. This comes close to euthanasia—a forbidden word in America at this time, but encompassed by many countries, with the Netherlands being prominent in the media of late.

On the subject of euthanasia, there is a valid distinction between active and passive, and between voluntary and involuntary. There is, however, no real question on philosophies and methods of abetting suicide.

Since its new measure of control over the death of the patient, embracing the various phases of CPR, the patient, through his or her physician or paramedical personnel, does have a degree of control.

Death is not optional. Certainly, there is no such thing as preventing death. There are only "untimely" and "timely" deaths. An in-depth understanding of the concept "Is there anyone who would be better off dead?" of necessity embraces the thoughts and wishes of the patient. The patient most often approaches this subject differently with the thought, "Could life ever be worse than death?" Comments I have heard from my patients over the last three decades, and increasingly in the last decade, include: (1) consider life without consciousness or intellect or ability to understand or perceive or enjoy what is going on outside, (2) consider life without control of self and of environment; for instance, the paralyzed quadriplegic individual whose life must be sustained on a respirator and who cannot speak, (3) consider life without communication; a substantially impaired body might be acceptable if two-way communication were possible, (4) consider life without pleasure—not speaking of hedonism, but of a life without constant, uncontrollable pain, and (5) consider life without dignity—not wanting to be reduced to a parasite on persons or society in general.

The thought of terminating life or of allowing the natural course to occur is more and more accepted when the physician is able to substantiate the patient's prognosis and concerns; that is, that death is imminent at some time in the near future and that the patient has a terminal, noncorrectable illness.

These concepts are valid in the competent adult and senior citizen. They are not, perhaps unfortunately, currently applicable to the newborn. Here, the "Baby Doe" rules exist, attempting to make sure that the quality of life is not taken into consideration in preserving the life of a deformed or otherwise abnormal infant.

Doctors have suggested that they have the capacity and duty to make life-and-death decisions for their patient. Nonmedical persons recite several reasons why doctors do not make the best decisionmakers. First, they are subject to biases based on the patient's class, race, age, disability, prognosis, and financial status. Second, doctors may have a preference to terminate a dying patient's care because of their own discomfort with death. Studies have shown that physicians are more afraid of death than patients or nonprofessionals. Doctors are not trained for "bringing moral and social guidelines to bear on particular disputes or situations," nor are they likely to have any special knowledge of the patient's life history, psychology, beliefs, and goals that would give them insight into the patient's best interest.[4] (*See* Appendix 3-1, Case 6.)

It is likely that doctors make most decisions to withhold treatment without input from patient or family. The decision to put a Do Not Resuscitate (DNR) order on a patient's chart is the most striking example of a decision to withhold treatment which often is made solely by the doctor. When a patient suffers cardiac arrest, something that inevitably happens in the process of dying, cardiac resuscitation (CPR) may restore life. Otherwise, the patient will die in a few minutes. Many doctors feel it is inappropriate to use CPR in their terminal patients and use a DNR order when they want to allow the patient to die. The American Health Association and the National

---

[4] Group for the Advancement of Psychiatry, Death and Dying: Attitudes of Patient and Doctor, 5 Symposium #11 634 (1965); Brennan, *Do Not Resuscitate Orders for the Incompetent Patient in the Absence of Family Consent,* 14 Law, Med & Health Care 13 (1986).

Academy of Science have stated, "Cardiopulmonary resuscitation is not indicated in certain situations, such as in the case of terminal irreversible illness where death is not unexpected."[5] (*See* Appendix 3-1, Cases 2, 3, and 5.)

There has been an increase in judicial intervention in matters of withholding or withdrawing medical treatment, tending to take the primary decision-making power away from the physician. The evidence shows that doctors routinely withhold or withdraw treatment and that these decisions rarely come to the attention of the family or court. In *State School v Salkewicz,* 373 Mass 728, 370 NE2d 417 (1977), the court noted that prevailing medical ethical practice does not, without exception, demand that all efforts toward life prolongation be made in all circumstances. Rather, as indicated in *Quinlan v Quinlan,* 70 NJ 10, 355 A2d 647, *cert denied,* 429 US 922 (1976), the prevailing ethical practice seems to be recognizing that the dying are more often in need of comfort than treatment. There are no reported studies of the practice of euthanasia in America, although evidence shows it is likely widely practiced. One court says, "recent surveys have suggested that a majority of practicing doctors now approve of passive euthanasia and believe that it is being practiced by members of the profession."

In a national survey in 1982, 84 per cent of doctors said they would likely give a patient pain-relieving drugs even though the dose was likely to be lethal. In a survey of 5,000 doctors in 1987, 70 physicians said they had performed active steps to terminate the lives of their patients. Of 588 respondents, 62 per cent stated they believed it was "sometimes right" for a doctor to take steps to bring about the death of a terminally ill patient.[6]

§3.07 Dealing with Impending Death of Patient

Of all the things a physician must do, telling a patient he or she is going to die, or telling the family that a loved one has expired, is the most difficult. This task may be even more difficult if questionable medical care is involved in the death. Certainly, the family must be approached honestly, discussing any care problem at an appropriate time. Cover-up and failure to disclose will amplify the family's distrust of the physician. In most death situations, it is important for the doctor and the patient's family to realize that modern medicine, with all its technology, cannot cure *all* illness or disease. There is little training in medical school to prepare the doctor for informing a family of death; it is mostly on-the-job training and is a test of the moral, ethical, and social background of the physician. Most good doctors agonize over whether they made the right decisions and did the right things. It is often difficult, because family members will sometimes turn on the doctor at the

---

[5] National Conference Steering Committee, *Standard for Cardiopulmonary Resuscitation (CPR and Emergency Cardiac Care (ECC),* 227 JAMA 837, 864 (1974).

[6] National Conference Steering Committee, *supra* note 5, at 837; Group for the Advancement of Psychiatry, *supra* note 4; Brennan, *supra* note 4.

very time the doctor is wondering "Did I use good judgment every step of the way?" Questions such as "Doctor, wasn't there something else you could do?" or "Why didn't you do something else?" are asked. On the other hand, many dying patients reassure their doctors and smooth the way for their demise.[7]

§3.08 Medical Directive

> Just as I choose a ship to sail in or a house to live in, so I choose a death for my passage from life.
>
> —Seneca 4 B.C. to 65 A.D.

As the citizens of this country, as well as others, become more informed as to the facts of life, the problems of illness, and the effect of illness on longevity and the quality of life, the patient is more involved, prior to his or her demise, in the disposition of his or her body. It has been well stated that the patient has an absolute right (when competent) to determine what happens to his or her body or its parts, and that no physician or court can or will abrogate that right. However, most patients have firm feelings about what will happen should they become disabled. It has been shown that most patients fear and reject the idea of being sustained on a respirator or undergoing mutilating procedures that will not improve the quality of life or reasonable longevity. It is possible, and in fact most desirable, for such patients to execute a *durable power of attorney,* which is accepted by statute in 38 states at this time. Such an instrument documents the patient's wishes as to what is to happen to him or her, to his or her body, and to his or her estate and finances if and when the patient becomes incompetent to make that decision. The durable power of attorney is not tolled by a change in the patient's mental status from competent to incompetent.

The *common law living will* is accepted in 17 states at this time. The same information can be directed to the physician or medical caretaker as in a durable power of attorney, but the living will is tolled if the patient becomes incompetent. Any patient at any time can revoke a living will or a power of attorney unless it specifically follows the methods set out in state statutes (varying somewhat from state to state). In this respect, the durable power of attorney is an extension of informed consent.

Living wills, as described above, do not address specific health problems and procedures, such as amputation, colostomy, or major mutilating surgery, and for this reason most doctors are not comfortable and often will not accept the living will as informed consent to a procedure. The living will is, however, a ticket to the doctor to talk with the patient about extraordinary illnesses and extraordinary treatments, and leads to the durable power of attorney, a device that all physicians are comfortable with.

---

[7] Keown, Daily Oklahoman, Feb 8, 1989, at 16.

Living wills have been strongly endorsed in principle. Unfortunately, existing living wills are rarely used in clinical practice because they are vague and difficult to apply. The American Medical Association's legal staff has prepared "The Medical Directive,"[8] which delineates four scenarios in which patients are to indicate their preferences regarding specific life-sustaining interventions. The Medical Directive also provides for designation of a proxy to make decisions in circumstances where a patient's preferences are uncertain. Finally, there is a section for a statement of wishes regarding organ donation. The American Academy of Family Physicians has informed its membership of advance directives. The Medical Directive provides an opportunity for significant improvement in documentation of the patient's preferences regarding life-sustaining care in states of incompetence. As an expression of a patient's wishes, the Medical Directive should be honored by courts and should facilitate physician-patient discussion of critical and terminal care, as often happens with the orthopedist who follows his or her patients through terminal injury or disease. (*See* Appendix 3-1, Case 7.)

§3.09 Incompetent Patients and Proxy Decisions

Competency is generally a legal term that describes the patient's ability to proceed or describe, or to be expert on a set of facts or a situation, within the judgment of the court.

Capacity, be it mental or physical, is a measurement made by a physician or similar person of the patient's ability to be competent, and includes mental status, physical examination, and the socioeconomic, environmental, and ethnic background of the patient. Capacity is a scientific judgment made by a professional. Physicians, in describing their patients appropriately, should not say that they are incompetent, but that they have or do not have the capacity to be competent, and they will both accurately and supportively describe the patient. The patient may have a limited capacity to understand. Many patients would not be informed or understand the complexities of the anatomy of the abdomen or of an extremity, yet would have the capacity to render competent consent based on a physician's description and the patient's combination of faith and understanding of the general problem, as well as understanding of alternatives to treatment.

Substituted judgment comes up occasionally; this is best exemplified by the Jehovah's Witness who refuses to accept a blood transfusion contrary to what the physician feels is in the patient's best interest. In situations like this, the physician is legally and ethically permitted to substitute the judgment of the otherwise competent and capable patient to refuse the transfusion based on religious beliefs. Although this opinion may well be contrary

---

[8] Emanuel & E.J. Emanuel, *The Medical Directive—A New Comprehensive Advance Care Document,* 261 JAMA 3288 (1989).

to the physician's belief, and contrary to the best interest of the patient, the physician's acceptance of the patient's wishes will ethically and legally exonerate the physician from negligent behavior if injury to the patient results.

§3.10 Ethical Basis for Refusal of Treatment

The ethical basis for refusing treatment to a patient or withdrawing treatment from a patient is part of the doctrine of informed consent. The real question is "Does the physician have proper permission to undertake treatment?" Wrongful treatment is just as negligent as wrongful death.

There are offers of treatment that the patient cannot refuse. Treatment that is dictated by statutory codes varies somewhat from state to state. Courts order treatments where they have taken into consideration the multiple facts of a case in which treatment is refused and is felt to be in the patient's best interest, or in which physicians want to terminate treatment but do not have adequate or competent consent by the patient, a guardian, or a similar person or family.

Finally, there are situations where the patient places an undue burden on the provider by refusing treatment. This is a slippery issue. It often arises when the patient's physician, in appropriate conscience, morality, religious belief, or soul-searching, is unable to comply with the request to refuse treatment.

Three different rationales for refraining from treatment include true medical futility; that is, the treatment—although it may prolong life for hours or days—offers no more than that, with no change in the patient's condition, no chance for improvement, and no relief of apparent pain or other discomforts. These rationales include a probable undesirable quality of life after treatment and/or not altering the undesirable quality of life that existed prior to treatment.

The problem with euthanasia and/or suicide arises in this area. The AMA has no problem with this doctrine if the patient is known by the physician to have been declared terminal in the near future or has no reasonable expectation of life.

Passive euthanasia is described as legally abetting the natural course of death. *Active euthanasia* is murder in our country. *Suicide* is the patient taking his or her life, and is considered murder. If the patient agrees and/or asks that his or her life be taken, that is suicide on the patient's part and murder on the physician's part, unless the behavior falls into the confines discussed above.

The Roman Catholic Church has a problem with this, in that its doctrine states that no taking of life is permissive and that the patient taking his or her life by act or by direction to another is suicide. Last year, a papal epistle categorized treatments to prolong life as "ordinary" and "extraordinary," pointing out that some treatments are so extraordinary that they are not elective and not suicide, with the basic philosophy that "God asks only so much."

§3.11 Facts and Fallacies About Life-Sustaining Treatment

"You can't quit once you start" is obviously a fallacy. In an old joke, the physician starts to operate on the wrong leg and the nurse asks "Doctor, is it possible you are operating on the wrong leg?" The doctor replies "Yes, but I've already started; I can't stop." This is a ridiculous concept and not factual. The doctor would most likely say "Thank you, nurse, I'll stop and proceed to the other side."

It is also a fallacy that it is illegal to stop life-sustaining treatment without a court order. A court order to stop life-sustaining treatment is necessary absent appropriate informed consent, such as a durable power of attorney.

The statement "I don't want to be the one to give the last dose of morphine" requires some reflection about why the physician or nurse is there. Somebody has to be the last one to do something, whether it is give a bath, give a shot, feed the patient, etc., not knowing the moment the patient is going to expire.

"A patient can't refuse treatment" (such as nourishment or IV medication)—the fact is, the patient can only be given medication or treatment of *any* sort with his or her permission. If he or she refuses, the treatment is withdrawn, if the patient is competent; if the patient is incompetent, a court order may be obtained.

"Let's put in an IV just for comfort" is a fallacy. In a large preponderance of cases, there is no discomfort in dying, yet the placing of an IV will make it less comfortable, the IV itself being substantially uncomfortable in many situations.

The fallacy that "A doctor can usually tell what a patient's wishes are" has repeatedly been shown to be false. Recent literature shows that quite the contrary is true; that the physician is often unaware of what his or her patient wants, often taking an incomplete history of wants and dislikes as well as many other features of the history—medical history, allergies, past history, and social and family history.

"They can't sue me for saving their lives." This may have been true in times past, but more and more litigation is brought against physicians who engage in the "game" of preserving life merely because it can be preserved, making a heart-lung specimen out of the patient when the patient has a terminal illness and death is imminent, but the exact time is not known. Litigation often uses the theory of medical battery or prolonging life unjustifiably, with depletion of the estate to the adverse interest to others. The "others" in this situation are the ones who receive the damages.

Most people die of a treatable disease. It is the timing of the treatment that may be negligent.

There is the emerging problem of the person who is dying of a disease which is treatable but not affordable. As medical technology advances, as the population gets older, and as more illnesses become treatable, although by expensive technology, there is no question that unaffordability will be an issue.

There is a strong statement in the philosophy "When there is nothing more to do, the physician's job has just begun." Included in this will be trying to facilitate financing or to somehow care for this group of treatable patients with an unaffordable treatment.

Colorado has been active in legislating medical treatment decisions. It is a model for most states. Briefly stated, the concept is that (1) the patient must be terminally ill, (2) the patient must be an adult, (3) viable pregnancy may invalidate many provisions, (4) witnesses cannot be employees; a patient's relatives sign a paper to withdraw treatment, (5) there is a seven-day waiting period, and (6) nutrition and hydration are optional.

In other words, it is not the treatment of the patient, but the context of the situation that requires elucidation. Following this road, the present Pope set out the doctrine of "proportionate benefit," which weighs the pain and suffering of the whole body and considers treatment that benefits or harms. The life-sustaining treatment that needs to be discussed, ideally with the patient—but, in the patient's absence, with his or her guardian, includes a wide range of treatments: (1) those which sustain circulation, such as CPR, blood transfusion, pacemakers, artery debridements or replacements, heart transplants, and even the use of Dopamine as necessary to maintain life indefinitely—not to change life, but to maintain it into a vegetative state, (2) those treatments sustaining respirations, such as administering oxygen, mechanical ventilation, tracheostomy, and extracaporial membrane oxygenation, (3) artificial nutrition and hydration, such as a feeding tube, intravenous feeding, gastrostomies, and total parenteral nutrition, (4) chemotherapies, including antibiotics, anti-neoplastic chemicals, anticonvulsants, anti-arrhythmics, and immunosuppressive drugs, (5) organ transplantation, use of critical organs, or blood elements, (6) benefit therapy—surgical and medical, such as amputation or renal dialysis, colostomy diuretics, use of AZT for AIDS (at this time), and such mutilating operations as mastectomy, head/neck dissections for malignancy, and removal of the larynx for malignancy, which permanently removes the ability to talk.

A physician may fail to acknowledge the wishes of a patient's living will if the physician is morally, secularly, or ethically in conflict with the patient's wishes. In such instances, the physician has a duty to refer the patient to another physician and to so inform the nearest of kin or guardian.

§3.12 Terminating Life; Do Not Resuscitate (DNR) Orders

Federal law requires administration of "appropriate nutrition, hydration, and medication," even in the extreme medical circumstances that justify the withholding of all other life-sustaining interventions. The meaning of "appropriate" is often unclear. (*See* Appendix 3-1, Cases 8 and 9.)

In withholding care, dehydration has been said to have a calming, pain-relieving effect on the patient. If the patient does not fall within the imminent death or terminal illness category, however, deliberate dehydration ordered by physician for this purpose is negligent practice.

The AMA says it is ethical, with the wishes of the nearest next of kin or family or guardian or following a durable power of attorney or living will that expresses the patient's wishes, to withhold fluids and nourishment. Adequate recording on the patient's record is essential in these instances to avoid charges of negligence or murder, as this is in effect a legal form of euthanasia.

A physician in most states is entitled to write a Do Not Resuscitate (DNR) document after adequately informing the nearest of kin or guardian and obtaining an agreement from them. The chart, of necessity, requires a justification for DNR, which comes under the general category of (1) terminal illness (no reasonable expectation of survival), or (2) imminent death. The timing of death is difficult to ascertain at times. These DNRs may require a daily update, particularly if the patient's condition changes for the better, and this update is the duty of the physician.

Orthopedists are faced, at times, with the question of whether a patient must be required to undergo treatment that will not cure or substantially improve the patient, but may well artificially prolong life, or whether the patient has an inherent right to refuse treatment. Many hospitals approach such problems with DNR or "No Code" orders.

DNR or NO CODE is the wrong statement when it is in answer to a question. This usually means no CPR, which is one simple treatment out of many. CPR is an interesting ritual. It is a symbolic measure to try to resuscitate breathing and a heartbeat. When in a hospital, a NO CODE is called under a number of rubics to not disturb other hospital patients, and at the same time all hospital patients know what a "Code Blue" or "Dr Blue" is, which is followed by a patient room number and the in-rushing of a structured treatment team, often with much confusion but always with an attempt to place an intratracheal tube by an anesthesiologist or his or her surrogate. The dancing around of physicians—typically young house staff, the whaling of nurses, and often other activities occur in CPR that are detrimental to the patient rather than supportive.

NO CODE, or no CPR, can easily be mistaken to mean global refusal of all types of care, so the patient's wishes must be clearly understood. This can only happen when a physician discusses with the patient the various treatments for life resuscitation, CPR only being one. In the experience of most physicians, the patient makes a statement something like "Do things that make me glad and better; do not do things that do not make me better and make me sad; do not diminish my quality of life, but do for me if the probability is that the quality of life or pain reduction will be improved." It is a rare CPR that prolongs the life of a hospital or nursing home patient who has other major terminal health problems, and should the patient survive, the quality of life is usually diminished. Those patients do not want to be subjected to useless, futile, or unwanted treatments. They do not want to be left in a state short of death, but also do not want to miss out on the possibility of beneficial treatments that would return them to a desirable quality of life. Therefore, it is incumbent on the physician to know his or her patient and to explain this to the patient in language that the patient can understand, or to the guardian or family of the patient who is not capable of understanding. Most often in our society today, these discussions are carried on with the next of kin, family, or significant others, as legal guardianship itself is a rare entity.

DNR orders should be in writing on the medical record of the patient. The physician should document on the chart that the patient has an irreversible illness and is considered terminal. In addition, it should be documented that the patient's condition and alternative prospects have been discussed with the patient and/or the appropriate family members or legal guardian, and that they understand the NO CODE or DNR concept and agree with it. The order should be placed in writing on the patient's chart (physician's or sheet or progress notes) and signed by the attending physician. A note at the nursing station or near the patient's bed, but not in a posture to alarm the patient or family, is helpful in curtailing uncertain behavior at the expiration of the patient.

A leading case which recites a legal basis for DNR and gives guidelines for therapeutic decisions is 6 Mass 466, 380 NE2d 134 *Dinnerstein* (1978). This case involved a 67-year-old widow with a diagnosis of Alzheimer's disease, which runs its course in five to seven years. It is a progressive disease leading to a vegetative or comatose state and then death. Falls with fractures, typically a hip fracture, are common and involve the orthopedist in patient care. At this time, Alzheimer's disease is felt to be incurable. At the time of this case, the patient had suffered six years and concomitantly suffered a stroke with severe residuals of that problem. She was confined to bed, tube fed, comatose, and incontinent of urine and bowel. Her condition was considered hopeless, with a life expectancy of one year on her present maintenance therapy.

The treating doctor recommended DNR and the patient's son and daughter agreed. The court was petitioned by the physician and hospital for a declaration that the physician could write such an order without specific advance judicial approval.

The court said that attempts to resuscitate will do nothing to cure or relieve the illness, which had brought the patient to the "threshold of death." The court then ruled that to issue a Do Not Resuscitate order is peculiarly within the competence of the medical profession in light of the patient's medical condition and history, as well as the expressed desires of the family. The court, citing the National Conference on Standards for Cardiopulmonary Resuscitation and Emergency Care, ruled that issuance of a DNR order is not a judicial decision, but one for the attending physician to address in keeping with the highest standards of the medical profession. The court said that "the law does not prohibit a course of medical treatment which excludes attempts to resuscitation in the event of cardiac or respiratory arrest and the validity of an order to that effect does not depend upon prior judicial approval." (*See* Appendix 3-1, Case 5.)

As a general rule, doctors believe that a DNR decision is a medical one, to be made by the doctor. Doctors may consult the patient and/or family before making a DNR decision, but these consultations are at the discretion of the physician. It appears that the "goal of promoting patient self-determination regarding resuscitation is not really being implemented in resuscitation decisions. It appears that the vast majority of these decisions are made with input from patient or family. . . ."[9]

In intensive care units of hospitals, most deaths can be anticipated and DNR orders can be reasonably given in the obvious fatal case. Moreover, complete withdrawal of intensive support should be considered an appropriate option in hopeless patients.[10]

Some scholars have suggested shifting the locus of decisionmaking to the hospital ethics committees. It is not clear that a committee of individuals would make better decisions than a doctor, judge, or family member. In practice, most committees are dominated by health care professionals, who will have the same biases as individual physicians. In practice, doctors do not necessarily follow hospital (ethics) policy. They guide their behavior by habits and patterns of the past. It is hard to change a doctor's behavior, unless something happens, like a lawsuit or a family member complaint.[11]

Even when doctors do involve family and significant others in decisionmaking, the consultation may be, and often is, shaped by the doctor's information and is apt to reflect the doctor's preference and bias more than a joint decision based on all facts. In making life or death decisions, the family is particularly vulnerable to what they perceive as the doctor's expertise. This is seen often in newborn children with defects that surgery may help somewhat, but will not cure. Aggressive medical treatment can help some of these children, such as those with spina bifida with meningomyelocele or other abnormal brain or spinal cord development. Untreated, the child may die or be more disabled. (*See* Appendix 3-1, Case 3.)

Traditionally, the courts have entrusted a great deal of decisionmaking to parents, as well as to doctors. Several cases of neglect or abuse have been reported, and the state has intervened to insist on appropriate treatment or to punish failure or abuse. (*See* Appendix 3-1, Case 10.)

§3.13 Do Not Admit Orders

Do Not Admit to Hospital orders are commonly used in nursing home environments and are an important document to have on the chart when the patient, as well as the family or guardian, understands and wishes to avoid prolonged terminal care. Again, the nursing home record must include a diagnosis that includes the statement that the illness is terminal with no reasonable expectation of survival, and that imminent death is apparent. In this way, the physician avoids a charge of abandonment.

---

[9] Evand & Brody, *Do Not Resuscitate Orders in Teaching Hospitals,* 253 JAMA 2236 (1985).

[10] Jean-Louis Vincent, *Terminal Events in Intensive Care Unit. Review of 258 Cases,* 17 Crit Care Med 530 (1989).

[11] Ikuta, *Dying at the Right Time: A Critical Legal Theory Approach to Timing-of-Death Issues,* 5 Iss in Law & Med 3, 64 (1989).

§3.14 Persistent Vegetative State (PVS)

A clear definition/diagnosis of the persistent vegetative state (PVS) is essential to rationally treating and prognosticating these patients. The following is the position of the American Academy of Neurology:

> The persistent vegetative state is a form of eyes-open permanent unconsciousness in which the patient has periods of wakefulness and physiological sleep/wake cycles, but at no time is the patient aware of himself or his environment. Neurologically, being awake but unaware is the result of a functioning brain stem, and the total loss of cerebral cortical functioning.
>
> No voluntary action or behavior of any kind is present. Primitive reflexes and vegetative functions which may be present are either controlled by the brain stem or are so elemental that they require no brain regulation at all. Although the PVS patient generally is able to breathe spontaneously because of the intact brain stem, the capacity to chew and swallow in a normal manner is lost because these functions are voluntary, requiring intact cerebral hemispheres.
>
> The primary basis for the diagnosis of PVS is the careful and extended clinical observation of the patient, supported by laboratory studies. PVS patients will show no behavioral response whatsoever over an extended period of time. The diagnosis of permanent unconsciousness can usually be made with a high degree of medical certainty in cases of hypoxic-ischemic encephalopathy after a period of one to three months.
>
> Patients in a persistent vegetative state may continue to survive for a prolonged period of time ("prolonged survival"), as long as the artificial provision of nutrition and fluids is continued. These patients are not "terminally ill."
>
> Persistent vegetative state patients do not have the capacity to experience pain or suffering. Pain and suffering are attributes of consciousness requiring cerebral cortical functioning, and patients who are permanently and completely unconscious cannot experience these symptoms. There are several independent bases for the neurological conclusion that PVS patients do not experience pain or suffering.
>
> First, direct clinical experience with these patients demonstrates that there is no behavioral indication of any awareness of pain or suffering. Second, in all PVS patients studied to date, post-mortem examination reveals over-whelming bilateral damage to the cerebral hemispheres to a degree incompatible with consciousness or the capacity to experience pain or suffering. Third, recent data utilizing positron emission tomography indicates that the metabolic rate for glucose in

the cerebral cortex is greatly reduced in PVS patients, to a degree incompatible with consciousness.[12]

(*See* Appendix 3-1, Cases 6 and 11.)

At times, hospitals and physicians will find themselves in situations where there are no guidelines. In such situations, the following questions should be answered before making a decision:

1. What is the state's definition of death?
2. Is the patient's condition terminal?
3. What is the overall prognosis of the patient?
4. Does the patient have a living will?
5. What is the state's law on durable power of attorney?
6. Is the patient competent?
7. If patient is incompetent, what are the state's guidelines for a family making a decision or a guardian being appointed?
8. What is the nature of the treatment which is being refused or asked to be withheld or terminated? Is it a respirator, feeding, medication, or surgical intervention?

Absent clear guidelines, the physician or hospital must seek the intervention and guidance of the court. The hospital may have to petition the court by an order to show cause or request an immediate hearing. In this event, the petitioners must be prepared to present evidence of the following: (1) the nature of the procedure, (2) the prognosis of patient with and without treatment, (3) the quality of life projected if the procedure is permitted, (4) pain and suffering, (5) activities the person was involved in prior to illness, (6) any wishes the patient made known to family members, and (7) the understanding of the family as to the outcome of treatment not rendered. Additionally, medical testimony regarding these factors, with medical details of the illness involved, may be required by the court.

In a case where a patient is not competent to make a decision and where there are no formal guidelines, the court may base its analysis on the overall best interests of the patient. However, this interest will be balanced with the state's interest in preserving life.[13]

§3.15 Death

In determining death, a President's Commission for the Study of Ethical Problems in Medicine and Biomedical and Behavioral Research (1981) set forth guidelines for the determination of death. Initially noting that a person with irreversible cessation of circulatory and respiratory functions is dead, the Commission emphasized that cessation is recognized by an appropriate

[12] *The Healing Ethics,* 2 Amer Acad Med Ethics 4 (1989).

[13] *Living Wills, Health Care and the Right to Die,* 11 Med Mal Law Strat 6 (1989).

clinical examination which reveals, at least, the absence of heart beat or respiratory effort or other evidence of responsiveness. Irreversibility is evidenced by persistent cessation of these functions during an appropriate period of observation. With respect to brain death, e.g., irreversible cessation of all functions of the entire brain, including the brain stem, the Commission provided the following guidelines:

> Cessation is recognized when clinical evaluation discloses absence of cerebral function (unreceptivity and unresponsivity) and absence of brain stem function (absence of reflexes); irreversibility is recognized when evaluation discloses that the cause of coma is sufficient to account for loss of brain function, the possibility of recovery of any such function is excluded and cessation of brain function persists for an appropriate period of time based on observation.

Clinical standards for assessing death and time of death will improve with technology.

§3.16 References

K. Mathis, M.D., J.D., Patient Rights, American Academy of Family Physicians and American Geriatric Society Meeting, Dallas Tex (Feb 21-25, 1990).

Winston & Landesman, *AIDS and a Duty to Protect,* 17 Hastings Center Report 22 (1987).

British Medical Association, Ad Hoc Committee on Medical Ethics, American College of Physicians, American College of Physicians Ethics Manual, *The Handbook of Medical Ethics,* 101 Ann Int Med 129 (1984), 101 Ann Int Med 263 (1984).

Gillan, *AIDS and Medical Confidentiality,* 294 Br Med J 1675 (1987).

R. Wasserstrom, The Legal and Philosophical Foundations of the Right to Privacy Biomedical Ethics (T. A. Mappes & J. S. Zembaty eds, 2d ed McGraw-Hill, New York, 1986).

Merritt, *The Constitutional Balance Between Health and Liberty,* 16 Hastings Cent Rep 2 (1986 Supp).

American Association of Retired Persons, American Bar Association, American College of Physicians, A Matter of Choice: Planning Ahead for Health Care Decision (AARP, Washington, DC 1986).

The Hastings Center, Guidelines on the Termination of Life-Sustaining Treatment and the Care of the Dying, The Hastings Center Manor (NY 1987).

The Institute for Society, Ethics and the Life Sciences, The Hastings Center's Bibliography of Ethics, Biomedicine, and Professional Responsibility (1984).

A. Jonsen, M. Siegler & W. Winslade, Clinical Ethics (1982).

President's Commission for the Study of Ethical Problems in Medicine and Biomedical and Behavioral Research, Deciding to Forego Life-Sustaining Treatment: A Report on the Ethical, Medical and Legal Issues in Treatment Decisions (U.S. Government Printing Office, Washington, DC 1983).

J.W. Ross, Handbook for Hospital Ethics Committees (1986).

Society for the Right to Die, The Physician and the Hopelessly Ill Patient: Legal, Medical and Ethical Guidelines (New York 1985).

Biomedical Ethics, 13 Primary Care 2 (M. Victoroff ed June 1986).

Annas, *Non-Feeding: Lawful Killing in California, Homicide in New Jersey,* 13 Hastings Center Report 8, 19-20 (Dec 1983).

Callahan, *On Feeding the Dying,* 13 Hastings Center Report 17, 22 (Oct 1983).

L. & Dornbrand, *Guiding the Hand that Feeds,* 311 NEMJ 402 (1984).

Lynn & Childress, *Must Patients Always Be Given Food and Water?,* 13 Hastings Center Report 17-21 (1983).

Paris & Fletcher, *Infant Doe Regulations and the Absolute Requirement to Use Nourishment and Fluids for the Dying Infant,* 11 Law, Med & Health Care 210 (1983).

Steinbock, *The Removal of Mr. Herbert's Feeding Tube,* 13 Hastings Center Report 13, 17 (1983).

Bross, *Medical Care Neglect,* 6 Child Abuse Negl 375 (1982).

N. Fost, How Decisions Are Made: A Physician's View, Decision Making and the Defective Newborn 220-30 (C.A. Swinyard ed 1978).

M. Victoroff, *The Ballad of Baby Doe: Parental Discretion or Medical Neglect?* 13 Primary Care 2, 217-283 (1986).

Appendix 3-1
Cases

1 ***Bowen v American Hospital Association,*** **476 US 610 (1986)** (Supreme Court said only the parents have the right to decide when to withhold treatment, that it would be a tort to operate on an infant without parental consent. The 1984 rules have been changed (minimally) and the Child Abuse and Prevention and Treatment Act is currently in effect. Researchers suggest that these rules are incapable "of providing meaningful guidance in the vast array of complex clinical situations faced by the physician . . ." Treatment cannot be withheld from an incompetent person unless there is clear and convincing evidence that the patient made a firm and settled commitment while competent to decline such treatment. The court reasoned that every competent person has a right to life and, because the patient's wishes were not clearly and convincingly expressed, it would be improper for the court to substitute its judgment. 15 AM J L & Med 149 (1989).

2 ***Petkus v Girzadas,*** **177 Ill App 3d 323, 532 NE2d 333 (1988)** (lower court held that pain and suffering refer to a patient's response to an injury, whereas loss of enjoyment measures the diminished quality of life. This established two causes of liability where one was present before. The New York Supreme Court reversed, holding that "loss of life's enjoyment is an inseparable part of pain and suffering." A number of New York cases were affected, and their awards will need revision).

3 ***Johnson v Sullivan,*** **No CIV-85-2434-P (WD Okla filed Oct 3, 1985)** (federal district court refused to dismiss a plaintiff's claims that the doctors and administrators at Oklahoma Children's Memorial Hospital had violated the plaintiffs' constitutional rights. The plaintiffs filed an action seeking to enjoin the myelomeningocele team, and others associated with it, at the Oklahoma Children's Memorial Hospital, from using nonmedical, social, and economic criteria—including the projected intellectual capacity, degree of paraplegia, family wealth and resources, and geographical location—to deny beneficial medical treatment to children born with spina bifida. Certain plaintiffs also sought damages against individual defendants who treated them. The plaintiffs include infants who were denied beneficial medical treatment, infants who were evaluated by the myelomeningocele team, their parents and guardians, and disability rights organizations. The complaint alleged violations of United States constitutional guarantees of due process and equal protection, of federal prohibitions against discrimination based on handicap by recipients of federal financial assistance, and of federal statutes regulating experimentation on human subjects. The complaint also sought damages for medical malpractice. Moreover, the plaintiffs sought associational standing and injunctive relief. On September 29, 1986, the co-defendants, officials of the state of Oklahoma and individual health care providers, filed motions to dismiss the plaintiffs' complaint).

4 ***Krygier v Airweld, Inc,* 137 Misc 2d 306, 520 NYS2d 476 (Sup Ct 1987)** (identifies of blood donors were protected by the Privacy Act, and a blood bank was entitled to an order precluding disclosure of the names and addresses of blood donors. The administrator for the estate of a patient who died due to receiving blood infected with the AIDS virus brought an action of wrongful death against the blood bank. The administrator sought to discover the names and addresses of donors whose blood was supplied to the hospital for transfusion. The blood bank sought a protective order, contending that the information sought was privileged and that disclosure would violate the donor's right to privacy. The administrator contended that the physician-patient privilege did not apply to voluntary blood donation and that the donor's identity was not protected by any privacy rights. The court said that even if the physician-patient privilege was held inapplicable, the blood bank's interest in maintaining the anonymity of donors, together with society's interest in maintaining a free flow of voluntary blood, far outweighed the reason to disclose all evidence necessary to prosecute the suit. The court found that the blood bank had persuasively argued that the disclosure of the donors' names would violate their right to privacy and that the blood bank was entitled to protect the donor).

5 ***Barber v Superior Court,* 147 Cal App 3d 1006, 195 Cal Rptr 484** (court dismissed murder charges against two physicians who had disconnected a patient's life-support system, allowing the patient to expire. Following successful surgery by one physician, the patient suffered cardiac arrest in the recovery room, and was resuscitated and placed on life-support systems. It was the opinion of the surgeon and attending internist that the patient had suffered irreversible brain damage, leaving him in a permanent vegetative state. The patient's wife and children were so informed, and at their request, the physicians removed the life-support system. Two days elapsed, during which the patient continued to breathe and after consultation with the family, the physicians ordered removal of hydration and nourishment intravenous tubes. In this case, the court agreed that the decision to disconnect all life support was proper due to the patient's hopeless condition. Evidence was presented that prior to incapacitation, the patient had expressed a desire not to be kept alive in a vegetative state. Again, this court held that the decision was medical and not judicial. The court concluded that the physician's "omission to continue treatment under the circumstances, though intentional and with knowledge that the patient would die, was not unlawful failure to perform a legal duty").

6 ***Westhart v Mule,* 261 Cal Rptr 640 (Ct App 1989)** (widow of a 74-year-old man, who was in an irreversible vegetative state prior to his death, contended that the placing of a feeding tube was contrary to her request for "no heroic measures" and violated their right to refuse life-prolonging medical treatment. The court of appeals found that the defendant's physicians neither acted outrageously nor intentionally inflicted emotional harm in deciding to order placement of the feeding tube. The decedent had suffered strokes and was deteriorating; would not eat or drink. The doctors placed the tube contrary to the widow's wish, which she alleged was outrageous behavior. The widow maintained that the right to continue medical treatment in a situation where the stomach tube placement would not alter the imminent demise of her husband was a decision not for doctors, lawyers, or the court, but for her, citing *Bouvia v Superior Court,* 179 Cal App 3d 1127, 1137, 225 Cal Rptr 297 (1986). The appellate court held that the placing of the tube was not outrageous and failed to substantiate a prima facie case. Further, the failure of the widow to take action to have the tube removed, through a request to doctor, hospital, or court, essentially foreclosed a case that the widow suffered severe emotional distress).

Comment: This decision seems to condone the doctors in contravening the patient's wishes for no "heroic" treatment, thus subordinating the patients' right to the opinion of the doctors.

7 ***Vassiliades v Garfinkel's Brooks Bros,* 492 A2d 580 (DC 1985)** (surgeon was liable, not for poor surgery, but for invasion of privacy in showing "before and after" pictures in an advertisement for his surgical services. The pictures were published without the patient's consent. The two issues which were decided against the surgeon were invasion of privacy and breach of privilege in the physician-patient relationship).

8 ***In re Harris,* 477 A2d 724 (DC 1984)** (patient should be examined by a physician and a psychiatrist of her choice before a court-ordered amputation of her leg, a District of Columbia appellate court ruled. The trial court authorized the hospital to schedule and perform the amputation of the patient's gangrenous right leg. On motion for a stay of the order, the court said that there was a conflict of psychiatric opinion as to whether the patient was competent to make a treatment decision. There also was a conflict of medical testimony that the gangrenous condition was so acute that amputation was necessary to save her life. In this situation, the appellate court said that there were not adequate findings of fact in the trial court record. It remanded the case to the trial court with the instruction that the patient be given an opportunity to undergo psychiatric and physical examinations by physicians of her choice. The trial court was then ordered to conduct a hearing and report the finding to the appellate court within 10 days, since it was not a "life or death" situation).

Comment: The competency of a patient is a difficult problem in many cases. Courts rarely take the posture of declaring competency or incompetency, but rely on competent medical opinion, yet courts must often weigh the opinions to select the one with the greatest probative value. This was the situation in *Harris.*

9 ***Elbaum v Grace Plaza of Great Neck, Inc,* 544 NYS2d 840 (1989)** (comatose patient's gastrointestinal tube could be removed without jeopardizing the integrity of the medical profession when there was adequate proof of the patient's wishes. The 63-year-old woman had been in a coma since a blood vessel in her brain ruptured in June 1986. Uncontroverted evidence at trial indicated that the patient was receiving nutrition and hydration through a gastrointestinal tube and was in a nursing home in an irreversible,

persistent vegetative state, with no hope of recovery. When her husband brought an action to have the gastrointestinal tube removed and to stop any other artificial life-sustaining treatment, a trial court refused under a 1988 ruling by New York's highest court that clear and convincing evidence of a patient's desire to decline medical assistance was required. On appeal, the major issue was whether there was clear and convincing proof that the patient had made a firm decision, when competent, to decline artificial life-sustaining treatment in her present condition. Testimony was given at trial by several family members to show the patient's pre-illness wishes about extraordinary or artificial life-sustaining treatment. Her husband and daughter had advised the medical director of the nursing home that the woman had previously stated that if she was ever in a "vegetable-like" state with no hope of recovery, she would not want to be kept alive, stating specifically she did not want a respirator, antibiotics, or tubes to keep her alive. The husband testified that his wife had expressed these views in the context of several highly publicized cases of comatose individuals. The patient's sister, as well as her adult son and daughter, also testified to the patient's similarly expressed views. The family's reluctance to consent to the 1986 gastrostomy had been overcome only by threats of legal proceedings. The trial court had reasoned that the patient's views were merely emotional responses to unsettling events, such as a friend's stroke, without true contemplation. The appellate court held, however, that the record established that the patient had reiterated her views, and had extracted renewed promises from family members that she would not be kept alive artificially, under less-emotional circumstances. The second issue on appeal was whether the patient's wishes could be overcome by the nursing home's interest in protecting what it perceived as the medical profession's, and its own, ethical integrity. The trial court had decided that the state's interest in preserving medical integrity outweighed the patient's interest in declining treatment. The court concluded that there was sufficient evidence of the patient's serious, consistent intent, and sufficient evidence that family members were not trying to impose their judgment. It also stated that maintenance of the medical profession's ethical integrity has been considerably lessened by prevailing ethical standards that do not require intervention at all costs. In reversing the trial court's decision, the court ordered that if a suitable facility that would accede to the patient's wishes could not be found within 10 days, the nursing home or a physician selected by the family must remove the patient's tube).

10 ***In re Gardner,*** **534 A2d 947 (Me 1987)** (patient who stated prior to an accident that he did not want to be kept alive in a persistent vegetative state, had the right to have life-sustaining procedures discontinued. The patient was in a truck accident and sustained irreversible head injuries, and life-sustaining methods, including a feeding tube, were used because the patient was spastic and could not chew. The court ruled that life-sustaining measures be discontinued, and the district attorney appealed. The high court said that the patient had a right to have life-sustaining procedures discontinued. The patient's right to refuse treatment was firmly anchored in the common law of informed consent, the court said. The patient had clearly and convincingly, in advance of treatment, expressed his decision not to be maintained on life-sustaining methods if he was ever in an irreversible vegetative state. Health care professionals must respect that wish, the court said, and a physician would be acting tortiously if he or she insisted on providing treatment against the patient's wishes. The court said there was no meaningful ground for distinguishing artificial nutrition and hydration through nasogastric tubes from other forms of life-sustaining procedures, such as a respirator or dialysis machine).

11 ***Cruzan v Harmon,* 760 SW2d 408 (Mo 1988) (en banc)** (guardians of a state hospital inmate in a persistent vegetative state did not have authority to order withdrawal of hydration and nutrition. The court held that the evidence of the patient's wishes was insufficient to support the guardians' claim of authority to exercise substituted judgement on the patient's behalf. The patient was in the vegetative state due to a head injury from an automobile accident, and had made no pre-injury living will or power of attorney, so her wishes should she ever be in a vegetative state were unknown).

12 ***Gallups v Cotter,* 534 So 2d 585 (1988), *rehg denied* (Nov 18, 1988)** (physicians who removed life-support system were not liable for outrage. A child suffered a head injury in an automobile accident, and was brain dead next day with death certified by a neurosurgeon. The child was kept on life-support systems at the insistence of the parents, although tested daily by the neurosurgeon and found dead. The surgeon daily asked consent to remove life-support, but was denied permission by the parents. On the 11th day, the parents allegedly expressed their agreement, but later denied it after the life-support system was terminated. The parents filed actions for wrongful death, breach of contract, fraud, and outrage. Summary judgment was entered for the physicians. The parents appealed only on the outrage allegation. The court stated that the surgeon's determination of death fulfilled the state's criteria of death, and that there was no evidence that the doctors acted recklessly or intentionally to cause the parents emotional harm. The court believed that consent was given on the 11th day, in the absence of any reckless or outrageous behavior by the physicians).

13 ***AB v C,* 477 NYS2d 281 (1984)** (court did not have jurisdiction to grant a patient's request for an order to allow her to refuse additional medical care. A 54-year-old patient fell and suffered a fracture and dislocations of cervical vertebrae. As a result, she was totally quadriplegic, confined to a wheel chair or bed and able to breathe only with the assistance of a ventilator. She characterized her condition as "living hell" and brought an action declaring herself competent. The Director-physician allowed her to refuse additional medical treatment and nourishment. The court expressed sympathy with the patient's plight, but said there was no justifiable controversy for it to decide. The court could not give an advisory opinion, and did not have jurisdiction over the claim. The patient was not in the hospital, and there was no controversy between her and the treating physician. She was not without recourse, however, the court said. She had already executed a

"Living Will" in which she directed that she be allowed to decide not to be kept alive by medication, artificial means, or heroic measures. She also planned to make a videotape of the request, so that if she became incompetent, her guardian could seek an appropriate order. In essence, the court could not require her to effect what would amount to legal suicide).

4

Physician Behavior

§4.01 Generally

The art of medicine is that quality which makes a doctor more than just a scientist—that quality which is cherished by those who are served. It establishes a bond between the physician and the patient that makes the practice of medicine satisfying and fulfilling as the wonders of science are brought forth to the patient, and has given generations of men and women the opportunity to be proud to be called "Doctor."

Medical organizations and state legislatures in the United States are looking for increasingly radical solutions to the loss of doctors in high-risk specialties because of the difficulties they face in obtaining malpractice coverage.

If the opposition of litigation lawyers can be overcome, some states may soon make headway with the new no-fault compensation schemes and provisions for arbitration. The problem is exemplified by Florida, where repeated attempts to reform the law have failed; a major malpractice insurer is threatening to withdraw coverage, and an unprecedented flight of doctors has forced the closure of accident departments and created large gaps in obstetric care.

A recent survey of obstetricians in Massachusetts reveals that one-fifth have quit obstetrics since 1984. An obstetrician in that state whose average net income is $100,000 pays $60,000 for $3,000,000 of malpractice insurance coverage.

Tort law in the United States is state rather than federal law. Most states have reviewed their existing legislation and, by 1987, more than 20 had made at least one reform, including capping noneconomic damages, limiting lawyers' contingency fees, or abolishing or modifying the rule of joint and several liabilities. About 15 states have abolished or modified the collateral source rule. In other states, limited tort liability has been fiercely contested by lawyers who have mounted successful legal challenges on the grounds that such limits are contrary to rights guaranteed in the states' individual constitutions.

A new element has entered the debate with the recent enactment by Virginia of a unique no-fault compensation scheme. The Virginia Birth-Related Neurological Injury Compensation Program will employ the state's existing Industrial Commission to determine claims for economic losses and the cost of therapy for infants injured while being delivered in hospitals by doctors participating in the scheme. Membership is voluntary and costs the obstetrician $5,000 for the first year, with future years' payments to be assessed on the basis of the individual physician's record. Doctors not normally engaged in obstetrics can pay $250 a year to be included for those cases they do handle. Hospitals pay $50 per delivery, not exceeding $150,000 in any one year.

The scheme began January 1, 1988, and as of January 1989 no applications for compensation had been made. The program has already attracted a lot of interest from state legislatures and medical associations, but it is too early to tell whether the scheme will succeed even if it survives.

Florida's latest attempt to end its medical crisis is a bill that includes a birth-related scheme like Virginia's, with provision for prompt resolution of all claims, a $40 million state subsidy to boost insurance premiums of doctors whose specialty is in short supply with doctor immunity from civil liability in emergencies except cases where there is gross negligence, and state assistance with professional quality control.

§4.02 Legal and Ethical Duties of Physicians

The role of the contemporary physician is evolving. Traditionally, doctors have defined their professional duties as care providers and counselors to their patients. The contemporary physician recognizes additional duties to the patient's family, to his or her peers, and to society in general. The performance of these new duties may conflict with the execution of his or her traditional duties causing the contemporary physician to be unsure as to the correct action he or she should take regarding patients.

Ethics refers to the moral principles that underly the rules of conduct of members of society. Ethics classifies right (morally acceptable) and wrong (morally unacceptable). In addition to proscribing wrong behaviors, ethics encourages good (beneficial) conduct.

Law is the body of authoritative rules by which a civilized society regulates, minimally, the conduct of its members. Law prescribes only the most unacceptable behaviors and usually does not require beneficial conduct by society members. Laws that regulate the professional behavior of physicians are evolving to include many ethical duties; fulfilling ethical standards remains more stringent than fulfilling legal standards.

Physicians have well-documented legal professional duties to their patients and to society. These legal duties arise from fiduciary, contractual physician-patient relationships. The *fiduciary* is a professional whom society has empowered with certain authority to make decisions in the best interest of the patient or client. A physician enters an unwritten contract with the patient. This contract carries several duties for the physician: (1) the duty of possessing the necessary knowledge and training to properly diagnose and treat, (2) the duty to exercise reasonable skill and care in his or her medical practice, (3) the duty to obtain the patient's informed consent for any course of diagnosis and therapy, and (4) the duty not to abandon the patient.

The few legally stipulated duties of physicians to society arise from his or her duty to protect persons other than their patients when they are known to be in clear danger. These involve the transmission of infectious disease—the quarantine doctrine—and the psychiatrist's duty to protect a potential victim from a known violent behavior potential in a patient. In *Tarasoff v Regents of the University of California,* 17 Cal Rptr 3d 425 (1976), the court held that a physician may not reveal the confidence entrusted to him in the course of medical attendance, unless he is required to do so by law or unless it becomes necessary to protect the welfare of the individual or community. (*See* Appendix 4-1, Case 1.)

§4.03 Contemporary Duty to Obtain Consent

The contemporary physician's ethical duties to the patient, the patient's family, colleagues, and society are a major professional responsibility. The principal ethical duty to the patient is to obtain a valid informed consent for any medical care and to follow the rational health care decisions of competent patients.

The physician must obtain the patient's valid consent. There are three essential conditions for a patient's consent to be valid. The patient must be furnished enough information; namely, that amount and type of information that a rational person would need before making such a decision. The patient must be competent to consent, meaning the ability of the patient to understand and act on the information given in the consent process. The patient must not be coerced into any decision.

Physicians have an ethical duty to follow the rational wishes of a competent patient, even if it leads to the patient's earlier death. According to the bioethical principle of autonomy or self-determination, only competent patients can determine what will be done with their body or body parts.

In *Schoelendorff v Society of New York Hospital,* 211 NY 125, 105 NE 92 (1914), Justice Cardozo held "Every human being of adult years and sound mind has a right to determine what shall be done with his own body." When patients become incompetent, the physician must identify and follow the patient's previously expressed wishes (preferably written). If a legal surrogate has been legally appointed, his or her decision is binding.

§4.04 Dying Patients

Dying patients or their surrogates additionally may request that the physician withhold fluid and nutrition to permit a rapid death. When this decision is made by a competent patient or legal surrogate, and when it is a rational decision (one that some other reasonable people would make in the same situation and which does not produce unusual distress), physicians have an ethical duty to follow it. Withholding food and fluids is controversial. Physicians have a moral obligation to relieve suffering, but this does not extend to putting patients to death.

Physicians have an ethical duty to answer questions, respond to concerns, and discuss the care of the patient as it relates to the patient's family. A satisfied, reassured family or caregiver enhances the therapeutic effect. Families also suffer, as well as the patient, and the physician has a duty to diminish suffering as best he or she can. (*See* Appendix 4-1, Cases 2 to 6.)

§4.05 Physicians' Duties to Other Physicians

Physicians have a duty to teach each other and share medical information, because patients in general are ultimately benefitted. Physicians have an ethical duty to help identify and rehabilitate impaired physicians. Helping rehabilitate peers with substance abuse or depression has the added benefit of protecting patients from physician error as a consequence of impairment. Physicians owe an ethical obligation to their colleagues to help remove incompetent physicians from the practice of medicine. The action protects the present and future patients of the physicians by preventing them from being harmed.

The physician has an ethical duty to testify as a plaintiff's expert in bona fide malpractice suits where it is clear that the defendant physician has been negligent in medical practice. If ordinary practicing physicians are not willing to accept this responsibility, plaintiff's counsel will retain professional witnesses who are willing to modify or slant their testimony favoring the plaintiff and not address the negligence as a negligent act.[1]

§4.06 What Constitutes Legal Cause

The physician's negligent conduct is a legal cause of harm to another if his or her conduct is a substantial factor in bringing about the harm. There is no rule of law relieving the physician from liability because of the manner in which his or her negligence has resulted in harm.

§4.07 Definition of Tort

A tort is not the same thing as a crime, although the two sometimes have many features in common. The distinction between them lies in the remedy afforded by law. A crime is an offense against the public at large for which the state, as the representative of the public, will bring suit in the form of criminal prosecution for purposes foreseen as protection, indicating the interest of the public as a whole, and punishing or rehabilitating the offender.

The civil action of tort, on the other hand, is commenced by the injured person, and its primary purpose is to obtain compensation for the damages suffered, at the expense of the wrongdoer. If successful, the plaintiff receives a judgment for a sum of money enforced against the defendant.

The same act may be both a crime against the state and a tort against an individual.

§4.08 Punitive Damages

The idea of punishment or of discouragement does not enter into tort law except insofar as it may lead the courts to tip the scale somewhat in favor of the plaintiff. If a tort has been committed in the first place, many of the decisions have rejected punitive damages entirely.

Where the defendant's wrongdoing has been intentional and deliberate and has a character of outrage frequently associated with crime, all but a few courts have permitted the jury to award *punitive* or *exemplary* damages. Such damages are given to the plaintiff over and above the full compensation

---

[1] Bernat, *Ethical and Legal Duties of the Contemporary Physician,* Pharos, Spring 1989, at 29; American Medical Association: Principles of Medical Ethics of the American Medical Association (§9), Chicago, American Medical Association, 1957, *cited in* T.L. Beauchamp & J.F. Childress' Principles of Biomedical Ethics (3d ed 1989); Schneiderman & Arras, *Counselling Patients to Counsel Physicians on Future Care in Event of Patient's Incompetence,* 102 Ann Int Med 693 (1985); Steinbrook & Lo, *Artificial Feeding—Solid Ground, Not a Slippery Slope,* 318 NEJM 286 (1988).

for injuries, for the purpose of punishing the defendant and teaching him or her not to repeat the action and deterring others from following that example.

Decisions have the additional purpose of reimbursing the plaintiff for illness or damages which are not legally compensable, such as the emotional damage, "wounded feelings," and the expense of the lawsuit.

Something more than a tort is required for punitive damages, such as circumstances of aggravation or outrage, spite, malice, a fraudulent or evil motive on the part of the defendant, or such a conscious and deliberate disregard of the interest of others that the conduct may be called willful and wanton.

In *Kelite Products v Binzell,* 224 F2d 131 (5th Cir 1955), the court held "the jury must find that he acted with malice (in the sense of ill-will) or conscious disregard in the consequences to others. The jury may infer this from circumstances of aggravation surrounding the tortious conduct."

There is general agreement that punitive damages will not stand absent malice or the other elements mentioned above; that mere negligence is not enough even though it is so extreme as to be characterized as "gross."

In the last two decades, more punitive as well as compensatory damages have been awarded against insurance carriers and others on the basis of ulterior misconduct in the handling of claims, and in some instances associated with tort actions, such as intentional infliction of mental distress. It is generally held that punitive damages are a windfall to the plaintiff, an honor and not a right, and that it is always within the discretion of the jury or the trial judge to withhold them.[2]

§4.09 What is Negligence?

For more than a century, negligence was recognized as an independent basis of liability with distinct features of its own, differing on the one hand from the intentional or unintentional torts, and on the other hand from those in which strict liabilities are imposed. The negligence theory at this time includes intentional and unintentional injuries, whether direct or indirect, grouped under distinct fields of liability and negligence. Negligence has developed into the main cause of action for accidental injury in America today.

The legal literature has produced a number of articles criticizing the negligence theory of liability. The cause of action from which liability derives requires more than conduct. The elements include (1) a duty or obligation recognized by law, requiring a person to conform to a certain standard of conduct, for protection of others against unreasonable risk, and (2) a failure of the persons to conform to the standard required—a breach of duty. These two elements go to make up what courts usually call negligence, but the term

---

[2] Duffy, *Punitive Damages: A Doctrine Which Should be Abolished,* Def Res Inst, No 4 (1969).

quite frequently is applied to the second alone. Thus, it may be said that the defendant was negligent but not liable because he or she was under no duty to the plaintiff patient. A third element is a reasonably close causal connection between the conduct and the resultant injury. This defines proximate cause for actual loss or damage resulting to the interest of others. Proof of damage is an essential part of the patient's case as an independent fact unrelated to negligence. The danger of future harm may in itself cause present damage. Foreseeability may be a factor converting negligence to actionable tort.[3]

§4.10 Negligence versus Unavoidable Accidents

An *unavoidable accident* is an occurrence which was not intended, and which, under all the circumstances, could not have been foreseen and prevented by the exercise of reasonable precautions—an accident is considered unavoidable or inevitable if it was not proximately caused by the negligence of any party to the accident. The precise definition varies from state to state. For example, if a driver suddenly loses control of his car because of a heart attack or stroke or an epileptic seizure, he may not be liable unless he knew he might become ill. Once his medical condition is revealed to him, he may be negligent in driving the car at all. In some circumstances, where he has prescribed a medication or has made a diagnosis of illness that puts a driver at risk of accidents, the physician may become involved in litigation through the doctrine of foreseeability. The same situation of unavoidable accident exists when a driver strikes a child or dog which has darted in front of his car when his attention is diverted by an unusual event, or for that matter, even when he is giving full attention to his driving but is already too close to avoid the accident. In *Yarborough v Berner,* 467 SW2d 1988 (1987), the defendant was entitled to unavoidable accident when a 4-year-old darted in front of the car. In *Alley v Siepman,* 87 SD 670, 214 NW2d 7 (1974), the defendant was not entitled to invoke the unavoidable accident doctrine when his accident occurred at a time and place where pedestrians crossed the road and it could well have been anticipated that somebody might step out in front of his vehicle. In *Seals v Morris,* 387 So 2d 1220 (La Ct App), *writ granted,* 397 So 2d 745 (1980), a green snake fell on the driver's shoulders, diverting his attention so that an accident was unavoidable. The case, however, was reversed at 410 So 2d 715 (La 1981) when it was shown that the driver was negligent when he left a window open under trees while fishing and permitted the snake to enter. Physicians are involved in unavoidable accident situations at times in the care of their patients, involving unexpected and unanticipated, very nearly unpreventable injuries. This is covered under

---

[3] O'Connell, Adding Insult to Injury—No-Fault Insurance for Products and Services (1977); Atiyah, Accidents, Compensations and the Law (3d ed 1980); Franklin, *Replacing the Negligence Lottery: Compensation and Selective Reimbursement,* 53 Va L Rev 74:774 (1967).

informed consent, so the patient understands this prior to assuming the risk of accidental injury.

§4.11 Unforeseeable Consequences

Negligence is conduct which falls below the standard established by law for the protection of others against unreasonable risks. It involves foreseeable risks, a threatened danger of injury, and conduct unreasonable in proportion to the danger. If one cannot reasonably foresee any injury as the result of an act or if conduct was reasonable in the light of what would be anticipated, there is no negligence and no liability.

If the physician unreasonably fails to guard against harm which he or she should foresee and the consequences could not have been anticipated, is there negligence? An early case offers an example: a defect on a railway platform creates, at most, the foreseeable possibility of a sprained ankle, but as a result of it, a passenger died of heart failure. *See Keegan v Minneapolis & St. Louis Railroad,* 76 Minn 90, 78 NW 965 (1899).[4]

The question of the liability from unforeseeable consequences never arises until causation has been established. In general, the limitation is to foresee consequences of liabilities restricted to the scope of the original risks created. The tests of responsibility, generally parallel the tests for negligence. In *Mauney v Gulf Refining Co,* 193 Miss 421, 9 So 2d 780 (1942), the court held the area in which liabilities impose is that which is within the circle of reasonable foreseeability, using the original point at which the negligent act was committed or became operative, and thence looking in every direction as to the semi-diameter of a circle. Those injuries which form from this point could or should have been reasonably foreseen as something likely to happen or within the field of liability which although foreseeable, were foreseeable only as a remote possibility, those only slightly probable, are beyond and not with the circle, in all of which time, place and circumstances play the respective and important parts.

In situations where the plaintiff's physical condition is weakened as a result of an injury and he or she contacts a secondary problem such as pneumonia or tuberculosis, it is generally held to be a normal consequence of the injury.

If the plaintiff's physical disability has weakened him or her while undergoing recovery and he or she falls and sustains additional injury, he or she may be able to recover damages if the accident was one that was normally expected in view of the patient's condition and due care to prevent that fall was not taken. On the other hand, if a second accident was such an abnormal consequence as drowning because a patient with a cast on a fractured arm fell out of a boat, that is held to be a superseding cause.

---

[4] Payne, *Foreseeability and Remoteness of Damage in Negligence,* 25 Mod L Rev 1 (1962).

§4.12 Insanity

Some orthopedic cases have been reported in which the injured patient has become insane and committed suicide. The prevailing view is that when insanity prevents one from realizing the nature of one's act or controlling one's act, suicide is to be regarded as the direct result for which the defendant would be liable. The situation is the same if one should hurt oneself during unconsciousness or delirium brought on by the injury or if one is sane or if suicide is during a lucid interval but one is in full command of all faculties, but life has become unendurable by reason of injury. It is agreed in negligence cases that the voluntary choice of suicide is abnormal superseding the defendant's liability. In *Trapani v State,* 23 AD2d 709, 257 NYS2d 224 (1965), it was held that "this is, of course, all but clear when the defendant knows the mental condition and should take precautions against suicide."

§4.13 Causes of Malpractice

Personality conflicts between doctor and patient are the most common cause of attorney consultation exploring the possibility of medical malpractice. Patients complain of the way they were "treated" by the physician and almost always they were talking most about the mistreating of, or failure to treat, emotional needs.

In one study by Rein, 10,000 medical malpractice cases were surveyed. He reported, "Most malpractice cases were started by unhappy patients who had no understanding of the technical aspects of their medical care, but sought legal advice because of the need to strike back, or because they have been made to feel impotent, insignificant and unimportant."

A second frequent cause of malpractice suits derives from adverse statements made by other doctors. Physician bias and jealousy (very common) come to the forefront here.

The physician's attitude is important as it relates to trivial aspects of care. To ignore patient comfort complaints or to give an impression of disinterest in pain control are often seen by the patient as an irreconcilable put-down. Arrogance, pomposity, fear, anger, inability to respond to pressure, or plain laziness, occasionally coupled with a dislike of people, are physician weaknesses that send patients to their attorney.

The doctor who does not respond often and earnestly to the needs of a patient who is in dire emotional distress or to the frightened patient, or fails to answer a question of a member of the family, and the patient then has an adverse result, is at high risk of suit.

When the doctor does not show up, does not respond, does not explain, does not show compassion, does not physically and emotionally relate to the patient after a bad result (whether that bad result derives from negligence or not) will be understood by the patient and his family as "hiding something." The physician-patient relationship is then tested.[5]

---

[5] Rein, *Are You Inviting a Malpractice Lawsuit?,* Orthop Today, Oct 1988, at 24.

§4.14 Psychological Causes for Malpractice

Jury Verdict Research reported in 1987 that the typical malpractice award more than doubled between 1984 and 1986. At the same time, the standard of cases increased throughout the country. There is much evidence to suggest the emergence of psychological bases for orthopedic symptoms which persist, basically bad results from surgical or medical treatment. In 1976, 12 per cent of all malpractice claims against physicians performing invasive procedures were against orthopedic surgeons, where 3.2 per cent of all practitioners are orthopedists. However, in mid-1988, 8.9 per cent of all claims, invasive or noninvasive, were against orthopedists.

Many psychological factors in orthopedic cases can magnify and prolong subjective complaints. The apparent suffering of the patient evokes sympathy from family and friends. Pain is a sensory experience. Suffering is an emotional response to pain. Disability is a psychosocial medicolegal situation with major financial ramifications. Issues in compensation neurosis, hypochondriasis, chronic tension, chronic pain, secondary gain, prescription abuse, medical dependence and anger are emotional and environmental factors which tend to intensify the patient's subjective complaints and may form a basis for a negligence claim against the treating physician.

The patient presenting to the orthopedist can belong to any one of three groups: (1) the organic group in which there are no psychological symptoms, (2) the purely psychological group in which there is no demonstrable organic basis for presenting complaints, and (3) the mixed group in which organic and psychological symptoms coexist.

There is a fundamental rule that psychological symptoms do not preclude organic symptoms but do prolong recovery, both physical and psychological. The triers of fact and third-party carriers must be sensitive to these concepts of all injured persons are receiving fair, equal, and adequate treatment. It is in this sensitive area that all too often the patient is a pawn of two adversarial sides that base their judgments on bias and/or medical opinions which stem from the wish to be a continuing consultant, overlooking these psychological facts rather than serving the injured patient. The other side of the coin is the physician who is inclined to overuse the psychological impairment.

§4.15 Low Back Cases

The need to recognize psychological factors has been emphasized by many currently actively practicing orthopedic surgeons. Waddell, *A New Clinical Model for Treatment Low Back Pain,* 12 Spine 632-644 (1987) makes a strong case for a need to recognize the psychological as well as the physical, aspects in diagnosis and treatment of low back pain patients. This task is hard for many (most) orthopedists who are trained in and live and breathe the hard sciences and may find it difficult to accept psychosocial concepts.

There is a distinction between low back pain, a self-limited condition, from low back *disability,* which is characterized by " . . . emotional distress, depression, failed treatment and adoption of the sick role." Some authors report 1 per cent success in treating the latter group of patients, primarily by not recognizing and treating the psychological aspect.

It is the psychological low back disability case following otherwise successful surgery that has resulted in significantly increased risks for litigation.

Several recent articles suggest that ample reason exists to conclude that the recent increase in malpractice suits is based on psychological factors in failed surgeries and in addictive personality stereotypes.

There seems to be an evolving standard of care that requires the operating surgeon to know his patient psychologically or to have another appropriate consultant opinion as part of the diagnostic work-up. There are problems in this area, for to deprive a psychologically-impaired person of surgeries that would help a less psychologically-impaired person is inconceivable. The problem is likely best resolved in the informed consent area that does not warrant results, although many outspoken orthopedists are saying that to do surgery on the psychologically-impaired patient smacks of unnecessary surgery. A bottom line, of course, is "how psychologically impaired" must the patient be and what criteria are to be used. One is reminded of psychological and psychiatric testimony in criminal trials and of the wide divergence of competent opinion and the apparent "bias" judgment in those areas.[6]

§4.16 Diagnosis Leading to Malpractice

In 1988, the most common causes for malpractice litigation were as follows:

1. Missed diagnosis of carcinoma of the breast, colon, lung, and prostate
2. Extremity injury, fracture, or vascular injury that was mismanaged
3. Need for consultation to manage special problems or complications, such as diabetic ketoacidosis or blood coagulation problems
4. Mismanagement or missed diagnosis of myocardial infarction
5. Drug injury—wrong medication, wrong dose, failing to update and reassess medication need and dosage and failure to warn patient of possible complications or problems to look for; these cases account for 10 per cent of all filed cases; the most common drugs involved are antibiotics, anticoagulants, analgesics, sedatives (including overdose), anticonvulsants, and hormones (estrogen- or testosterone-related drugs)
6. Obstetric problems
7. Low back pain, disc surgery problems, also missed pain causes such as ectopic pregnancy or pancreatitis

---

[6] Lobb, Elbaor & Lobb, *Observations and Psychological Factors in the Treatment of Difficult Orthopedic Patients,* 10 J Neurol & Orthop Med & Surger 231 (1989).

The above cases are not in order of frequency, but, in total, embrace over 90 per cent of the claims.[7]

§4.17 Anatomy of Malpractice Lawsuits

Many reviews of the subject point out that four categories of situations are at the root of most medical malpractice cases: (1) communication, (2) practicing beyond the physician's expertise, (3) inattention to practice detail, and (4) medical records, particularly in the doctor's office.

Under "communication," poor responses to telephone calls and messages from patients was a common theme running through many malpractice cases. The doctor has a duty to be available to patients under his or her care. Ignoring calls or an unreasonably slow response can result in injury to patients as well as put the doctor at legal risk. If the office staff prevents calls from reaching the doctor, the patient may assume it is by the physician's decision to be unavailable. Legally, this is patient abandonment.

Adequate communication entails providing sufficient advice for informed consent and informed refusal. In 1926, Justice Cardoza said "the patient has the right to be given reasonable medical evidence to decide what is done with his body." Current general advice is little different. Review of the risks, complications and expected results of treatment is necessary, as is answering questions and explaining the outcome if a particular procedure is refused.

Many physicians communicate inadequately when faced with complications or poor results. No doctor is pleased when these problems occur, but when they do, the patient needs extra attention—not less. Honesty and candor should be the rule, with precise record keeping indicating no conceivable fraud. (*See* Appendix 4-1, Cases 7 to 9.)

"Practicing beyond one's expertise" is a greater risk for physicians who fail to keep up with new knowledge, or for those who work in isolation, either because they are in solo practice or because they relate poorly with their colleagues. There are instances where orthopedic technicians are actually doing surgery under the tutelage of the orthopedist, an unethical practice. Other orthopedists run into trouble dealing with high-risk patients, handling cases when equipment or staff is inadequate, or inappropriately using consultants.

In the "neglect of detail" category, a number of small things may lead to big problems. High volume practitioners are at greater risk. Keep notes of talks regarding patients and telephone call information records. Curbstone consultations with a physician or nurse may be easily forgotten without notes. Adequate arrangement for patient coverage is essential, recorded in the office records. In *Smothers v Butler,* it was held that during the existence of the physician-patient relationship, a physician is under a duty to give all necessary care to the patient as long as he or she requires attention. Lack

---

[7] Persoff, Securing Informed Consent. Presented at the American College Legal Medicine—Mid-year Meeting, Oct 1989, Oklahoma City, Okla.

of diligence in attending to the patient after assumption of care renders the doctor liable.

In the area of office records, legible writing tops the list. Entering critical details in the record is vital, adequately detailing a patient's course, complications, treatments, and return appointments. Never alter records or, if necessary, date and sign the alteration. Medical records are evaluated for timeliness. If the operation report is dictated three weeks after the case, the attorney easily impeaches the surgeon; can he or she really recall everything that went on three weeks ago? A doctor who does not keep records up to date is more likely to be perceived as a doctor who is otherwise not up to date and careless.

Nurses' notes should always be read by the doctor making hospital rounds, as the nurse is often closer to the patient and more apt to record what the patient feels is wrong at any certain time—information vitally important to the physician.

Few patients seek out an attorney because of the prospect of a large award, but because they are mad at or disappointed with their doctor. They feel cheated, violated, or summarily dismissed without an explanation of what is next—dismissed with the thought that they are in pain, but that it is "all in their head." They feel diminished as a result of their physician contact; they feel a civic duty to correct a problem—to protect unsuspecting future patients who might come to their doctor.[8] (*See* Appendix 4-1, Case 10.)

§4.18 Settlements

More filed medical malpractice cases are settled than are tried in court. Where obvious negligence has occurred, settlement is based on damages and occasional consideration of punitive damages is had. More commonly, settlements are made based on criticism of what the surgeon did or did not do. The criticism can most often be defended, but at the risk of how a jury might interpret the criticism. Equally of weight in the settlement process is the expense of the defense and the personalities and reputations of witnesses. Although these factors do not test the facts of the practice of medicine, they enter the big unknown of how a jury may react.

In a malpractice action, unless res ipsa loquitur facts exist, it is necessary to have expert medical opinion to establish medical negligence. In times past, the "conspiracy of silence" practiced by most physicians frustrated plaintiff's attorneys in perfecting their cases. This behavior by physicians is much less prevalent these days. There are organizations which broker physicians willing and anxious to testify against their peers for a fee. Medical practitioners have typically been rugged individualists, at least in Europe and America. The change in social structure, in nearing total socialization of medical practice, has apparently produced a different behavior in the willingness of one

---

[8] Communication from T.C. Stafford & E.H. Neighbor, Medical Meeting Monitor, undated.

physician to impeach another in court. One of the positive things in the practice of the scientific aspect of medicine is that difference of opinion brings forth progress and benefits the patient. There is a strong tendency for one group of medical practitioners to espouse their belief as fact, and if another group has another legitimate posture of practice, adverse testimony now labeled malpractice by the first is offered. The trier of fact must realize that differences of opinion as to acceptable medical practice are the standard of practice and not the bias of a vocal or eschewed group. Aside from this scientific aspect of the practice of medicine, there lies the fact that dealing with and working with patients has a large "art" factor. It has been realized by most physicians that the active involvement of the patient in decisionmaking lessens the physician-patient conflict.

There exists an area of evaluation of the patient and then reporting to a third party that feels diagnosis is valid only if based on objective facts. This is particularly true in orthopedics and neurosurgery. It is good to have a fact situation that is scientifically reproducible. Then the diagnosis, and often the treatment, is readily verified. The truth of the matter is that this often does not happen, but the subjective issues prevail. A great disservice to the patient occurs when subjective symptoms are rejected, or as often happens, are considered fiction by the reporting practitioner. It is a fact that at least 70 per cent of all medicine practiced is based on subjective symptoms, and that that practice is well within the standard of care. Often in the opinion relating to "standard of care," idealist or biased rules are used to rate the defendant physician, are narrowly eschewed, and do not consider all facts of the patient at hand. It is then the attorney's job to develop "all" of the facts.

§4.19 Need for Patient Advocates

The intrusion of third parties into the practice of medicine confuses physicians and their patients. Patients with major diseases need more formal guidance at the outset than generally provided by medical caretakers. Some suggest an advocate plan to fill this need. It could strengthen the physician-patient relationship and promote an enlightened free choice of physicians. The plan should be insulated against the large institutional dominance of the health care system because it would be initiated by the patient under physician control. It would use valuable medical talent now being lost yearly by forced retirement.

There is pervasive concern on the physician's part of the waste of his or her talent in patient care restrictions and of his or her time by the tremendous "paperwork" load required by third-party carriers and agencies that dominate patient care. Currently, conversations among physicians are dominated by such expressions as "Medicine is no longer fun," "Every patient represents a lawsuit infringing on the very real good rapport that is the therapeutic value of the physician-patient relationship," and "It's just not worth the risk to practice medicine under the present environment."[9]

§4.20 Standard of Conduct

The standard of conduct may be (1) established by a legislative enactment or administrative regulation which so provides, (2) adopted by the court from legislative enactment or an administrative regulation which does not so provide, (3) established by a judicial decision, or (4) applied to the facts of the case by the trial judge or jury if there is no such enactment regulation or decision.

The court may adopt as a standard of conduct of a reasonable man the requirements of a legislative enactment or an administrative regulation. Its purpose is found to be exclusively or in part (1) to protect the class of person which includes one whose interest is invaded, (2) to protect the particular interest which is invaded, (3) to protect that interest against the kind of harm which has resulted, and (4) to protect that interest against a particular hazard from which the harm results.

In an action of negligence, the plaintiff has the burden of proving (1) facts which he or she attributes to a legal duty on the part of the defendant to conform to the standard of conduct established by law for the protection of the plaintiff, (2) failure of the defendant to conform to a standard conduct, (3) that such failure is a legal cause of the harm suffered by the plaintiff, and (4) that the plaintiff has in fact suffered harm of the kind leaving compensable the damages.

One who undertakes, gratuitously or as consideration, to render services for another is subject to liability for physical harm resulting from failure to exercise reasonable care to perform the undertaking if his or her failure to exercise such care increases the risk of such harm, or the harm is suffered because of the others' reliance on the undertaking.

§4.21 Functions of Court

In an action for negligence, the court determines (1) whether the evidence as to the facts raises an issue on which the jury may reasonably find negligent behavior, (2) whether such facts give rise to any legal duty on the part of the defendant, (3) the standard of conduct required of the defendant by a legal duty, (4) whether the defendant has conformed to that standard, (5) the applicability that any rules of law determine whether the defendant's conduct is a legal cause of harm to the plaintiff, and (6) for the harm suffered by the plaintiff is legally compensable.

In any action for negligence the jury determines, in any case in which different conclusions may be reached on the issues of (1) facts; (2) whether the defendant has conformed to the standards of conduct required by law;

---

[9] Moore, *Need for a Patient Advocate,* 262 JAMA 259 (1989).

(3) whether the defendant's conduct is a legal cause of the harm to the plaintiff and the amount of compensation for legally compensable harm.

§4.22 Standards of Care

If a person, in fact, has knowledge, skill, or even intelligence superior to that of the ordinary person, the law will demand that the person conduct consistent with it. Doctors must use all care which is reasonable in light of their superior learning experience and any special skills, knowledge, or training they may personally have over and above what is normally possessed by persons in the field.

A doctor, although he or she seldom does, may contract to cure a patient or accomplish a particular result, in which case the doctor may be liable for breach of contract when he or she does not succeed. In *McKinney v Nash,* 120 Cal 3d 428, 174 Cal Rptr (1981), it was held that the doctor's statement that the hernia operation would be simple and without problem was insufficient to qualify as a guarantee.

In the absence of an express agreement, the doctor does not want to insure either a correct diagnosis or a successful course of treatment. The doctor will not be liable for an honest mistake of judgment where the proper course is open to a reasonable doubt, but by undertaking to render medical service, even though gratuitously, the doctor will ordinarily be understood to hold him- or herself out as having a standard. The formula under which this is usually put to the jury is that the doctor must have and use the knowledge, skill, and care, ordinarily possessed and employed by members of the profession in good standing. The doctor will be liable if harm results because he or she does not have them. Sometimes, this is called the "skill of the average member of the profession," but this is clearly misleading since only those in good professional standing are considered and of these, it is not the middle but the minimum common skill which is to be looked at. If the defendant represents him- or herself to have greater skill than this, as where the doctor holds him- or herself out to be a specialist, the standard is modified accordingly.

There is an underlying assumption that two doctors practicing medicine in two different sections of America will prescribe the same treatment, but this is not true. Treatment patterns can vary among communities because doctors in different places have different acceptable methods. Within a given hospital, doctors tend to consult one another and reach a consensus on how to practice, that consensus being different in another community. The biases of stronger, more dominant physicians may influence which procedure or treatment is be favored or unfavored, and tends to cast a cloud on a physician who does a less locally-popular procedure. The consensus does not and should not be interpreted as a standard of care, but better describes what is locally "popular."

In some areas, certain operations are three times more frequently done than in other hospitals (i.e., hysterectomy). As this information becomes known, a question arises as to the scientific validity of the procedure. A major reason that medical practices vary so widely is that doctors suffer from a shortage of essential information. There is no comprehensive national collection of data concerning what treatments work best for what kind of medical or surgical problem. In reality, little medical research on the outcome of treatment is done. Do the patients get better or worse, live or die? With the increased reorganization of medical practices into institutionalized areas, government hospitals, HMOs, large clinics, and insurance or other third-party corporations, a data base is available for such research.

Lack of information about patient treatment outcome has several ramifications—physical, social, and financial. Not only do some patients have unnecessary surgery, but health care costs in America continue to rise. Current medical logic tells some doctors, "When in doubt, do it, making certain the patient is fully informed."

Outcome studies should not be used to ration medical care, in the opinion of most thoughtful citizens, but they represent a tempting tool. Many doctors fear that outcome research will demonstrate that a large percentage of what the physician does makes no difference. They fear that medical practice will be relegated to "cookbook mentality;" however, all physicians practice from established medical models which improve rather than restrict medical care. On the other hand, many (most) physicians would welcome standards of care that are universally accepted, although the patient at the edge of diagnostic criteria is apt to suffer.[10]

Several specialty groups have perfected "guidelines" for treatment of medical problems. For example, the American Academy of Orthopedic Surgeons (1986) issued guides. Subsequently, the "Academy" has modified its positions, saying these are "suggested" guides—not "absolute"—and that many "variables" may modify guides.

§4.23 Practice Guidelines

The Generic Practice Guidelines deal with such nonclinical issues as appointments and scheduling, telephone communications, billing and collecting, documentation, and patient records. They are developed by the Patient Safety/Risk Management Subcommittee of the AMA/Specialty Society Medical Liability Project.

The name "guideline" poses frightening legal worries for physicians who follow them. Many physicians find "great value" in guidelines to help them treat patients. Many comment that the guides present an educational aid in risk management and in loss prevention. Currently, the AMA plans to change "guidelines" to "parameters."

Much has been written in medical journals of the need for structured standards of care for physician to follow. The objection comes from physicians who feel that their individuality will become stifled and that progress, new ideas of diagnosis and treatment, and the essence of the physician-patient

---

[10] Ludtke, *Physician, Inform Thyself,* Time, June 26, 1989, at 71.

relationship will become things of the past, and that the physician, for the most part, will become a technician. Physicians favoring a structured standard of practice relative to their special field welcome it, feeling it would bring less uncertainty of patient and physician expectations.

§4.24 Medicine "By the Book"

Call them what you like—standards, guidelines, or parameters—they are beginning to define the way medicine is being taught, practiced, and paid for. One major impetus for the development of parameters is the consequence of the science of medicine outstripping the ability of individual physicians to know it all.

It is not feasible or appropriate to restrict physicians to one procedure or series of procedures for a specific condition. No two patients are exactly alike and no two conditions are exactly alike. Physicians will be best served by providing them with parameters that give them flexibility to utilize their skills within an acceptable range of options. This, in effect, is a modern definition of "standard of care." These types of flexible and updated parameters would be of advantage to physicians, patients, and third-party payers and should have a significant impact on professional liability problems.

As the parameters move forward, some outdated procedures should be dropped. This has been well demonstrated in laboratory tests that are obsolete and in pharmaceuticals that have been shown ineffective for their purported use. The growth of medical practice parameters will have an impact on malpractice. Just how much has spawned differences of opinion. Many malpractice problems today are not with "bad doctors." The problems are with good doctors who are on the front line and treating complicated cases using standard therapies, but often with unpredictable results. Every doctor in the country today is routinely doing things that he or she never heard of in medical school or residency training.

A major reason physicians fare poorly in court is that the self-acknowledged expert can say that the standard of care is whatever he or she thinks it ought to be. If you put two experts in a courtroom on opposite sides of the issue, who is the jury to believe? If you have an expert who says, "As determined by the American College of Surgeons (or the American Academy of Orthopedic Surgeons, or the American Medical Society), these are the options that could have been followed . . . " and the physician followed one of these options, a more viable "standard of care" is presented to the court.

In 1986, the American Society of Anesthesiologists set standards of practice for their members, adding two additional standards in 1988. The United States Government, through several agencies, is looking at practice guidelines (once maligned as "cookbook medicine") as a means of improving medical practice in the least objectionable way, as well as to help stem the rising cost of medicine.

A recently announced agreement between the American Medical Association and the Rand Corporation to develop "parameters" for medical practice is seen as even more significant, because it will bring together a highly reported team of Rand researchers and clinicians from a variety of specialties. Many point out that a physician is going to have problems if he or she agrees to be bound by these parameters and his or her care falls below certain treatment options. Using less pejorative words, such as "guides," the generalities of care would afford the physician a better negligence defense.

The area that a physician practices would come into gray areas with parameters set out by Harvard or Johns Hopkins doctors that would unduly or unrealistically suppress the small town doctor's practice. A question arises that, if the university center specialist makes the parameters, will it not be probable that the standard they set will oblige transfer of large groups of patients from the private practitioner to major medical centers to the practice disadvantage of physicians not privileged to practice in university centers? This would be much like the socialized medical practice in many countries that most American doctors resist.

It is probable that national standards would set the stage for testifying experts to base their opinions of breach of those standards, a difficult allegation to defend.

Many attorneys representing malpractice insurers say that physicians can benefit from practice standards that establish protocols for diagnosing illness, as well as for invasive patient procedures and for methods documenting patient records and obtaining informed consent. They say that they are not telling physicians how to practice medicine, but suggesting ways to lessen exposure to lawsuits.

Failure to follow the parameters does not indicate negligence per se, but would call for a reasoned explanation.

Medicare has gotten into the parameters of medication practice by setting up PROs, discussed above.[11]

§4.25 Guides Used in Practice

Considering the use and practicality of physician practice "guides," the following scenario is instructive. Mr. U.S. develops pain in his low back. Being a wise shopper, he goes to the library and checks out a medical article discussing his problem (although the article was out of date within one year of publication). He discovers the article was written in the 1980s and describes large variations in the use of medical care as a function of where one lives. He decides to experiment with his own health and consults several back specialists around the country. He finds out there is confusion regarding the correct diagnostic path to follow. More importantly, the patient determines that each orthopedist is firmly and unequivocally sure in his

---

[11] McGinn, *Practice Standards: MD's Shield or Plaintiff's Spear,* AMA News, Jan 6, 1988, at 25; Meyer, *Payers Reluctant to Tread Standards Waters,* AMA News, Jan 6, 1989, at 24; McGilrath, *Government Jumps on Bandwagon in Developing Practice Guides,* AMA News, Jan 6, 1989, at 3. Todd, *Only Parameters Will Give MD's Needed Flexibility,* AMA News, Jan 6, 1989, at 21.

recommendation. The therapeutic options are generally not given to the patient, and if given, the options are presented hurriedly and in abbreviated form as the orthopedist's pressure of time makes it impossible for a detailed, informed discussion to occur. The patient's own values regarding what components of his health he is interested in maximizing are not discussed. He leaves the last appointment confused. He makes the wrong decision, but lives anyway, although impaired.

This vignette relates to practice "guides." Physicians need to act. The financial forces on the health system and lack of minimal health insurance for many have all increased pressure for physician to define and justify what they believe and practice. When these changes are combined with changes in the technology of medicine, then the development of practice guides is felt to be necessary by many leaders in the health care arena; these are often nonphysicians.[12]

In respect to board-certified or board-eligible specialists, a national standard of care is increasingly employed. The effects of the use of a national standard of care are to hold the physician to a potentially higher standard of care than he or she might be held under a locality rule and permit the use of expert witnesses who did not practice in the community. With the expansion to a more national standard of care, the expert need only be familiar with the standard of care employed by physicians in the same specialty under similar circumstances.

The Committee on Professional Liability of the American Society of Anesthesiologists is presently studying and working on a "standard of practice." They have concluded from a review of 1,004 lawsuits for alleged anesthesia-related malpractice that the standard of care rendered to the patient significantly influences the amount of award to the plaintiff. If care was below standard, the likelihood of payment was 82 per cent; even if the care met standards, there was payment in 42 per cent of the cases. As of 1989, they concluded that the tort-based system of patient compensation for injury clearly favors payment to injured patients, but that inequities exist for both patient and physician.

Many physicians feel that the ability to monitor the effectiveness of efforts to reduce the risk of anesthesia will require a better data base than furnished by the insurance industry based on closed malpractice claims. Complete data can be provided only from a registry in which hospitals are required to report the number and types of anesthetics administered and predetermined information regarding adverse results. A national registry of anesthetic mishaps is suggested by many. There seems to be a trend to profile each physician in the country through licensure and disciplinary reporting. It is a short step to require reporting of all adverse results that patients sustain and make them part of a physician profile. The room for error and bias in such a system could be tremendous.[13]

---

[12] Brook, *Practice Guidelines and Practicing Medicine,* 262 JAMA 3027 (1989).

[13] Brunner, *Monitoring Anesthetic Care: New Directions,* 261 JAMA 1633 (1989); Cheney, *Standard of Care and Anesthesia Liability,* 261 JAMA 1599 (1989);

If the quality of care provided by a hospital affects its death rate, then some of the deaths are preventable. One large survey of cerebral vascular accident patients who died showed this to be true. A main criticism was incorrect diagnosis of patient illnesses. In retrospect, severity of illness can help a hospital identify probable preventable deaths. In this series, 42 per cent of low illness severity had probable preventable deaths, as compared to 11 per cent high severity of illness. The study suggests that this comparison would be valid to other severe illness or traumas.[14]

§4.26 Physician Duties Under the Standard of Care

The standard of conduct to which the physician must conform to avoid being negligent is that of a reasonable man under like circumstances, as stated in Restatement (2nd) of Torts. The physician is not required to render perfect care, provided he or she gave the highest possible degree of care available. Some jurisdictions state that the physician's duty is to render care exercising ordinary or reasonable care and diligence to apply his or her skill to the treatment of the case through application of his or her best medical judgment. There is substantial difference between "perfect-highest" and "ordinary-reasonable" care, and this often becomes an issue in evaluating standards of care in the eye of the medical expert who responds to interrogation by the questioner using "highest" or "ordinary." The issue comes close to "strict liability" and regresses to English common law. Many medical experts will express their opinion as to the standard of care based on their practice habits and biases and fail to recognize that "honest doctors have honest differences of opinion." This biased "perfect" theory is often proffered consciously or without in-depth thought, by the increasing number of professional university-based physicians who teach perfection practice in a controlled, structured environment. These teachings are often based on protocols that follow research or narrow beliefs and fail to recognize the total care situation of the physician "in the field," who practices prudent, reasonable, accepted medical techniques which may be different in some respects from the cloister. These physicians do not necessarily practice below the national standard of care when they differ from the teacher experts.

The plaintiff bears the burden of demonstrating that the treatment given was below the standard of care and skill expected from reasonable competent practitioners under similar circumstances. The duty to exercise such reasonable care applies, even when the physician renders this type of care on a regular basis. (*See* Appendix 4-1, Cases 11 and 12.)

Several states have enacted statutes defining the standard of care. North Carolina codes provide "the care of such health care provider must be in accordance with the standards of practice among members of the same

---

[14] Dubois, *Preventable Deaths: Who, How Often and Why?*, 109 Ann Int Med 582 (1988).

health care profession with similar training and experience situated in the same or similar communities at the time of the alleged act giving rise to the cause of action."

In Maryland, the M.D.-owned malpractice insurance groups issue insurance at a 35 per cent reduced premium if the insured agrees to follow certain "standards of care." The standards are categorized according to speciality, including methods of specific types of patient care and recordkeeping.[15]

Georgia courts have held that a medical malpractice cause of action lies where the physician fails to exercise the reasonable degree of care required in the profession. Quite simply, it must be realized that every successful malpractice case involves a successful demonstration that the appropriate standard has been breached; conversely, unsuccessful cases fail to prove that the conduct was substandard or that the conduct, even if below that required, caused the injuries complained of.

The minority view, at this time, is that the physician will be judged according to the acceptable standard of care exercised by practitioners in the same community when faced with similar circumstances. The trend is away from this "locality" rule, particularly in respect to specialists who practice under standards recognized and often certified by specialty boards, thus using a "national" rule.

North Carolina continues to apply the "locality" rule. Texas has held that the law imposes a duty on the treating physician to exercise the degree of skill and care which would have been exercised by a physician of ordinary prudence in the same locality under the same circumstances. Utah has similarly held specialists to the standard of care exercised by similar specialists in cities of comparable size.

There is authority expressly rejecting the locality rule, such as in Georgia, which provides that the standard of care for physicians is not based on a particular community, whereas the standard of care for hospitals is locality-oriented.

It seems that in courts that employ the locality rule, there is no uniform standard for determining what constitutes "the same or similar" community. The determination will vary with respect to the facts of each case, and should bear in mind the rationale behind the rule. In certain cases, the locality has been held to include the entire state.

The medical body of knowledge is an accumulation of individual experiences encompassing both the science and the art of medicine. Medicine is inexact, secondary to the endless variety of individual circumstances. The "science" is often anecdotal and opinionated, occasionally biased, which meld into a consensus of medical opinions, although hardly the absolute or gold standard of care of all patients with a similar affliction. The "art" of medicine is even more nebulous.

In a legal sense, the standard of care is different from the medical basis. The implementation of the legal "standard" is always retrospective, accepts

---

[15] Todd, *Only Parameters Will Give MD's Needed Flexibility,* Jan 6, 1989, at 21.

consensus opinion as fact (often not verifiable fact), considers the printed word as sacrosanct, and disregards in large part the intangible and interpersonal variables which so often affect the medical outcome. The physician realizes that deviation from the "standard" is often the vehicle of medical progress or even medical "breakthrough." A better understanding of "informed consent" by physicians and patients alike recognizes the new or experimental types of treatment, accepting that deviation from the standard is an absolute necessity in the development or improvement of diagnostic and therapeutic techniques.[16]

Many authors say that the "standard of care" is too vague. There are, however, basic concepts that apply to physicians throughout the country. The standard of care clearly requires a doctor to keep abreast of his or her practice of medicine, its changes, and to keep updated with regular continuing education. The standard of care requires the doctor to take a careful history, perform a careful examination, function within the confines of the physician's learning and capability, arrive at an appropriate diagnosis, prescribe and implement proper treatment, and refer for consultation when appropriate. It seems clear and not subject to controversy that the concept of standard of care requires the physician to be "careful."[17]

Generally speaking, the standard of care is nationwide rather than the local or community standard applied in years past. National standards exist because virtually all practicing physicians receive their education in a similar type of medical school with teachers from the country or world over; they read the same medical literature and they attend the same educational meetings if they keep current with their continuing medical education. There is little place for the community standard to supersede a national standard.

A question has arisen in a number of cases as to whether the standard of care required of a physician who holds him- or herself out as a specialist should be determined by the practice within his or her profession or by the practice among a geographically-circumscribed subset of his or her colleagues. In a number of cases, the courts have held a specialist to the standards of similar specialists practicing in the same community.

In an apparent compromise as to whether the local or national standard should be applied, courts have expanded the scope of geographical communities to include the entire state. In a number of jurisdictions, courts have taken varying positions over what standards should be applied.

As a general rule, the standard of care is assessed by qualified experts. At this time in history, the physician is under great pressure to keep medical costs down. Defensive medicine (although extremely difficult to define) practiced by physicians is decried. Several articles on this matter refer to Hellin v Casey, dealing with "what to do" if most other physicians are doing substandard practice. There appears to be no safe solution, but rationally, "when all else fails, practice good medicine."

---

[16] Nirschl, 9 Orthop Today 3 (1989).

[17] 1 Am Law Med Malpr 36-38 (Supp Nov 1989).

§4.27 Code of Hammurabi

The physician has been held to codes and rules of practice at least as long ago as 2000 B.C. when the "Code of Hammurabi" existed. This code states concern for the quality of health care. The code imposed strict rules on the physician and surgeon, and in effect made him or her a guarantor of his or her diagnosis and treatment. "If the surgeon has made a deep incision in the body of a man with a lancet of bronze and causes the man's death or has opened the carbuncle in the eye of a man and so destroys the man's eye, they shall cut off his forehand."

In early English common law, from which the concept of negligence arose, physicians were considered members of a public calling as were innkeepers and common carriers. Great public trust was placed in members of these professions, as persons using their services placed their lives in their hands. As the era of commercialism has developed, the physician's role is defined by rules of private contract with rights and duties established by society. Later in the 19th century, the tort concept of negligence and the reasonable man theory developed concomitantly, with the medical profession moving away from commercialism. Fault-based liability resulted.

Until the middle of the 19th century, a person was held liable for the injury that his or her behavior caused, regardless of the degree of care exercised. Strict liability was the code at this time. Due to the pressure of industrial expansion, liability concepts were changed so that the individual was held liable for negligently or deliberately caused injury.

In Losee v Buchanan, an early case in point, a steam boiler owned by the defendant exploded and damaged the plaintiff's property. The court held that fault must be shown before one can be held responsible for unintentional injury. The plaintiff could show no negligence on the part of the boiler owner, so the defendant prevailed.

In this era, negligence was treated as committing a legal wrong rather than as a separate, distinct legal theory. If a person (physician) was a member of a "public" calling, he or she could negligently breach a contract by failing to exercise due care. Public callings were those professions which required a great deal of trust by those utilizing their services, implying that a duty of carefulness and unusual skill existed, and thus an implied contractual duty of care.

Before the concept of negligence as a tort, medical malpractice was dealt with as a contract problem, the physician being held in breach of contract if he or she behaved negligently and the patient was injured thereby. As common law evolved, the courts increasingly treated malpractice as a tort, even if pled as breach of contract.

§4.28 Skill and Knowledge of Physician

One of the most difficult questions in connection with negligence is that of what the physician may be required to know. *Knowledge* is defined as the belief in the existence of a fact which coincides with the truth. It rests on the perception of the actor's surroundings, memory of what has gone before, and the power to correlate the two with previous experiences. This is quoted in the Second Restatement of Torts Section 289. Legal leaders in the late 1800's have concluded—and their legalese is true today—that there are no facts whatever which every person in the community is absolutely bound at his or her peril to know. This is also true in the practice of medicine.

§4.29 Differences of Medical Opinion

All jurisdictions realize that experts disagree. In medicine, there are different schools of medical thought and alternative methods of acceptable treatment that must be weighed by the opinions of medical experts. Generally speaking, the doctor is entitled to be judged according to the theories of the school the doctor professes to follow.

This doctrine does not mean, however, that any quack or "crackpot" can set him- or herself up as a "school" and apply individual ideas without liability. A "school" must be recognized as one with definite principles and must be in line with the thought of a respectable minority of the profession. In addition, there are minimal requirements of skill and knowledge for anyone who holds him- or herself out as competent to treat human ailments, regardless of his or her personal views on medical subjects. A physician is required to exercise reasonable care in rationally arriving at a diagnosis and is liable for failing to do so.

In times past, allowance was made for the community in which physicians practiced, and a country doctor was not expected to have the equipment, facilities, libraries, contacts, opportunities for learning, or experience afforded in larger cities. Since the standard of the "same" locality was obviously too narrow, this was commonly stated as "similar" localities, thus including other towns of the same general type.

The improvement of travel, communications, and the availability of continuing medical education have led most courts to abandon the fixed locality rule in favor of treating the community as merely one to be taken into account in applying the general professional standard. This is particularly true for physicians who are board-certified or board-eligible.

§4.30 Need for Expert Testimony

Because juries are composed of laypersons not competent to pass judgment on medical signs or techniques, it has been universally held that a finding in negligence cannot be had absent expert testimony. In the case of Cross v Huttenlocher, the court held, "To prevail in a malpractice case, the plaintiff must establish through expert testimony both a standard of care and the fact that the defendant conduct did not measure up to that standard." The necessary expert testimony to establish presence or absence of medical negligence may come from the defendant him- or herself.

With the continuing "conspiracy of silence," the well-known reluctance of doctors to testify against one another often works a hardship on the plaintiff, particularly in those jurisdictions that rely on the locality rule. In recent years, some doctors have been willing to testify for plaintiffs in cases where the evidence of actual negligence is quite clear. Medical school professors have become a pool of medical experts for the plaintiff. The matters regarded within the common knowledge of laypersons, as where the surgeon amputates the wrong leg, or where there is an injury to part of the body not within the operative field, is often held to permit the jury to infer negligence without the aid of any expert.[18]

§4.31 Types of Therapists

There are a number of medical disciplines involved in the diagnosis and treatment of soft tissue injuries. The following is a review of those disciplines, their usual training, and where they fit into the treatment pattern.

M.D.

Doctors of medicine in the United States are persons with college degrees who have an additional three or four years of training and who have graduated with credentialling from a medical school. Additionally, an internship is required. The requirements have changed in recent years. Most physicians practicing today have had a one-year internship and have either gone into the practice of medicine at that stage or gone into specialty training.

In the last few years, most medical schools continue an internship as the first year of a specialty training program as one option of ongoing training. Residency specialty training for a physician beyond internship is a training period practicing with and studying exclusively a specialty in medicine such as obstetrics, gynecology, internal medicine, pediatrics, general surgery, orthopedic surgery, psychiatry, etc. These residency periods range from three to five years after completion of medical school. Currently, it is common for a resident physician specializing to continue with additional training of a subspecialty such as spine surgery, hand surgery, vascular surgery, cardiology, nephrology, and other specialties.

From the point of internship forward of the M.D., he or she is duly licensed in the state of practice and must maintain that license during the period of practice in that or other states in the United States.

D.O.

A doctor of osteopathy is a person with training very similar to a medical doctor, using the same schooling techniques and the same residency opportunities. Additionally, osteopaths are trained as physicians who specialize in manipulative (mostly spine) therapies as an integral part of their training.

---

[18] Seidelson, *Medical Malpractice Cases and the Reluctant Expert,* 16 Cath U L Rev 1987 (1966); Marks, *Conspiracy of Silence,* 14 Cleve Marsh L Rev 520 (1965); Vogle & Delgado, *To Tell the Truth: Physician's Duty to Disclose Medical Mistakes,* 28 UCLA L Rev (1952).

D.C.

A doctor of chiropractic is a person with a training period that usually requires a college degree and then training in chiropractic medicine for two years. There are several schools of chiropractic, and the training periods are different. They become licensed by the state in which they practice, their training having been certified by their institution of education. A chiropractor manipulates segments of the body, usually the spine, believing that the root of most body complaints, illnesses, and resolution of injury are favorably affected by realigning or appropriately manipulating segments of the spine. This is done manually and by certain physical therapy techniques—massage, heat, etc. Chiropractic physicians do not prescribe medication other than health foods and vitamin compounds.

Physical Therapist

A physical therapist is a specially-trained individual with a college degree and three years (minimum) of post-college training in the art of physical therapy. Physical therapy deals with the manual treatment of patients to resolve pain complaints, increase motion to constricted joints, increase muscle strength when absent, and to facilitate the total rehabilitation of the patient. There is considerable education that the physical therapist imparts to the patient as part of his or her treatment technique. In some states, physical therapists are independent practitioners, owning and working in their own facility, but always working on a prescription from a physician. There has been a push in recent years by physical therapist lobbyists to become more independent, to see patients and make their own diagnosis, and to prescribe their own physical therapy treatment. Most physicians resist this.

Social Worker

These are college-graduated persons who specialize in diagnosing and consulting with patients and families regarding their social problems as they relate to lifestyle problems. There are many subdivisions of social workers that do not necessarily require specialized training but have a specialized interest, for instance those who deal with child welfare, unwed mothers, substance abuse, unemployment, housing, etc. Social workers frequently work with hospitals to place patients after discharge from the hospital if there is a specialized need such as a nursing home, etc. A special subdivision of social workers is the psychiatric social worker, who works closely with psychologically or psychiatrically involved patients, frequently working with and as part of the staff of a psychiatrist or psychiatric department in a hospital. Psychiatric social workers ordinarily have a Master's degree in social work which requires an additional one to two years of training beyond certification as a social worker. Social workers must be certified and licensed in the state of practice.

Psychologist

A psychologist is a medically-trained person with a Master's degree who may proceed to a Ph.D. Psychologists, like social workers, function in several areas of society, in industry, in conjunction with psychiatrists, and as independent practitioners. Also like social workers, they may be specific counselors to patients or families in need. Psychologists do not prescribe medication, which subserves some of the functions of a psychiatrist as far as diagnosis and treatment of a psychiatric illness, and often have fields of special interest such as pain control, substance abuse, family relations, or function in industry or commercial field of sales.

A psychologist is different from a psychiatrist; a *psychiatrist* is a medical or osteopathic doctor who has had additional residency training in the field of psychiatry, offers intensive psychiatric care for the patient, prescribes medication, and performs invasive procedures when indicated. These are not part of the training or the prerogative of the psychologist.

Vocational Rehabilitation Specialist

This is an individual with specialized training after a college degree in the field of vocational rehabilitation, with either a Master's degree or Ph.D. in the field, licensed by the state of practice. His or her function is to work with the patient and with industry in training, retraining, or facilitating the training of patients in need of a job change or skill training. These specialists subserve several groups, frequently as a government employee in one of their rehabilitative programs. They may also work in a specialized pain clinic group or other rehabilitation groups to facilitate rehabilitation of the impaired person during the process of post-injury or post-illness rehabilitative treatment.

D.D.S.

A dentist requires four years of dental school after completion of four years of college, and certification and licensure in the state of practice. Often a dentist will specialize in oral surgery, orthodontics, etc. The dentist is frequently involved in trauma situations, is called on to make a diagnosis, to perform treatment for the effects of an injury, to have a prognosis, and to participate in impairment evaluation of the injured person.

R.N.

A registered nurse is an individual who has completed high school and has participated in one of several methods of obtaining an R.N. These involve a college degree, nursing school training sufficient to meet state requirements (three years on the average), and then completion of state board examination, certifying him or her as a registered nurse. Persons with less academic training may qualify as LPNs or nurses' aides.

§4.32 What the Public Thinks of Physicians

It appears that most Americans feel that doctors "don't play fair." They do not explain themselves, in their opinion, because they feel doctors think that they do not need to. Also, there is a strong feeling that doctors are paid too much and contribute minimally to society and to charity, contrary to doctors' behavior 50 years ago.[19]

§4.33 Why Are Physicians Not Doing Well?

A recent review of what is going on with medical practice, particularly orthopedic practice, should be illuminating to orthopedists who realize that medical practice now is much different than it was 15 years ago.

Common doctor-to-doctor talk embraces comments that the climate of medical practice is "pretty bleak." The health atmosphere is changing; the government and lawyers seem to be increasingly taking over, and it is coming to light that something is going on that may or may not lie within the doctor's control—that the real dangers lie not "in the stars," but within the physician him- or herself—the natural human limitations of the physician and in the nature of our society. What is happening to physicians today is not and has not been something we can control—certainly not alone. No group of professionals could be expected to predict and control outcomes of the last 50 years of fantastic scientific and technological growth in medical diagnosis and treatment. This progress was achieved in a climate of massive increases in federal reimbursement, legislation, and litigation. This has progressively eroded the control that physicians have enjoyed in the past.

How does society perceive the physician? The orthopedist? It depends on where you look, what you are looking for, and who is doing the looking.

The Jobs Rated Almanac ranks the "best and worst" jobs using 12 criteria in terms of working conditions, and considers doctors as having chosen (out of the 250 occupations ranked) one of the 10 worst occupations in America, a status achieved "almost exclusively on emotional factors." Physicians are seen as having one of the five most stressful jobs; on a scale of one to 250, with one being easy, doctors rank 247, suffering less than astronauts, "Indy" racers, and firefighters.

In another study, the surgeon was not in the top 10 or even in the top 50 per cent of the "big picture." Hospital administrators are considered to have one of the most desirable jobs in America.

The media—movies and television—in the last 50 years has portrayed the doctor as individualistic, rational, and intelligent; possessing drive, exhibiting strong clinical skills, their work being the central part of their lives, and being greatly admired by other characters in the drama. Television, in particular, portrays the physician as being superhuman, a one-man band who single-handedly makes the diagnosis, determines the treatment, does the surgery, visits the patient at home, provides virtually all the emotional

---

[19] Brodie, *What the Public Thinks About Doctors,* 70A JBJ Surg 1119 (1988).

support to patients and their families, supervises the hospital nursing staff, and provides around-the-clock surveillance. It is easy to see why the American public is disenchanted when faced with the physician as he or she really is. The 1988 AMA Survey of Physicians and Public Opinion on Health Care Issues states that over one-half of the 1,500 surveyed felt that they (the patient) should be more involved in the diagnosis, and particularly the treatment plan. In other words, doctors are not communicating enough with their patients. One-third of those surveyed said that "doctors act like they are better than other people" and are "arrogant."[20]

§4.34 Physician Attitudes About Lying to Patients

"The man who wishes to make a profession of goodness," Machiavelli wrote, "must necessarily come to grief in a world where so many are not good."

In a recent survey of 407 practicing physicians, attitudes toward the use of deception in medicine was addressed. A questionnaire was used, seeking responses to difficult ethical questions potentially resolvable by deception, and asking general questions about attitudes and practices. Fifty-two per cent of the physicians responded. The majority indicated a willingness to misrepresent a screening test as a diagnostic test to secure an insurance payment and to allow the wife of a patient with gonorrhea to be misled about her husband's diagnosis if it were believed necessary to insure his treatment and to preserve a marriage. One-third indicated they would offer incomplete or misleading information to a patient's family if a mistake led to a patient's death. Very few physicians would deceive a mother to avoid revealing an adolescent daughter's pregnancy. When forced to make difficult ethical choices, most physicians indicated some willingness to engage in forms of deception. They appear to justify their decisions in terms of the consequences and to place a higher value on patient welfare and keeping patient confidences than telling the truth for its own sake. The American Medical Association's Principles of Ethics enjoins physicians to "deal honestly with patients and colleagues" without offering specifications. The American College of Physicians Ethics Manual advises physicians to act "with sensitivity and without duplicity" when forced to serve conflicting interests. These

---

[20] Surveys of Physicians and Public Opinion on Health Care Issues. American Medical Association 1, 15, 28 Chicago (1988); Charles, *A Comparative Analysis of Nurse and Physician Characters in the Entertainment Media,* 11 J Adv Nursing 179 (1986); L. Krantz, The Jobs Rated Almanac 3, 17, 225, 337, 339, 340 (1988); Wolf, *Conflict Between Doctor and Patient: A Review of Thinking by Jay Katz,* 16 Law Med Health Care 197 (1988); Meisel, *A "Dignitary Tort" as a Bridge Between the Idea of Informed Consent and the Law of Informed Consent,* 16 Law, Med Health Care 210 (1988); W. Osle, The Evolution of Modern Medicine Lectures Delivered at Yale University on the Sillman Foundation, Apr 1913 (1921).

documents do not discuss deception as a separate issue or emphasize telling the truth as an overriding moral imperative.[21]

§4.35 When Should a Physician Retire?

If a physician stops reading as soon as he or she closes the last examination book, he or she does not belong in front of patients at age 40 any more than at age 65. The brain, unlike the rotator cuff of the shoulder, does not wear out at age 33 or age 73. The currently-educated physician in good physical health does not need to retire at 60 to 65 years of age unless he or she wishes. Forced retirements by society stigma, bias, and economic threat are simply wrong. "The mind is a terrible thing to lose or sacrifice."[22]

§4.36 Quality of Care

In assessing quality of care, medical peer review groups have become a standard that physicians use to evaluate physicians. A medical peer review system that claims to adequately measure quality of care must be based on an adequate definition of quality.

Quality in a metaphysical sense is identical with properties of the object and does not imply preference. In contrast, quality in a preferential sense is identical not with the properties of an object but rather with the capacity of the properties to achieve a goal, this goal being a state of affairs that is preferred to other states. The highest quality medical care is that care that best achieves legitimate medical and nonmedical goals. These goals are set by the patient with the help of his or her physician. Medical goals are determined by the nature of the patient's illness and nonmedical goals by the need of the physician and the patient to maintain an acceptable relationship. (*See* Appendix 4-1, Case 13.)

The hospital chart review does not give the reviewer a complete assessment of quality. Nonmedical goals are rarely stated in the hospital or other medical record so that the peer review process may miss the fact that some unstated goals were met and others were not. The quality of care will be improved if patient and physician goals are mutually understood and pursued. The physician and patient must first discuss and agree on goals; second,

---

[21] Novack, *Physician's Attitudes Toward Using Deception to Resolve Difficult Ethical Problems,* 261 JAMA 2980 (1989); Connelly & DalleMura, *Ethical Problems in the Medical Office,* 260 JAMA 812 (1988); S. Bok, Lying—Moral Choice in Public and Private Life (1978); Weir, *Truth Telling in Medicine,* Perspect Biol Med 195 (Autumn 1980); Salzman, *Truth, Honesty and the Therapeutic Process,* 130 Am J Psychiat 1281 (1973); J. Katz, The Silent World of the Doctor and Patient (1984); Ad Hoc Committee on the Medical Ethics, *American College of Physicians Ethics Manual,* 101 Ann Int Med 129 (1984); Faden, *Disclosure of Information to Patients in Medical Care,* 19 Med Care 718 (1981).

[22] Silk & AMN Staff, *Senior Physicians Need Not Rush Into Retirement,* Amer Med News, July 14, 1989, at 28.

these goals must be recorded. In this connection, it is suggested that the standard history include a section on values that address such critical issues as the living will, resuscitation, religious beliefs that may influence medical care, and access to information. The list of goals will vary from patient to patient and physician to physician. Few physicians address these issues. It is a difficult and painful task to examine some of them and determine what values, if any, we have concerning them. Socrates said, "life without . . . examination is not worth living."

For many, quality is a "portmanteau concept." A portmanteau "carries a great many things, keeps them in no particular order, and does so in such a way as to conceal the contents."[23]

§4.37 Payment of Medical Bills

Medical claims for payment and a failure to authorize payment for care that was medically necessary would give rise to a cause of action against the utilization review system. In *Wickline v State,* 228 Cal Rptr 661, 670 (1986), *appeal denied,* 741 P2d 613, 239 Cal Rptr 805 (1987), *cert denied,* 484 US 1043 (1988), it was held:

> The patient who requires treatment and who is harmed when care which should have been provided is not provided should recover injuries suffered from all those responsible for the deprivation of such care, including, when appropriate, health care payers. Third party payers of health care services can be legally accountable when medically inappropriate decisions result from defects in the design or implementation of cost containment mechanisms as, for example, when appeals made on a patient's behalf for medical or hospital care are arbitrarily ignored or unreasonably disregarded or overridden. However, the physician who complies without protest with the limitations imposed by a third party payer, when his medical judgment dictates otherwise, cannot avoid his ultimate responsibility for his patient's care. He cannot point to the health care payer as the liability scapegoat when the consequences of his own determinative medical decisions go sour.

This seems to place a duty of advocacy on the physician. The physician who complies with the limitation made by a third party payer "without protest" has a direct obligation and liability to the patient.

This rule poses a duty of advocacy on the attending physician by the court. A physician who complies with a limitation imposed by a third party "with protest" has a direct obligation and liability to the patient. Medical schools

---

[23] *Council on Medical Service: Quality of Care,* 256 JAMA 1032 (1986). A. Donabedian, The Definition of Quality and Approaches to its Assessment 3, 5, 22-24, 27 (1980); Rutstein, *Measuring the Quality of Medical Care,* 294 NEJM 582 (1976); T.S. Beauchamp & J.F. Childress, Principles of Biomedical Ethics (3d ed 1989); Steffen, *Quality Medical Care,* 260 JAMA 56 (1988).

should institute courses for students in effective advocacy before utilization review tribunals. Courts have held that the system for reviewing medical necessity was "properly structured" because that system was based on an assumption that a conscientious physician would appeal all erroneous decisions by the lower levels of utilization review process.

§4.38 Continuing Medical Education

The medical community has taken an increased interest in improving the skills and competence of the physician. Continuing medical education is required in one form or another in most states and/or medical specialties. Recertification is another tool used. The malpractice lawsuit itself is a stimulus for better medical practice methods. Emphasis on patient participation—an expansion of informed consent—improves medical care. The nearly universal acceptance by jurists of national (rather than community) standards of medical care may be a protection to the practitioner. Iatrogenic (physician caused) injury or disease continues to be a significant problem. Some studies have shown that newly acquired medical knowledge does not necessarily improve patient care, the test coming in its use in a clinical setting. The plaintiff bar thus argues that the tort liability system would accomplish its social purpose if it could have both encouragement of continuing medical education and act as an accountability mechanism to insure that medical knowledge—newly learned and prior known—is applied in acute clinical settings. (*See* Appendix 4-1, Cases 14 to 16.)

§4.39 Quality of Physical Examination

In a study of the quality of physical examinations performed by interns and resident physicians in training, some striking results were obtained. Direct observation with medical students, interns, and residents showed errors in examinations with decreasing frequency with each added year of medical education, although errors in the final years were significant. Errors were made by the house staff in two-thirds of patients examined even though the house staff knew they were being evaluated. The resident with the best score made examination errors in one-third of the tests. Emphasis was made that those errors were not minor and that their correction frequently lead to changes in differential diagnosis and treatment. More emphasis of physical diagnosis is common at all levels of medical education at this time. Certainly, it is appropriate for the third party evaluating a medical report or related document to be aware and question the physical examination.[24]

---

[24] *Continuing Medical Education: A Dynamic Decade,* 243 JAMA 21 (1980); 80th Annual Report on Medical Education in the United States, 243 JAMA 2801 (1980); *Continuing Education Courses for Physicians,* 243 JAMA 1983 (1980); Praiss, *Cost Containment through Medical Education,* 244 JAMA 1 (1980); Race, *Continuing Medical Education. Current Legal Implications,* 1 J Legal Med 312 (1979); Trunet,

§4.40 Adverse Hospital Events

The majority of adverse hospital events are unrelated to lack of medical knowledge or failure to keep updated as to clinical advances. These adverse events are caused by ordinary mistakes or oversights, by the assumption that critical duties were performed by others, by distraction and disruptions, and by the dangerous casual attitude that can accompany repetitive chores.

A single act of negligence may create an event that is actionable, but obviously does not necessarily label the doctor negligent. Presumably, the negligent doctor is one who is negligent too often. The phrase "dangerous casualness" is relevant. Actionable events occur most often when health care providers are dealing with high-risk repetitive matters and allow themselves to become careless or preoccupied. Better trained physicians who limit their practice to areas they are very familiar with and do not become "too busy" have less likelihood of neglect with patient injury resulting. This is also true of physicians who keep abreast of current diagnostic and treatment modalities. The practice of medicine typically has good and bad days prone to repetitiveness resulting in "dangerous casualness." Minimizing human (physician) error would seem to depend on a combination of constant awareness along with an effective accountability mechanism. (*See* Appendix 4-1, Cases 17 to 46.)

Often, the physician is charged with poorly advising a patient or with conveying inaccurate advice as to patient care. Communication is a frequent problem, with the physician feeling that he or she has conveyed proper and sufficient information or advice and the patient disagreeing or perhaps at times not hearing or understanding. Written instructions are often used by physicians to avoid these allegations. Figure I is a typical good tool for emergency department patients. (*See* Appendix 4-1, Cases 47 to 68.)

The malpractice attorney is trained to analyze individual cases, rather than evaluate trends in cases. Insurance companies statistically evaluate risk; that is, which adverse events cost the most money. It is obvious that equally competent physicians are not equal insurance risks, depending more on the type of medical care problem involved.

§4.41 Referral

There is no physician duty to consult with a specialist on every potential complication in diagnosis or treatment. The duty to recommend and effect consultation depends on whether the physician knows or should know that the services of a specialist are required (following the standard of care philosophy). The physician must fully disclose all material information to allow

---

The Role of Iatrogenic Disease in Admissions to Intensive Care, 244 JAMA 23 (1980); Pinkerton, *Resident Physician Performance in a Continuing Education Format. Does Newly Acquired Knowledge Improve Patient Care?,* 244 JAMA 19 (1980); Wray & Friendland, *Detection and Correction of House Staff Error in Physical Diagnosis,* 249 JAMA 8 (1983); H.F. Wachsmand & S.E. Pegalis, American Law of Medical Malpractice 16 (Supp 1986).

the patient to make a reasonable decision whether to see another physician or specialist. It has been held that failure to make appropriate referral can only constitute negligence if referral would have resulted in treatment that would have produced a better result.

At times, there is a question as to the liability of the referring physician after the referral is made. There is authority that no joint duty exists between the practitioners that would hold the referring physician liable for the negligence of the specialist. However, the referring physician can be liable in making a referral to a physician who is unable to provide required care. The referring physician is held to know the impairments of a physician or hospital, whether the physician is competent in the areas of the patient's problems, and whether the physician is in adequate health and not incompetent by age, substance abuse, or mental illness. It has been held that the referring physical has a continuing duty to supervise the care of a patient following the referral to a specialist. (*See* Appendix 4-1, Cases 7 and 69 to 79.)

§4.42 Curbstone Consultations

> An Attorney or a physician who gives curbstone advice when it is requested by one who is not a client or patient is required only to give an honest answer. But where the representation, although in itself gratuitous, is made in the course of the defendant's business or professional relations, a duty is usually found.
>
> —C.W. Prosser, The Law of Torts, §107 at 706 (4th ed 1971)

In curbstone consultation situations, the courts are most likely to find a duty when gratuitous advice is given as part of a patient-professional activity. If friends or relatives of a patient have their own health adversely affected by erroneous information, a duty would exist on the part of the physician. A physician probably would not be responsible for telephone advice given to a nonpatient, but said doctor should avoid conduct that might be interpreted as a diagnosis.[25]

§4.43 Measuring Physician Performance

Orthopedists are beginning to look at and change their selection and evaluation processes when choosing and assessing other physicians. It is important that such evaluations not embrace a punitive tone without cause, or create an adversarial atmosphere and resentment or fear, as cooperation of the individuals will diminish. The method should increase performance and enhance education, leading to improved patient care.

The principal guidelines for determining and evaluating a physician are whether or not he or she is effective or ineffective in managing significant

---

[25] Stevens, *The Physicians Liability for Gratuitous Advice,* Med Trial Tech Quart, Summer 1980, at 99.

medical incidents. Effectiveness is defined as that quality from which others should copy and learn. Ineffective actions are those which lead to questioning motives, actions, behavior, and techniques of the physician, whether the result was good or bad. It is the act or incident evaluated as "We can learn from that and do it his way" or "There are better ways to do it, and I can tell you why." One university uses a model for evaluating medical professional personnel as follows:[26]

1. Conscientiousness
2. Recognition of individual limits
3. Confidence
4. The ability to handle a crisis
5. Integration of learned knowledge with the event and practice
6. Technical skills
7. Relationships with other physicians and patients
8. The ethics of an action or inaction
9. Others

For cases in which lack of diligence in orthopedic evaluation, treatment, or follow-up was alleged, (*See* Appendix 4-1, Cases 13 and 80 to 89.)

§4.44 Risks and Errors in Judgment

In trends where insurance companies evaluate risk, it is obvious that equally competent physicians are not equal insurance risks.

Most valid medical malpractice cases occur as a result of ordinary mistakes and oversights. A single act of negligence should not label the doctor as being "negligent." The definition of a negligent doctor is perhaps one who is negligent too often. The phrase "dangerous casualness" is one that is relevant and applicable. Dangerous casualness seems to occur most frequently among doctors who deal with repetitive high-risk circumstances. The better trained the physician or health care provider, the less likelihood there is for negligence. Physicians who limit the nature of their medical work and their patient load are less likely to be involved in malpractice litigation. The same is true for those physicians who keep current as to medical techniques and treatment modalities. Medical practice, however, is carried out by human beings who are prone to have good days and bad days, prone to distractions and disruptions, and prone to casualness with regard to repetitive routine. Minimizing human error depends on a combination of constant awareness along with appropriate accountability mechanisms.

The physician is not liable if he or she exercises the appropriate care but makes an error of judgment resulting in injury. If there are alternative

[26] Morton, *Duties of the Physician.* Presented at the American Academy of Legal Medicine Meeting, Oklahoma City, Okla (Oct 1989).

methods of treatment that are accepted by the profession, and the physician chooses one over another and the patient has been adequately informed, it is not a deviation from the standard of care. The physician gives the patient the benefit of his or her best judgment and cannot be liable for a "bad result" if that judgment is equal to that employed by other physicians in similar cases. The mere fact that another physician would have chosen another treatment plan is insufficient cause to hold the defendant liable. A general defense to medical malpractice actions where injuries occurred due to honest error of judgment is sound. This does not apply if the mistake constituted negligence. The failure to perform tests which would have permitted proper diagnosis, where the physician ignored the results of other tests and failed to refer the case, is not an error in judgment. The physician must use sound judgment and skill in the treatment of patients, and must possess and have access to medical knowledge customarily possessed by competent physicians so as to have a proper basis on which to base his or her judgment.

Problems often arise related to the manner in which the court instructs the jury on nonliability for an "error in judgment." The court should find the physician not liable for injuries arising out of error in judgment where he or she has exercised the requisite degree of care and skill in arriving at that judgment. The problem arises where the court adds the word "honest"—creating an "honest error in judgment." Such instructions have been found argumentative. It is also improper to add the words "good faith" to the error of judgment. The instruction can only be given after a factual basis for the error of judgment has been established by the evidence. At this stage, "honest" and "good faith" are unrelated to fact.

Often, there are two or more ways to diagnose or treat a problem. With expert testimony, the physician charged with a negligent error of judgment can successfully defend by showing "two schools of thought."

Failure to refer a patient as dictated by the applicable standard of care is a frequent charge levied against orthopedists whose patients are allegedly injured by that failure.

§4.45 The Bad or Unfortunate Result

A major problem facing the surgeon defending a lawsuit is that sometimes out of sympathy for the plaintiff a jury will assess liability when the evidence does not support malpractice. A jury can erroneously equate a bad result with negligence. By imposing liability based on bad results, even if reasonable care has been demonstrated through the use of an expert witness, the jury is tempted to impose a strict liability standard on the surgeon. The surgeon's best defense is finding and using the best available expert witness. (*See* Appendix 4-1, Cases 90 to 96, and 98.)

Consistent with the concept that the physician does not guarantee or warrant that he or she will effect a cure, the physician cannot be held liable merely because of a bad result. It must be shown that the physician's conduct failed to meet the standard of care. Negligence on the part of the physician is not inferred by a poor result.

The physician cannot insure the success of diagnosis and treatment, nor is he or she held to the highest degree of care known to the profession. The mere fact that he or she has failed to effect a cure or that his or her diagnosis and/or treatment have been detrimental to the patient's health does not raise a presumption of negligence. The plaintiff must establish not only that the defendant violated the applicable standard of care and was negligent, but that negligent acts constituted a proximate cause of the injury. The law does not require the plaintiff to prove to a certainty that the patient would have lived had he or she received more prompt diagnosis and treatment for the condition causing death.[27] (*See* Appendix 4-1, Cases 98 to 103.)

§4.46 Physician's Duty in Child Abuse Cases

The responsibility of a treating physician to treat, and then to report to proper authorities, cases of child or elder abuse is clear. Most large cities have medical examiners offices that have a protocol to ascertain child abuse deaths, but their reporting to authorities is "too late" in most abuse cases. Treating doctors are embarrassed in reporting and fear they might be mistaken, leading to another area of potential personal litigation. Some states, notably California, have developed a multidisciplinary protocol for the investigation of suspicious deaths that makes the personal element easier, but only in death cases.

Records show that in the last decade 11.2 per cent of child abuse cases are reported by physicians, although all states have laws requiring reporting. Many physicians, seeing few child abuse cases, lack confidence in making the diagnosis. The orthopedist often sees children with fractures that are difficult to explain and often should do a bone survey looking for other healed fractures. He or she is in better position to verify abuse suspicions. Many large hospitals have "second opinion" pain physicians ready to help in verification and reporting.

The conscientious physician has no trouble reporting known abuse; the big hindrance is the uncertainty of the fact of abuse.[28] (*See* Appendix 4-1, Cases 104 to 106.)

§4.47 Surgical Skills

A study was carried out at Peter Bent Brigham Hospital and Harvard Medical School, reviewing and identifying adverse outcomes due to error during care in general surgery. In two-thirds of the cases, the mishap was due to an unnecessary, defective, or inappropriate operative procedure. In attempt-

---

[27] Morton, *Duties of the Physician,* Presented at the American Academy of Legal Medicine Meeting, Oklahoma City, Okla (Oct 1989).

[28] Zylke, *Medical News and Perspectives: Child Abuse Problem Demands Much of Physician but Also of the Community and Its Officials,* 261 JAMA 2930, 2931 (1989); Krugman, Editorial, Child Abuse, 320 NEJM 531 (1989).

ing to identify the origin of the surgical errors, many facets were present and were recurrent. All of these factors were familiar to the experienced clinician. Leading the list was misplaced optimism. This took the form of misreading the early signs of peritonitis after colonic surgery (overestimating skill and underestimating the patient's fragility). A second common source of error appeared to be an unwarranted sense of urgency. The third source was the urge for perfection resulting in a wide-ranging operative manipulation considerably beyond the level needed for the relief of the patients's most important problem. A fourth error was referred to as "vogue therapy," with the performance of new, stylish procedures that have prestigious appeal. The predominant fallibility appears to be insufficient restraint and deliberation. Excessive haste, impatience, overconfidence, and inadequate peer group consultation were important influences in this regard.

The study recommended that hospitals continue to develop comprehensive methods to identify and prevent these events. Often, a distinction can be made between error in judgment (an error related to flawed reasoning) and error of negligence (error related to inattention or lack of obligatory effort). British courts separated the two situations, allowing malpractice to stand only on the error of negligence. American courts tend to combine the two, although in common law follow the British rule. It is often difficult to separate the two. (*See* Appendix 4-1, Cases 107 to 110.)

It has been repeatedly shown that surgeons who do a large volume of a particular operation have better results, fewer complications, and happier patients. Hospitals that have surgeons doing a large volume of a particular operation seem able to give better surgeon assistance and better postoperative care. Typical examples include open heart surgery, total hip or knee arthroplasties, spinal surgery, and hand and foot operations.

In one survey of 2,600 hospital admissions undergoing a surgical procedure, an evaluating group found that 36 injuries due to medical negligence occurred. These fell into two categories; undue haste in recommending the operation as opposed to further conservative care, and technical misadventures. Vogue surgeries seemed to have a higher complication rate.[29] (*See* Appendix 4-1, Cases 11, 62, and 111 to 145.)

§4.48 What is Board-Certified?

Physician advertising or letterheads identifying the physician as an expert witness, or physician self-credentialling in depositions as an expert witness is proscribed by most state licensing boards. Using "board-certified" as a cre-

---

[29] Garnick, *Surgeon Volume vs Hospital Volume: Which Matters More,* 262 JAMA 547 (1989); Couch, *The Cost of Misadventures in Colonic Surgery: A Model for the Analysis of Adverse Outcomes in Standard Procedures,* 135 M J Surg 64 (1978); Couch, *The High Cost of Low Frequency Events: The Anatomy and Economics of Surgical Mishaps,* 304 NEJM 634 (1981); Luft & Enthoven, *Should Operations be Regionalized? The Empirical Relation Between Surgical Volume and Mortality,* 301 NEJM 1364 (1979).

dential is similarly proscribed unless the board certification is given by a member of the American Board of Medical Examiners. This board represents 23 boards:

American Board of Allergy and Immunology
American Board of Anesthesiology
American Board of Colon and Rectal Surgery
American Board of Dermatology
American Board of Emergency Medicine
American Board of Family Practice
American Board of Internal Medicine
American Board of Neurological Surgery
American Board of Nuclear Medicine
American Board of Obstetrics and Gynecology
American Board of Ophthalmology
American Board of Orthopedic Surgery
American Board of Otolaryngology
American Board of Pathology
American Board of Pediatrics
American Board of Physical Medicines and Rehabilitation
American Board of Plastic Surgery
American Board of Preventative Medicine
American Board of Psychiatry and Neurology
American Board of Radiology
American Board of Surgery
American Board of Thoracic Surgery
American Board of Urology

Associate members include:

American Hospital Association
American Medical Association
Association of Medical Colleges
Council of Medical Specialty Societies
Federation of State Medical Boards of United States
National Board of Medical Examiners

There are many other credible medical specialty organizations that certify some of their members on completion of special training and expertise and passing peer reviews. They are given examinations, along with periodic recertification.

Orthopedists, as has been mentioned before, are regulated by local custom and by state board of licensure policy as to advertisement. Each state society should be consulted as to advertising policy. In general, the policy will permit a recitation of specialty board memberships. All certifications are recited with strict honesty as to the skill and procedures represented. False advertising is absolutely prohibited.

§4.49 Peer Review

A professional review performed to evaluate the conduct of a physician results in a "professional review action." This review is defined as a determination of whether a physician should be granted or allowed to maintain staff privileges based on the physician's competence and professional conduct. The competence and professional conduct of an individual physician refers to that conduct which affects or could affect adversely the health or welfare of a patient or patients and which could adversely affect the clinical privileges or the membership in a professional society by a physician. A professional review action also includes a formal decision of a professional review body not to take an action or make a recommendation.

The Health Care Quality Improvement Act of 1986 protects physicians who engage in peer review from the threat of lawsuits provided the peer review is done in good faith. The Act protects those involved with peer review if the professional action has been taken in the following manner:

1. In the reasonable belief that action was in the furtherance of the quality of health care
2. After reasonable effort to obtain the facts of the matter at hand
3. After adequate notice and a hearing are afforded to the affected physician or after such other procedures as are fair to the physician under the circumstances
4. In the reasonable belief that the action was warranted by the facts known

The Peer Review Process must follow fairness in due process and not violate a person's civil rights. An objective and fair credentialling system provides the physician under review an opportunity for a fair hearing process to permit him or her to defend against allegations that he or she feels are unjustified. The Health Care Quality Improvement Act of 1986 specifically provides that the professional review action will be presumed to have met these standards unless the presumption is rebutted by the affected physician based on a preponderance of the evidence. It does seem to assume that the physician is guilty until proven innocent.

Physicians who participate in peer review are immune from suit as long as the above guides are followed. This is guaranteed by the federal law of

November 1986. This immunity does not apply to information collected that is untrue and communicated with malicious intent or to actions based on discrimination. (*See* Appendix 4-1, Case 4.)

In *Patrick v Burget,* 800 F2d 1498 (9th Cir 1986), *revd,* 486 US 94, *rehg denied,* 487 US 1243, *remand,* 852 F2d 1241 (9th Cir 1988), the Supreme Court ruled that hospital peer review committees are not absolutely immune from federal antitrust suits under a state action defense. In this case, the motive of the action was anticompetitive in nature and not based on quality care.

§4.50 Peer Review Organization Oversight of Physicians

Peer Review Organizations (PROs), which look over the shoulders of physicians caring for Medicare's 31 million patients, are turning toward greater standardization regarding acceptable medical care. Under new rules set up by the Health Care Financing Administration (HCFA), Medicare PROs must keep a detailed quality profile on individual physicians and hospitals. The profiles are required in a job description or "scope of work" in effect by all the PROs. The rules require PROs to assign numerical severity ratings to each quality problem they detect and to identify the responsible hospital or physician for each case.

Scorecards would be kept on each hospital and physician, with certain scores triggering specific reactions by the PRO, resulting in recommendations for education, intensified review, notification to state boards, sanctioning, etc.[30]

§4.51 Data Banks

The Health Care Quality Improvement Act, 42 USC §§11101-11152, provides for hospitals to report professional review actions to state agencies; for state agencies, in turn, to report these to a national data bank and to report licensure action; and for insurance companies and health care facilities to report information about malpractice cases where amounts are paid by settlements or judgments.

Professional groups and health care entities will be required to report only adverse actions reached through a formal peer review process, and only when they are based on the practitioner's professional competence or conduct. The report may include only those actions that could adversely affect the health or welfare of the patient. Information must be reported to the data bank within 30 days of the action taken.

The information obtained by the data bank will be made available to licensing boards, hospitals, and other health care entities, and to persons

---

[30] McGinn, *PROs Step Up Watch Over MDs, Hospitals,* AMA Medical News, Jan 6, 1989, at 32.

who are the subject of the report. The latter will be able to find out who is requesting information about them.

According to the rules, all hospitals and health care entities that credential health professionals and have a formal peer review process must check with the data bank before granting clinical privileges and making staff appointments. They must review, every two years, the status of medical staffers and those to whom they have extended clinical privileges.

Attorneys who have filed malpractice claims against a hospital may request information about a specific health practitioner named in the suit. According to regulations, however, they will be given access to the information only if they submit evidence that the hospital failed to request information it was legally required to request from the data bank. Such information can be used by attorneys solely with respect to the malpractice action in question.

Procedures are established whereby health care practitioners can dispute information about themselves in the data bank. The bank secretary will automatically send physicians copies of reports filed about them, which will be held confidential for 30 days before being released to other parties, to allow the person to dispute the information.

According to the regulations, the bank will label information "disputed," stating that it provides "sufficient notice that the report is in question.." The regulations state that they "believe the potential threat to the public of withholding valuable information which may well be accurate is not outweighed by a possible detriment to the subject."

Initially, the data bank will be operated by UNISYS Corporation, funded by a $15.9 million contract. Information requests will be covered by user fees, probably $5.00 for each report. There will be no retroactive reporting.

The National Practitioner Data Bank tracking system for malpractice cases and disciplined physicians was expected to be on line by late 1990. The Department of Health and Human Services has given its final approval to the project under which doctors and dentists who settle or lose a malpractice case or who are censured will be routinely monitored.

Under the law, the health care providers, as well as malpractice insurance companies, must report settlements and liability verdicts. State licensing board officials must consult that data bank when a practitioner moves into their state.

Doctors can no longer move from state to state to escape disciplinary problems with impunity.

However, this may be the basis for the plaintiff's bar to move for disclosure of the data bank information in cases of negligent hiring and failing to properly investigate doctors who are on the attending staff of hospitals and other medical institutions. But the law does not require that the required review entities take any action if they discover that an individual has a poor record. Individual decisions will have to be made based on the facts of each case. The primary records kept in the data bank will be convictions, revocations, and suspensions by state licensing boards and malpractice verdicts and settlements. These, of course, may be matters of public record in each individual state where the action was tried.

Physicians have lobbied against public disclosure of the contents of the data bank because some feel pressured by insurance companies to settle lawsuits even though they feel there is no merit. They feel that the mere inclusion of their names in the bank as being parties to settlement will have an adverse effect on their career advancement, reputation, or ability to move from state to state. There is some merit to this fear. Presently, a consent to settle is not that difficult to obtain under our present system. Doctors are told that the legal significance of a settlement is that no liability is admitted, but the new law may make them more reluctant to settle, thereby creating a logjam in the courts. It may be the civil version of plea bargaining in the criminal courts.

There is merit to both plaintiff and defendant concerns. While consumers have a legitimate interest in knowing the records of the physicians who treat them, doctors also have a legitimate concern that their mere inclusion in the data bank not be an implication that they have been guilty of malpractice. We know that many physicians are sued quite often because of the nature of their practice, the types of patients they treat, or the venues in which they live. While doctors today must recognize that being sued in a case "goes with the territory," many patients may take it as a negative inference.[31]

§4.52 Risk Management

The goal of any individual or organization involved in the defense and/or prevention of the medical malpractice claim is to achieve the most efficient and effective result. That result may best be achieved through the coordinated efforts of the players.

Dramatic changes in the roles of the defendant physician, insurance representatives, and defense counsel are beginning to be made in an effort to achieve better results. The decade of the 1990s will be characterized by a significant increase in the level of participation of the physician in his or her own defense and the defense of others. Insurance representatives are becoming more proficient at investigating and resolving meritorious claims in the earliest stages, thereby reducing costs. Furthermore, insurance carriers are working more closely with defense counsel to contain costs and reduce average file life. The active participation of physicians and carriers is not intended to de-emphasize the role of defense counsel, but to complement it. The new decade will provide counsel with more opportunities to do what they do best—try cases. Fewer and fewer cases will settle on the courthouse steps after several years of preparation.

Each member of the defense team brings to the case a different area of expertise which has, to a great extent, previously been underutilized. Future

---

[31] Robertson, *Keeping Doctors on Their Toes,* 11 Med Malprac Law & Strat 3 (Nov 1989).

claims management methods will require the coordinated input of each individual working toward the same end result.

Risk management for the 1990s will focus largely on the issue of early reporting. The idea that, generally, claims do not improve with age, is a fact which needs to be understood, and this will be presented through educational seminars.

Another major area of interest in risk management is the effect of litigation on the defendant physician. Managing the stress associated with litigation has become a powerful issue for all those involved in the prevention and/or defense of malpractice claims. Numerous physician support groups have been formed as a means of addressing what may be, in certain cases, the most serious impediment to a successful defense.

Even the most coordinated efforts of the defendant physician, insurance carrier, and defense counsel, however, may still not be enough. Codefendants play a major role in the direction and ultimate outcome of a case. For this reason, the spirit of cooperation will extend in the 1990s to hospitals through formal cooperative and/or common defense and risk management programs. The "united defense" phenomenon, another of those elusive goals, is becoming more of a reality.

Various jurisdictions have succeeded in effecting important and vital tort reform; however, in spite of the best efforts, medical malpractice litigation will be a fact of life for several years. The establishment of the defense team for purposes of supsport, education, and expertise is a proven method for survival and success.

§4.53 Social Security Peer Review

At the present time, there are 48 separate places in the Social Security Medicare law where civil penalties may be imposed for noncompliance. The areas in which physicians are vulnerable are:

1. Nonparticipating physician charging a Medicare patient more than the Maximum Actual Allowable Charge (MAAC) limit
2. Failure to provide required notice for nonassigned elective surgeries where the fee will be more than $500
3. Failure to provide the required notice for services that might be declared medically unnecessary
4. Continuing to bill Medicare patients for in-office laboratory tests
5. Knowingly violating the Medicare Assignment Agreement
6. Making a claim to Medicare or Medicaid for services not provided as claimed or making false or fraudulent claims
7. Accepting a payment as an inducement to limit or reduce services to an individual under Medicare or Medicaid

8. Knowingly and willfully failing to furnish a diagnostic code when requesting payment for an item or service provided on assigned claim basis
9. Giving to any person information, with respect to Medicare coverage of inpatient hospital services, that is false or misleading and which could reasonably be expected to influence a hospital discharge

Recently, the Civil Monetary Penalties Law was amended to provide vicarious liability for a doctor's agent's actions.[32]

§4.54 Medical Quacks

Most people have a high priority for good health. Thus, the health field is, and has been, exploited by entrepreneurs who see fortunes to be made, generally by deception. The medical profession is partly to blame in failing to explain frankly the limitations of modern medicine. Many physicians unwittingly allow patients to assume that much more could be done for them, if they could find a miracle worker.

An ethical physician will not make extravagant promises of a cure; the quack has no such compunctions. If the physician would educate his or her patients and the public more thoroughly as to medical limitations, fewer "dupes" would turn to unproven, often dangerous remedies.[33]

§4.55 Physician Turf Wars

Not infrequently, the patient is adversely affected by "physician turf wars." These battles have been waged over the years, involving issues of patient welfare, access, availability and cost resources, economic interests of the doctor, and hospital and quality control. Often, where several medical specialties are competent to treat the same illness or injury, the decision becomes a medical staff—administrative staff decision, and is made without patient input or knowledge. In the era of increasing governmental involvement in the practice of medicine, turf battles are particularly devisive and counterproductive to medical professional stature and may not offer the patient the best care, but care dictated by a politically-ordered health care person.[34]

The same problem exists in the battle of who should treat protruded intervertebral discs (orthopedists, neurosurgeons, physiatrists, etc.), bunions and

---

[32] Kelsay, *Social Security Peer Review,* PLICO News, Jan 1989; M. Gaynes, Civil Money Penalties Reporter (Wilkes, Artis, Hedrick & Lane, 1666 "K" Street N.W., Washington, D.C. 20006)

[33] J. Randi, The Faith Healers (1987).

[34] Nelson, *Humanism and the Art of Medicine,* 262 JAMA 1228 (1989); Zarins, *The Vascular War of 1988: The Enemy is Met,* 261 JAMA 416 (1989); Wexler, *The Vascular War of 1988,* 261 JAMA 418 (1989).

foot surgery (orthopedist, podiatrist), and many other medical problems in which there is overlap in specialist training.

§4.56 Physician Emotional Reactions to Patients

The physician-patient relationship is central to the scientific and humanistic practice of medicine. The physician's contribution to the interaction should be the focus of medical educators who wish to improve this relationship. There is a wide range of physician response to patients; to know which are most troublesome and most persistent should lead to improvement of those behaviors that disrupt the physician-patient relationship. One large study showed that board-certified physicians reported the greatest of emotional reactions when patient behavior or circumstances actively threatened their integrity or self-esteem; the second greatest reaction occurred when undue demands were made on them by patients. These two observations did not decrease as the physician gained more experience. These investigators identified four groups of patients who were viewed negatively by physicians. Among them were patients exhibiting threatening characteristics similar to those who provoked the greatest degree of emotional response. Patients exhibiting several other characteristics also were perceived negatively. These include patients who caused the least degree of emotional reaction (poor historian, use of foreign language, and raising troublesome personal problems). Studies indicate that seasoned, highly-trained physicians harbor strong emotional reactions that may affect physician-patient relationships. It establishes that emotional responses are important considerations and that these emotions and causes must be addressed in medical school and continuing medical education. It is well known that contented patients rarely initiate litigation.

§4.57 Physicians and Dealing with Death

Of all the things a physician must do, telling a patient that he or she is going to die or telling the family that a loved one has expired are two of the most difficult. This task may be even more difficult if questionable medical care is involved in the death. Certainly, the family must be approached honestly, discussing any care problem at any appropriate time. Cover-up and failure to disclose will amplify the family's distrust of the physician. In most death situations, it is important that the doctor and the patient's family realize that modern medicine, with all its technology, is not going to be able to cure all illness or disease. There is little training in medical school to prepare the doctor for informing a family of death; it is mostly on-the-job training and is a test of the moral, ethical, and social background of the patient. Many good doctors agonize over whether they made the right decisions and did the right things. It is often difficult because family members will sometimes turn on the doctor, questioning if there was something else he or she could have done, at the very time the doctor is wondering whether he or she did use the best judgment every step of the way. At times, the dying patient reassures the doctor and smooths the way for his or her demise.[35]

§4.58 Helping a Patient to Terminate Life

The Georgia Superior Court has stated (forcibly) that physicians who help a competent patient terminate his or her life will be immune from prosecution. The case at point was a quadriplegic patient who had petitioned the court to be allowed to unplug his life-support system. His request was found consistent with a competent informed consent and his right to control his life. This decision, in relation to doctors, was to allow them to sedate the patient, smoothing his demise. The court held that patients have a right to refuse life-saving treatments when competent and fully informed. (*See* Chapter 6.)[36]

§4.59 Definition of Death

The President's Commission for the Study of Ethical Problems in Medicine and Biomedical and Behavioral Research (1981) has set the following guidelines for determination of death. Initially noting that an individual with irreversible cessation of circulatory and respiratory function is dead, the Commission emphasizes that cessation is recognized by an appropriate clinical examination which reveals, at least, absence of heart beat, respiratory effort, or other evidence of responsiveness. Irreversibility is evidenced by persistent cessation of these functions during an appropriate period of observation.

> With respect to brain death, that is, irreversible cessation of all functions of the entire brain, including brain stem, the President's Commission provides the following guidance: cessation is recognized when clinical evaluation discloses absence of cerebral function (receptivity and unresponsivity) and absence of brain stem function (absence of reflexes); irreversibility is recognized when an evaluation discloses that the cause of the coma is sufficient to account for loss of brain function, the possibility of recovery of any such function is excluded, and cessation of brain function persists for an appropriate length of time based on the observation.

Patients faced with a major loss, which is true of most who have been severely injured or those with a terminal illness, typically respond in a predictable psychological manner, known as the five stages of grief described by Elizabeth Kübler-Ross in Death and Dying.

---

[35] Gray, *They Shoot Horses That Have This,* Med Econ, Sept 4, 1989, at 61.

[36] *MDs Permitted to Help Patients End Life Support,* 12 Orthopedic Legal Letter 1, 6 (Nov-Dec 1989).

The first stage is denial and isolation. The first reaction may be a temporary state of shock from which the patient recuperates over time. Most people react to the first discovery of a terminal illness with the statement "No, not me, it can't be true." Most patients occasionally use denial as a buffer after unexpected shocking news to allow the patient to collect him- or herself and utilize other, less-radical defenses. Most usually, it is temporary and is replaced by partial acceptance.

Along with the partial acceptance come the feelings of anger, envy, and resentment—the second stage of grief. At this time, the question becomes "Why me?" This stage may be even more difficult to cope with, as anger is directed in all directions of the environment at random. Friends and relatives may have a hard time understanding the patient and should place themselves in the patient's position to comprehend his or her feelings.

Bargaining is the third stage. Because patients are unable to accept their destiny by denial and then by anger toward people and God, perhaps success will come by making some agreement that might postpone the inevitable. Most bargains are made with God and are usually kept a secret or are mentioned between the lines or in a chaplain's private office. Dr. Kübler-Ross reported over 200 interviews with dying patients and said none of them "kept their promise."

The fourth stage of grief is depression, both reactive and preparatory. When the patient can no longer deny illness and is forced to have more surgery or to be hospitalized, begins to have more symptoms, becomes weaker, and loses weight, he or she cannot "smile it off" anymore. Numbness, anger, and rage are replaced by a sense of great loss, loss of physical well-being and possibly loss of finances and/or job. Understanding the patient's depression and trying to encourage the patient of what may be unrealistic guilt or shame is possible during this depressive state. Preparatory depression occurs when the patient realizes his or her impending losses—everything and everybody he loves. If the patient is allowed to express his or her feelings of sorrow to family and friends, final acceptance will be easier for him or her.

The fifth and final stage of grief is acceptance. Eventually, after passing through the first four stages, the patient will reach a point where he or she is neither depressed nor angry about his or her "fate." It is a feeling of apathy. The patient will be tired and weak, but feels that the struggle is over and that "there comes a time for the final rest before the long journey," as one person described it. Although the patient finds peace and acceptance, interest in surroundings lessens. He or she may want to be left alone, or at least not bothered about distressing news or the problems of others, and if he the patient does have visitors, he or she may not want to talk.

§4.60 What Physicians Think About Physicians

In a recent spot check of more than 400 physicians, one of the requests was how doctors mishandle patients, often to the detriment of the medical profession. Answers ranged from the rather innocent (doctors fail to understand a patient's complaint) to childish vindictiveness (a pediatrician phoned parents about their child's lab report at 2 A.M. because he felt he had been harassed by them). Other responses were: "Doctors often don't communicate with their patients." "Some think they're God." "Most keep patients waiting too long." "Many don't empathize." "Some are plain insensitive. A few are unprofessional. Others are money-hungry."

These responses suggest two keys to good patient relationships for the physician. One is communication. Half of the battle is won if done properly. Most patients want to get along with their doctors, and will cut more slack than they deserve—providing they listen, and keep them tuned in to what the doctor is thinking and doing.

The other key is empathy—putting the doctor in the patient's place, recognizing the patient's needs as he or she perceives them and attending to them. The patient may not know to ask, but may well need help, understanding, respect, strength, reassurance, confidence, hope, or even just a dry shoulder, and it is up to the doctor to provide it. The most common physician faux pas in patient handling are discussed below.

Insensitivity

A surgeon, after removing a bowel obstruction, met with the patient's family to discuss the prognosis. In an ill-considered attempt to relieve tension, he joked "They shoot horses that have this." Insensitivity is probably the easiest interpersonal offense to commit—even when intentions are the very best. "Boy, how unfortunate," another doctor reportedly said to his pregnant, unmarried patient. "You must be miserable."

Another doctor who, after examining a patient, stated "You look as if you have cancer" then went to order studies, leaving the patient to deal with his shock by himself. Another recalls a colleague who, on finding breast cancer, told the patient bluntly "That has to come off." To any patient, learning of cancer is devastating. But sometimes, especially with a cancer, a medical problem can so preoccupy a doctor that he or she forgets that the "problem" is also a person. Sometimes, though, insensitivity is the result of less forgivable carelessness. A patient, waiting for her 2 P.M. appointment, overheard her doctor saying to a colleague "I've got to tell my 2 o'clock she's got lung cancer."

One respondent, a specialist who sees about 25 new referral patients daily, admits he grows weary of introducing himself and making small talk over and over again. "So sometimes I skip it, and get right to business" he explains. "I can't blame those patients if they think I'm a cold fish."

One doctor reportedly frightened the mother of a patient when he said, with some exasperation, "There is nothing, not a damn thing, wrong with your child."

Inconsideration

Over the years, probably nothing has done more to damage the medical profession's image than keeping patients waiting. One patient told another doctor about her own doctor: "An appointment for 1 o'clock means he'll see me at 2:30, but only if I get there at 1 and wait. If my appointment is for 1 and I get there at 2:30, then he'll see me at 4." Some physicians get so tied up with their various hospital duties that on some days they do not show up at the office at all. In past decades, patients tended to swallow this sort of waiting game. Today they are far more likely to figure "Hey, I'm paying this guy; I don't have to take this garbage."

Unprofessionalism

The public has traditionally granted almost reverential deference to doctors. But in return, patients are entitled to a deserving, respectable professional.

Unfortunately, some doctors regularly violate the standards. Many physicians berate nurses in front of patients or other doctors. Almost as bad is the habit of discussing patients in public, sometimes by name. One frustrated doctor blamed a patient for not recovering with standard treatment. "What can I do if you don't get better after all this?" he screamed.

Many physicians think nothing of criticizing other doctors to a patient. "Dr. Smith didn't handle this right" they will typically say. "If I had gotten to you earlier, I could have prevented the whole thing."

In a more substantial vein, the way the doctor practices speaks volumes about professionalism. One doctor tells of a colleague who insisted on performing surgery with his broken arm still in a cast. Another problem is with a specialist who is painfully slow with reports for referring doctors. That can be embarrassing when the primary-care doctor has to admit to a patient that he still has not seen the specialist's findings.

§4.61 Improper Treatment and Failure to Diagnose Fractures

A common cause of orthopedic negligence is failure to diagnose a fracture. Often, the physical finding at the fracture site is a subtle one, or one consistent with other than that pain complaint. A complete adequate physical examination, with x-rays, including special-view x-rays when indicated, and CT scans and MRI studies, is essential. Failure to use diagnostic facilities available to the orthopedist is a common negligent act.

In *Brazil v United States,* 484 F Supp 986 (ND Ala 1979), it was shown that a cursory and inadequate physical examination was carried out, and that a complete examination, particularly of the injured area (spine), would have revealed the fracture. In *Formont v Kircher,* 91 Idaho 290, 420 P2d 661 (1965), involved physician negligence for failing to adequately examine a leg for signs of infection (compound fracture), with the same result in *Hollis v Ferguson,* 244 Or 415, 417 P2d 146. (*See* Appendix 4-1, Cases 146 and 147.)

The basic tool of fracture diagnosis is the x-ray, which most often will demonstrate a fracture to the physician skilled in fracture care. The national standard of care is now that a physician who undertakes the diagnosis and treatment of fractures is held to the same skill as a board-certified orthopedist.

In *Pohl v Witcher,* 447 So 2d 1015 (Fla Dist Ct App 1985), a sprained ankle diagnosis was demonstrated incorrect when adequate x-rays, and x-rays taken at diagnostic angles, were taken. In *Baloney v Carter,* 387 So 2d 54 (La Ct App 1980), the hospital and physicians failed to x-ray a painful hip in spite of the patient's request for x-rays. In *King v Williams,* 276 SC 478, 279 SE2d 618 (1981), an ankle "sprain" did not heal and a diagnosis of fracture of foot bones was made after "proper" x-rays were taken. Foot/ankle injury fractures are often missed due to inadequate x-rays, which often should include anterioposterior and lateral and oblique views of the ankle as well as the same views of the foot.

Aside from ordering and taking inadequate x-rays, relying on "poor technique" can proximally lead to patient injury. In *Betenbaugh v Princeton Hospital,* 50 NJ 390, 235 A2d 889 (1967), the doctor and radiologist failed to diagnose a spinal fracture, as the x-rays taken failed to show the lower spine. In *Coyne v Cirilli,* 45 Or App 177, 607 P2d 1383 (1980), the foot fracture was "missed" because x-rays were "too light."

Failure to interpret x-rays correctly has led to missed fracture diagnoses and a resulting increase in injury and disability. In *Marino v Leonard,* 75 AD2d 639, 427 NYS2d 290 (1980), two physicians failed to diagnose a fracture of the patella. In *Vendette v Feinberg,* 125 AD2d 960, 510 NYS 355 (1986) the doctor admitted he misread a fractured radius when later films showed an incompletely healed fracture.

Often, the hospital radiologist will report a fracture to the attending physician that the emergency room physician had earlier missed. Failure in this communication is negligent and may lead to further patient injury. In *Keene v Methodist Hospital,* 324 F Supp 233 (ND Ind 1971), the radiologist failed to telephone an x-ray report to the attending physician, emergency room, or hospital administration when a skull fracture was present and the radiologist knew that reporting through "channels" would cause an unacceptable treatment delay for the injured patient. In *Phillips v Good Samaritan Hospital,* 65 Ohio App 2d 112, 416 NE2d 646 (1979), the radiologist diagnosed a forearm fracture requiring prompt orthopedic attention, but failed to promptly notify the attending physician.

The proper treatment for a fracture, if the bone fragments are displaced, is usually to manipulate the bone ends into satisfactory opposition so that they can heal in a functional position. At times, end-to-end apposition is not necessary or desirable, so that each fracture case needs to be evaluated alone.

The fracture usually must be immobilized using casts, splints, slings, etc., depending on the fracture location and type. If open surgery is used, internal fixation devices of appropriate size and strength must be applied to the bone.

If the treatment of the fracture is beyond the skill and knowledge of the patient, the doctor is obliged to place the patient in appropriate treating hands. In *Brazil v United States,* a patient with a fractured spine was sent home to his detriment, rather than being referred to a readily available orthopedist or neurologist. In *Villeto v Weilbaecher,* 377 So 2d 132 (La Ct

App 1979), the patient developed an unusual blistering under the cast that an orthopedist applied. The orthopedist was not familiar with the skin problem and should have referred the patient to a doctor who was familiar with the problem. In *Doan v Griffith,* 402 SW2d 855 (Ky 1966), the doctor discharged the patient from the hospital without advising him that surgery was appropriate treatment for his facial bone fractures.

A physician who undertakes the diagnosis and treatment of a fracture commits malpractice by choosing a medically unacceptable treatment. In *Weise v United States,* 724 F2d 587 (7th Cir 1984), the only proper treatment for knee fracture was open or closed reduction, not immobilization without fracture reduction. In *Marino v Ballestas,* 749 F2d 162 (3d Cir 1984), the expert testified that the treating doctor should have used external splints and observed humerus fracture initially, rather than open reduction early after the injury. In *Langley v Michael,* 710 SW2d 373 (Mo Ct App 1986), the surgeon reduced a compound fracture of the thumb with negligent cleansing, debriding, and doing the usual care for the open wound, and the patient had complications related to that non-cleansing.

Inappropriate treatment may include not hospitalizing a seriously ill or injured patient, as seen in *Baloney v Carter,* 387 So 2d 54 (La Ct App 1980) where a patient with a fractured hip was not initially hospitalized, delaying definitive treatment and causing the patient increased and prolonged pain. The proper treatment of a compound fracture may include use of antibiotics. In *Formont v Kircher,* 91 Idaho 290, 420 P2d 661 (1965), the surgeon failed to tell the patient to continue antibiotics to prevent infection after surgery for a compound fracture. In *Casey v Penn,* 45 Ill App 3d 573, 360 NE2d 92, *revd & remanded,* 45 Ill App 3d 1068, 362 NE2d 1373 (1977), the surgeon prescribed penicillin for an infection after reduction of a forearm fracture without doing bacteriological sensitivity tests to that antibiotic.

In *Deshotel v Aetna Casualty & Surety Co,* 269 So 2d 850 (La Ct App 1970), the orthopedist failed to order x-rays within 10 days after a fracture reduction, thus failing to show that the alignment of the wrist fracture had changed to an unaccountable position.

Charges of malpractice and maltreatment of a fracture frequently involve an allegation of failing to obtain proper apposition of bone fragments.

In line with a general rule of malpractice law is that a physician is presumed, in the absence of evidence to the contrary, to exercise the proper case and skill, and does not ordinarily guarantee a cure. It has been held that the attending physician cannot be held liable in the absence of evidence showing specific negligence causing failure of the bones to unite or for them to unite in mal-united posture. (*See* Appendix 4-1, Cases 26, 27, 45, 50, 55, 81, 90, 92, 111, and 146-198.)

§4.62 Potentially Addictive Patients

The physician is in a unique position to assess and advise the potentially addictive patient, and owes that patient the same duty to aid in correction. All too often, however, the doctor fails in this duty, and uses the easy way to "get the patient off his or her back" and avoid the persistent unremitting requests for more mind-altering medication without a clear medical reason. These patients are equally sick, are often undesirable to care for and easy to dismiss, and at times are at risk for medication withdrawal problems related to the drugs the doctor has prescribed. The need for physician diligence in care and avoiding liability is apparent.

Injuries that derive from prescribing the wrong drug or dose, or from the failure of the physician to know the possible adverse cross-reactions of the drugs prescribed account for many patient-engendered suits. (*See* Appendix 4-1, Cases 199 to 202.)

§4.63 References

Torry, *Insurer Adds Care Standards to Cut Premiums for Maryland MDs,* Amer Med News, Nov 3, 1989, at 23.

McGinn & AMN Staff, *MDs Fear Practice Guidelines Could Fuel Malpractice Suits,* AMA Medical News, July 14, 1989, at 24.

Spittel, Jr, *Where Does Peripheral Vascular Disease Belong?,* 12 J Am Col Cardiol 288 (1988).

Appendix 4-1
Cases

1 ***Dawson v Weems,* 352 So 2d 1200 (Fla Dist Ct App 1977)** (admitting physician who continued to care for the postoperative needs of a patient was not liable for the negligence of operating surgeons, where there was no evidence that he acted "in concert" with the operating surgeons in the surgery or postoperative complications).

2 ***Duval v Goldin,* 139 Mich App 342, 362 NW2d 275 (1984)** (suit alleged that doctor's epileptic patient negligently caused injury to the plaintiff. The theory of liability was that the doctor failed to prescribe, or failed to continue to prescribe, anticonvulsant medication and failed to instruct his patient not to drive an automobile after the medication was discontinued. The court held that the doctor had a special relationship with his patient which was sufficient to invoke the exception to the rule that no one has a duty to protect an individual who is endangered by the behavior of another person).

3 ***Welde v Kuzulla,* 140 Mich App 658, 365 NW2d 205 (1985)** (exception to the general rule that a physician may be liable for the injury or death of a nonpatient third party applied where the decedent died of injuries caused by a vehicle operated by the defendant's patient. The defendant had treated the driver with medication, and the theory of liability was that the medication was negligently administered. It was held that a special relationship exists when a physician determines or should have determined that his patient poses a serious threat to a third person. The court felt that insisting on compliance with the standard of care of the profession did not impose an unreasonable burden on the physician. It was held that liability would properly be imposed when a doctor's negligence is the proximate cause of injuries and the doctor is in the best position to prevent harm).

4 ***Clark v Hoek,* 174 Cal App 3d 208, 219 Cal Rptr 845 (1985)** (surgeon who, on behalf of a hospital and without compensation, acted as a proctor observing surgical procedures for the sole purpose of assessing the competency of the operating surgeon and reporting the same as part of the hospital's protocol in admitting a new physician to the hospital staff did not owe a duty of care to the patient in surgery that would render the proctor subject to liability for failing to intervene in the operation to prevent malpractice by the proctored surgeon).

5 ***Myers v Quesenberry,* Cal App 3d 888, 193 Cal Rptr 733 (1983)** (personal injury action arising out of an accident in which the automobile driver lost control of her car due to a diabetic attack, resulting in a collision with the plaintiff's automobile. The trial court erred in sustaining without leave to amend the doctor's demurrer to the plaintiff's complaint, where the plaintiff alleged that the doctor negligently failed to warn the patient against

driving in an uncontrolled diabetic condition, proximally causing the plaintiff's damages. The court held that a special relationship exists between a doctor and a patient which may support affirmative duties for the benefit of third persons. A doctor must warn the patient if a medical condition or medication renders certain conduct, such as driving a car, dangerous to others, but liability will only be imposed for those injuries which are the foreseeable consequence of the doctor's negligence. It could not be said that the dangers presented to the plaintiff and other persons by the patient's driving was unforeseeable to doctors).

6 ***Kirk v Michael Reese Hospital,*** **117 Ill 2d 507, 513 NE2d 387 (1987)** (Supreme Court of Illinois ruled that physicians are immune from liability attributable to a treated patient's driving, unless the injured party was specifically identifiable beforehand or had a special relationship with the patient. Two physicians gave antipsychotic medication to a patient, unaware that the drugs would cause drowsiness, especially when taken with alcohol. The patient lost control of his car and skidded into a tree, injuring a passenger in his car. The physician admitted responsibility to the patient, but not that it extended to anyone else. The majority of the high court found that a passenger does not fall into the class of persons to whom the duty of care is owed by the defendant doctors. The duty extended to any "specifically identifiable potential victim." A dissent argued that the opinion was "overly narrow").

7 ***Villetto v Weilbaecher,*** **377 So 2d 132 (La Ct App 1979),** ***amended*** **(Oct 15, 1979)** (patient slipped and fractured her left patella on October 12, 1973, and was admitted to a hospital where an open reduction and internal fixation of the patella was performed. A posterior plaster splint and bandages were placed on the leg. After operation, the patient complained of a burning sensation in the back of her calf. The surgeon's associate saw her the day after surgery and noticed swelling and blisters on the back of her leg and applied vaseline to them and rewrapped the leg. The surgeon continued treatment by applying sterile dressing. On October 26, the patient was treated with antibiotic ointment. On November 12, her treatment was changed to Elese to dissolve scars, and this was continued until December 27 when all open areas were closed. He advised her to use baby oil at that time. The trial court found the surgeon negligent in not calling a consultant or referring her to a specialist. The skin problem was herpes zoster (shingles). The proper treatment was application with topical steroid, which would have left her with less scarring, according to medical experts).

8 ***Kinzel v Messieh,*** **No S010875 (Cal Sup Ct)** (plaintiff contended that she was entitled to punitive damages because her surgeon was "malicious" in treatment by lying about her condition during her treatment of arthroscopic surgery, resulting in amputation of her right foot. The jury found simple negligence on the surgeon's behalf, but that malicious or oppressive behavior of the surgeon occurred when he lied or covered up what happened. He was negligent when he refused to return telephone calls from the nurses trying to tell him that his patient was in serious trouble, negligent when he failed to call a vascular surgeon until it was too late to save the foot, and negligent in refusing to allow a vascular surgeon to perform an arteriogram, causing additional delay in definitive treatment. The jury's punitive damage award was affirmed, this being the fourth attempt by the defendant to resist the punitive damages part of the award. Punitive damages are recoverable when a health care provider has acted with "requisite malice, fraud or oppression").

9 ***Bourassa v LaFortune,*** **711 F Supp 43 (D Mass 1989)** (anesthesiologist failed to discuss the cause of death, following a surgery, as a misplaced endotracheal tube, and that death resulted from lack of oxygen to the brain. The family was told that the death was due to cardiac arrest that resulted from the "cancer exploding." The defendant moved for summary judgment based on a three year statute of limitation in wrongful death actions, to which the discovery rule does not apply. The plaintiff opposed the motion, arguing that the statute of limitation was tolled under the fraudulent concealment doctrine. The court held that the surgeon and anesthesiologist had a fiduciary duty in their physician-patient relationship, imposing an affirmative duty to reveal the existence of facts which would support a malpractice action).

10 ***Hiser v Randolph,*** **126 Ariz 608, 617 P2d 774 (Ct App 1980), *overruled,* 688 P2d 605, 616 (Ariz 1984)** (physician conducted a pre-employment physical examination and certified the patient fit to drive a truck under ICC rules. The driver had a severe vision problem, as well as other physical problems. The question of fact sent to the jury was whether the physician's physical examination practice was below the standard of care (which it was), and whether the examination proximately related to the accident caused by the inadequately-examined truck driver).

Comment: In principle, an inadequate or false or misrepresented physical examination is negligent practice by a physician, and the reasonably foreseeable consequences of that negligence traced to the physician in *Hiser.*

11 ***Pelose v Green,*** **222 NJ Super 545, 537 A2d 745 (App Div 1988)** (court refused to believe that an orthopedic surgeon's relative lack of experience was proof of malpractice. The issue was whether poor results, after a cervical laminectomy, should be attributed automatically to the least experienced surgeon involved. In this case, the orthopedist, who was only qualified to perform lumbar laminectomies, assisted a neurosurgeon in removing lamina of the plaintiff's cervical spine. The patient developed quadriparesis. In this suit, patient alleged that the orthopedic surgeon's hand slipped while he was performing an unfamiliar procedure, damaging the spinal cord. An expert said that the mere fact that the orthopedic surgeon participated in the laminectomy indicated that he damaged the cord. The trial court dismissed the case because the patient was unable to provide direct evidence that the orthopedist erred. The Superior Court did not accept the argument that inexperience should necessarily be equated with incompetence).

12 ***Frick v Lee,*** **No 103054 (Mich Ct App)** (physician, an anesthesiologist, was having trouble inserting an endotracheal tube so that the surgeon called a second anesthesiologist to assist. One expert testified that the delay in administering (via endotracheal tube) adequate oxygen was the cause of the patient's worsened condition of brain damage and blindness in one eye. The court refused to allow evidence that the defendant had lost a lawsuit with similar facts in the recent past. The jury was instructed to presume the anesthesiologist, now deceased, exercised ordinary care and rendered adequate treatment in attempting to anesthetize the patient, who suffered brain damage and blindness in one eye).

13 ***Wickline v State,* 228 Cal Rptr 661 (1986), *appeal dismissed,* 239 Cal Rptr 805, 741 P2d 613 (1987), *cert denied,* 484 US 1043 (1988)** (female patient sued the state for negligence because Medi-Cal (State Health Care) granted only four of eight additional hospital days requested by her surgeon. She was discharged at the end of four extra days, but serious complications resulted and amputation of her leg was required nine days later. At trial, the physician testified that had she been allowed the full extension of eight days, her condition could have been monitored and her leg saved, although he and other doctors admitted that the patient seemed fit to release when she left the hospital. The jury found the state negligent, but the appellate court overturned the judgment against the state, finding that the denial of extension did not contribute to the amputation. The court noted that the physician should have protested the decision of Medi-Cal before releasing the patient and warned that doctors have "the ultimate responsibility" for their patients—a responsibility that cannot be escaped by a third-party payer when the physician's determinative medical decisions go sour. It is the physician's duty to be an advocate; it is also the doctor's responsibility to consider the economic impact of the decision).

14 ***Winston v Kaiser Foundation Hospital,* 93 Or App 528, 763 P2d 177 (1988), *modified,* 788 P2d 428 (Or 1989)** (doctors failed to diagnose liver disease and Vitamin A toxicity. According to experts, the diagnosing physicians violated the standard of care by not systematically ruling out each pathological possibility, and therefore missed the liver disease. The court held that a "proper set" of diagnostic tests would have led to the diagnosis and that proper medical management would have slowed the progress of the disease. A physician who negligently fails to diagnose a patient's disease may be held liable for such negligence, whether the negligence was in failure to take an adequate history, to order proper laboratory tests, or to do a biopsy (all acts of omission). A "neater" case results when specific allegations are made and proven. Proof of only negligent failure to diagnose the patient's condition without proof of particulars may not be a fatal flaw).

Comment: Currently, physicians are being pressured to reduce medical costs, to do fewer "tests," yet there seems (in part for the reasons alleged in *Winston*) that "defensive medicine" is increasingly practiced by physicians.

15 ***Sullinger v Setco Northwest, Inc,* 74 Or App 345, 702 P2d 1139 (1985)** (physician who declined a treating osteopath's offer to manage a sick child's case, stating that the child appeared to be recovering, but who assumed management of the case weeks later when the child was found to have suffered permanent damage from the illness (meningitis), was properly found not to have a physician-patient relationship that would be a basis for a duty owed the child).

16 *Bell v United States,* 854 F2d 881 (6th Cir 1988) (facts indicated probable negligent diagnosis by the first treating physicians where a 55-year-old man had been hospitalized most of the time for the prior three months with low back and radiating leg pain but, until prostate surgery, was never diagnosed. He became acutely ill with a fever and a 25-pound weight loss was noted. The patient complained of sacral pain and died the next day of a ruptured abdominal aortic aneurysm. An expert witness said that diagnosis of the aneurysm should have been made within a few days of the first care, that the symptoms of back and leg pains were consistent with a diagnosis of abdominal aortic aneurysm, and that a diligent diagnostician would have checked for and found the diagnosis earlier. The court found the physicians negligent in diagnosis, but that the patient had less than a 50 per cent chance of surviving aneurysm surgery).

Comment: Unless there are some circumstances not mentioned in the record, performance of abdominal aortic aneurysm surgery carries little risk to life, certainly a better than 50 per cent chance.

17 *Greco v Coleman,* 531 NE2d 46 (Ill App Ct 1988) (patient was in a vehicle accident sustaining several injuries, including fracture of the odontoid process of the cervical spine. The initial x-ray revealed no fracture, but the patient's neck was immobilized in a collar because of neck pain. Two weeks later, an orthopedist was called in consultation. He removed the cervical collar, reviewed x-rays, and found no fracture. Later, another physician found the odontoid fracture and performed surgery. At trial, the plaintiff claimed that the physician's failure to diagnose the fracture lead to his injuries, that follow-up x-rays or tomograms should have been taken to make the diagnosis, and that the orthopedist should have consulted with a radiologist. The first trial was a mistrial. The second trial resulted in a verdict of $35,000. A new trial on damages only was given to plaintiff. The third trial resulted in a verdict of $496,327.80, the amount of the physician's coverage as the doctor had declared bankruptcy before the suit was filed. The first treating orthopedist was the defendant).

Comment: Odontoid fractures of C2 often are difficult to diagnose, particularly if nondisplaced. The continuing pain in the upper neck was a clear clue that additional x-rays and CT scanning were indicated. Whether open surgery was necessary or external fixation with halo vest would have suffice is not discussed. Odontoid fractures often slip due to damage of the spinal cord, and potentially end catastrophically.

18 *Fourquet v Caledonia Hospital,* 82 AD2d 822, 439 NYS2d 435 (1981) (13-year-old youth fell, was taken to an emergency room, and x-rays showed a complete transverse fracture of the right radius with displacement. There was testimony that the plaintiff sustained a second fracture of his elbow that was neither diagnosed nor treated by the defendant physician.

As a result, the patient's elbow became subluxed with calcium deposits and marked limitation of motion. The judgment was in favor of the patient-plaintiff).

Comment: A fracture of the shaft of the radius, particularly in the proximal one-half, is frequently combined with a dislocation of the radial head, and is called a *Monteggia fracture.* Failure to diagnose fractures or dislocations on initial injury x-rays is a common source of medical negligence. Every part of each x-ray should be examined by the treating physician prior to treatment. If there is any question at all about negative x-rays, additional x-rays and comparative x-rays of the opposite extremity should be taken.

19 ***DeCosta v Champlain Valley Physicians Hospital,*** **537 NYS2d 665 (NY App Div 1989)** (patient went to emergency room with chest pain that was diagnosed as esophageal reflux. The patient had a history of high blood pressure and a normal stress test 10 months prior. An EKG was read as abnormal, but no specific defect was mentioned. The patient was discharged from the emergency room, and died 12 hours later. An autopsy showed an acute myocardial infarction. The jury awarded $53,000, and $4,847 funeral expenses. On appeal, the physician claimed that the verdict was excessive. The court disagreed, holding that negligent misdiagnosis was the proximate cause of death even though the patient would not have lived long due to his severe arteriosclerotic heart disease. Further, social security benefits of $616 per month were not an appropriate offset).

20 ***Datiz v Shoob,*** **125 AD2d 628, 509 NYS2d 850 (1986)** (orthopedist and pediatrician both failed to diagnose a congenital dislocation in an infant girl. On the day of birth, when she was seen in consultation, the orthopedist recognized that the child had the "floppy child syndrome." Nevertheless, he failed to see the hypotonia for detecting hip dislocation and did not make the diagnosis. Five months of treatment for knee and foot abnormalities were carried out by the orthopedist, but he continued not to recognize the congenitally dislocated hip. In fact, the diagnosis was not made by that surgeon until the child was three and one-half years old. A failure of diagnosis verdict was rendered against the orthopedist, verified by expert testimony).

21 ***Phillips v Good Samaritan Hospital,*** **65 Ohio App 2d 112, 416 NE2d 646 (1979)** (4-year-old child was taken to the emergency room following an accident, where x-rays were interpreted by the emergency room physician as negative for fracture of the arm or elbow. However, the next day, a board-certified radiologist indicated that there was a supracondylar fracture of the humerus with displacement. Due to failure of communication, neither the treating physician nor the family was advised of this finding. After several months, the infant's parents were advised of the fracture and it necessitated an open reduction by another physician. There was a verdict against both the radiology group and the first treating physician for failure to discover and failure to communicate the presence of a fracture which, when discovered, most probably could have been easily treated by a closed reduction).

22 ***Calvaruso v Our Lady of Peace Roman Catholic Church,* 36 AD2d 755, 319 NYS2d 727 (1971)** (child fell down steps and was brought to a hospital complaining of knee pain. X-rays were taken solely of the knee, although the patient had pain in the hip also. Diagnosis of the hip fracture was significantly delayed by failure to x-ray. The verdict for the plaintiff emphasized the need for adequate physical examination and adequate x-rays. Hip injuries frequently manifest with knee pain, and the reverse can be true).

23 ***Kenya v Williams,* 279 SE2d 618 (SC 1981)** (among other automobile accident injuries, a diagnosis of ankle sprain was made, with the report of a negative x-ray. The cast was removed one month later. The foot was swollen and blue. A second doctor took x-rays of the foot and diagnosed a fracture—dislocation of the foot—and corrective surgery was performed. A judgment against the first treating physician was affirmed on appeal. One test in the case was that x-rays were not taken of the foot, but of the ankle only, when the injury was to the foot).

24 ***Totten v Adongay,* 337 SE2d 2 (W Va 1985)** (negligence was alleged by an electrician in the treatment of his right wrist, which he injured while cutting firewood. When resulting pain interfered with his work, he went to his family physician, who could find no evidence of a fracture by physical examination or on x-rays, and prescribed heat and aspirin. After a month, the pain failed to ease. The patient returned to his doctor; again the doctor assured him there was no fracture. Five months later, he consulted with an orthopedist who quickly found a fracture of the navicular bone. It was plainly visible on x-rays taken by the first physician. The untreated fracture resulted in non-union, and was treated by implanting the non-union fragment with a prosthetic implant. He never fully regained the strength of his hand and pain persisted. It was held that there was enough evidence in the chain of events that a jury could make a decision about negligence without expert opinion. On the issue of the missed fracture and delayed treatment, pain and suffering attached, and possible loss of chance to avoid surgery).

Comment: Fracture of the navicular (scaphoid) occurs with what is frequently called a sprained wrist. Many times the fracture is not clear for seven to ten days. It is customary to treat such injuries expectantly; that is, as though there are fractures by the use of a thumb spica cast or splint and then repeat x-rays. If there is any question after the tenth day, obtaining a bone scan is helpful in delineating the fracture. Virtually all nondisplaced carpal navicular fractures held in a thumb spica cast for a sufficient time, although it may be three or four months, will heal, and virtually no impairment results. It is quite another story if non-union is allowed to occur. Frequently, open surgery and bone grafting is necessary. Arthritis frequently develops and a weakened, compromised wrist frequently results. Clearly, it is important to make the diagnosis of carpal navicular fracture early.

25 ***Greco v Coleman,* 138 Ill App 3d 317, 485 NE2d 1118 (1985)** (orthopedist was charged with the failure to detect a displaced fracture of the odontoid process of the second cervical vertebrae. His treatment included manipulating the neck when it should have been surgically stabilized. As a result, the patient sustained substantial impairment of spinal cord pressure and residual extremity impairments. An automobile accident was the cause of the injury in September 1973, and hospital emergency room x-rays revealed no indication of a fracture except for a clavicle fracture. After two weeks, when pain in the neck persisted, an orthopedist was called. He looked at the original x-rays and declared there were no fractures and discharged the patient from the hospital. Five weeks later, he went to a chiropractor who identified on his x-rays a displacement fracture of the odontoid and referred him to a second orthopedist. He used a brace for several months, but the fracture did not heal, so that in March 1974, bone grafting was carried out. He eventually stabilized with about 75 per cent loss of motion in the neck, as well as pain. There was a judgment against the first orthopedist).

Comment: Like several areas in the body, fracture of the odontoid may be a hidden or less obvious fracture soon after injury with persistent pain, so repeat x-rays, x-rays in different positions, a CT scan, tomography, and MRI are recommended. It has to be first thought of by the treating orthopedist, or cases just as this will be missed, much to the patient's disservice.

26 ***Kingston v McGrath,*** **232 F2d 495** (40-year-old lady in an automobile accident sustained injuries to her cervical and dorsal spine, was taken to the hospital, and had two x-rays taken of her chest and ribs. When placed in a private room, she complained bitterly of pain about her neck and about the mid-back. X-rays were sent out to a consulting radiologist who, four days later, returned the x-rays noting no obvious cervical spine fracture, but that there were six possible thoracic fractures, but that the latter could also be congenital abnormalities. The patient continued to complain bitterly of neck and back pain. No further x-rays, however, were taken for three weeks. The same set of x-rays showed multiple fractures of the neck and low back. She was immobilized in a body skull cast. She sustained permanent impairment with difficulty rotating her neck and pain and deformity of her mid-back. After extensive review of similar cases, the appellate court felt that, had the surgeons appropriately taken additional x-rays sooner, and been more responsive to her continuing severe pain complaints in specific locations, the mid-neck and mid-dorsal spine, prompt immobilization of the cast would have allowed for more prompt healing, less pain, and with reasonable probability, less permanent stiffness and deformity. The latter two observations of less stiffness and less deformity are more questionable than the former observation of less pain and more prompt care of her injury).

27 ***Rose v Hotel New Yorker,*** **1 AD2d 769, 148 NYS2d 204 (1956)** (there was sufficient evidence that the physician was not liable for missing a fractured wrist, in that there was sufficient evidence that the physician could not establish a diagnosis without X-rays. X-rays were apparently refused by the patient).

28 ***Bossard v McCue,*** **425 NE2d 682 (Ind Ct App 1981)** (patient consulted a neurosurgeon for leg and hip pain, and a diagnosis of ruptured lumbar disc was made. X-rays and a myelogram were taken and revealed nothing abnormal. The patient was put in traction, but agreed to undergo exploratory surgery when this failed to relieve pain. At surgery, the neurosurgeon found a ruptured fourth lumbar intervertebral disc, among other things. After surgery, the patient had severe pain in his back and lower extremities. The tests showed lack of sensation in his legs. Aortic thrombosis developed later, causing weakness, numbness, and pain down his legs, and ulcers on his feet and ankles. A vascular surgeon found a blockage of the aorta causing vascular insufficiency of his lower extremities. He performed a bypass operation to restore circulation to the area. The patient also required surgery to remove infectious tissue from the incision in his back. He was totally disabled, and suffered pain in his lower extremity. The patient and his wife filed a malpractice action against the neurosurgeon, alleging negligence and that the physician misrepresented his true condition, inducing him to undergo unnecessary surgery for a back disorder that damaged nerves in his back. They also alleged the physician was negligent in postoperative care. At trial, evidence included testimony by one physician that the neurosurgeon did a good job; other experts concluded that the diagnosis, care, treatment did not meet the minimal acceptable standards in that the diagnosis of the vascular problem was not made by the neurosurgeon and substantial disability resulted).

Comment: It is incumbent on all surgeons who operate the back to rule out vascular abnormalities prior to the surgery. The mistake in diagnosis and inappropriate treatment happens frequently enough that it needs to be a routine part of the diagnosing surgeon's thought process; that is, the possibility of circulatory abnormality in the pelvis and lower extremities.

29 ***Hermes v Pfizer,*** **Inc, 848 F2d 66 (5th Cir 1988)** (surgeon was held liable for $350,000 for the death of a patient due to a fractured trachea that caused a fistula with the innominate artery, which the surgeon apparently ignored, allowing bleeding and aspiration into lung and fatal aspiration into lungs).

30 ***Smallwood v Dick,*** **761 P2d 1212 (Idaho 1988)** (patient was injured in an automobile accident, taken to a hospital, and was x-rayed. A board-certified radiologist reviewed the x-rays the next day and ordered additional views, which were also read by radiologist. Later that day, the treating physician talked with the radiologist, telling him that the patient was complaining of low back pain. The radiologist said that arthritis was present and that additional x-rays were not necessary. The next day when getting out of bed, the patient had increased back pain and fell to the floor. It was then determined that the patient had a fracture of the D-10 vertebra that had slipped and caused severance of the spinal cord).

31 ***Braun v Rycyna,*** **100 AD2d 721, 473 NYS2d 627 (1984)** (appellate court ordered a retrial in a case stemming from the mishandling of a foot injury in 1979. The patient fell from a 15-foot ladder, and was brought to the emergency room where x-rays of the ankle were taken. He was referred to an orthopedist. In the emergency room, the orthopedist diagnosed a fracture of the ankle and applied a walking cast. Six weeks later, he removed the cast and noted that new x-rays showed that the ankle had healed satisfactorily. Nonetheless, the patient continued to complain of pain in his right foot. A second orthopedist was seen, ordered x-rays, and found that the foot also showed a fracture of the heel. The patient did not respond to conservative treatment for the heel fracture. Each of the medical experts for the plaintiff and medical malpractice board condemned the hospital and first orthopedist for not adequately examining and x-raying the patient. Part of the testimony was that it is well known that falls from heights will frequently fracture the os calcis in addition to other fractures. The decision held that the basic negligence was failure to take appropriate x-rays at the time of injury or soon thereafter—not to wait six weeks).

Comment: An os calcis fracture can be a hidden fracture and difficult to diagnose. The diagnosis is frequently based on the index of suspicion that they are present. Many orthopedists believe that, as a rule of thumb, the dorsal and lumbar spine should also be x-rayed with os calcis fractures because there is a high incidence of compression fractures of vertebral elements produced by the same mechanics that produce the os calcis fracture—the so-called "glider" injury.

32 ***Garrett v United States,* 667 F Supp 1147 (WD La 1987)** (there was no malpractice in the diagnosis of adult respiratory distress syndrome (ARDS) in a patient, rather than cardiogenic pulmonary edema, a federal trial court in Louisiana ruled. The patient was admitted to the hospital with a two-day history of vomiting, black stools, fainting episodes, and a nine-day history of nose bleeds. His condition improved, but five days later he again vomited. With consent of the patient's wife, an exploratory laparotomy and gastrectomy were performed, as well as surgery to restore blood flow to a blocked leg artery. The patient did well during and immediately after the operation, but later suffered a near respiratory arrest. On the basis of notes in the patient's chart and test results, the physician decided the problem was not of cardiac origin and made the diagnosis of ARDS. The patient's respiratory function improved after treatment. However, other organ systems began to fail, and the patient died less than a month after surgery. The patient's family filed a suit under the Federal Torts Claim Act, alleging wrongful death. They contended that the patient was given an excessive amount of intravenous fluids before, during, and after the operation, resulting in intravascular volume overload. They alleged that this resulted in the development of cardiogenic pulmonary edema, which was misdiagnosed as ARDS. The court disagreed with the family's allegation about the administration of fluids by treating physician. Expert testimony for the government justified the fluids given the patient at all times during his hospital stay. The family's expert who testified to the contrary had no expertise in surgery and did not demonstrate the scope of in-depth surgical knowledge possessed by the opposing experts and treating physicians. The court also disagreed with the family's expert that it was below the standard of care to diagnose ARDS instead of cardiogenic pulmonary edema. Even the family expert

admitted that pulmonary artery wedge pressure obtained the night of the patient's arrest and the next morning was inconsistent with the diagnosis of cardiogenic pulmonary edema. The court was unable to discover any evidence that should have alerted the hospital staff that their diagnosis was improper. Finding that the medical evidence supported the actions of the hospital physicians, the court entered judgment for the government).

33 ***Addison v Whittenberg,* 159 Ill App 3d 585, 512 NE2d 76 (1987), *revd,* 529 NE2d 552 (Ill 1988)** (physicians in a hospital radiology group were not entitled to summary judgment in a malpractice action against them for allegedly failing to discover a broken vertebra in the patient's neck, the Illinois Appellate Court ruled. The patient was admitted to the hospital on or about January 17, 1981 after involvement in an automobile accident. The physicians failed to discover and treat a broken vertebra in the patient's neck. Reversing the decision, the appellate court said that there was a genuine issue as to negligence and that summary judgment was improper. The court noted that the patient had not come forward with the opinion of an expert witness, in an affidavit or deposition, that the physician acted negligently. However, x-rays taken by the hospital the day of admission, on the day he was discharged from the hospital where he was first treated, disclosed he had a fracture of the cervical spine. A reasonable inference was that he suffered a fracture in the automobile accident. Because it was discovered a few days later, failure to discover on the date he was first taken to the hospital resulted in negligence. The appellate court's decision was reversed and the case was remanded).

34 ***Bauer v Friedland,* 394 NW2d 549 (Minn Ct App 1986)** (orthopedic surgeon placed four wires in reducing and stabilizing a fracture of the tibia following a motorcycle accident. A few years later when the orthopedist tried to remove the wires, three of the wires came out easily, but the fourth would not budge. Rather than make a cut in the bone and run the risk of fracture, the wire was left in place, but it was realized that there was a risk of it migrating. The risk of migration was not explained to the patient. Months later, the wire did migrate and damaged a branch of the posterior tibial nerve. It was held that medical testimony was not necessary to establish whether the case was worthy of trial, but that medical expert testimony was necessary on the question of whether leaving the wire in place was below the standard of care. Such testimony was not given).

Comment: It is not unusual for a metallic stabilizing device, when attempt to remove it, to be fraught with failure. Extensive and mutilating surgery has been carried out to the detriment of the patient for the removal of such wires. A better, and probably within the standard of care action, is to inform the patient of the presence of such foreign bodies and to periodically examine x-rays to see if they are moving. The fairly extensive destruction of bones to remove metallic fragments is frequently contraindicated, for there is increased risk of fracture to that area of bone.

35 ***Chasco v Providence Memorial Hospital,* 476 SW2d 385 (Tex Civ App 1972)** (general practitioner was not negligent in failing to recognize

symptoms of a subdural hematoma in an alcoholic patient, where findings on examination were equally consistent with the sleepy state of the sobering but intoxicated person).

Comment: These cases are often seen in the emergency room, on the street, and in jail. Repeated physical examinations and recording of findings are the standard of care. Failure to attend such patients regularly will allow subdural hematoma or other injuries to be missed and patient deaths to occur, when prompt diagnosis is often life-saving. Negligence in the form of lack of diligence in diagnosis or treatment is common in the care of these less-than-desirable patients.

36 *Weise v United States,* 724 F2d 152 (7th Cir 1983) (knee injury with a fracture was misdiagnosed as a sprain. Open reduction should have been carried out. One expert said that bed rest for twelve days followed by protected weight bearing was acceptable. The judge took medical literature furnished by the defendant home to study. Some literature taken home was not presented at trial, but the plaintiff did not object. The trial court's decision for the plaintiff was affirmed).

37 *Jones v Finley,* 170 Ga App 182, 316 SE2d 533 (1984) (patient continued to have pain after an injury. Initial x-rays viewed in retrospect by medical experts showed a faint line; however, this was admitted to being, in retrospect and as the case turned out, a "red herring." An osteochondral fracture of the left talus was eventually found when tomograms were taken. Both experts for the plaintiff admitted that missing a fracture such as this on original x-rays was not negligent because of its non-appearance, but that negligence derived from the failure to get different views and more adequate studies, including a CT scan).

38 *Lebrecht v Tuli,* 130 Ill App 3d 457, 473 NE2d 1322 (1985) (orthopedic surgeon and two internists failed to diagnose a herniated disc. The patient ultimately suffered partial paralysis and arachnoiditis. The medical facts were that the diagnosis was clearly missed, with the additional resentment on the patient's part that she was considered to be a psychiatric patient and that nervousness was the essence of her problem. All through the initial evaluation, the several physicians who saw her were convinced that her psychological state and her functional overlay masked, if not in fact explained, the symptoms, rather than a disc protrusion. She apparently presented several times with normal neurological evaluation. She then consulted a chiropractor who treated her for several weeks without success and referred her to a second neurologist. He did a cervical myelogram, found a protruded intervertebral disc, and performed surgery which relieved some of her pain. However, her symptoms recurred and five months later, a second myelogram revealed arachnoiditis, which resulted in eventual partial paralysis. Criticism in this case was that a myelogram was not done earlier, that when found, the disc protrusion was large enough that the flow of the Pantopaque dye used would not allow removal. Pantopaque is a known arachnoiditis-producing agent. Failure to complete a neurological examination and failure to refer to a neurologist was a criticism. The case really hinged on the credibility of the expert witnesses on the two sides, the one on the patient's side not prevailing in this case. The administration of the Pantopaque producing arachnoiditis was refuted by one credible witness who said that only patients with a peculiar sensitivity to Pantopaque develop arachnoiditis).

Comment: This case demonstrates a very commonly seen patient in whom there is a lot of anxiety, with what is called a nervous or hysterical overlay. Nevertheless, these anxious patients frequently do have significant organic pathology in an environment where the diagnosis is made—at least for medical expert purpose and disability evaluation purpose—based largely on objective evidence. This type of patient very frequently is unfairly placed into the category of "It's all in the patient's head." Each patient is entitled to a thorough history and repetitive thorough physical examinations to try to ascertain the basis of the complaints at the same time the treating physician is working with the emotional state. Descartes probably did a great disservice to patients and practitioners when he introduced the still largely accepted concept that patients are divided into a soma and a psyche; that is, physical symptoms and findings are one part of the problem, and psychological symptoms and findings are another part of the problem. In fact, they are always inextricably entwined.

39 ***Gomez v Long Island College Hospital,* 517 NYS2d 1985 (App Div 1987)** (patient suffered a fracture in her left little finger when she was mugged on February 2, 1980. She was 35 years old at the time and right-handed. The treating physician indicated her condition could be treated by physical therapy; however, she continued to have problems with her finger and visited a private physician who performed an operation to correct some of the problem. She spent three or four days in the hospital. The jury awarded a verdict in favor of the patient in the amount of $126,000, which was reduced by stipulation of the parties to $55,000. On appeal, the court said that the award should be reduced to $25,000. The fracture of the patient's left little finger had rotated as of February 27, 1980, as an unidentified physician made such a notation after examination and after reviewing the x-rays. The court said that it supported the patient's theory that the hospital failed to diagnose the rotation of her left little finger).

40 ***Perkins v Walker,* 406 NW2d 189 (Iowa 1987)** (patient was treated by an orthopedic surgeon for low back pain during the morning of September 5, 1979. He performed major surgery on her back. At 2:00 P.M. during postoperative care, the patient had a substantial drop in her blood pressure for a short period. Later in the evening, she suffered a stroke. In an action against the orthopedic surgeon, she claimed her stroke was caused by an adrenal crisis and that she had been treated previously with topical steroid cream for treatment of psoriasis. Her experts claimed that the side effect of long-term use of topical steroid was suppression of the adrenal gland. The adrenal gland would then not properly respond to stress, allowing the patient's blood pressure to drop, which in turn could result in a stroke. Her experts claimed that the surgeon should have either delayed surgery and tested for adrenal suppression or covered the patient immediately prior to surgery with an injection of cortisol to compensate for the gland's inability to function properly. The trial court ruled in favor of the surgeon, the appellate court affirmed the verdict in favor of the surgeon; the Iowa Supreme Court said that the trial court did not err in instructing the jury that a surgeon cannot be found negligent merely because he made a mistake in diagnosis and treatment of the patient. The court said that the instruction was proper because it questioned whether the surgeon should have covered by cortisol injection prior to surgery as a matter of judgment. There were clearly issues as to the surgeon's judgment in diagnosing whether the patient had suffered adrenal insufficiency or whether the cover with cortisol was appropriate).

41 ***Molien v Kaiser Foundations Hospital,* 27 Cal 3d 916, 616 P2d 813, 167 Cal Rptr 831 (1980)** (plaintiff went to her physician for a routine examination and was negligently diagnosed as having syphilis, and was so advised. She was treated with massive doses of penicillin and instructed to tell her husband about the diagnosis. The court held that a cause of action was stated for negligent infliction of serious emotional distress based on an erroneous diagnosis. In cases involving the failure to diagnose an incurable disease, it is difficult to prove what damages, if any, were suffered by the decedent or his or her survivors as a result of the failure to diagnose. If the disease was incurable and the decedent would have died regardless of the diagnosis and treatment, generally the courts have generally held that the incurability of a disease will preclude finding proximate cause in a wrongful death action, that there is some authority for allowing a finding of proximate cause in a survival action. The apparent reasoning is that the decedents's family would have suffered the same damages even if the disease had been properly diagnosed and treated, while the decedent might have endured long pain and suffering due to failure to discover the disease).

42 ***Adams v Luros,* 406 NE2d 1199 (Ind Ct App 1980)** (physician allegedly negligently failed to diagnose a tumor in the mid-region of the patient's spinal cord. The patient consulted the physician in January 1973 for lower back pain, partial paralysis of the right leg, and toe drop. The physician admitted him to the hospital twice and did extensive tests, but could not diagnose the problem. The patient stated that the physician told him to live with it until it got better or worse. In 1976, the patient began to experience additional difficulty with his leg. Eventually, in 1977, he consulted another orthopedist who gave him a diagnosis of tumor in the mid-region of the spinal cord. The tumor was removed by surgery, but the patient was left without use of his legs. The patient filed a suit against the physician on February 26, 1979, alleging negligence in failing to order a myelogram. A default judgment was entered. Reversing the decision, the appellate court said that the trial court should not have granted summary judgment to the physician. The new statute of limitation in the Indiana Malpractice Act did not apply to the patient's claim. The case was retried because the patient did not have knowledge of the negligence until March 1977, bringing the action within the statute of limitation).

Comment: In difficult diagnostic cases, rather than abandon and tell patients that they will have to live with their problem, it is prudent to continue to follow and continue to do appropriate diagnostic tests. It appears from the outset that myelography would have been appropriate in this case. In current time of practice, MRI studies and CT scanning would have demonstrated the tumor quite readily. Criticism of the evaluation of the patient in *Adams* is appropriate.

43 ***Aasheim v Humberger,* 215 Mont 127, 695 P2d 824 (1985)** (action against an orthopedic surgeon for diagnosing the plaintiff's knee condition as chondromalacia of patella without taking x-rays which, when later taken, showed a giant cell tumor that required excision of the knee joint and implanting of a total knee prosthesis. The trial court erred in failing to give "lost chance" instructions. Instead, the court instructed that the plaintiff was required to show only "that negligence on the part of the defendant deprived her of a reasonable medical probability of obtaining a better result." To do this, the plaintiff would have to establish that there was better than a 50 per cent chance of obtaining a better result).

Comment: Giant cell tumors of the bone embrace many tumor variations with difficulty in prognosis. Some are benign, others are malignant from the outset. Many benign tumors change in time to malignant.

44 ***Thome v Palmer,* 141 Ill App 3d 92, 489 NE2d 1163 (1986)** (action against an orthopedic surgeon, hospital, and two emergency room residents alleging that a dislocated elbow had gone unnoticed and that the patient's ulnar nerve had been damaged. The patient had a fracture of the wrist, but the elbow was not x-rayed inasmuch as it was not ordered. Acting on the information given by the resident and the x-rays available, the orthopedist reduced the wrist and did not examine the elbow. When the cast was removed two months later, the elbow was discovered to be dislocated. The orthopedist operated on the elbow, and the patient later reported numbness in her fingers. It was discovered that the ulnar nerve had been overstressed, necessitating a third operation by a neurosurgeon on the ulnar nerve. At trial, the residents claimed that they found no sign of dislocation of the elbow, although there was no record made of this. The court said that uncontroverted testimony was offered showing that normal findings in the patient are not usually noted in the record, although in this case, it might have spared the resident some anxious moments. The orthopedist was exonerated. The verdict was upheld on appeal).

Comment: The frequency of this type of problem, that is, wrist fracture with simultaneous elbow fracture, mandates consideration of x-rays in both areas on each injury, particularly in children. If the orthopedist had examined the patient, although she had a painful wrist, independent pain and deformity about the elbow should have been present. The decision handed down in this case probably would not have been the usual decision the country over in regard to the orthopedist's management of the case.

45 ***Pope v St Paul Fire & Marine Insurance Co,* 299 So 2d 863 (La Ct App), *cert denied,* 300 So 2d 496 (La 1974)** (surgeons who performed

a patient's posterior bilateral cervical facet fusion, using a fibular graft, failed to adequately take into account the patient's pre-fusion spinal condition, including bone spurs and cervical subluxation, and fused the spine in an excessive angle. The fact that the surgeons had not recognized the preoperative angulation as the possible cause of patient's paresis (which caused the patient to suffer from permanent partial paralysis of his upper extremities) in the medical literature did not remove it from realm of reasonably foreseeable harm).

46 ***Jackson & Jackson v United States,*** **577 F Supp 1377 (ED Mo 1983),** ***affd,*** **750 F2d 55 (8th Cir 1984)** (physician examined a patient stabbed by a fellow prisoner, but failed to make the diagnosis of a lacerated intercostal artery. The patient bled profusely and went into cardiac arrest and died four hours after the stabbing. The malpractice action the legal guardian brought alleged that the patient was in immediate need of blood and surgical intervention to halt the bleeding. However, this was contradicted by expert testimony. The court found that the physician who treated the prisoner failed to exercise the standard of care required by state law and failed to recognize clear symptoms of internal bleeding and to immediately give blood transfusions and perform surgery. The court stated that the guardian was entitled to damages for the death of the patient).

Comment: There was an obvious failure to do a complete physical examination, leading to the failure to administer appropriate treatment.

47 ***LeBlanc v Northern Colfax Country Hospital,*** **672 P2d 667 (NM Ct App 1983)** (patient was injured in a fight on February 15, 1978. He was kicked or hit in the stomach. He took Maalox and pain medicine, and went to the emergency room of a county hospital. A triage nurse obtained his history, examined him, and called a physician at home. They agreed it was not an emergency case and could wait until regular office hours four hours later. The physician prescribed Talwin and instructed the patient to see a physician in the morning if the pain continued. The patient was not examined by a physician until six days later when he was taken to the office of the physician who prescribed the Talwin. That physician had him admitted to the hospital immediately; the patient died the next day of bioperitonitis due to traumatic laceration of his liver. In an action against the hospital and physician, the trial court found that they were negligent, but that their negligence was not a contributing factor in the patient's death. The court granted summary judgment for the hospital and physician. Reversing the decision, the appellate court said it was a close case. An expert witness testified that the nurse's failure to recognize the potential dangers of the patient's condition fell below the standard of care. He also said there was enough indication of abnormalities to warn the physician of the need for further evaluation. The patient could not be faulted for delay in seeking medical attention since the instructions he received did not indicate the seriousness of his condition. The case was remanded to the trial court for a new trial).

48 ***Thompson v Sun City Community Hospital,*** **141 Ariz 597, 688 P2d 605 (1984)** (child was brought to an emergency room with injuries to his legs. In the process of transferring him from one hospital to another, the second hospital caused a delay in treatment, and the end result was diminished. The holding was that the child would have had a substantially better chance of full recovery had surgery been performed at once. This was the opinion of the medical experts. The medical evidence for the defense revealed an opinion that the child had only a 5 to 10 per cent chance of complete recovery as a result of the accident itself. The case was remanded to a jury to consider evidence of increase in chance of harm on the issue of causation).

49 ***Schultz v Tasche,* 166 Wis 561, 165 NW 292 (1917) and also 16 NCCA 1068** (where the negligent act of the plaintiff consisted chiefly of leaving the hospital prematurely and in conduct thereafter, and where the defendants were found negligent in the treatment of her fractured leg before she left the hospital, it was held that her acts amounted to negligent aggravation rather than contributory negligence, which, in that state at that time, would have operated to bar recovery).

50 ***Warren v Roos,* 127 Cal App 2d 224, 273 P2d 569 (1954); *DeHaan v Winter,* 258 Mich 293, 241 NW 923, *repealed,* 262 Mich 192, 247 NW 151** (plaintiff's evidence was sufficient to go to a jury where one of the negligent acts charged was recommending free use of a fractured limb. Competent expert testimony was necessary).

51 ***Massey v Litton,* 669 P2d 248 (Nev 1983)** (term "injury" used in medical malpractice statute of limitations meant "legal injury," the court ruled in this case. The patient underwent a hip replacement operation on July 27, 1976, with her legs placed in a traction device after surgery. When she complained of pain, the nurses told her that it was not unusual, that the device was not to be altered. In August, she discovered lack of sensation in her toes and lower leg. The toes curled down and she could not control her foot. She was told that this was not unusual or permanent. Her physician did not show concern until January, 1977 when he ordered an EMG. The patient received the test results two months later and a consultant diagnosed palsy with no evidence of renervation. In July, 1978, the patient's husband filed a complaint against the hospital and filed a petition to the State Medical Legal Screening, as required by law, alleging negligence by the physician. One year later, the panel found that the patient had failed to establish a reasonable possibility that the physician had been negligent. The patient joined the physician as a party suit against the hospital in August, 1979, filing an amended complaint in September. The trial court granted the physician's motion to dismiss the complaint as barred by the statute of limitation. On appeal, the patient contended that the term "injury" included not only the physical damage, but also the negligence causing the damage. The court agreed. The court held that a patient discovers a legal injury when he or she knows through the use of reasonable diligence, or should have known, the facts that would indicate to a reasonable person that a cause of action existed. In the present case, the patient's discovery of symptoms of drop foot did not necessarily mean that she had discovered or had cause to suspect

negligence. Her physician did not show concern until several months later, and the patient was entitled to rely on his professional skill and judgment while under his care. The case was reversed and remanded for further proceedings).

52 ***Commonwealth v Diaz,*** **19 Mass App Ct 29, 471 NE2d 741 (1984)** (orthopedic surgeon failed to tell a patient that the proposed operation was largely exploratory and that it might disclose a tumor. Lacking such information, the patient refused to undergo surgery. Eight months later, she had to undergo a below-knee amputation, a disaster she blamed on the surgeon who failed to operate earlier).

53 ***McAllister v Weirton Hospital,*** **312 SE2d 738 (W Va 1983)** (breakdown in communications between doctors began July 23, 1976 when a 15-year-old boy was brought to the hospital with a bullet wound in his right leg. The emergency room doctor said the bullet separated two main arteries supplying the right leg and foot. He administered a tetanus shot and applied a pressure bandage. X-rays revealed, in addition to arterial damage, a compound fracture of the leg and the patient was admitted. The local orthopedist telephoned, and precisely what was said on the telephone was disputed. The emergency room doctor recalled that he told the orthopedist that the patient had a gunshot wound and compound fracture of the leg. The orthopedist remembered the call, but nothing about a gunshot wound—just a simple fracture. The orthopedist told the emergency room doctor to have the patient ready for surgery at 10 A.M. the next morning. A little after midnight, though, the boy was in such pain that his family asked the nurse to call the orthopedist again. The nurse identified the boy with a gunshot wound and the orthopedist told her she must be mistaken because he had no patient with such a wound. After learning that the boy in question was indeed the orthopedist's patient, the nurse telephoned again at 1 A.M. and advised the orthopedist that he had said he would examine the boy at 10 A.M. When the orthopedist heard that, he remembered the boy, and ordered the boy transferred to another hospital with facilities capable of handling such an emergency. The emergency room doctor telephoned the hospital suggested by the orthopedist, and was told that the boy could not be accepted. Another hospital admitted the patient at 3:30 A.M. The operating surgeon, for reasons never made clear, did not attempt to restore the vascularization severed by the bullet. Three weeks later, after dry gangrene set in, the leg had to be amputated. A medical expert, a specialist in vascular surgery, testified that even prompt and skilled attention in this case probably would not have saved the leg, that there was obviously a breakdown in communication, but that the "die was cast" at the time of injury. Therefore, the orthopedist and emergency room doctor were held not to have been negligent).

Comment: The facts of this case suggest that the orthopedist was not giving clear and devoted attention to the emergency room doctor's call or that neither the emergency room doctor nor the nurse were adequately reciting the facts. It is not unusual for a busy surgeon awakened in the early hours of the morning to need to be called a second time or to have the call reinforced. In the series of calls that this orthopedist received, if he was clear and competent in his thinking, and it is presumed that he was taking calls, he assumed a major responsibility in the sequence of events in the care of this boy. The loss of chance to recover doctrine would be applicable here too, in that prompt repair of the artery gives much greater chance of salvation of an extremity than one delayed many hours.

54 ***Hungerford v United States,* 307 F2d 99 (9th Cir 1962)** (under the Federal Torts Claim Act, the patient charged government physicians with negligently failing to discover and inform him of his true condition. The diagnosis is not set out in the abstract of this case, but the court stated in passing that the government had a duty to communicate to the patient a correct diagnosis of his condition, as well as a duty to make a correct diagnosis and render proper care and treatment for the physical condition from which the patient was actually suffering).

55 ***Kady v Fraser,* 122 Colo 252, 222 P2d 422 (1950)** (patient asserted liability for failure of an orthopedist to inform him of the non-union of a fractured bone. The physician was found not to be liable for malpractice on the basis that the evidence showed that no damage to the patient resulted from the nondisclosure, and that there was no need for further treatment in that the non-union in itself constituted a satisfactory result).

56 ***Martisek v Ainswerth,* 459 SW2d 679 (Tex Civ App 1970)** (patient fell from a fire escape, but an orthopedist failed to inform him of injuries to his back or of precautions that should be taken, but told him that his back was "all right." Months later, the patient was injured while lifting a metal frame, sustaining a protruded intervertebral disc that required subsequent surgery and causing further disability. The court observed that the patient had introduced expert testimony to the effect that the physician, in failing to "disclose the situation" to the patient, fell below the ordinary standard of care and that the patient sustained injury by virtue of this negligence).

57 ***Sinkey v Surgical Associates,* 186 NW2d 658 (Iowa 1971)** (physician is not under an absolute duty to advise his patient of an unfavorable diagnosis. In this case, x-rays indicate an impression of appendicitis, but all other tests indicated tonsillitis. It was held that the one possible diagnosis as part of a differential diagnosis was not of such value to the patient to impose a duty on the physician to inform him).

58 ***Weil v Seltzer,* 873 F2d 1453 (DC Cir 1989)** (physician prescribed corticosteroid for an allergic condition, calling them antihistamines. In spite of progressive deterioration and ultimate demise from steroid-related complications, including several pathological fractures, and pulmonary embolus containing bone marrow and bone spicules, the lower court held the patient contributorily negligent for not finding out the medication he was taking. The basis of the suit was negligent long-term medical care, leading to known complicating fatal pulmonary embolus. The lower court awarded $4,000,000. On appeal, the defense pointed out that the current treating physicians were equally or perhaps even more negligent for not ascertaining that the patient had been taking steroid, and for poor communication between doctors in tak-

ing a medical history. The court held that the recent treating physicians could not be faulted, as they asked the patient what medicines the patient was taking. The real duty lay with the long-time steroid treating doctor for not informing the patient of his medication and risks. The case was remanded for errors in allowing lay (patient's) testimony regarding the defendant's prescribing habits).

59 ***Wilschimsky v Medina,*** **775 P2d 713 (NM 1989)** (physician who administers narcotic drugs in his office to a patient must take reasonable care to protect the general public against harm resulting from that patient's impaired ability to operate an automobile. This case involved a migraine headache patient, who regularly took Percodan for a severe headache. When a headache did not subside, the patient would go to the doctor's office and receive an injection of Demerol (a stronger narcotic). On the occasion which gave rise to this law suit, the patient became nauseated and a second drug was given for that problem. The patient drove her car toward home, but was involved in an automobile accident in which another was injured. The injured party filed suit, alleging in part that the physician was negligent in giving the drug to this patient that impaired her judgment and caused drowsiness. Evidence was in dispute as to whether the doctor had warned the patient of the side effects. The state high court ruled that a physician owes a duty of care to the general public when he administers drugs to a patient. In recognizing a duty toward third parties, the court observed that the recent growth in outpatient treatment for conditions that once would have been treated as hospital inpatients has increased the risk of injury to the public from patients driving under the influence of therapeutic drugs. In the administration of drugs in the doctor's office, the burden is slight in requiring the doctor to take preventive measures and give informed warning, require that another transport the patient, etc. The court said that the doctor should be held to prevailing standards in the medical community and that the ruling extended only to cases involving persons injured by patients driving from a doctor's office after being given drugs that might affect driving competence. The court held that what fulfilled these fact situations was a jury question. A dissenting opinion argued that the majority ruling would exacerbate the medical liability crisis by significantly extending a physician's potential liability).

60 ***Wilschinsky v Medina,*** **108 NM 511, 775 P2d 713 (1989)** (plaintiff was injured by an automobile driven by a patient of the defendant doctor, who had administered Demerol and later an anti-nausea medication. The patient was medically impaired by the injection. The patient had had a medical procedure performed at a hospital requiring the pain relief medication. The plaintiff alleged that the doctor was liable for not warning the patient not to drive and not preventing her from driving while under the influence of the drug. The defendant pled that New Mexico malpractice laws did not require him to keep the patient "off the roads." The highest court pointed out that those laws were written before outpatient surgery was "in vogue" and that those laws should be flexible, considering that outpatient surgery patients present a new risk to third parties. The suit was not dismissed on the defendant's objection. There was a firm objection by one justice).

61 ***Bullock v Newman,*** **378 SE2d 562 (NC App 1989)** (plaintiff was not informed of her cancerous condition for 87 days after her surgeon learned of the condition, alleged a compensible injury by stating that because her condition was allowed to persist throughout the delay in notification, she now suffers cancerphobia, the fear that cancer had spread throughout her body and may recur at some later date. The court held that summary judgment for the defendant was not proper, that there was a genuine issue of fact as to whether the delay caused the patient to continue in pain which could have been eliminated or lessened if treatment were stated earlier. Case set for trial on facts).

62 ***Roach v Hockey,*** **53 Or App 710, 634 P2d 249 (1981)** (two points are reinforced in this case: (1) the physician has a duty to use his or her best judgment based on available facts (although he or she may be negligent in not obtaining sufficient facts), and (2) the fact that an expert witness would or would not do a procedure differently than the defendant does not itself establish a departure from the standard of care).

63 ***Jozsa v Hottenstein,*** **528 A2d 606 (Pa Super 1987)** (this case hinged on the orthopedic surgeon failing to communicate to the patient that after carpal tunnel release surgery there is a four to five per cent recurrence rate (actually, it may be higher) and he further suggested that carpal tunnel release might ease her neck pain. After an auto accident, the patient had neck, shoulder pain as well as carpal tunnel pain. After carpal tunnel release as an outpatient under local anesthetic, her symptoms were essentially unrelieved. She brought suit claiming she had not been told the risk of recurrence and she had been misled about possible beneficial effects on her neck problems. The case was remanded by the appellate court because the jury was not given the right to decide whether failure to disclose a specific risk violated the patient's informed consent. Another part of the decision was that the defendant's "own admission that cervical pain can neither be caused by carpal tunnel syndrome nor alleviated by wrist surgery").

Comment: The statement above, by the defendant's own admission, is not true. A significant number of carpal tunnel compression syndromes also have cervical nerve root tethering, the so-called "double crush syndrome," that are substantially relieved at times by decompression of the medial nerve in the carpal tunnel.

64 ***Jenoff v Gleason,*** **215 NJ Super 349, 521 A2d 1323 (App Div 1987)** (orthopedist was ordered to stand a new trial, the higher court feeling that he was cleared of negligence in noticing and acting on x-ray reports. X-rays revealed a nodule in the lung that could have warned the patient and her physician of cancer. The malignancy proved fatal two years later. The radiologist who wrote the report initially is also joined in the suit because he failed to alert the orthopedist or the physician concerned with the patient. The case began in September, 1980 when the patient fractured her wrist. Standard preoperative x-rays were taken which revealed this mass. The radiologist recommended tomography for further delineation but did not communicate this to other physicians other than in the report. Two months later, a nurse reviewing hospital record for patient's insurance company saw the x-ray report and promptly reported it to the orthopedist, but it was another three months before the patient was informed. The court, in essence, held that the orthopedic surgeon, along with another consulting physician of the patient, had a duty to read the record of each of the tests that were pertinent to the patient, whether he ordered them or not, if they were available on the record (and in this case, they were), and further that the orthopedist must promptly act, not act three and one-half months after the fact on the suspect nodule).

65 ***Stager v Schneider,*** **494 A2d 1307 (DC 1985)** (as part of a workup for a foot case going to foot surgery, routine chest x-ray revealed a mass that was later shown to be adenocarcinoma of the lung. The orthopedic surgeon either missed the x-ray report or ignored the possibility of lung cancer and did not inform the patient prior to surgery, though the patient phoned the orthopedist the day of surgery cancelling the surgery because she was not feeling well. Once the surgery was cancelled, the orthopedist saw no reason to check the x-rays, so they were attached to the patient's chart in accordance with hospital rules. Nine months later, a second routing chest x-ray was carried out because her mother had died of lymphosarcoma and a half-sister had died of lung cancer. The tumor was re-identified and drastic lung surgery carried out on the patient at hand. The District of Columbia Court of Appeals agreed that a patient is obliged to cooperate in her treatment but added, "it is a quantum leap," from that adage to permitting a duty to be placed on a patient to call and inquire of test results under circumstances such as presented here. The fatal onus lay with the orthopedist in not reviewing the records and not reporting to the patient and not assuring appropriate follow-up care for the reported lung tumor nine months earlier).

66 ***Courteau v Dodd,*** **773 SW2d 436 (Ark 1989)** (plaintiff had sustained a broken neck in a diving accident. He was being maintained with trans-nasal endotracheal tube for breathing because he was bothered by a ventilator, shaking his head from side to side. X-ray report showed the tube was in esophagus, not trachea. The patient deteriorated with blood gas abnormalities due to inadequate respiration and had a heart attack from ischemia. The suit alleges that the radiologist had a duty to promptly inform attending physician that endotracheal tube was not in correct place to detriment of the patient. Two radiologist experts agreed that the defendant radiologist did promptly read and report in dictation the improper position of the tube and the probability that it should be replaced and his interpretation was within the standard of care. No physician expert addressed the issue of promptly reporting the mal-position of the endotracheal tube by radiologist to attending physician. A respiratory (non-physician) therapist testified that the behavior was below the "standard", but his testimony was not allowed on the issue of prompt reporting. The trial court found that without expert medical testimony from plaintiff, no genuine issue of material fact concerning defendant's alleged negligence existed. Defendant verdict).

67 ***Taber v Riordan,* 83 Ill App 3d 900, 403 NE2d 1349 (1980)** (action against a surgeon who damaged femoral nerve during operation, and failed to tell patient, failed to render proper post operative care or to obtain consultation, the court refused to allow issue of bad postoperative care to go to jury based on claim doctor had not told patient of femoral nerve problem; that standard of care must be established through expert testimony, that correctness of "handling of cases" required expert testimony unless matters involved are common knowledge or within experience of laypersons).

Comment: This case further says that failure to disclose may be malpractice, but it also may be fraud and even to the extreme of negligent outrage.

68 ***Stager v Schneider,* 494 A2d 1307 (DC 1985)** (case was filed against a radiologist and surgeon for failing to inform patient of "spot" on lung x-ray that was taken routinely before surgery on foot. Patient later had second surgery for removal malignant tumor of lung. Patient was not contributorily negligent in not inquiring about x-ray, but treating physicians owed patient duty to inform her).

69 ***Meinze v Holms,* 40 Ohio App 3d 143, 532 NE2d 170 (1987)** (an insurer's physician has a duty to disclose information to an insured which arises under circumstances which a reasonable physician or ordinary skill and diligence would disclose—a significant risk or danger to the person being examined, even though the doctor-patient relationship does not exist. The risk or danger may arise from the inadequacy of the treatment as well as the patient's condition. Unfortunately, this duty arises because the physician has examined the insured personally, or has reviewed his confidential medical records, and thus, assumed a professional and expert opinion with respect to the insured's physical condition and well being, even though a doctor-patient relationship has not been created).

70 ***Harwick v Harris,* 166 So 2d 912 (Fla Dist Ct App 1964)** (internal medicine specialist asked to take charge of a hip fracture was not responsible for selection of surgical procedure used by orthopedic surgeon, nor required to obtain the patient's informed consent).

Comment: The internist might be liable if he referred the fracture patient to a known incompetent orthopedist.

71 ***Stoval v Harms,* 214 Kan 835, 522 P2d 353** (attending physician was not vicariously liable for any negligence under doctrine of respondeat superior or agency where a fully-qualified psychiatrist was called in to examine patient and it was recommended that plaintiff/patient accept psychiatric treatment).

Comment: This is a common scenario and a typical court ruling.

72 ***Reed v Bascon,* 530 NE2d 417 (Ill App Ct 1988)** (doctor who refers a patient to another doctor is not liable for the second doctor's negligence in an operation if the first doctor continues to follow the patient postoperatively. The first doctor did not select the type of operation nor did he help with surgery and he was not negligent in his post-operative care. The first doctor did not know nor should not have known the second operating surgery was not a competent surgeon).

Comment: As a rule, if the first (referring) doctor retains control of a patient or fails any of the above tests, he or she may be jointly liable with the second doctor.

73 ***Reed v Gershwein,*** **772 P2d 26 (1989)** (physician was substituting for the patient/plaintiff's regular doctor when he examined the ears of the plaintiff. At first plaintiff asked not to see the substitute but later agreed to see him. Job security was an issue here. The physician sent a report to the employer without consent of plaintiff and contrary to plaintiff's interests. Patient's claim of breach of fiduciary duty of confidentiality as a result of the physician's unauthorized disclosure of the patient's records was an action in negligence, not malpractice, thus the statute of limitation for negligence was held, being three years, not a two-year statute for medical malpractice which would have tolled this action).

74 ***Lewis v Sorinao,*** **374 So 2d 829 (Miss 1979)** (the defendant, family physician of plaintiff, allegedly said he could achieve a good result in nonemergency treatment of a fracture dislocation of talus, and said that a recommendation that patient be sent to orthopedic surgeon was qualified rather than unequivocal. Plaintiff was entitled to judgment, not withstanding plaintiff's alleged refusal to leave hospital where he was being treated).

Comment: Fracture dislocation about the foot and ankle often requires experienced orthopedic management. When less experienced physician care is offered, complication rates are high. This case infers that the treating family physician did not possess, or should have known he did not possess, the skill to treat this type of injury. In doing so, he holds himself to have the degree of skill of an orthopedic specialist.

75 ***Kerkman v Hintz,*** **142 Wis 2d 404, 418 NW2d 795 (1988)** (court reasoned that a chiropractor has no duty to refer a patient who is not treatable through chiropractic means to a medical doctor. The court explains that this infers that the need for a chiropractor to refer patient to a medical doctor is an imposition on the chiropractor to make a medical determination that the patient needs medical care. Such determination could not be made without employing medical knowledge, and the chiropractor is not licensed to make such a determination).

76 ***Schnebly v Baker,*** **217 NW2d 708,** ***affd,*** **221 NW2d 739 (Iowa 1974)** (medical malpractice suit was filed against a pediatrician, a hospital and several hospital pathologists. The pediatrician appealed from the adverse judgment and from dismissal of his cross petition against both hospital and pathologist for indemnity or contribution indemnity or contribution as to the petition for contributions. The court reversed the holding that the pediatrician's negligent inattention to the patient superseded, and hence relieved the hospital laboratory and its negligence for incorrectly performing several of the tests upon which the pediatrician relied. Where the laboratory intended the report be relied upon where there were several incorrect reports, and where its role in the pediatrician diagnosis was vital and where the reports were not just erroneous to a degree but were completely wrong. The negligence of the pediatrician and that of the laboratory were concurring legal causes of injuries complained of, entitling the pediatrician to contribution).

77 *Graham v Roberts,* 441 F2d 995 (DC Cir 1970) (action against a dentist for malpractice. The dentist extracted the plaintiff's tooth. After extraction, the plaintiff developed a sinus condition which drained through the opening created by the extraction. The plaintiff's mouth became progressively worse, finally requiring surgery and further hospitalization. Plaintiff alleged the defendant was negligent by continuing to treat the condition over a four month period instead of referring the plaintiff to a properly-qualified specialist. In reinstating a jury verdict for the plaintiff, the court held that the question of whether the dentist had sufficient opportunity to see the progression of the plaintiff's infection so his failure to send the patient to a properly qualified physician constituted negligence, was for the jury to decide).

78 *Barth v Swedish Hospital Medical Center,* 81 Wash 2d 12, 499 P2d 1 (1972) (orthopedist and/or neurosurgeon referred the patient after biopsy showed Hodgkin's disease. Referral was to a radiologist who performed x-ray therapy. A year after treatment, patient became paralyzed from an injury to his spinal cord. There was a question among several pathologists as to the exact nature of the tumor, all agreeing that it was a malignancy involving the reticuloendothelial system in which Hodgkin's disease is one such tumor. There was a question of whether there was an excessive amount of radiation therapy given and did that cause the paraplegia. There were a number of expert testimonies on both sides of those issues. Judgment of the supreme court was that the case should be re-tried on the basis of informed consent, adjudicating the possibility that the patient had not been informed adequately of the risks of radiation therapy. Plaintiff also complained of res ipsa loquitur, and a strong descending opinion was held that the case heard by the supreme court had allowed judgment under the basis of res ipsa loquitur and should stand).

79 *Rahn v United States,* 222 F Supp 775 (D Ga 1963) (physicians at a government hospital were unable to correctly reduce and set fractures of both bones of the patient's right forearm. They were held to a breached duty of exercising reasonable care in their treatment because they knew that orthopedic specialists were available in the community but failed to seek their assistance, to the patient's detriment).

80 *Kobos v Everts,* 768 P2d 534 (Wyo 1989) (child was taken repeatedly to two pediatricians with one year old pain in hip complaint. They interpreted x-rays as "essentially" normal. The mother took the child to a third pediatrician, an orthopedist and a radiologist. These consultants found no abnormality. A diagnosis of osteomyelitis and septic arthritis was then made when child was taken to a Utah medical center. The patient was then returned home where a surgeon attempted to correct problem, but growth plate deformity and damage resulted. In the suit, plaintiffs alleged that deformity resulted from 2½ month delay in diagnosis. The pediatricians, orthopedist and radiologist said deformity stemmed from improper surgery. At trial, expert radiologist testified that defendant radiologist's care fell below acceptable standard. When the witness tried to elaborate, the judge cut him off. Plaintiff's attorney then tried to introduce testimony of orthopedist to establish the radiologist's duty, but judge excluded that testimony because it was a "waste of time." The plaintiff next tried to put the orthopedic expert's opinion that the defendant orthopedist should have read the x-rays and bone scan studies himself. Those views were discounted on the theory that "an orthopedic surgeon was not competent to express an opinion about x-rays." (By training and practice, orthopedists read x-rays, generally in concert with a radiologist). The pediatrician and pathologist likewise were barred from testifying. Finally, lawyers for plaintiff wanted to call the defendant physicians as adverse witnesses. The judge again said it would take too much time. From the limited testimony presented, it suggested that osteomyelitis is not diagnosable by x-ray alone, nor is septic arthritis. The judge concluded that the radiologist had no diagnostic duty and dismissed him from case. The state supreme court criticized the trial court for the repeated refusals to allow witnesses to testify, given his later granting a directed verdict for lack of proof. The supreme court noted that the law recognizes the expertise of orthopedists in interpreting x-rays. Next, the high court said the judge's opinion that the radiologist had no diagnostic duty as "directly contrary to common reasoning." Finally, the judge's jury instructions came under judicial fire. The proper test of negligence was not whether a physician had been reasonable and honest but rather whether he or she applied the skill and diligence used by most other doctors. Case was to be retried).

81 ***Burns v Haskel,*** **132 Me 74, 166 A 384** (medical testimony was that considering the severe nature of the injury, a Pott's fracture, a trimalleolar fracture of the ankle, and the fact that the patient was over 50 years old, 75 per cent recovery of function in his case was an excellent result, again saying that not all bad results are the result of negligent treatment).

82 ***Zachary v St Paul Fire & Marine Ins Co,*** **249 So 2d 273 (La Ct App 1971)** (it was not improper to refuse application of res ipsa loquitur to action for damages due to rupture of sclerotic artery, necessitating artery graft during operation on plaintiff's lower back, where plaintiff's circulation was restored following graft operating and there was medical testimony by doctors attending the operation that operating surgeon and assistants exercised the required degree of skill and diligence, did nothing unusual during surgery, applied no excessive force in removal of the disc material, used normal procedures, and stated that mere occurrence of rupture of artery is not evidence, per se, of lack of skill or utilization of improper procedures.

83 ***McCormack v Kindberg,*** **352 NW2d 30 (Minn Ct App 1984),** ***review granted,*** **363 NW2d 307** (action against surgeon removing the first rib for thoracic outlet syndrome. During the operation, subclavian was torn, causing massive hemorrhage requiring blood transfusions with complicating hepatitis and cirrhosis. The trial court erred in (1) refusing to allow plaintiff's counsel to cross examine defendant through use of medical journal article recognized by another expert as authoritative, and (2) restricting testimony of plaintiff's expert about first rib resection after he had testified he had no recollection of the operation performed on plaintiff).

Comment: Most surgeons are able to vividly recall their first operation in which a major complication arose, especially if it was the first time he or she performed the operation.

84 ***Bagherzadeh v Roeser,* 825 F2d 1000 (6th Cir 1987)** (orthopedist treated a teenage boy with two displaced femoral fractures, and one ended up substantially shorter than the other, though both healed without event. The boy was badly injured in an automobile accident, was brought to the emergency room with multiple injuries including these two fractures. The orthopedist treated him by using bilateral skeletal traction. Two months later the orthopedist outlined possible alternatives to the patient's family. The option of using a hip spica cast was discussed but quickly discarded by the family, and they decided on cast braces. It is known that cast braces, though they facilitate healing, will allow for shortening at times. This was explained to the family. The patient found the cast braces intolerable and they were removed after 11 days and the patient returned to traction. Later, while still in the hospital, the patient broke his left leg a second time necessitating open reduction nailing. Five months after he was brought to the emergency room, he left the hospital on crutches with the dismal knowledge that the right leg was shorter than his left and both are markedly bowed. An expert witness for the defense said the cast bracing was appropriate and they were more likely to prevent muscle wasting and joint stiffness than hip spica cast, an alternative cast treatment. The trial judge said "the difficulties and uncertainties in the practice of medicine are such that no one can be required to guarantee results." In determining what an orthopedic surgeon ordinarily learning judgment skill would do or not do, he should look at the evidence as it related to the standard of practice of orthopedic surgeons. The jury acquitted the defendant orthopedist and appellate court confirmed with the note that, "the law on the propriety of the judge's charge is not to be applied mechanically, but with due regard for the "personality" of a particular case").

Comment: This indeed is a complicated case in which one might have considered open reduction and internal fixation as the initial treatment. Traction treatment works well, but frequently leaves some deformity and is part of the risk of that technique, but it also avoids the complication of infection. It is the orthopedist's usual posture that a functional result is far superior to a cosmetic result. Each case of this sort needs to be evaluated and tried on the merits—as the judge said, the "personality"—of the case. It appears that the patient was uncooperative, quite demanding, difficult to maintain in traction, and, in fact, may well have introduced a substantial contributory negligence factor to the case.

85 ***Crawford County State Bank v Grady,* 514 NE2d 532 (Ill App Ct 1987)** (4-month-old child was taken to the hospital emergency room on

February 26, 1979. A diagnosis of viral gastroenteritis, dehydration, and acidosis was made. Family pediatrician attempted to perform a cut down on the right saphenous view of the right ankle to initiate and continue therapy to reverse dehydration. When the effort was unsuccessfully started, IV therapy in the right femoral area was begun, with the leg restrained and immobilized. On the evening of the day of admission, the child's chart indicated swelling and a hardness of hip and leg, leg was cold to touch and there were circulatory changes. The IV therapy was ended on February 28; records indicate that heat was applied to the leg at various times. On March 1, the child's right foot showed gangrene; on March 7, the child was returned to a children's hospital where the foot was amputated. The guardian of the child's estate brought an action of malpractice against the pediatrician and hospital. The trial expert for the child said that if the pediatrician was not informed of swelling of child's buttock and thigh indicated in the nursing notes of February 27, 1988, it was a breach of standard of care. He said that despite the documentation of the problem, nothing was done to treat it or prevent further problems. The jury rendered a verdict against the physician and the hospital. On appeal, the hospital contended, among other things, that the verdict was excessive and the record was devoid of any evidence of pain and suffering. The court found that the amount of verdict was amply supported by the evidence presented. The child had lost her foot and would require additional surgery to correct the varus deformity of her right tibia. She would always walk with a limp and uneven gait and probably have degenerative arthritic changes in the good knee because of increased pressure on it. The injury had denied her a normal childhood. He also would continue to have severe pain and suffering. The court concluded that the jury's verdict constituted reasonable compensation and affirmed the lower court's judgment).

Comment: It is essential that the physician read nurses' notes to be best informed and current regarding his or her patients.

86 ***Rigie v Goldman,*** **543 NYS2d 983 (App Div 1989)** (appellate court affirmed that evidence of habit and custom may be admitted in personal injury actions if that evidence "exhibits a uniformity of response to a recurring situation and there is a sufficient number of instances of repetitive conduct. The court concluded that although this evidence of habit and custom did not create a presumption that defendant followed this routine practice with plaintiff, the evidence was properly admitted to support an inference that he did so. The jury then is free to give what weight it wishes to that evidence).

87 ***Barnes v Schlein,*** **473 A2d 122 (Conn 1984)** (malpractice action against an orthopedic surgeon was barred by the statute of limitation. The patient was injured in a slip and fall December 20, 1972 and was treated by surgery December 20, 1972 and again February 20, 1973. In April 1973, the surgeon advised her that she needed extensive physicial therapy and further surgery to relieve the pain she was still experiencing. She obtained a second opinion from another physician-operator April 16, 1973. On

December 16, 1975, she filed against the first surgeon for negligence in treating her and causing her to endure further surgery. The trial court granted the physician motion of judgment on the grounds the action was filed more than two years after the patient discovered her injury. The case hung on the uncontradicted testimony of the patient that she was aware that something was wrong with her leg in April 1973 more than two years before the lawsuit was filed).

88 *D'Angelis v Zakuto,* 556 A2d 431 (Pa Super Ct 1989) (appellate court reversed a verdict (failing to diagnose pneumonia) ruling that trial court instruction of "two schools of thought" was in error. Jury instruction was, "A physician may rightfully choose to practice his profession in accordance with a school of thought which differs in concepts and procedures from another school of thought. Even though the school he follows is a minority one, he will not be deemed negligent or practicing improperly so long as it is reputable and respected by reasonable medical experts." Appellate court said, "Although a physician may not be liable for choosing among different acceptable methods of medical treatment, it was improper to give the "two schools of thought" instruction in this case without further explanation." Plaintiff's claim was based on the physician's failure to diagnose a well known disease, rather than on the propriety of a specific method of treating the disease, the court concluded that the "two schools of thought" instruction was misleading because it could have led the jury to believe that any expert validation of a physician's conduct would preclude negligence).

89 *Ames v Hehner,* No 96-915 (Neb Sup Ct Feb 1989) (court permitted a malpractice defendant to invoke continuous treatment doctrine to bar a claim which otherwise would have been timely under the discovery rule. The surgeon, in doing a thoracotomy in February 1981 sustained a complication of ongoing and worsening shoulder/arm pain in his patient. The surgeon continued treatment until December 1982 and allegedly assured her on several occasions that the pain complaint was temporary and would improve. The surgeon referred the plaintiff to several other physicians who were unable to diagnose the cause of pain. In August 1984, other physicians established a diagnosis of Klumpke's paralysis that was related to undue traction during surgery, the position of the arm during surgery being under control of surgeon. Trial court and supreme court held the continuous treatment doctrine, concluding that the plaintiff's cause of action accrued when her treatment by the defendant terminated in December 1981. The cases involving misdiagnosis a continuing tort for which the statute of limitations commences to run at the time the treatment ends. Since the plaintiff failed to file within two years of that time, her claim was time-barred. Although plaintiff was unable to discover her cause of action within two years of the surgery, the court noted, she did discover it within two years of the termination of the physician's treatment).

90 *Dewes v Indian Health Service,* 504 F Supp 203 (DSC 1980) (general surgeon had no duty to consult and refer instead of undertaking treatment of plaintiff's broken arm himself, where there was no proof that open reduction performed was beyond surgeon's competence or that the operation was negligently performed. Expert evidence indicated that method chosen by surgeon was a recognized one, even though several would not have used that technique themselves).

91 ***Taylor v Wilmington Medical Center Inc,* 577 F Supp 309 (D Del 1883)** (summary judgment stands in action where neurosurgeon was said by plaintiff to be negligent in failing to refer child to appropriate specialist or specialized institution. Expert testimony was without contradiction that standard of care did not call for referral and the treatment recommended by defendant would be essentially the same as referral to specialist or specialized institution).

92 ***Larsen v Yelle,* 246 NW 2d 841 (Minn 1976)** (physician treated a Colles' wrist fracture with circular cast not allowing for following up on undue swelling or fracture fragments moved to unacceptable position. When referred to orthopedic specialist, error in care was recognized and failure to refer case to specialist held below standard of care).

93 ***Kaplan v Berger,* 184 Ill App 3d 224, 539 NE2d 1267 (1989)** (neither defendant orthopedist communicated well with patient who had mass in right thigh. As a result, the patient was lulled into a state of false security and did not aggressively seek a diagnosis until metastatic schwannoma was later diagnosed. In 1981, the patient, who had a family and personal history of cancer (carcinoma of breast), consulted first orthopedist regarding mass in her right thigh; x-rays of thigh were negative. The orthopedist made appointment for patient to have ultrasound study, did not discuss why or possible diagnosis with patient, nor did he make return appointment with patient, so patient never obtained ultrasound study. Several months later, patient had lump removed from breast by another surgeon who found mass in thigh but said he did not do "leg work" though he had removed a mass from her leg in the past. In February 1983, a neurosurgeon removed mass from right thigh with malignant diagnosis and the tumor was noted to have spread to groin in August 1983. Patient sued the two orthopedists in March 1985; they claimed time was past statute of limitation with summary judgment for surgeons. The appellate court agreed that the patient could not know the nature of her problem until time of biopsy. Further, the higher court found that patient's failure to follow first orthopedist recommendations were based upon an understandable uncertainty caused by the orthope-understandable uncertainty caused by the orthopedist inaction. Although aware that the patient had a mass in thigh, the orthopedist did not take a family history (thought to be pertinent in this case) and did not tell patient to return or make appropriate referral; this court felt enough evidence existed for a jury to decide).

94 ***Gradel v Inouye,* 491 Pa 534, 421 A2d 674 (1980)** (verdict stood against an orthopedic surgeon who failed to timely diagnose cancer. A 5-year-old patient fell out of a tree, fracturing his left forearm in July 1964, and was treated by a board certified orthopedic surgeon. Cast was removed and patient was discharged from physician's care on October 31, 1964. In the year

after the cast was removed, patient's mother returned him to the surgeon on three occasions because of a lump at the fracture site which she had first noticed when the cast was removed. The lump gradually increased in size. The mother requested an x-ray each time; the surgeon did not x-ray the lump but diagnosed it as callous formation. Dissatisfied with surgeon's treatment, patient was taken to another physician in November 1965. X-rays revealed a soft tissue mass that invaded the bone at the point of the fracture. Biopsy showed fibrosarcoma. Amputation was necessary. Verdict was based on delay in timely diagnosis and treatment of the fibrosarcoma. Additional evidence was that part of the bone, along with the fibrosarcoma, was removed. A year later, the cancer recurred in the same site. It was at that time that amputation above the elbow was carried out. The charge was that had the diagnosis been made more promptly, there was a greater chance that second amputation would not have been necessary).

95 ***Harris v State,* 378 So 2d 383 (La 1979)** (action alleged plaintiff decedent contracted gas gangrene infection and died during operation. Therefore, evidence failed to indicate failure to adequately perform medical services or observation which led to inception of gas gangrene infection or failure to discover or diagnose by medical staff. Decedent was diabetic and obese with circulatory problems. She had a deep laceration from an accident and the family insisted on moving her from one hospital to another, though one factor in diagnosing gas gangrene is long term observation).

Comment: In this type of case, diabetic, obese, dirty wound, close and prompt attention may be life-saving, i.e., control of diabetes, administer antibiotic, clean wound as well as observe (as if looking for gas gangrene) and the prompt surgery may be life saving.

96 ***Quinlan v Brown,* 419 A2d 1274 (Pa 1980)** (physician was not negligent for treatment of a patient of a work related injury. A machinist received a continued shock from a direct electrical current when he grasped a lamp in the work area with his left hand. The current prevented him from removing his hand immediately. When he did remove his hand, he injured his left shoulder. He was taken to the hospital where he was treated by a specialist in general surgery and industrial injuries. The physician manipulated his injured shoulder but did not take x-rays. After his injuries to the rotator cuff, the patient underwent 14 physical therapy sessions. A month later, the patient consulted his family physician who ordered x-rays for the first time and then referred him to an orthopedic surgeon. The orthopedist operated and treated a posterior dislocation and discovered a stress fracture of the humeral head. The first treating physician was not held liable on the theory that the physician did not exacerbate the patient's injuries).

Comment: Posterior dislocation of the shoulder is a common occurrence with convulsive seizures and electric shock seizures and should have been picked up by the initial treating physician. A second criticism is that no x-rays were taken, which most probably would have shown the posterior dislocation, though occasionally posterior dislocations are difficult to see on routine x-rays. There were a number of alleged errors made in this trial, but the court's final comment was that whatever prejudicial effect the statements made by the physician's counsel in his closing arguments might have had on the jury, were amply cured by cautionary instructions given by the court. The criticism of the first treating doctor is appropriate.

97 ***Madere v Ochsner Foundation Hospital,*** **505 So 2d 146 (La Ct App 1987)** (action alleged negligence during performance of anterior cervical discectomy and fusion, during which the recurrent laryngeal nerves were damaged resulting in hoarseness to the plaintiff. When an expert testified that vocal cord paralysis is a known complication of this operation (when operation is performed through anterior neck approach), so its occurrence did not warrant inference that the surgeons necessarily were negligent. Negligence would have to be established by expert testimony).

98 ***Jordan v Long Beach Community Hospital,*** **248 Cal Rptr 651 (Ct App 1988)** (physician mistakenly removed wrong kidney when x-ray was read backwards. On x-ray, kidney studies, a tumor—probable carcinoma— of right kidney was demonstrated. The treating physician viewed x-rays that had been placed on view box backwards. A radiologist also viewed x-ray backwards and submitted report—tumor of left kidney. Before surgery, the operating urologist "thought he could feel a mass in left loin. Surgery for left nephrectomy was carried out and specimen put into formaldehyde so that it could not be reimplanted. When error was discovered, a second surgery to remove tumor (about 80% of kidney) was carried out. An award of $5,200,000 was given, eventually settled for $1,200,00).

Comment: This case is important to orthopedists who often have to be doubly certain that the correct side is being operated.

99 ***Shuffler v Blue Ridge Radiology Associates,*** **73 NC App 232, 326 SE2d 96 (1985)** (directed verdict for defendant was reversed on appeal. Plaintiff was in auto accident and taken to hospital. He was then sent for x-rays which were interpreted by one of the defendants. The x-ray technician could not properly position the patient and did not x-ray C-7/T-1 level of spine. The x-rays taken were read as showing no fracture. The patient was discharged from hospital but subsequently found to have fracture dislocation at C-7/T-1 after additional x-rays. Evidence at trial revealed that the radiologist did not inform the technician of the limited scope of the initial x-rays. Further proof established that failure to reveal this limited scope was a proximate cause of the delay in diagnosis of fracture dislocation. The patient fortunately suffered no permanent impairment but did have an increased period of pain and impairment).

100 ***Murdock v Thomas,*** **404 So 2d 580 (Ala 1981)** (emergency room physician and his attending consultant treated the decedent involved in a two-car accident, sending him home with pain medicine and no follow-up instructions. The patient had a ruptured spleen and died before definitive care could be given.

101 ***Miles v VanGelder,*** **1 Mich App 522, 1937 NW2d 292 (1965)** (after hemilaminectomy, the patient developed complications resulting from laceration of the dura occurring during surgery. A second surgery was performed to repair dural fistula. Jury found the operating surgeon was negligent in nicking the dura and not repairing it).

Comment: In surgery along the spinal cord, typically ruptured disc surgery, the dura is occasionally lacerated or torn in spite of the most careful techniques. Neurosurgeons will frequently deliberately cut into the dura to do their surgical techniques. The critical point is the repair of the dura when violated, suturing it tight enough so it does not leak and in a manner that does not entrap nerve fibers. Failure to do these things may well be a negligent surgical technique.

102 ***Young v Casper,* 249 NW2d 713 (Minn 1977)** (malpractice action against orthopedic surgeon for damages sustained when tip of knife broke off during laminectomy, migrated and lodged in retroperitoneal space, where a second operation was necessary for removal of knife fragment, expert testimony was that knife could only break if unusual force or bending or twisting of the knife blade would cause it to break, that "standard" use of knife would be a gentle straight cut, malpractice against surgeon stood, though expert testimony not necessary under these facts allowing res ipsa loquitur to stand).

103 ***Malone v Daugherty,* 453 So 2d 721 (Ala 1984)** (laceration of the common iliac artery and vein with pituitary ronguer during laminectomy operation was a "surgery accident," not equatable with negligence, and was not a departure from the "standard" in medical community in the field of orthopedic surgery).

Comment: There is ample expert opinion contrary to this view as to negligent surgical technique.

104 ***People v Jackson,* 18 Cal App 3d 504, 95 Cal Rptr 919 (1971)** (the court explained that the physician's diagnosis of battered child syndrome essentially means that the victim's injuries were not inflicted by accidental means and "this conclusion is based on an extensive study of the subject by medical science).

Comment: Trial courts have long recognized the "battered child syndrome," and it has been accepted as a legally-qualified diagnosis on the trial court level.

105 ***Johnfroe v Children's Hospital,* 537 So 2d 383 (La Ct App 1988)** (trial court properly dismissed a defamation action by the father and grandmother against the hospital that sent results of child abuse and sexual abuse examinations to law enforcement officials. The children were examined at the request of the mother to determine if they had been sexually abused by the father or grandmother. Results were inconclusive and were sent to law enforcement officials. The father was sent a bill from the hospital for examination. Under the category of "Principal Diagnosis," the notation "history of child abuse" appeared. Affirming dismissal of the defamation action, court said the inconclusive results of examination did not defame them. Bills were sent to the father only, and since they were not disclosed to any other third party, no defamation was present).

106 ***James v Maryland,* 248 A2d 910 (1969)** (for the first time, the court accepted the battered child syndrome, upholding the prosecutor's claim that the child had been physically abused by members of its family. The court decision said, "The State contends, on the other hand, that the evidence showed that Tracey was a "battered child;" that this is a term or art used by the medical profession to describe a specific condition or syndrome relating to a child who has been the victim of malicious assault by parental beating; that in other words, the "battered child" syndrome is a clinical condition in fact, who have received serious physical abuse; and that among the indices of suspicion which are designed to aid an examining physician in diagnosis of a "battered child," and which are pertinent in the present case are: (1) age usually under three years; (2) characteristic distribution of fractures; (3) disproportionate amount of soft tissue injury; (4) evidence of injuries occurred at different times and in different stages of repair; (5) cause of recent trauma doubtful; (6) suspicious family history and (7) previous similar episodes).

Comment: The above criteria are similar to the findings of a physician that alert him to, and by law compel him to, report to appropriate authorities, suspect "battered children." Resistance to reporting such incidents by the treating physician stem from his concern of engendering litigation against himself by the parents.

107 ***Songer v Jervis,* 763 SW2d 132 (Ky Ct App 1988)** (evidence of unnecessary surgery was sufficient to withstand defendant's motion for directed verdict. The plaintiff signed a permit for repair of navicular fracture and bilateral metatarsal osteotomies, but not including hammertoe operations. The podiatrist said the hammertoe surgery had been inadvertently left off of the permit, the patient testifying that she had not heard of hammertoe surgery until after surgery was done. The patient suffered persistent pain after operation. Patient was referred by family physician to an orthopedist who repaired non-union of fifth metatarsal bones. A suit for negligent and unnecessary surgery was brought against the family physician. The orthopedist, reviewing x-rays taken before first surgeries testifying that he saw no hammertoes, nor found indication for hammertoe surgery. He also found no navicular fracture bone fragments. The orthopedist disagreed with "floating osteotomy" method of operation done on the plaintiff and that such surgery was inappropriate for the plaintiff's foot problem. A podiatrist testified that operating to correct a nonexistent problem would be improper. Jury awarded $67,724 to plaintiff; appellate court affirmed, jury believing surgery was unnecessary, the defendant not presenting expert opinion to the contrary).

Comment: The case may have been better developed by the plaintiff. "Floating osteotomies" have a place in foot care surgery. The record is not clear on the thinking of the podiatrist.

108 ***Cotgeave v Public Administration of Imperial County,* 443 NYS2d 971 (1981)** (patient may introduce evidence that a physician had performed unnecessary surgery on other patients, ruled a New York trial court. The physician had performed lumbar and cervical laminectomies on a patient, who claimed the operations were unnecessary and surgery was contraindicated. Additionally, patient claimed he had done numerous unnecessary surgeries on other patients also. The court noted a dozen cases were pending against the physician's estate with similar allegations. Although the defendant's estate objected, the court said all evidence entered by the patient would not be used to prove that the operation on a patient was in fact unnecessary).

109 ***Puleo v Broad Street Hospital,*** **407 A2d 394 (Pa Super Ct 1979)** (patient filed a suit April 13, 1976 claiming the physician performed unnecessary back surgery on him May 30, 1973, and again on June 8, 1973. The physician argued that the suit was barred by the Statute of Limitations. Statute of limitation was felt not to be barred, based on the affidavit that he first discovered his injury May 16, 1974).

110 ***Ziegler v Superior Court,*** **134 Ariz 390, 656 P2d 1251 (Ariz Ct App 1982)** (hospital, with governing bodies, may be liable for injuries resulting from negligent supervision of members of the medical staff; where claim against hospital was caused by negligent supervision of members of the medical staff in allowing certain unnecessary surgical procedures (pacemaker insertion). The facts to be proven were actual or constructive knowledge and medical records of other patients, who might have had unnecessary pacemaker insertion, were held discoverable).

111 ***Slosser v Logorin,*** **44 Ohio App 253, 185 NE 210 (1933)** (in this 1933 case, the defendant physician purported to reduce a fracture of the arm, left the bones overlapping, put a cast on the arm in that condition, failed to take an x-ray to check the apposition of the bones before applying a cast or after applying a cast and continued treatment for an undue length of time without informing the plaintiff that he was unable to effect a cure. There was sufficient evidence here for the jury to decide the question of negligence by inept care of the fracture but also a second issue of failure to take x-ray before or after the application of the cast or timely x-rays during the course of the healing of the fracture).

112 ***Howard v Park,*** **34 Mich App 492, 195 NW2d 1939 (1972)** (in this case, the patient had been successfully treated with fracture of leg having had a boot cast applied. The surgeon, in removing the cast, using a vibrating saw, deeply cut and permanently injured the patient. It was held that the use of vibrating saw in producing the cut of this sort was not a usual risk that the patient assumed in the course of removing of a plaster cast).

113 ***Grewe v Mt Clemens General Hospital,*** **404 Mich 204, 273 NW2d 429 (1978)** (in this case, the plaintiff sustained a fracture and dislocation about the right shoulder. One of the defendant surgeons put his foot into the axilla pulling on the arm, an acceptable technique, but it was done in an unduly rough manner with multiple manipulations resulting in brachioplexus damage. The verdict was in favor of the plaintiff against hospital and its physicians. The technique of reduction of the dislocated shoulder is a standard accepted techniques; that is, foot in axilla, but the foot needs to be well padded and the technique does not use force of the foot into the axilla but rather the foot as a fulcrum to bring the arm at the shoulder away from the chest wall as the elbow is directed to the chest wall).

114 ***Basco v Sterling Drug,*** **416 F2d 417 (2d Cir 1969)** (product liability action against a drug manufacturer. Plaintiff contracted chloroquine retinopathy after using three different drugs. Court held that, assuming the risk of the condition did not become known until 1959 and that the plaintiff's blindness could have been caused by one of two drugs, for the jury could argumentatively find a breach of duty to warn with respect to one but not with respect to the other. It should have been instructed on the "substantial factor" test of multiple causation. Stroke has a well known reputation for causing eye problems. The prescribing physician has a duty to warn his patient and having written a prescription, may well be the first in line as an object of litigation).

115 ***Mueller v Mueller,*** **88 SD 446, 221 NW2d 39 (1974)** (jury found as a fact that the patient was addicted and the physician knew or should have known that she was addicted at the time, though he continued to administer medication (in this case, cortisone) and verdict for negligent treatment stood. In spite of the fact that the patient had inflammatory arthropathy for which cortisone relieved her pain, she was developing secondary effects of hypercortisonism to her detriment).

116 ***Ribando v American Syanamid Co,*** **37 Mich 2d 603, 235 NYS2d 110 (1962)** (action for injuries sustained when a needle broke off in the patient's buttock while the physician was administering Procaine (penicillin). The court affirmed judgment for the plaintiff on the grounds that evidence was sufficient to support the jury's finding that the physician was negligent either in the maintenance or use of the needle from the time of its purchase by him up to and including the time of injection. There was considerable testimony on how the physician, with reasonable medical probability, did not appropriately maintain his syringes and needles).

Comment: Current medical practice practically always includes use of disposable needles and syringes in sterile packets. Had the facts of this case occurred using such a needle/syringe packet, a question of strict liability against the manufacturers would be entertained.

117 ***Shoumatoff v Wiltbank,*** **226 NYS2d 576 (1962)** (plaintiff alleged that a broken needle, resulting from lack of skill on the part of the defendant and not using a longer needle and upon discovering the needle broken, the manner in which the defendant probed the needle in an effort to remove it, drove the needle deeper into tissue, making it extremely difficult, if not impossible to remove the needle. It was held that the one-inch needle was acceptable even though one and five eighths inch needle was more commonly used according to one expert. There was, in fact, no evidence that the probing to remove the needle fragment did drive the needle deeper into the tissue. The court went on to say that it could not speculate as to the reason of the needle breaking, nor could it subscribe the breaking to the technique or methods used by the defendant—that the evidence was insufficient to warrant a finding that the defendant acted without reasonable care and diligence in the exercise of his skill or without using his best judgment in applying his knowledge after discovery of the breakage).

118 ***Barber v Reinking,*** **68 Wash 2d 139, 411 P2d 861 (1966)** (nurse, following the instruction of her physician-employer gave the patient (a child) an intramuscular injection in the right buttock. The boy suddenly moved, and the needle was broken off into the soft tissues. The nurse was a licensed practical nurse—not a licensed registered nurse. The court held, in accordance with public policy, one who undertook to perform the services of a trained or graduate nurse must have the knowledge and skill possessed by a licensed registered nurse. The failure of the defendant to be so licensed raised an inference that she did not possess the required knowledge and skills to administer the inoculation in question. In respect to the issue of contributory negligence of the child, the court said this was attributed only in determining whether the practical nurse was negligent in failing to anticipate the sudden movement. A verdict against the nurse and her employer/physician held).

119 ***Herbert v Travelers' Indemnity Co,*** **239 So 2d 367 (La Ct App 1970)** (spinal anesthesiologist administered spinal anesthesia. When the point of the needle punctured the dura and entered the spinal canal, the patient gave a cry of intense pain and said his left leg felt as if it had been subjected to a severe electrical shock. Medical experts agreed that severe pain and a sensation of electric shock resulted from spinal needle coming in contact with a nerve root. One argument of the case was to justify what happened by a litany of excuses by the anesthesiologist. The court went on to state that facts were clearly evident from testimony of the experts that there was an injury to the nerve root and it was not incumbent upon the plaintiff to give a pathological explanation of the case. Whether the injection was made directly into the nerve roots was arguable, but the testimony left no doubt that injuries inflicted to the nerve roots would not have happened in normal routine spinal anesthetic procedure. A verdict against the physician stood).

120 ***Kalmus v Cedars of Lebanon Hospital,*** **132 Cal App 2d 243, 281 P2d 872 (1955)** (judgment was affirmed in favor of the plaintiff, holding that the evidence was sufficient to support a finding that a nurse not only used an infected needle, but also failed to follow standard hospital procedure in scrubbing the area to be injected, thereby causing staphylococcus infection. The employer/hospital, having been joined under respondeat superior doctrine, was held liable, in addition to the nurse).

121 ***Southern Florida Sanitarium & Hospital, Inc, v Hodge,*** **215 So 2d 753 (Fla Dist Ct App 1968)** (court affirmed judgment granted in favor of the plaintiff. Rejecting hospital's contention that evidence was insufficient to support a verdict, the court pointed out the testimony by the plaintiff's expert medical witness stated accepted medical standard required that sterility be maintained throughout the injection procedure, and where this standard was not departed from, infectious thrombophlebitis would not occur. In this case, a pyelographic mannitol concentration test was being conducted. In this case, the injection was by a technician employed by the hospital).

122 ***McCormick v Avret,*** **154 Ga App 178, 267 SE2d 759, *affd,* 246 Ga 401, 271 SE2d 832 (1980)** (action against physician alleging malpractice in using unsterile needle which caused radial nerve infection. A licensed nurse who had drawn over 2,000 blood samples was qualified to testify as expert as to keeping needles sterile when used for drawing blood. The plaintiff alleged that physician failed to follow standard procedures for keeping needles sterile, thereby causing severe infection involving radial nerve with permanent damage to plaintiff).

123 ***Baker v Chastain,*** **389 So 2d 932 (Ala 1980)** (physician was said to have treated bursitis at "back" of shoulder with injection using 1½" needle, after which the patient developed pneumothorax from punctured lung. Res ipsa loquitur was held improper as plaintiff's expert testified that it was "improper to ram a 1½" needle into the chest wall of such a thin person as the plaintiff).

124 ***Hove v McMaster,*** **621 P2d 694 (Utah 1980)** (doctor injected local anesthetic, injected directly into nerve causing partial loss of nerve function. Negligence was inferred from facts; however, law suit failed by passage of statute of limitation.

125 ***Horney v Lawrence,*** **375 SE2d 629 (Ga Ct App 1988), *rehg denied* (Nov 22, 1988)** (physician was negligent in allowing Valium to extravasate at venopuncture site on patient's hand while a gastroscopy was being done. The patient complained of severe pain in hand. After completing procedure, nurse found tender, swollen area at venopuncture site. She concluded it was caused by the escape of Valium into adjacent tissues. Permanent impairment resulted. The court held the standard of care required visual inspection of the injection site and evidence showed the physician did not do this at the time patient was complaining of pain and burning in her hand).

126 ***Sadnick v Doyle,*** **510 NE2d 603 (Ill App Ct 1987)** (surgeon sued for alleged negligence in severing nerve. Trial court wrongly prohibited a plastic surgeon from testifying about the standard of care for excising tattoos on the grounds that he was not familiar with local standards in trial court in Illinois. The patient consulted a general surgeon for removal of a nickel-sized, aged tattoo from the side of her neck. The surgeon informed her that the procedure would produce a hairline scar that would blend in the crease of her neck. Two days after he excised the tattoo, the surgeon said the incision looked fine but subsequently there was drainage. The patient's neck throbbed and swelled. The surgeon made two additional incisions, inserting drainage tubes and told the patient the incision would heal nicely and that her ear tingling and neck numbness would subside. The patient consulted a plastic surgeon because of loss of feeling in her neck and ear area and expanding swollen incision. Her neck stiffness subsided and a swollen discolored scar healed, but it caused her embarrassment and affected her manner of dress. The patient brought an action for malpractice against the general surgeon. She alleged negligence in removing her tattoo and failing to warn her of complications of insult to her greater auricular nerve and causing excessive scarring. A plastic surgeon who practiced primarily in another country testified what was the standard of care in excising a tattoo in the area where he lived. He testified that while he was not familiar with local standards, he was familiar with state procedures. He said that certain minimal uniform standards were applicable to tattoo excision regardless of locality. He was of the opinion that all alternatives should have been offered the patient because no tattoo treatment is ideal. He said any physician who excised tattoos who did not warn the patient of complications deviated from the standard of care. He also said the patient's nerve should not have been severed during the excision. The general surgeon testified that he had complied with the surgical standard of care by warning the patient of anticipated complications. After the court refused to allow the plastic surgeon's testimony because of unfamiliarity with local standard, the plastic surgeon who was an expert witness for the general surgeon was subpoened as an adverse witness to testify as the patient's expert. He said that a general surgeon in the area would be expected to mention scarring but not all possible risks and complications such as nerve damage. The court directed a verdict for the general surgeon. On appeal, the patient contended that the court inappropriately barred her expert testimony, and the appellate court said that a physician familiar with nationally uniform minimum standard of medical practice is considered knowledgeable of all localities. The court found that the trial court had wrongly prohibited the plastic surgeon's testimony about the relevant standard of care, its deviations and the relationship to the cause of the patient's medical problems. Holding that the lower court had erred in granting directed verdict, the court reversed and sent the case back to a new trial).

127 *Patten v Milam,* 480 A2d 774 (Me 1984) (the standard of care includes a physician putting on sterile gloves at least, and to wash his hands before making an incision when attempting to set a dislocated compound fracture. The fracture was a toe fracture but ended up infected and subsequently required amputation. The jury found him guilty of malpractice for not using standard sterile techniques in treating the fracture. As a fluke of justice, there was no medical witness who testified that such conduct violated the standard of care. Therefore, the case was dismissed. Appellate court held that "where the negligence is so dramatically evident, there is no need for medical expert to belabor the obvious negligence." The words "res ipsa loquitur" were not used, but this was that type of case).

128 *Blessing v Doctors Memorial Hospital, Inc,* 184 Ga App 737, 362 SE2d 394 (1987) (hospital was found not liable for negligence occurring after surgeon takes control of employees in operating room. A patient sued hospital and two physicians, seeking recovery for injuries and alleged suffering during an operation as a result of faulty equipment and improper positioning of his legs. He also sought to recover for an invasion of privacy because unauthorized visitors were allegedly permitted to enter the operating room and viewed his genitalia during the operation. The trial court granted summary judgment for hospital on both claims and partial summary judgment for one of the physicians under the invasion of privacy claim. On appeal, the court said the physician utilizing equipment in question stated it was in good working condition. The only evidence to the contrary was the patient's testimony as to statements allegedly made by unidentified operation room personnel during the course of the operation. In the absence of identification of those persons, the court said such testimony was insufficient to contravert the physician's testimony. The court said the evidence established that the positioning of the patient's leg was done under the physician's directions. Therefore, any negligent injury resulting from the physician would be imputed to the surgeon rather than to the hospital. The court further said that when a hospital yielded control of its employees to the surgeon in an operating room and the surgeon exercised immediate personnel supervision, he became their master and their negligence during his master-servant relationship would be imputed to him. The court found that the trial court did not err in granting summary judgment and affirmed the lower court's judgment).

129 ***Kortus v Jensen,*** **195 Neb 261, 237 NW2d 845** (plaintiff alleged negligence in injury to sciatic nerve during the course of total hip arthroplasty surgery, failed to show care below "standard" at the time surgery was done, requiring the sciatic nerve to be identified, dissected out and padded. Plaintiff's evidence did not support findings that defendant did not exercise degree of care and skill which law requires).

130 ***Berry v Rapides General Hospital,*** **527 So 2d 583 (La Ct App 1988)** (at times, a surgeon is faced with a request for his services in a less than satisfactory environment. The surgeon is responsible for knowing the locus where he works, and if obviously risky, to make other arrangements. The surgeon is held to know the personnel, the sterility of instruments and supplies as well as the competence of assistants and anesthesiologist. The surgeon was mitigated in emergency situations, however, the courts are more closely defining what an emergency is. In the case where a lady fell into a pit, impaled in the thigh on a wire producing a deep thigh wound, a neighbor/doctor told her that he had no facilities at his disposal to care for her and offered to drive her to the nearest hospital, some thirty miles off. The patient declined, went home and many hours later (2 A.M.) called another doctor to her home. He loosely sutured the wound, told the patient she should go to a hospital for definitive care. The second physician was sued and defended with the Good Samaritan statute which permits liability "only for gross negligence". The appellate court ruled it was not an emergency, the patient had not lost significant blood, no neurological loss and minimal pain, therefore only "ordinary negligence" need be shown. The supreme court favored the second doctor's care, feeling in fact, an emergency in the need for care but not life or death and the care rendered at two in the morning was negligent—proper first aid care and transfer to a hospital by car was standard as no ambulance was available. The operating surgeon knew the care he gave the patient put her at greater risk).

131 ***Pedersen v Vahidy,* 552 A2d 419 (Conn 1989)** (state supreme court granted defendant physician a new trial. In 1983, the defendant removed a lipon, while dissecting with scissors, he accidentally cut a nerve from part of brachial plexus. Trial jury awarded $300,000 in damages against physician. In reversing decision, trial court was said to have committed reversible error in its jury instruction. The surgeon never advised the patient of any risk of injury to the brachial plexus. That did not conclusively establish such a risk should have been disclosed to the patient, and the trial court's instruction to find for plaintiff on faulty informed consent was erroneous).

132 ***Swan v Wisdom,* 386 So 2d 574 (Fla Dist Ct App), *rehg denied* (Aug 12, 1980)** (29-year-old patient dislocated his right clavicle at the acromio-clavicular joint while playing football. The physician repositioned the patient's arm and stabilized it with a pin. The pin migrated and punctured the right lung. Blood and air accumulated in the cavity between the lung and chest wall. Additional surgery was required to drain the cavity. The physician presented evidence that the pin had migrated out of the bone while the patient was working on his truck without the arm immobilized, contrary to the physician's instructions. Expert testimony stated that pin fixation across the acromioclavicular joint is a risky procedure that close attention toward migration of the pin has to be had, that the pin in question was improperly placed without a hook on the end. A decision against the physician stood with the patient being contributorily negligent).

133 ***Bowie v Hearn,* 364 SE2d 469 (SC 1986)** (surgeon cut too deeply during a Cesarean section and lacerated the infant's face which the court held deviating from acceptable standard of care. The bottom line was that the surgeon moved through each surgical step in a careless manner or the mishap would have been avoided. The surgeon was in control of the instruments he was using and responsible for an injury that resulted from the negligent use of the instrument).

134 ***Rogers v Brown,* 416 So 2d 614 (La Ct App), *cert denied,* 422 So 2d 153 (1982)** (plaintiff had knee surgery during which the operation required exposure and manipulation of the peroneal nerve. Expert testimony agreed that the manner of doing surgery, including exposure and moving of the nerve was appropriate and well within the "standard". Verdict was for defendant).

135 ***Baker v Story,* 621 SW2d 639 (Tex Civ App 1981)** (surgical procedure was performed by a non-specialist under the supervision of a specialist surgeon. During the procedure, he cut a ureter instead of a nerve ganglia, incision of the ganglia being the purpose of the surgery. He was ultimately held not to be negligent. That accident was pursued against the supervising surgeon who moved to dismiss. The court held that while the physician actually performing the surgery was a non-specialist, the supervising surgeon was a specialist and would be held to the higher standard of care).

136 ***Bloskas v Murray,* 44 Colo App 13, 618 P2d 719 (1980)** (in March 1973, the plaintiff suffered a fracture, dislocation of right ankle after healing arthritis developed causing both pain and swelling. In March 1974, plaintiff

met with defendant doctor who suggested an ankle fusion to ease the pain. Surgery relieved pain temporarily but by that fall, patient was in pain again and returned to the defendant doctor. They decided that implanted artificial ankle would be the next course of action, but the ankle became infected and artificial parts were removed. Infection spread in July 1976 after four unsuccessful ankle fusions. The patient's right leg was amputated below the knee. Plaintiff brought medical malpractice suit claiming defendant had negligently failed to inform him of the substantial and specific risks associated with total ankle replacements and that he had negligently misrepresented the fact that amputation was a possible result of ankle replacement. The doctor had not told plaintiff that he had never performed ankle replacement. Trial court entered a judgment on a jury verdict for the defendant. On appeal, the court stated that all substantial risks significant in deciding whether or not to submit to surgery should be related to patient. The court held that the defendant had sufficiently fulfilled this requirement and there were no negligent misrepresentations. The court stated Colorado courts applied negligent misrepresentation only when the pecuniary loss if involved and that negligent misrepresentations that result in physical harm have not been recognized in Colorado. Plaintiff claims fell under the doctrine of informed consent in medical malpractice, both of which were correctly instructed to the jury. The court held there is no negligent misrepresentations so the lower court's judgment was affirmed).

137 *Moore v Averi,* 534 So 2d 250 (Ala 1988) (podiatrist cut through a metatarsal bone while treating foot problem. The osteotomy (cut through bone) failed to heal. Podiatrist had not immobilized the foot either with internal fixation or by cast. Improper healing was not discovered by surgeon and no x-rays were taken. Trial court found statute of limitation had run. Appellate court reversed, finding that continuing treatment rule includes patient visits after surgery, which in this case, brought filing date of negligence claim within the acceptable time frame. There was a "real" question by the court whether the podiatrist had breached his duty to exercise the degree of skill ordinarily used in his treatment of the plaintiff).

138 *Kalakowski v Voris,* 418 NE2d 1003 (Ill App Ct 1981) (in this malpractice suit, the trial court did not err in granting a new trial against two neurosurgeons in awarding a direct verdict in favor of the orthopedic surgeon. A myelogram of the patient's spine indicated a defect between two discs. The two neurologists recommended undergoing anterior disc removal and interbody fusion. The patient consented and they performed operation on August 24, 1973. After two neurosurgeons removed the infected disc, an orthopedic surgeon inserted bone plug into the space. After the operation, the patient suffered spasms in his legs, and his recovery was not proceeding as expected. A second myelogram performed three days after the operation revealed a complete obstruction between the sixth and seventh cervical vertebrae. The physician then performed a decompressed laminectomy and removed fragments of extruded disc. After the second operation, the patient still could not move his extremities. He received physical therapies and other treatments as an outpatient and gradually became able to assume some of the functions of daily living. The patient went to California where he underwent two additional operations. Afterward he had to use a permanent catheter for the first time. He suffered substantial loss of function of his right deltoid muscle. In an action against two the neurosurgeons and the orthopedic surgeon who performed the initial operation, the trial court granted a motion of direct verdict in favor of the orthopedic surgeon. The court also found the neurosurgeon not liable but granted the patient's motion for a new trial as to the neurosurgeon. On appeal, the trial court's decision was affirmed. Trial court judge was admittedly confused over the law which applied to subsequent aggravation of the patient's injuries, the court observed. The defense attorney also made improper remarks in the closing argument. The comment implied the effect of a verdict in favor of the patient would be an imposition of every conceivable surgical risk on surgeons which would force them out of work. As to a direct verdict for the orthopedic surgeon, the court said the evidence did not support the contention that disc fragments were in the surgical site when they inserted the bone plug).

139 ***Ralkey v Minnesota Mining & Manufacturing Co,* 492 A2d 1358 (Md App 1985)** (plaintiff suffered lacerations and permanent disfigurement when cast was removed using electric saw. Plaintiff reached settlement with physician, but filed products liability action against cast tape manufacturer, saying doctor followed manufacturer's instructions for removing cast but injury occurred. Language of the physician's release encompassed "all other tortfeasors").

140 ***Sammons v Smith,* 353 NW2d 380 (Iowa 1984)** (plaintiff underwent leg surgery under tourniquet control. Permanent damage to components of the sciatic nerve resulted. Expert testimony showed hospital was negligent in checking tourniquet pressure gauges before surgery, suggesting excessive tourniquet pressure as a cause of nerve damage (a well-known risk applies with pressure too high or for too long.) The court allowed action against surgeon under the res ipsa loquitur doctrine).

141 ***Jeffries v Murdock,* 74 Or App 38, 701 P2d 451 (1985)** (surgeon accidentally cut part of the nerve supply to plaintiff's vocal cords while repairing a subclavian artery aneurysm. Defendant said the aneurysm threatened loss of arm or life; plaintiff offered no rebuttal).

Comment: Cutting of nerves "accidentally," although easy to do in deep or blood-filled holes, represents less than perfect surgical technique. Often, nerve cutting at surgery reflects the surgeon's carelessness or lack of familiarity with surgical anatomy, and because they are a risk of surgery does not mean that they are not preventable misadventure.

142 ***Sigmon v Bullitt,* 39 Ohio App 3d 116, 529 NE2d 1388 (1987)** (breakage of possibly weak suture almost convicted a surgeon, with the plaintiff alleging that suture gave away, proving the surgeon did not know where to place suture. The Ohio Court of Appeals believed the patient had offered the surgeon a loophole. The suture breakage occurred several hours after a carotid endarterectomy, leading to severe brain damage. The plaintiff charged the surgeon with negligence handling of the suture and charged the manufacturer with providing "unreasonably dangerous suture" that would not withstand the normal pressures at the operative site. Both the trial court and later the appellate court pointed out that if the suture was substandard, the suture breakage could have occurred without any negligence on the surgeon's part. As far as the surgeon's negligence, the court held there was insufficient evidence of surgeon error).

143 *Sherrill v McBride,* 603 SW2d 365 (Tex Civ App 1980) (malignant melanoma was removed from patient's foot. Due to complications from catheter, a hemorrhage developed in the thigh requiring amputation. This remote complication was not told to patient and he sued for lack of informed consent. Expert testimony was that this complication was remote. Jury properly determined that there was no deviation from "standard" and finding for defendant was affirmed).

144 *Greenwood v Wierdsma,* 741 P2d 1079 (Wyo 1987) (action against surgeon and hospital where surgeon failed to scrub hands before a surgical procedure and failed to suture wound with only a nurse in attendance (removal of placenta after birth of child). Plaintiff further alleged hospital failed to properly investigate, certify and verify surgeon's skills and negligently allowed the surgeon to perform such surgery. There apparently was no injury to patient in spite of bad surgical technique. Court stated that there were ample facts for jury to consider and dismissal was not appropriate).

145 *Monahan v Weichart,* 93 AD2d 984, 461 NYS2d 633 (1983) (orthopedic surgeon was liable for doing surgery that was too drastic. The patient had rheumatoid arthritis of both knees. He could bend his knees but could no longer straighten the legs. The orthopedist was asked to do a supracondylar femoral osteotomy so the knees would come straight. He did both knees at the same surgery. After removal of cast in six weeks, both knees were stiffened by scarring. The question was whether the orthopedist had been reckless in the extent of the surgery and whether he should have done one knee at a time to see how it might have come out were keys to the judgment of the jury. There was enough expert testimony saying that one knee at a time was more within the standard of care than doing both at the same time in spite of the fact that the natural history of rheumatoid arthritis is one of progressive deterioration of joints and may well have led to a stiffened joint without surgery. The second, and perhaps dominating point, was that the deformity had been changed from one where the patient could sit with knees bent and now the knees would not bend at all. Additionally, there had been little improvement, if any, in the pain of the knees post-operatively compared to pre-operatively. The charge basically was recklessness in management of the case suggesting a more conservative approach was needed at the time and would have better fit the standard of care).

Comment: Cases like these are always judgment calls, and again, the judgment is based more on the outcome of the procedure. Had she not had the stiffened knees, very likely the procedure would have been considered by many orthopedists as being well within the standard of care.

146 *Fridena v Evans,* 622 P2d 463 (Ariz 1980), *rehg denied,* (Jan 13, 1981) (patient was awarded the verdict from the physician for negligence in an operation to lengthen her leg. A 15-year-old patient suffered serious fracture of her right femur in 1966. An orthopedic surgeon performed surgery and inserted a pin into her leg and hip. After surgery, the right leg was 1½″ shorter than the left leg. In January 1967, a second operation was performed by an osteopath. He attempted to lengthen the right leg by bisecting the middle of the femur and inserting a bone graft. Rather than lengthening the leg, however, the procedure resulted in further shortening, leaving the right leg 3″ shorter than the left. The award was made against the orthopedist based on expert medical testimonies that the surgical procedure was below the standard of care, and was in effect experimental surgery).

Comment: It is important that surgical procedures be the usual and acceptable procedures, that the physician not be innovative at the expense of the patient unless there is a clear understanding that this is an experimental type of procedure and that is included in the operative consent.

147 *Ogletree v Willis-Knighton Memorial Hospital, Inc,* 530 So 2d 1175 (La Ct App 1988) (patient sustained puncture wound of buttock in automobile accident. Surgeon cleansed and sutured wound, loosely leaving drains in wound. Patient did well for 24 hours when the nurses noted changes in vital signs and notified surgeon. The surgeon came to hospital, found wound massively swollen with blistered skin. He made diagnosis of gas gangrene, gave large doses of penicillin, took patient to surgery where wide debridement of dissecting infection was effected. Amputation was considered and rejected as infection had spread to abdomen. Patient died 11 hours later. Patient's family filed malpractice action but trial court found no liability. On appeal, the court pointed out that unsuccessful treatment, per se, is not malpractice. Experts pointed out difficulty in treating gas gangrene, with plaintiff's experts outlining steps for preventing gas gangrene. Surgeon had essentially followed these steps or had a rational explanation for reason of departure).

148 *Horton v Vickers,* 142 Conn 105, 111 A2d 675 (1955) (defendant physician treated a fractured hip by inserting a nail to hold the fragments together, but a urinary infection supervened and because danger from this, further attempts to maintain the fracture in apposition were abandoned after the fracture had separated. The plaintiff's hip was permanently disabled. The court, holding the testimony of the medical witness for the plaintiff that he considered procedures followed by the defendant as having been bad practice without further defining the phrase or relating it to reasonable care, skill or diligence exercised by how the physician and surgeon in the same general neighborhood did not require a finding of negligence).

149 *O'Grady v Cadwallader,* 183 Iowa 178, 166 NW 755 (1983) (in this 1918 case, a direct verdict was for the defendant was held. Medical expert said x-rays taken subsequent to initial treatment showed the bones not in good apposition. The plaintiff surgeon testified that there is nothing to support the finding of negligence, that he finally operated the arm. He testified that the physical examination of the bone showed that the x-ray gave the wrong impression—that the bones were in as good apposition as can be expected, and that there had been early healing of bone callous that precluded pronation and supination, that the callous was something that the treating physician had no control over and specifically was impossible to diagnose without making an incision. Further testimony was that good practice would not recommend open incision until adequate time had passed for the callous to mature. At that time, less than adequate apposition and malunion could be diagnosed and in fact was diagnosed and was appropriately treated by the physician).

150 ***Connelly v Cone,* 205 Mo App 395, 224 SW 1011 (1920)** (in this 1920 case, claim was made that defendant doctor failed to prevent defendant's fractured leg from setting in a position of mal-union. Facts showed fracture was a compound one with a contaminated wound and in such cases, infection frequently developed, the proper practice was first to treat the infection to get it under control and then to re-fracture the leg if it were malpositioned. In this case, the patient had recommended osteotomy (refracture) of the tibia but the patient refused).

151 ***Hollis v Ahlquist,* 142 Wash 33, 251 P 871 (1927)** (fractured tibia and fibula showed perfect alignment and apposition on first x-ray. After application of therapeutic cast, a second x-ray showed good alignment but that there was about ¼″ overlap. This was held not to justify the conclusion that the loss of apposition was caused by the treating physician's negligence. The Court held that a verdict was properly directed for the defendant upon evidence that observing the lack of apposition, that he decided against an attempt to re-set the leg, preferring to allow the natural processes to reduce the apposition by subsidence of swelling and relaxation of muscles, especially since the medical expert testified that x-rays taken before the trial indicated that a good union had been obtained).

152 ***Carraway v Smith,* 218 Ala 412, 118 So 758 (1928)** (plaintiff charged defendant with negligence in setting broken leg and leg did not heal. Evidence demonstrated the bone had healed in an overlapped position so the leg was shortened. There was failure of proof to support the complaint and a verdict for the plaintiff could not be sustained. Failure of proof amounted to not showing that the shortening was either unusual for this type of fracture nor excessive, nor is it the sort of shortening that would warrant in itself open operation).

153 ***Ayala v King Rider Lumber Co,* 146 La 536, 83 So 799 (1920)** (evidence was that the defendant used local anesthetic rather than general anesthetic setting the plaintiff's fractured femur which healed with an overlap. There was no evidence of negligence where the medical testimony was that the practice was proper; that is, overlapping the fracture fragments was proper in some cases. There is a factual medical idium that it is not proper

to treat the x-ray but is more proper to treat the patient as a whole rather than by x-ray).

154 ***Gebhardt v McQuillen,* 230 Iowa 181, 297 NW 301 (1941)** (this is a 1941 case charging that the defendant, while treating a patient's broken hip, allowed the leg to become shortened. In this case, the defense failed to show that it was not unusual, in spite of the best of treatments, for shortening of the leg to occur).

155 ***Harry v Sorensen,* 215 Iowa 1229, 247 NW 651 (1933)** (defendant's position was that he had thought he had corrected the fracture and x-ray facilities were not immediately available. Patient was placed in a trough splint, transferred to another town where x-rays showed the bones were not in apposition. After several attempts to reduce the fracture by the use of extension methods, the defendant was dismissed and another doctor called, who successfully treated the leg. Court noted that there was no expert testimony, that the defendant had not followed proper practice and saying the failure to effect a cure was not evidence of negligence).

156 ***Kinsley v Carravetta,* 244 App Div 213, 279 NYS 29, *affd,* 273 NY 559, 7 NE2d 691 (1935)** (in this 1935 case, the defendant was charged with negligence when x-rays first showed that the patient's broken leg bones were out of alignment and that the physician did not immediately take proper steps to correct this condition. Expert testimony for plaintiff admitted that the action to be taken was largely a matter of judgment and there was much evidence for the defendant because the fracture was infected. It would have been unwise to attempt further treatment at that time, especially since as far as the plate showed, there is a good chance for a good functional result with only minor deformity).

157 ***Kemp v McGillivray,* 129 Wash 591, 255 P 631 (1924)** (in this 1924 case, all the surgeons who testified, including the ones who performed a subsequent open reduction operation on the plaintiff's leg, testified that the defendant's treatment had secured a good functional result, although there would be some shortening and the ends of the bone were not in perfect apposition. The test here, as in many cases, has been assessing the functional result).

158 ***Derr v Bonney,* 38 Wash 2d 678, 231 P2d 637 (1951)** (this 1951 case claimed negligence in failing to attempt to reduce the swelling of the plaintiff's ankle before releasing her and placing the ankle in a cast immediately after the accident with swelling present. Findings were held not supported by medical evidence where the plaintiff's witness testified that the swelling was caused by a circulatory disturbance of the tissues in which, in his own opinion, nature might possibly take care of, but he did not testify that the defendant's procedure had been incorrect).

Comment: Often, in fractures about the wrist, foot and ankle, or other parts of the body, there is significant soft tissue swelling. If the fracture is one to be treated by closed reduction, use of a temporary splint, supporting the joint, allowing for expansion of swelling is appropriate. The use of compressive dressing, elevation, ice, etc., is also appropriate. Following reduction of the swelling, the fracture can be definitively held by an appropriate cast.

159 ***Olson v Weitz,* 37 Wash 2d 70, 221 P2d 537 (1950)** (court held that when the defendant physician removed a cast from the plaintiff's arm after treating a simple transverse greenstick fracture of the radius, the arm was in useless condition. It was subsequently found the jury could draw on an inference of negligence and went on to hold that the evidence was in conflict as to whether the arm was straight and in good condition at the time and had been subsequently re-fractured or whether, as several lay witnesses testified, it was crooked and useless immediately after the cast was removed. An issue of fact was presented for the jury whose verdict for the plaintiff would be sustained).

160 ***Kiekhoefer v Hilershide,* 104 Wis 126, 80 NW 62 (1899), *revd,* 113 Wis 280, 89 NW 189 (1902)** (in this case, 16 days after the physician had set a fracture of the plaintiff's wrist, the defendant had found that the broken ulna was slightly out of apposition but because partial union had taken place, refrained from attempting to re-set the bone and subsequently, because excessive development of callous of the hand was left deformed, it required surgery. This was held to be insufficient to support the jury's findings of negligence. While some expert witnesses had expressed doubt whether the union was difficult to break down to the deformity in such a short period, there was not sufficient evidence to raise as to the defendant's contention that a severe effort would have been necessary in order to correct the condition. It was pointed out that the excessive secretion of callous, according to the expert testimony, was not a consequence that the defendant could have anticipated as a result of a slight displacement. The case was reversed on later appeal, and a verdict for the plaintiff sustained, based on the court noting that in the second trial, there was medical testimony that from the subsequent examination, the displacement at the time of the examination by the defendant must have been much greater than he had previously admitted, and so great as to call for the resetting of the fracture and to account for the excessive flow of callous in the absence of such resetting).

161 ***Forman v Surber,* 113 Kan 42, 213 P 667 (1923)** (defendant had set the plaintiff's broken arm, and the plaintiff claimed parts of the broken bone were grating against each other. He reported this to the physician and after a cursory examination, physician assured plaintiff everything was all right and bone was straight. Doctor persisted with this attitude over the plaintiff's continuing complaints of feeling grating. When splint was removed, arm was crooked).

162 ***McMillen v Foncannon,* 127 Kan 573, 274 P 237 (1929)** (patient was discharged by the defendant as cured after treatment of fractured arm. However, the bones had not united and the arm would not support its own weight when extended—that is, it was flail. In this case, expert evidence that medical negligence existed was given. The judge said he felt there was negligence, even absent expert testimony).

163 ***Byrom v Eastern Dispensary & Casualty Hospital,*** **132 F2d 788 (DC Cir 1943)** (in this 1943 case, it was held that the jury could try the fact of negligence based on the issue that the physician failed to take further steps to secure union after the first attempt failed; that is, informed the patient that nothing further could or should be done, that he should accept the impairment that he had as a natural course following the injury he had).

164 ***Kernodle v Elder,*** **23 Okla 743, 102 P 138 (1909)** (this is a 1909 case in which the jury's verdict for the plaintiff was reversed. The plaintiff was treated for a fracture of the neck of the femur and later complained that his leg was shortened and he was lame. He attributed this to the treating physician's negligence. The court pointed out that the experts who testified all agreed in such cases with the plaintiff's age, a good result was extremely unlikely in about 80 per cent of these cases. This situation might be quite different currently with the present techniques of treating fractures of the neck of the femur; however, it still is a fact that a substantial number of fractured neck of femur treated by adequate open reduction and internal fixation proceed ahead to either shortening or failure of union or both).

165 ***Horn v Pope,*** **205 Ala 127, 87 S 161 (1920)** (in this 1920 case, plaintiff charged in general terms that the defendant, who had undertaken to treat the plaintiff's broken leg, negligently carried out the treatment so the bones failed to unite and the leg became crooked. This was held as the state of cause of action sufficient for the jury to try the facts and a verdict for the plaintiff was held supported by the evidence).

166 ***Merryman v Bunch,*** **24 Tenn App 408, 145 SW2d, 559 (1940)** (evidence was that neither the defendant physician, who originally undertook the care of the plaintiff's fracture nor the subsequent treating physicians were able to affect a cure. It was held that a directed verdict for the defendant was appropriate, stating clearing that the failure of the leg to heal could have been due to causes other than negligent or lack of proper treatment).

167 ***Butler v Molinski,*** **198 Tenn 124, 277 SW2d 448 (1955)** (this 1955 case held that in Colles' fracture, even with the best of cases, a silver fork deformity frequently resulted and that the defendant could not be held liable for alleged negligence in treatment. The court held that the mere fact treatment was not a success did not in any sense testify the conclusion of negligence).

168 ***White v Burton,*** **180 Okla 499, 71 P2d 694 (1937)** (evidence stated that the defendant had been negligent in delaying overnight before studying the plaintiff's fracture, was held to support the jury's verdict for plaintiff, despite medical testimony that the failure to unite was caused by the plaintiff's metabolic condition. In this case, as many, if it appears that the treatment complained of, even if improper, could have had no effect upon the failure of the bones to unite properly, there could be no recovery, though it might be held that there was a proximate cause in the fracture and end result the overnight delay contributed nothing to the probably outcome).

169 ***McDonnell v Monteith,*** **59 ND 750, 231 NW 854 (1930)** (it was error to direct for the defendant when there was conflicting evidence as to

whether the plaintiff, being treated for a broken arm, had followed the defendant's directions and whether any act on his part contributed to keeping the bone from uniting).

170 ***Lemon v Kessel,* 202 Iowa 273, 209 NW 393 (1926)** (when the plaintiff was released from the hospital, his fractured leg was substantially the same length as a normal leg, but thereafter, the leg presented an altogether different appearance and was in a different condition. The plaintiff was required to exercise ordinary care and to report change of condition to the doctors, even though he had not been instructed to do so. Failure on the patient's part to exercise such care prevented him from recovering damage).

171 ***Western Union Telegraph Co v Mason,* 232 Ky 237, 22 SW2d 604** (court said that conflicting medical testimony probably authorized a finding that a physician treating a fractured leg had been guilty of negligence in applying a cast improperly with the result that bones had jointed out of alignment. It takes an expert opinion to say that the case was improperly applied and a second opinion that the improperly applied cast resulted in the malunion).

172 ***Fowler v Burris,* 186 Mo App 347, 171 SW 620 (1914)** (in this 1914 case, the verdict for the plaintiff was reversed because of an error in instructions. They indicated there was evidence of negligence and that it should be tried by a jury. The alleged negligence stated that the defendant physician failed to properly splint a broken and dislocated wrist to prevent the deformity which resulted).

173 ***Parr v Young,* 121 Kan 47, 246 P 181 (1926)** (this 1926 case presented evidence sufficient for the jury to try the issue of negligence in connection with the splinting or casting of the injured member whether the defendant set the broken and dislocated wrist and when it was not straight after splints were removed, he told the patient to go ahead and use it. Further complaints developed; the physician re-broke and reset the wrist. On removal of the splint, it was again found to be brooked and not usable. The defendant again told him to use it and it would improve, though later, the physician proposed to again re-fracture and re-set the original fracture. The court said the evidence established that the plaintiff had been deprived of the use of his arm through improper splinting as was shown through expert testimony).

174 ***Davis v Wilmerding,* 222 NC 639, 24 SE2d 337 (1943)** (evidence was that after putting the plaintiff's broken arm in a cast, the defendant proceeded, by removing the cast once or twice a week and massaging the arm, not supporting the broken part of the bone during the process. This resulted with the bone healing out of alignment. Expert witness testified that the removal of cast at such intervals was bad practice and that massaging procedure was unusual. This was appropriately head by the jury as the proximate cause of the failure of union and the unusual technique used).

175 ***Hall v Nagel,* 139 Ohio St 265, 39 NE2d 612 (1942)** (this is a 1942 case in which the defendant, an osteopath, treating a broken humerus took an x-ray showing the fracture in good apposition. The next day, he applied an airplane splint and gave him no further treatment for a period of two weeks. Another x-ray showed the fragments mis-aligned and overlapping. The defendant testified he made no effort to treat the fracture because of the patient's general run-down condition and had so informed the plaintiff. The court said the question for jury was raised by testimony of medical witness that a fracture of this type could have been treated and good results obtained by manipulation in the use of airplane splint, and the plaintiff testified his physical condition was good. The court also held that it was reversible error to refuse to permit one plaintiff's medical witness to testify that the manipulation of the arm of the defendant implying the splint caused the bones to go out to apposition).

Comment: There are a number of ways to adequately treat the shaft of the humerus. Barring complicating situations, the use of an airplane cast is unusual. Hanging cast, stirrups, hemo-fracture splinters, and even sling and swath or sling alone are all accepted treatment as long as there is reasonably adequate position of the bone. Some overlap and minimal angulation are not unusual.

176 ***Olsen v McAtee,*** **181 Or 503, 183 P2d 979 (1947)** (this is a 1947 case where the physician placed a cast in the treatment of a fractured femur although x-rays showed the bone ends were overlapping. Part of the treatment included suspending weight from the cast. This treatment was persisted for over two weeks although subsequent x-rays showed the bones were still not in apposition. Medical witnesses testified that the bones began to knit in this position so that an open operation was required and that proper practice would have been to put a temporary cast on until the swelling went down and then taken proper steps to get apposition. Also, the cast applied by the defendant was improper in that it permitted the bones to rotate. Treatment in addition to the fracture caused the patient great pain. There was enough evidence in this case for the jury to try the question of negligence).

177 ***Person v Lilliendah,*** **118 Conn 693, 172 A 94 (1934)** (directed verdict for the defendant, as there was no expert evidence to support the plaintiff's contention that after her jaw was broken in the course of extraction, the defendant was guilty of failing to apply some kind of brace to keep the broken bones stable while healing).

178 ***Blackburn v Security Benefit Association,*** **149 Kan 89, 86 P2d 536 (1939)** (charge of negligence against a physician was made stating that the physician placed a cast on the plaintiff's injured leg in such a matter that the fractured portion of the leg was not covered. The court held that the claim was not supported by the evidence where there was nothing to show that it was not properly done. The testimony showed that because of other operative wounds, it is impossible to use a normal cast, and certain adjustments had been made to allow for these conditions. It, therefore, was held that the placing of the cast itself was not negligent treatment leading to the failure of adequate healing of the fracture, per se).

179 ***Lorenz v Lerche,* 157 Minn 437, 196 NW 564 (1926)** (in this 1926 case, six well-qualified experts for the defendant testified that the failure of the plaintiff's fractured leg to unite could not have resulted from tightness of the cast applied by the defendant and the alleged resulting ulcers on the flesh and only one comparatively inexperienced expert of another school testified this could have been the cause of the condition. It was held that the cast application as such did not produce the failure of healing and the verdict for the plaintiff was reversed).

180 ***Warwick v Bliss,* 46 SD 622, 195 NW 501, *appeal* 52 SD 107, 216 NW 865 (1923)** (case was brought with complaints that the defendant had been negligent in applying plaster cast too tightly to the plaintiff's fractured leg were held groundless. The evidence was that the tightness was caused by swelling which took place after the cast was applied, then on complaints of pain; the cast was first split a short distance and within a few days removed entirely. The court said that there was no showing that it was tighter than necessary to hold the bone fragments in place or sufficiently tight to do so in view of the fact that union failed to take place).

Comment: There is no comment on what additional future treatment was necessary to effect union of the fractured bones.

181 ***Kiley v Dervin,* 314 Mass 478, 50 NE2d 393 (1943)** (defendant was called to treat a broken arm which had been previously set and splinted directed that x-rays be taken and informed the technician that, if necessary, the splint and bandage could be removed for this purpose. There was a directed verdict for the defendant, although a medical witness for the plaintiff testified that x-rays showed that something had happened to the arm, a drop of about 10 per cent, and in his opinion, this was due to the fact that the splint and bandages were allowed to be taken off, and it was an error to allow such removal without giving the plaintiff anesthetic. The court said there was nothing to show that it was bad practice to have x-rays in question taken, and ordered to remove the splint or bandage in order to get adequate x-rays; that there was no direct evidence that the anesthetic was not in fact administered or that the defendant knew an anesthetic would not be administered if the condition required it; that there was no evidence that the technician was not a suitable person to entrust with the removal of the splint or damages; and as a matter of conjecture whether failure to give an anesthetic caused the bad result complained of, since several days had elapsed since the time the arm was set and the day the pictures were taken; and the plaintiff's medical witness testified that it was hard to tell whether removal of bandages caused the condition but it might be one of the causes. It was the court's opinion that there was no sufficient medical expert testimony to attach proximate cause to each of these items).

182 ***Sinz v Owens,* 33 Cal 2d 749, 205 P 2d 3 (1949)** (this 1949 case showed, upon medical testimony, that in treating a double comminuted fracture of the tibia and fibula, good practice required the use of skeletal traction to prevent angulation, that successive x-rays taken during the period of healing showed progressive angulation, that traction could have improved this condition even as late as the time the cast was removed from the patient's leg, and that it was the general custom of physicians in the vicinity to refer cases requiring skeletal traction to a specialist in a nearby city. A finding of causal negligence was justified, the court saying that the failure of the defendant to recognize inadequacy of treatment given under the circumstances was strong evidence of a breach of required standard or care).

183 ***Schanil v Branton,*** **181 Minn 381, 232 NW 708 (1930)** (this 1930 case states that the defendant treated a comminuted fracture below the knee by the use of a Thomas splint which was proper but there was evidence that insufficient traction was applied so that the foot was held loosely and it rotated and set in improper position).

184 ***Gunter v Whitener,*** **75 SW2d 588 (Mo 1934)** (this 1934 Missouri case held that there was sufficient evidence of negligence to go to a jury, the facts being that the defendant treated the fracture of the plaintiff's radius and ulna near the elbow by use of splints and pressure while several medical witnesses approved this, others testified that he should have proceeded either by the use of traction or by open reduction).

Comment: It is frequent that different surgeons of different schools will treat the same fracture by different techniques—some by open procedures, some by closed procedures. It is frequently difficult to get a concensus and equally difficult to get an unbiased opinion in these situations. Claims of negligence in connection with such operations have frequently been successful in cases where the plaintiff was complaining of the physician's failure to secure proper union.

185 ***Beauchamp v Davis,*** **209 Ky 397, 217 SW2d 822 (1948)** (in this 1948 case, it was noted that an orthopedic surgeon engaged by the defendant who had been originally called in the case to perform an open reduction on the plaintiff's leg had been found guilty of negligence in treating the leg by pins and an external plate which failed to achieve a union. The court held that the issue of the defendant's negligence and permitting the negligent act or in failing to preserve and prevent them should have been submitted to the jury. There are two issues here—one whether the defendant physician is liable for the action of the specialist that he calls in which, in fact, he is in many cases, and second, is the defendant operating surgeon's technique negligent?).

186 ***Furr v Herzmark,*** **206 F2d 468 (DC Cir 1953)** (defendant secured fracture of femur with four screws and plate. Femur failed to heal. Surgeon re-operated and placed six holed plate. The wound became infected in spite of antibiotics. Consultants said the metal plate and screws should be removed, but surgeon disagreed. Jury verdict for plaintiff).

Comment: The presence of metal internal fixing devices is not always thought to prevent infection from clearing, especially with current wide-range antibiotics. Each case must be evaluated individually.

187 ***Gleason v Bessinger,*** **708 F Supp 157 (SD Tex 1989)** (state-employed physicians are not entitled to "official immunity" from liability for medical malpractice. The plaintiff at a state park consulted staff physician who improperly treated a leg injury that resulted in severe infection and thereby sustained permanent additional impairment. The court reasoned that a physician must exercise judgment when treating a patient and that judgment is medical, rather than governmental, in nature. The court concluded that medical treatment is a profession ministerial act. Governmental immunity is designed to protect state employees from liability for harm resulting from policy-making actions. The court concluded that society's interest in effective government would not be significantly affected by holding state employed physicians responsible for their professional negligence).

188 ***Middlebrook v Imler,*** **713 P2d 572 (Okla 1985)** (patient was in an accident, sustaining fracture/dislocation of cervical spine along with multiple other injuries. He was treated initially by an orthopedist who put him in traction. A ruptured cecum was diagnosed and emergency surgery required taking the patient out of his traction. It was ascertained about that time that the traction was not effective. The patient was not able to stand or walk right after the injury but those soon ceased, and he was released from the emergency room. A day or so later, he began to feel pain in the right shoulder. It was at that time the fracture/dislocation of the cervical spine was diagnosed and the traction started. A neurosurgeon-orthopedic surgeon collaborated in surgical repair in which a strut bone graft operation was carried out. As the patient regained consciousness, he was unable to move his arms or legs, and his hands were numb. He was never to regain full use of his limbs. In the lawsuit, it was said no surgery had been called for since his condition was not one of progressive paralysis; that consideration of congenitally narrowed spinal canal was not attended to by the surgeons, and immediate re-operation to decompress the cervical spine when the first signs of neurological involvement appeared should have been carried out. The surgeons argued that the dislocated vertebra was an unstable situation, that the surgical crisis producing the quadriplegia was an unpredictable ischemic attack. Res ipsa loquitur was introduced. The final verdict was against the surgeons, but the basic thrust that the case had been equally well managed by closed skeletal traction, halo cast or some fixed skeletal traction technique, along with observing for worsening of neurological signs).
Comment: In cases like this, there are frequent differences of opinion. However, the non-operative approach suggested probably is the consensus at this time. The need for accurate recordkeeping as to whether there was in fact worsening of the dislocation and if there was any change of the neurological pattern (which can be monitored on an hourly basis if necessary) is a must. It should also be noted that use of skeletal traction, when the patient was transferred from his room to surgery and used at the time of surgery, would be appropriate in further protecting the cervical spine.

189 ***Sweat v Norman,*** **283 SC 443, 322 SE2d 478 (1984)** (plaintiff sustained fracture of right femur and patella resulting in 50 per cent loss of function of right leg. Additional multiple facial bone and mandibular fractures, with numerous lacerations about the face, left significant cosmetic defects in face. Jury award of $1,500,000 was held not excessive).

190 ***Rowan v Nassau Co,* 91 AD2d 608, 456 NYS2d 418 (1982)** (plaintiff sustained severe fractures of left forearm and left tibia and fibula, along with skull fracture, brain damage, loss of teeth, broken nose, all resulting in scarred deformed face. Award of $800,000 not excessive).

191 ***Rhoda v Aroostook General Hospital,* 226 A2d 530 (Me 1967)** (charge was made that a patient treated for a fractured leg with traction pin having been placed by an orthopedist, was handled and cared for in a negligent manner by unskillful and unprofessional employees. Court argued that the hospital was responsible for the action of its professional people and inadequate supervision and/or inadequate selection of employees are negligent acts. This case, however, was reversed on the basis that the hospital was an uninsured charitable hospital that could not be held liable on the basis of negligence in selecting an employee).

192 ***Jistarri v Nappi,* 549 A2d 210 (Pa Super 1988)** (orthopedic resident might be held to a lesser standard of care than a trained practicing orthopedic surgeon. In this case, the result is moot as case was dismissed by court for lack of expert testimony. The patient sustained fractured wrist that was set and placed in cast by resident and then checked four days later by staff orthopedist. The next day, patient had chest pain and cough and was hospitalized with Staphylococcus septicemia. One day later, cast was removed and a pressure area infected with Staph was found. The patient died of complications related to septicemia. The internist treating the infection deposed that infected ulcer at wrist fracture site was probable cause of septicemia. The internist was released from law suit and later refused to testify against orthopedists. The court held as a doctor no longer related to the case, he could not be forced to testify, thus case failed for lack of expert testimony. The question of negligence by the resident was unanswered, but probable cast complication (pressure point) led to infected ulcer which may well have been proximately related to septicemia leading to patient's demise).

193 ***Gladewater Municipal Hospital v Marashi,* 694 SW2d 619 (Tex Ct App 1985)** (patient filed a suit against an orthopedist alleging his osteomyelitis was due to the 39 days of bandages on his injured and operated leg that had only been changed twice. He was admitted to the hospital for a leg injury. Bandage for changed for the first in 13 days, although the wound had always drained with a strong offensive odor. The patient subsequently developed osteomyelitis requiring at least three operations. Expert testimony from a nurse stated that the hospital nurse had violated professional standards when they had failed to report to the doctor the wound was draining and neglected to change the bandages frequently. The surgeon was similarly criticized. The jury found the defendants guilty. There was some question whether expert nursing testimony should be allowed against a physician but it did stand. The facts were that it was a dirty compound wound that was healing slowly and that the tight dressing held infected material (pus) facilitating migration of infected material to bone, resulting in osteomyelitis).

194 ***Braun v Rycyna,* 473 NYS2d 627 (App Div 1984)** (orthopedist treated a patient who landed on his feet on a concrete surface. Multiple x-rays were taken of the ankle; no x-rays were taken of his foot. Injury diagnosis was fractured right ankle, and he was advised to go to an orthopedic specialist. He did so. The orthopedic surgeon applied a walking cast treating the ankle fracture, and took no additional x-rays. A month or so later, he removed the walking cast, x-rayed the ankle that showed the fracture healed despite the patient's continued complaints of pain in his right foot. The orthopedic surgeon never ordered x-rays of his foot. The patient finally consulted another physician who took additional x-rays. The new x-rays revealed a fracture of the right heel. Use of an orthopedic shoe failed to relieve his pain. He underwent bone fusion one and one-half years later. Surgery reduced his pain but also shortened his ankle. The trial court granted the hospital motion for directed verdict on the grounds the hospital's negligence was not the proximate cause of the patient's injury. The appellate court reversed the decision. The court noted that a medical malpractice panel unanimously recommended a finding of a liability against the hospital and the physician. Court said the opinion was supported by expert opinion of this medical member and required the case to be submitted to a jury. Although the jury returned a verdict in favor of the orthopedic surgeon, the court said it would be highly unfair to exclude him from a re-trial of the case).

Comment: Failure to x-ray areas of complaint is a frequent cause of negligence litigation. In this case, with repeated complaint by the patient of foot pain and failure to x-ray the foot by the surgeon was below the standard of care.

195 ***Martinez v First National Bank,* 755 P2d 606 (NM 1988)** (absence of evidence that the driver was laible for bike accident in which patient fractured elbow. The orthopedist saw patient in emergency room, ordered x-rays and diagnosed simple elbow dislocation. The surgeon "popped" the elbow in place and ordered further x-rays. He did not order x-rays before casting arm to see if manipulation had been successful, nor did he order x-rays four weeks later when cast was removed. The patient continued to complain of pain and limited motion at elbow, but was reassured by the first orthopedist that all was well. A second orthopedist took x-rays that showed elbow dislocation reduction to be unsuccessful and that there were three fractured bones and torn muscles and ligaments. The second surgeon testified that the time delay in removing bone chips was responsible for extensive damage to articular surface of the elbow. The patient and his parents brought a malpractice action against the first orthopedist. The jury awarded $115,000 and apportioned 20 fault to the victim, 35 per cent to orthopedist and 45 per cent to automobile driver who was not party to this suit. On appeal, the driver of the auto, being a non-party to suit, was exonerated and the case remanded to trial court to reconsider apportionment of damages).

196 ***Haney v Mizell Memorial Hospital,* 744 F2d 1467 (11th Cir 1984)** (patient was quite intoxicated and was involved in an automobile accident and was brought to the emergency room by the emergency team. He was treated for shoulder abrasion and put to bed, but several hours later nurses observed he was suffering congestion. As a precaution against vomiting, the emergency room doctor ordered no fluids or foods be given him. At 10:00 PM, the first signs of paralysis were noted. His neck was immediately immobilized, although no x-rays had been taken. After x-rays, cervical fractures were discovered. The injuries subsequently resulted in total and permanent paralysis of arms and legs. The initial treating surgeons were sued, with the argument that if early x-rays of cervical spine had been taken, the fracture would have been discovered and prompt immobilization might have prevented the quadriplegia. Experts for the defendants testified that the original damage probably would have had the same disastrous results. The fact that the patient was obnoxious as part of his intoxication was considered in the production of the end result of the quadriplegia. The physicians were released from negligence).

Comment: This is a close situation. Historically, intoxicated people with shoulder girdle, neck, and head injuries are suspect for fractures with potential catastrophic results. Managing them in that mode with protective splinting and prompt x-rays of the skull and cervical spine are routine procedures in many hospital emergency rooms. However, the jury in this case apparently agreed that the standard of care was not breached in not doing those studies and procedures.

197 ***Jackson v Huang,* 514 So 2d 724 (La Ct App), *rehg denied* (1987)** (damages were awarded for infant's injuries due to negligence during delivery. Trial judge erred in awarding infant damages for loss of future earnings but was correct in awarding damages for earning capacity in a court of appeals. The infant sustained a permanent injury of the brachioplexus and injured the right shoulder and arm during delivery. Parents sued the obstetrician who delivered the child. At the trial, an expert witness testified explained the procedure for delivering the infant when shoulder dystrocia is present as it was in this case. He believed the obstetrician failed to recognize the condition until he had already pulled so hard that the brachial nerve was injured. He said because of the normal delivery of the mother's first child, large size of second baby and slow down in active labor should have alerted the obstetrician to perform a Cesarean section. Trial court found that the physician was aware of the extended labor, large size of the infant and should have been aware of the possible consequence. The court found that the parent had established the standard of care, that the obstetrician had failed to use proper care and the injuries were the consequence of that and awarded the parents $467,000. On appeal, the court found that the trial court erred in making the award for loss of future income since he had never had employment and the court deleted $183,445 for loss of future earnings and increased the amount for loss of earnings capacity from $100,000 to $175,000).

198 ***Ohligschlager v Proctor Community Hospital,*** **55 Ill 2d 411, 303 NE2d 392 (1973)** (action against surgeon and hospital for injuries caused by perivascular extravasation during intravenous administration of drug intended to stop vomiting directed verdict for hospital that was improper. No sufficient evidence from which inference could be drawn that defendant hospital was negligent which contributed to plaintiff's injury. Testimony showed that nurses' aide was told of pain and swelling at injection site shortly before 8:30 P.M. but intravenous was not discontinued until five hours later. Nursing supervisor testified that it was the duty of nurses to make periodic checks and observe condition of needle and observe whether fluid was flowing, and that at hospital orientation programs, problems of infiltration and extravasation are discussed and nurses were warned of dangers accompanying administration of certain intravenous fluids, that if a patient complains of pain at injection site, the intravenous should be discontinued promptly. The doctor was excused as not being a proper party to the suit).

199 ***Oukrop v Wasserburger,*** **755 P2d 233 (Wyo 1988)** (doctor prescribed 25 times the usual dose of atropine to decrease saliva before oral surgery, despite being questioned by the pharmacist, and failed to advise patient or his parents of the error. The dentist realized an overdose had been ordered, called an internist friend who advised the dentist to call a poison control center for advice. Dentist went ahead with surgery, not advising patient or mother of overdose. After surgery, patient began to hallucinate. Mother called the dentist three times but was never told of the overdose. Dentist said dentist inferred the patient "probably" had been taking drugs. Patient ran away from home, slept in haystack, and operative site became infected. Months later, patient's personality changed with forgetfulness and temper outbursts. Testimony of a pharmacist that atropine overdose left permanent brain damage in mice was allowed. Dentist was assessed $750,000 in damages).

200 ***Stone v Smith, Kline & French Laboratories,*** **447 So 2d 1301 (Ala 1984),** ***affd,*** **731 F2d 1575 (11th Cir 1984)** (patient developed adverse reaction to Thorazine. Physician who prescribed it was said to have been adequately warned by manufacturer of certain hazards of Thorazine, that is, Thorazine-induced hepatitis. Patient did develop hepatitis and through she recovered, she had a period of increased impairment. In an action against the manufacturer of the drug, a federal court granted summary judgment for the manufacturer. On appeal, the court certified a question of law to the Alabama Supreme Court. The state court said that if warnings to the prescribing physician about an unavoidably unsafe prescription drug were adequate, even though the patient was not warned, then the warnings were sufficient as a matter of law. The patient conceded that her physician had adequately warned of adverse reaction including hepatitis problem. The supreme court affirmed summary judgment for the manufacturer).

201 ***McCarroll v Reed,*** **679 P2d 851 (Okla Ct App 1983),** ***rehg denied*** **(Jan 19, 1984),** ***cert dismissed*** **(Mar 13, 1984)** (patient claimed he became addicted to drugs prescribed by his physician treating him as an orthopedist and had a cause of action against him. The case was initially dismissed as there was no cause of action but it was then sent for re-trial after being heard by superior courts. The patient consulted a physician and osteopath for insomnia secondary to neck and back pain. He sold the patient some 1,125 units of Placidyl, Valium, Tuinal and Tenuate, all controlled drugs, over the next 13 months. The patient claimed as a result of this he had a severe addiction problem accompanied by an irresistible compulsion to commit crimes to finance his cravings for drugs. By the time he filed a suit against the physician for malpractice, he had been arrested seven times, lost two jobs, had four car accidents and three motorcycle accidents. He had been divorced, lost custody of his child and faced a prison term of more than 20 years. In reversing the trial court's decision, the appellate court said the patient stated a claim for medical malpractice, suggested also the punitive damage could be recovered if the patient could show oppression, fraud or gross negligence).

Comment: It is incumbent on the prescribing physician to know his or her patient and his or her behavior with the use of controlled substances. In patients with addictive tendencies, adequate control of the symptoms, pain, anxiety, etc., is appropriate, but recognize that addictive personality and addictive behavior is a separate illness in itself, requiring treatment. As part of the informed consent for treating the patient, informing the patient of his or her potential addictive problem is a must.

202 ***Young v Cerniac,* 126 Ill App 3d 952, 467 NE2d 1045 (1984)** (defendant physician prescribed one-half recommended dose of Heparin for pulmonary embolus. The court held the drug manufacturer's recommendation was "a standard against which the defendant's conduct could be measured." Directed verdict was reversed).

Comment: It appears here, as in other cases, that this standard is a measure subject to the explanation of the defendant and his expert.

5

Physician Education

§5.01 Generally

Physicians in this country are educated through a system that includes both formal classroom (didactics) and hospital-based (clinical) elements. They are then licensed by state governments, which can revoke or limit the licenses. Their ongoing performance is monitored through professionally supervised review of their practice and through governmental processes which rely on that professional review. Their work in hospitals undergoes professional peer review and is subject to scrutiny by other institutional committees (e.g., infection control and medical records) which may affect their behavior. Substandard performance may result in changes in practice privileges and, eventually, in licensure, and may require financial compensation to the injured patients through the professional liability system. Each instance is directed to the performance and qualifications of physicians, but they are distinct from one another and play different roles in the practice of medicine.[1]

Physician credentialing includes education, licensure, specialty certification, and hospital privileging; these are intended to assure physician competence. This system accredits programs for education and continuing education, evaluates physicians' competence to receive licenses and determines when those licenses should be revoked or modified, determines physician qualifications for specialty certifications, and specifies physician hospital privileges.

As a basic control on who practices medicine, physician credentialing plays a significant role in preventing substandard care and avoidable injury to patients; it aims to assure competence of physicians and to remove those who are incompetent.

Evaluation of the quality of care provided to individual patients is the quality assurance process. It contributes to the prevention of avoidable adverse outcomes by identifying substandard practices and imposing corrective measures, such as additional education, restrictions on practice, and loss of formal credentials.

The goals of the professional liability system are twofold: to compensate financially those who suffer harm through avoidable adverse outcomes, and to serve as a deterrent to such outcomes. It is related to the other systems discussed above; however, the purposes and processes of these various systems differ with respect to the agencies which conduct them, the types of behavior reviewed, the applicable standards, and the actions taken.

§5.02 Physician Credentialing

Physician credentialing consists of several processes, including physician licensure and discipline, hospital privileging, board certification, and certain federal activities.

Each state controls who may practice medicine by requiring licenses for the practice of medicine within that state. State licensure constitutes the principal governmental mechanism for controlling who practices medicine and is the public's main line of defense against unfit physicians. Although the federal government does not engage in physician licensing per se, it does play a role in protecting patients cared for under federal payment programs by determining who may be reimbursed under those programs.

As of 1985, there were approximately 535,000 licensed physicians in the United States, with approximately 513,000 having an M.D. degree (allo-

---

[1] United States General Accounting Office, Medical Malpractice, Characteristics of Claims Closed in 1984 (April 1987); Pennsylvania Medical Socy, Medical Malpractice in Pennsylvania (1985).

pathic physicians) and approximately 22,000 having a D.O. degree (osteopathic physicians).[2]

§5.03 Credentialing of Orthopedists

The credentialing of orthopedists has been part of the specialty since 1934. Credentialing is one important step in assuring the public that the treating orthopedist has had sufficient training and has the cognitive and technical skills to hold him- or herself out as a specialist in orthopedic problems. Practicing orthopedic medicine and surgery in a manner that describes the standard of care is an obvious result of such specialization with credentialing.

The credentialing process (1) assures the patient that the orthopedist has had adequate training, (2) provides the patient with information necessary to help him or her choose quality care, (3) serves the needs of the orthopedic community by establishing standards of training, education, achievement, and performance, (4) may serve as criteria for appointment to specific professional posts, and (5) prevents conflict of interest if the credentialing is granted by a professional, independent body recognized by both the government and the professional.

There are ways of achieving competent education, training, and ability to practice orthopedic medicine and surgery other than credentialing by a board such as the American Board of Orthopedic Surgery. All of the training and education opportunities to specialize in orthopedic medicine and surgery are available to any physician eligible by virtue of previous medical school/internship training and for those physicians demonstrating the required moral and ethical status. The taking of credentialing examinations is the physician's choice, and he or she may elect to practice orthopedics absent formal credentialing. The goal of credentialing is to unify community understanding regarding the background of the specialist, although that is not to say other physicians are not equally competent.

§5.04 Requirements for Licensure

All states require completion of a medical school curriculum and conferral of an M.D. or D.O. degree, and the passing of a comprehensive written examination for initial licensure. All require graduate clinical training consisting of a residency in a hospital. *Residency* refers to all graduate medical education immediately following medical school, including the one or more years required prior to licensure (formerly called internship) as well as extended specialty training traditionally designated "residency." States also have

---

[2] R. Shryock, Medical Licensing in American 1650-1965 (1967); Federation of State Medical Bds of the United States, Exchange (Section 1) and Exchange (Section 2) (1987); Federation of State Medical Bds of the United States, A Guide to the Essentials of a Modern Medical Practice Act (1985), and On the Assessment of Physicians (1985) (a formal policy statement of the FSMB); Office of Inspector General, United States Dept of Health & Human Servs, Medical Licensure and Discipline, An Overview (1986).

requirements for interviews, written references, and other review and screening mechanisms prior to issuance of a license.[3]

As the required comprehensive examination, states accept the results of two nationally-administered examinations. All states accept the Federation Licensing Examination (FLEX), a two-component examination comprised of multiple choice questions and patient management problems, developed by the Federation of State Medical Boards (FSMB), the national organization of state medical licensing boards. Some states require an examination before the graduate clinical training; others permit it during or after graduate training. All but two jurisdictions accept the National Board of Medical Examiners (NBME) certification as the basis for licensing a physician. NBME's certification requires satisfactory completion of a series of three examinations (one after the second year of medical school, the second during the fourth year of medical school, and the last during the first year of residency) plus other qualifications.

The majority of states require graduate clinical training before issuing a full license. The usual requirement is one year, but an increasing number of states require two or three years. All require that graduates of medical schools outside the United States and Canada complete at least one year of accredited United States or Canadian graduate clinical education before licensure, and many states require two or three years of such education.

Physicians licensed in one state may obtain licensure in another state on the strength of their earlier license, a process called *licensure endorsement* or *reciprocity*. The second state examines the credentials of the applying physician and, in cases where the applicant has not been formally tested for a period of time (usually 8 to 10 years), requires a formal examination. Some states use an oral examination while others use the second part of the FLEX examination and special examination (SPEX) designed for this purpose.

Following initial licensing, all states require physicians to renew their registrations at regular intervals. Twenty-four states require annual renewal, and the remaining states require renewal every two, three, or four years. Twenty-two states require continuing medical education credits as a condition of continued licensure. Generally, once a physician is licensed, meets continuing medical education requirements, and files any necessary reregistration forms and fees, the license is permanent as long as the state licensing board does not suspend or revoke it.

The periodic reregistration process provides an opportunity to review the qualifications of a physician to practice medicine. The FSMB recommends that boards require licensees to demonstrate their continuing qualifications for medical licensure. They recommend, as a minimum, having the physician

---

[3] R. Shryock, Medical Licensing in American 1650-1965 (1967); Federation of State Medical Bds of the United States, Exchange (Section 1) and Exchange (Section 2) (1987); Federation of State Medical Bds of the United States, A Guide to the Essentials of a Modern Medical Practice Act (1985) and On the Assessment of Physicians (a formal policy statement of the FSMB); Office of Inspector General, United States Dept of Health & Human Servs, Medical Licensure and Discipline, An Overview (1986).

complete a report on any adverse actions, such as malpractice suits or loss of hospital privileges. The board can then determine if the physician requires special attention or investigation. Boards are not limited to matters which are self-reported. Most states require reports about certain actions involving physicians, such as adverse privileging actions in hospitals and malpractice claims and judgments. With this information and the information reported under federal law, a board receives data about malpractice payments and hospital privileging information from a source other than the physician and uses the data in reviewing the physician at the time of reregistration. This has been accomplished by the recently enacted Professional Data Bank (1990).[4]

§5.05 State Licensing Boards

States exercise their authority to license physicians through state licensing boards.

A single board has jurisdiction over all physicians in most states, and about one-third of the states have separate osteopathic medical boards. In the majority of states, the boards have independent authority to issue and revoke licenses and to take other actions. In a few states, some other authority or official has the formal licensing power, and the medical boards serve in an advisory capacity.

Operation of the disciplinary system consumes most of the efforts of the state licensing board, but the routine examination and licensure activities described above also occupy them. General staffs range from 1 to 30, but California has about 170, including a large number of investigators. The boards also make use of consultants in reviewing medical evidence. In over one-half of the states, legal services are provided by the Office of the Attorney General. The others have their own staff attorneys or retain outside counsel.[5]

State medical boards have the authority to revoke licenses and impose other penalties on physicians. Most state boards describe the practice of medicine as a privilege granted by the state rather than as a right, with the clear understanding that the privilege can be revoked.

The boards may take disciplinary actions ranging from revocation, suspension of license, probation, stipulations, limitations, reprimands, letters of censure, and letters of concern. Sanctions are an important part of a board's armamentarium in dealing with disciplinary problems. Prior to instituting formal proceedings against a physician, the board investigative staff

---

[4] R. Shryock, *supra* note 3; Federation of State Medical Bds of the United States, Exchange (Section 1) and Exchange (Section 2) (1987); Federation of State Medical Bds of the United States, A Guide to the Essentials of a Modern Medical Practice Act (1985) and On the Assessment of Physicians (a formal policy statement of the FSMB); Office of Inspector General, *supra* note 3.

[5] Office of Inspector General, United States Dept of Health & Human Servs, Medical Licensure and Discipline, An Overview (1986).

examines complaints and determines whether to proceed formally. Many complaints do not warrant further board action.

For formal actions, boards are subject to the procedural requirements of state practice administrative procedure acts. The usual burden of proof for taking formal disciplinary action against a physician is clear and convincing evidence.[6]

Most states authorize boards to suspend a physician's license prior to formal hearing, when the board believes such action is required to protect the public health and safety. In some states, courts can set aside such summary suspensions, but the Federation of State Medical Boards (FSMB) recommends that court authority to stay such summary actions be eliminated.

Boards take many informal actions with respect to physicians, and such actions are significant to the disciplinary process. The pattern of procedural requirements for such informal actions differs among the states, but common features are no hearing before the board, no assurance of formal due process, and confidentiality. Much of the boards' impact on physician discipline is through these actions rather than through formal actions, and boards typically take several times as many informal actions as formal actions. These informal actions may, for example, direct a physician to avoid performing certain procedures beyond his or her competence, or to obtain further training. The board then monitors the physician to assure compliance, with the threat of formal action if the board's recommendation is not followed.[7]

It is difficult to say what the "correct" number of disciplinary actions should be; this calculation depends on knowing how many incompetent physicians there are, but there seems to be little reliable information about this independent of the actions of the disciplinary system itself.

Among the most frequent violations constituting grounds for discipline is the inappropriate prescribing of drugs (typically shown by the failure to keep adequate patient records to support the prescriptions written). About one-half of the disciplinary actions taken by states are for such offenses. A physician's personal drug or alcohol abuse is a second major source of disciplinary action. These two categories represent three-fourths or more of all disciplinary actions.[8]

§5.06 State Determination of Controlled Substance Abuse

Most states have statutory language to assess physician prescription practices. Illinois describes appropriate use in the Illinois Controlled Substances Act, Ill Rev Stat ch 56, §404:

---

[6] US Dept of Health, Educ & Welfare, Medical Malpractice, Report of the Secretary's Commission on Medical Malpractice (1973).

[7] Breaden & Galusha, *Official 1985 Federation Summary of Reported Disciplinary Actions,* 73 Federation Bull 300, 305 (1986).

[8] Federation of State Medical Bds of United States, A Mode for the Preparation of a Guidebook on Medical Discipline (1986).

"Good Faith" means the prescribing or dispensing of a controlled substance by a practitioner in the regular course of professional treatment to or for any person who is under his treatment for a pathology or condition other than that individual's physical or psychological dependence upon or addiction to a controlled substance, except as provided herein: and application of the term to a pharmacist shall mean the dispensing of a controlled substance pursuant to the prescriber's order which in the professional judgment of the pharmacist is lawful. The pharmacist shall be guided by accepted professional standards including, but not limited to the following, in making the judgment:

(1) Lack of consistency of doctor-patient relationship,
(2) frequency of prescriptions for same drug by one prescriber for large numbers of patients,
(3) quantities beyond those normally prescribed,
(4) unusual dosages,
(5) unusual geographic distances between patient, pharmacist and prescriber,
(6) consistent prescribing of habit-forming drugs.

Ohio has a similar code found in Ohio Rev Code Ann ch 119, §4731-11-02:

(A) A physician shall not utilize a controlled substance other than in accordance with all of the provisions of this chapter of the Administrative Code.

(B) Any other provisions of this chapter of the Administrative Code notwithstanding, a physician may utilize the schedule II controlled substance cocaine hydrochloride only as a topical anesthetic for mucous membranes in surgical situations in which it is properly indicated.

(C) A physician shall not utilize a controlled substance without taking into account the drug's potential for abuse, the possibility the drug may lead to dependence, the possibility the patient will obtain the drug for a nontherapeutic use or to distribute to others, and the possibility of an illicit market for the drug.

(D) A physician shall complete and maintain accurate medical records reflecting his examination, evaluation, and treatment of all his patients. Patient medical records shall accurately reflect the utilization of any controlled substances in the treatment of a patient and shall indicate the diagnosis and purpose for which the controlled substance is utilized, and any additional information upon which the diagnosis is based.

(E) A physician shall obey all applicable provisions of sections 3719.06, 3719.07, 3719.08 and 3719.13 of the Revised Code, and all applicable provisions of federal law governing the possession, distribution, or use of controlled substances.

(F) A violation of any provision of this rule, as determined by the board, shall constitute "failure to use reasonable care discrimination in the administration of drugs," as that clause is used in division (B)(2) of section 4731.22 of the Revised Code; and "a departure from, or the failure to conform to, minimal standards of care of similar practitioners under the same or similar circumstances, whether or not actual injury to a patient is established," as that clause is used in division (B)(6) of section 4731.22 of the Revised Code. A violation of paragraph (B) of this rule shall further constitute (sic) "selling, prescribing, giving away, or administering drugs for other than legal and legitimate therapeutic purposes," as that clause is used in division (B)(3) of section 4731.22 of the Revised Code. A violation of paragraph (C) of this rule, if committed purposely, knowingly, or recklessly, as those words are defined in section 2901.22 of the Revised Code, shall further constitute "selling, prescribing, giving away, or administering drugs for other than legal and legitimate therapeutic purposes," as that clause is used in division (B)(3) of section 4731.22 of the Revised Code.

Use of Drugs to Enhance Athletic Ability.

(A) A physician shall not utilize anabolic steroids, growth hormones, testosterone or its analogs, human chorionic gonadotropin (HCG), or other hormones for the purpose of enhancing athletic ability.

(B) A physician shall complete and maintain patient medical records which accurately reflect the utilization of any substance or drug described in this rule. Patient medical records shall indicate the diagnosis and purpose for which the substance or drug is utilized, and any additional information upon which the diagnosis is based.

(C) A violation of any provision of this rule, as determined by the board, shall constitute "failure to use reasonable care discrimination in the administration of drugs," as that clause is used in section 4731.22(B)(2) of the revised code; and "a departure from, or the failure to conform to, minimal standards of care of similar practitioners under the same or similar circumstances, whether or not actual injury to a patient is established," as that clause is used in section 4731.22(B)(6) of the revised code. A violation of paragraph (A) of this rule shall further constitute "selling, prescribing, giving away, or administering drugs for other than legal and legitimate therapeutic purposes," as that clause is used in section 4731.22(B)(3) of the revised code.

Texas, in Tex Public Health Code, tit 71, art 4405b, states that disciplinary action may be invoked for:

(C) writing prescriptions for or dispensing to a person known to be a habitual user of narcotic drugs, controlled substances, or dangerous drugs or to a person who the physician should have known was a habitual user of the narcotic drugs, controlled substances, or dangerous drugs. This provision does not apply to those persons being treated by the physician for their narcotic use after the physician notifies the board in writing of the name and address of the person being so treated;

(D) writing false or fictitious prescriptions for dangerous drugs as defined by Chapter 425, Acts of the 56th Legislature, Regular Session, 1959 (Article 4476-14, Vernon's Texas Civil Statutes), of controlled substances scheduled in the Texas Controlled Substances Act (Article 4476-15, Vernon's Texas Civil Statutes), or of controlled substances scheduled in the Federal Comprehensive Drug Abuse Prevention and Control Act of 1970, 21 U.S.C.A. Section 801 et seq (Public Law 91-513);

(E) prescribing or administering a drug or treatment that is nontherapeutic in nature or nontherapeutic in the manner the drug or treatment is administered or prescribed;

(F) prescribing, administering, or dispensing in a manner not consistent with public health and welfare dangerous drugs as defined by Chapter 425, Acts of the 56th Legislature, Regular Session, 1959 (Article 4476-14, Vernon's Texas Civil Statutes), controlled substances scheduled in the Texas Controlled Substances Act (Article 4476-15, Vernon's Texas Civil Statutes), or controlled substances scheduled in the Federal Comprehensive Drug Abuse Prevention and Control Act of 1970, 21 U.S.C.A. Section 801 et seq (Public Law 91-513).

Massachusetts sets out its policy in Mass Gen L ch 94C, §19(b):

Under Massachusetts law, physicians may not dispense controlled substances without a prescription except where the drug is being delivered or administered to the patient for immediate treatment. This prohibition applies to free samples of controlled substances which physicians keep in stock in their offices.

A physician registered with the proper agencies may deliver or administer controlled substances without a prescription to patients in a single dose or in such quantity as is, in the opinion of the physician, essential for the proper treatment of the patient. However, that amount or quantity of controlled substance shall not exceed the amount needed for the immediate treatment of the patient and all further controlled substances required must be dispensed by prescription. "Immediate treatment" is defined as "that quantity of a controlled substance which is necessary for the proper treatment of the patient until it is possible for him to have a prescription filled by a pharmacy."

A physician may not issue prescriptions to obtain controlled substances for the physician's supply for the purpose of giving out or selling those drugs to patients.

Where the physician does deliver controlled substances to a patient (and the substance is not administered by the physician or ingested in the physician's presence) the physician must package the controlled substance in a container and affix a label to the container which includes the following information: the physician's name and address, the date of dispensing, the name of the patient, the name, dosage and strength of the drug, directions for use, and any necessary cautionary statements.

> Physicians who stock sample controlled substances should be aware of the Prescription Drug Marketing Act of 1987, which imposes strict record-keeping requirements on physicians, restricts the manner in which drug samples may be acquired and authorizes heavy fines and prison sentences for violating its provisions.
>
> "A prescription for a controlled substance to be valid shall be issued for a legitimate medical purpose by a practitioner acting in the usual course of his professional practice. . . . An order purporting to be a prescription issued not in the usual course of professional treatment or in legitimate and authorized research is not a prescription within the meaning and intent (of this act)."
>
> This statutory language sets forth the minimum requirements that must be met in order for a prescription to be valid in the Commonwealth. In sum, the standard of conduct proposed by c 94C can be broken down into two requirements. To be valid:
>
> 1. A prescription must be issued for a legitimate medical purpose; and
> 2. By a practitioner in the usual course of his professional practice.
>
> The Board discussed these standards in depth in the disciplinary case "In the Matter of Arthur E. Baer, Adjudicatory Case No. 205, Board Decisions, Vol. 1 (1978)."

There have been a relatively small number of disciplinary actions for incompetence. However, this may not be a fair reflection of the prevalence of incompetence, since boards may be using more easily proven violations such as drug use or over-prescribing, which often coexist with incompetence, as the basis for their actions when they cannot secure sufficient evidence to support a charge of incompetence alone, or when the time and cost involved in demonstrating incompetence can be avoided by addressing other valid grounds for discipline.

Despite recent increases in pursuit of disciplinary actions, there seems to be general agreement that there is a need to increase efforts, through enhanced funding and staff, to seek out and discipline incompetent physicians. As indicated above, it is difficult to determine accurately the prevalence of physicians who should be disciplined. Additionally, the number of formal actions is not the only indicator of effectiveness of the disciplinary system in maintaining high standards. However, statements by leaders of the medical profession and studies, such as the Office of the Inspector General, United States Department of Health and Human Services (OIG) study, point to a need for continuing improvement in the disciplinary process.[9]

---

[9] Federation of State Medical Bds of United States, A Model for the Preparation of a Guidebook on Medical Discipline (1986).

The exchange of information about physicians who have been disciplined is an important safeguard against continued practice by sanctioned physicians. A physician who loses a license in one state may seek to obtain a license in another. A data exchange system, the Physician Disciplinary Data Bank (DDB) operated by the Federation of State Medical Boards (FSMB), serves to prevent this.[10]

§5.07 Federal Reporting Requirements

Recent federal legislation requires the reporting of certain information about physicians, similar to that reported to the DDB. The Health Care Quality Improvement Act of 1986 established a central, national data bank to be operated under the authority of the Secretary of Health and Human Services. This data bank contains information about all physicians who have been disciplined, who have had adverse privileging actions taken against them, and who have had malpractice claims paid on their behalf. Malpractice settlements or judgments must be reported to DDB and to state licensing board, all physician disciplinary actions must be reported by state licensing boards, and peer review committees must report to state licensing boards review actions that adversely affect the clinical privileges of a physician for more than 30 days. Professional societies with peer reviews must report actions adversely affecting membership. The state boards must pass these reports on to the data bank.

The information in the data bank is available to hospitals and other entities appointing physicians to staffs. Therefore, it is the duty of each hospital to query the data bank about any physician being considered for appointment, and to query the data bank every two years about all physicians on their staffs. If a hospital fails to do this, it is still presumed to have knowledge of information in the data bank. This information is also available for other limited purposes relating to physician competence.

The substantial information available to state licensing boards presents the boards with a serious challenge. They will have to develop ways to manage and use it productively, and will have to be funded adequately to do this. For adverse privileging actions by hospitals, there are established approaches. These actions are likely to represent a more comprehensive assessment of a physician's behavior than malpractice claim payments, and boards might treat them as equivalent to a complaint, triggering an investigation.

A report of a payment presents a somewhat different issue since such claims do not necessarily reflect a professional judgment concerning a physician's competence. Such information is already being collected by many state boards; 31 boards now receive reports of malpractice payments, malpractice claims, or both from liability insurers.

---

[10] US Dept of Health & Human Servs, Task Force on Medical Liability and Malpractice (Aug 1987).

The availability of this data on a nationwide basis will undoubtedly result in new ways to use it for physician discipline. A licensing board might conclude that any particular report indicates (1) a full investigation of the physician is warranted, (2) an investigation is not warranted, or (3) a pattern is emerging and needs to be monitored. Development of nationwide standards for review of data and criteria for classification may make a significant new contribution to this aspect of the work of the state licensing boards.[11]

Boards receive alerts of physicians in need of disciplinary action from many sources, including patients. Any person or organization may report to a board information which appears to show that a medical licensee is, or may be, medically incompetent, guilty of unprofessional behavior, or mentally or physically incapable of practicing medicine safely. Some individuals and entities are required by state law to make such reports. Mandatory reporting of some type exists in all but a few states, with civil penalties in many instance for failure to report. Those required to report vary by jurisdiction, but often include hospitals (which are required in 41 states to report adverse privileging actions), all licensees, and insurance companies for malpractice judgments, settlements, and claims. Much of this is in response to recommendations of the Federation of State Medical Boards (FSMB).

Despite the requirements for reporting, in one study the Office of the Inspector General (OIG) cited that "consumers and law enforcement agencies are the two most active sources of alerting boards of possible violations. . . ."

§5.08 Risk Management

Risk management refers to comprehensive loss prevention programs within institutions and is the process of applying sound management techniques to the identification, assessment, and resolution of problems to prevent medical mishaps and minimize the adverse effects of injury and loss to patients, employees, visitors, and the hospital corporation. There is increasing interest and activity in hospital risk management. Almost 4,000 full-time risk managers are now employed in the nation's hospitals.

Risk management and quality assurance are functions that overlap in many respects. Many consider quality assurance part of the larger issue of risk management. Risk management requires managerial skills, and is directed toward all persons, events, and activities in the health care setting; quality assurance requires clinical expertise and is primarily directed toward medical services to the patient.

---

[11] Eichorn, *Standards for Patient Monitoring During Anesthesia at Harvard Medical School,* 256 JAMA 1017 (1986).

§5.09 Peer Review Organization Activities

The federal government, peer review organizations (PROs), and state licensing boards should work together to develop systematic methods of exchanging information.

Utilization and quality control peer review organizations assure that medical services provided to Medicare beneficiaries meet professionally recognized standards of quality.

State licensing boards and PROs are both concerned with the quality of care, although their approaches differ. Evidence indicates that information on quality is rarely shared between these two entities. A report from the Office of the Inspector General (OIG) in June 1986 indicated that state boards do not typically inform PROs of their formal disciplinary actions and that PROs do not typically seek state board quality information. PROs do not usually disclose quality information to state boards without a formal request to do so.

Whatever the reason for the poor communication, sharing information must be encouraged to enhance the quality review and disciplinary efforts of both entities while reducing duplicate efforts.

Quality assurance activities aim at optimal delivery of health care to the individual patient. Quality assurance activities are performed by health care experts within health care institutions. Data is collected from adverse drug reactions reports, patient incident reports, medical chart audits, records review, and various committees—such as tissue, transfusion, infection control, morbidity and mortality, and utilization review. These data form the empirical foundation by which those responsible for quality assurance can formulate pragmatic programs for improvements in medical practice and patient care.[12]

§5.10 Professional Guidelines and Standards

Physicians, in their search for more effective treatments and better outcomes for their patients, have devoted increased efforts to gathering data and developing organized efforts to reduce or eliminate avoidable medical injuries. Part of the motivation has been the desire to avoid the financial effects of malpractice claims arising from such injuries. One institutional approach to this has been the development of standards for patient monitoring during anesthesia, for the nine component teaching hospitals of the Harvard Medical School. The suggestion for the standards came from Harvard's self-insurance entity, which expressed concern "about the number of incidents and claims and associated indemnity involving anesthesia care from 1976 through 1984." An article in the Journal of the American Medical Association explaining the standards, and a related editorial, acknowledged the traditional resistance of physicians to adherence to standards of practice that prescribe specific details of their day-to-day conduct of medical care.

---

[12] Eichorn & Hornbein, *The Setting of Standards of Care* 256 JAMA 1040 (1986).

Standards of this type are becoming relevant to the underwriting of insurance.[13] The Massachusetts malpractice insurer, the Medical Malpractice Joint Underwriting Association of Massachusetts, provides a premium discount for anesthesiologists who use certain equipment in all cases where its use is recommended by the standards of the American Society of Anesthesiologists.[14]

§5.11 Prescription of Drugs by Nurses

In the United States, the authority for licensing health professionals belongs to state governments. The purpose of professional licensure is to protect the public by requiring those providing health care services (for compensation or not) to demonstrate a minimum level of competency. Every state in the nation has enacted legislation to license physicians, nurses, and other health care professionals.

Nurse practice acts are state statutes that define the practice of nursing and set forth licensing requirements. Since World War II, nurses have increasingly performed tasks that were done by physicians prior to that era. Upgrading the educational requirements has made the nurse more competent to perform complex and specialized tasks. Nurses with advanced training are assuming primary medical care roles that formerly required a medical degree. Nursing specialization, such as in coronary care or orthopedic surgery, has become commonplace.

Nurse practitioners represent a group of specially-trained "physician extenders" who may practice independently or under physician supervision, depending on state statutes. The latter category has resulted in orthopedists being held vicariously liable for nurse negligence.

Twenty-six states have passed statutes allowing nurses to write and prescribe drugs, medications, and other treatments. No state authorizes all nurses to prescribe; only nurses who have met educational and other requirements that exceed minimal standards for licensure can prescribe drugs. Those jurisdictions are Alaska, Arizona, Connecticut, the District of Columbia, Florida, Idaho, Maine, Missouri, New York, North Carolina, Oregon, Pennsylvania, South Dakota, Tennessee, Texas, Utah, Vermont, Washington, and Wisconsin. In Rhode Island and Minnesota, prescribing authority is limited to licensed midwives.[15]

§5.12 References

The American Orthopedic Association International Conference of Certification and Credentialing, 71A JBJ Surg 1566 (1989)

---

[13] Hadley: *Nurses and Prescriptive Authority: A Legal and Economic Analysis* 15 Am J L & Med 245 (1989).

[14] Eichorn & Hornbein, *The Setting of Standards of Care,* 256 JAMA 1040 (1986).

[15] Hadley, *supra* note 13.

State of Illinois, Department of Professional Regulation, Illinois Controlled Substance Act (1989)

State Medical Board, Ohio's Medical Practice Act (Nov 1986)

Commonwealth of Massachusetts Board of Registration in Medicine, Prescribing Practices, Policy, & Footnotes, (Aug 1, 1989)

Texas State Board of Medical Examiners, Health-Public art 4495b

6

Physician-Patient Relationship

§6.01 Definition

The physician-patient relationship is a contractual one, implied in the behavior of the participants and rarely expressed in contract terms.[1] Whether or not consideration (money) is given to the physician does not lessen the contract or alter the doctor's duties, obligations, responsibilities, and liabilities. Whether a physician-patient relationship has been created, especially by implication, helps determine the physician's duty to the patient. The physician promises that he or she will practice the normal degree of skill, care, and knowledge, but gives no guarantee. Without a physician-patient relationship, no professional duty is owed to the patient. When a court attaches a legal duty, it is directly or indirectly traceable to a physician-patient relationship. Once the relationship is established, both the physician and the patient have duties. (*See* Appendix 6-1, Cases 1 and 2.)

Patients often allege breaches of duties when filing claims, using several theories; however, the physician-patient relationship is at the core of every medical malpractice action. This relationship is usually not expressed in formal contract terms, but is implied by the mutuality of the relationship. The

---

[1] D.T. Armitage & L.B. Vogt, Physician-Patient Relationship *cited in* Legal Medicine, Legal Dynamics of Medical Encounters 188, (1988).

physician is not an employee of the patient. The relationship is consensual, with the patient knowingly seeking the doctor's assistance. (*See* Appendix 6-1, Cases 3 and 4.)

The creation of a physician-patient relationship requires some form of physical contact with the patient. It may be created through a telephone call where professional advice is given by the doctor to the patient. (*See* Appendix 6-1, Case 5.) Physicians in certain specialities who have no personal contact with the patient, such as radiologists or pathologists, incur a professional duty to the patient by virtue of diagnosis via pathological studies or x-ray interpretations. (*See* Appendix 6-1, Cases 6 and 7.)

In the absence of a physician-patient relationship, the doctor is not legally obligated to treat strangers, even in emergency situations. Once established, however, the relationship, unless limited or conditioned by agreement, continues until medical services are no longer needed or are properly terminated. (*See* Appendix 6-1, Cases 9 to 12.)

Whether a physician-patient relationship exists legally is a factual determination; the court will determine whether the patient entrusted his or her care to the physician and whether the physician accepted that care. If the physician-patient contact caused the patient to have a reasonable expectation of treatment, or if the physician undertook to treat the patient, the court will usually find an implied physician-patient relationship. One legal definition is "the broad term covering all steps to effect a cure of an injury or disease." Realistically, courts tend to interpret almost any physician action as an undertaking to treat.

On rare occasions, a doctor will enter into a formal contract with a patient, guaranteeing some element of care and its result. When breached, this relationship is treated by the courts in the same manner as any contract.

In the physician-patient relationship, doctor availability may become an issue. No physician can be available to every patient 24 hours a day. The physician does have a duty, in most cases, to be available or to furnish suitable physician coverage when his or her absence places a patient in peril.

§6.02 Duties Imposed by the Physician-Patient Relationship

The courts generally are quick to establish a physician-patient relationship, but recognize the physician's ability to limit or qualify that relationship. The doctor may limit the relationship to the treatment of one problem—performance of a procedure or a one-time evaluation—and may limit his or her availability as to time and place. These limitations must be understood by the patient.

Physicians are free to choose their patients unless they have been employed by others and have previously agreed to be available to all comers, as might happen with an employed hospital emergency room physician. This principle is supported by the Principles of Medical Ethics of the American Medical Association and is supported by case law. (*See* Appendix 6-1, Case 13.)

Once the relationship is legally established, duties attach and the physician is liable for any damages legally caused by any breach of duty. The patient is obligated to participate and cooperate in treatment and to follow instructions for further evaluation and treatment. If the patient fails to do so, he or she may not be able to hold the doctor solely liable for any resulting injury. The physician's liability will be determined by an assessment of the facts by the trier of fact. Failure to follow the doctor's instructions does not automatically terminate the physician-patient relationship, but may be a bar to recovery or limit liability. The physician often has a duty to pursue a patient who fails in follow-up if the physician knows that such failure may result in injury to the patient.

When a physician examines a patient at the request of, and is paid by, a third party—such as an insurer, an attorney, or a governmental agency—the duty to the patient is different. The physician incurs no liability to the patient unless the examination is physically rough and injures the examinee or the doctor discusses diagnosis and gives professional advice to the examinee. (*See* Appendix 6-1, Cases 3, 4, and 13 to 17.)

§6.03 Litigation

A physician-patient relationship must exist before an action of negligence against the physician can stand. Frequently, defining this relationship is difficult. In a recent case reviewed by the Supreme Court in North Carolina, (*Easter v Lexington Memorial Hospital, Inc*, 303 NC 303, 278 SE2d 253 (1981)) it appears that the emergency room doctor did not see the patient prior to his being transferred to another hospital for treatment of a severe burn from which he subsequently died. There was an error in the hospital records, later rectified by the administrator and another doctor. There was a question of whether the emergency room doctor (who had signed out for the night and delegated his responsibilities to an obstetrician/gynecologist who was unskilled in the treatment of burns) could be held negligent for having his practice covered by a physician who was not competent to manage all types of emergency room patients, particularly a burn patient. A similar result was reached in *Nash v Royster*, 189 NC 408, 127 SE 356 (1925).

It is generally recognized that a physician-patient relationship exists as a result of mutual acceptance. The patient's acceptance is often assumed under the particular circumstances of the case (as where he or she sought treatment, for example), the courts typically focusing on the need for acceptance by the physician. (*See* Appendix 6-1, Case 19.)

In another case, the physician volunteered care or treatment or otherwise attempted to serve or benefit a worker and was accepted by the worker; this was considered a physician-patient relationship. (*See* Appendix 6-1, Case 1.) The court held in *Oliver v Brock*, 432 So 2d 1 (Ala 1976) that a physician has no obligation to engage in practice or accept professional employment, but that when the professional services of a physician are accepted by another person for the purpose of medical or surgical treatment, a physician-patient relationship is created. The relationship is a consensual one wherein the patient knowingly seeks the assistance of a physician and the physician knowingly accepts him or her as a patient. The court further stated that the relationship between a physician and a patient may result from an express or implied contract, either general or special, and that the rights and liabilities thereto are governed by the general law of contract, although the existence of the relationship does not need to rest on any express contract between the physician and the person treated. However, the voluntary acceptance of the physician-patient relationship by the affected party creates a prima facie presumption of the contractual relationship between them. The court also said that the physician may accept a patient and thereby incur the consequent duty, although his or her services are performed gratuitously or at the solicitation and/or on the guarantee of a third person. The court added that a physician-patient relationship depends on the facts in each case, but that some facts must be supplied to support the conclusion that the relationship has been created. *Id.* A claim for damages arising from medical malpractice is based on the assertion that the physician engaged to treat a patient or to make an examination for the purpose of treatment owes the patient a duty to use the requisite standard of medical skill to accomplish the objective for which he or she has been employed, which duty is owed to the patient by or for whom he or she is retained. This vocabulary is also used in *Davis v Tirrell,* 110 Misc 2d 889, 443 NYS2d 136 (Sup Ct 1981).

In *Hoover v Williamson,* 236 Md 250, 203 A2d 861 (1954), an action was brought against a physician who was employed by the plaintiff's employer to administer annual x-ray examinations, alleging the physician undertook to advise him of his condition of health as to lung infection, referred him to an expert, and after such consultation undertook to advise him and both wrongfully represented the seriousness of the condition and concealed from him that the consultant recommended he should discontinue his employment in his present environment. In this case, the court recognized that there is no doctor-patient relationship between (1) a prospective or actual insured and the physician who examines him for an insurance company, or (2) a prospective or actual employee and a doctor who examines him for an employer. In this case, however, the examining physician assumed to act additionally, even though gratuitously, in a manner he felt was in the interest of the patient, and the physician thereby incurred a tort obligation that was nonconsensual and independent of the physician-patient contract.

In *Rogers v Horvath,* 65 Mich App 644, 237 NW2d 595 (1975), a physician was held entitled to a summary judgment in a malpractice suit which alleged that a patient lost her workers' compensation benefits as a result of his report, which indicated there was nothing wrong with her. The court stated that the term "malpractice" denotes a breach of duty owed by one in rendering professional services to a person who has contracted for such services; in physician malpractice cases, the duty owed by the physician arises from the physician-patient relationship. The court pointed out that the physician was employed by the plaintiff's employer.

§6.04 New Duties of Physicians

As the practice of medicine becomes more complicated as the available treatment modalities expand, so does the risk of the treatments. The notion of strict liability being applied to the behavior of physicians and health care institutions has received moderate press. Hospitals and health care facilities are the most likely to have certain strict liability duties related to administrative capacities. Experts in the medical malpractice field report in their literature that the physician's liability is contained within the narrow confines of negligence and/or informed consent.

There are duties to warn patients and third-party carriers of foreseeable and serious dangers inherent in the care and management of the patient. The duty to recall past and present patients who have been exposed to potentially injury-invoking therapies has received wide coverage in the lay press as well as in the medical and legal literature. The classic case of *Tresemer v Barke,* 86 Cal App 3d 656, 150 Cal Rptr 384 (1978) relates to the duty of a physician to recall Dalkon shield patients. (*See* Annotation, *Application of Strict Liability in Tort, Two person or Entity Rendering Medical Services,* 100 ALR3d 1205.[2]

§6.05 Duty to Treat Patient; Less Common Situations

Ordinarily, the physician clearly has no duty to accept a patient for treatment, unless bound by an employment contract or similar agreement. In *Clark v Hoek,* 174 Cal App 3d 219, 219 Cal Rptr 845 (1985), the orthopedist was acting as an unpaid proctor, observing a new staff member pursuant to hospital bylaws. The proctoring doctor did not intervene during a surgery in which malpractice by the new operating surgeon occurred. The court held that the hospital, by its bylaws and at law, had a duty to monitor its physicians; a proctor such as the defendant was immune from liability in that no physician-patient relationship existed.

A physician has no duty to accept all persons presenting themselves for treatment. Physician liability can be imposed only when the physician has accepted a patient who has placed him- or herself under the physician's care.

In one case, a blind lady wished to be treated by the defendant physician. (*See* Appendix 6-1, Case 9.) Although she was blind, she was told she could not bring her Seeing Eye dog into the medical office. She sued because she was humiliated in front of other patients and felt her dog was entitled to special privileges. The court held that no physician-patient relationship existed.

In *Hastings v Baton Rouge General Hospitals,* 498 So 2d 713 (La 1986), the plaintiff was admitted to the emergency room with two stab wounds. The physician on duty resuscitated the patient, but the patient was not sta-

---

[2] S.E. Pegalis & H.V. Wachsman, *Medical Ethics (New)* 1 Amer Law Med Malprac 86 (Cumm Supp Nov 1989); Berg & Hirsh, *Duty to Recall,* 73 So Med J 1041 (1980).

ble. A consulting thoracic surgeon was called; he inquired whether the patient had insurance and, when informed the patient did not, asked that the patient be transferred to a public hospital. The emergency room physician felt that transfer would jeopardize the patient. The thoracic surgeon continued to refuse to accept the case. The hospital bylaws stated that, in such a situation, the chief of service was to be called when a patient could not be safely transferred. The emergency room doctor did not call the chief of service, and the patient died. The emergency room doctor and the hospital accepted the patient and a physician-patient relationship arose; therefore, they were held liable for the death. The thoracic surgeon who was called had not accepted the patient; therefore, he was not liable, but he may have breached his responsibility to the hospital by being on call and not accepting the patient.

Once the physician-patient relationship is started, the physician begins to attend the patient. The physician must give the patient all the necessary attention required by the patient's illness or injury. The physician cannot discontinue treating the patient without giving reasonable notice (by registered mail, return receipt requested) of that intention or making another physician available to continue treatment as necessary. Of course, the physician is not required to be in continual attention when such attention is not required. the physician's duty is the giving of ongoing instructions to the patient for any future care. Hospitals have policies (in bylaws) indicating how often an inpatient must be seen, generally at least every other day unless the illness is more serious.

In *Forstall v Hotel Dieu Hospital,* 429 So 2d 213 (La Ct App), *cert denied,* 433 So 2d 1054 (La 1983) the plaintiff required an arteriovenous fistula in the forearm (to facilitate dialysis). An artificial graft was used, became infected, and was removed by the defendant surgeon. The wound remained infected until a second surgeon removed retained graft material, after which the wound healed. The second surgeon testified that leaving the infected graft segment, which perpetuated the infection, was negligent surgery. The inference was that the patient was abandoned by the first surgeon, who did not intend to remove the remaining graft fragment. The case was returned for a jury determination of the first surgeon's intentions. In *Meeks v Coan,* 165 Ga App 731, 302 SE2d 418 (1983), a patient was left unattended without any covering physician. There may have been a lack of communication, but the physician intended no further treatment and did not notify the patient concerning arrangements for another physician.

§6.06 Medical Ethics

A common question of medical ethics is what information should be given to the patient or to the patient's family in particular situations. The underlying conflict is between the physician's duty to disclose information of value to the patient and the physician's duty to withhold information on the basis of its potential harmful effect on the patient.[3]

The President's Commission for Study of Ethical Problems in Medicine and Biomedical and Behavioral Research (1983) has made the following recommendations regarding the physician's dissemination of patient information. Althouth the informed consent doctrine has substantial foundations in law, it is essentially imperative to hae an ethically valid consent as a process of shared decisionmaking based on mutual respect and participation, not a ritual recitation of the contents of a form that details the risk of particular treatments. Much of the scholarly literature and legal commentary about informed consent portrays it as a highly rational means of decisionmaking about health care matters, thereby suggesting that it may be suitable for and applicable to well-educated, articulate, and self-aware individuals. Whether this is what the legal doctrine was intended to be or what it has inadvertently become, it is a view that the Commission unequivocally rejects.

In recent years, the physician in active practice and daily contact with patients has increasingly been faced with ethical and moral problems. It is apparent that when an ethical problem is properly identified, a process of resolution may begin. The physician may consult a variety of sources, including peers, medical schools, religion, philosophy, or law, and may find it necessary to apply the dicta of government, and to consider the code of a medical association or specialty association, health care policies, or third-party carriers. Medical codes of ethics generally derive from the acting principles for many or all of the other sources and may lack internal consistency or broad applicability as a result of having borrowed selectively from different value systems. In evaluating a medical ethics problem, a physician must be able to evaluate these various sources to arrive at the best resolution for the particular issue faced. A multitude of values, including the personal values and biases of the attending physician, are likely to play a role in any given case.[4]

The American Medical Association has stated:

> The confidentiality of physician patient communication is desirable to ensure free and open disclosure by the patient to the physician of all information needed to establish a proper diagnosis and obtain the most desirable clinical outcome possible. Protecting the confidentiality of the personal and medical information and such medical records is also necessary to prevent humiliation, embarrassment or discomfort of patient. The information disclosed to a physician during the course of the relationship between the physician and patient is confidential to the greatest degree possible. The patient should feel free to make a full disclosure of information to the physician in order the physician may most effectively provide needed services. The patient should be able to make this

---

[3] R. Beatch, Case Studies in Medical Ethics 137 (1977). Gadow, *Truth, Treatment of Choice, Scare Resource of Patients' Rights,* 13 J Fam Prac 857 (1981).

[4] Post, Peters & Stahl, *The Laws of Medical Practice in Pennsylvania and New Jersey,* L.C.P., (1984); S.E. Pegalis & H.V. Wachsman, *supra* note 2, at 87.

> disclosure with knowledge that the physician will respect the confident nature of the communication. The physician should not reveal confidential communications or information without the expressed consent of the patient unless required to do so by the law.[5]

Modern recordkeeping by computer technology permits instantaneous access to such information, which may facilitate the violation of physician-patient confidentiality. For the physician to take advantage of computer technology while maintaining an ethical standard of confidentiality, guidelines have been established for use of computerized data.[6]

---

[5] Current Opinions of Counsel on Ethical and Judicial Affairs of the American Medical Association §5.05 (1986).

[6] Hiller & Seidel, *Patient Care in Management Systems, Medical Records and Privacy: A Balancing Act,* 97 Public Health Reports 332 (1982); Watson, *Disclosure of Computerized Health Care Information: Privacy Rights Under Supply Side Competition,* 7 Amer J Law & Med 265 (1981).

Appendix 6-1
Cases

1 ***Keen v Wiggins,* 69 Cal App 3d 308, 138 Cal Rptr 3 (1977)** (physician-patient relationship existed where a physician volunteered care or treatment or otherwise attempted to serve or benefit a worker, and was accepted by the worker).

2 ***Oliver v Brock,* 432 So 2d 1 (Ala 1976)** (physician had no obligation to engage in practice or accept professional employment, but when the professional services of a physician are accepted by another person for the purpose of medical or surgical treatment, a physician-patient relationship is created. The relationship is a consensual one wherein the patient knowingly seeks the assistance of a physician and the physician knowingly accepts him or her as a patient. Moreover, the relationship between a physician and a patient may result from an express or implied contract, either general or special, and the rights and liabilities thereto are governed by the general law of contract, although the existence of the relationship does not need to rest on any express contract between the physician and the person treated. However, the voluntary acceptance of the physician-patient relationship by the affected party creates a prima facie presumption of the contractual relationship between them. The physician may accept a patient and thereby incur the consequent duty, although his or her services are performed gratuitously or at the solicitation or on the guarantee of a third person. Whether a physician-patient relationship exists depends on the facts in each case, but some facts must be supplied to support the conclusion that the relationship has been created. A claim for damages arising from medical malpractice is based on an assertion that the physician engaged to treat a patient or to make an examination for the purpose of treatment owes the patient a duty to use the requisite standard of medical skill to accomplish the objective for which the physician has been employed, which duty is owed to the patient by or for whom the physician is retained).

3 ***Willoughby v Wilkins,* 65 NC App 626, 310 SE2d 90 (1983), *rehg denied,* 315 SE2d 697 (NC 1984)** (emergency room physician on duty checked a patient's eyes, ears, nose, and throat and advised the patient to see her family physician. The defendant maintained that he did not accept the plaintiff as a patient because she was not in an acute emergency. The defendant claimed that when the patient was not in acute emergency, he wrote it up in a rejection book. He additionally claimed the plaintiff had an illness which had been going on for several days and was actually under the care of a family physician. Under the evidence presented, the jury was entitled to find that a physician-patient relationship was established and that the fact of rejecting the patient was not established. The patient's physical condition was evaluated by the physician who rendered medical advice to her, which would allow, although not compel, a jury to conclude that the

defendant had accepted the plaintiff as a patient and would undertake to diagnose and treat her. The defendant's statement that he did not accept the plaintiff as a patient did not have to be accepted as a legal conclusion binding on the plaintiff).

4 ***Easter v Lexington Memorial Hospital,*** **303 NC 303, 278 SE2d 253 (1981)** (patient was attended in an emergency room for second- or third-degree burns. Dr. C was the physician in charge of the emergency room; he moved for summary judgment stating that he never saw or treated the patient and did not have a physician-patient relationship, so that liability could not be imposed. The court held that summary judgment was inappropriate, as evidence showed that Dr. C was the physician in charge of the emergency room and assigned the treatment of the patient to another physician who had never treated major burns before. A material issue of fact was stated as to whether Dr. C, in assigning or permitting the physician untrained in the area of major burns to treat an emergency burn patient, was in fact negligent).

5 ***Clanton v Von Haam,*** **177 Ga App 694, 340 SE2d 627 (1986)** (physician-patient relationship was not created where the plaintiff telephoned the defendant physician, who had treated her previously for an unrelated condition. The physician listened to her late night recital of symptoms, told her she would have to wait to see him the next morning, and recommended that she continue the immediate course of treatment prescribed by another doctor).

6 ***Niccoli v Thompson,*** **713 SW2d 579 (Mo Ct App 1986)** (evidence was sufficient to establish a physician-patient relationship where an oncologist examined a patient at the treating doctor's request, suggested the type of surgery to be carried out, and charted the patient a fee).

7 ***Walters v Rinker,*** **520 NE2d 468 (Ind Ct App 1988)** (pathologist's act of examining and diagnosing a tumor from a patient for the purpose of diagnosis and treatment of the patient was sufficient to establish a physician-patient relationship between the pathologist and the patient, even though the patient did not personally seek the pathologist's assistance and the pathologist did not physically examine the patient or prescribe medication for him. The court stated that where health care services are rendered on behalf of patient, for the patient's benefit, a physician-patient relationship exists for the purpose of medical malpractice).

8 ***Craddock v Gross,*** **350 Pa Super 575, 504 A2d 1800 (1986)** (Workers' Compensation Court held that a physician examining a patient for purposes of assigning an impairment falls under the physician-patient relationship).

9 ***Lyons v Grether,*** **218 Va 630, 239 SE2d 103 (1977)** (physicians have no legal obligation to accept as a patient everyone who seeks their services. Whether a physician-patient relationship is created is a question of fact, depending on whether the patient entrusted his or her treatment to the physician and the physician accepted the case. The same result was reached in

Hiser v Randolph, 126 Ariz App 608, 617 P2d 774 (1980) wherein the physician simply did not agree and did not want to treat the patient, although the patient insisted that she become a patient; therefore, no physician-patient relationship existed. *See also Sendjar v Gonzalez,* 520 SW2d 478 (Tex Civ App 1975) holding that a physician-patient relationship did not exist where the physician refused to make a hospital call on an urgent basis to see a patient who was not under treatment at that time. Likewise, in *Duprey v Shane,* 39 Cal 2d 781, 249 P2d 8 (1952) the physician examined an employee, in a capacity other than that of a fellow employee. There was a physician-patient relationship established by a physician who examined the patient for another entity to establish a diagnosis but failed to pass to patient diagnosis of significant pathology. The court arranged follow-up medical care).

10 ***Ingber v Kandler,* 128 AD2d 591, 513 NYS2d 11 (1987)** (no physician-patient relationship existed where, at most, a physician gave an informal opinion to a fellow physician regarding a case with which the defendant had no connection whatsoever, and there was no showing that the defendant had any contact with the patient, saw any records relating to the case, or even knew the patient's name).

11 ***Chiesa v Rowe,* 486 F Supp 236 (WD Mich 1980)** (wife did not have a cause of action where the negligent act of a physician was carried out on her husband, because the requisite physician-patient relationship did not exist. The court held, however, that in a negligence action a physician's duty may extend beyond the interests of a patient to members of the immediate family who may be adversely affected).

12 ***Harper v Baptist Medical Center, Princeton,* 341 So 2d 133 (Ala 1976)** (plaintiff was treated on an emergency basis but was refused admission to the hospital because he did not have hospitalization insurance; no physician-patient relationship existed beyond the treatment for the non-hospitalized emergency).

13 ***Wilcox v Salt Lake City Corp,* 26 Utah 2d 78, 484 P2d 1200 (1971)** (no physician-patient relationship existed when a doctor, employed by a city to examine the chest x-rays of waitresses seeking the renewal of occupational permits, misdiagnosed an x-ray. The court held that the duty the doctor owed was to the city, not to the patient. A similar result was reached in *Hosel v United States,* 451 F Supp 1170 (ND Cal 1978), where the physician diagnosed the plaintiff as mentally unfit for duty. There was a duty owed to the United States, but not to the plaintiff).

14 ***Thomas v Kenton,* 425 So 2d 396 (La Ct App 1982)** (plaintiff who had a disease—Boek's sarcoid—alleged to have been contracted at a place of employment—could not recover in malpractice against a company physician who had examined plaintiff in that capacity every two years. The plaintiff alleged that the doctor misrepresented the nature of the plaintiff's condition and concealed from him the recommendations of other consultants, since no physician-patient relationship existed).

15 ***Tolisano v Texon,*** **144 AD2d 267, 533 NYS2d 874 (1988)** (physician could be held liable for the death of a witness whom he had examined and certified was physically fit to testify. The district attorney requested an examination of the witness to determine fitness to testify. The doctor examined the witness, who suffered from advance coronary atherosclerosis, and certified he could testify without "significant" risk to his life. The witness opposed his subpoena, but was ordered to appear. He appealed that order, but died while the appeal was pending. The family of the decedent filed a wrongful death action against the physician, who pled that no physician-patient relationship existed and moved to dismiss the complaint. The trial court denied the motion and the physician appealed. The appellate court affirmed the denial of the motion because an issue of fact existed as to the nature and extent of the doctor's duty to the witness. A duty arose when the doctor agreed to render an opinion, knowing it would be used to determine whether to subpoena the witness. Such a duty may exist outside of the realm of medical malpractice, the court concluded).

16 ***Ervin v American Guardian Life Assurance Co,*** **367 Pa Super 132, 545 A2d 354 (1988)** (where an insurance company employed a physician to examine the electrocardiogram of an applicant for insurance as part of a physical examination conducted to determine if the applicant was an insurable risk, no physician-patient relationship existed between the physician and the applicant; therefore, the defendant physician owed no duty to the applicant to discover his heart problem, or, having discovered it, to inform the applicant thereof).

17 ***Craddock v Gross,*** **350 Pa Super 575, 504 A2d 1300 (1986)** (a physician examining a patient at the direction of a workers' compensation carrier does not owe the patient a duty of care arising from a physician-patient relationship where the physician offers no advice, diagnosis, treatment, or prescriptions to the patient).

18 ***Betesh v United States,*** **400 F Supp 238 (DDC 1974),** ***disapproved, United Scottish Insurance Co*** **v United States, 614 F2d 188 (9th Cir 1979)** (preinduction physical examination was carried out by a government-employed physician who negligently failed to notify the examinee of an abnormality in an x-ray until six months later. A suit under the Federal Tort Claims Act prevailed, since there was not only a government regulation requiring physicians to notify rejected examinees who need medical attention to seek advice from a doctor, but there was a breach of common law duty under Maryland law to so advise the patient).

19 ***Gibbons v Hantman,*** **58 AD2d 108, 395 NYS2d 482 (1977)** (doctor who examined a patient after an operation and advised the patient to return to the surgeon had not established a physician-patient relationship).

20 ***Vassiliades v Garfinckel's Brooks Bros,*** **492 A2d 580 (DC 1985)** (surgeon was liable not for his surgical technique, but for an invasion of privacy where photographs were taken of a patient before and after surgery and used in a department store and in a television program without the patient's consent, publicizing private facts about the patient. Even without using her name, the surgeon was liable; the breach of confidentiality existing by virtue of the physician-patient relationship giving rise to a tort action. See also *Alberts v Devine,* 395 Mass 59, 479 NE2d 113 (1985), *cert denied,* 474 US 1013; *Watts v Cumberland County System,* 75 NC App 1, 330 SE2d 242, *review granted in part,* 74 NC App 769, 330 SE2d 256 *review denied,* 76 NC App 251, 355 SE2d 499, *review denied,* 314 NC 548, 335 SE2d 27 (1985)).

21 ***Olson v Western Airlines,*** **141 Cal App 3d 1, 191 Cal Rptr 502 (1983)** (examining doctor erroneously made a diagnosis of diabetes, which precluded the plaintiff from being a pilot, and, for the purpose of the effect of the negligent misdiagnosis, established a physician-patient relationship. The Olson decision was pointedly distinguished from Keen v Wiggins, wherein the examining physician was held to have established a physician-patient relationship when the physician undertook to professionally advise the examinee).

22 ***Rainer v Grossman,*** **31 Cal App 539, 107 Cal Rptr 469 (1973)** (no physician-patient relationship was created when a professor of medicine recommended surgery for the patient of a physician attending one of his lectures).

23 ***Barton v Owen,*** **71 Cal App 3d 484, 139 Cal Rptr 494 (1977)** (no physician-patient relationship was established through a telephone call to a physician, who told the wife of the ill person that the problem sounded like sinusitis, but refused to accept the person as a patient).

7

Contributory Negligence

§7.01 Generally

In many cases involving the orthopedist in which multiple allegations are made by the plaintiff patient, contributory negligence becomes an important defense. The patient has a real—not passive—part in the diagnosis, treatment, and rehabilitation from illness or injury.

§7.02 Defenses

Two of the most common defenses are contributory negligence and assumption of risk. The burden of pleading and proving the contributory negligence of the plaintiff is on the defendant. Contributory negligence is conduct of the plaintiff, contributing as a legal cause to the harm the plaintiff has suffered, which falls below the standard to which the plaintiff is expected to conform for his or her own protection.

Unlike assumption of risk, the defense of contributory negligence does not rest on the idea that the defendant is relieved of any duty to the plaintiff. Although the defendant has violated a duty and has been negligent and otherwise would be liable, the plaintiff is denied recovery in whole or in part because his or her own conduct disentitles him or her to maintain the action. In the eyes of the law, both parties are at fault. (*See* Appendix 7-1, Cases 1 to 8.)

The same intelligence, attention, memory, knowledge, and judgment are required of the plaintiff as are required of the defendant so far as facilitating healing and protecting against injury within the extent of the patient's abilities. Allowance is made for physical infirmity, for immaturity of children, and for the difference of information available to the defendant and the plaintiff. (*See* Appendix 7-1, Cases 9 and 10.)

The amount of information available to the physician and to the patient often varies. The physician owes a duty to the patient to be certain that the patient is informed on essential items of care to prevent injury and/or delay in healing. (*See* Appendix 7-1, Cases 11 to 14.)

§7.03 Patient Noncompliance

Patient noncompliance is a major medical and legal problem for orthopedists. In recent years, juries have had a tendency to impose a higher level of duty on the physician to obtain compliance.

In defense, when the patient leaves a hospital against advice or fails to follow instructions given by the orthopedist, the medical records must fully document these events and the apparent cause. Attempts to obtain follow-up compliance by the patient are often the physician's responsibility, and these attempts and their results must be recorded fully in the doctor's medical records. Failure to take medication or comply with consultations must also be recorded.

Those informed in office management point out that an office system will track all patients whose cases demand follow-ups with either referral or continued treatment. The doctor must have recorded in his or her records that the patient refused treatment or went elsewhere for treatment. Failure to have such information in the doctor's medical records tends to cause juries to believe, in fact, that those actions to follow-up the patient were not done.

Physicians who have real communication or incompatibility problems with their patients usually do not hesitate to terminate the relationship. To guard against charges of abandonment, the doctor must make his or her position clear in writing and send the letter by registered mail. Usually, a 30-day notice is sufficient protection against abandonment charges. The termination letter should note alternative practitioners or advise the patient to contact the medical society for referral.

Often, a patient will not return for follow-up because he or she has gone to another doctor. This situation may not be known to the first treating doctor until a lawsuit is filed. Try to avoid open-ended patient records. If a patient does not return for an appointment, try to find out why and record the attempt and the response. If a patient is referred, be certain that notation appears in the record. If the patient's care is at a plateau, indicate in the record that another appointment is not necessary. A complete medical record of the patient is never open-ended, but has a statement of what happened regarding the patient at the last appointment or missed appointment.

Good medical practice lessens patient noncompliance by establishing good rapport with the patient and giving a thorough explanation of what you feel is wrong with patient, of the treatment plan selected and why, of all medication, and of the prognosis. Ask the patient if he or she has any questions and record all of this data in the patient's medical record.

In contributory negligence, it is appropriate to use apportionment of the damages, when damages are appropriate. Many courts consider three types of comparative negligence—pure, modified, and slight to gross in allocating damages.

The American Medical Association has recommended shifting the resolution of medical malpractice cases from the civil justice to an administrative plan involving comparative fault. That formula states the plaintiff must prove that it is more likely than not that the physician's negligence was a contributing factor in causing the plaintiff's injury. If the physician's negligence was a contributing factor, his/her liability is limited solely to the extent of his/her responsibility for the injury. The physician will not be liable for the contributions of other individuals, including the patient or other factors such as the patient's preexisting medical condition.

Prior to 1975, juries did not apportion awards according to the degree of fault. Rather, under the concept of contributory negligence, a plaintiff who was even 1 per cent responsible for an adverse result could not recover from a culpable defendant. Additionally, under the theory of joint and several liability, any defendant who was found as much as 1 per cent liable might be held for the total award if other tortfeasors were insolvent. Moreover, the plaintiff had the right to decide which defendants would be sued. The rules were unduly harsh to all involved parties.

The comparative negligence rule was applied in the seminal case of *Li v Yellow Cab Co,* 13 Cal 3d 804, 532 P2d 1226, 119 Cal Rptr 858 (1975). The plaintiff was found 30 per cent responsible and the defendant could be held liable for up to 70 per cent of the total damages.

The American Medical Association v Superior Court abrogated the unilateral right of the plaintiff to select whom he or she could sue. California, in 1986, approved an initiative called The Fair Responsibility Act. It means that each culpable defendant is responsible for his or her share of pain and suffering or other noneconomic liability. New York, Florida, Oregon, and Illinois have similar laws. Kansas, Ohio, Colorado, Utah, and Vermont have abolished joint and several liability and have replaced it with a pure several liability rule, as the AMA has recommended.

Appendix 7-1
Cases

1 ***Clickner v Shanley,* 141 Misc 2d 600, 533 NYS2d 832 (Sup Ct 1988)** (verdict against a hospital and a physician upheld. The damages were assessed against the orthopedist and the hospital for malpractice in treating a motorcycle accident victim who sustained a compound leg fracture. He developed severe postoperative brain problems with significant permanent damage. Liability for the $1,500,000 verdict was divided between the auto driver who caused the accident and the medical caretakers. The court declined to reduce the amount by 10 per cent for contributory negligence, stating that the contributory negligence was not related to the malpractice, but to the causation of the accident).

2 ***Memorial Hospital of South Bend, Inc v Scott,* 300 NE2d 50 (Ind 1973)** (adverse verdict against a hospital and a surgeon for injuries which the plaintiff sustained while he was a patient. In successive petition, the trial court ordered a new trial on a motion to correct error. On appeal, the critical issue was whether the trial court properly applied the law when it absolved the plaintiff of contributory negligence. The court affirmed the order for a new trial, holding that the plaintiff was not contributorily negligent. This was the finding of the trial court, applying the standard that the plaintiff had to exercise conduct which would conform with his own protection, taking into account the physical infirmities which impaired his ability to function as "an ordinary reasonable man." The plaintiff was unaware of the danger of hot water being emitted from a flusher which was behind his back while using a hospital toilet. He could be excused from pulling the wrong lever due to his suffering from symptoms of multiple sclerosis as well as the effect of a thorazine injection that the physician had prescribed for him, and which rendered him incapable of driving an automobile for four hours).

3 ***Birk v Pritchard,* 33 Ohio App 2d 31, 291 NE2d 769 (1973)** (if a patient employs a physician to treat him and receives careful and skillful treatment and fails to return for treatment before discharge by the physician, and as a consequence suffers an injury, the patient is not entitled to recover against the physician despite malpractice on the part of the physician).

4 ***Quinone's v Public Administrator of County of Kings,* 49 AD2d 889, 373 NYS2d 224 (1975)** (although the facts were sufficient to hold a physician negligent in treating a patient, a verdict was rendered in favor of the physician because the patient failed to return for an appointment and removed a cast where there was non-union of an ankle fracture. The patient had been advised to place weight on the leg only while wearing the cast. The patient's contributory negligence barred recovery against the physician).

5 ***James v Karpan,* 116 Ariz 216 568 P2d 1114 (Ct App 1977)** (patient failed to return to her physician after he had asked her to return for

re-examination, despite her knowledge of the problem and of the need to evaluate her "bumps." The failure to keep appointments created a jury question on contributory negligence).

6 ***Mecham v McLeay,* 193 Neb 457, 227 NW2d 829 (1975)** (patient presented herself to a physician and later was referred to a neurologist for numbness and tingling of her arms and legs, fatigue, and weakness. A diagnosis of pernicious anemia was made. The patient left the hospital for unexplained reasons and did not return for one month, stating that she was too sick to come in sooner. It was held that the physician's care and treatment was within the standard of care and that the patient's deteriorating condition was due to her noncompliance).

7 ***Overstreet v Nickelson,* 170 Ga App 539, 317 SE2d 583 (1984)** (physician was negligent, but the patient also contributed substantially to the bad result that led to the suit. The patient cut her finger while slicing meat. A superficial laceration was sutured and she was sent home by the emergency room physician. Pain continued, and the following day she went to a family physician who seconded the diagnosis of superficial lacerations. She last saw her general practitioner 16 days after the injury. Pain persisted, so she consulted an orthopedist who discovered that the cut had damaged the flexor tendon sheath and radial digital nerve of one finger. Several additional operations failed to relieve the pain. Eventually, the finger had to be amputated. The allegations against the first treating physician were misdiagnosis, mistreatment, and abandonment. After 16 days, the family practitioner had told her there was nothing further he could do, which the plaintiff considered to be abandonment. The patient had been contributorily negligent for the delay in seeking additional consultation and for continuing to use the finger in spite of the fact it was painful. The neuromatous condition of reflex sympathetic dystrophy which developed was outside the control of either the physician or the patient. It simply occurs in a certain percentage of trauma cases—principally to hands and feet, but it can also occur in other areas of the body).

8 ***Schoonover v Holden,* 87 NW 737 (Iowa 1901)** (jury was instructed that it was the duty of an injured party to use all reasonable care for its own protection and that the jury might take into consideration the knowledge, if any, which the patient was shown to have had of the injury complained of and the condition of her dislocated knee after the defendant doctor had told her that he had reduced it. The jury was also instructed that it could consider whether or not the plaintiff made any effort to determine this was so, and whether or not she acted with the knowledge she had acquired to call other physicians and have the unreduced dislocation reduced. This instruction was held properly refused, the court stating that the patient had a right to rely on the defendant's possession of skill as a physician without calling others in to determine whether he really possessed it or not, and that he was not bound to consult other doctors unless he was fully aware that the defendant was not properly treating the injury).

9 ***Ostrowski v Azzara,*** **111 NJ 429, 545 A2d 148 (1988)** (New Jersey Supreme Court held that a patient's pre-treatment poor health habits may not be invoked as contributory negligence in a malpractice action against a physician whose negligence results in injury to the patient. The court further ruled that a patient's poor post-treatment health habits may serve to reduce damages but not bar any recovery. The court also held that patient failure to obtain follow-up medical care constitutes contributory negligence which may bar recovery from malpractice. The patient was a diabetic who consulted the surgeon for a sore toe. The patient was told by the doctor that she had severe peripheral vascular disease and was at risk of losing her leg, with control of diabetes being essential. The patient was also told that an increase in her insulin was needed. She said that she returned to the doctor and that the doctor said she did not need to regulate insulin doses. The defendant advised (inadvisedly) that the patient needed a toenail removed. Bypass surgeries failed following nail removal. The patient alleged that the removal of the toenail was too radical, necessitating bypass surgery, and that the surgeon did not treat her circulation before the nail surgery. The patient was a heavy smoker, another risk factor regarding her leg circulation. The court held the surgeon negligent, but that the plaintiff's fault exceeded that of the surgeon (51 to 49 per cent). The supreme court reversed, holding that the trial court had failed to properly distinguish between conduct which contributes to causing a patient's injuries—and thus may constitute comparative negligence—and conduct which serves only to reduce damages. The court observed that contributory negligence ordinarily consists of conduct occurring either before or concurrently with the defendant's negligent acts. On the other hand, a plaintiff's failure to exercise reasonable care following a defendant's negligent acts has generally been evaluated under the avoidable consequence doctrine, which has its roots in the law of damages. Noting that these two doctrines have been merged under New Jersey's comparative fault statute, the court concluded that it would be ironic if that statute—which was designed to ameliorate the harshness of contributory negligence doctrine—were interpreted to allow a failure of damages to rise to the level of comparative fault, which could bar recovery altogether, rather than merely reduce damages. The court then concluded that since tort law requires a defendant to "take his victim as he finds him," a patient's poor pre-treatment habits may not be viewed as comparative negligence in a malpractice action against a physician. However, the court stated, a physician will not be responsible for harm which results from a patient's pre-existing condition rather than malpractice. Once a patient comes under a doctor's care, the law justly expects the patient to cooperate with the physician in treating a medical condition. Thus, a patient's poor post-treatment health habits may be invoked by a malpractice defendant to reduce the amount of damages that may be recovered. Finally, the court concluded that the plaintiff's failure to consult her regular doctor prior to having the toenail removed could constitute comparative negligence which could bar recovery if that negligence exceeded the defendant's negligence).

10 ***Gillespie v Southern Utah State College,* 669 P2d 861 (Utah 1983)** (basketball player sprained his ankle and was treated by a school physician, and later by an orthopedist. The initial treatment was elevation and ice packs about the ankle after taping. The taping was too tight and gangrene developed in one toe, which had to be amputated. Although the patient's foot was also in danger, it survived. The patient developed thrombophlebitis, which required additional treatment. The thrombophlebitis was held related to the immobilization caused by the sprain and aggravated by the icing. Apparently, very vigorous icing, with frost bite, was part of the damage to the toes. The treating physicians were held liable, even though the facts of the case showed that the trainer was probably overzealous in tightening the tape and in persisting with the icing. Although he followed the physician's instructions, he actually exceeded them. There was, additionally, a question of whether it was the patient or the trainer who excessively applied the ice, so the contributory negligence of the player figured into the final settlement).

Comment: If a treating physician instructs others, be it athletic trainers or nurses, as to treatment—here, with respect to the sprained ankle—he or she is responsible for complications because the patient is under his or her care.

11 ***Warren v Roos,* 127 Cal App 2d 224, 273 P2d 569 (1954)** (Plaintiff's evidence was sufficient to go to the jury where one of the negligent acts alleged was recommending premature use of a fractured limb. Competent expert testimony was necessary. DeHaan v Winter 258 Mich 293, 241 NW 923 and later appealed 262 Mich 192, 247 NW 151 reached the same result).

12 ***Swanson v Hood,* 99 Wash 506, 170 P 135 (1918)** (question of the plaintiff's contributory negligence was held properly submitted to a jury, which found in his favor where, although there was evidence that he used his arm driving his automobile and when working about his store, he contradicted those charges and there was also evidence that the defendant had recommended moderate use of the arm and had himself at various times taken hold of it and rotated the forearm).

13 ***Schultz v Tasche,* 166 Wis 561, 165 NW 292 (1917) and also 16 NCCA 1068** (where the negligent act of the plaintiff consisted chiefly of leaving the hospital prematurely and in conduct thereafter, and the defendants were found negligent in the treatment of her fractured leg before she left the hospital, her acts amounted to negligent aggravation rather than contributory negligence which, in that state at that time, operated to bar recovery).

14 ***Harlow v Chin,* No S-4756 (Mass Sup Ct Nov 29, 1989)** (doctor's and hospital's petition for rehearing following the court's reaffirmation of $7,656,000 verdict in a suit alleging negligence leading to paraplegia was denied. In addition to other comments, the court indicated that the plaintiff's arguments using analogies of high salaries of sports figures, or the cost of one minute of advertising in Super Bowl promotions, was inappropriate).

8

Pleadings, Theories, and Defenses of Negligence Liability

§8.01 Generally

The attorney, as he or she contemplates filing suit in a malpractice case, has many considerations. He or she will take an exhaustive history of the potential client, assessing whether medical malpractice has occurred, if injury resulted, and to what degree the potential client may be contributorily negligent. The efficient (successful) malpractice attorney uses checklists extensively as part of case building. Medical records and other pertinent written information, x-rays, and other physical material that might become evidence are acquired.

The medical record can be obtained with a release of privacy from the patient, sometimes a slow process and often productive of incomplete records. If the case merits, and the court can be convinced, the plaintiff's attorney often obtains a petition for "impounding records," assuring that records will not be lost or altered. The attorney must convince the court that this is necessary to the case.

The physician has a duty to maintain a full record and not to alter records without noting the alteration and dating and signing same. The physician is the custodian of his or her records, and must guard them as part of the patient's privilege and release them only on competent release effected by the patient. The records are the physician's property, but a legible copy is adequate in most cases. The physician must be careful in releasing psychiatric records and is well-advised to counsel with an attorney should this problem arise.

The most central aspect of the doctor-patient relationship is the ability to talk freely and openly with each other. The medical profession recognizes the importance of confidentiality between the physician and the patient, and the law has historically protected this communication, understanding that confidentiality is needed for effective medical care. Just as the law has encouraged patients to be open with their physicians, it has also required physicians to share information with patients under the doctrine of informed consent. As the President's Commission for the Study of Ethical Problems in Medicine and Biomedical and Behavioral Research put it, "Ethically valid consent is a process of shared decisionmaking based upon mutual respect and participation."

If a physician is sued by a patient, in most jurisdictions he or she cannot communicate, including sending records, to subsequent treating physicians or talk with prior treating doctors or with adversary counsel without permission of the court. This is the legal position in which filing a medical malpractice action places the defendant.

Defendants argue that merely by virtue of starting a lawsuit and claiming a physical injury, the plaintiff waives physician-patient privileges, to allow private interviews with nonparty treating physicians. In *Koump v Smith,*

25 NY2d 287, 250 NE2d 857, 303 NYS2d 858 (1969), it was held that the commencement of a personal injury action waives the physician-patient privilege. It did not explicitly authorize interviews with a nonparty physician, but it did require the exchange of medical records.

Rejecting that interpretation, the court of appeals in *Steinberg v New York Life Insurance Co,* 263 NY 45, 48-49, 188 NE 152, 153 (1933) placed a high value on the physician-patient privilege "to protect those who are required to consult physicians from this disclosure of secrets imparted to them, to protect the relationship of patient and physician, and to prevent physicians from disclosing information which might result in humiliation, embarrassment, or disgrace to patients." The court also noted that the patient has a right to expect the physician to follow the Hippocratic Oath, which declares that "whatever in connection with my professional practice or not in connection with it, I may see or hear in the lives of men which ought not to be spoken of broad, I will not divulge, as reckoning that all such should be kept secret."

Defense representatives are not prevented from obtaining the patient's medical records nor are they precluded from interviewing the patient's physician privately, if the patient consents. Additionally, they are at liberty to seek the nonparty physicians' testimonies at depositions.

In those rare instances where defense representatives have interviewed a plaintiffs' physician without the knowledge and consent of the plaintiff, courts have suppressed the results of those interviews.

In *Anker v Brodnitz,* 98 Misc 2d 148, 413 NYS2d 582 (Sup Ct 1979), it was suggested that a doctor who discloses patient's confidences without authorization not only is open to a charge of professional misconduct, but that a cause of action exists against a doctor who breaches confidences. Furthermore, a cause of action has been recognized against an insurer who wrongfully induces the physician to breach confidences in the course of an interview.

In *Rea v Pardo,* 133 Misc 2d 516, 507 NYS2d 361 (1986), an attorney representing patient Rea wrote to the patient's physician, Dr. Pardo, requesting a copy of the patient's medical records and sending a proper authorization. Rather than complying with the attorney's request, the doctor referred the request to his insurer. The carrier asked the doctor to forward his records to them, and the doctor complied. Several months later, the plaintiff obtained the records from Dr. Pardo. Months after that, the plaintiff sued Dr. Pardo for malpractice and also for the "breach of confidentiality" involved in turning the records over to his insurer. The Erie County Supreme Court denied the defendant's motion for summary judgment dismissing the complaint, holding that the mere inference that a malpractice suit might be forthcoming in the future does not justify the physician's turning over the patient's records to the liability insurer. The court found that Dr. Pardo's "conclusion that he would be sued, although ultimately proved correct, was only conjecture at the time that he gave his patient's records to his insurer."

Courts that have permitted private interviews usually rely on the proposition that "no party to litigation has anything resembling a proprietary right to any witness's evidence." *Doe v Eli Lilly & Co,* 99 FRD 126, 129 (DDC 1983).

The defense argues that informal, private interviews reduce the cost of litigation, promote candor and spontaneity, permit defendants to quickly and inexpensively identify nonessential witnesses, and allow earlier evaluation of cases—all worthy policy goals. None of these arguments is affected in the least by the distinction of whether the case is in discovery or beyond that phase. (*See* Appendix 8-1, Cases 1 to 3.)

§8.02 The Complaint

In filing suits, methods of pleading include:

1. Pleading with specificity outlining a specific allegation of negligence and its subsequent injury is imperative
2. Pleading in general or vague terms, issued before knowing information in subsequent discovery depositions, but preserving the status of the suit
3. Amended complaint

§8.03 Theories of Liability Checklist

1. Negligence:
   a. Surgery misadventure, negligent techniques, unnecessary surgery
   b. Emergency room, failure to treat, misdiagnosis, improper transfer
   c. Excessive radiation treatment
   d. Failure to diagnose, missed fracture, uncorrected diagnosis
   e. Nursing care
   f. Failure to render timely care
2. Other Theories:
   a. Res ipsa loquitur
   b. Informed consent
   c. Battery
   d. Conspiracy
   e. Abandonment
   f. Willful wanton conduct
   g. Granting and reappointment of privileges
   h. Loss, alteration, or destruction of records
   i. Fraudulent concealment
   j. Intentional infliction of emotional distress
   k. Assumption of risk

l. False imprisonment
m. Agency, master-servant, respondent superior, borrowed servant
n. Outrageous conduct
o. Breach of contract
p. Lost chance
q. Statutes of limitation
r. Vicarious liability
s. "Good Samaritan" doctrine

§8.04 Motion Practice Checklist

1. Impounding of hospital records
   a. Petition accompanying documents
   b. Order to impound
   c. Notice of emergency motion—rule to show cause
   d. Motion—rule to show cause
   e. Order for sheriff to return and impound
   f. Notice of motion to release record for photocopying
   g. Order to release for photocopying
   h. Notice of motion regarding unexplained disappearance of records
   i. Motor for hearing regarding missing records
   j. Petition for order regarding unexplained disappearance of records
   k. Notice to produce records
2. Preliminary motions and forms
   a. Motion to transfer
   b. Motion to dismiss for failure to state a cause of action
   c. Motion to strike—res ipsa loquitur
   d. Motion to strike and dismiss
   e. Motion to strike portions of complaint, hospital, doctor
   f. Plaintiff motion for summary judgment
3. Discovery motions
   a. Notice of motion
   b. Proof of service by delivery
   c. Proof of service by mail
   d. Motion
4. Discovery notices to produce, motions and orders
   a. Notice to produce depositions

   b. Notice to produce
   c. Miscellaneous motions, orders, and procedures in malpractice discovery
   d. Barring a party or witness from testifying at the trial for failure to give deposition
   e. Motion to limit number of expert witnesses
   f. Motion to inspect specific areas, operation room, specific equipment, etc.
   g. Motion to compel parties to simultaneously disclose expert witnesses close to discovery
   h. Motion to leave to take audio visual deposition of plaintiff and plaintiff's expert witness
   i. Order for production and to establish sequence of discovery
   j. Motion to set discovery schedule
   k. Procedure to close discovery
   l. Motion to dismiss for plaintiff's failure to comply with court orders
5. Unusual orders
   a. Order to reappear for continuation of deposition and answer certified questions
   b. Motion regarding destruction of operative reports
   c. Order regarding neglect, loss, or destruction of exhibits
6. Trial forms
   a. Client's petition for change of venue
   b. Attorney's petition for change of venue
   c. Notice to produce at trial
   d. Motion in Limine

§8.05 Interrogatories Checklist

1. To doctors
2. To hospital
3. To defendant
4. Supplemental interrogatories
5. Request to admit facts
6. Notice to produce at deposition
7. Notice to produce at trial

§8.06 "Good Samaritan" Doctrine

The orthopedist, as all physicians are, is protected in most jurisdictions by the "Good Samaritan" doctrine—by statute, in most states. This doctrine generally provides that one who sees a person in imminent and serious peril through negligence of another (and, in fact, through no fault of another) when the rescuer has no duty to be the rescuer, cannot be charged with medical or contributory negligence, as a matter of law, in risking his own life or serious injury in attempting to effect a rescue or, in the physician's case, in the rendering of appropriate medical care, providing the care is not provided in a reckless or wanton manner. Under the doctrine, the rescuer may be considered negligent if the care markedly worsens the state of the person in peril and that worsening would not, in all probability, have occurred absent the rescue attempt.

The exact vocabulary of "Good Samaritan" codes varies from state to state, and most states tend to separate medical from nonmedical perils.[1] (*See* Appendix 8-1, Cases 4 to 13.)

§8.07 Abandonment

A frequent allegation in medical malpractice actions is patient abandonment. The physician-patient relationship is a contract to care for the patient until such time as one or both parties terminate the relationship, or such time that additional medical diagnosis or care is not necessary as related to the illness/disease that commenced the relationship. Often, more than one medical problem will cause a continuation of medical care by the physician, but when a negligent act by the doctor causes injury, the care of that injury, along with other medical problems, is often a point of controversy as to tolling the statute of limitations.

The physician or patient can terminate the physician-patient relationship by adequate notice. If the care is terminated by the physician, the notice should include assurance of notice (registered mail), record of notice in the physician's records, the giving of time to find alternative medical care, cooperation in furnishing and/or sending on medical records to a new health care provider, and making certain that the termination of medical care will not injure the patient while finding new medical care.

Abandonment of the patient by the physician is negligence, and a tort action will stand if the patient is damaged by the abandonment. Emotional stress caused by abandonment may be considered. Any adverse behavior of the defendant as such may add to the physician's negligence, which, if excessive, can lead to exemplary damages. (*See* Appendix 8-1, Cases 14 to 16.)

---

[1] L.S. Goldstein: Plaintiff's Perspective up to the Trial, Mid-Annual Meeting of the American College Legal Medicine, Oklahoma City, Okla, Oct 1989.

§8.08 Vicarious Liability

The orthopedist may become vicariously liable for the negligence of others, either under his or her control or ostensibly under his or her control. The term "liability" is a legal term that has been referred to as "of the most comprehensive significance, including almost every character of hazard or responsibility, absolute, contingent or likely." Vicariously, the doctor may easily be included in these parameters. In a memorandum opinion of the Court of Appeals of New York, an announcement that a referring physician cannot escape liability for negligence by showing negligence on the part of the treating physician to whom he referred the patient. Because there was sufficient evidence from which the jury could conclude that the defendant's negligence proximately caused the patient harm, the defendant may be found liable, regardless of the negligence of the treating physician. This decision means that referring physicians may be found liable for negligence if the treating physician was also negligent. Another well-established theory of vicarious liability is that a referring physician may be held liable if he or she knew, or should have known, that the physician he or she is referring patients to is habitually negligent or incompetent and negligently treats the referred patient.[2] (See Appendix 8-1, Cases 17 to 21.)

As an example, assume that A is negligent and B is not. *Imputed negligence* means that by reason of some relation existent between A and B, the negligence of A is charged against B, although B has played no part in it and has done nothing to aid or encourage it. Indeed, B may have done all that he or she can do to possibly prevent it. The result may be that B, in an action against C for his own injuries may be barred from recovery because of A's negligence to the same extent B has been negligent himself. This is commonly called *imputed contributory negligence.* The result may be that B and C's action against him becomes liable as the defendant foresees injuries on the basis of A's negligence. This sometimes is called *imputed negligence,* but is more often called *vicarious liability* or by the Latin name *respondeat superior.* (*See* **§8.18.**)

The foundation of the action is in negligence—not strict liability, as it may sound. The ordinary rules of negligence apply. Thus, the defense of contributory negligence and the assumption of risk are open to B, as well as A, and a judgment for A in an action brought against him by B is res judicata as to B's vicarious liability to C. The most familiar example is the liability of a master for the torts of a servant in the course of his or her employment.

§8.09 Deceit

The tort action for damages commonly referred to as an action for deceit is an ancient one going back as far as 1202. For a tort action to stand in deceit, the following must exist: (1) false representation made by the defendant; in an ordinary case, this representation must be one of act, (2) knowledge or

---

[2] Black's Law Dictionary 823 (4th ed 1968).

belief on the part of the defendant that the representation is false; this is often called *scienter,* (3) an intention to induce the plaintiff to act or refrain from an act, and reliance on misrepresentation, (4) justifiable reliance on the representation of the plaintiff in taking action or refraining from it, and (5) damage to the plaintiff resulting in such reliance.

Lawsuits against physicians for concealing medical malpractice fall under the general action of fraud. To prove such fraud, the plaintiff must show that the representation (1) was a misrepresentation of fact, (2) was false, (3) was a material fact, (4) was made willfully by the defendant, (5) was meant to be relied on by the plaintiff, (6) was known to be false by the defendant, (7) was not known to be false by the plaintiff, (8) was believed and relied on by the plaintiff, and (9) was the cause of the plaintiff's injury.

Where a physician has fraudulently concealed the existence of malpractice, the plaintiff's cause of action does not accrue until the plaintiff learns of the fraud. At times, there may be a basis for applying deceptive trade practice-consumer protection law to medical malpractice fraud. This theory is brittle and unsettled, but if applied would allow for treble damages.

§8.10 Estoppel

An *estoppel* is a rule which precludes a party from taking a particular legal position because of some impediment or bar recognized by the law. Estoppel comes from the French word "Estoupe," from which comes the English word "stopped." It is called an "estoppel" or a "conclusion" because a person's own act, or acceptance, stopped or closed his or her mouth to allege or plead the truth. This, at one time, was regarded as a rule of pleading or of evidence, but since it goes to the position taken on the merits, it clearly is a rule of substance at law.

§8.11 Nondisclosure

Nondisclosure can form a tort in negligence by passive failure of the defendant to disclose facts of which he or she has knowledge. A general rule is to find the duty of disclosure when circumstances are such that the failure to disclose something would violate the standard of practice by ordinary, ethical, competent physicians.

§8.12 Physician-Patient Relationship

A physician-patient relationship is an inviolate one in which the private rights, the privilege of the patient, is to be held confidentially by the physician or a medical agency who has such knowledge, unless a competent consent to release that information has been given by the patient. The three requirements listed by Prosser and Keaton are (1) disclosure of the private facts must be a public disclosure—not a private one, (2) the facts disclosed to the public must be private facts—not public ones, and (3) the matter made public must be one which would be highly offensive and objectionable to a reasonable person of ordinary sensibilities.

§8.13 Immunity

An immunity is a freedom from suit or liability generally grounded in the special status of the defendant as a governmental entity, an officer thereof, or a family member. Although immunity has traditionally been quite broad, it has been largely abolished at almost all levels, often through a complex process in which scholars, commentators, judges, and legislators all played an important role. Today, immunity, as traditionally known, no longer represents the first line of defense for governmental units. (*See* Appendix 8-1, Case 22.)

§8.14 Statutes of Limitation

In medical malpractice litigation involving the physician, a key element governing the viability of a suit is the applicable statute of limitation. These statutes limit the right of action on certain described causes; that is, they declare that no suit shall be maintained on a cause of action unless brought within a specified period after the right arises. Statutes of limitation are statutes of repose in civil matters, as opposed to acts of grace in criminal matters.

Tolling the statute of limitation is the goal of a large segment of medical negligence litigation, using a variety and increasing number of defense theories. All state and federal jurisdictions have in place statutes of limitation, the timing varying considerably. (*See* Appendix 8-1, Cases 23 to 35.)

§8.15 Lost Chance Doctrine

The *lost chance doctrine* permits payment for injury when a patient has been deprived of the opportunity to survive, improve, or recover. It also compensates a plaintiff who has had an impairment worsened by the acts of, or the failure to act by, the treating physician. (*See* Appendix 8-1, Case 36.)

In medical malpractice cases, there appears to be an increasing acceptance of potential negligence facts that possibly, not necessarily probably, occurred. The lost chance doctrine requires a possibility of what happened to be submitted to the trier of facts. The loss of chance to recover or survive does not depend on the patient's condition, but rests on the loss of opportunity to improve an impairment. As long as the proximate cause of the loss is proven, less than a 50 percent chance may be compensable. Expert testimony does not need to state that the negligence was probable for the lost chance doctrine to stand.

An instruction *directing* a jury to apply the lost chance doctrine in a malpractice action was erroneous, the Ohio Supreme Court ruled. The patient sued the physician, alleging negligence and failure to diagnose and treat osteomyelitis. The patient suffered several operations and a two-inch shortening of his leg. An arbitration board ruled in favor of the physician and a jury returned a verdict in his favor, but the appellate court reversed because of the alleged partiality of a physician member on the arbitration board. At a new trial, the patient was awarded $210,000 against the physician.

At the second trial, the patient asserted that the physician's alleged post-surgical negligence had caused him to lose a substantial chance of attaining a better recovery than actually occurred. The jury was instructed to apply the doctrine of "loss of substantial chance of recovery." The court said that the trial court erroneously concluded that the state had adopted the doctrine and the appellate court had found no error. The Ohio Supreme Court said both courts were in error. The patient contended that the loss of chance doctrine was recognized in the state and should be applied to the present case. The court said that even if the doctrine was recognized, the evidence did not support its application.

Testimony of the patient's two expert witnesses failed to show that the patient had a substantial possibility of a better result and was insufficient to permit a reasonable juror to find that he had the probability of a good recovery, the court said. Therefore, the loss of chance causation approach could not be applied. The patient had the burden of proving that he had a better than 50 per cent chance of full recovery in the absence of malpractice. The instructions did not make this point of law clear to the jury; therefore, the instruction was harmfully erroneous. The court reversed the appellate court's decision and sent the case back with directions to vacate the trial court's judgment and grant a new trial. (*See* Appendix 8-1, Cases 37 to 51.)

§8.16 Emotional Distress

A *duty* in negligence cases is defined as an obligation to which the law will give recognition; it is, in effect, a particular standard of conduct toward another. Liability is imposed with no great regard for the fault of the defendant. The definition of duty changes with social conditions, which constantly lead to recognition of new duties. No better general statement can be made than that the courts will find a duty where, in general, reasonable persons would recognize it and agree that it exists.

When the defendant's negligence causes only mental disturbance without causing physical injury, illness, or other physical consequence, in the absence of some other independent basis for tort liability most courts still hold that, in the ordinary case, there can be no recovery. The temporary emotion of fright does no physical harm and is so ephemeral that it is easily counterfeited and usually trivial, reason the courts.

Other unpleasant emotions, such as distress to a mother given the wrong baby at a hospital, have been dealt with on the same basis. Another case involves a physician or staff member negligently misinforming a patient of a dire situation (such as a physician misinforming a person that his or her mother died, or a physician not properly supervising transfer of a deceased patient to a funeral home or medical examiner facilities). There is very little litigation as to when the physician's responsibility to the patient terminates.

Prosser described emotional distress unintended as if the actor unintentionally causes emotional distress to another. (A) is subjected to liability to (B) for resulting illness or bodily harm if the actor should have realized his conduct (foreseeability) involved an unreasonable risk of causing the distress or harm. This has no application to the illness or bodily harm of another which is caused by emotional distress arising solely from harm or peril to the third party, unless the actor has otherwise created an unreasonable risk of bodily harm to the other.

If the actor intentionally and/or unreasonably subjects another to emotional distress which he or she should recognize is likely to result in illness or other bodily harm, he or she is subject to liability to the other for an illness or other bodily harm in which the distress is in legal cause (1) although the actor has no intention of inflicting such harm, and (2) irrespective of his or her act as directed against the other or third party.

Mental deficiency (as defined by Prosser) is (unless the actor is a child) insanity or other mental deficiency, and does not relieve the actor from liability for conduct which does not conform to the standards of a reasonable man under like circumstances.

The law has been slow to accept the interest in peace of mind as being entitled to independent legal protection even as against intentional invasions. It is only in recent decades that infliction of mental distress served as a basis of action apart from any other tort. In this respect, the law is clearly in the process of growth and the ultimate limits have not yet been determined.

An excellent summary of the progress of the law of infliction of mental distress from 1900 forward was reported by the New York State Law Revision Commission, in a study relating to liability for injuries resulting from fright or shock.

Current legal dicta suggest that mental suffering is scarcely more difficult to prove, and certainly no harder to estimate in terms of money, than the physical pain of a broken leg, which pain has never been denied.

Proximate connection between the act and patient's emotional distress is, at times, difficult to establish. Medical science has recognized that not only fright and shock, but also grief, anxiety, rage, and shame are "physical" injuries in the sense that they produce well-marked changes in the body and symptoms that are readily visible to the professional eye.

Emotional damages were allowed in *Savage v Boies,* 77 Ariz 355, 272 P2d 349 (1954), in which a woman suspected of insanity was decoyed to a hospital by a concocted tale of an injured husband and child. Other cases of emotional damages have been reported; in one case, the defendant was spreading false rumors that the plaintiff's son had hanged himself, and in another the defendant wrapped a dead rat into a loaf of bread, causing significant emotional distress. (*See* Appendix 8-1, Cases 52-62.)

§8.17 Mishandling Patient's Body After Death

Occasionally, orthopedists become involved in mishandling after a patient's death. Insisting on an autopsy at times evokes emotional distress; however, the mere asking for an autopsy is not reason for a claim. However, acting on the autopsy without a clear and informed consent is a tort.

Mental distress caused by a defendant's conduct which is not directed at the patient but at a third person causes other problems. The doctor transfers intent from a battery to be applied to a person, injuring another who deserves compensation. There seems to be little reason to allow recovery when the plaintiff suffers physical harm and to reject it when there is mental damage. Many courts have regarded the plaintiff's mental distress as certain to fall under circumstances that must have been intended and have allowed recovery on that basis.

There are cases in which recovery has been denied, usually on the grounds that mental disturbance is not reasonably anticipated. Recovery in such cases is ordinarily limited not only to plaintiffs who were present at the time, but who were known by the defendant so that the mental effect could reasonably have been anticipated by the defendant.

Some courts wrestle with the problem of whether recovery should be limited to near relatives or the person attacked or injured, or at least to close associates, where there is some additional guarantee that the mental disturbances is extreme. The easier cases are when a child of a third party is injured or killed. The case becomes more difficult as the relationship of the injured to the plaintiff dilutes.

Fault-based negligence and carelessness may be traced to Saxon law. The concept of negligence took shape as a social movement during the earlier part of the nineteenth century. A strong argument exists against taxing emotional interests that open the door to fictitious claims or to litigations in the field of trivialities or bad manners. The current legal argument opposing the "flood of litigation" theory is that the distinction of true clients from false ones requires careful scrutiny of the evidence supporting the claim, and that elimination of trivialities calls for nothing more than the same common sense which has distinguished serious from trifling injuries in other fields of law.

From the types of injuries addressed for emotional distress, it has been held that mere words, however threatening, violent, or insulting, do not constitute assault and afford no grounds for redress. This is in contrast distinction to body language, gesturing, pointing with hands, etc., which have been held as grounds for assault.

Because of these, legal arguments recognize there is no magic in the name given to a tort, and while the infliction of mental injury may be a cause of action, its limits are as yet ill-defined. It has been extended to its greatest length in the case of intentional infliction of mental suffering by conduct of a flagrant character. (*See* Appendix 8-1, Cases 58 to 66.)

§8.18 Respondeat Superior

The broad statement that an employer is liable to a third party for an injury which results proximally from the tortuous conduct of an employee acting within the scope of employment is applicable with respect to the liability of a hospital or doctor's office for the negligence of a nurse or other professional employee when that employee's acts result in injury to the patient. Whether, in a given case, a nurse is to be regarded as a servant of a hospital so as to bring the foregoing principal into play is often a question of some difficulty. Where it is established that the nurse was a servant or employee of the hospital at the time of injury to the patient as a result of negligence of the nurse, many cases expressly or impliedly recognize that the hospital is liable under the doctrine of respondeat superior. The same result, of course, holds in whichever environment the nurse may be employed—by a physician, by a clinic, or, more recently, by an outpatient, free-standing surgical facility.

Under the doctrine of respondeat superior, an employer is generally liable for the wrongful acts of its employees acting within the scope of their employment. In the medical context, a hospital typically employs nurses and other paramedical personnel and therefore may be held vicariously liable for negligent acts. This idea of strict liability has been justified for two reasons: it should lessen accidents by employees because there will be strict supervision, and it spreads the cost of operation. (*See* Appendix 8-1, Cases 67 to 68.)

§8.19 Breach of Contract

In usual practice, the orthopedist is not placed, and does not place him- or herself, in a breach of contract situation. A physician may warrant his or her medical care and create a contract that may be breached by negligent care, but this is an overt act between the patient and physician. Usually, a proper informed consent is the defense to actions for negligence which allege breach of contract.

By definition, breach of contract is the failure, without legal excuse, to perform any promise which forms the whole or part of a contract. Prevention by party to contract or occurrence of performance requisite under the contract may be actionable.

The physician-patient relationship is contractual in theory and negligent failure by the physician to perform may result in a tort action that the court treats like a contract in most cases. Therefore, it is wise to routinely allege an element of breach of contract in most medical malpractice actions. (*See* Appendix 8-1, Cases 69 to 70.)

§8.20 False Concealment

False concealment is alleged when the physician overtly conceals from the patient salient facts of care, injury, disease, and/or prognosis. This is usually fraudulent behavior and will toll the statute of limitation as well as allow consideration of punitive damages by the court if the patient was injured by the behavior. (See Appendix 8-1, Cases 71 to 88.)

§8.21 Battery

Battery is a harmful or offensive contact with a person, resulting from an act intended to cause the plaintiff or a third person to suffer such a contact, or an apprehension that such a contact is imminent. This is in contrast to assault, a term ordinarily used to refer to apprehension of imminent contact rather than to contact itself.

Although a contact of this type is essential, the intent element of the cause of action is satisfied only if the defendant intends a harmful contact, or an offensive contact, on the plaintiff or third person (all of which are battery-type consequences), but also if the defendant intends only to cause apprehension that such a contact is imminent (an assault-type consequence).

In defining battery, contact means not only touching or contact with a part of the person's body, but also touching or contact with the chair in which the patient is sitting or the car in which a person is riding. For an allegation of battery to stand, the defendant must have done some positive and affirmative act; the mere passive obstruction of a patient's passage, although it may constitute another tort, does not amount to a battery.

Courts have always given considerable weight to the element of personal indignity in battery cases. Consequently, the defendant is liable not only for the contacts that do actual physical harm, but for those relatively trivial ones that are merely offensive and insulting. This issue arises when patient body parts are exposed in the process of examination to the eyes of others not privy to the patient's care or where such exposure is excessive and not accommodated by the patient as part of the physical examination made for diagnostic purposes. In a case heard by the Ohio State Board of Medical Examiners, a complaint was heard against an optometrist who stripped his patients to the waist, exposing their breasts, when diagnosing eye problems. The optometrist said he was checking for scoliosis, as scoliosis at times affects eye function. Although the relationship between scoliosis and eye function exists in very few patients, it was sufficiently credible that the state board only reprimanded the optometrist, in spite of two expert witnesses who stated that such diagnostic behavior was unusual, not indicated, and unnecessary for the optometrist to arrive at his diagnosis.

The defendant may be liable even though a joke or a compliment was intended, such as an unappreciated kiss bestowed without consent or a misguided effort to render assistance. The plaintiff is entitled to protection according to the usages of a decent society and offensive contacts or those which are contrary to all good manners need not be tolerated. Taking indecent liberties without consent, of course, is battery, such as when a professional dismissed his patient from a consultation and slapped her on the buttocks.

Unless there is an expression to the contrary, consent is assumed to all those ordinary contacts which are customary and reasonably necessary in the common pursuit of life, such as a tap on the shoulder.

A stranger is not expected to tolerate the liberties which would be allowed an intimate friend, unless the defendant has special reason to believe that it would likely be permitted by the individual. The test is whether the contact would be offensive to an ordinary person not unduly sensitive to personal dignity. Intent requires the intent to bring about such behavior that would cause apprehension that imminent contact was forthcoming. This issue will and has arisen in physicians' examining rooms where physical examination or exposure is required, and is a reason to have a nurse in the examining room when a male physician examines a female patient.

§8.22 Assault

A person normally has an interest in freedom from apprehension of a harmful offensive contact with a person as distinguished from contact itself, which is protected by the tort action for assault. No actual contact is necessary. The patient may be assaulted by purely mental disturbances of this distinctive type. Assault is sometimes called "a touching of the mind if not the body."

An act of such a nature to excite apprehension of battery may constitute an assault. It is an assault to shake a fist under another's nose or aim or strike with a weapon, or to hold it in a position which threatens to rise and strike another, or to surround another with a display of force. In the physician's office, a nurse's threat to give a child patient a shot if she did not allow the doctor to examine her is an assault with sufficient threat to instill fear in the child.

Apprehension is not the same thing as fear and a plaintiff is not deprived of an action merely because of being too courageous to be frightened or intimidated.

The courts have been reluctant to protect extremely timid individuals from exaggerated fears of contact and have often stated that the apprehension must be one which would normally be aroused in the mind of a reasonable person. If the defendant physician has knowledge of the patient's peculiar abnormal timidity and intends to act on it, there should be a right to recover. This type of patient tests the physician's empathy and caring feelings. This is also where the busy physician—the assembly line physician—often is unable to spend sufficient time to garner the confidence, and then the consent, of the patient. Generally speaking, mere words, however violent, do not amount to assault unless they are accompanied with a threat by the defendant to carry through an act that is an assault or would be battery.

Assault and battery go together like apple pie and ice cream; the difference is mere apprehension versus physical contact. It is a battery to strike or otherwise touch a sleeping person—a person under anesthesia—although the person struck does not discover it until afterward. It is an assault to shoot at to frighten, but miss, a person. Except for this difference and the character of the invasion of the patient's interest, the two are, in all respects, identical. There is no apparent reason why the rules applied to battery, including the fiction of "transferred intent," should not also apply to assault. (*See* Appendix 8-1, Cases 89 to 94.)

§8.23 Outrageous Conduct

Often, the patient feels offended or slighted by his or her physician. This feeling may be due to a misunderstanding, but provides the underlying motivation for many malpractice suits. When the orthopedist is perceived to be indifferent, unkind, condescending, or is otherwise negatively perceived by the patient, patient discomfort, dislike, and antagonism often result.

Rarely is the behavior of the physician such that it is called outrageous and so contrary to good citizen or physician conduct that amplification of the patient's discomforture results. This is an area where punitive damages may be considered by the court. (See Appendix 8-1, Cases 95 to 102.)

§8.24 Extreme Outrage

The reasonable person in this country at this time is generally considered to be expected and required to be hardened to a certain amount of rough language and acts that are definitely inconsiderate and unkind. There is still in this country at least such a thing as the liberty to express an unflattering opinion of another, however wounding it may be to the other's feelings. In the interest of not only freedom of speech, but also avoidance of other more dangerous conduct, it is still very desirable that some safety valve be left in which the volatile temper may blow off relatively harmless steam. Petty insults or indignities lack, from their very nature, a convincing assurance that a certain mental distress is genuine or, if genuine, then serious and reasonable. As Prosser and Keeton on Torts 59 (5th ed 1984) state:

> when a citizen has been called an S.O.B. and testifies that the epithet has destroyed a slumber, wrecked his nervous system, and permanently impaired his health, other citizens who on occasion have been called the same thing without catastrophic harm have legitimate doubts that he was really so upset or if he were, doubts that his suffering could possibly be so reasonable and justified under the circumstances as to be entitled to compensation.

In special situations, extreme misconduct recovery is allowed. In *Wilkinson v Downton,* 2 QBD 57 (1897), a practical joker amused himself by telling a woman her husband had been smashed up in an accident and was lying in the road with both legs broken and that she was to go at once with two pills and fetch him home. The shock to her nerves produced serious and permanent physical consequences which at one time threatened her reason and caused weeks of suffering.

§8.25 Definition of Agency

The orthopedist often comes into situations where the legal concept of agency is pertinent. *Agency* includes every relation in which one person acts or represents another by the latter's authority, where one person acts for another, either in relationship of principal and agent, master and servant, or employer or proprietor, and independent contractor. Agency relates to business and commercial transactions.

Agency is a relation created by express or implied contract or by law, whereby one party delegates the transaction of some lawful business with more or less discretionary power to another who undertakes to manage the affair and render an account thereof.

Actual agency exists where the agent is employed by the principal. Agency by estoppel may arise where the principal, by negligence, in failing to supervise agent's affairs, allows the agent to exercise powers not granted to him or her, thus justifying others in believing that the agent possesses requisite authority. This may be true even if the principal has no notice of the agent's behavior.

Agency of necessity is a term applying to situations where one legally must provide for another who is the responsibility of a principal. A classic example is when a wife procures what is reasonably necessary for her maintenance and support when the husband fails to do so.

Ostensible agency exists where a principal intentionally, or for want of ordinary care, causes a third party to believe another is his agent who is really not employed by him. (*See* Appendix 8-1, Cases 103 to 112.)

§8.26 Borrowed Servant

A servant is a person employed to perform services in the affairs of another whose physical conduct in the performance of the services is controlled or is subject to the right of control by the other. In determining the existence of "control" or the right to have many factors taken into account or balancing against one another, the extent to which, by agreement, the employer may determine the details of work; the kinds of occupation and the customs of the community as to whether the work usually is supervised by the employer; whether the one employed is engaged in distinct business or occupation and the skill required of him, who supplies the place and is instrumental in the work, the length of time the employment is to last, the method of payment, etc. When the servant is borrowed by another for the purpose of performing specific duties for which duties he has control over, he (the borrower) becomes vicariously liable. This defines *borrowed servant.*

For an independent contractor to be distinguished from a servant, the general rule is that no vicarious liability is to be imposed on the employer by the action of an independent contractor.

The *borrowed* or *loaned servant doctrine* is a major exception to the doctrine of respondeat superior under agency law. Under the borrowed servant doctrine, when a special employer such as a physician "borrows" an employee from a general employer, such as a hospital, the special employer becomes liable for his or her negligent acts. Generally, the courts will not designate such an employee as a "borrowed servant" unless the special employer actually controlled or had a right to control the employee's acts. In essence, through this right of control, the special employer steps into the shoes of the general employer such that the logic under respondeat superior becomes applicable to the special employer. (*See* Appendix 8-1, Cases 113 to 115.)

A master is under a duty to exercise reasonable care to control his or her servant while acting outside his or her scope of employment as to prevent him or her from intentionally harming others or from so conducting him- or herself as to create an unreasonable risk of bodily harm to them if (1) the servant is on the premises in possession of the master or on the premises which the servant is privileged to enter only as his or her servant or his or her chattel of the master. The master knows or has reason to know that he or she has the ability to control his or her servant and knows or should know the necessity and opportunity for exercising such control.

§8.27 "Captain of the Ship" Doctrine

Colorado is the only jurisdiction that adheres to a pure "Captain of the Ship" doctrine, as in *Krane v St Anthony Hospital Systems,* 738 P2d 75 (Colo Ct App 1987) where the appellate court affirmed judgment for a hospital because of the alleged negligent act of its nurse which occurred during surgery in the presence of the operating surgeon. That court said that "once the operating surgery assumes control of the operating room, the surgeon is liable for the negligence of all persons working under his supervision." A recent comparable "Captain of the Ship" analysis has been employed by several jurisdictions in foreign body (surgical sponge) cases, reasoning in general that the surgeon is in charge of the case and cannot pass liability to a nurse who states that a sponge count is correct when, in fact, it was not. This vicariously held the surgeon responsible for the nurse's negligent act.

Although in recent years the "Captain of the Ship" doctrine has been abandoned in favor of a control test under agency law, "Captain of the Ship" language is prevalent. Many courts continue to refer to the "borrowed servant doctrine" as the "Captain of the Ship" doctrine. The surgeon by tradition, and probably by egocentricity, often refers to him- or herself as the "Captain of the Ship" in the operating room. The vocabulary in *Sparger* aptly explains that similes sometimes help to explain a factual situation, but in legal writing phrases have a way of being canonized and of growing until they can stand and walk independently of the general rules. The result in the case of the "Captain of the Ship" doctrine is that a surgeon or physician may be held liable, not as others on the basis of the general rule of borrowed servant, but as the "Captain of the Ship."

§8.28 False Imprisonment

False Imprisonment is alleged by a plaintiff when he or she, or a representative, feels that the plaintiff was restrained or imprisoned against his or her competent will. The problem occurs most often in criminal or psychiatric settings.

The orthopedist is rarely involved in situations where a patient claims false imprisonment. It does occur in emergency situations in which apparent psychotic peak has occurred in the patient or in situations where a patient is incompetent from intoxication or acute illness, such as acute toxic brain syndrome. The orthopedist most likely will not be the only physician involved in the care of such patients, but he or she may well share joint liability in the management of that patient. The tort of false imprisonment is designed to protect the personal interest of patients and to free them from restraint. "Imprisonment," although it seems originally to have meant stone walls and iron bars, no longer necessarily signifies incarceration. What does include restraint and impingement on a person's freedom of movement? It is generally held that the incarcerated individual does not need to be aware of incarceration or injury at the time of incarceration, that he or she may in fact be so toxic from a brain problem that he or she has no recall of the incident; nonetheless his or her person was incarcerated. The patient is entitled to compensation for loss of time for physical discomfort and inconvenience and any resulting additional physical injury or illness.

When restraining the patient against his or her wishes, a court order or, at the least, consultation of one or two other competent physicians as to the necessity of the restraint should protect the physician from adverse litigation. (*See* Appendix 8-1, Case 116.)

§8.29 Assumption of Risk

In an Oklahoma case reviewed on Certiorari, reversible prejudicial error was committed by using instruction No. 14 (Oklahoma Uniform Jury Instruction civil OUJI -CIV 9.14). Instruction 14 states, "A person assumes the risk of injury resulting from the negligence of another, if he/she voluntarily and unreasonably exposes him/herself to injury with knowledge and appreciation of the danger and risk involved." The assumption of risk is an affirmative defense that must be pled or it is waived, and not to be when defense was not the assumption of risk but that there was no negligence behavior.

The actor is required to recognize that his or her conduct involves a risk of causing an invasion of another's interest of a reasonable man would be so while exercising such attention, perception of the circumstance, memory, knowledge of other pertinent matters, intelligence and judgment as a reasonable man would have; and such superior attention, perception, memory, knowledge, intelligence and judgment as an actor himself has.

For the purpose of determining whether the actor should recognize that his or her conduct involves a risk, he or she is required to know the qualities and habits of human beings and animals, the qualities, characteristics, and capabilities of things and forces insofar as they are matters of common knowledge at the time and in the community, and the common law of common legislative enactment and general customs insofar as they are likely to affect the conduct of other or third persons.

Where an act is one which a reasonable man would recognize as involving a risk of harm to another, the risk is unreasonable and the act is negligent if the risk is of such magnitude as to outweigh what the law regards as the utility of the act or the particular manner in which it is done.

If the actor's conduct is a substantial factor in bring about harm to another, the fact that the actor neither foresaw nor should have foreseen the extent of the harm or manner in which it occurred does not prevent him or her from being liable. The actor's conduct may not be the legal cause of harm to another where, after the event and looking back from the harm to the actor's negligent conduct, it appears to the court to be highly extraordinary that it should have brought about harm. (*See* Appendix 8-1, Case 117 to 118.)

It is informative to consider assumption of risk cases from three different perspectives:

1. *Express consent* is a basic concept. Assumption of risk means that the plaintiff in advance has given his or her express consent to relieve the defendant of obligation conduct toward him or her and to take his or her chances of injury from a known risk arising from whether the defendant is to do or to leave undone
2. *Duty perspective* is a situation where the plaintiff voluntarily enters into some relationship with the defendant with the knowledge that the defendant will not protect him or her against one or more future risks that may arise from the relationship; he or she may then be regarded as tacitly or impliedly consenting to the negligences and agreeing to take his or her own chances
3. *Misconduct defense perspective* is the third type of situation where the plaintiff is aware of the risk that has already been created by the negligence of the defendant, but chooses to voluntarily proceed to encounter it

In all three of these situations, the plaintiff might be acting quite reasonably and not be at all negligent in taking the chance because the advantage of his or her conduct outweighs the risks.

Parties may expressly agree in advance that the defendant is under no obligation to care for the benefit of the patient. In this event, the defendant should not be liable for the consequences of his conduct which otherwise would be negligence. This rarely occurs in the practice of medicine but has applications in experimental medical procedures as long as it is not contrary to public policy. The knowledge and appreciation of risk is a title and the defense of assumption of risk is quite nearly confined and restricted by three elements or requirements. The plaintiff must know that the risk is present and understand its nature. Finally, his or her choice to incur must be free and voluntary since, in the ordinary case, there is no conclusive evidence against the plaintiff on these issues. They are normally for the jury to decide. "Knowledge of the risk is the watch word of the assumption of risk."

Appendix 8-1
Cases

1 ***Doe v Portland Health Centers, Inc,* 99 Or App 423, 782 P2d 446 (1989)** (hospital employee did not breach a physician's duty of confidentiality with regard to a patient's mother where confidential facts disclosed by the employee did not concern the mother and did not arise out of the mother's involvement with the patient's treatment. However, an issue of fact existed as to whether the hospital had contracted with the patient's mother, as opposed to the patient, to maintain the confidentiality of information regarding the patient. This precluded summary judgment for the hospital, the court said. The mother of a psychiatric patient brought action against a hospital employee for wrongful disclosure of confidential information. The employee disclosed to a third party that the daughter was hospitalized after a suicide attempt. The claim on the daughter's behalf was tried, and she was awarded damages. That judgment was not challenged. However, the mother, who was a psychologist, made five claims on her own behalf for the breach of confidentiality. She argued that as a result of the disclosure, she suffered business losses, loss of reputation and emotional distress. The circuit court dismissed the claims. The appeals court found that summary judgment on the invasion of privacy claim was proper. However, it reversed and ordered a new trial on the issue of breach of contract).

2 ***Anderson v Strong Memorial Hospital,* 542 NYS2d 96 (App Div 1989)** (neither a nurse, physician nor a hospital was liable for breach of confidentiality when they permitted members of the news media to be present in a waiting room, a New York appellate court ruled. An HIV positive patient claimed that they breached the physician-patient privilege of confidentiality. The mere fact that members of the news media and other members of the public were permitted to be in the hospital's infectious disease unit waiting room was not breach of the privilege, the court said. The patient did not claim that the physician or any other member of the staff identified him as a patient. That disclosure was made when the patient was in the examining room and was asked if he would consent to being photographed during his examination, the court said).

3 ***Howes v United States,* 887 F2d 729 (6th Cir 1989)** (plaintiff was the wife of a member of the military whose job required a high-level security clearance. She sought treatment from a civilian psychologist who was employed by the federal government at the Air Force base where her husband worked. The therapy consisted of several sessions and related to plaintiff's feelings about her husband's infidelity. Two years later, plaintiff returned to the psychologist to seek his intervention in her husband's excessive use of alcohol and marijuana. The psychologist advised plaintiff that such intervention was beyond his area of expertise and suggested she contact a social services office on base and told her he would seek consultation on

how to proceed with the case and they agreed to follow up on the matter at a later date. When the plaintiff returned with complaints that the problem had become worse, the psychologist told her that he would have to obtain clarification on security issues from other members of the staff. His notes indicated that plaintiff was seeking advice rather than treatment. He contacted his superiors and the social services office to discuss the case but did not mention plaintiff by name. One of his superiors told him that Air Force regulations required him to report suspected incidents of illegal drug abuse at the base. The psychologist then contacted plaintiff and informed her of his obligation to report the case to her husband's commander. When plaintiff complained that the psychologist had breached her confidentiality, he responded that he had consulted the others at her request. Plaintiff subsequently filed a complaint regarding the alleged breach of confidentiality. The complaint was referred to the psychiatrist who had instructed the psychologist to report the case to plaintiff's husband's commander. The psychiatrist contacted the psychologist, who then explained that plaintiff was the person whom they had previously discussed anonymously. During the investigation, the psychiatrist had access to medical records pertaining to plaintiff's sessions with the psychologist. Plaintiff later met with the psychiatrist regarding her complaint and reiterated her concerns about her husband's drug use. After informing plaintiff that the psychologist had not breached any duty of confidentiality, the psychiatrist proceeded to report the case, and this report led to proceedings against plaintiff's husband which resulted in a reprimand, revocation of his security clearance and mandatory drug rehabilitation. Plaintiff filed an action against the United States government, alleging that both the psychologist and psychiatrist had breached a duty of confidentiality owed to her. A federal magistrate dismissed the action and plaintiff appealed. The circuit court began its analysis by observing that Ohio law recognizes a cause of action against a physician for unauthorized disclosure of a patient's privileged communications. However, the court found that plaintiff's claim against the psychologist did not fall within this rule because plaintiff consented to the psychologist's consultation with his superiors. The court reasoned that the psychiatrist in the role as the psychologist's superior and investigator of plaintiff's complaint about the psychologist, properly had access to plaintiff's medical records. Regarding the claim against the psychiatrist, the court concluded that there was no cause of action for breach of confidentiality because plaintiff consulted the psychiatrist solely in connection with her complaint about the psychologist and never attempted to establish a physician-patient relationship with the psychiatrist. Finally, the court indicated that even if the reporting of plaintiff's husband to his commander had breached the physician-patient privilege, public policy would probably require the creation of an exception to the privilege due to the sensitive nature of plaintiff's husband's position).

4 ***Johnston v Matview,* 531 NE2d 970 (Ill App Ct 1988)** (appellate court held that a "Good Samaritan" statute which bars negligence claims against physicians who render medical treatment in response to emergency situations applies to hospital emergency rooms. In this case, an emergency

room patient sustained a cardiac arrest, a physician who was attending another patient, summoned by nurse instituted resuscitation. Shortly after, the patient's attending physician arrived and the first physician was dismissed. The patient died and autopsy showed pulmonary embolus. The first treating doctor was jointed in suit along with several other doctors and hospital. The first treating doctor was released using "Good Samaritan" doctrine, reasoning that statute applied to emergency care at the site of emergence which would equally well apply to emergencies occurring in the emergency room).

5 ***Colby v Schwartz,* 78 Cal App 3d 885, 144 Cal Rptr 624 (1978)** ("Good Samaritan" statute did not excuse physicians who render emergency aid as part of their normal course of practice from liability for negligence).

6 ***McKenna v Cedars of Lebanon Hospital,* 93 Cal App 3d 282, 155 Cal Rptr 631 (1979)** ("Good Samaritan" statute concerning non-liability of doctors for administering emergency care contained no limitation as to site of emergency, nor was there any legislative policy to accept hospital emergencies in its scope; in medical malpractice action against resident physician who responded to emergency all and instituted treatment to person who subsequently died, and against hospital respondeat superior, court correctly instructed jury that there could be no liability for civil damages as a result of acts or omissions of physician in rendering emergency care, even though emergency took place in a hospital where there was no showing that resident had any legal duty to respond to emergency call or did not care in good faith).

7 ***Burciaga v St John's Hospital,* 187 Cal App 3d 710, 232 Cal Rptr 75 (1986)** (court reasoned that statutes providing that no physician who renders emergency care at scene of an emergency or on request of another for medical complications arising from prior care by another will be liable for civil damages as a result of any act or omission in rendering such emergency care do not limit immunity only to a physician treating a patient outside his specialty. Thus, a staff physician of a hospital who treats another physician's patient at hospital in response to a medical emergency, is protected by the "Good Samaritan" laws. Pediatrician who responded to obstetrician's request to the delivery room "stat," was responding to an emergency within means of statute providing no physician who renders emergency care at scene of emergency will be liable for damages resulting from acts of omissions, and pediatrician was protected by Good Samaritan laws even though treatment was outside his specialty).

8 ***Wallace v Hall,* 145 Ga App 610, 244 SE2d 149 (1978)** (Georgia "Good Samaritan" law applies to any person who renders emergency care in good faith at emergency scene "without making charge," even if person rendering assistance was not a medical practitioner).

9 ***James v Rowe,* 674 F Supp 332 (D Kan 1987)** (action against physician and ambulance service by plaintiff who had incurred head injury in auto accident and who alleged defendants were negligent in treating him at accident scene and in transporting him to hospital, Kansas "Good

Samaritan" law would not warrant action since law did not extinguish common law negligence for all health care that might be given in an emergency. The court stated that "Good Samaritan" laws are not meant to exempt all medical personnel in every emergency situation but only those who happen across an emergency outside the normal course of their work and who otherwise have no duty to assist).

10 ***Markman v Kotler,*** **52 AD2d 579, 382 NYS2d 522 (1976)** (court held that application of "Good Samaritan" statute is not limited to situations where doctor administered emergency first aid to stranger; thus, court properly charged provisions of Good Samaritan statute in wrongful death action where jury might reasonably find, on basis of plaintiff's expert, that continuing emergency existed after decedent's onset of chest pain. The court further held that instruction was proper that defendant could not be held to a lesser "standard" under "Good Samaritan" law if emergency was self-created and jury could find for the plaintiff if defendant's conduct decreased decedent's chance of survival).

11 ***Orosz v Superior Court,*** **1990 Cal LEXIS 178** (emergency room physician, (defendant) plaintiff said he was only responsible for emergencies which occurred within the emergency room of San Pedro Peninsula Hospital and that the "Code Blue" emergency in this case took place in the hospital's intensive care unit. Western Steamship Lines filed suit against the hospital and (defendant) plaintiff for indemnification of a judgment recovered against it by a Western employee. In October 1983, assistant purser aboard one of Western's cruise ships became ill while on board. Eventually, she was taken to San Pedro Hospital where she suffered a cardiac arrest while in the intensive care unit. Although not part of the hospital's designated emergency response team which responds to Code Blue (cardiac arrest) alerts, (defendant) plaintiff responded to the emergency in the patient's case. He was an emergency room physician at the hospital at the time but his responsibilities for treating patients were limited to treating those in the emergency room. However, when not otherwise occupied in the emergency room, he sometimes responded to Code Blue alarms. (Defendant) plaintiff and a resident who also responded to the alarm attempted to intubate patient but allegedly performed the procedure improperly and she suffered permanent brain damage. Through her guardian, patient filed a complaint against Western and received a $7.75 million judgment. Western then filed the indemnity action. In August 1989, (defendant) plaintiff filed a motion for summary judgment claiming that he acted as a volunteer in responding to patient's Code Blue alarm and was thus entitled to immunity under California's Good Samaritan statute, Cal Bus & Prof Code §2395. Western opposed the motion, contending that (defendant) plaintiff was not immune due to the decision in *Colby v Schwartz,* 78 Cal App 3d 208 (1978). In that case, two emergency physicians who operated on the plaintiff in the course of their normal practice as members of the defendant hospital's "emergency call panel" were not entitled to immunity under the statute. In addition, Western contended that the hospital's by-laws created a pre-existing duty under which (defendant) plaintiff

was to treat the patient. The trial court denied the doctor's motion for summary judgment; defendant (plaintiff) filed a writ petition in a state Court of Appeals and that petition was also denied. In his supreme court petition, defendant (plaintiff) said if the court is going to base its decision on *Colby,* that opinion conflicts with that in *Burciaga v St John's Hospital,* 187 Cal App 3d 710, 232 Cal Rptr 75 (1986) which found that statutory immunity is not limited to doctors who respond to emergencies beyond their medical specialties. The doctor said that prior to his action, he understood that a physician who voluntarily responds to an emergency within his field of practice is protected under the Good Samaritan statute. On the issue of pre-existing duties, Western argued that the hospital by-laws constituted a contract between the hospital and defendant (plaintiff), imposing a duty upon him to assist someone in need of medical assistance. However, defendant (plaintiff) stated that *Colby* only mentioned the physician's "moral obligation to give emergency care" outlined in the Principles of Medical Ethics of the American Medical Association. "Nothing in *Colby* suggested that the Court meant to equate a 'moral obligation' to act to a legal duty to act, and Western provided no such authority," (defendant) plaintiff said. "None exists; the law recognizes legal obligations, not 'moral' ones").

12 ***Hamburger v Henry Ford Hospital,* 91 Mich App 580, 264 NW2d 155 (1979)** (physician attending emergency call, when he had no duty to, was exonerated from medical negligence by virtue of the Michigan Good Samaritan statute).

13 ***Higgins v Detroit Osteopathic Hospital,* 154 Mich App 752, 398 NW2d 520 (1986), *appeal denied,* 428 Mich 911 (1987)** (court of appeals reversed and remanded in part and affirmed in part that the trial court was correct in entering a directed verdict in favor of one defendant, a physician, based on Michigan's "Good Samaritan" statute which provides that when a doctor's actual hospital duty did not require a response to an emergency situation, a physician who in good faith responded to a life-threatening emergency within a hospital or other licensed medical facility, should not be liable for any civil damages as a result of or mission of case, except in which gross or deliberate negligence can be shown).

14 ***Huber v Aengst,* Docket NEC 12214 (Cal Super Ct, LA County May 17, 1973)** (plaintiff was the mother of a 3½-year-old child who aspirated and choked to death in the mother's arms in the office of the defendant physician following a surgical procedure. The mother claimed that on a previous day, the day following the boy's release from the hospital, she had twice called the doctor because of unusual bleeding. The calls were not returned, the mother recovered damages for the boy's death and her own emotional distress, the mother alleging substandard postoperative care and the surgery itself had not been necessary. Abandonment was the issue that sustained this case. Unnecessary surgery was apparently not considered by the court).

15 ***Therrell v Fonde,* 495 So 2d 1046 (Ala 1986)** (in this case, gross neglect was held discernible without expert witness. The company doctor and company nurse stood trial because they kept a worker waiting four

hours, even though they knew he had suffered a crushed hand and partial loss of finger. In remanding the case for trial, the Alabama Supreme Court overturned the lower court's decision declaring the defendant; the circuit court had dismissed the case because the injured worker had not produced a medical expert to testify on the standard of care said to have been violated. The plaintiff was working at a paper mill and his left hand was crushed. At the medical facility at the factor, one nurse gave him an analgesic, another filled out necessary insurance forms. The first nurse wrapped his hand with gauze and told him to take a seat. Some 35 minutes later, the company doctor arrived and asked the nurse about the patient's loss of finger. As the scene was later described, the company shook his head and walked into his office, did not unwrap or look at the hand or even talk to the injured worker. Transportation was difficult; ambulance was not permitted because insurance would not cover it, as the patient was to be transferred to the consultant's office. At the doctor's office, he was examined, x-rays were taken and then sent to a hospital where a 3½-hour surgery was carried out. Delay in time may not have had that great of impact on the end result; however, the decision based on evidence in court that "they were charged with conduct so gross, willful, wanton, and outrageous that it would be impossible for any ordinary person to bear up underneath, speaking of the company doctor and nurse).

16 ***Tripp v Pate,*** **49 NC App 329, 271 SE2d 407 (1980)** (patient injured her knee in a basketball game. Physician performed exploratory surgery and left town on vacation for a few days. He arranged for his two associates to attend her during his absence. The patient began to run an elevated body temperature, complained of pain in her leg, white blood count increased, and eventually she broke out in a red rash. After operating physician returned, the patient's condition was diagnosed as drug allergies. Certain medications were discontinued. She continued to suffer pain and swelling and her condition was diagnosed as post op infection of the knee resulting in a permanently stiff knee. The trial court affirmed a verdict in favor of the attending physician inasmuch as he had made appropriate arrangements to have her care followed, and it was her statement that she would have had the surgery done even if she knew the physician was leaving town in a few days. There is no evidence of abandonment. The court further noticed that there was absence of expert testimony that the medical care the patient had received was not in conformity with the approved medical practices).

17 ***Atkinson v Wichita Clinic PA,*** **763 P2d 1085 (Kan 1988)** (medical malpractice claimant who settles his claim against a physician whose negligence was proximate cause of injury leading to suit, may not proceed with a vicarious liability claim against the physician's employers. The case arose from the death of plaintiff's wife, allegedly due to anesthesiologist negligence. Claim was filed against anesthesiologist and the clinic that employed him. The clinic filed a cross claim against the anesthesiologist for indemnification of any loss the clinic might sustain. The anesthesiologist entered into a settlement agreement with the plaintiff, not a release, but a covenant not to sue. The presiding judge entered an order approving the settlement and explicitly stated that plaintiff would be permitted to proceed with suit against clinic. The judge also stated that the settlement would not toll the indemnification claim the clinic had against the anesthesiologist. The clinic moved for dismissal, arguing that because its purported liability as predicated on a vicarious liability theory, plaintiff's release of his claim against the anesthesiologist barred any further right of recovery against the clinic. This motion, heard by a different judge, was held in clinic's favor; plaintiff appealed. The state supreme court affirmed holding that plaintiff's settlement with the anesthesiologist precluded him from pursuing his vicarious liability claim against the clinic. The court acknowledged that the settlement was couched in terms to a covenant not to sue—which will ordinarily be interpreted not to release other joint tortfeasors—and that the agreement clearly reflected the parties intention to preserve the claim against the clinic. The court pointed out, however, traditional rules of vicarious liability authorize an employer to obtain indemnification from a negligent employee for damages assessed to employer based on respondeat superior doctrines. Thus, although plaintiff intended to retain his right to sue the clinic, the court reasoned that his agreement to hold the anesthesiologist harmless for the clinic's obligations should be construed as a relinquishment of that right, since an award against the clinics would lead to an award against the anesthesiologist on the clinic's indemnification claim. The plaintiff argued that this rule should not apply in medical malpractice action because state law required professional corporations and their employees to carry separate malpractice insurance. The court disagreed, finding that compulsory insurance laws did not alter traditional rule of respondeat superior).

18 ***Ordonez v Arizona Board of Regents,*** **No 207409 (Pima County Super Ct Ariz July 1987)** (decedent was taken to the doctor with increasing pain and signs of infection. The first doctor prescribed Gentamycin. After seven days, the patient was transferred to care of another resident physician's care. This resident consulted with staff members and prescribed Tobramycin, being unaware that the patient was already receiving Gentamycin. After three days on both antibiotics, the patient developed renal failure, a known side effect of either Tobramycin or Gentamycin. After two weeks of dialysis, the patient died. Plaintiff sued the first doctor, saying he was negligent in failing to monitor the decedent after transferring care to second doctor. Plaintiff contended that the attending physician was "Captain of the Ship" and responsible for coordinating efforts of other doctors who treated the decedent. Plaintiff then sued the general practitioner alleging negligence in failing to order blood tests to monitor patient's kidney condition while receiving Gentamycin. The plaintiff further alleged the first defendant doctor was negligent in failing to review the decedent's status with the second resident when he transferred the care to second resident, and sued the second resident for failure to review records, finding he was already receiving Gentamycin before prescribing Tobramycin. Finally, the plaintiff sued the university who employed the residents, alleging it was vicariously liable for negligence of its employees. Defense contended that the cause of death was due to intravascular coagulation, relating to Crohn's disease rather than renal failure. Settlement negotiations of plaintiff was a demand of $475,000. First doctor offered $10,000 and the University offered $50,000. Result was $993,000 with jury verdict finding the university and the two residents liable and exonerated the initial attending physician).

19 ***Boyd v Albert Einstein Medical Center,* 547 A2d 1229 (Pa Super Ct 1988)** (summary judgment was in error. The patient was a member in the HMO, the consulted primary care physician for lump in her breast which was suspicious and biopsy recommended. Patient was referred to HMO surgeon who was negligent in perforating patient's chest wall causing hemopneumothorax. Prolonged initial treatment and development of incapacitating chest wall pain (Tietz's syndrome) developed. Later, the patient died from a "heart attack." Husband sued the HMO on the grounds that they failed to supervise or qualify its physicians and that the hospital, who acted as its agent. On appeal, error by court was alleged in granting summary judgment, since a question existed as to whether the participating physicians were ostensible agents of the HMO. The patient and her husband had selected primary care physicians from a list provided by HMO and could not see a specialist without the primary care physician's (gatekeeper) referral. Since there was an issue whether the physicians were ostensible agents, the court reversed summary judgment and sent case for jury hearing).

20 ***Beauchamp v Davis,* 209 Ky 397, 217 SW2d 822 (1948)** (orthopedic surgeon was engaged by the defendant who had been originally called in the case to perform an open reduction on the plaintiff's leg had been found guilty of negligence in treating the leg by pins and an external plate which failed to achieve union. The court held that the issue of the defendant's negligence and permitting the surgeon's negligent act or in failing to preserve and prevent them should have been submitted to the jury. There are two issues here—one whether the defendant physician is liable for the action of the specialist that he calls in which in fact, he is in many cases, and second, is the defendant surgeon's technique negligent).

21 ***Reed v Gershwein,* 160 Ariz 203, 772 P2d 26 (Ct App 1989), *review denied,* (May 9, 1989)** (physician asked another to cover for him in his absence was not liable for malpractice, vicariously, of that physician as long as he exercised reasonable care in selecting the "covering" physician. The covering physician was not an agent, employee or under direct control of the doctor he was "covering" for).

22 ***Gargiulo v Ohar,* No 881291 (Va Sup Ct)** (plaintiff contended she was injured by an embolism resulting from the negligent insertion of a heart catheter by defendant. The alleged malpractice occurred when defendant was performing a test that was part of a study on the effect of nitroglycerine and nefedipine on the respiratory and cardiovascular systems of patients with scleroderma. In analyzing whether defendant was protected by sovereign immunity, the trial judge in Richmond and the state supreme court considered the nature of the function performed by the employee, the extent of the state's involvement in the function, the characterization of the act as judgmental or ministerial and the degree of control and direction the state exercised over the employee. Comparing the defendant to a physician in another case, five of the court's seven judges said both "were employees earning state salaries and receiving no compensation, directly or indirectly, from patients in state hospitals. Each was pursuing a course of education under the tutelage of other state employees. Neither was permitted to choose or to refuse patients. Both were required to obey state-established rules, to employ state-prescribed methods, and to follow state-standardized procedures. And, while each was entrusted with a measure of discretion in the performance of assigned duties, each functioned under the supervision and subject to the command of superiors employed by the state").

23 ***Eberhard v Harper-Grace Hospital,*** **No 103426 (Mich Ct App)** (statute of limitation may be tolled, reversing for discovery. The plaintiff, blind alleges he was told he was congenitally blind. The plaintiff had recently learned his blindness was negligently caused by hospitals not having oxygen monitoring and he received too high oxygen as post-delivery therapy, leading to his blindness. The court held that statute of limitation starts when patients know or should have known, the negligent act).

24 ***Otto v National Institute of Health,*** **815 F2d 985 (4th Cir 1987)** (doctrine of continuous care permits a patient to exhaust all possible treatment proposed by a government medical facility before bringing a malpractice action against it, despite the two year statute of limitation on such claims. The court concluded that under the Federal Tort Claims Act, a malpractice action against the United States does not accrue until the end of medical treatment, including treatment supplemented by private physicians. This extension of the period which government physicians are vulnerable to malpractice actions protects patient's right to place trust and confidence in their physicians, as it allows patients to complete this confidential relationship before challenging the quality of care).

25 ***Florida Patient's Compensation Fund v Sitomer,*** **524 So 2d 671 (Fla Dist Ct App 1988)** (Florida physician told his patient that nothing was wrong; he kept her from filing malpractice suit by simultaneously preventing the statutory clock from starting. The rule is that the statute of limitation starts at the time the patient learns of the injury or negligence or have reason to know of the cause. This is a breast surgery case with implants. She filed her case past the statute of limitation from the first surgery but not past the time after she learned that something else could be done. The first surgeon had told her that 18 months after the first operation, nothing could be done about the unsightly scars. The court pointed out that the surgeon kept reassuring the patient, that she had "complete confidence" in him and remained his patient for 17 months after the negligent surgery. The statute of limitation in this case would run in 18 months. The court emphasized, and this is the general rule, that the statute of limitation begins to run when the patient knows he/she has been injured by a negligent act. "It must be remembered, however, that the knowledge of an injury without more does not necessarily put the patient on notice that an injury was caused by the negligence of another," the court said).

26 ***Ellis v Lauter,* 287 NW2d 192 (Mich Ct App 1979)** (patient underwent surgery for a mass in the right posterior neck. The long thoracic nerve was severed. There was no question that the negligent severing of the nerve produced damage and it was a matter for the jury to assess damages. There was a delay in filing the suit that was alleged to bar the statute of limitation; however, it was pointed out that the patient did not find out the cause of her numbness and loss of use of the nerve until a later date that brought her well within the statute of limitation).

27 ***Clark v Hawkes Hospital,* 459 NE2d 559 (Ohio 1984)** (trial court improperly applied the termination of the physician-patient relationship as the accrual date for a medical malpractice cause of action. A patient was injured in an automobile accident on June 25, 1979, taken to a hospital emergency room where he was treated by a physician. Allegedly, as a result of the negligence, he contracted a staphylococcal infection. The patient also claims the physician negligently treated the infection and caused additional injuries and complications including staphylococcal endocarditis. The physician last treated the patient June 28, 1979. The patient filed a suit against the physician over a year after the statute of limitation had run. In reversing the decision, the supreme court said that the trial court improperly applied the termination of the physician-patient relationship as the time when the malpractice cause of action occurred. Using the new Ohio standard, the case was remanded to provide the patient an opportunity to show when he actually discovered, or should have discovered, his infection was the result of malpractice).

28 ***Rispoli v United States,* 576 F Supp 1398 (EDNY 1983)** (patient's action of malpractice was not filed by a two year statute of limitation. In October 1974, the patient's leg was crushed by an automobile. He was treated in a hospital for a severed femoral artery and open leg wounds. A month later, he was transferred to a Veterans' Administration hospital where he remained for five years. The physicians at the hospital performed a number of plastic surgical procedures in an attempt to close the patient's open leg wound. In October 1975, they began an abdominal flap procedure which involved the use of a cast. When the cast was removed in January 1976, the leg was successfully covered but the heel and top of the foot had "come off completely." The physician told him that the open wounds would be treated with wet dressings and the wound would heal. When healing did not occur, he was treated with many surgical procedures. Late in 1977, the patient went to see an outside plastic surgeon. As the case progressed, the court said it was clear that the patient's complaints as to his treatment at the time were not directed at the level of medical care but at one physician's allegedly abusive manner which was not sufficient to mark the accrual of a malpractice claim. Although he was aware in January 1976, when the cast was removed, that his heel and parts of his foot were missing, the patient had been warned to expect severe pain and complications and therefore was not alarmed when this occurred. Further, the physician assured him that the remaining open wounds would be treated and would heal. This did not happen after several

additional surgeries. The court said it was reasonable to conclude that it was not until the patient knew that the surgery was successful sometime after April 1976 that the patient should have developed the knowledge of his injury. Based on this, the court found that his claim was timely).

29 *Hoffman v Hospital Affiliates, Inc,* 652 SW2d 341 (Pa 1983) (patient fell at home, fracturing three bones. The next day she was examined by physician in the hospital emergency room. He consulted a radiologist to review the patient's x-rays and then told the patient she had no broken bones but a tendon sprain. One month later, a local orthopedic surgeon advised her that she could walk on her injured foot. She allegedly did not discover that the bones were broken until she visited her daughter in another city and had x-rays taken nearly four months later. Within one year after discovering her injury but 16 months after the alleged malpractice occurred, the patient filed a malpractice action. The physician moved to dismiss relaying on the one year Statute of Limitations and the court concurred. On appeal, the supreme court said that where the alleged injury was not discovered within the one year period, the statute of limitation was one year from the date of discovery with a three year ceiling on the date of discovery rule. The supreme court, therefore, found that the case was timely filed. The case was sent back for re-hearing on the issue of negligent treatment and damages).

30 *Osborne v County of Los Angeles,* 91 Cal App 3d 366, 154 Cal Rptr 129 (1979) (cause of action for failure to remove screw causing infection in hip did not accrue at the time of surgery removing other metallic devices; alleged negligence consisted of failing to remove screw while patient was under county care, and thus injury was a continuing one until plaintiff left hospital four years later. For purpose of statute of limitation, plaintiff neither knew or should have known of his cause of action prior to time he learned screw had been improperly left in hip, even though he knew it was there, in view of his declaration that he didn't know which devices were to be removed and which to remain).

31 *Rowell v McCue,* 188 Ga App 528, 373 SE2d 234 (1988), *rehg denied* (Sept 23, 1988) (orthopedist failed to adequately decompress median nerve, incompletely cutting the transverse carpal ligament, was testified by plaintiff's expert. negligence was affirmed against operating orthopedist, but suit failed due to statute of limitation passing and no evidence of fraud alleged).

32 *Johnston v Doctors Medical Center,* No S010223 (Cal Sup Ct) (defendant orthopedist performed several procedures including a lumbar discogram upon the plaintiff. Following this procedure, the plaintiff developed soreness at injection site and developed fever, the injection site showing signs of infection. Plaintiff was discharged from hospital with treatment for apparent infection and was alleged that the infection spread from disc space to adjacent vertebral body resulting in extensive osteomyelitis. The charge that defendants failed to properly diagnose and treat disc space infection was made but not tried due to delay in filing of suit past statute limitation).

Comment: Closed disc space infections after discograms are usually self-limited and heal spontaneously after several months of symptomatic treatment with bed reset, body cast, or brace. Empirical use of antibiotics, not knowing the nature of the infecting organism, is inappropriate in the eyes of most physicians familiar with the problem, although many doctors would prescribe antibiotics in "shotgun" fashion. When bone is involved and osteomyelitis is developing, an attempt to obtain a culture of the infecting bacteria by needle biopsy, or even open debridement and/or blood culture, should be considered, allowing specific antibiotic treatment.

33 ***Hart v Browne,*** **103 Cal App 3d 947, 163 Cal Rptr 356 (1980)** (plaintiff underwent multiple orthopedic procedures to improve function of a paralytic problem. The success was poor and amputation recommended and carried out. The plaintiff hired counsel to ascertain if care he received was with "standards." The plaintiff first only wanted an expert opinion ad if reviewing expert felt that no malpractice was present, he would not pursue action. The examining orthopedist found no negligent treatment by first treating orthopedist. The case was dismissed, statute of limitation subsequently expiring. Several years later, the plaintiff's attorney learned that second, the examining orthopedist was being sued in several similar cases. The plaintiff then brought an action in a malpractice against the reviewing orthopedist alleging fraud, deceit and negligence. Trial court entered a non-suit order. Court of appeals reversed. The appellate court held that the standard would be what a reasonable reviewing physician would do in the same or similar circumstances. Even though the physician in this case is not a treating physician, he is carrying out a medical function for which malpractice may stand).

34 ***Sharsmith v Hill,*** **764 P2d 667 (Wyo 1988)** (orthopedist's reliance on the pathologist diagnosis prevented the running of statutes of limitation. The surgeon removed a mass thought preoperatively to be a Baker's cyst. Frozen section was called benign. The pathologist, absent several days, examined the tissue and reported the tissue as benign neuilemoma. This occurred in May 1982. The patient returned to surgeon in December 1982 reporting pain and swelling, examined and told by surgeon to return in one month. In January 1983, the orthopedist wrote the pathologist and asked him to check on the original tumor and the pathologist assured the orthopedist the tumor was benign. In February 1983, a second surgeon removed two tumors in original operative site, diagnosis was malignant. The second set of pathologists reviewed original slides and diagnosed the original as well as new tumors as malignant Schwannoma. Above knee amputation was carried out. Court felt that statute of limitations ran as continuing treatment by the orthopedist occurred until he terminated treatment when patient went to second surgeon; however, the suit was not against the orthopedist as he appropriately relied on opinion of the first pathologist).

Comment: There is no evidence of lost chance pled. The treatment, above knee amputation, was the same treatment as it would have been had the malignant tumor been originally diagnosed. There certainly would be an ongoing "mental anguish" resulting from the question "Did she lose a significant chance of survival by delay in amputation?"

35 *Whitaker v Zirkle,* 188 Ga App 706, 374 SE2d 106, *cert denied,* 374 SE2d 106 (1988) (pathologist and hospital were not entitled to summary judgment and operating surgeon was absolved in action by patient alleging misdiagnosis of malignancy. A mole was removed 10 years before, interpreted by pathologist as not cancerous, tumor recurred and reoperated with diagnosis of malignant melanoma. Re-review of original tumor was interpreted as malignant. Statute of limitation was tolled by fact patient did not know of negligence until second surgery).

36 *Banta v Horton,* NEC 42447 (LA Sup Ct Cal Dec 1987) (plaintiff had a potentially cancerous or nerve absence lesion diagnosed by the radiologist and was referred to surgeon. Surgeon had not reviewed x-rays and phoned the radiologist's office for a report. Report given to him was different from original report in that the location of the tumor varied in distance from end of bowel. Surgeon, therefore, elected to approach the tumor abdominally, the patient having been inadequately prepared so far as bowel cleansing was concerned, and the surgeon did not find and remove the tumor diagnosed by the radiologist. Surgeon's note was confusing in that he said he had completely examined bowel (but he missed tumor). Five months later, patient was completely obstructed by rectal cancer, had liver metastasis and ultimately expired 15 months later. The surgeon's medical records never mentioned the original report of the radiologist, only his incomplete report from the radiologist's office, and no discussion between surgeon and radiologist. Plaintiff stated that the surgoen never advised her as what other tests might have been done to improve her chances of survival and she always had trouble getting to see surgeon postoperatively. Injury alleged was loss of chance of survival, emotional distress, pain and suffering and loss of earnings. Jury verdict for $666,000, reduced 45 per cent for comparative negligence, and further reduced as a result of statute of limitation, resulting in a net judgment of $173,000. A $100,000 settlement was reached with the surgeon. Jury returned verdict in favor of the radiologist).

37 *Finn v Schannel,* 412 NW2d 147 (Wis Ct App 1987) (physician was not liable for failure to reimplant fingers. Patient could not recover malpractice claim arising from failure for physician to re-implant four fingers he lost in an industrial accident. Patient severed three fingers on right hand and partially severed little finger with machine press. He was taken to the hospital but no attempt was made to retrieve the fingers from the press. They remained in the press overnight and became necrotic. The next morning, the physician removed tissue from patient's hand and amputated the little finger and remaining part of the others. The patient was left with a right hand having only an intact thumb and part of an index finger. The jury found that with reasonable certainty, re-implantation would not have been successful. It found no damages to patient's past loss of earnings or future loss of earnings but found $135,000 for his past and future mental and emotional distress. On appeal, court said that jury's conclusions were inconsistent in that reimplantation would have been unsuccessful. Court was required to strike jury's findings, two physicians in the hospital were negligent and dismissed the claim).

38 ***Finn v Schammel,*** **140 Wis 2d 763, 412 NW2d 147 (1987)** (worker lost two fingers in an on-the-job injury. The treating orthopedist elected not to reattach them because they were traumatized enough that any attempt would "probably have failed." The patient sued on the basis of lost chance, and the jury gave the verdict based on that theory. The court maintained that "negligence does not imply liability unless a causal connection with the loss has been demonstrated with reasonable certainty." The jury felt that even though the amputated fingers were irreversibly damaged, they nonetheless thought the physician should have tried to reattach them. The appellate court followed the jury's logic citing the "all or nothing" approach to personal injury cases. In this, the court insisted that the question of whether reattachment would have succeeded required a yes or no answer. If the jury, in effect, answered no, it could not then award damages based on a percentage chance of success).

39 ***Crisher v Spak,*** **122 Misc 2d 355, 471 NYS2d 741 (Sup Ct 1983)** (orthopedic surgeon treated a patient for complaints relative to the right foot in 1974. Surgery was recommended and performed. After the operation, the patient continued to have difficulty with her foot, continued to consult the surgeon through June 1975. In May 1975, elective diagnostic studies revealed nerve involvement. Surgeon advised that the patient had her pain discomfort because of a pinched nerve and the problem could be treated with surgery. At that time, the patient was in very little pain and decided not to undergo an additional operation. What the physician failed to advise his patient at the time was that he did not know the cause of what was causing the pinched nerve and surgery was necessary to make that determination. Further, he did not tell her that one of the possible causes of the pain was a tumor. The orthopedist testified that he did not even consider the possibility of a tumor. The patient ultimately had below knee amputation of the right leg, and a biopsy revealed she had a malignant tumor. In a malpractice action, the patient claimed the surgeon's failure to explain to her that surgery was necessary to determine the cause of her problem was a departure from the accepted standards of medical practice. Expert witnesses testified to that effect and additionally testified it was also a departure from accepted standards of medical practice for the physician not to advise her of possible causes of her difficulty including the fact that she might have a tumor. The jury found that the patient would have had an operation in 1975 if her surgeon had advised her that surgery was necessary to determine the cause of her pain and nerve involvement and had advised to the various causes of pain including tumor. The court said that negligence of the physician deprived her from a reasonable chance of avoiding amputation).

40 ***Mashburn v Hedrick,*** **305 SE2d 61 (NC Ct App 1983)** (trial court directed a verdict for a physician who was allegedly negligent in treating a patient with peripheral vascular disease. On March 25, 1977, the patient

was examined by his physician because of two purple toes and pain. The physician thought he had a bone spur and ordered an x-ray, and the x-ray showed the foot to be normal. The toes remained blue and pain continued for several days. Pain and discoloration reappeared two months later. The patient then went to an orthopedic surgeon who thought the patient had circulatory problems. The patient was referred to a vascular surgeon who diagnosed a clot or obstruction in the thigh at the popliteal area. The patient was hospitalized but did not improve. Arteriograms showed two of the three blood vessels in his lower leg had clotted. The surgeon performed a vein bypass operation but it clotted. He replaced it with a synthetic vein but that also clotted and gangrenous changes appeared. he finally had to amputate the leg below the knee. The Trial Court granted a verdict against the family physician. A jury found that if the physician had properly diagnosed the patient's circulatory condition or had referred him to a vascular surgeon earlier, there was a possibility that his leg could have been saved).

41 ***Wilson v Corbin,* 241 Iowa 593, 41 NW2d 702 (1950)** (failure to take proper x-rays of the patient's spine failed to diagnose compression fracture of third cervical vertebra reasoning that early diagnosis and treatment of this injury with appropriate stabilization treatment would result in essentially normal spine whereas three months plus delayed treatment allowed the formation of permanent deformity).

42 ***Rogers v Kee,* 171 Mich 551, 137 NW 260 (1912)** (physician was held liable for failing to properly diagnose a patient's broken leg that resulted in less than satisfactory recovery that have been likely with prompt treatment. This is a very old case, and it is likely that the techniques of treatment would differ now, but the philosophy of lost chance is legally valid).

43 ***Bryant v Rankin,* 468 F2d 510 (8th Cir 1972)** (applying Iowa Law) (this case was based on negligent diagnosis, delayed diagnosis and treatment of hip fracture and negligence in treating the attendant infection was proximate cause of greater degree of permanent impairment than had the fracture initially diagnosed and promptly treated. It was, therefore, loss of chance. However, the superior court, using Iowa law reasoned additionally that the patient might well have had the same degree of impairment in spite of the delay of treatment so there is a direct conflict in the fact situation as reported and the outcome).

44 ***Thompson v Sun City Community Hospital,* 141 Ariz 597, 688 P2d 605 (1984)** (child was brought to the emergency room with injuries to his legs. In the process of transferring him from one hospital to another, the second hospital causing delay in treatment, the end result was diminished. The holding was that the child would have a substantially better chance of full recovery had surgery been performed at once. This is the opinion of the medical experts. Medical evidence for the defense revealed an opinion that the child had only 5 to 10 per cent chance of complete recovery as a result of the accident itself. The case was remanded back to a jury to consider evidence of increase in chance or harm on the issue of causation).

45 ***Brozana v Flanigan,*** **309 Pa Super 145, 454 A2d 1125 (1983)** (surgeon's negligence either was a substantial factor in bringing about the loss of the patient's leg or increase the risk of losing the leg, and that increased risk was a substantial factor in the loss of the leg, this being caused by delay in diagnosis and treatment of a compound fractured tibia).

46 ***Reager v Anderson,*** **371 SE2d 619 (W Va 1988)** (patient was entitled to $1,250,000 for negligence leading to amputation of his fractured leg, and $22,938.33 was given to father. The jury found the first treating physician 45 per cent responsible and the orthopedic surgeon 55 per cent responsible. The patient was a 13-year-old who fell from a cliff, sustaining head injuries and fracture of left leg at knee. A general surgeon examined him in emergency room; three hours later nurse notes said toes of left foot were cold, white and numb. The surgeon was called two hours later. The circulatory problem in leg persisted with patient complaining of continuous leg/foot pain. The surgeon examined patient the next morning; an orthopedic surgeon looked at x-rays and confirmed nondisplaced fracture of tibia near the knee. The next day, the orthopedic surgeon was called in for formal consultation, who performed fasciotomy surgery (4 days after injury) for compartment syndrome at which time he noted, but did not debride necrotic muscle. Arteriograms were never performed to verify arterial circulation status. The next three days, nurses noted no pulse in left foot, cold and white. A vascular surgeon, though available, was not called. Six days after injury, a vascular surgeon was consulted and amputation was done above knee five days later. Pathology reported a 2 cm-long clot occluding popliteal artery).

47 ***Thornton v CAMC, Inc,*** **305 SE2d 316 (W Va 1983)** (court adopted a view that permitting recovery for loss of chance was compatible with application of test for proximate cause in an action which the defendant orthopedist negligently treated the fractured leg and that the negligence led to gangrene and eventual amputation. It was remanded in that the jury's instructions seemed to indicate that the doctor was not permitted that the amputation would have been necessary regardless of the doctor's negligence).

48 ***Roberson v Counselman,*** **235 Kan 1006, 686 P2d 149 (1984)** (plaintiff sued the physician alleging negligent failure to refer a patient to a cardiologist. The patient died of cardiac complications. One of the plaintiff's experts testified that the failure to hospitalized the patient increased the patient's chance of dying from 19 to 25 per cent. A second cardiologist testified the patient had a 40 per cent chance of survival with proper care but no chance with no care. The court rejected the greater than 50 per cent argument and held a question of fact was stated for the "loss of chance." The court held that absent such a rule health care providers would be free of liability even for the grossest malpractice if the patient only had a 50 per cent chance of surviving the disease or injury with proper treatment).

49 ***Mortensen v Memorial Hospital,*** **105 AD2d 151, 483 NYS2d 264 (1984)** (surgeon removed a Baker's cyst in the back of the knee, except at the time of surgery, it turned out to be a tumor mass. It was first held to

be benign, but pathologist later reported it to be malignant. It was a situation where the surgeon "did not want to be the one to tell the patient he needed his leg amputated." In a second operation three months later, the mass was found to be expanded a great deal and involved bone. Mid-thigh amputation was carried out. The malpractice action was based on the failure of the surgeon to inform the patient and family that there was a malignancy and amputation must be carried out before the second exploratory operation. The surgeon was exonerated on negligence so far as the surgery was concerned and an opinion that the surgery itself did not cause the need for amputation. The case was returned to the jury on the question of whether there was a "lost chance" and whether the delay in informing the patient made any difference as to the indication for amputation).

Comment: The patient is entitled to know from the onset the good as well as the bad aspects of his case, his prognosis, and what treatment alternatives are after a surgical procedure demonstrates a change in the apparent diagnosis such as in this case. There was an emotional trauma that the family experienced with this more than two-month delay; however, there was obviously no change in what operative procedure would be required for the initial lesion that the patient presented with to the first orthopedic surgeon.

50 *Jeffers v Weinger,* 132 Ill App 3d 877, 477 NE2d 1270, 87 Ill Dec 742 (1985) (patient was scheduled for a laminectomy for protruded intervertebral disc. She had some signs and symptoms of urinary and bowel loss of control. Surgery went well but in the immediate postoperative state, she developed complete loss of bowel and urinary control with progressive numbness. At this state, blood clotting tests were ordered. It was 24 hours before they returned while the patient was worsening from postoperative bleeding and blood clots. The second operation removed the blood clot, but there were permanent residuals to diminished control of bowel and urine and numbness in her leg. She developed a neurogenic ulcer on her heel due to lack of sensation. There were no allegations of negligence of either surgery. It was the delay in the surgery that was negligent. It should have been done as soon as the progressive symptoms were identified. The waiting for routine laboratory work was not appropriate).

51 *Garner v Lammico,* No 140 684 Div C (9th Jud Dist Ct Parish of Rapides La Aug 1988) (plaintiff was admitted with high fever and was given antibiotics. The work-up showed osteomyelitis in T8, T9, T10 area. Patient's condition deteriorated during the next three weeks, and then paraplegia developed. Myelogram showed complete block with compression of the spinal cord by an epidural abscess. The defendant surgeon continued to treat with steroids and antibiotics instead of immediately (after the paralysis) operating to decompress the spinal cord. No further diagnostic studies were performed. The patient became incontinent. She did regain some use of her legs but was unable to lift herself off the bed. After another nine days with worsening, defendant surgeon did decompressive surgery but patient remain paraplegic. In the allegation, plaintiff contended that a complete block on the myelogram required an immediate decompression of the spinal cord and a delay of nine days substantially reduced her chance for recovery. The defendant contended that the patient never had an epidural abscess and that all he found at surgery was "stained tissue," arguing that his treatment was proper. Plaintiff verdict of $350,000. Following the verdict, defendant settled for $500,000—verdict plus interest).

52 *DiGiovanni v Latimer,* 454 NE2d 483 (Mass 1981) (patient could not recover for damages for emotional distress caused by a physician's failure to inform her that he had removed her fallopian tube. As the ovaries were removed, it was bound in scar tissue and part of the fallopian tube was removed, verified by a pathologist. The patient contended that if she had known of the removal, she would have been able to have her physician take steps so she could conceive a child. She alleged that as a result of learning that the tube had been removed, she suffered severe emotional anxiety and depression. The trial court found that this was insufficient evidence to raise a legitimate question of liability. On appeal, the court found no error in the lower court's finding. She presented no evidence that procedures of treatment that might have increased the likelihood of conception. She further claimed that she had aggravation of epilepsy but did not prove a causal relationship between her alleged emotional distress and aggravation of her epilepsy).

53 *LeJeune v Rayne Branch Hospital,* 539 So 2d 849 (La Ct App 1989) (court held recovery against negligent hospital for wife's emotional distress resulting from patient's injuries. The suit arose from a stroke patient being bitten by rats, sustaining additional injury. The wife suffered significant emotional trauma and distress. The permission for recovery, limited to immediate family members, relied on the fact that virtually all courts have permitted third-party claims for emotional distress stemming from harm to family member, with some limitations. Some states bar recovery unless claimant suffers some direct physical impact as a result of tort feasor's action. This "impact rule" has been abandoned by many courts, using instead the "zone of danger" rule, which authorizes recovery by a third party who was personally endangered by the tortfeasor's action. Neither of these rules is appropriate in a medical malpractice context as the doctor rarely endangers persons other than the injured patient. This decision is based on statutory provisions which give the right to recover damages for tortuously caused injuries. The court found this statutory right extends to claims for emotional distress suffered by members of a tort victim's immediate family represents a significant departure from prior law, since the court's decision does not incorporate any of the limitations on recovery that have been imposed by other states).

54 *Schram v Memorial Hospital,* 115 AD2d 882, 496 NYS2d 577 (1985) (husband who witnessed child born but dying from umbilical cord strangulation could not recover from physician for alleged emotional distress he suffered absent showing that defendant's negligence exposed the husband to unreasonable risk of bodily damage or death).

55 *Halliday v Beltz,* 514 A2d 906 (Pa Super 1986) (daughter of patient who died following elective surgery could not recover against physicians and hospital for negligent infection of emotional distress where she did not view actual surgery and hence did not meet the requirement of sensory and contemporaneous observance of alleged negligence).

56 *Hensley v Heavrin,* 282 SE2d 854 (SC 1981) (patient's claim against a physician for malpractice for incorrect diagnosis of syphilis should not be dismissed. Based on laboratory blood samples, the physician diagnosed her as having venereal disease. The patient contended this caused her severe emotional distress and her husband struck her several times, fracturing her jaw in two places when he learned the test results. It was later discovered the test results were incorrect. She did not have syphilis. The court denied a motion to dismiss action against the physician when he appealed. Affirming the decision, the supreme court said the patient had a cause for action for mental distress. Whether the physician acts were so outrageous and extreme she was entitled recovery from him was a question to be determined by the jury. The patient had no cause of action against the physician for the injuries caused by her husband, for that was an unforeseeable intervening cause of injury).

Comment: A number of cases of this sort have been heard where hasty diagnoses or incomplete evaluation for diagnosis informing the patient of diseases that cause dire distress.

57 *Anderson v Prese,* 445 A2d 612 (DC 1982) (evidence is sufficient to support the finding of intentional infliction of emotional distress by a physician in this case. A physician who had been told by a patient of her history of depression cursed and screamed at her to leave his office. In a suit for intentional infliction of emotional distress, evidence was presented that the physician's conduct caused the patient to stay at home, discontinue working and later enter a hospital. The trial court entered judgment for the patient. On appeal, the court said the conduct may generally not be considered outrageous or extreme, but may be so characterized when the actor knows the other person is particularly susceptible to emotional distress. Because the physician had prescribed Valium for the patient many times, he apparently knew her fragile nervous state and that she would be susceptible to emotional distress. Therefore, his conduct was extreme and outrageous under the circumstances, and the evidence was sufficient to support the judgment of the trial court).

58 *Marlene F v Affiliated Psychiatric Medical Clinic,* No S003030 (Cal Sup Ct Apr 10, 1989) (psychologists sexually molested boys, causing great emotional distress to mothers. Mothers sued for emotional distress and favorable decision was upheld. The state supreme court held mothers were entitled to claim as their distress was direct result of psychologist behavior rather than "mere bystanders" to the jury).

59 *Hoffner v Hodge,* 407 A2d 940, *appeal dismissed,* 498 Pa 135, 445 A2d 104 (1979) (no recovery was allowed in malpractice action against physicians and hospital for allegedly negligent surgery resulting in injuries to identical twin who was not present at the time of negligent act. No exception was allowed for identical twin who alleged she was present with her twin at all times, albeit in a different physical location).

60 ***Grimsby v Samson & Ballard Community Hospital,* 85 Wash 2d 52, 530 P2d 291 (1975)** (plaintiff alleged the defendant physician's conduct in abandoning the patient and failing to provide her with medical care was reckless, wanton and outrageous in that the plaintiff was required to witness the pain and suffering of his wife when she died. Therefore, the defendant caused severe mental anguish resulting in physical injury. The elements of the tort were declared to be intentional or reckless infliction of emotional distress, outrageous and extreme conduct of defendant resulting in severe emotional distress, not necessarily resulting in bodily harm).

61 ***Uryasz v Archbishop Bergan Mercy Hospital,* 431 NW2d 617 (Neb 1988)** (new trial was ordered in a case where patient was injured by pain injection in groin. There was conflicting testimony as how an injection to a painful area in groin would result in leg pain, drop foot, and depression. There was little question that a latent psychological state became activated but jury believed the relationship between the injection and the symptoms. Court felt the award was excessive and sent the case back on that issue. The problem stemmed from difficulty in explaining how an injury to the femoral nerve would produce impairment below the knee as it has function only proximal to the knee, and how much such impairment would reasonably affect her wage earning ability).

62 ***Whetham v Bismarck Hospital,* 197 NW2d 678 (ND 1972)** (plaintiff's parents with a newborn child brought this action against the defendant hospital for damages for emotional and mental shock suffered by the mother when she witnessed her child being negligently dropped on the floor by a hospital employee. The plaintiff appealed from the dismissal of their complaint. The court confirmed the dismissal and held that the mother could not recover for emotional shock for the negligently inflicted injuries to her child unless the defendant negligence threatened the mother with harm or placed her within what is termed the "zone of danger." The court also noted that "we are today not adopting" the impact rule).

63 ***Kahla v Glosser Bros, Inc,* 326 F Supp 985 (WD Pa 1971), *affd,* 462 F2d 815 (3d Cir 1972)** (plaintiff administrator sought to recover wrongful death action that defendant security guard alleged made, though consented to search of the deceased. Medical testimony showed that the excitement caused the search so stimulated the heart of the deceased that she collapsed and died of a coronary occlusion. The court held that "impact rule" had not opened the door to allow recovery for injury solely resulting from shock, absence of physical injury or fear of immediate physical injury. The court granted a summary judgment to the defendant holding there is no reason to fear physical injury on the part of the defendant).

64 ***Owens v Children's Memorial Hospital,* 480 F2d 465 (8th Cir 1973)** (alleging that the defendants, a hospital and certain physicians, negligently failed to properly diagnose and care for their son who died after a

month of hospitalization, the plaintiff brought this action for physical and mental anguish and their great emotional disturbance and shock and injury to their nervous systems. The court affirmed the dismissal of this action on the grounds of failure to state a claim from which relief could be granted. Noting that the parents had alternative remedies under wrongful death statute, the court declined in absence of clear Nebraska precedent and in the face of adverse authority of the overwhelming majority of the courts in the United States to extend the liability of doctor and hospitals for malpractice beyond the individual patient involved where there is no impact or where the patients neither were in the "zone of danger" nor feared for their own safety and where the incident was slowly unfolding rather than traumatic).

65 ***Tobin v Grossman,*** **24 NY2d 609, 249 NE2d 419 301 NYS2d 554 (1969)** (this case points out the impact on the mother of a seriously injured child. Here, there are no new technological, economical or social developments which have changed the social or economic relationships. Therefore, there is no impetus for a corresponding legal recognition of such changes. If foreseeability is the sole test, then once liability is extended, the logic of the principal would not and could not remain confined. It would extend to older children, fathers, grandparents, relatives and others in similar situations. "Any rule based solely on eye witnessing the accident could stand only until the first case comes along in which the parent is in the immediate vicinity but did not see the accident").

66 ***Rockhill v Pollard,*** **259 Or 54, 485 P2d 28 (1971)** (child was hit by a car and was taken to a doctor's office. The physician initially declined to see the patient and then did a perfunctory exam. The child had a skull fracture which the physician did not find. Physician was alleged to be extremely rude and finally ordered the plaintiff out of the office into subfreezing temperature. The facts later showed that the child had not been adversely injured or further injured by the behavior. The court mentioned that the physician's rude conduct was inappropriate but malpractice as such was not committed).

67 ***Chavous v Richmond County Hospital Authority,*** **313 SE2d 492 (Ga Ct App 1984)** (hospital was found not liable for a surgery related infection. The patient had surgery on the lower two vertebra of the back and while recovering developed a staph aureus infection, effectively treated by antibiotics but took some time to heal. The patient alleged the hospital was negligent in failing to keep the operating room, dressing and sutures and other implements in sterile condition and the surgeon was negligent in using those. The hospital moved for summary judgments supported by affidavits by the director of nurses and by the operating surgeon that stated all professionals of standard of care were met and maintained in sterile position. The trial court refused to use res ipsa loquitur doctrine. The surgeon testified the patient's infection was from his own skin—not from unsterile conditions. Since the source of infection was not within the exclusive control of the hospital or surgeon, and the injury was one that does occur in the absence of negligence, res ipsa loquitur did not apply).

68 ***Brickner v Normandy Osteopathic Hospital,*** **746 SW2d 108 (Mo Ct App 1988)** (a hospital is liable for the malpractice of resident physicians in training at that institution. The court reasoned that the hospital must have given up all control over the resident in order to escape respondeat superior liability. The ruling in this case indicates that there will be great difficulty for teaching hospitals to insulate themselves from liability for mistakes made by their resident physicians).

69 ***VanZee v Witzke,*** **No 16343-a-REM (SD Sup Ct)** (in this case, it was alleged the orthopedist said that plaintiff's finger "would not be worse off after surgery" and "there will be no problem at all" and "there are no absolute guarantees" did not create a guaranteed contract between the patient and surgeon. The plaintiff had injured her finger in an accident as a child which caused it to lock up. The surgeon, it was alleged, was more interested in functional outcome. The surgery, and subsequent revision surgery, left the patient with an unsatisfactory result. The court held the viewing the claimed statements as detailed by the plaintiff in a light most favorable to her, the supreme court agreed they failed to express a contract on which to ground liability).

70 ***Steinbach v Barfield,*** **428 So 2d 915 (La Ct App 1983),** ***cert denied,*** **435 So 2d 431 (La 1985)** (court held that the plaintiff did not state a claim for breach of contract. The claim was that the defendant assured her she did not have cancer and had thereby contracted with her that she would not be discharged with evidence of cancer. The court held that the doctor's action could not be interpreted as a guarantee that she did not have cancer; he did what any other doctor does when attempting to diagnose a patient's condition, running diagnostic tests, interpreting results of those tests, based on his skill and experience, and attempted to discover the basis of the patient's problem. The facts did not support the theory of contract).

71 ***Tackleston v Abbott-Northwestern Hospital, Inc,*** **415 NW2d 733 (Minn Ct App 1987)** (evidence was insufficient to establish claim of fraudulent concealment against hospital or surgeon. Patient suffered a fall while patient in hospital in 1980, sustaining a severe ankle injury. A month later, another doctor, not related to the hospital told plaintiff that she should sue the hospital. In 1982, the hospital offered to forgive her bill if she would sign a release relieving hospital from liability, plaintiff refusing to sign. In January, patient commenced suit against hospital; the court denied summary judgment for plaintiff based on six-year statute of limitation for fraud, held two-year statute for medical negligence was appropriate and it had passed. Further, the court rejected attempt to waive bill as tolling statute as an attempt to conceal).

72 ***Trantafello v Medical Center of Tarzana,*** **182 Cal App 3d 315, 227 Cal Rptr 84 (1986)** (in this case, methylmethacrylate was used instead of bone to maintain space between the sixth and seventh vertebra where discs had been removed. The choice of material was not discussed with patient, but acrylic cement was unusual. Some nine months following surgery, patient began to experience neck pain and a choking sensation when he tried to swallow. He complained of stress to two orthopedists; they did not provide relief or mention the acrylic they had implanted. In March 1978, the orthopedist who had originally suggested surgery told the patient perhaps the operation was to blame for his discomfort, that there might be some protrusions anteriorly pushing on the esophagus. It was only when the patient consulted a third orthopedist that he learned the methylmethacrylate had been used. The surgeon removed the acrylic and fused to the bone to C6-7 with bone graft. The patient filed a malpractice action against the first two orthopedists. There was a statute of limitation problem. There was an allegation of fraud and concealment and the court held that informed consent and fraud and concealment are not synonymous. Further methylmethacrylate implants are not in the same foreign body category as sponges. There was expert testimony that methylmethacrylate was used as a "spanner," though unusual, and is used for stabilizing vertebral problems, fractures, instabilities, etc.).

73 ***Mann v Cracchiolo,*** **38 Cal 3d 18, 694 P2d 1134, 210 Cal Rptr 762 (1985)** (this case involved 54 physicians. The charges were fracture of the neck of the patient, concealing the offense, performing an operation to obtain Medicare funds, and then trying to kill her to hide the complicity in causing and concealing the fracture. The case began in November 1971 when the patient had her toes x-rayed in preparation for surgery and fell off the x-ray table. Skull x-rays were normal and initially there was no obvious evidence of fracture of the cervical spine. The fracture of the odontoid process was discovered at autopsy and re-review of the x-rays revealed the odontoid fracture possibly was there after the fall from the table. The neurosurgeon, who reviewed the records, felt that fracture of odontoid was present and it was recognized at the time of her initial care for the fall from the table; however, no open mouth view had been taken to confirm the fracture. The patient continued to complaint of head and neck pain. A year later, x-rays showed subluxation of C1 on C2. Although there was no history of intervening injury of the neck, there was an injury reported in which the hip was dislocated that was treated during this time frame. The supreme court held there was enough evidence that medical negligence may have been done by some of the treating physicians and that this was a jury question).

Comment: In retrospect, this lady should have had more adequate x-ray studies of her cervical spine, including tomograms and an open mouth view of the odontoid, if there was a reason to suspect she had a cervical spine fracture at that time. However, apparently another physician saw the x-rays and did not feel such was there, but no mention is made of listening to the patient's complaints and following up of persistent pain.

74 ***Watts v Cumberland County Hospital System,*** **343 SE2d 879 (NC 1986)** (woman lost a 4-year legal battle to prove malpractice and fraudulent concealment of spinal fractures against seven physicians. Her history compiled of seven years in visits to numerous orthopedists and neurologists was marked by the suggestion of a lingering somatization, hysterical personality, suspect adjustment to reaction about life, etc. The problem began in 1974 when she went to the emergency room following an automobile accident complaining of pain in her neck and back and several areas. No injuries were shown on x-rays. She had several hospitalizations with additional x-rays and myelograms and several orthopedic consultations. In 1977, an orthopedic surgeon operated her right wrist for carpal tunnel. A myelogram taken at that time to rule out cervical disc pathology showed "some degeneration of lumbar discs" which the orthopedist essentially discounted. In 1978, she was hospitalized for cervical and coccygeal pain. Discograms and myelograms were normal and the orthopedist re-emphasized that a considerable psychological overlay was present. In 1979, a radiologist reported what he thought he detected as "residual changes from previous vertebral fractures of L4 and L5." After a repeat study two years later, he retracted his findings, that they were nullified by technical problems on the original x-rays that he saw. Based on the radiologist's first opinion, a suit was filed. The North Carolina Supreme Court stated, "As for fraud, even if the missing x-rays had shown small lumbar fracture, there was no proof that any doctor had seen them." Since some of them had not been involved in the case at the time of the radiologist's disclosure).

75 *Wade v Tomasville Orthopedic Clinic, Inc,* 306 SE2d 366 (Ga Ct App 1983) (patient was under treatment for a complicated fracture, was hospitalized for 54 days and during this time had a Foley catheter in place. About a week before discharge, it was noted that she had infection. She had been placed on antibiotics; the record showed the organism present in the patient was resistant to the antibiotic. Subsequently, she developed back pain that the orthopedist felt was due to her injury. She did see a urologist, who felt she had a kidney infection and a stone and for reasons not disclosed, did a nephrectomy on her. The patient sued the doctors for fraud, alleging they should have told her about the infection she had. The doctors stated that they did tell her. It was the unsupported testimony of the patient that they did not. However, the fact that the patient had been placed on antibiotics tended to prove that the physicians were aware that an infection was present, even though it was an incorrect antibiotic. An action of fraud was dismissed, suggesting that if there was any action, it would be in negligence; however, the statute of limitation had run on that).

76 *Borderlon v Peck,* 661 SW2d 907 (Tex), *rehg denied* (1983) (state law did not abolish the doctrine of fraudulent concealment as a bar to the statute of limitation defense. When a suture needle broke during an operation, the physician purposely left the broken portion in the patient's abdomen but did not inform her of this decision. The needle was later discovered on x-ray and operation performed to remove it. The patient filed a suit against this surgeon six days after the two-year limitation period had run. The patient responded to motion for summary judgment by filing the response alleging fraudulent concealment. Trial court granted summary judgment and appellate court affirmed. Court held that fraudulent concealment of the defense had been abolished under the state Medical Liability Insurance Improvement Act, because the legislature intended to establish an absolute time limit of which suits must be filed. On review of the case, the Texas Supreme Court disagreed with the lower courts. The courts pointed out that it was not inclined a writ of recovery by the patient but merely permitting her to present evidence that, if believed, would stop the surgeon from pleading statute of limitation as a bar to her claim. Case was sent back for further proceedings. It is incumbent on the surgeon to inform the patient where there has been misadventure such as breaking of needle or instrument part. Failure to do so is contrary to customary practice as well as addressing the ethical and moral obligations of the physician).

77 ***Harris v Penninger,* 613 SW2d 211 (Mo Ct App 1981)** (patient filed malpractice for concealing that a dressing was placed too tightly on a wound. After an injury, a large hematoma appeared on patient's thigh. Surgeon aspirated a hematoma and applied a tight bandage. Three weeks later, necrosis developed in the skin edge of the hematoma and a second surgery by another surgeon was necessary. Patient sued the first surgeon for personal injury, alleging that it was caused by his negligence in applying a tight bandage after evacuation of the hematoma. The trial court dismissed the case; the patient appealed. The appellate court pointed out that all the patient alleged the surgeon fraudulently attempted to conceal his negligence. She did not assert that the alleged fraud caused her to suffer loss. It did appear that there was medical negligence but no loss was claimed).

78 ***Muller v Thaut,* 430 NW2d 884 (Neb 1988)** (supreme court adopted the fraudulent concealment doctrine in a wrongful death action based on medical malpractice, holding the statute of limitation would be tolled if the doctor concealed the cause of death. In this case, an infant died and the doctor told family infant died of respiratory disease. An investigation nine years later of death certificate revealed doctor had signed cause of death as trauma).

79 ***San Francisco 49's, Ltd v Milburn,* No 906795 (Cal Super Ct San Francisco)** (team physician was sued for negligence for allegedly withholding information concerning the condition of a football player's knee. Player stated had he been advised by management or physician not to continue to play football, he would have followed that advice. Football team was found guilty for failure to communicate to player the severity of his knee injury. The court held that the knee injury was caused entirely by the acts or omissions of defendants, in that defendants, as the plaintiff's team physician in charge of examining, diagnosis and treatment, were authorized representatives of the plaintiff for the purpose of communicating to the player the condition of his knee and probably effects on his knee if he continued to play).

80 ***Vall v City of New York,* 539 NYS2d 446 (App Div 1989)** (patient was seen in emergency room and admitted to hospital for repair of lacerations of right forearm including repair of ulnar and radial arteries, ulnar and median nerve and all flexor tendons. Patient made good recovery, a second surgery for tendon transfer being required. After second surgery, a clawed hand resulted. Surgeon present at both surgeries denied that either median or ulnar nerves were severed during operations. The description of

operations in hospital records was not complete for second operation, in violation of hospital regulation. Recovery room record, however, indicated that a separate procedure to repair median nerve had been performed during second surgery. Claw hand was reasonable result of injury to median nerve).

81 ***North America Co for Life & Health v Berger,*** **648 F2d 305 (5th Cir 1980),** ***rehg denied,*** **655 F2d 235 (5th Cir),** ***cert denied,*** **454 US 1084 (1981)** (building insurer brought an action against physicians seeking to recover disability benefits paid by the insurer to air traffic controllers, because of the physicians' allegedly fraudulent or negligent diagnoses. The lower court granted summary judgment in favor of the physician on the neglect count and the insurer appealed. This court found that the physician had used the insurers' form and had certified disability directly to the insurer and therefore knew exactly who would rely on his certification and for what purpose. The court, therefore held the physician was under duty to exercise reasonable care in performing medical services, making diagnosis and transmitting them to the insurer. The court held that summary judgment on the issue of negligence had been improper because of the duty to exercise reasonable care existed and genuine issues of fact remained to be resolved. Accordingly, the lower court judgment was reversed and the case was remanded).

82 ***Bloskas v Murray,*** **44 Colo App 13, 618 P2d 719 (1979)** (in March 1973, the plaintiff suffered a fracture, dislocation of right ankle after healing arthritis developed causing both pain and swelling. In March 1974, plaintiff met with defendant doctor who suggested an ankle fusion to ease the pain. Surgery relieved pain temporarily but by that fall, patient was in pain again and returned to the defendant doctor. They decided that implanted artificial ankle would be the next course of action, but the ankle became infected and artificial parts were removed. Infection spread in July 1976 after four unsuccessful ankle fusions. The patient's right leg was amputated below the knee. Plaintiff brought medical malpractice suit claiming defendant had negligently failed to inform him of the substantial and specific risks associated with total ankle replacements and that he had negligently misrepresented the fact that amputation was a possible result of ankle replacement. The doctor had not told plaintiff that he had never performed ankle replacement. Trial court entered a judgment on a jury verdict for the defendant. On appeal, the court stated that all substantial risks significant in deciding whether or not to submit to surgery should be related to patient. The court held that the defendant had sufficiently fulfilled this requirement and there were no negligent misrepresentations. The court stated Colorado courts applied negligent misrepresentation only when the pecuniary loss if involved and that negligent misrepresentations that result in physical harm have not been recognized in Colorado. Plaintiff claims fell under the doctrine of informed consent in medical malpractice, both of which were correctly instructed to the jury. The court held there is no negligent misrepresentations so the lower court's judgment was affirmed).

83 ***Sullivan v Birmingham,*** **11 Mass App 359, 416 NE2d 528 (1981)** (plaintiff physician had been sued for malpractice by the defendants, who

had included damages in their complaint. The newspaper then published the amount of damages of the defendant's claim. The plaintiff brought action against the defendants, alleging the inclusion of damages listed constituted an abuse of process, and liable negligence because malicious inclusion was intended to complete settlement for the defendant's unwarranted claims. The defendants asserted the defense by absolute privilege. Trial court granted the defendant's motion to dismiss the action and the plaintiffs appealed. The court stated that based on policy, absolute privilege applies to defamatory statements made during the process of litigation, as long as the challenge remarks are relevant or pertinent to the judicial proceedings and as long as the publication is not unnecessary or unreasonable. The court stated that the relevancy of the judicial proceedings is to be construed broadly so that the amount of damages claimed was pertinent to the malpractice action, notwithstanding any statutory prohibition. The court held that the defendant's statements were completely privileged and the defendant had the absolute privilege against all the plaintiff's claims. The lower court's decision was affirmed).

84 ***Cady v Fraser,*** **122 Colo 252, 222 P2d 422 (1950)** (patient asserted liability for failure of an orthopedist to inform him of the non-union of a fractured bone. The physician was found not to be liable of malpractice on the basis that the evidence showed no damage to the patient resulted from the nondisclosure, and there was no need for further treatment, that the non-union in itself constituted satisfactory results).

85 ***Lopez v Sawyer,*** **115 NJ Super 237, 279 A2d 116 (1971)** (a cancer case, the malpractice deals with the allegation that physicians had fraudulently concealed their negligence in the treatment of a patient rather than charge them negligent in failing to inform the patient of the diagnosis or test results showing cancer. The court observed that caution or empathy in telling the patient the diagnosis is appropriate to withhold but by doing so thereby jeopardizing treatment is negligent behavior).

86 ***Martisek v Ainswerth,*** **170 Tex Civ App 459, 459 SW2d 679 (1970)** (patient fell from the fire escape, but the orthopedist failed to inform him of injuries to his back or precautions that should be taken, but rather telling him that his back was "all right." Months later, the patient was injured while lifting a metal frame sustaining a protruded intervertebral disc requiring subsequent surgery and causing further disability. The court observed that the patient had introduced expert testimony to the effect that the physician, in failing to "disclose the situation" to the patient fell below the ordinary standard of care and injury had occurred to the patient by virtue of this negligence).

87 ***McDaniel v LaSalle Ambulance Service, Inc,*** **440 NE2d 158 (Ill App Ct), *rehg denied* (1982)** (physician did not fraudulently conceal a patient's malpractice claim against him. The patient fractured both of her legs in an accident Nov 6, 1975 and was treated by a physician. Seven weeks later while being transported by ambulance, her legs struck the pavement, and afterward she discovered she suffered a drop foot. Her attorney wrote

the physician asking whether the ambulance incidence might have caused the drop foot. He replied that the wheelchair incident was either a cause or an aggravating factor of the peroneal nerve injury. She filed against the ambulance company; three years later after statute of limitation expired, the physician stated in deposition that his earlier statement was inaccurate, that hospital records indicated that the patient had a drop foot condition about a month prior to the ambulance incident. The patient amended her complaint to include a negligence count against the physician. Trial court dismissed the claim against the physician as barred by the statute of limitation. Affirming the decision, the appellate court said the physician had not fraudulently concealed her claim of negligence. His earlier opinion was that the ambulance had either caused or aggravated the drop foot was covered by the statement "could be an aggravating factor" implying that the condition already existed. Therefore, he did not conceal cause of action).

88 ***Harkin v Culleton,* 141 Misc 2d 801, 544 NYS2d 204 (Sup Ct 1989)** (fraud claims against two physicians who allegedly concealed an incorrect diagnosis of a brain tumor were timely filed, a New York trial court ruled. In 1974, the patient began to suffer from headaches and occasional seizures. His treating physician suspected a brain tumor and called in a neurosurgeon for a consultation. He performed a craniotomy to determine the location and type of tumor but allegedly placed the bone flap in the wrong location. The mislocation of the opening prevented him from seeing the actual cause of the patient's seizures, a benign tumor (meningioma) in the tentorium section of the brain. Because no tumor was visible from the window he had formed, the neurosurgeon erroneously concluded that the patient had a deep-seated malignant tumor (glioma) which could not be viewed or excised. He closed the bone flap without taking further action and informed the patient that he had six months to live. Intensive radiation and chemotherapy were started, but the patient's condition soon deteriorated from both the unnecessary radiation and the failure to remove the meningioma. In November 1983, the physician who took over the patient's treatment after his first physician retired wrote to the neurosurgeon about the patient's most recent brain scan and its indication of a meningioma. In December 1984, the treating physician informed the patient for the first time that his condition was not terminal, that the diagnosis by the neurosurgeon and his first treating physician was incorrect, and that no biopsy had ever been performed. The patient then sought legal counsel and filed suit against the neurosurgeon and his first treating physician. On motions by the physicians, the trial court said that the malpractice and fraud claim against the treating physician were timely filed. The fraud claim against the neurosurgeon was timely filed, but the malpractice action was barred by statute of limitation. The summons and complaint first served on the neurosurgeon had been ruled invalid and proper service was not obtained on him until more than three years after the patient had discovered the alleged fraud).

89 ***Ebaugh v Rabkin,* 22 Cal App 3d 891, 99 Cal Rptr 706 (1972)** (surgeons operating on wrong person, while admittedly negligent, did not war-

rant award of punitive damages where surgeon did not know he was operating on wrong patient. Instruction allowing jury to award punitive damages if it were found that act of surgeon was willful or reckless or wanton or so recklessly done as to imply disregard for obligation and rights of plaintiff, upon whom wrong operation was performed, was prejudicially erroneous because, under trial court's reasoning, punitive damages would be allowable in any case or reckless act or conduct without required aggravating circumstances amount to malice).

90 ***Mann v Cracchiolo,*** **38 Cal 3d 18, 694 P2d 1134, 210 Cal Rptr 762 (1985)** (action based on death of plaintiff's decedent allegedly as a result of broken neck sustained in fall while being x-rayed at hospital and defendant's subsequent failure to diagnosis and treat injury, motion on summary judgment on punitive damage issues were properly granted; declaration of plaintiff's expert witness in opposition to motions at most made out a case for medical malpractice and did not claim for punitive damages. There was no evidence of conspiracy to conceal to decedent, of intentional performance of useless operation on the decedent, or of attempt to kill her; at most, all that was shown in opposition to motion was failure to observe, report or diagnose, which failure did not establish intentional misconduct).

91 ***Lane v United States,*** **25 F Supp 850 (ED Va 1964)** (patient consented to surgery on his left knee. The surgeon, in error, operated on the right knee. Court found battery applied (unauthorized touching), therefore the patient could recover in spite of no residual problems or limitations of the operated knee).

92 ***Guebard v Jabaay,*** **452 NE2d 751 (Ill App Ct 1983)** (trial court committed a reversal error in refusing to instruct the jury on res ipsa loquitur in an accident arising out of a Hauser knee operation following an injury treated by conservative treatment. The operation did not achieve the desired result; the surgeon performed a second one about three months later. The second one also was unsuccessful and patient claimed her knee was left in worse condition than it was before surgery. She filed an action against the orthopedic surgeon, claiming lack of informed consent of the first operation which was primarily performed by first year resident of the hospital, lack of informed consent to the second operation and doctor res ipsa loquitur. Jury returned a verdict in favor of physician; patient appealed. The appellate court said that the theory of lack of informed consent did not apply when the patient had consented to a procedure but was performed by somebody else. Court said the patient's informed consent based on second operation should also fail. Surgeon allegedly did not tell her that patellectomy was an option of treatment).

93 ***Perna v Pirozzi,*** **92 NJ 446, 457 A2d 431 (1983)** (surgical consent to attending physician, another surgeon did the surgery. Plaintiff verdict based on battery stood).

Comment: This issue of "ghost surgery" has been medically unethical and is legally battery, yet continues to occur. In this case, there was an error in that the surgeon assumed that the referring physician had obtained consent for the surgeon. Each physician is responsible for obtaining his or her own informed consent.

94 ***Oates v New York Hospital,*** **131 AD2d 368, 517 NYS2d 6 (1987)** (intoxicated man presented himself to emergency room with stab wounds in abdomen. Blood alcohol was more than twice the legal definition of intoxication. An orthopedist emergency room physician suspected the stab wound may have caused peritoneal injury and urged the patient to have an exploratory laparotomy. The patient adamantly refused. The physician then tried to gain consent from the patient's family who objected. Pleading the patient's alcohol consumption had rendered him incompetent, and his life might be in jeopardy, the physician obtained necessary permission from the hospital administrator and did the surgery. The suit alleged malpractice as well as assault against the physician. The action was dropped inasmuch as a medical expert felt the surgery was appropriate and well within the standard of care. however, the high court refused to accept dismissal of assault charge and indicated that evidence presented during the trial had not conclusively demonstrated the patient's life was in danger or that alcohol had sufficiently impaired his ability to judge the need for treatment. They found for the plaintiff on the basis of assault).

95 ***Mantz v Follingstaqd,*** **84 NM 473, 507 P2d 68 (1972)** (plaintiff had a mastectomy performed by the defendant surgeon and brought brought this action pressing numerous claims against the defendant. In affirming judgment, the defendant court held enter alia. That the defendant alleged failures of disclosure and diagnosis and diagnosis did not constitute "extreme and outrageous conduct" so as to entitle plaintiff to have a jury instructed on her claim of intentional infliction of severe mental suffering and anguish).

96 ***Shetter v Rochelle,*** **2 Ariz App 353, 409 P2d 74, *modified,* 2 Ariz App 607 (1965)** (plaintiff sought damages for negligence against defendant physicians for glaucoma that developed following eye cataract removal by a defendant. The court found the defendant not responsible since he made no fraudulent representation to the patient in obtaining his consent to operate or in disclosing possible detrimental results which were known to the plaintiff patient).

97 ***Vaughn v Langmack,*** **236 Or 542, 390 P2d 142 (1964)** (physician negligently left a surgical needle in the patient when he operated. The patient did not discover the negligence until the statute had run out. The court held that his cause of action was barred even though the statute only said that negligence must be brought "within two years." One of the descents said the legislature could not have intended to relieve doctors from their obvious duties of their patients by such a reading of the statute).

98 ***Greene v Belinkoff,*** **354 Mass 102, 235 NE2d 793 (1968)** (patient sued anesthesiologist for alleged malpractice when the doctor administered a spinal during the delivery of patient's baby. The plaintiff contended that the resulting pain was from an overdose of drug. Trial court gave instructions that the doctor be held to a standard of skill. An ordinary physician practicing in his community on an appeal rejected this community standard and substituted one for average qualified practitioner. Some allowances were made for the community in which he practiced with those standards).

99 ***Toth v Community Hospital,*** **22 NY2d 255, 239 NE2d 368 292 NYS2d 440** (plaintiff's twin premature baby girls received serious eye damage from oxygen treatment, and their father brought claim enter alia alleging the hospital was negligent because its nurses failed to follow their pediatricians' orders to reduce oxygen doses from 6 liters to 4 liters daily, but instead maintained a 6-liter dose for 30 days. It was alleged also the pediatrician was negligent for failing to discover deviation from his orders. The jury had determined the cost of 6 liters dose was in conformance with the standard medical practice at the time, and the pediatrician claimed that this finding insulated him from liability. The court, however, reversed the finding for the pediatrician on this claim, holding that having undertaken to act as a specialist, the pediatrician is under duty to exercise his superior qualities or special competence which may have rendered him negligent because he realized the special dangers from maintaining the 6-liter dosage and nevertheless failed to check on its discontinuance).

100 ***Kenner v Northern Illinois Medical Center,*** **164 Ill App 3d 366, 517 NE2d 1137, 115 Ill Dec 451 (Ill App Ct 1987)** (this case is based on a complaint by plaintiff claiming the physical restraints ordered by an on-call physician constituted battery. The patient won a retrial for his suit. The issue was whether informed consent granted to ône physician authorized treatment by his or her substitute. A patient was in the hospital with a fractured ankle. His wife signed consent on his behalf for treatment. On the fourth day, the patient became extremely restless; the nurse became alarmed and called the on-call doctor and received the order for the use of restraints. The patient's suit included battery and false imprisonment and he said he was disturbed enough by the continuing restraints that he left the hospital against medical advice, that he had suffered "grave personal damages, humiliation and mental anguish." The appellate court found that conduct of the on-call physician was not of such an outrageous nature to warrant punitive damages. There was medical evidence that the restraints represented appropriate treatment. The question of the position of the on-call physician was answered that the two physicians had regularly covered for each other. The hospital personnel knew this and it was part of the bylaws of the hospital that this was acceptable coverage of the patients, and that this chain of command included the implied consent of the spouse's consent was given also to the physician on call).

Comment: The question of substitute physicians treating under the consent and order of the first consented physician is frequently a question for the jury. It goes back to usual customs of patient care and hospital bylaws, and the competency of the covering physician.

101 ***Morgan v Shepard,*** **91 Ohio L Abs 579, 188 NE2d 208 (Ct App 1963)** (court held that "using customary methods generally employed by physicians and surgeons to diagnosis, care and treatment of patient, no matter how long such methods are continued to be employed, cannot avail to prove and establish as safe in law, methods and conduct which in fact are negligent").

102 ***Truman v Thomas,* 93 Cal App 3d 304, 155 Cal Rptr 752 *superseded,* 27 Cal 3d 285, 611 P2d 902, 165 Cal Rptr 308 (1979)** (court did not hold physician negligent for failing to perform Pap smear on a female above the age of 23. The court held that "common sense" will prevail. Obviously, the court should not impose a standard of care in medical profession unless common sense dictates that the profession is acting in a careless manner).

103 ***Hill v St. Clare's Hospital,* 67 NY2d 72, 490 NE2d 823, 499 NYS2d 904 (1986)** (hospital or clinic may be responsible to patient who sought care at the hospital rather than from any particular physician, although physician whose malpractice caused injury to patient was not an employee of the hospital. Physician who owned medical clinic which was held out to public as offering medical services could be vicariously liable for malpractice of treating physician, practicing on behalf of the owner physician who was ill at the time, even though the owner-physician neither participated in nor controlled diagnosis made or treatment prescribed—application of cast to plaintiff's foot without first having discovered three bone fractures and dislocation of great toe adding additional injury to the first injury precipitating the patient seeking medical care).

104 ***Barrette v Hight,* 230 NE2d 808 (Mass 1967)** (chief surgeon in a case assigned intern who was hospital employee to perform a preliminary cut down to assure adequate fluid inflow during operation. The intern was negligent and patient injured thereby. The court held that allowing an intern to do procedure was customary and chief surgeon had advisory control over the intern and action was independent of the chief surgeon, that the intern and employer was liable).

105 ***Fure v Sherman Hospital,* 55 Ill App 3d 572, 371 NE2d 143 (1977)** (court held that a shareholder in professional medical corporation was not liable for alleged negligence of another shareholder, as he did not participate in diagnosis, care or treatment given patient, but only signed insurance form on behalf of corporation).

106 ***Thompson v Presbyterian Hospital, Inc,* 652 P2d 260 (Okla 1982)** (surgeon who prescribed Demerol as pre-medication for spinal block anesthesia could not be held liable for death of patient who had cardiac arrest, where surgeon could not have reasonable anticipated either breach of duty of the anesthesiologist nor the ultimate harm to the patient).

107 ***Fanelli v Adder,* 516 NYS2d 716 (App Div 1987) and in *Zuckerman v Antenucci,* 124 Misc 2d 971, 478 NYS2d 578 (App Term 1984)** (usual rule, recognizing that where physicians enter into partnership for the practice of medicine, all are liable in damages for professional negligence of one of the firm, provided negligent act is within the scope of partnership business).

108 ***Sal v Ellfeldt,* 662 SW2d 517 (Mo Ct App 1983), and *Forray v New York Hospital,* 101 AD2d 740, 475 NYS2d 57 (1984)** (it was recognized

that an independently employee of independently acting is not liable for the malpractice of another surgeon, in the absence of evidence that he observed the wrongful act, or in the exercise of ordinary care should have observed).

109 ***Crump v Piper,* 425 SW2d 924 (Mo 1968)** (court reasoned that evidence supported inference that defendant doctors (one neurosurgeon and one orthopedist) were employed jointly to treat plaintiff for relief of back condition according to best judgment where they diagnosed his condition together, reaching same conclusion, both recommended back surgery. Although each performed that part of surgery for which his particular talents qualified him, they acted in concert to correct the defect and as postoperative treatment was by both doctors, doctors both were vicariously liable for the other's negligence and one not relieved of responsibility for the other's negligence simply because he left operating room when other doctor was closing the wound and forgot to remove a sponge).

110 ***Graddy v New York Medical College,* 19 AD2d 426, 243 NYS2d 940 (1963)** (court reasoned that although physicians employed together may be jointly liable for negligence, referral of patient by one physician to another competent physician, absent partnership, employment or agency, does not impose liability on referring physician).

111 ***McCay v Mitchell,* 463 SW2d 710 (Tenn App 1970)** (agency was a question of fact and there was ample evidence from which the jury could have concluded that substitute doctor was his agent acting within scope of authority and for benefit of his principal, when plaintiff called doctors' exchange to find their regular orthopedist and were referred to a substitute doctor because the regular doctor had left instructions to do so).

112 ***Latson v Zeiler,* 250 Cal App 2d 301, 58 Cal Rptr 436 (1967)** (physician or surgeon may be held liable for negligence or malpractice of a physician or surgeon acting in the case as his agent. A pathologist's lack of participation in preoperative examination and evaluation of the plaintiff did not absolve him from careless diagnosis made by another doctor acting as his agent).

113 ***Thoria v Ross,* 362 SE2d 390 (Ga Ct App 1987), *rehg denied,* (Oct 28, 1987)** (hospital is not liable for alleged negligence while the surgeon was in charge. Patient sued surgeon and hospital alleging an instrument was left in abdomen during operation. Trial court denied partial summary judgment to the hospital on the issue of liability to the patient under the borrowed servant doctrine. On intralocutory appeal, the court said the surgeon was not a hospital employee, although he had privileges at the hospital. During the operation, members of the hospital house staff and several nurses who were hospital employees, assisted him. In his deposition, the surgeon admitted he was in charge of the operating room during the surgery in question. Patient offered no evidence to rebut this, or that the surgeon was absent during any time during the hospitalization. Therefore, there was no question that the surgeon exercised immediate personal supervision over hospital employees who were present during operation. Since the surgeon conceded that instrument was left in patient's abdomen during surgery when he was in charge, court found the hospital was not responsible).

114 ***Beaches Hospital v Lee,*** **384 So 2d 234 (Fla Dist Ct App 1980)** (although duties of an assisting nurse involving professional skill are generally regarded as controlled by the surgeon, when nurse's services are simply ministerial in character she is not required as the doctor's borrowed servant but rather as a servant of the hospital so that the latter may be vicariously liable to the patient).

115 ***Truhitte v French Hospital,*** **128 Cal App 3d 332, 180 Cal Rptr 152 (1982)** (court held that a nurse who at the time of his/her negligent conduct injured a hospital patient, while assisting surgeon, could have been found to have been acting as servant of hospital when negligence occurred).

116 ***Johnson v Greer,*** **477 F2d 101 (5th Cir 1973)** (plaintiff sued administrator of a psychiatric clinic for damages alleging he had been falsely imprisoned, that he had been denied his constitutional rights, that he had been injured when orderlies attempted to administer medication to him. The plaintiff had entered the hospital pursuant a protective custody warrant issued by the justice of the peace under which he could have been held no longer than 24 hours; however, he was detained for five days. Trial court found for plaintiff on the first two charges and appellate court affirmed, holding the Civil Rights Act. However, the court reversed the plaintiff verdict on the personal injury count holding that the jury instruction on proximate cause which implied that the defendant could be liable even if the damages were not foreseeable, was improper in light of the defendant's lack of malice and lack of intent to injure the plaintiff. It should have been said that the defendant would be liable only if it were reasonably foreseeable that his improper detaining of the plaintiff could increase the risk of personal injuries. However, the court remanded, in addition to personal injury count, the damage issue under civil rights act since the jury's award for the latter could have been affected by the findings under the improper instruction).

117 ***Doss v Hartford Fire Insurance Co,*** **448 So 2d 813 (La Ct App 1984)** (in this case, the question is what surgical risks would a mailman be willing to incur to keep his feet in walking condition. The patient had metatarsalgia with painful callouses and osteotomies of the distal metatarsals were carried out, one of which ended in non-union. When it was explained that the chances of non-union were of the order of six to one, the court decided that the usual prudent mailman would opt to have the surgery. Before surgery, the orthopedist offered him an alternative by using metatarsal pads in his shoes. The orthopedist explained the surgery and what he told him was the subject of the controversy in this trial. Additional information provided by the surgeon with the possibility of anesthetic catastrophe, possibility of infection and possibility of pulmonary embolus. Also, the orthopedist testified there was a small percentage of osteotomies that fail to heal. The second surgery was carried out which was only partially successful. The pain in the foot caused the patient to fall, sustaining severe back injuries according to the plaintiff. After considerable discussion of what the patient should be expected to understand in the consent, the appellate court felt that a 10 to 15 per cent risk failure would not have deterred the mailman from having the surgery, even if he clearly recalled that part of the consent discussion. It further held that oral consent was just as valid as a written consent but more difficult to prove).

118 ***Faile v Bycura,* 374 SE2d 687 (SC Ct App 1988)** (plaintiff had "confused the concept of informed consent and assumption of risk." The plaintiff did not allege breach of informed consent but use of improper medical procedure. She did not cite a complication or risk that was disclosed to her. Assumption of risk was an appropriate defense for a podiatrist in light of evidence that a patient was advised of alternative treatment. The plaintiff had been receiving cortisone injections for heel pain for several years by the defendant podiatrist. X-rays showed heel spurs on both heels, though plaintiff said she never had pain about left heel. Defendant recommended and performed tenotomies and capsulotomies two to five toes, both feet. The plaintiff said no relief from surgery, in fact, then additional pain in balls of feet and toes, with continuing heel pain. Evidence showed that the defendant did offer alternative treatments and further, patient failed to comply in wearing orthosis inserted in her shoes. The verdict was for defendant considering the facts above).

9

Res Ipsa Loquitur

§9.01 Generally

It may be inferred that harm suffered by the plaintiff was caused by the negligence of the defendant when:

1. The event is of a kind which ordinarily does not occur in the absence of negligence
2. Other responsible causes, including the conduct of the plaintiff and of third parties, are sufficiently limited by the evidence
3. The indicated negligence is within the scope of the defendant's duty to the patient

It is the function of the courts to determine whether the inference may reasonably be drawn by the jury or whether it must necessarily be drawn. It is the function of the jury to determine whether the inference is to be drawn in any case where different conclusions may reasonably be reached. (*See* Appendix 9-1, Cases 1 to 7.)

§9.02 Definition

A legal dictum states that negligence must be proved and never presumed. The mere fact that an accident or injury has occurred is not evidence of negligence on the part of any person. Evidence is required from which a reasonable person may conclude on the whole that it is more likely than not that the event was caused by negligence. When it is a matter of mere speculation or conjecture, or where the probabilities are at best evenly balanced between negligence and its absence, it becomes the duty of the court to direct the jury that the burden of proof has not been sustained. (*See* Appendix 9-1, Cases 8 and 9.)

Negligence, like any other fact, may be proved by circumstantial evidence. (*See* Appendix 9-1, Case 10.) Like all other evidence, it may be strong or weak; it may be so unconvincing that it is quite worthless, or it may be irresistable and overwhelming. "Some circumstantial evidence is very strong, as when you find a trout in the milk." (Thoreau's Journal, Nov 15, 1850).

The circumstantial evidence must sustain the burden of proof by making it appear more likely than not to be factual. The inference must cover all the necessary elements of negligence and must point to a breach of the defendant's duty. The court must first determine whether the circumstantial evidence is reasonable before the jury can make its inferences.

Res ipsa loquitur is one type of circumstantial evidence which has generated considerable differences of opinion. The term is a Latin phrase meaning "It speaks for itself," first used in an 1863 trial in which a barrel of flour rolled out of a warehouse window onto passing pedestrians. *See Byrne v Boadle,* 2H CH & C, 722 159 Eng Rep 299 (1863); *Hake v George Widemann Brewing Co,* 23 Ohio St 2d 65, 262 NE2d 703 (1970); Annotation, *Hospital's Liability to Patient or Prospective Patient Injured as Result of Physical Condition of Premises,* 16 ALR3d 1237 (1967); 1 U Chi L Rev 519 (1934); 37 Calif L Rev 183 (1949); *Griffith v Griffith,* 48 Miss LJ 259 and expanded in 75 NW UL Rev 147 (1980). *See also* Restatement (Second) of Torts §328D.

A requirement that the occurrence be one that ordinarily does not happen without negligence is the only way of stating the principle of circumstantial evidence. The event must be such that, in ordinary experience, it gives rise to an inference that someone must have been negligent. This is the basis for the application of res ipsa loquitur. It defines comparable application in cases of objects such as bricks or window panes falling from a defendant's premises, falling elevators, loose livestock on the highway, escaped gas or water from mains, and lack of control of objects under the defendant's exclusive control. On the other hand, many accidents which, as a matter of common knowledge, occur frequently enough without one's fault, such as falling down stairs, an automobile tire blowout, or a staph infection from an operation do not justify the conclusion that negligence, per se, has occurred. *See Roark v St Paul Fire & Marine Insurance Co,* 415 So 2d 295 (La Ct App 1982).

It is not enough for the plaintiff to prove that he or she was injured by the negligence of someone; he or she must prove beyond reasonable doubt that there was a defendant who was negligent. It is necessary to link the defendant with the probability already established that the accident was negligently caused. *See Newing v Cheatham,* 15 Cal App 3d 593, 520 P2d 33, 124 Cal Rptr 193 (1975). The injury must be traced to a specific instrumentality or cause for which the defendant was responsible, or it must be shown that the plaintiff was responsible for all reasonably probable causes to which the accident could be attributed. The evidence must be sufficient to pass the test of greater probability, not of mere chance. General terminology states that the defendant must be in exclusive control of the instrumentality that has caused the accident. *See Markarian v Pagano,* 87 AD2d 726, 449 NYS2d 335 (1982).

Res ipsa loquitur leads to the conclusion that a defendant has not exercised reasonable care, and is not in itself any proof that the defendant was under a duty to do so. Thus, in medical malpractice, a physician-patient relationship must exist to involve the physician. *See Davis v Jackson,* 604 SW2d 610 1980 and *Beccue v Rockcord Park District* 94 Ill App 2d 179, 236 NE 105 (1968). It is in medical malpractice actions where the duty arises since a physician undertakes only to exercise a skill of care common to the profession. A mistaken diagnosis, the unfortunate choice of the wrong method of treatment, or the type of accident or undesirable result which happens despite all reasonable precautions is usually insufficient to show the necessary lack of skill or care. This means that ordinary laypersons are unqualified to say what a good doctor would not do wrong, and that expert testimony is indispensable before any negligence can be found. (*See* Appendix 9-1, Case 12.)

Of course, the unwillingness of the members a profession to testify against one another may impose a substantial burden on the plaintiff of which the courts will take notice. *See Vanzee v Sioux Valley Hospital,* 315 NW 489 (SD 1982) (one of four doctors testifying "pierce this conspiracy of silence").

There are medical and surgical questions which any lay-person is competent to judge and to conclude, from common experience, that certain things do not happen when proper skill and care have been exercised. The act speaks for itself when a surgeon leaves a sponge or implement inside a patient's body or removes an inappropriate part of the patient's anatomy, when a dentist drops a tooth down a patient's windpipe, when a patient suffers serious burns from a hot water bottle, or when instruments are not sterilized. (*See* Appendix 9-1, Cases 12 and 13.)

Medical experts may provide sufficient foundations for res ipsa loquitur on more complex matters, with testimony that the plaintiff's particular adverse reaction does not ordinarily occur when due care is used. (*See* Appendix 9-1, Cases 14 to 21.)

There is a small cadre of cases in which the defendant adopts a method of treatment, for valid and sound medical reasons, which is known to produce damaging results in a small percentage of cases. In spite of all professional care and skill, courts occasionally err, saying that no injury occurs in ordinary cases, so the jury must be permitted to conclude that there must have been negligence. This is clearly wrong, since the issue is the probability that an infrequent adverse result was caused by negligence, not the probability that it would happen at all.

§9.03 Statutory Elements

In most states, all statutory elements must be met for res ipsa loquitur to stand. In determining if res ipsa loquitur is applicable, the authorities are in harmony that the following three factors must be present:

1. The accident or occurrence producing the injury is of a kind which ordinarily does not happen in the absence of someone's negligence
2. The injuries are caused by an agency or instrumentality within the exclusive control of the defendant
3. The injury causing the accident or occurrence is not due to any voluntary action or contribution on the part of the plaintiff

Oklahoma Statutes tit 76, §21 (1981) entitled "Presumption of Negligence," contains the following typical provisions:

1. The plaintiff sustained an injury
2. Said injury was caused by an instrumentality solely within the control of the defendant or defendants
3. Such injury does not ordinarily occur under the circumstances absent negligence on the part of the defendant
4. If any fact requires a degree of knowledge or skill not possessed by the average person, such fact must be established by expert testimony

Appendix 9-1
Cases

1 ***Mote v Helmy,* 169 Ga App 475, 313 SE2d 493 (1984)** (plaintiff sued a hospital and an orthopedist where he had undergone a successful lumbar discectomy but developed a staph aureus infection in the incision site. The infection delayed his recovery substantially. Res ipsa loquitur was pled by the plaintiff. In addition, a general plea of negligence in failing to keep operating room instruments, dressings, sutures, etc., sterile was made. The res ipsa loquitur doctrine assumes that the negligence was so self-evident that a jury could decide the case by common sense. The surgeon told the court that staphylococcus is frequently found on a patient's skin, and that it may not be possible to remove all of it with preparation for surgery. Res ipsa loquitur cases must meet three criteria: the injury must be one that ordinarily does not occur without negligence, the injury must have been caused by something that was in the exclusive control of the defendant, and the injury must come about without any voluntary act on the part of the plaintiff. The plaintiff failed to satisfy the first two criteria).

2 ***Hoven v Rice Memorial Hospital,* 386 NW2d 752 (Minn Ct App 1986)** (action against surgeons and a hospital for an ulnar nerve compressed during the course of unrelated surgery. Res ipsa loquitur was relied on. There was proof of where or when the compression took place, and the surgeons had limited control of the patient other than the area of his body (hernia surgery) being operated on. Res ipsa loquitur was not applicable and expert assessment of the above facts was required).

3 ***Southern Florida Sanitarium & Hospital, Inc v Hodge,* 215 So 2d 753 (Fla Dist Ct App 1968)** (res ipsa loquitur was applicable where a patient allegedly sustained an infection, developing thrombophlebitis, after liquid was injected into her as part of a diagnostic test).

4 ***Little v Arbuckle Memorial Hospital Board of Control,* 665 P2d 1227 (Okla Ct App 1983), *cert denied* (June 28, 1983)** (Vistaril was injected into the arm of the plaintiff, resulting in an injury which required considerable treatment. There seemed to be no question that the negligent injection by a hospital-employed nurse was the cause. Res ipsa loquitur applied).

5 ***Adams v Leidholdt,* 563 P2d 15 (Colo Ct App)** (there was evidence that a plaintiff's injury occurred during or following hip surgery with injury to the peroneal nerve below the knee, that it was a rare injury, that nothing occurred during surgery to injure the nerve, and that wrapping the foot and positioning the leg in a traction device could have caused the injury. The plaintiff was entitled to invoke the doctrine of res ipsa loquitur).

6 ***Garrison v Hotel Dieu,* 319 So 2d 557 (La Ct App)** (res ipsa loquitur was not applicable against a hospital and an orthopedist in an action by a

patient who suffered an infection after back surgery. According to expert testimony, the infection was more likely due to a prehospitalization respiratory infection than to a shower the patient took the day after surgery).

Comment: Knowledge of a presurgical respiratory infection should be evaluated, and surgery should be delayed and prophylactic antibiotics should be administered, as necessary.

7 ***Rimmele v Northridge Hospital Foundation,* 46 Cal App 3d 123, 120 Cal Rptr 39 (1975)** (plaintiff sustained osteomyelitis of the spine (vertebra) allegedly resulting from a nurse-given, doctor-ordered injection. The doctor was released as a defendant, as it was clear that he personally gave no injection. There was no proof that the nurse's injection was negligent, yet osteomyelitis does not ordinarily occur absent negligence. Thus, the res ipsa loquitur doctrine could be invoked).

8 ***Hale v Heninger,* 87 Idaho 414, 393 P2d 718 (1964)** (res ipsa loquitur was not applicable in a malpractice action to recover for paralysis after a lumbar myelogram and laminectomy and fusion operation, since the plaintiff's affliction would not normally be caused by negligence. Expert testimony as to negligence was necessary).

9 ***Shurpit v Brah,* 30 Wis 2d 388, 141 NW2d 266 (1966)** (laypersons could not infer negligence from the fact that the plaintiff developed gas gangrene following the amputation of a hand. Expert testimony was necessary).

10 ***Keller v Anderson,* 554 P2d 1253 (Wyo 1976)** (inference of negligence sufficient to invoke res ipsa loquitur was not raised by the fact that a crushed leg resulted in an infection that eventuated amputation, in absence of evidence that the treatment and care caused the loss of the limb, notwithstanding that a fractured femur does not ordinarily result in amputation).

11 ***Stewart v New Orleans,* 418 So 2d 1389 (La Ct App), *cert denied,* 423 So 2d 1159 (La 1982)** (plaintiff alleged that his leg had to be amputated due to a hospital's use of "too tight" restraints as part of treatment of his psychosis. At the time the infection had already attacked the plaintiff's musculature system, the plaintiff's leg had drug track marks, the plaintiff's sickle cell trait would have aggravated the infectious condition, and the leg amputation was due to lack of blood supply resulting in gangrene. The preponderance of the evidence inferred the gangrenous leg had no relationship to the restraints, although the patient had a right to be protected against reasonable hazards to his health. Res ipsa loquitur was held inapplicable).

12 ***Congelton v Baton Rouge General Hospital,* 444 So 2d 175 (La Ct App 1983), *rehg denied* (June 19, 1984)** (res ipsa loquitur could not be applied where there was direct evidence to explain the activities leading to the injury. A woman suffered injury when she was donating blood at a blood bank. During the phlebotomy, a technician drawing the blood positioned the needle and adjusted the tourniquet when the woman complained of pain, and again when she complained of tingling and numbness. When the technician offered to remove the needle, the woman decided to complete

the procedure. After the phlebotomy, the woman complained that her arm was still numb, and the technician told her to call back the next day if her condition persisted. The woman called back the next day, and the supervisor told her to return for examination by the head of the pathology department. She was then advised to see a neurologist; he found an injury to the left antebrachial cutaneous nerve. Another neurologist did an EMG and confirmed the diagnosis. The woman sued the hospital to recover for her injury, testifying she had pain as soon as the technician started to draw the blood. The technician said the woman did not complain until the phlebotomy was almost completed. The trial court found that res ipsa loquitur was applicable in that the hospital failed to rebut the inference of negligence, and awarded for the patient. On appeal, the court said there was undisputed evidence that the injury was caused when the needle struck the nerve in the woman's arm, rendering the doctrine of res ipsa loquitur inapplicable. All of the medical testimony at trial indicated that the injury could have occurred in the absence of negligence. One physician testified that such an injury could happen even with the best medical technique, although testimony showed that the injury was highly unusual and extremely rare. The court said that this did not alone justify res ipsa loquitur. A greater weight of testimony showed that the hospital was negligent and was not the most plausible explanation of the injury. Finding the woman failed to prove negligence with a preponderance of the evidence, the court reversed the lower court's decision).

13 ***Kolakowski v Voris,* 415 NE2d 397 (Ill 1980) *rehg denied,* (Jan 29, 1981)** (case was allowed to proceed to a jury on a theory of res ipsa loquitur. In 1951, the patient began an extensive history of back problems. He underwent a laminectomy and fusion in 1956 after severe degenerative disease of the lumbar disc was diagnosed. He re-injured his back in an automobile accident in 1972. A myelogram performed in 1973 showed possible spinal cord impairment. His physician performed an anterior interbody discectomy and fusion. The physician informed him that possible complications of surgery included infection, quadriplegia, and quadriparesis. During the operation, a bone plug was implanted in the space left by the removal of the disc. Shortly after the patient was returned to his room, the nurse noted on his chart that he had stiffness and inability to move his legs. The surgeon diagnosed his condition as spastic paraparesis caused by spinal cord edema. The condition failed to improve with treatment and a myelogram indicated blockage of the seventh cervical vertebra. A laminectomy was immediately performed and fragments of extruded disc were removed from the fifth and sixth levels. No evidence of spinal cord compression or edema was found. The patient lost the use of his limbs and was virtually quadriplegic. A trial court granted summary judgment for the physician and hospital. The appellate court reversed. The supreme court found that res ipsa loquitur applied to the patient's claim. When he submitted himself to the care of a hospital and its staff and was rendered unconscious for surgery, the hospital and surgeon had complete control. The burden shifted to the hospital and the surgeon to dispel the inference that they did not exercise the control required to apply res ipsa loquitur. The fact that the patient presented expert testimony that his injury was the result of forcing the bone plug against the spinal cord after the disc was removed did not preclude the patient from relying on the res ipsa loquitur doctrine).

14 ***Killingsworth v Poon,* 167 Ga App 653, 307 SE2d 123 (1983), *cert denied* (Sept 6, 1983)** (patient had a myofascial trigger point of pain at the back of her shoulder girdle. An injection of local anesthetic and steroid was used; the needle passed too deeply and caused a pneumothorax (collapsed lung). There was no medical expert testimony, and although res ipsa loquitur was not invoked, the common knowledge doctrine was discussed. The example used by the court was "if a surgeon performs an appendectomy and unintentionally slits the patient's throat, the jury may not need the testimony of a medical expert to conclude the act was negligent." The court concluded, "It is widely known and generally understood by laymen that subcutaneous injections ostensibly given for the relief of muscular pain should not, if administered correctly, result in a puncture of the internal organs." The court referred to a Georgia Law Review that stated, "To put it more bluntly, medical defendants, as a class, are not deserving of any special dispensation from inferences of negligence that may be logically drawn from the circumstances. One suspects, but cannot prove, that the underlying judicial condemnation of res ipsa loquitur malpractice cases is the instinct to provide justified protection.").

15 ***Ballance v Wentz,* 22 NC App 363, 206 SE2d 734, *affd,* 286 NC 294, 210 SE2d 390 (1974)** (case alleged failure of fractured arm (humerus) to heal properly after a skin traction slipped off. Res ipsa loquitur was pled but no expert testimony was offered to show a breach of the standard of care).

Comment: The treatment of a fractured arm with a skin traction is unusual and may well have fallen below the standard of care, but this was neither pled nor proven.

16 ***Simar v Hartford Fire Insurance Co,* 483 So 2d 196 (La Ct App), *cert denied,* 485 So 2d 65 (1986)** (res ipsa loquitur was denied in an action based on a neurosurgeon's alleged negligence in the performance of a cervical laminectomy which rendered the patient paraplegic, where the patient had experienced two prior episodes of paralysis and experts agreed that his condition would have worsened without surgery because the lesion (spinal cord cyst) could have caused paralysis).

17 ***Haas v United States,* 492 F Supp 755 (D Mass 1980)** (knee surgery was carried out successfully in a Veterans' Administration Hospital, but the patient awoke from anesthetic with severe brain damage. It was held that the plaintiff sustained undisputed anoxic brain damage, that it is common knowledge from human experience that the brain of an unconscious person would not be deprived of oxygen unless someone caring for the patient was negligent, and that, where no counteraffidavit was filed, res ipsa loquitur would not stand; however, expert testimony as to negligence was necessary).

18 ***Oberlin v Friedman,* 1 Ohio App 2d 499, 205 NE2d 663** (plaintiff's expert testified that the defendant was negligent in injecting a neurolytic

substance (absolute alcohol) for anesthetic, which caused paraplegia. Defendant's expert produced substantial evidence that paraplegia was caused by thrombosis (transverse myelitis) disassociated from and not caused by the injection. Res ipsa loquitur had been pled, but was held inapplicable).

19 ***Graham v St Luke's Hospital,*** **46 Ill App 2d 147, 196 NE2d 355** (plaintiff received a therapeutic injection in a back muscle. The patient alleged that painful causalgia was caused by a negligent injection. Res ipsa loquitur was not applicable. The appearance of causalgia, absent expert testimony, was so remote from the injection that it was probably medically unrelated).

20 ***Drewry v County of Obion,*** **619 SW2d 397 (Tenn Ct App 1981)** (award for a plaintiff who alleged permanent partial loss of the use of a hand as a result of a nurse's negligence in administering calcium intravenously as ordered by a physician was reversed where the plaintiff introduced no medical evidence regarding the cause of her complaints or her alleged loss of use of her hand, and where the judge sitting without a jury awarded damages, relying on res ipsa loquitur. For the plaintiff to recover, the trier of fact would have to presume both negligence and causation. Proof of negligence supplied either by direct proof or by res ipsa loquitur establishes only negligence; it does not supply proof of causation).

21 ***Thomas v Corso,*** **265 Md 84, 288 A2d 379** (action for the failure of a physician on call to personally attend an automobile accident victim, causing injury to the victim, after being notified of the victim's condition on arrival at a hospital emergency room. The requirement of the physician's physical presence was a matter of common sense and expert evidence was not required to support an action for the death of the victim).

Additional Pertinent Citations

See Revels v Pohle, 101 Ariz 208, 418 P2d 364 (1966) (failure to steel-suture); *Fox v Cohen,* 160 Ga App 270, 278 SE2d 272 (1981) (burns on back); *LePelle v Grefenson,* 101 Idaho 422, 614 P2d 962 (1980) (dropped bone fragment during operation); *Pizzalotto v Wilson,* 411 So 2d 1150 (La Ct App 1982) (wrong diagnosis); *Zeno v Lincoln General Hospital,* 404 So 2d 1337 (La Ct App 1981) (nerves unavoidably severed during surgery); *Wells v Woman's Hospital Foundation,* 286 So 2d 439 (La Ct App), *cert denied,* 288 So 2d 646 (La 1974) (iodoform gauze left in closed surgical wound); *Suburban Hospital Association v Hadary,* 22 Md App 186, 322 A2d 258 (1974) (use of unsterilized instruments); *Wilson v Stilwill,* 411 Mich 587, 309 NW2d 898 (1981) (postoperative infection); *Higdon v Carlebach,* 348 Mich 363, 83 NW2d 296 (1957) (tongue cut); *Kim v Anderson,* 610 P2d 1270 (Utah 1980) (drill bit dropped down throat); *Butts v Watts,* 290 SW2d 777 (Ky Ct App 1956), *rehg denied,* (June 22, 1956) (portion of extracted tooth left in jaw); *Racer v Utterman,* 629 SW2d 387 (Mo Ct App 1981), *cert denied,* 103 S Ct 26 (1982) (surgical drape caught fire).

See also Powell v Mullin, 479 So 2d 1119 (Ala 1985); *Nelson v Parker,* 104 Cal App 770, 286 P 1078 (1930); *Timbrell v Suburban Hospital,* 4 Cal 2d

68, 47 P2d 737 (1935); *Borghese v Bartley,* 402 So 2d 475 (Fla Dist Ct App 1981); *Beaches Hospital v Lee,* 384 So 2d 234 (Fla Dist Ct App 1980); *Stringer v Zacheis,* 105 Ill App 3d, 434 NE2d 50 (1982); *Piacentini v Bonnefil,* 69 Ill App 2d 433, 217 NE2d 507 (1966); *Guilbeau v St Paul Fire & Marine Insurance Co,* 325 So 2d 395 (La Ct App 1976); *Tyler v Tauro Infirmary,* 254 La 204, 223 So 2d 148 (1969); *Bryan v Luverne Community Hospital,* 217 NW2d 745 (Minn 1974); *Hestbeck v Hennepin County,* 212 NW2d 361 (Minn 1973); *Jensen v Linner,* 260 Minn 22, 108 NW2d 705 (1961); *Rudeck v Wright,* 218 Mont 41, 709 P2d 621 (1985); *Martin v Perth Amboy General Hospital,* 104 NJ Super 335, 250 A2d 40 (App Div 1969); *Terhune v Margaret Hague Maternity Hospital,* 63 NJ Super 106, 165 A2d 75 (1960); *Becker v Eisenstodt,* 60 NJ Super 240, 158 A2d 760 (1960); *Tallarico v Nassau Hospital,* 115 AD2d 646, 497 NYS2d 483 (1985); *Wynn v Ricotta,* 101 AD2d 695, 476 NYS2d 36 (1984); *Harrison v Wilkerson,* 405 SW2d 649 (Tenn Ct App 1966); *Rodriquez v Montgomery,* 630 SW2d 826 (Tex Ct App 1982); *Worley Hospital, Inc v Caldwell,* 529 SW2d 639 (Tex Civ App 1975).

And see 12 Houston L Rev 1026 (1975); U Colo L Rev 182 (1965); Annotation, 82 ALR 1262 (1962) and Annotation, 9 ALR3d 1315 (1969).

10

Proximate Cause and Foreseeability

§10.01 Generally

It is essential for the plaintiff in a negligence action to reasonably connect the act or omission of the defendant to damage which the plaintiff has sustained. This defines a *proximate* or *legal cause.* There is perhaps nothing in the entire field of law which has called forth more disagreement or on which case law is in such a welter of confusion. Much of this confusion is due to the fact that no one problem is involved, but a number of different problems which are not distinguished clearly because the language or probative discussion of one is carried over to, or casts a shadow on, the others.[1]

It becomes a mental exercise of assessing what is thought to be fact, and weighing that with what would have happened had conditions contrary to the facts had existed; that is, would the injury have happened had there not been the alleged negligent action—if the defendant's conduct is a cause of the event—if the event would not have occurred but-for that conduct. Conversely, the defendant's conduct is not a causative event if the event would have occurred without it.[2] (*See* Appendix 10-1, Cases 1 to 4.)

The but-for rule explains the greater number of cases, but there is one type of situation that fails. If two causes concur to bring about an event and

---

[1] Prosser, *Proximate Cause in California,* 38 Calif L Rev 369 (1950); Morris, *Proximate Cause in Minnesota,* 34 Minn L Rev 1985 (1950); Green, *Proximate Cause in Texas Negligence Law,* 28 Tex L Rev 71 (1950); Thode, *Torte Analysis: Duty-Risk versus Proximate Cause of the Rational Allocation of Functions Between Judge and Jury,* 1977 Utah L Rev 1.

[2] Smith, *Legal Cause in Action of Tort,* 25 Harv L Rev 103 (1911); McLaughlin, *Proximate Cause,* 39 Harv L Rev 149, (1925).

either one of them alone would be a sufficient cause of the identical result, some other test is needed. The substantial factor formulation is applied here, which is an improvement over the but-for rule. If the defendant's conduct was a substantial factor in causing the plaintiff's injury, he or she will not be absolved from liability because another tortfeasor may also have been involved.

An important concept is that although causation is essential to liability, it does not determine it. Circumstantial evidence, expert testimony, or common knowledge may provide the basis from which a causal sequence can be inferred.

Proximate cause is often an issue when a physician fails to detect cancer or negligently delays the treatment of it—the decreased chance of survival or the diminished life span that the negligence causes under a "more probable than not" doctrine. There is a parallel between this type of negligence and liability for aggravation of an existing infirmity, and it is usually dealt with by the courts with awards proportionate to the degree of injury, injury being the probable lessening of the life span or the degree of aggravation of the infirmity.

For a physician to be liable for another's harm, it is necessary that his or her conduct be negligent toward the other and also that the negligence of the physician be the legal cause of the other's harm.[3] (*See* Appendix 10-1, Cases 5 and 6.)

Where a person has intentionally invaded the legally protected interest of another, the intention commits an invasion which, in the degree of his or her moral wrong and action, and the seriousness of the harm which was intended, are important factors in determining liability for his or her own unintended harm.[4]

A *superseding cause* is an act of a third person or other force which intervenes and prevents the physician from being liable for harm to another which is antecedent negligence as a substantial factor.[5] (*See* Appendix 10-1, Case 7.)

Paraphrasing Prosser and Keaton on Torts, 5th edition, this gives the medical and other professions the privilege, which is emphatically denied to other groups, of setting their own legal standard of conduct merely by adopting their own practices. It is sometimes said that this is because a physician has represented that he or she will follow customary methods and so has undertaken to do so. Another explanation—probably more valid—is the healthy respect that the courts have had for the learning of a fellow profession and the reluctance to hold physicians liable for actions taken on the basis of educated judgment. This is clearly related to the layperson's ignorance of medical matters and the necessity of expert testimony, since juries,

---

[3] Prosser, *Necessity of Adequate Causal Relation, Section 430,* 38 Calif L Rev 369 (1950).

[4] Prosser, *Unintentional Consequences of Intentional Invasions,* 34 Minn L Rev 1985 (1950).

[5] Prosser, *Superseding Cause,* 28 Tex L Rev 71 (1950).

when considered competent to do so, are permitted to find that a practice generally followed by the medical profession is negligent. This has frequently been done in cases where a sponge has been left in a patient's abdomen after an operation.[6] (*See* Appendix 10-1, Case 8.)

Negligence may arise as a result of the failure to prevent something from happening. Suppose that a patient consults an orthopedist with a contaminated wound, that the wound is managed locally, and that one week later he returns with signs of tetanus which, despite expert treatment, proves fatal. When the lawsuit is brought to trial, the doctor may argue that the treatment did not give the patient tetanus, but that the acquired contamination occurred as he was wounded and that the injury was the sole cause of his death. Medically speaking, that is correct. But, the law goes beyond either logical factor and assigns responsibility to other more tangential contributions. In this case, factual issues will involve how the physician cared for the local wounds and whether he sought to prevent tetanus by administering tetanus toxoid. If the doctor's evidence on this question is weak, he could be found liable for failing to prevent the condition from developing. (*See* Appendix 10-1, Cases 9 to 11.)

A similar case involved a patient who went to see a doctor with an acute femoral artery thrombosis which, if not managed properly, will lead to amputation of the leg. If this occurs and suit is filed, the doctor's testimony that he did not cause the thrombus will be of no consequence. What will count is whether appropriate steps were taken to prevent it, including instituting treatment promptly to revascularize the leg.[7]

In each of these cases, the legal concept of causation (proximate cause) extends far beyond the medical motion. Even when the two are more or less the same, physicians sometimes have difficulty understanding the imposition of liability. Suppose a total hip replacement has been performed and is complicated by deep venous thrombosis, and that despite all efforts, a secondary pulmonary embolus develops and the patient dies. In this case, the pulmonary embolus is the direct result of the venous thrombosis which clearly resulted from the hip surgery. The doctor feels that complication is one of the unavoidable risks of this procedure, and that it has been covered in the informed consent obtained from the patient. Indeed, that may be correct, but other issues must be considered. Was the procedure performed with adequate orthopedic indications? If so, was the patient exposed to unnecessary risks of thrombosis embolism and death, and as soon as indications were adequate, were there any contraindications to surgery? Suppose there was a pre-existing deep venous thrombosis that should have been managed before undertaking surgery, to prevent the sequelae that occurred here. The doctor's role in causing the patient's death would thereby be established. (*See* Appendix 10-1, Cases 12 and 13.)

---

6 James, *Particularizing the Standards of Conduct in Negligence Trials,* 5 Vand L Rev 697, 710 (1952); Morris, *Custom and Negligence,* 42 Colo L Rev 1147 (1942).

7 Mills, *Legal vs Medical Causation,* 8 Ortho Legal Let 8 1 (1985).

Certain conditions cannot be prevented. Even with proper management, some posterior hip dislocations will end in aseptic necrosis, but before the patient's attorney will accept a demand to desist, he or she will want to know about all aspects of management—such as a delay in reduction that might have played a part in the development of the necrosis. Did the physician's actions or failure to act contribute in some way to the outcome? In the instance of delay in treatment, the answer would be yes, and the doctor most probably would be legally responsible. (*See* Appendix 10-1, Case 14.)

§10.02 Foreseeability

Foreseeability is always an element of a physician's behavior when negligence is alleged. The action requires that the competence of the physician foresee the consequences of his or her actions even though those consequences may travel down a chain of several steps or involve several individuals. This includes the reasonably foreseeable consequences of rough or unskillful dissection during surgery, producing a trauma to unattended organs, nerves, or vessels, or hastily or incompletely scrubbing before surgery or causing a breach in sterile technique leading to infection in the patient's operative wound site. (*See* Appendix 10-1, Cases 15 to 18.)

In *Weil v Seltzer,* 873 F2d 1453 (DC Cir 1988), the plaintiff alleged that the proximate cause of her foot drop due to peroneal palsy was the result of the orthopedist's negligence in managing foot surgery. The plaintiff had foot surgery—a metatarsal osteotomy—initially supported by an elastic bandage. The orthopedist is said to have stated six weeks postoperatively that the osteotomy was healed and that the plaintiff was to bear full weight. A few weeks later, with pain persisting in the foot, repeat x-rays were taken and were reported to show failure of healing; a walking boot cast was applied. Six weeks later, the cast was changed and a second cast was applied. The orthopedist sent the patient to the hospital for a plaster technician to apply the cast. The cast applied pressure to the peroneal nerve, causing the foot drop condition. The hospital, as the employer of the plaster technician, settled the case for $20,000. The patient wanted more from the orthopedist. The lower court held that proximate cause had not been established, but the superior court reasoned that the causal link need not be explicitly established; that the exact import of the expert testimony was that the cast would not have been necessary but-for the postoperative treatment rendered by the defendant. A new trial was ordered. (*See* Appendix 10-1, Cases 19 to 21.)

In *Hammond v Fidelity & Casualty Co,* 419 So 2d 829 (La 1982), an orthopedist, general surgeon, and oncologist all offered prevailing medical views that cancer cannot be caused by orthopedic trauma. Nevertheless, the Louisiana Supreme Court held that physicians and jurists do not mean the same thing when they speak of "cause." It was ruled, in a five-four decision, that a sarcoma can legally be traced to an accident. The case involved a truck driver who sprained his arm when his truck dropped into a hole, bruising his arm. It did not heal. Ultimately, a sarcoma was identified and appropriate surgery was carried out for the tumor, although from a physician's point of view, this was a difficult case to understand. The majority of the nine justices acknowledged the weight of medical testimony, but noted that the lower court had failed to distinguish the "medical" meaning of cause from the "legal" meaning. A law review article was cited, "The doctor must realize that a determination of legal responsibility is not the same thing as a finding of a pathological cause or source for disease." (*See* Appendix 10-1, Cases 22 to 24.)

In *Blood v Lea,* the question was whether testimony as to the causal link between alleged malpractice and a child's injuries should be rendered merely speculative and thus inadmissible because the medical expert used the word "probably" in a letter concerning the care and treatment of a pregnant mother. The Supreme Judicial Court of Massachusetts held that the expert's assessment of a "probable" causal link between the alleged malpractice and the injury was sufficient evidence to submit the question to the jury.

On the issue of proximate cause and cast application, negligence in connection with the application or nonapplication of a splint or cast has frequently been held the proximate cause of the failure of bones to properly unite.

Is there proof that an attending physician's alleged negligence proximately caused the failure of the plaintiff's fractured or dislocated bones to properly unite? This has been the subject of considerable difficulty, and the absence of such proof has been fatal to the plaintiff's case in the absence of clear expert testimony. These difficulties have been apparent in cases where the defendant was able to produce medical testimony that the complaint was likely to result from the original injury, even with proper treatment. (*See* Appendix 10-1, Cases 25 and 26.)

Appendix 10-1
Cases

1 ***Murphy v Conway,* 360 Mass 746, 749 (1972)** (reciting the established doctrine that a plaintiff in a medical malpractice action has the burden of proving that the physician's negligence was the proximate cause of the plaintiff's injuries).

2 ***Beradi v Menicks,* 340 Mass 396 403 (1960)** (the causal link in proximate cause must be established by expert testimony that the injury was more probably than not the result of the defendant's negligence).

3 ***Mullins v Pine Manor College,* 389 Mass 47, 58 (1983)** (the question of causation is generally a question for the jury).

4 ***Colter v Barber-Greene Co,* 403 Mass 50, 54 (1988)** (to withstand a motion for a directed verdict on the issue of proximate causation, the plaintiff need only demonstrate that there was a greater likelihood that the harm of which the plaintiff complains was due to causes for which the defendant was responsible).

5 ***Malik v William Beaumont Hospital,* 168 Mich App 159, 423 NW2d 920 (1987), *appeal denied,* 431 Mich 875 (1988)** (a brother donated a kidney for his sister's transplant operation, the sister died, and the brother sought to recover for injuries inflicted on his sister. The brother claimed he should be compensated for the malpractice committed on his sister because it was foreseeable that he would be emotionally injured by her failure to recover, as well as suffer the needless loss of his kidney. The court viewed the transplant as two separate operations with separate physician-patient relationships arising from each. The court concluded that although the physician-patient relationship existed between the doctor and the brother as to the nephrectomy, and a physician-patient relationship existed between the physician who performed the surgery on his sister and the sister herself, no physician-patient relationship arose between the doctor and the brother as a result of the surgery he performed on the sister. The court held that since the brother sought to recover for injuries inflicted on him which resulted from the alleged malpractice committed on his sister, he failed to state a cause of action. The court also stated that even if the defendant had owed the brother a duty, he voluntarily agreed to give up his kidney regardless of the outcome of the transplant operation, and therefore the defendant's conduct did not proximately cause him to lose his kidney).

6 ***Heiser v Randolph,* 126 Ariz 608, 617 P2d 774 (Ariz Ct App 1980)** (patient was brought to an emergency room seriously ill with an injury and was also a "brittle" diabetic. The emergency room nurse recognized the serious condition and telephoned the on-call surgeon. The regular attending physician refused to come and directed the nurse to call the on-call physician. The on-call physician again refused to come and persisted in his refusal, even

after the hospital chief of staff personally called the on-call physician. The chief of staff himself arrived at the hospital, but the patient had died. The plaintiff sued the on-call physician, alleging that delay in treatment proximately caused the death. The defendant claimed there was no physician-patient relationship from which a duty arose to treat the patient. The court held, however, that serving as an on-call physician under hospital bylaws, the doctor was advised to treat all persons and that, as such, a physician-patient relationship existed).

Comment: The orthopedic surgeon often finds him- or herself on call in an emergency room as part of the responsibilities to the hospital in which he or she has staff privileges. The orthopedist's attention to telephone calls from emergency room physicians or nurses, conduct, and responses may legally involve him or her.

7 ***Dubak v Burdett Tomlin Memorial Hospital,* 559 A2d 424 (NJ Super Ct App Div 1989)** (doctrine of increased risk applied against a physician who failed to arrest a deteriorating condition—in this case, to do an abdominal tap for free blood, which would have indicated a ruptured viscus and the need to perform immediate surgery to arrest bleeding. Too long a delay in giving a whole blood transfusion was the second error. There was expert testimony that the patient's life could have been saved if the surgeon had been more diligent. The trial court provided the jury with alternative instructions, including (1) the surgeon's negligence was an efficient cause, or (2) the surgeon's negligence increased the risk of death, with the increased risk defined as a substantial factor in causing the death. The jury assessed fault 70 per cent to the patient's assailant, 20 per cent to the tavern where the assault occurred, and 10 per cent to the surgeon. The court held that the end result of the instructions was the same as proximate cause).

8 ***Derr v Bonney,* 38 Wash 2d 678, 231 P2d 637 (1951)** (claimed negligence in failing to attempt to reduce the swelling of the plaintiff's ankle before releasing her, and in placing the ankle in a cast immediately after the accident before the swelling was reduced, was not supported by medical evidence where the plaintiff's witness testified that the swelling was caused by a circulatory disturbance of the tissues in which, in his own opinion, nature might possibly take care of, and that he had recommended physical therapy, which was not effective. He did not testify that the defendant's procedure had been incorrect).

Comment: Often, in fractures about the wrist, foot, and ankle, or of other parts of the body, there is significant soft tissue swelling. If the fracture is one to be treated by closed reduction, use of a temporary splint, supporting the joint and allowing for expansion of swelling, is appropriate. The use of compressive dressing, elevation, ice, etc., is also appropriate. Following reduction of the swelling, the fracture can be definitively held by an appropriate cast.

9 ***Gebhardt v McQuillen,* 230 Iowa 181, 297 NW 301 (1941)** (count alleging injury to the patient's hip stemmed from the employed physician failing to place the fractured bones in their natural position and realigning

them as best possible, thus causing an impairment. There was sufficient evidence presented to allow a jury to try the issue of negligence. *Butler v Molinski,* 198 Tenn 124, 277 SW2d 448, (1955) held, in a case involving a Colles' fracture, that even in the best-managed cases a "silver fork" deformity frequently results and that the defendant could not be held liable for alleged negligence in treatment. The court said that the mere fact that the treatment was not a success did not in any sense justify the conclusion of negligence).

11 ***White v Burton,* 180 Okla 499, 71 P2d 694 (1937)** (evidence that the defendant had been negligent in delaying overnight before studying the plaintiff's fracture supported a jury verdict for the plaintiff, despite medical testimony that the failure to unite was caused by the plaintiff's rickets condition).

Comment: In *White,* as in many cases, if it appears that the treatment complained of, even if improper, had no effect on the failure of the bones to unite properly, there could be no recovery.

12 ***Rose v Hotel New Yorker,* 1 AD2d 769, 148 NYS2d 204 (1956)** (evidence was insufficient to establish that the defendant's physician was negligent in manipulating the plaintiff's arm so violently as to cause displacement of fracture fragments. The court said that it accepted the testimony of the plaintiff's own medical witness that, under the circumstances, such a violent manipulation was impossible and could not have caused the displacement, which must have stemmed from the original trauma).

13 ***DeCourcy v Trustees of the Westminister Presbyterian Church, Inc,* 270 Minn 560, 134 NW2d 326 (1965)** (burden was on the plaintiff to show that a fracture caused by the defendant's negligence and alleged subsequent treatment was either the originating cause of a pulmonary emboli, the immediate cause of death, or that it concurred with that cause as a substantial factor in producing death).

14 ***Thomsen v Rexall Drug & Chemical Co,* 235 Cal App 2d 775, 45 Cal Rptr 642 (1965)** (plaintiff alleged that she contracted vasculitis and became disabled because of an erroneous filling of a prescription. She had been taking cortisone for some time for an arthritis condition. Expert testimony showed that the cause of vasculitis is unknown but that either the cortisone or the erroneous prescription could have caused it. Therefore, the substantial factor test was applied and was for the jury to decide).

15 ***Merriman v Toothaker,* 9 Wash App 810, 515 P2d 509 (1973)** (court stated that medical testimony establishing causation between the liability-producing situation and the subsequent condition need only establish that the injury producing situation probably, or more likely than not, caused the subsequent condition, and that a doctor does not have to testify in terms of absolute certainty if, in his or her expert judgment, the causal relation is probably, or more likely than not, the cause of the injury).

16 ***Oko v Rogers,* 125 Ill App 3d 720 (1984)** (defendant admitted he held himself out as a specialist in surgery. The plaintiff argued, therefore,

that it was an error for the court to permit the jury to base its verdict on the standard of care by a general practitioner. The court noted that in most jurisdictions, it is an error to give an instruction which applies to a specialist the degree of skill and care required of a general practitioner. The plaintiff argued that a specialist is held to a higher degree of skill, care, and learning than the average practitioner. The court held, however, that the jury instruction was not in error, as Illinois is an exception to the general rule. The standard of care in Illinois was that the physician must employ reasonable skill, such as physicians in good practice ordinarily use and would bring to a similar case in that locality. The court had given the jury two different instructions. It gave an instruction as to the duty of care owed by a physician who held himself out as a specialist, but it also gave instructions as to the duty owed by a general practitioner. The trial court saw no conflict between the instructions and gave both. The appellate court concluded that the instructions were not in error).

17 ***Neese v Shawnee Medical Center Hospital, Inc,*** **626 P2d 1327 (1981)** (plaintiff underwent a laminectomy, and a part of a pituitary rongeur broke off in the patient's spinal column. The surgeon attempted to find it, but the effort was eventually abandoned without removing the metal fragment for fear of further damage. Postoperatively, the patient complained of pain and was ultimately advised by his physician of the circumstances and was told the foreign object would have to be left in for the rest of his life. At trial, the plaintiff's suit was dismissed for insufficient proof of negligence, and failure to prove that the alleged injuries were proximately caused by the acts of negligence of each defendant. The appellate court overruled, holding that while there is no generally recognized explicit presumption that an injury results from the presence of a foreign object left in the body during an operation, a conclusion of harm will be more readily supportable than in most other situations. The defendant contended that the plaintiff failed to prove, by medical evidence based on a reasonable medical certainty, that the patient's problems were caused by the presence of metal in the body. The court did not agree. Admittedly, the metal object remained in patient's body. The court concluded that the testimony produced at trial made out a prima facie case, warranting submission to the jury of the question of whether the plaintiff suffered detriment proximately caused by the presence of the metal jaw in his spinal column).

Comment: In *Neese,* an independent expert on behalf of the plaintiff rendered an opinion based on reasonable medical certainty as to the cause-and-effect relationship between the patient's pain and disability and the foreign object, which necessitated the above-described legal gymnastics. Essentially, the appellate court "saved" the plaintiff by, in effect, concluding that the jury could infer proximate cause based on the facts. *See* H. F. Walkman, 1 American Law of Medical Practice 44 (1989 Cumm Supp)

18 ***Brozana v Flanigan,*** **309 Pa Super 145, 454 A2d 1125 (1983)** (jury found negligence on the part of a physician in the treatment of a gunshot wound, but that such negligence was not the proximate cause of a leg ampu-

tation. The appellate court felt that, in its totality, the jury instructions on the issue of proximate cause were proper. The court stated that, taken as a whole, the trial court correctly informed the jury that the defendant could be liable if his negligence was either a substantial factor in bringing about the loss of the patient's leg, or increased the risk of losing the leg and that the increased risk was a substantial factor in the loss of the leg).

19 ***Davison v Mobile Infirmary,* 256 So 2d 14 (Ala 1984)** (plaintiff's action against a hospital was based on a radiologist's failure to report a stomach condition. The co-defendant treating physician stated that he would not have treated the patient sooner even if he had been advised of the x-ray findings. Therefore, the trial court concluded that the radiologist's failure to warn the treating physician was negligent, even though the negligence was not the proximate cause of the patient's injury. The appellate court reversed this decision, holding that the jury's prerogative had been usurped; the issue of the patient's credibility was for the jury. The jury concluded that the treating physician's statement that he would have done nothing sooner was made in his own self-interest. Otherwise, it would have been an admission of guilt. Here, the physician did nothing sooner or later to alleviate the patient's toxic condition).

20 ***Tobash v Jones,* 419 Pa 205, 213 A2d 588 (1965)** (patient alleged that a doctor's excision of a biopsy specimen from the spinal cord was a negligent act and the sole cause of disability. The patient alleged error in an instruction which made foreseeability the sole test in determining proximate cause. The court held that the jury was not misled on the weight to be given foreseeability in determining negligence when the instructions were read in their entirety).

21 ***Hastie v Handeland,* 274 Ca App 2d 599, 79 Ca Rptr 268** (wrongful death action against a driver and his employer and treating physicians. Evidence that the accident aggravated a pre-existing condition and brought symptoms of pain which resulted in the decedent's hospitalization for operation, and that the decedent contracted a fatal infection while in the hospital, created a jury question of the causal relationship between the accident and the decedent's death).

22 ***Lawlor v Cloverleaf Memorial Park, Inc,* 101 NJ Super 134, 243 A2d 293, *revd,* 106 NJ Super 374, 256 A2d 46 (App Div 1969)** (plaintiff's wife fell and was injured in a cemetery in 1964, and shortly thereafter she was treated in a hospital by a doctor. In 1965, she sued the cemetery for negligence. In 1966, before the trial, the cemetery filed a third-party complaint against the hospital and the doctor for malpractice. The plaintiff's wife also died in 1966. The husband pursued a survival and wrongful death action, moving to substitute the doctor and hospital as defendants in 1968. The court found that the latter parties were not joint tortfeasors with the cemetery. Any liability the cemetery would have had, for which it might have been indemnified, was because maltreatment was a foreseeable consequence of the tortious act, and the third-party complaint could not save the survival action from dismissal due to a two-year statute of limitation on such actions. The wrongful death action was reversed).

23 ***Landeros v Floor,* 50 Cal App 3d 189, 123 Cal Rptr 713, *superseded,* 17 Cal 3d 399, 551 P2d 389, 131 Cal Rptr 69 (1976)** (11-month-old child was brought to a hospital for treatment of a broken leg. The mother offered no explanation of how the break occurred. At that time, the child also had other cuts and bruises on her body. The child returned home with her mother and eventually sustained a permanent injury due to willful abuse by her parents. This malpractice action was initiated by the child's guardian against the doctor and the hospital for failure to diagnose the battered child syndrome and report it to proper authorities. The trial court dismissed the complaint based on the defendant's general demurrer, and the plaintiff appealed. The court stated that there was no common law malpractice action since the mere showing of the leg fracture in an infant without sufficient parental explanation did not impose on the defendant the duty to explore symptoms of battered child syndrome, and that without any duty, there can be no legal causation. However, the court said that the defendant's violation of a penal statute requiring a report involving nonaccidental injuries to minors survived the general demurrer, since a presumption of negligence arose in violation of a statute designed to protect the class to which the plaintiff belonged. Also, given the violation, the injury was foreseeable).

24 ***Johnson v State,* 37 NY2d 378, 334 NE2d 590, 372 NYS2d 638** (plaintiff daughter brought an action against a state hospital to recover funeral expenses and for emotional harm suffered, as a result of the hospital falsely advising the plaintiff that her mother, a patient in the hospital, had died. The court of claims awarded full recovery to the plaintiff, but the appellate court limited the award to funeral expenses only. On appeal, the decision was reversed and the plaintiff was held entitled to the entire recovery for emotional harm on the ground that the defendant's negligence for falsely reporting the mother's death was a proximate cause of the plaintiff's emotional injury, particularly where the plaintiff's claim for emotional harm was supported by objective manifestations of harm. That the defendant first sent a notification of death to the plaintiff's aunt, who in turn informed the plaintiff, did not absolve the hospital from liability because the hospital owed the plaintiff a duty to prevent such accidents).

25 ***McEwan v Ortho Pharmaceutical Corporation,* 270 Or 375, 528 P2d 522 (1974), *rehg denied* (Dec 10, 1974)** (action against two manufacturers of birth control pills was brought by a plaintiff who became blind in one eye and sustained injuries in the other. In affirming judgment in favor of the plaintiff, the court mentioned that, although the manufacturers contended that there was no evidence that the alleged failure to give adequate and timely warning of dangerous side effects caused the patient's injuries, this was not a contention that the intervening negligence of a physician exonerated them from liability owing to failure to warn).

26 ***O'Donahue v Riggs,* 73 Wash 2d 814, 440 P2d 823** (plaintiff patient and her husband sued a practical nurse at a hospital for negligence

for the injuries sustained when the plaintiff was pushed into a meal line by the nurse and fell. A judgment for the plaintiff was reversed because of prejudicial errors in the trial court's instructions. No error was found in the court's failure to submit the case solely on assault and battery rather than on negligence. To assert a causal action of negligence, the plaintiff did not need to establish that the defendant nurse intended to cause harmful or forensic contact with the patient, but that would have been required for the plaintiff to recover for assault and battery).

27 ***Murdock v Thomas,* 404 So 2d 580 (Ala 1981)** (automobile accident patient was taken to a hospital emergency room complaining of left rib and abdominal pain. The emergency room physician ruled out broken bones, heart attack, collapsed or contused lungs, and rupture of abdominal viscus through use of x-rays. He ruled out a ruptured spleen by physical examination. Pain medicine was given and the patient was released. Later, his family phoned the emergency room doctor reporting other symptoms which the doctor ascribed to the medication. The patient was brought back to the emergency room the next morning and died of hypovolemic shock. The cause of death was a ruptured spleen. The jury's verdict for the plaintiff was affirmed on appeal. The defense was that the patient died of a heart attack and that the spleen had been ruptured by emergency resuscitative activities (CPR pressure on the rib cage) the morning of the patient's death. On appeal, the court affirmed the decision, noting that if the evidence presented a mere gleam, glimmer, spark, or the smallest trace of scintilla to support the plaintiff's theory, then the court had to submit the case to the jury. The court said that the standard for determining the propriety of the submission of proximate cause to a jury does not encompass the probability of survival standard urged by the defense. If, in fact, there was a scintilla of evidence of proximate cause to warrant submission to the jury, then the verdict had to be sustained).

Additional Pertinent Citations

See Truhitt v French Hospital, 128 Cal App 3d 322, 180 Cal Rptr 152 (1982) (sponge removal; nondelegable duty of surgeon). See also *Dillon v Twin State Gas & Electric,* 85 NH 449, 163 A 111 (1932); *Mitzefelt v Kamrin,* 549 A2d 935 (Pa Super 1988); *Herskovits v Group Health Cooperative of Puget Sound,* 99 Wash 2d 609, 664 P2d 474 (1983); *Helling v Carey,* 83 Wis 2d 512, 519 NW2d 981 (1974).

11

Expert Witnesses

§11.01 Introduction

The orthopedist is often asked to evaluate a patient for litigation purposes. Some physicians find this a pleasant diversion from their regular practice, but many doctors resist and fear a court or deposition appearance regarding their patients. In fact, the physician may have a duty to aid a patient in litigation and to give related support. (*See* Appendix 11-1, Cases 47 and 48.)

The age of empirical jurisprudence appears to be upon us. This is seen at both at appellate level trials and in quantitative data gathered systematically for the purpose of characterizing one or more populations or phenomena. This generally excludes descriptive and anecdotal studies such as those that do not attempt to reduce their observations to quantitative form. It also excludes evidence that may be characterized as expert or scientific but which is not rooted directly in quantitative data. These data are playing more prominent roles in civil and criminal adjudication. Expert witnesses were once confined to a narrow class of forensic scientists, such as medical doctors. Today, psychologists, sociologists, statisticians, and other empirical researchers regularly testify in court. Attorneys are aware of the value of using empirical argument and hire expert witnesses to discuss and dispute vast bodies of data often generated precisely for the purpose of influencing legal decisionmakers.[1] (*See* Appendix 11-1, Cases 1 and 2.)

§11.02 Medical Expert Witnesses

The proposition that a medical doctor can be qualified by education and study to give opinion testimony regarding medical matters as to which he or she may not have had personal experience was established by the Supreme Court of Florida in *Copeland v State,* 58 Fla 26, 50 So 624 (1909). It is a well-recognized rule that unless the matter on which testimony is sought is within the comprehension of laypersons and requires only common knowledge and experience to understand, expert evidence on the issue of negligence is essential to support an action for malpractice against a physician or surgeon. Generally, to qualify as an expert witness for any subject, one must have acquired special knowledge of the subject matter. The determination of the competency and qualifications of a medical witness is in the first instance addressed to the judicial discretion of the trial judge before whom the testimony is offered, and the court's ruling in this regard will generally not be disturbed by a reviewing court unless the discretion has been abused or the error is clear and involves a misconception of the law.

Although the competency of a physician or surgeon who testifies as an expert on medical matters is sufficiently shown by the fact that the witness has been duly licensed to practice medicine and surgery, a more restrictive view has been taken by a number of courts which have considered the necessity of showing a medical witness's familiarity with a particular medical or surgical technique. Thus, he or she can testify that a medical or surgical technique was negligently performed by the defendant physician or surgeon.

While there is some authority to the contrary, those courts which have considered the question have generally expressed the view that, to qualify as an expert witness, the physician must be familiar with the medical or surgical techniques involved in the suit, unless the technique itself is so unique that the defendant is its sole practitioner and no witness familiar with it is available. (*See* Appendix 11-1, Cases 3 to 9.)

Some courts, while speaking in terms of an actual practical knowledge, define *occupational experience* as that which is usually done by a physician or surgeon in the performance of a particular technique, apparently holding that the witness must have performed the specific technique in question. Other courts have taken a broader view and have held that some familiarity with the technique is necessary, but might be gained through such other means as private study, observation, or consultation with other physicians or surgeons. (*See* Appendix 11-1, Case 10.)

---

[1] Monahan & Walker, *Social Frameworks: A New Use of Social Science and Law,* 73 Va L Rev 559, (1987) Monahan & Walker, *Social Authority: Obtaining, Evaluation and Establishing Social Science and Law,* 134 U Pa L Rev 477, (1986).

In many jurisdictions, the competency of a medical expert to testify about the standard of care to which physicians and surgeons are held has been stated to depend on the expert's familiarity with the standard of care in the defendant's community. The trend in an ever-growing number of jurisdictions is to allow an otherwise qualified medical expert to testify as to such standards, even though he or she is from a different locality than that in which the defendant practices. (*See* Appendix 11-1, Cases 11 to 25.)

§11.03 Standard of Care

As a general rule, expert testimony is required to establish the requisite standard of care, its breach, and the injurious effect of the breach. The expert witness' job is to educate the court of the medical facts in the case at hand and to explain the medical factors and their implications to a jury or judge who otherwise may not understand the intricacies of the medical situation. (*See* Appendix 11-1, Cases 26 to 29.)

The defendant physician may also testify as to the standard of care. A reputable medical journal or text may substitute for expert testimony where the issue is one which is within the common knowledge of jurors. In *Smith v Weaver,* 225 Neb 569 (1987), where the defendant failed to remove a surgical sponge from an operative site, the exception to the expert testimony rule based on the common knowledge of the jury was appropriate—where the negligent lack of care was apparent to anyone of average intelligence and ordinary experience. A medical article may be reinforcement, but most likely would not be allowed by the court as the sole expert evidence as it cannot be cross examined. Medical treatises are often allowed, if not objected to by the adversary. (*See* Appendix 11-1, Cases 30 to 36.)

The locality rule applies in certain jurisdictions and requires that the medical expert witness testifying in a medical malpractice case must either practice in the community or be able to testify as to the standard of care in the community. The physician-expert must be able to testify as to the standard applicable to the practitioner in the same field of medicine as the defendant. Although less of a problem in the last decade, there have been nonsuits or other trial errors or questions over the use of medical doctors to testify against osteopathic physicians, podiatrists, and chiropractors. Rarely is a chiropractor allowed to testify as to the standard of care of a medical doctor, osteopathic doctor, or podiatrist. Often, a medical or osteopathic physician is not permitted to testify against a chiropractor, as their schools of training and practice methods vary substantially. The training of medical doctors, osteopaths, and podiatrists is very similar, and the basic chiropractic training, at least as to the basic science, is similar to those other disciplines. (*See* Appendix 11-1, Cases 37 to 40.)

§11.04 Medical Evidence and Affidavits

Expert medical or rehabilitation testimony may be offered by (1) a verified or declared report, (2) a deposition, or (3) an oral examination in open court.

Courts take into consideration that it is both time-consuming and costly to have physicians actually appear at the time of trial to give live testimony, and encourage the production of medical evidence by a verified or declared report, generally containing the following:

1. Complete history of the claimant, including all previous relevant or contributory injuries with a detailed description of the present injury
2. Complaints of the plaintiff
3. Physician's findings on physical examination, including description of the examination and any diagnostic tests and x-rays
4. Date and cause of the alleged injury and whether, in the physician's opinion, it is job-related
5. Medical treatment already rendered and the treatment which the physician recommends for the future
6. Physical rehabilitation already rendered and the procedures the physician recommends for the future
7. The period during which the claimant was temporarily totally disabled; if the claimant remains disabled, the physician should so indicate; if temporary total disability has been terminated, date of termination must be indicated
8. Physician's evaluation of the extent of any impairment with a clear indication as to whether it is temporary or permanent in nature; in the event the injury occurred before July 1, 1978, the physician shall give an evaluation of the extent of the claimant's disability based on the capacity to perform ordinary manual mechanical labor
9. Any other factors on which the physician based permanent impairment, including a statement that the evaluation is in substantial accordance with the "Guides to the Evaluation of Permanent Impairment" adopted and published by the American Medical Association

§11.05 Conspiracy of Silence

In the 1950s and 1960s, the appellate and supreme courts of this country strongly denounced the medical profession for failing to provide expert testimony for injured patients. The concept of a "conspiracy of silence" was widely accepted by the courts, making it easier for patients to win cases without expert testimony. The doctrine of res ipsa loquitur expanded. Other theories of malpractice liability that did not require expert support were accepted by the courts. The most notable of these was the informed consent doctrine, under which the obligation to disclose risks is predicated not on the prevailing standard of practice but on court-established duties. Under this rule, if complications develop after a procedure is performed and the patient cannot demonstrate that it was negligently executed, he or she may still win the suit if it can be demonstrated that the physician failed to disclose material risks. As with res ipsa loquitur, no expert is required to help the jury decide on consent issues. The "conspiracy of silence" still exists, not so much in physicians' reluctance to testify in malpractice cases, but due to the physicians' fear of going to court. Even today, many doctors have an instinctive fear of the legal process. Most physicians become anxious if sued for malpractice, but rarely does fear constitute a conspiracy. (*See* Appendix 11-1, Cases 41 and 42.)

§11.06 Bias by Medical Experts

Personal injury and workers' compensation litigation rely heavily on medical testimony. In an adversarial system, medical opinion typically becomes polarized as to the involved parties. Attorneys want opinions that are both unbiased and favorable, and they view opposing opinions as both unfavorable and biased. Bias is a personal subjective viewpoint, as distinguished from "objective reality." (*See* Appendix 11-1, Case 43.)

Until 20 years ago, the "hard" sciences such as physics and mathematics held that absolute objective reality existed, independent of the perspective of any observer. This view is now obsolete; modern science recognizes that there is an inevitable, although at times subtle, relationship between the observer and what is observed. An observer witnessing an event, such as in a scientific evaluation of a patient, will influence the outcome (opinion). The significance of this updated view of science is that "bias" is an inevitable feature of all events that involve human beings. An example may be seen in the classic Japanese film *Rashomon,* in which four "observers" of a rape/murder testify to four entirely different sets of facts. An impartial, objective reality is impossible as long as human beings are involved in setting up, observing, and analyzing data. Since bias is inevitable, it must always be taken into account in the statements of experts.

Addressing the issue of bias in medical testimony, it is asserted that doctors serving as independent examiners avoid the contamination of bias. A closer look, however, fails to support this contention. The independent medical examiner's motivation is, first of all, to remain independent and to continue to be utilized in this capacity. His or her aim is to preserve neutrality, since favoring either side tends to result in losing independent examiner consultations. Independent medical experts typically "give" something to both sides, thus maintaining their independent posture. Such a procedure may be practical and expeditious in settling litigation, but may have little merit from a scientific point of view. Consistent impartiality by giving something to each side is subtle bias in itself.

Bias in physicians results from three sources—personal, technical, and environmental. As a human being, the physician is the product of childhood experience, schooling, neighborhood, parental influences, etc. The physician develops his or her personal philosophy, religious beliefs, and political views from life experience.

Issues of relevance in litigation include beliefs about the value of work and how responsible people should be for their lives, their minds, and their bodies. These personal viewpoints are usually held aside from conscious awareness, yet they influence the doctor's political preference as well as which side of a case he or she examines. If the doctor is a firm believer in individual responsibility, he or she may gravitate toward defense work. On the other hand, if the doctor believes that people are basically hapless victims of their environment and illness, he or she may favor plaintiff work.

Another source of bias is medical training. The medical and psychological theories that doctors learn determine how the doctor sees a patient. An orthopedist examining the back of a patient nearly always arrives at a different conclusion than a chiropractor. Freudian psychiatrists usually differ radically in their views from biochemically-oriented psychiatrists.

A subtle medical bias is the bias in favor of finding pathology. The doctor may tend to be conservative and prefer the risk of overdiagnosis and overtreatment to the risk of overlooking a disease. The consequence is significant in the evaluation and treatments rendered in a medical-legal context.

Traditionally, a medical view that rest is helpful for most illness, a standard in the past, is now a dangerous prescription for most medical problems.

§11.07 Environmental Factors

Environmental influences include factors such as the nature of the doctor's practice. From where do most of his or her referrals come? Does the doctor also render treatment? If so, there is often a bias in favor of finding something wrong to test.

Bias is a characteristic of human nature and cannot be eliminated. The nature of a doctor's bias can be established by looking at his or her "track record." However, this system may lead to a wrong conclusion. If an orthopedist examined 100 back pain patients and found that 80 per cent had pathology, does this establish the doctor as plaintiff-biased? To complicate matters, if 100 per cent of these patients really had pathology, then the doctor misdiagnosed 20 per cent of them. If, as an independent examiner, the orthopedist would have found that one-half had pathology, then he or she would have misdiagnosed the remaining 30 per cent.

In psychiatry, a well-known research study revealed that researchers simulating mental patients effortlessly escaped detection and were hospitalized as seriously mentally ill. Conversely, the same research team later sent patients with demonstrable psychiatric illness to a leading medical center where a significant number were diagnosed as faking. (*See* Appendix 11-1, Case 44.)

It is important not to take the credibility of experts at face value. The data on which physicians base their opinions should be carefully examined. We should not take for granted the scientific accuracy of the opinions and conclusions. It should also be remembered that "tried and true" medical treatments are continually evolving. Treatments once considered scientific are often later found meritless, perhaps even harmful or absurd. A skeptical mind coupled with reluctance to accept medical authority serves justice well.[2]

---

[2] Marcus, *Unbiased Medical Testimony. Reality of Myth,* 1 Expert Witness J 1 (1989).

§11.08 Physician's Role in Workers' Compensation

The physician is indispensable to the workers' compensation system and that role is not limited to diagnosis and treatment. Resolution of the great majority of issues that the system addresses, informally or formally, is based on medical opinion, usually presented in written form.

In compensation law, the problem of administrative law and evidence—as it relates to expert opinion and official notice—concerns principally the handling of medical facts. It has been assumed that when the medical testimony of one authority is in conflict with that of another, the compensation commission is upheld in its prerogative of choosing which medical opinion to accept, and that there is no significant difference between these competing items of medical evidence. This is not always true; there may be instances in which medical testimony that the commission relies on suffers from some flaw that disentitles it to acceptance when other more valid testimony stands in the record.

With the changing nature of injury and illness, physicians must be prepared to analyze the factual situation and, in difficult cases, assist in determining the degree to which the disorder is related to work.[3]

Courts are often asked to settle broad issues, including socioeconomic issues relating to damages in medical malpractice cases. The chain suggested above is the method of establishing socioeconomic as well as psychological emotions. The effects of negligent medical care are generally considered to be, per se, beyond the purview of the medical expert.[4]

[3] Larson, *The Role of the Physician in a Workers' Compensation Process,* 3 Occup Prob Med Prac 1 (1989).

[4] Appelbaum, *The Empirical Juris Prudence of the United States Supreme Court,* 13 Amer J Law Med 334 (1988).

Appendix 11-1
Cases

1 ***Sitts v United States,* 811 F2d 736 (2d Cir 1986)** (removal of ruptured disc was carried out at the wrong level. The patient had six functional vertebra. The S1-S2 was entered and disc material was removed. The involved area was actually L5-S1. When preoperative symptoms persisted, another workup demonstrated that the wrong level had been operated. The case was clearly one of medical negligence, yet for reasons unknown, the plaintiff failed to retain an expert witness. The case was decided in favor of the operating surgeon despite all of the evidence pointing to his negligence behavior).

Comment: To operate the wrong level is very easy and more frequent now. Particularly with the advent of image intensification, x-ray equipment is being used to localize the operating level at the time of surgery. This is true for all types of discectomies, be it percutaneous or chymopapain injection or using microsurgical techniques or the traditional open hemilaminectomy. The second most common cause of reoperation for protruded intervertebral disc symptoms is operating at the wrong level, the first being recurrent disc fragments from the appropriately operated level.

2 ***McNichols v Jersild,* 523 NE2d 1172 (Ill App Ct 1988)** (court refused to blame an orthopedic surgeon for selecting the plate of his choice to fix a fracture. The case hinged on the defense statement that an operative orthopedic textbook constituted the only acceptable medical practice. It recommended a different fixation device. The motorcyclist had a comminuted fracture of the right radius and ulna. The orthopedist used a five-hole, semitubular metal plate. The fracture angulated about six weeks. Although the fracture began to heal, the angulation prevented full pronation and supination. The patient did not return to the orthopedist for follow-up care, but consulted with another one who noted the plate was bent and the fracture not united. Two more operations were needed to correct the deformed arm. In a suit against the orthopedic surgeon, the patient named the second physician as his expert witness, but he could not state whether the operating orthopedist's treatment fell below the standard of care. To prevent summary judgment for the physician, the patient countered that according to Campbell's Textbook of Orthopedic Surgery, the orthopedist had placed at least one of the screws improperly and should have used a dynamic compression plate. The appellate court held that, although Campbell's preferred one type of plate, the treating surgeon was justified in using internal fixing devices that, by his experience and training, were acceptable devices. There was no allegation of experimentation in this case. The orthopedist was exonerated).

3 ***Kurynka v Tamarac Hospital Corp,* 542 So 2d 412 (Fla Dist Ct App 1989)** (laboratory data indicating cocaine use by a patient was not admissi-

ble merely because the expert based his opinion, in part, on that report. Although expert testimony may be admissible when based on inadmissible data, expert testimony may not serve merely as a conduit for the admission of inadmissible evidence).

4 ***Paternity of KG,* 536 NE2d 1033 (Ind Ct App 1989)** (experts may base their opinion's on reports not in evidence and reports inadmissible under the hearsay rule, where the witness is sufficiently qualified and credible to evaluate the report and its reliability, the laboratory report being of a type on which physicians regularly rely, in part, in formulating a diagnosis).

5 ***Earl v Cryovac,* 772 P2d 725 (Idaho Ct App 1989)** (substantial deference was to be allowed to expert internal medicine specialist's selection of data on which to form an opinion. An internist may qualify as expertly informed in another medical specialty field).

6 ***Richter v Northwestern Memorial Hospital,* 532 NE2d 269 (Ill App Ct 1988)** (neurosurgeon was competent to testify concerning the respiratory care of a patient. There was testimony that surgery is among the disciplines involved in respiratory care, and that decisions regarding respiratory care are among the regular duties of a surgeon).

7 ***Novet v Kishwaukee Community Health Services,* 531 NE2d 427 (Ill App Ct 1988)** (it was improper to allow a licensed occupational therapist to testify about the standards of care applicable to a physical therapist, given the significant differences in education, training, and licensing of the two professions as well as the occupational therapist's testimony that she had no training or education as a physical therapist and was not familiar with the standard of care applicable to physical therapists).

8 ***Williams v McClain,* 520 A2d 1374 (Pa 1987)** (surgery for total hip replacement for congenitally dislocated hip failed. A second hip surgery also failed and became infected and medical malpractice was alleged. As part of the evidence, a social worker's report was admitted, but she was not in court for cross-examination. Her report suggested a dominance of psychosomatic input to the disadvantage of the patient. The court held that expert testimony must be presented in an atmosphere where the expert may be cross-examined).

9 ***Evans v Ohanesian,* 39 Cal App 3d 121, 112 Cal Rptr 236 (1974)** (trial court entered judgment of nonsuit and the patient appealed. It was held that the trial court abused its discretion by precluding the patient from introducing expert opinion and other specialists, and even on the basis of the evidence already before it, the trial court should not have granted a nonsuit because testimony before the jury presented the elements of a prima facie case of actionable negligence. The question of whether the defendant's alleged maltreatment caused the plaintiff's permanent disability constituted a dispute about a factual matter and was for the jury to determine).

10 ***Morey v Harper,* 541 So 2d 1285 (Fla Dist Ct App 1989)** (action against an orthopedic surgeon; where evidence is presented that a per-

manent injury has been suffered based on a reasonable degree of medical probability, and that evidence remains uncontroverted, a jury verdict of no permanent injury was against the manifest weight of the evidence and the plaintiff was entitled to a new trial).

11 ***Pearce v Linde,*** **113 Cal App 2d, 627 248 P2d 506 (1952)** (in a malpractice action brought for alleged negligence in treatment involving bone grafting of the plaintiff's foot, the trial court properly refused to accept as an expert for the plaintiff a specialist in internal medicine who, although testifying that he had some knowledge of the proper professional treatment in such cases from what he had heard or read, had no experience in orthopedics. The testimony of the expert was not allowed).

12 ***Dow v Kaiser Foundation,*** **90 Cal Rptr 747 (Ct App 1970)** (an orthopedic surgeon who had never performed an anterior interbody fusion of the lumbar spine was not qualified to testify that complications, including kidney shutdown and thrombosis and swelling of the leg, do not occur in the absence of negligence. The court stated that the definitive criteria to be applied in determining whether a medical expert is qualified to testify in a particular case is measured primarily by "occupational experience" consisting of a basic educational and professional training as the foundation, but controlled by a practical knowledge of what is usually and customarily done by physicians under similar circumstances and which confronted the defendant charged with malpractice).

13 ***Swanson v Chatterton,*** **281 Minn 129, 160 NW2d 662 (1968)** (internal medicine specialist who was not engaged in extensive practice and who had never, in any way, participated in the reduction of a supracondylar fracture, who admitted he did not know any authorities and could not name any articles in books that he had read on the treatment of such fractures or the prevention of Volkmann's contracture, and who had no experience or expertise in the treatment of orthopedic patients, was properly excluded from testifying in an action brought against an orthopedic surgeon for malpractice in the treatment of a supracondylar fracture that resulted in a Volkmann's contracture).

14 ***Purtil v Hess,*** **111 Ill 2d 229, 490 NE2d 181 (1986)** (physician's conduct must be judged in light of the conditions and facilities with which he or she must work. If a plaintiff's expert is familiar with the standards of care applicable to the conditions and facilities available to the defendant doctor, then he or she is qualified to testify. If there are certain uniform standards that would be applicable to a given situation regardless of locality, then the lack of familiarity with practice in a particular locality will not disqualify the expert. However, if the conditions and facilities available are relevant, then before an expert can express an opinion as to the physician's conduct, the expert must be acquainted with the accepted standards of care under similar circumstances).

15 ***McCay v Mitchell,*** **463 SW2d 710 (Tenn Ct App 1970)** (trial judge did not abuse his discretion in refusing to allow a Pennsylvania doctor testify as to the standards of care and skill required of orthopedic surgeons and general practitioners in Tennessee, but did abuse his discretion in refusing to permit the same doctor to qualify on vascular spasm, as there is no difference between vascular spasms in Pennsylvania and Tennessee. The trial judge did not abuse his discretion in limiting a New York orthopedist's testimony as to standard of care and disallowing similar testimony relating to general practitioners).

16 ***Mitchell v Fire & Casualty Insurance Co,* 540 So 2d 352 (La Ct App 1989)** (patient had two accidents, after which a diagnosis of herniated intervertebral disc was made; the treating physician who saw and examined the patient several times was in a better position to have an opinion as to which accident caused the disc rupture).

17 ***Guentzel v Toyota Motor Corp,* 768 SW2d 890 (Tex Ct App 1989)** (surgeon, who was additionally qualified as to the safety engineering of automobile seat belts, was allowed to testify where it was more probable than not that injury to the plaintiff would have been lessened had the plaintiff worn seat belts at the time of the accident).

Comment: It is often overlooked that physicians have expertise in one or more fields other than their stated or regular practice. That serves them well as expert witnesses.

18 ***Strode v Lenzi,* 775 P2d 106 (Idaho 1989)** (Supreme Court of Idaho affirmed a trial court's finding that an out-of-state, board-certified orthopedic surgeon was not competent to testify with respect to the standard of care applicable to an Idaho orthopedic surgeon without first demonstrating that the expert possessed actual knowledge of applicable community standards. For an out-of-state expert to know of in-state standards, he or she must at least consult with an in-state specialist to determine whether the local community standard varies from the national standard for that board-certified specialty. A very strong dissent was written by Justice Huntley, chastising the majority for contributing to a "great deal of mischief and injustice" being perpetuated. It was pointed out that nowhere do Idaho statutes require an out-of-state expert to procure knowledge of a community standard by telephone. Justice Huntley further reasoned that there are certain things in the practice of medicine which by definition are the standards for all doctors and there are certain things that are the standards for all board-certified doctors, regardless of where they practice).

19 ***Petkus v Girzadas,* 532 NE2d 333 (Ill App Ct 1988)** (in medical malpractice action, an expert's lack of knowledge of another physician's advanced training will not disqualify the witness where certain minimal standards apply. Any difference of opinion becomes a question for the jury).

20 ***Harmon v Levenson,* 534 So 2d 486 (La Ct App 1988)** (expert's opinion as to matters within his or her field is entitled to greater weight than an opinion on the same issue by a specialist in another field. The weight given to an expert's testimony depends on qualifications and experience, as well as facts).

21 ***Dugan v Weber,* 530 NE2d 1007 (Ill App Ct 1988)** (medical expert may not rely on medical reports made in anticipation of trial. A rule allowing

experts to rely on otherwise inadmissible facts or data referred only to reports made and utilized during the course of medical practice).

22 ***Hill v Reynolds,* 557 A2d 756 (Pa Super Ct 1989)** (witness, a rehabilitation specialist, did not have to possess all the knowledge in his or her field of expertise to qualify as an expert for purposes of giving an expert opinion on an automobile passenger injury and the victim's potential future work capabilities. The expert in question was a nationally-certified rehabilitation counselor employed in assessing the residual physical capacities, vocational skills, and educational background of ill or impaired persons).

23 ***Allen v Turpin,* 533 So 2d 515 (Ala 1988)** (expert testimony is binding on a jury only when it concerns a subject exclusively within the knowledge of the expert and the testimony is uncontroverted).

24 ***Barr v Plastic Surgery Consultants, Ltd,* 760 SW2d 585 (Mo Ct App 1988)** (the rendering of a personal opinion by an expert witness which seems to contradict a professional opinion does not make that testimony inherently contradictory and thus proper for jury consideration).

Comment: It seems that courts allow expert witnesses to combine personal opinion with professional opinion only if substantial professional material is the basis of an opinion which answers the specific allegation. Personal opinion may be impeachable as bias.

25 ***Young v Stevens,* 132 NJL 124, 39 A2d 115 (Ct Err & App 1944)** (a medical doctor is competent to testify on all medical subjects on which he or she claims sufficient ability to express an opinion, and even though the physician does not hold him- or herself out as a specific specialist, he or she is competent to testify thereon with any objections going to the weight of his or her evidence rather than to his or her competency).

26 ***Sanchez v Derby,* 433 NW2d 523 (Neb 1988)** (trial court had discretion to allow a neuropsychologist to testify that a plaintiff's illness was caused by either a combination of posttraumatic stress disorder and reaction to pain, or organic disorder secondary to brain injury. Both would be compensable, and an absolute certainty as to a particular cause is not required).

27 ***Corbett v Weisband,* 551 A2d 1059 (Pa Super Ct 1988)** (expert opinion concerning the ultimate issue, in this case the unusual behavior of an orthopedic surgeon while performing a total knee replacement, is inadmissible as impinging on the duty of the trier of fact).

28 ***Williams v Naidu,* 168 Ga App 539, 309 SE2d 686 (1983)** (defendant physicians testified they had never been sued before, and a jury verdict for the defendant was reversed on appeal. The appellate court held that such testimony was tantamount to saying that the defendants had never been negligent as medical practitioners, from which it was inferable that they were not negligent in treating the plaintiff. The court noted that there was a presumption of due care and that this testimony unfairly enhanced the defendant's credibility).

29 ***Grant v Farnsworth,* 869 F2d 1149 (8th Cir 1989)** (doctor was not permitted to testify as to the extent and cause of the plaintiff's disability where the witness admitted that he would have to guess, as he lacked the necessary history of the plaintiff prior to the accident being litigated).

30 ***Mohn v Hahnemann Medical College,* 357 Pa Super 173, 515 A2d 920 (1986), *modified,* 527 A2d 542 (Pa 1987)** (amount of earnings of an expert as a medical-legal witness was an improper subject of questioning; rather, questions testing the credibility of the witness were the limit of permissibility).

31 ***Henning v Thomas,* 235 Va 181, 366 SE2d 109 (1988)** (trial court refused to permit a defendant to ask the plaintiff's medical witness whether he had entered the case through a national physician's medical referral agency for medical malpractice plaintiffs. The higher court reversed and pointed out that the bias of a witness, like prejudice and relationship, is not a collateral matter, and that the bias of a witness is always a relevant subject of inquiry when confined to ascertaining previous relationship feeling and conduct of the witness. On cross-examination, great latitude is allowed and the general rule is that anything tending to show the bias of a witness may be elicited).

32 ***Roof v Kimbrough,* 375 SE2d 318 (SC Ct App 1988)** (plaintiff brought a medical malpractice action against a surgeon for negligence in cutting the dura in back surgery, damaging nerves. On examination of the defendant, the surgeon's technique was extensively questioned and a text was introduced, Standard Orthopedic Operations by Dr. Jon Crawford Adams, which recited that it was a breach of surgical technique to "cut dura." The trial judge ruled that the book could not be read to the jury. Limited use of textbooks to impeach an expert witness was approved in Baker v Port City Steel Erectors, Inc, 261 SD 469, 200 SE2d 681 (1973). In Baker, however, the court noted that it is a violation of the hearsay rule to use scientific treatises in the cross-examination of an expert witness where the jury is likely to consider the treatise direct proof of an issue in the case. In this case, to allow the statement from the text would bias the jury that cutting the dura, per se, was negligent).

Comment: The cutting of the dura, in a scarred or anatomically abnormal low back, is not of itself negligent if recognized and repaired. Damage to nerve roots is another matter, and was not addressed in this case.

33 ***Stickney v Wesley Medical Center,* 768 P2d 253 (Kan 1989)** (a hospital may introduce impeaching evidence against a deceased doctor who had lost his hospital privileges if the plaintiff introduced his deposition. It was pointed out that the evidence would be prejudicial and damaging if used in live-witness testimony).

34 ***Reese v Winn-Dixie, Inc,* 542 So 2d 68 (La Ct App 1989)** (in a slip and fall case, the plaintiff was not permitted to cross-examine the defendant's expert medical witness using a previously published appellate opinion commenting on the witness' testimony as an expert. The orthopedist's qualifications were not called into question, and the jury was aware that the plaintiff was examined by the expert at the defendant's request and that the defendant was paying the witness).

35 ***Trower v Jones,* 121 Ill 2d 211, 520 NE2d 297 (1988)** (Supreme Court of Illinois allowed questioning of an expert medical witness in a medical malpractice case regarding the amount of annual income he earned from testifying and the frequency with which he provided testimony for plaintiffs. Considering the great latitude given expert witnesses during direct examination and the specialization of many experts as witnesses, the court reasoned this information would aid the jury in assessing the value of the testimony).

Comment: The *Trower* decision provides medical malpractice defendants with a method of impeaching unfavorable experts who may be biased in favor of the hiring party. Consequently, witnesses who testify less frequently and who do not depend on consulting services for a livelihood may prove more credible to jurors.

36 ***Combs v Hartford,* 544 So 2d 583 (Fla Dist Ct App 1989)** (hypothetical questions cannot be based on unproven facts. Questions posed to a plaintiff's expert sought to elicit from the witness a conclusion in the form of a diagnosis of the plaintiff's current condition, although the witness had not recently treated the patient. To justify the diagnosis, the witness would have had to assume that certain unproven facts were true without evidence offered to support those facts).

37 ***Martin v Mott,* 744 P2d 337 (Utah Ct App 1987)** (podiatrist was not negligent in diagnosing foot pain, and an orthopedist could not testify as to the breach of a standard of care by a podiatrist. When he testified, he did not know the standard of care expected of the podiatrist. The patient had consulted a podiatrist for treatment of foot pain. The podiatrist made a diagnosis of acute Achilles tendonitis and treated accordingly. When the patient persisted, the patient consulted an orthopedic surgeon. The surgeon diagnosed peripheral vascular disease and arterial occlusion. A cardiovascular surgeon was called to operate on the patient. The patient sued the podiatrist for malpractice for failure of diagnosis. In deposition, the physician admitted he had neither seen nor reviewed the podiatrist's medical records, with the exception of a bill listing the number of visits. He testified he did not know the standard of care for a podiatrist, but that the podiatrist had violated the standard of care for physicians. The podiatrist moved for a summary judgment; he submitted affidavits by two physicians who testified they were familiar with the standard of care for podiatrists and that he had fully complied with the standard of care. The trial court granted the motion. On appeal, the patient contended that the witness was qualified to testify as an expert in all fields of medicine. The court said that the party offering a witness must establish witness' knowledge in any area of the standard of care and treatment commonly practiced by those in the same specialty. In the present case, by the witness' own admission, he failed to establish by expert testimony the standard of care applicable to the podiatrist; therefore, the physician was not competent to testify about a breach of the standard of care. The court said that since the patient's evidence failed to raise an issue of fact as to negligence, summary judgment was appropriate).

38 ***Harris v Bales,* 459 SW2d 742 (Mo Ct App 1970)** (osteopath was qualified to testify as an expert in a malpractice action against an M.D. based on the improper reduction and treatment of a tibial fracture (leg bone), where the osteopath resided and practiced in the same area and community as the defendant doctor, was familiar with the procedure followed by both M.D.s and osteopaths in setting bone fractures, and testified as to matters of diagnosis and treatment known to every physician and practitioner of every school in the area).

39 ***Bethea v Smith,* 176 Ga App 467, 336 SE2d 295 (1985)** (in an action stating negligence by an orthopedist in treating an ankle fracture, the defendant's expert testified that there was no negligence, and where such testimony was not refuted by a podiatrist's affidavit that the orthopedist's care did not follow "the standard of care as it pertains to the medical profession generally," and where the record did not indicate that methods of diagnosis and treatment of ankle fractures were the same for orthopedists as for podiatrists, summary judgment was proper).

40 ***Anderson v Donis,* 541 NYS2d 25 (1989)** (trial court permitted an orthopedic surgeon and a podiatrist, both of whom had performed tenotomies during their careers, to testify as experts in the field of podiatry).

41 ***Maxey v Hubble,* 238 Va 607, *revd,* 385 SE2d 593 (Va 1989)** (action alleged malpractice in the perforation of esophagus due to the negligence of anesthesiologist. A $100,000 award was reversed. Before and during a two-week trial, the defendant contended that the physicians who treated her were bound by the physician-patient privilege and could not confer with the defendant's attorney or testify against her as a witness for the defense. The trial judge rejected that contention, but the defendant's attorney said that the testimony was improper in his opening statement, in his examination of the physicians, and in his closing argument. The defense attorney told the jury, "Physicians tend to close ranks in this type of situation, especially when they are all working together under the same circumstance . . . they have to work [together] every day . . ." He added, "These doctors are all under the gun in that type situation, and they don't come forth to volunteer to help the patient." In granting a new trial, the supreme court said, "Where counsel makes an improper statement and the court takes prompt action to remove it by appropriate instruction to the jury, it will ordinarily be presumed that the jury heeded the instruction and that no lasting harm was done. But where the prejudicial effect is so overwhelming that it cannot be removed by jury instruction, the injured party, if he asks, is entitled to a new trial." In this case, none of the defendant's attorney's allegations were proven, but were interpreted as the counsel's attempt to impress his personal ideas upon the jury).

42 ***Myer v McDonnell,* 40 Md App 524, 392 A2d 1129 (1978)** (malpractice action against an orthopedic surgeon alleged a spinal cord injury following surgery. The plaintiff's two experts were intimidated into refusing to testify by certain "behind-the-scenes activities" of the defendant physician. The trial court held that the evidence of witness tampering was admissible

to show that their testimony would be unfavorable to the defendant. The appellate court went further, stating that the evidence was admissible to establish that the defendant was aware of the weakness of his case, and that his defense would fail without "such improper and unfair tactics." The court noted that a growing concern within the professions and fermenting public opinion on doctors in general has forced state legislatures to investigate possible solutions to the impending health care crisis. State boards of medical examiners, or equivalent bodies, are bound by regulation or law to investigate this kind of physician and to enforce competent physician behavior).

43 ***Brousseau v Jarrett,* 73 Cal App 3d 864, 141 Cal Rptr 200 (1987)** (plaintiff injured in an automobile accident was treated by a physician who, by chance, had close ties with the insurance company representing the plaintiff. The defendant sent a report to the insurance carrier stating that no disability resulted from the accident when, in fact, there were significant injuries and disability. An original $7,500 offer by the insurance carrier was turned down, the carrier eventually offering $15,000, the policy limits, but at $3,800 additional legal costs to the plaintiff. The court held that an action in medical malpractice against the examining physician was appropriate. The result was not published).

Comment: The *Brousseau* court noted that the physician has a fiduciary duty to patients, and that the duty in this type of case includes rendering an appropriate, honest, and adequate report to the insurance company. If the physician cannot give an unbiased report, he or she has a duty to withdraw from that part of care or case evaluation.

44 ***Henry v Dean,* 310 NC 75, 310 SE2d 326 (1984)** (action alleging that three defendants conspired among themselves to alter and create false medical and hospital records for the purpose of frustrating the plaintiff's claim for wrongful death. The court held that a claim based on civil conspiracy seeking both compensatory and punitive damages was appropriate).

45 ***Hert v Gibbs,* 382 SE2d 191 (Ga Ct App 1989)** (court of appeals upheld a trial court's admission of expert testimony which, in response to a hypothetical question, stated that there was a causal relationship between a motor vehicle accident and a patient's brain injury. The plaintiff was in an automobile accident but appeared unhurt at the time. Six weeks later, he commenced having grand mal seizures, and underwent surgical removal of brain hematomata. In response to a hypothetical question, the surgeon said that he felt the hematoma resulted from the accident. An objection argued that the hypothetical question was based, in part, on facts and not on evidence. On questioning, the surgeon said he based his opinion on a behavioral change in the patient. The court held that admissible, and held also that the opinion was not speculative because "while the testimony as to the mere possibility of a causal relationship between a given event and subsequent physical or mental condition of an injured person will not establish the causal relationship . . . medical evidence which shows that possibility of a causal relationship in conjunction with other evidence is sufficient to establish the causal relationship." The court cited *Jacobs v Pilgrim,* 186 Ga App 260, 376 SE2d 49 (1988).

46 *Polo by Shipley Gotchel,* 542 A2d 947 (1987) (a contingent fee arrangement entered into between the plaintiff's attorney and a medical legal consulting service, providing for a 6 per cent contingent fee, payable by the client on successful disposition of the case, violated state public policy and was void).

47 *Spaulding v Hussain,* 229 NJ Super 430 551 A2d 1022 (1980) (a treating physician has a duty to render reasonably required litigation assistance to his or her patient, including testifying by deposition or by court appearance).

48 *Knight v Johnson,* No 88-619 (Mont Super Ct, Apr 27, 1989) (plaintiff was treated for injuries from an altercation. The defendant gave a deposition for defense counsel, and later received a letter telling him to appear at trial and that the plaintiff would be subpoenaed as his testimony was crucial. The physician never received the subpoena but said that, in any event, he would not testify in court. The plaintiff settled his case and brought suit against the physician, alleging breach of duty to appear and testify in court. The physician's previous failure to appear had forced a low settlement for the patient's injury. The trial court granted summary judgment for the physician, and the plaintiff appealed. The superior court concurred with the trial court, holding that in the absence of a subpoena, a physician has no duty to testify on behalf of a patient in a personal injury case. The court reasoned that the state subpoena process was efficient, orderly, and effective, and obviated the need to recognize a common law duty on behalf of physicians to aid their patients in litigation).

49 *Turgut v Levine,* 556 A2d 720 (Md App 1989) (physician appropriately testified and testimony was permitted in assessing the standard of care when his testimony was "buttressed" by an admission of the past rate of surgical techniques of the defendant).

50 *Foster v Greenville County Medical Society,* 367 SE2d 468 (SC App 1988) (medical society and individual members of a grievance committee owed no affirmative legal duty to a patient of one of the society's members and thus was not liable to the patient on a negligence theory. This decision will deter patients from suing medical societies for the tort of a society member. In this case, a child was injured by a physician who offered treatment while he was intoxicated. The medical society knew of the doctor's drinking problem, having been informed by the culpable doctor's former partner).

12

Medical Records

§12.01 Generally

For the medical doctor, the ethics of situations involving medical records are as important as the law. The Council on Ethical and Judicial Affairs of the American Medical Association is the body charged with interpreting the Principles of Medical Ethics. They have rendered many opinions. One such opinion states, "A Physician who formally treated a patient should not, for any reason, decline to make his medical record of that patient promptly available on request to another physician presently treating the patient—medical reports should not be withheld because of an unpaid bill for medical services."

The medical record is a detailed history of the patient's illness or injury and progress. It includes any information found in the physician's, hospital's, or other medical institution's file dealing with a particular patient. This includes not only the patient's medical chart, personal history, and financial information, but also other forms of clinical information, including x-rays, laboratory reports, prescriptions, notations in the narcotic log, and notations in the appointment book.

Ownership of the medical records is well settled in American law. While the physician or medical facility owns the physical record, the information in the record is the personal property of the patient. The right of the patient to have access to the information in the medical record is established by statute in most states. A model statement is found in the Oklahoma statute:

> Any person who is or has been a patient of a doctor, hospital or other medical institution shall be entitled to obtain access to the information contained in all his medical records upon request, and shall be furnished copies of all records pertaining to his/her case upon the tender of the expense of such copy/copies. The cost of each copy shall not exceed ten cents per page.

The statute that provides the right to access the information shall not apply to psychological or psychiatric records. It is recommended by legal authorities that such records not be withheld from the patient unless the information in and of itself would be damaging to the patient.

Refusing to allow a patient to see his or her record or to receive a copy of the record is a misdemeanor and punishable by fine in most states. Implied in the right of the patient to access the record is that the request be reasonable and the response of the office or institution be reasonable.

X-rays are also part of the medical record. Since they cannot be copied in the usual sense, the right of the patient to access the information becomes complicated. The Attorney General of Oklahoma has ruled that the patient has a right to a copy of any report based on x-rays, but does not have a right to take possession of x-rays as such. If the medical facility has x-ray copying equipment, there is no problem. Patients have a right to release medical information about themselves to anyone. The right to access medical information is routinely given to insurance companies for the purpose of claim payment, to attorneys for the purpose of conducting lawsuits, and to employers in pre-employment evaluation or for workers' compensation claims.

There are no laws stating how long a physician should retain patient records. It is recommended that all records be retained as long as possible. Records should be retained for a minimum of 10 years past the last time the patient was seen by the physician. There are two exceptions: a record may be safely destroyed five years after a patient's death, and the record of a minor should be kept until the patient has reached his or her 20th birthday, but it is better if it can be kept until he or she reaches the 30th birthday.[1]

The primary purpose of medical records is to document the course of the patient's illness and treatment (medical care) during particular periods and during any subsequent periods as an inpatient or outpatient. As such, these are important tools in medical practice. It primarily serves as a basis for planning patient care, evaluating its results, and for communication among physicians and other professionals contributing to the patient's care. A secondary purpose of medical records may be to meet legal requirements imposed on the hospital and the physician to provide clinical data of interest to researchers and to clinical data research systems. Medical records are the principle means of communication between physicians and nurses in matters relating to patient care. They reflect the extent and quality of medical care. Persistent failure on the part of the physician to appropriately make and complete hospital records has been deemed a sufficient basis for suspending staff membership.

§12.02 Patient's Duty to Return Records

In some situations, generally by court order, original medical records are required for review by the adverse party or by the patient. When such a situation exists, unless specified otherwise, the patient or the patient's representative is duty bound to return the records, unaltered, in an agreed to or timely manner. Failure to return records, particularly if such failure jeopardizes the other party's legal process, is tortious. (*See* Appendix 12-1, Case 6.)

§12.03 Physician's Duty to Testify for a Patient

In most jurisdictions, the physician can be held liable for failing to assist a patient in a lawsuit. This failure may take the form of failing to provide medical records, to fill out appropriate insurance forms or interrogatories,

---

[1] E. Kelsay, Medical Records: Law and Ethics. PLICO News. Oklahoma State Medical Society, March 1989.

or to appear at a deposition or trial for the patient. If the patient is damaged by such physician failure, the doctor may be liable. (*See* Chapter 10.)

§12.04 Diagnosis Method

Diagnosis is the identification of a disease by investigation of signs, symptoms, and other manifestations. In medical terminology, however, the precise meaning of the word is obscured by the many ways in which it is used, including clinical diagnosis, laboratory diagnosis, physician diagnosis, anatomical diagnosis, bacteriological diagnosis, x-ray diagnosis, electrocardiographic diagnosis, etc. In each of these cases, the word diagnosis denotes the appreciation of the meaning of the observations made by the particular methods used, but does not necessarily signify identification of a disease. For example, physical diagnosis comprises a group of procedures directed toward and determining the state of normality or abnormality of various organs. Anatomical diagnosis is employed in most pathological reports as a recapitulation of brief descriptive terms with principle anatomical lesions emphasized. The lesions that are noted may or may not identify the disease.

Important sources of error in the diagnostic process include incomplete data concerning the patient's illness. This can happen early in the illness before enough evidence has unfolded, or at any stage if the physician has not been thorough.

§12.05 Risk Management

In physician (as well as attorney) risk management, the necessity of complete, accurate, and current patient records is emphasized. The medical record is a reference document for designating personnel involvement in treating a patient or in communicating specific information to appropriate outside parties regarding a patient's condition. Medical records supply data for a variety of purposes, primarily for patient care but also for insurance companies, government agencies, and medical training and research. Several physicians may require access to a patient's records—primary care physicians, consulting physicians, and those seeing the patient on referral, as well as the new physician when the patient moves or changes doctors. (*See* Appendix 12-1, Cases 1 and 2.)

§12.06 Proper Maintenance of Records

"Do's and Don'ts" in medical record keeping include:

DO:

1. Use clear language; avoid vague references
2. Write legibly if notes are handwritten
3. Make sure records are complete

4. Record scheduled and missed appointments
5. Date and sign all entries, including corrections
6. Document what is said to the patient and what he or she says
7. Include emergency room and hospital stay and discharge summary records
8. File copies of consulting physician's notes, diagnosis, treatment, and recommendations
9. Include copies of disability reports and any other pertinent information from outside sources
10. Ask the patient to sign a release for prior or current medical records

DO NOT:

1. Alter records in any way that could be construed as deceptive
2. Abbreviate haphazardly
3. Sign reports, dictation, and staff notations until you have carefully reviewed them
4. Record personal opinions or unsubstantiated comments
5. Accept record release forms over 90 days old
6. Refill prescriptions over the telephone unless you have seen the patient or reviewed his or her chart

§12.07 History and Physical

Science uses two types of data—one for generating hypotheses, and a second for testing hypotheses. In clinical medicine, the history and physical examination generate the data used for making a hypothesis about what could be wrong with the patient. Laboratory testing, x-rays, and continued patient observation test the hypothesis and determine the problem(s) from which the patient is suffering. Although comparisons between physical examination maneuvers and imaging procedures may tell something about the precision of the former, such comparisons can tell little about the intrinsic worth of one versus the other, because these two different types of procedures generate data with two different types of usage.[2] (*See* Appendix 12-1, Case 3.)

In performing a medical examination, the physician begins a deductive process by which both objective and subjective information is obtained from the patient and related to recognized medical principles. The physician's primary concern is to identify or diagnose the condition and to develop an appropriate treatment plan. Information not important to the diagnosis or treatment plan is generally ignored. Information elicited by the doctor is

---

[2] Sapira, *Why Perform A Routine History and Physical Examination,* 82 South Med J 364 (1989).

presumed to be important to the physician's task and should not be casually discounted by the caretakers.

Initial examination typically consists of a history (which is the patient's own account of the events which led to seeking medical help), as well as a complete physical examination. After these steps, the physician reaches a working or tentative diagnosis, or if less certain, a differential diagnosis. At this point, a treatment plan may be suggested to the patient along with the reasoning as to its necessity, including a prognosis. Treatment often is part of diagnosis, carried out while other tests are ordered. (*See* Appendix 12-1, Case 4.)

§12.08 Medical Evaluation

Just as the cells of the body live in a fluid "milieu interieur," the physician works in a philosophical milieu that governs the interpretation of and response to situations encountered in practice. If the physician is to understand his or her role in society, and is to successfully deal with his or her professional sense of crisis, he or she must go beyond a patient-disease model. He or she must achieve a synthesis that relates the physician to the entire practice environment and its base knowledge. The metaphor of the animal organism as a machine was established by Descartes' Discourse on Method, probably outdated at the present time. The prevailing view of life as a mechanist process gives no room for the physician to interpret symbolic language. This is the current basis for objective and subjective findings that form the basis of fact-finding in respect to the patient's problem. Strict adherence to "objective" findings as more probative than subjective findings often does a disservice to that patient. In the day-to-day practice of medicine, subjective findings are the basis for 70 to 80 per cent of diagnosis and treatment.[3] (*See* Appendix 12-1, Case 5.)

§12.09 Altered Medical Records

In a medical malpractice case where health is a critical issue, a review of the medical records is essential. There are occasions when a record has been altered, although health care providers are expected to be objective and honest in their clinical findings. Personal opinions may be added as fact and become "defensive" recordkeeping.

Defensive recordkeeping, rationalization, and personal opinion are not illegal or unethical, although they place the physician in an uncomfortable position, particularly if the case is brought to litigation.

In most states, there is a code provision similar to the following:

---

[3] Bessinger, Jr, *Doctoring,* 81 South Med J 1558 (1988); J. Campbell, The Mythic Image (1974); R. Descartes, Treatise of Man (1972); J.O. La Mettrie, de L'Homme Machine, 1748 (1961) (historical notes by G.C. Bussey).

> Any person who is or has been a patient of a doctor, hospital or other medical institution shall be entitled to obtain access to the information contained in all his/her medical records upon request, and shall be furnished copies of all records pertaining to his or her case upon tender . . . ten cents per page.

If an alteration is suspected, it is wise for the attorney to examine the original documents, as it is a simple procedure to change something in the medical record and not have it be detected on a copy. Altered records may be detected by (1) a change made over correction fluid or an erasure, (2) additions or deletions made in a different ink and not dated and signed, (3) changes in the slant or pressure of handwriting, (4) impressions or the lack of a writing instrument on subsequent pages, (5) misaligned typed notations, and (6) writing crowded around existing entries. Substituted or rewritten records may be detected by (1) additions of different dates in different ink from the originals, (2) differences in folds, stains, offsets, holes, tears, impression, and type of paper, (3) intersecting ink entries of different dates that blend together, and (4) use of a later year, particularly if corrected more than once. (*See* Appendix 12-1, Cases 6 to 8.)

Often, words and terms in a medical record may have meaning only to the person writing them. A knowledge of words or abbreviations in the records is essential. What is normal for one professional may represent something different for another. For example, the physician has an opinion as to "impairment" of a patient while the trier of fact rates the "disability" of the patient.

Generally, progress notes and hospital discharge summaries are dictated within 24 hours of service and are typed promptly. Hospital records have a specific place on each page of the document for the date of dictation and the date of transcription. Delays in dictations on surgery reports or discharge summaries may provide an opportunity for record alteration. The Joint Commission on Accreditation of Health Care Organization (JCAHO) and/or State Board of Health have requirements that must be met by hospitals and other medical facilities. Records that are lost or misfiled are suspect for alterations or intentional concealment. In one case, May v Moore, an inference of guilt was found by the court after an infant died (from alleged improper treatment) and the medical records disappeared. Hospital personnel had copied the record, knowing that a particular physician frequently "lost" medical records. The court found that the habit of losing records admissible created an inference of negligence. The doctor later found the records, but they differed markedly from the hospital administrator's copy. The verdict was for the plaintiff. Civil conspiracy may exist when two or more join to alter records, as seen in Henry v Deen 310 SE 2d 326 (NC 1984).[4]

The medical record, of necessity, should be as complete as reasonably possible so as not to inadvertently exclude vital information. A frequent scenario

---

[4] McInnis, *Signs and Symptoms of Defensive Medical Record Keeping,* 60 Okla Bar J 1339 (1989).

in court is a physician alleging that he or she did something beneficial to the patient, but failed or forgot to write it in the medical record. Without fail, the courts reason that "If it is not in the record, it is presumed it was not done." (*See* Appendix 12-1, Cases 8 and 9.)

§12.10 Examining Room Procedures

It is the duty of the physician or nurse to assist patients while dressing or undressing.

In *Levett v Etkind,* 158 Conn 567, 265 A2d 70, the plaintiff fell while disrobing in the examining room and ultimately died from the injuries sustained in that fall. On appeal by the plaintiff, no error was found by the Supreme Court of Connecticut, which held that (1) the duty of the physician was to exercise a degree of skill and care that physicians in the same general neighborhood and in the same general line of practice ordinarily had and exercised in like cases, (2) the plaintiff could not prevail unless there was positive evidence of an expert nature from which the jury could reasonably and logically conclude that the defendant was negligent, (3) that the trial court correctly instructed that the defendant was responsible for any wrongful act on the part of the nurse in following his instructions, as well as for failure by her to follow such instructions, and (4) that the jury could have found that the plaintiff was chargeable with assumption of risk, since in this case the plaintiff had refused assistance.

Levett held that neither the defendant nor his nursing staff was negligent, and the strong point was the patient's refusal of assistance. According to the generally applicable standard of care and skill in this area, if the doctor believes the patient is in need of assistance and instructs a nurse to help the patient to dress or undress, then the physician has attempted to run his or her office according to the standard of care and skill of doctors who have nurses in their offices. Moreover, according to the generally applicable standard of skill for the care of the feeble and impaired, such patients should not be left unattended. In *Levett,* the defendant observed the patient's condition on that date and did not believe there was much risk in allowing the plaintiff to dress herself unassisted, and for that reason did not insist on the nurse being available to help the patient.

A similar result was reached in 2 Wash 2d 237, 97 P2d 689, in which a female patient fainted as she dismounted an examining table. The allegation here was not that the physician was negligent in not assisting her to dress, but in leaving her unattended. Again, applying the general medical malpractice rule, the physician's professional conduct is to be measured against the usual practice and cases in the locality and similar communities, and in particular, in that area at that time—in this case, Seattle. Since a nurse would not be in the room after this particular treatment was given, the physician was held not liable.

§12.11 Physician as Risk Manager

In an effort to lessen the risk of a malpractice suit in Kansas, the Professional Mutual Insurance Company is requiring physicians who deliver babies to keep a standardized form, a prenatal recordkeeping system that consists of a series of forms and flow charts that document the patient's medical history, schedule of physician's examinations, normal progress, complications, and patient education, to keep their malpractice insurance in force.

This is a step closer to third-party regulation of how the physician keeps records, and sets the standards of practice to be followed, under the guise of improving medical care. Strict regulation of physician practices by a peer group has many pluses, but it will meet the resistance of physicians who wish to protect their independence (and egos).[5]

§12.12 Computer Records

Computer-based medical records promise to solve many of the access and legibility problems of the traditional paper records. These can influence the quality of care by calling attention to adverse results and unattended medical problems reflected in the electronic chart. An increasing number of institutions are using computer-based medical record systems. Computer systems improve the availability of medical records from 85 to 99 per cent, according to one study. These systems do not save personnel time, but most informed users agree that the quality of care is improved. Physicians order 9 per cent fewer tests when the computer displayed the patient's logistic probability of having an abnormal result.[6]

§12.13 Uniform Medical Records

The Health Care Financing Administration is about to take the first step in extending Medicare Peer Review Organization (PRO) Review to office practices. The doctors will be asked to maintain uniform patient records. The PROs will require that records contain demographic and diagnostic data, treatment protocols, and any nursing, rehabilitative, or support services that have been prescribed.

§12.14 Diagnosis: Evaluation

Diagnosis is an issue of such heightened emotional experience to physicians that they may lose sight of its equal or greater significance to the

---

[5] Voelker-Amer Med News Staff, *'Insurer to Require More Record Keeping'*, Amer Med News (May 26, 1989).

[6] McDonald & Tierney, *Computer-Stored Medical Records: Their Future in Medical Practice,* 259 JAMA 3433 (1988); TG Tape, *Process in Ambulatory Care: A Controlled Clinical Trial of Computerized Records,* 12 Symp Comput Applic Med Care Proc 749 (1988).

patient. Physicians are taught the crucial importance of definitive knowledge of exactly what is wrong with the patient, while experience has repeatedly shown that a precise diagnosis often cannot be made. For physicians, diagnosis is an elusive ideal goal, ready to remind the doctor of his or her own limitations and to perhaps instill a feeling of guilt when he or she treats symptoms without knowing the cause.

In contrast, diagnosis for the patient is the appropriate self-centered issue for presenting him- or herself to the physician. The patient wants information about what is wrong, to remove the uncertainty of knowing that something is wrong without knowing what it might be. This uncertainty masks the fear, dread, and apprehension of the unknown, perhaps fatal, condition. Despite modern ideas of patient responsibility and holistic health, when sick or uncertain most patients desperately wish to place themselves under the care of potent authority. Diagnosis is the pivotal issue in the physician's exercise of this authority.

The physician's large emotional investment in diagnosis is hidden by the greater investment of the patient. Diagnosis is part of a process unfolding in time. It is preceded by the taking of a history from the patient, the performance of an adequate physical examination, and ordering and reviewing certain tests. These observations are followed by treatment and an outcome. Sometimes the diagnosis can be promptly made, such as in trauma with obvious injury. In other cases, the diagnosis unfolds gradually over several physician-patient consultations. Sometimes the diagnosis is accepted and other times it is rejected. It may satisfy or enrage the patient; it may promote collaboration or create alienation. (*See* Appendix 12-1, Cases 10 to 12.)

§12.15 Patient's Understanding of the Diagnosis

Despite the physician's satisfaction regarding the diagnosis and proposed treatment, a large minority of patients feel themselves underdiagnosed. Many of these patients fall into chronic pain syndromes, myofascial pain syndromes, headache problems, or cardiac and gastrointestinal disorders. The patient often overtly or covertly states, "No one has been able to tell what is the matter with me." This situation may be the end result of the physician candidly telling the patient that "I can't find anything wrong with you" or that "All tests are negative." Sometimes these physician statements are reassuring to the patient. It often means the diagnosis is incomplete. Often, the physician's reassurance is rejected by the patient.

These patients represent a specific category for therapy—the patient who has not accepted a diagnosis. They are often outspoken in their rejection and demand more tests and more treatment—often treatment that requires mind-altering drugs. Likewise, the patient who does not comply with treatment may be rejecting the diagnosis. Historically, these patients are frequently involved in litigation or compensation.

As a special category, patients who believe they are undiagnosed require special handling. Part of this revolves around the issue of responsibility.

Diagnosis is mostly the doctor's responsibility, and if the patient views him- or herself as underdiagnosed, he or she views the doctor as not adequately providing for him or her. From the patient's point of view, this means that the physician is responsible, even though from the doctor's point of view, the diagnosis proffered to the patient is his or her best effort and is likely accurate. If such a misunderstanding exists, good medicine dictates that it should be resolved.

There are other ramifications of diagnosis. Most often the patient accepts and works with the diagnosis, resulting in successful treatment. Sometimes the diagnosis is wrong. At times, the diagnosis is changed or elaborated on during the course of physician observation and treatment.

The physician often recognizes that the patient does not accept the diagnosis. His or her greatest usefulness is a willingness to work with the patient on that point. An example is the patient who has seen many doctors. In self-evident cases, collecting and reviewing the medical reports of other physicians is helpful and suggests another consultation to confirm or alter the diagnosis. With this, the patient may rationally yield to the weight of the evidence and proceed with a treatment plan. Unless a confident physician-patient relationship exists, most often treatment will subjectively fail.[7]

§12.16 Physician's Office Records

There is a broad range of styles and formats in physician medical records. These range from records which contain nothing more than handwritten notes for each office visit, to those prepared by a physician well-versed in litigation and which are usually more comprehensive. Handwritten notes are frequently less than legible and may require interpretation. On occasion, the doctor cannot "make out" written notes, which can become a point of physician impeachment.

It is common for all office records to be stored on computer discs, which will require print outs and verification by the physician or medical records librarian.

Not unusually, the patient will contend that the examining doctor did not do those parts of the physical examination that the doctor has recorded. This is a serious accusation which, if true, is deplorable and negligent behavior on the doctor's part. Proof of such behavior is difficult, but if the plaintiff is damaged by the behavior, it should be tried. Another error of physical examination is accepting examination results tendered by a physician who is not appropriately trained and specialized to do the examination, or who is incompetent for other reasons.

For many physicians, the malpractice crisis has long dominated their view of the legal context in which they practice. Today, legal pressures on the physician are increasing and compounding in their complexity. Direct practice regulation, reimbursement and income concerns, and pressures created

---

[7] Gaarder, *Diagnosis,* 82 South Med J 1153 (1989).

by the legal implications of clinical technology and the limits of medical practice have become significant forces in physicians' professional lives.

The physician-patient encounter has traditionally been a one-on-one relationship where the physician, using professional judgment, skill, and knowledge, makes a clinical decision based on the patient's individual condition, needs, and circumstances. While there have always been external constraints on treatment decisions, such as FDA approval of drugs before they can be prescribed, of late there are more players in the treatment room than ever before. Each views the clinical decision for the patient from a different perspective. (*See* Appendix 12-1, Cases 13 to 19.)

Follow-up visits should include pertinent information as to the patient's progress, new history or physical findings, and the results of additional tests. Notes should be made of complications or adverse results and that the patient has been informed of these and the prognosis.

§12.17 Taking a Medical History

The most important part of the medical record is the history. All physicians realize that a careful, complete, and accurate history is essential to a correct diagnosis and necessary to plan treatment for the patient. If a physician is superficial, casual, sloppy, or indifferent to obtaining the medical history, his or her credibility may be challenged. The validity of a physician's opinion depends, in large part, on the history obtained. The patient's credibility is critical, also, when giving the history. It is essential that the doctor mention that the patient is apparently competent, that there is no significant language or intellectual impairment, and that the patient realizes that full disclosure to the doctor is necessary. Credibility should not only focus on the patient's propensity for telling the truth, but on his or her ability to give an accurate history.

An initial or partial history may be obtained by requesting the patient to complete forms and/or have an office person ask preliminary questions. The physician must review and expand on this information for completeness.

§12.18 System (Symptom) Review

After obtaining information in the initial part of the history, the chief complaint and further information regarding the patient can be obtained through a system review. Information regarding illness, injury, and treatment of that area (or other areas) of the body has been noted. A complete system review includes head, eyes, ears, nose, throat, cardiovascular and respiratory system, gastrointestinal and genitourinary systems, spine, extremities, and joints. A mental history is essential and may require specialized skill to obtain.

In orthopedics, evaluation of a present injury requires knowledge of all previous injuries, treatments, and results. At times, knowledge of previous injuries is only available from the patient and is another test of his or her credibility.

§12.19 Physical Examination

The physical examination is often regarded by the attorney as the most important part of the medical record. The findings made by a physician on examination are extremely important to an accurate diagnosis, prognosis, and disability opinion; however, these findings alone are not sufficient to support a credible opinion regarding legal causation. Any inconsistencies between the history and the physical findings must be reconciled.

§12.20 Failing to Do Complete Physical Examination

As previously discussed, patients will often complain that the examining doctor did not perform parts of a physical examination described in the records. This is a serious accusation which, if true, is deplorable and negligent behavior by the doctor. Proof of such behavior is difficult, but if the plaintiff is damaged by the behavior, it should be tried. Another error in physical examination is accepting examination results tendered by a physician who is not appropriately trained and specialized to do the examination, or who is incompetent for other reasons.

§12.21 Differential Diagnosis

Differential diagnosis is the systematic utilization of a variety of information, including patient symptoms and medical tests, to diagnose an illness which is not immediately identifiable from unique symptoms.

Once the physician has taken the patient's history, system review, past history, and has reviewed tests and previous reports regarding the patient, a diagnosis may be appropriate. A clear medical problem (i.e., a fractured femur) makes the diagnosis apparent. More complex problems may suggest one or more diagnoses; thus, the differential diagnosis.

§12.22 Diagnostic Studies and Special Services

Diagnostic studies embrace a wide range of technical studies available to assist the doctor in his or her diagnosis and treatment. The physician is usually held to know the availability and understand the usefulness of tests. The physician who fails to use available appropriate diagnostic tests is vulnerable if a diagnosis is possible but is missed; thus "defensive medicine" is often practiced by using many tests that may overlap or may in fact be necessary to the diagnosis. The physician is often in a "Catch-22" situation, as medical payers object to or refuse to pay for certain tests or treatments while the physician feels that the diagnosis has been incompletely serviced.

The laboratory and other tests are typically recorded sequentially on their respective pages, available daily for the information of the treating medical personnel.

Special services, including respiratory, physical therapy, and occupational therapy, record treatments and observations on their hospital record forms.

The hospitalized patient may be well served by a consultation from one or more physicians called by the attending physician. The consultation is recorded on an appropriate page reflecting their opinion and recommendations. (*See* Appendix 12-1, Cases 20 to 22.)

§12.23 Prognosis

Prognosis is the physician's informed opinion of what the future of the patient holds, treated or untreated—whether the patient will heal, recover, deteriorate, die, etc. Part of the prognosis includes probable temporary or permanent impairment, future medical needs and costs, and pain and suffering. The physician realizes that every patient is different, and that the precise manner in which a condition may progress cannot be stated with complete certainty. If the doctor provides sufficient factual data in support of his or her prognosis, the legal standard of accuracy (reasonable medical certainty) should be met, and the trier of fact will have competent evidence to support a finding in this regard.

§12.24 Hospital Records

The physician's part of the hospital records of his or her patient is much like the physician's office record. It includes a present and past history, a system review, and a complete physical examination. It additionally includes a statement of the reason for hospital admission, a plan of treatment, and a short-term prognosis. The doctor also records daily progress notes stating what is going on with the patient, current test results, and additional plans. Nursing notes are recorded parallel to doctors' notes, recording vital signs (blood pressure, temperature, pulse, and respiration) and other significant observations regarding the patient. The physician who does not read and act on the nurses' notes daily may do his or her patients a disservice. Attorneys reviewing hospital records should be aware that nurses' notes are typically most informative.

Additionally, daily records are made by the doctor in the doctors' orders, along with a notation that the responsible nurse has seen and acknowledged the orders.

Vital signs such as blood pressure, temperature, pulse, respiration, fluid intake, and urine and bowel outputs are typically noted several times daily on a separate sheet—the vital signs sheet. (*See* Appendix 12-1, Cases 6 and 8.)

§12.25 Discharge Summary

When the patient is discharged, a record of his or her hospitalization is made by the treating and any other involved physicians. This summary repeats the purpose of admission to the hospital, the hospital course, what invasive testing or surgery was done, what medical treatments were carried out, and their results. A discharge plan is made for the patient, including follow-up by which physician and when. Discharge medication is noted. A specific note that the patient received information about diagnosis, discharge plans, return doctor visits, and medications is important, as well as required, as part of participation in many health plans (such as Medicare and Medicaid) and by the hospital itself.[8]

§12.26 Confidentiality of Medical Records

Medical records are strictly privileged between patients and physicians unless the patient has given competent, informed consent to their release to another. Failure of the physician to adhere to this duty places the physician at risk of a negligence suit. An exception to this rule is the presumed authorized release of medical information to another party when that party has arranged for and paid for the examination, usually in situations of obtaining disability information, pre-employment information, or second opinions desired by a responsible third party as to diagnosis and/or treatment.

At the time a patient signs a release to a third party, it should be understood that the release includes physical information, but excludes potentially sensitive personal and/or psychiatric information.

Privileged information in civil litigation is not used in the discovery process of litigation. Communications between patients and physicians are confidential and privileged and cannot be disclosed, with some exceptions. One exception occurs when a patient sues a physician. On filing such suit, the physician-patient privilege is either waived entirely or limited. The difference is defined by statute or judicial opinion. In many states, a codes of civil procedure provision governs the discovery of medical records, yet often fails to state in what fashion such discovery may proceed.

The Texas Rules of Civil Procedure Annotated Rule 166b (Vernon 1990) recites the following:

> Permissible forms of discovery are (a) oral or written depositions of any party or non-party; (b) written interrogatories to a party; (c) request of a party for admission of facts or identity of documents or things; (d) request and motions for production, examination and copying of documents or other tangible materials; (e) requests and motions for entry upon and examination of real property and (f) motions for a mental or physical examination of a party or person under the legal control of a party. Ex parte proceedings are not contemplated in these discovery rules.

---

[8] J.A. Tarantino & D.J. Oliveira, Litigating Neck and Back Injuries.

There are compelling reasons why the patient does not waive all privilege, as appears in the fundamental guarantee of the right of privacy.

Confidentiality is not an end in itself. Its importance resides in what it protects and what it makes possible. What it protects is privacy, a difficult concept. It is sufficient to make the point that having an appropriate degree of privacy is closely bound to an individual's self-image and sense of personal integrity. Confidentiality makes possible, with the professional relationship, an exchange of information of an intimate kind which might not otherwise take place. Confidentiality aids communication and within medical practice provides an essential basis for trust between doctors and their patients.

In protecting the physicians' right of privacy, a restricted medical authorization motion is filed and usually accepted. This will allow counsel to discover only matters germane to the malpractice action. These authorizations should specifically prohibit ex parte discussions with the plaintiffs' subsequent treating doctors. This presents a problem in the ethical practice of medicine, as the physician has a duty to pass to subsequent doctors, on appropriate request, the medical information he or she has regarding that patient. (*See* Appendix 12-1, Cases 18, 19, and 23 to 26.)

§12.27 Conspiracy of Silence Among Physicians

In the recent past, a "conspiracy of silence" existed which kept physicians from reviewing medical records and testifying against other physicians. This has eased a great deal in recent years, although surgical subspecialties still seem to be involved in this conspiracy. The medical-legal practice that many orthopedists are involved in as part of their practice does carry some medicolegal malpractice risk. The physician so reviewing and testifying is held to high ethical and integrity standards, even though he or she may be giving a professional opinion. The opinion must be reasoned, fair, and the same or similar to the opinion that most other similarly situated physicians would render.

In one case, *Agnew v Parks,* 172 Cal 2d 756, 343 P2d 118 (1959), the plaintiff alleged that failure to x-ray a hip injury led to an impairment and that the impairment resulted from negligence. The plaintiff's counsel contacted nine orthopedists, and each refused to testify. The plaintiff's counsel then approached a judge to intervene with the Los Angeles County Medical Society to find a disinterested witness. The physician appointed indicated that he did not know either party involved in the suit; however, it was shown that the appointed physician knew the defendant's physician and gave a favorable report for him. The trial court granted a nonsuit, but the appellate court overturned it and ordered a new trial. The court felt that there was "indirect and circumstantial" evidence linking all of the defendants to a conspiracy to defraud.

Comment: This case, along with medical reports of an apparent conspiracy among physicians in antitrust matters, demonstrated the risk of an attempted "conspiracy of silence" to deny a plaintiff his right to legal redress. There is little legal risk to reviewing and/or testifying physicians as long as the examining physician does not physically or emotionally harm the plaintiff patient. If the examining physician is not seeing the plaintiff for a third-party carrier or plaintiff's counsel, but as a treating physician requested to submit an evaluation report, the risk is greater. (*See* Appendix 12-1, Cases 27 to 29.)

§12.28 Medicolegal Report

For a variety of legal purposes, a medical report is necessary. One author, who may have a somewhat slanted view on the subject, makes a valid criticism: No medical school in the United States today offers a course in medical legal report writing, in spite of its obvious socio-economic importance and the billions of dollars in this type of claims. Little, if any, post graduate medical education on this subject is available.

If the report is on a patient being seen by other than the treating physician, the party who has requested the examination and the date of the examination should be named. When the report is the patient's own, written permission to release this information must be given.

It is crassly wrong for professionals to hold themselves out to as independent evaluators, or to be players on one side or the other of the adversarial system.

The report needs to contain an exhaustive and accurate history. Although the patient may give a lengthy report of the circumstances of the accident, only matters germane to the assessment of the injury should be included in the report, and certainly no judgment as to the cause should appear in the medical report. Although the patient's account to a physician of the circumstances of the accident is usually inadmissible as evidence bearing on the cause of action, it may be admissible to the extent that it is relevant to establishing the opinion on which the physician bases his or her opinion of what is going on, causation, effect, impairment, etc. If, in some way, these notes are erroneous, they may damage the credibility of the patient or in some way influence the outcome of the case.

The past history of the patient must be recorded, especially if previous injury or disease has a direct relationship in the production, aggravation, or acceleration of the impairment being assessed. If the report is on a patient the reporting physician has treated, a detailed report of the initial examination and subsequent treatment should be included. The patient should be questioned regarding his or her current condition and the severity, duration, and frequency of the specific complaints.

The clinical examination is carried out in a meticulous manner, notes being taken during the examination rather than depending on memory. Care should be taken to differentiate left from right, etc. In many jurisdictions, the medical witness is permitted to refer to these notes to refresh his or her recollection, provided the notes were made at the time of the examination or shortly thereafter.

Thorough notes can be invaluable for responding intelligently and consistently in far-reaching, extended cross-examinations. The sooner a formal report is dictated, the more accurate it will be. Measurements taken with a tape or goniometer, etc., should be done and recorded. Scars should be noted, especially when they interfere with function or cosmesis. Negative findings, where indicated, should be noted.

After describing the medical findings in technical terms, it is best to give a resume of the findings in lay terms for the benefit of those persons not familiar with medical terminology. This is very helpful to the recipient of the report if he or she is a lawyer or other medical layperson.

The examiner should express some opinion about the consistency of the patient's injuries with the patient's history and the flow of events from the time of injury through the problems and physical findings found at the time of the current examination. The comments should be based on the facts alone, as the physician perceives them, as reported by the patient. Statements as to causation need to be made with reasonable medical probability, substantiated by medical fact and by the experience of the examining physician.

In the event that the patient's condition is stable, and no further treatment is indicated, in many situations it is appropriate to assess the degree of, or make a statement concerning the presence or absence of, permanent impairment. The physician is rarely asked to rate disability; this is a prerogative of the trier of fact, utilizing several parameters, one of which is the impairment rating that the physician renders.[9] (*See* Appendix 12-1, Cases 18, 25, and 30 to 33.)

---

[9] H.H. Kessler, Disability — Determination and Evaluation (1970).

Appendix 12-1
Cases

1 ***Grant v Farnsworth,* 869 F2d 1149 (8th Cir 1989)** (doctor was not permitted to testify as to the extent and cause of the plaintiff's disability from an accident when he said that he would have to guess, as he lacked the necessary history of the plaintiff prior to trial).

2 ***Mackey v Greenview Hospital, Inc,* 587 SW2d 249 (Ky Ct App 1979)** (physician was liable for failure to take a careful history).

Comment: If a patient does not give a physician a full and accurate history, it may be a basis for finding the physician was not negligent. But, the physician must consider the history given by the patient, and failure to do so may constitute malpractice.

3 ***Daniels v State,* 532 So 2d 218 (La Ct App 1988)** (patient said her wrist was deformed as a result of treatment for a closed wrist fracture. Prior to administering treatment, the medical personnel asked the patient whether she had any allergies and whether she had been taking medication, and obtained the history of the injury. The court concluded that this history was adequate and that a more extensive history would not have lessened the severity of the patient's injury or disability).

4 ***Rivers v Kumar,* 500 NYS2d 39 (NY App Div 1986)** (familiar warning to maintain full and accurate records was underscored when a New York court levied against a neurosurgeon. The surgeon performed a cervical laminectomy on a 46-year-old lady with a permanently incapacitated leg. The result was not in itself negligent, since the surgeon pointed out that it is a known risk of such surgery. The most damaging factor in the case was the surgeon's admission that he performed surgery without taking a myelogram. He explained that the patient had refused to undergo myelography and consented to surgery without it. The patient insisted that a myelogram was never mentioned. Unfortunately, the neurosurgeon could not produce documentation, so the doctrine, "If it's not in the record, it wasn't done" was convincing in this case. The neurosurgeon further argued that the operation was necessary to release spinal nerve compression, but the hospital records failed to clearly state that such a diagnosis had been made. The verdict against the surgeon for medical negligence was upheld).

5 ***Welch v Chandler,* No 103544 (Me Ct App)** (patient's refusal to return medical records to the defendant physician prior to trial was fatal to the plaintiff's case as the defendant was unable to defend himself. In trial court, the plaintiff alleged that the defendant improperly prescribed Percodan and other narcotics during a six-year period, causing the plaintiff to become addicted. The plaintiff had obtained the defendant doctor's medical records for review before trial. Only five pages of the chart were returned and two discovery orders were entered and ignored. The plaintiff admitted

that some of the laboratory and x-ray files were missing, but denied retaining the remainder of the record. The court held that when the plaintiff took the records, he had control over them and had a duty to be able to return them on demand. The plaintiff's admitted failure to produce the file fatally compromised the defendant's ability to defend himself).

6 ***Fitzpatrick v Cummings,*** **No 85-40879 (Dade County Cir Ct 1988)** (police officer died after receiving an inadequate dose of Heparin in treatment of a pulmonary embolus. The decedent had undergone knee ligament surgery, was discharged from the hospital, and experienced severe chest pains 16 days later. A STAT (emergency) ventilation-perfusion lung scan showed probable acute pulmonary embolus, and intravenous Heparin was started but not in sufficient dosages to bring partial thromboplatin (PTP) blood tests within therapeutic levels. An action was brought against hospital and physician, alleging failure to give proper amounts of Heparin in the face of pulmonary embolus. The nurses' notes reflected that 2,000 units of Heparin were ordered and given, but the doctors' orders appeared to have been altered to show 20,000 units. A settlement of $280,000 cash, plus a lifetime annuity for the child was purchased at cost of $220,000 was obtained. The settlement was allocated $330,000 to the child and $170,000 to the wife).

7 ***Hurlock v Park Lane Medical Center, Inc,*** **709 SW2d 872 (Mo Ct App 1985)** (this case turned on the importance of medical records and on whether the nurses had scrupulously followed the doctor's instructions. The patient was a very fragile osteoporotic lady who was at risk for developing decubiti. She had a fractured femur and had been paralyzed in an accident some 20 years earlier, and had extensive emphysema. Her doctor's orders stated that she be turned every two hours. An accurate record of whether she was turned or not did not appear in hospital notes, nurses' notes, or progress notes. She would have been turned 117 times during a 10 day period, and there was a record of 18 turnings. She developed a large decubiti that eventually required amputation of her leg. The hospital was a prime target for this suit, although the doctors were also involved. The hospital staunchly maintained that, despite lack of documentation, the doctor's orders had been carried out. The trial court cleared the doctor from negligence, but not the hospital. The appellate court held that "not a scintilla of direct evidence" that the patient had not been turned was offered. The appellate court pointed out the legal frailty of the axiom "If it isn't written down, it wasn't done," since all of the witnesses who participated in the patient's care had taken part in the recordkeeping. On the question of whether the physician should have noted that the nurses' notes did not show a record of turning, it was held that it is appropriate for doctors to read nurses' notes, but that they may "also confirm obedience to the orders by observing the patient and nurses as they were").

Comment: The axiom "If it wasn't written down, it wasn't done" carries a great deal of weight in a number of malpractice cases. The obvious advice to both physicians and nurses, then, is to record as much as you can, as accurately as you can, and as frequently as possible. In these days when defensive medicine must be practiced, accurate recordkeeping is essential.

8 ***Boza v Schiebel,* 308 SE2d 510 (NC Ct App 1983)** (patient undergoing an orthopedic surgical procedure came out of surgery with one foot numb and a drop foot. Hospital records made it clear that the damage had been done by the negligent placement of a strap which exerted undue pressure on the peroneal nerve. The orthopedic surgeon was named as a defendant, but was able to clear himself by describing step-by-step how patients are put in position for the type of surgery he did, and showing that he, as the surgeon, had no part in the placement of the strap. The orthopedist was released, but the hospital was held responsible for the damages).

9 ***Bost v Riley,* 262 SE2d 391 (NC Ct App 1980)** (physician was negligent in his emergency evaluation of a patient involved in a bicycle accident. There apparently was some delay in making a diagnosis of a ruptured spleen, but that diagnosis was made and an emergency splenectomy was carried out. The physician left town on vacation the next day, leaving the care of the patient to a colleague. The patient developed peritonitis and later developed a volvulus, requiring emergency surgery and resection of three feet of gangrenous bowel. The patient did not do well and was eventually transferred to another hospital where three additional operations were carried out. The patient eventually died of liver failure induced by sepsis. The suit filed against the first physician alleged that he had left the patient to the care of incompetent personnel and physicians who did not know and understand the case, and that there was no conversation between the operating surgeon and the surgeon he was referred to. Inadequate progress notes were noted throughout the chart, so it was difficult for a third party to monitor the care the patient received. However, it was the judgment of the court that improper supervision postoperatively was not the cause of the death from sepsis and that the sepsis itself was appropriately treated under the circumstances).

Comment: *Bost* was a close case. A number of malpractice actions stem from incomplete or inadequate coverage by a physician seeing a patient in the absence of an operating or principal treating physician. Accurate hospital notes (progress notes in particular) are essential so that anybody following the patient can see what the problem has been, what is going on, and what the plan of treatment is. Anything less than this is negligent behavior on the part of the caring physician.

10 ***Thomas v United States,* 660 F Supp 216 (DC Cir 1987)** (patient went to a Veterans' Administration hospital with a hand injury. The emergency room physician recommended admission to the hospital in the orthopedic ward with a diagnosis of infection and directed the treating physician to rule out compartment syndrome. The patient was seen by several physicians over a period of one week. The infection worsened, but an abscess was not detected until one week after admission. Tingling was detected on the second day but was not followed up. When the physician cut open the patient's arm to drain the abscess, he found pus spreading through the fascial components, requiring decompression. The patient suffered permanent scarring and loss of function of the hand. The patient filed a malpractice action,

and the federal court said that the standard of care required the physician to act as a reasonably prudent person, and that this was not carried out. The JCAH required that certain standards be met so far as monitoring and keeping records on patients. The patient argued that, since the admitting physician had indicated in the records that compartment syndrome was to be ruled out, there should have been more extensive care, including more surgery if necessary. The court found that the medical records of the patient fell below the standard of care. They did not document the patient's condition properly, and did not provide the next attending physician with adequate information. There was an absence of detailed notes required by JCAH standards. Furthermore, the admitting physician made a notation to rule out compartment syndrome. The court said that the standard required reevaluation every four to six hours until the possibility of that condition was ruled out. The court concluded that the patient had clearly met the burden of showing that the hospital had breached this duty. Moreover, the court said that the hospital failed to treat the patient in a timely manner, which was not only a breach of the standard of care, but a proximate cause of the injury. The patient had proven loss of function of the hand, which limited his ability to accept certain employment opportunities and enjoy certain recreation and social activities. He incurred more pain and suffering and was facing future plastic surgery. Because of the patient's history of drug usage and inability to manage his life, the patient agreed that the payment should be partially made in the form of a lifetime annuity).

11 *McAllister v Weirton Hospital Co,* 312 SE2d 738 (W Va 1983) (this case is an example of a breakdown in communication between doctors. The misunderstanding began July 23, 1976 when a 15-year-old boy was brought to the hospital with a bullet wound in his right leg. The emergency room doctor said that the bullet separated two main arteries supplying the right leg and foot. He administered a tetanus shot and applied a pressure bandage. X-rays revealed, in addition to arterial damage, a compound fracture of the leg. The patient was admitted and the local orthopedist was telephoned, but precisely what was said over the telephone was disputed. The emergency room doctor recalled that he told the orthopedist the patient had a gunshot wound and compound fracture of the leg. The orthopedist remembered the call, but recalled nothing about a gunshot wound—just a simple fracture. The orthopedist told the emergency room doctor to have the patient ready for surgery at 10 A.M. the next morning. A little after midnight, though, the boy was in such pain that his family asked the nurse to call the orthopedist again. The nurse identified the boy with a gunshot wound, and the orthopedist told her she must be mistaken because he had no patient with such a wound. After learning the boy in question was indeed the orthopedist's patient, the nurse phoned him again and advised him that he was to examine the boy at 10 A.M. The orthopedist remembered that appointment and ordered the boy transferred to another hospital with facilities capable of handling such an emergency. The emergency room doctor telephoned the hospital suggested by the orthopedist and was told that the boy could not be accepted. Another hospital admitted the patient at 3:30 A.M.

The operating surgeon, for reasons never made clear, did not attempt to restore the vascularization severed by the bullet. Three weeks later, after dry gangrene set in, the leg was amputated. A medical expert, a specialist in vascular surgery, testified that even prompt and skilled attention probably would not have saved the leg, but that "the die was cast" at the time of injury. Therefore, the orthopedist and emergency room doctors were not liable).

Comment: The facts of this case suggest that the orthopedist was not giving clear and devoted attention to the emergency room doctor's call or that the emergency room doctor and nurse were not reciting the facts. It is not unusual for a busy surgeon awakened in the very early hours of the morning to need to be called a second time or to have the call reinforced. In the series of calls that this orthopedist received, if he was clear and competent in his thinking, and presuming he was taking calls, he assumed a major responsibility in the sequence of events in the care of the injured boy. The last chance doctrine would also be applicable, in that prompt repair of such an artery gives a much greater chance of saving an extremity than a repair delayed many hours.

12 ***Crippen v Charter Southland Hospital,*** **534 So 2d 286 (Ala 1988)** (testimony of treating psychologist and treating psychiatrist that unauthorized release of medical records had adversely affected patient, both emotionally and physically, raised an issue for the jury and precluded a summary judgment).

13 ***Fox v Cohen,*** **84 Ill App 3d 744, 406 NE2d 178 (1980)** (plaintiff alleged that a hospital deliberately misplaced her hospital records, and thus fatally impaired her malpractice action against a physician. The court held that a hospital owes a duty to its patients to use reasonable care to maintain medical records. The court, in dismissing the suit, noted that no injury had yet been suffered by the plaintiff because the malpractice action against the physician was still pending).

Comment: The *Fox* court infers that if the alleged information in the hospital records was necessary for a jury to reach a verdict, then an action against hospital would be appropriate. This is a "Catch-22" situation though, because either way the jury would have to speculate on the effect of the records.

14 ***GNOC Corp v Aboud,*** **715 F Supp 644 (DNJ 1989)** (two physicians might be held negligent, as well as liable in punitive damages, when they allegedly encouraged a patron of a casino to gamble, knowing that alcohol was contraindicated on top of the Percodan they had prescribed for him. The plaintiff alleged that the doctors knew or should have known that alcohol would be served and should not have prescribed Percodan, which the doctors had prescribed in treating knee, back, and jaw pain complaints. The plaintiff further alleged that the physicians were negligent in prescribing Percodan at the plaintiff's request without doing a physical examination, reviewing his medical records, taking a medical history, and consulting with prior treating doctors. The court denied the summary judgment request of the physicians. According to the court, punitive damages can be awarded to "punish doctors for aggravated or outrageous conduct and to deter similar conduct," and it is the jury's role, after hearing testimony, to determine if the physician's conduct warranted an award of punitive damages).

Comment: The above decision did not reach the question of negligence as it involved a hearing on motions, which were denied because a question of fact situation existed for a jury. Physicians, of course, are held to a standard of practice that includes adequate history taking, a review of available records, a consultation with prior doctors if important to the case at hand, and administration of adequate treatment. Prescription of the mind-altering drug Percodan should not be made on request of a patient who says that he forgot and left his prescription at home, particularly with the history and physical mentioned above. Doctors have a duty to warn patients of effects, side effects, and contraindications (such as the use of alcohol) when they prescribe a drug. It is improbable that doctors owe any duty to know and respond to the fact that casinos serve alcohol to their patrons.

15 ***Ortiz v City of Imperial,*** **No 88-6569, and 88-6681 (9th Cir)** (plaintiff was taken to an emergency room for suturing of a head wound. The defendants were given an "after care sheet" of instructions. The plaintiff fell again and was taken to jail infirmary where he was monitored by medical personnel who were unaware of his head injury; however, the plaintiff began to show warning signs given on the after care sheet, but the medical personnel did not call the emergency room or the attending doctor. Instead, they called another doctor who had previously prescribed sedatives for the plaintiff's alcohol withdrawal symptoms. According to the court, on the basis of expert testimony sedatives are appropriate for alcohol withdrawal symptoms, but inappropriate for head injury patients as they may obscure serious underlying head injury symptoms. The plaintiff died 10 days later from the original head injury. There was a verdict against the doctor and medical personnel for negligence in not reviewing records and for indifference to the patient's need).

16 ***Clanton v Von Haam,*** **340 SE2d 627 (Ga Ct App 1986)** (when a physician tells telephone callers that he will see them in the morning, the conversation does not establish a physician-patient relationship. The plaintiff patient had gone to the emergency room with severe back pain and numb legs. The physician on duty in the emergency room sent her home. The pain increased; she telephoned the hospital and was told that the doctor who had seen her had gone home. She recalled a team of two doctors whom she had consulted for a condition that had no relevance to her present back pain. She telephoned their office, got the answering service, left her number, and one of the doctors promptly returned her call and listened to her account of her symptoms, then told her she would have to wait until morning before he could see her. Later in the night, she found the pain unbearable, and went to another doctor who admitted her to the hospital. She ultimately had a permanently paralyzed left leg from an acutely extruded intervertebral disc. The trial judge found no grounds on which the physician could be held liable;

the physician was not obliged to see the patient merely because he had seen her for another disorder, because he returned her telephone call, or because he listened to her complaints).

Comment: This is a problem that physicians face frequently. It is important to make a record of every telephone conversation in which some comment was made or some advice was given. Had the physician in this case given advice over the telephone, he could have been held liable.

17 ***VanSickle v McHugh,*** **430 NW2d 799 (Mich Ct App 1988)** (physician-patient privilege does not apply to medical examinations that are not expressly for the purpose of rendering medical advice or care, at least when the patient lacks a reasonable expectation that a consultation will be confidential. A physician's examination of a patient on behalf of the patient's potential adversary in a personal injury suit removes that physician's testimony from the scope of the privilege. The decision allows damaging statements made by a plaintiff to a doctor during the examination to be admitted as evidence. The plaintiff sued for damages from an automobile accident. Her no-fault insurer, a potential defendant, had her examined by a surgeon. The defendant sought to depose that surgeon and the plaintiff sought a protective order, claiming the physician-patient privilege. The court held that the physician-patient privilege is inapplicable when the examination in question is "not conducted for the purpose of rendering medical advice or care to the person asserting the privilege, at least when that person lacks a reasonable expectation that the consultation is cloaked with vein of confidentiality." The court reasoned that because the potential defendant requested the examination, the doctor did not act within the traditional role of a treating physician. The court concluded that the examination of the patient could not have led the patient to "repose confidence in the doctor's treatment or expect confidentiality from information exchanged during the course of consultation").

Comment: This decision requires plaintiffs and their counsel to be aware of the dangers of consultations with defense physicians. Taken to its extreme, counsel may need to accompany plaintiffs to these medical examinations to avoid allowing plaintiffs to incriminate themselves while under the mistaken impression that they are protected by the physician-patient privilege.

18 ***Shankman v Axelrod,*** **535 NE2d 1323, 538 NYS2d 783 (1989)** (office records of an orthopedist could not be seized via an ex parte warrant issued by a state's department of health investigating staff. A medical consultant rendered an opinion that the doctor was negligent. The health department wrote the orthopedist requesting six additional patient charts and the doctor refused "because of pending litigation." The health department obtained a warrant and seized eight records. The high court affirmed an order to suppress use of the material seized and ordered the return of the records to the orthopedist. It held that the investigative agency had no implied power to obtain an inspection warrant for the sole purpose of seizing the physician's records).

19 ***Tams v Kolz,* 530 A2d 1217 (DC 1987)** (surgeon's failure to read the impression section of a radiology report was not the cause of a patient's injuries due to a retained surgical sponge. The patient went to surgery for removal of a cancerous tumor located between her bladder and vaginal wall. More than 400 items were used in the operation, including instruments, sutures, sponges, and lab pads. Four days following the operation, x-rays were taken of the patient's abdomen and a copy was forwarded to the surgeon. One month after discharge from the hospital, x-rays were again taken because of the patient's complaints of abdominal pain, and these showed a foreign object. At a second operation, the surgeon found a laparotomy pad that had adhered to an intestinal membrane. The damaged segment of the intestine was removed when the pad was extracted. The patient sued for malpractice, alleging negligence in failing to detect the pad before closing the first operation and failing to read the x-ray report which indicated the presence of a foreign object. At trial, the physician who testified for the patient indicated that the physician had a duty to read the x-ray report. He also indicated that it was the radiologist's duty to make it known to the surgeon that there was a foreign body present. He pointed out that it should have been noted under "Impression" on the x-ray report, although it had not been. The court entered a jury verdict for the surgeon. On appeal, the court pointed out that the patient's expert had effectively limited the surgeon's duty in studying the x-ray reading to the "Impression" section. Therefore, even if the surgeon had read that section, he would have remained unaware that the x-ray had disclosed the possible foreign object. Therefore, his failure to read the impression was not the cause of the patient's intestinal damage).

20 ***Gates v Jensen,* 92 Wash 2d 246, 595 P2d 919 (1979)** (liability was established on the basis of a doctor's failure to perform a spinal tap which the court noted was a simple, inexpensive, conclusive, and relatively risk-free procedure to determine the presence of a serious disease. The court noted that the test need only be used when other diagnostic procedures are inconclusive for some reason, or when the red flag of warning has been raised by some abnormality suggesting the risk of serious disease. When a patient's condition indicates a necessity for further examination, reasonable prudence requires the use of an alternative test; failure to do so is negligent practice of medicine).

21 ***Hughes v St Paul Fire & Marine Insurance Co,* 401 So 2d 448 (La Ct App 1981)** (the defendant was treating an obese 60-year-old patient suffering from long-standing chronic asthma. The patient was admitted to the hospital following an acute asthmatic attack, which was treated with antibiotics and then appropriate medication; following one week of mixed results, the patient had elevated carbon dioxide blood levels which threatened the patient's life. In spite of the use of oxygen, the patient suddenly became unresponsive and went into base and failed. The defendant performed a tracheotomy which failed, and the patient died. The plaintiff maintained that the defendant was negligent and failed to act in the face of the blood gas test showing the ominous rise in the level of carbon dioxide. The defendant main-

tained, however, that he first saw critical blood gas results after the final attempts were made to resuscitate the patient. The court concluded that, regardless of the exact time the blood gas results were first seen by the defendant, the defendant could rely on his clinical impression that the patient's condition was declined but not critical. Thus, the defendant was found not to be personally negligent).

Comment: In *Hughes,* the patient experienced progressive airway compromise. It is not clear what could constitute a "reasonable basis" for a physician to rely on a "clinical impression" in the face of contrary findings of laboratory tests. Blood gas studies demonstrated that the patient was "critical." The fact that the family physician was voluntarily ignorant of these critical values would not be negated by the physician's reliance on his "clinical impression." The laboratory tests, having been performed and available, should have been known to the attending physician. The failure to know was the physician's negligence.

22 ***Public Health Trust v Valcin,*** **507 So 2d 596 (Fla 1987)** (patient had undergone surgery that nearly caused her death. The patient and her husband brought an action against the hospital where the surgery was performed, alleging breach of the alleged warranty of effectiveness of the operation, lack of informed consent, and negligent surgery. The trial court held for the hospital on all claims. The court of appeals reversed the summary judgment in part; the supreme court approved part and quashed part of the appellate opinion. The supreme court held (1) that there was a substantial issue of material fact as to whether the plaintiff was adequately advised of the risk of surgery, (2) that there is a rebuttable, as opposed to a conclusive, presumption of negligence applicable when essential medical records are unavailable due to the adverse party's negligence, provided the plaintiff first establishes to the satisfaction of the court that the absence of the records hinders his or her ability to establish a prima facie case, and (3) that the hospital could properly be held liable for the significant omission committed by employee doctors within the scope of their employment).

23 ***Sweasy v King's Daughter Memorial Hospital,*** **771 SW2d 812 (Ky 1989)** (this action involved questions of infection allegedly occurring in the operating room at a hospital where the physician who was sued had privileges. The plaintiff sought to obtain various hospital records, incident reports, and peer review records regarding the defendant physician. The hospital refused, saying they were privileged under Kentucky law, which immunizes peer review reports and bars them from discovery. The trial court ordered the hospital to release the records, ruling that the privilege statute applied only to actions brought by physicians who apply for privileges. An appellate court reversed, and the plaintiff appealed. The state supreme court reinstated the trial court's order, showing that the privilege statute was part of a legislative act governing licensing and regulations of health care facilities and unrelated to medical malpractice actions. The court concluded that either the peer review privilege was limited to physician suits against peer review entities, or it violated a provision of the state constitution which prohibits laws covering more than one subject).

24 ***Rogers v Horvath,* 65 Mich App 644, 237 NW2d 595 (1975)** (physician was entitled to summary judgment in an employee's malpractice suit against him alleging she lost her workers' compensation benefits as a result of his report indicating that there was nothing wrong with her. The court stated that the term "malpractice" denotes a breach of duty owed by one in rendering professional services to a person who has contracted for such services. In physician malpractice cases, the duty owed by the physician arises from the physician-patient relationship. The court pointed out that the physician was employed by the employer).

25 ***Vassiliades v Garfinkel's Brooks Bros,* 492 A2d 580 (DC 1985)** (surgeon was liable not for poor surgery, but for invasion of privacy in showing before-and-after pictures in an advertisement for his surgical services. The pictures were published without the patient's consent. The two issues on which the case went against the surgeon were invasion of privacy and breach of privilege in the physician-patient relationship).

26 ***Chenoweth v Kemp,* 396 So 2d 1122 (Fla 1981)** (a fully-qualified medical specialist can testify as an expert as to the general presurgical behavior of another surgeon. A doctor did a physical examination before surgery consisting of listening to the patient's heart and lungs, and cleared her for surgery. The plaintiff complained of right arm pain and held her arm as it were in a sling. The doctor saw the patient the next day when she again complained of right arm pain. There was a question of whether the doctor examined the arm; he did not auscultate the neck looking for carotid artery bruit, admitting he never carried a stethoscope. The patient suffered a severe stroke. At trial, the defendant doctor was faulted by the expert for not obtaining a written consultation from a competent physician stating the risk or safety of the patient for surgery. The defendant doctor's choice was not competent, in that a complete neurological examination was not performed. One argument was that the plaintiff's expert did not "possess sufficient training, experience or knowledge to testify about defendant as the physician he chose to give presurgical physical examination").

27 ***Ravi v Williams,* 536 So 2d 1374 (Ala 1988)** (medical expert deposition was admissible even though the expert had not examined the patient and had not testified to hypothetical questions; opinions were properly based on a review of the medical records which were in evidence).

28 ***Hart v Browne,* 163 Cal Rptr 356 (Ct App 1980)** (consulting orthopedist was negligent for misrepresenting or inaccurately representing whether or not malpractice was indicated in another orthopedist's records, which he reviewed. A patient suffered partial paralysis after an automobile accident in 1962. After two operations on her back, she began seeing an orthopedic surgeon. On March 23, 1968, he performed five operations on her right leg and four operations on her left leg, necessitating hospitalization 11 times. Shortly after she began to recover, another orthopedic specialist recommended amputation surgery of her right leg in February 1969. After the amputation, she consulted a law firm about possible malpractice action against the orthopedist who performed the nine surgeries. The firm con-

ducted a detailed investigation, obtaining records of the orthopedist, hospitalization, and treatments. The firm contacted three local orthopedists who declined to be involved. An orthopedic surgeon willing to act as a consultant was finally located. After he reviewed all of the records, he advised the attorney that the orthopedist had conducted himself within the standard of care. The attorneys then advised the patient that she did not have a malpractice cause of action; no further action was taken. By February 1970, the statute of limitation had expired against the operating physician. Late in the summer of 1971, the attorneys learned that another attorney had a number of malpractice suits pending against the initial orthopedic surgeon. The attorney then filed a suit against the initial orthopedist; the suit was dismissed as barred by the statute of limitation. The patient then filed a suit against the consulting orthopedist. At the trial, three medical experts testified that the physician's care and treatment of the patient was negligent, and was the cause of amputation of her leg. The operating physician testified that his surgical privileges were revoked on June 4, 1970, and that his use of drugs in the years 1965 to 1968 may have affected his judgment. He also admitted he had performed several surgeries below the standard of care. The trial court granted a nonsuit on the claim of fraud and entered judgment on a jury verdict favoring the consulting physician. Reversing the decision, the appellate court found that the case should have been submitted to a jury. The evidence of malpractice on the part of the treating physician was sufficient to find that the consulting orthopedist had knowledge of the falsity of his representation. Therefore, the consulting physician was eventually found negligent).

29 ***Hiser v Randolph,*** **126 Ariz App 608, 617 P2d 774 (1980)** (physician conducted a pre-employment physical examination and certified the patient as fit to drive a truck under ICC rules. The driver had a severe vision problem, as well as other physical problems. Whether the physician's physical examination practice was below the standard of care and therefore proximately related to the accident caused by the inadequately examined truck driver was a question of fact for the jury).

Comment: In principle, an inadequate or false or misrepresented physical examination is negligent practice by a physician, and the reasonably foreseeable consequences of that negligence were traced to the physician in *Hiser.*

30 ***Sherrod v United States Fidelity Guaranty Co,*** **518 So 2d 640 (Miss 1987)** (orthopedic surgeon did not wrongfully and intentionally tell an insurance company that a patient was sufficiently recovered from a knee injury to return to work. The question facing the court was whether the surgeon should be held liable for his opinion, which cost the worker his disability benefits when another physician believed the man was still incapacitated. The orthopedic surgeon told the patient that despite a 5 per cent functional disability, he was well enough to return to work. At the same time, the man consulted a second physician who advised him that he needed a longer period to recover and that he continued to be temporarily totally disabled. The insurance company, by this time, had discontinued his benefits. The patient could not find other work. The patient sued the orthopedist, alleging that the orthopedist's action wrongly deprived him of compensation benefits. The orthopedic surgeon denied that his report to the insurance company had been any part of "any action of plan to inflict any mental, emotional, or any other distress" on the worker. Moreover, he insisted he had attempted in utmost good faith to fulfill and comply with any appropriate standard of care. The court held that a discrepancy of professional opinions is "no proof" that the orthopedic surgeon had formed his opinion maliciously).

Comment: It is well known that honest doctors have honest differences of opinion, based on their personal backgrounds, training, experience, and beliefs.

31 ***Aguiar v JR Simplot Co,*** **742 P2d 709 (Or Ct App 1987)** (workers' compensation case on appeal by the patient. The orthopedist who saw the patient discounted the sinus tarsae syndrome. One orthopedist gave a poor opinion. His testimony was found by the court to have been influenced by "personal sociological opinion." In the end, four different orthopedists reported that sinus tarsae surgery was rarely successful, whereas the original treating doctor reported that he had considerable success with the surgery and continued to recommend it. The court found personal bias in at least one of the physician's opinions. Another orthopedist based his opinion, in part, on his belief that the worker, who was an illegal alien, sought to continue medical treatment as a way to stay in the United States, and that he "could not afford to get completely well." The appellate court said that the case should be heard on its medical merits only, and offered the patient the option to have the surgery if he wished).

Comment: It is well known that orthopedic surgeons and other examining physicians frequently fall into one of two groups—one that tends to favor the plaintiff for the most part, and one that tends to favor the defendant for the most part. Often, examining physicians are involuntarily segregated into a class by limited referrals by the defense or plaintiff bar. There is no place for personal bias or advocacy in evaluating patients for diagnosis, treatment, and impairment. Given a chance, a great majority of examining physicians in this country render an unbiased opinion based on the facts as they see them. It cannot be denied, however, that examining physicians tend to slant their reports to favor the third party which is paying the physician's bill and which represents a source of continuing referrals.

32 ***Spaulding v Hussain,*** **551 A2d 1022 (NJ Super Ct App 1988)** (a physician has a duty to give reasonably required litigation assistance to his patient. This court upheld a suit filed by a patient against a physician who failed to appear on the patient's behalf at a personal injury trial. The patient was injured on the job. His attorney, in evaluating the case, felt that the appearance of the plaintiff's physician was essential to a favorable outcome of his case. The attorney met with the physician and alleged that the physician agreed to appear at trial. However, even after the attorney had obtained several continuances to accommodate the physician and both sides had presented their cases at trial, the physician did not appear in court. The attorney decided to accept what he considered to be an inadequate settlement and advised his client to file an action against the physician, and the plaintiff did. The suit alleged breach of contract, the physician having agreed to testify, and violation of a tort duty to testify at a plaintiff's trial. The physician pled medical emergency and further pled that the attorney should have asked for another continuance rather than accepting an inadequate settlement. An expert testified that the plaintiff's attorney exercised sound professional judgment in accepting the settlement offer. The jury found, using a special interrogatory, that (1) the company employing the plaintiff was liable for 65 per cent of damages from the on-the-job injury while the plaintiff was responsible for 35 per cent, (2) that the plaintiff had established a right to recover damages from the physician under a contract theory of promissory estoppel, and (3) that the plaintiff was entitled to recover from the physician under negligence principles, but that the recovery should be reduced by 45 per cent to reflect the negligence of the plaintiff's attorney in accepting an inadequate settlement. The court rendered a judgment notwithstanding the verdict on the issue of the attorney's comparative negligence, ruling that the physician was liable for 100 per cent of the damage the plaintiff sustained in accepting inadequate settlement. The physician appealed. The appellate court affirmed the trial court verdict, observing that prior New Jersey decisions had recognized, under contract principles, the enforceability of a treating physician's affirmative undertaking to testify. The court then ruled that a physician's tort duty to treat a patient in accordance with proper professional standards includes a duty to assist the patient's litigation. Noting that personal injury claimants cannot pursue their claims without the testimony of physicians, the court reasoned that a treating physician is not at liberty to refuse a patient's request for assistance in litigating a claim involving injuries which the physician treated. Although this duty may not require the doctor to testify in court, the evidence in this case supported the finding of liability, since the plaintiff had relied, to his detriment, on the physician's agreement to render specific litigation assistance.

Comment: Medical Liability Reporter 11;106, May 1989 pointed out that a number of courts have held that a physician has a duty to refrain from informally revealing information about his patient to the patient's legal adversaries. In *Spaulding,* the appellate court's discussion of the physician's duty to provide litigation assistance is "dicta," inasmuch as the trial court's instructions were not objected to by the defendant.

Appendix 12-2
Forms

Form 1
Back Pain Patient History Form

Name ______________________________ Age ______
Occupation ______________________________ Date ______

1. What date (roughly) did your present pain start? ____________

2. Mechanism of pain onset:

a.	Suddenly	____	g.	Injured at work	____
b.	Gradually	____	h.	Auto accident	____
c.	Lifting	____	i.	Pulling	____
d.	Twisting	____	j.	Fall	____
e.	Bending	____	k.	Hit in back	____
f.	Fall	____	l.	Sports	____

3. What activities make the pain worse?

a.	During exercise	____	f.	Bending forward	____
b.	After exercise	____	g.	Bending backward	____
c.	Sitting	____	h.	Coughing	____
d.	Standing	____	i.	Sneezing	____
e.	Walking	____			

4. What reduces your pain?

a.	Lying down	____	g.	Pain pills	____
b.	Sitting	____	h.	Muscle relaxants	____
c.	Standing	____	i.	Aspirin	____
d.	Walking	____	j.	Other ____________	
e.	Manipulation	____	k.	Nothing	____
f.	Physical therapy	____			

5. How long have you had back pain?

   ______ years ______ months ______ weeks

   How long have you had leg pain?

   ______ years ______ months ______ weeks

6. Have you had diagnostic studies other than x-rays?

   ______ yes ______ no

   a. Have you had a CAT scan? ____ yes ____ no ______ date
   b. Have you had a myelogram? ____ yes ____ no ______ date
   c. Have you had an EMG? ____ yes __ no ______ date
   d. Have you had a discogram? ____ yes ____ no ______ date

7. Have you been in the hospital for your back problem?

   ______ yes ______ no

   Number of times ______ Dates ____________________

8. Have you had neck or back surgery? _______ yes _______ no
Number of times _______ Dates ______________________________

9. Have you been in the hospital with other medical problems? _______ yes _______ no
Number of times _______ Describe reasons ____________________
____

10. Please list current medications: ___________________________
____
____

11. Do you take antacids? _______ yes _______ no

12. General medical problems:
    a. Stomach problems, ulcer, etc. ____
    b. Diabetes ____
    c. Arthritis ____
    d. Gout ____
    e. Sexual difficulties ____
    f. Bowel or bladder ____
    g. Cancer ____
    h. Heart ____
    i. Epilepsy ____
    j. Other ________________
    k. Loss of weight ____

13. Allergies? _______ yes _______ no Please list: ____________
____

14. Do you smoke? _______ yes _______ no How much? _______

15. Do you drink alcoholic beverages? _______ yes _______ no
How much? ____
____

16. What other types of doctors have you seen for this condition?
____

17. Do you want a report sent to your attorney?
_______ yes _______ no

18. Do you have additional information that might be helpful to understanding your problem? ______________________________
____

19. Please fill in last year of school: ________________________

20. To be sure paperwork is completed correctly, please check what applies to you:
Is this workers' compensation? _______ yes _______ no
Receiving disability income? _______ yes _______ no
Legal proceeding pending? _______ yes _______ no
Should report be sent to referring physician or family doctor?
_______ yes _______ no
Should report be sent to any other party? _______ yes _______ no

Form 2
Auto Accident Questionnaire
Composite Form

PERSONAL INFORMATION

Name ______________________ Date of Birth __________ Age ______
Social Security # __________ Address ______________________
City ______________________ State ______ Zip ______
Home Phone __________ Who referred you to our office? ______________
Height ______ Weight ______ White ☐ Negro ☐ Hispanic ☐ Asian ☐
Other ☐ Female ☐ Male ☐
Marital Status: Married ☐ Single ☐ Divorced ☐ Widowed ☐
Spouse's first name: __________
Occupation ______________________ Your employer ______________
Business address ______________________________
City ______________________ State ______ Zip ______
Attorney ______________________________
Address: ______________________ City __________ State ______
Phone __________

ACCIDENT INFORMATION

Date of Accident __________ Time ______ PM ☐ AM ☐
Reported to: Police dept ☐ Auto insurance co ☐
Please describe the accident: ______________________________
____
____
____
____

Were you: Driver ☐ Passenger ☐ In front seat ☐ In back seat ☐ Using seat belt ☐ On a motorcycle ☐
Insured person of vehicle in which you were riding: ______________
Driver of car: ______________________
Insurance company name: ______________________
Address ______________ Claims Adjuster __________ Policy # __________
Claim # __________ Name of insured person of other vehicle __________
Name of insurance company ______________________
Insurance company address ______________________
City ______________________ State __________ Phone __________
Claims Adjuster ______________ Policy # __________ Claim # __________
Driver of other vehicle ______________________
Were you on the job at time of accident: Yes ☐ No ☐

MEDICAL INFORMATION

What areas of your body were injured? ______________________
____

Did symptoms begin: Immediately ☐ Late same day ☐ Next day ☐ Next week ☐ Other ☐
Did you feel: Confusion ☐ Disorientation ☐ Memory loss ☐ Dizzy ☐ Blurred vision ☐
Were you unconscious? Yes ☐ No ☐ If so, for how long? ______
Have you been conscious since? ☐
Were you taken to hospital? ☐ Doctor's office? ☐ Emergency room? ☐ Home? ☐ Work? ☐
Were you hospitalized? Yes ☐ No ☐ If yes, at what hospital? ______
Were you examined? Yes ☐ No ☐ Doctor's name ______________
Medications? Yes ☐ No ☐

Name of medications? ______________________________
Did you have x-rays? ☐ Yes ☐ No ☐ What areas of your body? ______
____
What was the diagnosis? ______________________________
What treatment was given? ______________________________
Were you referred to this office? Yes ☐ No ☐ By whom? ________

AFTER ACCIDENT INFORMATION

What other doctors have you consulted?

Name	X-rays	Date	Diagnosis/Recommendations	Notes

Have you had the following examinations and/or tests?
Neurological ☐ Orthopedics ☐ CAT scan ☐ Myelogram ☐
Thermography ☐ Vascular Study ☐ EMG ☐
EEG ☐ EKG ☐ Arteriogram ☐ Other ☐

Have you had any of the following treatments?
Hot packs ☐ Cold packs ☐ Whirlpool ☐ Diathermy ☐
Orthotics ☐ Back Brace ☐ Neck Collar ☐

EFFECTS OF THE ACCIDENT

Lifting: Light ☐ Moderate ☐ Heavy ☐
Repetitive ☐ None ☐
Bending: Occasional ☐ Frequent ☐ None ☐
Twisting: Occasional ☐ Frequent ☐ None ☐
Standing: Short periods ☐ Prolonged periods ☐ Frequent ☐
None ☐
Walking: Short distances ☐ Excessive ☐ None ☐
Sitting: Short periods ☐ Excessive ☐ None ☐
Riding: Short periods ☐ Prolonged ☐ None ☐
Driving: Short periods ☐ Prolonged ☐ None ☐
Pushing: Short periods ☐ Prolonged ☐ None ☐
Pulling: Short periods ☐ Prolonged ☐ None ☐
Sleeping: Occasional ☐ Frequent ☐ Every night ☐
Never ☐
Concentrating: Short periods ☐ Prolonged periods ☐ None ☐
Weakness: Muscles ☐ Arms ☐ Legs ☐ General ☐
Occasional ☐ Frequent ☐
Balance: Occasional ☐ Frequent ☐ Constant ☐
Rising to walk after sitting: ☐ Occasional ☐ Frequent ☐ Never ☐
Reaching: Overhead ☐ Behind ☐ Ahead ☐
Lying on: Back ☐ Stomach ☐ Side ☐
Using fingers for fine manipulation: Writing ☐ Using buttons ☐ Other ☐
Using feet for levers: Brake ☐ Clutch ☐
Coughing Sneezing ☐ Straining at stool ☐
Judging distances: Occasional ☐ Frequent ☐ Unable ☐
Looking over your shoulder: Right ☐ Left ☐
Limbs: Falling asleep ☐ Numbness ☐ Tingling ☐
Weather: Wet ☐ Cold ☐
Squatting: Occasional ☐ Frequent ☐ Unable ☐
Kneeling: Occasional ☐ Frequent ☐ Unable ☐
Squeezing: Occasional ☐ Frequent ☐ Unable ☐
Pinching: Occasional ☐ Frequent ☐ Unable ☐
Pinching: Occasional ☐ Frequent ☐ Unable ☐

Climbing: Stairs ☐ Ramps ☐ Ladder ☐
Occasional ☐ Frequent ☐ Unable ☐
Feeling Tired: Occasional ☐ Frequent ☐ Constant ☐
Loss of sensation: Yes ☐ No ☐ Where? ________________
Increased: Anxiety ☐ Depression ☐ Irritability ☐ Forgetfulness ☐
Confusion ☐
Did you miss work? Yes ☐ No ☐ Have you returned to work? Yes ☐
No ☐ If so, what date? ________________
What duties at work, if any, aggravate your condition? ________________

____

What activities at home (or hobbies/sports) have you been unable to do? ________

____

What daily activities (home, hobbies, sports) aggravate your condition? ________

____

Please mark your areas of pain on the figures and list your current symptoms.

____
____
____
____
____
____
____
____
____
____
____
____
____
____
____

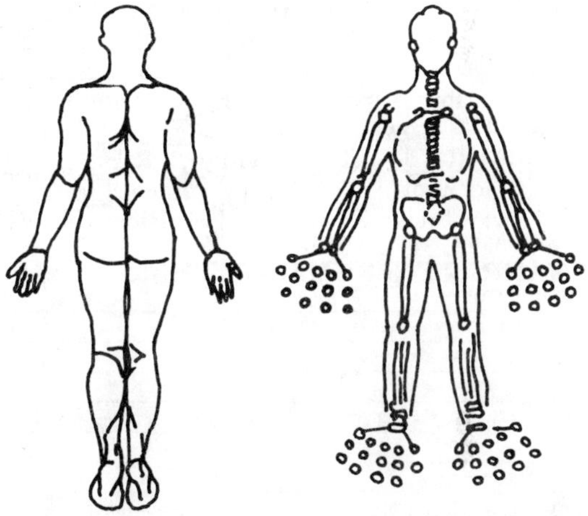

PAST HISTORY

Have you had previous symptoms or injury to the involved area? Yes ☐ No ☐

If so, describe injury and symptoms: ________________

____

When and how did injury/illness occur? ________________

____

What symptoms were you having in the involved area immediately before the present accident? ________________

____

Were you receiving treatment for symptoms of the involved area immediately before the present accident? Yes ☐ No ☐

Doctor's name: ______________________ Address ______________
Doctor's name: ______________________ Address ______________
What treatment, if any, has been given? ______________________
____
What was the diagnosis? ______________________________
Were x-rays taken? Yes ☐ No ☐ What areas? ______________
Has the present accident aggravated this previous condition? Yes ☐ No ☐

Time recorded: ________________
Doctor ______________________

PATIENT REPORT
Name ________________ Age ___ Sex ___ Next of Kin ________
Address ______ City ________ State _____ Zip _____ Phone _____
Situation and/or location taken from ______________________
Chief complaint: ______________________________

VITAL SIGNS
Time _____ Blood
Pressure _____ Pulse _____ Respirations _____ L.O.C. _____
Skin _____ EKG _____ Motor Function _____ Pupils _____

MEDICATIONS
Oxygen _____ I.V. rate _____ fluid _____ I.V. site _____ Medic Alert
Tag: _____ Current Meds ______________________
Allergies: ______________________________
Trauma found in: R ☐ L ☐ Shoulder; R ☐ L ☐ Upper Arm; R ☐ L ☐ Lower Arm; R ☐ L ☐ Hand; R ☐ L ☐ Hand; R ☐ L ☐ Hip; R ☐ L ☐ Thigh; R ☐ L ☐ Lower Leg; R ☐ L ☐ Ankle/Foot; ☐ Skull; ☐ Face; ☐ Neck; ☐ Upper Back; ☐ Mid Back; ☐ Lower Back; ☐ Chest; ☐ Ribs; ☐ Abdomen; ☐ Pelvis ☐

NARRATIVE SUMMARY (History, Assessment, Impression, Action)
____
____
____
____
____
____
____

Orders given by ______________________
Technician ______________________

HEALTH INFORMATION
What is your major complaint? ______________________
Other complaints: ______________________________
How long have you had this condition? _____ Have you had this or similar conditions in the past? ______________________
What activities aggravate your condition? ______________________
____
Is this condition getting progressively worse? Yes ☐ No ☐ Constant ☐ Comes and goes ☐
Is this condition interfering with: work ☐ sleep ☐ daily routine ☐ other ☐
How long has it been since you really felt good? ______________
Other doctors who treated this condition: ______________________

Drugs you now take: Nerve pills ☐ Pain killers ☐ Muscle relaxers ☐ "Pep" pills ☐ Tranquilizers ☐ Insulin ☐ Birth control pills ☐ Others ☐
How old is your mattress? _____ Is it comfortable? ☐ Uncomfortable? ☐
Are you wearing: heel lifts ☐ sole lifts ☐ inner soles ☐ arch supports ☐
Have you been in an auto accident: Past year ☐ Past 5 years ☐ Over 5 years ☐ Never ☐
If yes, describe: ____

____
Have you had any other personal injury or accident? Past year ☐ Past 5 years ☐ Over 5 years ☐ None ☐
Date of last physical examination ______________________

Family Health Information: (Many health problems are the result of hereditary spinal weaknesses; thus, information about your family members will give us a better picture of your total health picture).

Name Relation Past and Present Health Problems

____

____

____

____

X-ray Confirmation: This is to confirm that I have been advised by the doctor that x-rays can be hazardous to an unborn child. At this time, to the best of my knowledge, I am not pregnant, and I consent to spinographic pictures.

Date: ______________________ Signed: ______________________

Release of X-rays: I, __________, have requested the release of x-rays of __________ which are a part of patient records. I hereby acknowledge receipt of these x-ray films. I release and forever discharge the doctor from any and all responsibility or liability of any kind, nature or character whatsoever arising from said treatment.

Date: ______________________ Signed: ______________________
Witness: ______________________

Consent to Treat Minor Child: I hereby authorize the doctor to administer chiropractic as deemed necessary to my ______________________ (daughter, son).

Name: ______________________ Date: ______________________
Signed: ______________________

Form 3
Range of Joint Motion Evaluation Chart

Name ________________________

A/N ________________________

For each affected joint, please indicate the existing limitation of motion by drawing a line(s) on the figures below, showing the maximum possible range of motion or by notating the chart in degrees. Provide a complete description of all affected joints in your narrative summary. If range of motion was normal for all joints, please comment on that in your narrative summary. If joints which do not appear on this chart are affected, please indicate the degree of limited motion in your narrative.

BACK	EXTENSION	FLEXION
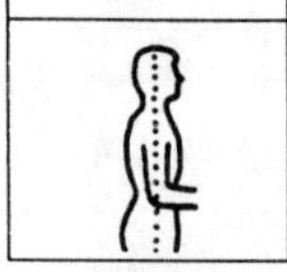	____°	____°

LATERAL (flexion)	LEFT	RIGHT
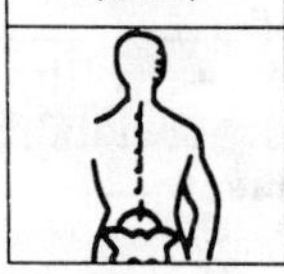	____°	____°

NECK	EXTENSION	FLEXION
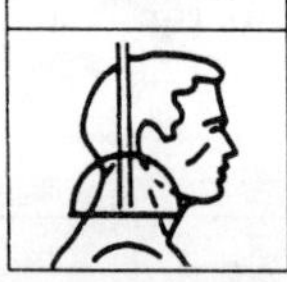	____°	____°

SHOULDER Abduction	LEFT		RIGHT	
	IN PRONATION	IN SUPINATION	IN PRONATION	IN SUPINATION
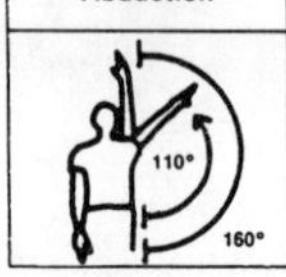	____°	____°	____°	____°

SHOULDER	LEFT		RIGHT	
	EXTENSION	FLEXION	EXTENSION	FLEXION
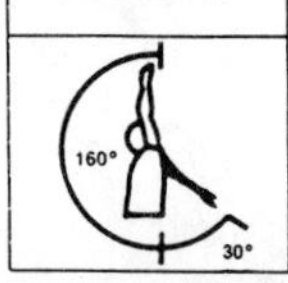	____°	____°	____°	____°

HIP	LEFT	RIGHT
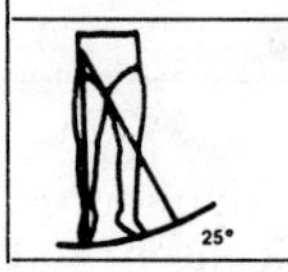	____°	____°

HIP FLEXION	LEFT		RIGHT	
	KNEE FLEXED	KNEE EXTENDED	KNEE FLEXED	KNEE EXTENDED
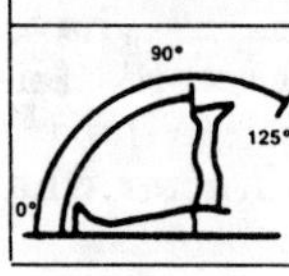	____°	____°	____°	____°

HIP	LEFT	RIGHT
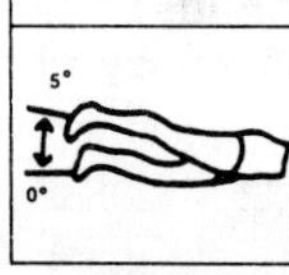	____°	____°

KNEE (flexion)	LEFT	RIGHT
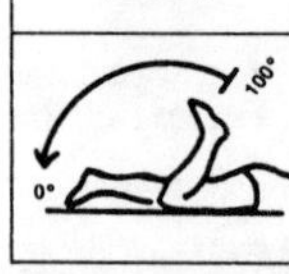	____°	____°

ANKLE	LEFT		RIGHT	
	INVERSION 35°	EVERSION 25°	INVERSION 35°	EVERSION 25°
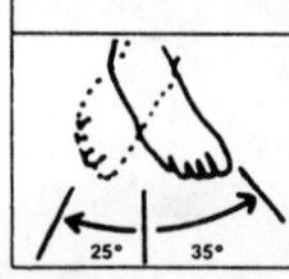	____°	____°	____°	____°

HIP	LEFT	RIGHT
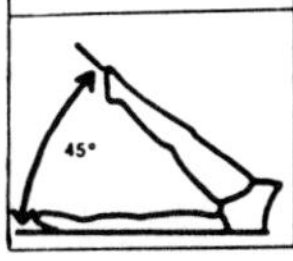	____ °	____ °

ANKLE FLEXION	LEFT		RIGHT	
	PLANTAR 40°	DORSAL 10°	PLANTAR 40°	DORSAL 10°
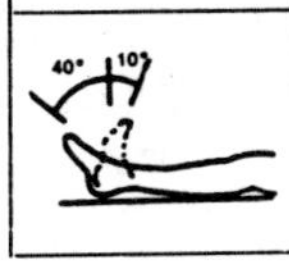	____ °	____ °	____ °	____ °

ELBOW	LEFT		RIGHT	
	FLEXION	EXTENSION	FLEXION	EXTENSION
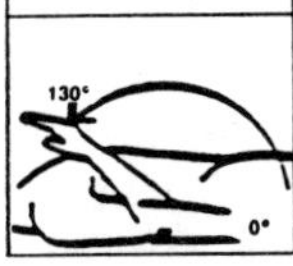	____ °	____ °	____ °	____ °

WRIST HINGE	LEFT		RIGHT	
	PALMAR 80°	DORSAL 70°	PALMAR 80°	DORSAL 70°
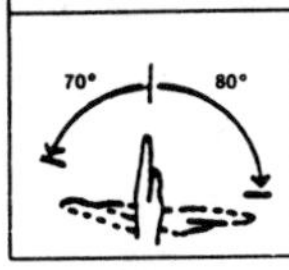	____ °	____ °	____ °	____ °

WRIST (rotation)	LEFT		RIGHT	
	PRONATION 90°	SUPINATION 90°	PRONATION 90°	SUPINATION 90°
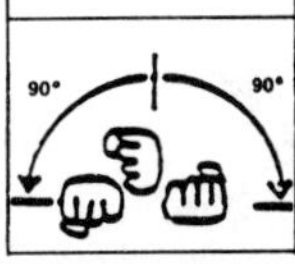	____ °	____ °	____ °	____ °

THUMB (proximal phalange)	LEFT	RIGHT
	FLEXION 70°	FLEXION 70°
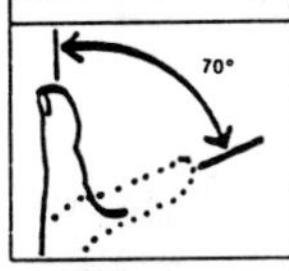	____ °	____ °

WRIST (radial, ulnar)	LEFT		RIGHT	
	RADIAL 10°	ULNAR 60°	RADIAL 10°	ULNAR 60°
	____ °	____ °	____ °	____ °

THUMB (distal phalange)	LEFT	RIGHT
	FLEXION 90°	FLEXION 90°
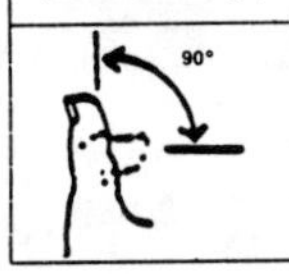	____ °	____ °

Date of Examination ____________ ____________________

(Examining Physician's Signature)

Date of Report ____________

Form 4
History

Chief Complaint:

Present Illness:

Allergies:

Past History:

Pertinent Family and Social History:

Review of Systems:

Form 5
Physical Examination

Vital Signs: BP: **Pulse:** **Respirations:** Temp:

General Appearance:

Skin:

HEENT:

Neck:

Chest:

Breasts:

Abdomen:

Genitalia:

Back:

Extremities:

Neurological:

Admitting Impression: 1)
2)

Plan of Treatment:

Form 6
Discharge Summary

Brief History:

Essential Physical Examination:

Pertinent Laboratory and Radiology Findings:

Consultation:

Hospital Course with Complications, If Any:

Condition, Treatment and Disposition on Discharge:

Principal Diagnosis: 1)
Secondary Diagnoses: 2)
3)

Principal Procedure: 1)
Secondary Procedures: 2)
3)

Form 7
Standards for Adequate Chart Documentation

The medical record must contain information to justify admission and continued hospitalization, support the diagnosis, and describe the patient's progress and response to medications and services.

All medical records must document the following as appropriate:

1. Evidence of a physical examination, including a health history, performed no more than 7 days prior to admission or within 48 hours after
2. Admitting diagnosis
3. Results of all consultative evaluations of the patient and appropriate findings by clinical and other staff involved in the care of the patient
4. Documentation of complications, hospital-acquired infections, and unfavorable reactions to drugs and anesthesia
5. Properly executed informed consent forms for procedures and treatments specified by the medical staff, or under federal or state law, if applicable, requiring written patient consent
6. All practitioner's orders, nursing notes, reports of treatment, medication records, radiology and laboratory reports, and vital signs and other information necessary to monitor the patient's condition
7. Discharge summary with outcome of hospitalization, disposition of care, and provisions for follow-up care
8. Final diagnosis with completion of the medical record within 30 days following discharge

Form 8
Strengthening the Office Medical Record Through Self-Assessment

The following questionnaire is designed to help you evaluate your charting strengths and weaknesses by conducting a brief self-assessment of your office medical records. Answer the questions based on your impressions of your current office medical recordkeeping practices. Try to be objective, and assign a plus (+) or minus (−) in the appropriate column. Then total your results.

PATIENT WORKUP	+	−
Do you chart the reason for the patient's visit, including all complaints?		
Do you chart patient's history, including past medical treatments, current medications, drug allergies, family history, etc?		
Do your patients fill out a questionnaire on their current complaints and previous history?		
If yes, do you document your review and follow-up on the questionnaire?		
Also, do you document your investigation of question marks and blank spaces left on the questionnaire?		
Do you chart all your physical findings?		
Do you chart negative findings?		
Do you diagram size and location of suspicious lumps and lesions?		
If yes, do your patients sign or initial these diagrams?		

DIAGNOSIS	+	−
Do you chart the data used to support your diagnostic impressions?		
Do you review and initial all path, lab and X-ray reports?		
Do you review available previous medical reports and then chart appropriate data?		
Do you chart discussions with other providers that lead to the diagnosis?		

TREATMENT	+	−
Do you outline a treatment plan that is supported by the findings in the workup and diagnosis?		
Do you chart obtaining the patient's informed consent?		

When appropriate, do you chart the patient's informed refusal?

Do you chart all instructions to the patient, including follow-up requirements?

FOLLOW-UP

+	−

Do you chart who is responsible for follow-up—patient or physician?

Do you chart recommendations for referral to outside care or follow-up?

Do you chart discussions with other providers about patient care?

Do you chart consideration of previous findings in follow-up?

Do you chart unchanged abnormal findings?

Do you chart review of subsequent lab/X-ray reports?

Do you chart patient compliance or non-compliance with recommendations?

OFFICE CHARTING PROCEDURES

+	−

Are missed/cancelled appointments (reason included, if known) noted on the chart?

Are all telephone conversations (physician and staff) regarding patient care noted on the chart?

Are all drug allergies noted prominently on the chart?

Are all lab/X-ray reports seen and initialled by the physician before placement in the chart?

Are signed, dated authorizations obtained and placed in the chart before copies of the chart are released?

Is it noted on the chart where the copy is being sent?

Is physician authorization required before records can be released?

Does your office follow a stated procedure for termination of care?

CHARTING HABITS

+	−

Are chart notes readable?

Are all chart entries signed and dated?

Are all no-shows/cancellations noted in the chart?

Are corrections and additions to the chart entered chronologically and dated and signed?

In your absence, could a colleague using information from the medical chart provide your patients with immediate and appropriate care?

TOTAL

To test your impressions, select a few office records which contain entries made in the last six months. Review them carefully. Answer each of the questions again assigning a plus (+) or a minus (−) where applicable and total your results.

When you are done, compare your "impressions" with "reality" and see where your office medical recordkeeping strengths and weaknesses lie. In today's legal climate, a deficiency involving any of the listed items could expose you to liability.

13

Hospitals

§13.01 Generally

The orthopedist needs to realize that virtually any negligence a hospital may be accused of may well involve the orthopedic patient, and thus, either directly or vicariously, involves the orthopedist. The physician has a duty to know the hospital, its personnel, and its strength and weaknesses. Based on this knowledge, the orthopedist has to decide whether to "risk" the hospital care of a patient. If negligent care or facilities are known to the orthopedist, he or she has a duty to inform and correct those problems as may relate to a patient. Failure to attempt correction, or ignoring a problem that leads to injury of a patient, is negligent behavior by the physician.

A government study of closed claims has shown that about 80 per cent of malpractice claims closed in 1984 involved injury occurring in a hospital. These data suggested the desirability of expanding hospital-based risk management programs.[1]

Hospitals are required to supervise physicians not only generally by limiting their privileges, but also directly and specifically through the authority of the medical staff. This is not an extension of medical malpractice liability, but a requirement to the judicial conservative who wants the law to be fair and efficient in providing guidelines to society and rules that will discourage the sort of conduct that leads to more litigation.

Determination of whether a particular physician is an employee or an independent contractor is the first consideration in defending the hospital-related physician negligence claim. When the physician in question does not clearly fit either category, the courts tend to ask "Whose patient was he?" This inquiry is the first step in determining whether the doctor was the ostensible agent of the hospital. There is no legal reason to insulate the hospital from liability for the negligence of those to whom it delegates duties. Finally, even if the subject physician was clearly not an employee in either the strict sense (such as a salaried employee) or in a legal sense (such as an ostensible agent), the court will investigate whether the physician was qualified to practice in the hospital at all or was qualified to perform the specific procedure at issue. The court should finally determine if the hospital breached its legal duty to use "reasonable care" in authorizing the physician to practice or perform the particular procedure in question.[2]

These problems occur with the physician knowing of, or participating in, both administrative hospital management and direct patient care. Common avenues that involve the orthopedist in litigation include (1) staff privileges and credentialling, (2) peer review, (3) facility committee participation, (4) patient admission-discharge requirements, including documentation, (5) knowing and following facility bylaws, (6) patient recordkeeping, with emphasis on adequacy and timeliness, (7) supervising personnel involved in

---

[1] US General Accounting Office Medical Malpractice — No Agreement on the Problems or Solutions (Washington D.C., USGPO, Feb 1986).

[2] Butler & Laszlo, *Hospital Liability for Physician Negligence in Georgia: A Realistic Approach,* 37 Mercer Law Rev 701 (1986).

his or her patient's care, assuring that orders are being carried out appropriately, (8) regular visitation to his or her patients and documenting and updating progress notes as required in bylaws, (9) behavior in the operating room, recovery room, intensive care unit, and other special care areas, and (10) behavior and patient care in emergency departments and many other areas.

In *Smothers v Butler,* it was held that the mere fact that a patient is in a hospital does not absolve a doctor from the duty to supervise care and to correct errors, if present. During the existence of the physician-patient relationship, a physician is under a duty to give the patient all necessary care as long as the case requires attention, and lack of diligence in attending to the patient after assumption of care renders the doctor liable. (*See* Appendix 13-1, Cases 1 and 2.)

An exhaustive discussion of hospitals' duties to patients, physicians, other professionals, employees, patients, and third parties would require volumes and is beyond the scope of this book. This chapter deals with typical physician-hospital relationships and pertinent law cases. For a more complete discussion, see the sources cited.

§13.02 Hospital Management

The Joint Commission on Accreditation of Hospitals (JCAH) was founded more than 60 years ago by the American College of Surgeons to help monitor and improve quality care in the nation's hospitals. As medical knowledge, practice, and technology exploded into broader and better treatment modalities, the JCAH had responsibility to provide mechanisms to evaluate these medical processes. This has sometimes been a stormy project, with some adversaries in respect to accreditation procedures, standards, and responsiveness. But, no one questions the need for establishment of certain standards with which hospitals must comply.

The JCAH's primary goal is to encourage hospitals and health care facilities to establish an environment supportive of a high quality of patient care. The entire accreditation process is designed to be consultative, educational, and to evaluate the system. The system results in recommendations to a hospital staff based on predetermined guidelines—the JCAH standards. JCAH has now changed its name to Joint Commission on Accreditation of Healthcare Organizations (JCAHO).[3]

As the Joint Commission enters the 1990's, it starts a new era of accreditation and service to health care organizations, their professional staffs, and the American public. Much of the groundwork for this new era was laid in 1986 with the introduction of the Agenda for Change initiatives. Through this innovative project, the Joint Commission once again set out to take the lead in improving the quality of health care in the United States. The Joint

---

[3] Affeldt, *JCAH Today: An Overview of the Joint Commission on Accreditation of Hospitals,* JCAH (Special issue) Surgical Rounds 16 (Mar 1981).

Commission's many decades of experience as a standard-setter of quality health care led to the identification of two critical factors—careful ongoing attention to the process and outcomes of care, and emphasis on continuous improvement in patient care services.

Full implementation of these objectives is still several years away, but the Joint Commission continues to progress steadily toward this goal. The 1990 Accreditation Manual for Hospitals (AMH) incorporates extensive standards revisions in several areas, important new glossary definitions, and significant changes in policies and procedures.

Among the key areas in which major changes have been made are monitoring and evaluation, hospital-sponsored ambulatory care services, infection control, decentralized laboratory testing, and patient care services for children and adolescents. Because a commitment to continuous improvement requires a strong, hospital-wide monitoring and evaluation program, the standards have been completely reformulated to clarify the steps necessary to support effectiveness of patient care. The new standard incorporates standards previously included in the "Medical Staff" and service-specific chapters. A simplified monitoring and evaluation standard now appears in those chapters.

A complete revision of the "Hospital-Sponsored Ambulatory Care Services" chapter was necessary because of the continuing evolution of ambulatory health care services. Important issues addressed by the new standards are (1) responsibility for the quality of care, (2) appropriate use of resources, (3) safety of the environment in which care is given, and (4) mental health services.

The new "Infection Control" standards include liberalized surveillance approaches to accommodate methods other than comprehensive surveillance, place greater emphasis on prevention and control of infection, and are less prescriptive regarding the structure of the infection control program. New standards have been added to address quality issues related to decentralized laboratory testing, covering qualitative and quantitative tests and readout devices designed to provide values for constituents in various body fluids or excretions.

New and revised standards addressing services for neonates, children, and adolescents received increased attention in the new edition of the AMH. These standards stress the importance of (1) the competency of individuals responsible for the assessment, treatment, and care of patients, (2) the family's and/or guardian's involvement in the treatment, (3) normalization of the patient's environment, rights, and responsibilities, (4) assessment and documentation of the patient's psychosocial needs, (5) documentation of relevant and age-appropriate social and family histories, (6) monitoring and evaluation, (7) education, and (8) continuity of care.

The board of commissioners directed that a definition of patient care quality be developed that could serve as a framework for the quality monitoring and evaluation activities required by the accreditation standards. After extensive deliberation, a definition of patient care quality was formulated.

The new definition is concise, focuses on the patient, and reflects the perspective of health care professions.

Policies and procedures that govern the accreditation process must also acknowledge increased public demand for both quality of care and accountability, while being responsive to an industry in the midst of dynamic change. To evaluate marginally performing accredited organizations, a new category, "Conditional Accreditation," has been established. The organizations that are found not to be in substantial compliance with Joint Commission standards but which are judged to be capable of expeditious resolution of performance deficiencies are identified. It is estimated, based on past surveys, that approximately 8 per cent of hospitals and 11 per cent of nonhospital mental health facilities would fall into this category. With the new policy change, these percentages are expected to shrink over time.

§13.03 Survey Eligibility Criteria

Any hospital may apply for a Joint Commission accreditation survey if the following eligibility requirements are met:

1. The hospital is located within the United States or one of its territories or possessions or is a United States military hospital
2. The hospital has all current licenses required by governmental authorities who have jurisdiction
3. The hospital provides treatment of such a nature that patients would not ordinarily be transferred to another organization for more intensive care, excluding convalescent homes, homes for the aged, or any establishment where custodial care only is provided; student health centers and offices or clinics providing ambulatory care patient services but not regularly admitting inpatients are not included
4. The hospital is currently in operation and actively caring for patients; when the hospital has been in operation for less than six months, the accreditation award includes a follow-up visit in approximately six months so the hospital's record of performance can be evaluated
5. The hospital has a governing body, an organized medical staff, and a nursing service
6. The hospital has the primary functions of diagnosis, treatment, and/or rehabilitation
7. The hospital provides the following services: diagnostic radiology services, dietetic services, emergency services, infection control, medical record services, nuclear medicine services, pathology and medical laboratory services, pharmaceutical services, plant, technology and safety management services, professional library services, quality assurance program, physical rehabilitation services, respiratory care services, and social work services

8. The hospital has at least one of the following acute care clinical services—medicine, obstetrics-gynecology, surgery (must have anesthesia services), pediatrics, child, adolescent, or adult psychiatric services, or alcoholism or drug abuse services
9. The hospital provides that each individual who has been granted clinical privileges by the governing body practices only within the scope of clinical privileges granted
10. The hospital provides registered nurse supervision at all times, as well as other nursing services necessary for continuous patient care
11. The hospital completes and returns an application for survey
12. The hospital completes presurvey materials as directed
13. The hospital operates without restriction by reason of sex, race, creed, or national origin

Hospitals that want to be accredited by the Joint Commission should begin by sending a request for an application for survey to the following address:

Joint Commission on Accreditation of Healthcare Organizations
Scheduling Department—Application Requests
875 N. Michigan Avenue
Chicago, IL 60611

The Joint Commission sends the hospital one application for completion. The application should be returned to the Joint Commission with a nonrefundable processing fee. The hospital should retain a copy of the application for its records.

When submitting its application, the hospital must provide (or authorize the Joint Commission to obtain) official records and reports of public or publicly-recognized licensing, examining, reviewing, or planning bodies.

Information obtained by the Joint Commission in the accreditation survey process, including the public information interview, and the results and recommendations of the survey, are confidential. The results and recommendations of the survey are provided only to the surveyed hospital, which may release them at its discretion. However, there are some exceptions. If a serious condition jeopardizing public safety or patient safety is found in a hospital, after the condition has been reported to the chief executive officer the relevant public authorities are notified of the problem in writing. For hospitals participating in Medicare that become conditionally accredited or nonaccredited, survey information will be provided to the administrator of the Health Care Financing Administration. For hospitals that become conditionally accredited or nonaccredited in states that recognize Joint Commission accreditation for licensure purposes, accreditation survey information will be provided to a licensing authority on its request. The organizational component(s) that contribute to a decision of conditional accreditation or nonaccreditation will be identified.

The Joint Commission provides the following information on request:

1. Whether a particular hospital has sent in a request
2. A list of organizations tentatively scheduled for survey with no indication of specific dates
3. Upcoming survey dates for a particular hospital after the hospital has been notified of the dates
4. Whether a survey was conducted
5. Whether a hospital is accredited, conditionally accredited, involved in an appeal, nonaccredited, or holds no accreditation status
6. The effective date of accreditation for a particular hospital
7. The accreditation history of a particular hospital (its status in the past)

§13.04 Hospital Peer Review

Hospitals have long been the setting in which physicians review the work of their colleagues and exercise control over it. Typically, committees have been established that review all deaths, monitor outcomes of surgery and other events, and notify the responsible physicians of any deficiencies detected by the reviews. The hospital privileging process provides a mechanism for disciplining those whose competence is below a standard acceptable to the physicians on the hospital's staff. Not only are these programs medical traditions, but they are now required by state law, imposing quality of care obligations to patients and to the accreditation standards of the Joint Commission and the requirements for participation in the Medicare and Medicaid programs.

§13.05 Quality Assurance Programs

To participate in Medicare and Medicaid, hospitals must have formal quality assurance programs. This requirement is imposed through accreditation standards of the Joint Commission and through conditions of participation for the Medicare program, established by the Secretary of Health and Human Services. There are approximately 6900 hospitals qualified for Medicare; about 5100 are accredited by JCAHO and by virtue of that accreditation are deemed to meet Medicare standards. All accreditation requirements and conditions of participation apply to the operation of the hospitals generally, not simply to care given to Medicare and Medicaid beneficiaries.

In surveying hospitals for compliance with accreditation requirements, the Joint Commission tailors its survey to the needs of each institution, so hospitals must be prepared to show evidence of compliance with standards, including the quality assurance standards. For hospitals not in the JCAHO program, state officials operating under contract on behalf of the Secretary of Health and Human Services perform compliance surveys. When deficiencies pose a serious or immediate threat to health, the offending facility is terminated from the Medicare and Medicaid programs. For lesser deficiencies, the hospital has a chance to submit a plan of action to correct the problem(s).

Conditions of participation required an "effective, hospital-wide quality assurance program to evaluate the provision of patient care" with a written implementation plan. Specifically, the hospital must evaluate all organized services related to patient care; it must evaluate all nosocomial infections and medical therapy; it must evaluate all medical and surgical services performed in the hospital in respect to correct diagnosis and treatment. Hospitals must document appropriate remedial action and the results of the action when they find deficiencies.

The federal government further ensures the quality of care rendered to Medicare beneficiaries through reviews of that care by Utilization and Quality Control Peer Review Organizations (PROs). Their quality assurance efforts consist principally in identifying, investigating, and correcting quality problems for inpatient hospital admissions. They have responsibilities in the area of quality assurance, and also in determining the medical necessity for an appropriateness of services and the need for inpatient care. Because of the concerns about the effects of the prospective payment system on quality of care, there has been an increase in the visibility and importance attached to the quality assurance responsibilities of PROs. They are also required to extend their review activities to competitive medical plans and health maintenance organizations, and to post-acute and ambulatory care settings.

In developing the PROs' tasks for initial contracts in 1984, Health Care Financing Administration (HCFA) had to balance two somewhat inconsistent objectives. It had to specify required tasks so the agency could monitor performance against explicit numerical goals, while at the same time allowing PROs enough flexibility to identify and attack local problems. HCFA's solution was to require PROs to propose one or more measurable objectives for each of five quality goals:

1. Reduce hospital readmissions resulting from substandard care provided during prior admission
2. Assure provision of medical services that, if not performed, have a "significant potential" for causing "serious patient complications"
3. Reduce avoidable deaths
4. Reduce unnecessary surgery
5. Reduce avoidable postoperative or other complications

To establish baseline figures, PROs sampled health care services statewide and chose procedures or conditions on which to focus, along with numerical targets, based on the five quality goals, providing validation of the local importance of each goal.

Objectives were chosen as to localities. There was a wide variation in proposed targeted procedures or conditions. Objectives were based on data about procedure use or specific practitioners in some cases; in other cases, such as "avoidable mortality," local rates were compared with national rates. In keeping with the intended local focus of the program, statewide PROs subcontracted with regional PROs and delegated some activities to individual hospitals.

In developing criteria, the PROs took national criteria for generally recognized services and care for specific diagnoses and procedures and adapted them to meet the needs of local practices. When adverse outcomes were observed, the patterns of care were compared to the typical patterns of treatment in the PRO area. A variety of strategies were then available to effect quality improvements, ranging from intensified review to formal sanctions.

§13.06 Privileges

The orthopedist, like all licensed physicians, must be competent in his or her art, remain competent, and live an appropriate lifestyle that is not adverse to his or her peers, including his or her hospital. Innumerable ethical, moral, and legal problems are possible; fortunately, in daily practice, few are tested.

The physician has a duty to formally apply for staff privileges, following hospital bylaws and completing the application accurately and honestly. Appropriate references are important credentialling requirements. The hospital will have a duty to contact the Physicians' Data Bank for a credentialling report. No licensed doctor can have hospital staff privileges reduced or withdrawn without the data bank having been informed. This is true of state boards of medical examiners (or the equivalent agency) when they discipline a licensed doctor. It is a violation of law for any of these groups, in any state in the United States, to fail to inform the Data Bank.

The hospital has a duty, through the physicians on its credentialling committee, to investigate each applicant thoroughly as to competence, morals, and ethics, in addition to reviewing Data Bank information. This has been, at times, a superficial process in many hospital credentiallings, leading to major hospital staff behavior problems. (*See* Appendix 13-1, Cases 3 to 10.)

Most hospitals require a new staff physician to serve a probationary period where his or her style of medical practice is monitored. Surgeons are often proctored in surgery by a senior staff surgeon. This proctoring surgeon is at times involved in litigation when the new surgeon commits malpractice and the plaintiff feels that the proctor should have prevented it. The holdings are most often in favor of the proctor, who is not doing the proctoring as a duty to the patient, but to the hospital. The hospital, in these situations, is often liable.

Once the new physician has successfully passed the probation period and has been granted full or active staff privileges, he or she becomes tenured and cannot be removed from the staff or have his or her privileges reduced without due process.

Most hospitals, including all hospitals certified by The Joint Commission of Healthcare Organizations (JCAHO), require recertification of physicians on the hospital staff annually or biannually. This assures that the hospital, credential, and executive committees review and approve the practice of each staff member. Some hospital bylaws allow renewal of staff privileges without due process; however, most require a due process procedure. It needs to be remembered that hospital staff privileges are a privilege rather than a right. (*See* Appendix 13-1, Case 1.)

§13.07 Hospital Duty to Patients

An extensive review of physician credentialling by hospitals and hospitals' duties to patients is outside of the scope of this book; however, a short overview should be helpful and informative to professional readers.

Various theories continue to be proffered by plaintiffs, and are often accepted by courts, that hospitals are liable for the acts of independent, private practicing physicians, even where the hospital has not negligently selected and retained the physician. *Pamperin v Trinity Memorial Hospital,* 423 NW2d 848 (Wis 1988) contains a typical discussion of the problem. In this case, the plaintiff argued that the hospital should be liable for a radiologist's negligence because state law required hospitals to have a qualified radiologist available to interpret films and to supervise the hospital's radiology department. The question here was whether the radiologist could delegate the statutorily required duty to another. The court held that he could not. Here, the orthopedist could not assume the hospital's x-ray film reading responsibility.

In *Johnson v Misericordia Community Hospital,* 99 Wis 2d 708, 301 NW2d 156 (1981), the court concluded that the hospital owed a duty to its patients to use care in selecting medical staff members and in granting privileges. The Wisconsin Supreme Court's holding probably reflects the national standard regarding this problem:

> In summary, we hold that a hospital owes a duty to its patients to exercise reasonable care in selection of its medical staff and in granting specialized privileges.
>
> The final appointing authority resides in the hospital's governing body, although it must rely on the medical staff, and in particular, the credentialling committee to investigate and evaluate an applicant's qualifications for the requested privileges. However, this delegation of the responsibility to investigate and evaluate the professional competence of applicants for clinical privileges does not relieve the governing body of its duty to appoint only qualified physicians and surgeons to its medical staff and periodically monitor and review their competency. The credentialling committee (or committee of the whole) must investigate the qualifications of applicants. The facts of this case demonstrate that a hospital, at a minimum, requires completion of the application and verify the accuracy of the applicant's statements, especially in regard to his medical education, training and experience. Additionally, it should (1) solicit information from the applicant's peers, (including

> those not referred to in his application) who are knowledgeable about his education, training, experience, health, competence and ethical character; (2) determine if the applicant is currently licensed to practice in the state and if his licensure or registration has been challenged, and (3) inquire whether applicant has been involved in any adverse malpractice action and whether he has experienced a loss of medical organization membership or medical privileges or membership at any other hospital. The investigating committee must also evaluate the information gained through its inquiries and make a reasonable judgment as to the approval or denial of each applicant for staff privileges. The hospital will be charged with gaining and evaluating the knowledge that would have been acquired had it exercised ordinary care in investigating its medical staff applicants; the hospital's failure to exercise that degree of skill and care and judgment that is exercised by the average hospital in approving an applicant's request for privilege is negligence. This is not to say that hospitals are insurers of competence of their medical staff for a hospital will not be negligent if it exercises the noted standard of care in selecting its staff.

In *Cronic v Doud,* 523 NE2d 176 (Mass Ct App 1976), the hospital bylaws contained a provision that the medical staff would conduct an ongoing evaluation of its members. From this, the court held that the hospital knew or should have known about the excessive number of rib resection surgeries a staff member was performing.

In *Pariser v Christian Health Care Systems,* 681 F Supp 1381 (ED Mo 1988), the physician lied on his application about whether or not he had lost staff privileges at another hospital. The court held that a lie on a medical staff application was sufficient grounds to suspend a physician under "the best interests of patient care" standard.

The emerging trend is to hold hospitals responsible for their physicians' actions and, at the minimum, to assure that the credentialling process of the physician on admission staff privileges and recertification of his or her privileges are attended to by adequate peer review. This emerging trend is further verified in *Purcell v Zimbelman,* 18 Ariz App 75, 500 P2d 335 (1972), *Beeck v Tucson General Hospital,* 18 Ariz App 165, 500 P2d 1153 (1972), and *Tucson Medical Center v Misevch,* 113 Ariz 34, 545 P2d 958 (1976). The verdicts, testing what constitutes malpractice, were part of these issues, following the logic that, if there is only one approved method of diagnosing or treating a particular condition or ailment, a physician is required to follow that method; if there are two or more approved methods for diagnosing or treating a particular condition or ailment, the physician is required to select and follow one of the approved methods; the mere fact that the plaintiff may not have attained the desired results from the defendant's treatment and care is not by itself to be taken as evidence of negligence on the part of the surgeon.

A new report claimed that thousands of United States hospitals are not correctly monitoring quality of care or safety standards. JCAHO found that most prevalent among hospitals was the failure to meet quality control standards designed to prevent unnecessary medical procedures. The report surveyed over 5,000 hospitals and found:

1. Over one-half (51 per cent) did not adequately review surgeries to see whether they should have been done or were done properly
2. One-half (50 per cent) did not properly monitor care in intensive and coronary care units
3. Approximately one-third (35 per cent) did not always evaluate blood transfusions patients to determine whether transfusions were necessary
4. Between one-fourth and one-third (29 per cent) did not adequately review the credentials of medical staff applicants[4]

§13.08 Hospital Administration

Patient safety is the responsibility of the hospital administration. The orthopedist is vicariously aligned to the hospital management and its potential errors. There are standards of care in respect to patients' safety, the breach of which imposes a tort liability. The American College of Surgeons has published a guide for establishing a patient safety system in a hospital. This guide recommends establishment of an office of patient safety, a patient safety system, and a safety self-audit system. Both physicians and nonphysicians have a duty to report instances that are both medically and not medically related. The goal of the hospital patient safety system is to improve the quality of patient care and reduce preventable risk to the patient, thereby meeting JCAHO standards.[5]

Care of patients in American hospitals is generally good, but not good enough. Malpractice in the last two decades seems to have contributed more to upgrading hospital quality assurance than anything the health care industry itself has initiated. There is an acute awareness that something must be done to decrease potential compensable liability events. This has resulted in risk management associations springing up throughout the country and in hospitals establishing their own risk management program. Risk management and quality assurance functions are essentially the same, designed to improve the quality of patient care.

Most hospital medical misadventures result from simple oversights, absentmindedness, or neglect. Most of the breakdowns occur because of patient care performance deficiencies, not because of lack of knowledge or training.

---

[4] Accreditation Manual for Hospitals, General Administrative Policies and Procedures (1990).

[5] American College of Surgeons, Patient Safety Manual (1979).

One of the more common hospital events is a patient fall, most often involving elderly patients.[6] The use of restraint devices (Posey belts and side rails) give hospital personnel a false sense of satisfaction that patients are secure. Patients can easily untie a Posey belt and then climb over side rails, resulting in a fall to the floor. Older patients or patients on medication are commonly disoriented. Patients also fall from unstable wheelchairs and bedside commodes. It has been suggested that high-risk patients not be left unattended and that there be a system of constant surveillance.

The fall injury is an area where the orthopedist can be, and most likely will be, more frequently involved in litigation. The physician who knows his or her patients knows the risk of the fall, the effect of the medication prescribed, and the risk it might introduce. If the physician fails to exercise sufficient supervision of hospital personnel assigned to protect the patient from falling, he or she may well be joined with the hospital in negligence actions.

The usual holding is that hospitals are required to use "reasonable care" to protect patients from falling, with due consideration to the patient's age, mental and physical condition, medications being taken, and how well the patient follows the physician's orders.

Carrying out medication orders by hospital personnel is another common source of error. An example is when a physician orders medication. It is frequently rewritten on a requisition that is sent by courier to the pharmacy. The prescription is filled by the pharmacist, but may be returned along with many other medications that the nursing unit can dispense, and may be followed by another shift. This system is fraught with potential error.

Transmittal of laboratory and radiology reports and other special procedure reports are often incompletely handled, mislaid, and tardy in arriving at the hospital floor area where the patient is, and where the physician reviews the chart. At times, reports or notations are not placed on the hospital record promptly, causing delays in diagnosis and treatment. The statement is often made that quality assurance must go beyond the passing, ritualistic, retrospective methods of patient care evaluations.

How a hospital operates in respect to written protocols may become a predictor of that hospital's liability. A hospital is supposed to have reasonable procedures and standards to ensure the quality of patient care. As mentioned earlier, JCAHO requires hospitals to have certain written protocols and to adhere to the regulations.[7]

It is possible for the physician to err in judgment, to be unsuccessful in treatment, or to disagree with others without being negligent.

Hospitals have a duty to review the quality of medical care performed within them. The duty is usually carried out through various committees of the hospital medical staff. The "work product" of the medical staff meet-

---

[6] American College of Surgeons, Providing Management Information for Patient Safety Programs (1980).

[7] Skillicorn, *Improved Quality Control in Hospitals: A Necessity,* J Leg Med 2471 (1981). S.E. Pegalis & H.V. Wachsman, 1 American Law of Medical Malpractice 112-13 (Cumm Supp Nov 1989).

ings are prohibited by statute against discovery as "peer review committee proceedings." Some states protect medical review activities as being either confidential or privileged; others allow limited protection with limited discovery.

In risk management, there is an ongoing question at this time of whether studying filed medical malpractice claims against a hospital is a useful quality assessment tool. Many have felt that medical malpractice claims are of limited value because filed malpractice claims represent only a small portion of medical misadventures in which malpractice occurred. It is common sense, of course, to use any took available to improve medical care and avoid medical misadventures.[8]

The orthopedist is often involved in the care of patients in emergency room facilities. Many misadventures and negligent actions have resulted in patient injury in the emergency environment. The "Good Samaritan" laws tend to protect the physician when responding to emergency situations if it was not his or her duty to do so.[9]

§13.09 Diagnostic-Related Groups (DRGs)

Hospitals and physicians face increasing constraints due to a variety of factors influencing quality of patient care. Federal and state diagnostic-related group (DRG) prospective hospital pricing has caused tremendous financial pressure on hospitals. In one large study analyzing the volume of orthopedic surgical procedures performed by an individual orthopedic surgeon for all patients, surgeons were arbitrarily categorized as high-volume and low-volume orthopedists. Patients of low-volume surgeons had longer hospital stays and hospital costs, greater financial risk under DRG's, and a poorer outcome compared with patients of higher volume orthopedic surgeons. Research says these findings are multifactorial, but they do raise important issues related to orthopedic surgical and hospital costs and quality of care.

The observation that high-volume surgical practices produce high patient outcome satisfaction has been reported in heart surgery patients, total joint replacement operations, hand and foot surgeries, and severely injured trauma patients. It is probable that complicated surgical care will become centralized, sharply limiting practice opportunities for a segment of orthopedists. This surgical restriction philosophy is seen in England, Canada, France, West Germany, and the Soviet Union at this time.[10]

---

[8] Krasak, *How to use Malpractice Data in Quality Assessment,* 9 Hospital Med Staff 28 (1980).

[9] Wiegenstein, *Emergency Medicine,* 243 JAMA 2182 (1980).

[10] Munoz, *Economics of Scale, Physician Volume for Orthopedic Surgical Patients, and the DRG Prospective Payment System,* 13 Orthop 39 (1990).

§13.10 Preventable Hospital Deaths

If the quality of care provided by a hospital affects its death rate, then some of the deaths are preventable. One large survey of cerebral vascular accident patients who died showed this to be true. A main criticism was incorrect diagnosis of the patient's illness. In retrospect, the severity of illness can help a hospital identify probable preventable deaths. In this series, 42 per cent of low illness severity had probable preventable death, as compared to 11 per cent of high severity of illness. The study suggests that this comparison would be valid for other severe illnesses or traumas.

§13.11 Employee Competence

The hospital has a duty to hire competent persons and to require personnel directors to review employee applications and to investigate and hire based as much on competence as on need—a major problem at this time in hospitals and nursing homes.

If the nursing staff does not have enough personnel to adequately serve the patient load, this may be a problem and a source of litigation. Although there are no set rules as to how many patients a nurse can care for, it is obvious that a realistic ratio of nurse to patients exists.

The nurses are divided into categories by skill, training, and state licensure: (1) registered nurses (R.N.), with full training and successfully completion of state licensure requirements, (2) licensed practical nurses (L.P.N.) with less training and fewer perceived nursing skills, (3) nurse aides with less nursing skill, who administer no medication and who are often trained on the job.

There are many areas where R.N.s and L.P.N.s can be additionally trained. As in the practice of medicine, the nurse is generally held to be competent and to have the skill of the level at which he or she practices, thus, an L.P.N. doing R.N. work is held to the duties of an R.N. (*See* Appendix 13-1, Cases 12 to 25.)

The nursing staff in a hospital functions by internally derived guidelines so that each job is spelled out, and the chief nurse is responsible to see that these duties are carried out. In cases of nursing malpractice, the plaintiff needs to look at the skills of the nurse and at whether he or she was functioning at an appropriate level, was supervised appropriately, and was hired appropriately.

Nurses are becoming more vulnerable to malpractice suits. According to an analysis of claims filed, nurses, not hospitals, have been held responsible in one-third of the cases in which an R.N. or a nursing service was named as a defendant. Eight per cent of malpractice suits, in one study, were filed against nurses. The common allegations were (1) patient fell/hospital negligence—21 per cent, (2) failure to monitor patient—20 per cent, (3) improper treatment/procedure/performance—14 per cent, (4) failure to insure patient safety—12 per cent, (5) medication errors—6 per cent, (6) failure to respond to patient—3 per cent, (7) improper techniques—3 per cent, and (8) failure to supervise treatment.

Although the nurse can be held individually liable, the hospital most often is liable as the employer under the doctrine of respondeat superior. (*See* Appendix 13-1, Cases 25 to 28.)

There are many problems of contract labor, agency, and unusual "Captain of the Ship" or "borrowed employee" doctrines considered in hospital liability cases.[11] (*See* Appendix 13-1, Cases 29 and 30.)

§13.12 Nurse Shortage

There is a known shortage of skilled nurses and related paramedical personnel. This increases the vulnerability of the physician who more often has to fend for him- or herself doing nursing work and/or having less-trained, less-competent paramedicals caring for his or her patients and carrying out doctor's orders. There appears to be little relief in sight, so the practicing physician must recognize the risk and structure his or her practice accordingly.[12]

§13.13 Patient Rights

The rights of patients have become a major consideration of patient care, in the hospital or in the physician's office. JCAHO has set forth a formal statement of "patients' rights."

The basic rights of human beings for independence of expression, decision, and action, and concern for personal dignity and human relationships, have always been of great importance in the United States. However, during illness, the presence (or absence) of these rights becomes a vital factor in recovery and survival. Therefore, this is a prime responsibility for hospitals to assure that these rights are preserved for their patients, although the hospitals have the right to expect reasonable and responsible behavior on the part of patients and their families and friends.

JCAHO has set forth the following basic rights of patients, to be applicable to all hospitals:

1. *Access to Care:* Individuals shall be accorded impartial access to treatment or accommodations that are available or medically indicated, regardless of race, creed, sex, national origin or sources of payment for care.
2. *Respect and Dignity:* The patient has the right to considerate, respectful care at all times with recognition of his personal dignity.
3. *Privacy and Confidentiality:* The patient has the right, within the law, to personal and informational privacy, as follows:

---

[11] Risk Management Foundation of the Harvard Medical Institutions, Inc (1989).

[12] Accreditation Manual for Hospitals, Rights and Responsibilities of Patients (1990); Curran, *Patients' Rights of Free Choice in Hospitals Power Over Staff Privileges: Conflict in the Courts,* 306 NEJM 1404 (1982).

(a) To refuse to see anyone not officially connected with the hospital, including visitors, or persons officially connected with the hospital but not directly involved in his care.

(b) To wear appropriate personal clothing and religious or other symbolic items if they do not interfere with diagnostic procedures or treatment.

(c) To be interviewed and examined in surroundings assuring reasonable visual and auditory privacy. This includes the right to have a person of one's own sex present during certain parts of a physical examination, treatment, or procedure performed by a health professional of the opposite sex and the right not to remain disrobed any longer than is required for accomplishing the medical examination.

(d) To expect that any discussion about his case will be conducted discreetly and that persons not directly involved in his care will not be present without his permission.

(e) To have his medical record read only by persons involved in his treatment or monitoring of its quality. Other individuals must have his written authorization or that of his legally authorized representative.

(f) To expect all communications and other records relating to his care to be confidential. This includes the source of payment for treatment.

(g) To request a transfer to another room if another patient or visitor in the room is unreasonably disturbing him by smoking or by other actions.

(h) To be placed in protective privacy when considered necessary for personal safety.

4. *Identity:* The patient has the right to know the identity and professional status of individuals providing service to him and to know which physician or other practitioner is primarily responsible for his care. He has the right to know of any existence of any professional relationship among individuals who are treating him, as well as the relationship to any other health care or educational institutions involved in his care. Participation by patients in clinical training programs or gathering of data for research purposes should be voluntary.

5. *Information:* The patient as the right to know the complete and current information concerning his diagnosis, treatment and any known prognosis. This information should be related in terms the patient can reasonably be expected to understand. When it is not medically advisable to give such information to the patient, the information should be made available to a legally authorized individual.

6. *Communication:* The patient has a right to have visitors and verbal and written communications. If the patient does not speak or under-

stand the predominant language of the community, he should have access to an interpreter. This is particularly true where language barriers are a continuing problem.

7. *Consent:* The patient has a right to reasonable participation in decision involving his health care. To the degree possible, this should be based on a clear, concise explanation of his condition and any proposed technical procedures, their risks, side effects, problems related to recuperation and probability of success. The patient should not be subjected to any procedure without his voluntary, competent, and understanding consent or the consent of his legally authorized representative. He should be infomred as to any medically significant alternatives for care or treatment. The patient has a right to know who is responsible for authorizing and performing procedures on him. The patient shall be informed if the hospital proposes to engage in any human experimentation or other research/educational projects affecting his care or treatment. He has the right to refuse to participate in any such activity.
8. *Consultation:* The patient has the right to consult with a specialist at his own request and expense.
9. *Refusal of Treatment:* The patient may refuse treatment to the extent permitted by law. When refusal of treatment by the patient or his legally authorized representative prevents the provision of appropriate care in accordance with professional standards, the physician-patient relationship may be terminated with reasonable notice.
10. *Transfer and Continuity of Care:* A patient may not be transferred to another facility unless he has received a complete explanation of the reason why and alternatives to such transfer and unless the transfer is acceptable to the other facility. The patient has a right to be informed of any continuing health care requirements following discharge from the hospital by the practitioner responsible for his care.
11. *Hospital Charges:* The patient has the right to request and receive an itemized and detailed explanation of his total bill for services rendered while hospitalized, regardless of the source of payment. He has the right to timely notice prior to termination of his eligibility for reimbursement by any third party payer for the cost of his care.
12. *Hospital Rules and Regulations:* The patient should be informed of the hospital rules and regulations applying to him, including mechanisms for the initiation, review and resolution of patient complaints.

§13.14 Patient Responsibilities

At the same time it established guidelines covering the rights of patients, JCAHO set up guidelines for patient responsibilities:

1. *Provision of Information:* A patient has the responsibility to provide accurate and complete information relating to his present complaints,

past illnesses, past hospitalizations, medications and any other matters relating to his health. He has the responsibility to report unexpected changes in his condition to the responsible practitioner. He is responsible for reporting whether he clearly understands a planned course of action and what is expected of him.

2. *Compliance Instructions:* A patient is responsible for following the treatment plan recommended by the practitioner responsible for his care. This includes following instructions from nurses or other health personnel as they carry out the coordinated plan of care, implement the responsible practitioner's orders and enforce the hospital rules and regulations. The patient is responsible for keeping appointments and notifying the responsible practitioner or the hospital.
3. The patient is responsible for his actions if he refuses treatment or does not follow the practitioner's instructions.
4. *Hospital Charges:* The patient is responsible for assuring the financial obligations of his health care are fulfilled as quickly as possible.
5. *Hospital Rules and Regulations:* The patient is responsible for following hospital rules and regulations affecting patient care and conduct.
6. *Respect and Consideration:* The patient is responsible for being considerate of the rights of other patients and hospital personnel and for assisting in the control of noise, smoking and the number of visitors. The patient is responsible for being respectful of the property of other persons and of the hospital.[13]

§13.15 Patient Care

Hospitals, with wide variations, are divided into sections (administratively) accommodating the various health problems for which patients are admitted. These sections typically include (1) general medicine-family practice, with its subsections of cardiology, infectious diseases, etc., (2) surgery, with its subsections of orthopedic, neuro, general, etc., (3) obstetrics, (4) pediatrics, and (5) psychiatry. In addition, patient service facilities are separate including diagnostic/therapeutic: (1) radiology, (2) laboratory (pathology), (3) physical therapy, (4) occupational therapy, (5) dietician (food services), and (6) pharmacy. (*See* Appendix 13-1, Cases 29 and 30.)

Each of these divisions is under supervision, with the supervisor being responsible for the carrying out of intra-institution protocols that have been established by the hospital administration. Thus, the hierarchy of responsibility is spelled out.

Ancillary divisions are of equal importance, such as building maintenance and housekeeping. These persons likewise can involve themselves and the hospital in negligence problems.

---

[13] Accreditation Manual for Hospitals, Rights and Responsibilities of Patients (1990); Curran, *Patients' Rights of Free Choice in Hospitals Power Over Staff Privileges: Conflict in the Courts* 306 NEJM 1404 (1982).

§13.16 Floor Care

Most hospitalized patients are cared for in hospital rooms fitted with hospital beds. The patients are not always restricted to the bed, but patient care usually centers around the room/bed unless special studies or invasive care is being done.

The patient arrives on the ward "floor" for diagnosis and care. The admitting doctor has a duty to promptly issue patient care orders, which are noted by an R.N. or L.P.N. Depending on the nature of care required, the charge nurse carries out the orders, or more often, delegates the orders to floor personnel assigned to that type of work and skilled in that type of care. The charge nurse remains responsible for supervising care, and if negligence occurs, he or she—as well as the tortfeasor—may be held liable.

Special problems centering on patient care currently require special care, such as postoperative or hospital-acquired infection. This is followed, reported, and recorded by hospital staff personnel as part of Infection Committee duties. This is preventive and as the therapeutic practice of medicine, often involves the orthopedist.

Patients who are less than competent mentally, those taking mind-altering (prescribed) medication, those who are physically weak from illness or injury, and elderly or demented patients require special care and the caretakers owe a duty to protect them from injury. This may take the form of assuring bed rails are in place, that restraints are in place (if ordered by the doctor), and that the room environment is not dangerous (such as a wet floor). In restless, incoherent patient care, a full-time "sitter" may be required. There are numerous negligence cases regarding these types of problems that often involve the orthopedist, as it involves his or her patient or involves the orthopedist's knowledge that less than adequate care is being given. The doctor is held to be knowledgeable as to the type and competence of care given, and is negligent if he or she fails to supervise or attempt to correct problems placing the patient at risk. (*See* Appendix 13-1, Cases 31 to 52.)

§13.17 Do Not Resuscitate (DNR) Orders

Do Not Resuscitate (DNR) orders are written by the physician who, in his or her medical judgment, along with family's request or consent, feels that heroic attempts to prolong life are medically, morally, and ethically inappropriate. These patients must be judged to have an incurable, fatal illness, and to be at the terminal stage of illness. These types of orders are in the news often, presenting unsolved legal and medical problems. The orthopedist who issues DNR orders must do so with all involved persons being fully informed and consenting; otherwise, he or she incurs the risk of negligence. (*See* Chapters 3, 4, and 14 on Patients' Rights, Physician Behavior, and Informed Consent, respectively.

Typical forms are instructional as to patient care and treatment flow methods. These forms and charts are essential to avoid some facets of care, as well as for recordkeeping.

§13.18 Living Wills

Recently, several surveys have shown that a substantial proportion of the population has prepared an advance directive. Studies of hospitals show varying policies for obtaining (from the patient) knowledge of the patient's advance directives or plans to obtain a living will or the existence of a durable power of attorney. One survey reports that 67 per cent have a formal policy in place. Most of these hospitals have a policy requiring the patient to notify them in advance or at the time of admission as to any advance directive and its location, while only 4 per cent actively inquire as to such directives—that is, the patient must initiate the information. Forty-six per cent of reporting hospitals have an active ethics committee, although this committee is not necessarily associated with advance directive policies.

Certainly, there appears to be a need for hospitals, as well as nursing homes, to have active policies and actively inquiring administrative personnel skilled in obtaining this information and in facilitating those patients wishing to formulate advance directives. The orthopedist can best serve his or her patient and family by being knowledgeable and helpful about these issues.[14] For a practical guide to drafting durable powers of attorney, including forms and coverage of the relevant laws of each state, see *Drafting the Durable Power of Attorney: A Systems Approach* by Francis J. Collin, Jr., John J. Lombard, Jr., Albert L. Moses, and Harley J. Spitler (Shepard's/McGraw-Hill, 1987).

§13.19 Discharge Planning

The physician has a legal duty when discharging a patient from the hospital or transferring the care of a patient to another doctor or facility to see that the patient understands what is happening. To discharge a patient from the hospital requires cooperation among the patient (or the legal representative of the patient), the primary physician, the hospital, and the insurance company, HMO, or government.

Discharge planning has been a requirement for hospitals participating in Medicare/Medicaid programs since mandated by the Omnibus Budget Reconciliation Act of 1986. This Act requires hospitals to provide Medicare patients, on admission, with a notice of the patient's discharge rights. The concept of discharge planning is not new; recently, New York State has implemented laws that impose regulations affecting the physician's determination for a patient's discharge. This law, as well as the Omnibus Act, ensures that the patient will not be prematurely discharged.

The hospitalized patient's discharge rights are summarized as follows:

1. The right to receive all hospital care that is necessary for proper diagnosis and treatment of the involved illness or injury, the discharge data

---

[14] Van McCray & Botkin, *Hospital Policy on Advance Directives, Do Institutions Ask Patients about Living Will?,* 262 JAMA 2411 (1989).

is determined solely by medical needs—not by DRG or by insurance payments

2. The right to be fully informed about decisions affecting inpatient health care coverage or payment for the hospital stay; a written discharge notice and a discharge plan must be received 24 hours prior to discharge
3. The right to appeal and written notice received from the hospital stating that inpatient services are no longer necessary
4. The right to receive a written discharge plan that insures a planned program of continuing care that meets the post-discharge need of the patient; discharge can be ordered only when services required in a written discharge plan are secured or determined by the hospital to be reasonably available
5. The right to appeal a discharge determination to a Professional Review Agent

The legal precedent for this group of patients (Medicare, Medicaid, and all New York State hospital patients) that will probably be rapidly adopted throughout the United States.[15]

§13.20 Hospital Costs for Postsurgical Infections

Postoperative infections in clean orthopedic cases occur in from .5 to 5 per cent of cases, according to many authors. Patients present with a wide variety of risk factors and hospitals and their operating rooms have their own risk factors. Postoperative infections can add $13,320 to $47,970 to routine hospital charges for laminectomies or total joint replacements.[16]

§13.21 Infection Control

Nosocomial infection—one which occurs in a patient who has been in a hospital for at least 72 hours and who did not have signs or symptoms of such infection on admission—is a serious problem in hospitals. Awareness of such problems has given rise to new types of medical specialists: infection control practitioners. These practitioners, be they physicians, nurses, or medical technologists, have initiated and supervised infection control programs. The JCAHO has required American hospitals to have infection con-

---

[15] J.E. Schutte, Medical Economics for Surgeons 67 (Dec 1988); §482.21, 51 Fed Reg 22043 (June 17, 1986); Pub L No 99-509, 9305 (amending the Social Security Act, 42 USC §1395).

[16] Pinner, *High-Cost Nosocomial Infections,* 3 Infection Control 143 (1982); W.A. Altemeir, Manual on Control of Infection in Surgical Patients (2d ed 1984); J.V. Bennett & P.S. Brachman, Hospital Infections (2d ed 1986); Condon, *Does Infection Control Control Infection?,* 123 Ann Surg 250 (1988).

trol committees since 1975. Many states have similar program requirements. More than 30 million patients are discharged from American hospitals each year. Of those, 3 to 15 per cent have acquired a nosocomial infection. The most realistic approach to the problem of in-hospital carriers is the epidemiological surveillance of nosocomial infection and intensive study of the problem as it presents. Often, sophisticated detective work is necessary.

A review of the various reported court decisions concerning alleged liability predicated on the contraction of nosocomial infection revealed that, in those cases where the plaintiff prevailed, evidence was presented that hospital policies had been violated during the care of the infected patient and that, as a result, it could reasonably be inferred that injury resulted from the violation of the hospital policy and rules of operation. Hospitals must have in place, and supervise closely, protocols to identify and control nosocomial infections, ascertain the mechanisms, and correct the same. A great deal of research appropriate to these discoveries and preventions appears in recent literature and is available to all medical personnel. Regular in-house, in-service instruction as to prevention, control, identification, and correction of nosocomial infection should be regularly imparted to all employees. It is necessary that each employee understand his or her role in the perpetuation and prevention of in-hospital infection, be it custodian, cook, or chief of staff. Increased awareness of infection control principles and aseptic techniques within the hospital requires daily reminders.[17]

§13.22 Venipuncture; IV Infection

Central vascular catheterization is an integral part of the care of critically ill patients, allowing hemodynamic monitoring as well as the administration of fluids, antibiotics, blood products, medications, and nutritional solutions. One of the most serious complications of intravenous needles or catheters is local infection leading to septicemia, which is often fatal. Recent studies have reported from 0 to 14.8 per cent of infections about venous catheters.

Many hospitals have rules stating that indwelling venous catheters must be treated as a recent surgical wound (dry sterile dressings, local antibiotics, and catheter changed every 48 to 72 hours). The patient requiring intravenous therapy is often the one in which placing an intravenous catheter may be difficult or impossible, due to the collapsed veins that are seen in the critically ill. This can lead to a "Catch-22" among the treating personnel.[18]

---

[17] S.E. Pegalis & H.V. Wachsman, 1 Amer Law Med Practice 88 (1986); Cram, *The Hospital's Obligations to Protect Patients from Carriers of Infectious Diseases,* Medic-Legal News, Fall 1979, at 8.

[18] Flowers, III, *Efficiency of an Attachable Subcutaneous Cuff for the Prevention of Intravascular Catheter-Related Infection,* 261 JAMA 878 (1989); Pinilla, *Study of Incidence of Intravascular Catheter Infection and Associated Infection in Critically Ill Patients,* 11 Crit Care Med 21 (1983); Linares, *Pathogenesis of Catheter Sepsis: A Prospective Study with Quantitative and Semiquantitative Culture of Hub and Segments,* 21 J Clin Micro Biol 357 (1985); Band & Make, *Safety of Changing Intravenous*

§13.23 Emergency Departments

Many hospitals have emergency care departments, which require great care in supervision by the hospital, with assurance of adequate and competent personnel. The same observation holds for intensive care units, special care units, urgent care units, and outpatient care facilities. The operating room, with its ever-expanding specialty areas, is another highly visible, vulnerable area, potentially exposing the hospital to negligence. See Chapter 16, Emergency Care.[19] (*See* Appendix 13-1, Cases 53 to 58.)

§13.24 Special Care Areas

Various special care areas, such as physical therapy or diagnostic x-ray departments, pose risk problems. The "floor" transfer of debilitated persons from bed, to litter, to x-ray table often produces injury when the transferring person is unskilled or uninformed as to special problems. All such transfers are initially the responsibility of the caretaker. Care continues to termination at the other end and the transfer person may be responsible for care at both ends of transfer as well as during transit itself.

The physical therapy area should be free of patient hazards, as directed by the department operating protocol. The x-ray department has special vulnerabilities, under the supervision of a radiologist and a department supervising technician. The examination rooms are often dark, hindering the patient's ability to help with examination, especially if the patient is also debilitated. Manipulating an injured or fragile patient onto or off of the examining table, or on an x-ray table to position the patient for a certain x-ray view, is often the source of a lawsuit for patient injury. Most of these injured patients are vulnerable by virtue of their injury/illness and unfamiliarity with x-ray facilities. These departments are often held to have a higher degree of duty to lessen a hazardous area of a hospital. (*See* Appendix 13-1, Cases 59 to 65.)

§13.25 Limited Capabilities

Hospitals that accept patients with injuries or health problems beyond the hospital's capabilities place themselves at risk of litigation. Hospitals

---

Delivery Systems at Longer than 24 Hour Intervals, 91 Ann Int Med (1979); Pruitt, Jr & Goodwin, Jr, *Current Treatment of the Extensively Burned Patient,* 15 Surg Ann 331 (1983); J.E. Edwards, Jr, *Candida Species,* in Principles and Practice of Infectious Diseases 1435 (2d ed 1985); Maki & Ringer, *Evaluation of Dressing Regimes for Prevention of Infection with Peripheral Intravenous Catheters: Gauze, a Transparent Polyurethane Dressing and an Iodophor-Transparent Dressing,* 258 JAMA 2396 (1987); B.H. Hamory, *Nosocomial Bloodstream and Intravenous Device Related Infections,* in Prevention and Control of Nosocomial Infections 283 (RP Wenzel ed 1987).

[19] Enfield & DP Sklar, *Patient Dumping in the Hospital Emergency Department: Renewed Interest in an Old Problem,* 8 Amer J Law & Med 561 (1988).

are held to accept only those cases for which they are equipped as a physical facility.

Transfer of patients from one hospital to another often presents problems. In situations where a patient or a patient's family wants a transfer, the attending physician should know the second hospital to be adequate, or, as the doctor, he or she may be negligent in transferring the patient to an at-risk situation. The same is true of referring a patient to another doctor who the referring physician knows (or should have known) is incompetent.

The hospital is at great risk, by COBRA laws, if it transfers a patient solely for financial reasons. A hospital cannot refuse to treat a nonpaying person, after he or she has been accepted, simply for financial reasons. The orthopedist may be pressured by a hospital administration to dismiss or transfer a patient for lack of pay considerations. The orthopedist becomes legally involved with the United States Government, as well as liable to the patient, if that patient is injured.

Alarm about the adverse effects of transferring emergency patients for economic reasons has resulted in federal legislation aimed at curbing the practice. This "dumping" of patients is an old practice receiving renewed interest, loading new risks of liability on the treating practitioner's shoulders. Many current authors conclude that currently proposed solutions to patient dumping will have limited effectiveness without more specific incentives for the provision of health care to the medically indigent.[20] (*See* Appendix 13-1, Cases 57 and 58.)

§13.26 Hospital Supplies

Routine hospital supplies like gloves, syringes, antibacterial scrubs, and surgical sponges have been implicated in deaths, and injuries such as paralysis, anaphylactic shock, cranial nerve damage, cancer, contact dermatitis and life-threatening infections should be included in the investation of hospital/doctor related complications.

Radio-opaque dyes used in IVP examinations, angiograms, catheterizations (vascular), and other diagnostic procedures (including myelograms) appear to break down plastic and rubber, causing both systemic reactions as well as the infiltration of breakdown debris into the circulation of the patient. Glass delivery systems are recommended to avoid most of these complications, a fact that is generally ignored by hospitals and in doctor offices in favor of the economic advantage of plastic (throwaway) materials.

Other devices to be investigated in the hospital as suspects for injuring patients include pacemakers, heart valves, catheters, x-ray tables, radiation therapy devices, surgical sponges, cotton platelets as used about the brain, spinal cord, or nerves, cryoprobes, intracerebral electrodes and pressure measuring devices, pneumatic (orthopedic) tourniquets, blood and body warmers or cooling equipment, electrocautery equipment, pressure body

---

[20] Powers, *Hospital Service and the Open Door,* 66 Mich L Rev 1455 (1968).

measuring devices in surgery or ICU, and respiratory equipment and anesthetic machines. All of these have been involved, at some time, in patient injury.

The hospital is in the posture of being a merchant in certain ways that can lead to litigation. The physician will order certain supplies such as splints, cast materials, sutures and suture needles, or other routine surgical supplies, which may be faulty. If the surgeon knowingly uses faulty supplies and patient injury results, he or she is liable. Similar situations occur with prescribed blood products and other medications with materials used in special diagnostic testing, such as myelographic "dye."

Equally important risk areas lie in equipment used for diagnosis or treatment, such as surgical cautery equipment, heating devices, and tables and devices to place patients in postures to administer treatment. Risk is involved in use of devices on the "floor," such as respiratory aids and oxygen and suction devices. The risk arises when these devices are faulty or fail to function and injure a patient.[21] (*See* Appendix 13-1, Cases 31 to 35, and 37 and 38.)

§13.27 Trauma in the Elderly

Trauma remains a leading cause of death and disability in America, consuming a large part of health care dollars. In the elderly, only 2 per cent of deaths among persons more than 65 years of age are related to trauma, but the death rate is much higher in this age group when they are traumatized.

When comparing injury severity scores, length of hospital stay, hospital charges, and mortality rates in 60 trauma patients over 60 years old with 60 trauma patients under 60 years old, the average hospital stay was four days longer and the charges were $15,769.55 more for those over 60 years.[22]

---

[21] Cruse, *Prospective Study of 20,105 Surgical Wounds with Emphasis on Use of Topical Antibiotics and Prophylactic Antibiotics,* presented at the Fourth Symposium on Control of Surgical Infections, American College of Surgeons, Washington, D.C. (Nov 10-11, 1972); Cruse & Ford, *A Five year Prospective Study of 23,649 Surgical Wounds,* 107 Arch Surg 206 (1973); Swartz, *Medical and Surgical Instruments and Devices,* in Fruner & M Friedman, 3 Products Liability 34A (1984).

[22] Ross, *High Cost of Trauma Care in the Elderly,* 82 So Med J 857 (1989).

Appendix 13-1
Cases

1 ***Rogers v Baptist General Convention,*** **651 P2d 672 (Okla 1982)** (plaintiff was admitted to a hospital for treatment of a heart condition, and walked out of the hospital and was injured when struck by a vehicle. The plaintiff's theory of liability was negligent failure to coordinate prior hospital records, which would have revealed that this patient required the level of care of an incompetent individual. The plaintiff had a qualified expert who stated that the failure of the hospital to cross-reference the patient's previous treatment with her current records was negligent. That conclusion was based on the standards developed by the Joint Commission on Accreditation of Hospitals (JCAH; now JCAHO). The impact of the testimony was to show that the hospital was negligent by not acquiring the data related to the patient's previous treatment. The testimony was allowed by the court).

2 ***McClaine v Alger,*** **150 Mich App 306, 388 NW2d 349 (1986)** (Michigan Appellate Court strongly suggested that a hospital or doctor's delay in forwarding an x-ray report to treating physicians who requested it may have been responsible for the mismanagement of a compression fracture. In this rather complicated case, the only physician who was exonerated was a second treating physician who finally took a second set of x-rays and testified as to what might have been done had the report on the first set of x-rays been given to the treating physician. The patient was a truck driver involved in a major accident and was seen in an emergency room. A radiologist noted "a slight loss of vertical height anteriorly at T-11 without buckling of anterior cortex" and that it was probably of no significance. The patient left the hospital while in significant pain, and signed a release for the hospital to forward his records and x-rays to a clinic in his home town. Based on the oral information from the patient, the next treating physician treated him as a lumbosacral sprain and prescribed rest for a period of time, followed by gentle exercises. Several calls were made to the hospital, but the x-rays did not arrive until some three months later. The second treating orthopedist who took his own x-rays noted that the fracture, which reported with a loss of height of T-11 without buckling of the anterior thorax, now had a loss of 70 per cent of the height. The hospital authorities argued that they were admittedly wrong in not sending the x-rays promptly, but that the deterioration of the vertebral body on the x-ray was not their negligence. The orthopedic expert testified that a hyperextension brace, if applied earlier, would have prevented the progressive collapse. There was a directed verdict for the hospital. The case was appealed and it was held that "reasonable minds could differ on factual questions" as to whether the hospital's negligence was unrelated to the patient's deteriorating spine. The case was remanded because of errors in the pleadings, with the court's opinion that it appeared

that the first treating hospital's and doctors' negligence in forwarding the x-rays adversely affected the patient, but that it was a jury question).

Comment: In the treatment of emergency patients, particularly transient people who will travel back to their home town when they are able, it is essential that the records clearly reflect the injury and the treatment. It is now standard practice in emergency rooms to give written instructions to the patients as to follow-up care and as to diagnosis. Additionally, a request to forward clinical records, laboratory reports, and x-ray reports should be promptly honored. In most jurisdictions, records cannot be withheld pending payment of a bill, for that compounds negligent behavior. Cases wherein psychiatric information is requested to be sent with the patient or to another physician may present problems that are best solved on an individual basis. On the other hand, doctors who are accepting a patient and who are waiting for records and x-rays have a duty to accept the patient as he or she is at the time of evaluation. Repeating x-rays is a feasible thing to do, rather than waiting three months for the others to be mailed. A telephone call to the treating physician is more promptly responded to, as to comments regarding diagnosis and treatment, so the second treating physician knows better what is going on after having contacted the first treating physician.

3 ***Sharsmith v Hill,* 764 P2d 667 (Wyo 1988)** (a hospital has a direct duty to its patients to supervise and review the treatment rendered by independent staff physicians, and a hospital may be vicariously liable for the malpractice of a staff physician. In this case, the plaintiff had a tumor removed from a leg by a staff surgeon; a section frozen at the time of surgery was called benign and was certified by a pathologist a few days later after review of permanent pathological slides. The tumor recurred several months later, and second biopsy reported malignancy, and amputation was necessary for adequate treatment. The claim against the hospital was based on (1) vicarious liability under an agency theory for the malpractice of the pathologists, who were independent staff physicians, and (2) direct negligence in failing to implement and pursue adequate peer review to monitor staff physicians. The trial court granted summary judgment. The State Supreme Court reversed, holding that a hospital holds itself out to the public as offering health services and may be held vicariously liable for the negligence of an independent staff physician who contracts with the hospital to provide those services. The court held that agency exists when patients hire the hospital, rather than a particular physician, and when the patient believes the physician is an agent of the hospital. The Supreme Court also held the hospital could be held liable for inadequately supervising and reviewing the care given by its physicians. Because a hospital has limited control over its doctors, the hospital's liability arises when it knows, or should have known, that a physician's conduct is deficient).

Comment: *Greenwood v Wiersma,* 741 P2d 1079 (Wyo 1987) reached the same result under facts similar to *Sharsmith.* Other recent decisions affirming the view that a hospital has a duty to its patients to screen staff physicians and/or closely supervise their patient care conduct include *Alford v*

Phipps, 523 NE2d 563 (Ill App Ct 1988); *Cronic v Doud,* 523 NE2d 176 (Ill App Ct 1988); *Reynolds v Mennonite Hospital,* 522 NE2d 827 (Ill App Ct 1988); *Thompson v Nason Hospital,* 535 A2d 1177 (Pa Super Ct 1988), *affd,* 542 A2d 1370, 1371 (Pa 1988); and *Sledziewski v Lutheran Hospitals & Homes Society of America,* 835 F2d 1250 (8th Cir 1987) (applying Nebraska law). For a thorough review of a hospital's duty in physician selection and supervision, see Mark S. Lindensmith, Causes of Action Against Hospital for Negligent Selection or Supervision of Medical Staff Member, 8 Causes of Action 427 (Shepard's/McGraw-Hill 1985).

4 ***Bost v Riley,* 44 NC App 638, 262 SE2d 391 (1980), *cert denied,* 300 NC 194, 269 SE2d 621 (1981)** (hospital breached its duty to oversee a physician practicing at the hospital and negligently failed to enforce its own rule requiring physicians to keep progress notes on a patient's condition. In this case, the court ruled that the negligence was not a contributing cause of the patient's death, and that the hospital, therefore, could not be held liable).

5 ***Elan v College Park Hospital,* 132 Cal App 3d 332, 183 Cal Rptr 156 (1982).** (citing annotation) (in a malpractice action against a surgeon, alleging negligent performance of an operation and breach of a hospital's duty to the patient of ensuring the competence of its staff physicians, granting summary judgment for the hospital was error where triable issues of fact existed—whether the hospital should have conducted an investigation through its peer review committee on notice of prior malpractice case involving the same surgeon, whether the committee had conducted its periodic reviews of the surgeon in a non-negligent manner assuming a review was made after notice of a prior malpractice case and if it had been made in a careful and proper manner, and whether the committee would recommend revocation or suspension of surgeon's staff privileges).

6 ***Johnson v Misericordia Community Hospital,* 99 Wis 2d 708, 301 NW2d 156 (1981)** (citing annotation) (hospital was negligent in granting orthopedic surgical privileges to a surgeon who unsuccessfully attempted to remove a pin, injuring the femoral nerve and artery, causing permanent paralysis of the quadriceps muscle and weakening knee function. Failure to investigate a medical staff applicant's qualifications for the privileges requested creates a foreseeable risk of unreasonable harm and a hospital has a duty to exercise due care in selecting its staff physicians).

7 ***Rule v Lutheran Hospitals & Homes Society of America,* 835 F2d 1250 (8th Cir 1987)** (Nebraska hospital was found liable for the malpractice of a staff physician whose qualifications had never been thoroughly investigated. A major complication occurred during the course of his performing operative procedures on a patient. This was an obstetrical case, and the physician had privileges to treat "major surgery." A check at hospitals where he previously practiced would have revealed that he lacked the necessary training and experience to deliver breech babies. He said that the hospital administrator had limited the investigation to asking the director of a family residency program whether he was qualified to practice in a rural setting. Thus, the hospital had broken its own bylaws. The appellate court concluded

that the damages occurred from "the natural and probable result" of permitting an inexperienced physician to perform the type of surgical procedures that he had been allowed to do).

8 ***Bauer v Friedland,* 394 NW2d 549 (Minn Ct App 1986)** (The patient had originally sought treatment for neck/shoulder pain and headache. After surgery for removal of a disc, the patient complained of numbness and tingling. Other physicians were not able to alleviate the pain. The charge was made that the operating neurosurgeon had overextended the patient's neck and failed to use a microscope during the course of surgery. A memo that the resident had written making the statement derogatory to the neurosurgeon was introduced and was a substantial factor in the jury's deliberations. The supreme court, however, said that the memo was hearsay and could not be considered. Therefore, there was a prejudicial error and the case was remanded for retrial).

Comment: All too often, physicians speak in a derogatory manner about other physicians, which is inappropriate. The ramifications of such a comment can be long-reaching and verification difficult, so that the outspoken physician makes such statements at his or her personal risk.

9 ***Fridena v Evans,* 127 Ariz 516, 622 P2d 463** (Supreme Court of Arizona entered a judgment in favor of a patient who brought a malpractice action against a physician's estate and a hospital for damages to the right leg caused by surgery performed by the physician. The court held that the hospital was negligent for failing to supervise a physician. The surgery resulted in an injury with the right leg three inches shorter than the left. An attempt was made to lengthen a shortened right femur that had occurred following a hip fracture that healed in a shortened position. There was expert testimony that the second operation was poorly founded and was not within the usual accepted standards of orthopedic management of this problem. There appeared to be no question that the physician had committed malpractice).

Comment: *See also Taylor v DiRico,* 124 Ariz 513, 606 P2d 3 (1980); *Harvey v Kellin,* 115 Ariz 495, 566 P2d 297 (1977); *Tucson Medical Center v Misevch,* 113 Ariz 34, 545 P2d 958 (1976); *Purcell v Zimbelman,* 18 Ariz App 75, 500 P2d 335 (1972); *Beeck v Tucson General Hospital,* 18 Ariz App 165, 500 P2d 1153 (1972).

10 ***Pickle v Curns,* 106 Ill App 3d 734, 435 NE2d 877 (1982)** (hospital was charged with failing to review and, in some instances, to supervise the medical care given by a staff physician within the hospital. The first complaint was that the doctor did not order a muscle relaxant (this is the doctor's choice, and he felt it was not necessary), and the second complaint was failure to do a physical examination as required by hospital bylaws. The court held that the hospital had not breached its duty by not supervising each act of the doctor; having not been put on notice, no investigation was indicated. The court held that a hospital administration cannot reasonably be expected to ensure that each of its staff physicians will always perform his or her duty of due care to a patient. The court stated that, having knowledge by innu-

endo, the hospital had duty to investigate and then perhaps to supervise or discipline).

11 ***Holbrooks v Duke University, Inc,*** **63 NC App 504, 305 SE2d 69 (1983)** (defendant hospital's nurse was held negligent for injecting medication in the "wrong" place, three inches above and anterior to a patient's knee).

12 ***Su v Perkins,*** **133 Ga App 474, 211 SE2d 421 (1974)** (doctor was not liable for a patient's injuries caused by a nurse's injection of a drug in subcutaneous tissue where the drug was in common use and had been given to the patient before. It was customary in hospitals to leave the administration of drugs to nurses. As the nurse knew the dangers of improper injection and that a longer needle should be used in obese patients, the doctor was under no duty to instruct the nurse in giving the injection or to personally supervise the injection).

13 ***Southwest Texas Methodist Hospital v Mills,*** **535 SW2d 27 (1976) (Tex Civ App)** (plaintiff alleged that preoperative medication was negligently given in the wrong part of the buttock, resulting in a sciatica nerve injury. Res ipsa loquitur did not apply where competent expert testimony pointed out at least eight possible causes of injury but did not negate any of them as a possible cause, and there was no testimony that the injury would not have occurred absent negligence).

14 ***Rimmele v Northridge Hospital Foundation,*** **46 Cal App 3d 123, 120 Cal Rptr 39 (1975)** (plaintiff sustained osteomyelitis of the spine (vertebra) allegedly resulting from a nurse giving a doctor-ordered injection. The doctor was released as a defendant as it was clear that he personally gave no injection. There was no proof that the nurse's injection was negligent, yet this type of problem (osteomyelitis) does not ordinarily occur absent negligence, thus the res ipsa loquitur doctrine could be invoked).

15 ***Lewis v Davis,*** **410 NE2d 1363 (Ind Ct App 1980)** (physician was held not liable for the action of a hospital nurse who improperly treated a patient's allergic reaction to a drug. The patient died of an allergic reaction to Triavil, which was prescribed by her physician. The physician had sent the patient to the hospital for the injection, as his own office was closed. The patient's estate filed a malpractice action against the physician, but the jury rendered in favor of the physician. There was no agency relationship between the nurse and the physician. The drug prescribed was appropriate and the nurse's immediate supervision of the patient in respect to the anaphylactoid reaction and death within minutes was below the standard of care).

16 ***Farrell v St Vincent's Hospital,*** **52 A2d 954 (Conn 1987)** (nurse and two orthopedic surgeons in a hospital were not negligent when treating a patient who suffered a re-fracture of a bone while the nurse was exercising his legs, according to the Connecticut Supreme Court. The patient was hospitalized as a result of multiple injuries suffered in an accident, including fracture of the shaft of the left femur, dislocation of the right hip, and fracture

of the left knee. Both legs were placed in traction for a few weeks until traction of the right leg was discontinued. The left leg remained in traction until December 1973. Traction was removed in favor of lifting and knee-bending exercises. A part-time nurse employed by the hospital was assigned by one of the patient's orthopedic surgeons to perform exercises on the patient. The patient claimed that during the process of exercising his left leg, the nurse re-fractured the femur. On appeal from a jury trial which rendered a verdict in favor of the nurse, two surgeons, and the hospital, the patient argued that the trial court erred in excluding all evidence of acts of malpractice occurring after December 15, 1973. The court noted that the initial complaint stated that malpractice occurred on or about December 17, 1973. Two days after the trial began, the patient filed a complaint alleging that the nurse had actually re-fractured his leg on December 15, 1973. The court said that since the patient's complaint never alleged negligence or wrongful conduct after the alleged fracture on December 15, 1973, the trial court was correct in excluding any evidence of alleged negligence or malpractice beyond that date. The trial court did not err in excluding the deposition of one of the patient's expert witnesses, a radiologist, who had died before the trial. The patient sought to introduce a deposition that had been taken prior to the trial, but the court ruled that the deposition was too confusing to be presented to the jury. The supreme court said that during the deposition, the radiologist had made reference to certain portions of the x-rays being analyzed by using the words "here, here and here" without any description as to where he was pointing. The jury at best would have to engage in speculation had that deposition been used as evidence. Finally, the court said it would not rule on the patient's claim that the trial court erred in prohibiting the orthopedic surgeon from testifying as to the standard of care owed by a nurse in the hospital).

Comment: Nothing in this case indicates what the negligence might have been, but it does point out the hazards of dealing with patients in long-term immobilization in rehabilitation. Bones are soft, muscles are tight and contracted, and they are easily fractured or torn, yet it is essential to go ahead with the patient as part of the rehabilitation.

17 ***Collins v West Lake Community Hospital,* 57 Ill 2d 388, 312 NE2d 614 (1974)** (in an action by a minor whose leg was amputated when ischemia developed after an operation to remove a blood clot from main artery, a directed verdict for the hospital was erroneous where the surgeon had ordered nurses to watch the condition of the toes, but the jury could have drawn the inference that those nurse observations were not made. The Loss of Chance doctrine—to timely re-operate the leg with possible salvage—was argued).

18 ***Gallagher v Detroit-Macomb Hospital Association,* 431 NW2d 90 (Mich Ct App 1988)** (hospital's internal rules and regulations could not be introduced to establish the applicable standard of care in an action alleging malpractice by a hospital nurse. Expert testimony was required that the nurse (or doctor) deviated from the standard of care of the community. Insti-

tutional rules are distinct from duties that the law requires; internal rules are mere day-to-day guidelines for operation of the institution).

19 ***Koeniguer v Eckrich,*** **422 NW2d 600 (SD 1988)** (in a new trial for a history in a case of fatal postoperative infection, the issue was whether a nurse is obliged to "go over the head" of a physician if he or she believes the doctor is wrong and harm will result. In this case, should the nurse have tried to prevent the discharge of a patient who had a temperature elevation that the physician felt was inconsequential? The Supreme Court of South Dakota ruled that "issues of material fact" remained unsolved. The major question was whether the standard of care required nurses to "independently evaluate a patient's condition prior to discharge, discuss their concerns with the doctor and go on to other authority if they believed that the physician's decision to release the patient was in error." An expert witness for the plaintiff testified that allowing a febrile patient to leave the hospital may have breached acceptable standards and that nurses have a duty to delay discharge pending administrative review. In this case, it was held that a jury must decide whether this testimony outweighed the hospital's contention that the physician's autonomy in this decision is absolute).

20 ***Rogers v Duke,*** **766 SW2d 547 (Tex Ct App 1989)** (surgeon left the operating room before a sponge count was tallied. The plaintiff said that the surgeon failed to oversee "every step" of the operation, including the sponge count. The surgeon left closure of the surgical wound to an assistant, a common practice. The defense maintained that the sponge count was the specific duty of the surgical nurses who were acting under the sole direction of the hospital. Charges against the surgeon were dropped. Before the court of appeals, the patient alleged that the nurses were acting as "borrowed servants" and that the surgeon as "Captain of the Ship" had absolute control over their actions in the operating room. The appeals court justice ruled against that argument. A nurse had testified that sponge counts were always done in accordance with established hospital rules, regardless of who performed the operation. Thus, the count was "an administrative function" and outside of the surgeon's exclusive control).

21 ***Pederson v Dumouchel,*** **72 Wash 2d 73, 431 P2d 973 (1967)** (patient had been involved in an automobile accident and was seen by a general surgeon and a dentist. Minor wounds were closed by the surgeon and a specific note was made that there was no evidence of a head injury. The patient was taken to surgery under the care of the dentist, who had the patient anesthetized by a nurse anesthetist who was an employee of the hospital. Hospital bylaws said that no surgery could be conducted under general anesthesia unless a physician was in the room. The physician had left the room with the dentist being in total charge of the operation of a patient who was having repair of a fractured jaw. The patient never regained consciousness. It was shown that there was severe anoxemia (diminished oxygen) due to the negligence of the nurse anesthetist. The patient had convulsions and became critically ill. He was transferred to another hospital where he was comatose for one month, and the record is not clear what happened to the patient after

that. The record further showed that the nurse anesthetist had been a narcotic user, had been committed to a state hospital for drug abuse treatment, and did not have a recollection of the incident other than what could be refreshed by viewing the hospital chart. The nurse anesthetist was clearly at fault and her treatment of the patient fell well below the standard of care. The physician had violated hospital bylaws and was technically negligent, although he had no direct contact with the care of the patient from the time the patient was transferred to the operating room. The dentist was held to have sufficient knowledge of anesthesia that he should have noted the nurse anesthetist's anesthesia and that the patient was "in trouble." All of the defendants—the nurse anesthetist, the initial treating surgeon, and the dental surgeon—were held liable. The case was dismissed on technical grounds to be re-tried, but not one attempt to reverse the adverse opinion against the three defendants was made. The hospital was also held liable, for not assuring that its bylaws were followed in having a licensed physician present during the course of the operation, and for the actions of the nurse anesthetist).

Comment: Res ipsa loquitur was held applicable in *Pederson,* using in part the argument from *Horner v Northern Pacific Beneficial Association Hospitals, Inc,* 62 Wash 2d 351, 382 P2d 518 (1963) in which the instructions to the jury declared

> Granting exclusive control of the instrumentality and eliminating voluntary participation or contribution by the respondent to the act producing the injury, we feel that negligence may be inferred in three situations without affirmative proof, that is, expert testimony. (1) When the act causing the injury is so palpably negligent it may be inferred as a matter of law, i.e., leaving foreign objects, sponges, scissors, etc., in the body, or amputation of the wrong member; (2) when the general experience and observation of mankind teaches that the result would not be expected without negligence and (3) when proof of experts in esoteric field creates an inference that negligence caused the injuries.

22 Jistarri v Nappi, 549 A2d 210 (Pa Super Ct 1988) (four surgeons and a hospital were not negligent in applying a cast to a patient's broken wrist. The complaint alleged that an orthopedic resident, a hospital employee, negligently applied the cast without adequate padding to an 85-year-old patient's fractured wrist. The patient developed a pressure ulcer under the cast, and the second treating orthopedic surgeon was negligent in failing to remove the cast and diagnose a Staphylococcus infection which entered her blood stream and heart. The weakened heart was susceptible to complications that caused her death. A verdict in favor of the defendants was appealed on the theory that the orthopedic resident should be held to the same high standard as a certified orthopedist, a standard substantially higher than for family practitioners. The court held that a standard of care higher than family practitioners, but less than a board-certified orthopedic surgeon, was appropriate, stating that a surgeon does not warrant a cure or guarantee the result of treatment).

23 **Keopel v St. Joseph Hospital & Medical Center, 8 Mich App 609, 155 NW2d 199 (1967)** (evidence was sufficient to make a prima facie showing that a nurse employed by the defendant hospital was negligent in the way she strapped a patient's arm to an operating table, resulting in an ulnar nerve palsy).

24 ***Koeniguer v Eckrich,* 422 NW2d 600 (SD 1988)** (question was raised if nurse, who knew of temperature elevation the day of discharge, should have contacted the surgeon to re-evaluate the patient. The patient had undergone implant surgery 10 days earlier and had a fever for several days, but the surgeon testified that there was no temperature recorded the morning he saw the patient and no fever reported the day before. It appeared that the temperature that the nurse knew of was not recorded for the morning of discharge. It further appeared that drainage from the wound was not reported by the nurse to the surgeon. The patient was readmitted three days later and died of sepsis six weeks later. Expert testimony indicated that nurses have a duty to question doctors' orders when those orders are not clear or are potentially incorrect, and also have a duty to inform the doctor of drainage from a wound. Therefore, the nurse's care was below the standard of nursing care. The physician was likewise negligent in not recognizing the change in the patient's condition and investigating and treating what later appeared as fatal septicemia. The court held that the hospital failed to demonstrate that the physician's alleged negligence superseded any negligence by the hospital, and that that alleged fact was for a jury to decide).

25 ***Hurlock v Park Lane Medical Center, Inc,* 709 SW2d 872 (Mo Ct App 1985)** (this case turned on the importance of medical records and whether the nurses had scrupulously followed a doctor's instructions. The patient was a very fragile osteoporotic lady who was at risk for developing decubiti (bed sores). She had a fractured femur, had been paralyzed in an accident some 20 years earlier, and had extensive emphysema. Her doctor's orders required that she be turned every two hours. An accurate record of whether she was turned or not did not appear in the hospital notes—the nurses' or progress notes. She would have been turned 117 times during a 10-day period, but there was a record of 18 turnings. She developed a large decubiti that eventually required amputation of her leg. The hospital was a prime target for this suit, although doctors were involved. The hospital staunchly maintained that despite lack of documentation, the doctors' orders had been carried out. The trial court cleared the doctor of negligence, but did not clear the hospital. The appellate court held that not a scintilla of direct evidence that the patient had not been turned had been offered. The appellate court pointed out the legal fraility of the axiom "If it isn't written down, it wasn't done." On the question of whether the physician should have noted that the nurses' notes did not show a record of turning, it was held that it is appropriate for doctors to read nurses' notes, but that they may "also confirm obedience to the orders by observing the patient and nurses as they were").

Comment: The axiom "If it isn't written down, it wasn't done" has carried a great deal of weight in a number of malpractice cases. The obvious advice to physicians, as well as to nurses, is to record as much as possible, as frequently as possible, and as accurately as possible. In the era of defensive medicine, accurate recordkeeping is essential.

26 ***Schmidt v St. Joseph's Hospital,*** **736 P2d 135 (NM Ct App 1987)** (patient's ulnar nerve was positioned on an operating table, apparently creating a pressure phenomena. She developed ulnar neuropathy. The surgery was a hydrocele surgery. The patient failed to respond to interrogatories and failed to present expert testimony that allowing her to develop the pressure phenomena affecting the ulnar nerves was below the standard of medical care. An attempt to invoke the doctrine of res ipsa loquitur was unsuccessful. The physician and hospital presented expert testimony that the physician adhered to community standards and that his actions were not the proximate cause of the patient's injury).

Comment: It is probable that nursing personnel and/or the anesthesiologist could be held responsible. This is one of the ever-present hazards with general anesthesia, and there is always a need to protect vulnerable areas—elbows, knees, etc., from pressure points that may produce neuropathies.

27 ***Goodenough v Deaconess Hospital,*** **637 SW2d 123 (1982)** (plaintiff alleged that a physician and hospital were negligent in positioning for a proctoscopic examination, thereby injuring the plaintiff's neck. Expert testimony was not necessary to establish a nurse assistant's negligence in failing to properly adjust the proctoscopic table, contrary to her specific instructions and duties. The jury had the right to draw the inference that the nurse's act or omission was the proximate cause of the neck injury).

28 ***Boza v Schiebel,*** **308 SE2d 510 (NC Ct App 1983)** (patient undergoing orthopedic surgical procedure came out of surgery with one foot numb and a drop foot. The hospital records made it clear that the damage had been done by the negligent placement of a strap which exerted undue pressure on the peroneal nerve. The orthopedic surgeon was named a defendant, but was able to clear himself by describing step by step how patients are put in position for the type of surgery he did and showing that he, the surgeon, had no part in the placement of the strap. The orthopedist was released, but the hospital was held responsible for the damages).

Comment: There has been a movement away from the surgeon's responsibility for placement of the patient; however, in most cases, he or she instructs that the patient be placed in the position desired for an area of the body to be accessible for the surgical incision, or for a part of the body to be free for movement during the operation so that the joint being operated on can be manipulated and tested. In many jurisdictions, the orthopedist in the case above would have been held responsible.

29 ***Blessing v Doctors Memorial Hospital, Inc,*** **362 SE2d 294 (Ga Ct App 1987),** ***rehg denied*** **(Nov 4, 1987)** (hospital was not liable for negligence which occurred after a surgeon took control of employees in an operat-

ing room. A patient sued the hospital and two physicians, seeking recovery for injuries and alleged suffering during an operation as a result of faulty equipment and improper positioning of his legs. He also sought to recover for an invasion of privacy because unauthorized visitors were allegedly permitted to enter the operating room and view his genitalia during the operation. The trial court granted summary judgment for the hospital on both claims and partial summary judgment for one of the physicians under the invasion of privacy claim. On appeal, the court said that the physician utilizing the equipment in question stated that it was in good working condition. The only evidence to the contrary was the patient's testimony as to statements allegedly made by unidentified operating room personnel during the course of the operation. In the absence of identification of those persons, the court said that such testimony was insufficient to controvert the physician's testimony. The court said that the evidence established that the positioning of the patient's leg was done under the physician's directions. Therefore, any negligent injury resulting from the physician would be imputed to the surgeon rather than to the hospital. The court further said that when the hospital yielded control of its employees to the surgeon in the operating room and the surgeon exercised immediate personnel supervision, he became their master and that their negligence during his master-servant relationship would be imputed to him. The court found that the trial court did not err in granting summary judgment, and affirmed the lower court's judgment).

30 ***Parks v Perry,* 314 SE2d 287 (NC Ct App 1984)** (after awaking from a general anesthetic, a patient persisted with ulnar nerve damage that was severe enough that she lost the function of her fourth and fifth fingers, and could not continue her job at a telephone company. The case was filed against the surgeon, the anesthetist, and the hospital. The anesthetist was a nurse-anesthetist employee of the hospital. The surgeon was excused inasmuch as it was not his responsibility, but the nurse anesthetist and hospital were held liable. The "Captain of the Ship" doctrine is no longer being followed in most jurisdictions. It was the responsibility of the anesthetist to so position the patient that the ulnar nerve could not be damaged. The ulnar nerve damage was caused by negligence on the part of the anesthetist).

31 ***Skelton v Druid City Hospital Board,* 459 So 2d 181 (Ala 1984)** (supreme court affirmed an implied warranty claim against a hospital that provided a surgeon with a defective suturing needle. The court reasoned that warranty provisions of the Uniform Commercial Code should apply to "hybrid" transactions which involve both services and sale of goods if the buyer relies on the seller's knowledge and skill in selecting the good used).

32 ***Podrat v Codman-Shurtleff, Inc,* 558 A2d 895 (Pa Super Ct 1989)** (during spine surgery, a pituitary roungeur broke and lodged in the plaintiff's intervertebral disc space. A second operation was carried out for removal of the broken instrument fragment, and the plaintiff sued under a strict liability theory on the basis that the hospital was the supplier of a defective medical instrument. Nonsuit was granted and appealed, and the appellate court affirmed. The court reasoned that the hospital was in the

business of providing services, rather than selling products. The instrument in question was incidental to providing a service. In response, the plaintiff countered that the hospital had charged him for the instruments. The court emphasized that the determination of whether a defendant provides a defective instrument, not whether a charge was made for the instrument, is crucial. A similar result would flow if the instrument was owned by the surgeon, which is often the case. Either the hospital or the owner surgeon may be negligent in malpractice for using equipment which it knew, or should have known, was defective. Liability can extend to the agency keeping, storing, and maintaining the instrument—ordinarily the hospital. Some courts have ruled that hospitals may be subjected to strict liability for injuries caused by defective products).

Comment: *See Cunningham v MacNeal Memorial Hospital,* 266 NE2d 897 (Ill 1970).

33 ***Redd v Adventist Health System/Sunbelt, Inc,* 353 SE2d 523 Ga Ct App 1987)** (action was brought against hospital personnel and operating surgeons for burns that a patient sustained during surgery to repair a fractured hip. The electrocautery apparatus malfunctioned, leaking current through the patient's knee and causing injury. The borrowed servant doctrine precluded recovery against the hospital where both the surgeon and his assistant were present and in control of operating room personnel during the entire operation. Even if the employees were found negligent, such negligence would be imputed to the surgeon as a matter of law. There was a question of the contributory negligence of the hospital in providing faulty x-ray or electrocautery systems).

34 ***Duff v Yelin,* 721 SW2d 365 (Tex Ct App 1986)** (this case involved a patient who developed ulnar nerve compression following cervical disc surgery, the compression being related to the position on the operating table. The question presented to the jury was whether the surgeon should have warned the patient of the possibility of malposition on the operating table. Because there was a sufficiently remote possibility of injury, the informed consent obtained was considered to be sufficient. Additionally, it was held that even if the possibility of injury existed and that information had been given to the patient, she would have gone ahead with the neck surgery because that was the primary reason for the neurosurgeon to be treating her, not the remote possibility of an elbow problem. However, the anesthesiologist was negligent in positioning the elbow, and there was a settlement on that issue by him).

35 ***Bergeron v Humana Hospital Corp,* 514 So 2d 492 (La Ct App 1987), *cert denied,* 517 So 2d 812 (La 1987)** (it was alleged that surgeons improperly placed a patients legs in a lithotomy position, applying pressure to the lateral aspect of knee and compressing the peroneal nerve, causing foot drop. Res ipsa loquitur was applicable against the surgeon, but not the hospital, where (1) foot drop would not ordinarily occur as a result of the surgery, (2) there was no direct evidence to explain how the foot drop

occurred, and (3) the position of the patient was under the total control of the surgeon).

36 *Spiritos v Temple Corp,* 466 NE2d 491 (1984) (convalescent home and its attending physician was not liable for a fractured hip sustained by a stroke patient while using the bathroom. Hearsay evidence supported the finding that the plaintiff fell while trying to get back to her wheelchair, although she had been told not to attempt it by herself).

37 *Schneider v Kings Highway Hospital Center, Inc,* 67 NY2d 743, 490 NE2d 1221 500 NYS2d 95 (1986) (prima facie case of a hospital's negligence was established by proof that a hospital rule required that bedside rails be up at all times for patients over 70 years of age, and by evidence from which the jury could conclude that it was more likely that hospital staff personnel had lowered the bed rails than the plaintiff's decedent—a weak, elderly patient who required assistance in and out of bed, who only remembered rolling over and landing face down on the floor parallel to the lowered bed rail. Moreover, releasing the bed rail required opening a latch at the foot of the bed which required moderate strength in excess of the patient's ability).

Comment: The orthopedist is regularly faced with the care of elderly, debilitated patients. He or she has a duty to place such patients in capable facilities and to check the patient for protective care as part of the "total" care. The surgeon incurs risk in knowingly referring patient to inadequate facilities (such as a hospital or nursing home).

38 *Washington Hospital Center v Martin,* 454 A2d 306 (DC 1982) (it was alleged that a hospital was negligent in permitting a 93-year-old postoperative patient, who had a history of slipping out of her restraints, to fall out of bed and be injured. The nursing protocol said that restrained patients should be "checked" every one-half hour. The verdict in favor of the plaintiff was upheld where the court found that (1) the issues before the jury as to whether the plaintiff was under restraint (as ordered by her physician) immediately prior to fall, and if not, as to whether the hospital was negligent in leaving her unattended, were not questions requiring expert testimony and (2) the giving of a res ipsa loquitur instruction, if error, was not prejudicial since the jury could readily have found negligence without the instruction).

39 *Bossier v DeSoto General Hospital,* 442 So 2d 485 (La Ct App), *cert denied,* 443 So 2d 1122 (1983) (hospital and attending physician were accused of negligence in offering only routine care to a patient who was receiving large doses of muscle relaxant and pain and anti-anxiety medication, and who fell from a bed, sustaining injury. The bedside rails were up at the time of the accident and the patient was "drugged" and confused and did not know how she fell. The court found that the hospital had a duty to take reasonable precautions to prevent or at least make it difficult for patients to attempt ambulating without assistance while under the influence of several medications).

Comment: In the usual hospital situation, a protocol exists under which a patient "at risk" as in *Bossier* is placed near a nursing station or in an observation area. Posey belt restraints are appropriate when properly used. A sitter is often necessary, as competent nursing personnel recognize how easily and how quickly these confused patients can accidently injure themselves. *See Polonsky v Ubion Hospital,* 11 Mass App 622, 418 NE2d 620 (1981) for similar facts and results.

40 ***Taylor v Beardstown,* 142 Ill App 584, 491 NE2d 803 (1986)** (action was brought against a hospital and a surgeon, alleging negligence in the bad result of a fractured hip repair. The hip fracture occurred when an epileptic patient with recurrent dizziness fell from a hospital bed. There was no proof that the accident would not have occurred absent a negligent act by a hospital employee, and it was held that the patient's inherent disease was the more probable cause of fall. The bad result of hip surgery was an independent issue not tried in this action).

41 ***Smith v Gravois Rest Haven, Inc,* 662 SW2d 880 (Mo Ct App 1983)** (nursing home was liable when a patient slipped out of an improperly applied, physician-ordered Posey belt, and fell and sustained a fractured hip. She was also under the influence of a sleeping pill).

42 ***Robbins v Jewish Hospital,* 663 SW2d 341 (Mo Ct App 1983)** (hospital was liable when a nurse left a bed rail down after a patient had taken a drug overdose and had chronic brain damage, necessitating the use of a leg brace. The patient fell and suffered a fractured hip. The court held that it was a jury question not requiring expert testimony).

43 ***Browne v MacCaulay,* 65 NC App 708, 309 SE2d 704 (1983)** (plaintiff, who was mentally competent, requested that his side rail be left down so he could change his pajamas after using the bathroom, at which time he fell and fractured a hip. The hospital was exonerated of liability).

44 ***Bland v King County,* 55 Wash 2d 902, 351 P2d 153 (1960)** (evidence did not show that a fracture sustained by a patient when hospital employees permitted him to fall while moving him from a bed to a wheelchair bore a causal relationship to his subsequent death from a coronary infarct).

45 ***Jarvis v St Charles Medical Center,* 77 Or App 353, 713 P2d 620 (1986)** (while a patient was undergoing surgery for a fracture of the tibia, an orthopedist noticed symptoms suggesting compartment syndrome, and he performed a fasciotomy to relieve potentially damaging pressure. He ordered the nurses to check the patient every hour and to call him if there was any sign of compartment syndrome. The following day, symptoms suggesting that such a syndrome had occurred; they promptly called the surgeon, who promptly relieved the pressure by spreading the cast. During the third postoperative night, the level of nursing alertness dropped dramatically. The nurses' log noted only sporadic checking of the patient, rather than the hourly checks requested by the surgeon. Early the following morning, the physician found the patient's foot blanched with no pulse. In surgery an hour later, he noted that some muscle necrosis had already occurred. The

patient underwent a series of procedures, but was left with a leg that had lost substantial function. Several experts appeared on both sides, one claiming that the orthopedist did not adequately spread the cast, although he had in fact done the other procedures anticipating the compartment syndrome, including the fasciotomy at the time of the surgery. Other experts said that the hospital nurses were negligent in not monitoring and not fulfilling the orders of the surgeon. The ultimate result was that the hospital and its nurses were held responsible and the orthopedist was not).

Comment: A compression syndrome such as this can rapidly occur after significant trauma to an arm or leg, and requires hourly observation to prevent just the type of complication that occurred in the above case. It did seem that the orthopedist was on the right track with his treatment plan, and that when the marked decrease of circulation to the foot was discovered, further decompression was carried out.

46 ***Rudolph v Iowa Methodist Medical Center,* 293 NW2d 550 (Iowa 1980)** (patient was entitled to damages from a hospital for the negligence of employees who injured him after an anterior cervical fusion, according to the Iowa Supreme Court. After an operation November 17, 1975, the hospital employees permitted the patient's head to drop sharply backward while transferring him from the hospital cart to a bed. The incident was not immediately reported to the operating neurosurgeon. During the next several hours, the patient became partially paralyzed and the neurosurgeon was finally notified. He performed a myelogram to find the site of the problem. After he re-opened the patient, he examined the surgical site and performed a decompression laminectomy to alleviate swelling and compression on the spinal cord. The patient remained in intensive care for eight days, with subsequent transfer from the hospital to a rehabilitation unit where he remained for three months. The patient made a good recovery except for some permanent disability. It was held that the hospital personnel were negligent and responsible for that degree of permanent impairment and the extensive postoperative hospitalization).

47 ***Garcia v United States,* 697 F Supp 1570 (D Colo 1988)** (physicians and nurses at a Veterans' Administration hospital were held negligent in managing a head injury patient. The patient was operated for bilateral subdural hematoma. He was allegedly showing no adverse symptoms postoperatively at 7 P.M. when a nurse went on break. Shortly after, the daughter, staying with the patient, reported to ward nurses that the patient was in respiratory distress, making snorting noises with "bubbling" from his mouth. When the nurse returned 30 minutes later, she found the patient unconscious with thick red blood draining from the operative site drains. Physicians responded to nurses' call 45 minutes later, with more time being lost in obtaining an emergency CT scan. The patient became permanently quadriplegic. At trial, a nurse who testified as an expert, stated that a "stat" call should have been made to the surgeons. A neurosurgeon and neurologist testified that if the patient had been promptly treated after showing signs of seizure, he would not have incurred these severe residual injuries which

were caused by a build-up of blood between his brain and skull. The court found that the nurses and physicians were negligent in failing to properly care for the patient, resulting in these complications, and that the plaintiff had proved that delay in treatment was the proximate cause of the injuries. An award of $1,300,000 was made for past and future economic losses (most of this being nursing care), and $550,000 for noneconomic losses for physical impairment, disfiguration, and pain and suffering. The wife was awarded an additional $15,000).

48 ***Uryasz v Archbishop Bergan Mercy Hospital,* 431 NW2d 617 (Neb 1988)** (new trail was ordered on the issue of damages where a patient was injured by a painful injection in the groin. There was conflicting testimony as to how an injection to a painful area in the groin would result in leg pain, drop foot, and depression. There seemed little question that a latent psychological state became activated, but the jury believed that there was a relationship between the injection and symptoms. The court felt that the award was excessive and sent the case back on that issue. The trial court awarded $195,000. The problem stemmed from (1) difficulty in explaining how an injury to the femoral nerve would produce impairment below the knee, as the femoral nerve has function only proximally to the knee, and (2) how much such impairment would reasonably affect the plaintiff's wage earning ability).

49 ***Battles v Aderhold,* 430 So 2d 307 (La Ct App 1983)** (patient had undergone thyroid surgery (the same general approach and postoperative status of anterior cervical disc surgery), awakened, and was returned to room. Some hours later, the patient developed breathing problem due to swelling in the neck, compressing the trachea. Some time was lost in finding a doctor to respond to the emergency, but eventually an endotracheal tube was placed after one failed attempt by another doctor. The patient was then returned to surgery where a tracheostomy was performed. Respiratory distress was corrected, but in the interim enough anoxia to the brain had occurred that permanent brain damage resulted. The litigation result was that each defendant did the best he could at the time he was present, yet postoperative care failed in monitoring this type of "at risk" patient in a hospital environment that could not offer effective emergency care without damaging injury).

50 ***Mellies v National Heritage, Inc,* 6 Kan App 2d 910, 636 P2d 215 (1981)** (directed verdict for a nursing center owner was precluded in an action alleging negligence in the care of a patient which caused and prolonged the patient's decubiti (bed sores), where the testimony of a nurse-instructor as to the standard of nursing care in preventing and treating bed sores raised jury questions. A nurse who has had extensive experience with bed sores is in fact an expert as to that problem, since their prevention, treatment, and cure are largely a nursing function; therefore, the expert testimony of a physician was not necessary).

51 ***Holbrooks v Duke University, Inc,* 63 NC App 504, 305 SE2d 69 (1983)** (defendant hospital's nurse was held negligent for injecting medication in the "wrong" place, three inches above and anterior to the patient's knee).

52 ***McWain & Tucson General Hospital,*** **137 Ariz 356, 670 P2d 1180 (1983)** (damage to a patient's sciatic nerve was caused by the faulty injection of medicine, according to a medical expert. He stated that there was a deviation from the standard of care, that the person giving the injection either did it improperly, injected the wrong site, or perhaps injected the wrong drug, and that the nerve damage was not the usual result of a therapeutic injection).

53 ***Brown v North Broward Hosptial District,*** **521 So 2d 143 (Fla Dist Ct App 1988)** (court found no inconsistency in the assignment of liability to a hospital, but not to a physician, for emergency room treatment that left a child paralyzed. The appellate court reduced the damages the hospital owed to 90 per cent. The patient was hit by and pinned underneath an automobile for several minutes. The child was carried to the emergency room where the physician suspected internal injuries and kept the child for observation. After five hours, the physician felt the child had only minor injuries and released him. When the child awoke the next day, his legs were paralyzed. Suit was filed for failure to discover and treat the paralysis caused by a spinal cord injury. The mother insisted that she had twice told the physician that the child could not move his legs, but received no response. The physician answered that he had never been told of any such difficulty, or he would have called a specialist in for consultation. The doctor further testified that his physical examination indicated that the patient could move his legs and that neurological testing was normal. The jury refused to fault the physician, but found the hospital liable for $1,100,000 damages. The hospital appealed, contending that the verdict made "no sense" since the liability of the hospital clearly derived from the conduct of the physician as an agent of the hospital. A review of the trial record, however, convinced the appellate court otherwise. Expert witnesses on both sides had testified that emergency room personnel were obliged to report any problems the patient had. The boy's paralysis may have first become manifest after the physician had given the discharge order and while emergency room personnel were moving him out of the emergency area. Thus, the verdict of separate negligence was not inconsistent with the available evidence. The verdict was reduced to $100,000, the statutory limit).

54 ***Moore v Brunswick Hospital Center, Inc,*** **540 NYS2d 794 (1989)** (patient expired when she went into cardiac arrest. The emergency resuscitation "crash team" placed an endotracheal tube into her esophagus rather than the trachea. The question of endotracheal cuff monitoring methods was crucial to establishing negligent placement of the tube; however, the proffered expert based her evidence on a conversation with others, not on personal knowledge or experience).

55 ***Jutzi v County of Los Angeles,*** **242 Cal Rptr 74 (1987)** (Hospital and physicians were not negligent in treating an emergency room patient who later had to have her leg amputated below the knee, the California Court

of Appeals ruled. The patient was a 30-year-old woman who was taken to the hospital emergency room for treatment of a broken ankle. X-rays of the tibia and fibula revealed fractures in the ankle joint. An emergency room physician who did not consider himself qualified for orthopedic care transferred the patient by ambulance to a county hospital. The emergency room physician at the second hospital—although not an orthopedist and although an orthopedist was available—treated the patient, reducing the fracture and applying a full leg cast. The physician had previously treated 50 to 60 similar patients. The patient was sent home in charge of the care of her leg and was advised to return to the hospital if there were complications. She was to return for a 24-hour cast check, but her mother could not take her to the hospital on that day. On her fourth day at home, the patient slipped and fell. She was in great pain by evening but did not seek medical care until the next day. At the hospital, it was found that the patient's lower leg circulation was impaired and that the tissue damage was irreversible. Gangrene developed, and 15 days later a below-the-knee amputation was carried out. The patient sued the county for malpractice involving medical services received at the hospital. At the trial, the patient's expert witness testified that the physician should have consulted an orthopedic specialist, asserting that the cast was too tight and contained a protruding ridge on the inside. He said that the patient's fall was not the cause of the complication. The hospital expert said that the fall and failure to immediately return to the hospital for treatment resulted in irreversible damage. It was pointed out that the patient's pain increased quickly and dramatically after the fall. The jury brought in a verdict for the county. On appeal, the patient contended that the trial court erred in applying a Health and Safety Code provision requiring additional qualifications of expert medical witnesses regarding emergency medical care. She contended that the physician of service did not constitute emergency medical coverage because, as such, it applied only to suits against physicians. The court disagreed. The court also said that since the testimony of the patient's expert indicated that her injury was such that there was a possibility of serious physical disability, this supported the finding that the physician's treatment constituted emergency care. Further, the court said that the patient's transfer to a second hospital did not preclude the finding that the medical services at the second hospital constituted emergency care. The court affirmed the lower court's judgment).

56 ***Mann v Cracchiolo,*** **38 Cal 3d 18, 694 P2d 1134, 210 Cal Rptr 762 (1985)** (action was brought based on the death of the plaintiff's decedent, allegedly as a result of a broken neck sustained in a fall while being x-rayed at a hospital, and defendant's subsequent failure to diagnosis and treat the injury. Summary judgment on punitive damage issues was properly granted where the declaration of the plaintiff's expert witness in opposition to the motions at most made a case for medical malpractice and not a claim for punitive damages. There was no evidence of conspiracy to conceal the injury, of intentional performance of a useless operation on the decedent, or of an attempt to kill her. At most, all that was shown in opposition to the motions was failure to observe, report, or diagnose, which failure did not establish intentional misconduct).

57 ***Ritter v Wayne County General Hospital,* 436 NW2d 673 (Mich Ct App 1988)** (two hospitals were not negligent in refusing to admit a patient. One hospital had no beds available. The second refused to accept him on transfer, but the third did admit him. The patient was a drug user who had an aortic valve replacement several years before. He required open heart surgery and died. The allegation was against the two hospitals for failing to admit, in violation of state and federal regulations. Affirming summary judgment, the court held that the first hospital had no duty to admit as it had no beds, and that the second hospital had no duty to provide emergency services as there was no indication that an emergency existed. The hospitals' behavior was not in violation of federal or state regulations).

58 ***Reid v Indianapolis Osteopathic Medical Hospital,* No IP88-1034OC (SD Ind Apr 13, 1989)** (federal district court held that actions brought under the federal "Anti-Dumping Act" (42 U.S.C. #1395 dd) are not controlled by state statutes which require prelitigation review of claims against health care providers. The court ruled that claims brought under that statute are governed by state legislation which limits the amount of damages that may be recovered in medical liability actions. In this case, the patient was taken to a hospital emergency room following an accident, was seen, "taken," and treated, and then was transferred to another hospital as there were no resources to pay. It was held that the patient was not adequately stabilized to be transferred without risk of death. The plaintiff stated that because the federal statute referred to damages under available state law for "personal injury," the statute incorporated only those state laws which applied across the board to all personal injury actions, not only to laws regarding medical negligence. There was a question of whether the state malpractice damage ceiling applied, with the court holding that the congressional intent was to incorporate that ceiling).

59 ***Chatham County Hospital v Ross,* 362 SE2d 390 (Ga Ct App 1987), *rehg denied* (Oct 28, 1987)** (hospital was not liable for a surgeon's negligence while the surgeon was in charge of an operating room, the Georgia Court of Appeals ruled. The patient sued the surgeon and the hospital, alleging an that instrument was left in the abdomen during operation. The trial court denied partial summary judgment to the hospital on the issue of liability to the patient under the borrowed servant doctrine. On appeal, the court said that the surgeon was not a hospital employee, although he had privileges at the hospital. During the operation, members of the hospital house staff and several nurses who were hospital employees assisted him. In his deposition, the surgeon admitted that he was in charge of the operating room during the surgery in question. The patient offered no evidence to rebut this, or that the surgeon was absent at any time during the hospital. Therefore, there was no question that the surgeon exercised immediate personal supervision over hospital employees who were present during the operation. Since the surgeon conceded that the instrument was left in the patient's abdomen

during surgery when he was in charge, the court found that the hospital was not responsible).

60 ***Krane v St Anthony Hospital,* 738 P2d 75 (Colo Ct App 1987)** (appellate court affirmed a judgment for a hospital because of the alleged negligence of its nurse occurring during surgery in the presence of the operating surgeon. The court said "once the operating surgeon assumes control of the operating room, the surgeon is liable for the negligence of all persons working under his supervision." A recent comparable "Captain of the Ship" analysis has been employed by several jurisdictions in a foreign body (surgical sponge) case, reasoning in general that the surgeon is in charge of the case and cannot pass liability to a nurse who states that a sponge count is correct when in fact it was not. This vicariously holds the surgeon responsible for the nurse's negligent act. Although the "Captain of the Ship" doctrine has been abandoned in favor of a controlled test under agency law, the "Captain of the Ship" language is prevalent. Many courts continue to refer to the "borrowed servant doctrine" as the "Captain of the Ship" doctrine. The surgeon, by tradition and probably by egocentricity, often refers to himself as the "Captain of the Ship" in the operating room. Similes sometimes help to explain a factual situation, but in legal writing, phrases have a way of being canonized and of growing until they can stand and walk independently of the general rules. The result of using the "Captain of the Ship" phraseology is that a surgeon or physician may be held liable).

61 ***Hollant v North Shore Hospital, Inc,* 24 Misc 2d 892, 206 NYS2d 177 (Sup Ct 1960)** (when an employee of a hospital assists a surgeon in an operation, a question of fact is presented as to whether the hospital has completely surrendered the control of the employee with the result that the employee becomes the special employee of the surgeon and the hospital is relieved of liability for his acts. If such questions were resolved adversely to the hospital, declared the court, notwithstanding the fact that the employee, in accordance with the policy of the hospital, followed the directions and commands of the surgeon, the hospital would be cast in damages due to the primary fault of the surgeon. Therefore, concluded the court, it was unable to hold that mere obedience by the hospital employee to the negligent direction of the attending surgeon exonerated the hospital from the effects of respondent superior).

62 ***Beaches Hospital v Lee,* 384 So 2d 234 (Fla Dist Ct App 1980)** (although the duties of an assisting nurse involving professional skill are generally regarded as controlled by the surgeon, when a nurse's services are simply ministerial in character, she is not the doctor's borrowed servant but a servant of the hospital, for which the latter would be vicariously liable). **Comment:** The following are in accord with *Beaches: Kitto v Gilbert,* 39 Colo App 374, 570 P2d 544 (1977); *Kohoutek v Hafner,* 366 NW2d 633 (Minn Ct App 1985); and *Synnott v Midway Hospital,* 287 Minn 270, 178 NW2d 211 (1970). But see *Swindell v St Joseph's Hospital, Inc,* 161 Ga App 290, 291 SE2d 1 (1982).

63 ***Duhon v State,* 516 So 2d 222 (La Ct App 1987)** (hospital was liable for the negligence of a technician. An award of $10,000 to a patient who was injured through the negligence of an x-ray technician was supported by the evidence. The patient had metastatic cancer of the breast, which was diagnosed in 1977. The cancer had begun to spread by 1980, affecting her bones. Even the slightest trauma would result in a fracture. In July 1982, the patient brushed against a door and fractured her shoulder. Surgery was performed and a subsequent x-ray showed satisfactory healing. She returned to the hospital on November 22, 1988. Her sister, who accompanied her, later testified that she herself had informed the x-ray technician that the patient could not help herself and required careful assistance. The technician refused to assist the patient. The sister said the patient complained of pain when she returned home and said that "the lady let her fall off the table." Her daughter testified that the patient had told them that the technician had dropped her, causing her to strike her back against the x-ray table. Five days later, the patient was taken back to the hospital because her back pain continued. The treating physician noted injuries in her records and that she had low back pain since she was helped onto the x-ray table. The patient returned home in pain, could not leave her bed, and died on December 29, 1982. Survivors brought a negligence action against the hospital. At trial, the hospital presented no evidence. The technician did not appear. The survivors were awarded $10,000 for the patient's pain and suffering. On appeal, the hospital contended that the hearsay by the patient's family was improper evidence, that neither negligence nor a connection between negligence and injury was proven, and that the damages awarded were excessive. The court said that, the patient's medical records, along with uncontradicted expert medical opinions, sufficed to establish the cause of the patient's injuries. The physician testified that the proper procedure in transferring the patient in such a fragile condition from a wheel chair to an x-ray table required more than one person. The patient's statements to her sister and daughters were accumulated. The medical records were not admitted erroneously, although the court considered that they were somewhat generous, but it was in the discretionary range, considering that the patient's injuries had caused her considerable pain and denied her the few simple pleasures she had in the last months of her life. The lower court's opinion was affirmed).

64 ***Austin v Sisters of Charity,* 470 P2d 939 (Or 1970)** (hospital x-ray technician, in attempting to position a patient on a table, grasped the patient beneath the arms and pulled, causing a back injury. The probability that the accident was caused by the negligent pulling of the technician was not greater than the probability of a non-negligent cause; therefore, res ipsa loquitur was inapplicable).

65 ***Fulton County Hospital Authority v Hyman,* 376 SE2d 689 (Ga Ct App 1988),** ***cert denied,*** **(Jan 19, 1989)** (plaintiff's infant child was taken to an emergency room for treatment of a thumb injury. The cut was repaired and dressed, and the patient was discharged from the emergency room with instructions as to the care of the wound. The patient was taken to a family doctor for follow-up care, and an infection was diagnosed, requiring two periods of hospitalization and partial amputation of the thumb. After several legal moves, the hospital was found liable and awards of $4,200 for unreimbursed medical expenses and $118,000 for pain and suffering were affirmed. Issues at trial included the alleged negligence of the parents in caring for the wound, timely response to a summons by the hospital (secretary was competent to receive the summons), and default judgment).

66 ***Nguyen v Los Angeles County Harbour/UCLA Medical Center,* No C537628 (Compton County Super Ct Cal Apr 13, 1989)** (six-month-old girl was being treated for a congenitally dislocated hip. A harness device to hold the reduced hip was not working; a hip arthrogram diagnostic study was proposed. In the x-ray department, a radiologist tried to locate the hip joint five times by injecting it. The patient suffered respiratory arrest. Because the radiology department had no emergency resuscitation equipment, the child was moved to pediatrics in its acute care unit one floor below, with some delay. On arrival at the unit, the child was in full cardiac and respiratory arrest. The heart beat was restored, but brain swelling ensued and the child was moved to intensive care. No intracranial pressure bolt was installed to monitor intracranial pressure; the brain herniated due to fluid overload. The plaintiffs alleged that air should not have been injected to outline the joint, as an air embolus explained the respiratory arrest. Further, negligence in overloading the child with fluids and failure to monitor intracranial pressure leads to brain herniation, and permanent brain damage, and a vegetative state. The defense responded that there was no air embolus, and that the problem was due to "sudden infant death syndrome," "near miss" sudden infant death syndrome (SIDS), a possibility that the child was a breath holder, "apnea of infancy," the child having a vaso-vagal nerve response during needling, causing respiratory arrest, and unknown causes. There was a jury verdict was for the plaintiff).

67 ***Schultz v Much,* 211 Cal Rptr 445 (1985)** (mother alleged that her baby was born quadriplegic and mentally retarded due to the negligence of several attending nurses and defendant physicians. The mother was involved in an emergency Cesarian section in which she received inadequate care. The jury awarded $480,000 in economic damages, which the appeals court affirmed. The court upheld the applicability of respondeat superior, citing the special relationship between a vulnerable hospital patient and the physician chosen by the patient. The court rejected the doctor's argument that the doctrine is outdated, noting the defenselessness of hospital patients, the element of choice of physicians, the inability of the patient to control what is happening, and the impersonal nature of hospital care. In this case, the nurses were under the control of the physician).

Comment: In most jurisdictions, respondeat superior would involve the hospital as responsible for nurses' negligence. The doctrines of master-servant and "Captain of the Ship" continue to be alleged, but rarely stand. The surgeon can be liable if he or she observes negligent nurse behavior and fails to correct it.

68 ***Pellitier v Kaiser Foundation Hospital,* No 8512-07970 (Multnomah County Cir Ct Portland Or 1988)** (plaintiff underwent arthroscopic surgery in which one blade of a special scissors broke, leaving a metal foreign body in the knee. Later, in the same operation, a chondrotome—a special cartilage cutting knife—broke into three pieces. The scissors blade was removed at the time of the first surgery; the knife fragments were discovered later. The plaintiff brought an action against the manufacturer, alleging that these products were unreasonably dangerous because they broke during the arthroscopic operation. The plaintiff alleged that the hospital was negligent in that the surgeon failed to recognize and remove broken objects during surgery and failed to inspect the instruments after surgery to see if they were intact. The manufacturer denied that its products were defective. It argued that the chances of two instruments breaking during a single operation were 1 in 100,000 and that a doctor could not be expected to look for broken instruments during a procedure. The patient had a 35 to 50 per cent disability to the knee, and claimed lost wages of $35,000 and medical expenses of $12,641. The defendants argued that most of the present knee pain was due to an inherent disease which was unaffected by the foreign bodies and that the foreign bodies were discovered while the patient was being evaluated for femoral bone tumor).

69 ***Richmond County Hospital Authority v Haynes,* 121 Ga 537, 174 SE2d 364 (1970)** (defendant hospital bound a patient in leather straps, restraining him while he was in a diabetic coma, under orders of his physician. Hospital rules regarding the use of padding and periodic removal for treatment of the affected area were not observed. As a result, the plaintiff suffered bruises and blisters which broke down and became infected. Nerve damage later occurred. The court affirmed the judgment for the plaintiff, holding that a res ipsa loquitur instruction was correctly given, and that the benefit of res ipsa loquitur was not lost because the plaintiff gave some evidence of the defendant's negligence and that the plaintiff's actions while in coma were not voluntary. The court also approved the exclusion of evidence that the plaintiff received social security. The evidence was offered to show a motive for not returning to work).

70 ***Wilmington General Hospital Association v Nichols,* 210 A2d 861 (Del Super Ct 1965)** (plaintiff had surgery, and postoperatively the surgeon prescribed two kinds of medicine to be given by injections in the buttock. On the morning in question, the nurse, employed by the defendant, gave the plaintiff two injections in his left buttock. The plaintiff testified that three to five minutes after injection, he felt a sharp pain down the back of his buttock, down his left leg on the outside, and across the top of his foot. The nurse stated that she gave the injection in the upper outer quadrant of the buttock to avoid injury to the sciatic nerve. The court held that evidence and direct testimony of the plaintiff was sufficient to establish that the injections were negligently given outside of the upper outer quadrant. The verdict was against the nurse and the hospital).

71 ***Kalmus v Cedars of Lebanon Hospital,* 132 Cal App 2d 243, 281 P2d 872 (1955)** (judgment was affirmed in favor of the plaintiff. The evidence was sufficient to support a finding that a nurse not only used an infected needle, but also failed to follow standard hospital procedure in scrubbing the area to be injected, thereby causing a staphylococcus infection. The employer hospital, having been joined under the respondeat superior doctrine, was held liable, in addition to the nurse).

72 *Williams v St Claire Medical Center,* 657 SW2d 590 (Ky Ct App 1983) (orthopedist was liable for failure to supervise a recently graduated nurse anesthetist. The surgeon was to do an arthroscopy of the knee, and spinal anesthetic was to be administered. The patient suffered cardiac arrest. The orthopedist was in the area, was called in to assist in resuscitation, and participated in a closed-chest massage. Although the orthopedist was not in direct control of the situation—he was off in emergency services—he did have control over the nurse anesthetist inasmuch as he was chairman of the department of surgery and, in that hospital, the department of anesthesia was a sub-unit of the department of surgery. There were no other physicians supervising the newly graduated nurse anesthetist. It was held that the orthopedist was vicariously in control of the situation, and participated in the negligence that occurred in the improper giving of a spinal anesthesia and in some errors in the resuscitation. The appellate judges agreed that this came within the "doctrine of apparent authority," although it was "indeed a radical departure from the established principles of malpractice liability").

73 *Harrington v Rush Presbyterian St Lukes Hospital,* No 79L15578 (Cook County Cir Ct Chicago Ill Oct 3, 1988) (25-year-old homemaker, badly injured in an automobile accident, became addicted to Darvocet pain medication. She was admitted to the psychiatric ward of the defendant hospital. Her attending physician ordered 42 tablets of Darvocet to be given, twice the dose the patient had ever taken. The patient received medication from a floor duty nurse, and was found dead several hours later. It appeared that no nurse checked in the interim, the patient being in rigor mortis when found. The plaintiff's allegations included improper monitoring on the part of the nursing staff. The result was a plaintiff verdict of $4 million. In the settlement negotiation, $750,000 was demanded by the plaintiff and $500,000 was offered by the defendant).

Comment: Implicit in this case is the duty of a nurse to recognize a probable error in physician orders (42 Darvocet tablets) and to contact the doctor or nursing supervisor to correct the error, or to refuse to give the medication as prescribed.

74 *Knuckles v Delman,* No SoC70429 (Los Angeles Super Ct Cal June 1988) (plaintiff, a 47-year-old warehouseman, alleged negligence in performing a spinal fusion and in postoperative care. The orthopedist diagnosed by x-ray a widening of interspinous distance and instability at the C3-4 level. Conservative treatment was ineffective, except that a Philadelphia brace decreased neck pain. A neurological consultation found no other neurological or physical problem, suggesting a myelogram or CT scan. The orthopedist did neither of these studies, but proceeded to operate and perform a

C3-4 fusion. On the day of surgery, the patient complained of weakness in his right arm and developed difficulty in urinary voiding. No neurological consultation or other examination was ordered by the surgeon. The next day, the patient complained to nurses of numbness in his hands and difficulty in moving them. By the third day, the patient was unable to move his hands, arms, or toes, and was unable to cough. The nurses did not attempt to reach the operating surgeon. On the fourth day, a neurologist was consulted and suggested a myelogram. A myelogram was done the next day and another doctor performed decompressive laminectomies. The plaintiff brought an action against the first surgeon alleging (1) inadequate preoperative indications for performance of the spinal fusion, (2) negligent performance of the surgical procedure, and (3) negligent neurological postoperative care based on failure to recognize emergency postoperative neurological complications. The hospital was part of the suit due to the alleged negligence of nurses in failing to timely inform the orthopedist. The injury that resulted from the medical malpractice was quadriparesis/quadriplegia. The plaintiff claimed $1,485,462; the result was a $525,000 settlement).

Comment: The negligent postoperative care—failure to examine the patient for three days—thus missing postoperative complications, and the nurses' failure to inform the doctor—is apparent. Less obvious are the criticisms of unnecessary surgery or surgical technique.

14

Informed Consent

But it does not matter to a man whether he acts at his own peril or not, unless harm comes of it, and there must always be someone within reach of the consequences of the act before any harm can come.

—Oliver Wendell Holmes, The Common Law and Other Writings, 164 (L. Adams ed 1982)

§14.01 Generally

The first record of the right of a patient to be informed comes from Kings Bench in 1767, which criticized a famed English surgeon and an apothecary for unwarranted experimentation. The first modern case involving informed consent was *Natanson v Kline* 186 Kan 393, 350 P2d 1093 (1959), *clarified & rehg denied,* 187 Kan 186, 354 P2d 670 (1960).

In 1987, the United States Court of Appeals upheld a judgment that gave doctors some comfort on the issue of consent. *Augustine v United States,* 810 F2d 991 (10th Cir 1987). The patient was advised by a gastroenterologist to undergo dilation of the esophagus. The doctor told the patient there was a 1 in 100 risk of rupture to the esophagus and drew a picture on the back of the consent form which the patient signed. During the procedure, the esophagus was perforated. The patient developed a mediastinitis and required major surgery. He recovered and sued the doctor for lack of informed consent and negligent misrepresentations.

At trial, the patient said he neither understood the risks nor was told of alternative forms of treatment available to him.

The court preferred the evidence of a doctor that great care had been taken in obtaining the consent of the patient. In reaching this conclusion, the Court of Appeals commented on the substantial evidence provided by the diagram on the consent form. The author does not believe that a doctor's reputation should hang on his artistic ability, but this case illustrates once again the importance of meticulous recordkeeping in accordance with good clinical practice.

§14.02 What is Informed Consent?

The doctrine of *informed consent* states the duty of a physician or surgeon to inform a patient of the risk involved in treatment or surgery. The earliest cases treated this as liability for battery. Beginning in the early 1960s, it began to be recognized that the matter was really one of standard professional conduct, so negligence has generally displaced battery as a basis for liability.

Informed consent is rooted in the fundamental recognition—reflected in the legal presumptions of competency—that adults are entitled to accept or reject health care interventions on the basis of their own personal values and furthering their own personal goals; that is, every person has a right to determine what should be done to his or her own body. (*See* Appendix 14-1, Cases 1 to 4.)

Patients are not entitled to insist that health care practitioners furnish them services when it would violate either the boundaries of accessible practice or a professional's own deeply held moral beliefs, or would draw on a limited resource of which the patient has no binding claim.

The fundamental values that informed consent is intended for most—self-determination and patient well-being—both demand that alternative arrangements for health care decisionmaking be made for individuals who lack substantial capacity to make their own decision.

Decisionmaking capacity is specific to each particular decision, although some people lack this capacity for all decisions. Many people are incapable of making some decisions but not others; the concept of capacity is best understood and applied as a functional manner.

Decisionmaking incapacity should be found to exist only when people lack the ability to make decisions that promote their well being and conformity with their own previously expressed values and preferences.

To the extent feasible, people with no decisionmaking capacity should still be consulted about their own preferences, out of respect for them as individuals.

Health care providers should not ordinarily withhold unpleasant information simply because it is unpleasant. The ethical foundation of informed consent allows withholding of information from patients only when they request it be withheld or when disclosure would cause substantial detriment to their well-being.

A shared decisionmaking based on mutual respect is ultimately the responsibility of individual health care professionals. However, health care institutions such as hospitals and professional schools have important roles to play in assisting health care professionals in this obligation. Although pieces of information may be provided with various people, there should be one individual officially charged with the responsibility for insuring that all necessary information is communicated and that the patient's wishes are known to the treatment teams.

Patients should have access to the information they need to help them understand their condition and make treatment decisions.

As cases arrise, new legislation is contemplated; courts and legislatures should reflect this view of ethically valid consent. Nevertheless, the Commission does not look to legal reforms as a primary means to bring about changes in the relationship between health care professionals and patients.

The Commission finds that a number of relatively simple changes in the practice could facilitate patient participation in health care decisionmaking. Several specific techniques, such as having patients express either orally or in writing their understanding of the treatment they are consenting to have, deserve further study.

Furthermore, additional societal resources need to be committed to improving the human side of health care, which has apparently deteriorated at the same time as there have been substantial gains in health care technology.

Because health care professionals are responsible for ensuring that patients can participate effectively in decisionmaking regarding their care, educators have a responsibility to prepare physicians and nurses to carry out this obligation.

The Commission recommends that health care institutions and professionals judiciously attempt to involve family members in decisionmaking for patients, with due regard to the privacy of the patients and for the possibility of cohesion that such practice entail.

The Commission recognizes that its vision of health care decisionmaking may involve greater commitments of time on the part of health professionals. Reimbursement of the professional should, therefore, take into account the time spent in discussion, rather than regarding it as a separate item for which additional payment is made.

The President's Commission in 1982 reported:

> As with 'medical paternalism,' the notion of patient sovereignty can be carried too far. Both positions attempt to best exclusive moral agency, ethical wisdom and decisionmaking authority on one side of the relationship while assigned the other side a dependent role . . . Neither extreme adequately reflects the current nature and needs of health care.[1]

(*See* Appendix 14-1, Cases 5 to 9.)

§14.03 Informed Consent Requirements

Common law requires that physicians obtain their patients' consent before treating them. To ensure that consent is informed, physicians must disclose the risks and benefits of alternatives, including nontreatment, to any intervention the doctor proposes. Ideally, disclosure promotes communication and fosters trust between patient and physician. When informed of risks and choices, a patient can tell the physician of his or her concerns, values, and wishes—these may modify the medical treatment the physician recommends.

Since the 1970s, the increased sensitivity of physicians to informed consent has promoted the autonomy and welfare of their patients. In spite of this, evidence suggests that full disclosure still occurs relatively infrequently, and not as contemplated by law. One report suggests that physicians sometimes couch their disclosures in terms to promote more costly procedures. Psychological studies also indicate that even with accurate disclosure, patients may not understand, because of poor communication, the information provided or its meaning. New information often does not lead patients to reconsider proposed treatments.

The detailed written forms used to obtain consent sometimes obscure understanding. Patients often treat them as meaningless paperwork and do not recall what they have signed. Even when doctors avoid making decisions, the patients typically choose what the physician wishes or suggests. It appears that full disclosure in obtaining informed consent does not always give the patient understanding or control, and without supervision, physi-

---

[1] M. Resoff, Making Health Care Decisions, a Report on the Ethical and Legal Implications of Informed Consent in Patient-Practitioner Relationship, 1 Presidents' Commission 36 (Oct 1982). Mid-year Meeting, American Academy of Legal Medicine, Oklahoma City, Okla (Oct 6-7, 1989).

cians generally do not disclose all pertinent information to their patients.[2] (*See* Appendix 14-1, Cases 10 to 17.)

§14.04 Forms of Consent

Constructive consent is understood without words, from the nature of the case or circumstances, as in a serious emergency and/or in cases of a patient's inability to speak or express him- or herself.

Implied consent is acknowledged without express statement, by the initial action of the patient and in response to a physicians' suggestions. For example, a person standing in a line of people receiving vaccinations gives implied consent when he or she holds an arm out.

Expressed consent is a clearly stated oral or written agreement to a proposed procedure based on information, comprehension, and a statement of approval, with or without limitations.

Informed consent must include:

1. The nature of the patient's illness and/or injury
2. The nature of the proposed therapy
3. Reasonable alternative therapies
4. Chance of success of the procedure proposed
5. Substantial risks inherent in therapies
6. Risk of refusing treatment
7. Statement that the patient has understood the procedure, alternatives, and risks, and has asked questions, if any

§14.05 Duty to Inform

As a general rule, the physician who intends to perform or supervise a treatment has the duty to obtain informed consent from the patient. This cannot be relegated to another person (such as a nurse or assistant, except to aid in explanation of the procedure). The physician has an independent duty and must personally obtain the consent or be assured (and assume the potential liability) that consent obtained by another is complete, accurate, and informed.

"I didn't understand," is a very common theory proffered by the plaintiff-patient. The patient may have signed the consent or listened to the surgeon's description, yet later will not recall the substance of consent or not recall the risks, if they were mentioned. Such patients argue that, had they known of the risk or limited probability of success, they would not have allowed the procedure to be performed. (*See* Appendix 14-1, Cases 5 and 18 to 27.)

In 1976, two busy thoracic surgeons (Robinson and Merav) conducted a survey with patients who were having a very major heart operation. They

---

[2] Rodwin, *Physician's Conflict of Interest,* 321 NEJM 1405 (1989).

were given an extensive informative dissertation containing all of the elements of a good informed consent. Four months after the consent was signed and the operation was completed, 33 per cent remembered the diagnosis and nature of their illness, 35 per cent remembered the major risks of the operation, 26 per cent remembered the proposed operation—that is, what was to have been done, 10 per cent remembered the potential complications, 29 per cent recalled the benefits, and 29 per cent remembered the alternative treatments available. The survey concluded:

> While patients were well informed and comprehended their situations prior to operation, they subsequently forgot most of what they understood and made other quantitative errors. We believe it is essential to document, in some way, the details of the informed consent so it becomes a permanent part of the clinical record, since memory of the event is unreliable.

§14.06 Methods of Documentation

A signature on a consent form is not enough; the consent form must indicate that the patient has read or been informed, is satisfied, has no unanswered question, and has agreed to the procedure by signing.

Other ways of documenting what the patient has been told and understands are:

1. Audiotaping or videotaping the information session
2. Written statements on the physician's letterhead with an outline of procedure, expected outcomes, potential complications, with the patient's signature on the patient's chart
3. Use of commercially available consent forms with patient signature
4. Sign-off or receipt for written or audiovisual material given the patient, indicating that the patient has received and understands the information

§14.07 Standards for Adequacy of Consent

The old rule was the "professional community standard." It is hard to get an expert witness to refute or support this standard.

The new rule is the "reasonable patient standard," which asks whether the patient would have gone through the procedure, or whether a reasonable person would undergo the procedure, knowing what was contained in the informed consent. This rule also includes a theory of causal relationship: is there a direct relationship between bad results and patient understanding? Would it have happened anyway? This is in addition to the question of whether the patient would have undergone the procedure if he or she had known of the bad result possibility?[3]

The Supreme Court of New Jersey adopted the prudent patient standard for determining whether a patient had given her informed consent to a medical/surgical procedure. The court reasoned that the prudent patient standard first announced in *Canterbury v Spence* better secures an individual's right of self-determination than the current professional standard. The professional standard asks whether the physician acted as a reasonable physician of similar training in the community would have acted in informing the patient of the risks involved in the procedure. In New Jersey, at least, future plaintiffs will have to establish that a reasonable individual in the plaintiff's position would not have chosen to undergo a recommended procedure after being advised of all significant risks. (*See* Appendix 14-1, Cases 1, 10, 13, 14, and 28 to 30.)

The operative or diagnostic procedure may be appropriately and skillfully performed. The doctor, however, may be liable for the adverse consequences about which the patient was not adequately informed.

A particularly vexing question is whether a patient needs to know about an undisclosed risk to make an informed decision. The courts often speak in terms of the materiality of the risk: the doctor's duty is to disclose all risks which are "material."

The extent of the duty to disclose is based on professional medical standards where a physician has customarily informed patients about the type of risk involved or whether a reasonable physician will make the disclosure under the circumstances.

A number of recent cases have defined the duty in informed consent in terms of the patient's need to know the information based on whether a reasonable person in the patient's position would attach significance to the information. "An unlimited discretion in the physician is irreconcilable with the basic right of the patient to make the ultimate informed decision. . . ."

In attempting to further describe the reasonable man, A. P. Herbert in Misleading Cases in Common Law 1741 (1930) says:

> He is an ideal, a standard, the embodiment of all those qualities which we demand of the good citizen. . . . He is one who invariably looks where he is going, and is careful to examine the immediate foreground before he executes a leap or a bound; who neither star gazes or is lost in meditation when approaching trap doors of life; . . . who never mounts a moving omnibus and does not alight from any car while the train is in motion and will inform himself of the history and habits of a dog before administered a caress . . . who never drives his ball until those in front of him have definitely vacated the putting green, who never from one year's end to another makes excessive demands on his wife,

---

[3] Arnold & M.M. Roseff, Informed Consent (1981); S.M. Torasa, Legal Guide to Physicians (1985); M.M. Resoff, Securing the Informed Consent Mid-year Meeting, American Academy of Legal Medicine Oklahoma City, Okla (Oct 6-7, 1989).

> his neighbors, his servants, his ox or his ass; . . . who never swears, gambles or loses his temper, who uses nothing except in moderate . . . even while he flogs his child he is meditating only on the golden mean . . . In all that mass of authorities which bears upon his branch of law, there is no mention of a reasonable woman.[4]

§14.08 Intent

In a loose and general sense, the meaning of "intent" is easy to grasp. Holmes said, "even a dog knows the difference being tripped over and being kicked. Of course, a cunning tripper might fool the dog—once, at least."

Intent is the key distinction between two major divisions of legal liability—negligence and intentional torts. Intent plays a key role in criminal law and elsewhere. (ALI Model Penal Code §2.02(2)(a) and (b) (1962) defining "purposely" and "knowingly.")

The three most basic ailments of intent are (1) state of mind, (2) consequences of an act or omission, and (3) belief that the consequences are substantially certain to result from the act.

Intent is broader than a desire or purpose to bring about a physical result. It extends not only to those consequences which are desired, but also to those which the actor believes are substantially certain to follow from whatever he or she does. For example, an actor fires a bullet into a dense crowd; he or she may pray that the bullet will hit no one, but if he or she knows the bullet will hit someone, he or she "intends" that consequence.

Intent, where tort liability is concerned, is not necessarily a hostile intent or a desire to do any harm. Rather, it is an intent to bring about results which will invade the interest of another in a way that the law forbids. The defendant may be liable although intending nothing more than a good-natured practical joke, honestly believing the act will not injure the plaintiff, or even seeking the plaintiff's own good. (*See* Appendix 14-1, Cases 3, 4, 10, 11, and 31 to 34.) This is also seen in medical practice when the physician does not warn a patient of the risk of causing damage to others. For example, substantial doses of muscle relaxants or tranquilizing or pain medication may render the patient less than competent and the patient may involve a third person in an automobile accident, injuring the third person.

§14.09 Assault and Battery

The intentional touching of another's person without authorization is a legal wrong, a *battery.* A threatening approach that puts a person in fear of battery is an *assault.* (*See* Appendix 14-1, Case 35.)

Lack of consent cases are tried on concepts of intentional torts, as opposed to negligence, and treat the presence or absence of consent as a simple yes-or-no question, rarely addressing the quality of care.

---

[4] *See also* Collins, *Language, History and the Legal Process: A Profile of the Reasonable Man,* 8 Rut Cam Law J 311 (1977).

§14.10 Competency

Three components are required for informed consent to a surgical procedure—knowledge regarding the procedure, voluntary agreement to the procedure, and competency in agreeing to the procedure. *Competence* is a legal concept that assesses the ability of the patient to know and understand what he or she is doing and what normally would be expected to result from his or her behavior.

The concept of competence can be separated into legal and actual components. Adults are presumed by society to be competent unless they are unable to understand what is going on and what the consequences of their behavior is. This inability may be congenital mental incapacity, or mental incapacity resulting from illness, injury, or toxic state. The adult may be unconscious and thereby incompetent to give consent. This gives rise to *actual incompetence.*

The *legally incompetent* are those who, due to a legal decision, have been adjudicated incompetent. Also included to varying degrees, based on age, are minor children under 18 years old.

The requirements of competency stem from contract and estate law. In contract law, there must be a meeting of the minds for a contract to be enforced. If one party to a contract cannot understand the contract or understand its consequences due to mental incompetence, no meeting of the minds occurs and the contract is void. The same logic flows in the making of a will; wills typically start "being of sound mind . . ." (*See* Appendix 14-1, Cases 7, 8, 30, and 36 to 39.)

In agreeing to a surgical procedure, the patient must be able to understand the reason and probable outcome for recommending an operation. Other factors of competence that might be applicable in other areas, such as the ability to manage money or know family relationships, are not necessary for consent to an operation.

In *Large v Superior Court,* 148 Ariz 229, 714 P2d 399 (1986), the patient sustained a fracture of the hip. Both the surgeon and the registered nurse in attendance felt that the patient understood her fracture injury, the need for surgery, and its consequences. Surgery went well. The patient died later, unrelated to her surgery, and her will was contested. The operative consent, as well as the will, was reviewed by the court. It was held that the operative consent was competent, but that the patient lacked testamentary competence which voided her will as she was not aware of the extent of her property and other money matters at the time she signed the will.

The refusal of a patient to consent to surgery, even though death would likely result if surgery was not carried out, does not indicate that the patient is incompetent.

In re Robert Quackenbush, 383 A2d 785 (NJ 1978), an elderly male with dry gangrene of legs to the knees due to peripheral vascular disease, who was septicemic and febrile, became afebrile by the use of intravenous antibiotics. The surgeon recommended above-knee bilateral amputations. The patient refused, stating he had been a "conscientious objector to medical care for more than 40 years." The surgeon and hospital felt that the patient was suffering from organic brain syndrome and petitioned the court for permission to perform amputations. The court, in hearing the evidence presented, found that although the refusal to accept surgery might interfere with accepted treatment, the patient did have an understanding of the proposed procedure with its risks and outcome. The patient had a valid concern about the risks of surgery, as well as with the difficulty of being rehabilitated and walking with bilateral prostheses. The court held, based on both prior case law and the right to privacy under the federal Constitution, that the patient was competent to refuse amputation.

There are exceptions to the competency rule, so each case is decided on its merits.

In *Younts v St Francis Hospital,* 469 P2d 338 (1986), a 17-year-old girl had a hand injury which required prompt surgery to prevent infection and deformity. The mother was in surgery and later was recovering from anesthetic drugs and semiconscious for 24 hours. The divorced father was 200 miles away and could not be contacted. The surgeon had hospital explain the injury, proposed surgery and described its consequences, and the patient agreed to surgery. This understanding by the patient, in light of the unavailability of either parent, was held to be a valid consent.

When a minor is not competent to make legal decisions regarding medical care, parents have the legal authority and obligation. This authority does not pass to such nonparents as caretakers, baby sitters, etc. The parents may, by written authority, direct another to assume the parental obligation to consent to medical treatment.

In *Zimmerman v New York City Hospital,* 91 A2d 290 (NY 1983), the patient, a child, had spondylolisthesis. Several surgeons recommended surgery. The mother gave consent. She was later shown to be mentally incompetent at the time of signing the child's operative consent. This mental incapacity was held "obvious." The child developed major permanent nerve damage postoperatively. This possible complication had been discussed with the patient and the mother before surgery. The court held that the surgery was performed without competent consent and that a battery with damage had been carried out by the surgeon.

§14.11 Informed Consent for Innovative Procedures

The need for clear and full disclosure to the patient by attending physicians is basic to an informed consent. What to disclose is, at times, a gray area and interpreted in various ways by the courts.

In innovative procedures, the patient is entitled to know the reasons and risks of the procedure as part of the informed consent. If techniques are in an evolutionary process (something past experimental and which other surgeons are also doing) the patient should understand and accept that. The surgeon naturally does not want a patient to feel that he or she is a guinea pig, so that the conversation will have to be artfully worded without being deceptive. The problem is further complicated by rapid development of new methods, devices, and drugs. Whether the procedure is innovative or experimental is often the key question.

Before 1900, there is no case law dealing with experimentation on human beings. The rule was that if the surgeon used an approved technique, it was negligence only if he or she deviated from the standard method of treatment.

The law does stay abreast of scientific as well as social progress, so a degree of human experimentation is logically accepted by the courts. The issue of experimentation on human beings has been a stimulus to informed consent, the experimental procedure necessarily being explained to, understood by, and accepted by the patient prior to the procedure.

The German atrocities—experimental medicine and surgery performed during World War II—became another stimulus to requiring consent to experimentation. The Nürenberg Code was accepted by most countries, including the United States. One part of this Code established the concept of human consent that should be followed when experimentation is done. The Code recites that the consent to experimentation must be voluntary and given by a patient who is competent and fully informed of the nature of the procedure and its risks and expected benefits. Moreover, the patient must be allowed to withdraw at any time. The experiment must be designed on scientific grounds, with a reasonable expectation for a successful or beneficial outcome.

The Federal Food and Drug Administration (FDA), using the Code's concept, has undertaken to monitor and control the development of medications and devices by use of rigid protocols for testing and investigation and moving slowly to approve medications or devices that may carry risks of human injury. Abuse of the stringent FDA rule did happen. In *Hyman v Jewish Chronic Disease Hospital,* 251 NY2d 818 (1964) a scientific study of the body's reaction to injected live liver cancer cells was done. No informed consent was obtained from the patients, and if a patient asked, he or she was told he was part of an experiment. The court, appalled, found that the patients had a right to be informed about experiments, informed of risks and possible benefits, and to give permission to participate in the experiment.

The drug or medicine package insert has become a mainstay of information from the drug manufacturer to the physician, patient, or interested third parties. Some courts have held that deviation from the package insert is negligence by the deviator, although most courts entertain a rebuttal by the user explaining the reason for the deviation.

In using orthopedic devices, the surgeon must fully explain the device, its purposes, and any alternative methods. If the device is new or innovative, the patient must know this. If it incurs unusual risk to life or limb, informed consent is mandatory.

In the early investigation of chemonucleolysis treatment of protruded lumbar intervertebral disc, a number of possible complications were recorded—most of them present today. The surgeon had a duty to inform the patient of each of these complications more accurately, as the procedure was new, innovative, and only recently released by the FDA.

In *Trantafell v Medical Center of Tarzana,* 182 Cal 3d 315, 227 Cal Rptr 84 (1986), a cervical discectomy procedure was performed in which a plug of bone cement was used as an intradiscal spacer rather than the more traditional bone plug. The cement spacer loosened and had to be removed, although the result of the first surgery was otherwise successful. The plaintiff alleged that there was no adequate disclosure of the bone cement method, that it was not universally accepted among orthopedists and neurosurgeons, and that it was experimental. The court held that, while not universally accepted as an operative method, it was innovative and scientifically based. It was not part of a research program, but for the benefit of the patient.

A rule seems to exist that if there is adequate scientific basis for a procedure, and the patient fully understands all parameters of the procedure, negligence in lack of informed consent will not stand.[5]

In a general way, consent to treat a patient, and the patient's acceptance of a treatment plan, are an off-shoot of a patient's (and the community's) desire to protect life, to protect against injury, and to improve the quality of life, tied in with the unwillingness of society, in general, to expose itself to experimentation or other uncertainties. One way of looking at the basis of this concept is to study three ethical legal problems generated by the failure of medical research or practice: (1) the failure to prevent or cure disease, as illustrated by AIDS, (2) the failure to provide benefits, as illustrated by the inappropriate continuation of life prolonging techniques—which has generated a growing support for active euthanasia, and (3) failure to rationalize health care, as illustrated by the failure to ensure adequate care at reasonable cost. The bottom line is that the days of the physician being infallible and of the patient necessarily accepting the risk of that infallibility, rather than participating in the decision of what happens to his or her body, have passed.

§14.12 Uniform Consent Laws

Some states have uniform consent laws, such as Louisiana. In *Hondroulis v Schuhmacher,* 521 So 2d 534 (La. Ct. App. 1988), cert. granted 522 So 2d 571 (La. 1988), affd; 531 So 2d 450 (La. 1988); mod. 533 So 2d 1221 (La. 1988); revd 553 So 2d 398 (La 1989) held that the "Uniformed Consent Law) can be rebutted by evidence that patient was not told of "known risks" with his medical treatment (death, brain damage, quadriplegia, paraplegia, loss of function of any organ or limb, disfiguring scar).

---

[5] Becker, Jr, *The Informed Consent for the Surgical Procedure: Consent Problems with Innovative Techniques and Experimental Procedures,* 18 Contemp Orthop 703 (1989).

§14.13 Ethical and Legal Ramifications

The ethical doctrine of informed consent is well established in modern medicine. Despite our philosophical and jurisprudential commitment to informed consent, a large amount of anecdotal evidence exists that significant medical interventions are sometimes imposed on patients in the absence of a voluntary, competent, and informed consent. Many of these incidents come within the legally-recognized exceptions to the usual informed consent requirements, such as life-threatening emergencies or when the patient knowlingly and competently waives the right. Medical interventions are imposed on patients in the absence of informed consent even where no valid exception to consent exists. This often occurs in life-sustaining situations. This happens, perhaps, because physicians and hospital administrators often harbor the impression that their realistic legal rights for imposing medical interventions without valid consent are considerably less than their potential civil or criminal liability for neglecting a patient's needs by withdrawing or withholding an unconsented treatment. In our present environment, it is unlikely that a physician will be sued or caused to pay a large fine exclusively for rendering medical treatment without first obtaining an informed consent.

Another important factor influencing physicians toward erring on the side of treatment even without a valid consent is the current system of financial reimbursement for medical care.[6] If a medical service is deemed necessary and within the standard of care, and if the service is covered under a third-party or insurance plan, those carriers routinely reimburse based on the claim that service was performed. Third parties do not investigate whether valid consent for the service was obtained.

The situation described above presents ethical, legal, and financial ramifications.[7]

§14.14 Patients' Rights

It was decided in 1982 by the Supreme Court that a patient has a constitutional right to treatment. Previously, Chief Justice Blackmun had felt that such a right was "frivolous." The constitutional issue was not properly before the court, but the Justice was prepared to assert that involuntarily committed or mentally retarded adults had a right to such training as is reasonably necessary to prevent a person's pre-existing self-care skills from deteriorating because of his or her commitment. This extends to nursing home care.

---

[6] Kapp, *Enforcing Patients' Preferences—Linking Payment for Medical Care to Informed Consent,* 261 JAMA 1935 (1989).

[7] Making Health Care Decisions: The Ethical and Legal Implications of Informed Consent in the Patient-Practitioner Relationship, President's Commission for the Study of Ethical Problems in Medicine, and Biomedical and Behavioral Research (1982); Kapp & Lo, *Legal Perceptions and Medical Decision-Making,* 64(2) Milbank Q 162 (1986).

In 1966, Dr. Henry Beecher of Harvard caused a stir in the medical world when he published an article cataloging abuses of human subjects in medical research reported in one year's issue of a leading medical journal. In 1969, the American Academy of Arts and Sciences issued a document, "Daedalus," on the subject of human experimentation which was the essence of formal and legal definition of informed consent given by patients to physicians. It was decided that the state had broad powers to limit reproduction for eugenic reasons rendered doubtful any notions of the right to reproduce, despite a subsequent decision in Oklahoma which could be read to merely insist that when sterilization is linked with criminal law, high standards of due process and equal protection must be applied. (*See* Appendix 14-1, Cases 7, 8, 29, and 36 to 39.)

§14.15 Foreign Bodies

Many surgeons are involved in medical malpractice actions which allege that foreign bodies were placed or left in their bodies without, or against, their consent. (*See* Appendix 14-1, Cases 40 to 48.)

Inadequate documentation of informed consent, particularly verifying that the patient was competent to understand, and did understand, all features of the consent, often makes it defective in the eyes of the court. A jury's reliance on actual documentation is not based merely on believability. If there is nothing in the medical record to say that the elements of informed consent were fulfilled, there is a legal presumption that no consent was given. In *Podvin v Eickhorst,* 128 NW2d 523 (Mich 1964), the plaintiff sustained a spinal cord injury, and was treated by a succession of physicians. There was no documentation in the chart regarding procedure indication or potential complications. This was allowed by the court to introduce "evidence of no consent given."

The following phraseology might be considered on an informed consent form:

> I have today discussed with the patient (and his or her family/responsible party/legal representative) his or her diseased state (the proposed treatment), the expected benefit, and the material risks of (that treatment) as compared with reasonable alternative forms of therapy, and what might be expected were there no treatment at all. The patient (and his or her family/responsible party/legal representative) consent to the treatment as proposed.

§14.16 Expert Testimony

In recent years, a number of cases involving informed consent have been brought on the basis of the patient's right to be reasonably informed of all material elements which may affect his or her decision as to whether to undergo the proposed treatment. A major issue in a number of informed consent cases has been whether it is necessary for the plaintiff to produce expert medical testimony to establish the existence and scope of the physician's duty to disclose the risk of proposed treatment. The necessity of expert testimony is linked to substantive law issues since, in view of difficulty of obtaining the testimony of doctors willing to testify against other members of their profession, the requirement of expert testimony can prevent recovery in many cases. This phenomena is commonly called the "conspiracy of silence."

Most cases involving informed consent have held that expert testimony is necessary to establish the existence and scope of the physician's duty to inform patients of the risks and options of treatment. In cases holding expert testimony to be essential, there is some variation as to whether the expert testimony should focus on the standard of practice of the physician, of physicians in the same locality, or of physicians of the same specialty. Some courts have taken the opposite position that expert testimony is not necessary on the informed consent issue.

Some jurisdictions hold that the physician has the duty to disclose risks of the proposed treatment unless that risk is obvious, but are more lax on other elements of informed consent; that is optional treatment or tests, etc.[8]

The physician-patient relationship is a consensual one, and in the absence of an emergency or other anticipated condition, a physician or surgeon must first obtain the consent of the patient if he or she is competent to give it, or of someone legally authorized to give it for the patient, before treating or operating on him.

§14.17 Treatment of Minors

In obtaining informed consent for treatment, the physician may find him- or herself treating a minor patient without the presence of parents to give consent. All states have statutes covering this problem.

Most states defined a minor as persons under 18 years of age, except those in active military service who are considered adults. Health workers included under the act include physicians, psychologists, dentists, podiatrists, chiropractors, registered or licensed practice nurses, and physician assistants.

The health services covered by the act include examination, preventative and curative treatments, surgical treatment, hospitalization, and psychological services. Abortion, sterilization, and medical research not necessary to preserve the life of a minor are not covered.

The right of a minor to give self-consent and the doctor-patient privilege allowed under these circumstances are also covered. Minors who are married or who have dependent children, or who are emancipated from their parent or legal guardian and who do not receive support from them, are allowed

---

[8] Silva, *Informed Consent in Human Experimentation: The Scientist Responsibility—the Subject's Right,* Trial 37 (Dec 1980); Cassileth, *Informed Consent—Why Are Its Goals Imperfectly Realized?,* 302 NEJM 900 (1980).

to give self-consent for most medical care, except abortion, sterilization, or life-threatening procedures.

When major surgery, general anesthesia, or life threatening procedures are planned, the surgeon must obtain agreement from another local physician (second opinion) to treat the self-consenting minor unless the problem is a true emergency and no other physician can be contacted within a reasonable period of time. A minor may also give self-consent for treatment of drug or alcohol abuse, or for its diagnosis or prevention.

If a minor has been or is pregnant, a physician may make diagnosis or treat or offer prevention (contraceptive advice) provided abortion or sterilization is not used. If a communicable disease, drug or substance abuse, or pregnancy is involved, the provider must offer counseling to the minor.

The act allows specifically for minor parents to give consent for diagnosis or treatment of their child or their minor spouse if the minor spouse is unable to give consent due to physical or mental incapacity.

Emergency care of a minor, where obtaining consent from a parent or legal guardian would unreasonably delay treatment or be life-threatening, can be self-consented by the minor. If such consent is obtained, a reasonable attempt must be made to notify the parents or legal guardians of the problem and treatment.

The physician is free from legal claims by the parents, spouse, or legal guardian of the otherwise authorized self-consenting minor for any treatment needed or provided under the act, except when negligence or intentional harm is done to the minor. The physician is protected by the act if the minor falsely represents his or her circumstances to give self-consent to the extent that the liability is limited to injury caused by negligence or intentional harm.

The minor may not invoke the common law right to revoke or disaffirm consent due to minority. Parents or guardians of minors consenting to treatment under the act will not be responsible to pay for such services. Several states list exceptions to the general rule the act promulgates. It is the physician's duty to know those exceptions. This information is available from state and country medical societies, or they can easily obtain it.

In emergency situations, the consent for care of minors too young or too incapacitated to give self-consent, minors who are wards of the court, and in cases where parents give divided consent, application to an appropriate court for consent can, and should, be utilized.[9] (*See* Appendix 14-1, Cases 28 and 49 to 51.)

---

[9] Jamir, *Children Health Services for Minors in Oklahoma: Capacity to Give Self-Consent to Medical Care and Treatment,* 30 Okla L Rev 385 (1977); Cohen, *Treatment of Minors Without Parental Consent: The Law in Oklahoma,* 82 J Okla State Med Assoc 471 (1989).

§14.18 Religious Beliefs

The orthopedist often treats patients with religious beliefs that conflict with normal medical practices. This is particularly true of the Jehovah's Witnesses, who will not consent to receiving a whole blood or a blood products infusion. Religious freedom is protected under the first amendment to the Constitution which states that United States Congress shall make no laws regarding the establishment of religion. The fourteenth amendment tells the states that they also must abide by the first amendment.

Jehovah's Witnesses affirms, under these Constitutional protections, that to accept blood transfusions would be against their religious beliefs. They rely on Old Testament scriptures: (1) "Only you shall not eat flesh with its life, that is, its blood. For your lifeblood I will surely require a reckoning . . ." (Genesis 9:4-5), (2) ". . . you shall eat neither fat nor blood." (Leviticus 3:17), (3) ". . . whoever eats any blood, that person shall be cut off from his people." (Leviticus 7:26-27), (4) "For the life of every creature is the blood of it . . ." (Leviticus 17:11) and (5) ". . . only be sure that you do not eat the blood, for blood is the life . . ." (Deuteronomy 12:23). In the New Testament, Acts 15:29 and Acts 21:25 support the admonition to avoid blood. Refusal to "take blood" is an expression of the Jehovah's Witness religious belief. The courts may not examine the rationality or logic of the belief, but can only affirm the Constitutional guarantee.

In *Schoendorff v New York Hospital,* 105 NE 92 (1914), Justice Cardozo stated that every competent adult has the right to determine what shall be done with his or her own body. Additionally, he said that when refusal to accept treatment is based on religious belief, interference with that belief may be a violation of his or her Constitutional rights. *In re Directors of Georgetown College,* 331 F2d 1000 (DC Cir 1964) and in *United States v George,* 239 F Supp 752 (D Conn 1965), the justices went to the patient and, when told by the patient that blood was refused, but that if ordered by the court, that the plaintiff and peers would be blameless in the sight of God, decided to "act on the side of life" and ordered blood transfusions. This inserted a variation in the consent rule relating to refusal of transfusion when having been fully informed of the risks of the refusal. The consent should include a statement that if a court orders a transfusion, the order will be resisted.

Of necessity, the consent must be flexible as the patient's condition worsens, or the patient's, family's, or peers' thinking changes. In these cases, a continuing dialogue with the patient and careful recording on the patient's chart is essential.

In *In re Osborne,* 294 A2d 372 (DC 1972), the patient who was severely injured refused blood transfusion, as did his wife, citing religious belief. They were fully informed of the risk, the patient stating he would prefer "everlasting life" over accepting a blood transfusion. The court, hearing the hospital request for a court-ordered transfusion, concurred with Constitutional rights and, further investigating family situation, found that the immediate family members would be cared for adequately, should the patient die.

In *Prince v Massachusetts,* 321 NJ 463 (1962), the court reasoned that competent persons (parents) may be martyrs, but they cannot cause their children to become martyrs. In *State v Perricone,* 37 NJ 463 (1962) the court held that court-ordered transfusions were valid in the case of children in eminent danger of death. In *Muhlenberg Hospital v Patterson,* involving post-partum bleeding with deterioration of the mother, the court held that allowing the mother's death impinged on state's right and interest in protecting the child's nurturing, and allowed transfusion. In *In re Sampson,* 317 NYS 2d 641 (1970), a child with severe facial deformity was denied access to blood transfusions necessary for elective corrective facial surgery. The patient was found to be a neglected child and ordered that blood be made available for corrective surgery. The court posited that the "state paramount duty is to insure his right to live and grow up without disfigurement, to grow up with sound mind and body." In *Green v Sanderson,* 286 A2d 681 (Pa 1971), similar logic was used in ordering transfusion for corrective surgery to a severely scoliotic child. The court declared the child neglected, and appointed a guardian who would authorize blood transfusion.

Physicians ask, "Can I be held liable for seeking a court order for my patient in these circumstances?" In *Harley v Oliver,* 404 F Supp 450 (WD Ark 1975) and in *Staelens v Yake,* 432 F Supp 834 (1977), the courts held that the physicians would be held free of liability in administrating court ordered transfusions.

§14.19 Third Parties

The intervention of third parties in the daily practice of medicine is expanding like the waves from a pebble thrown into a body of water. Some of this, in the minds of most physicians, is beneficial to patients and cost-effective, but to many it is an impingement on good medical practice and is changing the complexion of the daily practice of medicine to the point that many physicians are (or will) quit the practice of medicine. A significant drop in medical school applicants is being seen now as American rapidly approaches a totally socialized system with virtually no freedom on the patient's part of having the physician of his or her choice.

The medical literature frequently contains articles regarding informed consent. Several recent articles have suggested another way of enforcing informed consent by tying payment to the doctor to only those services specifically included in the informed consent. The opportunity for the less ethical doctors to obtain consent for a "laundry list" of informed judgments, as to which procedure would be paid and which not, in a way is a daily practice problem now. The arbitrary decision of a third party to refuse payment because a guideline suggests that too many, too long, or inappropriate procedures were done sets vocabulary in front of a patient that the insurer recognizes that a practice was below standard, and may well cause the patient to feel he or she has a cause of action against the physician.[10]

§14.20 References

Pinto, *Must You Bare Your Insurance Status to Your Patients?,* Leg Asp of Med Prac 43 (Jan 1980).

Dinman, *The Reality and Acceptance of Risk,* 244 JAMA 1226 (1980)

Grundner, *On the Readability of Surgical Consent Forms,* 302 NEJM 900 (1980)

Miller, *Informed Consent,* 244 JAMA 2100 (1980)

Douma, *Informed Patients and Physicians' Satisfaction,* 243 JAMA 2168 (1980)

Appelbaum & Roth, *Patients Who Refuse Treatment in Medical Hospitals.* 250 JAMA 1296 (1983)

Office of Technical Assessment, OTA-BA-306 Life-Sustaining Technologies and the Elderly (1987)

J. Katz, The Silent World of Doctor and Patient (1984)

---

[10] Kal, *Linking Payment for Care to Informed Consent,* 262 JAMA 2091 (1989); Kapp, *Response to Letter to Editor,* 262 JAMA 2091 (1989).

Appendix 14-1
Cases

1 ***Canterbury v Spence,* 464 F2d 772 (D.C. Cir. 1972), *cert denied,* 409 US 1064 (1972)** (action against surgeon for injuries resulting from laminectomy which resulted in paraplegia. The issue for the jury to decide was whether the surgeon's obligation to disclose information on risks was reasonably met or was excused by surrounding circumstances, where the patient testified the surgeon revealed to him nothing suggesting a hazard associated with the operation. The mother testified that the surgeon said that laminectomy was no more serious than any other operation, and it developed from the surgeon's testimony that paralysis could be expected in 1 per cent of cases).

2 ***Smith v Weaver,* 407 NW2d 174 (Neb 1987)** (physician was not liable for failure to warn a patient of drug side effects. The patient could not recover for the physician's alleged failure to obtain informed consent in the absence of evidence that the physician had not done that duty. The patient consulted the physician because of fatigue, itching, hair loss, and soreness of facial bones, among other things. After a week of hospitalization, the physical diagnosed possible systemic lupus erythematosus. Approximately two years later, the patient consulted the physician because of increased swelling of hands, feet, stiffness of her whole body, and lightheadedness and dizziness. The physician again diagnosed possible lupus, prescribed Clinoril, and allegedly advised the patient of the primary or common side effects of the drug. The patient later denied he told her of any side effects. The next day, the patient phoned the physician reporting that she had taken Clinoril tablets as instructed, but that her hands were swollen, she had vomited, and her entire body was swollen and itched. The physician felt these were problems caused by the disease process and advised the patient to continue taking the drug. A day later, the patient again reported problems. Since there were no tests detecting an allergic reaction to the drug, physician changed medications. The patient then reported improvement, but she still had pain in her hands. The patient sued the physician, alleging he was negligent in failing to warn her about the possible side effects of Clinoril. The patient contended that after her experience with the drugs, she lacked energy, had pain and sores, and that her ability to speak and to eat and to sleep had been adversely affected by the medication. The physician said he had exercised reasonable and the ordinary care and skill and knowledge of a member of the profession under the circumstances. A medial review panel confirmed this opinion and there was no counter expert evidence of record. The trial court then granted a summary judgment for the physician. On appeal, the patient contended that when it is claimed that a physician failed to warn of possible side effects of a drug, there is no requirement for specific technical and scientific knowledge. She contended that since her circumstances surrounded an injury, a

common experience and knowledge and observation, no expert was required. The supreme court said that the state was committed by the legislature to the court of professional theory under which expert evidence is necessary to establish what information would ordinarily be provided under prevailing circumstances by physicians in similar communities and similar counties. Therefore, in the present case, contradicted evidence that a physician followed the accepted standards rendered by factual issues of which physicians gave a patient a warning immaterial, there being no competent evidence that he was required to give any warning).

3 ***Harris v Smith,*** **372 F2d 806 (8th Cir 1967)** (action against an orthopedic surgeon for malpractice in the setting of a compound fractured arm accompanied by a dislocated elbow resulting in gas gangrene and necessitating the amputation of the arm. The court held that the trial court had committed prejudicial error in excluding the testimony of a general practitioner solely on the grounds that he was not a specialist in orthopedic surgery. It was held that he had sufficient general medical and surgical knowledge to appropriately evaluate and express an expert opinion in this case. In addition, having made an unfavorable diagnosis of his patient's condition or knowing of an unfavorable result of the diagnostic test, he becomes liable for malpractice where he then fails to notify the patient of this information. The relationship between the patient and physician is one of trust and confidence. The physician has a duty to reveal to the patient that which in his best interest he should know. The physician normally has a duty to disclose sufficient information regarding the hazards of the proposed course of treatment to enable his patient to make an informed and intelligent decision as to whether he wishes to undergo treatment or additional testing. There are, however, recognized limits to this required disclosure as in cases of emergency. The disclosure need not include slight or unusual risks of treatment proposed. The standard applied in measuring the physician's duty of disclosure is the information which a reasonable medical practitioner of the same school practicing in the same or similar communities under the same circumstances would disclose incident to the diagnosis or treatment. Some disclosures may disturb the patient to the degree that they serve as a hindrance to the diagnosis of treatment, and such disclosure may even constitute bad medical practice).

4 ***Babin v St Paul Fire Marine Insurance Co,*** **385 So 2d 849 (1980);** ***cert denied,*** **386 So 2d 358 (1980)** (an operative procedure was carried out by a surgeon who found a mass in the intestine during the course of the procedure, which he removed. Postoperatively, an intestinal leak was treated and formed a basis for lack of informed consent. It was determined that the consent form did cover procedures that being one of the "therapeutically necessary on the basis of the finding in the course of the operation").

5 ***Leonard v New Orleans East Orthopedic Clinic,*** **485 So 2d 1008 (1986)** (patient underwent a biopsy of spine to diagnose possible malignancy. Informed consent listed possible complications including paraplegia, quadriplegia, and death, but the patient denied that she read or that anyone discussed the risks with her. Nonetheless, she signed the permit. She developed a drop foot due to nerve damage. Expert evidence showed this to be a rare complication, with a 0.08 per cent occurrence with vertebral biopsy. The court held that a reasonable person would have undergone the procedure, even if the risk had been disclosed).

6 ***Congelton v Baton Rouge General Hospital,*** **444 So 2d 175 (La Ct App 1983),** ***rehg denied*** **(1984)** (doctrine of res ipsa loquitur could not be applied where there was direct evidence to explain the activities leading to the injury, according to a Louisiana Court. A woman suffered injury when she was donating blood at a blood bank. During the phlebotomy, a technician drawing the blood positioned the needle and adjusted the tourniquet when the woman complained of pain and again when she complained of tingling and numbness. When the technician offered to remove the needle, the woman decided to complete the procedure. After the phlebotomy, the woman complained that her arm was still numb, and the technician told her to call back the next day if her condition persisted. The woman did call back the next day and the supervisor told her to return for examination by the head of the pathology department. She was then advised to see a neurologist who found an injury to the left antebrachial cutaneous nerve. Another neurologist did an EMG and confirmed the diagnosis. The woman sued the hospital to recover for her injury, testifying she had pain as soon as the technician started to draw the blood. The technician said the woman did not complain until the phlebotomy was almost completed. The trial court found that res ipsa loquitur was applicable in that the hospital failed to rebut the inference of negligence and awarded for the patient. On appeal, the court said undisputed evidence of injury was caused when the needle had struck the nerve in the woman's arm rendering the doctrine res ipsa loquitur applicable. All the medical testimony at the trial indicated that the injury could have occurred in the absence of negligence. One physician testified that an injury of that type could happen even with the best medical technique, although testimony showed that the injury was highly unusual and extremely rare. The court said that this did not alone justify res ipsa loquitur A greater weight of testimony showed the hospital was negligent and was not the most plausible explanation of the injury. Finding the woman failed to prove negligence in a preponderance of evidence, the court reversed the lower court's decision).

7 ***Cross v Trapp,*** **294 SE2d 446 (W Va 1982)** (standard of care concerning physician disclosure or risk to an operative procedure would be based on the "patient need standard." When a particular medical risk should be disclosed by the physician to the patient under this standard will ordinarily depend on the existence and materiality of that risk with respect to the patient's decision relating to medical treatment, although medical expert testimony is not required to establish the scope of physician duty to disclose medical information under the "patient need standard." Expert medical testimony ordinarily would be required to establish such matters, including (1) the risk involved concerning a particular method of treatment,

(2) alternative methods of treatment, (3) risks related to such alternative methods of treatment and (4) results likely to occur if the patient remains untreated).

8 ***Alargey v Rothman,* 110 NJ 204, 540 A2d 504 (1980)** (court adopted the "prudent patient" standard for adequate disclosure which requires a physician to inform the patient of all "material risk" associated with the proposed treatment. The court also adopted an objective test to determine whether failure to comply with the applicable standard for disclosure proximately cause the patient's injuries, i.e., whether a prudent person in the plaintiff's position would have decided differently if adequately informed).

9 ***Doss v Hartford Fire Insurance Co,* 448 So 2d 813 (La Ct App 1984)** (what surgical risks would a mailman be willing to incur to keep his feet in walking condition? The patient had metatarsalgia with painful callouses, and osteotomies of the distal metatarsals were carried out, one of which ended in non-union. When it was explained that the chances of non-union were about 6 to 1, the court decided that the usual, prudent mailman would opt to have the surgery done. The orthopedists, before surgery, offered him an alternative by using metatarsal pads in his shoes or undergo surgery. The orthopedist explained the surgery and what he told him was the subject of the controversy in this trial. Additional information provided by the surgeon with the possibility of anesthetic catastrophe, possibility of infection, and possibility of pulmonary embolus. Also, the orthopedist testified that a small percentage of osteotomies fail to heal. The secondary surgery was carried out, which was only partially successful. The pain in the foot caused the patient to fall, sustaining severe back injuries according to the plaintiff. After considerable discussion of what the patient should be expected to understand in the consent, the appellate court felt that a 10 to 15 per cent risk of failure would not have deterred a mailman from having the surgery, even if he clearly recalled that part of the consent discussion. It further held that oral consent was just as valid as a written consent, but more difficult to prove).

10 ***Sherrill v McBride,* 603 SW2d 635 (Tex Civ App 1980)** (malignant tumor was removed from the patient's foot, with complications stemming from use of a catheter with a large hematoma occurring postoperatively in the patient's thigh. The hematoma became infected and, ultimately, the patient's leg had to be amputated. Expert testimony indicated that the risk of loss of a limb was a remote possibility. It was conceded that this was not told to the patient. The jury properly determined that there was no deviation from the standard of care and no deviation in the standard of informed consent in the community, and, as such, the finding for the defendant was appropriately affirmed. Expert testimony was that this was such a remote possible complication that the standard in the community at the time of the procedure was not to include that informed consent).

11 ***Leyson v Steuermann,* 705 P2d 37 (Haw Ct App 1985)** (corticosteroids were appropriately used but patient developed cataracts. The court held the "informed consent doctrine does not require the physician to dis-

close risks that are unexpected or immaterial nor even material risks where disclosure in precluded by emergency situations, by patient's incapacity, by patient's waiver of his right to receive information or where disclosure would be harmful to patient, nor need physician to disclose risks commonly understood, obvious or already known to patient." The court held this case should be held for a jury using the above criteria).

12 ***Dunham v Wright,*** **423 F2d 940 (3d Cir 1970)** (this ruling defined informed consent as "informed" only if the patient knows what is apt to happen to him, possible adverse results, and the dangers of the operation, and before a patient will be deemed to give an informed consent, it may be necessary to know the alternative methods of treatment available to him and the dangers and possible success of such alternatives).

13 ***Contrereas v St Luke's Hospital,*** **78 Cal App 3d 919, 144 Cal Rptr 647 (1978)** (physician fully informed plaintiff that one risk of surgery is infection, although the plaintiff was not told of the consequences of infection. Where there was no expert testimony that alternatives to operation were feasible or that any other practitioner in good standing would have given any additional information, it was held no negligence was had by the defendant hospital).

14 ***Harwell v Pittman,*** **428 So 2d 1049 (La Ct App 1983),** ***cert denied,*** **434 So 2d 1092 (1983)** (routine operative consent was had, but surgeon did not explain increased surgical and anesthetic risk attached to obese patients. Patient developed incision infection, hernia, and died. Failure to disclose these increased risks in obese patient was held negligent practice).

15 ***Grasser v Kitzis,*** **553 A2d 346 (NJ Super Ct App Div 1989)** (surgeon was negligent in not obtaining an informed consent. Twin fetuses were dead, and options for treatment were waiting for spontaneous miscarriage (pregnancy was in second trimester), attempting to induce labor, and cervical dilitation and sunction evacuation of uterine contents. The physician recommended later and patient accepted. During operation, uterine wall was perforated and a portion of bowel was suctioned into uterus that was repaired by abdominal surgery. In an action against the physician, the trial court returned defendant verdict. The appellate court reversed, saying that patient was not told of risks and had she been informed, she would not have consented to surgery. This established proximate cause to complication. The court, through expert testimony, said that the performing of dilatation and suction evacuation itself was not negligent).

16 ***Garcia v Meiselman,*** **220 NJ Super 317, 531 A2d 1373 (Law Div 1987)** (plaintiff alleged negligence and lack of informed consent. The plaintiff agreed to surgery to correct a prominent mandible, the surgery going well as to correcting deformity, but also leaving a numb hypersensitive lip due to injury to the medial mandibular nerve. This complication caused martial, as well as sensory, complications—the patient did not want his wife to kiss him. The lack of consent allegation stemmed from patient saying he was not told of risk of medial nerve damage. The court reviewed the doctrine of informed consent and found it to be a negligence concept in which a practi-

tioner fails to disclose a risk other reasonable practitioners would have disclosed. Proximate cause existed when the operation would not have taken place had the risk been disclosed; if the risk materializes with resultant injury, the practitioner is liable. The rationale for informed consent is that it enables the patient to evaluate options and attendant risks knowledgeably. Court noted that there were other options (other than no treatment) than surgery. The risk of corrective surgery could not be done without risk of damage to the medial nerve, causing risks and benefits to be inseparable. Accordingly, the court found the appropriate measure of damages should be arrived at by comparing condition the patient would have been, had there been no negligence with the condition the patient finds himself because of the negligence. If the operation was done as a result of the surgeon's failure to inform the patient of the risk the procedure entailed, then the condition the patient would have been without the operation should be compared with the condition he was in after surgery. In short, damages exist only if the patient's condition was worse than it would have been had the operation not been done).

17 ***Hondroulis v Schuhmacher, M.D.,*** **531 So 2d 450 (La 1988)** (Louisiana Supreme Court has found a signed form listing the major risks of laminectomy for ruptured disc surgery adequate evidence of informed consent, even though the surgeon failed to mention possible complications to the patient. The patient had leg and perineum numbness and urinary incontinence after surgery and filed an action based on lack of informed consent. The supreme court stated that the signed consent form created the presumption that the patient had been told everything she needed to know about the operation. In cross examination, the patient admitted she had been aware that complications can occur after "disc surgery").

18 ***Hondroulis v Schumacher,*** **521 So 2d 534 (La Ct App. 1988); 531 So 2d 450 (La. 1988); mod 533 So 2d 1221 (La. 1988); revd 553 So 2d 398 (La 1989)** (supreme court disapproved a lower court ruling that a signed consent for the medical procedure gave rise to a conclusive statutory presumption of valid consent. The case involves a patient who underwent lumbar disc excision, resulting in loss of bladder and bowel control and numbness in legs. Patient had signed a consent form preoperatively that recited risk of paralysis and loss of bodily function and stated that the patient had been informed of the procedure's risk. The consent form "tracked" the language of a Louisiana statute which requires written consent to a medical procedure set forth in general terms of any known risks of death, brain damage, quadriplegia, paraplegia, loss of body function or disfiguring scars. The consent form also must state that the patient has been fully advised about these risks. The statute says that, in absence of misrepresentations, such consent will be presumed valid. The patient brought her action alleging the surgeon failed to obtain informed consent for back surgery (laminectomy), stating that she would not have undergone the operation, had she been told of risk of loss of bladder of sphincter control. The court granted summary judgment in favor of physician, with appellate court affirming, based on there was no misrepresentation and the patient was bound by consent form she signed. The supreme court concluded that question of fact existed regarding the adequacy of the legislated permit form, with a principle objection that the form "merely stated" loss of function of bodily organs and did not address risk of sphincter or bladder control. Since most patients are aware that all surgeries have risks, the court reasoned that the general statement of risk of loss of bodily function—without mention of the risk or the organ threatened—had the effect of de-emphasizing the danger).

19 ***Archer v Galbraith,* 567 P2d 1155 (Wash 1977)** (permanent injury to recurrent laryngeal nerve followed neck surgery (thyroid node—same surgical approach used for anterior cervical disc surgery). A written consent was signed but no documentation that the information in the consent form was discussed with patient. At trial, the surgeon stated that he had discussed all usual risks of operation, including possible nerve damage. The patient said she received no information regarding possible complications, that the consent form was confusing, and that she did not understand what she was signing. This court held that the jury could not believe that the fact that nothing was in medical records to say that the doctor had explained complication possibilities was a presumption that such discussion was had. Nonetheless, the jury decided in favor of plaintiff based on the plaintiff and defendant's testimony).

20 ***Gouse v Cassel,* 561 A2d 797 (Pa 1989)** (jury was asked to respond to two interrogatories. One asked whether a patient was advised of the risks and alternatives to surgery, which a reasonable man would have considered significant in deciding whether or not to have the operation. The second asked if the jury found the patient had not been advised, would it find that a reasonable man in the patients' condition would have agreed to undergo the operation anyway. The jury answered that the patient had not been advised of the risks or alternatives. However, it answered the second question in the affirmative. On appeal, the court reversed and remanded for trial only to determine amount of damages to be awarded the plaintiff. A physician's liability for breach of the doctrine of informed consent's mandate for disclosure of risks and alternatives does not depend on the fact finder's determination that the patient would have declined the treatment had the disclosure been made).

21 ***Precourt v Frederick,* 395 Mass 689, 481 NE2d 1144 (1985)** (plaintiff sustained an injury to an eye by a foreign body. Four months later, metal was removed with the orthopedic surgeon saying there would be a 90 per cent chance of success, and vision was improved for a short period but the problem returned. A second surgery was recommended by the ophthalmologist for removal of scar at the back of the eye. The physician said there would be a 10 per cent chance of success. In fact, this did not work in both cases; a 90-day course of corticosteroid was part of the postoperative treatment. Following the second surgery, the patient developed aseptic necrosis of his hips and he became crippled, no longer able to work as an electrician. His suit was on informed consent, saying the risk of aseptic necrosis was never

discussed. The court held that this was a remote enough possibility of complication that the failure to disclose did not represent lack of informed consent. A verdict for the defendant physician was held by the supreme court. Part of the reasoning was that the risk of failure of the second operation was so high. The statement was "you must clearly inform the patients of the material hazard attendant from the anesthesia and the surgery involved in the operative procedure but "particularly in those cases with a small chance of success." In other words, requirement to disclose the potential risk of surgical procedure increases with the likelihood of failure).

Comment: This statement is in conflict with the verdict, but expresses the prevalent opinion the country over.

22 ***Mercer v Chi,* 282 NW2d 697 (Iowa 1979)** (there was evidence of informed consent to a lung scan, which was a test similar to the disputed venogram, and evidence that the patient's lack of physical resistance to the venogram test when the patient was awake and fully capable of resistance were admissable to refute the plaintiff's allegation that a venogram was performed without consent).

23 ***Ramos v Pyati,* 534 NE2d 472 (Ill App 1989)** (surgeon used a flexor tendon from ring finger as free graft to repair defect in thumb flexor. The surgeon found the palmaris longus tendon unsuitable. After surgery, the patient had trouble using tools, had poor flexion of ring finger and could not return to work as a mechanic. The plaintiff alleged no consent to invade palm for tendon graft harvesting, that the wrong type of tendon was harvested, that no consent and no discussion was had before surgery of harvesting ring finger tendon or of risk of weakening hand, making mechanical work impossible. Court affirmed and awarded $94,000. Defendant appealed and stated that according to medical literature, the flexor tendon was one of the acceptable tendon donors for tendon grafting (not necessarily thumb whose flexor tendon had less elastic material in it, thus ring finger flexor tendon inappropriate). Therefore, the defendant maintained his tendon donor was a matter of choice. The surgeon further asserted on consent issue that chance the ring finger flexor tendon would be used was so remote that he was not obliged to mention it and even if the operation exceeded the scope of the patient's consent, no prudent patient would have refused it. The appellate court rejected the orthopedist's argument, pointing out that the literature, in fact said flexor tendon could be used only if wrist, calf, toe extensor, and small or index finger flexor tendons were unavailable. By choosing tendon without exploring all other options, the surgeon failed to follow established protocol. According to expert testimony, the taking of ring finger tendon would weaken that finger without fully restoring the thumb, thus, why would a prudent patient accept such an arrangement. Trial court affirmed).

24 ***Daniels v State,* 532 So 2d 218 (La Ct App 1988)** (informed consent statute did not apply to routine nonsurgical treatments. Here the Colles fracture was somewhat displaced, but the orthopedist felt anesthetic and manipulation or open surgery would not improve the situation and treated fracture with splints. Plaintiff's expert verified deformity and pain in wrist resulting from fracture and that 30 per cent permanent impairment resulted. Affirming trial court's opinion, the court held that the informed consent statute did not apply to routine nonsurgical treatment).

Comment: A different opinion would stand in many jurisdictions as a patient is entitled to understand the injury and treatment options.

25 ***Dewes v Indian Health Service, Inc,*** **504 F Supp 203 (DSD 1980)** (plaintiff sustained a humeral fracture; bone plating surgery was carried out with plaintiff not knowing that non open surgery management by hanging arm cast was an acceptable (probable preferable) method of fracture treatment).

Comment: A big problem lies in the lack of a written record that the patient understands the informed consent and that any questions he or she had have been answered. The consent form should include a statement, a verification, which says that "I have reviewed the consent form and acknowledge that I understand the proposed procedure, its risks, and material or specific risks that may occur from the procedure. I have had an opportunity to ask questions about the procedure." The verification should be witnessed.

26 ***Edens v Kaplan,*** **No 106272 (Mich Ct App)** (plaintiff testified that she had not understood that removing her toenails would leave toes permanently without toenails regenerating. She said she had no conversation with the podiatrist to this end, though the operative permit that she signed did so state that this might be the case. The plaintiff admitted that she had not read the operative consent form. She did not provide expert testimony that the operation done was below the standard of care. The defendant prevailed. Also, a claim of battery was dismissed as the podiatrist had not exceeded the consent forms language).

27 ***Scott v Bradford,*** **606 P2d 554 (Okla 1979)** (scope of the physician's communication to a patient must be measured by the patient's need to know enough to enable him to make an intelligent choice. The disclosure must be sufficient for the patient to decide whether he is willing to have the procedure carried out. Full disclosure of all material risk incident to the treatment must be made. There is no "bright line" separating material from immaterial; it is a question of fact. A risk is material if it would be likely to affect the patient's decision. When nondisclosure of risk is open to debate, the issue is for finger of fact).

28 ***Cardwell v Bechtol,*** **724 SW2d 739 (Tenn 1987)** (minor girl experienced intermittent back pain. Two orthopedists diagnosed the problem of herniated disc. The parents refused to allow her to have a myelogram. Physical therapy did not improve the girl. In April 1982, the girl, who was then 17 years and 7 months old, visited an osteopath and told him her symptoms and the orthopedists' diagnosis. The osteopath, who was blind and confined his practice to manipulation, concluded she did not have a herniated disc and manipulative treatments were carried out with manipulations lasting about 15 minutes. Almost immediately after leaving the osteopath's office, the girl felt a tingling and numbing sensation which escalated into severe pain. Within the next few days, she developed bladder and bowel complications. Diagnostic tests confirmed herniated disc; a laminectomy was then performed. The patient's symptoms gradually improved. The girl and her parents sued the osteopath, alleging medical malpractice and failing to obtain informed consent, and because the treatment was given without parental permission, an allegation of battery was added. No expert testimony was given that the osteopath was negligent. The expert's opinion of the orthopedist and neurologist who had seen her before was not allowed, inasmuch as their statements were that they were not familiar with osteopathic standard of care. Because the patient did appear quite mature and was only a few months from majority, the exception was recognized that minors exhibiting varying degrees of judgment responsibility may have the capacity of consent. For more than a century, the common law has assumed that a rebuttable presumption of capacity exists in children older than 14 years of age).

Comment: Clearly, the manipulative therapy and the presence of protruded intervertebral disc symptoms is a risky business. It has been frequently recorded that manipulating osteopaths or chiropractors will change a protruded intervertebral disc into an extruded disc, in this case seemingly causing a cauda equina syndrome; that is negligent treatment.

29 ***In re Harris,*** **477 A2d 724 (DC 1984)** (patient should have been examined by a physician and a psychiatrist of her choice before a court ordered amputation of her leg, a District of Columbia appellate court ruled. The trial court authorized the hospital to schedule and perform the amputation of the patient's gangrenous right leg. On motion stay of the order, the court said that there was a conflict of psychiatric opinion as the patient was competent to make a treatment decision. There also was a conflict of medical testimony that the gangrenous condition was so acute that amputation was necessary to save her life. In this situation, the appellate court said there was not adequate findings of fact in the trial court record. It remanded the cast to the trial court with instructions that the patient be given opportunity to undergo psychiatric examination and physician examinations by physicians of her choice. The trial court was then ordered to conduct a hearing and report the finding to the appellate court within 10 days, again realizing it was not a life or death situation).

Comment: The competency of a patient is a difficult problem in many cases. The court itself rarely takes the posture of declaring competency or incompetency but relies on competent medical opinion, yet often the court must weigh the opinions with the greatest probative value. This is the situation in this case.

30 ***Crisher v Spak,*** **471 NYS 741 (Sup Ct 1983)** (orthopedic surgeon failed to tell a patient that the proposed operation was largely exploratory and that it might disclose a tumor. Lacking such information, the patient refused to undergo surgery. Eight months later, she had to undergo a below-knee amputation, a disaster she blamed on the surgeon who failed to operate earlier. The patient had come to the orthopedist complaining of foot pain.

Surgery was recommended. The patient continued to have trouble with her foot, and after seven months of unavailing treatment, the orthopedist referred the patient for a bunch of electrodiagnostic studies which revealed nerve involvement. She was told over the telephone that the problem was a pinched nerve and should be handled surgically. She did not, however, mention that the operation was required to identify the cause of the pinched nerve. In no great pain at the time, she decided against the surgery. Six months later, she consulted another co-defendant but returned to the original orthopedist who informed her she had a tumor. After biopsy revealed a malignancy, amputation was performed. In the negligence suit against the surgeon, as well as his colleagues, a medical expert testified that if the tumor had been discovered when the surgery was first proposed, amputation probably would not have been necessary. The witness testified had she been informed of the possibility of tumor, she would have accepted the surgery on the first recommendation. In affirming the verdict against the orthopedist, the tribunal suggested that the information could have been given to the patient in only a few minutes. The court suggested that the orthopedist may have said, "We do not know what is wrong with your foot. It may be many things, including a tumor, but it is important for your health to find out," rather than saying "You need surgery").

Comment: The doctrine of uninformed refusal of surgery or care is being heard more frequently. The concept has a widespread application in the practice or orthopedics. Patients have the right to refuse life-saving treatments, but if it is unclear whether they recognize the importance of an action, they should be warned.

31 ***Jeffries v Murdock,* 701 P2d 451 (Or Ct App 1985)** (orthopedic surgeon was cleared of medical negligence. He accidentally cut the nerve to the vocal cord. The patient had been in an automobile accident 20 years earlier which had produced an aneurysm in the neck, producing dense scarring. It was held that the case was difficult enough that the cutting of the nerve was a calculated risk. Informed consent had been given. The orthopedic surgeon sat down with the patient the next day and explained to him what went on and the nerve had been cut and he had worked to the best of his ability in a difficult operative site. The medical witnesses agreed there had been no negligence, only an unfortunate result of the difficult and hazardous operation).

Comment: Where there is a push for all adverse results to be considered negligent, there are often situations essentially out of the control of the operating surgeon, but which fall under the rubric of "assumption of risk" by the patient when he or she is appropriately informed prior to surgery.

32 ***Douget v Touro Infirmary,* 537 So 2d 251 (La Ct App 1988)** (surgeon proposed an anterior spinal fusion for chronic low back pain. He had done over 300 such procedures without major complications. He did warn patients ahead of time that her surgery would be difficult and more time consuming owing to adhesions from her several prior abdominal surgeries. At surgery, there were extensive adhesions, the renal vein was torn during dissection and repairs, but in repair process, the spleen had been damaged. The repaired vessels to the kidney did not leave adequate circulation to kidney so that removal of kidney and spleen was deemed necessary by surgeon and assisting surgeon who was a urologist. Patient had a complicated postoperative course with subphrenic abscess and bleeding peptic ulcers requiring partial gastrectomy as additional surgery. Two months after fusion surgery, patient died of Pseudomonas pneumonia and massive sepsis. The plaintiff widower based suit that he or plaintiff were not warned of risk of tearing renal vein and that unauthorized removal of kidney and spleen was battery. The appeals court saw no reason to overturn verdict. The surgeon did not mention renal vein tear as a risk as it had never occurred to him or others within his knowledge. He should not be expected to warn of a danger so rare that he had never encountered it in over 300 such operations. The routine operative permit that the patient signed specifically authorized the surgeon to perform "any additional operations or procedures beyond those . . . contemplated" that he judged necessary).

33 ***Spitzer v Ciprut,*** **437 NYS2d 27 (App Div 1981)** (arteriogram showed an aneurysm located in a blood vessel behind the right knee. When the operation was performed, the aneurysm was found to be in the blood vessel within the sciatic nerve in an extremely rare condition. The procedure performed to remove the aneurysm, but the 60-year-old patient suffered a drop foot. He filed a suit to recover damages on the theory of malpractice and lack of informed consent. The jury returned a verdict for the patient on malpractice and for the physician on informed consent. The trial court set aside the verdict for the patient on the grounds that he offered no expert testimony that the surgeon was negligent. In affirming the decision, the appellate court noted testimony by the surgeon's expert that the patient's drop foot was caused by the accumulated effect of the aneurysm and the unavoidable resection of tissues in tissues and handling the nerve during the operation. There was no proof that the surgeon was negligent. The surgeon was covered in part in the informed consent problem in that emergency type of care was necessary to remove the aneurysm, the surgeon realizing that damage to the sciatic nerve might well resolve. There was a close question whether in fact the surgeon, recognizing this potential risk of drop foot, would not more appropriately awaken the patient, discuss with the patient that particular risk and suggest alternative treatments if any were available).

34 ***Baltzell v Buskirk,*** **752 SW2d 902 (Mo Ct App 1988)** (surgeon was cleared after a fourth hearing. At issue was patient's claim that her consent to surgery could be disavowed at will. The facts of the case were not contested. The patient had previously undergone a breast lumpectomy by the same surgeon and went to him for mass in opposite breast. The surgeon obtained informed consent, removed mass which was benign. There were no postoperative complications but there was a small scar. The patient sued for battery and negligence as scar resulted in pain, mental anguish, and disfigurement. Hindsight convinced her that her informed consent should be disregarded, that the surgeon should have warned her of infection (there was a "simple suture irritation") and informed her of diagnostic alternatives such as mammography. A circuit judge dismissed the charges, an appellate judge ruled that the case should have gone to jury. The Missouri Court of Appeals faulted the patient's legal logic and evidentiary evaluation. First, the court noted that the charges made are mutually exclusive. Battery applies to situations which "an operation is performed without the patient's consent," noted the justices, where negligence suggests consent has been obtained without a complete description of the risks and alternatives. With those definitions in mind, the appellate court held the battery claim was groundless. The patient had "contended that her disavowal of the consent was sufficient . . . to entitle her to recovery under the theory of battery," noted the justices. But she could not merely "by her own retrospective appraisal," decide that it did not count. The only possible allegation was negligence, the court held. The justices then dismissed the negligence count, as the patient had proffered no expert testimony that the surgeon was required to disclose risk of infection or alternative treatments, while the expert did strongly support the need for biopsy in this type of case. Because the weight of the evidence was all on the surgeon's side, all charges were dismissed).

Comment: The innuendo is that retrospective disavowal is appropriate when a patient does not understand the risks of surgery or failure of disclosure or risks—it is a question of how complete the recital of rare complications must be.

35 ***Estra v Jacques,*** **321 SE2d 240 (NC Ct App 1984)** (patient gave informed consent for operation to a surgeon. A second surgeon performed the surgery without consent and complications arose. The first surgeon was negligent for breaching his duty to adequately advise the patient of all material facts that the patient might use in deciding whether or not to undergo the operation. One would expect, the court reasoned, that the patient's knowledge and trust in the surgeon would be a significant consideration in consenting to surgery. The second surgeon, who actually performed the surgery, was held liable for battery. The unauthorized touching was the negligent act).

36 ***Aponte v United States,*** **582 F supp 65 (DPR 1984)** (federal court in Puerto Rico ruled that a Veterans' Administration hospital and surgeons were negligent in operating a disabled schizophrenic patient without his wife's consent. The patient was hospitalized some 19 times for his schizophrenic problem. A benign lesion was to be operated, and without reading the schizophrenic reports, the chief of the hospital clinic explained to the patient that an operation was to be performed. The patient signed a consent form. His wife's consent was not requested. After the operation, the patient had a strong emotional reaction and required additional treatment on a permanent basis for significant depressed mood disorder. The government argued that the wife was not the patient's legal representative because she had not been fully appointed guardian in accordance to the law. The government also contended that the patient had consented in an informed manner. In the final judgment, the court said that the hospital and doctors were negligent in operating without a proper consent from the wife and, in particular, in not reading the patient's file).

37 ***Blitz v Boog,* 328 F2d 596, *cert denied,* 379 US 855 (1964)** (plaintiff entered Veterans' Hospital and was prevented from leaving by his doctor, although the plaintiff was competent and had requested to be discharged. This was a wrongful detention amounting to false imprisonment and since it was intentional, the government was not liable because of its sovereign immunity but the physician was personally liable).

38 ***Bonnie v Altman,* 683 F Supp 100 (DNJ 1988)** (person committed to a mental institution need not obtain the consent of his or her guardian to petition for release. The court reasoned that the consequences of wrongful commitment are so severe that "no impediment should stand in the way of its review").

39 ***In re Beth Israel Medical Center,* 136 Misc 2d 931, 519 NY2d 511 (NY Sup Ct 1987)** (court refused to order amputation of an elderly incompetent patient's leg to prolong life because it was not in her best interest. A 74-year-old, partially paralyzed aphasic woman was hospitalized after suffering a new stroke. After admission and occlusion of the left iliac artery, the vein resulted in a gangrenous condition of the foot which was spreading to the leg. If mid-thigh amputation was not performed immediately, she would be expected to die within a matter of weeks. The patient's sister opposed the amputation. She had a close relationship with the patient and stated unequivocally that the patient would refuse surgery. The hospital petitioned for authority to perform the amputation. The court heard testimony from the chief of surgery at the hospital and from an independent vascular surgeon. They agreed that without amputation, death was almost certain to occur in the next few weeks. The patient's internist agreed. The patient had no functioning intellect or meaningful awareness of life. She was not entirely comatose but could not understand or speak. She would never be able to move on her own, required nasogastric tube feedings because she could not swallow. Even with surgery, the patient's prognosis was poor. She was arteriosclerotic and a prime candidate for future strokes. Staff psychiatrist concluded that the patient was unable to understand the nature of the illness and make any reasonable adjustment as to her medical needs. The court found that a clearly convincing showing had been made, that the patient was mentally incapable of making a decision as to her medical care and that such incompetency was permanent. The court found that proposed surgery offered the patient no benefit other than potential for limited additional life. It would not return her to an integrated function but would at best prolong the natural dying process. The court said there was no human or humane benefit to be gained from subjecting patient to the pain and mutilation of surgery. She should be allowed to die with dignity).

40 ***Porter v Henry Ford Hospital,* 181 Mich App 706, 450 NW2d 37 (1989)** (patient underwent surgery and developed wound and bone infection which took 27 months to control after patient was transferred to Univer-

sity of Michigan Hospital. The cause of the infection was a felt pad left in operative site. The plaintiff filed a complaint alleging failure to take proper steps to prevent infection, failure to avoid or minimize development of osteomyelitis and failure to recognize symptoms of infection. Defense judgment was held, ruling the plaintiffs had failed to plead their allegations with requisite specificity and to present expert testimony on the standard of care. On appeal, the court held that enough specificity had been pled for the defense to adequately prepare its case).

41 ***Froh v Milwaukee Medical Clinic SC,*** **85 Wis 2d 308, 270 NW2d 83 (Ct App 1978)** (surgeon forgot a Penrose drain in a shoulder wound for two months before removing it. No injury resulted from the negligent act of surgery; therefore, the malpractice claim was denied by the court).

42 ***Ross v Chatham County Hospital Authority,*** **258 Ga 234, 367 SE2d 793 (1988)** (it was a surgeon's duty to assure himself and the patient that no foreign object remains within the body (intentionally placed part of the therapy) and the leaving of a foreign body in the patient's body is a negligent act of medical judgment and skill. The court held that a surgeon's failure to properly perform this act and impose liability on him without respect of the acts or the failure of acts of other personnel such as a nurse in the operating room who is also charged with a sponge count; the surgeon is primarily liable and his responsibility is not the vicarious responsibility of respondeat superior. The negligence is the surgeon's own negligence, and the surgeon's liability stems from his negligence. The court also concluded that the counting of sponges, instruments and other items which could be left in the patient during an operation is generally considered an administrative act rather than an act requiring exercise of professional skill or judgment for which negligence could be imputed to the surgeon).

43 ***Garrett v Brooklyn Hospital,*** **471 NYS2d 621 (App Div 1984)** (complaint of alleged malpractice in the failure to detect or remove a piece of glass from the patient's hand was properly dismissed. In October 1964, the patient underwent an operation to remove tissue from an area that had been lacerated when she fell on glass. Pathology reports that "no definite foreign body granuloma was identified." In August 1980, an x-ray of the patient's hand revealed a foreign body in the area of the operative scar, and a piece of glass was surgically removed. The patient filed a suit against the hospital and surgeon where the first operation was performed. The trial court dismissed the findings as barred by the statute of limitation. On appeal, the patient conceded that unless he was entitled to benefit of the foreign body exception, her action was barred by the statute of limitation. The appellate court agreed with the lower court that there was no basis of the discovery rule or foreign object exception. The patient entered the hospital with glass fragment already embedded in her hand. Thus, it was not introduced to her body as a result of any affirmative act on the part of a hospital employee. The court said the failure to detect or remove the fragment was made exclusively on diagnostic judgment or discretion. There was no clear fraudulent concealment. Statute of limitation applied).

44 ***Garrett v Brooklyn Hospital,*** **115 Misc 2d 933, 454 NYS2d 637 (2d Dept),** ***affd,*** **99 AD2d 541, 471 NYS2d 621** (glass left in a patient's hand after operation for its removal did not constitute a "foreign body or object" so as to come within the exception to statute of limitations permitting commencement of foreign object medical malpractice case within none year of date of discovery of foreign objects or facts of that would reasonably lead to such discovery).

45 ***Bauer v Friedland,*** **394 NW2d 549 (Minn Ct App 1986)** (orthopedic surgeon placed four wires in reducing and stabilizing fracture of tibia following a motorcycle accident. A few years later when the orthopedist tried to remove the wires, three wires came out easily; the fourth would not budge. Rather than make a cut in the bone and run the risk of fracture, the wire was left in place, but it was realized that there was a risk of it migrating. This risk of migration was no explained to the patient. Months later, the wire did migrate, damaged a branch of the posterior tibial nerve. It was held that medical testimony was not necessary to establish whether the case was worthy of trial, but the medical expert testimony was necessary on the question of whether leaving the wire in was below standard of care. Such testimony was not given).

Comment: It is not unusual for a metallic stabilizing device, when attempting to remove it, to be fraught with failure. Extensive and mutilating surgery has been carried out to the detriment of the patient for the removal of such wires. A better, and probably within the standard of care, action is to inform the patient of the presence of such foreign bodies and to periodically examine x-rays to see if they are moving. The fairly extensive destruction of bones to remove metallic fragments is frequently contraindicated, for there is increased risk of fracture to that area of bone.

46 ***Borderlon v Peck,*** **661 SW2d 907 (Tex 1983),** ***rehg denied*** **(1983)** (state law did not abolish the doctrine of fraudulent concealment as a bar to the Statute of Limitation defense. When a suture needle broke during an operation, the physician purposely left the broken portion in the patient's abdomen but did not inform her of this decision. The needle was later discovered on x-ray and operation performed to remove it. The patient filed a suit against this surgeon six days after the two year limitation period had run. The patient responded to emotion for summary judgment by filing the response alleging fraudulent concealment. The Trial court granted summary judgment and appellate court affirmed. The court held that fraudulent concealment of the defense had been abolished under the state medical liability insurance improvement act because the legislature intended to establish an absolute time limit of which suits must be filed. On review of the case, the Texas Supreme Court disagreed with the lower courts. The courts pointed out that it was not inclined a writ of recovery by the patient but mere permitting her to present evidence that, if believed, would stop the surgeon from pleading the statute of limitation as a bar to her claim. Case was sent back for further proceedings. It is incumbent on the surgeon to inform the patient where there has been misadventure such as breaking of needle or instrument part. Failure to do so is contrary to customary practice as well as to the ethical and moral obligations of the physician).

47 ***Pierson v Frontier,* 406 NW2d 56 (Minn Ct App 1987)** (surgeon was sued for leaving a metal clip in patient. Summary judgment for the surgeon was precluded because of an issue as to whether he and a treating physician participated in a joint enterprise with respect to operation. The patient consulted the physician because of epigastric pain. Physician diagnosed cholecystitis and contacted the surgeon to perform an operation to remove the patient's gall bladder and insisted that the physician and surgeon charge separate for their fees for the services. The surgical team left a metal clip inside the patient's abdominal cavity. The clip worked its way into the common bile duct and salts collected around it, forming a stone. The patient had a history of hiatal hernia. When he complained of chest pain and gastric pain, the physician contributed his pain over a six year period to either hernia or stress. Finally, a second physician diagnosed the problem as gall stones and operated, finding a metal clip inside the stone. Seventeen months after the second operation, the patient filed a complaint against the surgeon and the first physician, alleging negligence in that the clip was not removed during the first operation. The trial court granted a summary judgment to the surgeon finding he had no postoperative contact with the patient and that the action was barred over a two-year statute of limitation. On appeal, the patient contended the physician was in a joint enterprise in regard to the operation and because the negligent act was from out of the joint enterprise, the physician continued treatment after surgery and the patient claimed that his action was not barred. The surgeon admitted that he was the chief surgeon during the operation; however, he said he and the physician were acting as partners. The court said that if it was determined that a joint enterprise existed between the physician and surgeon, there would be an additional question whether the joint enterprise continued after the operation. The record indicated that postoperative contact between the two; the court said that more facts were necessary and reversed the lower court's judgment, sending the case back for further proceedings).

48 ***Puro v Henry,* 449 A2d 176 (Conn 1982)** (defendant was entitled to a new trial against the hospital and physician after the jury was unable to reach a verdict. The patient first consulted a physician in 1963 for abdominal problems. He sent him to a radiology group for x-rays who diagnosed gall bladder disease. On September 9, 1963, a cholecystectomy was carried out. Recurrent hernias necessitated three additional operations. During the third one, the surgeon inserted nylon mesh to reinforce the wound. After the third operation in May 1967, the patient began to experience severe pain in her abdomen, especially if she bent, stretched or twisted. On x-ray report in October 1969, by the same radiology group who took the earlier x-rays showed only radiopaque sutures. The patient continued to see the physician until 1972, when she terminated their relationship and consulted a general practitioner. He also had x-rays by the same group, but in the report dated October 1972, radiopaque needle-like object was disclosed. After one unsuc-

cessful attempt, the needle was later surgically removed. A malpractice action was filed in 1974. The patient claimed the hospital procedures for accounting for surgical needles were deficient and the physician was negligent for leaving the needle in her. The jury was unable to reach a verdict. The court ordered a new trial. On appeal, the decision was affirmed. There was expert testimony that the hospital failed to require needle counts and failed to execute its "one for one" procedure in the operating room. There is expert testimony tending to show that the physician was negligent. There is additional evidence that the physician was informed by the radiologist the presence of the needle in October 1969 and concealed it from his patient. Since there was sufficient evidence to warrant submitting the care to a jury, the trial court properly denied motions for judgment in favor of the physician and hospital).

49 ***Halley v Birbiglia,*** **390 Mass 540, 458 NE2d 710 (1983)** (action alleging negligence and failure to obtain informed consent of parents concerning risks associated with arteriogram given to child subsequently requiring amputation due to complicating thrombosis. Neurological consultation was not liable for negligence or for breach of disclosure duty where he was not agent of physician who performed the arteriogram; he was not the admitting or attending physician; he was not one of the medical personnel who spoke with parents and assured them of safety of test. The plaintiff's expert offered no opinion as to why duty to inform should be levied on defendant neurologist and plaintiff proffered no precedent to extend informed consent doctrine to individual so tangentially involved in performance of medical procedure).

50 ***Barth v Rock,*** **674 P2d 1265 (Wash Ct App 1984)** (5-year-old child broke her arm while riding a bicycle. Physician performed a closed reduction but later the arm began to swell so the cast had to be split. That altered the alignment of the fracture and a second operation was performed seven days later. There was a problem with the general anesthetic used in the second procedure and the patient ultimately died, with an autopsy diagnosis of cerebral anoxia and edema. Her parents filed an action for wrongful death against the operating physician and the nurse anesthetist in the hospital. After a three week trial, the jury returned a verdict in favor of the medical defendant. The trial court then granted a new trial on the basis that substantial justice was not done. In affirming the decision, the court noted that the testimony by the expert witness was clearly erroneous and misleading. He stated that a textbook he had relied on stated that there were 55 reported cases of allergic reactions to sodium pentothal. In fact, the textbook stated there were 55 reported cases of allergic reactions to barbituates. In addition, both nurse anesthetist and operating room physician admitted they had not informed parents of the risks of general anesthetic, because each believed the other had done so. The trial court promptly granted a new trial on the grounds that it was a matter of law that there was no informed consent).

51 ***Zimmerman v New York City Health & Hospitals Corporation,*** **458 NYS2d 552 (App Div 1983)** (spinal fusion was carried out on a 16-year-

old girl and there was no question that the child improved over what it would have been without the surgery. However, a substantial malpractice award was granted because of an incompetent consent. The girl was experiencing difficulty and pain in walking due to a low lumbar spondylolisthesis. The information that the mother received was that if spinal fusion was not carried out, she would be progressively unable to walk and probably would have severe nerve damage and be incontinent of urine. An attempt was made to get the mother's consent and testimony as that the mother seemed to be mentally sound at the time consent was written; however, it was found that the mother was mentally incompetent. The father was available for signing consent but had not been asked).

Comment: This information about the mother who signed the consent was known by the surgeon prior to the surgery but he operated anyway. Based on this, malpractice for lack of competent consent stood, with the original award being substantially reduced to a nuisance-value award.

Appendix 14-2
Forms

Form 1

Request and Consent for Surgical, Medical or Diagnostic Procedures and Acknowledgement of Receipt of Information

PATIENT: ______________________________

PATIENT NO.: ______________ DATE: __________ TIME: __________

The hospital and your physician are required by law to obtain your consent to perform the surgical, medical or diagnostic procedure(s) listed below. Signing this form will acknowledge that you request and consent to your physician performing the recommended procedure(s). Your signature also confirms that your physician has explained to you the procedure(s), the risks of the procedure(s), the alternatives, if any, and risks of the alternatives and the risks or consequences of foregoing all treatment. Please READ THIS ENTIRE FORM CAREFULLY and then before signing it, ask your physician any additional questions you may have. Your request and consent is valid until you withdraw it.

1. I hereby request and authorize __________ with hospital personnel and/or other trained persons of his/her choice to perform upon __________ (patient) the following surgical, medical or diagnostic procedure(s) ______________________________ to include any necessary or advisable anesthesia and disposal of tissue removed during surgery. I further request and authorize my physician and his assistant(s) to perform any other procedure that in his or their judgment is advisable for my wellbeing. This additional request and authority is extended as I recognize that during the above listed procedure(s), unforeseen conditions may require different or additional procedures.

2. I hereby request and consent to the administration of such anesthetics as are necessary. I further request that the choice of anesthetic to be used shall be made by professional anesthesia personnel.

3. I acknowledge that some of the risks known to be associated with surgery and anesthesia and which may be applicable to the proposed procedure(s) are:

   INFECTION
   SEVERE BLOOD LOSS
   IMPOTENCE
   DISFIGURING SCARS
   LOSS OF FUNCTION OF AN ORGAN
   LOSS OF FUNCTION OF AN ARM OR LEG
   LOSS OF AN ORGAN
   LOSS OF ARM OF LEG
   LOSS OF BLADDER FUNCTION
   LOSS OF BOWEL FUNCTION
   PARALYSIS BELOW THE WAIST
   PARALYSIS BELOW THE NECK
   BRAIN DAMAGE
   DEATH

4. I am aware that the practice of medicine and surgery is not an exact science and acknowledge that no guarantees or warranties have been made to me concerning the results of the procedure(s). I acknowledge that even though my physician has advised me of all known risks, up to and including the rare but possible severe risks as revealed in item 3 of this form, that additional unforeseeable and unpreventable situations could arise in the course of my care which might result in injury.

5. I HEREBY STATE THAT I HAVE READ AND UNDERSTAND THIS REQUEST AND CONSENT AND THAT ALL MY QUESTIONS ABOUT THE PROCEDURE(S), ALTERNATIVE PROCEDURE(S), AND RISKS OF EACH HAVE BEEN ANSWERED IN LANGUAGE THAT I UNDERSTOOD AND THAT ALL BLANKS WERE FILLED IN PRIOR TO MY SIGNATURE.

Signed: ______________________________

Patient or person authorized to request procedures for patient: ____________________

Relationship or Capacity: ____________________

Witness to signature: ______________________________

I have explained the procedure(s), alternative(s) and risks to the person or persons whose signature or signatures are affixed above.

____

(signature of physician)

Form 2
Hospital Evidence of Informed Consent to Operation or Other Procedure

1. I hereby certify that I have authorized Dr(s). ______________________ and/or such assistants as may be selected by him to perform the following procedure or operation: ____
____
____

2. I acknowledge that Dr. ______________________ has explained to me, in language that was easy to understand, the nature of my condition and the manner in which the operation or procedure is expected to remedy this condition. He has made no guarantee or assurances to me concerning the results of the operation or procedure(s). I have had explained to me alternative methods of treatment and agree to the above surgical approach.

3. I recognize that, during the course of the operation, additional or different procedures other than those described above may be necessary. I authorize such procedures as are, in my doctor's professional judgement, desirable to my health, including attempts to remedy any conditions that are not known at the time the operation is begun.

4. Dr. ______________________ has explained to me that there are substantial risks and consequences that may be associated with any surgical, medical, diagnostic, or anesthetic procedure. I understand that not every conceivable hazard can be listed, I realize the following possibilities exist, however INFREQUENT or rare: Excessive bleeding needing blood transfusion with its involved risks, infection of wounds and punctures, allergic reactions to medications, tape, etc; collection of blood or fluid requiring later drainage; and possible death. THESE ARE NOT PROBABLE RESULTS—THEY ARE STATISTICAL POSSIBILITIES.

5. I consent to the administration of anesthesia by or under the direction of an anesthesiologist or nurse anesthetist selected by my doctor, or to be administered by my doctor, his associates or assistants, and to the use of such anesthetics as may be advisable.

6. I consent to the above operation or procedure(s) being witnessed by students or practitioners in the health sciences in connection with their continuing education.

7. I authorize this hospital to preserve and examine for scientific, pathological, or teaching purposes or to otherwise dispose of, the tissue or organs resulting from the operation or procedure(s) authorized above.

8. Photographs: The undersigned hereby authorizes the taking of photographs or movies during a surgical or other procedure and during the subsequent treatment in Humana Hospital Dodge City. It is understood that said photographs will be used only for purposes of medical study or research, and that the name of the patient or undersigned will not be used to identify said photographs. This consent is expressly intended to release from liability all personnel of the hospital, as well as the operating physician, consultants and the attending physician.

9. I give my consent to Humana Hospital Dodge City to dispose of any tissue, parts or organs which may be removed as a result of the procedure(s) authorized above.

10. I certify that I have read, have had explained to me, and fully understand the above consent to operation or other procedure(s), and that it is my intention

to have the above carried out as stated, I verify that all blanks requiring insertion were completed, and any inapplicable paragraphs were stricken before I signed.

DATE: ________ TIME: ________ SIGNED: ______________________________
(patient)
WITNESS: ______________________________
(nearest relative)

Form 3
Consent for Operation or Other Procedure

Patient: ______________________________
Physician: ____________________________

1. I hereby authorize and direct Dr. ______________________, and such assistants, associates and designees as may be selected by him to perform the following procedures: ______________________________________

   ____

   and such additional procedures as are considered therapeutically and diagnostically necessary on the basis of findings during the course of diagnosis or treatment.

2. The nature of my ailment, the nature and purpose of the proposed procedure, possible alternative procedures, risks of unfortunate results, of possible complication, and of unforseen physical conditions within the body and the possibility of success have been explained to me.

3. I am aware that the practice of medicine and surgery is not an exact science and I acknowledge that no guarantees have been made to me as to the results that may be obtained.

4. I consent to the removal, use or disposal by the above named physician of any tissues or parts which may be removed.

5. I consent to the administration of anesthesia to be applied by or under the direction and supervision of Dr. ______________________ and to the use of such anesthesia as he may deem advisable, with the exception of

   ____
   (none, or a particular one if there is an exception)

I CERTIFY THAT I HAVE READ AND FULLY UNDERSTAND THE ABOVE CONSENT, THAT THE EXPLANATIONS THEREIN REFERRED TO WERE MADE, AND THAT ALL BLANKS OR STATEMENTS REQUIRING INSERTION OR COMPLETION WERE FILLED IN, AND INAPPLICABLE PARAGRAPHS, IF ANY, WERE STRICKEN BEFORE I SIGNED.

______________________ (date)	______________________ (patient signature)
__________ (time) ☐ A.M. ☐ P.M.	
______________________ (witness)	______________________ (address)
______________________ (witness)	______________________ (address)

(When patient is a minor, or incompetent to give consent, then consent is secured from parent, guardian, spouse, closest relative, or other person with relationship or authority.)

6. Patient is a minor, ________ years of age, or is unable to sign because ________________________________

________________ (date)	________________ (authorized signature)
________ (time) ☐ A.M. ☐ P.M.	________________ (relationship to patient)
________________ (witness)	________________ (address)
________________ (witness)	________________ (address)

Form 4
Admission Agreement

Please read and sign the following permits, release, and agreements. Delete or change any section you do not accept; please initial any change.

1. TREATMENT CONSENT: I, the undersigned, hereby authorize Valley View Hospital and the physicians in charge of the case of patient whose name appears on the reverse hereof to administer any treatment, or to administer such anesthetics, and perform such procedures as may be deemed necessary or advisable in the diagnosis and treatment of this patient. I understand my physician may order an "HIV Antibody" AIDS tests as part of this diagnosis and treatment.
2. RELEASE OF INFORMATION: It is agreed all records concerning my hospitalization remain the property of the hospital. I authorize the hospital to release to any insurance company, third-party payer, or their representative any copies or excerpts of records of this hospitalization which are necessary for payment of my account.
3. PERSONAL VALUABLES: It is understood the hospital maintains a safe for safekeeping of the patient's money and valuables. The hospital is not liable for loss or damage to any jewelry, glasses, dentures, furs, money, or other articles of usual value or size unless placed in the hospital safe. The hospital is not liable for any other personal property kept with the patient, including clothing, radios, and jewelry.
4. ASSIGNMENT OF INSURANCE: For the hospital services rendered, I assign and authorize direct payment of any hospital benefits, including major medical, due me from any insurance company or third-party payer. I further guarantee payment of any and all hospital charges not covered or paid by my insurance company. This assignment is irrevocable.
5. AVAILABILITY OF CHARITY CARE: I hereby acknowledge receipt of the Notice of Availability of Hill-Burton Charity Care.
6. BILLING PROCEDURE-PHYSICIAN SERVICES: I understand that some physicians furnishing services to me, including anesthesiologist, cardiologist, and radiologist, are independent contractors and are not employees of the hospital. These services will be billed directly to me by the specialist performing the service.

The undersigned certifies having read, and agrees to abide by, the foregoing treatments.

____________________ (patient's signature)　　____________________ (witness)

Patient is unable to sign at admission because ____________________,
or patient is a minor, ______ years of age.

____________________ (signature/relationship) (date)　　____________________ (witness) (date)

____________________ (INSURED (Assignment of benefits))　　____________ (account number)　　____________ (time/date of admission)

15

Patient Behavioral Considerations: Somatization

§15.01 Generally

Health is accorded a positive value in Western society, yet many persons choose illness as a way of life. This choice is usually, but not always, unconsciously determined, and the patient will state that health is preferable and seek medical care.

Somatization is a process by which the body is used for psychological purposes or for personal gain. Any one symptom or group of symptoms may serve one or more functions at the same time. These may include intrapsychic conflicts, interpersonal relationships, and responses to social, environmental, or economic problems. *See* Figure 15-1.

Examples of the psychological uses of somatization include (1) displacement of unpleasant emotions into physical symptoms, such as a preoccupation with bowel function instead of experiencing underlying depression, or (2) the use of the symptom to communicate, by symbolic means, an idea or emotion, such as hysterical paraplegia or hysterical blindness to symbolize and communicate the feeling of helplessness. (*See* Appendix 15-1, Case 1.) The alleviation of guilt through suffering, such as a pain syndrome experienced after the death of someone in the patient's life for whom the patient had mixed emotional feelings, is another example.

Personal gains may be obtained by somatization, and these include (1) the ability to manipulate relationships, or (2) the intention to obtain release from duties and responsibilities, such as absence at the place of employment or an excuse for not completing housework. Other examples are financial gain, such as disability payments or compensation payments for pain after a neck sprain, or perhaps a relationship or sympathy from another person, such as the concern and worry elicited in response to skin lesions that were surreptitiously self-induced.

Intrapersonal and psychic gains from somatization are similar to those observed in the factual organic illness. It is not unusual for persons with diseases of organic origin to capitalize on their illness to serve a variety of personal needs. However, there are some individuals who repetitively use their bodies as a means of handling life stresses. A person who uses physical symptoms as a lifestyle has somatoform disorders, such as hypochondriasis.

Although little attention is paid to the psychological ramifications to somatization in medical school training, patients with these symptoms occupy a significantly large proportion of the practicing physician's time. In several orthopedic studies, it has been found that 43 to 50 per cent of patients seen had organic disease alone, 13 per cent had organic and psychological problems, 6 per cent had no diagnosis, and 38 per cent had no disease, only psychological problems. When these patients were surgical patients,

Figure 15-1

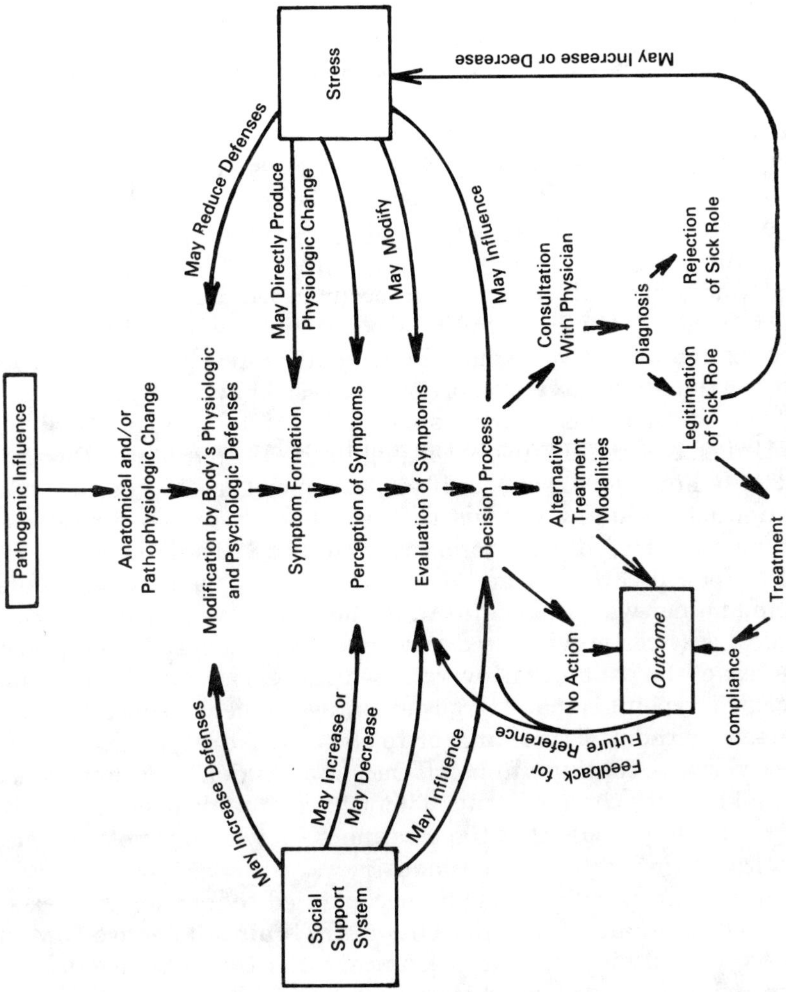

A schematic view of the process of illness and disease. Not all possible relationships are shown.

it was found that 66 per cent had organic diseases, only 16 per cent had both organic and psychological symptoms, 13 per cent had no diagnosis, and 5 per cent had only psychological symptoms. In another large study of nearly 700 patients, 37 per cent had organic disease, 40 per cent had a diagnosis of such functional disorders as depression or psychogenic back pain, and a diagnosis of functional disorder was implied additionally in another 23 per cent.

In another study, it was found that 50 per cent of all illnesses and injury episodes were accounted for by less than 25 per cent of the population. Illness or injury tended to occur in clusters and it was estimated that at least one-third of the illnesses were influenced to a significant degree by the patient's attempt to adapt to events and situations that he or she was presently encountering, frequently by somatization.

Another study of telephone company employees (Hinkle et al., 1956) revealed that over a 20-year period, 10 per cent of the men surveyed experienced 34 per cent of the total sickness disability—that is, days off from work, while the healthiest 10 per cent experienced only 1 per cent of sickness disability. The finding that illness does not occur in random distribution has also been confirmed in studies of military populations, where there is a consistent finding that a relatively small proportion of naval personnel account for a disproportionately large proportion of all sickbay visits.

The cost of medical care is an increasing portion of the gross national product in the United States. In 1980, according to the United States Bureau of Census, $200 billion was expended. If one assumes that 10 per cent of all medical care, not including psychiatric treatment, is provided to persons with no organic disease, then the total cost would be $20 billion yearly. That figure is for medical care only and does not include disability payments.

Viewed in another way, if 25 per cent of the people who used 50 per cent of the medical services provided reduced their medical care to the average rate of the rest of the population, overall medical services would be reduced by 25 per cent. The point is that a large percentage of medical care is directed toward persons without disease and/or to those who are overutilizing services. These services continue to be offered in a fashion consistent with a disease model because these patients do not have organic disease, and it is not unreasonable to propose that the treatment they have is not very effective. Somatization is indeed a large industry.

American medicine has increasingly become tied to technology. Tests or procedures such as organ transplants, CT, or MRI brain studies are now commonplace. Associated with these new technical skills, the cost of medical care has accelerated. Other surveys suggest that less technically sophisticated treatment or approaches may have equally satisfactory results in this group of patients. Increased attention by the orthopedist or examining physician to the relatively neglected somatization disorders becomes important in the evaluation and treatment of patients. Despite knowledge of somatization, physicians appear hesitant to alter the manner in which they practice medicine. Treatment failures, particularly surgical treatment, and more particularly surgical treatment of low back complaints, have their basis, in part, in the surgeon's failure to recognize and failure to understand the ramifications of somatization and other psychological impingements on the patient's illness. Failure to recognize the substantial effect of somatization on the prognosis of the injured patient by the examining and treating physician ultimately does a disservice to both the patient and society.[1]

Somatization disorder (SD) is defined as a syndrome whose criteria include the onset of symptoms before the age of 30 and complaints from a prescribed list of at least 14 unexplained symptoms for women, and 12 for men. These symptoms must not be caused by alcohol or drugs and must not be the side effects of medication. The symptoms must have caused the patient to consult a physician, to change his or her daily routine, and to take medication other than aspirin. (*See* Appendix 15-1, Cases 2 to 5.)

§15.02 Statement of the Problem

In October 1989, The American Academy of Pain Management made the following statement:

> The diagnosis, treatment, management, assessment, psychological and psychiatric restoration, vocational evaluation, and rehabilitation of chronic pain patients is unlike many other specialties in the field of the health sciences because of the heavy reliance on interdisciplinary team members from numerous and diverse backgrounds and training. What sets pain management apart is that team specialists frequently have to work with a pain patient cojointly to obtain a satisfactory and acceptable outcome. . . .
>
> Significant changes in health care have occurred during the last two decades. Basic science has introduced new technology. Social science has introduced and multidisciplinary medical management requires specialized skills. These skills include both clinical and management expertise. Complex health care needs now often elicit a team concept. . . .
>
> Board certified pain management specialists and, in some instances non-pain management specialists, may have to work cojointly to produce a desired and satisfactory outcome. It is best that as many of the therapists on each case be board certified in pain management.

§15.03 Psychological Treatment

For a total patient approach to the orthopedic patient in pain, a method of dealing with the psychological aspect of the problem is essential. Pain-prone patients must be oriented to the nature and treatment of their condition. Patients must understand that pain is not entirely or even substantially noiciceptive (due to mechanical factors) alone. They must learn that a chemi-

[1] C.V. Ford, The Somatizing Disorders. Illness as a Way of Life (1984).

cal imbalance is involved in pain perception, that tension and depression tend to be invariably associated with chronic pain and play an important role, and that antidepressant medication can be helpful in working through the psychological ramifications of the pain syndrome. The basic principle of the behavioral approach to chronic pain control (encourage activity and de-emphasize pain) may be combined with antidepressant medication. Explaining the treatment to and involving next of kin and a "significant other" in treatment is effective. Distraction from the pain, in the form of activity carried out at a reasonable pace or continuing to work in spite of pain, should be encouraged. Modifying the work environment to adapt to the physical impairment present should be part of the therapy plan along with vocational rehabilitation in many cases. In work hardening programs, where progressive work activities similar to the patient's job, become part of a conditioning rehabilitation. Often, however, duplication of the job activity leading to injury may set the stage for ease of re-injury. At this time, there is a degree of biased disagreement.[2]

§15.04 Psychological Basis of Malpractice Actions

Jury Verdict Research reported in 1987 that the typical malpractice award more than doubled between 1984 and 1986. At the same time, the standard of care cases increased the country over. There is much evidence to suggest that the emergence of psychological bases for many orthopedic symptoms which persist may reflect bad results from surgical or medical treatment. In 1976, 12 per cent of all malpractice claims against physicians performing invasive procedures were against orthopedic surgeons, where 3.2 per cent of all practitioners are orthopedists. However, in mid-1988, 8.9 per cent of all claims, invasive or noninvasive, were against orthopedists.

§15.05 Effect of Psychological Factors

Many psychological factors in orthopedic cases can magnify and prolong subjective complaints. The apparent suffering of the patient evokes sympathy from family and friends. Pain is a sensory experience. Suffering is an emotional response to pain. Disability is a psychosocial, medicolegal situation with major financial ramifications. Issues in compensation neurosis, hypochondriasis, chronic tension, chronic pain, secondary gain, prescription abuse, medical dependence, and anger are emotional and environmental factors which tend to intensify the patient's subjective complaints and may form

---

[2] Blumer & Heilbronn, *Treatment Outcome of 1,000 Patients with the Pain Prone Disorder,* 14 Psychia Annals 796 (1984); Engel, *Psychogenic Pain and the Pain Prone Patient,* 26 Am J Med 8 (1959); W.E. Fordyce, Learning Process in Pain, Psychology of Pain (R. Sternbach ed 1978), W.E. Fordyce, Behavioral Methods for Chronic Pain and Illness (1976); Krystal, *Alexithymia and Psychotherapy,* 33 Am J Psychother 17 (1979).

a basis for a negligence claim against the treating physician. (*See* Appendix 15-1, Case 1.)

The patient presenting to the orthopedist can belong to any one of three groups: (1) the organic group in which there are no psychological symptoms, (2) the purely psychological group in which there is no demonstrable organic basis for presenting complaints, and (3) the mixed group in which organic and psychological symptoms coexist.

There is a fundamental rule that psychological symptoms do not preclude organic symptoms, but prolong recovery—both physical and psychological. The triers of fact and third-party carriers must be sensitive to these concepts and insure that all injured persons receive fair, equal, and adequate treatment. It is in this sensitive area that all too often the patient is a pawn of two adversarial sides that base their judgments on bias and/or medical opinions that stem more from the physician wishing to be a continuing consultant, overlooking these psychological facts, than from serving the injured patient. The other side of the coin is the physician who is inclined to overuse the psychological impairment.

The need to recognize psychological factors has been emphasized by many actively practicing orthopedic surgeons. Wadell, writing in Spine (1987), makes a strong case for the need to recognize psychological, as well as physical, findings in the diagnosis and treatment of low back pain patients. This task is hard for many (most) orthopedists, who are trained to live and breathe the hard sciences and may find it difficult to accept psychosocial concepts.

Sometimes confusing or inappropriate behavior, such as a bad attitude, laziness, or extreme immaturity, can be a warning sign of something more serious—mental illness. We need to learn to recognize the following important warning signs. They can be the first step to healing the sickness.

1. Marked personality change over time
2. Confused thinking; strange or grandiose ideas
3. Prolonged severe depression, apathy, or extreme highs and lows
4. Excessive anxieties, fears, or suspicions; blaming others
5. Withdrawal from society, friendlessness; abnormal self-centeredness
6. Denial of obvious problems; strong resistance to help
7. Thinking or talking about suicide
8. Numerous, unexplained physical ailments; marked changes in eating or sleeping patterns
9. Anger or hostility out of proportion to the situation
10. Delusions, hallucinations, hearing voices
11. Abuse of alcohol or drugs
12. Growing inability to cope with problems and such daily activities as school, job, or personal needs

There is a distinction between low back pain, a self-limited condition, from low back *disability* which is characterized by "... emotional distress, depression, failed treatment and adoption of the sick role." Some authors report 100 per cent success in treating the latter group of patients, primarily by not recognizing and treating the psychological aspect. It is the psychological low back disability case following otherwise successful surgery that has resulted in significantly increased risks for litigation.

Several recent articles suggest that ample reason exists to conclude that the recent increase in malpractice suits is based on psychological factors in failed surgeries and in addictive personality stereotypes.

There seems to be an evolving standard of care that requires the operating surgeon to know a patient psychologically or to have another appropriate consultant's opinion as part of the diagnostic workup. There are problems in this area, for to deprive a psychologically-impaired person of surgeries that would help a less psychologically-impaired person is inconceivable. The problem is likely best resolved in the informed consent area that does not warrant results, although many outspoken orthopedists are saying that to do surgery on the psychologically-impaired patient smacks of unnecessary surgery. The bottom line, of course, is "how psychologically impaired" must the patient be and what criteria are to be used. One is reminded of psychological and psychiatric testimony in criminal trials and the wide divergence of competent opinion and apparent "bias" judgment in those areas.[3]

§15.06 Managing Difficult Patients

Often the orthopedist is faced with a difficult patient whose lack of cooperation or apparent misunderstanding of his or her care jeopardizes recovery. The problem may be fear on the patient's part, or anxiety over the injury or the financing of its care. The patient may be psychologically disturbed or demented. The dementia itself may be a marker of toxicity (perhaps from medication) or a sign of head injury. Sometimes patients generate problems by refusing treatment.

Following the doctrine of informed consent, the physician must explain the nature and risks of the proposed treatment, along with alternative treatments, to the patient. There is a legal trend obliging the doctor to explain to the patient the risks of noncompliance with the recommended treatment. In *Truman v Winter,* the patient prevailed because she had never been told why the test (a Pap smear) was important. She refused treatment and subsequently died from cervical cancer.

In another case, Moore v Preventive Medicine Medical Group, the patient was advised to see a specialist for a lesion on his ear. Months later, after the patient failed to follow his doctor's advice, he was diagnosed as having malignant melanoma and required disfiguring surgery. The appellate court reasoned that the first treating doctor could be found liable, even though he did not know the patient was noncompliant. This decision again stated

---

[3] Loff, Elbaor & Lobb, *Observations and Psychological Factors in the Treatment of Difficult Orthopedic Patients,* 10 J Neurol & Orthop Med & Surg 231 (1989).

that the doctor had a duty to provide enough information to the patient so that an informed consent could be made by the patient. A duty to follow-up a patient who is medically "at risk" was rejected by the court (not like an orthopedist failing to follow a newly-casted fracture). The lost chance of recovery doctrine was not, but could have been, appropriately pled.

In these sorts of cases, accurate legible office records stating the medical problem, the advice given for treatment, and containing a comment as to the potential problems that might derive from failure to comply are essential. Many recent cases employ the logic that when a doctor fails to tell the patient "why" a treatment is necessary, he or she is liable.

In cases of refusal of treatment, an appropriate standard followed by most physicians is to obtain a consultation for a second opinion, particularly if fear, anxiety, or a physician-patient conflict is present. The additional problem of breach of confidentiality should be considered, especially if the patient may face social, economic, or family loss, such as might occur with suspected AIDS or an illegitimate pregnancy.

Legal responsibilities are enforceable while ethical obligations to the patient, for the most part, are not.[4]

§15.07 Chronic Pain and Depression

Depression has been documented as a frequent concomitant of chronic pain. In reviewing recent literature, it is reported that the incidence of depression among chronic pain patients ranges from 10 to 100 per cent, with the majority reporting an average of 50 per cent. The direct link between pain and depression was found to be insignificant; however, measures of perceived life interference and self-control were found to be significant intervening variables between pain and depression. It is clear that psychological mediators may be involved in the development of depression secondary to chronic pain.

Once acute orthopedic injuries have progressed to chronic pain syndromes, ensuing psychiatric morbidity is likely, such as depressed mood disorder or secondary major depression. The prognosis for recovery in this group is guarded.[5]

§15.08 Stress and Impairment

Several studies indicate that stressful life events, particularly those events related to the injury and its consequences, increase the likelihood of depressive mood disorders. The physician treating these injuries (most back inju-

---

[4] Ills, *Managing Difficult Patients: Duties and Rights,* 12 Orthop Surg Leg Let 6 (1989).

[5] Rudy & Turk, *Chronic Pain and Depression: Toward a Cognitive-Behavioral Mediation Model,* 35 Pain 129 (1988); Atkinson, *Depressed Mood in Chronic Low Back Pain Relationship with Stressful Life Events,* 35 Pain 47 (1988).

ries) must be alert to those patients experiencing severe life stresses (at higher risk for chronic pain) and arrange for early psychologic or psychiatric intervention aimed in part at stress management. (*See* Appendix 15-2, Form 1).

In addition, effects of ethnic background, genetic variables, nutrition, substance abuse, smoking, and socioeconomic status are players in this high-risk group. A change or conflict in status and/or role constitutes one of the most severe forms of psychological stress. Physicians who fail to accept or utilize these concepts do their patient a disservice.

Stress-related disorders have been recognized as compensable under workers' compensation statutes, including the Federal Employees' Compensation Act (FECA), for many years. These impairments can be temporary or permanent, and are usually divided into three categories:

1. *Mental/physical:* Cases in this category involve a mental stimulus that causes a distinct physical injury to the injured person, such as a heart attack brought about by a stressful event. The mental stimulus may be of a sudden or relatively brief nature, such as a sudden explosion or witnessing a particularly violent injury to another. The stress may be gradual and sustained, such as that caused by long work hours, sustained harassment, and/or other forms of long-term personal friction.
2. *Physical/mental:* Conversely, a physical injury can result in a disabling emotional response. These problems are diagnosed as posttraumatic stress disorders, traumatic neurosis, conversion neurosis, or hysteria. Sometimes hysterical paralysis is a mental reaction to an injury, and may include aggravation of a pre-existing condition (i.e., nondisabling conditions that pre-existed the injury that were changed—aggravated, accelerated, or activated) to a new and disabling level.
3. *Mental/mental:* These cases involve a mental stimulus that results in a mental condition, such as psychoneurotic illness brought about by the condition of employment. As in mental/physical cases, the stress may be of a sudden or relatively brief nature, or may be gradual and sustained. The difference is in the resultant impairment being mental rather than physical.[6]

§15.09 Pain and Surgery

Complaints of unrelenting pain or recurrent pain are by far the more common incentive for surgical intervention. This presents unique difficulties to

---

[6] Rudy & Turk, *Chronic Pain and Depression: Toward a Cognitive Behavioral Mediation Model,* 35 Pain 129 (1988); Atkinson, *Depressed Mood in Chronic Low Back Pain Relationship with Stressful Life Events,* 35 Pain 47 (1988); Brown, *Life Events and Psychiatric Disorders Part 2 Nature of Causal Link,* 3 Psychol Med 159 (1973); Speculand, *Role of Recent Stressful Life Events in the Onset of TMJ Dysfunction Pain,* 12 Commun Dent Oral Epidemiol 197 (1984); M. Konner, Becoming a Doctor (1987); 1B Larson's Workman's Compensation Law §42.20 (Apr 1986).

the care provider, as there are no universally accepted techniques for measuring pain. The purely subjective character of pain embraces two areas. The intensity of the pain cannot be measured and no two patients have the same tolerance for the same pain complaint. If there is no basis for challenging the veracity of the patient's pain complaints, it is extraordinarily difficult to challenge the decision to perform surgery.

If chronic intolerable or recurrent severe pain in low back and/or legs continues in spite of good and cooperative conservative treatment, appropriate surgical intervention may be indicated. Surgery must be for a specific, demonstrable, irreversible lesion and must never be done on an "exploratory" basis. At this time, there are ample diagnostic tools available to the surgeon to make a verifiable diagnosis.

Some surgical indications are more urgent than the "standard" of two to six months of conservative treatment. Where there is a nerve root defect (muscle weakness, reflex and sensory change) with pain that is not improving or worsening, surgical nerve root decompression is suggested within two to four weeks by many surgeons. Another set of surgeons would still wait.

It is usual that the orthopedic surgeon can be faulted for delaying surgery and often that he or she will be criticized by a group of peers who do not follow his or her surgical indication reasoning.

A careful, conscientious surgeon experienced in the field is less apt to be critical than cloistered or biased individuals who are wed to their preferred management techniques and who discount those with another opinion.

Perhaps the bottom line in back surgery for unremitting, intolerable pain with a specific diagnosis in a psychologically stable patient is that reality testing is the probable chance of improving the patient's pain complaint.[7]

§15.10 Psychosocial Predictors of Disability in Low Back Patients

Education and self-rated health are important predictors of the degree of impairment perceived by the patient with low back pain. Little education, previous episodes of pain, and "always feeling sick" are recognized by most psychologists as significant factors when asked to prognosticate a patient with a low back pain outcome from treatment.

§15.11 Pain Clinics

Pain is one of the taboo words of modern medicine according to the pioneer pain management expert, Patrick Wall, M.D., who has dedicated his professional life to attacking the root causes of pain. He feels that treating chronic pain symptoms is regarded as second class medicine by many of the mainstream, objective-only minded physicians, and that this does a great disserv-

---

[7] Louis Harris & Assoc, The Nuprin Report (Oct 1985). Public Information Committee, PJ Vicente, Chairman, American Pain Society Newsletter.

ice to many patients. Even the phrase "quality of life" carries negative connotations, because it suggests what the pain management expert is unable to do for the patient-cure him or her.

Although there is some major truth in each of these formulations, it is believed that the *whole man concept* is the most attractive and useful in understanding and dealing with the psychological aspects of physical disability. The basis of this concept is that we do not treat disease and injuries but individuals who are suffering the effects of such disease and injuries and that these individuals may often have socio-economical, psychological, vocational, medical, and other problems which may profoundly affect the physical status.

According to this approach, successful rehabilitation may require evaluation using techniques of several disciplines and then manipulation of appropriate variables as needed to accomplish rehabilitation of the injury patient. An organic lesion, therefore, is but one of many factors influencing a likelihood of re-employment. Failure to consider a single crucial variable may lead to failure of the entire treatment program. It is most important to recognize the dynamic interaction of all of the variables affecting the patient's basic personality organization.

Most therapists recommend a holistic approach to rehabilitation. A total rehabilitation program dealing with musculoskeletally-impaired persons must include a full history and evaluation by the therapist in conjunction with the prescribing physician. In some states, registered physical therapists may independently prescribe and treat patients with a physician's prescription. Typically, the therapist will use diagnostic therapeutic techniques, such as isokinetics, isotonics, sports psychology, nutrition, education, pain and stress management, substance abuse, and spirituality. This is described as holistic, leading to an integrated wellness program. It often has been shown that a lesser program, a program using "bits and pieces" or the common "shake and bake" therapies is incomplete, frequently ineffective, and often not cost-effective.

The formation of multidisciplinary pain clinics is credited to John J. Bonica, M.D., opening first in Seattle in 1946. By 1969, there were 10 clinics, but because understanding of the merit of this pain management tool grew, there are over 700 such clinics now in America. The approach includes extensive review of prior records, an exhaustive history and physical examination (with a lot of patient interpersonal detective work), appropriate testing, and assurance that more invasive procedures, surgery, etc., might be helpful. The patient is introduced into a progressive, multifaceted self-help program. The well-motivated patient usually does well, becomes medicine-free, and moves toward a productive life. The poorly-motivated patient does poorly and often remains medication-dependent, and continues doctor shopping with great expense to the medical care system.[8]

---

[8] The Nuprin Report (Oct 1985); Public Information Committee, PJ Vincente, Chairman, American Pain Society Newsletter; Deyo, *Psychosocial Predictors of Disability in Patients with Low Back Pain,* 15 J Rheumatol 1557 (1988).

§15.12 Back Pain in Athletes

One of the biggest challenges for physicians treating athletes with spinal injuries is deciding which athletes should be allowed to return to contact sports and which should not. When athletes injure themselves in contact sports, they may suffer transient paralytic symptoms, such as quadriplegia, paresthesia, or hemiparesis, and some of these insults become permanent. Another group becomes at risk for reinjury.

Many such patients will have normal x-rays, CT scans, and MRI studies, yet have impairing temporary neurological findings. Trauma to the spinal cord producing these symptoms occurs with stretch, twist, concussion, and other mechanics.

The spine that is too narrow, as seen in development or congenital spinal stenosis, will set the stage for athletic injuries. Disc injury with or without herniation may be produced. Most athletes who have not sustained a fracture or dislocation of the spine and who do not have spinal canal compromising lesions can return to contact sports after a healing period, and, most important, after adequate soft tissue reconditioning. The "sports medicine" philosophy of rehabilitation is effective and perhaps the most effective tool to get the athlete (or any injured worker) back to the game (work). When to return to contact sports depends on many variables, including common sense, the goals and responsibility of the athlete, and the competence of the coaching and training staff.[9]

§15.13 Causes of Low Back Pain

Low back pain is a major source of morbidity. In the United States, impairments of the low back and cervical spine are the most common causes of long-term limitation of activity in persons less than 45 years of age. According to some studies, 80 per cent of the population will suffer at least one significant episode of low back pain during adult life.

The lumbar spine is a complex musculoskeletal system and the mechanisms operating in the low back are not completely understood. Many competing theories exist, and for each postulated mechanism, there is, in all probability, a group of patients whose pain is thus explained. The relative importance of these potential sources of pain, singly or in combination, is difficult to determine.

It is essential that patients with back pain be carefully evaluated during both the history and physical examination so the physician can be as precise as possible when making a tentative diagnosis. A detailed neurological examination is essential to detect and document involvement of spinal cord, nerve roots, rami, and other neural structures. Complete use of other diagnostic tests, such as x-rays, CT scans, MRI, electromyography, discography, and thermography, where appropriate, will facilitate a definitive diagnosis. Com-

---

[9] Bailes & Wilberger, *Managing Spine Injuries Can Be Tricky,* 7 Back Pain Monitor 1 (1989).

ments made about low back pain are equally appropriate for cervical or dorsal spine pain.

The difficulties of diagnosing and treating this problem are apparent in critical reviews of patients involved in litigation types of injury, such as workers' compensation or third-party liability claims where the possibility of secondary gain must be considered.[10]

§15.14 Failed Back Syndrome

The *failed back syndrome* is not a specific entity, but several continuing back pain problems that impair the patient after treatment. One group of patients includes those who have had surgery and still are nonfunctional because of pain. Some of these may be helped by additional invasive treatment; in others, further surgery may be inappropriate. Use of a diagnostic therapeutic algorithm is an excellent tool in these cases.

Other failed back patients include any patient who has not responded after six months of adequate conservative or surgical care in which the impairment returns soon after the treatment period. By use of a comprehensive algorithm, effective treatment of many chronic failed back patients can be had.

The usual conservative treatment modalities for pain reduction may include nonsteroidal anti-inflammatory medication, low-dose antidepressant medication, and transcutaneous electrical nerve stimulation along with "sports medicine" rehabilitative exercises. Evaluation of the degree of deconditioning to the area of the body using isokinetic equipment (such as Cybex or Lido) is appropriate, and concentration on muscle rebuilding at those areas of injury is important, as well as a tailored flexibility conditioning program. In most back pain patients, bed rest and spa-like therapies are not indicated and are often counterproductive.

There are doctors who use other methods, such as manipulation, sclerotherapy, or acupuncture, with reported success as ancillary treatment. But, it is essential to treat the whole person starting from the first visit—what the pain (impairment) means to the patient, what the patient's goals are, and how the patient's anger and/or disappointment relate to the pain complaint.[11]

---

[10] Lucas, *Low Back Pain,* 63 Surg Clin N Amer 515 (1983); Mixter & Barr, *Rupture of Intervertebral Disc with Involvement of the Spinal Canal,* 211 NEJM 210 (1934); Day, *Observation on the Treatment of Lumbar Disc Disease in College Football Players,* 15 Am J Sports Med 72, (1987); Blankstein, *Disc Space Infection and Vertebral Osteomyelitis as a Complication of Percutaneous Lateral Discectomy,* 225 Clin Orthop 234 (1987).

[11] Harsha, *What Does Pain Mean to the Patient in Treating His Back Pain,* 3 J Neurolog & Orthop Surg (1982); Harsha, *Patient Participation in His Low Back Care,* 5 J Neurol & Orthop Surg 17 (1984); Harsha, *Using Algorithm in Evaluating and Treating of Low Back Pain,* Presented at 8th Annual Meeting of the American Academy of Neurological and Orthopedic Surgeons, Las Vegas, Nevada.

§15.15 Chronic Pain

If we look at a cross section of any city in America, we find people wandering, searching for help. They appear confused, anxious, and depressed, and their accompanying family members are resentful, suspicious, and bewildered. The common complaint of the patient is "pain" that doctors have been unable to help. Their pain complaint is not acute like a kidney stone or abscess, but a chronic pain—unremitting and ever-present, bringing about dysfunctional changes in the musculoskeletal, digestive, cardiovascular, and respiratory systems.

Physicians, in medical school, are taught to gather data on which a diagnosis is made. Once made, the diagnosis will induce a therapeutic plan which varies slightly from doctor to doctor. If the pain follows an injury or disease, or is the byproduct of therapy, it is typically managed with analgesics or narcotics because physicians have been taught that when the problem is resolved, the pain will disappear. This model works for most acute pain syndromes, but never for chronic pain syndromes. The most comprehensive medical workup yields no useful information; therefore, the patient and family are informed that "nothing is wrong." Yet, the pain persists and often intensifies. The psychologically-oriented physician may then start patients on psychotropic drugs, although with little justification. When the pain persists, the doctor may be called a "quack." The drugs used may cause serious side effects. The wandering patient moves to another clinic or doctor, accompanied by family. *See* Table 15-1.

Table 15-1

Rehabilitation of the Patient with Chronic Pain: Difference in Treatment of Acute and Chronic Pain

Treatment	Acute Pain	Chronic Pain
Medication	Analgesics, anti-inflammatory and anxiolytic drugs	No analgesics and anxiolytic medication; antidepressants in selected patients
Physical Modality	Heat, massage, traction, and transcutaneous nerve stimulation used to relieve pain	None of the physical modalities used in acute pain physical modalities are used; transcutaneous nerve stimulation used in selected patients
Activity	Limit activity with total rest or rest to the part of the body; may involve time off from work or social role.	Increase activity and resumption of work/ social role

Treatment	Acute Pain	Chronic Pain
Psychological	Attention to pain behaviors provided	No attention to pain behaviors; reinforcement of activity and well behavior; instruction in stress and anxiety reduction skills (biofeedback, autogenics) and coping skills

The chronic pain patient may seek out a specialist, who may find a minor deviation from normal in his or her evaluation, giving the patient a ray of hope, only to be snuffed out when the new treatment fails. Psychiatric help is often sought or referred by a physician, implying to the patient that the problem is "in your head." The patient feels that it is bad enough to hurt, but is further traumatized when labeled "a little off." Depressive mood disorder may result.

In all of these patients, positive findings are present, yet the level of injury does not reflect the level of suffering or the dysfunction present. Often, the medical report of the patient at this stage recites that the professed pain cannot be verified by objective findings or that there is incapacitating functional overlay. The net result of the ever-increasing pain is to make patients more depressed with their lot in life and angry at doctors for not helping. The patient feels rejected by family members who declare that "The doctor says all tests are normal—they can't find anything wrong, and you will just have to learn to live with it."

Chronic benign pain patients have a behavior problem which changes their activities of daily living, making them restricted and impaired. Their use of medical services far exceeds normal illness use. They may have an organic disorder combined with their psychological impairment—the two being inseparable from a cause or treatment point of view. Typical markers of chronic benign pain patients include: (1) they have "a nickel's worth of disease and a dollar's worth of physical disability," (2) the patient's pathology has been corrected but pain is still present, (3) the patient is nonfunctional, but there is no apparent organic cause, and (4) the patient has extreme somatic preoccupation.

"It's always surprising to me that the chronic pain patient spends a great deal more time worrying about health and pain than the dying cancer patient." "Chronic pain patients are obsessed with their bodies and how they are functioning." These scenarios are often repeated and are the impetus for the formation of multidisciplinary pain management centers. The concept of caring, rather than curing, is the basis for these clinics.[12]

---

[12] Letter to the Editor, *The Management of Chronic Pain,* 5 Clin J Pain 128 (1989). Taylor, *Early Dementia Presenting as Chronic Intractable Pain,* 4 Clin J Pain 129 (1988); P.D. Wall & R. Melzack, Textbook of Pain (1989); Bhala, *Shingles and Post-therapeutic Neuroalgia,* 4 Clin J Pain 169 (1988).

§15.16 Evaluating Chronic Pain; Psychological Perspective

The Minnesota Multiphasic Personality Inventory (MMPI) has been a standard psychological test to evaluate chronic pain. Most chronic pain patients have elevated scores in the depression and hysteria sectors of the test, but so do many non-pain patients. Strong reliance has been placed on the diagnostic reliability in assessing psychological versus organic pain, but many practitioners are unwilling to accept MMPI testing.

The MMPI shows that a small percentage of patients with elevated scores do not benefit as much from treatment and have continued psychological disturbance. Thus, in the chronic pain population, the entire spectrum of psychological symptoms (reflected in the clinical scores of the MMPI) can be associated with chronic illness and should be treated in the context of an intense, behaviorally-oriented pain management.[13]

The Melzak and Million self-administered pain questionnaires are popular diagnostic tools also. *See* Appendix 15-2, Forms 2 and 3.

§15.17 Measurement of Pain

It has become clear that to further the scientific understanding and clinical knowledge of the chronic pain syndrome and its treatment, data using such a set of reliable measures must be collected. Furthermore, these data should be analyzed using current multivariate methodology which gives attention to measurement error as well as to causal interactions and control issues. Fortunately, the tools are becoming available, just as consumers and certifiers of chronic pain treatment are demanding careful program evaluation and result accounting.

There are several ways to document pain. The pain drawing popularized by Mooney is widely used by orthopedists. Having the patient keep a daily diary that records difficulty in performing activities of daily living and why is helpful. The patient typically records difficulty getting out of bed and performing household chores or work activities (reciting which activity—bathing, sweeping, or other tasks). Use of a pain allogram scaling pain from 0 to 10, with 10 being intolerably painful, has been accepted by most physicians who treat chronic pain. Both visual analogue and verbal descriptors may provide sensitive tools for separating unpleasantness from intensity of

---

[13] Naliboff, *MMPI Changes Following Behavioral Treatment of Chronic Low Back Pain,* 35 Pain 271 (1988); Bradley, *Multivariate Analyses of the MMPI After Low Back Surgery,* 1 J Behav Med 253 (1978); Love & Peck, *The MMPI and Psychological Factors in Chronic Low Back Pain,* 28 Pain 1 (1987); Herron & Pheasant, *Changes in MMPI After Low Back Surgery,* 7 Spine 591 (1982); McGill, *The Relationship of Minnesota Multiphasic Personality Inventory (MMPI) Profile Clusters to Pain Behaviors,* 6 J Behav Med 77 (1983) R.A. Sternback, Pain Patients: Traits and Treatment (1974).

pain. This is helpful when working with the patient's pain coping skills.[14]

§15.18 Prejudices Toward Pain

There are three prejudices that hamper the assessment and treatment of pain. The first involves the authority struggle between the health team and the patient. The bottom line is that the patient must be believed. Pain is whatever the experiencing person says it is, existing when he or she says it does. Many nurses and medical personnel are fearful that the patient is, or will become, an addict, perhaps desiring pain medication to satisfy craving for a drug. Research indicates that the percentage of patients who are true addicts is 3 per cent. The risk is not so high that you are apt to give medication to somebody who should not have it. Most patients, if asked, would emphatically tell you that if they were not in pain, they would not be taking this drug. Therefore, they are not, and will not, become addicts.

The second prejudice involves a known physical cause of pain versus an unknown cause. Just because a cause cannot be determined does not mean that the pain is imaginary. Most pain is the combination of physical and emotional or mental stimuli.

The third prejudice involves the acute pain model versus adaptation. It should be understood that physiological and behavioral adaptation occurs, leading to periods in which the patient exhibits minimal or no signs of pain and requests no pain medication. As soon as the adaptations leave, the patient begins to behave as though in pain and requests medication for it. We might jump to the conclusion that it is emotional, whereas it may simply be distraction or adaptation.

§15.19 Longevity of Chronic Pain

There is impressive evidence that a large percentage of patients with postoperative pain, posttraumatic pain, severe pain associated with visceral disease, and post-burns are inadequately relieved. Moreover, many patients with nonmalignant chronic pain do not respond to the usual medical therapy

---

[14] J.A. Tarantino & D.J. Oliveira, Litigating Neck and Back Injuries (1988); Duncan, *Comparison of Verbal and Visual Analogue Scales for Measuring the Intensity and Unpleasantness of Experimental Pain,* 37 Pain 37 295 (1989); Williams, *Toward a Set of Reliable and Valid Measures for Chronic Pain Assessment and Outcome Research,* 35 Pain 239 (1988); Bergner, *The Sickness Impact Profile, Development and Final Version of a Health Status Measure,* 19 Med Care 787 (1981). S.F. Brena & S.L. Chapman Pain and Litigation in Textbook of Pain (P.D. Wall & R. Melzack eds 1979); Dworkin, *Unraveling the Effects of Compensation, Litigation and Employment on Treatment Response in Chronic Pain,* 23 Pain 49 (1985); Edwards, *Familial Pain Models: The Relationship Between Family History of Pain and Current Pain Experience,* 21 Pain 379 (1985); Jaegger & Reeves, *Quantification of Changes in Myofascial Trigger Point Severity with the Pressure Algometer Following Passive Stretch,* 27 Pain 203 (1986); Kames, *The Chronic Illness Problem Inventory: Problem Oriented Psychological Assessment of Patients with Chronic Illness,* 14 Int J Psychiat Med 65 (1984).

and many are exposed to the high risk of iatrogenic complications including drug toxicity, drug dependence, and multiple operations. A significant number of these patients give up medical care, and consult quacks who not only deplete their economic resources but also do them harm.

Patients with cancer pain fare no better, and indeed there are numerous reports indicating that many patients with advanced cancer live their last months of life with unrelieved severe pain.

Experiences of managing chronic pain patients in World War II prompted an increased interest in the study of chronic pain and pain therapy. They pointed out several deficiencies that have been noted a number of times in the literature in the last three decades. The main reasons these deficiencies remain the same can be grouped into three major categories: (1) inadequate or improper application of knowledge and therapies currently available, (2) great voids and knowledge about pain in mechanisms due to insufficient research in the past, and (3) problems with communication.[15]

§15.20 Pain Perception

The International Association for the Study of Pain (IASP) has defined pain as "an unpleasant sensory and emotional experience associated with actual or potential tissue damage, or described in terms of such damage." IASP states "pain is always subjective," affirming that pain cannot be assessed independent of a patient's self-report.

Pain beliefs represent a patient's own conceptualization of what pain is and what pain means for him or her. Such beliefs may be discordant with current scientific understanding and may adversely affect compliance with modern methods of chronic pain treatment. Understanding the dimensions around which pain beliefs develop and that relationship with pain beliefs explains behavioral manifestation of pain experiences. These core beliefs have been found to be predictive of subjective pain intensity, multidisciplinary chronic pain treatment compliance, poor self-esteem, somatization, and psychological distress, and are associated with attributions about health locus of control.

Although pain is a subjective experience, any physician who evaluates pain should be dissatisfied with the exclusive emphasis on subjectivity. There is a growing consensus among researchers and pain physicians that there are multiple components to pain experiences.

One component of pain is the physical-organic-medical basis which can be revealed by history, physical examination, laboratory testing, and various imaging techniques, including x-rays, myelograms, CT scans, and MRI studies.

---

[15] J.J. Bonica, Pain, Discomfort and Humanitarian Care J. References Proceedings, National Conference at National Institute of Health, Bethesda, Md (1979); J.J. Bonica, Mechanism of Pain and Analgesic Compounds 13-31, 97-105 (R.F. Beers & E.J. Bassett 1979); Bonica, 20 Triangle 1-6 (1981) (editorial).

This basis does not give a reproducible pain model. Two different patients with exactly the same workup experience pain differently. Thus, these determinants of pain must be supplemented by at least two other components, one observable and one more subjective.

Among the observable manifestations of pain "behaviors" are groans, grimaces, rubbing, limping, and other signs of pain and its negative impact. Additional behaviors include pain medication use, altered posture and mobility, time spent lying down during the day, and use of a cervical collar, back braces, and other pain paraphernalia. More subjective is the evaluation of the patient's verbal, written, and/or drawn pain report, assessing the degree of anxiety, depression, and hostility.

The suspicion that some patients with chronic pain may be intentionally producing or exaggerating pain stems from several sources. One is the difficulty in finding a physical basis that adequately explains the pain complaint. Another is that patients who complain of pain are undoubtedly influenced by altered patterns of family responsibilities, avoiding unpleasant work situations, and increased availability of support and attention. These behaviors are inherent in all people and an exclusive emphasis on such factors is simplistic and often detrimental to the patient.

Many of these patients are involved in compensation and disability claims, as well as litigation, stemming from accidents or malpractice allegations. This has led some to suggest that patients who are receiving benefits or who have a lawsuit report a greater level of pain and suffering and distress and are less likely to respond to treatment because of their presumed incentive to pain. Recent research, however, has not consistently supported such claims, and current thinking emphasizes the beneficial effects of treatment of chronic pain patients, whether or not they are receiving benefits or involved in litigation. Factitious disorders are rare pain syndromes, but do occur, as the Munchhausen syndrome, and should be part of the differential diagnosis.

Multiple components of pain complaints—physical contribution, observable impact on behavior, and subjective reports of pain and distress—must each be rated in dimension from high to low. This multidimensional approach comes closest to addressing the sensory and emotional aspects of pain according to IASP definition.

Some pain management physicians, in working with chronic pain patients, believe that the complaints of pain and physical limitations, numerous doctor contacts, drug usage, and suffering behavior are all behavioral and can be changed as a result of alterations in reinforcers and efforts by the patient.[16]

---

[16] Seres & Newman, *Negative Influences of the Disability Compensation System: Perspectives for the Clinician,* 3 Sem in Neurol 360 (1983); Lazarus, *Munchausen's Syndrome,* Pharos, Summer 1989, at 34; Demjen & Bakal, *Subjective Distress Accompanying Headache Attacks: Evidence for Cognitive Shift,* 25 Pain 187 (1986); Dworkin, *Severity of Pain: Can It Be Judged Without a Subjective Report?,* 4 Led Dialog Pain 1 (1988); Fishbain, *Munchausen Syndrome Presenting with Chronic Pain: Case Report,* 35 Pain 91 (1988).

§15.21 Pain Pathways

Pain can be defined as the perception of a sensory phenomena associated with tissue damage. All surgical procedures cause tissue injury which results in the production and release of chemical mediators that are thought to be responsible for activating pain pathways.

When a tissue is injured by trauma, inflammation, or ischemia, the pain pathway is activated. If the tissue injury is sufficient, the perception of pain is reported by the patient.

Under normal circumstances, the cell membrane has a bipolar lipoprotein configuration with phospholipid sequestered in its membrane. With tissue injury, the cell membrane is disrupted and previously inaccessible phospholipid is exposed to the enzyme phospholipase A2, which catalyzes its conversion to arachnoidic acid. Arachnoidic acid is then converted by the enzyme cyclo-oxygenase (prostaglandin synthetase) into shortlived endoperoxide. These intermediate compounds are metabolized to stable prostaglandins and thromboxanes by tissue isomerase enzymes. Arachidonic acid is also converted via the lipoxygenase enzyme system into a variety of leukotreins, some of which are important mediators involved in pain production.

The sensory transmission of noxious stimuli is called nociception and specialized receptors, which are free nerve endings of primary sensory afferent fibers, are referred to as nociceptors. These receptors are classified according to the type of energy that activates the nerve ending receptor—chemical, mechanical, thermal, or polymodal (responds to several types of stimuli).

Prostaglandin-sensitized chemical nociceptors which can be directly activated by bradykinin. Other chemical activators and sensitizers play a part in the total pain mediation schema. Once the nociceptor is activated and the intensity of the electrical stimulus is sufficient, transmission of pain impulses from the nociceptor proceed along the A-delta or C-fiber afferents. A-delta fibers are myelinated and conduct sharp, well-localized pain, whereas C-fibers, which have polymodal receptors (nociceptors) are unmyelinated and are thought to transmit dull, poorly-localized pain. The cell bodies of the nerve fibers are present in the spinal cord ganglia, communicating with fibers from various lamina of the substantia gelatinosa in the spinal cord. The dorsal horn of the spinal cord is an area of intense neurotransmitter activity, modulating or augmenting pain pathways, partly under the influence of descending pain-modifying nerve tracts. Pathways can be stimulated by activation of the opiate receptor system by a wide variety of neurotransmitters. The widespread distribution of opiate receptors in the brain and spinal cord has provided an appreciation of the range of effects of opiates on the pain pathway at both perceptual and "preperceptual (spinal cord) levels." The dorsal horn and cord-brain pathways are the sites for the hypothetical Melzac-Wall gate control mechanism of pain. Pain perception consists of a complex inter-reaction of several pathophysiological mechanisms. A useful classification is as follows:

1. Nociceptor pain based on excitation of pain receptors in joint structures (except cartilage) and in the periarticular area as in tendons, bone, and muscle. Inflammation sensitizes receptors, so responses are elicited by joint movements within normal range for that joint.
2. Neurogenic inflammation induced by release of substance P and other neuropeptides from sensory nerve endings and probably contributing to nociceptive pain.
3. Neuropathic pain occurs after lesions of nerve fibers by transection, compression, stretch, metabolic, or toxic disturbances. The anoxal membrane becomes excessively excitable, so that slight mechanical or chemical stimuli can elicit nerve impulses. There is impairment of the whole neurone, including its peripheral and central targets of neuronal and trophic control.
4. Deafferentation pain involves hyperexcitability of sensory neurones in the central nervous system (CNS). It probably occurs after partial destruction of the presynaptic excitatory of inhibitory inputs, leaving the deafferented neurone in a state of pharmacological supersensitivity. Phantom limb pain, post-herpetic neuralgia, and trigeminal neuralgia are examples.
5. Reactive or deregulatory pain involves dysfunction of efferent control loops. If mononeurone output results in excessive muscle tone or if there is poor sympathetic control pain receptors in muscle, tendon and joints may become excited. Disturbed spinal reflex transmission from the somatosensory afferants to motor and sympathetic output as the consequence of long-term peripheral trauma may explain many symptoms of pain in the musculoskeletal system (trigger points, pain referral, pain associated with muscle spasm) may be attributed to abnormal control mechanisms in a complex cybernetic system.
6. Psychosomatic pain is a relevant factor to all chronic pain in the musculoskeletal system which may be associated with abnormal motorneuronal or sympathetic outflow under inadequate brain commands.[17]

---

[17] Zimmerman, *Which Type of Pain?,* 6 Intern Back Pain News 5 (1988); Flower & Blackwell, *The Importance of Phospholipase A2 in Prostaglandin Synthesis,* 25 Biochem Pharmacol 285 (1976); E.R. Perl, Afferent Basis of Nociception and Pain Pain 19-46 (J.J. Bonica ed 1980); Battista, *Neurologic Aspects of Pain and Recent Development in the Management of Pain,* 17 Contemp Orthop 28 (1988); Chahl & Iggo, *The Effects of Bradykinin and Prostaglandin E1 on Rat Cutaneous Afferent Activity,* 59 Br J Pharmacol 343 (1977); F.W.L. Kerr, The Structural Basis of Pain; Circuitry and Pathways Pain, Discomfort and Humanitarian Care 61-62 (L.K. Ng & J.J. Bonica eds 1980); Dodd, *Neurotransmitters and Neuronal Markers at Sensory Synapses in the Dorsal Horn,* 6 Adv Pain Res Ther 105 (1984); Honig, *Nonsteroidal Anti-Inflammatory Drugs as Post-Operative Analgesic,* 18 Orthop Rev 30 (1989).

§15.22 What is Pain?

Pain in the normal course of events signals a need for attention to a problem that needs a solution—it may be a life-saving experience. Acute pain is usually perceived as a response to a peripheral stimulus related to, or thought to be in relationship to, tissue damage. Acute pain serves a purpose to the person. Chronic pain, on the other hand, is inexplicable—it serves no purpose to the person and is counterproductive to a satisfying way of life. The same treatment, such as medication and surgeries, which relieves or improves acute pain syndromes, quite often results in physical and emotional deterioration in patients with chronic pain. Chronic pain is a persistent and useless burden for the patient and presents out of proportion to any discoverable pathology.

One of the more important developments in the last three decades has been the recognition that pain is an unpleasant emotional experience and not purely a physiological sensation. Chronic pain is properly recognized as a psychophysiological experience. It involves not only nociception, the portion of noxious stimuli, but also the interpretations of those sensations as "painful" and an evaluation of the pain as creating "suffering." The physical discomfort is often aggravated or improved by psychological (perpetual, cognitive, emotional, and behavioral) factors. Experts in the field consider chronic pain of this sort a "learned pain syndrome." Acute pain is self-limited and related to the healing or relief of tissue damage or alteration producing the pain. Chronic pain, on the other hand, presents with features out of proportion to tissue damage and is unrelieved by traditional pain therapies.

Traditional pain is thought to be a distinct sensation with its own set of receptors and neuroanatomic pathways in the peripheral and central nerve system. A most significant contribution to the understanding of pain was made by Melzak and Wall in 1965 as they proposed the "gate control theory." It has been revised minimally, but proposes modulation of peripheral noxious input in the central nervous system, and has provided better understanding of several pain syndromes and the development of useful treatment. The role of "endorphins and other neurotransmitters" in the central nervous system has been a second advance, starting in early 1970. This has led to the use of several classes of neurotransmitter-manipulating chemicals therapeutically.

In considering acute versus chronic pain, acute pain is a constellation of unpleasant perceptual and emotional experiences and certain associated anatomic, psychologic, and behavioral responses. The patholphysiology of acute pain is fairly well understood, as is its management. Acute pain has an important biological function, warning the patient that something is wrong; for example, acute left chest pain warning of a heart attack.

Chronic pain is defined as lasting beyond the period of injured tissue healing or recurs at intervals for months or years. The physiologic effects and behavioral responses to chronic pain are quite different than that of acute pain. Experts emphasize that chronic pain never serves a biological function and that it imposes severe emotional, physical, economic, and social stresses on the patient and caretakers. Many patients with chronic pain deteriorate, showing sleep disturbances and appetite alterations, decrease in physical activity, and often excessive medication intake. Patients with chronic pain manipulate their environment (family, job, peers, etc.), require multiple drugs from their physicians, and occasionally receive surgeries of questionable indication. Social and family isolation, with reduced physical activity, are common markers. This describes the "chronic benign pain syndrome."

It is important to understand that the chronic pain syndrome patient has learned behavior and a pain behavior personality, and the perceptual, effective motivational factors of pain experience.

The physician charged with testing the chronic patient must understand that the patient is best dealt with using a multifaceted treatment model. It may be that one discipline is more involved with a particular patient than another, but the patient needs to be evaluated and treated assessing physical, emotional, social, vocational factors, and often from a pharmacological, dietetic, legal, and spiritual point of view. Factors above that perpetuate the pain syndrome are equally important to a physical or psychological defect that might be addressed from a one- or two-mode treatment perspective.

The traditional physician approach to pain management relies on the biomedical model of disease. These include: (1) elimination of the source of noxious sensations by means of rest and/or medical or surgical approaches to underlying pathology, (2) use of analgesic and other medications to change behavioral response to noxious stimulation, and (3) alteration of the nervous system with drugs and surgeries, modifying or interrupting pathways responsible for the patient's pain perception. These include nerve blocks and neurosurgical procedures. These treatments are accompanied with attention to the pain, providing comfort to the patient and reinforcing the attitude that the pain is the impairment.

There is a fundamental difference in rehabilitation of the chronic pain patients, as using acute pain approaches to treat chronic pain often makes the chronic pain patient worse and more recalcitrant to treatment. Tremendous problems arise in the treatment of any pain using only the biomedical model.

The diagnosis of the patient with chronic pain not only involves medical assessment, but a multidisciplinary evaluation of the treatable physical and psychological problems. The evaluation of the patient addresses the meaning of the chronic pain to the patient, and the reason for the patient's perception or display of disability due to the pain which seems out of proportion to discoverable pathology. Treatment of patients with chronic pain syndromes should be provided in an integrated, coordinated fashion so several alterations of the patient's lifestyle can be worked with. Treatment programs address issues of remediation of the deficits in the patient's "well behavior" repertoire so that he or she can handle well-being again. Treatment must also re-engage the patient in the life role which constitutes well behavior by reinstituting the vocational and avocational activities appropriate to the patient and addresses the contingencies prevailing in the patient's environment which perpetuate or reinforce his or her chronic pain behavior.

The chronic pain management team uses the same types of practitioner as any other rehabilitation facility, but these professions have a clear and working understanding of the multifaceted problem peculiar to the chronic pain syndrome patient. These include physicians, most often anesthesiologists, neurologists, neurosurgeons, orthopedists, physiatrists, psychiatrists and psychologists, social workers, physical and occupational therapists, vocational rehabilitation workers, and others. The patient must have an active role in achieving a level of function as near to normal as possible.

The major strategy is to reduce medication and to give medication on a regular basis, not pro re nata (prn). Inpatient detoxification is often necessary to get the patient off of medications that are self-defeating.

Use of diagnostic and therapeutic blocks of nerves and myofascial or enthetic trigger points is helpful, often facilitating physical therapies designed to increase areas of flexibility as well as strengthen supportive muscles in areas of physical impairment. General body condition is virtually always indicated in these individuals, as they have been involved in long periods of inactivity and are generally or locally (as to parts of the body) deconditioned.

The transcutaneous stimulator is a physical modality based on gate control theories using high frequency stimulation of large pain mediating fibers, modulating the more impairing pain conducted through small-diameter fibers. In addition, acupuncture-like stimulation has been shown to be effective and is probably based on the alteration of neurotransmitters, specifically endorphins, in the brain. Transcutaneous nerve stimulation has not only been used in acute pain, but can be helpful in chronic pain patients in deference to drugs. The transcutaneous stimulator is cost-effective, with a proven efficiency of 30 to 70 per cent in several studies for both acute and chronic pain relief or attenuation, with 30 to 35 per cent obtaining long-term (over three months) relief.[18]

§15.23 Pain Control in the Hospital

Hospitalized patients (and office-treated patients) rarely become addicted to narcotic medication when supervised by diligent physicians. There is a

---

[18] Harsha, *Patient Participation in His Low Back Care,* 5 J Neurolog & Orthop Surg 17 (1984); Harsha, *Using Algorithm in Evaluating and Treating of Low Back Pain,* presented at 8th Annual Meeting of the American Academy of Neurological and Orthopedic Surgeons, Las Vegas, Nevada; Harsha, *What Does Pain Mean to the Patient in Treating His Back Pain,* 3 J Neurol & Orthop Surg 3 (1982); J. Barber & C. Adrian, Psychological Approaches to Management of Pain (1982). S.F. Brena & S.L. Chapman, Management of Patients with Chronic Pain (1983). H. Carron & R.E. McLaughlin, Management of Low Back Pain (1982); B.J. Crue, Chronic Pain: Further Observation from City of Hope National Medical Center (1979); 4 L.K. Ng & J.J. Bonica, Pain, Discomfort and Humanitarian Care. Developments in Neuorlogy (1980). Harsha, *Trigger Point Myofascial Pain Syndrome,* 3 J Neurol and Orthop Surg 181 (1982); Harsha, *What Does Pain Mean to the Patient?,* 74 J Okla State Med Assn 145 (1981).

great tendency for nurses, supervised by physicians, to undertreat pain complaints, to the disservice of the patient. There is a pervasive view among physicians that minimal pain control, even in the patient who continues impaired by pain, is better than running a risk of addiction. In several large series of cases receiving pain medication, this was shown not to be true. In the Boston Collaborative Drug Surveillance Program, 11,882 patients were studied; only four became dependent (if they were not already dependent). Of 10,000 burn patients in severe pain, none became dependent when adequate but well-controlled opioid medication was given.[19]

§15.24 Back School

The idea of "back school" is appealing, and only in recent years has the value of the concept become established. There is the problem that everyone recognizes the need, but it has been difficult to quantify the results.

To gauge the value of back school, we must take into account the natural recovery of back pain which, even in the most pessimistic reviews, approaches 85 per cent over a a three-month period.

Back schools may be directed at a wide range of patients, and it is important to accept the difference between acute and chronic pain. We must also take into account the patient's age, sex, and occupation, as well as his or her workers' compensation status or the presence of pending litigation.

Back schools have a variety of main focuses. Some emphasize ergonomics, particularly in the work place. Others concentrate on fitness and exercise, while a third approach stresses the psychological aspect of pain control.

A combination of these approaches has been shown to be the most effective. Class size varies and therefore so does the cost-effectiveness of the program. Specific interest in a treatment modality may dominate the program and destroy objectivity. There is a question about how many hours of back school education are necessary before back schools work, and of the frequency and number of classes. There is a wide range of charges for back education, back training, and pain management programs. In the United States at this time, they range from $50 to $1,500.

In the evaluation of the deconditioned patient commonly encountered in orthopedic practice, there is a need for understanding the status of the patient—whether his or her condition is acute, sub-acute, or chronic. The principles of physical training for the deconditioned patient include an understanding by the physician and the patient of the ranges of motion of the affected body area, evaluation of isolated trunk strength, evaluation of the aerobic capacity of the patient, and evaluation of the ability of the patient to participate in such functional task performances as lifting, carrying, climbing, kneeling, and crawling.

An integral part of the deconditioned patient, as is true of all pain patients, is identifying barriers to functional recovery, including the financial disin-

---

[19] Portenoy, Sports Medicine News, May 1989, at 5.

centive problems. The deconditioned patient who is about to have surgery will benefit with a conditioning program ahead of time to understand the surgery, the groups of muscles or parts of the body that are now deconditioned and may be further deconditioned by the surgery, and what treatment modalities the patient can engage in to lessen those.

The value of back education programs can be measured in many ways. The patient acceptance and assessment value is nonscientific but more than 90 per cent of participants consider back school beneficial. That number certainly says something about the lack of communication in the ordinary treatment of back pain by patient-physician visits alone. The value of back education can be measured through reduction in pain.

Most clinics report that 70 per cent of the attendees learn to control pain. The differentiation must be made between acute and chronic pain patients and between clients dealing with primary physical problems and those treating chronic pain syndromes.

In the latter group. a success rate of 30 per cent is considered excellent. Return to work is an excellent measure of effectiveness. The more successful programs return from 50 to 90 per cent of their participants to gainful employment. Once again, the percentage varies between short-term and long-term problems. Perhaps the most interesting statistic is the recurrence rate following return to work. Contrary to popular belief, chronic back pain sufferers who complete an effective back education program generally retain adequate function. Fewer than 10 per cent develop chronic absenteeism.

Based on statistical analysis of patients completing a back education program, several factors appear to be important:

1. Patients who perform regular exercise show greater improvement
2. Patients who practice regular back care had greater pain relief
3. Patients who restricted their activities, avoided most activities, or used back braces on a regular basis did poorly
4. Patients who felt they understood their diagnosis did better

A back school should eliminate common misconceptions and make the patient aware that the severity of back pain does not reflect the nature of the physical problem. Most of all, an effective back school must take the responsibility for the care of the painful back away from the doctor and return it to the patient where it rightfully belongs.

§15.25 Behavioral Principles and Treatment of Low Back Pain

Major behavioral learning principles include classical conditioning, operant conditioning, and observational learning-modeling-education.

The multimodal behavioral treatment philosophy includes selecting one of many techniques is better than relying solely on one technique. Multibehavioral treatment versus traditional psychological treatment approaches seem more effective. The multimodal disability management protocol includes individual and group crisis intervention counseling, family crisis intervention counseling, behavioral stress management, and cognitive-behavioral skills training.

Major barriers to recovery from a psychological point of view include the patient's inherent inability to understand or accept the psychological issues present. Also, compliance and resistance and denial issues invariably arise and must be overcome before a patient can be psychologically oriented and understand and profit from this type of therapy.

Financial disincentives are always a tough problem. It is difficult to have a patient accept that he or she will make less money or will need to give up disability benefits if participating in a self-help rehabilitation program.

The problem that the psychological therapist has is having the patient understand the somatization that occurs with increased stress and that symptom magnification, although perhaps "natural," is self-defeating. Each patient needs to be studied and treated individually. The therapist needs to understand the barriers to recovery, and the patient needs to understand this same issue and deal with it.

§15.26 Behavior Treatment

Using a total patient approach to the orthopedic patient, a method of dealing with the psychological aspect of the problem is essential. Pain-prone patients must be oriented to the nature and treatment of their condition. Patients must understand that pain is not entirely, or even substantially, noiciceptive (due to mechanical factors) alone. They must learn that a chemical imbalance is involved in pain perception, that tension and expression tend to be invariably associated with chronic pain and play an important role, and that antidepressant medication can be helpful in working through the psychological ramifications of the pain syndrome. The basic principle of the behavioral approach to chronic pain control (encourage activity and de-emphasize pain) may be combined with antidepressant medication. Explaining the treatment to the next of kin and involving them in the treatment is effective. Distraction from the pain, in the form of activities carried out at a reasonable pace or continuing to work in spite of pain, should be encouraged. Modifying the work environment to adapt to the physical impairment present should be part of the therapy plan along with vocational rehabilitation in many cases. Work hardening programs which utilize progressive work activities similar to the patient's job become part of a conditioning rehabilitation. Often, however, duplication of the job activity leading to injury may set the stage for ease of re-injury. At this time, there is a degree of biased disagreement.

Helping chronic pain patients to change adverse behaviors is a major challenge to all involved, yet it is necessary and rewarding. Physicians possess great understanding of disease, but prevention and treatment relies on the patient's ability and motivation to implement medical and lifestyle changes. Adherence to any medical regimen that a physician prescribes occurs about

50 per cent of the time, with substantial alteration of such ingrained behavior as smoking, excessive eating, and alcohol use being maintained in only 5 to 10 per cent of patients.

Most physicians do not feel comfortable and confident about motivating patients to engage in health-promoting behaviors, in part because of the difficulty of the task and in part because of lack of training in that task. The multifaceted chronic pain clinic fits this area of treatment.[20]

§15.27 Family Therapy

Involving the family in the treatment of chronic pain syndromes is essential to improvement. The patient involved in the pain syndrome has a great impact on his or her family, with substantial change in family function and stability resulting. Gestalt therapies seem most popular at the present time, with a formula for those involved with pain patients to understand the problems they face, adjust to them when necessary, but more importantly to become empathetic while having "tough love." The need for expert family counselors or similar credentialled persons to participate in this type of family intervention cannot be overemphasized. Many well-meaning, relatively uninformed advisors (ministers, relatives, attorneys, insurance claims adjusters, and employers) have complicated the treatment of the chronic pain patient.[21]

§15.28 Drug and Alcohol Pain versus Trauma Pain

Often there is an interface between chronic pain patients and substance abuse patients. Alcohol abuse is well documented in trauma patients. Previous non-abusers may become alcoholic as part of their chronic pain syndrome and many drug or alcohol abusers become involved in accidents that lead to a chronic pain syndrome. Treatment of the chronic pain syndrome must first include withdrawal on a permanent basis from all mind-altering drugs. This ordinarily requires in-house detoxification, treatment, and an afterhour outpatient treatment program. The chronic pain syndrome can be addressed at the same time. Some experts have observed that the addicted chronic pain patient treated as above has a better prognosis than the nonaddicted.[22]

---

[20] Nartin & Coates, *A Clinician's Guide to Helping Patients Change Behavior,* 136 West J Med 751 (1987).

[21] Jaffe, *The Role of Family Therapy in Treating Physical Illness,* 29 Hosp & Community Psychiatry 169 (1978); Harsha, *Low Back Pain is a Family Affair,* 8 J Neurol & Orthop Med & Surg 147 (1987); Swanson & Maruta, *The Family's ViewPoint of Chronic Pain,* 8 Pain 163 (1980).

[22] Soderstrom, *Mayland Institute for Emergency Medical Services Systems,* Surgical Rounds, Sept 1988, at 75; Williams & Thorn, *Am Empirical Assessment of Pain Beliefs,* 36 Pain 351 (1989).

§15.29 Guided Imagery

Therapeutic guided imagery offers a variety of opportunities for a patient to gather information about the unconscious, physical processes within his or her physical body and how to alter them. These methods are particularly useful as an extension of other chronic pain management methods.[23]

§15.30 References

W.E. Fordyce, Behavioral Methods for Chronic Pain and Illness (1976).

Pain Management: A Handbook of Psychological Treatment Approaches. (A.D. Holzman, D.C. Turk eds 1986).

Linton, *Behavioral Remediation of Chronic Pain: A Status Report,* 24 Pain 125 (1986).

Jessup, Neufeld & Mersky, *Biofeedback Therapy for Headache and Other Pain: An Evaluative Review,* 7 Pain 225 (1979).

Turk, Meichenbaum & Berman, *Application of Biofeedback for the Regulation of Pain: A Critical Review,* 86 Psychol Bull 1322 (1979).

Holroyd, Penzien & Hursey, *Change Mechanisms in EMG Biofeedback Training: Cognitive Changes Underlying Improvements in Tension Headache,* 52 J Consult Clin Psychol 1039 (1984).

Hoffman, Benson & Arns, *Reduced Sympathetic Nervous System Responsivity Associated with the Relaxation Response,* 215 Science 190 (1982).

E. Jacobson, Progressive Relaxation (1938).

Borkovec & Sides, *Critical Procedural Variables Related to the Physiological Effects of Progressive Relaxation: A Review,* 17 Behav Res Ther 119 (1979).

Ferguson, Marquis & CB Taylor, *A Script for Deep Muscle Relaxation,* 38 Diseases of the Nervous System 703 (1977).

Keefe, Block, Williams & Surwit, *Behavioral Treatment of Chronic Low Back Pain; Clinical Outcome and Individual Differences in Pain Relief,* 11 Pain 221 (1981).

Melzack, *Prolonged Relief of Pain by Brief, Intense Transcutaneous Somatic Stimulation,* 1 Pain 357 (1975).

Thorsteinnson, Stonnington, Stillwell & Elveback, *The Placebo Effect of Transcutaneous Electrical Stimulation,* 5 Pain 31 (1978).

Rosenberg, Curtis & Bourke, *Transcutaneous Electrical Nerve Stimulation for the Relief of Postoperative Pain,* 5 Pain 129 (1978).

Fordyce, Fowler, Lehmann, *Operant Conditioning in the Treatment of Chronic Clinical Pain,* 54 Arch Phys Med Rehabil 399 (1973).

---

[23] Jaffe & Bresler, *The Use of Guided Imagery as an Adjunct to Medical Diagnosis and Treatment,* 20 J Humanistic Psychol 45 (1980).

Fordyce, Roberts & Sternbach, *The Behavioral Management of Chronic Pain: A Response to Critics,* 22 Pain 113 (1985).

N.H. Hendler, D.M. Long & T.N. Wise, Diagnosis and Treatment of Chronic Pain (1982).

M. Stanton-Hicks & R.A. Boas, Chronic Low Back Pain (1982).

M. Swerdlow, Relief of Intractable Pain (1983)

V. Janda, Muscle Function Testing (1983).

P.D. Wall & R. Melzack, Textbook of Pain (1984)

J.F. Lehmann, Therapeutic Heat and Cold (3d ed 1982).

J.S. Mannheimer & G.N. Lampe, Clinical Transcutaneous Electrical Nerve Stimulation (1985).

Mannheimer & Carlson, *The Analgesic Effect of Transcutaneous Electrical Nerve Stimulation in Patients with Rheumatoid Arthritis. A Comparative Study of Different Pulse Patterns,* 6 Pain 329 (1979).

P.M. Scott, Clayton's Electrotherapy and Actinotherapy (7th ed 1975).

Paris, *Mobilisation of the Spine,* 59 Phys Ther 988 (1979).

R.A. McKenzie, Treat Your Own Back (3d ed 1985).

R.A. McKenzie, The Lumbar Spine, Mechanical Diagnosis and Therapy (1981).

Janda, *Postural and Phasic Muscles in the Pathogenesis of Low Back Pain,* Proceedings of the XIth Congress of the International Society for Rehabilitation of the Disabled (Dublin, 1969).

Porter & Paris, *The Role of Back Education in the Prevention and Treatment of Back Pain* Proceedings of the Vth International Conference of the International Federation of Orthopaedic Manipulative Therapists (Vancouver, 1984).

Hoberman, *Discussions of a Paper by J.O. Sullivan, "Psychiatric Factors in Low Back Pain in New York State Journal,"* 55 J Med 231 (1955).

Beals & Hickman, *Industrial Injuries of the Back and Extremities,* 54A JBJ Surg 1593 (1972).

Appendix 15-1
Cases

1 ***Mueller v Lose,*** **No 132030 (Sonoma County Super Ct Cal Oct 1987)** (plaintiff had been partially paralyzed on her left side since birth. She developed severe back pain when she was 32 years old, was hospitalized by her family doctor, and four days later saw a consulting orthopedist. She was incontinent of urine and was thus referred by the orthopedist to a urologist, who diagnosed a neurogenic bladder. The orthopedist contended that he recommended to the family doctor that the patient be transferred to another facility for a myelogram to see if a central lesion was present. The family doctor denied that the recommendation was made. The family physician had a neurosurgical consultation made, which expressed the opinion that the patient could be discharged from the hospital as she was neurologically improving and that her pain was largely "psychological." The patient refused to undergo an "extensive" neurological examination. Several days later, the patient was again hospitalized with a diagnosis of ruptured disc, and cauda equina syndrome was diagnosed. Two urgent disc removal surgeries were done 48 hours apart. The plaintiff sued the family doctor and the neurosurgeon (the case against orthopedist was dropped due to his death). The plaintiff alleged that the family physician diagnosed and did not understand the significance of the plaintiff's symptoms and failed to follow the orthopedist's recommendation. The plaintiff alleged that the neurosurgeon failed to realize the classic symptoms of cauda equina syndrome, that he was negligent in diagnosing the situation as hysterical, and that he ignored the urologist's and orthopedist's recommendation to perform a myelogram. The family doctor argued that he could not be expected to diagnose cauda equina syndrome in that it was so rare. The neurosurgeon argued that the plaintiff's changing neurological signs were inconsistent with a ruptured intervertebral disc, that the plaintiff's chart indicated a hysterical personality, that the plaintiff refused to allow a rectal examination, and that the childhood stroke she had suffered made it difficult to do an adequate neurological examination. Prior to the back incident, the patient had substantial impairment from her childhood stroke. After the back incident, the patient was additionally nearly paraplegic and without control of bladder or bowel. The plaintiff alleged $30,000 in medical expenses, past and future medical expenses of $360,000, future lost wages of $350,000, and future attendant care of $1 million. The result was an award of $3.2 million and that the family practitioner was not liable. The jury apportioned 40 per cent negligence to the neurosurgeon and 60 per cent to parties other than the family practitioner, but attributed the entire amount to the neurosurgeon).

Comment: Hysterical patients often have organic pathology.

2 ***Werdin v RHN Fielden,*** **406 NW2d 89 (Minn Ct App 1987)** (claim for negligence against a physician stemming from what the patient

considered to be forceful manipulation of her neck during an examination for a foot problem. The patient subsequently presented herself to a neurosurgeon four months later with neck pain, making no complaint about her foot. She was in a bus accident seven years previously, and the neurosurgeon felt that the existing complaints were an aggravation of arthritic changes in her neck. The patient was quite uncooperative, not allowing an adequate physical examination or x-rays. However, she allowed a CT scan to be run, which was normal. The examining physician felt that she was a "highly emotional, suggestable individual" and that the symptoms in her neck, and later in her legs and feet, were similarly highly exaggerated. There was "no objective evidence of neurological abnormalities." The patient was unable to find a physician to testify for her within a two-year time frame; the case was tried on the res ipsa loquitur rule and dismissed by the judge. The trial court's decision was upheld by the appellate court).

Comment: The presence of somatic complaints that are out of proportion and unexplainable by virtue of physical examination and other testing is a common experience for the orthopedic surgeon. To routinely say that such a patient is emotionally unstable and that there is therefore nothing wrong does a great disservice to the patient. Additional patient evaluation is important to understand what the pain means to the patient and what other social and economic problems play into the patient's complaints. Additionally, the fact that there are no objective findings in no way means that there is no organic pathology. Further testing may elicit such findings, and many of these cases go basically undiagnosed, with the patient continuing to be disabled. The trier of fact is hard pressed to make an evaluation. The very essence of legal training is that there is a provable fact at the basis of a problem. Absent that demonstrable verifiable fact, the law tends to rule against the person with the unverifiable situation. The practice of medicine, on the other hand, takes the patient as a whole, accepts his or her symptoms as a problem to the patient, and attempts to explain them in a rational manner. If there is an objective basis, that is fine; if not, it is no less a problem to the patient and treatment is instituted as appropriate.

3 *Lebrecht v Tuli,* 473 NE2d 1322 (Ill App Ct 1985) (orthopedic surgeon and two internists failed to diagnose a herniated disc. The patient ultimately suffered partial paralysis and arachnoiditis. The diagnosis was clearly missed, with the additional resentment on the patient's part that she was considered to be a psychiatric patient and that her nervousness was the nexus of her problem. All through the initial evaluation, the several physicians who saw her were convinced that her psychological state and her functional overlay masked, if not in fact explained, the symptoms, rather than disc protrusion. She apparently presented several times with a normal neurological evaluation. She then consulted a chiropractor, who treated her for several weeks without success and referred her to a second neurologist. He did a cervical myelogram, found a protruded intervertebral disc, and performed surgery, which relieved some of her pain. However, her symptoms recurred and five months later a second myelogram revealed arachnoiditis, which resulted in eventual partial paralysis. The plaintiff argued that a myelogram should have been done earlier, and that, when found, the disc protrusion was large enough that the flow of the pantopaque dye would not allow removal. Pantopaque is a known arachnoiditis-producing agent. Failure to complete a neurological examination and failure to refer to a neurologist was also alleged. The case really hinged on the credibility of the expert witnesses on the two sides, the one on the patient's side not prevailing in this case. The administration of Pantopaque, producing arachnoiditis, was refuted by one credible witness, who said that only patients with a peculiar sensitivity to Pantopaque develop arachnoiditis).

Comment: This case demonstrates a commonly seen type of patient in whom there is a lot of anxiety, with what is called a nervous or hysterical overlay. Nevertheless, these anxious patients frequently have significant organic pathology in an environment where diagnosis is made, at least for medical expert purposes and disability evaluation purposes, largely on the basis of objective evidence. This type of patient very frequently is unfairly placed in the category of "It's all in the patient's head." Each patient is entitled to a thorough history and repetitive thorough physical examination to try to ascertain the basis of the complaints at the same time that the treating physician is working with the emotional state. Descartes probably did a great disservice to patients and practitioners when he introduced a concept that still is largely accepted: that patients may be divided into a soma and a psyche; that is, physical symptoms and findings are one part of the problem, and psychological symptoms and findings are another part of the problem. In fact, they are always inextricably entwined.

4 ***Anderson v Prese,* 445 A2d 612 (DC 1982)** (evidence was sufficient to support the findings of intentional infliction of emotional distress by a physician. A physician who had been told by a patient of her history of depression cursed and screamed at her to leave his office. Evidence was presented that the physician's conduct caused the patient to stay at home, to discontinue working, and to later enter a hospital. The trial court entered judgment for the patient. On appeal, the court said that the conduct may generally not be considered outrageous or extreme, but may be so characterized when the person knows that the other person is particularly susceptible to emotional distress. Because the physician had prescribed Valium for the patient many times, he apparently knew of her fragile nervous state and that she would be susceptible to emotional distress. Therefore, his conduct was extreme and outrageous under the circumstances, and the evidence was sufficient to support the judgment of the trial court).

5 ***Sanchez v Derby,* 433 NW2d 523 (Neb 1988)** (trial court had discretion to allow a neuropsychologist to testify that a plaintiff's illness was caused by either a combination of posttraumatic stress disorder and reaction to pain, or organic disorder secondary to brain injury. Both would be compensable, and an absolute certainty as to a particular cause was not required).

6 ***Nyhof v North Dakota Workmen's Compensation Bureau,* 325 NW2d 239 (ND 1982)** (ongoing pain was traced to the concept of "secondary

gain" in this case. A sanitation man collected disability benefits for four years after a back sprain suffered while heaving a garbage can. The patient persisted with unremitting pain, seemingly disproportionate to the injury, until medical experts became suspicious of secondary gain. In this case, the pain management experts and pain evaluators working with this patient commented that "It is the overall impression of the staff that this is going to be a difficult case for several reasons. The patient is now making 25% more per week than he did when he was working, as his income now is tax-free." He was able to perform household duties and his wife was able to make a living on her own; therefore, their financial situation appeared to be locked in, and it was extremely doubtful that he could be budged unless his financial situation was altered in some manner. None of the orthopedists treating him found any objective reason for the continuing pain, and all suggested some work rehabilitation. One underscored the urgency of fitting him into some active program, "because he can't go on like this the rest of his life." The patient did not indicate that he would like to try. He said he feared another injury and also loss of his benefits. The compensation bureau finally expressed the opinion that he had received four years of compensation and had been adequately compensated, and the payments were discontinued. The Supreme Court of North Dakota affirmed the Bureau's action).

Comment: Occasionally, a patient receiving disability payments falls into the category of the patient in the case above, and it is difficult for the trier of fact to come up with an equitable solution, considering the fact of secondary gain.

Appendix 15-2
Forms

Form 1
Life Events Scale

Below is a list of events that you may have experienced during the past year. In the left hand column, please check off those events that did occur. In the right hand column, please rate how stressful you perceived each event to have been, on a scale of 1 to 5. (Scale values: 1—not at all stressful; 2—slightly stressful; 3—moderately stressful; 4—somewhat stressful; 5—extremely stressful). Ignore the numbers to the right of each event. They will be used in analyzing your life events scale during the program session.

Personal	____	Personal injury or illness (53)	____
	____	Outstanding personal achievement (28)	____
	____	Revision of personal habits (24)	____
	____	Change in recreation (19)	____
	____	Change in church activities (19)	____
	____	Change in sleeping habits (15)	____
	____	Change in eating habits (15)	____
	____	Christmas (12)	____
Family	____	Death of a spouse (100)	____
	____	Divorce (73)	____
	____	Marital separation (65)	____
	____	Death of a close family member (63)	____
	____	Marriage (50)	____
	____	Marital reconciliation (45)	____
	____	Change in health of a family member (44)	____
	____	Pregnancy (40)	____
	____	Gain of new family member (39)	____
	____	Change in number of arguments with spouse (35)	____
	____	Son or daughter leaving home (29)	____
	____	Trouble with in-laws (29)	____
	____	Wife begins or stops work (26)	____
	____	Change in number of family get-togethers (15)	____
Financial	____	Change in financial state (38)	____
	____	Mortgage over $40,000 (31)	____
	____	Foreclosure of mortgage or loan (30)	____
	____	Mortgage or loan of less than $10,000 (17)	____
Social	____	Jail term (63)	____
	____	Sexual difficulties (39)	____
	____	Death of a close friend (37)	____
	____	Begin or end school (26)	____

	____	Change in living conditions (25)	____
	____	Change in schools (20)	____
	____	Change in residence (20)	____
	____	Change in social activities (18)	____
	____	Minor violations of the law (11)	____
Work	____	Fired at work (47)	____
	____	Retirement (45)	____
	____	Business readjustment (39)	____
	____	Change to a different line of work (36)	____
	____	Change in responsibilities at work (29)	____
	____	Trouble with boss (23)	____
	____	Change in work hours or conditions (20)	____

Form 2
Back Pain Questionnaire
Adapted from Million Visual Analog

Name: ______________________ Date: ______________________

Please make an "X" along the line to show how far from normal toward the worst possible situation your pain problem has taken you.

1. How bad is your pain?

   ____

   No pain — Worst possible

2. How bad is the pain at night?

   ____

   No pain — Worst possible

3. Does the pain interfere with your life-style?

   ____

   No problem — Total change in life-style

4. How good are pain killers for your pain?

   ____

   Complete relief — Cannot walk

5. How stiff is your back?

   ____

   No stiffness — Worst possible

6. Does your pain interfere with walking?

   ____

   No problem — Cannot walk

7. Do you hurt when walking?

   ____

   No pain — Worst possible

8. Does your pain keep you from standing still?

   ____

   Can stand as long as I want — Cannot stand at all

9. Does your pain keep you from twisting?

   ____

   No problem — Cannot twist

10. Does your pain allow you to sit in an upright hard chair?

    ____

    Can sit as long as I like — Cannot sit in a hard chair at all

11. Does your pain allow you to sit on a soft chair?

    ____

    Can sit as long as I like — Cannot sit in a soft chair at all

12. Do you have back pain when lying in bed?

    ____

    No pain — No relief at all

13. How much does your pain limit your normal life-style?

    ____

    No limit — Cannot do anything

14. How much does your pain interfere with your work?

    ____

    No problem — Totally—cannot work

15. How much have you had to change your workplace because of back pain?

    ____

    No change — So much that I cannot keep a job

Form 3
Pain Questionnaire

Name: ________________________________

Is anyone in your family, including yourself, experiencing chronic pain of any sort? Yes ____ No ____

If yes, who? ____ Age ____
Male ____ Female ____

Using the following table, please rate the pain as best you can from your experience or observation.

	None	Mild	Moderate	Severe
Throbbing				
Shooting				
Stabbing				
Sharp				
Cramping				
Aching				
Burning				
Heavy				
Tender				
Splitting				
Tiring				
Sickening				
Fearful				
Punishing				

No Pain __________________________ Worst Possible Pain

0 No pain
1 Mild
2 Discomforting
3 Distressing
4 Horrible
5 Excruciating

16

Emergency Care

§16.01 Generally

Emergency health care exists for the benefit of the patient or family who needs emergency medical care and for society's benefit in mass casualty incidents. In America, an emergency facility is expected to be staffed by medical, nursing, and ancillary personnel who are trained and experienced in the treatment of emergencies.

Approximately 80 million visits are made each year to emergency facilities by patients who expect to be seen promptly, to have appropriate medical treatment and nursing care, and to link that care with secondary and tertiary care when needed.

Emergency medicine encompasses the immediate decisionmaking and action necessary to prevent death or any further disability for patients in health crises, a life- or limb-threatening situation. It is practiced by physicians trained to engage in the recognition, stabilization, evaluation, treatment, and disposition of patients in response to acute illness and injury. It is practiced primarily in emergency facilities and includes extensive responsibilities for community disaster preparedness and emergency medical services (EMS).

The patient determines what constitutes an "emergency." The patient defines the reason, time, and point of entry into the system, regardless of ability to pay, age, or the nature of illness/injury.

§16.02 Emergency Guidelines

Emergency guidelines are set out in three sections: (1) emergency physicians, (2) emergency nurses, and (3) facility administrators. These are intended to guide the planning and measuring ability to meet objective criteria in preparing to treat critically ill or injured patients.

The first section outlines the responsibilities of emergency care providers and acknowledges the public's expectations (1) that they be able to evaluate and treat all life- or limb-threatening conditions, (2) that the emergency care be available to all patients without regard to ability to pay, (3) that evaluation, management, and treatment be appropriate and timely; and (4) that emergency care will be constantly available.

The next section sets out the physical bounds of the emergency facility; specifically, those components required to help the patient from the time he or she enters the facility until care is transferred to another physician or until the patient is transferred. The section includes guidelines for administration, staffing, facility design, equipment, and drugs.

The third section encompasses the relationship between the facility and those entities with which it must interact. Emergency care begins in the prehospital setting by emergency medical technicians, continues in the emergency facility, and ends with follow-up care by other appropriate health professionals. The emergency physician and emergency nurse are the central figures in this concept of patient care, as they are responsible for facilitating relationships that ensure continuity of care.

These guidelines are a statement of suggested capability, they are advisory and are not written to be interpreted as mandatory by legislative, judicial, or regulatory bodies. They are designed to assist a facility's planners in offer emergency care that meets the public's expectations of receiving prompt and appropriate health care for life- or limb-threatening conditions. The American College of Emergency Physicians and the Emergency Nurses Association believe the patient has the right to have these guidelines met or exceeded.

§16.03 Professional Responsibilities

Emergency care, by definition, includes the immediate evaluation of and intervention in life- or limb-threatening situations. The nature of these services creates public expectations and professional responsibilities on the part of the care providers. Conditions necessary to meet those responsibilities are as follows:

1. Facilities using the term "emergency," "emergent," "emergi-," should have the physical design, equipment, and personnel to evaluate and stabilize patients with life- or limb-threatening illnesses or injuries
2. Emergency care providers should have the knowledge and skills necessary to provide evaluation, management, and treatment to patients with life- or limb-threatening illnesses or injuries

3. Timely emergency care should be available 24 hours a day, seven days a week; that is, 24-hour access to emergency care should be available in each community, although not all facilities must operate continuously
4. Emergency care should be given to all patients, without regard to ability to pay for the services, but with the understanding that they are financially responsible for charges incurred
5. Facilities should have a public education program that describes the capabilities of the facility, hours of operation, and a list of other facilities available if that particular facility is not open on such a basis

§16.04 Principles of Emergency Care

Facility administration, staffing, design, and materials essential to the treatment of life- or limb-threatening conditions are as follows:

1. *Administration:* The emergency facility should be organized to meet the health care needs of its patient population. Quality, safety, and appropriateness of emergency care should be continually evaluated by the medical director, along with the director of emergency nursing and ancillary services, with the personnel maintaining skills and knowledge in treating life- or limb-threatening conditions, with the duties of each defined in writing. Appropriate triage of patients should be determined by trained personnel using guidelines established by the medical director and director of emergency nursing. The physician will ultimately examine the patient in a timely manner with diagnosis and recommended treatment. Emergency facility operations should have written guidelines of its policies and procedures, made available to the new staff members who will provide patient care. New staff members must attend a formal orientation program. A permanent medical record should be established on every patient seen in the emergency facility.
2. *Staffing:* The emergency facility should be staffed by emergency care professionals, including a physician during hours of operation, with the patient care directed by a physician. The medical director of emergency services should possess training and/or experience in emergency medicine sufficient to meet qualifications for taking the American Board of Emergency Medicine certification examination or equivalent. The American College of Emergency Physicians believes that certification of knowledge and skill in emergency medicine can result only from successful completion of examinations administered by a recognized board. Successful completion of any course or series of course may serve as evidence of knowledge and skill of a certain sub-area within emergency medicine, although the completion of such does not serve as an acceptable substitute for certification of knowledge and skills required to practice the specialty of emergency medicine. The medical director

must be competent in the management and administration of clinical services, ensuring that the staff is adequately qualified and educated. Staff physicians should possess training and/or experience in emergency medicine sufficient to evaluate, manage, and treat all patients with life- or limb-threatening conditions. Nursing care provisions in the emergency facility should be directed by a registered nurse with education and/or experience in emergency nursing sufficient to meet the qualifications for taking the Certified Emergency Nursing examination, as well as to be competent in management and administration of clinical services, ensuring nursing and ancillary staff are qualified and educated. Staff nurses should possess adequate emergency or critical care experience or have completed an emergency care education program, be competent in advanced life support, and possess knowledge/skills to evaluate, manage, and educate patients in accordance with the Standards of Emergency Nursing Practice.

3. *Equipment and Supplies:* An emergency facility should have equipment and supplies of high quality and suitable for all patients. All reusable patient care medical equipment should have documentation of a preventive maintenance schedule to ensure patient safety. All necessary equipment and supplies should be available in the facility during hours of operation.
4. *Medications and Drugs:* Appropriate drugs and agents should be available in the emergency care facility during hours of operation.
5. *Facility:* The emergency facility should be designed to provide safe and effective care with convenient access to treatment areas for all patients anticipated, with provisions to give the patient visual and auditory privacy. Radiological services should be available during the hours of operation to provide diagnostic imaging of patients with life- or limb-threatening conditions. Laboratory services should be available during hours of operation to provide diagnostic tests for patients with life- or limb-threatening conditions. Appropriate signs should indicate the direction of the emergency facility from major thoroughfares, indicating if the facility is a specialized emergency care center.

§16.05 Patient Care

Emergency care begins in the prehospital setting, continues in the emergency facility, and concludes when the patient is transferred to another physician or is discharged. The transfer of responsibility should be in an effective and efficient manner. For proper continuity of care, certain relationships must exist, as set out below.

1. *Prehospital Providers:* Emergency care prior to reaching the emergency facility should be consistent with the American College of Emergency Physicians' position paper, "Medical Control of Prehospital Emergency Medical Services." The local emergency medical services

(EMS)/disaster coordinating body should determine each emergency facility and its role in the local EMS/disaster plans. Accordingly, patients should be transported to the nearest appropriate emergency facility. When ambulance services are used to transport patients to an emergency facility, a communication system, such as a two-way radio, should be available to allow for notice of arrival or advance information concerning critically ill or injured patients. A written documentation of all prehospital care provided should be made immediately available on transfer of care and should be made part of the patient's emergency facility permanent record.

2. *Emergency Facility Care Providers:* Emergency facility personnel should be familiar with the protocol followed by prehospital providers in their community. A qualified physician, nurse, or other appropriately trained person should conduct initial assessment of all patients with life- or limb-threatening illnesses or injuries transported to the facility.
3. *Referral:* Appropriately qualified physicians who are willing to accept inpatient and/or outpatient responsibility should be identified in advance for referral.
4. *Transfer:* Emergency facilities should have a written plan for transferring patients by a vehicle that has appropriate life support capabilities, if such transfer is necessary. A patient with a life- or limb-threatening condition should not be transferred from an emergency facility until appropriate evaluation and stabilization have been instituted. Arrangements for transfer should include communication between physicians involved, exchanging clinical information, and ascertaining that the receiving physician will accept the patient, that the receiving institution has appropriate anticipated facilities, and that space is available at the receiving facility. The patient should be transferred from one physician directly to the care of another physician. Documentation of patient care, including laboratory tests and radiology test results, should accompany the patient. The medical responsibility of the patient being transferred should be established before the transfer begins. Transfer agreements should be made with those institutions providing definitive care not available at the transferring facility.[1]

---

[1] Special Contribution, Emergency Care Guidelines (Revised). *Definition of Emergency Medicine and the Emergency Physician,* 15 Ann Emer Med 133, 153, 159 (1986); American College of Emergency Physicians: Section of Certification, in ACEP Position Summaries 9 (1986); Emergency Department Nurses Association, Standards of Emergency Nursing Practice (1983); American College of Emergency Physicians, *Definition of Emergency Medicine,* 10 Ann Emer Med 385 (1981); American College of Emergency Physicians, *Medical Control of Prehospital Emergency Medical Services,* 11 Ann Emer Med 387 (1982); American College of Emergency Physicians, *Emergency Ambulance Transport to Medical Facilities,* 12 Ann Emer Med 187 (1983); Committee on Trauma, American College of Surgeons, *Hospital and Pre-hospital Resources for Optimal Care of the Injured Patient,* 68 ACS Bulletin 11 (1983); American College

§16.06 Initial Care of Patient with Multiple Injuries

Care of the multiply-injured patient requires the input of many physician specialties, including orthopedics. It is essential that all medical personnel be familiar with the care of the multiply-injured patient, to understand priorities of diagnosis and treatment and the probability of associated injuries that may be present.

Many studies have documented that approximately 30 per cent of trauma fatalities are preventable and result from negligent care of the patient. Knowledge of the mechanics of injury and an organized informed assessment of the patient at the injury scene, or more often in the emergency room, results in fewer iatrogenic injuries to the patient. The American College of Surgeons Advanced Trauma Life Support (ATLS) Course has established standards and priorities in the initial care of the injured person.

The mechanism of injury is early essential information for the treating physician. Much of this initial information under ideal and usual circumstances is transmitted to emergency room staff by radio when called by the emergency treating ambulance transport personnel. Knowledge of the mechanism of the injury allows the medical personnel to predict what major injuries may be present and to be "set" for them. As an example, blunt injuries require more evaluation than penetrating trauma. Management depends largely on which area of the body was injured and the energy of the injury force incurred. (Tissue damage is proportional to the mass and velocity of the injuring impact). If the patient has suffered blunt injury in an automobile accident, knowing the impact point of the vehicle, the position of the injured patient, and what happened to that body (was seat belt on, was window broken by body part, was patient thrown from auto, did auto turn over) helps the initial assessment. Frontal impact increases the likelihood of intracranial or cervical spine injury, cardiac contusion, thoracic or abdominal injury, and knee/hip injury. Impact on the side of a vehicle may produce cervical spine injury, or chest injury with spleen injury on left side impact, and liver injury with right side impact.

Seat belts are life-saving devices (if worn), particularly with frontal impacts, and prevent ejection of those wearing them from the vehicle. Seat belts are less effective in lateral impacts. Rear-end impacts typically produce cervical spine injuries and injuries associated with steering wheel impact.

The risk of major injury is highest when a person is ejected from a vehicle or when a motorcycle rider is thrown off. Head and spine injuries are often fatal under those circumstances.

Knowledge of the patient's vital signs at the scene of the accident is helpful to the emergency room physician, and he or she will have the emergency transport crew institute appropriate treatment enroute to the emergency room. The initial assessment of the acutely injured patient is probably best

---

of Emergency Physicians, *Patient Transfer Guidelines,* 14 Ann Emer Med 1221 (1985).

achieved by a protocol or flow sheet. A number of trauma scoring methods for injuries are helpful, both in triage and in prognosis. The ABCD for examining and diagnosing acute or comatose patients is (A) airway, (B) breathing status, (C) circulation status, and (D) disability (meaning neurological status, state of consciousness). AVPU is used in the neurological examination: (A) alertness, (V) not alert, responds to vocal stimuli, (P) responds only to painful stimuli, and (U) unresponsive. (AVPU can also mean awake, vomiting, pupil reaction, and urination, signs important in evaluating brain function.) In the awake, alert patient, AMPLE is a useful mnemonic: (A) allergies, (M) medications, (P) previous major illness, (L) last meal, and (E) events leading to injury. (*See* Appendix 16-1, Cases 1 to 12.)

In the initial assessment of the trauma patient, four major steps may be followed: (1) primary survey, (2) resuscitation, (3) secondary survey, and (4) definitive care. Every trauma resuscitation needs to follow a structured, systematic plan, supervised by the most competent person at the scene. This will direct proper priorities in early trauma care and help avoid missed injuries.

The primary survey is to detect life-threatening injuries and immediately treat each as they are identified. The primary survey must include (1) airway with cervical spine control, (2) breathing and ventilation, (3) circulation with hemorrhage control, (4) neurologic status, and (5) patient exposure.

The trauma team leader should perform the primary survey. A brief history of the accident and its mechanics are quickly reviewed as follows:

1. *Airway:* Securing the airway is always the first priority. Due to the risk of associated cervical spine injuries, this has to be done as though the neck is "fragile." This is particularly true if there is evidence of head injury. The airway must be established by moving the cervical spine.
2. *Breathing:* Establishing an airway, placing an endotracheal tube does not ensure that the patient is breathing. Pneumothorax, hemothorax, flail chest, or massive pulmonary contusion may impair adequate ventilation.
3. *Circulation:* Blood volume and peripheral perfusion must be assessed. The most common cause of death in patients in emergency room of hospital is bleeding with uncorrected hypovolemia. Rapid pulse is often an early clue to unrecognized internal bleeding. The blood pressure is a less accurate guide to blood loss, as 20 to 25 per cent of the body's blood volume may be lost with altering blood pressure. Active bleeding sores must be controlled. Tourniquet use is discouraged and risky; bleeding can virtually always be controlled with pressure dressings. Use of a tourniquet may further impair a circulation-deficient extremity.
4. *Neurological Examination:* A rapid neurological examination is essential, with careful recording on the patient's record, to be compared with

later assessments. The neurological exam assesses the patient's level of consciousness, pupil response, eye opening, verbal response, and movement of all extremities. Use of the Glascow or similar coma scale is indicated here.

5. *Expose the Patient:* The patient must be totally exposed in the search for injuries. Hypothermia as an existing problem or induced by exposure in the emergency room must be remembered.
6. *Resuscitation:* This phase of initial assessment is performed by another member of the trauma team while the primary survey is being accomplished. Oxygen is administered to each patient. Intravenous lines with large bore needles are placed (two lines minimum). If intravenous access cannot be achieved, "cut down" exposure of a peripheral vein, using saphenous vein or gaining central access can be life-saving. Placing a central line initially should not be done due to the risk of the procedure. The needle catheter should be 14-gauge or larger, as the flow of fluids and medications follow Poiseuille's law, which says that flow is pro-portional to the inner radius of the catheter to the fourth power and the pressure gradient across the catheter. Flow is also related inversely to the length of the catheter and the viscosity of the infusate. Diligence in increasing pressure to "speed up" catheter inflow must be followed as pressures over 300 mm/Hg run a risk of air embolus. If the patient has a penetrating chest wound, intravenous lines should be placed above and below the thorax.

Volume replacement should be adequate to maintain urine output. Aggressive and early fluid replacement is essential to avoid later complications, related to inadequate resuscitation and hypoperfusion. If Ringers and glucose solutions are inadequate, a whole blood transfusion may be necessary. It is preferable to use fully cross-matched blood, but it may take one to two hours to obtain, so using type-specific blood is acceptable in emergency situations. If type-specific blood is unavailable, O− blood should be used for women and O+ blood for men. Laboratory tests should be drawn as intravenous catheters are being placed. The only mandatory blood test is type and cross-match.

The goal of the primary survey is to identify life-threatening injuries and treat them as they are identified. The primary survey usually takes less than two minutes.[2]

§16.07 Secondary Survey

This survey is a more complete physical examination, again done by the team leader. This must be a head-to-toe survey with examination devices in every body aperture. Further history is obtained, including other

---

[2] AB Peitzman & AO Udekwu, *Initial Care of the Multiple-Trauma Patient,* Surg Rounds for Orthop, June 1989, p. 61.

diseases, allergies, medications being taken, and last meal taken in case a general anesthetic becomes necessary.

X-rays of appropriate areas are taken at this stage, with a survey, lateral cervical spine being taken on all head injuries or spine injuries. Complete spine (cervical, dorsal, and lumbar) and pelvis x-rays are taken for multiple body trauma, such as a pedestrian injury or a vehicle ejection patient. This secondary physical examination must include a complete neurological examination, including updating the Glasgow Coma Scale.

A nasogastric tube would be passed. If nasal or cribiform fracture is reasonably suspected, the nasogastric tube should be passed orally. Heart evaluation, assessing heart size, rate, murmurs, and all records on the patient's chart is important.

Abdominal examination will miss 40 per cent of visceral pathology in blunt injury cases. This is due to the abdominal examination being done under less than ideal circumstances when head injury or restlessness or intoxication is present in patient. The most reliable diagnostic modality to evaluate the abdomen is diagnostic peritoneal lavage. Peritoneal lavage is generally performed through a small infra-umbilical incision under local anesthesia. A catheter is passed intraperitoneally and aspirated. If no blood is withdrawn, one liter of saline is placed intraperitoneally and is again aspirated. The effluent is sent to the laboratory for cell count, Gram strain, bilirubin, and amylase determination. If pelvis fracture is suspected, the catheter should be passed through a supra-umbilical incision.

The pelvis should be rocked to determine instability. The perineum must be examined for laceration, hematoma, or urinary meatus. If gross blood is found on rectal examination, proctoscopy is essential. If a pelvic fracture is present in a male patient, a urethrogram should be done followed by placement of a Foley catheter. Bimanual pelvic examination in women is necessary.

The secondary survey attempts to ascertain life-threatening or debilitating injuries. During the secondary evaluation, fractures and/or dislocations of major and minor bones/joints should be diagnosed and a treatment plan established. The emergency orthopedic situation, such as compound fracture/dislocations and those injuries that interfere with extremity blood supply, should be diagnosed and promptly treated.

§16.08 Persistent Shock

If a patient is unresponsive to fluid replacement during the secondary survey, reassessment for tension pneumothorax, cardiac tamponade, ongoing blood loss, or spinal cord injury should be ruled out. Military antishock trousers (MAST) are used extensively by the Armed Forces and many EMT care people. It has not been shown that they affect the outcome in most shock patients, yet their use is medically/physiologically sound. Use of the MAST device has caused some injury, such as deep vein thrombosis and thigh or calf compartment compression syndrome. Definitive care is usually carried out in the operating room or intensive care unit.

Close cooperation, the diligent, repeated evaluation of the multiply-injured patient, and the institution of prompt, appropriate treatment is the secret to minimizing death in this group of patients. The liberal use of medical consultants is equally important for these patients. If the principal physician is uncertain or overloaded, he or she has a duty to get help.[3] (*See* Appendix 16-1, Cases 13 to 23.)

§16.09 Trauma Scores

Assessing the severity of illness or injury is best achieved with an objective system, utilizing a standard "language" for the purpose of communication. Indices of severity are numerical ratings attached to selected patient characteristics to provide a means of assessing mortality and morbidity resulting from injury or illness.

For trauma patients, these scoring systems are essential techniques for (1) improving field triage, (2) planning, allocating, and evaluating medical resources, (3) assessing the effectiveness of medical care in reducing morbidity/mortality, and (4) institutional auditing. There is no single index of severity that meets all of these requirements, but a combination of both anatomic and physiologic scales provides the desired information. The injury severity score developed by Baker is the most widely used. The *injury severity score* is defined as "the sum of the squares of the highest AIS grades in each of the three most severely injured areas." Including more squares produced no significant increase in the correlation between total injury severity and mortality.

In scoring, the first step in systematically using the trauma chart is to grade all injuries for a given patient. The injury severity scoring regions include:

1. Head or neck injuries, including any injury to the cervical spine and cervical cord, skull, brain, and ears
2. Injuries to the face, including mouth, eye, nose, and facial injuries
3. Chest injuries include internal chest cavity organs, diaphragm, thoracic spine, and rib cage
4. Abdominal or pelvic contents include injuries to all internal abdominal organs and the lumbar spine
5. Injuries to the pelvic girdle and extremities include sprains, fractures, dislocations, and amputations, except those to the skull, spinal column, and rib cage
6. External injuries include all contusions, abrasions, burns, and lacerations

---

[3] American College of Surgeons, Advanced Trauma Life Support Course for Physicians (1989); Champion, *Trauma Score,* 9 Crit Care Med 672 (1981); Champion, *Trauma Severity Scoring to Predict Mortality,* 7 World J Surg 4 (1983); McSwain, Jr *Pneumatic Antishock Garment: State of the Art 1988,* 17 Ann Emer Med 506 (1989).

When all injuries have been graded, the AIS code of the most severe injury in each of the regions is recorded under the AIS score in the scoring table. The injury severity score is obtained by summing the squares of the highest AIS code in each of three most severely injured regions. The highest score is 75.[4]

§16.10 Quality of Care

It is increasingly apparent that the quality of the initial care of the injury directly impacts on the morbidity and mortality of the injured. There are numerous examples of poor or misguided treatments at the site of injury which worsen the condition of the patient. No person should attempt medical assistance to the injured unless capable and informed. The injury site is not the place for mythical aids or treatments to be performed by persons as part of an ego trip.

Basic first aid is helpful and is usually limited to assurance of an adequate airway for the patient, maintenance of body temperature, and control of excessive bleeding by "pressure only." Common sense, "cautious" removal of the patient from life-threatening environments such as fire or water are most important, and obtaining help is the job of the person rendering first aid.

The most competent persons should remove the patient to a more definitive care environment. Emergency medical services (EMS) are available in most areas in America. As in any system, elements of the EMS system must work together smoothly. A basic life-support system is a minimum combination of interacting elements and personnel. It should have (1) programs to train the citizen in the emergency care of the sick and injured, and to inform the public how to summon an ambulance, (2) easy and quick telephone access by which the public can obtain aid rapidly (within a designated area), (3) coordinated dispatch of an ambulance from the call-receiving point on a 24-hour basis by dispatchers trained to analyze the severity of the medical occurrences, (4) a dedicated radio network which allows communication between ambulances, hospitals, physicians, and other medical and public safety resources, (5) ambulance personnel trained in emergency procedures who can stabilize the patient at the scene and maintain the stable condition while transporting the patient, (6) vehicles designed specifically for the transport of the critically injured and sudden illness patient, and adequately equipped with life-supporting supplies to sustain the patient while enroute

---

[4] Baker, *The Injury Severity Score: A Method for Describing Patients with Multiple Injuries and Evaluating Emergency Care,* 14 J Trauma 187 (1974); Baker & O'Neill, *The Injury Severity Score: An Update,* 16 J Trauma 882 (1976); Barancik & Chatterjee, *Methological Consideration in the Use of the Abbreviated Injury Scale in Trauma Epidemiology,* 21 J Trauma 627 (1981); Greenspan, *Abbreviated Injury Scale and Injury Severity Score: A Scoring Chart,* 25 J Trauma 60 (1985).

to the hospital, and (7) physicians in charge of the medical operations and in control of medical decisions.[5]

Patients seen in the emergency room need to be fully informed (or a responsible person accompanying the patient) as to their ailment and the treatment recommended, as well as follow-up appointments and plans. It is desirable that the patient further know the consequences of not following instructions and choices to seek other follow-up if desired, but not to ignore follow-up instructions. The format of these patient care tools (instructions) are much like the informed consent information. *See* Appendix 16-2 for sample forms to be given to the emergency department patient after a treatment plan has been established. (*See also* Appendix 16-1, Case 24.)

§16.11 Working Relationships Within Hospital

Effective working relationships between the emergency department and other hospital departments involved in the care of the acutely ill or injured patient are essential. To promote effectiveness, the American College of Emergency Physicians has recommended the following guidelines:

1. The emergency physician's primary legal, moral, and ethical responsibility is to patients he or she sees and treats in the emergency facility. It is understood that the physician may be consulted to answer questions about emergency medical care in other areas of the hospital, although there is a question of how much response is sound if there is no back-up support in the emergency room. An emergency physician is legally vulnerable to action by emergency patients who may require his or her services. Of course, every physician must determine his or her own legal, moral, and ethical responsibilities, but it is clear that the emergency department patient is the first priority.
2. The hospital and medical staff have the primary responsibility of providing adequate physician coverage for all hospital departments involving direct patient care. It is noted in the AMA Guidelines for Categorization of Hospital Emergency Capabilities that "the same physician should not take emergency department and in-hospital emergency calls." Therefore, the primary responsibility is placed on the hospital administration and medical staff to ensure that adequate physician coverage is available in all patient care areas where emergency medical care may be needed.
3. It is essential that all equipment, procedures, and training of hospital personnel be standardized to provide continuity of effective medical care in all areas of the hospital. It is also desirable that personnel be cross-trained in both emergency and acute care departments to prepare them for the safe and efficient transfer of patients. To

---

[5] Roberts Woods Johnson Foundation Special Report on EMS (1977).

accommodate effective transfer, a series of protocols should be developed and implemented by the staff members of all departments involved.[6]

§16.12 Medical Staff Responsibilities

The American College of Emergency Physicians believes that the best patient care occurs when there is no ambiguity as to who is the physician responsible for the patient. Medical orders establish which physician is in charge of a patient's care. Therefore, the College endorses the following principles:

1. Emergency physicians should not be involved in writing any orders that extend, or appear to extend, control and responsibility for the patient beyond treatment in the emergency department to the inpatient setting.
2. Hospital and emergency department policies should clearly delineate responsibility for writing admission orders. Policies should also guarantee that the patient be seen in a timely manner.
3. Patients needing urgent medical attention should receive an appropriate medical evaluation and stabilization of any emergency medical condition by competent emergency physicians and consultant physicians, without consideration of ability to pay for these services.
4. Hospitals and their medical staffs have an obligation to provide for consultative services by qualified, on-call physicians who will respond in a reasonable period of time to requests for assistance by physicians in the emergency department.
5. Written policies and procedures should be in place to delineate clearly the qualifications and responsibilities of on-call physicians.

Telephone orders dictated by physicians from outside of the emergency department for patients who are currently in the department can result in serious lapses in the quality of the medical care the patient receives. Therefore, the American College of Emergency Physicians endorses the following principles:

1. Emergency department patients should be examined and evaluated by a physician in the emergency department prior to carrying out telephone orders.
2. Hospital and emergency department policies should specify the criteria for dictating and accepting telephone orders.
3. Drug Enforcement Administration regulations prohibit dispensing controlled substances from emergency department stocks for treat-

---

[6] Special Contribution, *Relationship Between the Emergency Department and Critical Care Units,* 6 Ann Emer Med 273 (1977).

ment of patients by telephone order. Hospital and emergency department policies should prohibit telephone orders for medications on the controlled substances list.

§16.13 Recordkeeping

The formation and completion of precise and accurate records of emergency department patients is part of practicing good medicine within the standard of care. The physician finds it a chore at the time, but invaluable in the follow-up of these patients or when review or legal actions are considered or pursued. (*See* Appendix 16-1, Cases 25 to 31.)

In an effort to lessen the risk of malpractice suits in Kansas, the Professional Mutual Insurance Company is requiring physicians who deliver babies to keep a standardized form—a prenatal recordkeeping system that consists of a series of forms and flow charts which document the patient's medical history, schedule of physician's examinations, normal progress, complications, and patient education—to keep their malpractice insurance in force.

This is a step closer to third-party regulation of how the physician keeps records and sets the standard of practice to be followed under the guise of improving medical care. The thought of strict regulation of physician practice directed by a peer group has many pluses, but it will be met with resistance by physicians who wish to protect their independence (and egos).[7] (*See* Appendix 16-1, Case 30.)

§16.14 Keeping Patient Charts

There are advantages and disadvantages to a dictated chart in the emergency department. If developed properly, a transcribed emergency department record has many advantages over a written chart and very few disadvantages. When organizing this system, only qualified medical transcriptionists should be used to maintain the same high quality professional reports found elsewhere in the hospital. The transcriptionist should be physically located in the emergency department so the chart is typed in a matter of minutes and prior to the patient's discharge from the department. The transcriptionist may be part of a medical typing pool, but the immediate priority should always be the emergency department. Because the transcriptionist can "pick up the slack" in typing non-emergency charts, it cuts the backlog of medical records that often exists and the typist is busy throughout her working hours, making this method quite cost-effective.

---

[7] Voelker-AMN Staff, *Insurer to Require More Record Keeping,* Amer Med News, May 26, 1989; Ervin, *Q&A,* ACEP News, Dec 1983, at 4.

The dictated chart has many advantages, including:

1. Efficiency of the physician is increased; he or she can see more patients in the same time frame or spend more time with patients, improving patient care.
2. Documentation is improved in that it enhances follow-up care. It is easier to read by the follow-up physician, increasing relations between the emergency department and the attending physician. Additionally, a better legal defense can be made, if needed. Lack of documentation is one of the biggest problems faced in malpractice cases. Suits often are won or lost solely on the basis of what is (or is not) in the chart, and physicians generally will go into more detail when dictating rather than writing the notes.
3. Billing is easier; both detailed description and clarity of the report greatly help the billing department. Often, insurance companies will reimburse better on a typed note than on a handwritten note.

The only disadvantage is the need for the chart to be checked for accuracy, which often does not occur in a busy emergency department, another reason to have qualified transcriptionists who will type the chart correctly the first time.

A recent review of malpractice cases arising in emergency departments underscored the importance of dictated records. In every case where the question was one of informed consent or clinical judgment, records were handwritten with no mention of what was told the patient or of the factors used in making the judgment call. Even when the illegible handwriting of most physicians is ignored, rarely does a handwritten record convey the physician's analysis or document the patient's informed consent. As important as the record is, fully informing the patient is a paramount consideration.

The consent to allow treatment that is signed on admission to an emergency department is valid for the life- or limb-threatening situation, but it does not excuse the physician from obtaining specific informed consent for procedures and treatment that are not for life- or limb-threatening conditions.

Emergency records are not private medical documents, but legal records of the physician-patient encounter. If they become public because of a lawsuit, they are assumed to be accurate, complete, and a reliable source of what occurred during the emergency visit. From the court's perspective, the medical record accurately reflects the health care the patient received. "If it isn't written down, it didn't happen." Explanations in court of what was done but not recorded are often assumed to be self-serving. In the adversarial legal system, the court will consider the facts from the point of view most favorable to each side. The plaintiff cannot dispute the medical record, and the jury will believe the record every time. If records are not dictated to record what was done, the physician is vulnerable if a suit is filed.

There are three strong arguments for dictation. The first is quality assurance. Federal law requires hospitals to review cases in the emergency department, and an adequate mechanism of screening by nonmedical personnel is not possible with scrawled notes in the record. The next is reimbursement. Third-party payers require documentation that the care rendered equals the level of service charged, particularly at the higher levels. Each Medicare reviewer, for example, correlates charges with the actual medical record several hundred times a day. Payment is routinely denied when they are unable to read a chart or when they feel the documentation does not support the amount charged. With a legible typed record, the hospital will collect more than enough to offset the cost of dictation. Third, most hospitals self-insure for the first $20,000 to $30,000 of each malpractice suits (a deductible). If dictation prevents one suit a year from being filed, the hospital will benefit. Some knowledgeable sources are predicting that, in the near future, malpractice carriers will decline to insure emergency department groups who do not dictate.[8]

An alternative method for rapidly producing accurate medical records is the nurse-scribe method. We now have several years of experience with a non-nurse scribe system. Prerequisites for hiring are knowledge of medical terminology and anatomy and good penmanship. This system has proven effective in generating accurate and complete medical records. The primary responsibility of the scribe is to record all pertinent data in an accurate, legible manner on the patient's emergency medical record. This information includes discharge instructions and prescriptions for medications. At the time of discharge, the physician need only sign the prescription and review the recorded information.[9] (*See* Appendix 16-1, Cases 32 to 36.)

Another system that might be used to improve emergency records is the new voice-activated computer that allows physicians to dictate patient reports into a handset and get a printout seconds later. Diagnostic protocols are programmed into the software with blank spaces where the physician insets the information describing the case. These show on the screen as he or she goes along. Additionally, there is a list of options in certain areas; the physician has a choice from among a dozen discharge instructions, ranging from "admit to hospital" to "send home with medication."

Although the unit price is expensive, this system would cut down on turnaround time for transcriptions and would eliminate high transcription costs, as well as provide accurate reports which would not have to be proofread. However, this is most likely to save money as a barrier against frivolous malpractice litigation. As defense lawyers have been saying for years, the best defense against such suits is complete, accurate, legible, immediately-available patient records.[10]

---

[8] George, The ED Record—Friend or Foe, 5 JACEP 535 (1976); Roussi, *An Improved Record System for the Emergency Department,* 4 JACEP 419 (1975); Witt & Haedtler, *Nurse-Scribe System Saves Time in the ED,* 1 J Emer Nurs 23 (1975); JACH, Accreditation Manual for Hospitals Emergency Services Standard VIII (1983).

[9] Lynch, *An Emergency Department Scribe System,* 3 JACEP 302 (1974); Hixson, *Scribe System Works Like a Charm in Sarasota ED,* 2 Emer Dept News 4 (1981); Alfred, *Improved Emergency Department Patient Flow: Five Years of Experience with a Scribe System,* 12 Ann Emer Med 71 (1983).

[10] Welker, *New Voice-Activated Computer Saves Time, Ensures Accuracy,* Emer Med & Ambul Care News (Jan 1988).

§16.15 Observation Units

There are three categories of patients that may require extended services in the emergency department (ED) or hospital as an alternative to routine hospital admission or ED discharge. They include (1) less than 24-hour stays for Medicare patients who do not meet established criteria for hospital admission (called Medicare 23-hour patients), (2) observation of patients on an indefinite basis while waiting for an available bed (holding patients), and (3) patients requiring prolonged treatment or observation in the ED (observation patients).

Medicare 23-hour patients should generally be admitted as a regular hospital admission and become the responsibility of the admitting physician. Holding patients may occupy a bed in an ED observation unit, with the same regulations, orders, and procedures that will be followed on transfer to a regular hospital bed. These patients should be managed by their admitting physician, but if he or she is not available, will become the responsibility of the emergency physician.

There are a number of features that should be part of any observation unit:

1. The goal of all observation units should be to improve the delivery and quality of medical care to all patients
2. Each unit should have a designated physician and nurse responsible for the unit and its conduct
3. All patients should be evaluated at least at the time of admission and at the time of discharge, and at the time of any change of condition, if indicated
4. All units should follow the standards of the Joint Commission on Accreditation of Healthcare Organizations (JCAHO)
5. Equipment and supplies should be appropriate for patients' needs and should be kept in a designated place
6. Units should be available adjacent to the ED if an emergency physician is to be responsible for patient care
7. Guidelines for nursing staff should be delineated
8. Standard protocol for transfer in and out of ED should be established and followed
9. The patient's private physician should be notified regarding care and disposition
10. Emergency physicians should be reimbursed for patient care in the observation unit
11. Written policies and procedures should be specific as to admission to the unit, including diagnostic and therapeutic categories. They should describe which types of patients are not appropriate for monitoring (usually determined by medical staff and based on observation unit capabilities), and criteria for discharge or admission to a regular hospital bed and when such decision should be made. Minimum staffing

requirements and delineation as to which physician is responsible for each patient should be specified. Requirements for documentation of the patient's stay in the unit should be clearly defined, including reason for admission, diagnostic goals, vital signs, written orders, progress notes, nursing notes, procedure notes, and disposition. Finally, policies should include a carefully defined program for quality assurance and utilization review.[11] (*See* Appendix 16-1, Case 31.)

§16.16 Emergency Surgery in Trauma Centers

As trauma systems develop, more patients may benefit from immediate surgery. With in-house surgeons available, enthusiasm for direct transfer from the accident scene to the operating room is now a fact in many hospitals. Ideally, a board-certified surgeon and a resuscitation team will meet the field transport team in surgery. Patients with prehospital hypotension unresponsive to fluid replacement indicate a need for rapid reparative operation. Penetrating injuries to the chest and abdomen with hypotension are the primary indication for emergency surgery, and it can be anticipated that survival will be enhanced.[12] (*See* Appendix 16-1, Case 37.)

§16.17 The High Cost of Trauma

Each year in the United States, injuries result in 3.6 million hospital admissions, accounting for 1 out of 10 admissions. Orthopedists are involved in the care of approximately 70 per cent of these cases.

The per-case hospital charge averages $8,100 for minor injuries and $105,350 for major injuries, with head and spinal cord injuries sustaining the highest cost. The total cost amounted to $109 million in 1983, 1984, and 1985.[13]

Trauma remains a leading cause of death and disability in America, consuming a large part of the health care dollar. In the elderly, only 2 per cent of deaths among persons more than 65 years of age are related to trauma, but the death rate is much higher in this age group when they are traumatized.

When comparing injury severity scores, length of hospital stay, hospital charges, and mortality rates in 60 trauma patients over 60 years old with

---

[11] Special Contribution, *Emergency Department Observation Units,* 17 Ann Emer Med 153 (1988).

[12] Hoyt, *The Impact of In-House Surgeons and Operating Room Resuscitation On Outcome of Traumatic Injuries,* 124 Arch Surg 906 (1989).

[13] Editorial, *The Cost of Trauma Injuries,* Surg Rounds for Orthop, July 1989, at 23.

60 trauma patients under 60 years old, the average hospital stay was four days longer and the charges were $15,769.55 more.[14]

Trauma is the leading cause of childhood mortality. In most series of polytrauma, musculoskeletal injuries predominated. Head injuries accounted for most fatalities, with blood loss and hypovolemia shock next. As in adults, stabilization of fractures, blood loss replacement, and early mobilization lessened morbidity. Internal or external fixator fracture stabilization is frequently indicated in these patients, rarely being in the same fracture as an isolated injury.

Musculoskeletal trauma is generally not the cause of death in children, but in those with multiple injuries that survive the episode, the orthopedic sequela are the cause of long-term disability.

§16.18 Emergency Transport of Young Child

Younger children have more cervical kyphosis when supine. There is a normal disproportion between head size and thorax in children up to seven years of age compared to adults. When on a flat back board, the head of a young child is forced into flexion, potentially displacing an acute unstable fracture-dislocation. To prevent this flexion in acutely injured necks of young children, a back board with a recess cut out to accommodate the head, so the neck will stay in neutral position, should be used, or a small roll should be placed under the shoulders to accomplish the same position.[15]

§16.19 Farm Accidents

High-impact vehicle and farm machinery injuries in children may present unique problems of treatment for the orthopedist. The emergency care frequently involves multiple system care, frequently life-saving. Identification of tetanus and/or gas gangrene with prompt treatment can be life-saving. Prevention of tetanus and gas gangrene by appropriate toxoids and antitoxoids are routine considerations. Realizing that delay in long bone fracture healing occurs in these cases with soft tissue damage, leg length discrepancy needs to be dealt with. Epiphyseal damage frequently occurs after high-velocity trauma about joints and corrective measures appropriately timed must be carried out in those cases.[16]

---

[14] Ross, *High Cost of Trauma Care in the Elderly,* 82 South Med J 857 (1989).

[15] Hensinger, Emergency Transport and Positioning of the Young Child with a Cervical Spine Injury—The Standard Backboard May be Hazardous, Presented at the Scoliosis Research Society, 22nd Annual Meeting, Vancouver, British Columbia, Canada (Sept 15-19, 1987).

[16] Cogbill & Busch, *Farm Accidents in Children,* 76 Pediatr 56 (1985); Lewallen & Peterson, *Nonunion Long Bone Fractures in Children,* 5 J Pediatr Orthop 135 (1985).

§16.20 Pedestrian Injuries

The incidence of pedestrians involved in automobile mishaps is significantly higher than car occupants or motorcyclists. The principal determinant of death is the weight of the vehicle. The most common site of injury is the head, causing periods of concussion, but the most common site of *serious* injury is the leg. Injuries to all areas of the body increase with age and weight of vehicle, with accidents most frequent in children and the elderly.[17]

§16.21 Informed Consent

The orthopedist is often faced with emergency situations in which prompt care of the patient is indicated. The patient may be incompetent due to injury, and no legal representative is available to give consent. In valid emergency situations, the physician is well protected against negligence actions based on lack of informed consent. A valid emergency must exist and immediate treatment must be necessary for this exception to stand. *Emergency* is defined as including any situation in which a delay in the prompt provision of medical and/or surgical care could reasonably be expected to result in loss of life or limb, result in significant impairment to function, or allow probable significant disfigurement.

The determination of the existence of emergency is a medical decision. Although not required in most jurisdictions, the opinion of a second physician strongly reinforces the existence of an emergency.

This principle was established in *Luka v Lowrie,* 136 NW 1106, (Mich 1912), in which a child sustained a crushed foot. Nobody could be contacted to give consent; amputation was felt to be life-saving and was successfully carried out. The surgeon and four other physicians agreed on the emergency status. The court held that, had the parents been available, being reasonable persons they would have agreed to the operation.

On the other hand, the physician who undertakes the care of a patient and fails to act with due diligence to save life or limb in an emergency situation is equally medically negligent.

According to established legal principles, one who is mentally competent can refuse life-saving measures, but one who is "incompetent" has no similar legal capacity. Problems arise not only when a physician determines that life-saving measures are indicated despite a valid refusal, but also when a physician provides treatment with consent, but capacity to give that consent is in doubt.

In the emergency room, the thinking and the reason for its existence is to save lives. Often, there is no time to sift through the fine points of law or ethics. Emergencies provide neither time nor opportunity for clear cut and definite choices.

Emergency rooms will become increasingly important as the site for urgent interventions. Increasingly, emergency rooms are perceived as

---

[17] Atkins, *Injuries to Pedestrians in Road Accidents,* Br 297 Med J 1431 (1988).

readily available and accessible to provide crisis care. As a result, the legal implication of receiving that care is exposed. Regular tortfeasance is always potentially present, but specific problems also regularly present themselves to the emergency room physician. These problems include assessing the patient's competency and legal ability to refuse or give informed consent, assessing the legal and policy determinants of suicide attempts, and how to deal with hostile patients and family and the duties to, and obligations of, involved third parties.

A patient's rights in the emergency room are compromised, particularly if there is a mental, drug-induced, or other impairment of the cognitive ability of the patient. The doctor's dilemmas are increased. The law is settled in this area, although it does not always solve the physician's problem.[18]

§16.22 Determining Competency of Patient

Determination of patient competency is a challenge to physicians who see patients in emergency situations. If life, death, or a significant impairment will result from failure to treat, then the physician may comfortably treat. In less urgent situations, where the patient needs to consent competently and informed, the issue may be problematic. Many psychiatrists recommend a method such as the Mini Mental Status Exam (MMSE) (see Form 22). In a large series of patients, the MMSE was combined with formal psychiatric consultation. The MMSE was carried out using Cognitive Status Examination (CSE), requiring 95 minutes to conduct and interpret. The MMSE takes only a couple of minutes. The two tests were felt comparable, disagreeing in 17.2 per cent of cases. The examining physician must have an educated opinion as to the competency of the patient before the signing of informed consent and commencement of treatment.[19]

§16.23 Pneumatic Antishock Trouser Garment

The pneumatic antishock garment (PASG) is an inflatable three-chambered polyvinyl device that can be rapidly applied around each lower extremity and lower torso to increase blood pressure and/or splint underlying fractures. There are synonymous terms for the device—G-suit and MAST (military antishock trousers).

When applied in the field, the PASG should be placed first on a backboard to be used for patient transit and then the board should be placed under the patient while great care is taken to protect the spine. The garment is then

---

[18] Feldman, *Patient's Rights: A View from the Emergency Room,* 16 Leg Aspects Med Prac 11 (1988); Becker, *The Informed Consent for Surgical Procedure: The Exceptions to the Rule,* 18 Contemp Orthop 138 (1989).

[19] Phillips & Burch, *The Neurobehavioral Cognitive Status Exam as a Measure of Competency in Medically Ill Patients,* 82 So Med J (abstract) 29.

fastened and inflated. All the while, the patient's airway is checked and maintained. The patient is transported to definitive care as soon as possible. Sudden removal or deflation of the PASG must be avoided, as irreversible shock may occur.

In the past decade, the pneumatic antishock trouser suit has been used with increasing frequency in treatment of blood loss shock and blood loss in a multiply-fractured pelvis. Relatively few complications have been attributed to these devices and many lives have been saved.

Compartment compression syndromes with thigh and calf soft tissue damage resulting, requiring emergency fasciotomy, have been reported. All personnel using antishock trousers should be alert to these possible complications. It appears that injured persons with antishock pants in place for over 120 hours are at risk for compartment syndromes.[20]

§16.24 Hypovolemic Shock

The usefulness of measuring skeletal muscle PO_2 in monitoring patients at risk of hypovolemic shock is of value. PO_2 assessment enables the determination of the severity of shock and determination of the risk of shock in critically ill patients, improving treatment and lessening morbidity.[21]

§16.25 Fluid Requirements in Trauma Patients

The fluid required for initial resuscitation of trauma patients should reflect at least, in part, the severity of the original injuries and shock. Severe shock and trauma lead to extravasation of plasma into the interstitium and intracellular sequestration of water and electrolytes. When it is necessary to infuse more than three liters of fluid to maintain blood pressure during the first 24 hours after trauma, there is a strong association with pulmonary failure and death in the high-risk patient.[22]

§16.26 Shock

Burn patients often lose substantial blood volume through the burned areas and as a result of surgical debridement and skin grafting. Irreversible shock, which persists despite fluid resuscitation, remains a significant cause of early mortality in thermally- and/or multiply-traumatized children (often

---

[20] Lieberman & Maull, *Use of the Pneumatic Antishock Garment in Trauma: A Crucial Review,* 18 Contemp Orthop 431 (1989); Bass, *Thigh Compartment Syndrome Without Lower Extremity Trauma Following Application of Pneumatic Antishock Trousers,* Ann Emerg Med, June 26, 1983, at 382.

[21] Beerthuizen, *Early Detection of Shock in Critically Ill Patients by Skeletal Muscle PO_2 Assessment,* 124 Arch Surg 853 (1989).

[22] Vassar, *Early Fluid Requirements in Trauma Patients,* 123 Arch Surg 1149 (1988).

adults). Lethal circulating products of tissue damage (not yet specifically identified) have been implicated in the shock pathophysiology. Some surgeons and therapists have found exchange blood transfusion life-saving, applying the above hypothesis.

As in all hypovolemic shock states, appropriate fluid replacement is essential; however, when replacement is adequate, further fluids are self-defeating, leading to pulmonary edema and heart failure.

Diagnosis of what additionally is perpetuating the shock picture, and treating it, is essential. Septic shock, due to bacterial infestation, or more likely due to bacterial toxins, is another area of concern.

These problems are rarely best handled by the orthopedist, but care in concert with a physician specializing in emergency, cardiovascular pulmonary is more appropriate.[23] (*See* Appendix 16-1, Cases 21 and 32.)

§16.27 Domestic Violence

In the course of care of trauma victims, the orthopedist may see and treat abuse victims, children and adult. These patients, on the average, present with typical symptoms and behavior. Experts say physicians should be alert to the following clues of an abused woman, a common abuse problem:

1. *Somatic Complaint:* Headache; insomnia; choking sensation; hyperventilation; chest, back and pelvic pain
2. *Other Signs, Symptoms or Situations:* Shyness; fright; embarrassment; evasiveness; jumpiness; passivity; frequent crying; patient often accompanied by male partner who wishes to be with her when she is seen by physician; drug or alcohol abuse, often with overdose; injuries[24]

§16.28 Head Injury

Head injuries account for a substantial proportion of all persons admitted to a hospital for brain trauma. In one large series, 80 per cent of all persons hospitalized for an acute brain injury had a mild uncomplicated brain injury. More than 40 per cent of cases of mild brain damage were caused by automobile accidents. The most common diagnosis was cerebral concussion, with other "intracranial injury" next (14 per cent). Medical length of stay in a hospital was three days and depended on a brain injury diagnosis and Glascow Coma Scale score. In this series, 50 per cent were tested for blood alcohol levels and two-thirds of those had blood levels over 100 mg/cc. In hospital treatment costs for concussion, diagnosis only exceeded $6 million in that

---

[23] Stratta, *Exchange Transfusion Therapy in Pediatric Burn Shock,* 12 Circul Shock 203 (1984).

[24] Medical News & Perspectives, *Campaign Alerts Physicians to Identify, Assist Victims of Domestic Violence,* 261 JAMA 963 (1989).

year (San Diego County in 1981).[25] (*See* Appendix 16-1, Cases 8 and 32 to 34.)

§16.29 Seizure Disorders in Trauma

In the general population, 0.5 to 2 per cent of persons have seizure disorders. Most are controlled medically, yet unpredictable seizures occur with a head injury. The whole gamut of potential injuries from a violent fall may present in the seizure patient. The orthopedist often sees these patients in the postictal state for evaluation. Treatment methods are no different from nonseizure patients, except a clear knowledge of status and of the cause of the seizure may prevent complications, such as a recurrent seizure displacing a reduced fracture or dehiscing an operative wound. Seizure patients also involved in metabolic imbalances or drug/alcohol usage may present special problems that may involve the orthopedist expertise.[26]

§16.30 Spleen Rupture

In the emergency room, the acutely injured patient often cannot tell of abdominal pains. If lower rib or upper abdomen blunt trauma is noted or suspected, or if lower ribs are broken, spleen or liver laceration is suspect. It is easy to overlook the life-threatening bleeding that may occur. Peritoneal taps and serial blood count in the comatose patient are the necessary diagnostic tests. The patient who is awake may be dismissed from the emergency room prematurely to exsanguinate at home. Precautionary periods of in-hospital observation may be the standard.[27]

§16.31 Treating Fractures in the Emergency Department

A child's bone differs biomechanically from adult bone. The cortex is more porous and, when subjected to forces leading to fracture, plastic deformation is greater prior to fracture than in the adult bone. In children, the bone often bends without fractures being noted on x-rays. A child's bone heals quickly and remodels well. Knowledge of these factors is necessary in judging how much angulation, displacement, or shortening is acceptable. Remodeling is greater the younger the child, and is best in the plane of motion of the joint. Displacement or angulation of the proximal humerus/humeral head with its multiple planes of motion is better tolerated than at the knee where there is one principal plan of motion. Non-union of fracture is rare in the pediatric group of patients.

---

[25] Kraus, *The Epidemiology of Mild Uncomplicated Brain Injury,* 28 J Trauma 1637 (1988).

[26] Fallon, *Seizure Disorders and Trauma,* 82 So Med J 1093 (1989).

[27] Beal & Spisso, *The Risk of Splenorrhaphy,* 123 Arch Surg 1158 (1988).

Manipulation of injuries that involve the epiphysis should be done one time only with adequate anesthesia; repeated manipulation risks significant physis injury. Open reduction in those situations is preferable. A fracture that involves the epiphysis should be followed until a growth pattern is established, as growth irregularity is common. The family needs to be warned of these complications as part of the informed consent.

The highest risk of vascular problems in pediatric fractures is in supracondylar fractures of the humerus, vertical shear fractures of the pelvis, distal femoral and proximal tibial physeal fractures, tibial shaft fractures, and fracture-dislocation of the talus. Those injuries with high risk of neurologic complications include supracondylar fractures of the humerus, spiral fractures at the mid-distal one-third of humerus, distal radius with displacement, vertical shear fractures of the pelvis, posterior hip dislocations, proximal tibial-fibular fractures, and unstable vertebral injuries.

In the emergency treatment of fractures, there are several important considerations. The fractured extremity must be protected (splinted) until definitive treatment is effected. Significant additional injury may occur to the extremity if the fractured bone ends are not protected. Expert testimony may be necessary to establish that the failure to immobilize did cause negligent additional injury. Typical "additional" injuries include additional or new damage to blood vessels, nerves, or muscle, or converting the original closed fracture into an open fracture.

The timing of the definitive repair of acute fractures may be negligent. The usual negligence stemming from delay is failure of the surgeon to definitively treat a fracture that involves circulatory compromise, or delay in the repair of a compound fracture that becomes infected when it was probable that it would not if cared for in a timely manner.

Post-repair management of the fracture is often vitally important. Most fractured extremities swell after fracture reduction and the fracture is often held in position with a cast. Circulatory compromise in the cast frequently occurs and must be promptly corrected, often by splitting or removing and replacing the cast. Often, time is of the essence here to prevent gangrene, skin ulceration, or loss of deep soft tissues due to ischemia. The circulatory problem will often present at times inconvenient for the surgeon to attend, such as the middle of the night. (*See* Appendix 16-1, Cases 35 and 36.)

To avoid delays and missing spinal fractures and their complications, x-rays of the entire spine are now recommended when a fracture at any other level is found. Dura tears are common, but not thought of if occult fracture is present. In reviewing a large number of cases, one author found a second (unsuspected) fracture in 6.5 per cent of the cases, which needed individual evaluation and treatment.[28]

---

[28] Trauger, *Dural Tears, Second Fracture Sites Often Accompany Spinal Injury,* 9 Orthop Today 35 (1989).

§16.32 Multiple Organ Failure

Much is unknown regarding multiple organ failure and/or the adult respiratory syndrome that follows multiple body trauma (MOF). It is known that humeral factors, not normally present in the homeostatic body, appear after trauma and that the degree of hypovolemic shock does not parallel blood loss. The current theory is that there is a generalized action of inflammatory mediators after multiple body trauma. Although some of these mediators are chemically immeasurable and others present by extrapolation, their effect is to close down function of one or many major body organ systems that lead to death. Pulmonary edema occurs after total body trauma, and at times after removal of lower torso-extremity pneumatic trousers during the reperfusion process. Release of chemoattractants leukotreine B_4 and thromboxane which increases pulmonary capillary permeability and pulmonary edema, are probable causative mechanisms.

The treatment is supportive; that is, to maintain and/or correct those homeostatic defects that can be identified. This requires a highly skilled, knowledgeable medical care team and constant diligence.[29]

§16.33 Whole Body Inflammation in Fatal Trauma Cases

In a large number of autopsied patients who died from trauma, generalized inflammation of non-traumatized organs was found, with hypovolemic shock listed as the cause of death. Multisystem failure and adult respiratory syndrome seem to be the cause of death. In trauma centers, it is now being realized that addressing the multi-organ failure before it appears, if possible, improves survival. In many of the above patients, head injury only was present.[30]

§16.34 Frost Bite; Hypothermia

Nearly 7,000 deaths due to cold exposure have occurred in the United States in the last 10 years, many of these seen in emergency rooms and by orthopedists. Death due to hypothermia is common; more common are complications from cold tissue damage to the extremities—frostbite. It is important that cold tissue damage and hypothermia be promptly recognized and treated by the doctor. Gradual body warming with appropriate supportive care of the hypothermia may be life-saving. If the attending physician is not

---

[29] Pruitt, *The Pathogenesis of Multiple Organ Failure,* 123 Arch Surg 1518 (1988); Nuytinck, *Whole Body Inflammation in Trauma Patients: An Autopsy Study,* 123 Arch Surg 1517 (1988); Trunkey, *Inflammation and Trauma,* 123 Arch Surg 1517 (1988); Klausner, *Reperfusion Pulmonary Edema,* 261 JAMA 1030 (1988).

[30] Nuytinck, *Whole Body Inflammation in Trauma Patients: An Autopsy Study,* 123 Arch Surg 1517 (1988).

familiar with total hypothermia care, immediate consultation with an informed doctor is the standard of care.

Frostbite is the freezing of the body's outer tissues or "shell." Whereas superficial frostbite can be reversed with swift thawing, deep frostbite kills tissue and may produce gangrene. Gradual warming of deep tissues, aseptic protection, and "wait and see" are the treatment standards. This is a situation when delay in amputation or debridement until clear demarcation is appropriate care. It is important not to do a mutilating surgery when a lesser procedure next week might work. Attending to infection and nutrition and general health are supplemental therapies.

The orthopedist, as he or she deals with emergency situations, will see frostbite patients. Frostbite is not a major problem until the wind chill temperature falls below 20° F. The face and peripheral areas such as fingers, toes, ears, and nose are most susceptible, as peripheral blood is shunted to deeper tissues to maintain their homeostasis. Mild frostbite is characterized by very pale skin with random splotchiness. Often, the area will sting and burn. With more severe cases, the skin will appear gray or ashen, and will feel numb. With the first sign of suspected frostbite, the area should be warmed. Hands and feet can be immersed in water at 108 to 113°, measured by a thermometer. Do not massage the area, as further damage to the skin may occur.

Hypothermia is a progressive condition in which the body's heat production cannot keep up with heat loss. Hypothermia must be part of the orthopedist's differential diagnosis as he or she assesses the injury patient from a prolonged cold environment. Conditions such as fatigue, dampness, or ethynol intoxication will enhance heat loss and quicken the hypothermic onset. As the patient's core temperature drops, various physiological responses take place. Slurred speech, loss of motor coordination and strength in the upper limbs, lethargy, and excessive shivering are signs that body temperature has dropped as much as 2° F. A further drop in body temperature will result in irregular heartbeat, loss of consciousness, and death by heart failure. Emergency treatment is removal of all cold wet clothes, wrapping in warm blankets, and restoration of fluid balance by giving warm IV fluids and a warm drink, if the patient is able to drink.[31]

§16.35 Adult Respiratory Syndrome

The adult respiratory distress syndrome (ARDS) and transfusion related acute lung injury (TRALI) are characterized by diffuse, acute lung injury. The pathophysiology of these entities appears to relate to endothelial injury

---

[31] Steel, *Management of Frostbite,* 17 Phys & SportsMed 135 (1989); Kilbourne, *Illness Due to Thermal Extremes,* J.M. Last & Maxey-Rosenau's, Public Health and Preventive Medicine (12th ed 1986); H.K. Collins, Hypothermia: The Facts (1983); Mills, Jr, *Summary of Treatment of the Cold Injured Patient: Frostbite,* 25(2) Alaska Med 33 (1983); McCauley, *Frostbite Injuries: A Rational Approach Based on Pathophysiology,* 23 J trauma 143 (1983).

of lung vessels by a variety of traumatically or foreign material induced chemotaxic medicated changes. For those interested, Swank and Moore have extensively researched the subject. ARDS continues to be causative of death in a high proportion of multiply-injured patients and patients with sepsis, as well as those involved with multi-organ failure syndrome.[32]

ARDS is an acute respiratory failure due to non-cardiogenic pulmonary edema. It is a sequelae of shock, systemic sepsis, trauma, viral respiratory infection, and many other traumatic insults.

This disorder is particularly tragic because it affects young healthy patients. ARDS is common and lethal, affecting an estimated 150,000 people a year. The mortality rate is 50 per cent, despite supportive therapy. This syndrome occurs in approximately 2 per cent of all patients who have sustained trauma. Rapid pulse, dyspnea, hypoxemia, and decreased compliance are resistant to routine methods of oxygen administration. The patients also exhibit restlessness, anxiety, cough with significant pulmonary excretions, and often an expiratory wheeze. In later stages of the disease, almost complete consolidation of lung fields may occur.

The cause is multi-factorial—fluid overload, lung emboli, aspiration of gastric contact, shock, and clotting factors such as platelet aggregates. Fibrin thrombi passing through standard blood transfusion filters and loading in pulmonary capillaries have been suggested has etiologies. Sepsis is thought to be a major factor.

Early diagnosis is essential for management. The earlier the diagnosis is made, the greater the chance for survival. Mechanical ventilation may be successful treatment. In addition, these patients require adequate blood volume replacement and the use of cardiotonic drugs, if necessary, to maintain heart function. Use of methyl prednisilone therapy is controversial. Also, it has been shown that patients on steroid therapy have an increased risk of infection.

Fat embolus syndrome is a clinical symptom complex consisting of tachypnea, tachycardia, fever, mental status changes, and petechia. It appears more commonly in adults than in any other age group. This incident correlates positively with a number of long bone fractures, open fractures, or fractures caused by vehicular or other accidents.

It was believed that fat emboli syndrome was caused by alteration of pulmonary function brought on directly by fat emboli from fractured bones. Although fat emboli are found in the lungs when the patient sustains fractures and other musculoskeletal trauma, there is now evidence that fat emboli occur immediately following intra-medullary nailing of the femoral shaft. Any delay greater than 24 hours is associated with a five-fold increase in incidences of ARDS, the greater risk to life.

Similar fat emboli syndromes have been reported after total hip arthroplasty and femoral prosthesis, placement using methymethacrolate bone

---

[32] Swank & Moore, *Roles of the Neutrophil and Other Mediators in Adult Respiratory Distress Syndrome,* 64 Mayo Clin Proc 1118 (1989).

cement. Less commonly, the syndrome occurs with total knee replacement, usually with the use of a long-stem prosthesis.

Maintenance of normal blood volume and proper oxygenation are important in preventing the clinical manifestation. Treatment includes blood volume replacement, cardiotonic drugs, and respiratory support. Oxygen delivered by mass is adequate in many patients, but some will require positive pressure breathing. It has been noted that patients with low blood alcohol, .02 or less, are more likely to develop fat embolus. On this basis, intravenous alcohol has been recommended as treatment at times. Again, the use of steroids has been recommended, and again the increased risk of pulmonary infection presents.

Respiratory complications after spinal fusion for scoliosis are increased in patients who have non-idiopathic curves, mental retardation, anterior spinal fusions, and relative arterial hypoxemia with an obstructive component in pulmonary function. Pulmonary function is normal on routine testing in young adults with scoliosis with curves up to 45°, although there are some reports of small titled volume in scoliosis patients with high respiratory frequency in order to maintain adequate ventilation. In severe thoracic scoliosis, respiratory failure, a restrictive lung pattern, polycythemia, corpulmonale, and abnormal blood gas values are present. If acute respiratory failure develops, successful management is possible, long-term survival is expected, and pulmonary function will deteriorate slower than an expected rate.

Spontaneous pneumothorax bullae can be caused by Marfan's syndrome as well as other entities. The frequency of spontaneous pneumothorax over 12 years of age with Marfan's syndrome is nearly 5 per cent. Definitive surgical treatment should be formed at the first occurrence of pneumothorax because of the high rate of recurrence after chest tube. This is true with Marfan's syndrome only; pneumothorax otherwise is frequently spontaneous and cared for with chest tubes, yet a high percentage of the cases will resolve; however, if repeated pneumothorax occur, surgical ablation of the bullae may be necessary.

Atelectasis occurs frequently in patients treated with ventilation for respiratory failure due to neuromuscular disease and infections occurring soon after intubation are a principal co-factor—aspiration pneumonitis, focal lung infections, and the types of recurrent lung infiltrates seen in bronchietasis and in cystic fibrosis.[33] (See Appendix 16-1, Case 37.)

---

[33] *Id.* Bass, Allison, Jr., Reins, & Yeager, *Thigh Compartment Syndrome Without Lower Extremity Trauma Following Application of Pneumatic Anti-shock Trousers,* 12 Ann Emer Med 382 (1983); Jardon, Wingard & Barak, *Malignant Hyperthermia, a Potentially Fatal Syndrome in Orthopedic Patients,* 61A JBJ Surg 1064 (1979); Lawhon, Kahn & Crawford, *Controlled Hypotensive Anesthesia During Spinal Surgery. A Retrospective Study,* 9 Spine 450 (1984); Modig, *Advantages of Dextrone 70 over Ringer Acetate Solution in Shock Treatment and in the Prevention of Adult Respiratory Distress Syndrome,* 10 Resuscit 219 (1983); Rovner, Bard & Malerich, *Fatal Toxic Shock Syndrome as a Complication of Orthopedic Surgery,* 66A JBJ Surg 952 (1984); Stock, *Transcatheter Embolization for Control of Wound Hemorrhage Follow-*

§16.36 Corticosteroids

The prospective, randomized, double-blind placebo-controlled clinical trial remains quintessential in resolving often complex, controversial clinical problems. Its importance is epitomized in the resolution of the age-old debate over the roles of corticosteroids in septic shock and adult respiratory distress syndrome (ARDS).

Corticosteroids do not help; they may hurt. ARDS as a systemic disease has its morbidity and mortality related to inadequate tissue oxygenation.[34]

§16.37 Fat Embolism

Post-traumatic fat embolism has been a subject of confusion and controversy for over 100 years. Hundreds of papers have been published on the subject, only recently clarifying its pathophysiology.

Fat embolism syndrome may be defined as a complex alteration of homeostasis which occurs as a complication of fracture of the pelvis and/or long bones and multiple body trauma. It manifests itself as acute respiratory insufficiency. Florid, symptomatic life-threatening fat embolism occurs in 1 to 10 per cent severe body traumas, and to a lesser extent presents in subclinical form in all long bone fractures.

Adult respiratory syndrome has similar presentations, usually related to soft tissue trauma, and is part of disseminated coagulopathies. In each syndrome, end arteries in multiple organs are involved with either fat globule embolism or coagulopathy clots which impair small vessel perfusion. The lung acts as a filter of these clots, so its function is often dangerously impaired.

Treatment of fat embolus syndrome, as well as adult respiratory syndrome, is (1) supportive respiratory care, oxygen, maintenance of the airway including mechanically-maintained intratracheal respiration and appropriate medication; the service of specialists in pulmonary medicine may be lifesaving, and (2) control or correction of the cause—if infectious, prompt antibiotic administration; if multiple fracture, prompt stabilization with immobilization of the patient.[35] (*See* Appendix 16-1, Case 19.)

---

ing Hip Surgery, JBJ Surg 1000 (1980); Stratta, *Exchange Transfusion Therapy in Pediatric Burn Shock,* 12 Circulat Shock 203 (1984); Anderson, *Post-Operative Respiratory Complications in Non-Idiopathic Scoliosis,* 29 ACTA Anest 186 (1985); Gosling, *Fat Embolism Syndrome,* 165 Clin Orthop 63 (1982); Johnson, *Incidence of Adult Respiratory Distress Syndrome in Patients with Musculoskeletal Injuries,* 25 J Trauma 375 (1985).

[34] Weng, *Critical Care Medicine,* 261 JAMA 2836 (1989); Bone, *Early Methyprednisolone Treatment for Septic Syndrome and Adult Resporatory Distress Syndrome,* 92 Chest 1032 (1987); Shumacker & Cain, *The Concept of a Critical Oxygen Delivery,* 13 Intens Care Med 223 (1987); Mohsenifar, *Dependence of Oxygen Consumption on Oxygen Delivery in Patients with Chronic Heart Failure,* 92 Chest 447 (1988).

[35] Gossling & Pellegrini, Jr, *Fat Embolism Syndrome,* 165 Clin Orthop & Rel Res 68 (1982).

§16.38 Electrical Injuries

Most victims of high-voltage electrical injuries can be treated successfully. Treatment principles include fluid resuscitation to promote vigorous diuresis, and bicarbonate administration to alkalinize the urine to protect against renal tubular damage. Compartment pressure monitoring with early fasciotomy when indicated contributes to low amputation incidence. Because neuromuscular, ophthalmologic, and psychiatric complaints may appear later, routine follow-up for at least one year is important in a total care program. Aggressive rehabilitation contributes to a higher percentage of the injured returning to work.

§16.39 Blunt Trauma and Cardiac Contusion

The initial physical examination is frequently unreliable in the diagnosis of blunt trauma at high-risk intra-abdominal injury or cardiac contusion. Early use of abdominal lavage, CT scanning, and ultrasound devices to aid in diagnosis can be life-saving. There is always a risk to "watchful waiting." The examining physician must use all diagnostic tools available.[36]

§16.40 AIDS

Emergency room personnel must realize that they are at increased risk of AIDS exposure. The only proven cases of infection of health care persons has occurred when an inadvertent penetration (needle stick, scalpel injury) has occurred. Great care in patient contact is encouraged. Use of gloves during patient examination is routine, although they will not protect against penetrating wounds.[37]

§16.41 Duties to Patient

The physician in charge of emergency situations in or outside of the hospital is held responsible for knowing the quality of emergency transport services and their personnel. If he or she refers patients to another hospital, he or she is held responsible for knowing the quality and level of care offered by that institution. Patient dumping from one hospital to another has been a recent problem and is a disservice to the critically injured or ill patient. COBRA laws are in place in many states to limit patient dumping. Dumping occurs when a patient presents to an emergency room critically ill, and is stabilized and sent off to another hospital because the patient does not meet the admitting requirements of the first hospital. Dumping often follows

---

[36] Miller, *Myocardial Contusion,* 124 Arch Surg 805 (1989); Mackersie, *Intra-abdominal Injury Following Blunt Trauma,* 124 Arch Surg 809 (1989); Mizrahi, *Posttraumatic Autotransplantatikon of Spleen Tissue,* 124 Arch Surg 863 (1989).

[37] Kelen, *Unrecognized Human Immunodeficiency Virus Infection in Emergency Department Patients,* 318 NEJM 1645 (1988).

when a patient cannot provide financial assurance for ongoing care. Often, a dumped patient will be sent to another hospital which has not agreed to accept him or her. Referring a patient to another hospital which does not have the facilities, personnel, or medical staff to handle the medical at hand is culpable. (*See* Appendix 16-1, Case 38.)

In August 1986, anti-dumping provisions of the federal Combined Omnibus Budget Reconciliation Act of 1985 (COBRA) went into effect. The COBRA amendments to Medicare require all hospitals receiving Medicare funds to adequately screen all patients seeking Medicare and to refrain from "inappropriately transferring a woman in active labor." Under these provisions, a hospital can only transfer a patient who is critically unstable when the patient or guardian requests a transfer or when it is in the best interests of the patient. Hospitals and physicians found guilty of violating this law would be subject to money fines ($25,000 to $50,000 per incident) and loss of participation in Medicare.[38]

Transfer of the emergency patients from field to hospital or from one hospital to another is often a life-saving process, but is fraught with risks. Excellent training and care by the emergency personnel is essential. Equally important is the equipment used by the transferring services. Ambulances and their emergency equipment are used many times daily and rapidly wear and may be faulty. A protocol that tests all essential life-saving equipment daily to be assured of function and safety is basic. There is nothing more tragic than being in the field, needing a resuscitator or suction device or medication, and finding it unavailable or nonfunctional.

Air transportation presents a particular problem. These vehicles must meet all standards for ground ambulances and be adequately staffed with competent, rested pilots capable of flying the various types of missions they must complete. Helicopter pilots additionally often land in areas not designed for aircraft; they must be particularly familiar with terrain, air traffic control areas, and program policies relating to night flying and landing.

Safety must be an institutional priority. No mission should be undertaken unless weather, equipment, and personnel are suitable. Regular safety meetings should be scheduled and all personnel should attend. Crew members should be able to cancel any mission at any time, with suitable after review. The pilot (or ground vehicle operator, if applicable) must have the last word on aircraft safety and weather conditions and no pressure should be applied to change his or her decision to undertake. The orthopedist/emergency room

---

[38] Berliner, *Patient Dumping—No One Wins and We All Lose,* 78 AJPH 1279 (1988); Kellermann & Hackman, *Emergency Department Patient Dumping,* 78 AJPH 1287 (1988); Equal Access to Health Care: Patient Dumping, 37th Report by the Committee on Government Operation, House of Representatives, 100th Cong, 1st Sess 149, 216 (July 22, 1987) (US Govt Printing Office, Washington, DC 1988); Schiff, *Transfers to a Public Hospital: A Prospective Study of 467 Patients,* 314 NEJM 552 (1986); Himmelstein, *Patient Transfers: Medical Practice as Social Triage,* 74 AJPH 494 (1984); Ginsberg, *The Destabilization of Health Care,* 315 NEJM 757 (1986); Reinhardt, *Health Insurance of the Nation's Poor,* 6(1) Health Aff 101 (1987).

physician is involved in this process, for the currently stabilized patient may have tertiary care delayed, calling for intensive patient care, perhaps in a less desirable environment. The physician is held to know if the transport service chosen is less than competent. Although the physician does not often travel with the patient being transferred, he or she is responsible for organizing care (writing orders) for the patient.[39] (*See* Appendix 16-1, Cases 17, 21, 31, and 39 to 43.)

Alarm about the adverse effect of transferring emergency patients for economic reasons has resulted in federal legislation aimed at curbing the practice. This dumping of patients is an old practice receiving renewed interest, but not loading new risks of liability on the medical practitioner's shoulders. Many current authors conclude that currently proposed solutions to patient dumping will have limited effectiveness without more specific incentives for the provision of health care to the medically indigent.[40]

§16.42 Principles of Appropriate Patient Transfer

Quality emergency care should be available to all who seek it. For that care to be provided, patients are sometimes transferred to another health care facility from the emergency facility where they sought care. To ensure access to emergency care and patient safety when transfers occur, the following principles regarding patient transfer are indicated:

1. The health and well being of the patient must be the main concern when patient transfer is being considered
2. Emergency physicians and hospital personnel should comply with state and federal regulations regarding patient transfer; a medical screening exam mandated by federal law should be performed by a physician; in the event a physician is not physically present in the emergency department 24 hours a day, the screening exam may be performed by properly trained ancillary personnel according to written policies and procedures
3. The physician should inform the patient or responsible party of the reasons for, and the risks and likely benefits of, transfer, and document this in the medical record; the competence of the patient to agree or refuse to be transferred should be assessed prior to obtaining consent; if the patient is incompetent to make this decision, a person legally responsible for the patient should make this decision on behalf of the patient

---

[39] Laufer, *Emergency Medicine transports by Resident Physicians,* 262 JAMA 2052 (1989).

[40] Enfield & Sklar, *Patient Dumping in the Hospital Emergency Department: Renewed Interest in an Old Problem,* 8 Amer J Law 7 Med 561 (1988); Powers, *Hospital Service and the Open Door,* 66 Mich L Rev 1455 (1968).

4. The hospital and medical staff should identify individuals responsible for transfer decisions and clearly delineate their duties in that process
5. The patient should be transferred to a facility appropriate to the medical needs of the patient, with adequate space and personnel available
6. A physician or other responsible person at the receiving hospital must agree to accept the patient prior to the transfer
7. The patient transfer should not be refused by the receiving hospital when the transfer is indicated, and the receiving hospital has the capability and/or responsibility to provide care for the patient; economic reasons should not be the basis for transferring or refusing to accept a medically unstable patient
8. Communication to exchange clinical information between responsible persons at the transferring and receiving hospitals must occur prior to transfer
9. An appropriate medical summary and other pertinent records should accompany the patient to the receiving institution
10. The patient should be transferred in a vehicle that is staffed by qualified personnel and contains appropriate equipment
11. When transfer of patients is part of a regional plan to provide optimal care for patients at specialized medical facilities, written transfer protocols and interfacility agreements should be in place[41]

§16.43 Emergency Department Overcrowding

Many Americans face a crisis in health care that is widespread and continues to grow. Hospital overcrowding, and the resulting congestion and holding of patients that occurs in emergency departments in many parts of the country, is severely limiting the public's right to timely access to emergency medical care and the quality of medical care.

There are many factors contributing to the emergency department overload problem, including a shortage of health care professionals (especially nurses), increased numbers of uninsured patients, and hospital or emergency department closures. Underlying many of these factors is inadequate funding of health care services. The emergency department is generally the first area compromised when hospitals do not have adequate beds for patients requiring hospital admission; the patients remain in the emergency department.

Emergency physicians and nurses, therefore, are called on to provide ongoing inpatient and intensive care (ICU) in the emergency department, in addition to their responsibilities to other emergency patients, limiting their capacity to provide safe and efficient medical/nursing care. The overburdened resources of crowded emergency departments have forced staff to

---

[41] American College of Emergency Physicians, Principles of Appropriate Patient Transfer Position Statement Approved Sept 8, 1989.

delay basic emergency care to sick and injured individuals. In some areas, the health care system has become so overcrowded that there are prolonged delays for prehospital providers to find available emergency departments for ambulance patients. These delays further decrease the availability of emergency medical services (EMS) vehicles and manpower, and therefore lengthen EMS response times. In the interest of every citizen of this nation, this trend cannot be allowed to continue.

Emergency physicians and nurses cannot control the factors that impair the availability, timeliness, and quality of emergency care by themselves. While they are working to improve the efficiency of hospital admission and discharge procedures, facilitate communication between hospitals and prehospital providers regarding hospital and emergency department bed availability, and to standardize policies that regulate regional emergency department availability and ambulance diversions, these are only stopgap measures; long-term solutions are urgently needed.[42]

§16.44 Urgent Care Facilities

Because emergency rooms are frequently overloaded and doctors offices are not always convenient to the patient or are not open when a patient needs urgent (yet not emergency) care, a new type of facility has evolved—urgent care facilities—either as part of hospital outpatient services or free-standing operating facilities with a physician staff. Patients with injury problems are often referred to an orthopedist. As in emergency rooms, orthopedists will work part-time or see patients in the urgent care environment, and should therefore understand the urgent care philosophy and administration. Rarely will an urgent care facility see a nonpaying patient, which is likely to be tested legally.

Two common types of non-emergency department immediate care facilities are (1) fast track "convenience care" for emergency departments, and (2) minor immediate care facilities.

§16.45 Minor Immediate Care Facility

This is a program were patients with minor medical problems can come to a hospital emergency department with the assurance that they will be seen quickly, without an appointment, and at a fee significantly lower than the usual emergency visit charge. It is designed to appeal to the working person who cannot get a convenient appointment with a local physician and who generally stays away from hospital emergency departments because they realize that the minor nature of their complaint means that they will be the last one treated. The program is designed to compete with urgent care

---

[42] American College of Emergency Physicians, Emergency Nurses Association Position Statement, Hospital and Emergency Department Overcrowding Jointly Approved Sept 1989.

centers, after hour clinics, etc., and to appeal to patients that would otherwise not come to the facility because of high cost and/or time delays.

Benefits include:

1. Patient volume—brings patients to emergency department that otherwise would not go
2. Increases visibility of the hospital, as well as emergency department
3. Enhances image of the hospital, showing the community that the hospital wants to provide convenient care at low costs
4. Reduces cost and paperwork in billing, since there will be no billing, no collection, and no bad debt
5. Creates "spill over" lab and x-ray for patients who do not qualify for the program; may generate an admission out of visit or from subsequent visit

Qualifications include:

1. Patient must have a minor medical problem that does not require lab or x-ray studies (colds, sore throats, earaches, flu, food poisoning, fever in children, puncture wounds, skin rashes, minor wounds not requiring surgical repair, wound cleansing, tetanus injection)
2. Patient usually requires an examination and a prescription
3. Patient may pay for services prior to being seen with cash or credit card; checks may be accepted during hours when banks can be called to verify; patients will be provided an appropriate form to obtain reimbursement from an insurance carrier; no special insurance form will be prepared

§16.46 Fast Track Convenience Care for Emergency Departments

As emergency departments have developed over the past 10 years, the care they have provided for the community has evolved into three major categories: (1) major/critical care, (2) intermediate/emergent care, and (3) minor/convenient care.

The care of the critically ill or injured patient has been addressed by the medical and political groups of each community. Out of this evolution has developed a major reclassification of hospitals into a broad spectra of facilities ranging from tertiary care (Level I and II) facilities to community hospitals (Level III and IV) for each of the major categories of medicine. As each hospital has fit into this classification, the emergency department and staff for that facility has evolved upward or downward to meet the needs of the patients it serves.

The intermediate/emergent care consists of the patient who, because of the nature of the medical problem, time of day or night, or lack of unavailability of a private physician, goes to the emergency department for immediate care. This category of patient is best seen in the emergency department where delays are minimal, where lab and x-rays are immediately available, where specialist consultation is readily available, and where direct admission and/or surgery can be obtained without transfer to another facility.

The minor/convenience care patient is initially seen in the emergency department so he or she can be seen at his or her convenience, at any hour, without having a private physician, without an appointment, and with a good probability that the patient's insurance will cover costs. This has been acceptable to private physicians, as the patients are referred to them for consultation or follow-up, making this an excellent source for building a practice.

Evolution has greatly altered minor/convenience care. As emergency departments have grown busier with emergent and/or critical patients, the minor care patients have had increasing delays in care. These delays have resulted in the loss of the convenience they initially provided. The increased number of private physicians has offered the minor/convenience care patient significant alternatives for care in the form of (1) private physician availability on a no appointment or shorter delay basis, (2) extended private physician hours, (3) freestanding ambulatory care centers, and (4) emergency departments developing a second or "fast track."

The rationale for emergency departments developing a "fast track" is high volume, loss of patients, or both. Departments with high patient volume are experiencing long delays in seeing emergency (as well as non-emergency) patients. Poor traffic flow resulted from these delays. Dissatisfaction was voiced by patients, their families, and medical staff. Teaching hospitals found that house staff only added to these delays.

Many emergency departments experienced a lack of anticipated growth—a plateau or an actual decline in emergency patient visits because of alternatives for minor health care expanding in their catchment areas. Faced with internal problems of high volume, poor traffic flow, long delays, or external threats of pleasant, friendly, efficient, quality alternatives, emergency departments began to explore their alternatives. Many hospitals purchased or constructed their own freestanding ambulatory care centers to protect their turf. To become more competitive, emergency departments developed tiered-facility fee structures and began utilizing the standardized CPT-4 (current procedural terminology) professional fee codes to graduated fees according to the complexity of medical problems or the amount of services rendered. Adjacent ambulatory care centers were developed, offering lower than emergency department rates for patients with minor medical problems.

As creative minor/convenient care has evolved, beneficial and untoward trends have developed. Included in the beneficial trends are (1) consumer rather than physician orientation, (2) patient advocate, (3) convenience, (4) ambience, (5) speed, (6) minor medical problems having their priority, (7) need of medical staff support, and (8) "marketing" is possible.

The untoward trends include (1) inappropriate direction or triage, requiring transfer to a full-service emergency department, (2) the high cost of freestanding facilities with low inpatient referrals, (3) private freestanding facilities self-referring and thus "stealing patients" from medical staff, (4) private medical plans and insurance companies discouraging or penalizing their subscribers for utilizing emergency departments rather than an alternative, (5) industrial accident patients directed to industrial clinics to avoid delays, unnecessary sick time, and unnecessary costs, and (6) advertising that can alienate the medical community.

As a second generation alternative for minor/convenience care utilizing the knowledge of the beneficial, as well as the untoward, trends, emergency departments have developed the fast track "convenience care" concept for their facilities.

Fast track convenience care is simply this:

1. *Primary purpose:* The primary purpose for convenience care is to better treat and better serve the segment of the emergency patient population with minor medical problems without sacrificing the care to the more seriously ill or injured patient.
2. *Express line:* An express line convenience care for customers who have few (or minor) medical problems that can quickly and efficiently be seen and treated in a short, predictable period of time.
3. *Common entrance:* The facility and entrance are the same for convenience care as well as ambulatory emergency patients. The patient does not have to choose or make the decision. Once inside, the patient is directed (triaged) to convenience care or to emergency care, depending on the complexity of the medical problem.
4. *Facility:* A specific ward or area (four to six beds) in the emergency department is dedicated to convenience care patients during the designated hours of operation. After hours, this area can be double-utilized by the emergency department for overflow.
5. *Hours of operation:* The hours of operation are based on consumer need. Ultimately, salary costs for the convenience care medical team will be the deciding factor. However, if marketing is planned, a "brand name" and broad hours of operation (12 hours a day) are preferred. If medical staff acceptance is a concern, then weekday evening (5 P.M. to 11 P.M.) and weekends (11 A.M. to 11 P.M.) hours may be a necessary compromise.
6. *Medical team:* A separate medical team is in-house and dedicated to convenience care during the hours of operation. The team should initially consist of "known commodities" such as an emergency department physician, an emergency department RN, and an emergency department clerk/technician, who will deliver the product desired. Substitution with non-emergency department personnel (P.A., nurse practitioner, LPN, other primary care or house staff physician) should be avoided until convenience care is up and running and justifies each member of the team.

7. *Put-through times:* The "put-through" time for convenience care patients should be 30 minutes to a maximum of one hour. This should include acute URIs, UTIs, minor pediatric illnesses, ENT, and eye problems. Minor extremity injuries should be included if x-ray delay is minimal. Illnesses requiring lab (except strep screen or chemical UA) should be directed to emergency care unless arrangements for priority can be made with the laboratory. No patients with abdominal pain should be triaged to convenience care.
8. *Fees.* The fees for minor medical care should be the same throughout the department. Total visit fees and lab and x-ray fees should be competitive with alternative care facilities. It is important to remember that any professional fee differences will alter the physician provider's medicare (CPT-4) profile.
9. *Mis-triage:* Should a convenience care patient get mis-triaged to emergency care, he or she would not be penalized as the facility and professional fees for minor medical problems are the same in both tracks.
10. *Physician referrals:* The referral back to the private physician as well as the on-call schedules utilized in the emergency department should also be adhered to in convenience care. Patient convenience services (i.e., initial burn dressing changes, suture removal, weekend wound, or eye checks) need to be studied closely, and depend on patient requests and other available resources in the community.

See Appendix 16-2 for example emergency room care and aftercare forms.

Appendix 16-1
Cases

1 ***Methodist Hospital v Bell,* 362 SW2d 475 (1961)** (given comments by emergency room personnel that patient was "only drunk," absence of physical examination, and patient's death from injuries, the doctor in charge was negligent, as his duty was the care of the emergency room patients).

2 ***Jackson v United States,* 577 F Supp 1377 (ED Mo 1983)** (federal prisoner was stabbed by a fellow prisoner. A physician examined the patient but failed to make the diagnosis of a lacerated intercostal artery. The patient bled profusely and went into cardiac arrest and died four hours after the stabbing. The malpractice action that the legal guardian brought alleged that the patient was in immediate need of blood and surgical intervention to halt the bleeding. This was uncontradicted by expert testimony. The court found that the physician who treated the prisoner failed to exercise the standard of care required by state law and failed to recognize clear symptoms of internal bleeding and to immediately give blood transfusions and perform surgery. The court stated that the guardian was entitled to damages for the death of the patient).

Comment: There was an obvious failure to complete the physical examination, leading to the failure of appropriate treatment.

3 ***Lawrence v Rubio,* 406 NE2d 946 (Ill App Ct 1980)** (patient went to the hospital emergency room after injuring the lower part of his leg. The physician tested the patient's ability to manipulate his foot, palpated the ankle, and ordered x-rays. The physician and chief radiologist interpreted the x-rays as showing no bony abnormalities. The physician diagnosed a severe sprain and treated the patient in his office on four occasions. The patient did not return for more than a year after injury. At that time, the physician diagnosed a rupture of the Achilles tendon. When his leg appeared not to be healing, patient consulted an attorney who arranged an appointment with an orthopedic surgeon. The surgeon confirmed the physician's latter diagnosis and told him the injury was too old to be treated successfully. At trial, it was held that had the orthopedist examined the patient initially, the standard of care would be that he make a diagnosis of tear or rupture of Achilles tendon; however, the treating physician was a general practitioner and was not held to the same standard of care that the orthopedist would have been).

Comment: The general rule is that when a family practitioner holds himself out to treat what is clearly an orthopedic problem, he is held to the same standard of care that the orthopedic surgeon would have been. Unless there are extenuating circumstances in this case that are not recorded, a different result probably would be had in most jurisdictions.

4 ***Salcedo v Diaz,* 647 SW2d 51 (Tex Civ App 1983), *revd,* 659 SW2d 30 (1983)** (patient was brought to the emergency room with chest pains and pain radiating into the arms suggestive of myocardial infarction. An EKG was misread as normal. The patient was sent home only to return later with continuing symptoms and subsequently died. Judgment for negligence stood based on the misreading of electrocardiogram and missed diagnosis with resulting inappropriate treatment).

5 ***Jutzi v County of Los Angeles,* 242 Cal Rptr 74 (Ct App 1987)** (30-year-old lady was taken to the hospital emergency room for treatment of a broken ankle. X-rays of tibia and fibula revealed fractures in the ankle joint. Emergency room physician who did not consider himself qualified to give orthopedic care transferred the patient by ambulance to a county hospital. The emergency room physician at the second hospital, though he was not an orthopedist, and though orthopedists were available, treated the patient, reducing the fracture, applying a full leg cast. The physician had previously treated 50 to 60 similar patients. The patient was sent home in charge of the care of her leg and advised to return to the hospital if there were complications. She was to return for a 24-hour cast check but her mother could not take her to the hospital on that day. On the fourth day at home, the patient slipped and fell. She was in great pain by evening but did not seek medical care until the next day. At the hospital, it was found that the patient's lower leg circulation was impaired and that tissue damage was irreversible. Gangrene developed and 15 days later, below knee amputation was carried out. The patient sued the county for malpractice involving medical services received at the hospital. At the trial, the patient's expert witness testified that the physician should have consulted an orthopedic specialist asserting that the cast was too tight and containing a protruding ridge on the inside. He said the patient's fall was not the cause of the complication. The hospital expert said the fall and failure to immediately return to the hospital for treatment resulted in irreversible damage. They pointed out that the patient's pain increased quickly and dramatically after the fall. The jury brought in a verdict for the county. On appeal, the patient contended that the trial court erred in Health and Safety Code Section requiring additional qualifications of expert medical witnesses regarding emergency medical care. She contended that the physician of service did not constitute emergency medical coverage because it applied only to suits against physicians. The court disagreed. The court also said that since the testimony of the patient's expert witness indicated her injury was such that there was a possibility of serious physical disability, this being supported by the finding that the physician's treatment constituted emergency care. Further, the court said that the patient's transfer to a second hospital did not preclude the finding that the medical services at the second hospital constituted emergency hearing. The court affirmed the lower court's judgment).

6 ***Allen v State,* 535 So 2d 903 (La Ct App 1988)** (woodcutter fell onto a stack of wood, went to emergency room with back pain, pain in buttocks and hips. The resident doctor diagnosed muscle strain and gave him a pre-

scription for muscle relaxant. Pain in left hip persisted and patient was returned to emergency room three days later in septic shock. The doctor noted severe spasm of anterior and posterior thigh muscles. Pain was not relieved by injection of Diazepam (Valium), patient's pain worsened; "shock" state continued and he returned to the emergency room. At that time, presence of gas gangrene was obvious and hip joint disarticulation amputation was carried out as an emergency life saving surgery. The patient filed a suit, alleging the resident should have made diagnosis of gas gangrene more timely, perhaps preventing amputation. Plaintiff's expert pointed out that the muscle spasms following blunt trauma would be prompt (day of injury) and not present three to five days after injury as doctor reported in his examination of patient. The low blood pressure along with spasm anterior and posterior (unusual pattern for muscle spasm) should have alerted doctor to another serious diagnosis, infection being high on that list. Defendant's experts explained blood pressure as low normal for hard working man, and other signs (spasm in thigh) warranted no further investigation and finally that gas gangrene (when present) will be fatal within 48 hours without radical surgery. The trial court held for plaintiff with $250,000 award holding a slow onset of infection in an otherwise healthy man was most probable).

7 ***Wisker v Hart,* 766 P2d 168 (Kan 1988)** (plaintiff was involved in motorcycle accident, went to emergency room where diagnosis of fracture of right ninth rib was made, along with internal visceral contusions. Peritoneal tab showed no internal bleeding. He was discharged from emergency room with strong instruction to be quiet, avoiding work or stress for a week. Patient went home, and five days later changed a truck tire and "wrestled" with a tight wheel nut. He had the onset of abdominal pain, would not lie down, and his wife took him to the emergency room three hours later in shock. At surgery, a 1″ laceration of the liver was seen and repaired with loss of estimated 7,000 cc's blood. Repeated surgeries to stop bleeding failed and patient died. The widow said all physicians should have made diagnosis the day of injury and physicians countered patient died because he failed to follow medical advice. Jury said physicians were 40 per cent liable and patient 60 per cent liable by virtue of his non-compliance. The Kansas Supreme Court held physicians were not liable in that Kansas statutes say that in medical malpractice cases, physician must be more than 50 per cent negligent to be liable).

Comment: The medical errors made were that physicians should have been alert to liver tear with isolated ninth right rib fracture in a patient who has significant abdominal signs (enough to do peritoneal tap) and other tests such as regularly following blood county to assess possible internal bleeding—the patient of this sort is best hospitalized, albeit in a known non-complaint patient.

8 ***Blackman v Rifkin,* 759 P2d 54 (Colo Ct App (1988)), *cert denied* (1989)** (evidence was accepted by jury to effect that patient's brain damage resulted from her intoxication and subsequent aspiration of vomitus leading to anoxia and brain injury. The surgeon was alleged negligent as he sutured

her lacerated head incurred in a fall as a result of intoxication. The plaintiff positioned that the surgeon and emergency room team gave substandard care. Jury held for physician. On appeal, the plaintiff argued that trial court erred in not instructing jury to the effect that her intoxication was not a defense that she was negligently treated. Expert witness for doctor testified that intoxicated people were at greater risk for aspiration as well as brain damage, absent any injury or surgery, that the aspiration may happen so quickly that no one could anticipate and prevent. The appellate court said that the patient was seeking to insulate her own conduct in becoming intoxicated from the jury's consideration as being a possible cause of her brain damage. As to jury instruction, the court said that if the requested instruction had been given, it would be in irreconcilable conflict with the correct view of law).

9 *Distad v Cubin,* 633 P2d 167 (Wyo 1981) (plaintiff decedent entered emergency room complaining of obesity of many years duration. The emergency room doctor, advised of the problem, arranged to see patient the next morning. Patient died during the night of pulmonary edema and heart failure. Court noted that there were state and federal regulations requiring the hospital to render emergency services to all patients, that these regulations were to protect those requiring "truly" emergency services. There was no clear evidence that this patient was in need of emergency care. The court held that these statutory regulations could not be used as a basis for establishing negligence).

10 Nash v Royster, 189 NC 408, 127 SE 356 (1925) (physician-patient relationship must exist before an action of negligence against a physician can stand. Frequently, defining this relationship is difficult. The emergency room doctor did not see the patient prior to his being transferred to another hospital for treatment of a severe burn from which he subsequently died. There was an error in hospital records, later rectified by administrator and another doctor. There was a question whether the emergency room doctor who had signed out for the night and delegate his responsibilities to another doctor who was an OB/GYN specialist, unskilled in the treatment of burns, could be held negligent in having his practice covered by a physician who knew or should have known was not competent to manage all types of emergency room patients, particularly a burn patient. It is generally recognized that the physician-patient relationship exists as a result of mutual acceptance. The patient's acceptance is often assumed under the particular circumstances of the case (as where he sought treatment, for example), the courts typically focusing on the need for acceptance by the physician).

11 *Buck v United States,* 433 F Supp 896 (MD Fla 1977) (emergency room physician and his supervising surgeon were negligent in treating a rattlesnake bite victim. Neither had experience or knowledge of snake bites; neither attempted to recommend consultation (which was the main error) with a physician experienced in the knowledge of snake bite care. As a result, patient's condition deteriorated and significant complications resulted).

12 ***Citizens Hospital Association v Schoulin,*** **48 Ala App 101, 262 So 2d 303 (1972)** (hospital emergency room personnel were negligent when an automobile accident patient, brought to the emergency room after two orderlies placed him on a stretcher, then refused to admit him though he was complaining of severe back pain. Patient went to a second hospital, was x-rayed, a fractured spine was diagnosed and appropriate treatment was instituted).

13 ***McAllister v Weirton Hospital Co,*** **312 SE2d 738 (W Va 1983)** (There was a breakdown in communications between doctors. The misunderstanding began July 23, 1976 when a 15-year-old boy was brought to the hospital with a bullet wound in his right leg. The emergency room doctor said the bullet separated two main arteries supplying the right leg and foot. He administered a tetanus shot and applied pressure bandage. X-rays revealed, in addition to arterial damage, a compound fracture of the leg. The patient was admitted. The local orthopedist was phoned but precisely what was said on the phone was disputed. The emergency room doctor recalled he told the orthopedist the patient had a gunshot wound and compound fracture of the leg. The orthopedist remembered the call but nothing said about a gunshot wound, just a simple fracture. The orthopedist told the emergency room doctor to have the patient ready for surgery at 10 the next morning. A little after midnight, though, the boy was in such pain that his family asked the nurse to call the orthopedist again. The nurse identified the boy with gunshot wound, and the orthopedist told her she must be mistaken because he had no patient with such a wound. After learning the boy in question was indeed the orthopedist's patient, the nurse again phoned the orthopedist at 1 A.M. and advised the orthopedist that he had said he would examine the boy at 10 A.M. the next day. At that time, he did remember the boy and ordered that he be transferred to another hospital with facilities capable of handling such emergency. The emergency room doctor phoned the hospital suggested by the orthopedist and was told the boy could not be accepted. Another hospital admitted the boy at 3:30 A.M. The operating surgeon, for reasons never made clear, did not attempt to restore the vascularization severed by the bullet. Three weeks later, after dry gangrene set in, the leg had to be amputated. A medical expert, a specialist in vascular surgery, testified that even prompt and skilled attention in this case probably would not have saved the leg, that there obviously was a breakdown in communications but the die was cast at the time of injury. The orthopedist and emergency room doctor were acquitted in the claim).

Comment: The facts of this case suggest that the orthopedist was not giving clear and devoted attention to the emergency room doctor's call, or the emergency room doctor and nurse combined were not reciting all the facts. It is not unusual for a busy surgeon awakened in the wee hours of the morning to need to be called a second time or have the call reinforced. The series of calls that this orthopedist received, if he were clear and competent in his thinking (and it is presumed he was to be taking calls) was that he assumed a major responsibility in the sequence of events in the care of this boy. Last chance doctrine would be applicable here too, in that prompt repair of the artery gives much greater chance of salvation of extremity than one delayed many hours.

14 ***Jackson & Jackson v United States,* 577 F Supp 1377 (ED Mo 1983)** (federal prisoner was stabbed by a fellow prisoner. A physician examined the patient but failed to make the diagnosis of a lacerated intercostal artery. The patient bled profusely and went into cardiac arrest and died four hours after the stabbing. The malpractice action that the legal guardian brought alleged that the patient was in immediate need of bleed and surgical intervention to halt the bleeding. This was uncontradicted by expert testimony. The court found that the physician who treated the prisoner failed to exercise the standard of care required by state law and failed to recognize clear symptoms of internal bleeding and to immediately give blood transfusions and perform surgery. The court stated that the guardian was entitled to damages for the death of the patient).

Comment: There was an obvious failure to complete physical examination leading to the failure of appropriate treatment.

15 ***Thomas v Corso,* 265 Md 84, 288 A2d 379 (1972)** (action involving failure of physician on call to personally attend automobile accident victim, causing injury to victim, after being notified of victim's condition on arrival to hospital emergency room, requirement of the physician's physical presence is a matter of common sense and expert evidence was not required).

16 ***Laugharn v Savoie,* 480 So 2d 325 (La Ct App 1985)** (until recently, industrial surgeons on duty in factories have usually been immune to malpractice suits because workers injured on the job required recovery through the workers' compensation court. However, more states are pointing out that such immunity cannot be taken for granted and that negligent behavior of the employee physician can stand personally in respect to the physician. The problem case was that a hospital nurse accidentally jabbed her thumb with a contaminated needle, continued to work for three days and the thumb became very tender. She went to the emergency room where the emergency room physician prepared to operate on the thumb and forced irrigation fluid into the tendon sheath destroying the tendon sheath resulting in gangrene. Hand surgeon performed surgery to "save the thumb" but its function was impaired. Expert testimony was held that the emergency room surgery was meddlesome and not within the standard of care for that type of wound. Although the case was initially denied on the theory of immunity of industrial physician, that was reversed).

Comment: Inferred in this case was the standard rule of care frequently recited as part of the Hippocratic Law, "To the patient, do no harm." To do so is negligent behavior. That is not a strictly applicable rule as many of the major procedures require some harm to be done as they try to affect global improvement.

17 ***Ebarb v Insurance Co of N America* 424 So 2d 1266 (La Ct App 1982)** (68-year-old man died of an acute myocardial infarction (heart

attack). He had been involved in an accident in which his right hand had been severely mangled. Emergency surgery for the hand was carried out. The patient had a history of prior heart disease. The question was whether there was a causal relationship between the hand injury and the heart attack. Citing present medical legal thinking, recognition of stress is a factor of myocardial infarction. The appellate judge affirmed a ruling that there was a direct relationship and that the myocardial infarction in fact was a reasonable consequence of the injured hand).

18 ***Normand v Hartford Fire Insurance Co,*** **538 So 2d 632 (La Ct App 1988)** (court refused to penalize a patient for preferring the opinion of one orthopedist over another. As a result, damages against emergency room physician have trebbled. At issue was whether the patient had contributed to poor outcome by rejecting one orthopedist's opinion that surgery was indicated to repair injury incurred at hand of emergency room doctor. The patient had presented to emergency wound with puncture wound and lacerated extensor tendon, which, finding no functional defect, the emergency room doctor repaired by suturing tendon and splinting forearm-hand. Two days later, patient complained of weakness and pain in wrist, saw an orthopedist who prescribed antibiotics and revised splint. Two weeks later, the wound was healed and wrist had normal range of motion. Three months later, the patient returned with recurrence of pain and weakness attributed to partially ruptured extensor tendons—he prescribed conservative therapy, markedly improving patient condition. Several months later, a second orthopedist recommended tendon graft with comment that disability could "probably" be reduced from 15 per cent to 5 per cent. The patient refused and filed claim against the emergency room physician. The trial court felt that emergency room doctor's care was negligent, but that plaintiff contributed to impairment by refusing surgery. The Louisiana Appellate Court felt that plaintiff's refusal of surgery was reasonable, citing the first orthopedist's opinion that in "terms of benefit versus risk" because the muscles were so scarred and weak." That court pointed out the plaintiff cannot be penalized for not accepting one orthopedist's opinion over another if both were competent. That court further increased the award from $4,000 to $15,000).

19 ***Kuchak v Lancaster General Hospital,*** **547 A2d 372 (Pa Super Ct 1988)** (estate of 15-year-old who died from fat emboli was awarded $121,000 in damages from delay in treatment. The youth had multiple fractures with fat emboli resulting in lungs and brain. The patient was receiving oxygen by ventilator and Valium was ordered for restlessness. At one period, patient became restless with increased heart rate, the ordered Valium being given "too late" according to expert, so that patient involuntarily pulled oxygen tube out and could not be resuscitated. The damages awarded were for delay in treatment only).

20 ***LeBlanc v Northern Colfax County Hospital,*** **672 P2d 667 (NM Ct App 1983)** (patient was injured in a fight on February 15, 1978, being kicked or hit in the stomach. He took Maalox and pain medicine, went to the emergency room of a county hospital. A triage nurse obtained his history, examined him, and called a physician at home. They agreed it was not an emergency case and could wait until regular office hours four hours later. The physician prescribed Talwin and instructed the patient to see a physician in the morning if the pain continued. The patient was not examined by a physician until six days later when he was taken to the office of the physician who prescribed the Talwin. He had him admitted to the hospital immediately; the patient died the next day of bioperitonitis due to traumatic laceration of his liver. In an action against the hospital and physician, the trial court said they were negligent but their negligence was not a contributing factor in the patient's death. The court granted summary judgment for the hospital and physician. Reversing the decision, the appellate court said it was a close case. An expert witness testified that the nurse's failure to recognize potential dangers of the patient's condition fell below the standard of care. He also said there was enough indication of abnormalities that the physician should be warned of the need for further evaluation. The patient could not be faulted for delay in seeking medical attention since the instructions he received did not indicate the seriousness of his condition. The case was remanded to trial court for a new trial. On appeal, the court affirmed, noting that if the evidence presents a "mere gleam, glimmer, spark or the smallest trace or scintilla to support the plaintiff's theory, then the court must submit case to jury. The standard for determining the propriety of the submission of proximate cause to the jury does not encompass the "probability of survival" standard urged by the defense. If, in fact, there was a scintilla evidence of proximate cause to warrant submission to the jury, then the verdict must be sustained).

21 ***Murdock v Thomas,*** **404 So 2d 580 (Ala 1981)** (patient in an automobile accident was taken to emergency room complaining of left rib and abdominal pain. The physician ruled out broken bones, heart concussion, collapsed or contused lungs and rupture of abdominal viscus through use of x-rays. He ruled out rupture spleen by physical examination. Pain medicine was given, family phoned emergency room doctor later with other symptoms that the doctor related to mediation. The patient was returned to the emergency room the next morning and died of hypovolemic shock. Cause of death was ruptured spleen. Jury verdict for plaintiff was affirmed on appeal. The defense of the case was that the patient died of a heart attack and the spleen had been ruptured by emergency resuscitative activities on the rib cage the next morning).

22 ***Harper v Baptist Medical Center, Princeton,*** **341 So 2d 133 (Ala 1976)** (plaintiff was taken by ambulance to hospital emergency room; orthopedist examined patient and diagnosed laceration of popliteal artery at knee. Emergency room treatment was provided by the hospital but hospital would not admit patient because he had no health accident insurance. After remaining in the emergency room for four hours, plaintiff was transferred to another hospital where surgery was carried out. First hospital and orthopedist were not liable to plaintiff based on its refusal to treat injuries; hospital did not owe duty to plaintiff to provide him with medical care since they had not accepted him as a patient before sending him on to another hospital).

Comment: A potential fault was the four hour delay in transfer, placing the ischemic leg at peril as a major part of its blood supply may have been compromised by peroneal artery severance.

23 ***Bennett v Winthrop Community Hospital,*** **21 Mass App 979, 489 NE 2d 1032 (1986)** (expert evidence was not necessary in finding that it was a jury question as to whether or not emergency personnel were negligent, knowing of plaintiff's drugged and drunken state that required restraint in ambulance, in leaving plaintiff unattended, unrestrained. The patient left bed, fell and knocked out teeth and lacerated face).

24 ***Banks v St Mary's Hospital & Medical Center,*** **558 F Supp 1334 (D Colo 1983)** (this was an action against the hospital and physicians arising over the death of the plaintiff's daughter in the emergency room. The hospital could not be held liable for alleged negligence in permitting physicians to practice in the emergency room where they worked under hospital training program, in that the training program was not under control of the hospital but had the effect of being an independent contractor).

25 ***McAllister v Weirton Hospital Co,*** **312 SE2d 738 (W Va),** ***rehg denied*** **(1983)** (patient was brought to the emergency room with gun shot wound to his leg with obvious loss of arterial function and severe pain. The emergency room physician gave preliminary treatment, admitted the patient to the hospital and called the orthopedist on call. Although the patient suffered a compound fracture, when he questioned the orthopedist, it was reported to him the patient had a simple fracture and did not mention gun shot wound. Thus, the orthopedist issued orders for treatment of closed fracture. The patient was scheduled for surgery the next day. The patient complained of severe pain during the night and the family transferred to another hospital at 2:30 A.M. He was operated by another surgeon at 5:30 A.M. Those surgeons did not attempt to re-vascularize the severed arteries. Three weeks later, gangrene required amputation of the leg below the knee. In an action against the first hospital and the orthopedist alleging negligence in the delay by transferring him while the required surgery could be performed and alleged improper treatment of his injuries. Asked the question whether negligence was being addressed, though expert testimony said it was, the first treating emergency room physician being negligent in his assessment of the situation and he being an employee of the hospital brought the hospital into liability. However, there were errors in the instructions to the jury. The court's opinion was that the court found reasonable men could draw different conclusions from the evidence which presented the jury question. The crux of the case heard hinged on the fact that the jury was not presented with the issue of damages making the question of negligence moot).

Comment: Question of proximate cause was not addressed. It is probable in a case of this sort that sufficient trauma at the time of injury that any emergency or definite treatment such as arterial repair is a very real risk of subsequent gangrene and the result as this patient had. In this sort of case, the theory of "lost chance" needs to be addressed. Several of these issues did not appear to be completely researched.

26 ***Delisi v St Luke's Episcopal-Presbyterian Hospital, Inc,* 701 SW 2d 170 (Mo Ct App 1985)** (patient was seen in an emergency facility by a surgeon treating a knife wound. The testimony was that the physician was informed the wound was made with an "old rusty knife." He debrided the wound, washed it out, sutured the wound, dressed it but did not prescribe antibiotics. An infection did develop, was subsequently treated successfully with antibiotics. The testimony was that it was customary to use antibiotics to knife wounds. The physician testified that it was a clean wound and that antibiotic therapy is not always indicated and that there is some risk for routine use of antibiotics. No expert told the court that any specific antibiotic would have prevented the infection.

Comment: The problem of when to prescribe antibiotics in the face of wounds is a common one. It is easy to routinely prescribe antibiotics for every suspicious wound; however, antibiotics are not free from complications themselves. Plus, routine prescription for antibiotics changes the bacteria flora so the appearance of bacteria that are resistant to antibiotics is common. In many centers, wounds of this sort are cleaned and then cultured and then treated appropriately, sutured or not. If there is any question, it is better to leave the wound open or at least sutured loosely so that infections that might develop will drain readily. If the cultures return the pathogen 48 hours or so later when the information is available, calling the patient in at that time is appropriate. The best judgment is frequent dressing changes, daily if there is suspicion of infection, culturing at that time and dealing with the antibiotic situation. This in in the acute clean injury; if it is a dirty wound, a contaminated wound, prophylactic antibiotics are appropriate initially. Which antibiotic is used depends on the experience of the physician.

27 ***McKellip v St Francis Hospital, Inc,* 741 P2d 467 (Okla 1987)** (jury should determine the proximal cause issue in a medical malpractice case involving loss of less than even chance of recovery or survival, the Supreme Court said. On July 12, 1981, a 61-year-old patient was taken to an emergency room operated by the city. Patient was moderately obese with a family history of heart disease though he, himself, did not have a history of heart disease. He complained of pain in his chest. The emergency room diagnosed gastritis. Sometime later, the patient suffered cardiac arrest, returned to the hospital and at 9:30 P.M. was pronounced dead. Two years later, medical malpractice suit was filed with federal court against emergency room physician and hospital. Board-certified emergency room physician testified the treating physician and hospital were negligent in diagnosing gastritis instead of heart attack and in releasing him rather than keeping him for observation for a reasonable period of time. In the expert's opinion, the patient's heart attack was probably well under way when he came in to the emergency room the first time; admitting him to the hospital for observation would not have prevented the heart attack. He also testified

unquestionably that there was a chance he would have been significantly improved had he been kept in the hospital for observation. The trial court granted in favor of the physician and hospital on the grounds they failed to prove elements of claim. Federal appellate court certified two questions of law to the Oklahoma Supreme Court for resolution: (1) In medical malpractice action under Oklahoma law, absent evidence that the patient more likely than not would have survived with proper treatment, if patient established a causation under the law the loss of chance doctrine by presenting the evidence that the alleged negligence lessened the chance for survival, and (2) if the loss of chance doctrine is recognized in Oklahoma, would the deceased's chances have been significantly improved had he been hospitalized. The supreme court said that in a medical malpractice suit, where the claimant shows that a physician's conduct causes substantial reduction in the patient's chance of recovery or survival, regardless of the statistical evidence, the question of proximal cause is for injury. Expert testimony that unquestionably a patient's chance would have been significantly improved had medical malpractice not occurred was sufficient under the loss of chance doctrine to create a jury question, even though the expert cannot qualify the increased chance of survival. It was the task of the jury to determine whether the alleged negligence was the cause of the patient's injury. The court said damages must be limited to only those proximally caused by the breach of duty, the amount of damages that could be recovered in malpractice action under the loss of chance doctrine was the percent of chance loss multiplied by the total amount of damages that would ordinarily be allowed in wrongful death accident).

28 ***Albertstett v Country Mutual Insurance Co,*** **398 NE2d 611 (Ill App Ct 1979)** (9-year-old boy fell, lacerating his left knee while doing chores on his grandfather's farm. He was taken to a health center where the wound was cleansed and sutured. A day later, another physician advised the patient to loosen the bandages and gave him some aspirin. The next evening the patient was taken to the emergency room and was admitted with a diagnosis of cellulitis. The day following, gas gangrene was diagnosed and he was transferred to another hospital. The patient died five days later. In a malpractice action, the court held that there was medical negligence in that the physician did not prescribe tetanus antitoxin in a notorious situation (farm wounds) which carries a high risk for this type of infection, and that timely emergency surgery to drain the area of gas gangrene was not carried out).

29 ***Clanton v Von Haam,*** **340 SE2d 627 (Ga Ct App 1986)** (when a physician tells telephone callers that he will see them in the morning, does the conversation signify a physician-patient relationship? The answer is no. The patient who brought charges had gone to the emergency room with severe back pain and her legs feeling numb. The physician on duty in the emergency room sent her home. The pain increased; she telephoned the hospital and was told the doctor who had seen her had gone home. She remembered a team of two doctors who she had used for a condition that had no relevance to her present back pain. She telephoned their office, got the answering service, let her number and one of the doctors promptly returned her call and listened to her account of her symptoms, then told her she would have to wait until the morning before he could see her. Later in the night, she found the pain unbearable, went to another doctor who admitted her to the hospital. She ultimately had a permanently paralyzed left leg from an acutely extruded intervertebral disc. Trial judge felt no obligation on any grounds that the physician was liable. He was not obliged to see her because he had seen her for another disorder or because he returned her phone call or because he listened to her complaints).

Comment: This is a problem that physicians face frequently. It is important for him/her to make a record of every telephone call on which some comment, some advice was made.

30 ***Bost v Riley,*** **262 SE2d 391 (NC Ct App 1980)** (patient was negligent in his emergency evaluation of a patient involved in a bicycle accident. There was apparently some delay in making a diagnosis of a ruptured spleen but diagnosis was made and emergency splenectomy was carried out. The patient left town on vacation the next day, leaving the care of the patient to a colleague. The patient developed peritonitis and later developed a volvulus requiring emergency surgery and resection of three feet of gangrenous bowel. The patient did not do well and was eventually transferred to another hospital where three additional operations were carried out. The patient eventually died of liver failure induced by sepsis. The suit filed against the first physician alleged that he had left the patient to the care of incompetent personnel and physicians that did not know and understand the case, that no conversation between the operating surgeon and the onset he was referred to was had. Inadequate progress notes were noted throughout the chart so it was difficult for a third party to monitor the care the patient had. However, it was the judgment of the court that improper supervision postoperatively was not the cause of the death from sepsis, that the sepsis itself which was appropriately treated under the circumstances).

Comment: It was a close case. A number of malpractice actions stem from incomplete or inadequate coverage by a physician seeing a patient in the absence of an operating or principal treating physician. Accurate hospital notes, progress notes, in particular, are essential so that anybody following the patient can see what the problem has been, what is going on and what the plan of treatment is. the patient was taken to the emergency room and was admitted with a diagnosis of cellulitis. The day following, gas gangrene was diagnosed and he was transferred to another hospital. The patient died five days later.

In a malpractice action, the court held that there was medical negligence in that the physician did not prescribe tetanus antitoxin in a notorious situation (farm wounds) which carries a high risk for this type of infection, and that timely emergency surgery to drain the area of gas gangrene was not carried out.

31 ***Brown v North Broward Hospital District,* 521 So 2d 143 (Fla Dist Ct App 1988)** (Florida court held that the first treating physician in the emergency room was responsible for the problems that left a child paralyzed. The case started when a 5-year-old boy rolled down the street while lying on a skate board. He slid under a slowly moving car, was pinned in the exhaust pipe for several minutes until his stepfather and driver were able to extricate him. He was taken to the emergency room, physician suspected an intra-abdominal trauma, kept him for observation. After five hours, physician concluded the boy had only minor injuries and authorized his release. When the child awoke at home the next day, he was unable to move his legs. The physician was sued for failure to find a spinal cord injury. The mother insisted she twice told the physician he could not move his legs but received no response. The physician answered he had never been told he was having difficulty; if he had, he would have called a consulting neurologist. He said his observation of the boy was that he was able to move his legs and peripheral nerve function had been normal. Expert witnesses on both sides testified that emergency room personnel were obliged to report any problem the patient had. The boy's paralysis may have first become manifest after the physician had been given a discharge order or while hospital personnel were removing him in and out of the emergency room).

Comment: The case does not record the cause of the paralysis—spinal cord contusion, fracture of spine with spinal cord compression, trauma to the anterior spinal artery, etc., would be suspect. Certainly, a complete physical examination recorded on the record is essential in this type of case, as well as changes in the physical condition during the period of observation and again recorded on the record.

32 ***Rogers v Kasdan,* 612 SW2d 133 (Ky), *revd,* 449 US 39 (1981)** (physician and hospital were negligent in that there was sufficient evidence to support a jury finding that negligence was a substantial factor in causing the patient's death. The patient died of brain damage seven days after suffering injuries in an automobile accident. Her death was allegedly from the result of an untreated water intoxication caused by the intravenous administration of more fluids administered for shock than the body could handle. The hospital was involved with evidence showing procedures were not followed and input-output records for fluid were not accurately kept. Further, emergency room records were not adequately complete and various sets of records showed discrepancies, and there were many illegible and incomplete words. Additionally, there was a probability according to medical experts, that the trauma of the impact at the time of the accident was sufficient to require consultation by a plastic surgeon which was not had. The treating physician additionally admitted that a drug he prescribed was inappropriate for a patient who had injuries. Two expert witnesses stated that the patient's death was caused in part by deficiencies in medical care by physicians in the hospital).

33 ***Henry v Felici,* 758 SW2d 836 (Tex 1988)** (court attributed the child's death to hospital's poor staffing and equipment. The child, injured,

was taken to a local hospital emergency room where diagnosis of skull fracture was made. Suspecting a brain "bleed" the treating pediatrician ordered a CT scan of skull and neurosurgical consultation. Neither was done as CT scanner was broken and neurosurgeon was out of town. The pediatrician checked out to his partner as it was his weekend off. The partner and a neurologist who also had been called felt the child needed immediate surgery and transferred the child by ambulance to a hospital 45 miles away. A nurse who could intubate, if necessary, went along with the child. Those doctors then turned the care of the patient to resident doctor. Two hours later, ambulance equipment suitable for this type of emergency was finally obtained and child transferred where definitive care was rendered but the child died. The family settled for $250,000 with hospital, then sued pediatrician and partner, but lost through supreme court. It was the court's feeling that, although the doctors were negligent, the fault lay with the hospital. "The reason the child was not transferred within a reasonable time was due to the hospital's failure to provide equipment, medication, qualified personnel and an ambulance." They held that the hospital alone should bear the blame).

34 ***Chasco v Providence Memorial Hospital,*** **476 SW2d 385 (Tex Civ App 1972)** (general practitioner was not negligent in failing to recognize symptoms of subdural hematoma in an alcoholic patient, where findings on examination were equally consistent with sleepy state of sobering intoxicated person).

Comment: These cases are often seen in the emergency room, on the street, and in jail. Repeated physical examinations and recording of findings are standard of care. Failure to attend such patients regularly will allow subdural hematoma or other injuries to be missed and patient death to occur when prompt diagnosis is often life-saving. Negligence in the form of lack of diligence in diagnosis or treatment is common in the care of these less than desirable patients.

35 ***Thompson v Sun City Community Hospital,*** **141 Ariz 597, 688 P2d 605 (1984)** (child was brought to the emergency room with injuries to his legs. In the process of transferring him from one hospital to another, the second hospital causing delay in treatment, end result was diminished. The holding was that the child would have a substantially better chance of full recovery had surgery been performed at once said medical experts. Medical evidence for defense revealed an opinion that the child had only 5 to 10 per cent chance of complete recovery as a result of the accident itself. The case was remanded back to a jury to consider evidence of increase in chance or harm on the issue of causation).

36 ***Alfonso v Lund,*** **783 F2d 958 (10th Cir 1986)** (alleged malpractice occurred in December 1978 when a 17-year-old boy was brought to the hospital with index and middle finger on dominant right hand completely severed and the ring finger badly lacerated by a power saw. The surgeon stated that too much time had elapsed to successfully reattach the severed fingers. Although arrangements had been made to transfer him to a hand surgeon by helicopter, the loss of time was such that the surgeon convinced the parents to do the repair of the hand accepting amputation. A few months later, the plaintiff moved to another state. The patient had complaints of pain in the stumps of amputated fingers, restricted motion of his ring finger. He consulted the head of the reimplantation services of the board-certified plastic surgeon and general surgeon. The surgeon told him that the initial treatment had been badly flawed. The surgeon should have referred him to somebody who could reattach fingers if he, himself, was unable to do the job. He also described the techniques that was used to close the stumps and straighten the ringer finger as "improper." That specialist testified the same in deposition. The specialist was not able to answer with reasonable medical probability that reimplantation would have been successful not knowing the condition of the fingers, of the vessels, etc. The lost chance theory was considered. The U.S. District Court of Appeals agreed with the District Court that although a complicated situation, there was no medical negligence based on the lack of "probability" testimony).

37 ***Richter Northwestern Memorial Hospital,*** **532 NE2d 269 (Ill Ct App 1988)** (neurosurgeon was competent to testify concerning the respiratory care of patient. There was testimony that "surgery is among the discipline involved in respiratory care" and decisions regarding respiratory care were among regular duties of a surgeon).

38 ***New Biloxi Hospital, Inc v Frazier,*** **146 So 2d 882 (Miss 1962)** (in an emergency, a patient should not be permitted to leave the hospital until he has been seen, examined and offered reasonable first aid. In undertaking to do so, the hospital and examining orthopedist must exercise due care. The hospital and doctor rendering emergency care is obliged to do that which is immediately and reasonably necessary for preservation of life, limb or health of the patient and that the hospital or doctor must not discharge patient in critical condition without furnishing or procuring suitable care).

39 ***Middlebrook v Imler, Tenny & Kugler, M.D.s, Inc,*** **713 P2d 572 (Okla 1985)** (patient was in an accident, sustaining fracture/dislocation of cervical spine along with multiple injuries. He was treated initially by an orthopedist who put him in traction. A ruptured secum was diagnosed and emergency surgery required taking the patient out of his traction. It was ascertained about that time that the traction was not effective. The patient was not able to stand or walk after the injury but that soon ceased and he was released from the emergency room. A day or so later, he began to feel pain in the right shoulder. It was at that time a fracture/dislocation of the cervical spine was diagnosed and traction started. A neurosurgeon and orthopedic surgeon collaborated in surgical repair in which a strut bone graft operation was carried out. As the patient regained consciousness, he was unable to move his arms or legs and his hands were numb. He was never to regain full use of his limbs. In the lawsuit, it was said no surgery had been called for since his condition was not one of progressive paralysis, that consideration of congenitally narrowed spinal canal was not attended to by the surgeons, and that immediate re-operation to decompress the cervical spine

when the first signs of neurological involvement appeared should have been carried out. The surgeons argued that the dislocated vertebra was an unstable situation, that the surgical crisis producing the quadraplegia was an unpredictable ischemic attack. Res ipsa loquitur was introduced. The final verdict was against the surgeons, but the basic thrust that the case had been equally well managed by closed skeletal traction, halo cast or some fixed skeletal traction technique, along with observing for worsening of neurological signs).

Comment: In cases like this, there are frequent differences of opinion. However, the non-operative approach suggested probably is the consensus over the country at this time. The need for accurate record keeping as to whether there was in fact worsening of the dislocation and if there was in fact any change of the neurological pattern which can be monitored on an hourly basis if necessary and a necessity accurately recorded. It should also be noted that use of skeletal traction, when the patient was transferred from his room to surgery, and used at the time of surgery would be appropriate in further protecting the cervical spine.

40 ***Wisker v Hart,*** **766 P2d 168 (Kan 1988)** (two physicians were absolved of liability. The plaintiff was involved in motorcycle accident, went to emergency room where diagnosis of fracture of right ninth rib was made, along with internal visceral contusions. Peritoneal tab showed no internal bleeding. He was discharged from the emergency room with strong instruction to be quiet, avoid work or stress for a week. Patient went home, five days later changed a truck tire and "wrestled" with a tight wheel nut. He had onset of abdominal pain, would not lie down, and his wife took him to the emergency room three hours later in shock. At surgery, a 1" laceration of the liver was seen and repaired with loss of estimated 7,000 cc's blood. Repeated surgeries to stop bleeding failed and patient died. The widow said all physicians should have made diagnosis the day of injury and physicians countered patient died failing to follow medical advice of the physicians. The jury said that the physicians were 40 per cent liable and the patient 60 per cent liable by virtue of his noncompliance. The Kansas Supreme Court held the physician not liable in that Kansas statutes say that in medical malpractice cases, the physician must be more than 50% negligent to be liable).

Comment: The medical errors made were that the physicians should have been alert to liver tear with isolated ninth right rib fracture in a patient who has significant abdominal signs—enough to do a peritoneal tap and other tests, such as a regularly following blood count to assess possible internal bleeding. A patient of this sort is best hospitalized, albeit in a known non-compliant patient.

41 ***Williams v Hospital Authority of Hall County,*** **119 Ga App 626, 168 SE2d 336 (1969)** (when a hospital maintains first aid facility furnishing emergency care to injured persons, it cannot arbitrarily refuse its facilities to a member of the public in obvious need).

42 ***Hammond v Grissom,* 470 So 2d 1049 (Miss 1985)** (patient was brought to the emergency room with a skull fracture and other injuries. The emergency room was busy; she was checked in but was not afforded definitive treatment for two and one-half hours. A cursory examination by an emergency room physician was such that an opinion as to consulting a neurosurgeon was that there was no hurry, he could finish office hours and then stop by and see her. She was transferred to ICU and died en route. Autopsy showed subdural hematoma bilaterally. There were some errors in the trial proceedings so it was remanded for a jury to hear again, but the basic facts were that there was a negligent delay by the emergency room and a misdiagnosis by the emergency room physician. She had bleeding from her ears. There was an odor of alcohol on her breath. The Supreme Court said she should have been more promptly and more adequately attended).

43 ***Haney v Mizell Memorial Hospital,* 744 F2d 1467, 16 Fed R Evid Serv (Calaghan) 1220 40 Fed R Serv 2d (Calaghan) 338 (11th Cir 1984)** (action against the hospital and emergency room physician also involving the attending orthopedist where the plaintiff claimed negligence in diagnosis and treatment following an automobile accident, resulting in quadriplegia. The verdict for the defendants was sustained where evidence pointed to abuse of alcohol and drugs and defense counsel's statement that the plaintiff was "stoned out of his mind" at the time of the accident, and regardless of medical care given, patient could have encouraged irreversible spinal cord damage either during the wreck itself, while being assisted to the side of the road, or while being transferred to the hospital and to show that because of the plaintiff's intoxication, combativeness and unwillingness to cooperate with the medical personnel, it is nearly impossible to properly diagnose him).

Appendix 16-2
Forms

Form 1
Care of Minor Head Injury

Our Medical Evaluation indicates that you have sustained an injury to the head which is not serious enough to require hospitalization. However, following a head injury, signs may appear that call for further examination.

If any of the following signs should appear, call your doctor or the Emergency Department for advice:

1. Continued nausea or vomiting
2. Severe or increasing headache lasting longer than 24 hours or becoming more intense after 12 hours from injury
3. Drowsiness or difficulty waking up (the patient should be aroused every hour for 12 hours after the injury
4. Bleeding or watery discharge from nose, ears, or throat
5. Fever
6. Unusual behavior:
   a) Inability to sleep
   b) Inability to concentrate
   c) Dizziness, weakness, trouble walking
   d) Seizures, blackouts, loss of bladder control
7. Unequal pupils; your pupils should be the same size; they will be small in bright light, and large in dark light, but they should be equal

Take only aspirin for headache or discomfort. *No Alcohol.* Limit activity for 24 hours after injury.

Form 2
Vomiting and/or Diarrhea

FOR 24 to 48 HOURS:

1. No milk, solids, or juices
2. Give clear fluids only (start with small amounts frequently)
   a. Initially, small sips of water (for infants ½ to 1 oz. every hour)
   b. Then 7-Up, Coca-Cola (stir or shake to remove gas)
   c. Sugar water: One (1) teaspoon of sugar or honey for each 4 ounces of water
   d. Jello or Jello water: Made by adding extra water and NOT allowing the jello to set *The stools will take on the color of the jello given (that is, cherry jello will give a red stool)
   e. Tea with sugar: (1 teaspoon/ 4 oz); only after 24 to 48 hours
   f. Gatorade

AFTER 24 to 48 HOURS:

If the vomiting stops and the stools are less frequent, add ½ strength skim milk (made by mixing equal parts of water and skim milk and bringing to a boil. Allow to cool to room temperature before giving to the baby).

AFTER 48 to 72 HOURS (and the child continues to improve):

1. For infants six weeks old, continue the clear fluids and ½ strength skim milk for another 1 to 2 days before trying the baby back on the formula
2. For children six weeks to two months, you may also add rice cereal
3. For children two months to one year, add rice cereal, bananas, toast
4. Older children may have bananas and toast

If after 4 to 5 days the child's stools are soft-to-formed:

1. Infants up to 3 to 4 months may be tried back on the formula (starting with ½ strength at first)
2. Children older than 3 months may be given yellow vegetables, carrots, and the like
3. Older children may have bananas, apple sauce, rice, tea, toast, and bouillon.

Form 3
Care of Lacerations

1. Keep the wound elevated above the level of the heart when practical; this will help reduce swelling and speed wound healing
2. Keep the wound clean and dry for 48 hours
3. Keep the dressing on for 48 hours if possible, then clean the wound 3 times a day with peroxide: no dressing should be necessary after this time

Some localized swelling, redness, pain, and even drainage may occur after a wound is sutured. Any increase in any of these symptoms suggests the possibility of infection.

Call the doctor:

1. If you have a fever
2. If red streaks appear running from the area of the wound
3. If there is excessive bleeding or swelling of the wound

Return to your private physician, company clinic, or referred physician to have the stitches removed.

If the stitches are in your face or hand, return to your private physician, company clinic, or referred physician within 48 hours to have the wound checked. This is very important.

If the stitches are anywhere else but the face, return to your private physician, company clinic, or referred physician in 7 days to have stitches removed.

Form 4
Care of the Burn Wound

1. Keep the dressing dry to avoid infection
2. If the burn is left exposed, cleanse it gently with cotton balls, soap and water, or as directed by the doctor
3. If your burn is covered with the white cream Silvadene, you should remove the protective dressing and cleanse the wound thoroughly (being especially careful to remove all the old Silvadene Cream) two times per day; then you should re-apply Silvadene Cream and a dry dressing; burns are best cleaned in a shower; even gentle cleansing may hurt, but you must do this to remove all the old medicine
4. Some swelling, redness, pain, and drainage are expected; any increase in any of these, the second day suggests the possibility of infection—it should be reported to your doctor or the Emergency Department; evaluation may be recommended sooner than scheduled
5. Fever over 100 degrees should be reported to a doctor within hours of its appearance
6. Your wound should be inspected by a doctor within 24 hours

Form 5
Treatment of Fever

1. Fever indicates that the body's defenses are fighting infection; in itself, fever is not a bad thing, but it is uncomfortable, and may serve as an important warning of a worsening condition
2. Children tend to run much higher fevers in response to infection than adults; therefore, a temperature of 104 degrees in a child may be comparable to a temperature of 102 in an adult
3. There are two common ways to reduce fever:
   a) Medicine (aspirin or a substitute)
   b) Lukewarm baths

Aspirin

a) An excellent drug for reducing fever, but can be quite dangerous if used unwisely. Follow this chart closely:

	1¼ grain (75 mgm) Baby Aspirin	5 grain (300 mgm) Regular Aspirin
One year & over	1	¼
Two & a half & over	2	½
Five years & over	4	1
Twelve years & over	8	2

If the person is very small for his or her age or if there is any question, give a smaller dose. Aspirin may be given every four hours.

Acetaminophen—Tylenol, Tempra, Liquiprin—may be used as an aspirin substitute.

b) Just as effective as aspirin in decreasing fever or pain, but not as dangerous, and it is available in liquid form. Follow the chart closely:

	Mgm	Drops	Syrup	Tablets
Under 10 lbs	30	.3cc	¼ tsp.	Depends
Under 1 year	60	.6cc	½ tsp.	upon
1-6 years	120		1 tsp.	the
6-12 years	240		2 tsp.	tablet
Older	300–325		2½ tsp.	

c) If aspirin or Tylenol does not reduce the fever below 104 degrees, then one should resort to cooling methods.

1. Place the baby in lukewarm (not cold) water—this usually works quite well; do this 15 to 20 minutes or until the temperature is below 104 degrees
2. DO NOT USE ALCOHOL RUBS—this can be very dangerous

3. Give the child lots of fluids (Kool-Aid, Jello, water, Gatorade, pop, weak tea, etc.) as long as he runs a fever
4. Afterward keep the baby dressed lightly—diaper and T-shirt—he will not freeze or catch cold. He may shiver, but that is only a reaction to the air around him being much cooler than he is

d) If all the above things fail, bring the child to see a doctor

Form 6
Care of Low Back Pain

General Instructions:

1. Bedrest may be prescribed; if it is, you should not leave your bed except to go to the bathroom
2. Do not lift anything (even light items)
3. Heat in any form is helpful—for example, heat lamps, diathermyultrasonic treatments, towels wrung out in hot water, warm baths, or liniments. It is suggested that treatments be performed 3 to 4 times per day and last at least twenty minutes
4. A corset support may be prescribed
5. Medications: Your medicines must be fitted to your particular needs. Do not take any medicine (not even medicine you buy without prescription) without telling your doctor. If medicines are prescribed, carefully follow the instructions on the label.

NOTE: Many weeks may pass before you get complete relief from low back pain. Even then, exercises, firm bed, and good physical conditioning are all required to prevent recurrences. So, please be patient. The results that you obtain will be directly influenced by the amount of effort you exert to help yourself.

Form 7
Emergency Department
Aftercare Instructions to the Patient

NOTE: The examination and treatment you have received in the emergency department have been rendered by the emergency physician on an emergency basis only and are not intended to be a substitute for, or an effort to provide, complete medical care. The emergency physician feels that your problem can be treated adequately on the outpatient basis at the present time. Your family doctor (or follow-up physician named below) will receive a copy of your record and all test reports. It is important that you be checked again and that you report any new or remaining problems at that time. It is impossible to recognize and treat all elements of injury or illness in a single emergency department visit. Meanwhile, follow the instructions below as they pertain to you.

General Instructions

1. You may have been given a prescription for medications in the emergency room. Follow the label instructions.
2. If you had x-rays taken, they have received an emergency reading only. The radiologist will make the final interpretation of your x-rays. If you have any questions concerning his or her reading, you may call your family doctor (or follow-up physician named below).
3. If your problem continues to exist, or worsens, it is recommended that *YOU SEE YOUR FAMILY DOCTOR*. If you do not have a family doctor, you may follow-up with the following staff doctor:

   Dr. ______________________________
   Office Address: ____
   Office Phone: ______________________

You will need to call to arrange an appointment *at his or her office* for follow-up care.

Form 8
Emergency Department
Aftercare Instructions to the Patient

NOTE: The examination and treatment you have received in the emergency department have been rendered by the emergency physician on an emergency basis only and are not intended to be a substitute for, or an effort to provide complete medical care. The emergency physician feels that your problem can be treated adequately on the outpatient basis at the present time. Your family doctor (or follow-up physician named below) will receive a copy of your record and all test reports. It is important that you be checked again and that you report any new or remaining problems at that time. It is impossible to recognize and treat all elements of injury or illness in a single emergency department visit. Meanwhile, follow the instructions below as they pertain to you.

Head Injuries

1. Report to your doctor immediately if anything listed occurs (even within several months):

   a. Persistent vomiting, stiff neck, or fever
   b. Unequal pupils (one pupil small, one large)
   c. Confusion or unusual drowsiness
   d. Convulsions or unconsciousness
   e. Stumbling or other problems with normal use of arms or legs

2. Waken the patient hourly the first night to check for the above signs.
3. Aspirin or Tylenol may be given for headache; however, if the headaches persist, or are not relieved by aspirin or Tylenol, you should be examined again by your family doctor. If you do not have a family doctor, you may follow-up with the following staff doctor:

Dr. ______________________________
Office Address: ______________________________________
Office Phone: _______________________

You will need to call for an appointment *at his or her office* for follow-up care.

4. If you have had x-rays, they have received an emergency reading only. The radiologist will make the final interpretation of your x-rays. If you have any questions concerning his or her reading, you may call your family doctor (or follow-up doctor as named above).

Form 9
Emergency Department
Aftercare Instructions to the Patient

NOTE: The examination and treatment you have received in the emergency department have been rendered by the emergency physician on an emergency basis only and are not intended to be a substitute for, or an effort to provide complete medical care. The emergency physician feels that your problem can be treated adequately on the outpatient basis at the present time. Your family doctor (or follow-up physician named below) will receive a copy of your record and all test reports. It is important that you be checked again and that you report any new or remaining problems at that time. It is impossible to recognize and treat all elements of injury or illness in a single emergency department visit. Meanwhile, follow the instructions below as they pertain to you.

Back and/or Neck Injuries

1. Use heat or cold on the injured area—whichever seems to help the most. Be careful not to burn yourself.
2. Rest as much as possible until you are improved. Rest on a firm mattress—not a soft sofa.
3. Avoid positions and movements that make the pain worse.
4. Relax emotionally—if you are tense, the problem will only be worse.
5. Gentle but firm massage will increase circulation in sore muscles, and so will help to clear the soreness.
6. You may have been given a prescription by the emergency physician for pain and/or muscle relaxant medication. Follow the label instructions.
7. If you had x-rays taken, they have received an emergency reading only. The radiologist will make the final interpretation of your x-rays. If you have any questions concerning his or her reading, you may call your family doctor (or follow-up physician named below).
8. If your discomfort continues over 72 hours, it is recommended that you see your family doctor. If you do not have a family doctor, you may follow-up with the following staff doctor:

Dr. ______________________________
Office Address: ______________________________________
Office Phone: ________________________

You will need to call for an appointment *at his or her office* for follow-up care.

Form 10
How to Get Along with Your Back

Sitting: Use a hard chair and put your spine up against it; try and keep one or both knees higher than your hips. A small stool is helpful here. For short rest periods, a contour chair offers excellent support.

Standing: Try to stand with your lower back flat. When you work standing up, use a footrest to help relieve swayback. Never lean forward without bending your knees. Ladies take note: Shoes with moderate heels strain the back less than those with high heels. Avoid platform shoes.

Sleeping: Sleep on a firm mattress; put a bed board (¾″ plywood) under a soft mattress. Do not sleep on your stomach. If you sleep on your back, put a pillow under your knees. If you sleep on your side, keep your legs bent at the knees and at the hips.

Driving: Get a hard seat for your automobile and sit close enough to the wheel while driving so your legs are not fully extended when you work the pedals.

Lifting: Make sure you lift properly. Bend your knees and use your leg muscles to lift. Avoid sudden movements. Keep the load close to your body, and try not to lift anything heavy higher than your waist.

Working: Don't overwork yourself. If you can, change from one job to another before you feel fatigued. If you work at a desk all day, get up and move around whenever you get the chance.

Exercise: Get regular exercise (walking, swimming, etc.) once your backache is gone. But start slowly to give your muscles a chance to warm up and loosen before attempting anything strenuous.

See Your Doctor: If your back acts up, see your doctor; don't wait until your condition gets severe.

Form 11
Emergency Department
Aftercare Instructions to the Patient

NOTE: The examination and treatment you have received in the emergency department have been rendered by the emergency physician on an emergency basis only and are not intended to be a substitute for, or an effort to provide complete medical care. The emergency physician feels that your problem can be treated adequately on the outpatient basis at the present time. Your family doctor (or follow-up physician named below) will receive a copy of your record and all test reports. It is important that you be checked again and that you report any new or remaining problems at that time. It is impossible to recognize and treat all elements of injury or illness in a single emergency department visit. Meanwhile, follow the instructions below as they pertain to you.

Sprains and Severe Bruises

1. Elevate the injured part to lessen swelling and help reduce pain.
2. Ice packs applied during the first 48 to 72 hours will lessen swelling and help relieve discomfort. Apply ice for 20 to 30 minutes three or four times a day.
3. An elastic bandage may have been applied to provide support. Rewrap it if it becomes too tight or too loose.
4. Avoid use of the injured part during the first 48 to 72 hours. After that time, limit the use until there is no more pain.
5. Follow label instructions for any prescription(s) given to you by emergency room physician.
6. If you had x-rays taken, they have received an emergency reading only. The radiologist will make the final interpretation of your x-rays. If you have any questions concerning his or her reading, you may call your family doctor (or follow-up physician named below).
7. If your problem continues for over 72 hours, it is recommended that *YOU SEE YOUR FAMILY DOCTOR.* If you do not have a family doctor, you may follow-up with the following staff doctor:

Dr. ______________________________
Office Address: ______________________________
Office Phone: ______________________________

You will need to call to arrange an appointment *at his or her office* for follow-up care.

Form 12
Emergency Department
Aftercare Instructions to the Patient

NOTE: The examination and treatment you have received in the emergency department have been rendered by the emergency physician on an emergency basis only and are not intended to be a substitute for, or an effort to provide complete medical care. The emergency physician feels that your problem can be treated adequately on the outpatient basis at the present time. Your family doctor (or follow-up physician named below) will receive a copy of your record and all test reports. It is important that you be checked again and that you report any new or remaining problems at that time. It is impossible to recognize and treat all elements of injury or illness in a single emergency department visit. Meanwhile, follow the instructions below as they pertain to you.

Wound Care (Lacerations)

1. Keep dressings clean and dry.
2. Elevate wound to help relieve soreness and help speed wound healing.
3. Avoid use of injured part.
4. Change dressings in 36 to 48 hours.
5. Despite the greatest care, any wound can be infected. If your wound becomes red, swollen, shows pus or red streaks, or feels more sore instead of less sore as days pass, report to your doctor immediately.
6. If you have stitches: They are not absorbable and must be removed in _______ days. Go to your family doctor to have your stitches removed. If you do not have a family doctor, you may follow-up with the following staff doctor:

Dr. ______________________________
Office Address: ____
Office Phone: ______________________

You will need to call to arrange an appointment *at his or her office* for follow-up care.

7. If you had x-rays taken, they have received an emergency reading only. The radiologist will make the final interpretation of your x-rays. If you have any questions concerning his or her reading, you may call your family doctor (or follow-up physician named above).

Form 13
Emergency Department
Aftercare Instructions to the Patient

NOTE: The examination and treatment you have received in the emergency department have been rendered by the emergency physician on an emergency basis only and are not intended to be a substitute for, or an effort to provide complete medical care. The emergency physician feels that your problem can be treated adequately on the outpatient basis at the present time. Your family doctor (or follow-up physician named below) will receive a copy of your record and all test reports. It is important that you be checked again and that you report any new or remaining problems at that time. It is impossible to recognize and treat all elements of injury or illness in a single emergency department visit. Meanwhile, follow the instructions below as they pertain to you.

Eye Injuries

1. Various medications may have been used during the examination of your eye(s). And a patch may have been applied. If so, you should leave it on for at least four hours, longer if removal results in increased pain.
2. Pontocaine may have been placed in your eye for immediate relief of pain. DO NOT RUB your eye or you may be additional harm. You will not be given a prescription for this medication because of the complications which occur from prolonged use.
3. Avoid bright lights or sunlight, watching TV, or reading very much while your eyes are healing.
4. Antibiotic eye drops may have been prescribed. If so, you should use them at least every 3 to 4 hours, every hour if a severe eye infection is present. They must be continued for at least three days after all evidence of infection is absent.

Dr. ______________________________
Office Address: ______________________________
Office Phone: ______________________________

You will need to call to arrange an appointment to see an eye specialist *at his or her office* for follow-up care.

Form 14
Emergency Department
Aftercare Instructions to the Patient

NOTE: The examination and treatment you have received in the emergency department have been rendered by the emergency physician on an emergency basis only and are not intended to be a substitute for, or an effort to provide complete medical care. The emergency physician feels that your problem can be treated adequately on the outpatient basis at the present time. Your family doctor (or follow-up physician named below) will receive a copy of your record and all test reports. It is important that you be checked again and that you report any new or remaining problems at that time. It is impossible to recognize and treat all elements of injury or illness in a single emergency department visit. Meanwhile, follow the instructions below as they pertain to you.

Gastric Reflux Instructions

1. Avoid excessive fluids with meals.
2. Avoid carbonated drinks.
3. Remain upright one hour after meals.
4. Avoid gas-producing foods (legumes, beans).
5. Avoid tight-fitting belts and clothes.
6. Use antacids every four hours as needed.
7. Avoid excessive alcohol, cigarettes, aspirin, coffee, and other irritants.
8. If your problem continues to exist or worsens, it is recommended you see your family doctor. If you do not have a family doctor, you may follow-up with the following:

Dr. ________________________________
Office Address: ____
Office Phone: ____________________________

You will need to call to arrange an appointment to see an eye specialist *at his or her office* for follow-up care.

Form 15
Emergency Department
Aftercare Instructions to the Patient

NOTE: The examination and treatment you have received in the emergency department have been rendered by the emergency physician on an emergency basis only and are not intended to be a substitute for, or an effort to provide complete medical care. The emergency physician feels that your problem can be treated adequately on the outpatient basis at the present time. Your family doctor (or follow-up physician named below) will receive a copy of your record and all test reports. It is important that you be checked again and that you report any new or remaining problems at that time. It is impossible to recognize and treat all elements of injury or illness in a single emergency department visit. Meanwhile, follow the instructions below as they pertain to you.

Blood Pressure Check

During your emergency department evaluation, your blood pressure reading was noted to be higher than average. This does not mean that you have high blood pressure (also known as hypertension), which is blood pressure that is persistently elevated over normal. Several measurements may be necessary to evaluate your blood pressure and decide what treatment, if any, is appropriate for you. A normal blood pressure in an adult is generally considered to be 140/90 or below, although blood pressure gradually rises as we grow older and a somewhat higher reading may be acceptable in older people. The examination and treatment you received in the emergency department was on an emergency basis only and is not intended to be a substitute for or an effort to provide complete medical care. You should follow-up with your physician for further evaluation. If you do not have a physician, you may follow up with:

Dr. ______________________________
Office Address: ______________________________
Office Phone: ______________________________

You may bring this form to the emergency department for one re-check of your blood pressure between 7 A.M. and 10 A.M. from Monday through Friday.

Today's Date__________ BP______________________________
Re-check Date__________ BP______________________________

Form 16
Emergency Department
Aftercare Instructions to the Patient

IMPORTANT: We have examined and treated you today on an emergency basis only. This is not a substitute for, or an effort to provide, complete medical care. In most cases, you must let your doctor check you again. Tell your doctor about any new or lasting problems. It is impossible to recognize and treat all injuries or illnesses in a single emergency department visit. If you had special tests such as EKG's or x-rays, we will review them again within 24 hours. We will call you if there are any new suggestions. After leaving, you should FOLLOW THE INSTRUCTIONS BELOW.

Right shoulder contusion, soft tissue knee injury, lumbosacral strain with right sciatica

Contusions (bruises):

Contusions are injury to a body part caused by a blunt object. The force of the injury breaks some of the tiny blood vessels in and under the skin. Leaking blood from these broken vessels causes the swelling and the blue color. As the bruise heals, the swelling will go away. The bruise will change as the blood is washed away from the inside. Its color will change from blue to yellow-green and later to a faint brown. It should disappear completely in about three weeks.

Ice packs are helpful to keep the swelling down in the first two days after a contusion injury. After that, it should get steadily better. If it worsens at any time, if you have new symptoms, or if you still have pain in a week, CALL YOUR DOCTOR.

Muscle strain:

If you overstretch a muscle, or work it too hard, you will strain it. Muscles are made up of thousands of tiny fibers. When you strain a muscle, a few of these fibers break. Your muscle will feel better when these damaged fibers heal. That will happen during the next week or two.

In the first 48 hours after injury, use an ice pack to the strained area for 20 minutes four times daily to fight the swelling. Rest is important as well, especially during the first few days. After that, gently stretch the muscles. That will help them start working normally again. Do not use the muscle so much that it hurts. Avoid full strength use of the muscle until pain-free.

After the first 48 hours, you may begin to use heat to the injured area. Try applying a warm, moist towel or washcloth to the affected area for 20 minutes three times daily. Use extreme caution with a heating pad; it can cause severe burns.

Hydrocodone and acetaminophen (Vicodin 5 mg):

This is a strong narcotic pain medicine. We give it for severe pain. Its main side effects are sleepiness, and less often, stomach upset. DO NOT DRIVE

OR OPERATE MACHINERY while taking it. Other side effects are rare. CALL YOUR PHYSICIAN RIGHT AWAY if you have any new or severe symptoms.

Take Vicodin in the following dose: 1 tablet every four hours as needed for pain.

Some: 1 by mouth four times daily.

AS ALWAYS, YOU ARE THE MOST IMPORTANT FACTOR IN YOUR RECOVERY. Please follow the instructions above carefully. Take your medicines as prescribed. Most important, see a doctor again as discussed. If you have problems that we have not discussed, CALL OR VISIT YOUR DOCTOR RIGHT AWAY. If you cannot reach your doctor, contact the Emergency Department.

I understand the instructions above, and discussed in the Emergency Department.

____

Patient or responsible person

____

M.D. or R.N.

Cigarette smoking:

This is surely your greatest health problem! The facts are clear that cigarette smoking will shorten your life. It will cause a great deal of illness along the way. If you need help quitting, talk to your regular doctor.

Seat belts:

There is no doubt that seat belts save lives. Every day in the emergency department we see how people without seat belts are more severely hurt. We always buckle up! Please do the same!

Form 17
Fever—Children's Therapy

Facts about fever:

It is common for children to run fever even with minor illnesses such as colds and other viral infections. Fever tells you that your child is sick but not how sick he or she is. The way the child acts—fussiness, loss of appetite, drowsiness, or not wanting to play—are better signs of how sick he or she is. If the child appears unusually ill, or if you cannot lower the temperature, or if fever persists, consult your physician promptly.

Therapy:

Fluids—give fluids frequently to replace the increased water loss caused by the fever and make the child more comfortable.

Clothing—dress the child lightly. Using heavy clothing or blankets will prevent heat loss and temperature may go higher.

Use of medications for fever—using acetaminophen (Tylenol or other acetaminophen products) for fever does not cure the cause of the fever but may make the child more comfortable. Remember to return the medication bottle after each use to a safe place out of the child's reach.

Doses of Tylenol (doses of other acetaminophen products should follow package recommendations):

Age	0-3 mos.	4-11 mos.	12-23 mos.	2-3 yrs.	4-5 yrs.	6-8 yrs.	9-10 yrs.,
Drops	0.4 ml	0.8 ml	1.2 ml	1.6 ml	2.4 ml	No	No
Elixir	No	½ tsp.	¾ tsp.	1 tsp.	1½ tsp	2 tsp	2½ tsp
Chewable Tabs	No	No	1½	2	3	4	5

Tylenol may be repeated in 4 to 6 hours, but do not exceed five doses in 24 hours.

Sponging for fever—if you are unable to control the fever with the above measures, you may sponge the child with lukewarm (neither hot nor cold) water. Do not use alcohol. Do not sponge for longer than 20 minutes at a time or more frequently than every two hours.

Doctor: ______________________________

Office: ____

Office Phone: ________________________

Form 18
Acknowledgment of Patient Instructions

I acknowledge that I have been informed and understand that I have this date received emergency medical care and not necessarily definite diagnosis or treatment, and I have been instructed to contact a physician as soon as possible for continued medical diagnosis and care if indicated. I also acknowledge receipt of the below listed instructions. I understand that any x-ray reports or laboratory tests, if taken, are available to my doctor.

______________________________	______________	__________
Signature of patient or representative	Witness	Date

All x-rays taken in the emergency department are reviewed by a radiologist within 24 to 48 hours. You will be notified by telephone if the radiologist's report has additional findings from the emergency physician's report.

HEAD INJURY:

1. Allow patient to sleep as he normally does; however, awaken him every _______ hour(s) and make sure he knows his name, the date, where he is, etc.
2. Observe for persistent nausea and/or vomiting
3. Observe for weakness or lack of coordination in his arms and/or legs
4. Observe for blurred or double vision
5. Observe for persistent or increasing headache or unusual restlessness
6. Observe for any abnormal drainage from the ears or nose
7. Observe for convulsions or seizures
8. Observe for unequal pupils

If any of these symptoms should occur in the next 24 to 36 hours, please contact your family doctor at once or return to the emergency department.

SUTURES & CUTS:

1. Keep the dressing dry; if it should become wet, have the dressing changed immediately with dry dressing or call your family physician
2. If there is unusual pain, bleeding, swelling, and/or redness of the wound, report to your doctor or return to the emergency department
3. Keep your wound comfortably elevated as much of the time as possible for the next few days
4. Have your sutures removed in _______ days
5. Apply ice as needed

6. Wash with soap and water, apply antibiotic ointment after dressing is removed

Other____

SPRAINS AND FRACTURES:

1. Keep injured part elevated on two pillows while lying down for 24 to 48 hours
2. Apply ice bags intermittently to the injured area for the first 24 hours; use a towel or cloth between the ice bag and skin to prevent frostbite
3. Persistent pain and disability for more than 72 hours are caution signs indicating that you should see a physician for further evaluation
4. If you have an *elastic bandage* on, rewrap it if too tight or too loose
5. If you have *cast,* keep it perfectly dry at all times; *allow cast to harden 48 hours before putting pressure or weight on any part of it*
6. Wiggle toes or fingers to help prevent swelling in the cast; do this as often as possible
7. If the part swells anyway or gets cold, blue, numb or if pain increases markedly, have it checked promptly
8. Remove ace/splints: _____ when comfortable without it; _____ days; _____ only when your follow-up doctor instructs you
9. Stop using crutches: _____ when able to walk without pain; _____ days; _____ when follow-up doctor instructs you

FEVER:

1. Do not dress or cover warmly
2. Encourage to drink clear fluids
3. Give a lukewarm bath for fever above 102°F; DO NOT GIVE ALCOHOL BATH
4. Antibiotics do not cure fever
5. Fever medication may need to be taken for at least two more days
6. Do not give aspirin

NAUSEA, VOMITING AND DIARRHEA:

1. After vomiting ceases, start with small sips of clear fluids
2. Take all liquids in small amounts
3. Encourage __________ for babies—give 1 oz every 30 to 60 minutes for the first 12 hours
4. Gradually increase amounts of fluids and soft foods, jello, crackers for adults; cereal, banana baby food for infants; Pedialyte is available for infants—this contains essential vitamins and minerals

MEDICATION:

1. Your medication may impair the mental and/or physical abilities required for the performance of potentially hazardous tasks such as driving a car or operating machinery
2. This medication should not be combined with alcohol, tranquilizers, and other central nervous system depressants

WOUND CHECK ON:____________________

OTHER INSTRUCTIONS: __________________________________

____

We are rendering emergency service only. It is important to follow-up with your personal doctor without fail within ______ days. If your condition worsens, call your personal doctor or return to the emergency department. It is your responsibility to call and arrange for appointment in advance. If you have any questions, call the emergency department at ______.

BACK AND/OR NECK INJURIES:

1. Use heat or cold on the injured area—whichever seems to help the most; you may want to alternate the hot and cold
2. Rest as much as possible until you are improved; rest on a firm mattress—not on a soft sofa
3. Avoid positions and movements that make the pain worse
4. Relax emotionally; if you are tense, the problem will only be worse
5. Gentle but firm massage will increase circulation in sore muscles and that will help soreness
6. Follow label instructions for medications you may have been given for pain or muscle relaxant
7. If your discomfort continues over 72 hours, it is recommended you see a physician; if you do not have a family physician, call or return to the emergency department

GASTROENTERITIS (Acute Vomiting and Diarrhea):

1. Diet:
   a. First 24 hours. Clear liquids only (such as tea, broth, Coke, 7-Up, ginger ale, Jello, apple juice, Kool-Aid, or popsicles
   b. Second day: Continue clear liquids; add skimmed milk and crackers; gradually advance diet as tolerated; do not force patient to eat
2. If vomiting persists, give small amounts of clear liquids or ice chips frequently, beginning about 3 to 4 hours after the last vomiting episode

3. Follow label instructions for medications prescribed
4. Your family doctor should be consulted if the diarrhea persists or becomes bloody, or if dehydration develops, if fever persists over 101 degrees, or if any new symptoms develop; if you have no family doctor, call the emergency department at ______

Additional instructions: ____

____.

Form 19
Aftercare Instruction Sheet

PATIENT NAME: ______________________

Below is a list of follow-up instructions. Please follow carefully those instructions printed next to the blocks marked by an X. This is vital to the improvement of your condition.

FOLLOW-UP INSTRUCTIONS:

Within the next ____ days, check with your family physician or the physician to whom you are being referred for:

____ Examinations and further treatment
____ Re-evaluation and further treatment
____ Results of tests done
____ Suture removal
____ Further Tetanus Immunization

WOUND CARE:

1. Keep dressings clean and dry
2. Elevate the wound area to help relieve soreness, help speed wound healing and reduce swelling
3. Despite the greatest care, any wound can become infected; if your wound becomes reddened, swollen, shows pus or red streaks, or feels more sore instead of less as days go by, you must report to your family physician immediately

DRESSING INSTRUCTIONS:

____ Do not change your dressing. Keep it clean and dry until you see your family physician or the physician to whom you are being referred
____ Change your dressing once every ________
____ 1. Remove dressing carefully
____ 2. Cleanse area with ________
____ 3. Apply ________ to the wound
____ 4. Follow with application of a clean and preferrably sterile dressing or bandage

MEDICATION INSTRUCTIONS:

Any medication has the potential to disagree with you. If you notice any unusual side effects, contact your family physician, the physician to whom you've been referred, or the emergency department immediately.

_____ Take medication as prescribed

_____ Take medications prescribed until conditions improve

_____ Be sure to finish *all* the medication prescribed

_____ Your medication may cause drowsiness; do not drive a motor vehicle or work around any dangerous machinery while taking this medication

SPONGE FOR TEMPERATURE TECHNIQUE:

For a temperature above 102 degrees, place child in tub of luke warm water for 20 minutes. Pour the water over the child. The child may begin to chill, this is a normal response. After 20 minutes, recheck childs temperature. It should be reduced. If not contact your physician.

GENERAL INSTRUCTIONS:

_____ Ice to injured area

_____ Heat to injured area

_____ Ice to the injured area for the first 24 hours than heat thereafter

_____ Elevate injured area

_____ Soak injured area in warm water and detergent

_____ Take aspirin or Tylenol for temperature/pain _____ every four hours as needed

_____ Stay off your feet and in bed until condition improves

_____ Do not return to school or work until __________

_____ Encourage clear fluids

_____ If your ace bandage is too tight remove and rewrap it

CAST AND FRACTURE CARE:

Your cast will not be dry for a period of 48 hours and can easily be broken or damaged. Put the injured area to rest for this period of time. Keep the injured area part elevated above the rest of the body for 24 hours. Keep your cast dry at all times. If you have a walking cast on your leg (i.e., one with a rubber heel on it), it is imperative that you do not put any weight on it for 48 hours or it will break. Return to the hospital immediately if any of the following signs become evident.

1. If your fingers or toes become swollen, numb, blue, or paralyzed
2. If pain does not greatly subside in 12 hrs
3. If pain becomes worse than at the time of casting

HEAD INJURY INSTRUCTIONS:

Observe the patient for 24 hours. Contact your family physician or return to the emergency department immediately if any of the following are observed:

1. Repeated vomiting
2. Confusion, delirium, or disorientation
3. Blurred vision or double vision
4. A difference in pupil size comparing left to right
5. Twitching or convulsions
6. Clear or bloody fluid from the nose or ears
7. Persistent headaches
8. Weakness of face, arm, or leg muscles
9. Difficulty in rousing patient (the patient should be awakened every 2 hours during the first night)

IMPORT NOTICE:

Your x-ray has been interpreted by the Emergency Department physician. Your x-ray will be reread by a radiologist in 24 hours. If his interpretation differs from what you have been told, the attending physician will be notified.

AFTERCARE OBSERVATION:

Return to your family physician or to this emergency department if your condition gets worse or does not improve.

OTHER INSTRUCTIONS: ______________________________________

____

PLEASE NOTE:

Treatment given in the emergency department is offered as emergency first care only. Follow-up treatment by a physician may be important for your safety. You are urged to follow carefully the instructions marked on this sheet.

REFERRED TO:
Physician ______________________________

Treated By:
Physician ______________________________

Treated On:
Date ________________________

I have read and acknowledge receipt of the above printed instructions.

Form 20
Aftercare Instruction Sheet

PATIENT NAME:__________________________________

Below is a list of follow up instructions. Please follow carefully those instructions printed next to the blocks marked by an X. This is vital to the improvement of your condition.

FOLLOW-UP INSTRUCTIONS:

Within the next _____ days, check with your family physician or the physician to whom you are being referred for:

______ Examinations and further treatment
______ Reevaluation and further treatment
______ Results of tests done
______ Suture removal
______ Further Tetanus Immunization

WOUND CARE:

1. Keep dressings clean and dry
2. Elevate the wound area to help relieve soreness, help speed wound healing and reduce swelling
3. Despite the greatest care, any wound can become infected; if your wound becomes reddened, swollen, shows pus or red streaks, or feels more sore instead of less as days go by, you must report to your family physician immediately

Form 21
Work/School Release

Patient's Name:________________________ Date:________________

Specific Limitations: ____

____

Diagnosis: ____

____ Return to work/school today

____ Return to work/school ______ (date) or in ______ days

____ Light duty until ______ (date) or in ______ days

Physician Signature:________________________

Referred to:________________________

Form 22
Mini-Mental State Examination (MMSE)

Add points for each correct response.

		Score	Points
Orientation			
1. What is the:	Year	____	1
	Season	____	1
	Date	____	1
	Day	____	1
	Month	____	1
2. Where are we?	State	____	1
	County	____	1
	Town or city	____	1
	Hospital	____	1
	Floor	____	1
Registration			
3. Name three objects, taking one second to say each. Then ask the patient to repeat all three after you have said them. Give one point for each correct answer. Repeat the answers until patient learns all three.		____	3
Attention and calculation			
4. Serial sevens. Give one point for each correct answer. Stop after five answers. Alternate: Spell WORLD backwards.		____	5
Recall			
5. Ask for names of three objects learned in question 3. Give one point for each correct answer.		____	3
Language			
6. Point to a pencil and a watch. Have the patient name them as you point.		____	2
7. Have the patient repeat "No ifs, ands, or buts."		____	1
8. Have the patient follow a three-stage command: "Take a paper in your right hand. Fold the paper in half. Put the paper on the floor."		____	3
9. Have the patient read and obey the following: "CLOSE YOUR EYES." (Write it in large letters.)		____	1

10. Have the patient write a sentence of his or her choice. (The sentence should contain a subject and an object and should make sense. Ignore spelling errors when scoring.)	____	1
11. Have the patient copy the design. (Give one point if all sides and angles are preserved and if the intersecting sides form a quadrangle.)	____	1

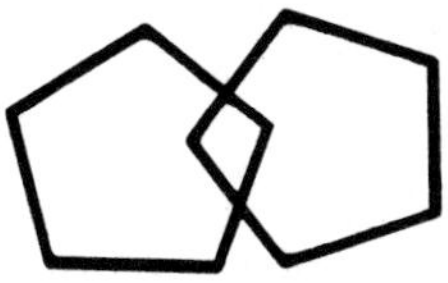

____ = Total 30

In validation studies using a cut-off score of 23 or below, the MMSE has a sensitivity of 87%, a specificity of 82%, a false positive ratio of 39.4%, and a false negative ratio of 4.7%. These ratios refer to the MMSE's capacity to accurately distinguish patients with clinically diagnosed dementia or delirium from patients without these syndromes.

SOURCE: Courtesy of Marshall Folstein, MD. Reprinted with permission. For additional information on administration and scoring refer to the following:

1. Anthony JC, LeResche L, Niaz U, et al: Limits of "Mini-Mental State" as a screening test for dementia and delirium among hospital patients. *Psych Med* 1982; 12:397-408.
2. Folstein MF, Anthony JC, et al: Meaning of cognitive impairment in the elderly. *J Am Geriatr Soc* 1985;33(4):228-235.
3. Folstein MF, Folstein S, McHugh PR: Mini-Mental State: A practical method for grading the cognitive state of patients for the clinician. *J Psych Res* 1975; 12:189-198.
4. Spenser MP, Folstein MF: The Mini-Mental State Examination, in Keller PA, Ritt LG: *Innovations in Clinical Practice: A Source Book* 1985; 4:305-310.

17

Testing

§17.01 Generally

The orthopedist often relies on tests to aid diagnosis. This chapter reviews the principal tests used, their value, and their risks.

X-rays and related tests are standard diagnostic tools, without which sophisticated diagnosis of orthopedic problems, treatment, and follow-up would not be possible. Some of these tests are life-saving, and many are essential to the disability evaluating process.

A great deal appears in current medical literature on quality assurance in testing—its reliability and reproducibility. In x-ray type techniques, reproductibility is well-standardized, with poor techniques being apparent and a red flag to the interpreting physician, who should insist on quality films before making a diagnosis. The physician is responsible for knowing poor techniques and knowing that he or she is basing a diagnosis on suspect results.

The same quality considerations apply to laboratory testing. Those results depend on the skill and integrity of the laboratory technician. The physician must use laboratory results as part of the patient examination, but not make a diagnosis based exclusively on a laboratory finding. When a laboratory finding is inconsistent with a tentative diagnosis, repeating that laboratory test is warranted. Throughout the country, there are reports of laboratory technicians falsifying or "dry labbing" tests—to the detriment of the patient. The doctor can be held liable for misdiagnosis based on poor laboratory work done by facilities he or she has referred to, when the doctor knew, or should have known, of the laboratory's work.

Most laboratories and all x-ray facilities have physician directors responsible for the reporting of results. Delay in furnishing results to the treating physician can impair the patient's treatment, at times risking more injury or death. The physicians involved have a duty to operate their laboratory, x-ray, or other diagnostic facilities carefully in each facet of the facility's purpose.

§17.02 Failure to Diagnose Fracture

A common cause of orthopedic negligence is failure to diagnose a fracture. Often, the physical findings at the fracture site are subtle or nonexistent other than pain complaints. A complete adequate physical examination is needed, in addition to x-rays, including special view x-rays, CT scans, and MRI studies, when indicated. Failure to use diagnostic facilities available to the orthopedist is a common negligent act. Aside from ordering and taking inadequate x-rays, relying on "poor technique" can proximally lead to patient injury. Failure to interpret x-rays correctly has led to a missed fracture diagnosis resulting in increased injury and disability. Often, the hospital radiologist will report a fracture to the attending physician that the emergency room physician had earlier missed. Failure in this communication to the treating doctor is negligent and may lead to further patient injury.

The basic tool of fracture diagnosis is the x-ray, which most often will demonstrate a fracture to the physician skilled in fracture care. The standard of care now is that a physician who undertakes the diagnosis and treatment of fractures is held to the same skill as a board-certified orthopedist. X-rays are usually held to be essential for diagnosis of fractures unless they are otherwise visible, i.e., compound fractures. (*See* Appendix 17-1, Cases 1 and 2.)

§17.03 Diagnostic Studies

In addition to x-ray studies, more recent diagnostic advances include:

1. Magnetic Resonance Imaging (MRI) is the diagnostic imaging study of choice in patients who have lumbar disc herniations with clear signs and symptoms, failing to respond to conservative treatment, claudication, spinal stenosis—including lateral recess stenosis, and "far out syndromes" and tumors
2. Computerized Tomography (CT) is still used by many physicians as the diagnostic imaging modality of choice for the same indications given for MRI; however, CT better defines bone, but more poorly defines soft tissue interfaces
3. Myelography is rapidly being replaced by MRI; indications have been about the same as for MRI, but does not show nerve root sleeves, lateral recesses, and nerve root tunnels; some experts prefer myelography to evaluate spinal stenosis
4. Discography is used by many spine surgeons to diagnose and verify painful symptomatic intervertebral discs by duplicating the patient's pain; it is becoming more popular with spine surgeons, particularly

those using spinal fusion for degenerative disc disease that remains impairing in spite of good conservative treatment and without other pain explanation

5. Discogram-CT may be useful in identifying the cause of low back pain in some patients, particularly those with radiculopathy and negative MRI
6. Bone scans are most useful in patients who have a known primary tumor with suspected osseous metastases (MRI is more sensitive than bone scan in evaluating infections)
7. Thermography remains highly controversial; it does not identify verifiable pathologic anatomy except as reflected by changes in autonomic (sympathetic or parasympathetic) enervated areas

§17.04 High Tech Testing

In the interest of providing a clearer understanding of back and other pain pathologies for the physician and patient, as well as presenting objective (and often pictorial) evidence of pathology, new sophisticated computerized devices have recently been developed. These devices, as well as video recordings and other animated displays, have changed the courtroom to reflect these high technology advances.

In the case of low back pathology, the ability to measure specific muscle weaknesses, areas of soft tissue contracture, endurance, and reproducibility, and to record via computer techniques on screen/paper print-out, is a big step forward in diagnosis and treatment.

In the use of the newer computerized diagnostic devices, the user (physician/attorney/trier of fact) must be able to document that: (1) the high tech equipment is scientifically accepted, (2) the operator of equipment was qualified, (3) the equipment was in proper working order and currently standardized, and (4) the test was properly administered.

Using the computerized diagnostic equipment, the measuring process works as follows: the patient is placed in a restraint system that limits movement of the lumbar spine and performs a series of standardized tests against varying loads and at various speeds at various angles (ranges) of spine motion. This information is summarized on a computer-generated report, and individual results are compared to a data bank of thousands of patients in comparable populations.

Because the machine produces objective, qualifying measurements, test results are less dependent on subjective interpretations of medical experts than evidence taken from other types of equipment. The measurements recorded are large enough to make it almost impossible for the patient to fake the results of an evaluation. Typical accepted testing equipment includes Cybex and Lido devices.

A typical case involved a 32-year-old railroad man claiming total and permanent disability from back injury. Experts testified that plaintiff's economic loss amounted to $600,000, with wage loss to time of trial of $75,000.

The defense counsel had reason to believe that the patient was exaggerating his symptoms, but testing by medical experts was inconclusive. When the patient was tested on computerized isokinetic diagnostic equipment, the interpretation by the evaluator and independent expert revealed signs of symptom exaggeration. The evidence was admitted, defeating a motion to deny, and resulted in only a $21,500 award.

Once the computerized information is admitted, even objective evidence is subject to the vagaries of expert analysis and interpretation, with trial battles hinging on the credibility of the experts. The jury's decision is often made on objective evidence subjectively analyzed.

These credibility problems have been seen in other "objective testing results," as in cases using thermography. Courts have established a set of criteria for a "medically necessary test" which include, at a minimum:

1. The test be widely accepted by the practicing peer group
2. The test be based on scientific criteria accepted by the majority of that peer group
3. The test is not of an experimental or investigational nature[1]

§17.05 X-Rays

X-rays are invaluable studies in the practice of orthopedics, as well as other medical disciplines. Their value is in diagnosis, treatment, and follow-up of orthopedic problems. There are several important guidelines that should be followed to maximize yield and minimize radiation risk:

1. At least two perpendicular views should be obtained in spine and extremity problems, as fractures or other lesions may be obscure in one plane
2. Proper patient positioning, following protocol in standard reference books, should be followed to maximize demonstration of lesions
3. If standard views raise diagnostic suspicions, but are not definitive, multiple additional views and comparative x-rays of opposite extremities are necessary to avoid missing a diagnosis
4. In fracture or suspect fractures, x-rays should be repeated in 7 to 14 days as follow-up of fracture healing, or verifying fracture, is not obvious on first film or to better evaluate suspect infection
5. Analgesia may be required to permit proper positioning or permit performance of stress testing; great care must be taken to avoid injury to a patient who may fall or otherwise be injured in the x-ray department (*See* Appendix 17-1, Case 3.)

---

[1] Beam, *High-Tech Evidence in Back Injury Cases,* Case and Comment, Nov-Dec 1989, at 29; Ash, *The Misuse of Thermography in the Courtroom,* Insurance Counsel Journal Oct 1986, at 601.

6. Treat the patient, not the x-rays; it is more prudent to treat the suspect pathology pending further studies or consultation than to rely only on conventional x-rays

Recent advances of CT scanning and MRI studies provide detail of bone, articular cartilage, tendons, vessels, and nerves, giving a more global feel for the degree of injury.

In suspected reflex sympathetic dystrophy, isotope bone scans are quite helpful. Commonly, x-rays may show patchy osteoporosis (Sudek's atrophy), particularly if the dystrophic process has been going on for several weeks. Radioisotopes show an increased flow during the radionucleotide angiogram phase of the bone scan, and may show early activity; however, the most sensitive indicator of reflex sympathetic dystrophy is increased tracer in the delayed image.

Post-traumatic changes on a bone scan usually involve focal areas of increased uptake, whereas changes related to reflex sympathetic dystrophy often involve diffuse uptake in all the bones of the hand and wrist. Thermography is useful in demonstrating reflex sympathetic dystrophy, comparing one side to the opposite side.[2]

§17.06 Errors in X-Ray Interpretation

The radiologist is a key person in interpreting the x-rays, myelograms, arthrograms, CT scans, and MRI studies, and may have expertise in discography and ultrasound studies. Ordinarily, a physician trained in thermographic studies is responsible for interpreting thermograms. The orthopedist, by tradition and training, also reads his or her own x-rays. In recent years, orthopedic training has included interpretation of CT scans, MRI studies, and the newer studies that have been developed. This leaves a large segment of older orthopedists untrained in the high techniques and tests unless they have sought additional training.

Radiologists have a duty to timely inform the treating physician, either by written or oral report, of findings in these studies. A number of lawsuits have centered around injuries that have occurred because of a breakdown of communication. Failure to report completely, and occasionally failure to forward reports or x-rays when requested by patient, physician, attorney, or court, has also resulted in litigation.

Error in interpretation or failure to find significant pathology that results in further injury to the patient is another avenue of tort action against the radiologist, orthopedist, or hospital if the physician is an employee rather than an independent contractor.

Hospitals that offer x-ray services to their physicians have a duty to place a radiologist in charge of the x-ray department to assure adequate and safe performance of radiologic procedures, as well as to interpret them and

[2] Symposium on Diagnostic Radiology, 64 May Clinic Proc 962 (1989).

report in a timely manner. X-ray technical personnel have a duty to perform their functions safely and to prevent injury to the patient. The responsible physician has a duty to inform his or her patient of radiation hazards. (*See* Appendix 17-1, Cases 3 to 20.)

Thirty million x-rays are taken yearly in the United States. It is prudent to limit x-rays to actual need and to take views most likely to be diagnostic. A review of tort literature does not show litigation claiming damage from routine x-rays, although claims have been filed for possible damage to an unborn fetus when the mother was negligently given spine x-rays and another when a multiply x-rayed scoliosis patient was sterile as an adult.[3]

§17.07 Radiation Risks to Physicians

Several studies have shown that orthopedic surgeons and their assistants receive substantial radiation while doing orthopedic operations that require guidance by fluoroscopy or C-arm, image-intensification x-ray equipment. The day of the surgeon holding a fractured arm under a fluoroscope to set a fracture is past, but similar techniques using image intensifiers are commonly used by the surgeon or an aide. Substantial and cumulative radiation sets on the surgeon. The surgeon runs the risk of complications of excessive prolonged radiation if he or she acts carelessly. The same may be true of assistants. The surgeon certainly is responsible for personal safety, but owes a duty to those nearby as he or she knowingly allows their exposure.

Many operating rooms have a radiation protocol that requires use of lead aprons and gloves, that insist on techniques that distant all personnel from the radiation source (x-radiation absorption decreases by the square root of distance from source, thus distance is protective), and require the wearing of x-ray exposure badges or meters.[4]

§17.08 Hazards of Ionizing Radiation

Patients and medical personnel are exposed to ionizing radiation frequently during daily medical practice. Physiological changes in man considered harmful are characterized by observable signs or symptoms. These symptoms are the same in all respects whether caused by radiation or some other agent.

Ionizing radiation damages cells, usually in nonspecific ways. Exposure to other physical or chemical substances will cause the same effects, because the body will respond in the same way to certain cell damage.

---

[3] Post & Sledge, *Orthopedic Surgery,* 261 JAMA 2869 (1989); *Symposium on Diagnostic Radiology,* 64 Mayo Clinic Proc 962 (1989).

[4] Levin, *Radiation Exposure to the Surgeon During Closed Interlocking Intramedullary Nailing,* 69A JBJ Surg 761 (1987).

The process of ionization and its ability to cause cell damage warrants understanding and application of the knowledge by physicians who diagnose, treat, and operate using radiating agents.

Ionizing radiation is that form of radiation which can potentially disrupt biological function by removing electrons from neutral atoms and molecules as it enters or passes through the body. As ionizing radiation passes into or through tissues, it transfers energy by the ionizing process. The intensity of radiation to which a body is subjected is referred to as the radiation field. The term "dose" usually expresses a measure of radiation that a body absorbs when exposed to a radiation field.

§17.09 Types of Radiation

Radiation is a means of propagating energy and ionizing radiation can transfer its energy two ways—either as electromagnetic waves, or as energetic atomic particles. The two electromagnetic forms of ionizing radiation are gamma rays and x-rays.

Gamma rays are pure energy, possessing no mass. They are emitted from the nucleus of an atom during the disintegration of an element. Gamma radiation is one of the most penetrating types of radiation emitted from radioactive substances. Because of its penetrating capability, gamma radiation emitted from a given radionucleotide presents a potentially serious external exposure problem.

In terms of physical characteristics, energy levels, and penetrating capability, x-radiation is basically the same type of radiation as gamma radiation, although x-rays are often produced by a machine and are emitted from the atom's electron shell rather than its nucleus.

Ionizing radiation can be particulate. Three of the more significant particles are formed during radioactive decay of elements. Alpha particles are positive charged electrons and beta particles are negative charged electrons and interact electrically within the body.

§17.10 Acute Radiation Exposure

One of the factors affecting radiation injury is dose rate, or the time span over which a certain exposure is received. Since the body will recover somewhat between successive exposures to radiation, an acute (rapid) exposure will have more drastic effects than the same total dose spread over a longer time frame. While the exact effects of an acute radiation exposure cannot be accurately predicted, some factors are known.

1. *The specific amount of radiation absorbed:* The larger the amount of radiation absorbed by living tissues, the greater the biological damage.
2. *The depth of penetration:* Some types of radiation, such as x-rays and gamma radiation, have great penetrating ability and can thus affect certain vital organs. Other types of radiation may cause only surface damage or no damage.

3. *Area of application:* As in thermal burns, the area of exposure is important. An exposure of several thousand rads to a given location is often used in radiation therapy. The same exposure to the whole body would be fatal. In a radiation accident, personnel are often partially shielded from direct radiation, and this may radically affect the outcome of exposure.
4. *The age of the person:* Young people seem to be more radiosensitive than the mature, perhaps because the cellular activity is greater. For this reason, the United States Nuclear Regulatory Commission will not permit any person under 18 years old to be occupationally exposed to ionizing radiation.
5. *Sex:* Male reproductive organs are more sensitive to radiation than female tissues. In part, this is because the testicles of the male are located externally, and are more subject to radiation exposure.
6. *Nutritional and general health status:* A healthy, well-nourished individual can generally withstand a greater radiation exposure than a sickly, mal-nourished person.

§17.11 Acute Radiation Sickness

There are four categories of radiation sickness. No obvious disease can be attributed to acute exposure of 100 rem or less. A small percentage of persons may become nauseated and minor blood laboratory changes may be noted.

As the 100 rem level is exceeded, the hematopoietic category is entered, where people show clear evidence of radiation sickness. In doses between 100 and 1,000 rem, the most significant damage is to bone marrow/blood forming organs. About 80 per cent of persons acutely exposed to 1,000 rem will die. White blood counts fall progressively with opportunistic infections, frequently causing death.

In exposures from 1,000 to 5,000 rem, the hematopoietic changes occur as well as serious damage to the gastrointestinal tract, with ultimate necrosis and slough of intestinal lining. Death is usual in one to two weeks.

In exposures of over 5,000 rem, the above changes start but central nervous system changes, with seizures and death, usually occur in 24 to 48 hours.

In chronic total or extensive body exposure up to 100 rem, the following may occur: (1) nausea, (2) vomiting with dehydration, (3) fever—probably related to secondary infection due to impaired immunity, (4) malaise, (5) diarrhea, (6) bleeding from mouth and gums, bowels, or under skin when enough radiation has been received to affect blood clotting mechanisms, (7) convulsions and irrational behavior, (8) blood changes with drop in white blood cells, (9) loss of hair, (10) secondary infections, (11) psychological disturbances, and (12) death. (*See* Appendix 17-1, Case 21.)

§17.12 Densitometry

Dual photon absorptiometry is a method of assessing bone mass, of predicting the degree of osteopoenia and the risk of fracture. It is not experimental, but also is not universally accepted as a standard to measure treatment. It also appears useful in predicting stress fractures after certain types of exercise.[5]

§17.13 Dualphoton Absorptiometry Osteoporosis—Femur

Early diagnosis of post-menopausal osteoporosis can be facilitated by use of dualphoton absorptiometry. When used in examination of the proximal femur, prediction of hip fracture is remarkably accurate. Femora at risk for fracture is 45 per cent less in young women and 25 per cent less in age-matched controls. An automated version of dualphoton absorptiometry is practical for this use as an automated procedure and is used in over 1,000 hospitals in America.[6]

§17.14 Computerized Axial Tomography

CT scans have proven invaluable as an adjunct to radiography in orthopedic diagnostic conditions. The image of CT scanning makes three-dimensional studies practical, such as assessing pelvic fractures, joint dislocation, and the extent of bone tumor or osteomyelitis involvement. CT scanning depends on fat to delineate nerves and vessels, and thus may not be as accurate in emaciated persons. These sharp anatomical details obtained with CT scanning is useful in determining the existence of metastasis or infectious lesions. Where bone scanning with radioisotopes is 78 per cent accurate, CT scanning allows definitive diagnosis between infection and tumor.

The musculoskeletal applications of computerized axial tomography (CAT or CT) are numerous. The value of CT scan and diagnosis of neoplasms, trauma, infections, and other lesions has been well demonstrated in the last decade.

It is now possible, using improved software, to have images that are formatted in the coronal and sagittal planes, as well as in three-dimensional reconstruction.

The best results with CT scanning come with using very thin slices (2 mm). Thicker slices (4 to 10 mm) have been used for larger areas of the body, such as the pelvis or torso. Three dimensional images are quite useful in the studying and planning of complex fractures about the pelvis, shoulder, wrist, foot, facial bones, and areas where the anatomy is complex.

---

[5] Haak, presented at the 30th Annual Society of Military Surgeons Meeting, San Anthonio, Texas, *as reported in* 9 Orthopedics Today 1 (1989).

[6] Mazess, 8 Orthop Today 11 (1988).

Digital subtraction is a technique for removing unwanted information from the image used to study vascular structures by use of contrast medium instead of arteriography. Because of problems such as mis-registration, cardiac output variables, and the lack of small vessel details, arterial as well as venous route administration is being used. More recently, techniques have been used with arthrography.

Subtraction techniques require expensive equipment and skilled technical help. A digitized computer system allows real-time visualization of images produced. The advantages of digital subtraction are speed, real-time visualization, permanent disk storage, ease of differentiation of Barium and impregnated cement from contrast material, and intravenous contrast for study of arterial venous structures. The disadvantages are costs and problems with mis-registration in moving areas such as the abdomen, thorax, or close to the heart. There is some discomfort to the procedure; the patient needs to be absolutely immobilized longer than with conventional subtraction as for arthrography.

The use in orthopedics is most apparent in arthrography, particularly in total joint replacements and in preoperative planning of surgeries for neoplasms.

CT scanning can characterize the nature of acute fractures-dislocations in regions difficult to examine by conventional x-rays, such as the skull, spine, and pelvis. CT of the spine is useful in the evaluation of patients who have previously been treated by lumbar or cervical interbody fusion. It allows uncontrovertible evidence of failure of bony union at arthrodesis site, and may define major causes of residual or recurrent symptoms.

In the extremities, CT will define intra-articular extension of fractures, post-traumatic ossecus and cartilaginous fragments within joints, soft tissue injury, and secondary manifestations of trauma. Multiplanar reformation and three-dimensional image reconstruction of axilly-acquired CT data can provide preoperative and postoperative information valuable in surgical postoperative management.

Interbody fusions are difficult to evaluate on routine x-rays, and it is often important, both medically and legally, to know if a previous interbody fusion is solidly fused.

CT discography is a valuable method of identifying the cause of discogenic pain. Patients with positive clinical pain provocation but no pathology seen on CT discography remain problematic. Standard diagnostic procedures are often used to identify protruded discs while intradiscal lesions are ignored even though the latter have been found to correlate with discographic pain reproduction. Most often, the CT discographic scanning will show degenerative changes to some degree. All such degenerative discs, however, do not reproduce the patient's pain pattern.[7]

---

[7] Mooney, *Disc Deterioration in Low Back Syndromes,* 13 Spine 1349 (1988); Weinstein, *The Pain of Discography,* 12 Spine 1344 (1988).

§17.15 Indications for CT Scan

Major indications for CT scan following musculoskeletal trauma include:

1. Trauma to base of skull
2. Maxillofacial injury
3. Evaluate cervical, dorsal, lumbar spine fracture/dislocations
4. Identification of occult pelvic fractures
5. Pre- and post-reduction evaluation of hip dislocation
6. Tibial plateau fractures
7. Evaluate calcaneal fractures
8. Talar and midfoot injuries
9. Injuries to glenohumeral and sternoclavicular joints
10. Determination of extent of hematoma
11. Diagnosis of post-traumatic myositis ossificans.[8]

§17.16 CT in Blunt Soft Tissue Trauma

In blunt soft tissue trauma cases, it may be difficult to assess progress of bleeding or other soft tissue traumas. CT scanning has been so refined that accurate diagnosis of bleeding in muscle, muscle compartment distortion, hemorrhage in areas vulnerable to nerve compression, or evaluation of bleeding in or about viscera, such as splenic rupture, can be noninvasively evaluated and progressively followed.[9] (*See* Appendix 17-1, Case 12.)

§17.17 Imaging of Joint Replacements in Reconstruction Procedures

Imaging of patients with arthroplasty, particularly using metallic implants, can be difficult. The configuration of components, the differentiation between component, bone cement, and bone may require special techniques. CT scanning is frustrated with metal because of the scattered radiation caused by the metal.

Pain is usually the reason that imaging studies in joint replacements are carried out, looking for infection or loosening.

Routine x-rays provide valuable information so far as position of the prosthetic devices and presence or absence of bone cement radiolucencies.

---

[8] Sartoris & Resnick, *Evaluating Musculoskeletal Trauma with Computed Tomography,* Comp in Orthop, May-June 1989, at 74; Wolock, *Clinical Application of Volumetric Three-Dimensional Imaging,* 18 Orthop Rev 787 (1989); Rothman & Glenn, *CT Evaluation of Interbody Fusion,* 193 Clin Orthop Rel Res 47 (1985).

[9] Elmore, *Selective Non-operative Management of Blunt Splenic Trauma in Adults,* 124 Arch Surg 581 (1989).

Subtraction arthrography is a valuable tool in evaluating a painful prosthesis, especially in the hip joint. Other causes of pain, such as bursitis or non-union of the greater trochanter, can also be detected with arthrograms. Diagnostic and therapeutic injection of an anesthetic agent, aspirating for culture or other analysis as part of the arthrographic study, is possible and helpful.

Using x-ray plain films, arthrography, and radioisotope studies, the detection of loosening and/or infection of total hip arthroplasties varies between 94 to 96 per cent accuracy.

Bone scans themselves are less accurate than the combination of the studies. Several studies favor Gallium scans for suspect infection.

Radioactive bone scanning with diphosphonates has been used for evaluation of painful hips. Minor increases of activity can be seen in asymptomatic hips more than a year after implantation. Marked changes of activity compared to adjacent or contralateral sites suggests loosening. In patients with painful hip prostheses, a degree of uptake has not been helpful in differentiating loose aseptic prostheses from infected prostheses. The studies are more accurate in total hip replacements and are most accurate there with the acetabular component.

Small amounts of radioisotope Technetium 99 can be added to the contrast agent at the time of arthrography and may be more sensitive than routine arthrography for the detection of femoral component loosening. Sequential radioactive isotope scanning and use of labeled radioactive leukocytes are additional techniques in trying to decide whether the pain about a hip prosthesis is loosening or infection, with label leukocytes having a greater sensitivity in some studies.

§17.18 Magnetic Resonance Imaging (MRI)

MRI has revolutionized many aspects of radiologic diagnosis. It employs a strong magnetic field to polarize cellular nuclei in an elevated energy state. On release of the electromagnetic field, specific amounts of energy are released by the tissue in which the magnetic field has passed. The variation of energy release can be computed and imaged on a television screen, showing soft tissue planes in fine detail.

Because of the natural contrast between bone and soft tissue or tumor and infected areas, MRI is a natural method for assessing the musculoskeletal system. It has become the procedure of choice in preoperative evaluation of malignant tumors of soft tissue and bone. MRI is the most sensitive test available to demonstrate aseptic necrosis, particularly in the femoral head. MRI has shown high accuracy in diagnosis of shoulder rotator cuff, knee meniscal, and Achilles tendon tears. Contraindications to MRI are pregnancy (although MRI is safer than x-rays), pacemakers, cochlear implants, and claustrophobic patients (the test requires patient to be perfectly still in a tunnel-like chamber for 15 to 20 minutes). MRI has largely replaced myelography and arteriography.

MRI is one of the newer techniques used to study the anatomy of the body. Unlike images in traditional x-rays, or computerized tomography (CT), MRI studies are created by using a static magnetic field, magnetic gradients, and radio frequency pulses. MRI does not require ionizing radiation.

Nuclei with uneven atomic numbers, such as hydrogen, sodium, and potassium, have spin and charges and act like small magnets. Hydrogen is the atom currently used for MRI studies because of its abundance and relatively strong signal. In the body, these nuclei are normally randomly oriented.

When patients are placed in a static magnetic field, the nuclei tend to align themselves parallel to it. Application of radio frequency pulses induce the nuclei to rotate into the transverse plane, that is, 90 degrees to the plane of the magnet. This produces a signal that is detectable. Different information and image features are obtained, depending on the pulse sequence used. More physiological information is obtained with MRI studies than with conventional CT scanning.

The spin-lattice relaxation time (T-1) is the time it takes the nuclei to return to the axis magnetic field. The spin-spin relaxation time is due to nuclear interactions that result in the return of the transverse magnetization to equilibrium. The relaxation times are prolonged in abnormal tissues, which assists in the detection of pathology. Utilizing this information, biochemical materials have been analyzed for years in the laboratory. Only recently have similar applications through the tissues of the body, viewing them as biochemical materials, been utilized as the current MRI techniques.

The information seen on imaging the body is affected by the pulse sequence. Inversion recovery and partial saturation sequences are T-1 weighted. In these sequences, pathological lesions appear darker than normal tissue. Spin-echo sequences, with long repetition and echo times, are T-2 weighted and abnormals have a high signal intensity which appears as white. Images can be obtained in any plane, typically using axial, coronal, or sagittal planes. There are no hazards to the MRI studies such as can occur with ex-irradiation studies.

Images on the normal musculoskeletal anatomy demonstrate high signal white intensity with fat, marrow, and nerve tissue. Muscle is intermediate in density. Cortical bone ligament tendon menisci look black. Articular cartilage appears gray. There is more water in articular cartilage than there is in menisci. Normally, flowing blood does not produce a signal. Therefore, vessels generally appear black.[10] (*See* Appendix 17-1, Cases 8 and 9.)

MRI is superbly suited to the depiction of a wide spectrum of injuries to bone and articular cartilage. MRI has proven capable of depicting abnormalities ranging from clinically innocuous bone bruises to post-traumatic osteonecrosis. Many of the abnormalities that have been detected by MRI have

---

[10] Pykett, *Principles of Nuclear Magnetic Resonance Imaging,* 143 Radiol 157 (1982); Berquist, *Magnetic Resonance Imaging: Application in Musculoskeletal Infection,* 3 Magnetic Resonance Imaging 219 (1985); Modic, *Magnetic Resonance Imaging of Intervertebral Disk Disease,* 103 Radiol 103 (1984); Wimmer, *Bone Tumors: Magnetic Resonance Imaging Versus Compound Tomography,* 155 Radiol 709 (1985).

been radiographically occult and often clinically unsuspected. MRI has become established in assessment of chondral injuries, insufficiency and stress fractures, occult proximal femoral fractures, tibial plateau fractures, and scaphoid (wrist or foot) injuries.

The FDA has classified MRI scanning as a Class II device and issued guidelines for its safe clinical use. The safe levels of exposure are much greater than when first used, with requirement that radiofrequency magnetic field must both produce a core increase of temperature greater than 1° C or heat greater than 38° in the head, or 39° in the trunk or 40° in the trunk. No long-term hazards have been observed, nor are any expected with the MRI scanners in current use.[11]

The Council on Scientific Affairs of the American Medical Association found that MRI is superior to CT scanning for lesions that involve brain or spinal cord white matter, for early hypoxic changes, and for delineating the extent of tumor invasion. It is superior to myelography, particularly at the base of the brain and the upper cervical spinal cord.

Transcranial ultrasonography is a useful non-invasive method to monitor intracranial circulation, to assess arterial flow velocity. Positron emission tomography is experimental, but soon to become clinical as a tool to determine patterns of brain and spinal cord metabolism. As a serendipidity, positron emission clearly demonstrates tumor from radiation necrosis.

Single photon emission computed tomography, along with various radionuclide, helps assess hemodynamics and metabolism. It is particularly useful in monitoring cerebral perfusion after head injury.

§17.19 SPECT

Single Photon Emission Computed Tomography (SPECT) has received increasing attention as radiopharmaceutical that reflects perfusion, metabolism and receptor and cellular function have become widely available. Perfusing SPECT of the brain provides functional information useful for the diagnosis and management of stroke, dementia and epilepsy. SPECT has been applied to myocardial, skeletal, hepatic and tumor scintigraphy, resulting in increase diagnostic accuracy over planar imaging because background activity from the target structure when tomographic techniques are used. SPECT is less expensive and far more accessible than positron emission tomography and will become an increasingly attractive alternative for transferring the positron emission tomography technology to routine clinical use. SPECT has unique applications that are increasingly finding their way into routine practice of clinical nuclear medicine.

MRI studies of the acutely injured spinal cord patient is of great value in assessing soft tissue injury, particularly the status of spinal cord and nerve roots. These are very ill patients, so that a resuscitation team and physician

---

[11] Shellock & Bierman, *The Safety of MRI,* 261 JAMA 3412 (1989).

to supervise movement of unstable spine segment patients are essential. MRI studies of these patients are of great prognostic value in assessing recovery potential, in staging possible spinal surgery. In intervertebral disc protrusion, MRI studies are about 90 per cent accurate, where CT scans are 75 per cent accurate when compared with surgical findings.[12]

§17.20 False Positive MRI Studies

It is well known that 24 to 37 per cent of persons who have never experienced back pain or sciatica have been found to have abnormal myelograms, CT scans or discograms (looking for disc rupture, not pain assessment).

Recent studies have shown that 28 per cent of asymptomatic individuals have significant discal changes or spinal stenosis when assessed with MRI. Abnormal findings are greater in persons over 60 years of age.

The significant incidence of abnormal MRI findings in asymptomatic persons reinforces the dangers of predicting surgical decisions on diagnostic tests without precise correlation with clinical signs and symptoms—even when using state of art imaging modalities.[13]

MRI studies of the acutely injured spinal cord patient is of great value in assessing soft tissue injury, in particular the status of spinal cord and nerve roots. These are very ill patients, so a resuscitation team and physician to supervise movement of unstable spine segment patients are essential. MRI studies of these patients are of great prognostic value in assessing recovery potential, and in staging possible spinal surgery. In intervertebral disc protrusion, MRI studies are about 90 per cent accurate, where CT scanning are 75 per cent accurate when compared with surgical findings.[14]

---

[12] Council on Scientific Affairs, *Magnetic Resonance Imaging of Central Nervous System,* 259 JAMA 1211 (1988); Grolimund, *Evaluation of Cerebrovascular Disease by Combined Extracranial and Transcranial Doppler Sonography,* 18 Stroke 1018 (1987); Doyle, *Differentiation of Cerebral Radiation Necrosis from Tumor Recurrence by (18) FDG and 82RB Positron Emission Tomography,* 11 J Comput Assist Tomogr 563 (1987); Abdel-Davem, *Changes in Brain Perfusion After Acute Head Injury: Comparison of CT with Tc-99HM-PAO SPECT,* 165 Radiol 221 (1987); Stroller, *Magnetic Resonance Imaging of the Spine and Joints,* 18 Orthop Rev 4 (1989).

[13] Boden, *The Incidence of Abnormal Lumbar Spine MRI scans in Asymptomatic Patients: A Prospective and Blinded Investigation,* 82 So Med J 55 (Supp (Abstract) 1989); Miller, *Magnetic Resonance Imaging of the Spine,* 64 Mayo Clinic Proc 986 (1989).

[14] Cotler, *Magnetic Resonance Imaging of Acute Spinal Cord Trauma Preliminary Report,* 2 J Orthop Trauma 1 (1988); Forristall, *Magnetic Resonance Imaging and Contrast CT of Lumbar Spine: Comparison of Diagnostic Methods and Correlation with Surgical Findings,* 31 Spine 1049 (1988); Goldberg, *The Impact of Magnetic Resonance on the Diagnostic Evaluation of Acute Cervico-thoracic Spinal Trauma,* 17 Skeletal Radiol 89 (1988).

§17.21 MRI Findings in TMJ Syndrome

MRI is an established method for demonstrating internal derangement of the temporomandibular joint. It does not demonstrate the static status of the joint in motion. A simulated motion study using serial images with the mouth in varying degrees of opening is beneficial. The sequential opening images are viewed on a monitor using a cine loop computer sequence to simulate the opening and closing phases of the temporomandibular joint. This type of information has the advantage of virtually eliminating the need for invasive techniques (arthrography).[15]

§17.22 MRI versus Arthroscope

Arthroscopic surgery is currently the most accurate diagnostic modality for knee joint pathology, with a 95 per cent accuracy rate. However, it has drawbacks including invasiveness, pain and complications. MRI evaluation of the knee joint in several studies has been shown to be comparable to arthroscopic examination. For many orthopedists, it has become the gold standard for diagnosis of internal derangement of the knee. When combined with clinical and x-ray examination, MRI provides the most accurate noninvasive source of information for pathological findings in the menisci and anterior cruciate ligament.[16]

§17.23 Myelography

Myelography is a test that allows x-ray visualization or photograph (generally both) of the spinal canal after injection in intrathecal space of a radiopaque dye. This procedure allows checking of the entire spinal canal for intra- or extradural lesions. There are complications including post spinal headache which may be very persistent but may be helped by blood patch application over myelographic hole in dura. Twenty cubic centimeters of the patient's blood in place by spinal needle in epidural space at effected area may help. Other complications include trauma to nerve or nerve roots, intrathecally, arachnoiditis, intrathecal bleeding (perhaps the cause of arachnoiditis) infection and dye allergy.

Until recent years, Pantopaque was the standard myelographic dye. It was oil-based and caused a significant number of arachnoiditis complications. Currently, it is rarely used, though arachroiditis complication is rare,

---

[15] Miller & Bell, *Cine MRI of the Tempomandibular Joint: The Oshsner Experience,* 82 So Med J 83 (supp (abstract 1980).

[16] Kelly, *Magnetic Resonance Imaging of the Knee: A New Gold Standard?,* Orthop Rev, Mar 1988, at 328. Glasgow, *Double-Blind Assessment of the Value of Magnetic Resonance Imaging in the Diagnosis of Anterior Cruciate and Meniscal Lesions,* 71A JBJ Surg 113 (1989); DeHaven & Collins, *Diagnosis of Internal Derangement of the Knee. The Role of Arthroscopy,* 57A JBJ Surg 802 (1975); Galimore, Jr & Harms, *Knee Injuries: High Resolution MR Imaging,* 157 Radiol 23 (1985).

perhaps occurring only when intrathecal bleeding occurred as a complication of the needle passed during myelography. Arachnoiditis is usually in lumbar area and is thought to be more intense when the lumbar spinal puncture is bloody.

The adverse reaction to myelographic use of iophendylate has been known to manufacturers, but no adequate warnings have been given to orthopedists, neurologists, neurosurgeons or radiologists who perform myelograms. Total removal of the dye after completion of the myelogram and instilling dexamethasone lessens arachnoiditis complication risk. Use of safer dyes and currently use of non-invasive CAT scans or MRI studies replace need of myelography in most cases.

Metrizamide (Amipaque) is a water based myelographic dye that has lower dye study complications and also fills nerve root sleeves more effectively than Iophendyate, and is the usual myelographic dye used at this time. Its complications are the same as any myelogram, with less arachnoiditis complications but with reports of brain irritability with seizures and comas. (*See* Appendix 17-1, Cases 22 to 26.)

Both Iophendylate and metrizamide are iodine compounds and must be avoided in iodine sensitive patients unless they have been pretreated with corticosteroids and antihistamines. Emergency resuscitation equipment must be at hand in all occasions when myelography is being performed. Myelography is a painful test. All of the above problems with myelography show the value of MRI testing, at least as an initial study, with myelography being used when surgery is contemplated and precise diagnosis is uncertain.

The indication of myelography includes diagnosing tumors, protruded intervertebral discs, infection (abscess), fracture fragment impingement of dura or nerve root, spinal stenosis, nerve tunnel stenosis (not well studied by myelography) and certain vascular deformities. Myelography is carried out in a darkened room and patient is often sedated, so that x-ray department and personnel must be alert to patient injury from falls or positioning where breathing is difficult.

Contraindications to myelography include patients at risk for seizure, severe cardiovascular disease, alcoholism, multiple sclerosis, iodine allergy and patients using Phenothiazine tranquilizer drugs as they lower seizure threshold.

The dye use in intravenous pyelography often gives clues to contraindications for use in myelography when adeverse reactions to iodine-containing dye occur.

§17.24 Discography

Intervertebral disc injection of radio-opaque dye outlines the intervertebral disc. The normal and abnormal conditions are of diagnostic significance; a protruded intervertebral disc can be demonstrated. Easier, less invasive methods, however, (MRI, CT, myelography) are preferred by most orthopedists. Injecting a symptomatic degenerative disc with duplication of the patient's pain complaint is the real current value of the discogram and helps planning definitive treatment of the patient's pain complaint. Discitis, which may be infectious due to break in aseptic technique or hematogenous spread of bacteria or discitis due to chemical reaction, is rare and usually self limiting. Treatment is largely supportive, bed rest, corset, brace, or body cast until healing occurs. Antibiotic treatment initially without a bacterial culture and sensitivity may be inappropriate. Chemically induced discitis is inappropriately treated by "shotgun" antibiotic.

There is rarely any impairment following healing of discitis. If the process does not improve or resolve in a few weeks, needle aspiration of the disc space for culture and sensitivity is indicated. MRI study of the disc area will ascertain if abscess or bone invasion is occurring.

It has been shown by discography as the gelatinous material moves posteriorly in patients with nerve root irritation. Pain on coughing is found in disc rupture, the gelatinous contents of the nucleous pulposus being squeezed out of disc and spreading around nerve root where it causes aseptic inflammation.

Sciatica consists of two elements—syndrome of nerve root irritation (radiculitis) and the syndrome of nerve compression that may eventually require surgery. It is not necessary to do discograms to make this diagnosis, but discogram studies verify this. When coughing causes sciatica, the above also is verified for the most part.[17]

§17.25 Diagnostic Injections

Diagnostic injections as part of diagnostic testing for discogenic pain syndromes are described in this section.

Epidural (Caudal) Block

This is carried out when there is suspect abnormality in the spinal canal as source of pain. That pain ordinarily is irritation of either nerve root or of dural tissues. The techniques is usually instilling hydrocortisone compounds in the epidural space either with a small amount of local anesthetic or, in the case of caudal blocks, with a larger amount of isotonic saline. Ordinarily, large amounts of local anesthetic are not used because of the risk of obtaining spinal anesthetic and its attendant problems.

The rationale for epidural blocks using steroids is to reduce inflammation in the local area. Some physicians believe the mechanical distention of the epidural space will break down adhesions which may participate in the pain causing process. An attempt is made to concentrate the steroids at the area of irritation. The technique is valuable to identify symptomatic discogenic disease, disc protrusions and to treat localized lumbar spinal stenosis.

---

[17] Walk, *Diagnostic Lumbar Disc Puncture: Clinical Review and Analysis of 67 Cases,* 66 Arch Surg 232 (1953); Fraser, *Discitis after Discography,* 69B JBJ Surg 26 (1987); L. Walk, Lumbar Diskography and Its Clinical Evaluation (1962)

Discography

This is used, for the most part, to evaluate the symptom status of degenerative discs. Rarely is it used to identify protruded intervertebral discs, for other techniques are readily available, less expensive and carry lower morbidity. Discography also carries an increased radiation exposure.

Discographic techniques are most useful in problem cases. The technique is carried out by ordinarily using a posterior lateral approach and 8 to 10″ spinal needle under fluoroscopic control to enter the centrum of the suspect intervertebral disc to instill a small amount of radiopaque material. The information derived under fluoroscopy and by permanent x-ray is by obtaining a picture of the intervertebral disc, comparing it with normals.

Degenerative discs have characteristic patterns as do normal disc spaces. If there is an extrusion or an extension of disc material into a protruded area, this diagnosis can also be made with discographic dye. Important information can be had with the patient's unsolicited response to the injection of the dye. If the patient reports exact duplication of the type of back pain and/or scleratomal leg radiation that he is complaining of, this is clear evidence that internally deranged disc participates in his pain pathology.

Discograms at this time are complimentary to MRI studies showing deterioration of disc spaced in assessing whether that deterioration is in fact symptomatic.

Complications include discitis, both sterile and pyogenic, and nerve root injury or vessel/viscus injury due to improperly placed discogram needle.

In cases of suspected joint infection or other pathologies, direct needle puncture and aspiration of joint or bursal cavity may be necessary to obtain organisms for culture. At the same time, placing radio-opaque dye in space will delineate area suspect and form a map for surgery as these bursae may dissect to area remote from joint. Incorrect or unnecessary surgery can be avoided with this information.[18]

§17.26 Arthrography

Arthrography is a technique to visualize changes in the anatomy of inside a joint. Radiopaque dye is instilled into the joint and sometimes additional air is introduced for contrast. Multiple x-rays in various positions to outline the joint are taken. A skilled radiologist is required to interpret the findings. Arthrograms were popular before advent of arthroscopy, but have been virtually replaced by MRI studies. The knee joint, followed by shoulder, hip and ankle are the joints most often studied. There are some risks of infection and chemical synovitis or joint bleeding as complications; it also is a painful test.

In the hip, arthrograms may show incomplete reduction or interposed tissue. In the ankle, they may show ligament disruptions and in the shoulder,

---

[18] Steinbach, *Bursae and Abscess Cavities Communicating with the Hip,* 156 Radiol 303 (1985).

they show rotator cuff tears. MRI studies will do the same thing, but may not be available and arthrograms are less expensive.

Vibration arthrography is a diagnostic study, but basically research at this time. Vibration sensors are attached to strategic areas of the joint (usually knee) and a controlled vibration is passed through joint and recorded on a graph or TV screen. Gross pathologies display typical patterns on the screen, but small defects are missed at times. The advantage is that it is non-painful and non-invasive. The procedure is not ready for general physician use at this time and may remain a research tool.[19]

§17.27 Tenography

Tenography, the injecting of radiopaque dye into tendon sheaths and x-ray imaging of the area, is useful in diagnosing tendon ruptures or scarring about the ankle.[20]

§17.28 Arthroscopy and Bursoscopy

Shoulder arthroscopy is becoming an acceptable means of diagnosis, clinical documentation and in some cases, treatment for pathological states in and about the glenohumeral joints. Because of the variation in soft tissues about the shoulder, a systematic, yet safe (so nerves or vessels will not be injured) plan to place scope portals is necessary. A reproducible operating room routine of patients' placement and extremity movement by assistant is more important than might be in arthroscopic examination of knee or ankle. Special techniques are done to examine and treat the subacromial space (bursoscopy). There are some real risks to shoulder arthroscopy.[21]

§17.29 Arthroscope

The *arthroscope* is an instrument designed to look into and operate within a joint. The knee joint is most commonly investigated, though arthroscopic examinations are now being done on hip, ankle, shoulder and wrist.

Arthroscopy has become a subspecialty in orthopedics. Although not complicated, the technique requires instruction in its uses and requires a remarkably high degree of hand-eye coordination. All surgeons do not have this coordination, making arthroscopy impractical or risky. Insufficient attention to the development of basic arthroscopic skills may result in higher

---

[19] McCoy, *Vibration Arthrography as a Diagnostic Aid in Disease of the Knee,* 69B JBJ Surg 288 (1987).

[20] Gilula, *Ankle Tenography: A Key to Unexplained Symptomology,* 151 Radiol 581 (1984).

[21] Stephen, *A Complete System for Arthroscopy and Bursoscopy of the Shoulder,* Surg Rounds Orthop, July 1989, at 57.

complication rates. Careful preparation is the cornerstone of satisfactory arthroscopic execution by the orthopedic surgeon.

Good diagnostic skills come before good surgical skills. It is important for the orthopedist embarking on arthroscopic diagnosis and treatment to visit with and work with a skilled arthroscopist or attend instructional courses to learn the skill.

In reviewing the pitfalls of arthroscopic examination, improper placement of ports is commonly seen. It is easier to look up with a scope, so port placement should accommodate that. Some arthroscopists say if you cannot do the operation in "your mind" with a spinal needle, you will likely have problems with the more complicated surgical arthroscopic instruments.

The arthroscope is introduced into the sterile (and generally anesthetized) patient, first by making a small skin puncture wound at the appropriate site (called ports). A pointed metal probe ensheathed with a slightly larger tube is gently passed into the joint, the probe is withdrawn and a second device containing an optic system and small tubes for passing irrigating solutions in and out is inserted. A bloodless field is important; a tourniquet is used often. Prior to inserting the trocar device ultimately receiving the optical unit, another probe with tube is inserted and attached to a fluid (saline) inflow reservoir. The joint is distended by gravity flow with reservoir five to eight feet above operative table height.

The optical system is passed into several areas of the joint, using predetermined desirable port, thus virtually all of the interior of the joint can be visualized. Visualization of the joint interiorly can be done by the surgeon using the eye piece, or by attaching the optical system to a video camera so that all in operating room can see the interior and also allowing a permanent record to be made of pathology.

Through additional ports, additional tubes can be inserted through which operating instruments can be passed. Using bimanual technique, the surgeon manipulates the instruments to site of operation, using the optical system as a guide. This maneuvering requires a high degree of hand-eye coordination that all surgeons do not have.

Operative procedures in the knee and parallel procedures in other joints include (1) synovial biopsy, (2) drainage and gavage of joint for infection or removal of arthritic debris, (3) trimming, cutting, partial or complete removal of damaged meniscus, (4) participate in essentially an arthroscopic secondary repair of torn anterior cruciate ligament, (5) lateral patellar expansion release, and (6) severance of impinging synovial bands or adhesions.

There are risks to arthroscopy that the patient should be informed of as part of informed consent. These include (1) infection, (2) intra-articular bleeding, (3) severance of a vessel in cutting that may bleed into outside the joint, (4) breakage of instrument parts that become a foreign body in the joint, requiring removal (the fault of breakage may be defect in instrument or surgeon using instrument too forcefully), (5) cutting too deeply injuring ligament or perforating posterior capsule and damaging vessels or nerves, (6) damage, scuffing, of articular surface potentially leading to cartilaginous degenerative changes, (7) damage to intact meniscus or cruciate ligaments, and (8) herniation of synovia through operating port and/or impingement of sensory nerve leading to painful neuroma. The neuroma problem is avoided by appropriate placement of ports. the use of a tourniquet has inherent risks independent of the arthroscope. A tourniquet for too long or excessive pressure of tourniquet inflation will cause muscle and nerve damage distal to the tourniquet site in susceptible patients. Many times, tourniquet damage is subtle, not gross, but with careful measurement muscle/nerve dysfunction (which may or may not recover) can be demonstrated.

One of the types of arthroscopic instruments is a motorized shaver or cutter that presents additional risk of inadvertent joint perforation injuring tissues, or articular scuffing or debridement that is too deep. Arthroscopic surgery takes great and specialized surgical skill, should not be done by a surgeon unfamiliar and unexperienced with technique.

Contraindications to arthroscopy include (1) skin infections, and (2) acutely injured blood-filled joint as blood will impede examination and forcing irrigating fluid into joint runs risk of extravasating fluid into tissue planes—including increase of compartmental pressures leading to compartment compression syndromes with potential compartmental muscle-nerve damage necessitating fasciotomy surgery.

Arthroscopic examination and surgery represents one of the great advances in orthopedic diagnosis and treatment. The techniques most often are superior to open arthrotomies, or lesser the extent of arthrotomy, thereby lessen morbidity, speeding convalescence. Open arthrotomy has a place, often done by orthopedists not skilled in arthroscopic surgery or for larger knee reconstruction operations. This is an area where the surgeon should know and respect his limitations.[22]

§17.30 Scintigraphy

Scintigraphy or *bone scanning* has a variety of orthopedic uses. When certain radionucleotides are injected in the blood stream, they will concentrate in areas of increased circulation, making diagnosis of inflammatory lesion, tumors, infection and occult fractures possible.

Nuclear medicine techniques, including dual-photons, absorption for the measurements of spinal and hip bone mineral, use of radioisotopes such as Indium-111 labeled leukocytes for detection of musculoskeletal infection and lymphoscintigraphy to map the lymphatic drainage sites from tumors are typical examples.

---

[22] Coutts, *Symposium: The Diagnosis and Treatment of Injuries of Cartilage,* 19 Contemp Orthop 401 (1989); R.D. Altman, *Arthroscopy and Synovial Biopsy,* Primer on the Rheumatic Diseases (H.R. Schumacher 9th ed 1988); K. Hughes, Arthroscopy: Looking Into Your Knee. A Pictorial Review. (1987); Understanding Arthroscopy: Diagnosis and Surgical Treatment of Joint Problems. A Patient Oriented Seminar of Arthroscopic Usage (1987); M.A. Moskowitz & M.E. Osband, The Complete Book of Medical Tests (1984).

Other techniques that provide useful information but are still in the research mode are radiolabeled antibodies for detecting metastatic sites and single photon emission, CT, for accurate location and detection of ossecus abnormalities.

Techniques to measure bone density and mineral content, using single photon absorption, of forearm bones or lumbar spine or femoral neck, evaluate osteopenia. There is controversy in the literature as of this date as to which technique is superior, but there is no controversy to the value of the procedure in assessing bone mineral content, in diagnosis and follow-up for osteoporosis.

Techniques have been recently introduced that allow the labeling of various cellular components of blood with Indium-111 while preserving their structure and their function. There are several methods for labeling leukocytes, all which begin with a Volex-induced electo-sedimentation rate to yield leukocyte rich plasma. Leukocytes can be further separated by centrifuge to obtain a purer granulocyte preparation that can be obtained by layering leukocyte rich plasma. On different densities of Ficol-Hypaque solution, the resulting leukocyte pellet is incubated with Indium-111 for 10 to 20 minutes at room temperature. The cells then are injected back into the patient who provided the cells. Leukocytes tend to concentrate in areas of acute osteomyelitis and some research laboratories are reporting good results in outlining areas of chronic osteomyelitis.

The use of radio-labeled monoclonal antibodies is currently being investigated. It is possible with this technique to outline tumors by attaching radio isotopes to associated antigens.

Lymphoscintigraphy

Technetium-32 labeled colloids can be injected interstitially to determine lymph drainage from a specific primary tumor. This is useful when radical dissections for lymph bone tumors, such as melanomas, are planned.[23]

§17.31 Nuclear Medicine

The use of skeletal imaging agents such as Technetium (Tc-99m) is based on knowledge that bone is a dynamic tissue that serves two essential functions—skeletal remodeling to provide support and protection and mineral homeostasis (maintaining mineral content). The rate of blood flow is the main determinant of short-term uptake of the radioisotope, but areas of rapid turnover seen in tumors and healing fractures and infections are easily demonstrated by bone scanning.

Bone x-ray techniques are rather insensitive in evaluating metabolic change unless significant demineralization is present. Usually, loss of 30 to 50 per cent of bone mineral is necessary to be seen on routine x-rays, where

---

[23] Wukich, *Diagnosis of Infection by Preoperative Scintigraphy with Indium-Labeled White Blood Cells,* 69A JBJ Surg 1353 (1987).

bone scanning will reveal much less if the demineralization is accompanied with increased blood flow. Bone scanning is diagnostically nonspecific, thus results must be correlated with x-rays, physical findings, history and other tests.

Bone scans are useful as baseline studies in tumor assessment with periodic follow up of metastatic lesions. Eighty per cent of skeletal metastasis locate in the bones of the trunk, 10 per cent in skull, and 10 per cent in appendicular skeleton (extremities).

Bone scanning is valuable in demonstrating benign bone lesion, tumor or infection. Gallium isotopic bone scanning is useful in separating infection from noninfected lesions. Aseptic necrosis shows by contrast in bone scanning, by virtue of decreased blood flow.

The test entails intravenous instillation of an isotonic solution containing a radioisotope. The radionuclide concentrates at areas of inflammation, demonstrating the pathologic lesions. There fractures are suspect, but occult or hidden; bone scanning is particularly helpful.

Triple phases of bone scanning is a useful indicator of tissue viability as early as two days after injury. It has a role in clinical evaluation of extremities at risk from a circulation point of view, such as in frostbite or diabetic pregnancies.[24]

In infants under six weeks of age, the diagnosis of osteomyelitis is difficult. Bone scans using Ga-67 were most effective, but a high rate of positive diagnosis using Tc-99m was found. An ill patient with fever and local extremity swelling with pain are severe physical markers of acute osteomyelitis.[25]

In acute osteomyelitis, Technetium phosphate radionuclide bone scanning is between 85 to 95 per cent accurate. It is a simple, fairly noninvasive nontraumatizing test. Diagnosis of osteomyelitis in children is often difficult. Initial x-rays are often negative up to 10 days from infection onset. Blood cultures are positive in about 50 per cent of patients and elevated white blood counts and sedimentation are suggestive, they also are nonspecific. The bone scan, therefore, is an important diagnostic tool and is available to most practitioners.[26]

Gallium-67 scan is a useful diagnostic tool, especially in localizing deep infection. The interpreter of the test must recognize false positive tests in patients with pancreatic disease.[27]

---

[24] Krasnow, *False-Negative Bone Imaging Due to Etidronate Disodium Therapy,* 13 Clin Nucl Med 264 (1988); Schneider, *Unsuspected Sacral Fractures: Detected by Radionuclide Bone Scanning,* 144 AJR 337 (1985).

[25] Bressler, *Neonatal Osteomyelitis Examined by Bone Scintigraphy,* 152 Radiol 685 (1984).

[26] Wilson, *The Technetium Phosphate Bone Scan in the Diagnosis of Osteomyelitis in Childhood,* 65A JBJ Surg 431 (1983).

[27] Maderazo, *The Influence of Various Factors on the Accuracy of Gallium 67 Imaging for Occult Infection,* 29 J Nucl Med 608 (1988).

§17.32 Positron Emission

A rapidly expanding diagnostic tool is the positron emission device (PET). Use of PET expands the value of radiodiagnostic and MRI studies as well as expand effectiveness of EMG and other brain mapping methods. Measures of blood flow to any part of the body is possible along with precise (with some limitations) assessment of metabolism and functional activity of cells and organ systems.[28]

§17.33 Pulmonary Function Tests

Valid pulmonary function data require that attention be paid to issues that can lead to errors in measurement or in interpretation. Routine procedures designed to reduce errors should be established. Among the most important are (1) assuring accurate measurement and calculation of lung function parameters, which requires attention when measuring machine is brought into service and again when it is updated, (2) selecting reference equations and lower limits of normal apprpriate for the patient being studied and equipment being used, (3) avoiding errors introduced by using excessive number of measurements in generating an interpretation, and (4) avoiding interpretation of results without considering the clinical setting and pertinent elements of a complete data base.[29]

§17.34 Medical Laboratory Results Protection

There has been much discussion between consumers and providers of laboratory service as to providing standards assuring the consumer of accurate and reproducible results of the laboratory tests he is paying for. The United States Congress has passed a bill (HR 5471) that mandates more regulation of Pap smear testing. This will likely be a model for most laboratory procedures. Inaccurate results of lab testing can have adverse and even fatal effects on the patient. The physician using laboratory results to guide his treatment can be held liable for knowing the accuracy of the laboratory producing those results and for the injury that might stem from inaccuracy.[30]

§17.35 Thoracoscopy

Expeditious surgical management in serious chest injury improves survival chances. Emergency thoracotomy can often be avoided by the use of a simple procedure—thoracoscopy. The thoracic cavity can be readily

---

[28] Wagner, Jr, *Peace Through Mind/Brain Science,* 262 JAMA 625 (1989).

[29] Crapo & Morris, *Pulmonary Function Testing: Sources of Error,* 82 So Med J 875 (1989).

[30] Gianell, *Concerns Over Lab Errors Lead to Federal Legislation,* AMA Medical News, Jan 6, 1989.

examined under local anesthetic, and chest tube placed in 15 minutes if open surgery is not indicated. About 50 per cent of emergency open surgeries are avoided by this method.[31]

§17.36 Arteriography

Arteriography is a diagnostic test to study the patency of arteries. It is used in the extremities to study blood flow, to demonstrate occlusions, aneurysms and also aids in evaluating collateral circulation. This test is also commonly used to diagnose arterial problems in brain, lung, heart and kidney. The risks of arteriography includes bleeding at needle injection sites, with extravasation of dye that may be irritating, inflammatory response in vessel leading to further occlusion and dye allergy (should be ascertained before testing by history). In the case of allergy history, skin testing and preparing with corticosteroids and antihistamine medication. Infection in or about the artery is an absolute contraindication. (*See* Appendix 17-1, Cases 27 and 28.)

§17.37 Venography

Venography is a testing method by injecting radio-opaque dye in veins distally to suspect pathology and taking x-rays visualizing area of problem. Occlusion and blood clots are diagnosable. Complications include leaking of dye about venipuncture site with irritation, chemical phlebitis causing pain and at times occlusion of the vein. Reports of worsening thrombophlebitis, particularly in the calf, have been made. Allergy to the dye should be ascertained before the study and if completion of the venogram is essential, pretreating the patient with corticosteroid and antihistament medication is indicated. Infection in or about the vein is an absolute contraindication to the test. (See Appendix 17-1, Cases 29 to 31.)

§17.38 Plethysmography versus Venography

Impedence plethysmography is a non-invasive method measuring blood flow. Its greatest value is in demonstrating deep vein thrombosis, particularly when iliofemoral blood clots are forming, as these clots are high risks of migrating to lung as pulmonary emboli.

The clinical signs of acute deep vein thrombosis, local increase in temperature, positive Homan's sign (pain in calf when foot is dorsiflexed) and venous dilitation are notoriously unreliable. Ascending venography is the present standard of demonstrating deep vein thrombus, but is invasive, painful and often difficult to do in obese patients and/or patients with edema of foot. To do a venogram, a catheter must be passed into a foot vein, often requiring a surgical procedure under local anesthesia and often with enough swelling

---

[31] Jones, *Emergency Thoracoscopy: A Logical Approach to Chest Trauma Management,* 21 J Trauma 280 (1981).

and unavailability of a vein that procedure cannot be completed. In some patients, the venographic dye will produce a secondary chemical phlebitis, further complicating problem and frustrating diagnosis.

Negative factors in diagnosis of deep vein thrombosis include the necessity of having plethysmography equipment and skilled technician and with venography, availability of adequate x-ray equipment and a radiologist to do and interpret the venogram. One series reports 3.9 per cent iliofemoral venous thrombosis at high risk of producing pulmonary emboli.[32]

§17.39 Special Procedures

Other procedures which may be carried out, which are not necessarily testing, but of diagnostic importance, are discussed in this section.

Transcutaneous electrical nerve stimulation (TENS) is a procedure of applying control, low voltage pulses to the nervous system by passing electricity through electrodes attached to the skin. TENS is used for analgesia to manage and relieve pain. The procedure is non-invasive and non-addictive.

TENS devices are available only on prescription by a licensed physician. Most TENS devices are compact, portable and easy to operate with professional guidance. The portable devices are battery powered and about the size of a package of cigarettes. TENS devices that require alternating current (AC) power sources are considered clinical devices that are primarily used in hospitals or physicians' offices.

An electrical current is transmitted from the TENS devices by wire leads that are connected to electrodes placed on the skin. The electrodes are covered with a conductive gel and are taped to the patient's skin. Most devices have either one or two—many up to four—channels, permitting stimulation of multiple sites at the same time.

There are several different types of modes of stimulation used by TENS units. Laboratory studies have demonstrated that different nerves have different response characteristics and the degree of pain relief depends upon the type of stimulation applied. The effect of TENS on pain depends on several factors such as the nature and sensitivity of the patient, the patient's pain threshold and the intensity of stimulation.

Common TENS stimulation modes include:

1. Conventional (this is the most common TENS mode because it is tolerated best by a larger number of patients). It uses a high rate, narrow pulse width and modern intensity stimulation. When effected, the conventional offers a fast onset of pain relief but has a relatively short after effect, which generally does not exceed the length of the initial stimulation.
2. The acupuncture-like TENS mode uses a low rate, high pulse width and high intensity stimulation. An induction period at least 20 to 30

---

[32] Brown, *Impedence Plethysmography,* 68B JBJ Surg 264 (1987).

minutes is required. Acupuncture-like TENS produces strong visible muscle contraction, and in many cases is not well tolerated by patients. Consequently, it should not be continued for more than 30 to 45 minutes during each session. This mode many provide a long after-effect of pain relief.

3. The Burst TENS mode is a burst or pulse train stimulation. It employes a wide pulse width, high intensity and a combination of pulses that give high frequency burst with each low pulse rate. Muscle twitches, rather than muscle contractures, are produced for this mode. It is considered clinically similar to conventional TENS.
4. The brief intense TENS mode most closely proximates the burst mode. it utilizes a high rate, wide pulse width and high intensity for a period of five to 15 minutes with off periods of two to three minutes. Brief intense TENS has been found to be a benefit in wound debridement procedures and extremity mobilization. This is the least commonly used form of TENS.

A careful evaluation of the patient before initiating TENS therapy is essential. This evaluation should include detailed history of condition including the chronology of the pain and its onset; location of pain (deep, superficial, radiating); measurement of the pain intensity by use of allogram or similar tool and any emotional responses that may affect the pain (anger, frustration, helplessness, anxiety or suicidal ideation). Other factors that may modify the patient's loss of pain are medications, diet, posture and activity.

A trial TENS treatment should be given to all patients considered for this form of therapy. Following the trial period, the patient is assessed to determine whether he or she is able to tolerate TENS, if symptomatic relief occurred, and whether or not side effects were exhibited. After trial period and decision is made to continue, alter or discontinue TENS therapy. If continued, TENS therapy should be provided as often as required to maintain reduced pain or pain free state. The device is portable and assuming the patient is adequately informed and capable, it is common to send the device home with the patient with instructions for using it varying periods of time, depending on the patient's problem.

The effectiveness of TENS varies with many factors such as those mentioned above. Often, it is very effective for a period of time, three months or so, then becomes less effective. Several reports have pointed out that TENS unit is an effective tool for acute and chronic pain in about one-third of patients, moderately effective in about one-third and ineffective in about one-third. There may well be a placebo effect which, of course, makes no difference if there is pain relief as long as the patient is apprised that the placebo effect is part of any treatment. The use of placebos fraudulently or by concealment is poor practice, unethical and contraindicated. However, the use of the concept of placebo medication with the patient understanding clearly how it works is appropriate and often beneficial.

Caution of the use of TENS units with pregnant patients, patients with epilepsy, patients with TIA and stroke-like situations of the brain have been suggested. These are precautionary behaviors; no strict contraindication is recited by the developers and for long term users of TENS.

There is virtually no complications of TENS. Those that do occur most often are related to sensitivity of the electrodes, the gel or the electric transmission across the skin.

§17.40 Thermography

Clinical thermography is used to measure temperature variation at the surface of the body to obtain diagnostic images. Issues related to the clinical use of thermography are safety, sensitivity, specificity and predictive value, as well as deciding whether the information derived is necessary in clinical decision making.

Thermography as a diagnostic imaging device is safe, non-invasive and non-manipulative. It does not subject the patient to radiation or any extraneous medication. Thermography for conditions with nervous system involvement has commanded much attention, particularly nerve root pressure causing neck and back pain and peripheral nerve involvement in radicular pain. Additionally, interest has focused on its use in evaluation of deep venous thrombosis of legs and cerebrovascular patency. Finally, thermography continues to be used for certain non-nervous, non-vascular lesions such as thyroid disease or arthritis.

The conclusions reached in these widely separate clinical situations show that most investigators recommend thermography only as a screening tool, as an adjunctive diagnostic device, but not as a primary diagnostic guide. Evidence of the technology's clinical effectiveness has not been tested rigorously in prospective, controlled clinical trials and while comparative series and case reports have been reported, most have been retrospective and not blinded. Thermography is a well-known technology, but it does not appear to have achieved universal clinical acceptability as a clinically effective diagnostic procedure. Its effectiveness as a diagnostic test in clinical situations remains controversial, and evidence for its clinical application has not been "convincing to the clinical community."

NIH has advised that further studies are required to validate the efficacy of thermography, that it may prove confirmatory as an adjunctive but not as an isolated diagnostic tool, and that there is need for well designed studies to validate its usefulness. FDA published proposed classifications for telethermographic systems and LCT systems. In that public notice, the FDA recommended that nonpowered LCT systems be classified into Class I (General Controls) and AC powered LCT and thermographic systems be classified into Class II (Performance Standards). FDA also recommended that any thermographic system intended for sole diagnostic screening be classified into Class III (Premarket Approval). To date, no thermographic device has been thus classified. (Taken from Public Health Service in Health Technology

Assessment Reports, 1989, National Center for Health Services, U.S. Department of Health & Human Services.

Thermography seems to be slowly establishing a niche as a diagnostic test. Its obvious worth is in evaluating automonic nerve responses and this nerve system component accounts for skin temperature change. Such entities as reflex sympathetic dystrophies and other causalgia-like problems are nicely outlined by thermography.

Where there are nerve root displacement lesions, some authors have correlated skin temperature changes with lumbar CT scan results. Presently, thermography is most useful as an adjunct to other testing such as physical examination with history, x-ray and CT scan.

Thermography is a safe adjunctive physiological procedure which may be useful in the diagnosis of selected neurological and musculoskeletal conditions. It is non-invasive and does not involve the use of ionized radiation.

Thermography may facilitate the determination of spinal nerve root and distal peripheral nerve dysfunction. It also contributes to the evaluation of possible autonomic nervous system dysfunction and of spinal disorders.

Thermography may be useful in documenting peripheral nerve and soft tissue injuries such as muscle ligament sprain, inflammation, muscle spasm, and myositis.

Liquid crystal thermography measures temperature via infrared radiation emitted from object being studied. Thermography is capable of detecting very small temperature changes but is totally without specificity as to the cause or meaning of the measured changes.

Over the years, thermography has been considered for a possible role in screening for several medical conditions. After evaluation, however, its use was discarded because of one or more of the following limitations: absent specificity, excessively high incidence of both false positive and false negative results, low sensitivity for a core mass temperature and readings that could be influenced by poor user technique and/or intestinal or unintentional bias. Any or all of these characteristics affect thermography test results and make interpretation very difficult. Thermography has been tried and either discarded or relegated to secondary diagnostic role for mammography (looking for cancer) deep vein thrombosis and determining amputation level for a circulation-impaired extremity. Thermography has gained attention as a diagnostic test for low back pain and other musculoskeletal symptoms. In patients whose symptoms are supported by objective measures determined by CT, MRI and clinically observed motor/sensory changes, the non-specific thermography readings are often confirmatory of the diagnosis established by these other modalities.

For musculoskeletal injury claims seeking monetary compensation, thermography has been used in patients who had equivocal or negative results from more specific tests. In these instances, a thermogram has been offered by attorneys to support or refute the plaintiff's subjective complaint. The technique is particularly susceptible to all the biases and vagaries mentioned above. Many of these cases have been reported anecdotal and poorly controlled, therefore, lacking scientific credibility.

Neurothermography, which is a newer method for detecting dysfunction of the peripheral autonomic nervous system, measures surface temperature asymmetry. This method of testing is useful in patients with compressive neuropathy like the median nerve compression in carpal tunnel syndrome. In these patients, nerve impairment can be shown before muscle wasting from motor nerve compromise has occurred. Reflex sympathetic dystrophies can be diagnosed earlier, facilitating more successful long-term treatment.[33]

In *Thermographic Diagnostics, Inc v Allstate Insurance Co,* 219 NJ Super 208, 530 A2d 56 (1987), the use of neuromuscular thermography was found to be sufficiently supported by credible expert testimony to have a medical value by a New Jersey trial court in recent cases involving payment for medical services under New Jersey's no-fault auto accident statute.

The accident was taken by provider of the thermograms (TDI) against the insurance company on assignment of the insured. Plaintiff said that it took the thermograms as ordered by treating physicians who considered the study necessary for diagnostic purposes. The defendant's insurance company, who refused to pay over $150,000 of the patient's bills maintained that thermography is not a necessary medical expense, because it still is experimental of dubious value. They also contended the charges were excessive compared to other more conventional diagnostic tests.

After hearing extensive expert testimony of both sides of the issue, the court concluded that the thermography as an additional means of undermining, whether there is an organic basis for the patient's complaint and to indicate the need for more invasive diagnostic test was legitimate as supported by expert testimony.

The court then examined the New Jersey no-fault insurance statute and its legislative history and concluded that the charges of the plaintiff were both reasonable and necessary within the meaning of the statute and therefore, were compensable medical expenses in this case.

The issue of the malpractice procedure has left New Jersey legislature which examined the possibility of medical fee schedule for automobile liability. The court therefore ordered payment of the fees unless the defendant showed excessive bills and abuse in individual cases.

The New Jersey Court joined the Florida District Court of Appeals to find in favor of reimbursement for the use of diagnostic thermography. *Palma v State Farm Fire & Casualty Co,* 489 So 2d 147 (Fla Dist Ct App 1986) These decisions, however, do not indicate a general acceptance of the use of diagnostic thermography by insurance companies around the country. The continued likelihood of nonpayment in other states remains high and requires close monitoring by interested parties.

---

[33] Perry, Jr, *Thermography Reveals Change in Temperature, but not in Meaning of the Change,* J Musculoskeletal Dis, Apr 15, 1989, at 15. Herrick & Herrick, *Thermography in the Detection of Carpal Tunnel Syndrome and Other Compression Neuropathies,* 12A J Hand Surg 943 (1987); Greene, *Neuropathy,* 7 Seminars in Neurology 313 (1987).

For the most lengthy opinion, Judge Talbot seems to consider the issue a factual one. Judge Talbot set forth the issue with the opinion, "In essence, this court must decide whether thermography is a necessary and reasonable diagnostic test qualifying for the patient under the statute." 530 A2d at 58.

"To answer this question, it is necessary to review the extensive medical testimony concerning neuromuscular thermography presented by both parties." 530 A2d at 58. Judge Talbot proceeded with an exhaustive summary of the expert testimony and concluded, "When used with limitations, this court finds neuromuscular thermography sufficiently supported by creditable expert testimony to have medical values."

Having posed the issue of the validity of thermography and answer in favoring of the plaintiffs, the court turned around and decided it had no business considering the scientific validity of thermography. The court turned to legislative history of the New Jersey no fault accident and concluded that it must deliberately construe such legislature. Citing the Florida case, *Palmer v State Farm Fire & Casualty Co,* 489 So 2d 147 (Fla Dist Ct App 1986), the court ruled that only the treating physician, preferably a neurologist, should decide the reasonableness or necessity of any medical treatment, including "minority medical viewpoints." 530 A2d at 66.

The court explained that it was not "her problem" to determine what she had just spent 20 pages deciding. The opinions state:

> Under the New Jersey No Fault Act, the necessity of medical expense must be decided by the treating physician, the one most qualified to make such a judgment. It should not be the providence of the judiciary to decide in the face of conflicting expert medical testimony, highly complex questions of medicine and science. Surely the legislature could not have intended for the judiciary to sit in the capacity of a medical board review. Therefore, this court holds that need is shown if it is the treating physician's sincere believe that the procedure will further the diagnosis and treatment of its patient.

This case, if followed up on an appellate level, would eliminate the statutory requirement that a medical diagnostic test be both necessary and reasonable. The physician or chiropractor could perform and charge for any test regardless of acceptance or lack of acceptance of that test by the medical community. Consequently, under this opinion (had it ended at this point) over treatment and unnecessary testing would be limited only by the physician's imagination.

It is submitted that this is neither a "liberal" construction nor a workable rule. The court rebels at the idea of a judge having to rule upon "highly complex questions of medicine and science." In a medical malpractice case, the same judge empaneled jurors with far less education and knowledge to decide complex questions of science and medicine.

In the final paragraph in the course of opinion, Judge Talbot seems to have changed her mind again, having pronounced that only the treating physician, rather than the court, can rule on the validity of diagnostic tests. The court returns to its earliest thesis and makes the facts of determination that thermography is useful: "In conclusion, this court finds that thermography has a firm scientific basis. It is beyond the period of initial research."

One can be certain that the court ruled in favor of the plaintiff, but in my opinion, the basis of the court's ruling is no clearer than a thermogram. On March 23, 1988, the District Court of Appeals of Florida decided in *State Farm & Casualty Co v Palma,* that $253,500 were fair in reasonable attorney's fees to contest the State's denial of a $600 bill for thermography. In its opinion, Judge Downey states that "It appears that State Farm decided to go to the mat over the bill for thermographic studies because, apparently, it is a diagnostic tool which is becoming more widely used, contrary to State Farm's view of what is necessary medical treatment, as provided in the statute. Having chosen to stand and fight over this charge, State Farm, of course, made a business judgment for which it should have known a day of reckoning would come should it lose in the end.

The court recognized the great disparity between the medical bill and the attorney fees. However, the judge commented that the parties had elected to go toe to toe over the issue. He further recognized that the real issue was not an incidental medical bill. The record is clear that State Farm hoped to prove a point in a case regarding bills for this medical procedure that would avail it in other cases nationally. Those stakes were high and the issue became complex justifying the legal effort. These Citations were found in *State Farm Casualty Co v Palma,* 13 FLW 742 (Fla Dist Ct App 1988).[34]

§17.41 Ultrasound

Ultrasound is useful in skilled hands for demonstrating soft tissue lesions. Soft tissue masses can be identified and biopsied. Lesions of joints and capsules, ligaments and internal soft tissues can be evaluated, perhaps not as accurately as with MRI, but at much less cost. Tears of the shoulder rotator cuff can be seen with ultrasound. Measurement for spinal stenosis has been reported.

The use of ultrasound to evaluate osteoporotic fragility of bone is a valuable test. Ultrasound measures both bone mass and a component of bone fragility distinct from decreased mass.

Another increasing popular use of ultrasound is in measurement of spinal canal size. It is a useful, economic, noninvasive and non-radiation using test. Screening for spinal stenosis is the principal use.[35]

Ultrasound is very useful in detecting congenital dislocated hip. It can be repeatedly used without danger to patient or family, unlike x-ray, though the examination does take longer than x-ray. The real time images will not

---

[34] Perlman, *Thermography: A Diagnostic Test in Search of its Place,* 10 J Neur and Orthop Med and Surg 15 (1989); Green, *Infrared Electronic Thermography (ET): A Noninvasive Diagnostic Neuroimaging Tool,* 11 Contemp Orthop 39 (1985).

[35] Chovil, *Ultrasonic Measurement of Lumbar Canal Diameter,* 82 So Med J 977 (1989).

eliminate the need for x-ray to relate femoral head position to rest of pelvis on a permanent record. Ultrasound requires a skilled technician to get reproducible results. Ultrasound testing requires good cooperation between pediatrician, orthopedist and radiologist who does the ultrasound as all three are important in assessing the situation.

At this time, Doppler examination, impedence plethysmography and triplex scanning (ultrasound) are often used to diagnose deep vein thrombosis with ultrasound scanning in the hands of a skilled examiner, providing the most useful information as to presence and extent of deep venous thrombosis.

Clinical symptoms and signs are 50 per cent accurate in diagnosis of deep venous thrombosis in the lower extremity. Although venography using contrast material has long been considered the "gold standard" for diagnosis, it is expensive, causes discomfort, is often difficult to obtain (because of difficulty in finding a vein in edematous foot) and carries some risk of producing chemical phlebitis in an already compromised venous system. Some noninvasive diagnostic techniques correlate well with venography but do not demonstrate the extent of vein involvement.[36]

Ultrasonic evaluation of the moving shoulder is a new effective method for evaluation of integrity of rotator cuff. Contrast arthrography is the only other non-operative technique to demonstrate shoulder intra-articular pathology. Ultrasound of moving shoulder is noninvasive and preferred by many radiologists, also is more cost effective.

Recent advances in ultrasound have made the development of diagnostic instruments that combine cross-sectioned imaging and Doppler analysis. These instruments have expanded the role of diagnostic ultrasonography to the assessment of vascular disease. The current applications of duplex Doppler and color Doppler imaging in evaluating extracranial carotid and vertebral arteries and peripheral arterial or venous systems are noninvasive, safe and diagnostic.[37]

Ultrasound, in different administration modes, is used as a therapeutical, producing deep heat without burning in controlled application.

§17.42 Electromyogram (EMG)

The electromyogram (EMG) is used often in diagnosis of orthopedic problems. The test measures nerve function and is useful in assessing nerves, nerve roots and spinal cord damage, both acute (but less reliable) and chronic. The EMG is helpful in following the progress of nerve lesion, both assessing improvement of injury or disease or its worsening.

Nerve velocity measurement, assessing speed of a stimulus moving across a nerve, is diagnostic of some nerve compression syndromes, though a

---

[36] Persson, *Use of Triplex Scanner in Diagnosis of Deep Venous Thrombosis,* 124 Arch Surg 593 (1989).

[37] Lewis & James, *Current Applications of Duplex and Color Doppler Ultrasound Imaging: Carotid and Periphenal Vascular System,* 12 Orthopedics 1147, 1158 (1989).

negative result does not exclude a compression syndrome. (*See* Appendix 17-1, Case 32.)

Evoked potential EMG are nerve velocity tests measuring conduction speed from a distant point to a selected area in brain measure with overlying electrodes. This test is useful in assessing peripheral nerve and/or spinal cord function.

EMO studies are usually conducted by placing fine needle electrodes in predetermined muscles at known anatomical points and administering a small electric current and obtaining a measurement that is compared with known standards. The test is painful, patient often complaining. The empathetic orthopedist, as well as the neurologist of physiatrist who performs the test, should forewarn the patient. Infection at needle electrode site has been reported but is rare.

A new diagnostic tool utilizing EMG is making it possible to more precisely diagnose a number of psychiatric problems which are related to brain dysfunction. In working with a new area of medicine, known as neurometrics, physicians are utilizing brain mapping to quantitatively diagnose brain pathology—including schizophrenia, alcoholism, dementia and certain types of cognitive impairment and memory loss.

Before this testing, it was difficult to separate psychiatric or psychological problems (which had a biological component and thus might be treatable with medication) from those which are behavioral. Brain mapping, or quantitative electroencephalography (QEEG) utilizes a computer to analyze the electrical activity of various regions of the brain. This data, along with a computer generated color-coded picture of the brain, can often determine whether or not a patient's psychiatric problem has a biologic component related to brain dysfunction.

Neurometrics can be used in evaluating head injuries when recovery is delayed longer than expected. Neurometrics is especially useful in differentiating disorders which may have similar symptoms—simple depression and bipolar depression or dementia and depression in older patients.

§17.43 References

M.A. Moskowitz & M.E. Osband, The Complete Book of Medical Tests (1984)

S.D. Sobel & T. Ferguson, The People's Book of Medical Tests (1985)

R.K. Ausman & D.E. Snyder, *Medical Library, Lawyer's Edition,* 3 Orthopedics 193 (1989)

Joynt, *Neurology,* 261 JAMA 2859 (1989)

Leonidas, *Ultrasound Examination May be Best Way to Check for Congenital Hip Dislocation in Infants,* presented at Spring Session of the American Academy of Pediatrics, New York City (1988), *as reported in* Edelman, 8 Orthopedics Today 7 (1988)

Appendix 17-1
Cases

1 ***Shuffler v Blue Ridge Radiology Associations PA,* 73 NC App 232, 326 SE2d 96 (1985)** (directed verdict for the defendant was reversed on appeal. Plaintiff was in auto accident and taken to hospital. He was then sent to x-ray department which were interpreted by one of the defendants. The x-ray technician could not properly position the patient and did not x-ray C7-T1 level of the spine. X-rays taken were read as showing no fracture. The patient was discharged from hospital but subsequently found to have fracture dislocation at C7-T1 after additional x-rays were taken. Evidence at trial revealed that the radiologist did not inform the technician of the limited scope of the initial x-rays. Further proof established that failure to reveal this limited scope was a proximate cause of the delay in diagnosis of fracture dislocation. The patient fortunately suffered no permanent impairment but did have an increased period of pain and impairment).

2 ***Addison v Whittenberg,* 512 NE2d 76 (Ill App Ct 1987)** (physicians in hospital radiology group were found negligent for allegedly failing to find broken vertebra in the patient's neck, ruled the Illinois appellate court. The patient was admitted to the hospital on or about January 17, 1981 after involvement in an automobile accident. The physicians failed to discover and treat a broken vertebra in the patient's neck. Reversing the decision, the Appellate Court said there was a genuine issue as to negligence and summary judgment was improper. The court noted the patient had not come forward with the opinion of an expert witness in an affidavit or deposition who believed the physician acted negligently. However, x-rays taken by the hospital the day of admission and on the day of discharge revealed he had a fracture of the cervical spine. A reasonable inference was that he suffered a fracture in the automobile accident. Because it was discovered a few days later and failure to discover on that date he was first taken to the hospital resulted in negligence. Appellate Court's decision was reversed and case remanded).

3 ***Phillips v Good Samaritan Hospital,* 65 Ohio App 2d 112, 416 NE2d 646 (1979)** (four-year-old child was taken to the emergency room following an accident where x-rays were negative for fracture of the arm or elbow, so emergency room physician interpreted. However, the next day, a board-certified radiologist indicated that there was a supracondylar fracture of the humerus with displacement. Due to failure of communication, neither the treating physician or the family was advised of this finding. After several months, the infant's parents were advised of the fracture and it necessitated an open reduction by another physician. There was a verdict against both the radiology group and the first treating physician for failure to discover and failure to communicate the presence of a fracture which, when discovered, most probably could have easily been treated by closed reduction).

4 ***McClaine v Alger,*** **150 Mich App 306, 388 NW2d 349 (1986)** (Michigan appellate court strongly suggested a hospital or doctor's delay in forwarding an x-ray report to treating physicians who requested it may have been responsible for mismanagement of a compression fracture. In this rather complicated case, the only physician who was exonerated was a second treating physician who finally took a second set of x-rays and testified as what might have been done had the report on the first set of x-rays been given to the treating physician. The patient is a truck driver in a major accident, was seen in an emergency room. A radiologist noted that "a slight loss of vertical height anteriorly at T-11 without buckling of anterior cortex and therefore probably of no significance. The patient left the hospital while in significant pain, signed a release that the hospital forward his records and x-rays to the clinic in his home town. Based on the oral information from the patient, the next treating physician treated him as a lumbosacral sprain and prescribed rest for a period of time followed by gentle exercises. Several calls were made to the hospital but the x-rays did not arrive until some three months later. The second treating orthopedist who took his own x-rays noted that the fracture that was reported noting a loss of height of T11 with buckling of the anterior cortex now had a loss of 70% of the height. The hospital authority argued that they admittedly were wrong in not sending x-rays promptly, that the deterioration of the vertebral body on x-ray was not their negligence. The orthopedic expert testified that a hyperextension brace, if applied earlier, would have prevented the progressive collapse. A directed verdict for the hospital was had. The case was appealed and the Court of Appeals of Michigan found that "reasonable minds could differ on factual questions" as to whether the hospital's negligence was unrelated to the patient's deteriorating spine. The case was remanded because of errors in the pleadings with the Court's opinion that it appeared the first treating hospital and doctors' negligence in forwarding the x-rays adversely affected the patient. The amount was undetermined. That was a jury question).

Comment: In the treatment of emergency patients, particularly transient people who, when they can, will travel back to their home, it is essential that records reflect clearly what the injury was and what the treatment was. It is standard practice in emergency rooms now to give written instructions to the patients as to follow-up care and diagnosis. Additionally, a request to forward clinical records, laboratory reports, and x-ray reports should be promptly honored. In most jurisdictions, records cannot be withheld pending payment of a bill, for that compounds negligent behavior. In some cases where psychiatric information is requested to be sent with the patient or to another physician, there may be problems that are best solved on an individual basis. On the other hand, doctors accepting a patient and waiting for records and x-rays have a duty to accept the patient as he or she is at the time of examination. Repeat x-rays are feasible rather than waiting three months for them to be sent. A telephone call to the treating physician helps the second treating physician better understand what is going on with the patient.

5 ***Totten v Adongay,* 337 SE2d 2 (W Va 1985)** (question was raised whether negligence occurred in a suit brought by an electrician who injured his right wrist while cutting firewood. When resulting pain interfered with his work, he went to his family physician who could find no evidence of fracture by physical examination or on x-rays, and prescribed heat and aspirin. After a month, pain failed to ease. Patient returned to his doctor; again the doctor assured him there was no fracture. Five months later, he consulted an orthopedist who quickly found a fracture of the navicular bone. It was plainly visible on x-rays that were taken by the first physician. The untreated fracture resulted in non-union and was treated by implanting the non-union fragment with a prosthetic implant. He never fully regained the strength of his hand and pain persisted. It was held there was enough evidence in the chain of events that a jury could make a decision without expert opinion on the issue of missed fracture and delayed treatment, pain and suffering attached to that and possible loss of chance to avoid surgery).

Comment: Fracture of the navicular (scaphoid) occurs with what is frequently called a sprained wrist. Many times the fracture is not clear for 7-10 days. It is customary to treat such injuries expectantly; that is, as though there are fractures, treating with thumb spica cast or splint and then repeat x-rays. If there is any question after the tenth day, obtaining a bone scan is helpful in delineating the fracture. Virtually all non-displaced carpal navicular fractures held in thumb spica cast for a sufficient time, though it may be three or four months, will heal and virtually no impairment results. It is quite another story if non-union is allowed to occur. Frequently open surgery and bone grafting are necessary and arthritis frequently develops and a weakened compromised wrist frequently develops. It is an important concern to make the diagnosis of carpal navicular fracture early on.

6 ***Hart v Eldridge,* 282 SE2d 369 (Ga Ct App), *rehg denied,* (1981)** (hospital employee was sent to the emergency room for examination and x-ray when he complained of low back pain. A radiologist reviewed the x-ray and reported it to be normal. Over a year later, the employee collapsed at work and emergency surgery was performed for ruptured abdominal aortic aneurysm. He died two days later because of complications. Subsequent examination of the first emergency room x-rays showed the aneurysm. The suit was filed against the radiologist and examining physician for wrongful death. The first was held that Statute of Limitations had run but Appellate Court later amended the Statute inasmuch as the victim did not and could not have known of the faulty x-ray reading until about the time of surgery and subsequent death. Supreme Court then reversed the charge indicating the radiologist should be held liable).

7 ***Breining v United States,* 861 F2d 1342 (5th Cir 1988)** (patient hired defendant physician to have x-rays taken to satisfy requirement of his employer, the school district. The court held that the defendant physician had a duty to inform the plaintiff of his abnormal chest x-ray because the school district did not retain the defendant physicians and when the plaintiff retained the physician he created a physician patient relationship).

8 ***Tams v Kolz,* 530 A2d 1217 (DC 1987)** (surgeon's failure to read impression section of radiology report was not the cause of a patient's injuries due to a retained surgical sponge. The patient went to surgery for removal of a cancerous tumor located between the bladder and the vaginal wall. In the operation, more than 400 items were used, including instruments, sutures, sponges, and lab pads. Four days following the operation, x-rays were taken of the patient's abdomen and a copy forwarded to the surgeon. A month after discharge from the hospital, x-rays were again taken because of patient's complaints of abdominal pain and these showed a foreign object. At a second operation, surgeon found a laparotomy paid that had adhered to an intestinal membrane. Damaged segment of the intestine was removed when the pad was extracted. The patient sued for malpractice alleging he was negligent in failing to detect the pad before closing the first operation and failing to read the x-ray report which indicated the presence of a foreign object. At trial, the physician who testified for the patient indicated the physician had a duty to read x-ray report. He also indicated it was the radiologist's duty to make it known to the surgeon that there was a foreign body present. He pointed out that it should have been noted under "Impression" on the x-ray report, though it had not been. The court entered a jury verdict for the surgeon. On appeal, the court pointed out that the patient's expert had effectively limited the surgeon's duty in studying the x-ray reading to the Impression section. Therefore, even if the surgeon had read the section, he would have remained unaware that the x-ray had disclosed the possible foreign object, so because he failed to read the impression was not the cause of aggravation of the patient's intestinal damage).

9 ***Smallwood v Dick,* 761 P2d 1212 (Idaho 1988)** (patient was injured in an automobile accident and was taken to a hospital for x-rays. A board-certified radiologist reviewed the x-rays the next day and ordered additional views, which were also read by the radiologist. Later that day, the treating physician talked with radiologist telling him the patient was complaining of low back pain, but radiologist saying arthritis was present and additional x-rays were not necessary. The next day, the patient was getting out of bed, had increased back pain, and fell to the floor. It was then determined that the patient had a fracture of the D-10 vertebral that had slipped and severed the spinal cord. The plaintiff sued all concerned. The treating physician and hospital settled for $375,000. After completing trial, the patient's damages were set at $777,500. The jury awarded judgment of $259,162.12 against radiologist in favor of plaintiff and $97,552 in favor of wife. The plaintiff and wife filed to increase verdict. After reviewing evidence, the trial court concluded it would have awarded damages in excess of $1,000,000. The supreme court said the trial court did not abuse its discretion in ordering new trial on damages, as it had that authority and also could grant a new trial on liability if asked).

10 ***Greco v Coleman,* 138 Ill App 3d 317, 485 NE2d 1118 (1985)** (this case concerned an orthopedist who was charged with failure to detect displaced fracture of the odontoid process of the second cervical vertebra. His

treatment included manipulating the neck when it should have been surgically stabilized. As a result, the patient sustained substantial impairment of spinal cord pressure and residual extremity impairments. An automobile accident was the cause of the injury in September 1973, and hospital emergency room x-rays revealed no limitation of fracture except for a clavicle fracture. After two weeks when pain in the neck persisted, an orthopedist was called. He looked at the original x-rays and declared there were no fractures and discharged him from the hospital. Five weeks later, he went to a chiropractor who identified on his x-rays displacement fracture of the odontoid and referred him to a second orthopedist. The patient used a brace for several months but the fracture did not heal so in March 1974, bone grafting was carried out. He eventually stabilized with about 75% loss of motion in the neck, as well as pain. Judgment against the first orthopedist held).

Comment: Like several areas in the body, fracture of the odontoid may be a hidden or not obvious fracture soon after injury with persistent pain. Repeat x-rays, x-rays in different positions and CT scan or tomography are important, for this can be a life-threatening fracture and easy to miss. It has to be first thought of by the treating orthopedist or cases just as this will be missed, doing the patient a disservice.

11 521 A2d 1323 (NJ Super Ct App Div 1987) (orthopedist was ordered to stand a new trial, the higher court ruled. The case began in September 1980 when the patient fractured her wrist. Standard preoperative x-rays were taken which revealed this mass. The radiologist in that film recommended tomography for further delineation but did not communicate this to other physicians other than in the report. Two months later, a nurse reviewing hospital records for an insurance company saw the x-ray report and promptly reported to the orthopedist, but it was another three months before the patient was informed. The malignancy proved fatal two years later. The radiologist who wrote the report initially was part of the suit because he failed to alert the orthopedist or the physician concerned with the patient. The court, in essence, held the orthopedic surgeon, along with another consulting physician, had a duty to read the record of each test that was pertinent to the patient, whether he ordered it or not, if they were available on the record. Further, the orthopedist must promptly act, not act 3½ months after the fact, on a suspect nodule).

12 *Wilson v Corbin,* 241 Iowa 593, 41 NW2d 702 (1950) (failure to take proper x-rays of the patient's spine led to failure to diagnose compression fracture of third cervical vertebral. The reasoning was that early diagnosis and treatment of this injury with appropriate stabilization treatment would result in essentially normal spine whereas three months plus delayed treatment allowed the formation of permanent deformity. Loss of chance doctrine in addition to negligent diagnosis and treatment applied).

13 *Bachman v Butler,* 288 SW2d 597 (1956) (physician failed to diagnose a skull fracture. The failure was based on the fact that the physician was of the eclectic school and did not have training or use x-rays. The patient expired from a complication of a severe skull fracture. The physician was held liable).

14 ***Kingston v McGrath,* 232 F2d 495 (9th Cir 1956)** (40-year-old lady in an automobile accident sustained injuries to cervical and dorsal spine, was taken to the hospital, had two x-rays of chest and ribs. When placed in a private room, she complained bitterly of pain about her neck and about the mid back. X-rays were sent out to consulting radiologist who, four days later, returned x-rays saying no obvious cervical spine fracture and possible six thoracic fractures, but that the latter could also be congenital abnormalities. The patient continued to complain bitterly of neck and back pain. No further x-rays, however, were taken for three weeks. The same set of x-rays showed multiple fractures of neck and low back. She was immobilized in a body skull cast. She sustained permanent impairment with difficulty in rotating her neck and pain and deformity of her mid-back. After extensive review of similar cases, the Appellate Court felt the surgeons appropriately would have taken additional x-rays sooner, being more responsive to her continuing severe pain complaints in specific locations, that is, mid neck and mid dorsal spine, reasoning that more prompt immobilization of the cast would allow for more prompt healing, less pain and (with reasonable probability) less permanent stiffness and deformity. The latter two observations of less stiffness and less deformity are more questionable than the former observation of less pain and more prompt care of her injury).

15 ***Brazil v United States,* 484 F Supp 986 (ND Ala 1979)** (physician at a Veterans' Administration hospital failed to diagnose and treat a fractured spine. A 53-year-old patient involved in a head-on collision on 8/21/77 was taken to the hospital. X-rays were ordered but no thoracic spine x-rays were ordered. The two physicians attending found an arthritic condition known as ankylosing spondylitis but did not find fractures of the patient's thoracic spine. Orthopedic and neurological consultations were available at the hospital. The patient was not admitted. He was discharged shortly after midnight. The family was told to check him every hour to determine whether he was coherent. Lack of coherence would indicate brain damage. The patient continued to suffer a great deal of back pain. The next day he went to the emergency room at the university hospital where he was examined for about an hour but no x-rays were taken. He returned home where he began losing feeling in his legs and had trouble walking. On May 24, three days after the accident, he returned to the Veterans' Administration hospital. X-rays were taken which revealed a "sharp subluxation" of T9. Because of a heart condition, surgery was not performed. The attending physician prescribed a steroid to reduce swelling, told the patient to lie flat on his back and if he moved he would become paraplegic. Despite the warnings, the patient continued to thrash around more than the average person. He sat up and once got out of bed and cranked his bed to change positions. On May 29, both legs were paralyzed. A laminectomy was performed and decompression and spinal fusion were carried out. By the time of trial, the patient had only partial paralysis of his legs. Negligence against the physician and

hospital were levied on the first treating physician because symptoms were present in the dorsal spine but x-rays were not taken. Similarly, negligence was levied against the second treating physicians for not taking x-rays and adequately examining him—"not even palpating" the patient's back. There was an offset in contributory negligence on the patient's part).

16 ***Mann v Cracchiolo,* 38 Cal 3d 18, 694 P2d 1134, 210 Cal Rptr 762 (1985)** (this case involved 54 physicians. The charges were fracturing the neck of the patient, concealing the offense and performing a useless operation to obtain Medicare funds, then trying to kill her to hide the complicity in causing and concealing the fracture. The case began in November 1971 when the patient had her toes x-rayed in preparation for surgery and fell off the x-ray table. Skull x-rays were normal and initially there was no obvious evidence of fracture of the cervical spine. The fracture of the odontoid process was discovered at autopsy and re-review of the x-rays revealed the odontoid fracture possibly was there after the fall from the table. The neurosurgeon, who reviewed the records, felt the fracture of the odontoid was present and it was recognized at the time of her initial care for the fall from the table; however, no open mouth view had been taken to confirm the fracture. The patient continued to complain of head and neck pain. A year later, x-rays showed subluxation of C1 or C2. Though there was no history of intervening injury of the neck, there was an injury reported in which the hip was dislocated that was treated during this time frame. The supreme court held there was enough evidence that medical negligence may have been done by some of the treating physicians and that this was a jury question).

Comment: In retrospect, this lady should have had more adequate x-ray studies of her cervical spine, including tomograms, open mouth view of the odontoid, if there was reason to suspect a cervical spine fracture at that time. However, apparently another physician saw the x-rays and did not feel such was there, but no mention is made of listening to the patient's complaints and following up of persistent pain.

17 ***Stager v Schneider,* 494 A2d 1307 (DC 1985)** (as part of a workup for a foot case going to foot surgery, routine chest x-rays revealed a mass that was later shown to be adenocarcinoma of the lung. The orthopedic surgeon either missed the x-ray report or ignored the possibility of lung cancer and did not inform the patient prior to surgery, though the patient phoned the orthopedist the day of surgery cancelling it because she was not feeling well. Once the surgery was cancelled, the orthopedist saw no reason to check the x-rays, so they were attached to the patient's chart in accordance with hospital rules. Nine months later, a second routine chest x-ray was carried out because her mother had died of lymphosarcoma and a half-sister had died of lung cancer. The tumor was re-identified and drastic lung surgery was carried out on the patient. A principal question in this case was whether it was the duty of the orthopedic surgeon to inform the patient of abnormality on x-rays with a degree of contributory negligence on the part of the patient for not requesting that information. The District of Columbia Court of Appeals agreed that a patient is obliged to cooperate in her treatment

but added, "It is a quantum leap," from that adage to permitting a duty to be placed on a patient, to call and inquire of test results under the circumstances presented here. The fatal onis lay with the orthopedist in not reviewing the records and not reporting to the patient and not assuring appropriate follow-up care for the reported lung tumor nine months earlier).

18 ***Jenoff v Gleason,* 215 NJ Super 349 (App Div 1987)** (plaintiff underwent orthopedic surgery which referred her to defendant internist. He ordered a chest x-ray because the hospital required it and anesthesiologist wished it as part of his pre-anesthetic work-up. The defendant didn't review x-rays, though he had cleared patient for surgery if x-rays were normal. When the defendant went to check x-ray, it already was in surgery with the patient, so he never saw the x-ray. Two months later, during a health insurance examination, another chest x-ray showed lung cancer that eventually caused patient's death. The defendant was held negligent by the court, also liable under lost chance doctrine. The orthopedist likewise was held as he operated the patient responsible for her physical status, though he had diluted his liability in relying on defendant's clearance for surgery, except for abnormal x-ray, which was known (or could have been known) before surgery. The surgery itself had no apparent effect on the lung tumor. The hospital has a duty as well as the radiologist, but they were not joined in this suit. The radiologist owed a duty to report to the physician ordering x-ray but not to report to patient).

19 ***Jones v Finley,* 170 Ga App 182, 316 SE2d 182 (1984)** (fractured ankle was missed by a number of physicians. The patient continued to have pain after an injury. Initial x-rays viewed in retrospect by medical experts showed a faint line. However, this was admitted to being in retrospect and as the case turned, that line was a "red herring." An osteochondral fracture of the left talus was eventually found when tomograms were taken. Both experts for the plaintiff admitted that missing the fracture such as this on original x-rays was not negligent because of its non-appearance, but the negligence derived from the failure to get different views and more adequate studies, including CT scan).

20 ***Braun v Rycyna,* 473 NYS2d 627 (App Div 1984)** (orthopedist treated a patient who landed on his feet on a concrete surface. Multiple x-rays were taken of the ankle; no x-rays were taken of his foot. Injury diagnosis was fractured right ankle, and he was advised to go to an orthopedic specialist. He did so. The orthopedic surgeon applied a walking cast treating the ankle fracture, and took no additional x-rays. A month or so later, he removed the walking cast, x-rayed the ankle that showed the fracture healed despite the patient's continued complaints of pain in his right foot. The orthopedic surgeon never ordered x-rays of his foot. The patient finally consulted another physician who took additional x-rays. The new x-rays revealed a fracture of the right heel. Use of an orthopedic shoe failed to relieve his pain. He underwent bone fusion one and one-half years later. surgery reduced his pain but also shortened his ankle. The trial court granted the hospital motion for directed verdict on the grounds the hospital's negligence was not the

proximate cause of the patient's injury. The appellate court reversed the decision. The court noted that a medical malpractice panel unanimously recommended a finding of a liability against the hospital and the physician. The court said that the opinion was supported by expert opinion of this medical member and required the case to be submitted to a jury. Although the jury returned a verdict in favor of the orthopedic surgeon, the court said it would be highly unfair to exclude him from a re-trial of the case).

Comment: Failure to x-ray areas of complained about is a frequent cause of negligence litigation. In this case, with repeated complaints by the patient of foot pain, the surgeon's failure to x-ray the foot fell below the standard of care.

21 ***ZeBarth v Swedish Hospital Medical Center,* 81 Wash 2d 12, 499 P2d 1 (1972)** (orthopedist and/or neurosurgeon referred the patient to a radiologist after hospitalization and biopsy showed Hodgkin's disease. The radiologist performed x-ray therapy. A year after treatment the patient became paralyzed from an injury to his spinal cord. There was a question among several pathologists as to the exact nature of the tumor, all agreeing that it was a malignancy involving the reticulcendothelial system in which Hodgkin's disease is one such tumor. There was a question of whether there was an excessive amount of radiation therapy given and did that cause the paraplegia. There were a number of expert testimonies on both sides of those issues. Judgment of the supreme court was that the case should be re-tried on the basis of informed consent, adjudicating the possibility that the patient had not been informed adequately of the risks of radiation therapy. The plaintiff also complained of res ipsa loquitur and a strong descending opinion was held that the case heard by the supreme court had allowed judgment under the basis of res ipsa loquitur should stand).

22 ***Woods v United States,* 720 F2d 1451 (9th Cir 1983)** (negligent administration of a cervical myelogram was alleged. The patient claimed that the physicians in an Army Medical Center failed to aspirate all the contrast medial and residual Pantopaque caused brain damage. A trial court ruled that the patient failed to prove the use of Pantopaque caused her seizures. On appeal, the court agreed with the lower court's decision on a claim based on negligence of administration of cervical myelogram. A claim of assault and battery (based on diagnostic procedure) was made but the court said that there was no intentional wrongful act by the physician).

23 ***Schaecher v Reinwein,* 41 Ill App 3d 1055, 355 NE2d 351 (1976)** (orthopedic surgeon did a partial lumbar myelogram but did not carry myelogram to first cervical level, did not order bone scan or electromyelogram and performed laminectomy in lumbar area without finding cancerous tumor of thoracic spine. Plaintiff's expert did not testify as to standards of care in defendant's community; there was no evidence that bone scans and electromyelograms were not available and expert offered no opinion as to existence of tumor at time of diagnosis and treatment by defendant. Defendant was entitled to directed verdict).

Comment: This scenario happens often in orthopedic practice. Currently, most communities have or are close to having sophisticated diagnostic facilities (CT scan, MRI, bone scanning, and electromyelograms). The bottom line is awareness of the possibility of a cervical or dorsal lesion explaining lumbar-suspected pathology.

24 ***McClane v United States,* 490 F Supp 485 (ED Wis 1980)** (patient's brain stem injuries were the result of negligence during a myelogram. The patient was admitted to the hospital complaining of hip pain. Routine x-rays of the spine and pelvis produced a tentative diagnosis of ankylosing spondylitis. The patient also was diabetic. A lumbar myelogram was unsuccessful because of ossification and calcification; therefore, a neuroradiologist performed a cisternal puncture cervical air myelogram. During the procedure, the patient suffered brain stem injury and became 100 per cent totally and permanently disabled. The question of fact lay between whether the radiologist damaged the spinal cord or whether there was spontaneous unavoidable stroke. The court found a preponderance of the evidence that supported the conclusion of spinal cord trauma by the radiologist).

25 ***Pratt v Stein,* 298 Pa Super 92, 444 A2d 674 (1982)** (plaintiff underwent a lumbar myelogram and disc surgery in lumbar spine. Post-operative infection developed, leaving patient with significant lower extremity deficit. A plaintiff verdict was sustained. The plaintiff claimed that the myelogram showed a mid cervical block and examination suggested upper cervical nerve involvement. Plaintiff maintained that lumbar surgery was contraindicated and that failure to explain and treat the cervical lesion was a departure from standard of care. Postoperative wound infection and draining sinuses were stated by plaintiff to be below standard of care as wound was not drained earlier. There was not adequate rebuttal to plaintiff's allegation).

Comment: The failure to deal with the cervical problem and the probable impropriety of doing lumbar spine surgery are most probably negligence. The delay in surgical drainage of disc space infection will resolve with rest and antibiotics when identified, with surgical interference risking worsening of condition. If a wound abscess is identified, incision and drainage of that abscess is appropriate.

26 ***Cox v Haworth,* 283 So 2d 392 (NC Ct App 1981)** (hospital had no duty to obtain a patient's informed consent for a myelogram. The patient entered the hospital for a myelogram. During the procedure performed by his personal physician, who was assisted by hospital personnel, used hospital facilities and administered drugs provided by the hospital. The patient alleged that because the physician failed to remove all the Pantopaque dye that was injected in his spinal cord, he suffered incapacitating pain and arachnoiditis. The patient filed a suit against the hospital for failing to obtain this consent. Also, he alleged the hospital was liable under theories of battery and res ipsa loquitur. The trial court granted a summary judgment for the hospital affirming the decision. The court said the patient failed to prove the physician was an agent of the hospital. The patient was admitted by his private physician; the hospital had no duty to properly inform and

advise the patient the nature of the procedure being performed. The physician, on the other hand, does have a duty to get an informed consent from the patient and does have a legal responsibility to respond to the allegation that the Pantopaque did produce arachnoiditis).

Comment: There are papers in medical literature that state Pantopaque does produce arachnoiditis, particularly if there is bleeding in the spinal canal at the same time. Pantopaque has been largely replaced by Metrizamide.

27 *Karibjanian v Thomas Jefferson University Hospital,* 717 F Supp 1081 (ED Pa 1989) (federal district court, applying Pennsylvania law, ruled that a hospital may be subject to strict liability and informed consent for injury caused by an x-ray dye (Thoratrast) that was injected during a test of artery damage, an arteriogram. The patient died. The plaintiff alleged that the defendant hospital failed (1) to undertake or support research to find a remedy for Thorotrast complications; (2) to obtain informed consent for administration of Thorotrast and (3) was subject to strict liability because Thorotrast was a defective product. On issue of informed consent, the hospital said the duty for obtaining informed consent lay with the doctor. The court refused, based on recent decisions that the hospital is responsible for supervising its staff physicians. The hospital argued that informed consent is limited to surgical procedure and does not extend to the administration of drugs or other substances. In this case, the court noted one of plaintiff's allegation was that injection was not necessary and in an alternative, using a chemical other than Thortotrast be used. In this way, it appears the court by-passed the question, "Is informed consent necessary only for surgical procedures?" The court then refused to dismiss the strict liability claim, ruling the plaintiff should be permitted to pursue her contention that the hospital was a seller of Thorotrast. This holding rejects the hospital's contention that strict liability should not be applied to hospitals that provide medical products as a part of providing services to the patient such as arteriograms. The court noted the hospital provided Thorotrast from its inventory, thus the plaintiff should be allowed to attempt to establish strict liability theories to this case. The court did dismiss the claim for failure to attempt to find a remedy for the complications of Thorotrast, finding no basis for imposing a burdensome duty for hospitals to do or support research).

28 *Cress v Mayer,* 626 SW2d 430 (Mo Ct App 1981) (defendant performed surgery to remove part of first rib for thoracic outlet syndrome. The plaintiff says that surgeon said it was a simple operation without risk and that physical therapy would not help her shoulder/arm pains and numbness. The surgeon offered no alternative treatment. A major injury occurs during surgery leaving the arm partially paralyzed. The defendant physician argued that the plaintiff had the burden of proof through expert testimony of what a reasonable specialist surgeon should have told the plaintiff as to risks and treatment options. On appeal, the court noted that two experts said the plaintiff was mis- or under-informed, that physical therapy was treatment of choice and that indication for surgery was rare. Further, no diagnostic testing, such as arteriogram, was done to verify that arterial impingement (diagnostic of thoracic syndrome) was present. It was held that informed consent was inadequate and question of unnecessary surgery).

29 ***Brown v Koulizakis,* 331 SE2d 440 (Va 1985)** (orthopedic surgeon and consulting internist were sued by the state. A patient suffered a fatal pulmonary embolus. The patient came to the hospital complaining of low back pain. He was hospitalized and had a series of tests, including epidural venography. As a complication of the venography, pulmonary embolus did occur (one of the risks of venography). The onset of chest pain is when the internist was called in. Additional diagnostic studies including a discogram were cancelled. Chest x-ray was normal. No additional testing for pulmonary embolus such as radioisotope testing was carried out. No anticoagulant therapy was started. Autopsy showed "massive, acute" with a "secondary saddle type" pulmonary embolus occurring as a terminal event and associated with recurrence of low back pain. Medical experts harshly criticized the orthopedist for doing venography. Though not unaccepted, it is rarely a useful test for low back pain when other is less invasive, more diagnostic tests such as CT scan and MRI studies could be used. Although the court has ordered a new trial because of some technical errors, the supreme court has stated that a jury must hear evidence that the patient "was at risk and there were clear danger warnings of pulmonary embolism and that prompt actions might have saved the life of the patient").

Comment: In current medical practice, an attempt to diagnose pulmonary embolus promptly and treat it with anticoagulants can be life-saving. The recognition of thrombophlebitis is a risk of venography and must be covered with informed consent. Informed consent problems were not mentioned in this particular case.

30 ***Brown v Koulizakis,* 331 SE2d 440 (Va 1985)** (epidural venogram was performed on a 31-year-old man in an attempt to diagnose the cause of back pain. Seven days later, the patient experienced severe right upper quadrant pain. A lung scan confirmed pulmonary embolus, but the patient experienced acute respiratory distress and died within hours. The plaintiff's expert maintained the possibility of blood clots from a venogram and the extended period of bed rest required the use of heparin. The plaintiff's expert also maintained there was a delay in ordering the lung scan. An expert gave the patient of better than a 95 per cent chance of survival. The trial court's dismissal was reversed. The appellate court reasoned if the physician's action of inaction destroys a "substantial possibility of patient survival." Such conduct is the proximate cause of the patient's death. Patient is not required to prove to a certainty that the patient would have survived with more prompt diagnosis and treatment. The appellate court noted that the patient died of the condition which would have been discovered by more prompt diagnosis and treatment by the physician).

31 ***Smith v Luckett,* 155 Ga App 650, 271 SE2d 891 (1980)** (fact that plaintiff developed phlebitis, a known complication of venogram and where

there was no proof of negligent performance of the venogram or other deviation from the standard of care, justified defendant verdict).

32 ***Lipsius v White,* 91 AD 271, 458 NYS2d 928 (1983)** (plaintiff's expert testified that good medical practice required EMG and nerve conduction studies be performed of both upper extremities, prior to surgery, in order to make diagnosis of median nerve compression at wrist by carpal tunnel syndrome, and also to judge its severity. he testified that it was improper to operate without having done these tests. The expert said that post-operative symptoms resulted in division or injury to a branch of the median nerve during operation. The court held that a prima facie case based on negligence as well as informed consent).

Comment: It may be that the defendant surgeon was under represented holding that EMG is necessary to make and essential before surgery recommended. This may be the view of some but by no means all or even a preponderance of surgeons doing this kind of operation. To wait for EMG changes means the nerve is already damaged and much less likely to sustain a good pain relief, functional repair with median nerve neurolysis and carpal tunnel release. There is abundant literature to support this observation.

33 ***Peace v Weisman,* 186 Ga App 697, 368 SE 2d 319 (1988)** (plaintiff had applied for social security disability benefits. The Georgia Department of Human Resources required him to undergo a medical consultation and examination. The defendant physician conducted the examination of the direction of DHR for the sole purpose of rendering a medical opinion to DHR concerning the plaintiff's ability to work. Plaintiff states that defendant physician committed medical malpractice by failing to diagnose his lung cancer in a timely manner, thereby allowing the malignancy to progress to its terminal stage. The court held that no physician patient relationship had existed between the plaintiff and the defendant during the physical examination and therefore the plaintiff could not recover on the basis of professional malpractice. The court further stated that in the absence of physician patient relationship, the defendant's only duty to the plaintiff was to conduct the examination in such a manner not to injure the patient).

34 ***McPherson v Ellis,* 302 NC 266, 287 SE2d 892 (1982)** (action against neuroradiologist and surgeon for failing to inform risk of arteriogram which, in this case, resulted in paralysis over 45 per cent of body and rated as 40 per cent impairment of upper and 5 per cent of lower extremities. The trial court erred in instructing jury to consider remoteness of this complication and to determine whether relating such a risk was required under standard medical practice in neuroradiology and neurology at the relevant time in the community or similar communities; uncontroverted evidence indicated that standard of care required advising the patient of risk of paralysis).

18

Physical Medicine

Introduction

§18.01 Generally

Physical medicine can be defined as that branch of medical practice which uses physical agents, such as light, heat, water, electricity, and a variety of mechanical and physical agents, in the management of injury or disease. *Rehabilitation* is a combined treatment and training protocol designed to improve the patient's functioning in his or her society. Rehabilitation is appropriately divided into physical, psychological, social, and vocational components. Rehabilitation is a creative procedure which includes the cooperative efforts of many medical specialists and their aides in other fields to improve or stabilize the physical, mental, social, and vocational abilities of handicapped persons, with the objective of preserving or improving their ability to live happily and productively on the same level and with the same opportunities as their neighbors or peers.

Community health services have defined rehabilitation as "the process of decreasing dependence of the handicapped or disabled person by developing to the greatest extent possible, the abilities needed for adequate functioning in his individual situation."[1]

The importance of physical medicine and rehabilitation medicine has been repeatedly demonstrated in the successful assessment and treatment of patients through the last three decades. What may have started as a nursing or comforting method for patients with pain or impaired movement, largely using laying-on-of-hands treatments, has now evolved into a highly skilled, quite technical medical discipline. One has only to travel to areas in the world where rehabilitative methods are unknown or unavailable to the disabled patient to see the devastation that adequate rehabilitation could have prevented.

It is known today that the care of the sick and disabled must go beyond the antiquated approach in which the physician only concerns him- or herself with the diagnosis of static pathologic processes, provides a necessary operation or medication, and dismisses the patient as treated, after which the treating physician's responsibility has ended. The modern accepted approach realizes a dynamic approach to the study of disorders of physiologic processes which are constantly changing and that concern with the physical, psychological, and social ramifications is a duty owed the patient at all stages of care. Instead of providing episodic care for specific diseases, the modern physician must take a holistic approach in which he or she strives to maintain the patient in the best possible health physically and mentally, even though the patient may be severely impaired. There is a growing realization that interrelated social factors outside of the physical or chemical aspect of the patient are involved with health. The amount of chronic illness among aging persons is increasing. The medical problem of chronic illness is a major one, deserving as much (or more) concern as acute illnesses. Each time a surgeon saves a life or repairs a crippled joint, or each time a medical practitioner prevents death in a paralyzed patient, a triumph over death and crippling is achieved. At the same time, though, these physicians have created new problems for managing chronic impairments.

Twenty-five years ago, a major report said that three million persons in the United States could be rehabilitated and returned to useful lives, provided we had the facilities and personnel. Facilities and personnel have increased, but the number of chronically ill persons has also increased tremendously, leaving many uncared for or incompletely cared for at this time.[2]

The physical medicine aspect of medicine should be a multifaceted group of professionals. The orthopedist needs to know where to tap into this group and use appropriate team members or refer a patient to a rehabilitation specialist and/or facility. The active, informed orthopedist is up to date on the

---

1 Community Health Council of the United Community Fund of San Francisco, Report on Rehabilitation of Chronically Ill and Disabled Persons in San Francisco 1960, at 4.

2 Foster, Jr, *Neuroses and Trauma,* 32 Clin Orthop 54-59 (1964).

rehabilitation techniques and facilities available to him or her and the patient. Ideally, the orthopedist (or other treating physician) should be an active partner in the rehabilitation of his or her patient.

Because of the tremendous national and international interest in rehabilitation as a mass humanitarian endeavor, there has been an unfortunate tendency for professional groups and for many individuals to assume that they know all there is to know about rehabilitation. They tend to set themselves up as experts in rehabilitation and to assume that their small segment of rehabilitation is the whole of rehabilitation.

Each rehabilitation group that is really qualified to handle any one of the four major phases of rehabilitation—physical, psychological, social, or vocational—has developed a body of knowledge and programs applying that knowledge and has trained expert professionals to administer or supervise the programs. Such professionals are those who carry on effective production rehabilitation. The less-trained, less-conscientious therapist, or one who uses one or two modalities in the name of rehabilitation, likely does his or her patient a disservice.

The chronic pain clinic, the sports medicine clinic, and successful goal-directed back clinics which operate on a multifaceted approach using those professional disciplines needed by patients are currently returning more orthopedic patients to work or productive lives with acceptable comfort and function. This is the real criteria for the successful rehabilitation of the orthopedic patient.

Early involvement in an adequate rehabilitation program is most productive of satisfactory outcomes as opposed to delaying indicated therapies for months or years, for whatever reason. A pioneer in rehabilitation medicine, Howard Rusk, has pointed out:

> Rehabilitation of the chronically ill and disabled is not just a series of restorative techniques; it is a philosophy of medical responsibility. Failure to assume the responsibility means to guarantee the continued deterioration of many less severely disabled persons until they, too, reach the severely disabled and totally dependent category. The neglect of disability in its early stages is far more costly than an early aggressive program of rehabilitation which will restore the individual to the highest level of physical, economic, social and emotional self-sufficiency.[3]

The physical medicine/rehabilitation specialist is typically represented by a physician called a *physiatrist*. The physiatrist has first become a licensed physician and then has completed specialty training as a physical medicine

---

[3] Rusk, Preventive Medicine, Curative Medicine—The Rehabilitation, 13 New Phys 165 (1964); F.H. Krusen, Handbook of Physical Medicine and Rehabilitation (2d ed 1971).

specialist.[5] Generally, working with the physiatrist is a registered physical therapist. In most states, the physical therapist must work under a prescription from a physician, although in some states registered physical therapists can practice independently, examine patients, prescribe a treatment plan, and participate in disability evaluations. This is a state-legislated program, for which strong physical therapist lobbying for the privilege is being voiced.

In addition to physiatrists and registered physical therapists, there is a wide range of disciplines participating in rehabilitation, including (1) therapy aides largely on-the-job trained, working under registered physical therapists or licensed physicians, (2) social workers, usually postgraduate-trained and state-licensed, (3) occupational therapists, postgraduate-trained and state-licensed, (4) speech therapists, (5) exercise therapists, (6) dieticians, (7) psychologists, postgraduate-trained and state-licensed and (8) vocational rehabilitation specialists, postgraduate-trained and state-licensed. Each of these disciplines, as well as others not mentioned, must participate in patient care only under prescription by, or via consultation with, a physician, or in some states a registered physical therapist.

There are certification avenues for rehabilitation facilities, but none required by states (except Florida). CARF is one certifying agency following the same basic techniques for certification as the Joint Commission on Accreditation of Health Care Organization. Their requirements are rigorous and beyond most facilities that do good rehabilitation work; thus, a void is present at this time in credentialling rehabilitation facilities or physician in-office treatment plans. There is a need for such evaluations, some of which are done through rules of Medicare and/or Medicaid and other third-party carriers. There is a real need to separate the laying-on-of-hands, "shake and bake" therapies from the organized holistic programs geared to improving the patient's control of self as much as possible.[6]

Typical services offered by registered physical therapists, along with or under prescription by an orthopedist, are:

1. Treatment of neck and back disorders or deformities
2. Management of motor unit pathologies
3. Rehabilitation of the stroke or brain-injured plegic patient
4. Treatment of soft tissue nonarticular and articular pathologies
5. Treatment of congenital and traumatic spinal cord lesions
6. Aftercare of fracture
7. Postsurgical rehabilitation after joint arthroplasties
8. Cranial nerve and central nervous system diseases

---

[5] Hirschfield & Behan, *The Accident Process. Etiological Consideration in Industrial Injuries,* 186 JAMA 193-99 (1963).

[6] Roundtable Discussion, American Back Society Spring Symposium, Cambridge Mass, Apr 1989.

9. Decubitus ulcers, burns, and other skin loss contracture problems
10. Cerebral palsy and rehabilitation of children
11. Postoperative care of reconstructive surgeries to extremities, tendon transfer, joint fusions, skin grafting, etc.
12. Hand injuries and surgeries
13. Chronic benign pain management
14. Care and training of the amputee

The therapist is additionally trained in a wide variety of disorders not mentioned above, but which are often helpful to the orthopedist. These include:

1. Disorders of respiration (pulmonary function)
2. Cardiovascular problems
3. Auditory disorders, evaluation, and treatment
4. Psychiatric rehabilitation, including the mentally retarded
5. Rehabilitation of the blind
6. Speech and language disorders
7. Training of patient and family in transfer, standing, and walking with or without assistive devices (cane, walker, crutches, wheelchair)
8. Bed position; decubitus prevention
9. Training in functional and homemaking activities

Total patient care requires consideration and help in psychosocial, vocational rehabilitative, dietary, and often substance abuse problems.

It is important for the physician and therapist to know their skills and rehabilitative limitations and to seek appropriate consultation early. Time lost in rehabilitation often prolongs or reduces the maximal improvement that the patient is entitled to.

In the laying-on-of-hands therapies that the physical therapist may use, there are ever-expanding and innovative methods of treatment. These include therapeutic heat and cold, diathermy, ultrasound and other deep heat modalities, electrical stimulation, hydrotherapy, and massage.

Exercise therapy is rapidly becoming a sub-rehabilitation specialty with the realization that the function and improvement of physical capacity and endurance are largely related to both musculoskeletal flexibility and muscular strength—often retraining specific muscles. These deficiencies can be assessed by skillful muscle testing and a study of joint system range of motion. To better evaluate, record, and compare these data with an expanding data bank, new assessment and treatment devices studying isokinetic-isotonic strengths as well as testing patient compliance are available.

Chronic benign pain management is another rapidly expanding rehabilitation tool, often carried out in chronic pain clinics. Many rehabilitation facilities combine traditional physical therapies, particularly exercise, with chronic pain management methods, and better approach holistic care with better patient outcomes.

Many chronic pain management clinics are set around one or two treatment modalities, such as myofascial trigger point or other nerve type injection, tending to ignore the social and other physical, vocational, and psychological ramifications of the patient's chronic pain syndrome. This may represent inadequate or incomplete chronic pain management.

§18.02 History and Physical Examination

When a patient is first seen by the physiatrist or physical therapist, a complete history and previous records, tests, surgeries, and their results are reviewed. The patient is interviewed as to what his or her goals in treatment are, and is assessed as to how he or she views the problems to be treated. A complete physical examination of the areas to be treated and observation of general health problems are assessed. If any contraindications to a specific treatment modality appear in the history or if the therapist ascertains any contraindication, these must be noted.

A diagnosis is made by the therapist, often similar to the diagnosis of the referring physician, but couched in the expertise of the physiatrist or physical therapist. If there are major deviations or disagreements in the diagnosis and proposed treatment, the referring physician must be contacted by the therapist.

The diagnosis is always made known to the patient; an explanation of "what" and "why" are important therapeutic tools, because much of rehabilitation is educational in nature.

In chronic (and acute) back pain patients, it has been found that a formal dissertation, including anatomy, physiology, biochemistry, as well as treatment techniques and their anticipated effects, is very helpful as a therapeutic tool for the patient. Often, the physician ignores his or her patient's "need to know."

A large percentage of the orthopedic patients referred for rehabilitation fall into frequent categories. The back pain patient, the postoperative arthroplasty or joint reconstruction patient, the injury-healing partially immobile (or paralyzed) patient, the non-injured musculoskeletal pain patient, the arthritic patient, and the post-illness infirm patient each has different, yet at the same time overlapping, needs.

It seems tradition for the physiatrist/physical therapist to address the organic/physical problem first, and the psychological/social and parallel problems secondarily. Ordinarily, this presents no problem as long as all are assessed and treated.[7]

---

[7] Krusen & Ford, *Compensation Factor in Low Back Injuries,* 166 JAMA 1128-33 (1958).

§18.03 Physical Therapist

The *physical therapist* is a highly-trained paramedical person who specializes in the mechanical, and to some extent the chemical, aspects of rehabilitation of patients. His or her skills lie in excellent knowledge of the anatomy and pathology of the body, and should include a high degree of empathy for the patient and charismatic characteristics that motivate patients to help themselves. This can be a difficult and frustrating job.

The therapist does very little laying-on-of-hands therapy that is curative. The therapist applies modalities that relax the patient, that stretch the patient, and, at times, that change the chemistry of underlying tissues.

Patient compliance is always the "bottom line" to physical therapeutic techniques. It is important that the patient understand what therapies are being administered and what the purposes are. The physical therapist also is in an excellent position to observe, understand, and treat any psychological ramifications of the pain syndrome.

From a training point of view, the physical therapist is a college graduate with two or more years of specialized training in a school of physical therapy, ordinarily university bound. The therapist has completed examinations by her peers and has obtained a license of certification.

The *registered physical therapist aide* has similar skills but less training, and has a lesser credential. Both disciplines require a state license by a division of the state board of medical examiners, a license that is subject to peer review and periodic renewal. Most states require continuing medical education as part of the continuing license or certification.

§18.04 Rehabilitation

Many methods are utilized for the physical treatment of disabilities, including low back pain, and they all have their advocates. Most base their beliefs on the fact that a particular patient recovered or improved with a specific treatment. However, the majority of patients with acute injuries, including those with acute low back pain, will recover with no treatment at all.

A general review of physical therapy treatment options reveals that most have no scientific basis and are passed from one clinician to another by what has been described as "Ecclesiastical Succession."

Analyzing the literature carefully, as we must, we find very few studies that are properly designed and therefore very little valid guidance in selecting appropriate treatment regimes. Even studies frequently quoted fall short on important study criteria, leading to invalid conclusions.

A few properly designed research studies do help with decisionmaking concerning treatment of low back pain:

1. Two days of bed rest was found to be as effective as seven, and two days reduced the time lost from work by 45 per cent compared to seven days
2. There appears to be short-term, but no long-term, benefits from immobilization and manipulation types of therapies

3. Back school (lecture) is as effective as a form of physical therapy that included manipulation, and both were found to be more effective than no treatment at all
4. McKenzie individualized exercises were found to be more effective than back school or 90-90 traction in acute/chronic lumbar pain patients
5. Posture correction is beneficial during the early treatment of low back pain

Since the anatomic cause of the majority of low back pain cases cannot be objectively evaluated or visualized, an individualized treatment program based on each patient's self-report of pain in response to mechanical examination would seem to directly affect the underlying abnormality.

There are many examples of this type of approach in solving other more familiar painful situations. This would appear to be a partial explanation for the apparent success of the McKenzie approach.

Most physical therapy options offer but one mode of treatment for all patients; that is, traction, modalities, corsets, etc., as though all low back pain had the same underlying cause. Only manipulation and an individualized exercise rehabilitation program allows for customized treatment for each patient's presentation.

While the vast majority of low back pain episodes resolve with little or no treatment, at least 60 per cent of patients have recurrent symptoms in one year. Patient education as part of the treatment for the initial acute episode appears to be helpful as a deterrent of recurrences.

Millions of American workers are injured in industrial accidents every year. Currently, 1.25 million Americans sustain injuries to their back or spine. Back injuries, therefore, represent a substantial percentage of total injuries. Of those back injuries, 65,000 have some permanent disability.

At the present time, approximately 2.5 million Americans have permanent impairments of their back as a result of injury.

Physicians are traditionally concerned with pathological lesions, yet have long recognized that certain environmental and psychological characteristics influence the prognosis following any injury, perhaps back injuries in particular. Many observers have suggested that disability payments alter the response to treatment of injured patients. It is well known that therapy successful for non-compensation patients is not satisfactory for those receiving compensation. In particular, patients with complaints referable to the lower part of the back responded less favorably to appropriate treatment when disability payments are involved.

One study found that those receiving compensation demonstrated 33 per cent less objective evidence of impairment, received nearly twice as many physical therapy treatments, and experienced 44 per cent less long-term improvement compared with patients not receiving compensation.

Several studies of a large number of patients operated on for protruded intervertebral discs found that private, non-compensable patients fared much better.

All explanations for less favorable results among patients receiving compensation have indicated a psychological factor. Multiple pathogenic mechanisms and behavioral syndromes have been suggested, including such concepts as accident neurosis secondary gain, the accident process, acute traumatic neuroses, and other psychological explanations.

Although there are some major truths in each of these formulations, it is believed that the whole man concept is the most attractive and useful in understanding and dealing with the psychological aspects of physical disability. The basis of this concept is that we do not treat disease and injuries, but individuals who are suffering the effects of disease and injuries, and that these individuals may often have socio-economical, psychological, vocational, medical, and other problems which may profoundly effect the physical status.[8]

§18.05 Key to Rehabilitation

The key to rehabilitation is to understand the patient's physiological, physical, and mental capacities and whether these capacities meet the demands of the workplace. To achieve this, the physician must be acquainted with the demands at work and the complexity of the tasks; for example, the loads imposed, the patient's strength and endurance, the range and coordination of motions required, and the environmental stresses. The reporting physician cannot render an accurate work ability or impairment report without knowing these elements, and places him- or herself in an impeachable position if he or she renders opinions absent these considerations.

This approach has been highly developed in the area of sports medicine, where the aim is to match the player's ability to the demands of the playing field. In a similar manner, the abilities of the patient must be matched to the demands of the workplace. More importantly, the work place should be matched to the worker, as the work place may be compared to a "chronically diseased" environment in many cases, which, however, is very treatable. It is in this arena that the worker, the employer, and the physician must be ergonomically oriented to best serve the patient-worker.

Most therapists recommend a holistic approach to rehabilitation. A total rehabilitation program dealing with musculoskeletally impaired persons must include a full history and evaluation by the therapist in conjunction with the prescribing physician. Typically, the therapist will use

---

[8] F.H. Krusen, Handbook of Physical Medicine and Rehabilitation (2d ed 1971; Hirschfield & Behan, *The Accident Process: Etiological Consideration in Industrial Injuries,* 186 JAMA 193-99 (1963); Krusen & Ford, *Compensation Factor in Low Back Injuries,* 166 JAMA 1128-33 (1958); Hirschfield, *Some Thoughts on Disability,* 6 J Occupat Med 267-70 (1964); Miller, *Accident Neurosis,* 1 Brit Med J 992-98 (1961); Solomon, *Low Back Pain: The Psycho-Somatic Viewpoint,* 18 Indus Med 6-12 (1949); Yochelson, *Psychiatric Aspect of Backache,* 3 Curr Prac Orthop Surg 253-72 (1966); Beals & Hickman, *Industrial Injuries of the Back and Extremities,* 54A JBJ Surg 1593 (1972).

diagnostic/therapeutic techniques such as isokinetics, isotonics, sports psychology, nutrition, education, pain and stress management, substance abuse, and spirituality. This is described as holist leading to an integrated wellness program. It has often been shown that a lesser program, a program using "bits and pieces" or the common "shake and bake" therapies, is incomplete, frequently ineffective, and often not cost-effective.[9]

Back Pain

§18.06 Structures Which Hurt in the Low Back

Back strain is one of the most common diagnoses resulting from injury. The knowledgeable physician will pinpoint where he or she feels the area of painful injury is located as the diagnosis. Back strain is no more a diagnosis than whiplash, but is merely a description of the mechanics of insult.

Back muscles are susceptible to strain, but this is virtually always self-limited, as are trigger point problems unless fibromyalgia or myofascial pain syndromes develop. These later conditions are very common and rank high in the differential diagnosis of post-injury back pain that does not promptly resolve.

The facet joints are infrequent areas of acute pain from acute injuries. Some orthopedists say that 20 per cent of chronic back pain emanates from facets; most believe facet pain is part of discogenic pain complex.

When low back strain is diagnosed, most orthopedists believe that deep structures account for ongoing pain (three weeks or longer; less may well be entirely muscle strain). "When you think of low back pain, think annulus," is the message of many. The supraspinous ligament cannot be the cause because it does not exist at K4-5 or L5-S1 and the interspinous ligament is barely developed, not a true ligament. The iliolumbar ligament does not exist until 30 years of age, being attached to quadratus lumborum muscle to pelvis until the enthetic attachment metamorphosis into myotendinous tissue. The longitudinal ligaments are so intimately associated with the annulus of the intervertebral disc that it is impossible to distinguish them. There is no research to show that the ligamentum flavus can be a pain source. The disc can be the source of pain even when it is intact, which is the usual situation. Common compression injuries (lifting, jumping, jerking insults) can cause end plate fractures which, if not fully repaired, can trigger a series of inflammatory and immune responses that erode the matrix of the nucleus, causing pain (particularly with loading) and leading to disc rupture. There is no pain when the nucleus alone is injured, as there are no nerve endings in the

---

[9] Nordin, *Orthopedics, Physical Rehabilitation and Ergonomics,* 18 Orthop Rev 67 (1989)

nucleus. Pain occurs as the lesion approaches the periphery—the annulus—as these structures are richly supplied with nerve endings. Normal discs burst only after a fracture of the vertebral end plate occurs.[10]

§18.07 Measuring Spinal Disorders

Accurate measurement of the motions and stretch of the trunk is limited by landmarks that rarely remain constant, a shifting axis of rotation and dual roles of muscles that act as both extensors and flexors. *Goniometers* are devices that measure angles and can be used in measuring degrees of motion in one plane at a time. Electronic devices are now available to facilitate this type of testing. These angular motions are the basis for much of the American Medical Society's Guides for Impairment. The goniometer gives no information about muscle strength or endurance. *Dynometers* are devices that measure forces, based on several measurement methods, such as strain gauges, sprain-loaded devices, pressure measuring instruments, simple free weights, and highly sophisticated, computer-operated devices that combine several methods.

The evolution of the "back examination" is evolving from an unstructured history and physical into a collection of qualitative and quantitative data that can greatly expand the understanding of low back pain.[11]

§18.08 Failed Back Patients

Several large studies using low back pain patients in which repeat low back surgery has been carried out reported poor results. Beyond two operations, more patients are likely to be made worse than helped. In general, in compensation patients the second operation should be regarded as the last chance.

Good results of repeat surgery are associated with at least 6 to 12 months of relief following previous operation, sciatica predominating over back pain and a recurrent prolapsed intervertebral disc. Bad results of repeat surgery were associated with scarring and neurolysis, previous infections, and repair of pseudarthrosis.

Psychological and social elements of anxiety, depression, hypochondriasis, conversion mechanisms, assuming the disability role, and family, employment, and financial concerns contribute substantially to low back pain impairment. All of these entities need evaluation before recommending repeat low back surgery. Most important is rigorous patient selection. Proper

---

[10] N. Bogduk, Strained Ligament—Think Annulus Presented at the International Back Pain Society Montreaux (1988) *reported in* 6 Int Back Pain News 4 (1988).

[11] Allen, *Clinical Kinesiology: Measurement Techniques for Spinal Disorders,* 17 Orthop Rev 1097 (1988); Gerhardt *Goniometry and Precision Measuring Devices,* 10 J Neurol & Orthop Med & Surg 5 (1989).

surgical indications should be strictly adhered to and all patients should routinely have formal psychological assessment before repeat low back surgery.[12]

§18.09 Which Back is Prone to Pain?

In recent years, parameters to assess potential low back patients have emerged. Body build (except gross obesity), body weight, age between 18 and 45 years, intelligence, ethnic background, and sex have little predictive value. Back and shoulder girdle muscle mass, strength, and endurance are most predictive. Testing these factors by isokinetic and isometric devices are becoming increasingly popular. Monitoring muscle performance using electromyographic techniques are additional new helps.[13]

§18.10 Myofascial Pain and Trigger Points

A very common source of skeletal pain is the *myofascial pain syndrome.* These are soft tissue pain complexes involving muscle fascia and their attachments at musculotendinous junctures or to bone (enthetic attachments). The muscles in certain areas of the body seem vulnerable to becoming painful after overload or injury, along with nutritional and postural deviations. The myofascial structure will often develop "trigger points" in predictable areas and, when stretched or compressed, will produce a significant local pain and often refer a pain complaint to a remote (but again predictable) area of the body.

Myofascial trigger points are easy to find. By definition, they are self-sustained, hyper-irritable foci located in the skeletal muscle of its associated fascia. A trigger point is a pathological entity. When muscles have been disturbed, when trauma is involved, trigger points are pathological with release of calcium ions that combine with adenosine triphosphate to give uncontrolled contraction, which ends up as muscle contraction. This is different from muscle spasm, in which a muscle goes in and out of contraction. In myofascial contracture, shortening of muscles across the joints they serve produces mechanical inefficiency and pain in a predictable manner. Decreased range of motion and muscle atrophy with weakness and loss of endurance of that muscle group may occur. The referral patient with the myofascial trigger point may mimic a radicular (nerve or nerve root) pattern. Similarity of referred trigger point pain to nerve compression syndromes must be recognized.

It is essential to consider myofascial pain syndromes with their attendant

---

[12] Waddell, *Failed Lumbar Disc Surgery and Repeat Surgery Following Industrial Injuries,* 61A JBJ Surg 201 (1979).

[13] Lewyn, *Insurer Researches Lower Back Pain* USA Today Jan 5, 1989, at 7B.

trigger points in the differential diagnosis of a musculoskeletal pain complaint. Misdiagnosis, mistreatment, and inappropriate surgery may be done to the detriment of the patient.[14]

§18.11 Phantom Pain

Patients who experience phantom pain can be relieved temporarily by segmental spinal anesthesia, suggesting some spinal cord participation in phantom pain. The same narcotics given intravenously, going then equally to the brain, does not have the phantom pain relieving ability. Epidural administration of local anesthetic often triggers phantom pain. The whole group of phantom pain, causalgia, and reflex sympathetic dystrophy is unexplained from a pathophysiology point of view, although no question exists concerning the tremendous disability of these problems.[15]

§18.12 Treating Chronic Back Pain

Recurring low back pain is often related to the work place. Heavy work and awkward constrained positions are associated with a high incidence of back pain. The physician informed as to the work place, one who has seen his or her patient at work, is in a better position to assess the cause and effect of work and to be more ergometric in solution suggestions.

The key to the patient's rehabilitation is to understand his or her physiological, physical, and mental capacities, and to achieve this the physician needs to be acquainted with the demands of the work loads involved—the strength, endurance, range, and coordination of motions required and the environmental stresses.

An algorithm must be used to evaluate back pain patients. Goals must be set and measurements established for assessing improvement. Thorough evaluation is important to rule out any other diseases, such as gynecological disease, rheumatic disease, or congenital or posttraumatic states or depression. The algorithm must take into consideration that both the patient and the work task need evaluation, particularly if the patient has been away from the work task for more than two months.

Stretching exercises to increase the extensibility of muscles and soft tissues have not alone been proven effective. They are, however, part of the key to restoring the functional range of joint motion. Stretching exercises are generally felt to be injury-preventing.

Range of motion measurements of trunk flexibility are routinely used in clinical evaluation. Little is known about how different variables affect range of motion. Trunk flexibility decreases with age and pain. To be

---

[14] Rosomoff *Surgeon Blames Many Failed Backs on Trigger Points,* 11 Back Pain Monitor 1 (1988).

[15] Jacobson, *Relief of Persistent Post-Amputation Stump and Phantom Limb Pain with Intrathecal Fentanyl,* 37 Pain 317 (1989).

meaningful, the data must take into account age, sex, height, obesity, and other physical attributes.

Fitness is a broader term for the ability to perform strengthening and endurance exercises. Cady (1979) showed that an increased level of fitness reduced the amount of musculoskeletal impairments among fire fighters. Others have shown that cardiovascular fitness tends to prevent chronicity in low back pain patients. It is unclear whether strength or endurance is more important.

Trunk strength needs to be measured by several parameters, as there is a correlation between isokinetic, isometric, and isodynamic trunk strength and endurance. One strength measurement in terms of lifting capacity is not able to predict the occurrence of low back injury, but there has to be enough strength capability for the work requirement. It is, therefore, important to look at work requirements and to train the patient to an acceptable level of ability. Rehabilitation training must include strengthening, endurance, and stretching exercises simulating work task requirements.

§18.13 Work Hardening Programs

Work hardening programs performed by specialized groups led by an orthopedist, physical therapist, and a specially-trained nurse seem most effective, returning acute and subacute back pain patients to work in 15 weeks. The treatment provided is adequate evaluation, positive reinforcement to return to work, education, physical reconditioning, and work place evaluation. The best reconditioning is similar to aggressive sports medicine.[16]

§18.14 Meeting Chronic Pain Needs

The medical profession is deficient in meeting the needs of pain sufferers. "I don't think there is a medical school in the world where more than four hours out of four years are spent in teaching students to diagnose or treat pain problems," says John Liebeskind, Ph.D., past president of the International Pain Foundation. "That's a primary reason why most pain problems are mismanaged or ignored, with tragic, unnecessary consequences." René

---

16 M. Nordin, Dynamic Measurement of Trunk Movements During Work Tasks Proceedings of the First International Ergonomics Symposium, Zadar, Yugoslavia *in* N. Corlett, The Ergonomics of Working Postures, Models, Methods and Cases (1986); Mooney, Symposium: Occupational Orthopedics 18 Contemp Orthop 377, (1989); Cady, *Strength and Fitness and Subsequent Back Injuries in Fire Fighters,* 21 J Occup Med 269 (1979); Anderson, 6 *Epidemiological Aspects on Low Back Pain in Industry* Spine 53 (1981); R. Hazard, "A One Year Prospective Study of Chronic Low Back Pain Patients, Presented at International Society for the Study of the Spine (ISSLS) Miami, Fla (1988); Keyserking, *Isometric Strength Testing as a Means of Controlling Medical Incidents on Strenuous Jobs,* 22 J Occup Med 332 (1980); TG Mayer, *Objective Assessment of Spine Function Following Industrial Injury,* 10 Spine 482 (1985).

Descartes, the French philosopher of 300 years ago, stated his conviction that mind and body are separate entities, a dualism that has greatly influenced the practice of medicine and from which knowledgable physicians are only now beginning to escape. We know the mind influences body and that physical pathology has a profound effect on mind and mood.[17]

§18.15 Chronic Benign Pain

Chronic, intractable, benign pain is defined as *non-neoplastic pain*, greater than three months duration without objective physical findings and/or known noiciceptive peripheral input. A significant number of patients suffering from chronic low back pain or neck pain do not fit into known diagnostic (organic) categories. As many as 30 per cent of chronic low back pain patients have no organic findings on physical examination.

A careful, all-inclusive physical examination is a basic initial requirement in classification of chronic benign low back pain. It is particularly important for the orthopedist not to quickly diagnose chronic benign low back pain, or somatization disorder, or a more pejorative label, based on the fact that he or she has not exhausted all diagnostic resources. This area is a real test of the diagnostic (very nearly detective work) skill of the physician.[18]

§18.16 Muscle Pain

Tenderness is one of the most commonly reported signs of musculoskeletal dysfunction and chronic pain. Tenderness on palpation is either assessed by the examiner or by the patient, although the subjectivity of these observations is often criticized.

Pressure algometers are pressure sensitive devices in which pressure on a muscle site is recorded and related to pain onset and intensity, an improvement over the sole report of the patient.[19]

§18.17 Physiotherapy Diagnostic Scale Muscle Strength

It is important that the examining physician or therapist have standards to measure the strength of individual muscle groups. In this way, the status and responses to treated muscle groups can be recorded and therapeutic

---

[17] Schechter, *Conquering Pain,* Modern Maturity, June-July 1989, at 72; Kirkaldy-Willis, *Discussion at North American Pain Society Spring Symposium,* Cambridge, Mass (Apr 13-16, 1989).

[18] Rosomoff, *Physical Findings in Patients with Chronic Intractable Benign Pain of the Neck and/or Back* 37 Pain 279 (1989).

[19] Ohrbach & Gale, *Pressure Pain Thresholds in Normal Muscles: Reliability, Measurement Effects and Topographic Differences* 37 Pain 257 (1989).

plans made. A universally accepted scheme is presented by Csuka, called Objective Gradation of Muscle Strength:[20]

1. 5 (normal) Motion against considerably applied manual force
2. 4 (good) Some motion possible against manually applied load
3. 3 (fair) Motion possible against gravity, but not against applied load
4. 2 (poor) Motion possible with elimination of gravity as a factor
5. 1 (trace) Palpable or visible contraction but no motion
6. 0 (none) No evidence of muscle contraction

§18.18 Causes of Back Pain

Back pain has a profound social, psychological, and economic impact on our ability to perform basic social tasks. Chronic back pain can seriously disrupt activities of daily living, including earning capacity. In terms of lost work days, inefficient work patterns, absenteeism, and compensation payments, the cost of back pain is enormous.

While back pain is a common ailment, there is a very little agreement as to its cause or prevention. This is due, in part, to conflicting interpretation of clinical data. Nearly all studies, though, conclude that there is no one specified cause associated with back pain, but that it most often manifests itself in work or work-like environments.

Generally accepted data indicate that 60 per cent of all workers (including homemakers) report having experienced low back pain. Almost 20 per cent of these claimed that back pain was a constant factor in their lives, and most reported its occurrence, but at infrequent intervals.

An important observation is that most low back pain is not medically diagnosed, and that in those cases in which a diagnosis was made, most were associated with muscle strain, disc derangement, and skeletal degeneration.

One-half of those experiencing low back pain had noted it between 1 and 5 years after starting work, one-third for at least 6 to 10 years, and one-fourth for more than 10 years. Sixty per cent of those reported having significant pain at least five times per year, most often during winter months and humid days.

In more detailed studies of back pain, it has been demonstrated that it is usually accompanied by other related pains, particularly combined neck/shoulder and low back/thigh pain. Pain syndromes that couple neck and low back pain have a greater adverse effect on work ability.

Basic age and sex differences appear, with young workers reporting a 25 per cent lower incidence of low back pain than those about to retire. However, persons 35 to 45 years old had back pain nearly as frequently as the oldest age group. The older persons reported greater frequency (five times per year—chronic) and increased severity of pain with lost work time.

---

[20] Glad & Kirschenbaum, *Study Shows Work Environments, Job Tasks May Cause Back Pain,* Occup Health & Safety, Feb 1989, at 44.

There was much less effect of gender in most surveys, yet when critically analyzed, a different picture is noted. Among those suffering chronic back pain, males exceeded females by two to one. In those experiencing low back pain sporatically, females only slightly outreported males. The key factor in determining the catalyst for low back pain is the work environment. Forty per cent blamed their general working conditions for the onset of their pain. An additional 50 per cent pinpointed specific work tasks as pain triggers. A substantial number of workers reported pain onset unrelated to sudden moves or unusually heavy incidents. Apparent specific catalysts are multivariate, accumulative, and linked to work risk factors.

Tenure in a job is related to increased chronic pain complaints, with more frequent complaints during the end of a work schedule, the highest being among workers doing the same repetitive job occasionally and those working overtime.

Among the chronic sufferers, there may be a self-selection process involved, in which the impediment caused by back pain weeded out the more severe cases from the regular eight-hour shift and concentrated them in a less work hour group. The relationship of depression and pain is that the depressed person perceives that he or she is incapacitated and rendered dysfunctional by the types of aches and pains that most persons have all the time, and the depressed patient becomes an invalid at that point. Once depression is treated, they can better tolerate their pain and the treatment is made more effective. No specific link can be made between rates of back pain and occupational status. Rates of pain occurred at equally low levels among both professional and semi-skilled workers. The highest rates are found among lower white collar clerical and unskilled workers.

There are extreme differences in the rate of back pain for persons in varying work tasks and settings. Back pain occurs in commercial drivers less often than in those engaged in service and maintenance. Factory workers report less back pain than metal shop or office workers, but all report substantially greater pain than commercial drivers. These reports are contrary to the earlier, often-reported notion that back pain is experienced in proportion to strenuous work.

It is much more probable that the well-conditioned worker is at less risk of back pain doing the same job, protecting his or her back, than the poorly-conditioned person doing occasional jobs in varying uncontrolled environments. Unusual work positions, such as bending sideways, and to a lesser extent bending forward, while sitting or standing, are frequently related to the onset of back pain. Those who "never" sit at work have high back pain reports, while those who sit some and walk some have less. Those who sit the entire work day are also at risk. It has been shown that the sitting posture loads the lumbar discs the most, particularly if in a slouched posture, and sitting still is nearly as adverse for the same reasons.[21]

---

[21] Glad & Kirschenbaum, *Study Shows Work Environments, Job Tasks May Cause Back Pain,* Occup Health & Safety, Feb 1989 at 44; Comments at American Back Society Spring Symposium, Cambridge, Mass, (Apr 13-16, 1989).

§18.19 Causes of Low Back Pain

Low back pain is a major source of morbidity. In the United States, impairment of the low back or cervical spine is the most common cause of long-term limitation of activity in persons under 45 years old. By some studies, 80 per cent of the population will suffer at least one significant episode of low back pain during adult life.

The lumbar spine is a complex musculoskeletal system and the mechanisms operating in the low back are not completely understood. Many competing theories exist, and for each postulated mechanism, there is in all probability a group of patients whose pain is thus explained. The relative importance of these potential sources of pain, singly or in combination, is difficult to determine.

It is essential that patients with back pain be carefully evaluated during both history and physical examination so that the physician can be as precise as possible when making a tentative diagnosis. A detailed neurological examination is essential to detect and document involvement of the spinal cord, nerve roots, rami, and other neural structures. Complete use of other diagnostic tests, such as x-rays, CT scanning, MRI, electromyography, discography, and thermography, where appropriate, will facilitate a definitive diagnosis. The comments made about low back pain are equally appropriate for cervical or dorsal spine pain.

The difficulties of diagnosing and treating this problem are apparent in critical reviews of patients involved in litigious types of injury, such as workers compensation or third-party liability claims where the possibility of secondary gain must be considered.[22]

§18.20 Mobilizing Joints; Frozen Shoulder Syndrome

The physical therapist frequently is called on to improve function and reduce pain. Among the problems to be dealt with is limited motion due to the frozen shoulder syndrome.

This entity, although not well understood pathologically by the orthopedist, is one where there is frequently a sudden onset of painful limitation of motion. It tends to occur in certain personality types that are high on the anxiety scale—compulsive, obsessive individuals.

Manual manipulation for a frozen shoulder under anesthesia is not universally accepted, although it has its advocates. Manipulation under anesthesia followed by intensive physical therapy probably does shorten the overall

---

[22] Lucas, *Low Back Pain,* 63 Surg Clin No Amer 515 (1983); Mixter & Barr, *Rupture of Intervertebral Disc with Involvement of the Spinal Canal,* 211 NEJM 210 (1934); Day, *Observation on the Treatment of Lumbar Disc Disease in College Football Players,* 15 Am J SportsMed 72 (1987) A; Blankstein, *Disk Space Infection and Vertebral Osteomyelitis as a Complication of Percutaneous lateral Discectomy,* 225 Clin Orthop 234 (1987).

period of recovery of the frozen shoulder. There is, however, a natural tendency for the frozen shoulder to resolve itself in a period of time, although two or three years is not unusual.

§18.21 Therapy Modalities

Physical therapy programs are guided passive and active range of motion, and gentle manipulations by the patient and by the therapist. Techniques of improving extension and abduction by wall crawling on notched boards and/or using a shoulder wheel are helpful. These techniques are most often used after a period of heating the shoulder. In the most acute case, starting with pendulum exercises may be the first step.

In posttraumatic situations, fractures, or dislocations where there is limitation of motion, where there has been sufficient time for soft tissues to heal, the physical therapist has an essential part in rehabilitation. In the usual situation, passive pendulum exercises to increase range of motion are first used. It is important to protect soft tissues or bony structures that are not healed well enough to tolerate active manipulation. Most soft tissue injuries are healed well enough in three weeks and fractures are stable enough in four to six weeks that progressive active range of motion is started. It is important to obtain full range of active and passive motion as rapidly possible. This may be a moderately painful experience for the patient. This is an area where the physical therapist is important, with his or her skills, charisma, and utilization of the concept of "No pain, no gain."

On the issue of pain control, the physical therapist has a variety of tools that are helpful. Deep heat modalities, transcutaneous electrical nerve stimulation (TENS) units, alternate hot and cold packs, and ice massages are frequently helpful. If the patient describes an acute change in the pain pattern, suggesting disruption of soft tissue or bone, the physical therapist must immediately report this to the treating orthopedist.

Physical therapy rehabilitation of the elbow requires early mobilization as soon as soft tissues or bony structures heal to permit this. Again, three weeks for soft tissue healing such as posterior dislocation of the elbow, and four to six weeks with internally-fixed supracondylar, epicondylar, or olecranon fractures, are usually sufficient to allow active mobilization. Overstretching the elbow actively in extension in particular is contraindicated, because there is a tendency for a contracted brachialis muscle to overstretch too quickly and a complicating myositis ossificans frequently occurs.

The functional range of motion 20 to 30 degrees of extension and 120 to 130 degrees of flexion is a goal that physical therapy should achieve for the patient. Pronation and supination of 50 to 60 degrees are likewise important to achieve useful function. In patients who have persistent flexion and extension contractures after a sufficient period of physical therapy, usually four to six months, the orthopedic surgeon should be informed so the surgeon can consider open capsulotomy or other soft tissue releases.

In the care of patients, humane acts—touching and stroking—not directly affecting "the care" (a word meaning neither more nor less than medical and surgical intervention for the purpose of favorably altering the course of an illness) are in short supply in the hospital world; that the patient's mental status is only marginally relevant to the effort, yet helpful verbal or nonverbal communications are helpful to the patient; and that far from being embarrassed by brusqueness, residents are more likely to be embarrassed by (and considered not quite professional) acts or gestures that are other than completely instrumental.

§18.22 Conservative Back Care

In the soft tissue injured low back, the painful discogenic or facet deranged low back, or in spondylolisthesis, accomplishing clinical stability of the motion segments is the first order of treatment. This results in 90 per cent or greater alleviation of, or reduction to acceptable levels of, the pain from the impairment. Surgery is appropriate for a certain group of unremitting pain complaints based on motion segment "instability." Surgery is admittedly a big price to pay, and is frequently less than successful. Surgery for the sharply localized nerve root impingement, such as unremitting protruded intervertebral disc, is the most successful surgical candidate, but even here well-controlled studies of operated and unoperated patients show similar end results three to five years after symptom onset.[23]

Exercise

§18.23 Why Exercise?

There is general acknowledgment that physically fit people are much better able to deal with life's physical and emotional demands. In addition, adequate levels of fitness are necessary to participate in many sports safely with optimal performance and enjoyment. The same situation exists for most work activities. It is important that patients understand that they should become physically fit before attempting a high level of sports participation or participation in some strenuous work activities.

Endurance exercise calls forth complex metabolic, cardiovascular, pulmonary, neurological, and hormonal adjustments that allow the body to respond to the demands of the working muscle.[24]

Exercise has been shown to be an effective adjunct to good health and the rehabilitation of deconditioned patients. Exercise should be prescribed by the physician in a specific manner, to avoid injury or other complications. Supervised exercises are effective and predictable. To tell the patient "Go exercise" is less than professional, if it is a therapeutic prescription. The

---

23 White, *Conservative Treatment Considered Best Course for Spondylolisthesis,* 3 Orthop Today 6 (1989).

24 Van Camp, *Your Patient Asks: Why Exercise,* 3 Your Patient & Fitness 13 (1989).

effects of different exercises, the neutral spine, and the need for strength and flexibility are concepts that apply to all back pain sufferers except acute fractures or sprains. The choice of exercises and the rate of progression will depend on the patient's individual problem. Each person needs individually tailored exercises. Handing someone a generic set of exercises is not good treatment and does the patient a disservice. Physicians must be cautious with sedentary patients who are at risk of the ravages of inactivity. When these people need an exercise plan, a pre-exercise physical examination is appropriate and medically necessary. A proper evaluation will answer (1) what conditions in patients are contraindications to physical activity, (2) what conditions must be stabilized before beginning, or monitored during, an exercise program, (3) what is the patient's overall health status is, and (4) whether other health problems need treatment to the patient's health benefit.

Contraindications to physical activity include absolute and relative contraindications and are distinguished by their severity. Absolute contraindications include (1) severe coronary heart disease and acute myocardial infarction, (2) unstable angina pectoris, (3) congestive heart failure, uncorrected, (4) uncontrolled high-grade ventricular or atrial arrhythmias, (5) severe valvular heart disease, including severe aortic or mitral stenosis, (6) uncontrolled hypertension systolic over 200 or diastolic over 105 mm Hg, (7) pulmonary hypertension, and (8) recent pulmonary embolus or deep vein thrombosis.

Certain medical conditions must be treated or stabilized prior to beginning an exercise program. These are less severe than absolute contraindications to exercise, but must not be overlooked. Usually, the final decision regarding exercise will depend on the severity of the medical problem. Relative contraindications include (1) congenital heart disease, (2) congestive heart failure, (3) significant valvular heart disease, (4) cardiac arrhythmias, including heart block, (5) hypertension, (6) fixed-rate artificial pacemaker, (7) cardiomyopathy, (8) peripheral vascular disease, (9) possible digitalis or other drug toxicity, (10) electrolyte, particularly hypokalemia abnormalities, (11) uncontrolled metabolic disease, (12) serious systemic disease, such as mononucleosis or hepatitis, (13) neuromuscular or musculoskeletal disease in which loading or overloading would directly cause injury, or in the compromised person would increase risk of inadvertent injury, (14) marked obesity, (15) anemia, and (16) psychosis.

The above restrictions can only be assessed by adequate history and physical examinations. Injudicious exercise prescriptions by an uninformed or careless physician places the patient at risk of preventable injury.

It has been shown that, in any exercise program, physiologic warming up and warming down protects the exercised muscle from injury.[25]

---

[25] Safran, *The Role of Warmup in Muscle Injury Prevention,* 16 Am J Sports Med 123 (1988); Stamford, *How Much Should I Exercise,* 17 Phys & SportsMed 150 (1989); Goldstein, *Clinical Applications for Exercise,* 17 Phys & Sports Med 83 (1989); Van-Camp, *The Preexercise Evaluation and Contraindications to Exercise,* 2 Your Patient

Despite increasing evidence that regular aerobic exercise yields many benefits for patients with arthritis, patients are often advised to restrict physical activity. Findings from patient studies with rheumatoid arthritis or osteoarthritis who participated in an aerobic exercise program show that the subjects made significant gains in strength and other aspects of performance. In addition, they improved subjective aspects that might have a positive impact on the quality of life, including pain tolerance, joint pain, mood, and social activity.

§18.24 Islamic Prayer Exercise

Flexion and extension exercises have been suggested for disc rupture and disc decentralizing pain syndrome. McKenzie has championed the idea during the last decade with remarkable success. Using the Islamic prayer exercises is a variation on this theme. This method includes different spinal movements of flexion, mild extension, and deep knee bends. The aim is to reduce lumbar lordosis. The reversal of the lumbar curve and full flexion of the lumbosacral joint will accomplish this goal and will also strengthen abdominal muscles and flexors of the spine.

The Islamic prayer (knee chest posture) and Paul Williams exercises tend to ignore value of strengthening lumbar extensor muscles. Isometric dynamic tests of lumbar flexor and extensor muscles virtually all show that, in low back pain syndromes, lumbar extensor muscles are 20 to 50 per cent weaker than flexors.[27]

§18.25 Treating Asthma Patients

The orthopedist often treats and is involved in the rehabilitation of asthmatic patients. Until recently, many patients with asthma have been advised to restrict participation in exercises because of concerns that exercise might trigger bronchospasm. Currently, greater understanding and effective treatment for asthma show that such exercise limitation was poorly founded and unnecessary. Most pulmonary specialists believe that the asthma, not the patient's lifestyle, should be altered. The exercise plan should be tailored to the patient's cardiorespiratory reserves, as it is for any systemic disease.[28]

& Fitness 12 (May/June 1989); Huston, *The Athletic Heart Syndrome,* 313 NEJM 24 (1985).

[27] Elzayat, *Microsurgical Lumbar Disc Removal (Elzayat's Approach) with Islamic Prayer-Position Exercises,* 10 J Neurol & Orthop Med & Surg 223 (1989).

[28] Schroeckenstein & Busse, *Exercise and Asthma: No Incompatible,* J Musculoskel Med, June 1989, at 63.

§18.26 Back School

Back school is an educational program that is very helpful to back injured patients. It takes several forms, and is usually given by a treating physician or one of his or her back-treating personnel with a special skill. Anatomy, physiology, pharmaceutics, and physiotherapy are common subjects, with the botton line being that the patient understand him- or herself, the injury, what to expect, and most importantly, what he or she can do to help him- or herself.

Relaxation therapy can be important in allowing the patient to help his or her pain complaint. One such relaxation technique is an exercise involving the patient lying supine, alternately tensing and relaxing each muscle group of the body, starting at the toes and ending in the scalp, while breathing deeply and using the abdominal muscles to their fullest. There is an element of self-hypnosis in the procedure, so some people are inherently more successful than others. When somebody is very relaxed, he or she can use his or her left brain with his or her imagination to almost feel as if he or she can go inside his or her body to the spot that is causing pain, and feel that he or she is relaxing the muscles or applying the kind of heat deep inside that he or she desires. One author says "tension melts away, more or less, like a mental massage."[29]

Physical therapists find instability in the spine by careful examination and treat them by gentle digital and body-positioning techniques. The abnormality they find is usually segmental and also involves rotational (facet displacement) pathologies. Many patients are improved with this method, combined with rehabilitation posturing, stretching, and strengthening exercises.

The manipulative therapies above are different in method from chiropractic and osteopathic, which represent a slightly different approach to a similar problem.[30]

§18.27 Feldenkrais Exercise

In the use of exercise plans for the rehabilitation of back injuries, techniques to teach the patient posturing tailored to the patient at hand is another rehabilitation concept of importance. The Feldenkrais method does this. If one has little awareness of the lower back's relationship to the forward movement of the head on getting out of a chair, and does not understand how that affects hip and knee extension at exact moments, a person who suffers damage or disability from any source may find rising to a standing posture difficult or impossible. So, those not aware of rigidity and com-

---

[29] Holzman, *Back to School for Aching Backs,* Insight, Jan 9, 1989, at 54.

[30] Paris, *Physical Signs of Instabilities,* 10 Spine 277 (1985); Gaymans & Lewit, *Mobilisation Techniques Using Pressure (Pull) and Muscle Facilitation and Inhibitation, reprinted in* Rheumatol Res, Prague, Czechoslovakia, Dr. A. Susta, CSC, Director.

pression in the muscles of the trunk can often perceive nothing but pain. The increased sensory acuity through precisely programmed motor responses give the patient increased sensory awareness of where the body is in space and how to move it. The Feldenkrais therapist, rather than working exclusively on a problem area as though it were a mechanical entity operating independently, would look comprehensively at how the patient arranges his or her body in movement and rest, working therapeutically from there.

The Feldenkrais method is an ingenious approach to improving a patient's ability to function through stimulating the exploratory style of learning, which is natural for infants. At its heart is the overwhelming human need and capacity for learning.

§18.28 Overuse Syndromes

Many physical therapists and physiatrists feel vigorous physical therapy is the cornerstone in management of overuse syndromes that affect muscles and tendons. Early rest intervention to heal the inflamed tissues is necessary. Prevention of injury or recurrence is essential. Classification of overuse pain is important. The pain of tendonitis is usually classified as (1) pain after activity only, (2) pain during activity that does not restrict activity, (3) pain during activity that restricts performance, and (4) chronic unremitting pain.

The first type is treated with relative rest with a 25 per cent reduction in work load. The second type is treated the same way, but with a 50 per cent reduction and the addition of nonsteroidal medication. The third type by definition precludes competitive athletic performance. The patient should be encouraged to refrain from all activity loading the pain area. Judicious use of corticosteroid injection may be considered, taking great care not to inject into a musculotendinous juncture. The direct injection of corticosteroid into a muscle tendon interface has been shown to result in microstructure disarray and can lead to rupture.

The fourth type should be treated with long-term physical therapy. Many of these patients have developed scarring about musculotendinous areas and degenerative changes within these units. Surgery may be necessary.[31]

§18.29 Strengthening Thigh Muscles

The average orthopedist, in prescribing specific exercises, will be treating back pain patients most often, but a second group—knee complaints—embraces a large group of patients. Strong thigh muscles are needed by the running, jumping, and cutting athletes to be effective as well as to protect their knees. The more sedentary majority of walking people need strong

---

[31] Puffer & Zachazewski, *Vigorous Physical Therapy Crucial for Overuse Injuries*, Orthop Product News, Mar 1989.

thighs to get up from a chair, out of an automobile, or up and down inclines or stairs.

Specific anterior and posterior thigh exercises, aerobically done tc build strength and endurance, should be part of every exercise plan, including low back therapies, for general conditioning effects and to emphasize that the rehabilitation that works best is a total body commitment. Failure to use muscles actively is known to be detrimental to health. The loss of strength of muscle and bone mass had been shown in astronauts even with a rigorous exercise plan when in flight.[32]

§18.30 Muscle Stretching

The understanding of muscle physiology is a rapidly expanding field. It is well understood that underused muscles become weak and lack endurance, and that optimally exercised muscles gain strength and endurance. The rehabilitation of deconditioned patients is not a rapid process, but is in proportion to the resistance that the muscle works against, as well as frequency. Equally important is the state of health of the person increasing muscle power. Age, nutrition, lack of toxic chemicals in the system (alcohol or drugs), as well as the increased presence of some hormones have their positive or negative effects. Gender has something—but relatively little—to do with muscle mass building.

Muscle soreness is less well understood and may be a sign of overload. Overloading muscle masses with little or no reserve or muscles with limited nerve input (i.e., post-stroke, post-polio, etc.) can cause permanent damage.

The repetitive small trauma overload syndromes, as seen in repetitive upper extremity work requirements on the job, probably do not permanently injure muscle fibers, but the muscle fibers often respond with reflex weakness and lost endurance and strength, producing (often intolerable) pain. Attempts to overdevelop these sore muscles occasionally lessen those impairments, but are not routinely successful.

Conditioning exercise programs, under the supervision of, and prescribed by, orthopedists or other physicians who understand exercise physiology and therapy, remain a major therapeutic tool.

Pre-exercise stretching of muscles lessens muscle injury, but usually has no effect on post-exercise pain. That pain lessens as muscle becomes stronger.

Exercise training improves lipoprotein lipid profiles in patients with coronary artery disease. Although the patient needs medical supervision, the "heart" patient ordinarily is benefitted by supervised exercise. The same patient with deconditioned back, leg, and shoulder girdle muscles (which is nearly always true of the "heart" patient) is likewise helped in ambulation ability and pain control with a regular, supervised, tailored exercise program.

---

[32] Pine, *How Will Astronauts Stay Fit During Long Space Flights,* 17 Phys & SportsMed 175 (1989).

Moderate endurance exercise training lowers blood pressure and can be an initial treatment for mild hypertension.[33]

The key to rebuilding bone mass and strength is achieving the proper training level and then to continue the exercise. The same philosophy is valid for increasing and maintaining muscle strength and endurance. Strict adherence to a program of simple exercise, such as walking, jogging, and stair climbing, increases bone mass and muscle strength. It is important to attend to diet, obesity, and calcium intake. It has been further shown that the exercising patient will reach a plateau of bone mass and muscle strength after several months, but promptly lose both if he or she stops the exercises.

Several recent studies have shown that both flexion and extension lumbar spine exercises, when done in a sports medicine aerobic fashion, lessen mechanical low back pain in the majority of patients. Patients doing flexion exercises gained more motion, but then the flexion range in the normal low back is two to three times greater.

The hypothesis is that increasing the flexibility of mechanically-deranged, painful lumbar segments is at least as important as developing muscular strength and endurance. Most rehabilitation experts and low back treating physicians see the best result in patients who achieve greatest flexibility. Those patients who also gain most in muscle strength (body in general and low back, in particular) have least low back symptoms and best work potential. The exercise program works best in a back school environment addressing psychological problems, if present.[34]

Other Treatments

§18.31 Hyperthermia

For the sports medicine physician, dealing with outdoor sports or poorly ventilated gymnasiums, hyperthermia is a condition which must be understood, diagnosed, and treated. See Chapter 19, Figure 1 for diagnosis and treatment.[35]

---

[33] Heathe, *Exercise Training Improves Lipoprotein Lipid Profiles in Patients with Coronary Artery Disease,* 105 Am Heart J 889 (1983); Hagberg, *Effect of Exercise Training on the Blood Pressure and Hemodynamic Features of Hypertensive Adolescents,* 52 Am J Cardiol 763 (1983); Brown & Myles, *The Relationship Between Aerobic Fitness and Certain Cardiovascular Risk Factors,* Aviation, Space & Environ Med, June 1983, at 543.

[34] Boone, 59 Phys Ther 965 (1979); Ponte, *Orthopedics and Sports,* 6 Phys Ther 130 (1984); Kendall, *Simple Apparatus for Assessment of Stiffness,* 9 Annals Physical Med 203-205 (1968). P.C. Williams, Low Back and Neck Pain (6th ed 1982); DN Buchalter, Trends in Ergonomics/Human Factors III 727 (1983);

[35] Hubband & Armstrong, *Hyperthermia: New Thoughts on an Old Problem,* 17(6) Phys & SportsMed 97 (1989).

§18.32 Manipulation

The orthopedist does not often use spinal manipulative therapy, although its utility is recognized at times. The osteopathic physician may often use spinal manipulation as therapy. The chiropractor, by training, uses manipulative treatment of the spine, hoping to cure or improve many of the body's ailments.

It is essential for each disciple who does in fact manipulate a patient to know that patient from an anatomical point of view, to have a verifiable diagnosis, and to know when spinal manipulation is appropriate and when it may injure the patient.

Around the world, the medical literature reports injuries, some devastating, following spinal manipulation. The patient with an incipient extruded nucleus pulposus or, in fact, an extruded disc should not have vigorous spinal manipulation. Patients with weakened annulus fibrosa, with incipient protruded intervertebral disc, may be converted into a frankly protruded disc patient by spinal manipulation.[36]

Manipulation is a skillful use of the hands. It is not the purview of any particular profession or group and is not a panacea for all back pain. Manipulation is associated with a crack or cavitation of the joint which is based on carbon dioxide out of solution, and results in some improvement of the passive and active range of motion of that joint. Manipulation does not put bones back in place. Manipulation does have an affect on altered physiology, including range of motion and pain. Manipulation is a most effective and cost-effective form of treatment for dysfunctional problems in the cervical, thoracic, and lumbar spine. Manipulation is an end-range, passive motion with high velocity and short amplitude. This can be accomplished by the patients themselves through active exercise. The patients, therefore, can bring about their own recovery. Patients should be allowed to generate their own forces and then the therapist should carefully assess which patients require manipulation and which do not. Most patients will not.[37]

§18.33 Electrical Muscle Stimulation

Rehabilitation specialists have expressed interest in the application of electrical current to the musculoskeletal system to improve muscle strength and endurance, as well as to facilitate nonunion of bones. As a result, there has been a proliferation of electrical devices for which favorable results are claimed.

There is a controversy as to whether electrical stimulation alone is capable of strengthening normal skeletal muscle. Many authors report this to be

---

[36] Dan & Saccasa, *Serious Complications of Lumbar Spinal Manipulation,* Med J Aust Dec 10-24, 1983, at 672; Gallinaro & Cartesegna, *Three Cases of Lumbar Disc Rupture and One of Cauda Equinae Associated with Spinal Manipulation (Chiropraxis),* The Lancet, Feb 19, 1983, at 411.

[37] Roundtable Discussion, American Back Society, Spring Symposium, Apr 1989.

true; others seem skeptical. Most studies, though, indicate that under proper conditions, a specific transcutaneous electrical stimulator can produce a statistically significant change in the strength of the muscle. If electrical stimulation is to be accepted, the claims made for the various devices must be reliably verified, and the medical community must be made aware of the differences in muscle stimulators.[38]

§18.34 Geriatric Rehabilitation

Geriatric rehabilitation has come to the forefront in medicine as the aging population increases. Much of patient care of the elderly is furnished by family practitioners and internists; however, rehabilitation falls to the orthopedist or physiatrist, if available. Nursing home care of senior citizens is much more frequent with the decreasing availability of hospital beds for long-term care.

The orthopedist is often called on to make functional assessments of the patient and to supervise a program of habilitation, if not rehabilitation, to improve strength, mobility, and overall function of this population.[39]

§18.35 How TENS Works

Transcutaneous electrical nerve stimulation (TENS) has been effective in controlling acute and chronic pain in about one-third of patients for prolonged periods. Its effect relates to the ability to increase Substance P and endorphin concentrations as measured in plasma and cerebrospinal fluid. A newer modification of TENS using strength duration modulation in altering the TENS-induced wave configuration has been shown to further increase P substance and endorphin level, felt to more favorably control chronic pain.

Posterior spinal cord stimulation is carried out by surgically implanted TENS-like devices. By selective stimulation of the posterior spinal cord level, a subset of chronic pain patients may have their low back and leg pain reproduced. This group of patients may benefit by neurosurgical implantation of an electrostimulating electrode on dura at the appropriate level with stimulation via a remotely implanted battery. Many neurosurgeons are enthusiastic about this pain control method. Complications include adverse tissue reaction to device components, infection, electrode displacement, and wire breakage. Paresthesias and disturbing numbness may occur in the area of pain being treated. Varying degrees and lengths of time have had favorable results.

Most physicians using TENS therapy believe that pain relief is greatest when the TENS unit induces paresthesias into the pain site. Many patients

---

[38] Laughman, *Strength Changes in the Normal Quadriceps Femoris Muscle as a Result of Electrical Stimulation,* 63 Phys Ther 494 (1983).

[39] Smith & Grabois, *Physical Medicine and Rehabilitation,* 261 JAMA 2876 (1989).

find the paresthesias a distasteful trade-off for their pain. The fact that paresthesias do not occur with TENS stimulation of the spinal cord indicates that the TENS effect is not through the dorsal nerve root and that peripherally originating pain is best treated with TENS placed peripherally, not at the spinal cord.

It appears that pain relief afforded by TENS is derived in part from shifting the balance of excitation between large and small afferent fibers in favor of the former. Changing of the spatiotemporal pattern of neural input also is changed with TENS therapy.[40]

A wealth of information is available on the clinical application of TENS for pain management. The most successful use of TENS is in the control of postoperative pain. In chronic pain, manipulating the intensity and frequency of electrical input produce favorable results in 50 to 60 per cent of patients, with the benefit being short-lived at three months or less in one-third of patients. Addition of acupuncture types of TENS probes increased effectiveness and several studies in specific back pain patients. The physiology of how TENS works is complicated and uncertain, but is believed to be primarily involved with blocking of pain fiber transmission, following the Melzack-Wall theory. More recently, variations on endorphin stimulation in the brain have been popularized.[41]

§18.36 Acupuncture

There is an important difference between traditional Chinese medicines and scientific acupuncture. Most physicians fail to recognize the difference. Traditional Chinese acupuncture is based on "meridian theory," a metaphysical concept that originated 4,000 years ago. It postulates a mysterious body energy called "chi" which traverses hypothetical meridian pathways to the surface at some 361 acupuncture points on the skin. International researchers have rendered these theories obsolete. It is now recognized that acupuncture is a technique for getting a stimulus, preferably a pulsing DC current, into the central nervous system. The best points to use are those where fibers are most easily accessed, such as motor, Golgi tendon apparatuses, or adjacent to a nerve or nerve root.

The current theory is that the acupuncture stimulus stimulates appropriate areas of the brain, increasing chemical brain pain modulators (endor-

---

[40] Melzack, *Prolonged Relief of Pain by Brief, Intense Transcutaneous Somatic Stimulation,* 1 Pain 357 (1975); Smith, *Alleviation of Deafferentation Pain by Posterior Spinal Cord Stimulation Without Development of Paresthesias in Area of Pain,* 4 Clin J Pain 157 (1988); Katz Melzack, *An Association Between Phantom Limb Sensations and Stump Skin Conductance During Transcutaneous Electrical nerve Stimulation (TENS) Applied to the Contralateral Leg: A Case Study,* 36 Pain 367 (1989); Berlant & Lampe, *How TENS Work,* 4 Clin J Pain 191 (1988), Willer, *Human Noiciceptive Reactions: Effects of Spatial Summation of Afferent Input from Relatively Large Diameter Fibers,* 201 Brain Res (465, 1980).

[41] Gersh & Wolf, *Applications of Transcutaneous Electrical Nerve Stimulation in the Management of Patients with Pain: State of the Art,* 65 Phys Ther 315 (1985).

phins). The intensity of pain gradually abates with repeated acupuncture in susceptible treatment. A strong faith that it will help is an important concomitant of successful treatment and likely explains the high degree of good results in the Orient in years and centuries past. Pain relief, if effective with acupuncture, is usually cumulative, and with an irregular course. If there is no improvement in 8 to 10 treatments, acupuncture is probably an inappropriate modality for that patient.[42]

§18.37 Iontophoresis

Iontophoresis is one of the physical therapy tools used to deliver drugs to tissues about the body, passing corticosteroids to inflamed areas and local anesthetic to painful areas. One study showed that antibiotics could be passed into burns. The technique has its advocates and carries a low risk of infection, but is fairly expensive.[43]

§18.38 Group Therapies

A group therapy approach to the psychosocial treatment of chronic pain problems is currently popular. The purpose of the group is to (1) encourage communication among patients, families, and physicians, (2) improve education of physicians concerning the emotional impact of chronic pain syndromes, (3) present factual material about chronic pain behavior to patients and families, and (4) enable patients to live with their pain problem more realistically and comfortably.[44]

§18.39 Pain Opioids; Drugs

Patients with severe, nonmalignant pain who fail to be relieved by nonopioid medications and other analgesic chemicals are considered for long-term opioid medication when treated by informed physicians who are familiar with chronic pain management as a subspecialty in medical practice.

These physicians maintain that addiction, tolerance, and toxicity in patients is exaggerated. These adverse expectations have persisted in spite of accumulating evidence that these complications seldom occur.

There is no known cure for chronic pain and many patients continue to suffer, despite the "best" physicians have. Extensive experience has been

---

[42] Ulett, *Scientific Acupuncture Peripheral Electrical Stimulation for Relief of Pain. Part II,* Pain Management, July-August 1989, at 185; Ulett, *Scientific Acupuncture Peripheral Electrical Stimulation for Relief of Pain. Part I,* Pain Management, May-June 1989, at 126.

[43] Harris, *Iontophoresis: Clinical Research in Musculoskeletal Inflammatory Conditions,* J Orthop & Sports Phys Ther Fall 1982, at 109.

[44] Portenoy & Foley, *Chronic Use of Opioid Analgesics in Nonmalignant Pain: Report of 38 Cases,* 25 Pain 171 (1986).

gained in the use of long-term narcotic medication in cancer patients, so the long-term risks of this type of therapy are known. Much societal negative input in treating chronic pain patients with opioids is voiced in the current "war on drugs" social climate.

The toughest issue for treating physicians is the term "addiction," because the wrong definition of addiction is used. *Addiction,* which in some circles has been replaced by the term "psychological dependence," is a psychologic and behavioral syndrome characterized by compulsive drug use, overwhelming interest in securing a supply and recidivism after drug detoxification. Among medical patients, aberrent behavior is drug hoarding, acquisition of drugs from multiple sources, drug sales, and unsanctioned dose escalation. But, drug addiction is seldom observed.

The preponderance of current data suggests that the causes of addiction lie more in the psychopathology of the patient and the environment than in the reinforcing qualities of the drug.

Accepted guidelines for treating selected chronic pain patients with opioid drugs include:

1. This therapy should be considered only after all other reasonable attempts at pain control using non-narcotic analgesics have failed
2. A history of substance abuse is a relative contraindication
3. A single physician should be responsible for all drug prescriptions
4. The patient's informed consent should be obtained before starting therapy; points to be covered include recognition of the low risk of psychologic dependence as an outcome, potential for cognitive impairment with drug use alone and in combination with sedative/hypnotics, and an understanding by women that children born when the mother is on opioid maintenance therapy are likely to be dependent at birth
5. After drug selection, a dose should be given on an around-the-clock basis; several weeks should be agreed on as an initial period of drug titration (establishing the least effective drug dose)
6. Failure to achieve at least partial analgesia at relatively low initial doses in nontolerant patients raises questions about the potential treatability of the pain syndrome with opioids
7. Emphasis should be given to attempts to capitalize on improved analgesia by gains in physical and social function
8. In addition to the daily dose determined initially, patients should be permitted to escalate the dose temporarily on days of increased pain; two acceptable methods are (1) prescription of an additional four to six "rescue doses" to be taken as needed during the month, or (2) instruction that one or two extra doses may be taken on any day, but must be following by an equal reduction of dose on subsequent days
9. The patient must be seen and the drug prescribed on a monthly basis
10. Exacerbations of pain not effectively treated by transient, small increases in dose are best managed in a hospital where dose escalation,

if appropriate, can be observed closely and return to the baseline dose can be accomplished in a controlled environment

11. Evidence of drug hoarding, acquisition of drugs from other physicians, uncontrolled dose escalation, or other aberrant behavior should be followed by tapering and discontinuance of opioid maintenance therapy[45]

§18.40 Placebos

A clear understanding by the physician of the placebo response of patients is essential. The term "placebo" carries a pejorative connotation among uninformed or biased medical workers, causing a disservice to the patient. Measurement of the placebo factor by physicians and psychologists has been difficult and inconsistent. Like many areas of the practice of medicine, clear explanations of "why" and "how" are difficult and often anecdotal; the placebo response is not denied by any practitioner who regularly attends patients.

The *placebo response* may be defined as a favorable response by a patient after administration of a medication or treatment (including an operation) which is based on the patient's wishes and belief that the treatment will be beneficial. Acupuncture is thought by many to fit here. The placebo response may be long- or short-lived, again often based on the patient's wishes and belief. It is well known that many medications or treatments fit the one-third, one-third, one-third paradigm in which the treatment is effective for one-third of patients, somewhat effective for another one-third, and ineffective for the balance.[46]

§18.41 Prolo Therapy

Problems other than anterior primary rami syndromes can cause radiculopathy and sciatica-like pain syndromes, but the physician must understand and look for these entities to avoid misdiagnosis and/or mistreatment. Local pathology involving spinal ligaments, facet joints or their ligaments, sacroiliac joints, or myofascial syndromes need to be considered as etiological sites.

The myofascial model of pain production can be dealt with as Travell and Simons suggest—with passive stretch and/or injected or sprayed agents, along with identifying the culprit causing the recurrence (posture, work position, etc). This can be a real detective job, but rewarding. In the ligament model, it shows that injury or relaxation of these structures (supraspinous

---

[45] Portenoy & Foley, *Chronic Use of Opioid Analgesics in Non-malignant Pain: Report of 38 Cases,* 25 Pain 171 (1986); R.K, Portenoy, Opioid Therapy in the Management of Chronic Low Back Pain. Interdisciplinary Rehabilitation of Low Back Pain (CK Tollison ed 1989).

[46] Voudouris, *Conditioned Response Models of Placebo Phenomena: Further Support,* 38 Pain 109 (1989).

and interspinous ligaments, facet capsules and the heavy posterior sacroiliac, the sacrospinous and sacrotuberous ligaments) can produce local pain as well as radicular pain patterns. Prolotherapy (also called sclerotherapy and proliferent) is used by some surgeons to cause scarring and thickening of injured ligaments. Other physicians prevent changing the load on the painful ligaments by exercise plans, changed lifestyle, and other physical therapy modalities.[47]

Many prolotherapists additionally use manipulative treatments to first place incompetent ligaments in a more anatomical position. Throughout the country, prolotherapy is not widely accepted and is rejected by many as non-therapeutic, with several risks. The risks are infection, permanent alteration of soft tissues producing scar that is not adapted to the local functional homeostasis, and pain—severe at times.[48]

§18.42 References

R.A. McKenzie, The Lumbar Spine: Mechanical Diagnosis and Therapy Waikanae, New Zealand (1981).

A.L. Nachemson, Lumbar Intradiscal Pressures, The Lumbar Spine and Back Pain 341 (K Jayson ed 1980).

P.C. Williams, Low Back and Neck Pain: Causes and Conservative Treatment (1974).

G.S. Hackett, Ligament and Tendon Relaxation Treated by Prolotherapy (3d ed 1958).

F.C. Yeomans, Sclerosis Therapy (1939).

---

[47] Mayer, *Using Physical Measurements to Assess Low Back Pain,* J Musculoskel Med, June 1985, at 44; R.A. McKenzie, The Lumbar Spine: Mechanical Diagnosis and Therapy (1981); A. White, Back School and Other Conservative Approaches to Low Back Pain (1983); Spengler, *Chronic Low Back Pain: The Team Approach,* 179 Clin Orthop 71 (1983).

[48] Onglery, *A New Approach to the Treatment of Chronic Low Back Pain,* The Lancet, July 18, 1987, at 143; Naeim, *Treatment of Chronic Iliolumbar Syndrome by Infiltrating the Iliolumbar Ligament,* 136 West J Med 372 (1926); Bunting, *The Effects of Mechanical Tension Upon the Polarity of Growing Fibroblasts,* 44 J Exp Med 147 (1926). YK Liu, *An In Situ Study of the Influence of a Sclerosis Solution in Rabbit Medial Collateral Ligament and its Junction Strength,* 11 Conn Tiss Res 95 (1983).

Appendix 18-1
Cases

1 ***Novet v Kishwaukee Community Health Services,* 531 NW2d 427 (Ill Ct App 1988)** (it was improper to allow a licensed occupational therapist to testify about the standard of care applicable to a physical therapist, given the significant differences in the education, training, and licensing of the two professions, as well as the occupational therapist's testimony that she had no training or education as a physical therapist and was not familiar with the standard of care applicable to physical therapists).

2 ***Tart v McGann,* 697 F Supp 627 (ED Mo 1985)** (court reasoned that inadequate physician monitoring of exercise testing contributed to and led to a post-test myocardial infarction. The case was settled for $50,000).

19

Sports Medicine

§19.01 Generally

Sports medicine became one of the "buzz words" in orthopedics in the 1980s. For more than two decades, orthopedists, calling themselves sports medicine physicians, have cared for an elite subset of orthopedic problems. This furnished a format for research and improvement in that category of injury resulting from contact sports or overload situations. Epidemiology and prevention of injury are natural spin-offs of these studies and favorably affect the athlete. It may be important to realize that sports medicine deals with all sports injuries, from the professional athlete, to the out-of-shape, to the sports buffs. Equally important is the pre-activity physical examination now recommended for all competitive athletes before they participate, be this the six-year-old youngster or the seasoned professional athlete.

Emphasis on activity, exercise, and relaxation, rather than the competitive value of sports activity, is useful in most therapeutic situations. The concept of getting and staying "in shape" is a natural result of sports medicine philosophy—well shown to prolong and improve the quality of life.

§19.02 Sports Medicine Physicians

The orthopedist or other physician who practices sports medicine is of a special type:

1. There is an inherent love of the sport and the competition, and it usually has been present since childhood

2. The team physician is typically outgoing and is comfortable with athletic field visibility
3. The team physician typically experiences emotional "highs" and "lows" as the team does well or falters; the physician must be on guard not to medically compromise, where playing an "at risk" player might favor the game outcome at the expense of the player
4. The team physician must be financially secure enough to block out significiant periods of time from his or her practice for little or no remuneration
5. Liability by the physician is a concern at all levels, and increases as the physician cares for highly paid professional athletes

§19.03 Physician-Team Relationship

Working for a professional team is basically a triangular arrangement, comprising the doctor, the player, and the management, whereas in private practice it is merely the physician and the player. That situation can theoretically lead to trouble, as has been verified by a few involved physicians. The care includes the physician-patient relationship, with all of its duty of appropriate care and confidentiality. Information release regarding player injury and rehabilitation is best forwarded to management to let them disburse and assume liability, if any.

In professional sports, each player is typically attached to an agent who most often is an attorney. The agent's role is to keep the player's money coming in, so if a player's ability to perform athletically is diminished, the agent typically goes for money another way. Most team physicians are aware of this and tend to go the extra mile with diagnostic testing and the liberal use of consultants.

Team physicians are advised to become intimately informed about the specific sport they are involved with, as knowledge of the mechanisms of injury and potential re-injury is critical to prescribing appropriate therapy. The team doctor usually supervises the trainers and should be familiar with the training rooms and methods that the players use.

The active sports medicine physician, working with the team—be it amateur or professional—tends to practice in a "fishbowl." The physician's name may be in the paper often, and the player and coaching expectations are high with their respective future often resting on the ability to produce and the timeliness of the injured patient's ability to return to the game. The doctor must regularly deal with the injured player's parents at the amateur level, and the public relations person in the professional arena.

Sports are beneficial because people know how to be competitive within set guidelines, how to apply themselves, how to work on their weaknesses and overcome limitations, and how to work as team members. When the sports medicine doctor is dealing with athletes, he or she wants to give them the best opportunity to excel without injury, as they are stressing their bodies to the maximum. This general philosophy is basic to the practice of medicine by the physician, but more tempered.

Athletic medicine is all-encompassing, much more than treating an injury. Sports medicine should be largely preventive of injury. The team doctor must be well informed as to electrolyte balance, emotional balance, and conditioning physiology. The team doctor should be a skilled family physician and a skilled psychologist.[1]

§19.04 Duties of Sports Medicine Physicians

When becoming a team doctor, the physician assumes a wide range of duties and liability risks. His or her prime function, of course, is the health of the patient/athlete. The team doctor needs to participate in the medically sound training of the coaching staff, paramedical aides, trainers, etc.

Football has been the highest risk sport. Using NCAA sponsored protocol, serious injury has been dramatically reduced in recent years. In that sport, the following rules, under supervision of the team doctor, have helped reduce injuries and the severity of injury. The team doctor should participate with the team staff in the following:

1. Working with coaches to drill players in proper conditioning exercises to strengthen the neck so the athlete will be able to hold his head firmly erect while making contact in blocking and tackling
2. Working with team staff in drilling players in the proper execution of the fundamentals of football; players should use a shoulder for blocking and tackling and not use the head as a battering ram
3. Make rules against "spearing" in practice and in games; the player needs to be taught that the helmet is a protective device, not a weapon
4. Team trainers, doctors, and coaches should all be knowledgeable about protective equipment and regularly check for safety and state of repair
5. The physician should be on the field of play during games and practice sessions; when not on the field, arrangements for the doctor's immediate availability must be made; each team should have its own well-trained trainer, supervised by the team doctor
6. Coaches and trainers must be alert to catastrophic injury situations, such as head and neck injuries, and must be skilled in CPR and airway evaluation
7. The team physician should understand the special problems associated with each sport, directing his or her expertise to conditioning and preventing particular injuries[2]

---

[1] D. Macleod, *The Team Doctor,* 23 Brit J SportsMed 211-12 (1989).

[2] Rund, *Airway Obstruction: Recognition and Immediate Management,* 17 Phys & SportsMed 173 (1989).

In transferring injured players from the athletic arena, reasonable care and expertise is expected of team caretakers. If the doctor is in attendance, he or she may be held liable for transfer injury. The doctor may be also held liable if not present for failing to adequately train the coaches, trainers, etc., if that was considered to be one of his or her duties and an athlete is injured by the negligence of the poorly trained. (*See* Appendix 19-1, Case 1.)

In *Kersey v Harbin,* 591 SW2d 745 (Mo Ct App 1979), the court held those who provide medical assistance to the injured on the field must satisfy three elements. The first requires that the person conducting the sports activity appreciate the severity of the athlete's injury. The second element requires a determination that one or more of the persons conducting the sports activity has the skill to provide adequate medical care, including ability to safely, and without further injury to the athlete, get the injured player to an adequate medical care facility. In an emergency situation, it may be necessary for the coach not only to contact a physician and ambulance, but also to pay for these services. Most states have laws entitling a coach to be reimbursed by the team-sponsoring entity, or from parents or guardians. The last element is the question of whether the medical care, if provided, would have avoided the ultimate additional injury.

§19.05 Sports Injuries

The increasing participation in organized sports has been paralleled by an increasing number of sports injuries. An exact diagnosis of the injury and an understanding of the mechanisms of injury are essential for proper management, relief of pain, and restoration of function. These injuries can be classified in two categories: (1) macrotrauma, and (2) repetitive microtrauma. Overuse injuries, which result from repetitive microtrauma, are caused by the interaction of a number of risk factors. Determining the etiological factors present is essential for proper management and prevention of overuse injuries. The roles of non-narcotic analgesics, muscle relaxants, and non-steroidal anti-inflammatory drugs (NSAIDs) in aiding recovery and restoration of function in sports injuries have been extensively studied. NSAIDs have been demonstrated in clinical and laboratory studies to speed recovery from overuse sports injuries. Their place in acute sports injuries due to single impact macrotrauma is more controversial.[3]

§19.06 Athlete Nutrition

The physician involved in the care and treatment of athletes is often responsible for nutritional advice, as with any other patient. Doctors must be informed of the patient's physiological need in order to properly advise. Fadism on sports nutrition will continue as long as athletes aspire to succeed.

---

[3] J.L. Micheli, *Common Painful Sports Injuries,* 2 Clin J Pain §43-50 (Supp 5 1989).

Dietary manipulation and nutritional supplements potentially provide athletes with a performance advantage as well as a psychological boost. However, certain dietary practices pose nutritional and health-related risks.

Vegetarian eating styles can adequately meet athletes' nutritional needs and can successfully support vigorous training schedules. High carbohydrate diets used by endurance athletes can enhance performance, but at the expense of protein reserves in some persons, which comes from muscle mass. Certain nutritional fads present risks of nutritional inadequacy and adversely affect performance as well as being detrimental to health. The supervising health care person must be knowledgeable in this area.[4]

§19.07 Risk Factors in Young Athletes

Many children and adolescents participate in sports which put them at risk for musculoskeletal injury. Underlying physical conditions or risk factors may predispose them to particular types of sports injuries. Research shows that these risk factors fall into five categories: (1) body type, (2) flexibility, (3) muscle strength, (4) inadequate rehabilitation of previous injury, (5) skeletal malalignment, and (6) congenital abnormalities.

Heavy football players are at the greatest risk for injury; sprains and strains are less common in flexible athletes. Patellar pain syndromes often relate to malalignment situations.[5]

§19.08 Problem Areas for Older Athletes

The orthopedic injuries of senior athletes stem from a variety of factors, including their more-frequent degenerative joint disease, whose root cause may be former injuries.

As an example, a younger athlete with a pronating foot may experience an increase in pronation as he or she gets older. He or she starts developing a bit of strain along either the plantar fascia or the talonavicular joint. The pain progresses to the posterior tibialis and may eventually end with a complete rupture of the posterior tibialis tendon. The point is, if you have a perfect shape you can be athletic to a very old age without having these degenerative changes occur; however, many of us are not that fortunate.

---

[4] Short & Short, *Four Year Study of University Athlete's Dietary Intake,* 86 J Am Dietetic 632 (1983); Burke & Read, *Diet Patterns in Elite Australian Male Triathletes,* 15 Phys SportsMed 140 (1987); PWR Lemon, *Protein and Exercise: Update,* 19 Med Sci Sports Exer 179 (Supp 1987); Brownell, *Weight Regulation Practices in Athletes: An Analysis of Metabolic and Health Effects,* 19 Med Sci Sports Exer 546 (1987); O'Neil, *Research and Application of Current Topics in Sports Nutrition,* 86 J Am Diet A 1007 (1986); Applegate, *Fad Diets and Supplement Use in Athletics,* 1 Sports Sci Exch 1 (1988).

[5] Moskwa & Nichols, *Musculoskeletal Risk Factors in the Young Athlete* 17 Phys & SportsMed 49 (1989).

The decreased elasticity that comes with age takes its toll on senior athletes. Most orthopedists agree that muscle pulls and tears and ruptures of the Achilles tendon, patellar tendon, quadriceps tendon, and lumbar dorsal fascia, as well as rotator cuff tears, are all more common in older athletes.

The good news is that senior athletes suffer fewer acute or traumatic injuries than younger athletes, and their symptoms are more often related to overuse or improper training. It is very important that senior athletes emphasize stretching before and after all sports activities, as well as warm up and cool down.

Protective muscle strength is another important factor in a senior athlete's health and fitness. Many older athletes already have early degenerative changes so muscle strength of the joints is a greater factor in protecting them from major trauma, such as severe ligament disruptions.

§19.09 Causes of Sports Injuries

Most sports injuries are caused by (1) poor training methods, (2) weak tissue, and (3) biomechanical factors. Training should involve varied workouts—not the same thing day after day. As a result of poor training, injuries generally occur because of (1) failure to follow 48-hour recovery rule, and (2) failure to stop with onset of pain. Pain is your body talking to you. Patients should be taught that when a localized discomfort worsens as they go along, they should stop the activity. An intelligent program includes vigorous exercise, but no more often than every 48 hours. Certain biomechanical abnormalities cause an athlete to put greater stress on certain parts of the body, or the athlete may have weak tissues more susceptible to injury. With an increased work load, the weakest link eventually breaks.

§19.10 Treatment of Sports Injuries

Treatment for all sports injuries includes (1) ceasing the sport that caused injury until it can be engaged in without pain, and (2) trying an alternate sport that will not stress the injury site. If injury is in the lower leg or lower back, cycling or skiing might be an alternative; if in the upper leg, jogging in place might be another choice; if in the shoulder or arm, lower body exercise might be an alternative, starting with no strengthening exercises until the injured tissue is recovered, then doing three sets of 10 (lift weights, rest, lift weights, rest, lift weights, rest). (*See* Appendix 19-1, Cases 2 and 3.)

§19.11 Runner's Knee

When running, you land on the lateral heel, and roll medially toward the big toe. This pronation causes the lower leg to twist inwardly. The most common sports injury is "runner's knee," caused by the patella rubbing against the femur when the lower leg twists inward and the patella moves laterally. The person most likely to get runner's knee is the one with flatfoot. Most of these patients have normal arches, but excessive pronation. The key is to assist patient to attain the proper amount of pronation. Some is necessary to distribute the shattering force of body weight, but too much causes inward twisting and all kinds of problems. Treatment for runner's knee includes proper inserts in shoes and having shoes which limit pronation, and then strengthening the vastus medialis, along with an exercise program.

§19.12 Plantar Fasciitis

Plantar fasciitis occurs most commonly when the fascia is torn at insertion on the heel. This may be caused by stiff soles or ones that bend in the wrong place so that excessive force is used to come up onto the toes. Anterior shin splints are caused by damage to the anterior tibial group of muscles, and posterior shin splints by damage to the attachment of the posterior tibial muscle on the interosseous membrane between the tibia and the fibula. It is necessary to stop running until pain is gone, then use the shoe inserts and conditioning exercises.

Occasionally, pain occurs on the lateral side of the knee; this seems to represent an irritation to the popliteal tendon and should be treated like a muscle injury. A more common problem is Achilles tendonitis, which represents a tear. Patients should be warned NOT to attempt to run through that pain, as this will cause permanent damage.

§19.13 Sports Medicine Negligence

The sports medicine physician may be liable for negligence in several ways not common to other physicians. The sports physician often wears two hats—one representing the player patient, and the other representing the competitive, or, at times, financial interest of the team management. The more professional the sport, the more obvious this is. Often the patient will feel uninformed about his or her injury or its prognosis and will file a cause of action. An action may also be brought if the athlete feels he or she was returned to the game too soon, was uninformed of the severity of the injury, or has a great risk of reinjury. (*See* Appendix 19-1, Case 3.)

Liability may stand when a physician identifies a medical problem or potential problem, fails to warn the patient/athlete of the nature of the problem, and then fails to recommend further diagnosis or treatment. In the case of the sports team physician, the courts have distinguished between liability of the physician and liability of the team for failure to refer. A similar division of referral responsibility may occur when two or more health caretakers are attending the patient at the same time. Often, this type of case turns on the degree of control the party—the doctor or the team—has, and whether the physician is serving the interests of the athlete or the team, particularly in allowing the player to play without informing him or her of the risk of injuring the injured body part.

§19.14 Disclosure of Confidential Information

Disclosure by physicians who have information relating to the physical or mental condition of patients to an unauthorized third party is negligent and tortious. This is particularly true where great damage to earning capacity might arise, as with the professional athlete.

If the physician communicates information concerning a patient to a third party, with or without consent, the physician may be liable for defamation, invasion of privacy, or breach of the physician-patient fiduciary relationship. Further, disclosure made in the absence of consent may subject the doctor to potential liability if one relies on the physician's statement, and it is subsequently proven inaccurate. Generally, a physician may avoid liability by restricting his or her statements to the nature of injury and general method of treatment. The physician must strictly avoid opinions as to prognosis and "how the patient is taking it."

§19.15 Sports Injuries Resulting in Death

Most athletes are in prime physical health; even so, they should not participate in sports unless so certified by a qualified physician. The side line paramedical personnel, such as the coaching staff and trainer, should be trained by a professional to the extent that they can care for the injuries and recognize health problems that the athlete may present. Often, the team doctor vicariously assumes responsibility for the knowledge and care given to the athlete by the team personnel, also assuming liability for their treatment negligence. This vicarious team physician liability is now common enough that many team physicians insure themselves.

Examples of emergency situations that may face the team trainer/coaching staff is the suddenly unconscious player, one who has had a sudden cardiac arrest. At this time, it is a rare side line person who tries CPR, or is even capable of doing it, and the patient dies.

A common injury during game activities is an acute head injury. To recognize that a head/neck injury may be present may save a life or prevent quadriplegia (in the case of an unstable neck injury). The coaching staff must have basic knowledge about assessing mental status and the cursory neurological signs that may indicate head injury.[6]

§19.16 Spine Injuries

One of the biggest challenges for physicians treating athletes with spinal injuries is deciding which athlete should be allowed to return to contact sports. When athletes injure themselves in contact sports, they may suffer transient paralytic symptoms, such as quadriplegia, paresthesia, or hemi-

---

[6] Thompson, *Seventeen Players Die in Football Last Year,* 17 Phys & SportsMed 37 (1989); Saunders & Harbaugh, *The Second Impact in Catastrophic Contact - Sports Head Trauma,* 252 JAMA 538 (1984).

paresis. Some of these insults may become permanent and some become "at risk" for reinjury. Many such patients will have normal x-rays, CT scans, and MRI studies, yet have impairing, temporary neurological findings. Trauma to the spinal cord producing these symptoms occurs with stretch, twist, concussion, and other mechanics.

The spine that is too narrow, as seen in developmental or congenital spinal stenosis, will set the stage for injuries. Disc injury with or without herniation may be produced by athletic injury.

Most athletes who have not sustained fractures or dislocations in the spine and who do not have spinal canal compromising lesions can return to contact sports after a healing period and, most importantly after adequate soft tissue reconditioning. The sports medicine philosophy of rehabilitation is perhaps the most effective tool to get the athlete (or any injured worker) back to the game (work). To return to contact activities depends on many variables, but includes the goals and responsibility of the athlete, the competence of the coaching and training staff, and common sense.[7]

§19.17 Horseback Injuries

Severe horseback riding injuries are common. One-third of these injuries are to the spine and involve nerve injury. Emergency transport of the injured is often difficult, due to the remote site of the accident. Knowledge and skill in emergency care and excellence in diagnostic/therapeutic care by the definitive caretaker minimizes permanent impairment.[8]

§19.18 Growth Plates Fractures in Athletes

Isolated avulsion fractures of various growth plates in adolescents are common occurrences among young athletes. Active muscle contractions, particularly in light of forced muscle stretching, are usually the cause. Occasionally, the force of the muscle contraction itself will cause the avulsion. Most of these avulsions do not require surgical intervention. Pelvic avulsion fractures can usually be handled with rest and crutches. Recovery and return to competition is usually rapid. Growth disturbances are rare, because these types of injuries tend to occur in older adolescents. Tibial tubercle avulsions, and often displaced avulsions of the tibial eminence in the knee, require open reduction and internal fixation.[9]

---

[7] Bailes & Wilberger, *Managing Spine Injuries Can be Tricky,* 7 Back Pain Monitor 1 (1989).

[8] Brooks & Bixby-Hammett, *Prevention of Neurological Injuries in Equestrian Sports,* 16 Phys & SportMed 84 (1988).

[9] Blantz, *Multiple Epiphyseal Fractures in an Athlete,* 28 Orthop Rev 980 (1989).

§19.19 Classification of Epiphyseal Injuries

Clinically, the Salter-Harris classification of physeal injuries is most useful:

1. *Types I and II Injuries; Metaphyseal:* Usually easily reduced and have the fewest future complications. The patient's family must be advised, however, that despite anatomic reduction, growth disturbance may occur later, particularly at the distal radius. In the metacarpal or phalanx, complete displacement, lateral or severe dorsal or palmar angulation, and mal-rotation must be corrected.
2. *Types III and IV Injuries; Articular:* If displaced, must be reduced, often surgically, and temporarily fixed in a manner to avoid injury to the physis. The most common location of these latter injuries includes the thumb proximal phalanx base (reversed gamekeeper's thumb) and distal phalanx (mallet finger).
3. *Type V Injuries; Physeal:* Often severely traumatizes growth center, causing abberant cessation of growth.

Discretion and experience are paramount in managing a malunited injury to decide which lesions are best treated surgically and which can be treated by watchful waiting for known effects of growth remodeling and Wolff's law.[10]

§19.20 Overuse Sports Injuries in Children

Overuse injuries are the result of repetitive forces that exceed a person's ability to withstand them. Typical overuse injuries in adults involve bone (stress fractures) and tendon (Achilles tendonitis of fascia or plantar fasciitis).

Athletic injuries to the musculoskeletal systems of children are both similar and different from the adult. The epiphyses in children are weaker than bone, so slip or fracture of the cartilaginous interface of bone occurs with injury before bone fracture happens. A small beak of bone attached to the physis is where the fracture often occurs—Salter IV type.

The physes where muscle attaches are particularly vulnerable to injury. Repetitive stretching, as in pitcher's elbow, may be the site of traction epiphysitis, with more forceful insults resulting in physis avulsion.

Overuse syndromes in children and adolescents occur in the areas of active cartilage growth, including the physis (growth plate), the growing articular cartilage, and the cartilage of the apophysis at the tendon-bone junction. Injuries to these tissues include patello-femoral syndrome, shin splints, impingement syndromes, and later epicondylitis of elbow.

---

[10] S.C. Sandzen, Complication of Physeal Injuries of the Hand and Wrist. Presented at the Piedmont Orthopaedic Society Annual Meeting, Longboat Key, Florida (May 20-24, 1987).

The epiphyseal overuse syndromes are usually easily treated by reducing or avoiding the stress involved in the injury. Premature or injudicious return to the injuring sports activity can lead to permanent physeal injury, leaving life-long impairments. The orthopedist/sports medicine physician may incur legal liability if he or she allows such a patient to return to the game too soon and unconditioned. Resisting the pressure of coaches and parents may be the hardest part of the treatment of the young athlete.[11]

§19.21 Shin Splints

A common sports-related leg pain complaint is often called *shin splints*. A number of problems may cause shin and anterior ankle pain in the athlete, usually overload or stress-related problems. Exercise-induced leg pain is a frequent complaint in running athletes. The name shin splint has confused orthopedic/sports medicine literature. The AMA standard nomenclature says it is "pain and discomfort in the leg from repetitive running on hard surfaces or forceful excessive use of foot dorsiflexor muscles. The diagnosis of 'shin splint' should be limited to the musculotendinous inflammations excluding fracture and ischemic disorders. Shin splints are more correctly labeled *medial tibial stress syndrome.*

Overuse of the leg may present a variety of diseases in which shin splints is only one cause. It may be difficult to differentiate shin splints from a stress fracture or an exertional compartment syndrome. Tumor must be ruled out by taking an x-ray of the leg. Often, bone scanning will show the inflammatory phase of shin splint or stress fracture.

In the medial tibial stress syndrome, the pain is located over the border of the distal one-third of the tibia. Pain is usually induced by activity and relieved by rest. Pain can be produced by resisted active plantar flexion and inversion of the foot. On bone scan, a linear increase uptake is often found along the posterior edge of the medial border of the tibia. Treatment is decreasing cyclic loading of the leg. Non-impact forms of exercise, bike riding, and swimming are recommended to keep the muscle "in shape." Shoe orthoses to correct foot pronation are often helpful, along with softer running surfaces. There is rarely an indication for operation.

Compartment syndromes occur, not unlike those complications of leg trauma/fracture. When the pressure in a muscle compartment enclosed by a fascial sheath increases enough, neurovascular compromise results. Early pain is manifest, but later muscle necrosis and vascular impairment of the foot may ensue. During exercise, muscle compartment pressure increases. If symptoms are severe or chronic enough, surgical fasciotomy usually lessens pain and impairment, and in emergency states may prevent muscle necrosis/leg amputation.

Stress fractures of the tibia, rarely of calcaneus, usually present with localized bone pain, worsen with ambulation, and lessen with rest. Diagnosis by

---

[11] Clain & Hershman, *Overuse Injuries in Children and Adolescents,* 17 Phys & SportsMed 111 (1989).

routine x-ray is difficult in the early stage. Bone scans are the current standard of early diagnosis. Like any fracture, immobilization until x-ray evidence of healing is the recommended treatment.

In all leg compartment periostitis (shin splint) problems, as well as with healed stress fractures, an ongoing rehabilitation program is important. Maintaining or regaining muscle strength and joint flexibility is important. Close attention must be paid to the cause of the problem, such as improper shoe wear, uncorrected foot postures, and over-enthusiastic activity on hard, stressful surfaces.[12]

§19.22 Muscle Cramps

Muscle cramps during or following sports activities sharply limit sports efficiency and comfort. The cramps are a marker of overuse, perhaps in undeveloped or strengthened muscles. "Charlie horse" muscle cramps, however, often occur in the most seasoned athlete. There may be a genetic tendency for certain persons to develop muscle cramps. The physiology is muscle overload, with chemical products of metabolism such as lactic acid. Bruised muscles may be more vulnerable.

The treatment is stretching of the cramping muscle and local heat—not ice, which may slow muscle clearance of metabolites by locally decreasing circulation. Return to activity should include stretching and attempting to avoid overload.[13]

§19.23 Compartment Syndrome

In a distance runner who developed a shin splint, a posterial fascial compartment release was performed using a 2 cm incision and blind severence of fascia with scissors. However, pain persisted and worsened, and arteriovenous fistula was diagnosed by arteriogram. Repair of the fistula was carried out several months later. The patient much improved, but was unable to run at the prefasciotomy level, an unusual complication.

To diagnose and treat this syndrome, it is necessary to (1) assess bleeding and perform appropriate hemostasis with deflated tourniquet, (2) carefully place fasciotomy incisions away from high risk to local neurovascular structures, (3) make skin incisions that are adequate to visualize adjacent neurovascular structures, and (4) monitor the patient closely after surgery.[14]

---

[12] Brown & Braley, *Differential Diagnosis and Treatment of Shin Splints,* Surg Rounds for Orthop, Sept 1989, at 27.

[13] Benda, *Outwitting Muscle Cramps—Is It Possible?,* 17 Phys & SportsMed 173 (1989).

[14] Amrotta & JC Richmond, *Arteriovenous Fistula After Posterior Compartment Fasciotomy to Treat Shin Splints,* 16 Phys & SportsMed 55 (1988).

§19.24 Chronic Exertional Compartment Syndrome

The diagnosis of chronic exertional compartment syndrome is not often considered in the evaluation of chronic leg pain, although the syndrome has been well documented since 1956. There has been controversy as to the value of measured intracompartmental pressures. Most physicians agree that the patient's history is most important. Clinical clues to the diagnosis include a feeling of fullness or tenseness with activity in the effected compartment, relation of pain to a certain length of activity or distance running, and relief with rest. Physical examination, by contrast, is variable, showing no consistent positive findings. One consistent negative finding is absence of tenderness over the tibia, as seen in shin splints or stress fractures.

Therapists agree that an increase in intracompartmental pressure exists in the patient with this problem. The use of pressure measurements is controversial. Measuring a compartment pressure before, during, and after pain-producing activity should produce diagnostic information, but in one large series it was felt useful in only 70 per cent of athletes.

Intracompartmental pressures during exercises greater than 75 mm/Hg are usually significant when demonstrated. Many surgeons recommend fasciotomy in patients who develop 40 to 45 mm/Hg during activity, if there is also pain. Higher resting and post-resting intracompartmental pressures are usually considered more important (diagnostically) than during exercise pressure if under 70 mm/Hg.[15]

§19.25 Osteopenia and Athletic Amenorrhea

Approximately one-fourth of women over 60 years of age have osteoporosis; in post-menopausal women with previously documented osteopenia, regular exercises have been found to increase the mineral content of the vertebral bodies, in contrast to a continuing loss of bone in non-exercising controls.

Despite this beneficial effect of exercise on bone and mineral content, recent studies have shown that pre-menopausal women who are amenorrheic lose cancellous bone at rates similar to those who are post-menopausal, despite, or perhaps due to, the intense exercise. It has also been shown that high exercise levels in women tend to lead to oligomenorrhea or amenorrhea. The treating physician needs to be informed and to inform patients appropriately that exercise is good, but that over-exercise creates potential hazards.

Giving attention to the endocrinological status of the patient undergoing rehabilitation following disease or injury is important. Pituitary axis abnormalities, hypo- or hyperthyroidism, and testicular or ovarian abnormalities all influence muscle strength and muscle endurance as well as ligamentous support strength. To oblige a patient with endocrinological imbalance to

---

15 Mannarino & Sexson, *The Significant of Intracompartmental Pressure in the Diagnosis of Chronic Exertional Compartment Syndrome,* 12 Orthop 1415 (1989).

exercise maximally may well cause damage to the patient—a situation that could be predicted by the treating physician.

§19.26 Prophylactic Braces and Devices

Sports regulatory bodies have made strides toward limiting biomechanically inadequate protective devices, establishing standards and understanding the relationship of footwear to turf and surface fixation. Adverse effects of rigid protective equipment, such as football helmets, remain a problem. Vital and vulnerable areas such as the head, eyes, neck, kidneys, genitalia, and teeth must be protected during contact sports activities. Bracing of knees that have been injured or protecting knees from being injured by various types of accidents with polycentric-hinged or plastic shell braces, circumferential plastic shells, straps that encircle brace components on thigh and calf, shoe inserts, and exercising with heel controls, sprains and straps, have been tried and have their advocates. However, there have been no definitive reports that show that any type of bracing either prevents injury in contact sports activities or offers significant protection against re-injury.

In motor vehicle accident prevention, safety belts have been shown, without question, to substantially reduce injuries at the time of accidents, albeit there are a few specialized injuries that are precipitated by seat belts. These injuries are those in which the seat belt produced an injury on the forward-backward acceleration-deceleration phases of accidents, producing certain fractures about the spine. That tendency is lessened by wearing shoulder straps.

Large advances have been made in the construction of automobiles—such as proper positioning or elimination of knobs, handles, and protuberances on the dashboard. Air bags are relatively new and shield the body in the forward acceleration phase as the body responds to the force of the accident. Advances in plastic, non-lacerated inner surface windshields has lead to fewer severe facial lacerations.[16] (*See* Appendix 1, Case 4.)

---

[16] Brown, Myles & Allen, *The Relationship Between Aerobic Fitness and Certain Cardiovascular Risk Factors,* 54 Avia Space Environ Med 543 (1983); Hagberg, *The Effect of Exercise Training on Blood Pressure and Hemodynamic Features of Hypertensive Adults,* 52 Amer J Cardio 763 (1983); Heath, *Exercise Training Improves Lipoprotein Lipid Profiles in Patients with Coronary Artery Disease,* 105 Amer Heart J 889 (1983); Paffenbarger, Hyde & Wing, *Physical Activity, All Cause Mortality and Longevity of College Alumni,* 314 NEJM 605 (1986); Sedgwick Davidson & Taplin, *Relationship Between Physical Fitness and Risk Factors for Coronary Heart Disease in Men and Women,* 14 Aust New Zeal J Med 208 (1984); Hammond & Froelicher, *Exercise Testing for Cardiorespiratory Fitness,* 1 Sports Med 234 (1984); Tanaka, *A Longitudinal Assessment of Anaerobic Threshold and Distance Running Performance,* 16 Med Sci Sports Exer 178 (1984); Laughman, Youdas & Garrett, *Strength Changes in Normal Quadriceps Femoris Muscle as a Result of Electrical Stimulation,* 63 Phys Ther 494 (1983). Cox & Lens, *Women Midshipmen in Sports,* 12 Amer J SportsMed 241 (1984); Drinkwater, *Bone and Mineral Content of Amenorrheic and Eumenorrheic Athletes,* 311 NEJM 277 (1984); Krolner, Toft & Nielsen, *Physical*

§19.27 Knee Braces

Many athletes wear what they hope is a prophylactic knee brace in an attempt to prevent knee injuries. This is especially true in football where the knee is the most frequent site of injury and the medial collateral is the most often injured ligament.

There are indications that knee braces neither serve to reduce injuries nor lessen the severity of injuries. The concept of prophylactic knee braces is intuitively logical, but the results seem to indicate that more developmental work must be done before there will be any prospect of significant impact on injury reduction.

Prophylactic knee braces are designed to protect against damage to the medial collateral ligament caused by lateral blows. After the first brace appeared in 1979, it and other variations gained popularity after anecdotal testimonials supported their ability to reduce the number of injuries. Some colleges now require all football players to wear them.

In 1986, the Athletic Injury Monitoring System began gathering injury data from a national sample of college football teams. As this was an observational study, the decision as to which players wore braces was under local control, based on policies at individual institutions.

During the study on knee braces, data was collected on 8,325 collegiate football players. The trainers who made the reports noted the type of injury, circumstances, type of playing surface, lost playing time, whether a prophylactic knee brace was worn, and, if so, what brand. A total of 3,744 injuries were reported during the observation period, and 714 involved the knee. One-half of the 407 knee injuries reported in 1987 and 1988 involved the medial collateral ligament. Players who wore braces had more injuries than expected, and players who did not wear braces had fewer injuries than expected. Critics say there could be selection bias. Additionally, when injuries did occur, it did not appear that braces reduced the severity; there was no significant difference in the distribution of the three grades of injuries or in the useful days lost because of injury.

The final chapter on prophylactic knee-bracing has not been written. Meanwhile, the sports medicine physician is confronted with conflicting clinical, cadaveric, and biomechanical studies, manufacturers' claims, and a public that wants to do whatever is possible to limit career-ending knee ligament injuries. To further complicate matters, more than 30 prophylactic knee braces are now marketed across the country, although it is still considered investigational.[17]

Although two of the most common injury sites are at the patella and the meniscus, determining which is involved is central to providing effective

---

Exercise as Prophylaxis Against Involutional Vertebral Bone Loss. A Controlled Trial, 64 Clin Sci 541 (1983).

[17] Cowart, *Bracing Those Knees: How Effective?,* 263 JAMA 201 (1990); McCarthy, *Prophylactic Knee Braces: Where Do They Stand?,* 16 Phys SportsMed 102 (1988); Paulos, France & Rosenberg, *The Biomechanics of Lateral Knee Bracing. Part I: Response of the Valgus Restraints to Loading,* 15 Am J SportsMed 419 (1987).

treatment and helping patients resume normal activities with minimal delay. Subjective factors such as the ability to get into and out of a squatting position provide clues to meniscal versus patellar involvement. Objective factors such as anatomic knee variations do likewise.

§19.28 Diagnostic Algorithms

The use of algorithms and patient assessment forms are very useful in diagnosing any orthopedic joint or soft tissue problems and are no less useful for the sports medicine physician. (*See* Appendixes 19-2 and 19-3.)

Because of arthroscopic surgery and other improved techniques, the future looks brighter for patients with knee injuries; however, there apparently is no perfect substitute for natural knees and no remedy to return them to a natural state once degeneration has begun.

§19.29 Knee Collateral Ligament Injuries

In the sports medicine field, the automatic surgical intervention of major knee ligament injuries is no longer accepted. There are many situations where major injuries can be treated and rehabilitated by noninvasive methods.

In medial collateral ligament tests, early arthroscopic examination to rule out anterior cruciate ligament tears is a recommended diagnostic tool. Absent anterior cruciate ligament tear, a three-phase treatment protocol plan for complete medial collateral ligament tear is recommended. The first is the fitting of an orthosis with 30 degrees of flexion, partial weight bearing with crutches, and strengthening exercises. The second phase allows knee motion from 30 to 90 degrees, followed by the addition of isotonic and isokinetic exercises and full weight bearing without crutches, if tolerable. The third phase includes removal of orthosis, continuing exercise activity, and the addition of a running program.

Critical treatment depends on arthroscopic confirmation of an intact anterior cruciate ligament. If this ligament is torn, early repair surgically in the active young athlete, followed by a similar protocol as set out above, is a satisfactory method. All orthopedists/sports medicine physicians do not believe that early or frequent repair of the anterior cruciate ligament is best. They may recommend the above medial collateral ligament conservative, noninvasive method and see if the knee is stable and useful to the injured sports person. A secondary repair of the anterior cruciate ligament, using a combined inter-articular and extra-articular procedure with adequate protection early during healing, and then an equally adequate rehabilitation program, provided a useful knee as often as doing an early open repair.[18]

---

[18] Wasilerwiski, *Rehabilitation After Arthroscopic Lateral Tetinacular Release*, 28 Orthop Rev 1011 (1989).

In the sports medicine field, the automatic surgical intervention of major knee ligament injuries is no longer accepted. There are many conservative treatments.

§19.30 Rehabilitation After Lateral Release

Emphasis on rehabilitation after operation is equally important to the surgery when it is done well. This is particularly true of knee surgeries, including open or arthroscopic techniques. The knee muscular supports lose mass and power rapidly after disuse for any reason, and require energetic supervised resistive exercises to achieve maximum recovery. Use of an isokinetic knee rehabilitation machine can be very helpful.[19]

§19.31 Foot Orthotics

Biomechanical foot orthotics relieved lower extremity pain in 96 per cent of recreational athletes who wore permanent orthotics for three months to two years, according to a study done at Emory University and Georgia State University in Atlanta. To obtain such a high level of effectiveness, it is believed that the patient must undergo (1) a thorough biomechanical evaluation, (2) gait analysis, and (3) a trial period with temporary orthotics to guide the clinician in making a permanent orthotic specific to the patient's deformities.[20]

§19.32 Running and Osteoarthritis

There is a question of whether the impact of running produces osteoarthritis in weight-bearing joints. Sports medicine physicians who have studied this issue generally feel that the running, per se, does not induce osteoarthritis, but may well aggravate or accelerate the arthritic symptoms, and jogging or other activities that are high impact to weight-bearing surfaces should be reasonably curtailed if osteoarthritis is present. At the same time, non-impact aerobic exercising improves function, mood, and pain control in a symptomatic arthritic (either osteoarthritic or rheumatoid) joint. It has been shown that running or low-impact aerobic activity may well slow the functional aspects of musculoskeletal aging.[21]

---

19 Wasilerwiski, *Rehabilitation After Arthroscopic Lateral Tetinacular Release,* 28 Orthop Rev 1011 (1989).

20 Indelicato, *Nonoperative Management of Complete Tears of the Medial Collateral Ligament,* 18 Orthop Rev 1947 (1989).

21 Pascale & Grana, *Does Running Cause Osteoarthritis?,* 17 Phys SportsMed 157 (1989). Eichner, *Does Running Cause Osteoarthritis?,* 17 Phys SportsMed 147 (1989).

§19.33 Arthroscopy

Arthroscopy has become a subspecialty in orthopedics. Although not complicated, the technique requires instruction in its uses and requires a remarkedly high degree of hand-eye coordination. All surgeons do not have this coordination, making arthroscopy impractical and high risk. Insufficient attention to the development of basic arthroscopic skills may result in higher than necessary complication rates. Careful preparation is a cornerstone to satisfactory arthroscopic execution by the orthopedic surgeon.

Good diagnostic skills come before good surgical skills. It is important for the orthopedist embarking on arthroscopic diagnosis and treatment to visit and work with a skilled arthroscopist or to attend instructional courses to learn the skill.

In reviewing the pitfalls of arthroscopic examinations, improper placement of ports (the site where the arthroscope pierces the joint) is commonly seen. It is easier to look up with a scope, so port placement should accommodate that. The port, in the knee, should be at the edge of the patellar tendon, not the joint line, to increase the area of view. In making a second opening into the joint, using a spinal needle to locate where the surgeon wants the second port is helpful. Some arthroscopists say that if you cannot do the operation in your mind with a spinal needle, you will likely have problems with the more complicated surgical arthroscopic instruments. Care in the use of the instruments is necessary, as the surgeon may lever, bend, or twist excessively (and easily), breaking off part of the instrument into the joint. Postoperative hemorrhage into the joint or effusion usually follows long and/or difficult procedures; drainage of the joint with a closed drain system, when appropriate, is recommended by many surgeons to avoid this problem.[22]

§19.34 Peroneal Nerve Palsy

In the treatment of athletes with bruises and extremity sprains, application of pressure dressings, splints, and use of heat or cold are common emergency treatment modalities. A knowledge of the anatomy of the area treated by the team physician or the paramedical (trainers-coaches) staff is essential. Often, the training of side line personnel is not under the control of the team or treating physician, but it is often a short step from mismanagement of an athlete's injury at the side line by a trainer, to the orthopedist/sports medicine physician.

Wrapping an extremity with a pressure pad or ice pack, using an elastic bandage, has caused permanent injury. This situation is most often seen when a pressure paid is placed over the peroneal nerve at the lateral knee.[23]

---

[22] Drez, Jr, Presented at Arthroscopic Surgery Meeting, Scottsdale, Ariz (1989).

[23] Green, *Peroneal Nerve palsy Induced by Cryotherapy*, 17 Phys SportsMed 63 (1989).

§19.35 Median and Ulnar Nerve Injury

Many sports activities require prolonged repetitive usage of the upper extremities. These may present as an overuse syndrome that involves altered peripheral nerve function. Typical is the professional bicyclist who holds the handlebars without changing position. Electrodiagnostic studies are helpful in these problems, showing impaired nerve function. The symptoms may vary from numbness and weakness of the forearm/hand to cramping of forearm/palm musculature. In patients who present with nerve entrapment syndrome, changing position while doing the activity is more likely to relieve symptoms than resorting to surgical decompressions. Surgery should be reserved for the recalcitrant case which is unresponsive to all noninvasive treatments.[24]

§19.36 Acute Brachial Neuropathy in Athletes

Acute brachial neuropathy (ABN) is an uncommon cause of pain and weakness in the upper extremity. It should, however, be included in the differential diagnosis of shoulder pain in the athlete. This disorder consists of an acute or insidious onset of shoulder pain that is intense and lasts for hours to weeks. The etiology is unknown, but viral and allergic causes have been implicated. ABN occurs in both contact and noncontact sports. Weakness of the extremity occurs most often in the shoulder and upper arm and may occur in conjunction with pain or as a second stage when the pain has diminished. Winging of the scapula is frequently observed secondary to weakness of the serratus anterior muscles. The patient should be informed that some residual weakness and scapular winging may persist. There may also be an associated sensory loss, most commonly occurring over the lateral deltoid region. The diagnosis is confirmed by the history and physical exam, along with electromyography and nerve conduction studies. Treatment includes an initial period of rest, use of analgesics and occasional use of a sling. After the pain resolves, rehabilitation of the entire extremity and upper body should be instituted.[25]

§19.37 Seizures

When the athlete, or any patient, develops seizures, traditionally the doctor looks for a cardiac or pulmonary problem, reasoning that there is a temporary decrease in brain oxygen as the seizure trigger. The experienced

---

[24] Jackson, *Electrodiagnostic Studies of Median and Ulnar Nerves in Cyclists,* 17 Phys SportsMed 137 (1989).

[25] Hershman, Wilbourn & Bergenfled, *Acute Brachial Neuropathy in Athletes,* 17(5) Am J Sports Med 665 (1989).

sports medicine doctor has also learned that this may be an early manifestation of focal brain disease and looks for the same.[26]

§19.38 Psychological Variables

There is increasing evidence of the role of psychological variables in the risk factors of experiencing injury in sports participation and in rehabilitation of sports-incurred injuries. The failure of medical personnel, coaches, parents, and the athlete to recognize this interaction places the athlete at greater risk. In a society where there is still a stigma attached to needing help for so-called "head problems," and especially in the athletic environment where toughness and other ego defenses are the rule rather than the exception, the social support system is of critical importance.

The athlete must be taught that seeking help to cope with the psychological aspects of an injury is in the same category as seeking help to improve physical performance, endurance, or for honing fine points or participation in his or her sport. It is also important that the medical and sports communities make available this sports-supporting network.[27]

§19.39 Sports Emotions

Several psychological studies have addressed subjects of emotional trauma resulting from sports-related injury in the athlete. Studies show no gender difference, but show greater depression with or without anxiety occurring in the injured athlete as compared to the injured non-athlete peer. The most seriously injured group experienced significantly more tension, depression, and anger, and less vigor, than peer norms, a mood disturbance that often lasted over one month.

Emotional disturbance can occur after a sports-related injury, and its prompt recognition may facilitate the athlete's optimal rehabilitation and a safe return to participation in sports.[28]

§19.40 Sports and Steroids

Self-destructive behavior, such as smoking, on the part of the patient presents the doctor with a dilemma. The physician may well feel anger and frustration at a patient whose behavior undermines potential excellence as an athlete, yet the doctor usually is unwilling to alienate that athlete, further complicating the care.

When the physician knows of or suspects that the athlete is taking potentially harmful medications, such as androgenic steroids, to enhance the ath-

---

[26] Simpson & Grossman, *Seizures After Jogging,* 321 NEJM 835 (1989).

[27] Pease, *Athletic Injuries and Psychological Variables,* Surg Rounds for Orthop, Nov 1989, at 63.

[28] Smith, *Emotional Responses of Athletes to Injury,* 65 Mayo Clin Proc 38 (1990).

letic performance, the situation is further complicated by not intervening, giving the inference that the physician condones the steroid use. One solution is to refuse to serve patients who use these (or other) drugs; however, such a threat carries little weight with the athlete who is convinced of a personal need for the steroids. A more viable solution is establishment of a close physician-patient relationship that will have a better therapeutic effect on the patient. It probably is better for physicians to treat patients taking harmful medications to the best of their mutual abilities (albeit unsuccessfully at times) than to refuse them. A close comparison with the AIDS patient and the doctor's refusal to treat can be made. Recordkeeping is important to both patient and physician in these cases, reciting the problem and the treatment rationale.[29]

§19.41 Anabolic Steroids

Much has been written in the lay press regarding the use of anabolic steroids by athletes to improve their physical abilities. Anabolic steroids, used regularly and in combination with physical activity, will increase muscle mass, strength, and endurance, thereby improving physical capabilities. A continuing aerobic exercise training program is essential for maintenance of the effects.

The side effects of anabolic steroid use far outweigh the above advantages in the eyes of most physicians. The use of androgenic steroids (testosterone) adversely affects the heart in many persons, leading to heart muscle ischemia which may lead to cardiac failure or coronary occlusion; death may result. Premature aging, including premature growth arrest in adolescents, with shortened stature, may occur. Sterility is reported. Gynecomastia with breast cancer has also been reported. A variety of psychotic symptoms are seen in patients who abuse anabolic steroids. Many frightful, self-destructive behavior problems, including suicide, are described. The physician who prescribes steroids to increase athletic prowess must do so only for a patient who has been informed of and accepts the risks. Many physicians prescribe anabolic steroids in good faith to help the athlete to excel, but do so at the peril of the athlete and the negligence exposure of the prescriber.

Anabolic steroids have been outlawed for use in virtually all competitive sports, as they present an unfair, unethical competition advantage.[30]

---

[29] Cristofar, *Steroids, the Athlete and the Physician,* J Musculoskel Med, Nov 1989, at 3.

[30] Friedl & Yesalis, *Self-Treatment of Gynecomastia in Bodybuilders Who use Anabolic Steroids,* 17 Phys SportsMed 67 (1989); Cowart, *Steroid in Sports: After Four Decades, Time to Return These Genies to Bottle,* 257 JAMA 421 (1987); Haupt & GD Rovere, *Anabolic Steroids: A Review of the Literature,* 12 Am J SportsMed 469 (1984); Nagelberg, *Cerebralvascular Accident Association with Testosterone Therapy,* 314 NEJM 649 (1986); Pope & Katz, *Steroid Abuse May Prompt Severe Psychiatric Symptoms,* 145 Am J Psych 487 (1988); Lenders, *Deleterious Effects of Anabolic Steroids on Serum Lipoproteins, Blood Pressure and Liver Function in Amateur Body Builders,* 8(1) Int J Sports Med 19 (1988).

§19.42 Erythropoientin

In athletics, the use of androgenic steroids and reinfusion of patients stored blood to enhance athletic prowess have been universally described as physiologically dangerous and unfair from a sportsmanship point of view. Erythropoientin is a new drug that stimulates the bone marrow to rapidly produce more red blood cells. Its use in treating anemia is very beneficial and has been approved by the FDA for this purpose. Erythropoietin might be used by an athlete to increase endurance by increasing the body's blood oxygen transport ability. There is clear evidence that excessive or inappropriate use of erythropoietin presents health risks.[31]

§19.43 Bone Scans

Overload muscle injury or overstretching seen in athletic or similar injuries can be difficult to diagnose. Simple overload of a muscle mass may present as muscle belly soreness, pseudoweakness, and functional deterioration. If injury to muscle fibers or muscle attachment to bone through Sharpy fibers is present, the treatment may be different and more prolonged. Use of radio-isotope bone scanning can be helpful when diagnosis of a skeletal or muscle injury is difficult. A total body scan can be used to evaluate the entire musculoskeletal system; specific views can confirm the diagnosis. This imaging technique can also differentiate between skeletal and muscle injury, and between myocardial and skeletal muscle in injuries with chest pain which have equivocal EKG studies but elevated serum enzymes, marking muscle damage.[32]

§19.44 Bone Tumors versus Sports Injuries

One of the great fears of a physician is missing an important diagnosis, for humane as well as medicolegal ramifications. The loss of time from treatment and further progression of the illness can be catastrophic. Most traumatic sports injuries are strains, sprains, and contusions, and a large number of these are overuse injuries. Because symptoms are nonspecific and similar to other conditions, and because soft tissue and bone tumors occur in the same areas as sports injuries, delay in treatment of a tumor occasionally occurs because it is thought to be a sports injury.

Appearance of sports injuries can be deceiving. Often, the first examiner does not feel the clinical picture is of sufficient severity to pursue an indepth

---

[31] Cowart, *Erythropoietin: A Dangerous New Form of Blood Doping,* 17 Phys SportsMed 115 (1989); Eschbach, *Correction of the Anemia of End Stage Anemia With Recombinant Human Erythropoietin,* 31 NEJM 118 (1989); Mayer, *Working Capacity is Increased Following Recombinant Erythropoietin Treatment,* 34 Kidney Int 525 (1988).

[32] Martin, *Bone Scanning for Detection of Exercise-Induced Musculoskeletal Injury,* 17 Phys SportsMed 125 (1989).

diagnosis or follow-up. Follow-up of these sports injuries is essential and should be the duty of the coach, trainer, and physician. The most commonly missed diagnoses are osteogenic sarcoma, myositis ossificans, osteoid osteoma, periosteal calcification, and fibrosarcoma. Delay in benign disease treatment is not significant for survival, but the contrary is true in malignancy. The following rules of thumb may be helpful:

1. If a patient does not respond to the initial treatment, assume the condition is more complicated than originally thought
2. If the original x-rays are of poor quality or were taken a long time ago, repeating them is indicated
3. If the patient has not responded to treatment despite normal-appearing x-rays, other diagnostic tests and consultation should be sought[33] (*See* Appendix 19-1, Case 5.)

---

[33] McKirgan & Steingard, *Bone Tumors Masquerading as Traumatic Injury,* 17 Phys SportsMed 121 (1989).

Appendix 19-1
Cases

1 ***Hart v Schutt Manufacturing Co,* No C456-012 (Pasadena City Super Ct, Cal 1988)** (football player was caught at the bottom of a pileup. When attendants reached player, the face mask of his helmet was stuck in the turf. The patient was removed by medical personnel, allegedly with inadequate immobilization, resulting in incomplete quadriplegia. The state was held medically responsible for negligent player transfer, as the accident occurred in the Rose Bowl).

2 ***Guebard v Jabaay,* 452 NE2d 751 (Ill App Ct 1983)** (trial court committed a reversal error in refusing to instruct the jury on res ipsa loquitur in an accident arising out of a Hauser knee operation. The patient injured her knee in downhill skiing in 1971, and was treated by an orthopedic surgeon. Conservative treatment failed to relieve her condition, so he performed a Hauser operation June 2, 1971. When the operation did not achieve the desired results, he performed a second one about three months later. The second one also was unsuccessful, and the patient claimed her knee was left in worse condition than it was before surgery. She filed an action against the orthopedic surgeon, claiming lack of informed consent to the first operation which was primarily performed by a first-year resident of the hospital, lack of informed consent to the second operation, and doctor res ipsa loquitur. The jury returned a verdict in favor of the physician, and the patient appealed. The appellate court said that the theory of lack of informed consent did not apply when the patient had consented to a procedure, but it was performed by somebody else. The court said that the proper cause of action would have been battery. The patient had withdrawn her claim based on battery and had chosen to rely on the wrong theory of informed consent. The court said that the patient's informed consent claim based on the second operation could also fail. The surgeon allegedly did not tell her that patellectomy was indicated).

3 ***Mikkelsen v Haslam,* 764 P2d 1384 (Utah Ct App), *rehg denied,* (1988)** (plaintiff underwent a hip replacement for a congenitally dislocated hip. After six months, the patient had no symptoms. The orthopedist testified that he had told the patient not to run, twist, or lift, to protect the hip. The patient testified that the orthopedist told her she could skip, play tennis, or do anything she wished. Five years after the operation, the patient called orthopedists to see if it was safe for her to go skiing; others verified the telephone call, saying that the orthopedist endorsed skiing for the patient. The next year, the patient fell, fracturing the femur about and distal to the hip prosthesis in a manner that no re-repair of the total hip could be carried out, causing the patient to be a crutch or wheelchair ambulator for life. In the malpractice action, the plaintiff contended that the orthopedist failed to adequately advise her of the physical limitations imposed by the hip

replacement. She also contended that she should have had regular, ongoing follow-up examinations offered to her by the orthopedist. At trial, five orthopedists testified that failure to advise not to ski in this type of case was below the standard of care for orthopedic surgeons. The trial court found for the plaintiff, dividing damages 50 per cent to defendant and 50 per cent to patient, thus awarding no damages to the plaintiff. They found that failure to warn not to ski was a cause of the patient's injury, but also found that the patient was negligent or assumed the risk, and that that was a cause of injury. On appeal, the patient contended that the trial court erred in not giving her requested jury instruction limiting contributory negligence and/or assumption of risk defenses. These instructions would have clarified that those defenses were appropriate only if the jury found that the defendant had not advised the patient that she could ski. If he told her she could ski or did not advise her of specific risks, the court said that the jury should have been instructed that, to find the patient contributorily negligent, she must have been negligent in her manner of skiing. The appellate court agreed with the plaintiff and remanded for a new trial).

4 ***Allen v American Baseball Cap, Inc,* No 2918 (Philadelphia Ct CP Pa)** (plaintiff, a high school student, was hit in the head by a hard baseball during a varsity game. The protective helmet was alleged to have insufficient padding to protect the wearer's head from baseball blows. Expert medical testimony was that the particular helmet had been previously tested, found unsafe, and that recommendations made to increase padding were not followed. This fault was corrected by the manufacturer only two years later, when the same recommendations were made by the National Operating Committee for Standards in Athletic Equipment).

Comment: The team doctor possibly incurs liability in these cases as advisor for protective equipment—he or she, as a professional, must be adequately informed before advising. In this case, permanent injury from intracerebral hematoma, requiring surgery, resulted in permanent injury—memory loss and paralysis of the right arm and leg.

5 ***Crisher v Spak,* 471 NYS2d 741 (Sup Ct 1983)** (orthopedic surgeon treated a patient for complaints relative to her right foot in 1974. Surgery was recommended and performed. After the operation, the patient continued to have difficulty with her foot, and continued to consult the surgeon through June 1975. In May 1975, elective diagnostic studies revealed nerve involvement. The surgeon advised that the patient had pain discomfort because of a pinched nerve and that the problem could be treated with surgery. At that time, the patient was in very little pain and decided not to undergo an additional operation. The physician failed to advise his patient at the time that he did not know what was causing the pinched nerve and that surgery was necessary to make that determination. Further, he did not tell her that one of the possible causes of the pain was a tumor. The orthopedist testified that he did not even consider the possibility of a tumor. The patient ultimately had a below-knee amputation of the right leg and a biopsy revealed she had a malignant tumor. In a malpractice action against the orthopedic surgeon,

the patient claimed the surgeon's failure to explain to her that surgery was necessary to determine the cause of her problem was a departure from the accepted standards of medical practice. Expert witnesses testified to that effect and additionally testified that it was also a departure from accepted standards of medical practice for the physician not to advise her of possible causes of her difficulty, including the fact that she might have a tumor. The jury found that the patient would have had an operation in 1975 if her surgeon had advised her that surgery was necessary to determine the cause of her pain and nerve involvement, and had advised as to the various causes of pain including the tumor. The court said that the negligence of the physician deprived her of a reasonable chance to avoid amputation).

6 ***Dugan v Hillmer,*** **No 87 CV 24 (La Plata County Dist Ct Nov 1987)** (36-year-old attorney stepped into a hole while training for a marathon and strained his Achilles tendon. After unsuccessful conservative treatment, the plaintiff consulted an orthopedist who held himself out as a sports medicine specialist. On April 22, 1986, the orthopedist examined the patient and put him into a walking boot cast. The plaintiff began to feel pain in his calf and returned to the defendant's office. The defendant's associate removed the cast on May 7 and instructed the plaintiff to see the defendant on May 9. The defendant's examination revealed exquisite tenderness in the calf and a positive Homan's sign; the diagnosis was phlebitis. A venogram was not performed. The defendant was told to elevate the leg and apply hot soaks, to take Motrin, and to wait three to six weeks. The plaintiff followed instructions, but two weeks later presented to an emergency room as pain had migrated to the groin. A venogram then showed complete obstruction of the deep veins of the calf and thigh. The plaintiff brought an action, saying that on May 9th the defendant negligently failed to diagnose deep venous thrombosis. He further alleged that the two and one-half week delay in diagnosis caused a severe post-phlebitic syndrome and reflex sympathetic dystrophy).

Appendix 19-2
Tables

Table 1
Diagnosis and Treatment of the Most Common Heat Illnesses*

	Diagnosis	Treatment
Heat cramps	Associated with whole-body salt deficiency. Cramps occur in abdominal wall and large muscles of the extremities but differ from exertion-induced cramps; entire muscle not involved; cramp appears to wander because individual muscle bundles contract. Plasma Na+ deficit; urine NaCl concentration from a trace to 3 gm/L; 51 mEq/L, with specific gravity > 1.016. Observed mostly in unacclimatized individuals.	Oral 0.1% saline solution (two 10-grain salt tablets in 1 L water) or IV 0.5-1.0 L normal saline solution. IV solutions, used when symptoms include nausea and vomiting, bring rapid relief with no lasting sequelae.

* Abbreviations

ALT: alanine aminotransferase
AST: aspartate aminotransferase
BP: blood pressure
BUN: blood urea nitrogen
CNS: central nervous system
CPK: creatine phosphokinase
DIC: disseminated intravascular coagulation
Hct: hematocrit
IV: intravenous, intravenously
LDH: lactate dehydrogenase
Tre: rectal temperature

	Diagnosis	Treatment
Heat exhaustion	Inability to continue activity in the heat. Symptoms may include nausea, vomiting, irritability, headache, "heat sensations" on head and trunk, orthostatic changes, syncope, dyspnea, weakness, piloerection. Tre up to 39° C, depending on the physical activity that preceded overt illness and the point at which temperature was first recorded. Sweating is profuse. Mental function and thermoregulation are mildly impaired. Acclimatization reduces incidence of symptoms. There are three types of heat exhaustion; the first two involve peripheral vascular collapse: 1. Water depletion. Hypohydration, prominent thirst; cramps seldom seen; onset possible with a few hours of exercise. 2. Salt depletion. Prominent fatigue, cramps, vomiting, progressive weakness; thirst seldom observed; onset within 3-5 days. 3. Nonclassic exercise-induced. Tetany, carpopedal spasms, abdominal cramps, syncope, respiratory alkalosis (all induced by	Type 1 and 2: Rest and cooling increase venous return to heart. Mixed salt/water depletion is usually seen. Replace water and electrolytes based on measures of serum Na+, protein, BUN, Hct, pulse, BP, or orthostatic changes. After the duration of exercise and heat exposure and the amount of fluid intake are determined, water and electrolyte loss may be estimated as 1.5 L water and 2 gm NaCl per hour of continuous, moderate to heavy exercise. (Typical losses during a 4-hr work shift in harsh conditions are 6.0 L water and 8 gm NaCl.) Type 3: Rest, cooling and rebreathing of expired air. The prognosis is best when mental acuity is not altered and when serum enzymes are not elevated. Immediate return to work/exercise is inadvisable, except in mildest cases; allow 24-48 hr for recovery.

	Diagnosis	Treatment
	hyperventilation); absence of primary salt or water depletion; onset of overt symptoms is acute.	
Exertional heatstroke	Thermoregulatory failure. Tre of 39.4°-40.6° C or higher. Other symptoms include elevated serum enzymes (AST, ALT, LDH, CPK), hypotension, vomiting, diarrhea, coma, convulsions, and frank impairment of mental function and temperature regulation. Sweating may or may not be present. Onset may be rapid in patients who have been exercising.	A true medical emergency. Intubate patient if comatose or convulsing. If cardiovascular difficulties are severe or if peripheral blood flow is compromised, use conductive cooling by immersing the patient in ice water. Immersion therapy not only provides the fastest cooling rate when Tre is > 40.6° C, but also improves venous return and cardiac output via skin vasoconstriction and the effects of hydrostatic pressure. Seek a cooling rate of 0.15° C min^{-1} until Tre reaches 37.88° C, then monitor. In most cases the Tre reaches 37.8° C within 30 min. Monitor Tre for rebound hyperthermia at regular intervals for 24-48 hr. Administer IV fluids judiciously (1.0-1.5 L); consider possible pulmonary edema. Analyze serum enzymes and coagulation factors for seven days. Monitor renal and acid-base status. Complications may include CNS damage, renal failure, rhabdomyolysis, DIC, and hepatic or myocardial necrosis. The prognosis is

Diagnosis	Treatment
	best when peak Tre is < 42.2° C, serum AST < 1,000 U/L in the first 24 hr, and duration of coma is > 2 hr. The mortality rate (10%-80%) is directly related to the duration and intensity of hyperthermia as well as to the speed and effectiveness of diagnosis and treatment.

Table 2
Objective Factors in the Differentiation Between Meniscal and Patellar Pain

Exam	Meniscus	Patella
Knee effusion	There are intermittent effusions with twisting re-injury episodes	Effusion is much less common at the anterior joint
McMurray test	Joint line pain and clunk best elicited with the 'grind test' variant of the McMurray test	Subpatellar pain. Palpate for crepitus occurring at the patella rather than at joint line
Tenderness	Should be localized to the medial or lateral joint line along with pain	Subluxate the patella medially and laterally to palpate under the medial and lateral facets for tenderness and palpate at the distal pole for patellar tendon origin pain (jumper's knee)
Quadriceps atrophy	Usually significant atrophy, especially at the vastus medialis	Occasionally there is atrophy but it is less significant
Preexisting variations	Not usually or necessarily present	Look for hip anteversion, genu valgum, Q sign, lax joints, small patella, low- or high-riding patella, and multiple ossification centers
Pain on collateral ligament testing	Grind test produces pain and a clunk more consistently than McMurray test	No pain
Diagnostic Procedure		
Routine x-rays	Joint line narrowing or degenerative change on a weight-bearing film	Signs of patellofemoral instability or erosion of the articular surface
Nuclear scan	Often increased activity at the joint line	Often increased activity at the patella

Exam	Meniscus	Patella
Arthrogram	Often positive	Usually not helpful
MRI scan	Often positive for meniscal tear or pretear degeneration	Cross-section may show patellar instability and articular damage
Surgery	Usually definitive treatment	Palliative treatment, risky

Appendix 19-3
Forms

Form 1
Knee History

Name: ____________________ D.O.B.: __________ Sex: _____ Date: _______

Referring Physician: ____

Occupation: ______________________________ Date of injury: __________

Height: ______ Weight: ______ Athletic event and position played: ______

____

Chief Complaint: ____

____

____

History of Injury: ____

____

____

Was swelling: Immediate? ______ Late? ______ Degree of swelling: ______

Was knee locked? ______ Lose motion: Quickly ______ Slowly ______
Not at all ______

Was knee aspirated? ______ Was fluid bloody? ______

Initial Diagnosis: ____

____

Initial Treatment: ____

____

Past History of Knee Injuries: ______________________________________

____

____

Prior surgeries and dates: ____

____

Who did surgeries? ____

____

Form 2
Present Status

Symptoms are: Acute____ Chronic____ Constant____ Intermittent____

What makes symptoms worse? ____

____

What relieves them?____

____

Pain: Location__________ Type________________________

Severity:____________________ Night________ Day________

Does pain increase with: Sitting________ Standing________ Squatting________ Kneeling________ Sprinting________ Jogging________ Pivoting________ Cutting________ Ambulating________ Climbing stairs________ Climbing hills________ Going down stairs________ Going down hills________

Does your knee have a history of: Locking________ Popping________ Catching________ Giving away________ Grinding________ Clicking________ Swelling________

How long does swelling last?________ Degree of swelling________________

Loss or limitation of motion:________ In flexion________ In extension________

Does your knee give away?________ Is there knee weakness?________________

Is knee unstable?________ Has your (patella) knee cap ever dislocated or subluxed?______ How many times?______ Is there pain at those times?______

Gait in: Walking________ Jogging________ Running________

What worsens the pain or brings it on? ____

____

Are there other medical problems related to the knee problem? ________

Are you an athlete?________ What is your motivational level? __________

20

Surgical Care

§20.01 The Hazards of Surgery

General surgeons, trauma surgeons, and orthopedic surgeons may not regard themselves as belonging to one of the high-risk specialties, but in recent years the number of claims against them has risen steadily, as have all claims for medical negligence. Claims are now varied, but there are certain features common to all, and some of the problems are still seen all too often. Operations on the wrong patient or limb, retained swabs, sponges, instruments, or parts of instruments are frequently reported.

Problems often arise when young surgeons or inexperienced surgeons are left to perform operations for which they are not sufficiently experienced. Clearly, broad practical experience is an essential part of surgical training, but it is a matter to be judged when a surgeon in training is left on his or her own. Ideally, the surgical trainee will perform a procedure under supervision on several occasions, and then be left unsupervised but with expert help easily available should it be needed.

Unfortunately, cases have been reported where inexperienced surgeons are getting into difficulty when they have been elected to perform procedures on their own and cannot quickly or easily obtain experienced help. The chiefs may have left the operating room to attend a meeting or a surgeon with commitments at two hospitals may be at one of them while his or her junior is performing a procedure at another hospital. In these circumstances, when the problem arises, it is difficult to obtain help quickly and damage is done before the senior surgeon can reach the operating room to help the junior surgeon.

When a postoperative complication occurs, it is incumbent on the surgeon to take a close personal interest in the patient's management, to explain carefully what has happened, and to perform any further operative procedure him- or herself. If, for any reason, this is impossible—for instance, if the surgeon is ill or on leave—it is vital that clear arrangements be made with a colleague to cover, so that the surgeon in training knows who to turn to for advice.

Being on call for another surgeon's patients is another common source of claim. The incidence of complications rises while a member of the surgical team is primarily responsible for patients while the attending physicians are off duty or out of town. It is essential to inform those taking over about ill patients or unresolved pain syndromes. A covering surgeon must visit these patients and not rely on nurses to call them if they are worried.

Delays in diagnosis may occasionally occur. Acute low back pain or joint pain syndrome continues to be a source of difficulty and errors in judgment have had fatal consequences. However, if a doctor takes proper steps to try to reach a diagnosis and keeps good records, his or her management can be defended if he or she reaches the wrong conclusion. An error in judgment is not necessarily negligent. This is part of common law in the United States. This principle is hardly ever applied when there has been an obvious mistake in diagnosis that should not have been missed.

Delays in diagnosis of cancer, particularly sarcomas and bone cancers, are common causes of claims. Some cannot be defended and others are defensible because even the most sophisticated investigation can produce inconclusive or false negative results.

Diagnostic investigations may be hazardous. As physicians perform more sophisticated procedures on patients, the investigation itself may bring to light entirely new potential medical-legal problems. Endoscopic procedures, arthroscopies, myelograms, discograms, venograms, and selective injections for pain control are all procedures at risk. Provided the complications are recognized and treated promptly, it should be possible to mount a strong defense in such cases. It is assumed that an informed consent has been signed by the patient prior to the procedure.

Complications of surgery are sometimes inevitable, and rarely cause claims if the patient is fully informed about what happened and is treated correctly and sympathetically. Nevertheless, some complications, such as femoral vein damage during varicose vein surgery or total hip arthroplasty, can be difficult to defend.

Other mishaps are well recognized and occur occasionally despite steps that have been taken to avoid them, including recurrent laryngeal nerve damage during anterior cervical discectomy or peroneal nerve damage during total knee replacement surgery. Consideration should be given to warning the patient about these potential complications. Sometimes, when a claim is made and investigation reveals that appropriate steps have not been taken to avoid the problem, a settlement is necessary. The plaintiff will often obtain an opinion from another orthopedist who has particular expertise in the field of concern who affirms the procedure should only be performed by a specialist surgeon with specialized training in that field. It may be difficult to defend the operating surgeon if something goes wrong during an elective operation of this sort if that surgeon has not had what is considered to be adequate training.

It is becoming increasingly common for patients to sue their surgeons when complications develop after surgery, such as wound drainages, wound infections, incisional hernias, etc. Such claims are usually strongly defended and are often abandoned by the plaintiff who has not obtained expert opinion. Sometimes settlement is necessary if there has been a breakdown in communication between the patient and surgeon or if poor records make it difficult to provide information necessary to defend the claim. This is often made a considerable time after the event.

Wise old surgeons say that there is no such thing as a minor operation, and minor operations frequently cause claims. Biopsy of lymph nodes in the posterior cervical triangle is a common site of injury to the spinal accessory nerve. Subcutaneous lumps excised under local anesthetic can be close to nerves such as neurofibromata or synovial cyst (ganglia). It is essential to bear in mind the anatomy of the cutaneous nerve when performing such minor operations.[1]

Medical-legal claims are made only by a tiny fraction of patients treated and most can be defended. When claims arise, however, they can cause an enormous amount of anxiety and shame, and it is only by constant vigilance that they can be avoided. There is no practicing surgeon who hears of a malpractice suit filed against a colleague who does not think "But for the Grace of God, there go I." (John Bradford, 1510-1555.)

§20.02 Diagnosis

Diagnosis is an issue of such heightened emotional experience to physicians that they may lose sight of its equal or greater significance to the patient. Physicians are taught the crucial importance of definitive knowledge of exactly what is wrong with the patient while experience repeatedly has shown that a precise diagnosis often cannot be made. For physicians, diagnosis is an elusive ideal goal ready to remind the doctor of his or her own limitations and perhaps a feeling of guilt when he or she treats symptoms without knowing the cause.

In contrast, diagnosis for the patient is the appropriate self-centered issue for presenting him- or herself to the physician. The patient wants information about what is wrong with him or her, to remove the uncertainty of knowing something is wrong without knowing what it might be. This uncertainty masks the fear, dread, and apprehension of the unknown, perhaps fatal, condition. Despite modern ideas of patient responsibility and holistic health, when sick or uncertain, most patients desperately wish to place themselves under the care of potent authority. Diagnosis is the pivotal issue in the physician's exercise of this authority.

The physician's large emotional investment in diagnosis is hidden by the greater investment of the patient. Diagnosis is part of a process unfolding in time. It is preceded by the taking of a history from the patient, performance of an adequate physical examination, and ordering and reviewing certain tests. These observations are followed by treatment and an outcome. Sometimes the diagnosis can be promptly made, such as in trauma with obvious injury. In other cases, the diagnosis unfolds gradually over several physician-patient consultations. Sometimes the diagnosis is accepted and other times it is rejected. It may satisfy or enrage the patient; it may promote collaboration or create alienation.

---

[1] Keddie, *The Hazards of Surgery,* Intl J Med Def Union 2 (Spring 1988).

Despite the physician's satisfaction regarding the diagnosis and proposed treatment, a large minority of patients feel themselves underdiagnosed or undiagnosed. Many of these patients fall into chronic pain syndromes, myofascial pain syndromes, headache problems, as well as cardiac and gastrointestinal disorders. The patient often overtly or covertly states "no one has been able to tell what is the matter with me." This situation may be the end result of the physician candidly telling the patient "I can't find anything wrong with you" or "All tests are negative." Sometimes these physician statements are reassuring to the patient, but they often mean that the diagnosis is incomplete. The physician's reassurance is often rejected by the patient.

These patients represent a specific category for therapy—patients who have not accepted their diagnosis. They are often outspoken in their rejection and demand more tests and more treatment—often treatment that includes mind-altering drugs. Likewise, the patient who does not comply with treatment may be rejecting the diagnosis. Historically, these patients are often involved in litigation or compensation.

As a special category, patients who believe they are undiagnosed require special handling. Part of this revolves around the issue of responsibility. Diagnosis is mostly the doctor's responsibility and if the patient views him- or herself as underdiagnosed, he or she views the doctor as not adequately providing for him or her. From the patient's point of view, this means that the physician is responsible, even though, from the doctors's point of view, the diagnosis proffered to the patient is a best effort and likely accurate. If such a misunderstanding exists, good medicine dictates that is should be resolved.

There are other ramifications of diagnosis. Most often the patient accepts and works with the diagnosis, resulting in successful treatment. Sometimes the diagnosis is wrong, or at times it is changed or expanded during the course of observation and treatment.

Often, the physician recognizes that the patient does not accept the diagnosis; his or her greatest usefulness is a willingness to work with the patient on that point. An example is when a patient has seen many doctors. In self-evident cases, collecting and reviewing medical reports of the other physicians is helpful. Often, insisting on another consultation to confirm or alter the physician's diagnosis is helpful. With this, the patient may rationally yield to the weight of evidence and proceed with a treatment plan. Unless a confident physician-patient relationship exists, most often treatment will subjectively fail.[2]

§20.03 Surgery Mishaps

In a report from the Peter Bent Brigham Hospital and Harvard Medical School, a study was conducted for a one-year period to identify adverse

---

[2] Gaarder, *Diagnosis,* 82 So Med J 1153 (1989).

outcomes due to error during care in general surgery. In two-thirds of the cases, the mishap was due to an unnecessary, defective, or inappropriate operative procedure. In attempting to identify the origin of surgical errors, many facets were present and recurrent. All of these factors were familiar to the experienced clinician. Heading the list was misplaced optimism. This took the form of misreading the early signs of peritonitis after colonic surgery, an example of over-estimation of skill with under-estimation of patient's fragility. A second common source of error appeared to be unwarranted sense of urgency. The third source of error was the urge for perfection that resulted in a wide range of operative manipulation considerably beyond the level needed for relief of the patient's most important problem. A fourth error was referred to as "vogue therapy," the performance of new, stylish procedures that have prestigious appeal. The predominant fallibility appears to be insufficient restraint and deliberation. Excessive haste, impatience, overconfidence, and inadequate peer group consultation were important influences in this regard. The study recommended hospitals continue to develop comprehensive methods to identify and prevent these events.[3]

§20.04 Physiology

The practicing orthopedist has seen a different type of patient in the last decade or more. The patient is more sophisticated as to body anatomy and physiology. The typical patient is inquisitive about what is going on with him or her and is entitled to an explanation of what may be happening with his or her body. The orthopedist, appropriately so, is more of a teacher to patients, involving the patients in decisionmaking as to the types of treatment, but also involving the patient with a commitment to understand himself and treat himself more appropriately.

There are many fads that are involved in the practice of medicine. Patients read of new treatments, of new explanations, of new problems that they are facing, are constantly exposed to media descriptions of hazards they are exposed to, and the physician is no longer considered the "bottom line" so far as informing the patient about illness or injury. The physician, the patient, the paramedical personnel, and society in general are all partners in diagnosing and treating the patient's ails.

A good deal of medicine has always been practiced based on statistics on what happened to the larger percentage of patient groups with similar symptoms, similar diseases, and similar injuries. The media reports of these percentages—good or bad—are mentioned by the patient as he or she visits the physician.

Physical fitness is an area of increasing interest by society as a whole and very appropriately is a field of understanding and duty to inform so far as the patient is concerned. Failure of the physician to impart to a patient the essentiality of fitness and wellness is a disservice to the patient.

---

[3] Couch, *The High Cost of Low Frequency Events: The Anatomy and Economics of Surgical Mishaps,* 304 NEJM 634 (1981).

Measurement of fitness is a technical issue, but verifiable information and quantifying physical fitness are increasingly available. Some of those currently used are (1) asking the subject's opinion, (2) measuring the maximum rate of oxygen consumption (VO_2 Max), and (3) measuring the anaerobic thrust and estimated endurance on a bicycle ergometer or treadmill.

The mortality rate from heart disease has reduced about one-third in the last 15 years. This dramatic result appears to be related to improvements in lifestyle and decreases in cardiovascular risk factors such as smoking, high blood pressure, excessive body fat, and increased serum cholesterol, triglycerides, glucose, and uric acid value. Coincidentally, the fitness factors mentioned above have also steadily improved in the last 15 years. Working with these risk factors and informing patients as to what they can do to help themselves is part and parcel of the concept of rehabilitation. Wellness is appropriately one parameter of rehabilitation. The orthopedist, as a rehabilitation specialist, is a prime deliverer of this service. If the orthopedist fails to be interested or is not informed on the principles of fitness and risk factors, or lacks the communication skills to convey these to a patient, the service rendered the patient is incomplete.

Strong muscles are commonly touted to be more resistant to strains, and more likely to endure prolonged exercise. At this time, opinions vary regarding the best techniques for strengthening these muscles and for measuring muscle strength. Standards for increasing muscle strength are those techniques that include isometric, isotonic, and isokinetic resistive exercises. There is some evidence that electrical stimulation of the muscle also improves muscle strength. Isotonic and isokinetic exercises applied across irritated or damaged joint surfaces increase compressive forces on those joint surfaces. More recent studies have shown that isometric and/or isometric with electrical stimulation increases muscle strength with minimal compressive forces across the joint.

Spas and other exercise facilities have expanded rapidly in the last 20 years. Many groups of self-help type enterpreneurs who instruct patients frequently seem to overload muscle groups, so that muscle re-education and muscle strengthening is not improved and is perhaps damaged. The scientific community feels that well-trained medical personnel skilled in exercise and muscle physiology are the appropriate personnel to supervise muscle rehabilitation and muscle strengthening, and additionally to instruct on appropriate postures and positions for the use of strengthening muscles so they will not become otherwise damaged. The orthopedic surgeon, the physiatrist physician, and the registered physical therapist are the appropriate professionals for that type of patient care at this time.

Men typically have greater muscular strength than women. This may be due to behavioral influences, or it may due to the greater size, the greater lean body mass, and the increased number of muscle fibers that are present in a man. Upper body strength in women is reported to be 50 to 60 per cent of that in men. Trunk strength is about 64 per cent of men and lower body strength is about 72 per cent compared to men.

Exercise-related injuries are similar in women and men. In training facilities such as the United States Naval Academy in Annapolis, women midshipmen at first had more overuse injuries. However, as they proceeded with the same training, the same exercises, and the same measuring techniques, men and women became the same so far as ease of injury.[4]

§20.05 Preparation for Elective Surgery

The orthopedist is often called on to perform surgery. Operative procedures are classified as emergency (potentially life- or limb-saving) and elective. Adequate preparation of the patient before elective surgery and as much as possible before emergency surgery is the standard of care to be exercised by competent orthopedists as well as any other surgeon. Failure to adequately "work the patient up" before surgery often leads to preventable complications, including death from surgery. The best surgical candidate is, of course, the patient who is in good physical condition.

Preoperative planning for an elective operation begins with a history and physical examination. These much evaluate the presenting complaint and screen for related problems and assess risk factors. Laboratory testing to further evaluate risk are essential. The minimum preoperative, pre-anesthetic laboratory tests include a complete blood count, urinalysis, and blood electrolyte studies. If the patient is over 35 years of age, an electrocardiogram and chest x-rays are advisable. If significant blood loss is anticipated during operation, blood type and cross-matching with arrangement to have adequate replacement blood available before surgery commences, is necessary.

Long-range preparation for surgery includes stabilization of pre-existing health problems, such as cardiac, pulmonary, or renal diseases. A smart move for major and/or high-risk surgery is to have the patient evaluated and "cleared" for surgery by an internist or cardiologist. There is no reason for the surgeon to cut corners in this area, placing the patient at unnecessary risk.[5]

---

[4] Brown, Myles & Allen, *The Relationship Between Aerobic Fitness and Certain Cardiovascular Risk Factors,* 54 Avia Space Environ Med 543 (1983); Hagberg, *The Effect of Exercise Training on Blood Pressure and Hemodynamic Features of Hypertensive Adults,* 52 Amer J Cardio 763 (1983); Heath, *Exercise Training Improves Lipoprotein Lipid Profiles in Patients with Coronary Artery Disease,* 105 Amer Heart J 889 (1983); Sedgwich, Davidson & Taplin, *Relationship Between Physical Fitness and Risk Factors for Coronary Heart Disease in Men and Women,* 14 Aust New Zeal J Med 208 (1984); Hammond & Froelicher, *Exercise Testing for Cardiorespiratory Fitness,* 1 Sports Med 234 (1984); Tanaka, *A Longitudinal Assessment of Anaerobic Threshold and Distance Running Performance,* 16 Med Sci Sports Exer 178 (1984); Laughman, Youdas & Garrett, *Strength Changes in Normal Quadriceps Femoris Muscle as a Result of Electrical Stimulation,* 63 Phys Ther 494 (1983).

[5] Hampton, *Relative Contributions of History Taking, Physical Examination and Laboratory Investigation to Diagnosis and Management of Medical Out-patients,* 2 Br Med J 486 (1975).

Hypertension is often associated with increased peripheral-vascular resistance and/or cardiac muscular hypertrophy. Sudden increase in blood pressure in patients otherwise well-controlled on medication or poorly-controlled patients should have elective surgery deferred until blood pressure is stabilized.

§20.06 Outpatient Surgery

In recent years, much of orthopedic surgery is done on an outpatient basis. The laboratory and x-ray testing must be reviewed before the patient is admitted as an outpatient to see if additional testing or examination is necessary. Some patients are not appropriate outpatient candidates, such as cardiac risk patients who will require monitoring postsurgically. Nowadays, hospital costs may interfere with ideal patient care or a third-party carrier may limit the surgeon; however, the surgeon's obligation is to the patient, and the surgeon incurs potential liability if he or she places the patient "at risk" for financial expediency. Communication with the patient and family at all stages of operative planning, performance, and postoperative care has been shown to be the most efficient diluent of physician/surgeon criticism. The inner operative risk soft myocardial infarction is three times higher in patients who have had recent myocardial infarcts, with incidence reduced to 15 per cent when surgery was delayed three months and 4 to 5 per cent when delayed six months.[6]

Preoperative planning for an elective operation begins with a history and physical examination. These must evaluate presenting complaints and screen for related problems and assess risk factors. Laboratory testing to further evaluate risk is essential. Despite preoperative planning and treatment, the physical condition of some patients presents unacceptable anesthetic/surgical risks. These patients should have surgery cancelled, continue nonoperative (medical) care, and be re-evaluated later. Often, family and patient counselling is helpful and therapeutic. Communication and hope have repeatedly been shown to be of great importance in treating the patient and dealing with family, and become the duty of competent physicians in all medical disciplines.[7]

§20.07 Preparation of Patient for Operative Procedure

All preparations and draping of the operative patient are designed to (1) present the surgeon with an operative field that presents the least risk of infection, and (2) give the operative surgeon ample room to perform the

---

[6] Krieg, *Why Are Clinical Laboratory Tests Performed?*, 233 JAMA 76 (1975); Kaplan, *The Usefulness of Preoperative Screening,* 253 JAMA 3576 (1985).

[7] L Goldman, Cardiac Risks and Complications of Non-Cardiac Surgery, 98 Ann Int Med 504 (1983).

procedure without encumberance by drapes or disturbing heights of draped material or folds that block the use of hands or instruments, etc.

Standard surgical techniques are well known to operating room personnel—from physician to technician. These include first positioning the patient in an appropriate manner on the operating table, so that the operative site will be exposed to its greatest advantage to the surgeon. Very often, the consideration of having a joint, such as a knee, hip, or shoulder, be freely mobile presents special prepping problems.

There have been arguments through the years as to which are the better techniques for preparing the skin. Some surgeons believe that the operative site should be shaved the night before and then prepped and put in sterile drapes, and others feel that the shaving of the operative site hours before the operative procedure enhances the risk of infection.

In a general way in prepping extremities, the entire extremity is prepped well above the operative site to the tip of the toe or fingers. Extremities should be prepped in such a way that the tourniquet is well out of the field and in a manner that the preparation material used on the skin does not drip down into or underneath the tourniquet. The lengths of time for skin preparation and materials used are in a state of flux. Most surgeons believe that a bactericidal chemical—iodine, merthiolate, or zephryn—should be used at the area of operation and that the area distal to the operation should be prepped for a set period of time, the most conservative believing 10 minutes is appropriate and others believing that 5 to 7 minutes is adequate. The prepped area, then, is draped in a manner using sterile drapes, so that no unprepped skin is exposed if the extremity is move.

Some surgeons feel that the draping should continue to the edge of incision. Others feel that the operative site should be covered with a plastic barrier that has a contact cement on one side, so that the incision is made through the barrier. There has been no proof that either of these techniques mitigate against infection more than if the operative site is squared off, not covered by a plastic barrier, with the edge of the drapes being some inches away from the incision line.[8]

§20.08 Surgical Techniques

A surgical approach should provide an easy access to all the structures sought. The incision should be long enough not to hinder any part of the

---

[8] Estrera, King & Platt, *Massive Pulmonary Embolism—A Complication of the Technique of Tourniquet Ischemia,* 22 J Trauma 60 (1982); Jackson, Pollock & Tindal, *The Value of a Plastic Adhesive Drape in the Prevention of Wound Infection, A Controlled Trial,* 58 Brit J Surg 340 (1971); Scherr & Dodd, *In Vitro Bacteriological Evaluation of the Effectiveness of Anti-Microbial Irrigating Solutions,* 58A JBJ Surg 119 (1976); Scherr, Dodd & Buckingham, Jr, *Prophylactic Use of Topical Antibiotic Irrigation in an Uninfected Wound—A Microbiological Evaluation,* 54A JBJ Surg (1972); Slocum, O'Neal & Allen, *Neurovascular Complications from Mal-positioning on the Operating Table,* 86 J Gyn Obstet 7-9 (1948).

operation. When practical, it should parallel or at least take into consideration the natural creases of the skin and looser lines. This makes the chances of a cosmetically aesthetic scar more realistic.

Longitudinal incisions on the flexor or extensor surface of the joint may cause an unsightly scar. It may restrict motion of the joint. A longitudinal mid-lateral excision, especially on the finger or the thumb or on the ulnar border of the hand, usually produces little scarring because it is located where movement of the skin is least. The approach should do as little damage as possible to deeper structures. It should follow a line of cleavage and planes of separation between muscle and fascia. It should pass between muscle bellies rather than through them.

The location of nerves and blood vessels must be known by the surgeon at all times, and, when possible, they must be preserved. Preserving veins may be as important as preserving arteries. If a nerve, artery, vein, or important structures are "at risk," that area should be fully exposed anatomically before proceeding with the operation, to protect the "at risk" structure.

A keen knowledge of anatomy is an essential attribute of an orthopedic surgeon. The practiced orthopedist will regularly look up and have available atlases or diagrams of the anatomy of the operative site, if there is any uncertainty at all, rather than call on memory from past surgeries or past anatomical dissections. It does not diminish the orthopedist to have an anatomical textbook in the operating room on an easel, readily available for reference.

Unnecessary scarring and disfigurement in making surgical approaches is to be avoided. A number of years ago, it was established that making a long incision parallel to the scar of a previous incision is unjustified. An incision through an old scar will heal as well as a new incision, and even though the scar may not be ideally located, the deeper structures may be reached by retracting the skin and subcutaneous tissue. Furthermore, a second incision made parallel to an old scar may impair circulation and allow a necrosis to occur in the strip of skin between two incisions.

The position of the patient for surgery is important. It should be properly established before the operation is begun and provisions must be made to prevent the position from changing during the operation. Braces, sand bags, and tape splints are helpful.

Control of blood loss is important in any operative procedure. This is particularly true in orthopedic surgeries, and perhaps more so in hand and foot work. A properly applied tourniquet helps in this regard. Absent tourniquet control, meticulous hemostasis during the operative procedure is important. For more specific observations on operative approaches, dissection techniques, hazards that may be present, and techniques to avoid, reference should be made to the appropriate area of the body.[9]

In addition to the standard operative techniques of making the incision in the appropriate area, understanding the anatomy well, avoiding undue risks to underlying tissues to affect exposure, which are true of any operative

---

[9] Compere, *Avoiding Unnecessary Scars,* 91 Clin Orthop 13 (1973).

procedure, there are frequently additional considerations in orthopedic surgery. The fixation of the various tissues is different from the problems seen in general surgery.

The fixation of tendon to bone is a basic orthopedic concept. Principal tendon sutures are well understood by the orthopedic surgeon. In suturing tendon-to-tendon to repair a laceration tendon or put in a tendon graft from one end to another end of a tendon, end-to-end smooth suturing with sutures buried into the interstices of the tendon with nonabsorbable suture is the preferable way.

In suturing tendon-to-bone, however, it is preferable to bring the tendon into roughened up bone or to window the bone or pull the tendon through a hole in the bone and suture it on itself. Tendon-to-bone heals more solidly than tendon-to-soft-tissue adjacent to the bone. A variety of fixing techniques is used to fix tendon to or into bone. These techniques include the use of stainless steel wire in a pull out manner so that the wire is brought out through the skin and later withdrawn by a special disengaging technique. Additional techniques include the use of pins or screws or buried wires or buried nonabsorbable suture to bring the tendon into and/or hold the tendon onto bone.

The fastidious accomplishment of tendon-to-bone or ligament-to-bone stabilizing techniques may be the difference between the failure and success of the transplanted or attached tissue.

Surgical approaches are important in the successful invasive care of orthopedic problems. The last few decades, a number of new surgical approaches has been described, but few are truly original. Many are modifications of old approaches rediscovered, or modifications of present approaches.

§20.09 Needlestick Injuries in the Operating Room

The surgeon may become responsible during an operation if an assistant or a nurse is injured by needlestick or scalpel cut. These persons, as well as the surgeon, are "at risk" for hepatitis B and immunodeficiency virus. Vaccines have been developed against the former; barrier methods have remained the preventative mainstay. Puncture wounds of the hands are potential sources of contamination. In a recent study, gloves from 280 orthopedic operations for acute trauma were tested for perforations; one or more was found in 30 per cent of the gloves worn by surgeons or scrub nurses. About 60 per cent of the perforations were noticed at the time of penetration, with the index finger and thumb the most often affected. When double gloves were used, 19 per cent of outer gloves, and 6 per cent of inner gloves, were found perforated. The study shows that gloves function poorly as a needlestick barrier, especially in difficult lengthy procedures and/or open fracture cases, which may also present with sharp bone spicules. Double-gloving offers increased, but incomplete, protection. Modified surgical technique and instrument handling designed to protect members of the surgical team is a better answer.[10]

Examination of 582 surgical gloves, packaged and ready for operating room use, showed 34.5 per cent had perforations prior to surgery, and 74 (12.7 per cent) which were unperforated before surgery became perforated at that time. Only 50 per cent of these perforations were noted by surgeons. Glove perforations did not influence bacterial counts on the surgeon's hands or on the outside of the gloves. The conclusion is adverse to glove makers and a challenge for improvement; however, it further supports the preoperation handwashing efficiency of the surgeon. There were no wound infections in the series reported above.[11]

Using a "leak detector" that he developed, Maurice Albin, anesthesiologist at the University of Texas Health Science Center in San Antonio, found that 58 per cent of gloves used during surgery suggested an infection risk in addition to potential surgeon injury.[12]

§20.10 Surgical Wound Irrigation

Irrigation of surgical wounds in the operating or emergency room is necessary to remove debris which adds to the infection risk and also to wash out or dilute the bacterial content, which also reduces the risk of infection. A variety of antimicrobial solutions have been used. Povidone iodine solution is probably the most popular, showing good wound clearance of debris and bacteria, actually sterilizing operative sites with a 25 per cent solution. Various antibiotic solutions are also frequently used. Both povidone iodine and antibiotic solutions at times produce allergic reactions, so that an essential part of preoperative history is the allergy history.[13]

§20.11 Surgeon's Liability

The orthopedic surgeon may be negligent in respect to operative judgment or operative technique. In unnecessary surgery cases, the plaintiffs' bar usually does not have much trouble finding a physician who will disagree with the operation as to whether it was indicated or performed satisfactorily. This is a rich ground for differences of opinion between plaintiff and defense expert witnesses, with allegations by the plaintiff that the operation was unnecessary because it was out of date, or that other options were better, safer, or had a better track records. (*See* Appendix 20-1, Cases 1, 2, 3.) In

---

[10] McLeod, *Needle Stick Injuries at Operations for Trauma: Are Surgical Gloves an Effective Barrier?,* 71B JBJ Surg 489 (1988).

[11] Dodds, *Surgical Glove Perforation,* 75 Br J Surg 966 (1988).

[12] Health Briefing, *A Leak Detector for Surgical Gloves,* Insight, Nov 6, 1989.

[13] Scherr & Dodd, *In Vitro Bacteriological Evaluation of the Effectiveness of Anti-Microbial Irrigating Solutions,* 58A JBJ Surg 119 (1976); Scherr, Dodd & Buckingham, Jr, *Prophylactic Use of Topical Antibiotic Irrigation in an Uninfected Wound—A Microbiological Evaluation,* 54A JBJ Surg (1972).

operations with known risks of injury to adjacent or more remote tissue, it is imperative that the patient understand the informed consent form. The question comes down to whether the damaged tissue (often a nerve, vessel, or viscus), although known to the patient as a risk, was in fact caused because the surgeon was careless. (*See* Appendix 20-1, Cases 3, 4, 5, 6, 7, 8, and 9.)

The above questions of fact require expert testimony. Observations of contiguous personnel, such as a nurse or anesthesiologist or surgical assistant who saw the operative technique and its competence, may help the jury understand. (*See* Appendix 20-1, Case 10.)

There are instances when the surgeon is not experienced in the operation. With the operation new to him, he has made a hasty decision to operate without absolute indications, and should have proceeded with a trial at nonoperative treatment or, in reverse, should have proceeded with surgery or other intervention, but was unskilled and frightened of the problem (often an emergency problem). It is helpful to know the surgeon's ego level and biases, as well as his skill background. (*See* Appendix 20-1, Cases 7, 11, and 12.)

In the areas of affirming the physician's competence by those closest at hand to the possible negligent act, the "conspiracy of silence" is often present and impenetrable.

The surgeon may engage in substandard operative techniques by poorly tying sutures, or by handling the tissue at the operative site too roughly, leading to sutures or tissue failure. (*See* Appendix 20-1, Cases 13, 14, 15 and 16.) Improper usage of operative instruments, causing them to break and leave foreign objects in the operative site, may sometimes occur. The problem of sutures or device or implant failure and the problem of leaving foreign bodies in the patient present difficult evidentiary problems at times. (*See* Appendix 20-1, Case 17.) The discovery of a foreign body may be delayed by years if the surgeon did not inform the patient. If the foreign body causes injury, allegations of fraud may be brought against the surgeon.

The joint responsibility of the surgeon, hospital, and manufacturer of a failed device is often tested in court, and again this is a question for expert testimony on the issue of device failure; at times there is a res ipsa loquitur argument on the issue of injury solely under the control of the defendants (doctor, hospital, or manufacturer). (*See* Appendix 20-1, Case 18.)

§20.12 X-Rays in the Operating Room

It is often necessary to make x-rays during an orthopedic procedure. Radiographic technicians who work in operating rooms must wear the same clothing (masks, etc.) as surgical personnel and must be fully apprised of aseptic techniques.

Portable x-ray units used in operating rooms must be cleaned regularly, and are ideally not used in any other area of the hospital. Special techniques of cleaning the x-ray unit are essential when the portable x-ray unit is used in infected orthopedic surgeries.

The placing of the unsterile x-ray cassette is a potential surgical contamination problem. Special, double-thickness plastic cassette holders are available and can be handed from an unsterile person by unwrapping out of its wrapper to a sterile person, taking an unsterile x-ray and over-folding it in the edges of the cassette holder, so that a sterile device is in fact had.

Many x-ray tables are fitted with cassette trays so an unsterile personnel can place the x-ray cassette in the appropriate position underneath or to the side of the operative site, not disturbing the sterile operative field.

A great deal of time can be lost in the taking and developing of x-rays during the operative procedure to the disservice of the patient, increasing operative time, blood loss, and risk of infection in the open wound. Therefore, every attempt should be made in the orthopedic operating theatre to facilitate the speedy taking and development of film.

Image intensifier, television fluoroscopy, commonly called a C-arm portable x-ray unit, is available in most orthopedic theatres now. This rapidly speeds up the x-ray control of an operative procedure. It does introduce its own special sterility problem in covering the rotating x-ray arm, but ample draping techniques and supplies are available at this time so that no greater risk is presented by the use of C-arm x-ray intensifier devices in the operating room.

§20.13 Surgical Environment

The operating room should provide an environment that is safe for the patient and efficient for personnel who work there. This requires close attention to many details on a daily basis. The physical features of the operating room, the equipment in the room, and the procedures performed by surgeons, anesthesiologists, nurses, and other personnel need accommodation. These considerations need to be evaluated for cost-effectiveness, litigation potential, tradition, and personal preferences.

Orthopedists usually require a larger room than some specialities because of need for special machines and equipment. Rooms and orientation to accommodate special operating tables, fracture tables, C-arm x-ray units, along with bulky anesthetic machines and monitors, are minimal requirements. Breaks in sterile techniques and prevention of adequate control of the patient may occur in cramped quarters.

Many of the devices used in surgery can be hazardous to the patient or personnel. All persons involved are held to understand risks and take steps to cope with the hazard. X-ray equipment exposes operating room personnel as well as patients; the cumulative effect of irradiation is a potential risk to those involved. Protective aprons, gloves, body positioning behind a lead shield, and distancing from the x-ray unit are protective.

Anesthetic gases escaping into the room is risky to some. HIV infection is a concern to all who deal with patients' body fluids. Double gloving, frequent glove changes, precise surgical technique, and protecting all sharp instruments and needles from all who may come in contact are essential. Hepatitis B virus infection potential is lessened by the same precautions. Most physicians feel that all hospital personnel should receive hepatitis B vaccine.

Electrosurgical devices can burn the patient or surgeon if the surgeon has a hole in his or her gloves.

Prevention of infection is one prime concern in all operating theatres; it is the joint responsibility of all persons in the room, generally supervised by the senior nurse in the room. All persons entering the operating suite must change all outside street clothes, don operating room attire, and change shoes or use protective shoe covers, lessening the chance of bringing infection from the street to the operating suite.

Standard protocols for setting up surgical instruments and maintaining them sterile and accommodating the surgeon is the full-time job of "scrub" nurses or technicians who are (or should be) highly trained in this discipline. (*See* Appendix 20-1, Case 19.)

Positioning of the anesthetized patient on the operating table to prevent pressure areas, skin breakdowns from pressure, pressure neuropathy, or skin burns is the joint responsibility of the anesthesiologist, operating room nurses, and surgeons. Many operating room supervisors insist on a regular protocol, checking each vulnerable "pressure point" area after anesthesia, but before patient skin preparation and sterile draping.

All operating room personnel must wear face masks at any time they are in the room, and have their head covered so no hair is exposed. All personal touching the patient or surgical instruments must be appropriately gowned and gloved.

All persons who participate in the touching phase of the operation or touching of instruments must appropriately scrub their hands before each operation, before gowning and gloving.

Skin preparation to reduce surgical infections requires performance by a skilled person, and although techniques vary, shaving and scrubbing the skin with antiseptic solution for sufficient time (up to 10 minutes per operative site) are usual. There is ongoing research and advancement in antiseptic chemicals to improve this phase of surgery.

The "prepped" patient's operative site is outlined by a series of sterile drapes to lessen spread of infection from the unprepared area. Barrier drapes that will not transmit moisture are "state of the art."

Sales of disposable operating room supplies totaled approximately $1.8 billion in 1988, according to a recent Frost & Sullivan report. Disposable supplies are popular because they allow budget analysts to identify and isolate specific item costs, and costs in other areas such as sterilization and laundry can be eliminated.

Additionally, disposable products offer better protection to both patients and surgical staff, with two groups dominating the disposable supply market—wound closure products (suture and stapling device sectors) and non-woven linen products (surgical apparel and surgical packs and parts).

Large growth will be seen in grafts and mesh products, material used to patch or repair vessels and tissues such as arteries or valves.[14]

---

[14] *Disposable Surgical Products on the Rise,* Occ Health & Safety News, June 1, 1989.

Airflow in the operating room is important for the comfort of operating room personnel, maintenance of the anesthetized patient, and to reduce infection. Many surgical infections have been shown to come from operating room personnel, from traffic flow, and from excessive conversation. These situations should be tightly controlled; they are an area of infection prevention under the control of those in the operating room.

Breaks in sterile techniques also lead to wound infection. These breaks are potentially numerous, but can be minimized by diligent, well-trained personnel and are, in large part, the responsibility of the operating room supervisor.

Adequate lighting is essential in the operating room. Errors are made when lighting is inadequate to show the operative site. Often, specialized lighting and magnification on, and managed by, the surgeon is essential.

Infection surveillance programs are important to record and improve prevention. Most hospitals require this as part of recordkeeping and appropriate administration of the hospital. Some infections, as well as other surgical misadventures, are preventable and under the control of the surgeon, operating room personnel, and hospital administration, so that continual surveillance is standard operating room procedure. Some infections and surgical misadventures are not preventable and should be considered in the patient's informed consent. Researching the misadventures may be a fruitful exercise in the event the patient feels damaged.[15]

§20.14 Anesthetic and Intraoperative Deaths

Estimates of the death rate in the first 48 hours after operation is 0.3 per cent in many studies. Of these deaths, about 10 per cent occur during induc-

---

[15] Laufman, *The Control of Operating Room Infection: Discipline, Defense Mechanisms, Drugs, Design and Devices,* 54 Bull NY Acad Med 465 (1978); Hanbraus, *Bacterial Contamination in a Modern Operating Suite: Effect of Zoning System on Contamination of Floors and Other Surfaces,* 80 J Hyg (Camb) 57 (1978); Ritter, *Street Shoes Versus Surgical Footwear in the Operating Room,* 3 Infect Surg 81 (1984); Belkin, *Clean Room Technology and Aseptic Practices in the Surgical Suite,* 27 J Environ Sciences 30 (1984); Walter & Kundsin, *The Airborne Component of Wound Contamination and Infection,* 107 Arch Surg 588 (1973); Cruse & Foord, *The Epidemiology of Wound Infection: A 10 Year Prospective Study of 62,939 Wounds,* 60 Surg Clin N Amer 27 (1980); Maki, *Relation of the Inanimate Environment to Endemic Nosocomial Infection,* 30 NEJM 1562 (1982); Chinyanga, *Temperature Regulation and Anesthesia,* 26 Pharmacol Ther 147 (1984); AORN Recommended Practices, *Electrosurgery,* 39 AORN J 248 (1984); AORN Recommended Practices, *Radiation Safety in the Operating Room (including lasers),* 42 AORN J 920 (1985); Linos, *Radiation Hazards to Operating Room Personnel During Operative Cholangiography,* 115 Arch Surg 1431 (1980); Burig, *Health Experiences of Operating Room Personnel,* 62 Anesthes 425 (1985); Lifson, *National Surveillance of AIDS in Health Care Workers,* 256 JAMA 3231 (1986).

tion of anesthesia; 35 per cent occur intra-operatively and 55 per cent in the first 48 hours. Failure to maintain adequate ventilation and aspiration of gastric contents are preventable causes of anesthetic death. Sudden unexpected cardiac arrhythmias or asystole, drug-induced myocardial depression and progressive hypotension (often from surgical blood loss) are responsible for 10 to 15 per cent of deaths in the first 48 hours. Constant diligence on the part of the anesthesiologist allows him or her to deal with these problems early, avoiding catastrophe in most cases.

Improvements in risk assessment for short-term morbidity have led to physician changes in clinical behavior. In reviewing five large studies in tertiary care facilities, the clinician appears to be sensitized to specific cardiac risk issues, many of which can be corrected before surgery, lessening operative risks.

These changes in clinical approach require a new set of weighted cardiac factors to predict operative events so that additional improvement is a goal. Objective forms of assessment and clinical judgment can function well in concert.[16]

§20.15 Nutrition

Appearing more frequently in the medical literature are articles relating the nutritional and immune status of the patient to clinical care and surgical care, exploring its effects on postsurgical complications. The operating surgeon is responsible to assess these factors and utilizes available diagnostic and therapeutic information, to initiate this knowledge before surgery. The metabolically-compromised or poorly-nourished patient is a surgical risk. These problems continue into the postoperative period, and if not adequately dealt with, will predictably adversely affect the patient's convalescence. The same logic applies to the immunosuppressed patient, the patient with chronic infection, or the patient with other systemic states that adversely affect infection prevention or control. Postoperative wound infection occurs in 3 to 5 per cent "clean" cases in hospitals across America. Urinary tract, pulmonary, and venipuncture site infections, however, add another substantial trough of hospital/surgery-related infections, many of which relate to the care and diligence of patient care offered by the caregivers.[17]

---

[16] Moyer, *The Assessment of Operative Risk,* Surgery: Principles and Practice (J.F. Rhodes ed 4th ed 1970), at 232; Del Guercio & Cohn, *Monitoring Operative Risk in Elderly,* 243 JAMA 1350 (1980); Hooton, *The Joint Association of Multiple Risk Factors with Occurrence of Nosocomial Infection,* 70 Am J Med 960 (1981). WD Owens, et al, ASA Physical Status Classification: A Study of Consistency of Ratings, Anesthesiol 239 (1978).

[17] Baker, *Nutritional Assessment: A Comparison of Clinical Judgment and Objective Measurements,* 306 NEJM 969 (1982); Champion, *Assessment of Injury Severity: Triage,* 8 Index Crit Care Med 201 (1980); Knaus, *Relationship Between Acute Physiologic Derangement and Risk of Death,* 38 J Chronic Dis 295 (1985).

§20.16 Suture Techniques

At times, failure of a surgically tied knot during or after operation adversely affects the surgical outcome. In orthopedic cases in particular, it is common to fix tendons or other soft tissues to bone, capsule, or ligament under tension, as part of the surgical correction. Failure of these sutures often nullifies the purpose of the surgery. A wide variety of suture materials are used in operations; most are synthetic or biodegradable. Monofilament sutures are often preferred, under the belief that they are less irritating and less responsive to infection. Surgical wire and steel staples are commonplace. The weight of suture (size) may be considered in preventing complications. The larger the diameter of the suture, the greater the tissue necrosis and infection risk; also, resulting scar is heavier.

In tying sutures, it has been shown that instrument tying using forceps weakens the sutures by crushing the fibers; thus hand tying of sutures may be preferred. Use of continuous suturing is preferred in some circumstances, particularly when approximating long, contiguous wounds. Interrupted sutures make a stronger closure and, with fine sutures, make less of a scar. The tying of suture knots is part of the surgeon's skill; he or she must know the suture material and what its propensity for unknotting is. The square knot is stronger than the "granny" knot. The square knot several times looped is less apt to untie.

Some patients are allergic or sensitive to certain sutures, at times developing sterile abscess and requiring deep suture removal. The surgeon should always ask the patient if he or she has a suture allergy before performing an operation.[18]

§20.17 Tourniquet Ischemia

One research study showed (1) significant changes which may lead to cell death occur after, but not before, three hours of tourniquet ischemia in monkeys, (2) changes in ultrastructure appearance of mitachondria and sacroplasma are the best way to assess the effects of ischemia were the best way to assess the effects of ischemia in muscle, (3) no significant changes relative to ischemia were seen in muscles of human subjects at the end of two hours, (4) restoration of circulation after a period of ischemia has a myo (muscle) protective effect and the changes in the muscle thought to be pathological may have been present in the patient before ischemia was produced.

This argues against the common belief that tourniquet ischemia over 90 minutes to 2 hours often causes muscle damage. Nerve injury is often seen after tourniquet inflation.[19] (*See* Appendix 20-1, Case 20.)

---

[18] Stamp, *Surgical Suture Strength,* 54 Amer Surg 300 (1988); Jenkins, *Surgical Wound Dehiscence,* 63 Brit J Surg 873 (1987); Poole, Jr., *Suture Techniques,* 6 Surg 631 (1985).

[19] Tountas & Bergman, *Tourniquet Ischemia: Ultrastructural and Histochemical Observations of Ischemic Human Muscle and of Monkey Muscle Nerve,* 2 J Hand Surg 31 (1977).

§20.18 Tourniquet Hemostasis

Studies using a Doppler stethoscope to measure the pressure at which peripheral pulses disappeared have shown that tourniquet pressures well below those currently used will produce a bloodless operative field. On the average, pressure 189 ± 24 mm/Hg produces a bloodless field in the upper extremity and 231 ± 26 mm/Hg for lower extremity. Another method to more safely have a blood field is to inflate the tourniquet 25 mm/Hg above the patient's systolic blood pressure.[20]

§20.19 Tourniquet Cast Application

Several orthopedists have shown that the intracompartmental pressure of the anterior tibial compartment so that limb volume increases over 7 per cent for the first five minutes after tourniquet pressure releases. This is important, as a cast applied immediately after tourniquet decompression would produce a risk of too tight a cast unable to accommodate a post-tourniquet increase leg volume, risking significant compartment compression syndrome.[21]

§20.20 Anesthesia

The orthopedic surgeon has daily contact with the anesthesiologist. The "Captain of the Ship" doctrine is rarely followed by the current jurist, yet the orthopedist is involved with the anesthetic of a patient and is legally vulnerable in several areas.[22]

§20.21 Recovery Room Care

As the surgical patient leaves the operating room, he or she is most often transferred to the recovery room, a specialized area staffed with highly-trained personnel skilled at monitoring the awakening patient. Close attention to the patient is required, maintaining the various life-support systems—IV tubes, endotracheal tubes, oxygen flow, etc. Constant monitoring of blood pressure, pulse, respiration (checking for airway patency), and managing the patient so he or she does not injure him- or herself during the awakening process.

Negligence occurs in the recovery room when the staff is not appropriately diligent, when the staff is overloaded, and when monitoring of life-saving equipment fails. Careless movement of patients in precarious states so far

---

[20] Reid, *Tourniquet Hemostasis,* 177 Clin Orthop Rel Res 230 (1983).

[21] Ayoub & Bennt, *A Study of Cutaneous and Intracompartmental Limb Pressures Associated with the Combined Use of Tourniquet and Plaster Casts,* 68B JBJ Surg 497 (1986).

[22] Critical Care Clinics: Systemic Responses to Anesthesia and Operation (K. Waxman ed 1987).

as body positioning or restlessness has produced injury while under the control of recovery room personnel. (*See* Appendix 20-1, Cases 21 and 22.)

§20.22 Postoperative Care

Complications that follow operations are usually related to the surgery, although unexpected nonsurgery-related problems may develop. Meticulous postoperative care can decrease the incidence of complications and facilitate the patient's convalescence. Advances in medical technology have brought a steady decrease in postoperative complications. Aggressive monitoring is now more often employed, particularly in the use of intensive care units, ventilatory support, arterial lines, and central venous catheters. These measures are extremely valuable in minute-by-minute assessment of the patient's physiological status and allowing rapid corrective measures or medications to be used.

The physician communicates the specific postoperative order as written orders on the patient's chart. This, along with the nursing staff and physician's daily (or more often) progress notes, provides a written document of the patient's problems and orders for care. It is essential that these notes be legible and complete, or the patient's care may suffer for lack of communication. Some uniformity of orders and the physician's understanding of what care devices and personnel are available will make the care process more smooth—still avoiding routine orders that may exclude a need of the patient.

Selection of postoperative monitoring is guided by a thorough understanding of the patient's preoperative condition and reasoning behind the surgery being carried out. The vital signs are regularly monitored and recorded on the patient's chart. These typically include temperature, pulse rate and blood pressure, respiratory rate, urine output (often at hourly or more frequent timings, depending on the patient's condition), central venous pressure (CVP), weight (daily), and fluid intake/output.

As the patient leaves the recovery room, he or she is most often is transferred to an intensive care unit or to the general surgical nursing unit. Here the patient is cared for using a standard protocol with a nursing supervisor, floor charge nurse, general patient care nurse, medication nurse, and nurses' aid (or some general variation of this plan) in direct charge of patient care.

The surgeon owes the patient a duty to protect him or her, to be aware if errors are being made, and to determine that nursing staff is adequate. The surgeon has a further duty to timely visit the patient (most hospital bylaws say daily visits) to assess health status, review nursing notes, and make appropriate "order" changes in the best interest of the patient.

In intensive care settings, additional monitoring is often required, including measurements by arterial line, continuous pressure recording (CVP) monitoring of rightsided pulmonary pressures via Swanz-Gantz catheters, continuous monitoring of oxygen saturation of the blood via pulse oximetry, and electrocardiography monitoring. With all of these data, a clear knowledge of the patient's physiological status and need on a minute-by-minute basis is obtained. Fever in the postoperative period is usual for the first 48 to 72 hours, usually below 38C (100.4F) and usually not spiking. Fever from septic sources usually lasts four to six days, tending to be spiking and associated with such apparent causes as wound infection or lung or urinary tract infection. The most common cause of postoperative infection is atelectasis, pneumonia, urinary tract, septic and non-septic phlebitis, drug allergies, wound infection, and other deep infections. The diligent surgeon will search out the cause with appropriate and repeated physical examination and laboratory or x-ray testing, and institute treatment.

Emperic use of antibiotics without identifying sources of infection and offending organism with its sensitivity studies is inappropriate. Having identified an infected site, ordering wide-range antibiotics most likely to cover the infection until culture/sensitivity studies are available is the current standard. Postoperative wound infection should be treated as any other closed-space infection with wound opening, culture/sensitivity tests, and appropriate antibiotics.

It has been emphasized in recent years that toxic shock syndrome infections may stem from postoperative wounds that early after surgery (up to five days) do not appear infected, painful, red, or swollen, but then suddenly explode into a life-threatening situation.

§20.23 Pain Relief

Pain relief is often a problem postsurgically. There is a great hesitancy among surgeons prescribing, and nurses giving, adequate pain relief medication, in the service of preventing addiction. Narcotic addiction is rare indeed in the postsurgical patient not already addicted. That addiction should be treated later as a separate illness. In recent years, special pumps containing pain medication that the patient self-administers have been very effective and usually show the patient using less total pain medication.

§20.24 Deliberately-Placed Foreign Bodies

A variety of drains may be used postsurgically and require special attention. The Penrose drain is a small type of dental rubber placed in or adjacent to a surgical drain to inhibit collection of serum or other fluids and lessen infection. These drains should be removed as soon as possible, as soon as drainage abates, as increasing infection along the drain may occur. For deeper wounds, such as spinal fusion or total joint site, closed-suction drain systems (hemovac or Jackson-Pratt) may be helpful in reducing fluid accumulation, facilitate less painful leaking, and lessen the infection risk. These are ordinarily removed in 48 to 72 hours. Another frequently used tube drain is the Foley catheter in the urinary bladder. It facilitates urine output knowledge and drainage of the urinary bladder with temporary postsurgical control, and keeps dressings dry. Foley catheters are a cause of infection (which is true of all types of urethral catheters) and require a rigid protocol of aseptic insertion, regular cleansing, frequent (at least weekly) changing, and regular culture/sensitivity testing of urine, with antibiotic coverage when indicated.

§20.25 Venipuncture

A common and often unrecognized cause of postoperative (on any patient with venipuncture) is the infection that occurs about the hub of a venipuncture needle or plastic intravenous catheter. Many hospitals have instituted a rigid protocol similar to urethral catheter care. Many (probably most) venipuncture catheters are superficially infected within 24 to 48 hours, leading to septic phlebitis or septisemia. Patients with central venous catheters are at high risk of infection, especially triple lumen catheters. Several studies have shown 5 to 6 per cent infection in 48 hours in single lumen and as high as 19 per cent in triple lumen catheters. The treatment includes removal of the catheter, with culture/sensitivity studies and replacement at a remote area if necessary. Flushing the catheter with appropriate antibiotics was recommended by one surgical group, but this would also introduce other risks. Venipuncture catheter or needle infection should be under the control of health care persons doing the venipuncture therapy or testing.

Respiratory infections and impairment occur frequently after surgery with lung anesthesia in the preceding 24 hours. With deep breathing and coughing, the atelectasis reverses to minimal to none in most patients. Patients "at risk" of substantial atelectasis (with pneumonia risk) are elderly with poor chest wall muscle strength, patients with chest wall trauma or surgical incision due to painful breathing, and obese persons that are not rapidly ambulated.

§20.26 Central Venous Catheters and Complications

Three million central venous catheter (CVC) procedures conducted in the United States annually are associated with a significant incidence of complications, including infection, pneumothorax, hemothorax, hydrothorax, vessel and cardiac perforation, cardiac tamponade secondary to pericardial effusion, dysrhythmia, and air embolus.

Complications occur in 5 to 20 per cent of CVC procedures. Many of these are attributable to user technique and are possibly preventable. The FDA task force recently recommended the following ways to minimize these problems:

1. CVC should only be performed when potential benefits appear to outweigh risks.
2. Except for pulmonary artery catheters, the catheter tip should not be placed in, or allowed to migrate into, the heart.
3. Catheter tip position should be confirmed by x-ray and be periodically checked.
4. CVC must be performed only by trained personnel well-versed in anatomical landmarks, safe techniques, and potential complications.
5. Before being allowed to perform these procedures independently, those in training must be closely supervised by qualified personnel.

Experienced trainees should also be monitored to ensure continuing competence.

6. Those placing CVC should be familiar with the specific equipment used as well as proper selection of insertion site and catheter type, size, and length.
7. Those caring for indwelling CVCs should be well-informed about care and must be aware and alert to possible CVC complications.
8. Manufacturers should include specific labeling, addressing the potential complications of CVC use.
9. Users must read such labeling as it contains instruction, warnings, and other information essential to safe and effective placement of the catheter.
10. CVC, except in emergency, must be done with strict aseptic technique, using sterile gloves, skin preparation, etc. In those instances were emergency placement is absent sterile techniques, replacement into a sterile field with a new sterile catheter into a sterile field must be effected.[23]

§20.27 Thrombophlebitis

Preventable postoperative complications should be addressed. Deep venous thrombosis is a major threat in many "at risk" patients. Those patients who are, or will be, immobile, those with lower extremity surgery, and those with a previous history of thrombophlebitis are "at risk." Prophylactic treatment with anticoagulative therapy or use of mechanical alternating compressive dressing to legs are recommended by most physicians for their "at risk" patients.

Informed consent of patients and adequate explanation to the family are important presurgical obligations of the surgeon, and more so in our present informed society.[24]

§20.28 Postoperative Nutrition

A variety of pathologic and homeostatic changes can occur after major surgery. These include utilization of muscle store for gluconeogenesis and protein synthesis in injured and starved patients in the postoperative period.

---

[23] Scott, *Complications Associated with Central Venous Catheters,* 91 Chest 121 (1988); Langston, *The Aberrent Central Venous Catheter and Its Complications,* 100 Radiol 55 (1971); Dave & King, *Fatal Cardiac Tamponade and Other Mechanical Complications of Central Venous Catheter,* 62 Br J Surg 610 (1975); Sznajder, *Central Venous Catheterization: Failure and Complication Rates by Percutaneous Route,* 146 Arch Int Med 259 (1986); Ryan, *Catheter Complications in Total Parenteral Nutrition,* 290 NEJM 757 (1974).

[24] Russell, *Prophylaxis of Post-operative Deep Vein Thrombosis and Pulmonary Embolism,* 157 Surg Gynecol Obstet 89 (1983).

In most postoperative patients, the period of starvation does not present a major problem and does not mandate nutritional intervention. Many patients are chronically ill, borderline malnourished, and/or are unable to take nutrients by mouth for days or weeks. Closely monitor metabolic and/or electrolyte defects and correct them, often by aggressive parenteral nutrition. A skilled nutrition expert is very helpful here. Failure to recognize the importance of the nutritional parameters of our patients (and we often fail to do so) leads to slow impaired healing, increased complications, and decreased patient comfort (and often mood).[25]

Nutrition problems, including weight loss of greater than 10 to 12 per cent of body weight in the last six months, include faulty wound healing and wound disruption. The same observations are made in patients with unexplained low white blood count, low serum protein values, and persons who are presently taking, or who have currently taken, corticosteroids.

The patient's medications should be known to all medical personnel involved in the operation, as well as knowledge and chart recording of allergies. A careful social history, including smoking, alcohol, or other substance abuse possibilities are important parts of the preoperative history.

Metabolic problems such as diabetes mellitus must be evaluated and be under control before operation. Signs or symptoms of tumor spread should be assessed in cancer patients.[26]

§20.29 Trauma Patients

An often overlooked and criticized problem in the care of traumatized patients, and others subject to prolonged hospitalization, is malnutrition. One-third of orthopedic trauma patients were found malnourished in one large study. The facts are that trauma patients have a high catabolic rate early after injury, their metabolic rate can increase by 50 to 55 per cent, depleting glycogen, fat, and protein reserves. This, in turn, slows soft tissue and bone healing and impairs the immune system's ability to resist infection. Treating and avoiding malnutrition is an essential treatment modality in these patients, and must not be ignored by the treating physician.

§20.30 Special Problems Relating to Surgical Patients

Diabetes Mellitus

Diabetes mellitus (as distinguished from diabetes insipidus) notoriously complicates wound healing by decreasing micro-vascularity and adversely

---

[25] Jewell & Persson, *Preoperative Evaluation of the High Risk Patient,* 65 Surg Clin N Amer 3 (1985); S.L. Gorbach, Surgical Infections 301 (1984); J.J. Bonica & C. Benedetti, Post-Operative Pain. Surgical Care (1980).

[26] Jewell & Person, *supra* note 25 and S.L. Gorbach, *supra* note 25.

affecting the homeostatic sequence of tissue healing. Twenty per cent of persons are suspect diabetics, many with the diagnosis being made at the time of surgery. Patients who are not known diabetics and who have preoperative hyperglycemia can generally be classified as having impaired glucose tolerance (secondary diabetes mellitus) or gestational diabetes, based on the history of past medical illness and a detailed description of current medications. However, if the patient's history does not suggest a diagnosis of impaired glucose tolerance or gestational diabetes, and the patient is not stressed at the time of evaluation, the surgeon should suspect the presence of diabetes mellitus and treat the patient accordingly.

The classic sign of diabetes mellitus in an unstressed person includes excessive thirst (polydipsia), frequent urination (polyuria) and weight loss with a fasting blood sugar test over 140 mg%. The known or suspect diabetic should have insulin in doses to maintain blood sugar between 100 and 250 mg%.

There are two non-gestational types of diabetes mellitus requiring the same treatment protocol in surgical patients. Type I or juvenile diabetes mellitus, and Type II or adult onset diabetes mellitus usually related to obesity. Many diabetics can be treated with diet and oral hypoglycemia medications. More severe cases, and those with significant reduction of insulin output or insulin receptors, may require parenteral insulin. Complications, other than impaired wound healing, include a hyperglycemia crisis leading to coma and severe dehydration. Diabetic ketoacidosis acidosis may complicate hyperglycemia in susceptible patients and be life-threatening. Insulin shock from overdose of insulin likewise may be lethal.

Renal Dysfunction

Renal failure is defined as renal (kidney) failure with significant alteration in blood electrolytes and waste products. Clinical manifestation may vary on the extent of renal disease and is often asymptomatic, diagnosis by routine laboratory abnormality. The chemical abnormalities present in renal failure are an index to its treatment, which is often dramatic when the metabolic defect is corrected. This must be done before additional body stress, including anesthetic/surgery, is carried out. Renal failure may worsen uncontrollably, leading to renal shutdown and death. "Kidney" death is a common consequence of trauma, shock, overwhelming infection, uncontrolled metabolic disease or bold transfusion reaction, or any combination. The surgeon has a duty not to overlook renal failure and to proceed with invasive procedure cautiously. Kidney failure is often called *uremia* by the lay public.

Heart

Cardiac status must be known to all involved in a surgical procedure—the surgeon and operating room and recovery room/intensive care personnel—as they all participate in diagnosis of sudden changes in heart function and emergency resuscitation. The presurgical evaluation of the heart is an essential part of the history, physical examination, and laboratory evaluation. Defects in cardiac circulation, arrythmias, diminished heart muscle function, and changes in coronary artery and peripheral vascular resistance are essential to understanding cardiac function and assessing the risk of anesthesia and/or surgery. Often, surgery should be delayed until adequate cardiac function is demonstrated, many times after consulting with a cardiac specialist.

Pulmonary

Lung function is essential to provide oxygen to the blood circulation in concert with the heart pump. Diminished pulmonary function occurs when lung alveolae are impaired by scar, pulmonary edema, diminished alveolar blood supply, or inadequate lung expansion due to rib cage or thoracic muscle pathology. The lungs also contribute to removal of toxic chemicals (CO_2, alcohol, etc.) with homeostatic upset when lungs function inadequately.

Brain

Impaired brain function can influence risk of surgery. Recent head injury, suspicion of intracranial bleeding or bleeding risk, and anoxic states are often worsened by anesthetic and/or surgical manipulation. Brain tissue that is diseased or recently injured is further "at risk" when exposed to many anesthetic/pain relief chemicals.

The surgeon/anesthesiologist must accept a risk if it unnecessarily puts the heart, kidney, lungs, brain and/or other tissues at further risk by an operation that might be appropriately delayed until the impaired vital organ improves. In emergency surgical situations, these risks are often a factor weighed against the potential benefit of the emergency operation. These considerations and risks must be conveyed to the patient and/or the person giving proper informed consent.[27]

§20.31 Respiratory Failure in Surgical Patients

Acute respiratory failure is the inability of the lungs to oxygenate blood. Synonyms are non-cardiogenic pulmonary edema, permeability pulmonary edema, or interstitial pulmonary edema.

---

[27] Tilney & Lazarus, Surgical Care of the Patient with Renal Failure (1982); Shaw, *Cardiac Output and Pulmonary Wedge Pressure: Use for Evaluation of Fluid Replacement in Trauma Patients,* 12 Arch Surg 1161 (1977); Davis, *Acute Oliguria After Cardiopulmonary Bypass: Renal Functional Improvement with Low-Dose Dopamine Infusion,* 10 Crit Care Med 852 (1982); Rasmussen & Ibels, *Acute Renal Failure: Multivariate Analysis of Causes and Risk Factors,* 73 Am J Med 211 (1982); Brenowitz, Williams & Edwards, *Major Surgery in Patients with Chronic Renal Failure,* 134 Am J Surg 765 (1977); Widmer, *Serum Electrolyte and Acid Base Composition: The Influence of Graded Degrees of Chronic Renal Failure,* 139 Arch Int Med 1099 (1979); Harter, *Review of Significant Findings from the National Cooperative Dialysis Study and Recommendations,* 13 Kidney Int S107 (Supp 1983); Drucke, *Dialysis Osteomalacia and Aluminum Intoxication,* 26 Nephron 207 (1980).

The diagnosis of acute respiratory failure includes increased respiratory rate over 20 per minute, hypoxemia with decreased PO_2 below 60 mm/mercury on an inspired oxygen concentration above 50 per cent; hypercapnia with carbon dioxide concentration above 60 mm with a pH of more than 7.35.

Respiratory failure commonly results from altered ventilation-perfusion ratios leading to hypoxemia, hypo- or hypercarbia, and decreased pulmonary compliance. Adult respiratory distress syndrome (ARDS) is the result of a number of direct or indirect pulmonary insults showing up as diffuse pulmonary infiltration on x-ray, impaired effective compliance, marked impairment of oxygen transport, and pulmonary congestion. It is frequently a fatal problem.

The physiological abnormalities of decreased functional residual capacity, increased lung water, and pulmonary hypertension are similar to those found in other forms of respiratory failure. Alterations of alveolar ventilation exist in nearly all situations of respiratory insufficiency, either as a primary mechanism or as a secondary phenomena.

Ventilation of the alveoli is impaired, both in the amount of air inhaled with each breath and the residual retained air products in the alveoli. Changes in alveolar ventilation result from alteration in central and peripheral pulmonary receptor stimulation. These receptors may respond to alterations in the pulmonary interstitium from inflammation and fluid accumulation.

Dead space ventilation may result in hypercapnia even in the face of increased ventilation. Dead space ventilation is caused by elevated arterial carbon dioxide tension and can be determined by measuring arterial and mixed expired carbon dioxide to determine presence of dead space ventilation or increased carbon dioxide. The culprit should be identified. Decreased minute ventilation commonly follows narcotic-induced central nervous system depression and can be reversed if they are opioid drugs by use of that Naloxone, an opioid antidote. If respiratory acidosis is part of the anesthesiologist's care, there are a number of drugs available to aid the problem depending on the chemicals in the anesthetic agent. Chronic respiratory acidosis is seen in hypothyroidism, in renal failure with electrolyte abnormality, and in metabolic alcolosis.

Airway obstruction is the most correctable of all causes of impairment of ventilation. It is the common cause of anesthetic catastrophe. Correction of increased dead space ventilation may be challenging. A series of drugs is available to aid in bronchodilation. If airway edema is present, attempting to deal with it chemically is appropriate. Most important, however, is relief of mechanical obstruction by adequate clearing of the bronchial airways of secretions and maintenance of the patient's intra-tracheal tube.

The placement of the intra-tracheal tube can be difficult at times, both by virtue of the obtundent state of the patient and/or anatomical variations of the nasopharynx and upper respiratory tree. Prompt tracheostomy can be life-saving. The intra-tracheal tube placer is extremely important for assuring that the intra-tracheal tube is in fact in the tracheal and not in the esophagus, for many anesthesia CPR-related demises have found the intra-tracheal tube in the esophagus, serving no function toward aerating the lungs.

§20.32 Immune Mechanisms

The orthopedist is held to understand normal immune mechanisms of the body, to best serve the patient. The immune system of the body substantially contributes to the patient's ability to heal wounds, deal with infections, handle cancer, and accept or reject bone graft or other implants.

Host defense mechanisms are divided into local and systemic. *Local host defenses* include epithelial coverings, specialized cells, and secretions. *Systemic defense mechanisms* include phagocyte cells and complement, humoral, and cell-mediated immune mechanisms. There are major interactions at many levels between the various local and systemic immune processes. Many of these interactions are poorly understood.

Immunodeficiency may be primarily or acquired, secondary to illness or iatrogenic intervention. In most cases of primary immunodeficiency diseases, defects in systemic host defenses can be clinically detected. They have a predictable relationship to the kinds of infection the patient may be "at risk" of getting. In the more common acquired immunodeficiencies, the relation of host defense defects to the pathogenesis of infections is less clearly defined.

The human body is a complex tube covered by skin and lined with mucosa. Various mechanical, cellular, microbiologic, and biochemical properties of these account for local host defense mechanisms. When these coverings are broken, the defense mechanisms may be compromised. Evaluation of breaks in local host defenses begins by locating the breaks or disruptions of the skin. These might include endotracheal tubes, tracheostomies, nasogastric tubes, and catheters in bladder or intravenously. Other disruptions include intracranial pressure monitors, chest tubes, external fixators, and muscle compartment pressure catheters. Implanted prostheses can produce changes in local host defenses. Burns, draining sinuses, pressure sores, and surgical wounds should also be noted.

Changes in local microflora are important considerations in evaluating local host defenses, especially in hospital or nursing home patients. Prolonged hospitalization often results in change of flora or overgrowth by gram negative bacteria. Prolonged use of broad spectrum antibiotics often leads to fungal/yeast overgrowth.

Although changes in local bacterial flora can be evaluated by culture of body fluids and mucosal surfaces, the status of many other important aspects of local immunity cannot be determined reliably by means presently clinically known.

For purposes of study, systemic immunity may be classified as either antigen-specific or nonspecific. Humoral immunity and cell-mediated immunity provide antigen-specific immunity, whereas phagocytes and complement provide nonspecific immunity. At the present, there is little therapy available for most of the deficiencies, but the orthopedist should understand these deficiencies as they often interfere with treatment outcome. The most spoken immunodeficiency at this time is acquired immunodeficiency syndrome (AIDS) which fits in the discussion above.

§20.33 Obesity

Many surgeons hesitate to operate on the obese patient, due to increased operative risk of morbidity and mortality. This is especially true of the morbidly obese—100 pounds or greater overweight. Although the morbidity and mortality is greater, this risk can be reduced by attention to detail in pre- and postoperative care. The increased risks include wound infection, wound dehiscence or hernia, thrombophlebitis or pulmonary embolus, anesthetic calamities, acute postoperative asphyxia in patients with obstructive sleep apnea syndrome, acute respiratory failure, cardiac failure, and missed abdominal catastrophe, such as perforated viscus. Adult onset diabetes mellitus is common in the obese. A high degree of suspicion for peritonitis must be maintained after abdominal viscera surgery or after lumbar discectomy where inadvertent slipping of disc while removing instrument anteriorly may have perforated a viscus. Awareness of the problems associated with respiratory insufficiency on obese patients should enable surgeons to avoid pitfalls when managing patients with obstructive pulmonary disease.

The risk of deep vein thrombosis and pulmonary embolism is high, but use of intermittent pressure boots and early postoperative ambulation can minimize this risk.

Weight reduction by diet is associated with 95 per cent failure. Most studies show that morbidly obese patients can lose two-thirds of their excess weight with one year after gastric bypass or gastric stapling surgery. This weight loss usually is associated with correction of adult onset diabetes, many problems associated with obstructive pulmonary disease, hypertension, chronic venous stasis ulcers of legs, stress incontinence, gastric reflux and hiatal herniation, and a number of female hormone-related problems. Weight loss is a beneficial prescription by the orthopedist who should not hesitate to consider gastric bypass surgery as a good treatment in this situation, but the surgeon must be skilled in the procedure and current in the management of its physiological complications.

§20.34 Hypovolemic Shock

Hypovolemic shock is classified as mild, moderate, and severe. In mild shock, there is 20 to 25 per cent loss of blood volume, and it manifests itself with slight rapid pulse, mild hypotension, and mild vasoconstriction. In moderate shock, the blood loss is 25 to 35 per cent, resulting in a thready pulse, tachycardia, hypotension, marked vasoconstriction, diaphoresis, restlessness, and decreased urine output. In severe shock, there is 35 to 50 per cent loss of blood volume with severe hypotension, tachycardia, vasoconstriction, obtundation, and absence of urine output.

The body's normal responses to restore normal volume are inadequate. Restoration of exogenous volume in the form of intravenous administration of fluids is the only treatment. Changes secondary to low perfusion rate result in decreased oxygen delivery to vital organs and a consequent shift from aerobic to anaroebic metabolism, with eventual organ failure.

One important change is that eventually there is a period of complete micro-circulatory arrest in skeletal muscle, followed by destruction of many capillaries and leukocytes when re-perfusion is started. This results in local variations of hypoxic injury of muscle.

Patients who eventually die of shock have ischemic myocardial damage. Treatment includes vigorous ventilatory circulation, maintenance of an airway, and equally vigorous circulatory support. The placing of a large-bore venous catheter, or, if necessary, a surgical cut-down and canulating a vein, blood replacement if available, and crystalloid solution administration are the most important treatment for hypovolemic shock. Lactated Ringer's solution is isotonic and administration of it appears to decrease the requirement for whole blood. However, it may contribute to acidosis. Dextrane 70 has been shown to decrease the total fluid requirement and maintain the urine output, and was associated with a lower incidence of adult respiratory distress compared to the use of Ringer's solution. The effectiveness of synthetic, oxygen-carrying blood replacement products in patients who sustained blood loss is presently being evaluated.

Pneumatic anti-shock trousers are often used in the immediate resuscitation of a severely injured patient. Thigh compartment syndromes may result from these trousers unless their pressure is elevated only high enough to restore adequate blood pressure and the duration of application is no longer than clinically necessary.

After minimal resuscitation of the patient, the orthopedist is often faced with treatment of multiple fractures which may be associated with significant hemorrhage. Hemorrhage remains the most common cause of death after pelvic fractures.

Direct angiography identifying areas of bleeding and embolizing of those bleeding vessels with autologous clot or gelatin sponge has been successfully used recently.

Toxic shock does occur in the traumatized patient. It is a little later in onset, ordinarily, from the initial trauma. It also occurs after elective surgery. Staphococcal aureus wound infections are the culprits with their toxic production, and although predominantly seen in menstruating women, it occurs in post-menopausal women and some men as a postoperative complication. The wound may be benign, but it should be explored in the operating room. High-dose antibiotic therapy and multi-organ system support are necessary.

Septic shock continues to remain a major clinical problem. The best means of resuscitation remains uncertain. A combination of antibiotics, 3 per cent solution corticosteroids result in proven long-term survival in experimental septic shock, is not proven in humans.

Irreversible burn shock that persists despite fluid resuscitation remains a significant cause of mortality in thermo-injured children. Because circulatory serum factors have been implicated in the pathophysiology of burn shock, exchange transfusion has been tried and reported successful in patients not responding to conventional volume therapy.

§20.35 Surgical Blood Transfusions

Whole blood transfusions are rarely used in surgical or traumatic situations, because packed red blood cell transfusions are more practical, safer, and more economical. Still, a certain percentage of transfused patients develop complications. Virtually all complications can be avoided by use of predeposit autologous blood transfusion programs, intra-operative blood salvage programs, selection of patients for intra-operative isovolemic hemodilution, pharmacological approaches to blood loss, and directed donations.

An *autologous transfusion* is one in which the blood recipient serves as his or her own donor. This may occur in elective or planned surgery when the patient is able to have blood withdrawn by a blood bank and stored until the surgery date. The average "well" a person can donate is four units of blood per four weeks. In emergency situations, there is not enough time before transfusions to prepare autologous transfusion and still allow the patient to have sufficient blood reserves at the time of surgery.

There are several advantages in a patient donating his or her own blood: (1) there is no chance that the transfusion will infect the patient with any diseases, such as hepatitis, AIDS, or malaria, unless the patient already has them, (2) the patient will not suffer any immune reactions against transfused blood, and (3) the patient, by prior donation of his or her blood, stimulates the body to make more blood at the time of the operation.

Autologous donation of blood requires the cooperation of the patient and the physician, and the medical direction of the hospital or independent blood bank. The surgeon must request the donation and specify how many units will probably be needed. In usual circumstances, the patient's hemoglobin level must be 11 gms/cc. The patient is placed on oral iron to stimulate blood regeneration.

A system to collect blood for subsequent reinfusion following major operations, such as total hip or knee replacements, is available and was recently approved by FDA. It is available through Richard Medical Corporation, Memphis, Tennessee. The blood is collected as it is lost during surgery, is filtered, and is reinfused at a substantial advantage to the patient. There are no allergic reactions, no virus disease transmissions, and the need for blood bank blood is reduced. Relatively little instruction to operating room personnel is needed. Reinfused blood has been shown to have better oxygen-carrying capacity than bank-stored blood.

§20.36 Postoperative Instruction

Postoperative instruction, as any treatment instruction, should be given to the patient in an affirmative manner, depending on the patient. Patients often do not see postoperative risks the same way as the surgeon. The patient often assumes that these instructions are little more than conservative concern on the part of the doctor. Many malpractice lawyers advise surgeons not to cushion such advice. It is imperative to establish ground rules before performing a procedure, perhaps with vocabulary like "I will not operate unless you do as I instruct. If you are not willing to give me your word on that, you should find another surgeon." This approach may be necessary for a noncompliant patient, but may be unnecessary with a patient the surgeon knows to be compliant.

On follow-up, the surgeon should not tolerate noncompliance. When the first sign appears, send the patient a certified letter specifying how he or she has failed to follow-up instructions and may thereby be jeopardizing a good result, and urging the patient to make another return appointment soon. If that appointment is missed, consider dismissing the patient from care but not abandoning him or her. Give the patient time to find other medical care and cooperate with that doctor in terms of sending records, etc. Leaving a noncompliant patient unhealed and "at risk" for ease of re-injury can be interpreted as abandonment. "Getting tough" with a patient often has a positive, "public relations" type of effect—it shows concern for the patient and strengthens the physician-patient relationship. (*See* Appendix 20-1, Case 23.)

§20.37 References

S.W. Banks & H. Laufman, An Atlas of Surgical Exposure to the Extremities (1953).

S. Hoppenfield & P. deBoer, Surgical Exposure in Orthopedics: The Anatomic Approach (1984).

Requirements of Construction and Equipment for Hospitals and Medical Facilities. Health and Human Services Publication HRS-M-HF-84-1, Rockville, MD (1984).

A.K. Weiss, The Physiology of Aging. Surgery in the Aged (L.J. Greenfield ed, 1975).

Silberman, *Renal Failure and the Surgeon,* 144 Surg Gynecol Obstet 775 (1977).

Detsky, *Evaluating the Accuracy of Nutritional Assessment Techniques Applied to Hospitalized Patients: Methodology and Comparisons,* 8 JPEN 153 (1984).

Pettigrew & Hill, *Indicators of Surgical Risk and Clinical Judgment,* 73 JBJ Surg 47 (1986).

Windsor & Hill, *Weight Loss with Physiologic Impairment: A Basic Indicator of Surgical Risk,* 207 Ann Surg 290 (1988).

Collins, *Clinical Judgment Versus the Laboratory,* 306 NEJM 987 (1982).

Christou, *Host Defense Mechanisms in Surgical Patients: A Correlative Study of the Delayed Hypersensitivity Skin-Test Response, Granulocyte Function and Sepsis,* 28 Can J Surg 39 (1985).

Casey, *Correlation of Immune and Nutritional Status with Wound Complications in Patients Undergoing Vascular Operations,* 93 Surg 882 (1983).

Stratton, *Waterless Agents for Decontamination of the Hands,* 7 Infect Control 186 (1986).

Larson, *Handwashing and Skin—A Review: Physiologic and Bacteriologic Aspects,* 6 Infect Control 14 (1985).

P.F. Millington & R. Wilkinson, Skin (1983) Oxygen Transport in the Critically Ill (M.R. Pinsky & J.V. Snyder eds 1987).

Problems in Anesthesia: Perioperative Problems/Catastrophes, Vol 1, No 2 (R.W. Vaughn ed 1987).

Kenean, *Fever Following Orthopedic Operations in Children,* 6 J Pediatr Orthop 139 (1986).

Galicier & Richet, *A Prospective Study of Post-Operative Fever in a General Surgical Department,* 6 Infect Control 486 (1985).

Drag, *Elevated Temperature in the Post-Operative Patient,* 21 J Foot Surg 269 (1982).

Siegman-Igra, *Late Post-Operative Fever—Viral Infection Following Multiple Blood Transfusion,* 19 Isr J Med Sci 267 (1983).

Holland, *Epidural Morphine and Post-Operative Pain Relief,* 28 Can Anaesth Soc J 453 (1981).

P.R. Bromage, Epidural Analgesia (1978).

Sobel & Kaye, *Urinary Tract Infections,* Principles and Practice of Infectious Diseases (G.I. Mandell ed, 2d ed 1985).

Ramsye-Stewart, *The Perioperative Management of Morbidly Obese Patients (A Surgeon's Perspective),* 13 Anaesth Inten Care 399 (1985).

Moss, *Risk of Seroconversion for AIDS in San Francisco Health Workers,* 28 J Occup Med 821 (1986).

Spence, *Environmental Pollution by Inhalation Anaesthetics,* 59 Brit J Anaesthesia 96 (1987).

Selwyn, *Skin Preparation, the Surgical "Scrub" and Related Rituals,* Surgical Sepsis 23 (S.J. Karran & C.W. Walter eds 1980).

Seropian & Reynolds, *Wound Infections After Preoperative Depilatory Versus Razor Preparation,* 121 Am J Surgery 251 (1971).

Schwartz & Saunders, *Microbial Penetration of Surgical Gown Materials,* 150 Surg Gynecol Obstet 507 (1980).

Steere & Mallison, *Handwashing Practices for the Prevention of Nosocomial Infections,* 83 Ann Intl Med 683 (1975).

Beck, *Aseptic Barriers in Surgery,* 116 Arch Surgery 240 (1981); Ha'eri & Wiley, *Wound Contamination Through Drapes and Gowns: A Study Using Tracer Particles,* 148 Clin Orthop 160 (1980).

Alexander, *Development of a Safe and Effective One-Minute Preoperative Skin Preparation,* 120 Arch Surgery 1357 (1985).

McCue, *Efficacy of Double-Gloving as a Barrier to Microbial Contamination During Total Joint Arthroplasty,* 63A JBJ Surg 811 (1981).

Orr, *Is a Mask Necessary in the Operating Theater,* 63 Ann R Col Surgery Eng 390 (1981).

Olson, *Surgical Wound Infections: A 5-Year Prospective Study of 20,193 Wounds at the Minneapolis VA Medical Center,* 199 Ann Surgery 253 (1984).

Kaul & Jewett, *Aents and Techniques for Disinfection of the Skin,* 152 Surg Gynecol Obstet 677 (1981).

O'Donohue, Jr, *National Survey of the Usage of Lung Expansion Modalities for the Prevention and Treatment of Postoperative Atelectasis,* 87 Chest 76 (1985).

Wang, *The Management of Central Catheter Infections,* 3 Pediatric Infec Dis 110 (1984).

Verghese, *Central Venous Septic Thrombophlebitis—the Role of Medical Therapy,* 64 Med 394 (1985).

Ducatman, *Catheter-Induced Lesions of the Right Side of the Heart: 141 Autopsies,* 253 J AMA 791 (1985).

E.E. Peacock, Wound Repair (3d ed 1984).

Yue, *Effects of Experimental Diabetes, Uremia and Malnutrition on Wound Healing,* 36 Diabetes 295 (1987).

Church, Choong & GL Hill, *Abnormalities of Muscle Metabolism and Histology in Malnourished Patients Awaiting Surgery: Effects of a Course of Intravenous Nutrition,* 71 Brit J Surg 563 (1984).

Fletcher, *A Comparison of Parenteral Nutrition and Early Postoperative Internal Feeding on the Nitrogen Balance After Major Surgery,* 100 Surgery 21 (1986).

F. Vincent, *Preoperative and Postoperative Care: Renal Disease,* Handbook of Surgery, (T.R. Schrock ed 1985).

W.M. Bennett, *Altering Drug Dosage in Patients with Diseases of the Kidney and Liver,* Clinical Uses of Drugs in Patients with Kidney and Liver Disease (R.J. Anderson & R.W. Schrier eds), at 16.

Appendix 20-1
Cases

1 ***Herman v Milwaukee Childrens Hospital* 121 Wis 2d 531, 361 NW2d 297 (Ct App 1984)** (after an operation (splenectomy), the patient went into shock. A first-year surgical resident was called but was unable to place a venous catheter for blood transfusion. There were more experienced residents and surgeons in the hospital, but they were not called. Later, the chief of surgery arrived and got the transfusion started, which reversed the hypovolemic shock. The shock was sufficient to cause the patient permanent brain damage. A plaintiff's award, based on nursing and resident physician delay, was $3,000,000, which was later reduced as excessive).

2 ***Horney v Lawrence,* 375 SE2d 629 (Ga Ct App), *rehg denied* (1988)** (physician was negligent in allowing Valium to extravasate at a venopuncture site on patient's hand. A gastroscopy was being done; the patient complained of severe pain in his hand. After completing the procedure, a nurse found a tender swollen area at the venopuncture site. She concluded it was caused by the escape of Valium into adjacent tissues, and applied hot packs. Tissue damage required corrective surgery, and permanent impairment resulted. The court held that the standard of care required visual inspection of the injection site and that the evidence showed the physician did not do this at the time the patient was complaining of pain and burning in her hand).

3 ***Woitalewicz v Wyatt,* 428 NW2d 216 (Neb 1988)** (numbness was a compensable disability after closure of traumatic and postsurgical wounds from open surgery to repair a fractured jaw. Postoperative swelling and drainage occurred. The surgeon failed to obtain cultures, but prescribed antibiotics, with subsequent osteomyelitis developing. A second surgery, removing dead bone and teeth, with bone graft taken from hip, was carried out. Expert testimony showed that the first surgeon was negligent, with substandard care leading to infection, numbness of skin, and necessitating subsequent surgery. There was an award of $185,000 for the plaintiff. In rebuttal, defendant argued that economic loss attributed to numbness was not a disability as a wage earner. The court held that disability alone was compensable totally separate from wage earning capacity, therefore the jury could find numbness (and the patient's tendency to bite the mouth, with infected ulcers resulting) compensable).

4 ***Smith v Gottsegan,* 535 So 2d 1330 (La Ct App 1988)** (court rejected the plaintiff's argument that would have expanded grounds for proving malpractice and impose a non-discriminatory conformity on the practice of medicine. The threat was the contention by experts that the surgical approach to the first rib was unusual; it was by definition a deviation from standard of care. The plaintiff did not respond to conservative care for a problem

termed "thoracic outlet syndrome" and resection of the first rib to make more room for nerves and vessels in the thoracic outlet was recommended by the surgeon. He elected to approach the first rib through an unusual posterior incision. The patient developed a "winged scapula" due to damage to the long thoracic nerve. A wound dehiscence and spontaneous expression of a hematoma occurred a few days postoperatively, and the defendant's expert testified that pressure on the long thoracic nerve by hematoma caused the problem. A pretrial medical board and the court found that wound dehiscence or hematoma was not peculiarly caused by the unusual incision. The surgeon testified that he chose the posterior approach in the best interest of his patient, a very large, muscular person. The court found this the most reasonable argument in that there were three experts for the defendant saying about the same thing, and three experts who indicated that, by choosing the less popular posterior route, the surgeon had not lived up to the standards of his peers).

5 ***Pelose v Green,* 222 NJ Super 545, 537 A2d 745 (App Div 1988)** (court refused to believe that an orthopedic surgeon's relative lack of experience constituted self-evident proof of the malpractice at issue, that a poor operative result after cervical laminectomy should be automatically attributed to the least experienced surgeon involved. The case started when the orthopedist who was qualified to perform a laminectomy only in the lumbar spine assisted a neurosurgeon in removing a lamina of the patient's cervical vertebra. The patient developed quadriparesis. In the subsequent suit, the patient alleged that the orthopedic surgeon's hand had slipped while performing the unfamiliar procedure, thereby damaging the spinal cord. According to an expert witness, "the mere fact that the orthopedic surgeon participated in a laminectomy indicated he did not damage the cord." The charge was dismissed because the expert witness did not prove that the orthopedic surgeon had erred. Moreover, they were unwilling to accept the argument that inexperience should necessarily be equated with incompetence).

6 ***Turgut v Levine,* 556 A2d 720 (Md Ct Spec App 1989)** (physician appropriately testified, and his testimony was permitted in assessing standard of care, when the testimony was "buttressed" by an admission of the past rate of surgical technique problems of the defendant. In this case, methods of suturing were in question).

7 ***Bowie v Hearn,* 364 SE2d 469 (SC 1986)** (surgeon cut too deeply during a Cesarian section and lacerated the infant's face, which the court held deviated from the acceptable standard of care. The bottom line was that the surgeon moved through each surgical step in a careless manner, or the mishap would have been avoided. The surgeon was in control of the instruments he was using and was responsible for the injury which resulted from negligent use of the instrument).

8 ***Dow v Kaiser Foundation,* 90 Cal Rptr 747 (Cal Ct App 1970)** (orthopedic surgeon who had never performed an anterior interbody fusion of the lumbar spine was not qualified to testify that the complications, including kidney shut-down and thrombosis and swelling of the leg, that

resulted from the operation performed by the defendant surgeon, do not occur in the absence of negligence. The court stated that the definitive criteria to be applied in determining whether a medical expert is qualified to testify in a particular case is measured primarily by "occupational experience," consisting of a basic educational and professional training as the foundation, but controlled by a practical knowledge of what is usually and customarily done by physicians under similar circumstances, and which confronted the defendant charged with malpractice).

9 ***Quintal v Laurel Grove Hospital,* 62 Cal 2d 154, 397 P2d 161, 41 Cal Rptr 577 (1964)** (judgment against a surgeon who failed to perform an open heart massage because he did not feel competent to do so when cardiac arrest occurred during anesthetic from a minor operation, resulting in a child patient becoming spastic, quadriplegia, blind, and mute. The jury found that the injury was the result of negligence, even though another surgeon performed open chest surgery approximately four minutes after the heart stoppage).

10 ***Inouye v Black,* 238 Cal App 2d 31, 47 Cal Rptr 313 (1965)** (neurosurgeon used wire to stabilize vertebral surgery. The wire was defective. The surgeon had tested the wire ahead of time and had used the wire before, and it was of the proper size and consistency to use in accordance with good neurosurgical practice. The fact that the wire failed was not sufficient evidence to hold the surgeon negligent).

11 ***Utzler v Medical Center Hospital,* 540 A2d 652 (1987)** (verdict for a surgeon was proper in light of the patient's failure to provide expert testimony that there was a deviation from the standard of care and concerning causation of the injury. In this case, postoperative infection fell within the reasonable risk attached to the surgical procedure itself, and questionable postoperative management by the surgeon was not below the standard of care, although it was not the technique that some criticizing doctors might have used).

12 ***Dewes v Indian Health Service, Public Health Service,* 504 F Supp 203 (DSD 1980)** (general surgeon had no duty to consult and refer instead of undertaking treatment of plaintiff's broken arm himself, where there was no proof that the open reduction performed was beyond the surgeon's competence or that the operation was negligently performed; expert evidence indicated that the method chosen by the surgeon was a recognized one, even though several would not have used that technique themselves).

13 ***Runnells v Rogers,* 596 SW2d 87 (Tenn), *rehg denied* (1980)** (medical malpractice was based on the physician's failure to remove a piece of wire from a patient's foot. On April 14, 1979, the physician examined the patient and x-rays were taken. An unsuccessful attempt to remove the wire was made. He was given antibiotics, was told to stay off his feet, and to come back in two days. Over the next four weeks, the physician made no attempt to remove the wire. He continued to prescribe antibiotics. The patient's foot turned from red to blue to black, and became grossly infected. A second physician removed the wire. A medical malpractice review board found that the

physician did not conform to reasonable standards when he failed to recommend appropriate consultation after several visits).

Comment: Failure to consult with appropriate specialists in dealing with a patient's problems is a frequent cause of negligence. The practice of medicine does not allows a physician's ego to dictate that he or she can handle any problem, to the detriment of a patient.

14 ***Hertgen v Weintraub,* 29 Misc 2d 396, 215 NYS2d 379 (1961)** (allegation was that the physician had contracted to treat and care for the patient. Following the surgical procedure, a surgical needle was permitted to remain in the patient's body, which is the basis for a malpractice action rather than for a breach of contract action. It was shown that there was neither pain nor suffering, and that the patient's decision not to probe for the needle but to observe it was not negligence per se. In this case, negligence for malpractice was not present, according to the court, for there were no demonstrable damages that had not been addressed by care that fell within the standard).

15 ***Buzan v Mercy Hospital, Inc,* 203 So 2d 11 (Fla Dist Ct App 1967)** (damages from defendant hospital and surgeon were sought, alledging that a nurse, employed by the hospital, and who assisted in the operating room, was negligent in improperly counting sponges. A sponge was left inside the patient. It was held that, where during the course of an operation, a laparotomy square was left in the patient's abdomen, and where it appeared that nurses employed by the hospital in which such operation was performed assisted in the operation, and one of the duties was the making and recording of the accounts of the laparotomy square, the hospital was liable).

16 ***Furlong v Stokes,* 427 SW2d 513 (Mo) (1968)** (defendant orthopedist had performed surgery on the plaintiff's knee. In the course of surgery, for reasons not explained, a "hot portable lamp" came into close proximity with the plaintiff's knee, causing a burn. The surgeon was in control of the operating room and the equipment being used, including the light. The burn was not disputed. It was held that (1) there was no direct evidence, and insufficient circumstantial evidence showed the lamp could have caused the burn, and (2) the plaintiff failed to make a submissible case under res ipsa loquitur. It was a five-hour operation and the lamp was used at times to illuminate the back of the knee when normal lighting was inadequate. It was shown that the light was always five feet or more from the leg and that burning was improbable. There was expert testimony to show that the area called a burn had in fact been devascularized from loss of collateral vessels. A circulation complication at the site of skin closure does not in itself reflect negligent surgical technique).

Comment: When a surgeon has been sued for malpractice because a patient was injured by hospital equipment, courts have generally applied the general rule that liability will attach only if the doctor failed to use reasonable skill, care, or diligence. Often, the doctrine of res ipsa loquitur has been applied, not against the surgeon but against the hospital, as it maintains exclusive control over the equipment in question. It is usually held that when a physician finds an operating room apparently ready for the operation, and nothing puts him or her on notice of any neglect on the part of the hospital in setting up the room, he or she is not required to inspect or review the performance of the hospital's duty in preparing the room for surgery.

17 ***Richardson v Sun,* 505 NE2d 374 (Ill App Ct 1987)** (surgeon performed surgery using chromic cat gut sutures, knowing (or should have known, as it was in the history) that the patient was allergic to it. The patient's wounds healed "poorly," leaving substantial disability. There was a summary judgment for the plaintiff).

18 ***Sheperd v McGinnis,* 257 Iowa 35, 131 NW2d 475 (1964)** (case was brought against an operating surgeon who knew the sutures he had used might be infected or would cause unusual irritation, but proceeded to use them anyway without waiting for other sutures. He was liable for the infection to the patient, as was the hospital).

19 ***Sammons v Smith,* 353 NW2d 380 (Iowa 1984)** (plaintiff underwent leg surgery under tourniquet control, and permanent damage to components of the sciatic nerve resulted. Expert testimony showed that the hospital was negligent in checking tourniquet pressure gauges before surgery, suggesting excessive tourniquet pressure as a cause of nerve damage (a well-known risk when pressure is too high or is applied for too long a time). The court allowed action against surgeon under the res ipsa loquitur doctrine).

20 ***Johnson v Hermann Hospital,* 654 SW2d 124 (Tex Ct App 1983)** (postoperative patient was moved to ICU with an endotracheal tube in place. The routine nurse responsibility was to keep the airway open at all times by deep and thorough suctioning of the endotracheal tube. The patient became cyanotic two to three hours after ICU admission, and minutes later a new endotracheal tube was inserted as the patient had cardiac arrest; he was resuscitated but suffered permanent brain damage. The jury, by expert testimony, accepted that the attending nurse was not experienced and did not suction the first endotracheal tube adequately. A plaintiff's verdict was remanded for retrial due to technical errors).

21 ***Hooker v Headley,* No A89A1192 (Ga Ct App July 1989)** (defendant surgeon had not negligently performed surgery, but was negligent in not admitting his patient to ICU, leading to the patient's death. A gastric stapling procedure had been done without complication and patient was doing well coming out of surgery. The ICU was full, so the surgeon placed the patient on ward. Twelve hours later, respiratory arrest leading to death occurred. The allegation of the plaintiff was that the patient was very high-risk and that arrangements should have been made to put her in ICU, reasonably assuring that her complications would be promptly addressed and that she would survive. An expert testified that he would have admitted her to the ICU, which was not a sufficient test of the standard of care, but he also said that admitting her to the ICU was one of the proper parameters of care

for high-risk patients, which indicated that the surgeon's management of this patient was below the standard of care).

22 ***Rudolph v Iowa Methodist Center,* 293 NW2d 550 (Iowa 1980)** (patient was entitled to damages from a hospital for the negligence of employees who injured him after an anterior cervical fusion. After an operation November 17, 1975, the hospital employees permitted the patient's head to drop sharply backward while transferring him from a hospital cart to a bed. The incident was not immediately reported to the operating neurosurgeon. During the next several hours, the patient became partially paralyzed and the neurosurgeon was finally notified. He performed a myelogram to find the site of the problem. After he reopened him, he examined the surgical site and performed a decompression laminectomy to alleviate swelling and compression on the spinal cord. The patient remained in intensive care for eight days, with subsequent transfer from the hospital to a rehabilitation unit where he remained for three months. The patient made a good recovery except for some permanent disability. It was held that the hospital personnel were negligent and responsible for that degree of permanent impairment and for the extensive post-operative hospitalization).

23 ***Heller v Medine,* 50 AD2d 831, 377 NYS2d 100 (1975)** (action against a surgeon for medical malpractice in which the patient claimed medications used in postoperative care were contraindicated. The trial court held that the patient was to first establish that she was not contributory to negligence by reason of either the failure to follow doctor's instructions or the failure to keep two appointments. The court stated that the patient's failure to follow instructions did not defeat an action for malpractice where there was improper professional treatment, but that, under the circumstances, damages would be reduced to the degree of the patient's negligence).

24 ***Garrett v United States,* 667 F Supp 1147 (D La 1987)** (there was no malpractice in a physician's diagnosis of adult respiratory distress syndrome (ARDS) rather than cardiogenic pulmonary edema. The patient was admitted to the hospital with a two-day history of vomiting, black stools, and fainting episodes, and a nine-day history of nose bleeds. His condition improved, but five days later he again vomited. With the consent of the patient's wife, an exploratory laparotomy and gastrectomy was performed, as well as surgery to restore blood flow to a blocked leg artery. The patient did well during and immediately after the operation, but later suffered a near respiratory arrest. On the basis of patient notes and tests, the physician decided that the problem was not of cardiac origin and made the diagnosis of ARDS. Respiratory function improved after treatment; however, other organ systems began to fail and the patient died less than one month after surgery. The patient's family filed a suit under the Federal Torts Claims Act, alleging wrongful death. They contended that the patient was given an excessive amount of intravenous fluids before, during, and after the operation, resulting in intra-vascular volume overload. They alleged that this resulted in the development of cardiogenic pulmonary edema, which was misdiagnosed as ARDS. The court disagreed with the family's allegation as to

the administration of fluids by the treating physician. Expert testimony for the government justified the fluids given the patient at all times during his hospital stay. The family's expert who testified to the contrary had no expertise in surgery and did not demonstrate the in-depth surgical knowledge possessed by the opposing experts and treating physicians. The court also disagreed with the family's expert that it was below the standard of care to diagnose ARDS instead of cardiogenic pulmonary edema. Even the family expert admitted that pulmonary artery wedge pressure obtained on the night of the patient's arrest and on the next morning was inconsistent with the diagnosis of cardiogenic pulmonary edema. The court was unable to discover any evidence that should have alerted the hospital staff that their diagnosis was improper. Finding that the medical evidence supported the physicians and the hospital, the court entered judgment for the government).

25 ***Cotgeave v Public Administration of Imperial County,*** **443 NYS2d 971 (1981)** (patient may introduce evidence that a physician had performed unnecessary surgery on other patients. The physician had performed lumbar and cervical laminectomies on a patient, who claimed the operations were unnecessary and that the surgery was contraindicated. Additionally, the patient claimed he had also done numerous unnecessary surgeries on other patients. The court noted that a dozen cases were pending against the physician's estate, with similar allegations. Although the defendant's estate objected, the court said that all evidence entered by the patient would not be used to prove that the operation on the patient was in fact unnecessary).

26 ***Racer v Utterman,*** **629 SW2d 387 (Mo Ct App 1981)** (patient was badly burned as a result of an operating room mishap. A disposable drape caught fire. Neither the surgeon nor the operating room personnel knew, nor had any way of knowing, of the flammable nature of the drape. The surgeon was released from liability, while the surgical drape manufacturer was not).

27 ***Forstall v Hotel Dieu Hospital,*** **429 So 2d 213 (La Ct App 1983)** (orthopedist was unable to convince a jury that he had paid daily postoperative visits to a surgery patient on whom he had done an osteotomy. The hospital records and nurses' notes did not show visits, but the orthopedist stated that he visited daily. The orthopedic surgeon was aware of the possibility of compartment syndrome; this developed and necessitated a fasciotomy on the fifth day. The postoperative fasciotomy wound was left open, which is well within the standard of care, but became infected. The wound eventually healed, but was quite scared and there was a moderate drop foot due to scarring. Expert testimony was against the orthopedist on the point that he attempted to close the operative wound before the infection was under control. A second criticism was his inability to verify that he made daily hospital visits, which, according to hospital bylaws, were required).

28 ***Tripp v Pate,*** **271 SE2d (NC Ct App 1980)** (patient injured her knee in a basketball game. A physician performed exploratory surgery and left town on vacation for a few days. He arranged for his two associates to attend her during his absence. The patient began to run an elevated body temperature, complained of pain in her leg, her white blood count increased, and eventually she broke out in a red rash. After the operating physician returned, the patient's condition was diagnosed as drug allergies. Certain medications were discontinued. She continued to suffer pain and swelling and the condition was diagnosed as postoperative infection of the knee, resulting in a permanently stiff knee. The trial court affirmed a verdict in favor of the attending physician inasmuch as he had made appropriate arrangements to have her care followed, and it was her statement that she would have had the surgery even if she knew the physician was leaving town in a few days. There was no evidence of abandonment. The court further noticed that there was no expert testimony that the medical care the patient received was not in conformity with approved medical practices).

29 ***Galloway v Ioppolo,*** **464 So 2d 386 (La Ct App 1985)** (surgeon performed an anterior cervical discectomy; postoperative bleeding occurred, followed by respiratory arrest and death. An autopsy verified the collapse of the trachea from postoperative bleeding. The court reasoned that such postoperative bleeding can occur absent negligence, relying on expert testimony. That was only issue pled, so the case was dismissed).

Comment: Accepting that postoperative bleeding can occur without negligence, some error must have been committed, with inadequate postoperative patient monitoring being apparent. Bleeding is rarely massive; thus, slow occlusion of the trachea would lead to signs observable by medical personnel monitoring. All such patients should have a tracheostomy tray at bedside for emergency use. The importance of close postoperative monitoring and recording cannot be over-emphasized to surgeons and nursing personnel.

30 ***Monk v Doctors Hospital,*** **403 F2d 580 (DC Cir 1968)** (hospital and physician were negligent in their use of a electrosurgical machine in a surgical procedure. The evidence revealed that a machine was used in a manner inconsistent with the manufacturer's instruction manual. It was noted that the physician was independently liable because he saw where the machine was placed, and through his familiarity with the proper operation of the machine, he should have known that it was placed in an improper area of the plaintiff's body, resulting in a burn injury).

31 ***Steinberg v Indemnity Insurance Co,*** **364 F2d 266 (5th Cir 1966)** (plastic surgeon applied a plaster cast too tight, producing necrosis of underlying skin and partially defeating the purpose of the surgery. Medical negligence was alleged, but the expert witness was a general practitioner, unskilled in the application of casts and splints, so his testimony was not allowed).

32 ***Marvin v Talbott,*** **316 Cal App 2d 383, 30 Cal Rptr 893 (1963)** (physician was charged with breach of warranty to successfully perform an operation and cure his patient. The patient stated that the physician's conversation included the statement, "I will make a new man out of you." The court held that the promise was impossible of performance, or so ambiguous,

vague, and uncertain in meaning as to foreclose reliance, and was therefore not a warranty and did not give rise to an enforceable agreement).

21

Pain Diagnosis and Treatment

The diagnosis is in the history if we but choose to listen. Unfortunately, we are deaf.

—Sir William Osler, M.D.

§21.01 Generally

Pain is one of the taboo words of modern medicine, according to the pioneer pain management expert, Patrick Wall, M.D., who has dedicated his professional life to attacking the causes of pain. He feels that treating chronic pain symptoms is regarded as second class medicine by many "main stream, objective-only minded" physicians, and this does a disservice to many patients. Even the phrase "quality of life" carries negative connotations, because it suggests what the pain management expert is often unable to do for a patient—cure him or her.[1]

Most Americans experience physical pain; most experience three or four different kinds of pain every year. Headaches are the most common type of pain, with three-fourths of all adults suffering from one or more headaches a year.

Among those suffering multiple pains, the types of pain frequently described as "most troublesome" in adults are (1) backaches (16 per cent), (2) headaches (15 per cent), (3) joint pains (11 per cent), (4) stomach pains (6 per cent), (5) muscle pains (5 per cent), (6) premenstrual pain (3 per cent), and (7) dental pain (3 per cent).

Over one-half of American adults have suffered from backaches (56 per cent), muscle pains (53 per cent), or joint pains (51 per cent) in the last year. In addition, 46 per cent have complained of stomach pains and 40 per cent of women have had menstrual or premenstrual pain. The least common type of pain is dental, with 27 per cent of all adults reporting this pain; however, this percentage represents 47 million Americans.

---

[1] Williams, *Toward a Set of Reliable and Valid Measures for Chronic Pain Assessment and Outcome Research,* 35 Pain 239 (1988).

Pain ranks as the most frequent cause of suffering and impairment and remains one of the most perplexing problems the orthopedist faces. Pain, in the normal course of events, signals the need for attention to a problem needing resolution. Acute pain is usually perceived in response to a peripheral input, often related to tissue damage. Chronic, persistent pain, however, defies medical knowledge and current treatment modalities. Acute pain serves a useful, sometimes life-saving purpose. Pain lasting beyond its time of signalling value (chronic benign pain) serves no useful purpose and impedes rehabilitation; it becomes one of the most difficult and complex problems to live with and treat. Paradoxically, the same therapeutic intervention, such as drugs and surgeries that seem to relieve painful experiences associated with well-defined biological disorders of acute pain, quite often results in physical and emotional deterioration in chronic benign pain patients.

§21.02 Acute Pain

Acute pain consists of a constellation of unpleasant perceptual and emotional experiences and certain associated autonomic, psychological, and behavioral responses. The pathophysiology of acute pain is fairly well understood and its diagnosis is not difficult. Treatment of acute pain syndromes is usually effectively carried out by the health care system. Acute pain has an important biological function of warning the individual that something is wrong and usually prompts him or her to seek medical counsel, and is used by physicians as a diagnostic aid.

§21.03 Chronic Pain

Chronic pain is defined as pain which persists beyond the usual course of an acute disease or a reasonable time for an injury to heal. The physiologic, effective, and behavioral responses to chronic pain are quite different than those of acute pain. Chronic and persistent pain never has a biologic function and imposes physical, economic, and social stresses on the patient and family. Many chronic benign pain patients undergo (1) progressive physical deterioration characterized by disturbances in sleep and appetite, (2) a decrease in physical activity, and (3) often have excessive medication intake, all of which frequently contribute to accompanying depression.

Managing chronic pain patients in World War II prompted an increased interest in the study of chronic pain and pain therapy. Physicians pointed out several deficiencies that have been noted a number of times in the literature in the last three decades. The main reasons these deficiencies remain the same can be grouped into three major categories: (1) inadequate or improper application of knowledge and therapies currently available, (2) great voids in knowledge about pain mechanisms due to insufficient research in the past, and (3) problems with communication.

To further the scientific understanding and clinical knowledge of chronic pain syndrome and its treatment, data using a set of reliable measures must be collected. Furthermore, these data should be analyzed using current multifaceted methodology, which gives attention to measurement error as well as to causal interactions and control issues. Fortunately, the tools are becoming available, just as consumers and certifiers of chronic pain treatment are demanding careful program evaluation and results.[2]

§21.04 Pain Perception

The International Association for the Study of Pain (IASP) has defined *pain* as "an unpleasant sensory and emotional experience associated with actual or potential tissue damage, or described in terms of such damage." IASP states "pain is always subjective," affirming that pain cannot be assessed independently of a patient's self-report. See Figure 21-1.

Pain beliefs represent the patient's own conceptualization of what pain is and what pain means for him or her. Such beliefs may be discordant with current scientific understanding and may adversely affect compliance with modern methods of chronic pain treatment. Understanding the dimensions around which pain beliefs develop and that relationship with pain beliefs explains behavioral manifestation of pain experiences. These core beliefs have been found to be predictive of subjective pain intensity, multidisciplinary chronic pain treatment compliance, poor self-esteem, somatization, and psychological distress and are associated with attributions about health locus of control.

Although pain is a subjective experience, any physician who evaluates pain should be dissatisfied with the exclusive emphasis on subjectivity. There is a growing consensus among researchers and pain physicians that there are multiple components to pain experiences.

One component of pain is the physical-organic-medical basis which can be revealed by history, physical examination, laboratory testing, and various

---

[2] Williams, *Toward a Set of Reliable and Valid Measures for Chronic Pain Assessment and Outcome Research,* 35 Pain 239 (1988); Bonica, *Editorial,* 20 Triangle 1-6 (1981); VanderDoes, *Patients' and Nurses' Rating of Pain and Anxiety During Burn Wound Care,* 39 Pain 95 (1989); Zimmerman, *Which Type of Pain?,* 6 Intl Back Pain News 5 (1988); Flower & Blackwell, *The Importance of Phospholipase A2 in Prostaglandin Synethesis,* 25 Biocgem Pharmacol 285 (1976); Perl, *Afferent Basis of Noiciception and Pain* in Pain (J.J. Bonica ed 1980); Battista, *Neurologic Aspects of Pain and Recent Development in the Management of Pain,* 17 Contemp Orthop 28 (1988); Chahl & Iggo, *The Effects of Bradykinin and Prostaglandin E1 on Rat Cutaneous Afferent Activity,* 59 Br J Pharmacol 343 (1977); Bergner, *The Sickness Impact Profile, Development and Final Version of a Health Status Measure,* 19 Med Care 787 (1981); Otsuka & Takahasi, *Putative Peptide Neurotransmitter,* 17 Ann Rev Pharm & Toxico 425 (1977); Stewart, 3 *A Fragment of Substance P with Specific Central Activity,* 3 Peptides 551 (1982); Yanaihara, *Substance P Radioimmunoassay Using N-alpha-tyrosyl-substance P,* 23 Endocrinologia Japonica 457 (1976); Seres & Newman, *Negative Influences of the Disability Compensation System: Perspectives for the Clinician,* 3 Seminars in Neurol 360 (1983); Lazarus; *Munchausen's Syndrome,* The Pharos, Summer 1989, at 34; Demjen & Bakal, *Subjective Distress Accompanying Headache Attacks: Evidence for Cognitive Shift,* 25 Pain 187 (1986);

Figure 21-1

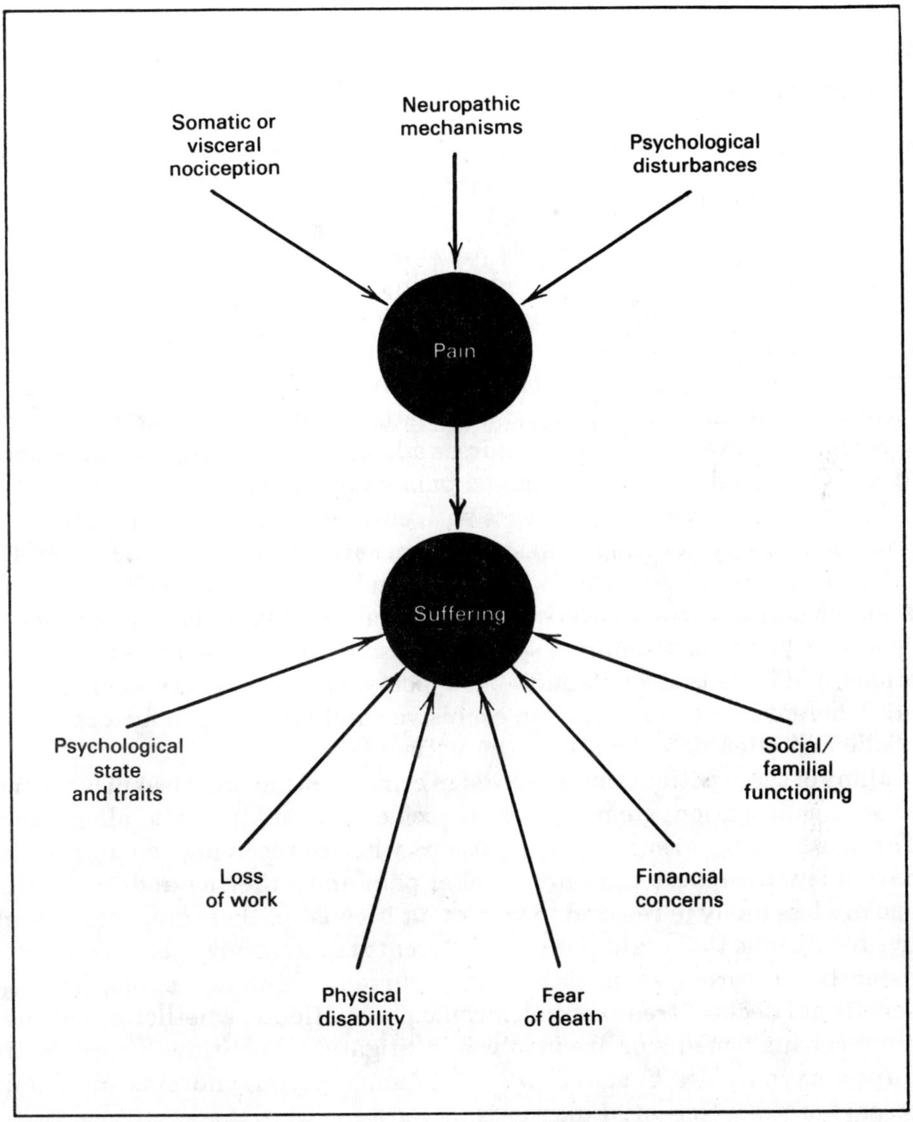

Model of the pain diagnosis, representing the multifactorial nature of pain and its associated symptoms. The diagnosis must be determined prior to the development of a therapeutic strategy. (With permission, CA-A Cander Journal for Clinicians, Vol. 38, No. 6, Nov-Dec 1988, Russell K. Portenoy, M.D.)

imaging techniques—including x-rays, myelograms, CT scans, and MRI studies.

This basis does not give a reproducible pain model. Two different patients with exactly the same workup experience pain differently. Thus, these determinants of pain must be supplemented by at least two other components, one observable and one more subjective.

Among the observable manifestations of pain "behaviors" are groans, grimaces, rubbing, and limping. Additional behaviors include use of pain medication, altered posture and mobility, time spent lying down during the day, and use of a cervical collar, back braces, and other pain paraphernalia. More subjective is the evaluation of the patient's verbal and/or written or drawn pain report, assessing predictable areas of pain in the body as well as the degree of anxiety, depression, and hostility.

There is a significant relationship between nurses and patient pain ratings. Patients' ratings of tension correlate with the amount of analgesic medication used. Pain-related behavior, coping mechanisms, and effects of treatments are similarly affected by a patient's attitude, anxiety, age, and previous pain experience, where nurses add bias to their pain rating report. Most nurses underrate the patients' pain experience.

The suspicion that some patients with chronic pain may be intentionally producing or exaggerating pain stems from several sources. One is the difficulty in finding a physical basis that adequately explains the pain complaint. Another is that patients who complain of pain are undoubtedly influenced by altered patterns of family responsibilities, avoiding unpleasant work situations, and increased availability of support and attention. These behaviors are inherent in all people and an exclusive emphasis on such factors is simplistic and often detrimental to the patient.

Many of these patients are involved in compensation and disability claims, as well as litigation, stemming from accidents or malpractice allegations. This has led some to suggest that patients who are receiving benefits or who have a lawsuit report a greater level of pain and suffering and/or distress and are less likely to respond to treatment because of their presumed incentive to continue their pain complaint. Recent research, however, has not consistently supported such claims, and current thinking emphasizes the beneficial effects of treatment of chronic pain patients, whether or not they are receiving benefits or are involved in litigation. Factitious disorders are rare pain syndromes, but do occur as the Munchhausen syndrome and should be part of the differential diagnosis.

Multiple components of pain complaints—physical contribution, observable impact on behavior, and subjective report of pain and distress—must each be rated in dimension from high to low. This multidimensional approach comes closest to addressing the sensory and emotional aspects of pain according to the International Associaton for Study of Pain (IASP) definition.

Some pain management physicians, in working with chronic pain patients, believe the complaints of pain and physical limitations, numerous doctor contacts, drug usage, and suffering behavior are all behavioral and can be changed as a result of alterations in reinforcers and efforts by the patient.[3]

In a demographic profile of pain sufferers, there are many differences in the prevalence and severity of different pains among different demographic groups.

Young people are more likely to experience pain than older people. The younger they are, the more likely they are to suffer pain. This is true of each type of pain mentioned above except joint pains, which are far more common in older persons. Women are somewhat more likely than men to complain of pain, particularly headache. Headaches occur more frequently in women but they usually cope better. White Americans are more likely to experience pain than Hispanic or black Americans, particularly suffering more often with back, muscle, or joint pains. White women experience fewer days of premenstrual or menstrual pain than black or Hispanic women.

There are also striking differences between the prevalence of pain in different income groups. Those with household incomes under $15,000 are more likely to have joint pain, while those with incomes of $50,000 or more are more apt to have muscle pain.

There is a strong familial link with pain. Those with parents who have suffered severe pain are more likely to experience backaches, muscle pain, or joint pain. Second or third generation Americans experience headaches, backaches, muscle pains, and stomach aches more often than the first generation. Dental pain appears just the opposite.

Americans with only "occasional pain" (one to five days a year) report little impact on their lives. Persons with more than occasional pain (more than six days per year) may experience significant interruption of daily routine, including loss of work and sleep. Among full-time working people, 550 million days are lost—approximately five days per person. Those numbers reflect a massive loss of production.

The more stress a person experiences, the more likely he or she will experience pain. Persons under great stress seem to have more and greater pains in each of the above areas. Stress is a fact of modern American life. Fully 45 per cent of all Americans report stress one or more times per week, 35 per cent report stress less than one time per week, and 15 per cent of Americans say they never experience stress. Pain sufferers are well aware that stress often causes their pain.[4]

---

[3] Zimmerman, *Which Type of Pain?,* 6 Intl Back Pain News 5 (1988); Flower & Blackwell, *The Importance of Phospholipase A2 in Prostaglandin Synthesis,* 25 Biocgem Pharmacol 285 (1976); Perl, *Afferent Basis of Niociception and Pain in Pain* (J.J. Bonica ed 1980); Battista, *Neurologic Aspects of Pain and Recent Development in the Management of Pain,* 17 Contemp Orthop 28 (1988); Chahl & Iggo, *The Effects of Bradykinin and Prostaglandin El on Rat Cutaneous Afferent Activity,* 59 Br J Pharmacol 343 (1977).

[4] Bergner, *The Sickness Impact Profile, Development and Final Version of a Health Status Measure,* 19 Med Care 787 (1981).

§21.05 Pain Pathways

Pain can be defined as the perception of a sensory phenomena associated with tissue damage. All surgical procedures cause tissue injury, which results in the production and release of chemical mediators that are thought to be responsible for activating pain pathways.

When a tissue is injured by trauma, inflammation, or ischemia, the pain pathway is activated. If the tissue injury is sufficient, the perception of pain is reported by the patient.

Under normal circumstances, the cell membrane has a bipolar lipo-protein configuration with phospholipid sequestered in its membrane. With tissue injury, the cell membrane is disrupted and previously inaccessible phospholipid is exposed to the enzyme phospholipase A2, which catalyzes its conversion to arachnoidic acid. Arachnoidic acid is then converted by the enzyme cyclo-oxygenase (prostaglandin synthetase) into short-lived endoperoxide. These intermediate compounds are metabolized to stable prostaglandins and thromboxanes by tissue isomerase enzymes. Arachnoidic acid is also converted via the lipoxygenase enzyme system into a variety of leukotreins, some of which are important mediators involved in pain production.

Substance P is an amino acid through which to relate to pain impulse transmission and serves in the brain as a nerve transmitter. The function and concentration of Substance P is paradoxical, being high in plasm, spinal fluid, and saliva of some chronic pain patients, and low in others as compared with non-chronic pain patients. Elevated Substance P in cerebrospinal fluid however, may be a significant marker in chronic pain patients; an elevated Substance P is not found in other identified, known pathological states.[5]

The sensory transmission of noxious stimuli is called *nociception,* and specialized receptors, which are free nerve endings of primary sensory afferant fibers, are called *nociceptors.* These receptors are classified according to the type of energy that activates the nerve ending receptor—chemical, mechanical, thermal, or polymodal (responds to several types of stimuli).

Prostaglandin-sensitized chemical nociceptors which can be directly activated by bradykinin. Other chemical activators and sensitizers play a part in the total pain mediation schema. Once the nociceptor is activated and the intensity of the electrical stimulus is sufficient, transmission of pain impulses from the nociceptor proceed along the A-delta or C-fiber afferants. A-delta fibers are myelinated and conduct sharp, well-localized pain, whereas C-fibers, which have polymodal receptors (nociceptors) are unmyelinated and are thought to transmit dull, poorly-localized pain. The cell bodies of the nerve fibers are present in the spinal cord ganglia, communicating with fibers from various lamina of the substantia gelitinosa in the spinal

---

[5] Otsuka & Takahasi, *Putative Peptide Neurotransmitter,* 17 Ann Rev Pharm & Toxico 425 (1977); Steward, 3 *A Fragment of Substance P with Specific Central Activity* 351 (1982); Yanaihara, *Substance P Radioimmunoassay Using N-alpha-tyrosyl-substance P,* 23 Endocrinologia Japonica 457 (1976).

cord. The dorsal horn of the spinal cord is an area of intense neurotransmitter activity, modulating or augmenting pain pathways, partly under the influence of descending pain modifying nerve tracts. These pathways can be stimulated by activation of the opiate receptor system by a wide variety of neurotransmitters. The widespread distribution of opiate receptors in the brain and spinal cord has provided an appreciation of the range of effects of opiates on the pain pathway at both perceptual and preperceptual (spinal cord) levels. The dorsal horn and cord-brain pathways are the sites for the hypothetical Melzac-Wall gate control mechanism of pain. Pain perception consists of a complex inter-reaction of several pathophysiological mechanisms. A useful classification is as follows:

1. *Nociceptor pain* is based on excitation of pain receptors in joint structures (except cartilage) and in the peri-articular area, as in tendons, bone, and muscle. Inflammation sensitizes receptors so responses are elicited by joint movements within normal range for that joint.
2. *Neurogenic inflammation* is due to release of Substance P and other neuropeptides from sensory nerve endings, probably contributing to nociceptive pain.
3. *Neuropathic pain* occurs after lesions of nerve fibers by transection, compression, stretch, metabolic, or toxic disturbances. The anoxal membrane becomes excessively excitable so that slight mechanical or chemical stimuli can elicit nerve impulses. There is impairment of the whole neurone, including its peripheral and central targets of neuronal and trophic control.
4. *Deafferentation pain* involves hyperexcitability of sensory neurones in the central nervous system (CNS). It probably occurs after partial destruction of the presynaptic excitatory of inhibitory inputs, leaving the deafferented neurone in a state of pharmacological supersensitivity. Phantom limb pain, post herpetic neuralgia, and trigeminal neuralgia are examples.
5. *Reactive* or *deregulatory pain* involves dysfunction of afferent control loops. If mononeurone output results in excessive muscle tone or if there is poor, sympathetic control pain receptors in muscle, tendon, and joints may become excited. Disturbed spinal reflex transmission from the somato-sensory afferants to motor and sympathetic output as the consequence of long-term peripheral trauma may explain many symptoms of pain (trigger points, pain referral, pain associated with muscle spasm) may be attributed to abnormal control mechanisms in a complex cybernetic system.
6. *Psychosomatic pain* is a relevant factor to all chronic pain in the musculoskeletal system which may be associated with abnormal

motorneuronal or sympathetic outflow under inadequate brain commands.[6]

§21.06 Cumulative Repetitive Trauma Pain

Neck/shoulder/arm pain related to repetitive minor injuries at work or home frequently presents a controversial problem in assessing proximate cause and the degree of injury-related impairment.

A survey by the United States Health and Nutrition Examination of 6,913 people over the country showed that 80 per cent had musculoskeletal pain in the preceding 12 months. All respondents who could recall at least one month of regional musculoskeletal pain were asked about its site, quality, and impact on function. Forty per cent had neck and shoulder pain, but only 6 per cent were disabled enough to take time off. These findings confirm the nature of memorable neck/arm pain. How do we deal with arm pain in our daily living? Most people who recalled neck/arm pain said they did not have other symptoms or impairments about their bodies. Men tended to ascribe arm pain complaints to injuries, while women felt it related more to overload. Most reported symptoms as not very serious 42 per cent of the time, while 8 per cent said the pain was serious. Only 3 per cent sought medical advice. Others used no treatment, or home remedies such as heat, limited movement, aspirin, or NSAIDS (non-steroidal anti-inflammatory drugs).

In the above survey, nearly all the symptoms that related to low back pain with neck/shoulder/arm pain complaints lasting one month or more represented 6 of those surveyed.

Cumulative trauma disorders (CTDs) were often felt to be a significant etiologic factor in persons with neck/arm pain. The United States Surgeon General's Office and the National Institute of Occupational Safety and Health appear to accept the CTD theory, stating "When job demands repeatedly exceed the biomechanical capacity of the worker, those activities become trauma producing. Hence, traumatogens are work place sources of biomechanical strain that contribute to the onset of injuries affecting the musculoskeletal system."

The above dictum is opposed by many physicians and workers representing third-party or self-insured carriers. They point out that any upper extremity task poses a challenge to workers who experience any arm or neck discomfort. The challenge may prove insurmountable if there is no flexibility

---

[6] Seres & Newman, *Negative Influences of the Disability Compensation System: Perspectives for the Clinician,* 3 Seminars in Neurol 360 (1983); Lazarus, *Munchausen's Syndrome,* The Pharos, Summer 1989, at 34; Demjen & Bakal, *Subjective Distress Accompanying Headache Attacks: Evidence for Cognitive Shift,* 25 Pain 187 (1986); Fishbain, *Munchausen Syndrome Presenting with Chronic Pain: Case Report,* 35 Pain 91 (1988); Kerr, *The Structural Basis of Pain: Circuitry and Pathways,* in Pain, Discomfort and Humanitarian Care (L.K. Ng & J.J. Bonica eds 1980); Dodd, *Neurotransmitters and Neuronal Markers at Sensory Synapses in the Dorsal Horn,* 6 Adv Pain Res Ther 105 (1984); Honig, *Nonsteroidal Anti-Inflammatory Drugs as Post-Operative Analgesics,* 18 Orthop Rev 30 (1989); Dworkin, *Severity of Pain: Can it be Judged without a Subjective Report,* 4 Ed Dialog Pain 1 (1988).

on the job. Under the banner of worker comfort and satisfaction, labor and management should seek redress in job flexibility, task design, and proper remuneration.

The examining physician, in evaluating CTD trauma cases, must be informed of work environment, as well as the psychosocial ramification of his or her opinion, and that examiner may make him- or herself vulnerable to criticism. Honest doctors have honest differences of opinion, but opinion must be rationally based and not biased.[7]

§21.07 Chronic Pain Evaluation

If we look at a cross section of any city in America, we find people wandering, searching for help. They appear confused, anxious, and depressed, and their accompanying family members are resentful, suspicious, and bewildered. The common complaint of the patient is "pain" that their doctors have been unable to help. Their pain complaint is not acute like a kidney stone or abscess, but chronic pain—unremitting and everpresent, bringing about dysfunctional changes in the musculoskeletal, digestive, cardiovascular, and respiratory systems. A spinal pain algorithm shows an acceptable organized plan to assess acute/chronic pain. See Figure 21-2.

In medical school, physicians are taught to gather data on which a diagnosis is made. This includes a therapeutic plan that varies slightly from person to person. If the pain follows an injury/disease or is the byproduct of therapy, it is typically managed with analgesics or narcotics, because physicians have been taught that when the problem is resolved, the pain will disappear. This model works for most acute pain syndromes—never for chronic pain syndromes. The most comprehensive medical workup yields no useful information; therefore, the patient and family are informed that "nothing is wrong." Yet, the pain persists and often intensifies. The psychologically-oriented physician may then start patients on a variety of psychotropic drugs, although with little justification. When the pain persists, the doctor may be called a "quack." The drugs used may cause serious side effects. The wandering patient moves to another clinic or doctor, accompanied by family.

The chronic pain patient may seek out a specialist who may find a minor deviation from normal, giving the patient a ray of hope, which is only to be "snuffed" out when new treatment fails. Psychiatric help is often sought or referred by a physician, implying that what is wrong is "in your head." The patient feels that it is bad enough to hurt, but is further traumatized when labeled a "little off," and depressive mood disorders often result.

In all these patients, positive findings are present, yet the level of injury does not reflect the level of suffering, the dysfunction present. Often, the medical report of the patient at this stage recites that professed pain cannot be verified by objective findings or there is incapacitating functional overlay. The net result of the ever-increasing pain is to make patients more depressed

---

[7] Hadler, *Arm Pain and the Workplace,* Medilegal Bull, Fall 1988, at 7.

Figure 21-2

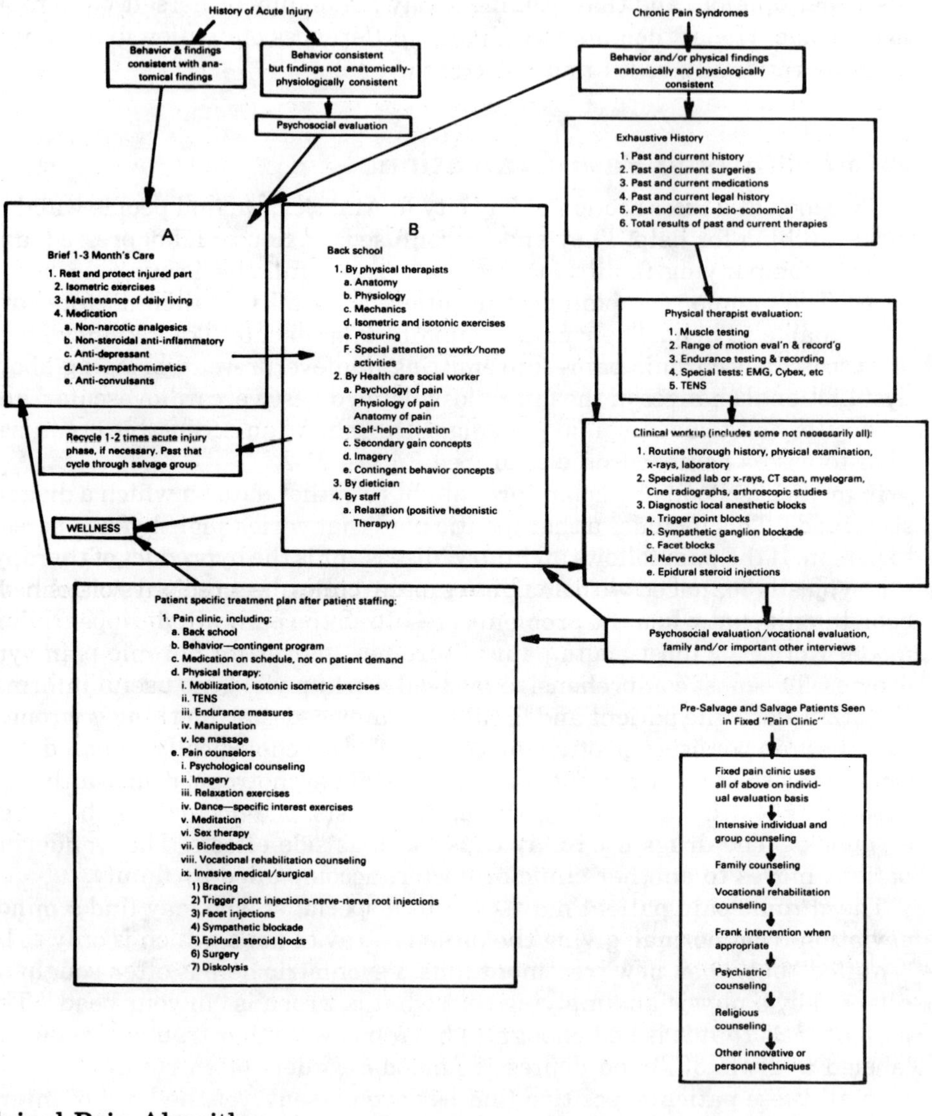

Spinal Pain Algorithm.

at their lot in life and angry at doctors not helping him. The patient feels rejected by families who report "The doctor says all tests are normal—can't find anything wrong, and you will just have to learn to live with it."

Chronic benign pain patients have a behavior problem which changes their activities of daily living, becoming restricted and impaired. Their use of medical services far exceeds those with normal illnesses. They may have an organic disorder combined with their psychological impairment—the two being inseparable from a cause or treatment point of view. Typical professional comments regarding markers of the chronic benign pain patients include (1) they have a "nickel's worth of disease and a dollar's worth of physical disability," (2) the patient's pathology has been corrected but pain is still present, (3) the patient is non-functioning, but there is no apparent organic cause, and (4) the patient has extreme somatic preoccupation.

Further comments include "It's always surprising to me that the chronic pain patient spends a great deal more time worrying about health and pain than the dying cancer patient" and "Chronic pain patients are obsessed with their bodies and how they are functioning." These scenarios are often repeated and are the impetus for the formation of multidisciplinary pain management centers. The concept of caring for, rather than curing, is the basis for these clinics.

§21.08 Pain Clinics

The formation of multidisciplinary pain clinics is credited to John J. Bonica, M.D., opening first in Seattle in 1946. By 1969, there were 10 clinics, and as understanding of the merits of this pain management tool has grown, there are now 700 such clinics in the United States. The approach includes extensive review of prior records, exhaustive history and physical examination (with a lot of patient interpersonal detective work), appropriate testing, and assurance that more invasive procedures—surgery, etc., might be helpful. The patient is introduced into a progressive multifaceted self-help program; the well-motivated patient usually does well, is medicine-free, and moves toward a productive life. The poorly motivated patient does poorly and often remains medication-dependent and continues "doctor shopping," with great expense to the medical care system. (*See* Appendix 21-1, Case 1.)

Major behavioral learning principles include classical conditioning and observational learning-modeling-education. The multi-model behavioral treatment philosophy includes selecting many techniques, which is better than relying solely on one technique. Multi-behavioral treatment versus traditional psychological treatment approaches seem more effective. The multimodal disability management protocol includes individual and group crisis intervention counseling, family crisis intervention counseling, behavioral stress management, and cognitive behavior skills training.

Many pain clinic treatment protocols emphasize "feeling better in spite of pain" or "better cope with pain." More successful programs emphasize a highly-structured and goal-oriented program, overcoming disability through systematic restoration of functional ability. The multidisciplinary approach using this concept with chronic benign pain patients is more effective than using a more narrow approach, such as work hardening, or simple physical therapy, such as monotherapy. Chronic pain specialists are increasingly recommending the functional ability, goal-oriented multidisciplinary approach to these recalcitrant chronic pain syndrome patients, even though it is initially more expensive.[8]

Major barriers to recovery, from a psychological point of view, include the patient's inherent inability to understand or accept the psychological issues. Compliance, resistance, and denial issues invariably arise and must be overcome before a patient can be psychologically oriented and understand and profit from this type of therapy.

Financial disincentives are always a strong problem. It is difficult to ask a patient to accept that he or she will make less money or suggest he or she give up disability benefits while in a self-help rehabilitation program.

One problem the psychological therapist has is the patient understanding the somatization that occurs with increased stress and that symptom magnification, although perhaps "natural", is self-defeating. Each patient needs to be studied and treated individually. The therapist, as well as the patient, must understand the barriers to recovery and must deal with it then.

The typical chronic pain clinic includes the following:

1. Physical therapy services (evaluation, consultations, and therapeutic techniques) by registered physical therapists and frequent re-evaluation. Daily observation by the treating physician in the physical therapy area greatly aids in learning and understanding the patient.
2. Nerve blocks (trigger point injections, sympathetic nerve blocks, epidural blocks—with or without steroids) are helpful as evaluation and/or treatment. Acupuncture in skilled hands may also be helpful.
3. Evaluation by pain counselors (in-depth psychological, social, and spiritual) skilled in techniques of empathy and "tough love." A clinical psychologist is a regular part of the treatment program. Psychiatric liaison is most helpful.
4. Classes, including back school, discuss the anatomy of injured areas and healing process. The need of techniques to be used are explained to the patients. Emphasis is placed on muscle re-strengthening and remobilization (as soon as the physician permits) of tight myofascial joint systems. Tailored exercise routines and the self-help approach are taught. The patient is taught to anticipate the effects of mind-altering chemicals which may be judiciously prescribed on a regular schedule and in reasonably tailored decreasing doses. Emphasis is placed on achieving a lifestyle free from using medications that diminish brain function. Development of a sense of patient control over pain reduces the level of perceived pain. The patient is informed as to current

[8] Bonica & Black, *The Management of a Pain Clinic,* 1 Excerpta Medica Amsterdam 116 (1974).

neuropsychology as it applies to pain perception. The patient learns relaxation, diversion, response to increased physical activity, imagery, biofeedback, meditation, and auto-hypnosis. Discussions of research are part of the program. Physicians, physical therapists, and pain counselors all participate in these classes.

5. Stress control. Ramifications of the various lifestyle stressors related to pain perception and its resultant impairment are taught. The number of sessions depends on the patient's needs, abilities to apply techniques of stress control, and the number and types of stressors present in the patient's environment. Often, the motto "I may not be responsible for my pain, but I am responsible for the treatment of my pain" is invoked. The knowledge that one is able to do something about pain can bring marked reduction in the anxiety associated with pain.
6. Nutrition counseling is employed for patients with nutritional problems, obesity being the most common.
7. Social readjustment counseling. The ability to live successfully with people in their community is a potent tool for chronic pain patients. Part of this may include active vocational counseling.
8. Spiritual counseling is a frequent and valuable asset to the problem for many patients.

Regular re-evaluation and frequent physician-patient contacts are necessary for this program to work. As the patient changes, the revision of treatment makes this program flexible. A trust-alliance between the patient and therapist is essential.

Results of this type of program have been satisfactory to patients and physicians in most instances. Benefits include lifestyle changes, self-image improvement, and decreased usage of medical services. This method is often appropriate for the acute pain patients, resulting in shorter disability periods, decreased total medical usage, and may prevent catastrophic changes in the patient's lifestyle.

§21.09 Pain Management, Generally

Three general methods of treatment of pain are pharmacologic, physical, and psychological. The goal of medical management of the patient with pain and inflammation is to relieve these symptoms with minimal side effects and inconvenience. Pain associated with inflammation may be relieved with nonsteroidial anti-inflamatory drugs (NSAIDS), including aspirin. All of these agents relieve pain and stiffness in a similar manner. Their primary action seems to be the inhibition of the cyclo-oxygenase system in the arachnoidonic acid cascade. When prescribing NSAIDS for orthopedic pain and inflammation, it seems sensible to start with aspirin because of its low cost and safety at analgesic doses. If safety and low incidence of side effects are the most important factors, however, the newer NSAIDS, such as ketoprofen, will be preferred. The relief of pain is an important aspect of postoperative care. Parenteral and oral opiates serve as the standard against which other therapies for severe pain are compared. When pain cannot be adequately controlled with intra-muscular or subcutaneous opiates, intravenous opiates controlled by the patient are often useful. Relatively small doses of epidural or intrathecal opiates can also be used to achieve postoperative pain relief. Thus, treatment for orthopedic pain begins with NSAIDS, followed by an oral opiate combined with acetaminophen, aspirin, or another NSAID. If these regimens are ineffective, oral opiates followed by parenteral opiates may be tried.[9]

§21.10 Surgical Indications

Complaints of unrelenting pain or recurrent pain are by far the most common incentive for surgical interventions. This presents unique difficulties to the care provided as there are no universally accepted techniques for measuring pain. The purely subjective character of pain embraces two areas. The intensity of the pain cannot be measured and no two patients have the same tolerance for the same pain complaint. If there is no basis for challenging the veracity of the patients' pain complaints, it is extraordinarily difficult to challenge the decision to perform surgery.

If chronic intolerable or recurrent severe pain in the low back and/or legs continues, in spite of good and cooperative conservative treatment, appropriate surgical intervention may be indicated. Surgery must be for a specific demonstrable irreversible lesion and should never be done on an "exploratory" basis. At this time, there are ample diagnostic tools available to the surgeon to make a verifiable diagnosis.

Some surgical indications are more urgent than waiting for the "standard" two to six months of conservative treatment. Where there is a nerve root defect (muscle weakness, reflex, and sensory change) with pain that is not improving or worsening, surgical nerve root decompression is suggested within two to four weeks by many surgeons. Another set of surgeons would wait, considering that only certain acute fracture dislocations, severe infection, or compound wounds as an emergency surgical situation.

It is common that the orthopedic surgeon is faulted for delaying surgery or is criticized by a group of peers who do not follow his or her surgical indication reasoning. A careful, conscientious surgeon experienced in the field is less apt to be critical than cloistered or biased individuals wed to his preferred management techniques and discounting those with another opinion. The only emergency surgery indicated for lumbar disc operation is cauda equina syndrome with urinary bladder/bowel paresis.

Perhaps the bottom line in back surgery for unremitting, intolerable pain with a specific diagnosis in a psychologically stable patient is reality testing—is there probable chance of improving the patient's pain complaint?

---

[9] Tollison, *Comprehensive Pain Center Treatment of Low Back Workers' Compensation Injuries,* 13 Ortho Rev 1115 (1989),

§21.11 Stress Pain

In recent years, the relationship between the summation of life events (stress) and the quality, severity, and response to treatment of pain complaints has been medically accepted. Additional effects of ethnic background, genetic variables, nutrition, substance abuse, smoking, and socio-economic status are players in this global understanding of patients. Physicians who fail to accept or utilize these concepts do patients a disservice. A change or conflict in status and/or role constitutes one of the most severe forms of psychological stress.[10]

Stress-related disorders have been recognized as compensable under workers' compensation statutes, including the Federal Employees' Compensation Act (FECA), for many years. These impairments can be temporary or permanent, and are usually divided into three categories:

1. *Mental/physical:* Cases in this category involve a mental stimulus that causes a distinct physical injury to the injured person, such as a heart attack brought about by a stressful event. The mental stimulus may be of a sudden or relatively brief nature, such as a sudden explosion or witnessing a particularly violent injury to another. The stress may be gradual and sustained, such as that caused by long work hours, harassment, and/or other forms of long-term personal friction.
2. *Physical/mental:* Conversely, a physical injury may result in a disabling emotional response. These problems are diagnosed as post-traumatic stress disorders, traumatic neurosis, conversion neurosis, or hysteria. Sometimes, hysterical paralysis is a mental reaction to an injury and may include aggravation (i.e., non-disabling conditions aggravation, acceleration or activation of a pre-existing condition) to a new and disabling level.
3. *Mental/mental:* In this group, cases involve a mental stimulus that results in a mental condition, such as a psychoneurotic illness brought about by the conditions of employment. As in mental/physical cases, the stress may be of a sudden or relatively brief nature, or may be gradual and sustained—the difference is that the resultant impairment is mental rather than physical.

§21.12 Stress Management

Stress costs American third-party payers approximately $150 billion a year. Stress is a problem for the sufferer, but is economically "killing" the competitiveness of the United States, according to many economists.

---

[10] Brown, *Life Events and Psychiatric Disorders. Part 2. Nature of Causal Link,* 3 Psychol Med 159 (1973); Speculand, *Role of Recent Stressful Life Events in the Onset of TMJ Dysfunction Pain,* 12 Commun Dent Oral Epidemiol 197 (1984); M. Konner, Becoming a Doctor (1987).

Stress is a natural and necessary part of life, without which the human would accomplish little. The way a person responds to stress can cause stress-related illness. Learning pain and stress-controlling techniques is an essential part of rehabilitation of many chronic, as well as acute, pain syndromes. Because the adverse reaction to stress experienced by many is viewed as counterproductive to traditional American work ethics, persons unable to handle stress well are frequently denigrated and labeled with a number of pejorative terms.

A variety of therapeutic methods are used by pain therapists to lessen stress, including relaxation techniques, imagery, massage, specific exercises, and humor workshops. It appears that methods that elevate the body's endorphin output decrease the adverse effect of stress, and that the reverse is true. It must be recognized that each injured person is unique, special, and different, and is rarely dishonest and malingering—these labels represent adversive stress.

Every physician knows that some patients handle stress better than others, often depending on the situation. The reason is that each person has a unique stress response pattern that determines responses to stress. Two individuals can be subjected to the same stressful problem; one will wilt, and the other may seem to thrive on it. It appears that each person has a stress-related "Achilles heel." It has often been observed that, because of this "Achilles heel," a patient will fall into repeating self-defeating patterns. In teaching the patient to reinforce strong stress coping skills and bolster weak skills, the patient often can adopt pain and stress coping methods that will work for him or her.

Psychologists point out that thinking/processing of information by the brain falls into predictable types:

1. *Grounding energy people* obtain information primarily through their senses. They are practical, realistic, detail-oriented, and predictable. Their life focuses on the present.
2. *Creative energy persons* have dominant creative energy and receive information from intuition rather than senses. They are often visionary, looking for new ideas. They are focused on the future.
3. *Logic energy persons* are objective, quantitative, and "cause and effect" oriented. For them, time is sequential. Their mode asks the question "Why?"
4. *Relationship energy persons* are especially sensitive to others. They often make decisions based on their emotions and usually have strong likes and dislikes.

Once patients are understood by their energy types, treatment strategies can be formed. Relationship energy patients generally need more analysis and more objectivity. They need help to make better decisions. High logic patients improve when they become sensitive to the needs of others. Grounding energy patients need to look at options and possibilities of a problem, for their mode is to see a problem only one way. Creative energy people generally need to learn to focus on the present problem and work with it. Logic patients are stressed by illogical persons, open-ended questions, disorganization, and hasty decisions. Relationship energy patients become stressed by rejection, isolation and criticism, trying to please others who may not be listening. Creative energy patients are stressed by detail, rigid rules, negative people, unproductive meetings, and people who are resistant to change.

It is said that there is not a "best" or "ideal" profile, but it is helpful to learn skills for compensating for weak areas. Energy profiles are not changed without conscious effort, since they are formed in childhood and continue to develop through life unless altered.

A formula for change includes awareness, knowledge, skills, continual practice, and mastery. Consultation with pain management experts to supervise this important part of pain control is appropriate and effective therapy.

Holmes-Rahe created a stress scale that predicts health problem probability based on the patient's life changing problems. They rate such events as death of a spouse—100; divorce—73; marriage—50; retirement—45, and pregnancy—40. The higher the score, the greater the probability of accident or illness.

Carrying an extra load at work is not nearly as stressful as conflict with a colleague, neighbor, or clerk. Work overloads have been overstated as a contributor to poor mental health, viewed by many industrial psychologists. The problems at work that the worker (patient) does not have the "tools" to handle are more stressful, unless the worker has learned how to manage. Conflict with a superior is especially stressful, where as fights at home are less stressful if the participants have experience "dealing with problems later."

People get used to continuing hassles that do not involve personal friction, such as unusual work weeks. The strain of having problems with others, particularly with persons who are part of daily life, is not relieved until the conflict is resolved. Men are more likely to stay angry with their kids or with their hassling superior at work. Women are able to cope with fighting with their children, but do equally poorly with work-related personnel.

In a personal dispute, middle-aged persons favor compromise more than younger or older people. Young workers tend to be brash and challenging and older people tend to think they know everything.

Uncompromised stress related to work may impinge on the chronic pain patient, causing the pain complaint to worsen, and the impairment to worsen and prevent improvement until the situation is resolved.[11]

§21.13 Documenting Pain and Suffering

There are several ways to document pain. The pain drawing popularized by Mooney is widely used by orthopedists. Having the patient keep a daily diary that records difficulty in performing activities of daily living and why

---

[11] Kessler, *Study Reveals Surprise Stressors,* Occupat News, Oct 1989, at 23.

is another popular technique. The patient typically records difficulty in getting out of bed and performing household chores or work activities, reciting which activity—bathing, sleeping, or doing other tasks—is the most painful. A pain allograph scaling pain from 0 to 10 based on 10 being intolerably painful is widely used among orthopedists also.[12]

§21.14 Neuropathic Pain

There appears to be a special category of pain that patients may experience which is central (within the brain) in origin. Many authors feel that neurotropic pain is poorly relieved by narcotic medication, to the point where patients are deprived of the pain relief they might have. Other authors have shown some pain relief with large doses of narcotics but, here again, practitioners hesitate, fearing narcotic addiction. Many neuropathic pain patients seem undertreated, perhaps at the expense of the biases of the physicians. Anti-depressant medication is frequently helpful with or without narcotic medication. Accurate history and physical examination, as well as care by an informed, empathetic physician, frequently sets the course to improved pain control in neurotropic pain patients. Patients with reflex sympathetic dystrophy, causalgia, and phantom pain may well be variations of neurotropic pain patients. Dysethetic pain is still another descriptor.[13]

§21.15 Pain Evaluation, Psychological

Healing or successful intervention usually leads to resolution of pain. In some patients, biologic or psychologic symptoms associated with pain persist despite treatment or apparent healing. In cases where the etiology is unknown, persistent pain is categorized as a clinical syndrome known as "chronic pain." Organic, psychologic, and socio-environmental factors contribute to the development of chronic pain. Major organic illnesses leading to chronic pain include headaches, back problems, arthritis, and cancer. Significant psychological reactions occur in many pain patients, with depression being the most common. Pain is often seen in patients with psychiatric disorders such as depression, anxiety, and somatization, as well as in substance abusers. Before successful management can begin, the major etiologic factors and sequelae of the chronic pain syndrome must be understood. Antidepressants, neuroleptics, anticonvulsants, nonsteroidal anti-inflammatory drugs, and hydroxyzine have been proven effective in the

---

[12] Dorken: *Workers' Compensation Opening up a Major Market for Psychological Practice,* J Prof Psychol, Dec 1979, at 835; J.A. Tarantino & D.J. Oliveira, Litigating Neck and Back Injuries (1988).

[13] Fields, *Can Opiates Relieve Neuropathic Pain?,* 35 Pain 365 (1988); Tasker, *The Problem of Deafferentation Pain in the Management of the Cancer Patients,* 2 J Palliat Care 8 (1987); Max, *Antidepressant Medication in Neurotrophic Pain Management,* 32 Neurol 589 (1987); Max, *Neuropathic Pain Management with Antidepressant Medication,* 4 Pain 348 (1987).

treatment of pain syndromes. Treatment of patients who present with chronic pain must be individualized based on a comprehensive understanding of the factors underlying the chronic pain syndrome of each patient.[14]

The Minnesota Multiphasic Personality Inventory (MMPI) has been a standard psychological test to evaluate chronic pain. Most chronic pain patients have elevated scores in the depression and hysteria sectors of the test, as do many pain patients. Strong reliance has been placed on the diagnostic reliability in assessing psychological versus organic pain until recently when many practitioners are unwilling to accept MMPI testing by itself.

The MMPI shows a small percentage of patients with elevated scores who do not benefit as much from treatment and who have continued psychological disturbance. Thus, in the chronic pain population, the entire spectrum of psychological symptoms (reflected in the clinical scores of the MMPI) can be associated with chronic illness and should be treated in the context of an intense, behaviorally-oriented pain management.[15]

In the psychological assessment of chronic pain patients, many workers feel that the MMPI gives less than accurate or even incomplete information. Other tests, more specifically designed to evaluate pain, have been developed and are used with MMPI studies for a more complete evaluation.

The McGill Pain Rating Scale developed by Melzac (a pain management pioneer) is a subjective pain rating scale that amplifies the MMPI.

Rorschach tests the patient's cognitive interpretations in all life experiences, including pain. There is evidence that the MMPI can be "faked," whereas it is believed to be impossible to fake Rorschach testing.

Although the courts vary, more credence ("moral weight") is attached to psychological evaluations using two or more testing techniques. One report states that MMPI combined with Rorschach testing is widely accepted by jurists when administered and interpreted by expert professionals.

§21.16 Pain Drawings

Pain drawings are a valid and often used tool to assess how a patient perceives his or her pain problem and assesses the patient's coping skill when the pain drawing projects pain experience and location.

Examples of pain drawings appear in Figures 21-3 to 21-11.[16]

---

[14] France, *Psychiatric Aspects of Pain,* 5(2) The Clin J Pain 535 (1989).

[15] Herron & Pheasant, *Changes in MMPI After Low Back Surgery,* 7 Spine 591 (1982); Love & Peck, *The MMPI and Psychological Factors in Chronic Low Back Pain,* 28 Pain 1 (1987); Astrom & Uden, *Drawing Out the Cause of Chronic Back Pain When Diagnosis is Difficult,* Intl Back Pain News, Issue 8, Sept 1989, at 4. Loper, *Paralyzed with Pain: Need for Education,* 37 Pain 315 (1989); Lewyn, *Insurer Researches Lower Back Pain,* USA Today, Jan 5, 1989.

[16] McGill, *The Relationship of Minnesota Multiphasic Personality Inventory (MMPI) Profile Clusters to Pain Behaviors,* 6J Behav Med 77 (1983); Naliboff, *MMPI Changes Following Behavioral Treatment of Chronic Low Back Pain,* 35 Pain 271 (1988);

§21.17 Which Back Is Prone to Pain?

In recent years, parameters to assess potential low back patients have emerged. Body build (except gross obesity), body height, age between 18 and 45 years, intelligence, ethnic background, and sex have little predictive value. Back and shoulder girdle muscle mass, strength, and endurance are most predictive. Testing these factors by isokinetic and isometric devices is becoming increasingly popular. Monitoring muscle performance using electromyelographic techniques is an additional help.[17]

§21.18 Failed Back Pain Patient

Several large studies of low back pain patients in which repeat low back surgeries have been carried out indicate poor results. Beyond two operations, more patients are likely to be made worse than helped. In general, in compensation patients the second operation should be regarded as the last chance.

Good results from repeat surgery are associated with patients who achieve at least 6 to 12 months of relief following the previous operation, patients in which sciatica predominates over back pain, and patients with recurrent prolapsed intervertebral discs. Bad results from repeat surgery were associated with scarring and neurolysis, previous infection, and repair of pseudarthrosis.

Psychological and social elements of anxiety, depression, hypochondriasis, conversion mechanisms, and assuming the disability role, and family, employment, and financial concerns contribute substantially to low back pain impairment. All of these entities need evaluation before recommending repeat low back surgery. Most important is rigorous patient selection. Proper surgical indications should be strictly adhered to and all patients should routinely have formal psychological assessment before repeat low back surgery.[18] See "Failed Back Surgery Algorithm," Figure 21-12.

§21.19 Sports Injuries

One of the biggest challenges for physicians treating athletes with spinal injuries is deciding which athletes should be allowed to return to contact sports. When athletes injure themselves in contact sports, they may suffer

---

Bradley, *Multivariate Analyses of the MMPI Profiles of Low Back Patient,* 1 J Behav Med 253 (1978); Herron & Pheasant, *Changes in MMPI After Low Back Surgery,* 7 Spine 591 (1982); Love & Peck, *The MMPI and Psychological Factors in Chronic Low Back Pain,* 28 Pain 1 (1987); Astrom & Uden, *Drawing Out the Cause of Chronic Back Pain When Diagnosis is Difficult,* Intl Back Pain News, Issue 8, Sept 1989, at 4; Loper, *Paralyzed with Pain: Need for Education,* 37 Pain 315 (1989).

[17] Lewyn, *Insurer Reaches Lower Back Pain,* USA Today, Jan 5, 1989.

[18] Bailes & Wilberger, *Managing Spine Injuries Can Be Tricky,* 7 Back Pain Mon 1 (1989).

Figures 21-3 to 21-5

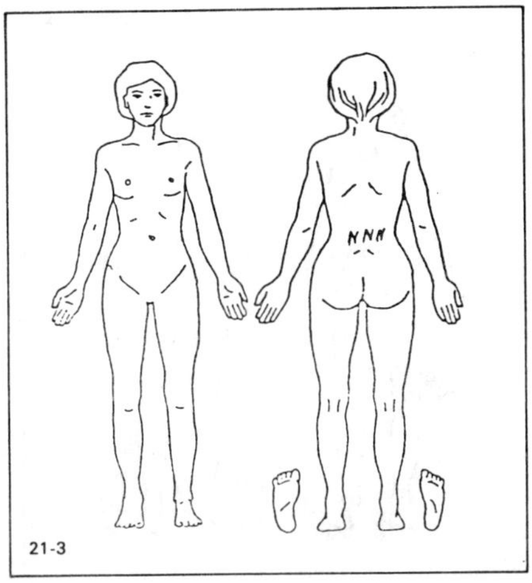

21-3

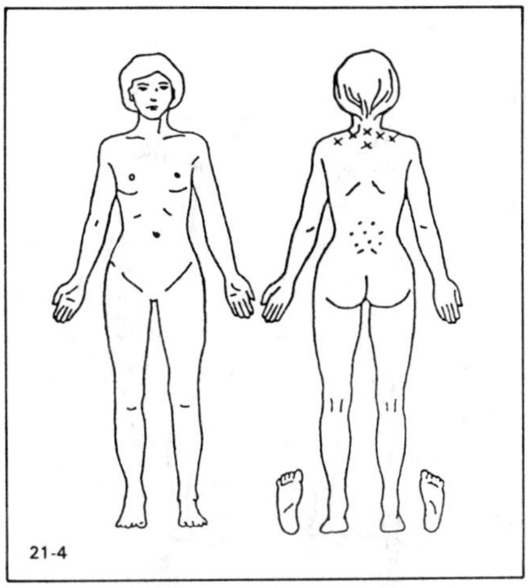

21-4

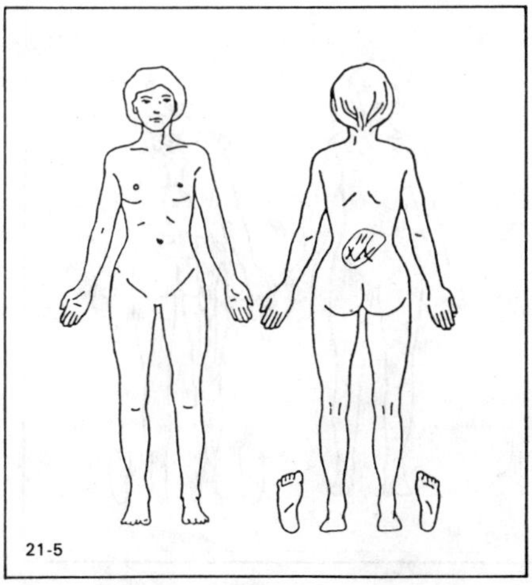

21-5

Organic pain drawings. The pattern is crisp and clear, strictly localized to relevant anatomic structures. Multiple pain symbols and circling of the painful area in Figure 21-5 may indicate nonorganic pain, but is outweighted by a very limited extension within an area commonly afflicted with pain.

Figures 21-6 to 21-8

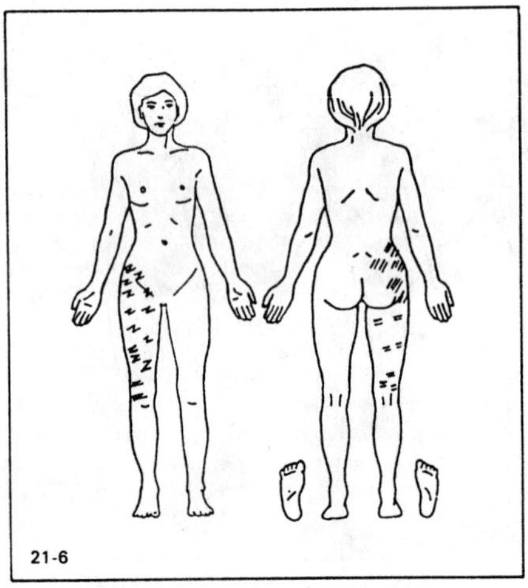

21-6

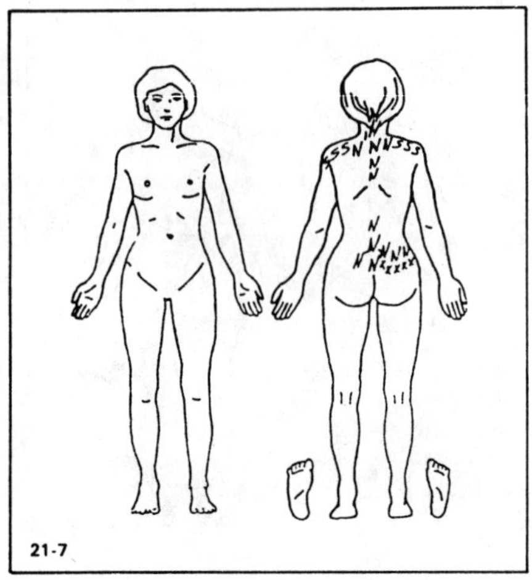

21-7

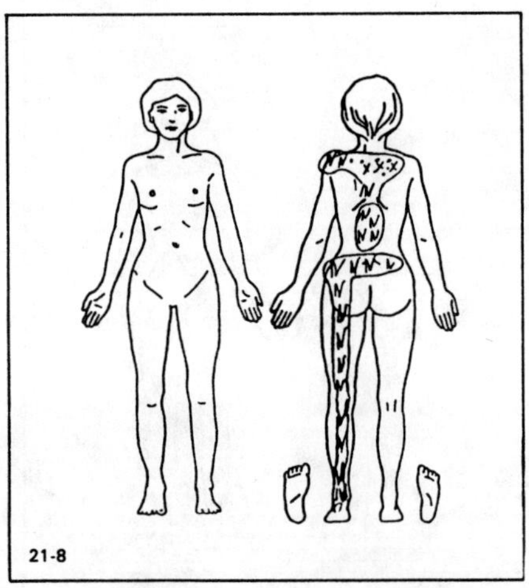

21-8

Possibly nonorganic pain. Pain is fairly anatomic but tends to expand or displays irregular features such as ventral thigh pain in Figure 21-6. Pain radiating down the left leg as in Figure 21-8 could be a perfect representation of a herniated disc but circled areas of pain expanding along the entire vertebral column merit a guarded rating. Multiple pain symbols are used.

Figures 21-9 to 21-11

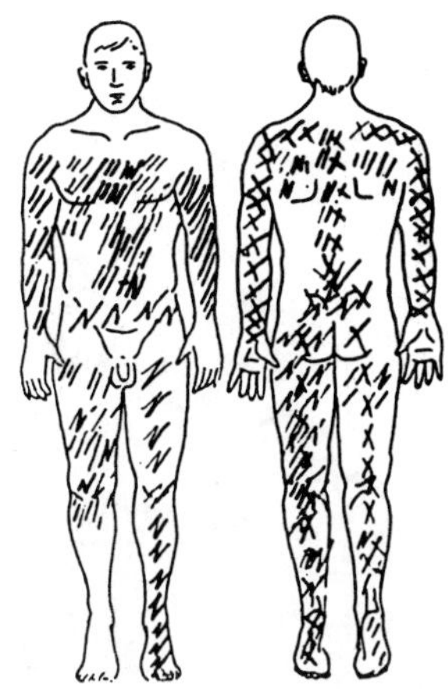

21-9

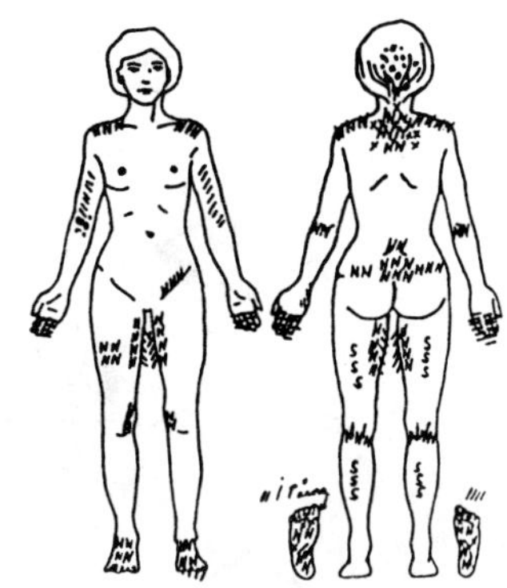

21-10

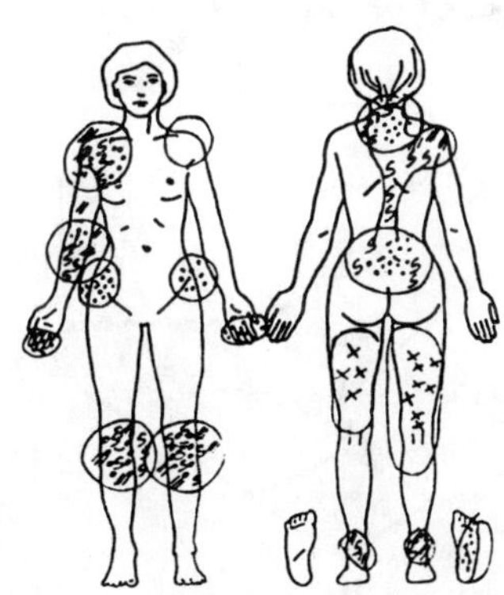

21-11

Nonorganic pain drawings. Observe "total body pain" as in Figure 21-9 or multiple discrete areas of pain distributed in a random or bilateral fashion. Several pain symbols are used, sometimes forming a disorganized pattern. Circled areas (Figure 21-11), explanatory remarks (Figure 21-10), or pain symbols outside the body outline (Figures 21-10 and 21-11) are noteworthy features.

Figure 21-12

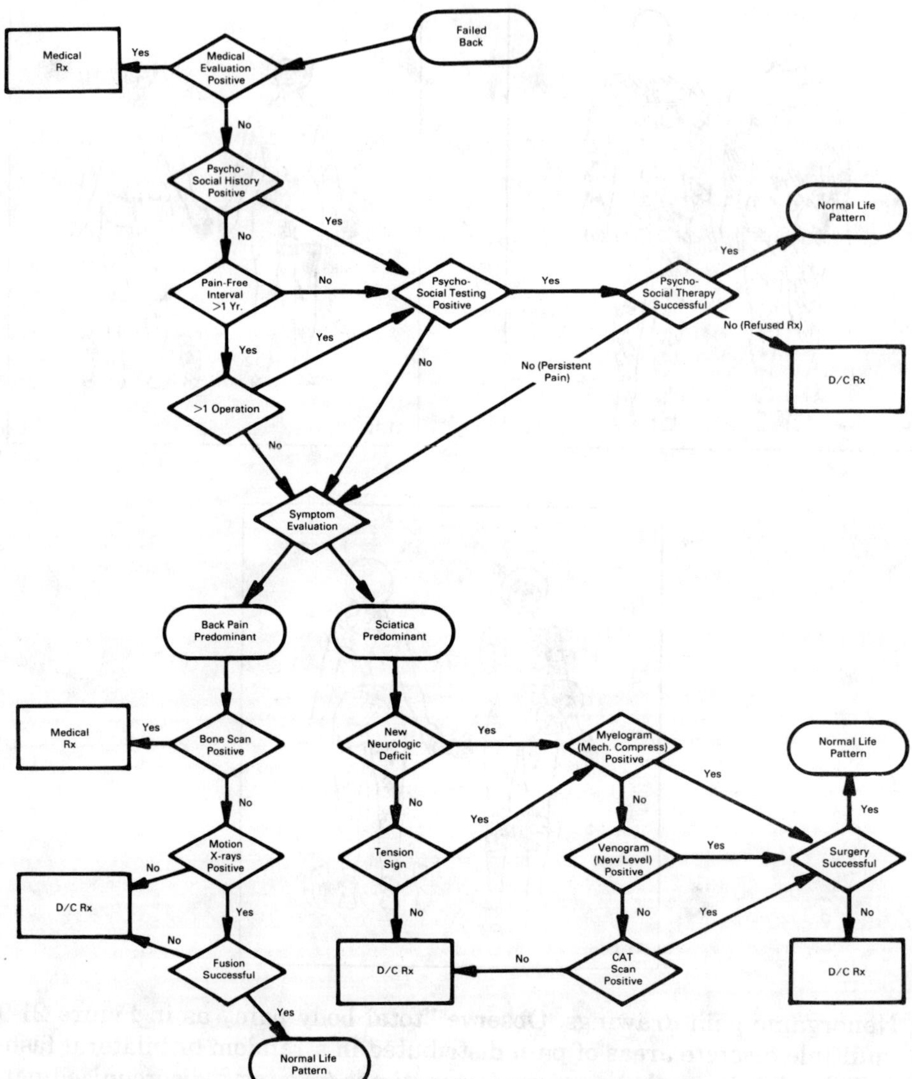

Failed back surgery algorithm. (From: Rothman and Simeone: "The Spine", 1982, The W.B. Saunders Company, West Washington Square, Philadelphia, PA 19105, page: 638: *Reprinted with Permission.*)

transient paralytic symptoms, such as quadriplegia, paresthesia, or hemiparesis. Some of these insults may become permanent and some become "at risk" for reinjury. Many such patients will have normal x-rays, CT scans, and MRI studies, yet have impairing temporary neurological findings. Trauma to the spinal cord produces these symptoms with stretch, twist, concussion, or other mechanics.

The excessively narrowed spine seen in developmental or congenital spinal stenosis will set the stage for injuries. Disc injury with or without herniation may be produced by athletic injury.

Most athletes who have not sustained a fracture or dislocation in the spine and who do not have spinal canal compromising lesions can return to contact sports after a healing period and, most importantly, after adequate soft tissue reconditioning. The sports medicine philosophy of rehabilitation is perhaps the most effective tool to get the athlete (or any injured worker) back to the game (work). To return to contact activities depends on many variables, including "common sense" goals, the responsibility of the athlete, and the competence of coaching and training staff.[19]

§21.20 Somatization Disorder

Health is accorded a positive value in Western society, yet many persons choose illness as a way of life. This choice is usually, but not always, unconsciously determined, and the patient will state that health is preferable and seek medical care.

Somatization is a process in which the body is used for psychological purposes or for personal gain. Any one symptom or group of symptoms may serve one or more functions at the same time. These may include intra-psychic conflicts, interpersonal relationships, and responses to social, environmental, or economic problems.

Examples of the psychological uses of somatization include (1) displacement of unpleasant emotions into physical symptoms, such as a preoccupation with bowel function instead of experiencing underlying depression, or (2) the use of the symptom to communicate, by virtue of symbolic means, an idea or emotion, such as hysterical paraplegia or hysterical blindness to symbolize and communicate the feeling of helplessness. The alleviation of guilt through suffering, such as a pain syndrome experienced after death of someone in the patient's life for whom the patient had mixed emotional feelings, is another example.

Personal gains may be obtained by somatization, and these include (1) the ability to manipulate relationships, such as "Not tonight dear, I have a headache," or (2) the intention to obtain release from duties and responsibilities such as absence at the place of employment or an excuse for not completing housework. Other examples are financial gain, such as disability payments

---

[19] Bailes & Wilberger, Managing Spine Injuries Can Be Tricky, 7 Back Pain Mon 1 (1989).

or compensation payments for pain after a neck sprain, or perhaps a relationship or sympathy from another person such as concern and worry elicited in response to skin lesions that were surreptitiously self-induced. (*See* Appendix 21-1, Case 2.)

Intrapersonal and psychic gains from somatization are similar to those observed in the factual organic illness. It is not unusual for persons with diseases of organic origin to capitalize on their illness to serve a variety of personal needs. However, there are some individuals who repetitively use their bodies as a means of handling life stresses. A person who uses physical symptoms as a lifestyle has a somatoform disorder such as hypochondriasis.

Although little attention is paid to the psychological ramifications of somatization in medical school training, patients with these symptoms occupy a significantly large proportion of the practicing physician's time.

In several orthopedic studies, it was found that 43 to 50 per cent of patients seen had organic disease alone, 13 per cent had organic and psychological problems, 6 per cent had no diagnosis, and 38 per cent had no disease, only psychological problems. When these patients were surgical patients, it was found that 66 per cent had organic diseases, only 16 per cent had both organic and psychological symptoms, 13 per cent had no diagnosis, and 5 per cent had only psychological symptoms. In another large study of nearly 700 patients, 37 per cent had organic disease, 40 per cent had a diagnosis of functional disorders such as depression or psychogenic back pain, and a diagnosis of functional disorder was implied additionally in another 23 per cent.

In another study, it was found that 50 per cent of all illnesses and injury episodes were accounted for by less than 25 per cent of the population. Illness or injury tended to occur in clusters, and it was estimated that at least one-third of the illnesses were influenced to a significant degree by the patient's attempt to adapt to events and situations that he or she was presently encountering, frequently by somatization.

Another study of telephone company employees (Hinkle et al., 1956) revealed that, over a 20-year period, 10 per cent of the men surveyed experienced 34 per cent of the total sickness disability—that is, days off work—while the healthiest 10 per cent experienced only 1 per cent of sickness disability. The finding that illness does not occur in random distribution has also been confirmed in studies of military populations, where there is a consistent finding that a relatively small proportion of naval personnel account for a disproportionately large percentage of all sickbay visits.

The cost of medical care is an increasing portion of the gross national product in the United States. In 1980, according to the United States Bureau of Census, $200 billion was expended. If one assumes that 10 per cent of all medical care, not including psychiatric treatment, is provided to persons with no organic disease, then the total cost would be $20 billion yearly. That figure is for medical care only and does not include disability payments.

Viewed in another way, if 25 per cent of the people who use 50 per cent of the medical services reduced their medical care to the average rate of the rest of the population, overall medical services would be reduced by 25 per cent. The point is that a large percentage of medical care is directed toward persons without disease and/or those who are over-utilizing services. These services continue to be offered in a fashion consistent with a disease model because these patients do not have organic disease, and it is not unreasonable to propose that the treatment they have is not very effective. Somatization is indeed a large industry.

American medicine has increasingly become tied to technology. Tests for procedures such as organ transplants and CT or MRI brain studies are now commonplace. Associated with these new technical skills is the accelerated cost of medical care. There are other surveys suggesting that less technically-sophisticated treatment or approaches may have equally satisfactory results in this group of patients. Increased attention by the orthopedist or examining physician to the relatively neglected somatization disorders becomes important in evaluation and treatment of patients. Despite knowledge of somatization, physicians appear hesitant to alter the manner in which they practice medicine. Treatment failures, particularly surgical treatment and, more particularly, surgical treatment of low back complaints, have their basis, in part, in the surgeon's failure to recognize and understand the ramifications of somatization and other psychological impingements on the patient's illness. Failure to recognize the substantial effect of somatization on the prognosis of the injured patient by the examining and treating physician ultimately does a disservice to both the patient and society.

There is a prevalence of somatization by patients with back pain. In the evaluation of the low back or neck/shoulder or headache patient, it is necessary to have or obtain a reliable feel of the patient's psychological status. Somatization disorders are common in daily medical practice but are frequently unrecognized. Somatization Disorder (SD) is defined in the Diagnostic and Statistical Manual of Mental Disorders, 3rd Edition (DSM111) as a syndrome whose criteria include symptoms onset before age 30 and complaints from a prescribed list of at least 14 unexplained symptoms for women and 12 for men. These symptoms must not be caused by alcohol or drugs and must not be the side effects of medication. The symptoms must have caused the patient to consult a physician, to change his or her daily routine, and to take medication other than aspirin. Resolution of, or continued recognition of, the effect of the physiological ramifications to the patient is an essential part of the evaluation and treatment.[20]

§21.21 Pain Treatment with Medications

The treatment of acute pain is directed toward the cause of pain, combined with pain relief methods to make the acute pain experiences more comfortable during the healing phase. These methods include use of appropriate medication, prescribed with full knowledge of its effects and side effects. There is much in the medical literature regarding the dosage of potentially

---

[20] DeGruy, *Somatization Disorder in a University Hospital*, 25 J Fam Prac 579 (1987); Ford, The Somatizing Disorders: Illness as a Way of Life (1984).

addicting medications being too liberally prescribed. This issue is, in some areas, nearly a discipline directed by custom. A physician may have a strong bias toward a duty not to allow addiction, even at the expense of patient comfort. This duty is reasonable, but is so engraved that the fear of addiction outweighs reasonable therapeutic dosing.

There is evidence that a large percentage of patients with postoperative pain, post-traumatic pain, severe pain associated with visceral disease, or post-burns are inadequately relieved by treatment. Moreover, many patients with non-malignant chronic pain do not respond to the usual medical therapy, and an impressive number are exposed to a high risk of iatrogenic complications, including drug toxicity, drug dependence, or multiple operations. A significant number of these patients give up medical care and consult "quacks," who not only deplete their economic resources but also do them harm.

Since the introduction of curare into clinical practice, muscular paralysis has mistakenly been interpreted as a calm and painless state. Often, curare-like drugs are administered to ventilate patients to facilitate patient respiration and nursing care with administering concomitant analgesic and/or anti-anxiety agents. This unkindly and negligently allows the patient to suffer, and may well reduce survival chances.

Benzodiazepines have no analgesic effect, so while patients are paralyzed and may be sedated, they may experience significant pain. Nursing surveillance and physician acumen must extend to patient comfort as well as diligence against mechanical failure.

In one large hospital, there were serious pharmacologic misconceptions among ICU staff members regarding the effects of neuromuscular blockers and benzodiazapines. It is probable that the same problem exists throughout the country.[21]

Patients with cancer pain fare no better. There are numerous reports indicating that many patients with advanced cancer live their last months with unrelieved severe pain.[22]

Cancer patients may experience acute or chronic pain caused by tumor infiltration of pain-sensitive structures or related to surgery, radiation, and chemotherapy. Acute bone pain is a common cause of intractable pain in cancer patients, with or without the associated neurologic deficits resulting from tumor metastasis to bone and contiguous neural structures, such as large peripheral nerve trunks or the spinal cord. Treatment of bone pain most often involves the concomitant use of focal radiation therapy and analgesic drugs, particularly steroids, NSAIDS (sometimes combined with opioids), and adjuvant analgesic agents, such as levodopa and calcitonin. Pharmacologic therapy, however, is not always efficacious and may have significant side effects. Less commonly, invasive therapies such as resection of

---

[21] DeGruy, *Somatization Disorder in a University Hospital,* 25 J Fam Prac 579 (1987).

[22] Bonica, *Pain, Discomfort and Humanitarian Care,* J Ref Proc, National Conference at National Institute of Health, Bethesda (1979); Bonica, *In Mechanism of Pain and Analgesic Compounds* (R.F. Beers & E.J. Bassett eds 1979).

vertebral body tumor with spinal reconstruction or pituitary ablation and intraventricular opioid administration (for diffuse bone pain) are offered.[23]

§21.22 Particular Medications

There are at least 20 NSAIDS under investigation by the Food and Drug Administration, some of which hold promise to overcome undesirable effects of narcotic medications used for pain control. Some are injectable and others can be used transdermally.

It appears now and in the foreseeable future that dependence lability and analgesia are linked at specific brain receptor sites, meaning that, for most patients, effective pain control by narcotic agents carries the risk of undesirable side effects such as addiction. Close monitoring is the standard.[24]

Because the intensity of pain (mild, moderate, and severe) is critical to the appropriate choice of drugs, one should avoid unnecessarily potent drugs in situations where weaker analgesics are sufficient. Non-opioids (e.g., acetaminophen) are used in mild/weak opioids (codeine or codeine derivatives) and their combination with non-opoids are used in moderate pain; strong opioids (morphine and related drugs) are used in more severe pain.

A thorough understanding of specific pain syndromes is of particular importance in identifying the situations where the initial use of co-analgesics and/or analgesic adjuvants is warranted. These medications include non-steroidal anti-inflammatory agents, mild tranquilizer medication, and muscle relaxant chemicals.

Patients with severe non-malignant pain who fail to be relieved by non-opioid medication and other analgesic chemicals are considered for long-term opioid medication when treated by informed physicians who are familiar with chronic pain management as a subspecialty in medical practice. These physicians maintain that addiction, tolerance, and toxicity in appropriate patients are exaggerated. These adverse expectations have persisted in spite of accumulating evidence that these complications seldom occur. There is no known cure for chronic pain and many patients continue to suffer despite the "best" treatment offered. Extensive experience has been gained in the use of long-term narcotic medication in cancer patients, so the long-term risks of this type of therapy is known. There is much negative input in treating chronic pain patients with opioids, as voiced by the current "war on drugs" social climate.

The toughest issue for treating this type of patient is the term "addiction," because the wrong definition of addiction is often used. Addiction—in some circles, "psychological dependence," is a psychological and behavioral syndrome characterized by compulsive drug use, overwhelming interest in securing a supply, and recidivism after drug detoxification, with withdrawal symptoms during detoxification.

---

[23] Payne, *Pharmacologic Managment Cancer Pain,* 5 Clin J Med 543 (1989).

[24] Kantor, *The Management of Pain by Pharmacological Agents,* 5 The Clin J Pain 121 (1989).

Among most medical patients, abberant behavior such as drug hoarding, acquisition of drugs from multiple sources, drug sales, and unsanctioned dose escalation, suggesting drug addiction, is seldom observed.

Current data suggest that causes of addiction lie more in the psychopathology of the patient and the environment than in the reinforcing qualities of the drug.

§21.23 Treatment without Narcotic Medication

In the management of benign pain with medication, there are a number of narcotic and non-narcotic analgesics available for oral and parenteral administration, but less than one-half of the pharmacies stock all of them on a routine basis. Despite the utility of oral morphine and methadone in severe cancer pain, less potent compounds are used for the "routine" pain complaints.

The choice of drug should be based on assessment of the patient's medical status and a thorough assessment of pain. The medical status of the patient is important in the choice of drugs in that the actions of certain analgesics are more confounded by disease than others. The side effect potential of certain drugs may be altered by renal dysfunction—the excitatory effect of meperidine on the central nervous system, for example.

§21.24 Narcotics in Pain Control

Physician prescriptions have been under surveillance for years regarding narcotics and other mind-altering substances. The general rule is to assess each case on an individual basis, using guidelines but considering what are called the "usual and customary standards based on patient diagnosis." A notice was recently issued by the State of Washington Department of Health regarding narcotic prescription for chronic pain patients. This is a patient group that the orthopedist frequently sees. In September 1987, the Medical Disciplinary Board issued the following bulletin to physicians licensed in the State of Washington:

> CHRONIC PAIN
>
> Many cases reviewed by the Washington State Medical Disciplinary Board involve inappropriate prescribing of controlled substances. A significant number of these are related to the use of narcotics as a method to manage chronic pain. During fiscal year 1987 the Board experienced nearly a 100 per cent increase in disciplinary actions related to prescribing of controlled drugs for chronic pain. The Board does not recognize repeated prescribing of controlled drugs as appropriate therapy for chronic pain.[25]

---

[25] *Policy Statement,* State of Washington Department of Health (1989).

Accepted guidelines for treating selected chronic pain patients with opioid drugs include:

1. This therapy should be considered only after all other reasonable attempts of pain control have failed using non-narcotic analgesics.
2. A history of substance abuse is a relative contraindication.
3. A single physician should be responsible for all drug prescriptions.
4. Patients should be given informed consent before starting therapy; points to be covered include recognition of the low risk of psychological dependence as an outcome, potential for cognitive impairment with drug use alone and in combination with sedative/hypnotics, and an understanding by women that children born when the mother is an opioid maintenance therapy are likely to be dependent at birth.
5. After drug selection, the dose should be given on an around-the-clock basis; several weeks should be agreed to as an initial period of drug titration (establishing the least effective drug dose).
6. Failure to achieve at least partial analgesia at relatively low initial doses in a non-tolerant patient raises a question about the potential treatability of the pain syndrome with opioids.
7. Emphasis should be given to attempts to capitalize on improved analgesia by gains in physical and social function.
8. In addition to the daily dose determined initially, patients should be permitted to escalate the dose temporarily on days of increased pain; two methods are acceptable: (a) prescription of an additional 4 to 6 "rescue doses" to be taken as needed during the month, or (b) instruction that one or two extra doses may be taken on any day, but must be followed by an equal reduction of dose on subsequent days.
9. The patient must be seen, and the drug prescribed, on a monthly basis.
10. Exacerbations of pain not effectively treated by transient small doses: increased doses are best managed in hospital where dose escalation is appropriate and can be observed closely. Return to the baseline dose can be accomplished in a controlled environment.
11. Evidence of drug hoarding, acquisition of drugs from other physicians, uncontrolled dose escalation, or other abherrent behavior should be followed by tapering and discontinuance of opioid maintenance therapy.[26]

In industrialized countries throughout the world, much greater quantities of narcotic medications are used than in less-developed countries.

---

[26] Portenoy & Foley, *Chronic Use of Opioid Analgesics in NonMalignant Pain: Report of 38 Cases,* 25 Pain 171 (1986); Portenoy, *Opioid Therapy in the Management of Chronic Low Back Pain,* Interdisciplinary Rehabilitation of Low Back Pain, (C.D. Tollison ed 1989).

§21.25 Psychological Treatment of Pain

Using a total patient approach to the orthopedic patient includes dealing with the psychological aspect of the problem. Pain-prone patients must be oriented to the nature and treatment of their condition. Patients must understand that pain is not entirely or even substantially nociceptive (due to mechanical factors). They must learn that a chemical imbalance is involved in pain perception, that tension and depression tend to be invariably associated with chronic pain and play an important role. Additionally, antidepressant medication can be helpful in working through the psychological ramifications of the pain syndrome. The basic principle of the behavioral approach to chronic pain control (encourage activity and de-emphasize pain) may be combined with antidepressant medication. Explaining the treatment to and involving the next of kin and significant others in the treatment is effective. Distraction from the pain in the form of activities carried out at a reasonable pace and continuing to work in spite of pain should be encouraged. Modifying the work environment to adapt to the physical impairment should be part of the therapy plan, along with vocational rehabilitation in many cases. In work hardening programs, progressive work activities similar to the patient's job become part of a conditioning rehabilitation. Often, however, duplication of the job activity leading to injury may set the stage for ease of re-injury. At this time, there is a degree of biased disagreement.[27]

§21.26 Patient-Controlled Analgesia (PCA)

Many orthopedic patients fail to gain satisfactory analgesia from the regularly scheduled administration of intramuscular analgesic medication. Patient-controlled analgesia (PCA) has become more popular.

The effectiveness of patient-controlled analgesia (PCA) depends on the patient's appropriate response to pain with subsequent reinforcement (narcotic injection). Each patient has psychological characteristics that modify response to treatment. Patients, particularly women, with external locus of control had higher levels of pain and greater dissatisfaction with PCA. Those with an internal locus of control predicted lower pain controls and increased satisfaction with PCA.

Chronic pain patients spent more time in "moderate" pain than acute pain patients. While patients with a history of chronic pain had higher scores on an hourly pain scale compared to acute pain patients, there is no difference between the two groups on overall testing measures (a psychological measurement method). Most chronic pain patients reported the same pain levels

---

[27] The Nuprin Report; Blumer & Heilbronn, *Treatment Outcome of 1,000 Patients with the Pain Prone Disorder,* 14 Psychiatric Ann 796 (1984); Engel, *'Psychogenic' Pain and the Pain Prone Patient,* 26 Am J Med 899 (1959); Fordyce, Learning Process in Pain, Psychology of Pain (R. Sternback, ed 1978); Fordyce, Behavioral Methods for Chronic Pain and Illness (1976); Krystal, *Alexithymia and Psychotherapy,* 33 Am J Psychother 17 (1979).

with PCA as they did during its use, in contrast to acute pain patients who were higher than during PCA use.

Children learn use of PCA quickly, making it an effective and efficient way to manage acute/chronic pain problems.

Effective postoperative pain control contributes to patient comfort and facilitates healing. The tendency for physicians/surgeons to underuse analgesic often does the patient a disservice, prolonging convalescence. Use of PCA requires skilled nursing personnel and cooperative patients. See Tables 21-1 to 21-4 for typical hospital guides in using PCA.

Table 21-1
Patient-Controlled Analgesia (PCA)

History of Pain Control

A patient who receives a p.r.n. pain medication by intramuscular injection inevitably gets caught up in a cycle of alternative pain and analgesia. He or she feels pain and asks for the medication. About 30 to 60 minutes later, he or she experiences a period of analgesia. This may last for 30 minutes to one hour. For the next hour or so, the patient will experience a reawakening of the pain (from the analgesia or over-sedated feeling to one of discomfort, and then to full-blown pain). Then, at some point, a pain medication is again requested, starting the cycle over.

Variables that have to be considered are:

1. How long was the time of the onset of pain and the response of the nurse to medicate, and then that patient's response to the medication administered. In other words, how long did it take for the patient to absorb the medication?
2. Each patient's management, or their pain tolerance
3. Levels that occur in either a peak or a valley, without a constant type level

Purpose

PCA has been designed to overcome the above disadvantages, which allows for better pain control by giving small doses at short intervals, stabilizing the serum narcotic concentrations and allowing the patient to maintain therapeutic levels. The PCA system delivers medications intravenously, so relief comes faster than with the I.M. route. Because the patient controls his or her own pain, he or she does not have to depend on the nurse availability.

Considerations

The PCA unit includes an infusion pump, a timing device, a display panel, and a call cord. To use it, first set the dose and the time interval. For example, a patient may need 1 mg of morphine sulfate in dilution every 6 minutes. This would recommend the maximum dose allowed. After the dose and time interval has been set, the patient would be instructed to push the button at the end of a cord whenever he or she feels pain. This will make a bell sound, and one dose of medication is released by the machine into the I.V.

tubing which has been inserted in the patient's vein. As long as the patient has not pushed the button in the last 6 minutes, he or she will receive the medication. If he or she has already received the medication less than 6 minutes before, the bell will sound and the patient will receive a placebo effect. The unit display panel tells you how long the patient has been using the system, how many times he or she has pushed the button, and how many doses the patient has actually received. The panel also shows you how much medication is left. It is tamper-proof. To change the interval and dose settings, you need the key which is kept on the narcotic ring. If the patient tries to change the settings, an alarm will sound and the display panel will give the message "Unauthorized entry attempt."

Table 21-2
Policy for Use of Patient-Controlled Analgesia (PCA) Pump and Nursing Accountabilities

Definition

PCA is a safe and controlled method of patient-induced intravenous delivery of analgesic drugs utilizing the PCA infuser.

Purpose

The PCA is used primarily for the control of postoperative pain. Other suitable candidates are as follows:

1. Patients in need of parenteral analgesic treatment
2. Trauma patients who have a clear sensorium
3. Patients suffering from chronic pain, such as those with a terminal disease
4. Male or female patients between the ages of 18 and 70
5. Mentally alert patients; they must be able to understand and comply with instructions and procedures
6. Patients without a history of allergies to the proposed analgesic (morphine)

Policy Responsibilities

Physicians are responsible for ordering the PCA pump. The order must include:

1. Intravenous keep-open fluid compatible with analgesic (D5W or N.S.)
2. Analgesic: Morphine Lmg/ml prefilled syringe
3. Dosage to be delivered: MI given each time the patient activates PCA
4. Frequency: The interval between injections (LOCKOUT)
5. Four-hour limit: The maximum amount that can be delivered in a 4-hour period
6. Loading dose optional

Pharmacy

The pharmacy is responsible for acquiring the medication and making it part of the floor stock narcotic, and for:

1. Reconciling the usage
2. Disposing of any narcotic left in the cylinder that is returned by nurses for disposal
3. Making the charge for the drug

Nursing

1. A charge nurse (preferably an R.N.) will be responsible for instructing the patient/family about the PCA pump, including the purpose, benefits, technique, alarms, safety mechanism and the need for the IV line; where possible, these will be done preoperatively
2. Two nurses, one of which must be an R.N., are responsible for initiating the pump and setting the program according to the physician's orders; from that point forward, the medication nurse who is responsible for control medications will be responsible
3. If the PCA is discontinued, then the med nurse will document the used/unused portion on the flow sheet and the narcotic sign-out sheet, then return the unused portion to the pharmacy
4. Maintain the pump key on the narcotic key ring; this key is counted with the narcotic count
5. All patients who are on a pump will have that balance of medication left in the pump charted on the flow sheet by the off-going and the on-coming medication nurse, and so documented
6. Maintain an open IV line
7. The PCA tubing is changed at least every 48 hours and should be tagged accordingly
8. Monitoring the patient every four hours; this is documented on the flow sheet as to the following:
    a. Sedation level
    b. Analgesic level—record the patient's response to pain
    c. Total doses of drug delivered since last notation and the amount, in mg, delivered
    d. Signed name, according to that on nursing license
9. Vital signs are to be taken at least every four hours and more often if fresh post-op
10. Responsible for the control substance, as with all control substance protocol

Recovery Room

1. Will initiate the use of the pump according to orders on fresh post-op patients
2. May need to give the loading dose if so ordered
3. Follow physician's orders according to dosage, volume, and interval, and set machine
4. Responsible for keeping an adequate supply of medication in narcotic inventory
5. Responsible for acquiring a machine for ready hookup when ordered
6. Stamp the flow sheet according to procedure
7. Signing out the medication, as with any other control substance
8. Responsible for signing over the pump to the floor during transfer and also the key

Nurse Who Notes the Initial Order for the PCA Pump

1. Notes the order/stamps the flow sheet
2. Flags the chart for PCA Pump
3. Notifies the charge nurse, who will orientate the patient to the PCA pump
4. Either puts the flow sheet in the front of the chart for Recovery if the patient is to have the device started in that area, or places it in the MAR medication cardex
5. The charge nurse after the instruction will get the patient to sign the bottom of the flow sheet

Patient's Responsibility

1. The patient will have a thorough understanding of the concept
2. Must be able to push the button as the medication is needed
3. Must sign the permit of understanding the PCA system prior to the initiation of the pump

Table 21-3
Procedure for Initiating the Patient-Controlled Analgesia (PCA) Pump

Equipment

1. Lifecare patient-controlled analgesia (PCA) infuser
2. PCA set stored on an exchange cart in the recovery room
3. Primary IV line
4. Prefilled vials of analgesic (stored in the narcotic cabinet on the unit or in the recovery room

Initiation of the Pump

1. Requires a physician's order, preferably preoperatively, which includes:
   a. Intravenous fluid compatible with analgesic ordered
   b. Analgec concentration (morphine sulfate)
   c. Dosage/ml given each time the PCA patient activates the PCA patient control
   d. Four-hour limit—total amount that can be delivered by the PCA pump in a 4-hour period
2. A charge nurse (preferably the R.N.) will explain the concept to the patient before the PCA pump is started; if a surgical patient, this would be done preoperatively
3. The patient is requested after the explanation to sign the flow sheet for the pump service
4. Recovery room personnel will initiate the use of the PCA pump on all surgical patients; this machine will in the onset be used only for postoperative patients
5. The recovery room R.N. will give the loading dose where ordered by the surgeon or the anesthesiologist
6. There must be an established IV line to act as the carrier for the medication; PCA cannot be used with a heparin lock; the line must be a primary line that is compatible with the analgesic ordered
7. The narcotic that is used in the PCA pump is signed out in the recovery room or the unit in which the medication is being used
8. To initiate the pump, the RR nurse or the unit nurse will sign out the narcotic in the usual method; the flow sheet will be started and contain the patient's name, room number, physician, drug ordered, date and time the syringe was started, and your signature; this flow sheet is kept in the med profile and is to be charted on from there, unless ordered otherwise
9. Enter the patient's name on the narcotic sheet in the usual sign-out method
10. Connect the PCA tubing and prime the set using the prescribed analgesic
11. Document on the PCA flow sheet that is kept with the MAR in the med cardex
12. Administer a loading dose, if ordered, and then set pump according to the physician's order
13. When the patient is transferred from the recovery room to the patient's bed, the flow sheet will be on the front of the patient's chart; this will be signed by the nurse bringing the patient to the floor as to how much of the medication was given in the recovery room and how much is left in the machine

14. The key to the machine will then be given to the receiving nurse, who will sign the flow sheet as to the amount of medication left in the machine
15. The receiving nurse should be the medication nurse, who will then carry this key and care for this medication delivery for the remainder of that shift
16. When the vial of the analgesic is empty, record the amount of analgesic delivered, the total number of doses, and your signature; discard the vial; if a new vial is being initiated, start a new narcotic flow sheet and then remove the the previous sheet and put this in the patient's chart under "Medications"
17. Partially-full vials that have been discontinued are to be sent to the pharmacy for wasting; a notation is to be made of the amount used and the amount returned to the pharmacy; this notation is made on the flow sheet and on the sign-out narcotic sheet (on the sheet, it would be the same documentation as any other wasted control medication, the only difference being that the remaining solution is returned to the pharmacy)
18. When the PCA pump is discontinued, the infusion set must be taken to the med room or to any sink, with the contents in the tube drained into the sink and then washed down the drain
19. Remember to document well on the flow sheet; this includes an entry on the flow sheet at least every four hours, with more documentation as needed to assess the level of analgesia
20. WHEN COUNTING THE NARCOTICS AT THE END OF THE SHIFT, THE MEDICATION NURSE REPORTING OFF AND THE ONE REPORTING ON GOES AND CHECKS THE PUMP AND SIGNS OFF THE AMOUNT USED AND THE AMOUNT IN THE MACHINE; THIS BECOMES PART OF THE NARCOTIC COUNT-OUT PROCEDURE

Table 21-4
Patient-Controlled Analgesia (PCA) Patient Education Plan

Purpose

The success of the PCA delivery system depends on the patient's ability to use the device. A thorough explanation and demonstration of how it works is essential. If it is to be used to manage postoperative pain, then the system is to be explained before surgery so that the patient has a clear mind and comprehends the management points.

1. Do not mention the time interval. Just stress that he or she should push the button as often as necessary to relieve pain. Explain that the patient may not be completely free of pain, but should be comfortable.
2. The charge nurse must inform the patient of the PCA concept (after it has been ordered by the physician) and the infuser operation prior

to installation of the PCA pump. This should be done before surgery. This should allow the patient to ask questions as you share this information. This should allay fears and apprehension.

3. Have the patient sign the written statement of instruction on the bottom of the PCA flow sheet behind the MAR in the patient's Cardex.

In this, the patient is able to control the amount of medication given both as to dose and timing, but the apparatus is set so that excessive doses of either Morphine or Demerol, which are the more commonly used drugs at this time, cannot occur.

The traditional method of administering analgesic drugs is in moderate doses separated by structured periods of time in the hospital or other environments, such as nursing home extended care facilities. A nurse usually gives drugs orally or parenterally, either IM or IV, only when the patient requests it and then only if sufficient time has passed since the last dose, in compliance with the physician's order.

Physicians skilled in pain management have repeatedly pointed out that pain medication is most effective and used in lesser doses when given on a regular schedule, not on patient demand. Physicians are often guided in giving orders for pain medication by concerns for addiction and overdose which may relieve the respiratory depression or other life-saving events.

Additionally, nurses are typically sensitive to inducing addiction and are fearful of administering an overdose, even though their actions are within the parameters of physician orders. For these reasons, the patient is often undertreated for a pain problem. This undertreatment perhaps reflects inadequate understanding on the part of the prescribing physician or the delivering nursing personnel.

Patient-controlled analgesia (PCA) was devised to transfer responsibility for pain relief from the nurse to the patient, using an electronic or mechanical means to safeguard against overdose. The technique uses an IV access to which a PCA device is attached. This is loaded with a narcotic analgesic and is activated by the patient when pain or discomfort arises to an intolerable level. Morphine or Demerol are the usual analgesic agents. The device is programmed with a lock-out, a timer where no drug will be delivered by activating a switch normally used to inject the dose. Other features available on some PCA machines include programming for dose activation and total dose for an extended period of time—four to five hours.

Initial studies show that PCA is enthusiastically received by patients. Comments were uniformly favorable compared to other forms of analgesia the patients experienced. More recently, careful studies have compared the efficacy of PCA in achieving successful analgesia to IM administration of narcotic analgesia and lumbar epidural administration. The findings were (1) better analgesia was obtained from epidural injection narcotics with their potentially serious side effects, such as respiratory depression, (2) patient-controlled analgesia works uniformly well, and (3) traditional routes of administration of doses are usually inadequate, leaving the patient with significant periods of pain.

After the intermittent technique for PCA was established, continuous mode techniques were designed to meet the theoretical need to maintain a narcotic blood level. Break-through pain was treated by patient activation by the PCA bolus mode.

In the use of PCA, there is a difficulty in assessing the changes in narcotic metabolism which occur in both normal and ill persons. With specific delivery rate, it may be acceptable for the patient's pain need. However, changes in the patient's metabolism may cause slowing of narcotic dissipation rate in the blood resulting from accumulation of narcotic and insidious onset of adverse effects. The patient becomes somnolent and continues to receive continuous infusion of narcotics, even though the pain threshold has been overcome. Nurses and attendants may presume the patient's need for pain relief is satisfied and reduce their attentiveness accordingly. This cycle continues with infusion of narcotics and decreased attention until the patient reaches the extreme of respiratory depression or cardiac function depression, and disaster follows. The continuous infusion mode patient monitored is potentially dangerous unless the drug in use has no likelihood of accumulation in blood or tissue. If the continuous infusion mode is selected, the nursing attention to the patient must be consistent, persistent, and vigilant, with the caregivers understanding the signs and symptoms the patient may exhibit when too much narcotic has been given. Special in-service training must be given. In some larger hospitals, there is a pain control service generally headed by a registered nurse trained in anesthesia techniques. The principal function of such a nurse is to supervise ongoing in-service instructions to nursing personnel as well as physician staff.

Several lawsuits involving PCA and altered narcotic toxicity have arisen. In these cases, the physician, the nurse, and the manufacturer of the device have been named defendants. A few cases have been settled; others are in various stages of litigation. A thorough understanding of narcotic pharmacology and what factors are important to evaluation of PCA negligence becomes a duty to each professional that deals with PCA. The following is paraphrased from a large hospital anesthesia in-service training in the use of PCA.

1. Pharmacology: Morphine is an opiate (narcotic) analgesia. It interacts with opiate receptors of the central nervous system (CNS) and other tissues. It may cause intense itching. Analgesia occurs with altering other senses or mental function. Antitussive effect (cough suppressant effect) occurs at lower doses than analgesic effect.
2. In treatment of acute pain, tolerance and dependence are not a problem when the right dose and frequency are used in postoperative settings. The goal is pain relief. Continuous infusion and on-demand analgesic can improve pain control. Unacceptable side effects necessitate change to another opioid drug.

3. In treating chronic pain, distinguish between terminal and non-terminal pain. For terminal pain, adjust the dose for optimal analgesia without concern for possible dependence. For non-terminal pain, use as a last resort, because tolerance dependence and addiction can happen. Goals are (1) pain prevention—not pain relief, as total pain elimination may not be possible, and (2) reaching an acceptable level of activity and alertness. Solutions with more than one active ingredient, such as the "Brompton cocktail" which has several analgesic agents co-mixed, should be avoided. Be alert to severe pain which requires higher doses to maintain steady pain relief. Add other medications as needed, i.e., stool softeners (as narcotics cause constipation) or anti-depressant medications, NSAIDS, amphetamine-like chemicals to reduce sedative effects of opioids, steroids used to treat pain associated with nervous spinal cord compression; compazine, haldol, or thorazine.
4. Monitor the effect of morphine thoroughly and frequently to assess pain intensity and the benefit, if any, the analgesia is providing.
5. Adjust dose requirements, being aware that these vary with weight, severity of pain, age, incidence of side effects, and concomitant disease, and that they must be titrated to response. Significant tolerance does not occur when treating cancer pain. Pain is an antagonist to adverse effects of opioids. As tolerance develops to analgesia, it also develops to respiratory, depression, and somnolence. The average oral dose is 8 to 30 mg every 4 hours; oral extended release products; 30 mg every 12 hours and Titrate to pain relief. Some patients require an 8-hour regime. Subcutaneous or intramuscular dosing is usually 5 to 15 mg every 4 hours; 10 mg doses are adequate only in 70 per cent of patients with moderate to severe pain. Rectally, the average dose is 10 to 20 mg every 4 hours.

   Intravenous dose is 4 to 10 mg and injected slowly over a 4 to 5 minute period. Continuous intravenous fusion is 1 to 10 mg per hour. Some patients with chronic pain may require up to 40 to 95 mg per hour. Intravenous patient-controlled anesthesia is usually 1 mg per activation.

   Epidurally, 5 mg initially, repeated 1 to 2 mg after one hour to a maximum of 10 mg per 24 hours is the standard. Continuous epidural is 2 to 4 mg per 24 hours initially, repeated with 1 to 2 mg. Intrathecally, use .1 epidural dose.

   Reduce dose in elderly, poor risk patients, patients receiving other central nervous system depressants, and patients with hypothyroidism. Prolonged dosages may be necessary in patients with renal dysfunction and hepatic insufficiency.
6. In evaluation of pain, site intensity, quality, variation, and time interval until pain recurs in response to prior therapy should be considered. Adverse effects include respiratory or cardiovascular depression (monitored for a minimum of 24 hours after epidural or intrathecal doses), sedation, nausea and vomiting, and constipation.

7. In using pharmokinetics, the onset is 15 to 30 minutes with a 10 mg subcutaneous dose, with peak analgesic effect, intravenous, within 20 minutes. Duration effects are four to five hours with 10 mg subcutaneously, two to three hours with intravenous administration. Absorption is rapid, with a three to four fold variation between patients occurring in absorption. A substantial amount of narcotic is released from the blood as it passes through the circulatory tree. There is rapid disappearance from plasma, with 93 per cent being eliminated within five minutes of administration. The active drug is attached to brain receptors producing its effect there.
8. Adverse reactions include respiratory depression (which occasionally occurs with therapeutic doses), circulatory depression, signs of overdose (small eye pupils, drowsiness, decreased rate of respiration, slow pulse, and hypotension), sedation, dizziness, nausea, vomiting, sweating, and constipation. Occasional reactions include euphoria, dysphoria, dry mouth, biliary tract spasms, postural hypotension, syncope, tachycardia, brady-cardia, urinary retention, and allergic reactions.
9. Precautions should be taken with pregnancy, intracranial injury or space-occupying lesions within the brain, acute asthma, chronic obstruction pulmonary disease or respiratory disease with hypoxia, inability to maintain adequate blood pressure, prosthetic hypertrophy or uretheral stricture, elderly and debilitated patients, and acute abdominal pain.
10. Significant drug interactions include Tagamet, Breviblock, Atarax, Visteril, Benzodiazapines which improve sedation and relieve preoperative anxiety, and phenothiazines with possible increased central nervous system and respiratory depression and hypotension. Laboratory interactions include serum amylase increased five to 10 times, serum creatinine, and serum lactate decreased.

The above scheme of evaluation of morphine is applicable to any drug that the physician uses and can serve as an algorithm showing what the physician's duty to the patient is when prescribing various medications.

In patient surveys, this manner of pain medication is practically always enthusiastically accepted by patients. The nursing staff is satisfied as less nurse attention is required; however, the apparatus is a bit complicated and requires familiarity by hospital personnel.[28]

---

[28] Ready, *Pain Service Held Key to Optimal Care,* 3 Pain Topics 1 (1989); Means, *Studies Show PCA May Allow Children to Safely Control Own Post-op Pain,* 3 Pain Topics 1 (1989); Jonson, *Modifiers of Patient-Controlled Analgesia Efficiency — Locus of Control,* 39 Pain 17, 23 (1989); Raj, Knar, Runyon & Hopson, *Patient Controlled Analgesia for Post-Operative Pain in Orthopedic Patients,* 16 Orthopedic Rev 953 (1987).

§21.27 Depression

Depression has been documented as a frequent component of chronic pain. In reviewing large series, the incidence of depression among chronic pain patients ranges from 10 to 100%, with the majority of reports giving an average of 50 per cent. The direct link between pain and depression was found to be non-significant; however, measures of perceived life interference and self-control were found to be significant intervening variables between pain and depression. It is clear that psychological mediators may be involved in the development of depression secondary to chronic pain.[29]

§21.28 Assessment and Treatment of Pain Patients in Emergency Center

A broad spectrum of painful conditions presents to the modern emergency center (EC). Three of the most common categories are (1) acute, self-limited disorders, (2) chronic medical or surgical syndrome with acute exacerbation, and (3) psychic pain syndromes in which etiology cannot be easily ascertained. Many factors may differentiate pain from suffering, and physicians should educate patients not only about the nature of their condition and its prognosis, but also about anticipated discomfort. Concerns in the EC include the tendency to undertreat or even ignore pain, the need for appropriate but flexible dosage schedules, and physicians' concerns with masking important signs and symptoms.

NSAIDS are currently the safest and most effective group of oral analgesics. Important factors for selection of medications are efficacy, dosage, lack of side effects, and cost. Two special groups of patients—those with psychic pain syndromes and those with drug-seeking behavior—can create problems for the physician. Patients with chronic pain syndromes need special follow-up, but do not benefit from additional analgesic drug therapy. Patients who seek and abuse drugs can be difficult to identify, may have true underlying medical pathology, and should not be given narcotic prescriptions.[30]

§21.29 Placebo

A clear understanding by the physician of the placebo response of patients is essential. The term "placebo" carries a pejorative connotation among uninformed or biased medical workers, causing a disservice to the patient. Measurement of the placebo factor by physicians and psychologists has been difficult and inconsistent. Like many areas of the practice of medicine, clear explanations of "why" and "how" are difficult and often anecdotal, but the

---

[29] Rudy & Turk, *Chronic Pain and Depression: Toward a Cognitive-Behavioral Mediation Model,* 35 Pain 129 (1988).

[30] Boisaubin, *Assessment and Treatment of Pain in the Emergency Room,* 5 The Clin J Pain 519 (1989).

placebo response is not denied by any practitioner who regularly attends patients.

The *placebo response* may be defined as the favorable response by a patient after administration of a medication or treatment (including operations) based on the patient's wish and belief that the treatment will be beneficial. Acupuncture is thought by many to fit in this category of medicine.

The placebo response may be long- or shortlived, again often based on the patient's belief/wish. It is well known that many medications and treatments fit the one-third, one-third, one-third paradigm in which the treatment is effective for one-third of patients, somewhat effective for another one-third, and ineffective for the balance.[31]

§21.30 Acupuncture

There is an important difference between traditional Chinese medicine and scientific acupuncture. Most physicians fail to recognize the difference. Traditional Chinese acupuncture is based on "meridian theory," a metaphysical concept that originated 4,000 years ago. It postulates a mysterious body energy called "chi" which transverses hypothetical meridian pathways to surface at some 361 acupuncture points on the skin. International researchers have rendered these theories obsolete. It is now recognized that acupuncture is a technique for getting a stimulus, preferably a pulsing DC current, into the central nervous system.

The best points to use are those where fibers are most easily accessed, such as motor, Golgi tendon apparatuses, or adjacent to nerve or nerve root.

The current theory is that the acupuncture stimulus stimulates appropriate areas of the brain, increasing chemical brain pain modulators (endorphins). The intensity of pain gradually abates with repeated acupuncture in susceptible treatment. A strong faith that "it will help" is an important factor of successful treatment and likely explains the high degree of good results in the Orient in years and centuries past.

Pain relief, if effective with acupuncture, is usually cumulative and with an irregular course. If there is no improvement in 8 to 10 treatments, acupuncture is probably an inappropriate modality for that patient.[32]

§21.31 History and Theory of TENS

Transcutaneous electrical nerve stimulation (TENS) began with the formulation of the "gait control theory" by Melzac and Wall in 1965. The theory states that there are cells in the brain and spinal cord whose purpose is to receive injury signals, which are transmitted via the thinly-myelinated A

---

[31] Voudouris, *Conditioned Response Models of Placebo Phenomena: Further Support*, 38 Pain 109 (1989).

[32] Ulett, *Scientific Acupuncture Peripheral Electrical Stimulation for Relief of Pain, Part I and Part II*, Pain Management (July-Aug 1989).

delta and C fibers system. Impulses are conducted to the dorsal horn cells in the spinal cord. These cells are profoundly influenced by input from two other sources: non-noxious events (touch and position) and inhibitor impulses from high levels of the nervous system, including rostral brain stem and medulla.

The potency of inhibitory influence from the brain stem was demonstrated by Reynolds, who was able to block pain input impulses by stimulating certain parts of the mid-brain. This blocking of pain was sufficient that surgery can be carried out without other anesthesia. The descending inhibitory system has been called "stimulation-produced anesthesia." There are two neurotransmitter chemicals in the brain involved in the effect: serotonin and endorphin.

The first applications of TENS clinically was in 1967. TENS therapy has come a long way since then. The original pulse generators were bulky, the electrodes were placed on the skin, and brittle conduction wires were placed onto the electrodes. Electronic miniaturization has reduced the size of the pulse units and carbon electrodes have improved the skin interface performance. Another improvement has been the addition of more channels, which allows the patient to stimulate larger areas. A patient with low back pain and sciatica can place one channel on the back and one on the leg.

Vital to recent advances in TENS is the ability to determine the pulse wave form by adjusting controls to change wave amplitude, width, and frequency. This control allows for stimulating specific function, such as certain pain fibers, but also sympathetic nerve input.[33]

§21.32 How TENS Works

TENS has been effective in controlling acute and chronic pain in about one-third of patients for prolonged periods. Posterior spinal cord stimulation is carried out by surgically implanted TENS-like devices. By selective stimulation of posterior spinal cord level, a subset of chronic pain patients may have their low back and leg pain reproduced. This group of patients may benefit by neurosurgical implantation of electrostimulating electrodes on dura at the appropriate level with stimulation via remotely implanted battery. Many neurosurgeons are enthusiastic over this pain control method. Complications include adverse tissue reaction to device components, infection, electrode displacement, and wire breakage. Paresthesias and disturbing numbness may occur in the area of pain being treated. However, results are reported by varying degrees and length of time.

Most physicians using TENS therapy believe that pain relief is greatest when the TENS unit induces paresthesias into the pain site. Many patients

---

[33] De Moore & Blaker, *How Effective is TENS for Chronic Pain?,* Am J Nursing, Aug 1983, at 1176. Shealy, *The Pain Game,* Millbrae Cal, Celestial Arts 1976, at 72; Melzac & Wall, *Pain Mechanisms: A New Theory,* 150 Sci 971 (1965); Wall, *The Gate Control Theory of Pain Mechanisms. A Re-examination and Re-Statement,* 101 Brain 1 (1978).

find the paresthesias a distasteful trade-off for their pain. The fact that paresthesias do not occur with TENS stimulation of the spinal cord indicates that the TENS effect is not through the dorsal nerve root and that peripherally originating pain is best treated with the TENS placed peripherally, not at the spinal cord.

It appears that pain relief afforded by TENS, in part, is derived from shifting balance of excitation between large and small afferent fibers in favor of the former. The spatiotemporal pattern of neural input is also changed with TENS therapy.[34]

§21.33 Corticosteroid Injections

Both intra-articular and extra-articular injections of hydrocortisone are frequently used by physicians for pain control. These steroids exert strong anti-inflammatory effects and represent great therapeutic benefit. These same steroids have adverse side effects. They can cause skin depigmentation if injected subcutaneously. They cause wakening and rupture when injected into a tendon or ligament. These steroids can cause cartilage breakdown, particularly in weight-bearing joints. These tissue breakdowns seem to be dose-related. It appears that hydrocortisone injections may be safely placed in a paraligament or tendon. It is the intra-ligament an intra-tendon injection that alters the collagen homeostasis, leading to tissue disruption.[35]

---

[34] Reynolds, *Surgery in the Rat During Electrical Analgesia Induced by Focal Brain Stimulation,* 164 Sci 444 (1965); Melzac, *Prolonged Relief of Pain by Brief Intensive Transcutaneous Somatic Stimulation,* 1 Pain 357 (1975); Smith, *Alleviation of Deafferentation Pain by Posterior Spinal Cord Stimulation without Development of Paresthesias in Area of Pain,* 4 Clin J Pain 157 (1988); Katz & Melzac, *An Association Between Phantom Limb Sensations and Stump Skin Conductance During Transcutaneous Electrical Nerve Stimulation (TENS) Applied to the Contralateral Leg: A Case Study,* 36 Pain 367 (1989); Almay, *Substance P in CSF of Patients with Chronic Pain Syndromes,* 33 Pain 3 (1988); Berlant & Lampe, *How TENS Work,* 4 Clin J Pain 191 (1988); Shealy & Maurer, *Transcutaneous Nerve Stimulation: A Preliminary Technical Note,* 2 Surg Neurol 45 (1974); Berlant, *Method of Determining Optimal Stimulation Sites for Transcutaneous Nerve Stimulation,* 64 Phys Ther 924 (1984).

[35] Willer, *Human Nociceptive Reactions: Effects of Spatialation of Afferent Input from Relatively Large Diameter Fibers,* 201 Brain Ros 465 (1980); Fitzgerald, Jr, *Intrasynovial Injection of Steroids — Uses and Abuses,* 51 Mayo Clin Proc 655 (1976); Gray & Gottlieb, *Intra-articular Corticosteroids — An Updated Assessment,* 177 Clin Orthop 235 (1983); Balch, *Repeated Corticosteroid Injection into Knee Joints,* 16 Rheum Rehabil 137 (1977); Bedi & Ellis, *Spontaneous Rupture of the Calcaneal Tendon in Rheumatoid Arthritis after Local Steroid Injection,* 29 Ann Rheum Dis 494 (1970); Ford & DeBender, *Tendon Rupture after Local Steroid Injection,* 72 S Med J 827 (1970).

§21.34 Epidural Steroid Therapy

The use of epidural corticosteroids often lessens low back and leg pain in several chronic low back syndromes. Also, it is useful in acute discogenic syndromes. The theory follows that the pain, in part at least, has an inflammatory component and that steroid injection reduces this. The procedure is done in an epidural space at the intervertebral level or by a caudal route. Complications include dural penetration with dural leak, which can be controlled by blood patch, the patch technique being done prophylactically by some surgeons/anesthesiologists.

Epidural opiates are used at times for more prolonged low back/leg pain control and are used by some as postoperative pain control. Complications include respiratory depression, hypotension, nausea-vomiting, and itching. Fatal reactions to epidural narcotic usage have been reported. This is a recovery room/ICU procedure, where epidural steroids therapy can safely be done on an outpatient basis.[36]

§21.35 Phantom Pain

Severe, unremitting phantom pain felt in the amputated part of the body is the most formidable and dreaded complication of major amputations. Incapacitating phantom pain occurs in from 2 to 15 per cent of lower extremity amputations.

Phantom pain has been reported since 1551. A classical description by Mitchell of Civil War amputees reads:

> A person in this condition is haunted, as it were, by constant or inconstant fractional phantom of so much of himself as has been lopped away—an unseen ghost of the lost part, and sometimes a presence made sorely inconvenient by the fact that while but faintly felt at times, it is at others acutely called to his attention by the pains or irritations which appear to suffer from a blow on the stump or a change in the weather.

In phantom pain, the amputated part—generally the more distant part (foot or hand)—is perceived to be present, moves with body activity, and responds to ambient temperature. The etiology of phantom pain has been the subject of years (centuries) of study. It represents a deafferenting phenomena and disassociation between peripheral afferent input and central afferent pain control.

Phantom pain is rarely improved by surgeries. Therapies may include

---

[36] Kennedy & Willis, *The Effects of Local Steroid Injections on Tendons: A Biochemical and Microscopic Correlative Study,* 4 Am J Sports Med 11 (1976); Rocco, *Epidural Steroids, Epidural Morphine and Epidural Steroids Combined with Morphine in the Treatment of Post-Laminectomy Syndrome,* 36 Pain 297 (1989).

drugs, ultrasound, and TENS. Psychotherapy may likewise help. The best results seem to come from multifaceted pain clinic types of care.[37]

§21.36 Malingering

It is often difficult, but important, for physicians—or any person representing the patient—to determine if the patient is malingering. It is inaccurate and potentially risky to label the person as a malingerer based on bias or "gut" reaction. There are more creditable ways of evaluating such individuals.

The American Psychiatric Association lists in its Diagnostic and Statistical Manual of Mental Disorders, under "Index of Suspicion of Malingering," as:

1. The patient is attorney-referred
2. The patient complains of illness or injury that far exceeds objective findings
3. Lack of patient cooperation in treatment, monitoring, and diagnosis
4. The patient appears to manifest an antisocial personality disorder

In another study, a physician researching the malingering problem suggests that the following may be malingering:

1. The patient with vague complaints
2. The patient with ill-defined complaints
3. The patient who is reluctant to accept a favorable or improving prognosis
4. The person who purposefully alters test results
5. The patient who dramatizes complaints
6. The patient who insists on receiving addicting or commonly abused drugs

---

[37] Sjogren, *Lumbar Epidurography and Epidural Analgesic in Cancer Patients,* 36 Pain 305 (1989); McCollough, III, *Complications of Amputation Surgery,* Complications in Orthopedic Surgery (C.H. Epps ed 1978); Aftana & Zubek, *Cutaneous Sensitivity of Unilateral Arm Amputees,* 18 Canadian J Psychology 101 (1974); Farley, *Painful Stump Neuromata Treatment,* 48 Minn Med 347 (1965); Harris, *Prosthetic Management of Lower Limb Amputation,* Modern Trends in Vascular Surgery (1970); Krainick, *Spinal Cord Stimulation in Post Amputation Pain,* 4 Surg Neurol 167 (1975); Melzack, *Phantom Limb Pain: Amputation for Treatment of Pathological Pain,* 35 Anest 409 (1971); Weaver & Marshall, *A Functional and Social Review of Lower Limb Amputees,* 60 Brit J Surg 732 (1973).

There are many tests available to detect malingering. These tests are best done by psychologists testing for simulated mental disorders.[38]

§21.37 Treating the Person As a Whole

Although there is some major truth in each of the above formulations, it is believed that the "whole person" concept is the most attractive and useful in understanding and dealing with the psychological aspects of physical disability. The basis of this concept is that we do not treat disease and injuries, but individuals who are suffering the effects of such disease and injuries, and that these individuals may often have socio-economical, psychological, vocational, medical, and other problems which may profoundly affect their physical status.

According to this approach, successful rehabilitation may require evaluation using techniques of several disciplines and then manipulation of appropriate variables as needed to accomplish rehabilitation of the injured patient. An organic lesion, therefore, is but one of many factors, influencing a likelihood of re-employment. Failure to consider a single crucial variable may lead to failure of the entire treatment program. It is most important to recognize the dynamic interaction of all of the variables affecting the patient's basic personality organization.[39]

§21.38 References

Beals & Hickman, *Industrial Injuries of the Back and Extremities,* 54A JBJ Surg 1593 (1972).

Brena & Chapman, *Pain and Litigation,* in Textbook of Pain (P.D. Wall & R. Maizack eds 1984).

B.L. Crue & J. Pinsky, Chronic Pain (1979).

Dworkin, *Unraveling the Effects of Compensation, Litigation and Employment on Treatment Response in Chronic Pain,* 23 Pain 49 (1985).

Edwards, *Familial Pain Models: The Relationship Between Family History of Pain and Current Pain Experience,* 21 Pain 379 (1985).

Jaegger & Reeves, *Quantification of Changes in Myofascial Trigger Point Severity with the Pressure Algometer Following Passive Stretch,* 27 Pain 203 (1986).

Kames, *The Chronic Illness Problem Inventory: Problem Oriented Psychological Assessment of Patients with Chronic Illness,* 14 Int J Psychiat Med 65 (1984).

---

[38] Silivial, *Defense of Harrassment. Intentional Infliction of Emotional Harm and Employment Related Claims of Anxiety and Depression,* The Law Def Bull, Sept 1987; Tarantino & Oliveira, *Determining Personal Injury Damages,* Litigating Neck and Back Injuries (1988).

[39] Tarantino & Oliveira, *Determining Personal Injury Damages,* Litigating Neck and Back Injuries (1988).

J. Barber & C. Adrian, Psychological Approaches to Management of Pain (1982).

S.F. Brena & S.L. Chapman, Management of Patients with Chronic Pain (1983).

H. Carron & R.E. McLaughlin, Management of Low Back Pain (1982).

B.J. Crue, Chronic Pain: Further Observations from City of Hope National Medical Center (1979).

Ng & Bonica, *Pain, Discomfort and Humanitarian Care,* Developments in Neurology, Vol 4 (1980).

Ng, *New Approaches to the Treatment of Chronic Pain: A Review of Multidisciplinary Pain Clinics and Pain Centers,* National Institute on Drug Abuse, Research Monograph #36, May 1981.

Ketrum, *Management of Pain in Orthopaedics,* 5 (2) The Clin J Pain 526 (1989).

Waddell, *Failed Lumbar Disc Surgery and Repeat Surgery following Industrial Injuries,* 61A JBJ Surg 201 (1979).

Appendix 21-1
Cases

1 ***Hughes v Webster Parish Police Jury,* 414 So 2d 1353 (La Ct App 1982)** (45-year-old man was injured when working beneath a police vehicle. A clutch and pressure plate weighing a total of 40 pounds fell on his chest. He said he experienced sharp pain on his lower back, went blind for a moment, rested for about 30 minutes after the accident, and then left the job to see his family physician. An orthopedist saw him on referral and noticed lumbosacral tenderness, prescribed a brace, and indicated he would be ready for duty in 12 days. The patient, however, was treated for several days, unimproving, with a variety of treatments, including steroid injections, topical anesthesia, excercises, corset, psychological evaluation, and two additional orthopedists. He was seen at a pain center that noted only "mild back spasms." Three possible diagnoses were suggested: (1) malingering, considered to be unlikely, (2) psycho-physiological musculo-skeletal disorder, and (3) hysterical neurosis conversion. The psychiatrist said he could not sort out the orthopedic and emotional factors in the pelvic pain. The patient was somewhat socio-economically deprived, had a seventh-grade education, and limited experience at any job other than the type of work he was doing. He was still unable to be gainfully employed four years after the accident. The employer stopped disability payments. The Louisiana District Court rejected the injured man's plea for benefits on the basis of permanent and total disability. The Court of Appeals noted, however, that there had been no evidence of a rehabilitation program, which had been suggested to the employer 14 months after the accident. The case was remanded with orders to pursue a special pain clinic approach, designed to deal with the combination of orthopedic and emotional disabilities).

Comment: This is a common sort of case where a minimal injury will produce pain of an incapacitating nature. There are many headache problems that fall into this category. The vocabulary used to describe this situation is difficult in itself, with each specialist seeming to favor his or her terminology. It basically falls into the category of somatization disorder. Very rarely are there significant objective findings of injury, or if they existed, they have healed. There is, however, a profound impairment that manifests itself by loss of endurance, ease of fatigue, and a pain complaint that is interpreted as overwhelming. Each case must be evaluated on its own merits, considering all factors of the case—physical, psychological, spiritual, socio-economical, ethnic, etc. It is certain that some of the patients are malingerers, but this is generally considered to be a minority. This is the sort of case in which third-party carriers and a number of orthopedists, as well as physicians in general, take the rather biased or arbitrary view that if there is not an objective finding, the odds are that the impairment is more related to the patient's lack of will power or willful misconduct, which very often works a disservice to the patient).

2 ***Nyhof v North Dakota Workermen's Compensation Bureau,* 325 NW2d 239 (1982)** (ongoing pain was traced to the concept of "secondary gain." A sanitation man collected disability benefits for four years after a back sprain suffered while heaving a garbage can. The patient persisted with unremitting pain, seemingly disproportionate to the injury, until medical experts became suspicious of secondary gain. In this case, the pain management experts and pain evaluators working with the patient commented "It is the overall impression of the staff that this is going to be a difficult case for several reasons. The patient is now making 25 per cent more per week than he did when he was working, as his income now is tax-free." He was able to perform household duties and his wife was able to make a living on her own; therefore, their financial situation appeared to be locked in, and it was extremely doubtful he could be budged unless his financial situation was altered in some manner. None of the orthopedists treating him found any objective reason for continuing pain and all suggested some work rehabilitation. One underscored the urgency of fitting him into some active program, "because he can't go on like this the rest of his life." The patient did not indicate he would like to try. He said he feared another injury and also loss of his benefits. The compensation bureau finally expressed the opinion that he had four years of compensation and had been adequately compensated and payments were ceased. The Supreme Court of North Dakota affirmed the Bureau's action).

Comment: Occasionally, a patient receiving disability payments falls into the category as above, and it is difficult for the trier of fact to come up with an equitable solution, considering the fact of secondary gain.

22

Disability Evaluations

§22.01 Generally

The practice of medicine and of law often operates from incompatible bases. Physicians must work with lawyers and reconcile medicine to the legal work. This interrelation often happens in disability evaluations of patients carried out by physicians.

While disability is a legal term, each year American physicians receive hundreds of thousands of requests to determine it.

Physician misunderstanding of disability evaluations is common, inviting accusations of bias, lackeyism, and malpractice. Disability evaluation involves determining if the worker can do his or her job or if a parallel, non-work ability exists. Payments may be made for partial or total, temporary or permanent disability.

The physician enters the evaluation scene through requests from the patient, insurance companies, military service, vocational rehabilitation agencies, labor unions, employers, attorneys, and state or federal government agencies.

Because claims can be made to so many different agencies, and because each jurisdiction (usual state) has its own, frequently changing rules and procedures, there is no one situation a physician can anticipate in evaluations. In every case, however, a worker contends he or she is unable to do his or her usual work and appeals to some outside agency for compensation. Attorneys may be hired by the worker, the employer, or a funding agency if a claim is contested, with any of the parties involved seeking a separate medical opinion.

A successful claimant usually receives disability payments from one of three sources: workers' compensation, non-occupational insurance, or social security. Each state has its own workers' compensation program and policy, separate from the military or federal government. In some states, workers' compensation covers only prescribed occupational illnesses or injury; in others, it covers all work-related illness or injury. Usually, there is a monetary limit on the amount paid to any one worker. In very small companies without workers' compensation insurance, injured employees may file suit in civil court.

Many companies and many individuals have some form of non-occupational disability insurance that covers injuries or illnesses unrelated to work activities. Premiums may be paid by the employer, the employee, or both.

In a case where a worker is declared totally and permanently disabled, uncovered by workers compensation or non-occupational insurance, or when maximum benefits have been paid, the worker can, in many instances, apply for social security disability insurance.

Disability evaluation often begins with a patient's visit to his or her private physician, although certain agencies such as workers' compensation boards or insurance companies may have physician consultants available. In some states, the physician must determine the percentage of impairment and give an opinion regarding its permanence. When the report is filed with the proper paying agency, a medical evaluation may be required for which the physician may be paid a fee.

Many claims are contested; thus, after evaluation, the physician may be asked to give written responses, depositions, or courtroom testimony explaining and rationalizing the evaluation. There are real problems between initial evaluation and courtroom, including (1) lack of physician education as to the evaluation process, (2) lack of uniformity of standards and procedures for recording and assessing the evaluation, (3) unsuitable questions on a standard form as it applies to the patient at hand, and (4) subjective and biased judgments about impairment.

The AMA Guides to Evaluation of Permanent Impairment (last revised in 1988) stress the difference between disability and impairment. Permanent impairment is purely a medical condition indicating "any anatomic or functional abnormality or loss" while disability is an administrative adjudication indicating a patient's "actual or presumed ability to engage in gainful activity." Although permanent impairment is always considered in determining disability, other factors such as patient's age, sex, education, and economic and social environment must be considered by the trier of fact.

The doctor is rarely exposed in medical school to classes about impairment evaluation, special circumstances related to such examinations, or skills in report writing. Many informed individuals feel that medical school is not the appropriate forum for this knowledge, but that disability evaluation is a postgraduate endeavor. Although extensive research relating to pathophysiology of "physical strength and/or work capacity or the performance of certain physical motions" has appeared in ergonomic and physiology and exercise journals, most physicians are unfamiliar with the literature.

Many disability forms ask unanswerable questions, such as "Can the patient stand or sit for 2, 4, or 6 hours? Continuously? Intermittently?" Or, "How much weight can the patient lift or push? Occasionally? Often? Infrequently?" Many (most) physicians are not only ignorant of the basic research to answer these questions, but are "ignorant of their ignorance." Most physicians make disability evaluations their lowest concerns in patient care, thus reinforcing their ignorance of the subject.

Unfortunately, many doctors find themselves telling lawyers or insurance companies what they think the third party wants to hear, resulting in increased and repeat evaluations, leading to greater fees. This is one descriptor of the "medical prostitute."

Having "expert" objective opinions judged by a jury of laypersons, with attorneys for both sides, may present a problem. Doctors and lawyers are realizing that there is a basic difference in their philosophy of practice, with physicians basically interested in reality and lawyers basically interested in the appearance of reality.

There are set guidelines for the observation and reporting of physical impairment, except those predicated on restrictive data, i.e., the AMA Guides (1984) basing impairments largely on loss of range of motion of the joint system, neurological defects, and measures of cardiac/pulmonary function. These leave a multitude of impairments unattended, such as pain, loss of endurance, ease of fatigue, and weakness.

At this time, the physician must be educated and the attorney equally informed in the legal process of claims handling so that they know what their role is and how to answer questions carefully and cautiously, so that answers are not misleading or carry a double meaning so they will not be compromised or legally vulnerable. Doctors are well advised to recall that they are called on to give expert medical opinions, not to act as persuaders (McCahan). The proper role of the physician in this situation on impairment is indicating how, in his or her opinion, this could affect an individual's ability to work.[1]

§22.02 Disability Evaluation

Although medicine and law often operate from an incompatible basis, physicians must work with attorneys in the process of reconciled medicine in our present legal climate. Nowhere is this more evident than in disability evaluation, and almost every physician at some point in his or her career is called on to do one. The orthopedic surgeon probably renders disability impairment opinions more frequently than most other medical disciplines.

To accurately understand, analyze, and describe a disability claim or situation, one must be aware of factors impinging on a case from its medical onset to its legal conclusion. Some of these subjects are learned in traditional medical training or continuing education, but others are not. In chronologic sequence, these include:

1. Pre-existing medical conditions, both physical and psychological
2. Pre-existing vocational status, employment, and training
3. Type of illness or injury and its natural history
4. First aid and emergency care
5. Personality and psychological reactions
6. Primary follow-up care (diagnosis and treatment)
7. Support staff services; e.g., physical therapy, work hardening, etc.
8. Clinical management, consultant specialist opinions
9. Vocational rehabilitation (availability, personnel, and services)
10. Work availability within physical restrictions
11. Employer practices regarding rehiring or return to work

---

[1] Heibert, *Disability Evaluation: A Fledgling Science? Medical News,* 250 JAMA 873 (1983); Guides to the Evaluation of Permanent Impairment. American Medical Association, Chicago (A.L. Engelberg 3d ed 1984 1988).

12. Administrative system incentives to (or not to) return to work
13. Insurer approach to claim (denial, obstruction, facilitation)
14. Attorney presence, orientation, etc.
15. Disability evaluation or similar assessment
16. Legal system, its efficiency, incentives, precedents, and complexity

Many different individuals are involved in these components of the disability determination process. The skills, attitudes, experiences, talents, and personalities of each will impact the process.

It is important to separate disability, which is a legally-mandated professional opinion, from impairment, which is the opinion of an examining physician as to the degree of loss of function of part or all of the human body, but physician misunderstanding of disability evaluations is rampant. Such misunderstandings have been plaguing such professional groups as the American Academy of Compensational Medicine, the American Academy of Occupational Medicine, and the American Occupational Medicine Association for years.

Disability evaluation involves determining whether a worker can do his or her job. Payments may be made for either partial or total, temporary or permanent disability. Permanent disability ordinarily is a disability that lasts a year or more.

Because claims can be made to so many different agencies, and because each jurisdiction (usually a state) has its own (frequently changing) set of rules and procedures, there is no one situation a physician can anticipate in a disability evaluation. In every case, however, a worker contends he or she is unable to do his or her usual work and appeals to some outside agency for compensation. Attorneys may be called in by the worker, the employer, or funding agencies if the claim is contested, and any of the parties involved may seek separate medical opinions. The successful claimant receives disability payments from one of three sources: workers' compensation, non-occupational insurance, or social security.

Social security disability insurance is a federally created and regulated insurance plan. The definition of disability as it relates to work capacity is exclusively the purview of the government administrators. The primary physician's opinion has little, if any, impact on the decision. Administrating this insurance scheme requires the quantification of illness as it relates to the work capacity (disability). What has evolved is a program that insures for the amount of "disease." The assumption is that with more disease, there is a greater likelihood of illness, even illness manifested as work incapacity. Leaving this underlying assumption tacit is responsible for the adversary climate that envelopes the physician, the patient claimant, and the administrators. It is also the responsibility for the paucity of clinical investigation into critical issues of the amount and form of illness a diseased person will have.

In a case where a worker is declared totally and permanently disabled but not covered by workers' compensation or non-occupational insurance, or if he or she exceeded maximum workers' compensation benefits, he or she can apply for social security and disability insurance.

In any event, disability evaluation often begins with a patient's visit to his or her private physician, although certain agencies like the workers' compensation boards or insurance companies may have physician consultants available. In some states, the physician must determine the percentage of impairment and give an opinion of the permanence of it. When the report is filed with the proper paying agency, such as the Social Security Administration, a medical evaluation is required for which a patient is often paid a standard fee.

§22.03 Disability versus Impairment

Disability is defined as inability to engage in any substantial gainful activity by reason of any medically-determined physical or mental impairment, or impairments which can be expected to result in death or which have lasted or can be expected to last for a continuous period of no less than 12 months (20 CFR §404.1501).

Impairment results from anatomical, physiological, or psychological abnormalities which are demonstrable by medically-accepted clinical and laboratory diagnostic techniques. Statements of the applicant, including his or her own description of the impairment (symptoms), are alone insufficient to establish the presence of a physical or mental impairment. *Id.*

§22.04 Who Determines Disability?

In social security disability evaluation, the government administrative office is solely responsible for the ultimate decision in disability determinations. Primary considerations given to the severity of the individual's impairment—age, education, and work experience. Medical considerations alone (including the psychological and physiological manifestations of aging) can justify a finding that an individual is under disability where the impairment is one that meets the duration of the requirement and is listed (20 CFR §404.1502).

The function of deciding whether or not an individual is under a disability is the responsibility of the secretary. The weight to be given to such a physician's statement depends on the extent to which it is supported by specific and complete physical findings and is consistent with other evidence as to severity and probable duration (20 CFR §404.1526).

The Guides promulgated by the Social Security Administration require a case be documented so any physician or reviewing component would reach the same conclusion as the examining physician. Since the social security examiner does not see the patient face to face, the medical report needs to give that examiner an accurate mental picture of the disability claimant. The examiner must be able to determine how the patient can function, given the limitations imposed by the impairment.

A recent newsletter (NADE Advocate) gives an example. "The physician's record may indicate that the patient has arthritis of the right knee with limited motion." While this certainly may be sufficient information for the physician to diagnose and set a treatment plan, the Social Security examiner needs to know how the patient gets about with arthritis. Does he just have a stiff painful knee or can he only walk with a cane? That makes a difference when assessing a client's ability to work. Social Security Administration's Handbook for Physicians has a listing of accepted diseases, illnesses, and injuries that, when sufficient, qualify for Social Security disability consideration. Impairments not listed in the appropriate sections of that handbook may be considered to be the medically equivalent of an impairment listed only if medical findings are equivalent in severity and duration to the listed findings. A decision shall be based on medical evidence demonstrated by medically-acceptable clinical and laboratory diagnostic techniques (20 CFR §404.1505).[2]

§22.05 Chronic Disabilities

Multifaceted problems test the doctor's wisdom in treating chronic disability. That's the challenge! Is a different kind of thinking required in treating people with chronic disabilities as opposed to acute injuries or disorders? Excerpts taken from an interview of Charles H Epps, Jr, MD, Professor of Orthopedics and Chief, Division of Orthopedic Surgery, Howard University, comes from 11 Legal Letter, 1988, at 3. In orthopedics, the major goal is to restore a person to as great a functional level as possible. There are many times when this is not possible. The orthopedist has to recognize and try to direct the patient into treatment areas that will improve his or her lifestyle, and recognize patients who cannot realistically be helped. In chronic disability, the physician has to picture the patient in a global manner, in how the patient appears from his or her physical injury as well as how the patient presents to his or her socioeconomic environment, and consider ethnic backgrounds and goals. Sometimes an operation which will improve one person

---

[2] Ruggles, *Why Don't They Believe Me When I Say He's Disabled?*, 5 The NADE Advocate 6 (1989). E.E. Witte, The Development of the Social Security Act (1963). Bartel v Cohen, 445 2d 80-84 (1971). Bishop v Weinberger, 380 F Supp 293-98 (1974). Varney v Weinberger, 373 F Supp 678-83 (1974). Department of Health, Education & Welfare Publication No (SSA) 79-10089, Disability Evaluation Under Social Security: A Handbook for Physicians Washington, DC United States Government Printing Office (1979); Mooney, *Amer Acad Orthop Surg Bull,* Apr 1988, at 14. Gold v Secretary of Health, Education and Welfare, 463 F2d 38-44 (1972), Klein, *Assessment of Workers' Compensation Claims for Back Strains/Sprains,* 26 J Occup Med 443 (1984); Hadler, *The Socio-Political Climate Surrounding Low Back Pain,* 2 J Occup Med 681 (1979). Kalsey, White, Pastides & Bisbee, *The Impact on Musculoskeletal Disorders on the Population of the United States,* 61A JBJ Surg 959-64 (1979); Magora, *Investigation of the Relation Between Low Back Pain and Occupation,* 5 Scand J Rehab Med 191-96 (1973); Ad Hoc Committee on Medical Ethics, American College of Physicians: American College of Physicians Ethics Manual, 101 Ann Int Med 129 (1984).

would be a disservice to another with the same problem. Accurate diagnosis of the patient's psychological make-up is important.

In major joint replacement surgery, such as hips and knees, one of the main considerations as to indication is whether the patient will be substantially improved in ability to ambulate. If he or she is not an ambulatory patient, such major surgery is rarely indicated. There are many situations where reconstructive surgery is anatomically appropriate but is not appropriate from a rehabilitation point of view. Such cases as marked club feet in severely mentally retarded patients or patients with meningomyelocele at times cannot be rehabilitated. Otherwise, correcting club feet or dislocated hips is appropriate. Frequently, great pressure is brought by the family to do these operations when the end result will not be a rehabilitated person.

Pain can be another reason for doing major joint surgeries in an otherwise bedfast patient. If the arthritic process of a hip or knee precludes the patient from moving well in bed and otherwise interferes with the quality of his or her life, joint resection or hemi- or total hip replacement or some procedure on the knee is justified.

Patients who have severe medical problems and also have appropriate indications for reconstructive surgery to the spine or to weight-bearing joints present a decision problem. This is a multifaceted problem in which the evaluation of the medical problem by the appropriate discipline takes priority. At times, severe scoliotic patients can have their cardiopulmonary deficiencies improved by appropriate surgery, even though the anesthetic risk at the time of surgery is increased over a more normal patient.

Where there are treatment options available, financial considerations often come into play. In a situation such as prescribing a wheelchair, a motorized wheelchair might be more convenient for the patient, but he may be able to function in a non-motorized wheelchair. There are many situations such as this. A physician must do the best he or she can for the patient with what is available to the patient. If you need transportation, you can get a bicycle, a Ford, or a Mercedes—all three will get you where you are going. The prescribing and fitting of braces and prosthetic devices fit into this same category. A very simple stirrup brace made out of reinforcement rods works well for a patient in Central Africa with no other resources, but is generally rejected by a patient in the United States knowing that more sophisticated hinged braces (sometimes even computerized devices) are available. Inevitably, a cost factor arises that the orthopedist is called on to participate in, along with what is necessary and what is convenient.

Many orthopedic patients have long-term problems. Most other medical disciplines have finished with the patient once the surgical suture is removed. The orthopedist frequently treats fractures that take weeks or months to heal. Impaired children are followed for years or for life, as are chronically disabled patients. It is common for the orthopedist to establish a long-term (many years) relationship with this type of patient. The longer a physician practices, the more he or she realizes the importance of treating each patient as a whole, not as an isolated segment or disease entity. It is important that the orthopedist treating the long-term patient, as well as the acute patient, be concerned with the patient as a whole. This does not mean that he should be skilled in regulating various medications (or be obliged to do this) such as digitalis or insulin. They must understand though, that if a patient has other major elements (such as a heart attack three or four years ago), the patient may have such a fear of having another one that it may affect how he or she responds to the rehabilitative process as a whole. It is equally important that the orthopedist know the family situation, such as whether the spouse of a patient with a chronic lower back problem is an invalid, or if that man who injured his back at work continues to have a job that he dislikes and feels unappreciated or threatened.

Knowledge of superiors' and employers' behavior can radically affect how a patient does in a rehabilitation program. Commonly, if work is fun the patient heals readily and returns to work responsibly. Conversely, when the job is threatening, the supervisor is abusive or demanding, or if there is a "lot of hassle" (which is common), patients do not rehabilitate as well and return to gainful employment less frequently.

§22.06 Medical Evaluation

Just as the cells of the body live in a fluid "Milieu interieur," so does the physician work in a philosophical milieu that governs interpretations of and response to situations encountered in practice. If the physician is to understand his or her role in society and if he or she is to successfully deal with his or her professional sense of crisis, he or she must go beyond a patient disease model. He or she must achieve a synthesis that relates the physician to the entire practice environment and its base knowledge. The metaphor of the animal organism as a machine was established by Descartes' "Discourse on Method." The prevailing view of life as a mechanist process gives no room for the physician to interpret symbolic language. This is the current basis for objective and subjective findings that forms the basis of fact finding in being more probative than subjective, and often does a disservice to the patient. In day-to-day practice of medicine, subjective findings are the basis of 70 to 80 per cent of diagnosis and treatment.[3] Eighty per cent of all diagnoses are based on the physician's interpretation of what the patient says. Again, the physician is challenged to listen to patients to better prepare to make an appropriate diagnosis.

§22.07 Medical-Legal Obligations of the Orthopedist

For a variety of legal purposes, a medical report is necessary. Some do not support the convention that medicine is a learned physician. R.M. Fox, a personal injury attorney, who has a somewhat slanted view of these matters,

---

[3] Bessinger, *Junior Doctoring,* 81 So Med J 1558 (1988). J. Campbell, The Mythic Image (1974).

makes a valid criticism: "No medical school in the United States today offers a course in medical legal report writing, in spite of it obvious socioeconomic importance and the billions of dollars in this type of claim. Little, if any, post graduate medical education on this subject is available."[4]

If the report is on a patient who is being seen by other than the treating physician, the party who has requested the examination and the date of the examination should be noted. When the report is the patient's own, written permission to release this information must be given.

The report needs to contain an exhaustive and accurate history. Although the patient may give a lengthy version of the circumstances of the accident, only what is germane to the assessment of his injury should be included in the report, and certainly no judgment as to the validity should appear in the medical report. Although the patient's account to a physician of the circumstances of the accident is usually inadmissible as evidence bearing on the cause of action, it may be admissible to the extent that it is relevant to establishing the bases on which the physician formed an opinion of what is going on, causation, effect, impairment, etc. If, in some way, these notes are erroneous, they may damage the credibility of the patient or in some way influence the outcome of the case.

The past history of the patient must be recorded, especially if previous injury or disease is a direct concern in the production, aggravation, or acceleration of the impairment being assessed. If the report is on a patient whom the reporting physician has treated, a detailed report of the initial examination and subsequent treatment should be included. The patient should be questioned regarding his or her current condition, and the nature, severity, duration, and frequency of the specific complaints.

The clinical examination is carried out in a meticulous manner, notes being taken during the examination rather than depending on memory. Care should be taken to differentiate left from right, etc. In many jurisdictions, the medical witness is permitted to refer to these notes to refresh his or her recollection, provided the notes were made at the time of the examination or shortly thereafter.

Thorough notes can be invaluable for responding intelligently and consistently in far-reaching, extended cross-examination. The sooner a formal report is dictated, the more accurate it will be. Those measurements which will be taken with a tape or goniometer, etc., should be done and so recorded. Scars should be noted, especially when they interfere with function or cosmesis. Negative findings, where indicated, should be noted.

After describing the medical findings in technical terms, it is best to give a resume of the findings in non-technical lay terms that translate the technical language for the benefit of those persons of non-medical training who will read them. This is very helpful to the recipient of the report if he or she is a lawyer or other lay medical person.

The examiner should express some opinion about the consistency of the patient's injuries with his or her history and the flow of events from the time

---

[4] R.M. Fox, The Medical Legal Report Theory and Practice (1969).

of injury through the problems and physical findings at the time of the current examination. The comments should be based on the facts alone, as the physician perceives them, as reported by the patient. Statements as to causation need to be made with reasonable medical probability, substantiated by medical fact and by the experience of the examining physician.

In the event that the patient's condition is stable and no further treatment is indicated, in many situations it is appropriate to assess a degree or make a statement concerning the presence or absence of permanent impairment. It is not often that the physician is asked to rate disability. This is a prerogative of the trier of fact, utilizing several parameters, one of which is the impairment rating that the physician renders.[5] (*See* Appendix 22-1, Cases 1 to 13.)

§22.08 Examination

In performing a medical examination, the physician begins a deductive process by which both objective and subjective information is obtained from the patient and related to recognized medical principles. The physician's primary concern is to identify or diagnose the condition and to develop an appropriate treatment plan. Information not important to the diagnosis or the treatment plan is generally ignored. Information elicited by the doctor is presumed to be important to the physician's task and should not be casually discounted by the care takers.

The initial examination typically consists of a history (which is the patient's own account of the events which led to his or her seeking medical help), as well as a complete physical examination. After these steps, the physician reaches a working or tentative diagnosis, or, if less certain, a differential diagnosis. At this point, a treatment plan may be suggested to the patient along with reasoning as to its necessity, including a prognosis. (*See* Appendix 22-1, Cases 14 to 19.)

§22.09 Confidentiality

The orthopedist is often faced with a confidentiality as he or she examines and treats a patient. Some areas are covered by law, such as knowledge that the physician's patient is a wanted criminal—appropriate reporting of this person is necessary. Suspicion of child abuse is legally reportable. In cases of certain infectious diseases, reporting is again regulated by law. If the patient has an infectious venereal disease, confidential reporting is in order, but conveying that information to a third party without the patient's consent breaches the patient's privilege. If a patient with syphilis or AIDS knowingly proposes to potentially infect another, the question of privilege is weighed against the public good.

---

[5] H.H. Kessler, Disability—Determination and Evaluation (1970).

In this category of problems, with various states having different laws, counsel with another physician, or perhaps even better, with an informed attorney, will dilute the physician's liability. (*See* Appendix 22-1, Cases 20 and 21.)

§22.10 Fraudulent Reporting

Most orthopedists see patients for the purpose of disability (impairment) evaluation. This is, in essence, a subspecialty and for many orthopedists represents a substantial amount of their practice time and income.

This type of practice is exacting, requiring the doctor to know the patient being examined in as many ways and as completely as possible to produce a complete, fair, unbiased, and honest evaluation. There have been many suits alleging incomplete history-taking or physical examination, and many suits alleging fraud, bias, incomplete examination, concealment, and complicity with a third party. The making of an incorrect diagnosis, or expressing an evaluation result different from the patient's wishes, unless bound in fraud or similar behavior, is rarely held negligent.[6]

Just as the physician is bound to help a patient with timely reports or form completion, the physician has a duty to be scrupulously honest and complete with the evaluation. (*See* Appendix 22-1, Cases 22 to 27.)

§22.11 Use of Forms in Evaluation

In the process of examination and recording of observations relating to impairment, an organized, pictorial scheme is helpful. This is conducted by using a variety of forms that convey the examiner's observation to the reviewer.

§22.12 Honest Doctors' Honest Differences of Opinion

Neck, shoulder, and arm pain related to repetitive minor injuries at work or home frequently presents a controversial problem in assessing proximate cause and the degree of injury-related impairment.

A United States Health and Nutrition Examination Survey of 6,913 people throughout the country showed that 80 per cent had musculoskeletal pain in the preceding 12 months. All respondents who could recall at least one month of regional musculoskeletal pain were asked about its site, quality, and impact on function. Forty per cent had neck and shoulder pain, but only 6 per cent were disabled enough to take "time off." These findings confirm the ubiquitous nature of memorable neck and arm pain. How do we deal with arm pain in our daily living? Most people who recalled the days they

---

[6] S. Bok, Secrets: On the Ethics of Concealment and Revelation (1982).

had neck and arm pain did not have other symptoms or impairments about their bodies. Men tend to ascribe arm pain complaints to injury while women feel it more often relates to overload. Most reported symptoms as "not very serious" 42 per cent of the time, while 8 per cent said remedies such as heat, limited movements, aspirin, or NSAIDS (nonsteroidial anti-inflammatory drugs), were sufficient to control symptoms.

In the above survey, nearly all the symptoms related to the low back, with neck/shoulder/arm pain complaints that lasted one month or more representing 6 per cent of those surveyed.

Of the neck/arm pain, persons with cumulative trauma disorders (CTDs) were often felt to be a significant etiologic factor. The United States Surgeon General's Office and National Institute of Occupational Safety and Health appear to accept the CTD construction, stating "when job demands repeatedly exceed the biomechanical capacity of the worker, those activities become trauma producing. Hence, traumatogens are workplace sources of bio-mechanical strain that contribute to the onset of injuries affecting the musculoskeletal system."

The above dictum is opposed by many physicians and workers representing third-party or self-insured carriers. They point out that any upper extremity task poses a challenge to workers who experience any arm or neck discomfort. The challenge may prove insurmountable if there is no flexibility on the job. Under the banner of worker comfort and satisfaction, labor and management should seek redress in job flexibility, task design, and proper renumeration.

The examining physician in evaluating CTD-type cases must be informed of work environment, as well as the psychosocial ramification of his or her opinion and that the examiner may make him- or herself vulnerable to criticism. Honest doctors have honest differences of opinion, but opinion must be rationally based and not biased.[7] (*See* Appendix 22-1, Cases 28 to 29.)

§22.13 Psychosocial Predictors of Disability in Low Back Patients

Education and self-rated health are important predictors of degree of impairment perceived by the patient with low back pain. Little education, previous episodes of pain, and "always feeling sick" are recognized by most psychologists as significant factors when asked to prognosticate a patient with low back pain outcome from treatment.[8]

---

[7] Hadler, *Arm Pain and Workplace,* Med Leg Bull, Fall 1988, at 7.

[8] Deyo, *Psychosocial Predictors of Disability in Patients with Low Back Pain,* 15 J Rheumatol 1557 (1988).

§22.14 Malingering

It is often difficult, but important, for the physician or any person representing the patient, to determine if the patient is malingering. It is inaccurate and potentially risky to label the person as a malingerer on the basis of a "gut" reaction. There are more creditable ways of evaluating such an individual.

The American Psychiatric Association lists in its Diagnostic and Statistical Manual of Mental Disorders (DSM III R) an Index of Suspicion of Malingering:

1. The patient is attorney-referred
2. The patient complains of illness or injury that far exceeds objective findings
3. Lack of patient cooperation in treatment, monitoring, and diagnosis
4. Patient appears to manifest an antisocial personality disorder

In another study, a physician studying the malingering problem suggests:

1. The patient has vague complaints
2. The patient has ill-defined complaints, not conforming to anatomical location
3. The patient is reluctant to accept a favorable or improving diagnosis
4. The patient dramatizes complaints
5. The patient insists on receiving addicting or commonly-abused drugs

There are many tests available to detect malingering. These tests are best done by psychologists testing for simulated mental disorders.[9]

§22.15 Stress

Stress-related disorders have been recognized as compensable under workers' compensation statutes, including Federal Employees' Compensation Act (FECA), for many years. These impairments can be temporary or permanent and are usually divided into three categories:

1. *Mental/physical:* Cases in this category involve a mental stimulus that causes a distinct physical injury to the injured person, such as a heart attack brought about by a stressful event. The mental stimulus may be of a sudden or relatively brief nature, such as a sudden explosion or witnessing a particularly violent injury to another. The stress may be gradual and sustained, such as that caused by long work hours, harassment, and/or other forms of long-term personal friction.

---

[9] Silvial, *Defense of Harassment, Intentional Infliction of Emotional Harm and Employment Related Claims of Anxiety and Depression,* Law Def Bull, Sept 1987.

2. *Physical/mental:* Conversely, a physical injury can result in a disabling emotional response. These problems are diagnosed as post-traumatic stress disorders, traumatic neurosis, conversion neurosis, or hysteria. Sometimes hysterical paralysis is a mental reaction to an injury and may include aggravation of a pre-existing conditioned (i.e., non-disabling conditions that pre-existed the injury that were changed—aggravated, accelerated, or activated—to a new and disabling level.
3. *Mental/mental:* In this group, cases involve a mental stimulus that results in a mental condition, such as a psychoneurotic illness brought about by the conditions of employment. As in mental/physical cases, the stress may be of a sudden or relatively brief nature, or be gradual and sustained—the difference is that the resultant impairment is mental rather than physical.[10]

§22.16 Work-Related Stressors

Carrying an extra load at work is not nearly as stressful as a conflict with a colleague, neighbor, or clerk.

Work overloads have been overstated as a contributor to poor mental health, as viewed by many industrial psychologists. The problems at work that the patient/worker does not have "tools" to handle are more stressful, unless the worker has learned how to manage through experience. Conflicts with superiors are especially stressful, whereas fights at home are less stressful if the participants have experience with dealing with them later.

People get used to continuing hassles that do not involve personal friction, like irregular work weeks. The strain of having problems with others, particularly with persons who are friends, does not let up until the conflict is resolved. Men are far more likely to stay angry with their kids or with their hassling superior at work. Women are more used to having fights with their children and do well with that stress, but do equally poorly with work-related personal hassles.

In a personal dispute, middle-aged persons favor compromise more than younger or older. Young workers tend to be brash and challenging and older people tend to think they know everything.

Uncompromised stresses related to work may impinge on the chronic pain patient, causing his or her pain complaint to worsen, the impairment to worsen, and the impairment not to improve until work situations (or other stressful problems) have resolved.[11]

---

[10] 1B Larsons Workman's Compensation Law §42.20 (Apr 1986).

[11] Kellser, *Study Reveals Surprise Stressors,* Occup News, Oct 1989, at 23.

§22.17 Work Ability Testing Devices

The testing devices that are available today do not tell anything about work capacity. The patient must be taken to the workplace if a valid work capacity evaluation is to be completed.

There is no legally defensible scientific data available to physicians with which they can screen patients in terms of strength and flexibility testing. A great deal of useful data is accumulated by the use of isometric low back testing equipment, from which the knowledgeable physician can say that the datum—the patient's work capacity—is "consistent with," but not "with reasonable medical certainty." That day may well be coming in the next few years. Additional testing with MRI, bone scanning, ultrasound, EMG, etc., can confirm diagnosis, but does not judge work capacity.[12] (*See* Appendix 22-1, Case 29.)

§22.18 Biased Medical Testimony

Personal injury and workers' compensation litigation necessarily rely heavily on medical testimony. In an adversarial system, medical opinion typically becomes as polarized as the involved parties. Attorneys want opinions that are both unbiased and favorable, and they view opposing opinions as not only unfavorable but biased.

Bias is a personal subjective viewpoint as distinguished from "objective reality."

Until 20 years ago, the "hard" sciences such as physics and mathematics held that absolute objective reality existed, independent of the perspective of any observer. This view is now obsolete. Modern science recognizes that there is an inevitable, although at times subtle, relationship between the observer and what is observed. An observer witnessing an event, such as in a scientific evaluation of a patient, will influence the outcome (opinion). The significance of this updated view of science is that "bias" is an inevitable feature of all events that involve human beings. An example is seen in the classic Japanese film *Rashomon* in which four "observers" of a rape/murder testify to four entirely different sets of facts. An impartial, objective reality is impossible as long as human beings are involved in setting up, observing, and analyzing data. Since bias is inevitable, it must always be taken into account in the statements of experts.

Addressing the issue of bias in medical testimony, it is asserted that doctors serving as "independent examiners" avoid the contamination of bias. A closer look, however, fails to support this contention. The independent medical examiner's motivation is, first of all, to remain independent and continue to be utilized in this capacity. His or her aim is to preserve neutrality. How can he or she accomplish this, since favoring either side tends to result in losing "independent examiner" consultations? Independent medical

---

[12] Nordin, *From Round Table Discussion, American Back Society, Spring Symposium,* Cambridge, Mass (1989).

experts typically "give" something to both sides, thus maintaining their independent posture. Such a procedure may be practical and expeditious in settling litigation, although from a scientific point of view may have little merit. Consistently being impartial by giving something to each side is subtle bias in itself.

Bias in physicians results from three sources: personal, technical, and environmental. As a human being, the physician is the product of childhood experience, schooling, neighborhood, parental influences, etc. The physician develops his or her personal philosophy, religious beliefs, and political views from his or her life experience.

Issues of relevance in litigation include beliefs about the value of work and about how responsible people should be for their lives, minds, and bodies. These personal viewpoints are usually held aside from conscious awareness, yet they influence the doctor's political preference as well as which side of a case he or she usually examines for. If the doctor is a firm believer in individual responsibility, he or she may gravitate toward defense work. On the other hand, if the doctor believes that people are basically the hapless victims of their environment and illness, he or she may favor plaintiff work.

Another source of bias is medical training. The medical and psychological theories doctors learn determine how the doctor sees a patient. An orthopedist examining the back of a patient always arrives at a different conclusion from a chiropractor's opinion of the same patient. Freudian psychiatrists differ radically in their views from biochemically-oriented psychiatrists.

A subtle medical bias is the bias toward finding pathology, the doctor tending to be conservative and preferring to risk overdiagnosis and overtreating than to miss disease. The consequence is significant in evaluation and treatments rendered in a medical-legal context. Traditionally, rest was viewed as helpful for most illnesses; a "standard" in the past is now a dangerous prescription for most medical problems.

Environmental influences include factors such as the nature of the doctor's practice. From where do most of his or her referrals come? Does the doctor also render treatment? If so, there is often a bias in favor of finding something wrong to test.

Bias is a characteristic of human nature and cannot be eliminated. The nature of a doctor's bias can be established by looking at his or her "track record." However, this system may lead to a wrong conclusion. If an orthopedist examined 100 back pain patients and found that 80 per cent had pathology, does this establish the doctor as plaintiff-biased? To complicate matters, if 100 per cent of these patients really had pathology, then the doctor misdiagnosed 20 per cent. if, as an independent examiner, he would have found that one-half had pathology, then he would have misdiagnosed the remaining 30 per cent.

In psychiatry, a well-known research study revealed that researchers simulating mental patients effortlessly escaped detection and were hospitalized as seriously mentally ill. Conversely, the same research team later sent patients with demonstrable psychiatric illness to a leading medical center, where a significant number were diagnosed as faking. It is important to not take the credibility of experts at face value. The data on which physicians base their opinions should be carefully examined. We should not take for granted the "scientific" accuracy of the opinions and conclusions. It should also be remembered that "tried and true" medical treatments are continually evolving; treatments considered "scientific" are later found meritless, perhaps even harmful or absurd. A skeptical mind coupled with reluctance to accept medical authority serves justice well.[13]

The physician is indispensable to the workers' compensation (WC) system and his or her role is not limited to diagnosis and treatment. Resolution of the great majority of issues that the system addresses, informally or formally, is based on medical opinion, usually presented in written form.

In compensation law, the problem of administrative law and evidence—as it relates to expert opinion and official notice—concerns principally the handling of medical fact. It has been assumed that when medical testimony of one authority is in conflict with that of another, and the compensation commission is upheld in its prerogative of choosing which medical opinion to accept, there is no significant qualitative difference between these competing items of medical evidence. This is not always true. There may be instances in which medical testimony suffers from some flaw that disentitles it to acceptance when other, more valid testimony stands in the record.

With the changing nature of injury and illness, physicians must be prepared to analyze the factual situation and, in difficult cases, to assist in determining the degree to which the disorder is related to work.[14]

§22.19 Physician Prejudices

All physicians have prejudices if they are honest with themselves. Doctors who treat low back pain patients often group their patients when evaluating them for disability. Patient motivation to return to work is a large factor in any person's impairment. The motivation is blunted by the prospect of losing money while disabled. It has been shown that the greater the monetary advantage to remain off work or at limited work, the less the motivation to return to work.

In this situation, the examining physician should accurately assess impairment, allowing the trier of fact to ascertain disability. It is equally important for the examining physician to do his or her assessment without bias. At this time, examining physicians are often adversarial in reporting. Unfortunately for the patient, non-medical parties to the adversarial evaluations are confused to the detriment of the patient, with pejorative or demeaning comments, and even give advice to the patient regarding one or more of the evaluating physicians.

---

[13] Marcus, *Unbiased Medical Testimony: Reality or Myth,* 1 Expert Witness J 1 (1989).

[14] Larson, *The Role of the Physician in the Workers' Compensation Process,* 3 Occup Prob in Med Prac 1 (1989).

The skillful examining physicians recognize and understand resistant behaviors in patients being evaluated. The importance of sensitive understanding and performing detailed profiles of the shaping of behavior in these patients helps the study. Resistance, noncompliance, and functional overlay often present in varying degrees. Behavioral signs of resistance include (1) argumentative/manipulative behaviors, (2) withholding vital information, (3) overt attempts to misunderstand feedback and questions, (4) and incoherent vague responses.

These acts of deception of self and/or others, whether consciously contrived or silently held, remain an act of self-disclosure and a vital part of the claimant's symptoms. Resistance is a maladaptive reaction against loss (or perceived impending loss) and is a manifestation of conflicting emotions. These behaviors should be regarded as an informative exposé which is to be respected and accepted instead of being regarded as an act of deception. Resistant behavior, when encountered, should be engaged in neutral tone. The professional examining physician should keep constant vigilence for behavioral signs of resistance:

1. Patient unwilling to remove clothes; act is performed grudgingly or refuses
2. Argumentative/defensive—raises unfounded claims
3. Manipulative—makes demands; changes subject when adverse subject discussed
4. Withholds vital information when such information is readily available
5. Constantly changing visual focus; episodic or persistent aversion glance; fluttering, batting eyelids
6. Easily distracted or superattentive to details
7. No-show, tardy, or reschedules evaluations
8. On manual muscle testing, "give away" weakness in lower extremity, with no corresponding gait abnormality
9. Exaggerated subjective symptoms inconsistent with objective symptoms, testing, and statistical variables
10. Performance discrepancies—physical capacity not performed with maximum effort; capacity demonstrated by distraction maneuvers or by vicarious observation

The examiner's attitude is important, a terse or put-down effect by the examiner or retort in response to a hostile challenge by the patient may add fatal stress to the evaluation. A kindly, even straightforward, nonjudgmental attitude on the part of the physician is quite workable and disarms hostility, not dishonesty.[15] (*See* Appendix 22-1, Cases 19 and 28.)

---

[15] Washington, *Deception: An Informative Exposé in Disability Evaluations,* 1 Disability Evaluating News 1 (1989).

§22.20 Work-Related Accidents

A national survey shows the 10 leading work-related diseases and injuries to be:

1. Occupational lung disease
2. Musculoskeletal disease
3. Occupational cancers
4. Amputations, fractures, eye loss, lacerations, and traumatic death
5. Cardiovascular disease
6. Reproductive disorders
7. Neurotaxic disorders
8. Noise-induced hearing loss
9. Dermatological conditions
10. Psychological disorders

Another survey polling several thousand workers asked what they believed to be the biggest problem in maintaining good health. The response was:

1. Lack of exercise: 42%
2. Eating too much: 28%
3. Smoking too much: 10%
4. Drinking too much: 4%

When physicians were surveyed, the same items were reported, although smoking and drinking were rated much higher and drinking was construed to include illicit drug usage.

In comparing the injuries and health problems, a relationship between the lifestyle and health behavior of the worker and on-the-job injuries is probable. The relationship between a neglected body, poor nutrition, effect of drugs, and respiratory diseases aggravated by smoking and the direct results on accidents and diseases is unmistakable.

To a large measure, the solution lies in part of the basic concepts of a sports medicine clinic or a working back clinic rehabilitation; that is aerobic exercise, conditioning, and musculoskeletal flexibility is good for injury prevention as well as for therapy when injured.[16]

---

[16] Allers, *Work Place Preventive Programs Cut Cost of Illness and Injuries,* Occup Health and Safety, Oct 1989, at 26; Haddad, *Analysis of 2,932 Workers' Compensation Back Injury Cases,* 12 Spine 756 (1987).

§22.21 Work Ability Work Releases

Physicians have become part of an ongoing problem dealing with ethical and probative issues in respect to certifying disability. The problem comes frequently in requests by the patient for a "note"—a certificate for illness. Variations on the following scenario appear in the doctor's office daily.

A 48-year-old construction worker presented to a doctor seeking a work release for the previous four days. He reported being ill with fever and sore throat, although now recovered without treatment by a physician. An examination revealed that the patient was free of illness. His wife and children were regular patients, but this was his first visit to the doctor. Should the doctor sign his work releases for four prior days?

These cases place the physician in the awkward position of judging the veracity of the claims of a stranger, with little evidence on which to base the judgment. The physician's decision says more about his or her mood or beliefs about human nature than about the legitimacy of the claim. The worker has few incentives to tell the truth and the doctor has few incentives to ascertain the truth. The worker who may not be truthful can look forward to financial benefits based on the doctor's "note." If the doctor questions the truth or the patient's illness, loss of patients or continuing treating this family under unpleasant stress can be anticipated. This physician is, in this set of facts, no longer practicing medicine, but is judging human character. Every time a physician makes a judgment not based on medical expertise, medical practice is demeaned and the doctors' credibility is vulnerable. In 1980, the American Medical Association revised its Principles of Medical Ethics to include the statement that physicians should "deal honestly" with patients and colleagues (and triers of fact). The physician who misrepresents the truth to the patient (or others) is not subject to medical and legal censure.[17]

§22.22 Emergency Room Visits

In a recent survey, musculoskeletal injuries accounted for 580,000 (18 per cent) of the estimated 3.2 million emergency room-treated occupational injuries in the United States. Manual handling of materials, repetitive motions, and vibrations are especially important etiological factors.

Injuries associated with manual handling (unaided lifting and lowering) cause low back injury, the largest single subset of musculoskeletal injuries. Low back injuries account for one in five of all occupational injuries.

Repetitive motion associated trauma (cumulative trauma disorders) are common and include carpal tunnel syndrome, tendonitis, ganglionitis, tenosynovitis, bursitis, and epicondylitis. These injuries may be caused or aggravated by repeated twisting or awkward positions of work.

---

[17] Hollerman & Hollerman, *School and Work Release Evaluations,* 260 JAMA 3629 (1988). T.L. Beauchamp & J.F. Childress, Principles of Biomedical Ethics 223 (2d ed 1983).

Vibration-associated injuries are seen in vehicle operations (truck, automobile, taxi driving). The effects of vibration are poorly understood, but an increasing body of data suggest that low back pain, vertebrogenic pain, and degenerative disc disease may be vibration-associated and/or vibration-aggravated.

An estimated 1.2 million workers are exposed to segmental vibration, i.e., vibration principally of a part or parts of the body, such as hand-held power tools, chain saws, jack hammers, etc. Often, the extremities exposed to segmental vibration present with numbness and/or blanching of fingers, with reduced sensitivity to heat, cold, or pain. Occasional increased sensitivity is noted.[18]

§22.23 Early Intervention

Vocational rehabilitation has attracted increasing attention in more and more states as advocates and detractors debate the appropriate use of this potentially beneficial, yet costly, workers' compensation benefit. The stated purpose of rehabilitation is to return the worker to a job as promptly as possible. In states with strong vocational rehabilitation programs, early intervention after injury and obtaining medical and vocational suggestions for planning a program of rehabilitation has been most productive. On the average, about 70 per cent of all injured workers, early intervened and felt to be candidates for vocational rehabilitation, returned to work (not necessarily the same work) within two years of injury. Early intervention and management of workers by medical and rehabilitation personnel knowledgeable about this type of care has been shown cost-effective. Intervention in cases within between 80 and 160 days from injury seemed most effective timing in one state (Minnesota).[19]

Health selection, which transfers workers with health problems from occupations with heavy physical demands to occupations with light physical demands, may be a factor contributing to excessive morbidity in the latter group. For all disease and functional disorders that have been studied, an increased risk for future health problems was greatest in those who switched jobs for medical reasons. This relationship was most apparent in musculoskeletal disorders and impaired working capacity. The consensus indicates clearly that there is a negative health selection in physically light occupations.

---

[18] Division of Surveillance, Hazard Evaluation and Field Studies. Div Safety Research, National Institute for Occupational Safety and Health as reported in 249 JAMA 2301 (1983).

[19] Rehabilitation in the Minnesota Workers' Compensation System, 4 Workers Compensation Research Institute Brief (1989); Magora, *Investigation of the Relation Between Low Back Pain and Occupation,* 5 Scand J Rehab Med 191-96 (1973); Williams & Hedlar, *Musculo-skeletal Components of Decrepitude,* 11 J Semin Arth Rheum 248 (1981).

§22.24 Back Injuries

It is important that workers' compensation treating physicians be informed of the social economics of on-the-job low back injuries. In most ways, injuries to other areas of the body follow the same route. The general observation throughout the country is reflected in New York. In 1982, the Workers Compensation Board of New York State authorized payment of $42,084,999 for closed cases of spinal injuries. In the same year, 30 states paid a combined $1.9 billion for medical treatment and/or compensation for back injuries. Analysis of 2,932 spinal injury cases evaluated for disability in a seven-year period showed a mean of 23.4 months of medical treatment and 1.706 cases concluded with no disability. Also, 91 per cent of the claimants represented by counsel were not working, whereas 77 per cent not so represented were working. Most of the consultants' reports to insurance carriers and the claimants reports veered toward an adversarial position which favored the respective interested party. The cost of workers' compensation back injury is very high. The conclusion is obvious that iatrogenic and jurisgenic factors directly prolong the medical care, creating delay in returning to work.

Several authors have observed that (1) most back injury patients under treatment for two months or less return to work, (2) of back injury patients treated for three to six months, one-third will return to work, (3) of those back injury patients treated for 6 to 18 months, fewer than 50 per cent will return to work, and (4) of those on-the-job back injury patients receiving treatment 18 months or more after their injury, fewer than 10 per cent will return to regular gainful employment. The above percentages are altered favorably by aggressive patient participation programs, both physical and vocational.[20]

§22.25 Pre-Employment Examinations

Many orthopedists have work relationships with large companies that require pre-employment examination as part of the physician duties. The purpose of the examination is not limited to the employability of the person, but to understand his or her physical condition. A complete history along with a complete (not superficial or limited) physical examination is essential. The report of this examination must be made to the employer factualy and unbiased, just as any other examination—disability examination, etc. When pathology is found, the physician has a moral and generally a legal duty to inform the examinee; failure to do so may be negligent. Ordinarily, the examining physician does not become the treating physician, but returns the examinee to a family physician or arranges consultation when abnormalities are found. Employability and work limitations are part of the evaluation; thus, many entities become interested in the health of the examinee. Com-

---

[20] Haddad, *Analysis of 2,932 Workers' Compensation Back Injury Cases,* 12 Spine 756 (1987).

munication with all interested parties is essential for a smooth and effective evaluation. The prospective employee, as well as the already employed employee, has a legal right to be informed of the hazards of the work place. The employer must conform with hazard communication standards implanted by OSHA in 1983. It may be negligent behavior on the part of the employer (or a physician if he or she follows employer orders not to inform) who fails to do so.[21]

§22.26 Company Doctors

The industrial physician or industrial doctor who examines an employee for pre-employment purposes or disability examination, in most jurisdictions, cannot be held liable for a negligent observation or for missing a diagnosis as long as the doctor's examination was not physically injurious to the employee. The industrial doctor, unless an independent contractor, is a company employee. There have been cases where the examination was "rough" and the employee was injured—cases in which emotional trauma or fraud was alleged.

The industrial surgeon who treats an injured employee negligently has been immune to personal suit in the past if the doctor was an employee of the company. Recent cases have held that an employee physician working for the company, who negligently injures an employee, can be held liable for the examination injury unrelated to preceding workers compensation claim. (*See* Appendix 22-1, Cases 22 and 23.)

Company health care employees, such as a nurse assisting or reporting to a company-employed physician, are rarely held liable for acts of negligence. The "Captain of the Ship" applies here less frequently than in hospital nurse-physician relationships.[22]

§22.27 Completing Reports and Forms

The treating physician has a legal duty to assist a patient with completing insurance forms and disability forms, and submitting reports of the patient's history, physical condition, treatment, and results, along with an opinion

---

[21] Strasser, *Preplacement Exams Assess Workers' Medical Ability to Perform a Task,* Occup Health & Safety, Mar 1989, at 16. Krueger, *Expanded Right-to-Know Laws to Affect 4.5 Million Work Places,* Occup Health & Safety, Sept 1988, at 10.

[22] *Rehabilitation in the Minnesota Workers' Compensation System,* 4 Workers Compensation Research Institute Brief 1 (1989); Magora, *Investigation of the Relation Between Low Back Pain and Occupation,* 5 Scand J Rehab Med 191-96 (1973); Williams & Hedlar, *Musculo-skeletal Components of Decrepitude,* 11 J Semin Arth Rheum 248 (1981); Haddad, *Analysis of 2,932 Workers' Compensation Back Injury Cases,* 12 Spine 756 (1987); Strasser, *Preplacement Exams Assess Workers' Medical Ability to Perform Task,* Occup Health & Safety, Mar 1989, at 16; Krueger, *Expanded Right-to Know Laws to Affect 4.5 Million Work Places,* Occup Health & Safety, Sept 1988, at 10; Hadler, *Medical Ramifications of the Federal Regulation of the Social Security Disability Insurance Program,* 96 Ann Int Med 665 (1982).

as to the patient's impairment and the cause of the impairment. For the orthopedist to fail to do this without cause is culpable in most jurisdictions and the patient has a cause of action.

Withholding reports until a bill is paid is below the standard of care, although a reasonable report fee, absent any prior agreement or statutory exclusion, can be requested. If a patient is presenting for disability evaluation, an understanding prior to examination as to payment of a fee for the report can be reached; if the patient refuses to pay, the physician has not established a physician-patient relationship and is not bound to evaluate the patient.

The orthopedist is often asked to testify by deposition or court appearance. If he or she agrees, or is legally subpoenaed, he or she cannot avoid appearing and expressing a medical opinion. Payment for deposition or court appearances is the patient's responsibility in most states, although it is common to effect an agreement between the physician and attorney, with the attorney guaranteeing the doctor's reasonable fee. If the physician fails to appear, he or she may be held liable for the amount of damages caused by his failure to appear. (*See* Appendix 22-1, Cases 26 and 27.)

§22.28 Social Security Guidelines

Social security disability insurance is a federally created and regulated insurance plan. The definition of disability, as it relates to work capacity, is exclusively the purview of government administrators. The primary physician's opinion has little, if any, impact on decisions. Administering this insurance scheme requires the quantification of illness as it relates to work capacity (disability). What has evolved is a program that insures for the amount of "disease." The assumption is that with more disease, there is a greater likelihood of illness, and that illness manifests as work incapacity. Leaving this underlying assumption tacit is responsible for the adversary climate that surrounds the physician, the patient claimant, and the administrators. It is likely also responsible for lack of clinical investigation into critical issues of amount, form, and direction of illness that a diseased (and, by corollary, disabled) person has.

In addressing chronic pain complaints, the Social Security Administration has proposed expansion of regulations pertaining to evaluation of symptoms including pain (52 Fed Reg 35516 Nov 14, 1988). Physicians treating chronic pain problems generally believe that social security administrators should recognize expert evaluation and treatment of relative pain prior to final disability evaluation. The present disability system rewards sick behavior and impedes rehabilitation in many cases, and a tool to recognize this and treat is essential.

At the present time, there are 48 separate places in the Social Security Medicare Law where civil penalties may be imposed for noncompliance. The areas in which physicians are vulnerable are:

1. A nonparticipating physician charging a Medicare patient more than the Maximum Actual Allowable Charge (MAAC) limit
2. Failure to provide required notice for non-assigned elective surgeries where the fee will be more than $500
3. Failure to provide the required denial notice for services that might be declared medically unnecessary
4. Continuing to bill Medicare patients for in-office laboratory
5. Knowingly violating the Medicare Assignment Agreement
6. Making a claim to Medicare or Medicaid for services not provided as claimed, or making a false or fraudulent claim
7. Accepting a payment as an inducement to limit or reduce services to an individual under Medicare or Medicaid
8. Knowingly and willfully failing to furnish a diagnostic code when requesting payment for an item or service provided on assigned claim basis
9. Giving to any person information, with respect to Medicare coverage of in-patient hospital services, that is false or misleading and which could reasonably be expected to influence a hospital discharge

Recently, the Civil Monetary Penalties Law was amended to provide vicarious liability for a doctor's agent's actions.[23]

§22.29 Disability Ratings

The Social Security Administration has forms setting out work-related impairments. Additionally, the United States Department of Labor uses a set of forms that sets out limitations. The following work classifications are defined in the Dictionary of Occupational Titles from the United States Department of Labor:

1. *Very heavy:* Lifting objects in excess of 100 pounds with frequent lifting and/or carrying of objects weighing 50 pounds or more
2. *Heavy:* Lifting 100 pounds maximum with frequent lifting and/or carrying objects weighing up to 50 pounds
3. *Medium heavy:* Lifting 75 to 80 pounds maximum with frequent lifting and/or carrying objects weighing up to 40 pounds
4. *Medium:* Lifting 50 pounds maximum with frequent lifting and/or carrying of objects weighing up to 24 pounds

---

[23] Hadler, *Medical Ramifications of the Federal Regulation of the Social Security Disability Insurance Program,* 96 Ann Int Med 6654 (1982); Schuster & Hamaty, *Legal Issues: Social Security Disability Regulations,* 3 Natl Pain Mgmt Update (So Pain Society) 1 (1989); Kelsay, *Medicare Civil Monetary Penalties Law,* PLICO News, Jan 1989, at 5-8; M. Gaynes, Civil Money Penalities Reporter (1989).

5. *Light:* Lifting 20 pounds maximum with frequent lifting and/or carrying of objects weighing up to 10 pounds
6. *Sedentary:* Lifting 10 pounds maximum and occasionally lifting and/or carrying such articles as dockets, ledgers, and small tools[24]

§22.30 References

Winston & Landesman, *AIDS and a Duty to Protect,* 17 Hastings Cent Rep 22 (1987).

J.C. Bruce, Privacy and Confidentiality of Health Care Information (1984).

J.F. Monagle & D.C. Thomasura, Medical Ethics: A Guide For Health Professionals (1988).

Gillan, *AIDS and Medical Confidentiality,* 294 Br Med J 1675 (1987).

R. Wasserstrom, The Legal and Philosophical Foundations of the Right to Privacy, Biomedical Ethics (T.A. Mappes & J.S. Zembaty 2d ed McGraw-Hill, New York, 1986).

Merritt, *The Constitutional Balance Between Health and Liberty,* 16 Hastings Cent Rep 2 (Supp 1986).

[24] United States Department of Labor, Dictionary of Occupational Titles App D at 101-102 (4th ed Supp 1986); Chaffin, *Pre-employment Strength Testing,* J Occ Med, June 1978, at 403-08; D.W. Kyserling, Isometric Strength Testing in Selecting Workers for Strenuous Jobs Ph.D. Dissertation, Industrial and Operations Engineering and Industrial and Health Science, University of Michigan (1979); Kyserling, *Establishing an Industrial Strength Testing Program,* 20 Amer Ind Hyg Assoc J 6 (1978); Harber & Soohoo, *Static Ergonomic Strength Testing in Evaluation of Occupational Back Pain,* 26 J Occup Med 877 (1984).

Appendix 22-1
Cases

1 ***Sears Roebuck & Co v Murphy,*** **508 NE2d 825 (Ind App Ct 1987)** (case presented a question of whether a torn medial meniscus and loss of cartilage can be considered permanent impairment if no functional loss is present. In a worker's compensation claim, the claimant was installing air conditioning, had to kneel and lift, and sustained discomfort in his knee, feeling a pop. The diagnosis was a torn medial meniscus that was successfully operated and a torn part of cartilage was removed. An orthopedist testified that he had no functional loss, but 5 per cent impairment was given because he lost part of the medial meniscus. There was some question of whether it was due to an on-the-job injury, but this was resolved in favor of the patient. On the question of permanent disability for the loss of cartilage, two of the three judges felt there was no permanent impairment, inasmuch as there was no functional loss, and the third felt that because there was loss of tissue and a natural history of meniscectomy, the patient was apt to develop degenerative arthritis later in life, so there was impairment).

Comment: This is a typical situation showing the difference between impairment, which is the evaluation that a physician does, and disability, which is the decision of the trier of fact, in this case falling within the state workers' compensation law of Indiana.

2 ***LoDico v Caputi,*** **517 NY2d 640 (App Div 1987)** (in May 1983, a patient noticed a sudden onset of numbness in his right thumb and first and second fingers. Several days later, he noticed his entire right arm was weak and experienced tingling in his fingers. The arm/hand symptoms continued to persist for several days, and he noted pain in the posterior aspect of his neck. On May 9, 1983, he sought medical treatment from an osteopathic physician. He diagnosed the patient's condition as cervical-dorsal strain and treated him with oral medication as well as manipulation. Seven weeks later, the patient was seen by a neurologist who found no neurological abnormalities. Since the patient was not able to work after the onset of symptoms, he filed for workers' compensation benefits and directly reported to a physician for examination of disability. On September 9, 1983, a physician examined him and forwarded a report to the employer's workers' compensation company that said, in his opinion, that the patient had recovered from the alleged injury of May 1983, had no evidence of intervertebral disc injury or disease or peripheral damage, and should be able to return to his usual work without restrictions and limitations. Sometime after examination, the patient was diagnosed as suffering from a brain stem tumor. The patient filed a malpractice action against several physicians, including the one who examined him for workers' compensation. The trial court denied that physician's motion to dismiss the claim against him. He argued that there was never a physician-patient relationship. The appellate court said that the physician who

had conducted the examination of the patient solely for the purpose of rating the injury for the insurance company for workers' compensation was not liable to him for failure to properly diagnose a latent brain tumor. The physician neither offered nor intended to treat or care for the patient, and he had no reason to believe that the patient would rely on the report to the insurance company).

3 ***Keene v Wiggins*, 69 Cal App 3d 308, 138 Cal Rptr 3 (1977)** (physician submitted a copy of a medical report to plaintiff's workers' compensation carrier for the purpose of evaluating a claim for workers' compensation benefits, on which the patient relied to his detriment. The physician was not liable to the patient for negligence in making the report, where the doctor made the examination solely for the purpose of rating injury for an insurance carrier, neither offered nor intended to treat or otherwise care for the patient, and had no reason to believe the patient examined would rely on the report).

4 ***Johnston v Siblay*, 558 SW2d 135 (Tex Civ App 1977)** (physician-patient relationship was insufficient based on the nature of the examination. The physician conducted the examination of an injured employee for the purpose of evaluating the employee's disability for an insurance carrier after a claim for workers' compensation had been filed. It was further noted that the physician did not injure the employee during the course of the examination).

5 ***Hughes v Webster Parish Police Jury*, 414 So 2d 1353 (La App 1982)** (45-year-old man was injured when he worked beneath a police vehicle. A clutch and pressure plate weighing a total of 40 pounds fell on his chest. He said he experienced sharp pain on his lower back, went blind for a moment, resting for about one-half hour after the accident, and then went to his family physician, who referred him to an orthopedist. The orthopedist noticed lumbosacral tenderness on examination, prescribed a brace, and indicated the patient would be ready to return to work in about 12 days. The patient, however, was treated for several years, unimproving, with a variety of treatments, including steroid injections, optical anesthesia, exercise regime, corset, and psychiatric consultation. He was also seen by two additional orthopedists. He was seen at a pain center that noted only "mild back spasms." There were three possible diagnoses: (1) malingering (considered to be unlikely), (2) psychophysiological-musculoskeletal disorder, or (3) hysterical neurosis conversion. The psychiatrist said he could not sort out the orthopedic and emotional factors in the pelvic pain. The patient was somewhat socioeconomically deprived, had a seventh grade education, and limited experience at any job other than the type of work he was doing at the time of the accident. He was still unable to be gainfully employed four years after the accident. The employer stopped disability payments. The Louisiana District Court rejected the injured man's plea for benefits on the basis of permanent and total disability. The Court of Appeals noted, however, that there had been no evidence of a rehabilitation program, which had been suggested to the employer 14 months after the accident. The case was remanded,

with an order for a special pain clinic approach, designed to deal with the combination of orthopedic and emotional disabilities).

Comment: This is a common sort of case where a minimal injury will produce pain of an incapacitating nature. There are many headache problems that fall into this category. The vocabulary used to describe this situation is difficult in itself, with each specialist seeming to favor his or her own terminology. It basically falls into the category of somatization disorder. Very rarely are there significant objective findings of injury, or if they existed, they have passed the healing period. There is, however, a profound impairment that manifests itself by loss of endurance, ease of fatigue, and a pain complaint that is interpreted as overwhelming. Each case must be evaluated on its own merits considering all factors of the case—physical, psychological, spiritual, socioeconomical, ethnic, etc. It is certain that some of the patients are malingerers, but this is generally considered to be a minority. This is the sort of case in which third-party carriers and a number of orthopedists, as well as physicians in general, take the rather biased or arbitrary view that if there is not an objective finding, the odds are that the impairment is more related to the patient's lack of willpower or willful misconduct, which very often works a disservice to the patient.

6 ***Ferguson v Wolkin,* 131 Misc 2d 304, 499 NYS2d 356 (Civ Ct 1981)** (judgment for defendant orthopedist was upheld in an action alleging malpractice in reporting that the plaintiff, whom the defendant had examined for the purpose of determining whether she was able to return to work after an automobile accident, was fit to work. The plaintiff returned to work and suffered a back injury a month later. Although the physician-patient relationship was applicable, the defendant could only be liable for breach of duty in conducting the examination, not beyond that, and not even if the conclusions based on the examination were wrong).

7 ***Parker v St Elizabeth Community Health Center,* 226 Neb 526 412 NW2d 469 (1987)** (if a handicapped worker's recovery from knee surgery was poorer than average but within normal limits, can the subsequent impairment be attributed to the underlying impairment? In this case, they were residuals of polio. Under statute, employees are liable only to the degree of injury that the accident would have caused in an unimpaired person; that is, the increased amount of impairment that the accident produced. At the time he was hired, the hospital x-ray technician could walk only by putting all of his weight on his left leg, swinging his atrophied right leg forward. A fall from a ladder in the hospital tore the medial meniscus in the left knee, and despite arthroscopic surgery he found walking and standing difficult and pushing x-ray equipment almost impossible. He began to submit poor quality x-rays. His performance deteriorated so much that he lost his job. It was successfully argued by the patient's counsel, with medical expert evidence, that a patient with an impaired right leg would be slower and less completely rehabilitated than the left leg, the argument being he could not fully develop his quadriceps muscles. That, however, is not the only test. The residual synovitis and internal derangement pain would, with reasonable

medical probability, be greater in the normal knee in a patient who had an impaired opposite knee because the normal knee is always in an overloaded position protecting the abnormal knee).

Comment: In a case like this, it is very important to accurately assess what is the cause of the ongoing pain. The fact that there may be a wasting of the quadriceps muscle to a degree is not the only cause of ongoing pain.

8 ***Laberge v Lancleave,* 534 So 2d 1176 (Fla Dist Ct App 1988)** (question of whether a plaintiff had suffered permanent injury was for the jury to decide, regardless of the quality of the expert's testimony).

9 ***Tolisano v Texon,* 533 NYS2d 874 (App Div 1988)** (physician could be held liable for the death of a witness whom he had examined and certified was physically fit to testify. The district attorney requested an examination of the witness to determine fitness to testify. The doctor examined the witness, who suffered from advanced coronary atherosclerosis, and certified he could testify without "significant" risk to his life. The witness opposed his subpoena, but was ordered to appear. He appealed that order, but died while the appeal was pending. It was alleged that death resulted from stress. The appellate court dismissed his appeal. The family of the decedent filed a wrongful death action against the physician, who pled that no physician-patient relationship existed. The physician moved to dismiss the complaint on the grounds above, plus public policy grounds. The trial court denied the motion and the physician appealed. The appellate court affirmed the denial of the motion. An issue of fact existed as to the nature and extent of the doctor's duty to the witness. A duty arose when the doctor agreed to render an opinion, knowing it would be relied on to determine whether to subpoena the witness. Such a duty may exist outside of the realm of medical malpractice, the court concluded, without expanding on the nature of that duty).

10 ***Davis v Tirrell,* 110 Misc 2d 889, 443 NYS2d 136 (Civ Ct 1981)** (student had been examined by a physician who was hired by the school for evaluation of her mostly handicapped status. The court emphasized that there was no treatment or expectation of treatment and no diagnosis for the purpose of treatment, and that the report of the examination was given to the employee and the doctor—not to the patient. An analogy was made to the personal injury litigation situation where the plaintiff submits to an examination by the defendant's doctor in order that the plaintiff's claim for damages may be rebutted at trial. The court stated that the insufficient examination might affect the weight of the professional opinion expressed at trial, but did not give rise to a claim for malpractice because no physician-patient relationship existed).

11 ***Spaulding v Hussain,* 551 A2d 1022 (NJ Super Ct App 1988)** (physician has a duty to give reasonably required litigation assistance to his patient. This court upheld a suit filed by a patient against a physician who failed to appear on the patient's behalf at a personal injury trial. The patient was injured on the job. His attorney, in evaluating the case, felt that the appearance of the plaintiff's physician was essential to a favorable outcome. The attorney met with the physician and alleged that the physician agreed to appear at trial. However, even after the attorney had obtained several continuances of trial to accommodate the physician, and both sides had presented their cases at trial, the physician did not appear. The attorney decided to accept what he considered to be an inadequate settlement and advised his client to file an action against the physician, which the plaintiff did. The suit alleged breach of contract, the physician having agreed to testify, and violation of a tort duty to testify at the plaintiff's trial. The physician pled medical emergency and further pled that the attorney should have asked for another continuance rather than accept an inadequate settlement. An expert testified that the plaintiff's attorney exercised sound professional judgment in accepting the settlement offer. The jury found, using a special interrogatory, that (1) the company employing plaintiff was liable for 65 per cent of damages from the on-the-job injury while the plaintiff was responsible for 35 per cent, (2) that the plaintiff had established a right to recover damages from the physician under a contract theory of promissory estoppel, and (3) that the plaintiff was entitled to recover from the physician under negligence principles, but that the recovery should be reduced by 45 per cent to reflect the negligence of the plaintiff's attorney in accepting an inadequate settlement. The court rendered a judgment notwithstanding the verdict on the issue of the attorney's comparative negligence, ruling that the physician was liable for 100 per cent of the damage the plaintiff sustained in accepting an inadequate settlement. The physician appealed. The appellate court affirmed the trial court verdict, observing that prior state (New Jersey) decisions had recognized, under contract principles, the enforceability of a treating physician's affirmative undertaking to testify. The court then ruled that a physician's tort duty to treat a patient in accordance with proper professional standards includes a duty to assist the patient's litigation. Noting that personal injury claimants cannot pursue their claims without the testimony of physicians, the court reasoned that a treating physician is not at liberty to refuse a patient's request for assistance in litigating a claim involving injuries which the physician treated. Although this duty may not require the doctor to testify in court, evidence in this case supported the finding of liability, since the plaintiff had relied to his detriment on the physician's agreement to render specific litigation assistance).

Comment: 11 Medical Liability 106 (May 1989) pointed out that a number of courts have held that a physician has a duty to refrain from informally revealing information about a patient to the patient's legal adversaries. In *Spaulding,* the appellate court's discussion of the physician's duty to provide litigation assistance is "dictum" inasmuch as trial court's instruction were not objected to by the defendant.

12 ***Mackey v Greenview Hospital, Inc,* 587 SW2d 249 (Ky App 1979)** (failure to take a careful and accurate medical history was the basis for liability. It was pointed out, on the other hand, that if a patient does not give a physician a full and accurate history, that may be a basis for finding the physician not guilty of malpractice. The physician must consider the history given by the patient, and failure to do so may constitute malpractice. Con-

ducting a careful and complete physical examination is equally important for the physician to avoid negligent practice. The minimal or "clothes on" examination reported by a physician to be a "complete" physical examination is culpable, although patients often report that the doctor "didn't touch me" in the physical examination. It needs to be remembered that skilled practitioners can make many diagnostic points by observation of the patient without the laying on of hands or requiring the patient to be fully unclothed. Further, the complete physical examination of a part of the body often does not require a complete body examination; in fact, such examination may be inappropriate).

13 ***Millison v EI duPont deNemours & Co,*** **545 A2d 213 (NJ Super Ct App Div 1988)** (company physician and company were liable for concealing asbestos-related disease from an employee who was examined and diagnosed by the physician. Several widows filed suit against company physicians for failure to warn of the risks of working with asbestos. Each employee received an annual physical examination and chest x-ray, but was not told if there was anything wrong. On remand, the court awarded $1,382,500 in compensatory and punitive damages. The highest court found evidence sufficient to show the company and its physicians engaged in a deliberate strategy to conceal the employee's asbestos-related diseases).

14 ***Craddock v Gross,*** **350 Pa Super 575, 504 A2d 1300 (1986)** (workers' compensation court held that a physician examining a patient for the purpose of assessing impairment creates a physician-patient relationship).

15 ***VanSickle v McHugh,*** **430 NW2d 799 (Mich Ct App 1988)** (physician-patient privilege does not apply to a medical examination that is not expressly for the purpose of rendering medical advice or care—at least when the patient lacks a reasonable expectation that the consultation will be confidential. The court found that a physician's examination of a patient on behalf of the patient's potential adversary in a personal injury suit removed the physician's testimony from the privilege scope. The decision allows damaging statements made by a plaintiff to a doctor during an examination to be admitted as evidence. The plaintiff sued for damages from an automobile accident. Her no-fault insurer, a potential defendant, had her examined by a surgeon. The defendant sought to depose that surgeon and the plaintiff sought a protective order, claiming the physician-patient privilege. The court held that the physician-patient privilege is inapplicable when the examination in question is "not conducted for the purpose of rendering medical advice or care to the person asserting the privilege, at least when that person lacks a reasonable expectation that the consultation is cloaked with a veil of confidentiality." The court reasoned that because the potential defendant requested the examination, the doctor did not act within the traditional role of a treating physician. The court concluded that the examination of the patient could not have led the patient to "repose confidence in the doctor's treatment or expect confidentiality from information exchanged during the course of consultation").

Comment: This decision requires plaintiffs and their counsel to be aware of the dangers of consultations with a defendant's physician. Taken to its extreme, counsel may need to accompany plaintiffs to these medical examinations to avoid allowing plaintiffs to incriminate themselves while under the mistaken impression that they are protected by the physician-patient privilege.

16 ***Patterson v Workmen's Compensation Appeal Board,* 554 A2d 614 (Pa Commonw Ct 1989)** (while adjusting brakes on his truck, the claimant was struck by a car. He complained of intractable neck pain, receiving total disability payments for two years. When the employer's examining doctor found no "hard core" evidence of disease or injury, the workers' compensation board agreed and all benefits were cut off. An MRI was taken before an appeal could be heard; the test showed a herniated intervertebral disc at C5-6 and C6-7. The board, however, refused to hear the appeal. The Commonwealth Court of Pennsylvania disagreed. "The MRI scan, bolstered by the opinion of two board certified specialists, confirms that the plaintiff's pain is caused by 'soft tissue' injury not readily disclosed by routine physical examination or x-rays." In the "interest of justice," the board was instructed to rehear the case).

17 ***Lotspeich v Chance Vought Aircraft,* 869 SW2d 705 (Tex Civ App 1963)** (physician who gave a pre-employment examination and read chest x-rays failed to disclose that probable pulmonary tuberculosis was present. The physician was exonerated under the logic that he did not have knowledge of the tuberculin condition alleged, shown by the x-ray, and further that the physician was not under a duty to the patient to disclose the condition. His employment, in this regard, was the sole benefit of the examination).

Comment: It is easy to see where the opposite opinion could be reached, but apparently not under Texas law at the time of *Lotspeich.*

18 ***Hoover v Williamson,* 236 Md 250, 203 A2d 861 (1954)** (action by an employee against a physician who was employed by the employer to administer an annual x-ray examination, alleging that the physician undertook to advise him of his condition of health as to lung infection, referred him to an expert, and after such consultation undertook to advise him and both wrongfully represented the seriousness of the condition and concealed from him that the consultant's recommendation was to discontinue his employment in his present work environment. In this case, the court recognized that there was no physician-patient relationship between (1) a prospective or actual insured and the physician who examined him for an insurance company, or (2) a prospective or actual employee and a doctor who examined him for an employer. However, in this case, the examining physician assumed to act additionally, even though gratuitously, in a manner he felt was in the interest of the patient, and the physician thereby incurred a tort obligation that was non-consensual and independent of the physician-patient contract).

19 ***Willitzer v McCloud,* 453 NE2d 693 (Ohio 1983)** (independent physician examining a workers' compensation claim at the request of an industrial commission was not immune from civil suit based on the examination. The supreme court pointed out that a physician's potential liability is not based on furnishing testimony in an adjudicatory proceeding or on a submission of a medical report, but on the manner in which he conducts examinations of claimants for the purpose of reporting their conditions to the commission. The facts showed that the physician's examinations had been inadequate and incomplete, and that the reports of examination contained intentional misrepresentations that resulted in a denial or reduction of benefits. The court said that the physician's examinations were an investigative, medical factfinding function, and not a quasi-judicial function, as he was not a witness furnishing testimony at a trial).

20 ***Dornak v Lafayette General Hospital,* 399 So 2d 168 (La 1981)** (when a physician employed by an employer performs a physical examination, he or she ordinarily is not required to disclose the results. However, the court held that such a duty existed to inform the prospective employee that he probably had tuberculosis, based on the physician's examination).

21 ***Ruffin v Strange,* 434 So 2d 1200 (La Ct App 1983)** (patient filed a claim against her treating physician for failure to release medical reports to her personal physician. The patient filed a claim for workers' compensation benefits based on a wrist injury. She later filed an action against the treating physician for refusing repeated requests to furnish a narrative report to her or her personal physician or her attorney. A trial court dismissed the action, but the appellate court reversed. The court said that the patient's personal physician needed the reports to properly examine and evaluate her injuries. The court said that she had a cause of action separate from the workers' compensation claim).

22 ***Budzichowski v Bell Telephone Co,* 445 A2d 811 (Pa Super Ct 1982)** (two industrial physicians were charged with mismanaging an orthopedic injury. The patient was a telephone installer and, in the line of duty, was attacked by a dog. He was seen by two company doctors who gave him a diagnosis of hip strain, and another told him he had inguinal strain. He was sent back to work with muscle relaxants. Nine months later, however, the claimant sought the advice of a non-company orthopedist because of continuing pain. X-rays showed aseptic necrosis of the right femoral head. Bone graft surgery was carried out. The patient was improved, but still had significant disability. The court held that there had been negligence on the part of the physicians in that there was no initial x-ray, and no ongoing follow-up treatment other than "pills." In spite of the persistent pain complaint, no repeat x-rays were taken, and then an obvious significant pathology was found by the treating orthopedist. There was a question of whether the company doctors had immunity, but it was held that this was the second issue unrelated to the negligence of the physicians).

23 ***McNeil v Diffenbaugh,* 434 NE2d 377 (Ill App Ct 1982)** (company physician was not subject to a malpractice action by a fellow employee who

claimed the physician failed to diagnose multiple myeloma while treating him for a work-related back injury. The employee injured his back while unloading his truck, and was treated by a physician at the company facility. The employee alleged that the physician failed to diagnose and treat an existing tumor in the same upper mid-back region as the injury and had failed to diagnose multiple myeloma. The employee became paralyzed and terminally ill from the myeloma. He filed a malpractice action against the physician to cover for the deprivation of support and parenteral care and companionship. On appeal from dismissal from those claims, the appellate court affirmed the decision, holding that the employee's action against the physician was barred by the Workers' Compensation Act. The employee and physician were co-employees and the Act provided exclusive remedy for his injury to the Workers' Compensation Court. The doctrine said that the dual capacity doctrine did not apply because the employer was providing medical services required by the Act. The medical services were provided in his capacity as an employer and did not have a second capacity toward the employee).

Comment: This result would not have been reached in all jurisdictions. Again, whether the physician should have diagnosed the multiple myelomas as part of his care and treatment of the industrial accident is a matter of speculation, but is certainly not beyond the realm of possibility. Again, this shows the necessity for a physician to take a full complete history, do a complete examination, and order appropriate tests as part of his evaluation.

24 ***Thomas v Kenton,* 425 So 2d 396 (La App Ct 1982)** (plaintiff who had Boek's sarcoid, alleged to have been contracted at place of employment, could not recover in a malpractice action against the company physician who had examined him in that capacity every two years. The plaintiff alleged that the doctor misrepresented the nature of his condition and concealed from him recommendations of other consultants since no physician-patient relationship existed).

25 ***Panaro v Electrolux Corp,* 545 A2d 1086 (Conn 1988)** (malpractice action against a plant nurse alleging that the nurse negligently delayed and evaluated a patient, causing the disability from a stroke to be worse. The court dismissed the malpractice action, saying the worker's sole remedy was the workers' compensation award, and that the nurse was not an independent contractor subject to separate liability as the plant doctor might be, but was a full-time plant employee, with regular hours, salary, and benefits).

26 ***Chew v Paul D Meyer,* 527 A2d 828 (Md Ct Spec App 1987)** (patient sued a surgeon for not completing insurance forms. An employee's loss of his job was not a medical injury under the Health Clinic Practice Act, the court ruled. The surgeon was informed that insurance forms had to be completed and returned to the employer promptly. It enabled him to collect sick pay as well as to document a legitimate excuse for absence from work. His employer required that a written explanation for absence from work be signed by a physician and be produced in 15 days or less. On the day following the operation, the employee gave the form to the surgeon and insisted he

complete it immediately. The surgeon refused, but accepted it for completion by his secretary. The patient allegedly told the surgeon that the papers should go in within the next week, or it would cost him his job. However, the employer did not receive the form until 18 days after he was admitted to the hospital and the employee was discharged. The employee filed suit against the surgeon, claiming he was fired for unexcused absences from work because the surgeon failed to send the form to the employer in a timely manner. The surgeon moved for dismissal, contending that the patient's claims were not properly before the court, but should have been filed for the health arbitration office. The trial court granted the surgeon's motion to dismiss, finding the claim was essentially for malpractice. The court also granted its motion for summary judgment as to all counts except for one breach of contract. On appeal, the court said that the employee's injury could not have been characterized as having resulted from the rendering or failure to render health care. The employee said he was entirely satisfied with the surgeon's performance in that regard. The complaint was for the surgeon's failure to perform a clerical task, collateral to health care. Therefore, the court found that the case was properly before the trial court. As to the breach of contract claim, the court said that the employee's claim that the services of the surgeon's contract included the completing and submission of the forms in question, combined with an allegation of failure to complete that form, stated a probable cause of action for breach of contract. The court said that summary judgment on this count was correctly denied. The court said that the combination of either a contractual obligation or a conflict arising from a physician-patient relationship, coupled with the employee's reliance on the risk of harm and the surgeon's knowledge of these factors, gave rise to the duty to act reasonably in fulfilling the obligation. The court reversed the lower court's judgment and remanded for further proceedings).

27 ***Roth v Makay,* 664 P2d 1299 (Wash Ct App 1983)** (patient sued an orthopedist for failure to file his workers' compensation form. It was held that the negligence action against the physician for not filing the form should not have been dismissed. The physician treated the worker for a back injury. The worker gave the claim form to the physician for completion, believing that the physician would file it for him. When he discovered the claim had not been filed within the required period, the worker sued the physician. The trial court dismissed the suit and held that it was the worker's nondelegatable duty to file the claim form. The appellate court reversed and remanded the suit. The physician's statutory duty that he lend "all necessary assistance" to the worker could include following the instructions on the form that he should detach and send specific parts to the Department of Labor).

28 ***Hart v Browne,* 163 Cal Rptr 356 (Ct App 1980)** (consulting orthopedist was negligent for misrepresenting or inaccurately representing whether or not there was malpractice when he reviewed records. A patient suffered partial paralysis after an automobile accident in 1962. After two operations on her back, she began seeing an orthopedic surgeon. On

March 23, 1968, he performed five operations on her right leg and four operations on her left leg, necessitating hospitalization 11 times. Shortly after she began to recover, another orthopedic specialist recommended amputation surgery of her right leg in February 1969. After the amputation, she consulted a law firm about a possible malpractice action against the orthopedist who performed the nine surgeries. The firm conducted a detailed investigation, including obtaining hospital records and records of the orthopedist, hospitalization, and treatments. The firm contacted three local orthopedists who declined to get involved. At final count, an orthopedic surgeon was willing to act as a consultant. After he reviewed all the records, he advised the attorney that the orthopedist had conducted himself within the standard of care. The attorneys then advised the patient she did not have a malpractice cause of action; no further action was taken. By February 1970, the statute of limitation had expired against the operating physician. Late in the summer of 1971, the attorneys learned that another attorney had a number of malpractice suits pending against the initial orthopedic surgeon. The attorney then filed a suit against the initial orthopedist; the suit was dismissed as it was barred by the statute of limitation. The patient then filed a suit against the consulting orthopedist. At the trial, three medical experts testified that the physician's care and treatment of the patient was negligent, and was the cause of amputation of her leg. The operating physician testified that his surgical privileges were revoked on June 4, 1970, and that his use of drugs in the years 1965 to 1968 may have affected his judgment. He also admitted he had performed several surgeries below the standard of care. The trial court granted a nonsuit on the claim of fraud and entered judgment on a jury verdict favoring the consulting physician. Reversing the decision, the appellate court said that the case should have been submitted to a jury. The evidence of malpractice on the part of the treating physician was sufficient to find that the consulting orthopedist had knowledge of the falseness of his representation. Therefore, the consulting physician was eventually found negligent).

29 ***Sherrod v US Fidelity & Guaranty Co,*** **518 So 2d 640 (Miss 1987)** (in this case, the question was whether the surgeon "wrongfully and intentionally" told the insurance company that a patient was sufficiently recovered from a knee injury to return to work. The question facing the court was whether the surgeon should be held liable for his opinion, which had cost the worker his disability benefits when another physician believed the man was still incapacitated. The orthopedic surgeon told the patient that, despite 5 per cent functional disability, he was well enough to return to work. At the same time, the man consulted a second physician who advised him that he needed a longer period to recover and that he was temporarily totally disabled. The insurance company, by this time, had discontinued his benefits and the patient could not find other work. The patient sued the orthopedist, alleging that the action had wrongly deprived him of compensation benefits. The orthopedic surgeon denied that his report to the insurance company had been any part of any action or plan to inflict any mental, emotional or any other distress on the worker. Moreover, he insisted that he had attempted in utmost good faith to fulfill and comply with an appropriate standard of care. The court held that a discrepancy of professional opinions is "not proof" and that the orthopedic surgeon had formed his opinion maliciously).

Comment: It is well known that honest doctors have honest differences of opinion based on their personal backgrounds, training, experience, and beliefs.

30 ***Nyhof v North Dakota Workmen's Compensation Bureau,*** **325 NW2d 239 (ND 1982)** (in this case, ongoing pain was traced to the concept of "secondary gain." A sanitation man collected disability benefits for four years after a back sprain suffered while heaving a garbage can. The patient persisted with unremitting pain, seemingly disproportionate to the injury, until medical experts became suspicious of secondary gain. In this case, the pain management experts and pain evaluators working with this patient commented "It is the overall impression of the staff that this is going to be a difficult case for several reasons. The patient is now making 25 per cent more per week than he did when he was working as his income is now tax-free." He was able to perform household duties and his wife was able to make a living on her own; therefore, their financial situation appeared to be locked in, and it was extremely doubtful if he could be budged unless his financial situation was altered in some manner. None of the orthopedists treating him found any objective reason for continuing pain and all suggested some work rehabilitation. One underscored the urgency of fitting him into some active program "because he can't go on like this the rest of his life." The patient did not indicate that he would like to try. He said he feared another injury and also loss of his benefits. The compensation bureau finally expressed the opinion that he had had four years of compensation and had been adequately compensated, and the payments were discontinued. The Supreme Court of North Dakota affirmed the bureau's action).

Comment: Occasionally, a patient receiving disability payments falls into the category as above, and it is difficult for the trier of fact to come up with an equitable solution, and the fact of secondary gain has to be considered.

23

Medications

§23.01 Generally

Like other areas of medical practice, negligent prescription of medication occurs. It seems more likely to happen to the very busy practitioner—the doctor who delegates prescription writing to the office nurse, who refills many prescriptions or initiates them to the pharmacist over the phone, or who simply lacks diligence. Prescribing the wrong drug or the wrong dosage and failure to inquire about prior drug usage or adverse/allergic reactions are common litigation allegations. The pharmacist is a most valuable colleague of the physician, who alerts the doctor to questionable prescription doses and has a duty to check with the doctor if prescriptions are unclear (often illegible). In most states, the pharmacist has no duty to warn the patient of risks (although this seems to be changing), but if the pharmacist warns or advises a patient, he or she does so at legal peril.

§23.02 Drug Technology

Electronic instrumentation, scientific instrumentation, chemical sophistication, and drug development have become active participants in the day-to-day practice of medicine, including orthopedics. The role of these medical products and procedures in medical injuries is a separate area of investigation in the litigation process. Questions may be asked regarding care in design, sales, installation, and maintenance of these products, and as to whether error was the cause of injury claimed. Questions are asked regarding the diligence of the manufacturer in reducing the known or possible risk, about medical and paramedical personnel's manner of usage of the device/equipment, as to whether instructions were followed, and as to whether due care in application was carried out.

Safety in the design and proper use of medical products is a sophisticated business and is usually beyond the training of hospital administrators, purchasing agents, and clinical physicians and their patients, all of whom must rely on designers, manufacturers, and suppliers.

It is frequently recognized that a patient's injury or death cannot be traced to the negligence of a physician or hospital personnel to unforeseen acts of God, or to the patient's underlying disease or injury, but can be traced to the unexpected byproduct of faulty design, defective manufacturing and assembly, or inadequate operating instructions.

In these cases, liability for injury or death lies with the manufacturer, but proof of the responsibility involves understanding the participation of each person involved in the procedure.

Medical and surgical instruments are tools of a profession dedicated to healing ill or injured persons. The fact that these tools or devices are used with laudable intent does not change the fact that they are mechanical, electrical, or chemical tools used daily in many nonmedical aspects of society. They are subject to defects in design, manufacture, or distribution, as all tools are, and when damage results from negligence in those areas, product liability theories apply.

These same concepts apply to drugs, dyes, chemicals, anesthetics, and medications used in medical practice, although tort law has lagged behind in adjudicating these types of cases.

By definition, a *device* is an "instrument, apparatus, implement, machine, contrivance, implant, in vitro reagent, or other similar or related article, including any component, part or accessory related to the above. It is further defined as (1) recognized in the official National Formulary or the United States Pharmacopedia, or any supplement to them, (2) intended for use in the diagnosis of disease or other conditions or in the cure, mitigation, treatment, or prevention of disease or injury in man or animals, (3) intended to affect the structure and/or function of the body of man or animals and which does not achieve any of its intended purposes through chemical action within or on the body of man or animal and which is not dependent on being metabolized for the achievement of any of its intended purposes.

Under the federal act, drugs are defined nearly identically, but are further subjected to certain technicalities of batch certification and premarket clearance under 21 USC §321(g).

Drug manufacturers have attempted to shield themselves with legal doctrines (generally written about as "misconstrued"—the so-called "learned intermediary"). The misconstruction was carried to the interpretation of FDA regulations, as well as Restatement (Second) of Torts §402A comment k. Misapplications in the court studies deal largely with inaccurate or incomplete instructions for use, or failure to provide proper warning.

In assessing hospital-based patient injuries, the possibility of misuse of diagnostic tools and devices or of improper drug administration must be considered. In four large studies, 36 per cent of patients were found to have iatrogenic illness. In 9 per cent of these, the illness was life-threatening. In 2 per cent, iatrogenic negligence was felt to be the cause of death. In these studies, university hospitals reported that exposure to drugs was a particularly important factor in determining which patients had complications. Given the increasing number and complexity of diagnostic procedures and therapeutic agents, monitoring of untoward events is essential. The education of all related medical personnel (including the patient) is an important preventive measure.[1]

§23.03 Principles of Drug Therapy

Because all patients respond differently to medications, individualization of dosage is required so therapy will be effective and nontoxic. A basic tenet of pharmacology is that a closer relationship exists between the concentration of a chemical in the blood stream and the drug's effect, than between the drug dose and the effect. Rational drug therapy requires an understand-

---

[1] Steel, Gertman, Crescenzi & Anderson, *Iatrogenic Illness on a General Medical Service at a University Hospital,* 304 NEJM 638 (1981); Atkinson, *Medical Misadventure: Always Operator Error,* Trial, Nov 1984, at 46.

ing of *pharmacokinetics*—the study of drug movements through the body. In this way, the amount of drug delivered to the target tissue can be controlled within a definable and safe range. The basic pharmacokinetic principles embrace (1) drug absorption, (2) drug distribution, (3) loading doses, (4) elimination-drug clearance, (5) drug accumulation, (6) maintenance doses, (7) drug removal following overdose, (8) dose dependent pharmacokinetics, (9) therapeutic window, (10) dose alteration produced by disease states, and (11) drug interactions.

§23.04 Drug Interactions

Drug interactions are a modification of the effect of a drug when used in association with another drug. These interactions can result in augmentation or diminution of pharmacologic activity and may account for a significant proportion of adverse reactions. *Hypersensitivity* (signs and symptoms resulting from an immune response to a standard dose of a drug), *idiosyncrasy* (inordinate response to a standard dose), and the *predictable response* (toxicity expected from an overdose) account for less than one-half of drug reactions.

The treatment of many pathological states, such as hypertension, arthritis, congestive heart failure, depression, cancer, infections, and inflammatory diseases, involves use of multiple drug therapy. The trend in America toward simultaneous use of increasing numbers of pharmacologic agents over long periods of time is causing great concern.

Since the efficiency and toxicity of a new drug is ascertained by testing the sole drug used, testing may not be valid in treating a patient receiving several medications. The time course of drug activity is determined by its pharmacokinetic characteristics: (1) absorption, (2) distribution, (3) metabolism, and (4) excretion. Absorption is usually by mouth, although injection, lung aerosol, and sublingual and percutaneous routes are often used. Distribution is important in getting the drug to the target tissue. Metabolism occurs mostly in the liver and kidney, as well as through the bowel and skin. Excretion is mostly via kidney, but also through bile and expired air. Many medications bind to serum protein, lessening their relative activity. (*See* Appendix 23-1, Case 1.)

§23.05 Adverse Reactions

Quinine is a commonly prescribed drug to alleviate leg cramps. It has been recently reported to cause potentially fatal thrombocytopenia an idiosyncratic adverse reaction. These patients develop antibodies attaching to and destroying platelets. One fatal subarachnoid hemorrhage case has been reported. An adverse reaction to use of medication receives much attention as to incidence, nature, and cost. The legal ramifications of drug reaction are often tested in court. Adverse drug reactions are a major cause of acute and chronic hospital admissions. Practical drug use recognizes the risk-benefit ratio. Many ill patients are treated with multiple drug therapy and may be expected to experience drug-drug interaction. They may (perhaps all patients do to a certain extent) experience a placebo response. It is said that one-third of all favorable responses to treatment are based on the placebo effect.[2] (*See* Appendix 23-1, Cases 2 to 6.)

§23.06 Placebo Response

A clear understanding by the physician of the placebo response of patients is essential. *Placebo* carries a pejorative connotation among uninformed or biased medical workers, causing a disservice to the patient. Measure of the placebo factor by physicians and psychologists has been difficult and inconsistent. Like many areas in the practice of medicine, clear explanations of "why" and "how" are difficult. Often anecdotal, the placebo response is not denied by any practitioner who regularly attends patients.

The placebo response may be defined as a favorable response by a patient after administration of a medication or treatment (including operation) which is based on the patient's wishes and beliefs that the treatment will be beneficial. Acupuncture is thought by many to fit here. The placebo response may be long or short-lived, again often based on the patient's beliefs/wishes. It is well known that many medications and treatments fit the one-third, one-third, one-third paradigm in which the treatment is effective for one-third of patients, somewhat effective for one-third, and ineffective for the last one-third.[3]

§23.07 Randomized Trial of Drugs

There is increasing recognition that major therapies should be rigorously evaluated before they are put into general clinical use. Randomized, controlled trials present the most unbiased assessment of risks and benefits of such therapy. Understanding the application of randomized studies includes (1) blinding of therapy, (2) types of measure and outcome that can be used, (3) aspects of sample size calculation, (4) analysis of data, and (5) ethics of randomly-controlled trials.[4]

§23.08 Prescription Practices

On the prescriptions written by physicians today, 99 per cent involve drugs that were not on the market a generation ago. New and contradictory infor-

---

[2] A.S. Nies, Principles of Therapeutics, Cecil Textbook of Medicine (J.B. Wyngaarden & L.H. Smith eds 1982).

[3] Voudouris, *Conditioned Response Models of Placebo Phenomena: Further Support,* 38 Pain 109 (1989).

[4] Laupacis, *Randomized Trials in Orthopedics: Why, How, and When,* 71A JBJ Surg 535 (1989).

mation about uses, effects, risks, and adverse exposures to drugs appears often. Doctors regularly testify that the source of information they rely on as a major influence is the industry-supported pharmaceutical detail person. These detail personnel are not toxicologists, physiologists, pharmacologists, or epidemiologist competent to analyze raw data about the drug they push to the physician to prescribe for patients.

Manufacturers' documents show that detail personnel are given "twisted" promotional techniques that obscure risk factors and are trained to turn aside questions of adverse effects. The Ohio Supreme Court, in one case, dealt with the issue by saying "Where scientific or medical evidence exists tending to show that a certain danger is associated with use of a drug, the manufacturer may not ignore or discount that information solely because he finds it to be unconvincing."

A Boston study ranked drugs most frequently associated with untoward events in a hospital setting as: nitrates, digoxin, lidocaine, aminophylline, quinidine/disopyramide/procainamde, heparin/warfarin, penicillin, benzodiazepine hypertensives, and Propranolol.[5]

§23.09 Physicians' Desk Reference

The Physicians' Desk Reference (PDR), an annual text, is a compendium of a wide range of information regarding virtually every medication in use in America. Each medication is described in common form, discussing (1) drug description "chemically," (2) clinical pharmacology, (3) indications and usage, (4) contraindications, (5) warnings, (6) precautions, (7) adverse reactions, (8) contraindications, warnings, and overdose, and (9) how the medication is supplied. The information in the text is supplied by the manufacturer of the drug. The PDR is published by Medical Economics, Oradell, New Jersey 07649.

Many courts have used the information in the PDR, with expert witness support, to determine the standard of care regarding the use, abuse, and efficacy of a medication. Other text sources of drug usage are available in medical libraries. Most pharmacists are well-informed as to drug usage, adverse reactions, and contraindications. (*See* Appendix 23-1, Cases 8 to 10.)

The PDR also is used as the standard of care in many states, for indications and dosages of medications, unless the prescribing physician has a reasonable basis for deviating. Ordinarily, the court or jury does not accept the fact that the doctor has not read the PDR as a reason for not using it as the authority for his or her drug usage. Some states, on the other hand, do not accept the PDR as the only authority for drug usage, but rely on the expert opinions of practicing physicians. Occasionally, the opinion of a pharmacist regarding the doses of medication is accepted. Most often, however, the

---

[5] Woods, Katz & Winger, *Use and Abuse of Benzodiazepines: Issues Relevant to Prescribing,* 260 JAMA 3476 (1988); Marks, *Techniques of Benzodiazepine Withdrawal in Clinical Practice: A Consensus Workshop Report,* 3 Med Toxicol Adverse Drug Exp 324 (1988).

pharmacist is not an acceptable adverse witness in medical malpractice cases. (*See* Appendix 23-1, Case 11.)

One of the very common risks that the modern physician faces is failing to inform patients of drug reactions. The prudent physician practices with a limited armamentarium of drugs for which he or she knows the risks and contraindications and can easily so inform a patient from recall. When the doctor uses a new or unfamiliar drug, he or she must be informed of the risk and convey this to the patient. This information is readily available to the physician in the PDR or through computer services or a call to the pharmacy. The area of drug prescription is high risk and is all too often overlooked by the busy practicing orthopedist. (*See* Appendix 23-1, Cases 9 and 12 to 17.)

§23.10 Consent

Many courts have held that informed consent deals with surgery, with invasive procedures—not with informing patients of the good and bad about prescribed medication. More recently, courts have held physicians liable for not informing patients of the possible adverse effects of the medication prescribed. (See Appendix 23-1, Case 18.)

The physician is in a unique position to assess and advise the potentially addictive patient and owes that patient the same duty to aid in correction of addiction. All too often, however, the doctor fails in this duty and avoids the patient who has persistent unremitting requests for more and more mind-altering medication. These patients are sick, are often undesirable to care for and easy to dismiss, and at times are "at risk" for medication withdrawal problems related to the drugs the doctor has prescribed.[6]

§23.11 Anaphylaxis—A Liability Risk

Physicians who use injectable medication occasionally see a patient with an anaphylactoid reaction that can be fatal. The more diverse the drugs injected, the more often the risk of anaphylaxis. The physician must be informed of the actions of the medication he or she injects. The physician must also be prepared and update his or her facility to handle the unusual, but life-threatening anaphylactoid reaction. The following guides have been suggested by the Executive Committee of the American Academy of Allergy and Immunology:

1. After injection, patients should wait in the doctor's office for twenty minutes for physician observation.
2. Trained personnel should be available who can recognize anaphylactic reactions and initiate treatment; they should be trained in basic cardiopulmonary resuscitation.

---

[6] Physicians Desk Reference (1989).

3. Appropriate equipment and medications should be available, including stethoscope and sphygmometer; tourniquets, syringes, hypodermic needles, and large bore needles (14 gauge); aqueous epinephrines HCL 1:1000; equipment for administering intravenous fluids; injectable diphenhydramine (Benadryl) or similar antihistamine; aminophyllin for intravenous administration; corticosteroids for intravenous administration and vasopressors. The proper use of these materials should provide effective initial treatment for acute systemic allergic reactions. Prompt recognition of systemic reactions and the administration of epinephrine are the mainstays of therapy.
4. Rarely, invasive procedures such as direct laryngoscopy, direct current cardioversion, tracheostomy, and intracardiac injection of drugs may be needed. Those procedures are not usually done in a doctor's office, as appropriate facilities are not typically available.
5. Physicians should be alerted to the fact that beta-adrenergic blocking drugs are not likely to respond to epinephrine. The initial treatment of anaphylaxis is the same, but if unresponsive, immediate transport to a hospital emergency room is necessary.[7] (See Appendix 23-1, Case 15.)

§23.12 Warning Patients and Third Parties of High Risk

Although not often litigated in the past, an increased duty is being placed on the physician if he or she recognizes that the recipient of services poses a risk of injury to a third person. The wise physician goes out of his or her way to tell a patient about the medication prescribed, why, what effect is hoped for, and what adverse reactions may occur. Often, the drug will produce drowsiness or interfere with cognitive ability. The physician has a duty to warn the patient to avoid dangerous situations, such as driving a vehicle, climbing to heights, working dangerous equipment, swimming, etc. This duty is to protect the patient and third parties from being injured by the patient. (*See* Appendix 23-1, Case 19.) Many suits allege the vicariously liability of a physician for negligent prescribing drugs and negligently failing to warn and control a patient.

Typical drugs warranting counseling of the patient and family include sedatives, tranquilizers, sleeping medication, alcohol, antileptic drugs, antipsychotic drugs, and insulin.

---

[7] Executive Committee American Academy of Allergy and Immunology. Position Statement, *Personnel and Equipment to Treat Systemic Reactions Caused by Immunotherapy with Allergic Extracts,* 77 J Allergy Clin Immunol 271 (1986).

§23.13 Tranquilizers

Unmonitored tranquilizer usage can be damaging to the nervous system. Tranquilizers can impair the immune system, weakening the body's defenses against a wide variety of illnesses that lie in wait for an opportunity to take hold and propagate. In every hospital in America, there are patients who have been admitted due to drug misuse (including deliberate substance abuse) and there are likely to be patients who have an extended hospital stay or who die as a consequence of drug therapy. Every medication carries a risk with it—some drugs are dangerous enough to cause major physiological or psychological problems. Several reports say that 10 per cent of hospital admissions are attributable to improper drug use.

Many patients on tranquilizers, pain medication, or other mind-altering medication have learned the trick of asking their pharmacist to telephone the physician's office for renewal of the prescription. Often, this type of patient will telephone the doctor at home after hours, weekends, or holidays with urgent requests, saying their prescriptions were lost, stolen, or otherwise misplaced. The physician must always be on guard, dealing only with patients over the telephone who are known to be and making a note to enter in the patient's file.

Since their introduction almost three decades ago, the benzodiazepines have become one of the most widely prescribed group of drugs in the history of medicine. Despite periodic trends criticizing the broad use of benzodiazepines, their popularity seems to be well-deserved, when one considers the many thousands of references in the worldwide medical literature that clearly reflect the significant benefits realized with these agents. In addition to their more familiar applications in anxiety, insomnia, and preoperative sedation, administration of the benzodiazepines extends to certain life-saving uses as well (i.e., control of the muscle spasms of tetanus and other conditions often seen in certain Third World countries).

The potential for abuse and the occurrence of dependence during benzodiazepine therapy has prompted numerous studies and reports. Although physiologic dependence can develop in some patients, available evidence does not appear to support the wide occurrence of abuse in the general population. However, it is critically important that health care professionals be able to recognize and treat benzodiazepine dependence when it occurs. To assist physicians in this effort, a workshop was held in Basle, Switzerland in September 1987. Experts gathered there to evaluate their experiences and establish guidelines for managing benzodiazepine-dependent patients.[8]

Another area of third-party concern (as well as for the patient) is the care, control, and counseling of epileptic and diabetic patient, those weak from malignancy or anemia, those with severe angina "at risk" for heart attack, and psychologically-impaired patients with impulse behavior disorders. Part of the standard medical care of these patients is informing them of their illness, of what it does to them as a person, of what the risks of taking and

---

[8] *Id.* Shemonsky, *Critical Cases,* 14 Legal Aspects of Med Prac 4 (1986).

not taking the medication are, and of the patient's responsibility to manage him- or herself with the physician's help. The epileptic who fails to take medication may have a seizure and, if driving a car, may injure third parties. If the epileptic has a dose of medicine that is too large, he or she may be drowsy and fall asleep. The diabetic patient with too much insulin may become hypoglycemic, faint, and injure others or him- or herself.

§23.14 Written Notification to Patient

An effective and legal insulation for the physician is to provide written documentation of a patient's illness, treatment, and the risks attached to the illness and the medication prescribed, along with instructions for follow-up care.

Orthopedists are additionally vulnerable at times by allowing patients who are impaired by pain and/or external supportive devices (casts, braces), or who are insufficiently rehabilitated, to drive, climb ladders, or exit from an emergency situation. (*See* Appendix 23-1, Cases 14 and 20 to 25.)

§23.15 Non-Narcotic Analgesias

Pain-relieving medications are generally divided into *narcotic* (tending to be habit forming) and *non-narcotic* (usually not habit forming).

Typical non-narcotic analgesics include aspirin, acetaminophen (Tylenol), and non-steroidal anti-inflammatory agents. Aspirin and acetaminophen are often combined with stimulants, mild narcotics, and tranquilizer compounds. Contraindications include known hypersensitivity, blood coagulation problems, and gastrointestinal problems such as peptic ulcer.

Typical narcotic medications include: codeine, hydrocodonone, dihydrocodeine (Vicodin, Synalgos-DC, Darvon, Darvocet, Percodan and Tylox). Potential narcotic agents include Demerol, Morphine, Dilaudid, Pentazocine (Talwin), and Numorphan.

Analgesia is one of the most often prescribed medications used by orthopedists for pain complaints. Most physicians have pain control routines and biases. It has been shown that pain medication prescriptions are often underused and that the addiction that is commonly alluded to is infrequent. There is, however, a concern by physicians and nurses in giving potentially addictive drugs. (*See* Appendix 23-1, Case 26.)

§23.16 Narcotics and Mind-Altering Drugs

The orthopedist is faced daily with patients who are in pain, who are anxious, who are depressed, or have trouble sleeping. These symptoms have to be addressed by the physician. (*See* Appendix 23-1, Case 27.) In day-to-day conversation and in the writings of many orthopedists, negative thoughts are apparently directed toward patients who use narcotics and physicians who prescribe these medications. (*See* Appendix 23-1, Case 28.) Those attitudes have an altruistic flavor, but it is in fact a rare, actively-practicing physician who does not prescribe mind-altering drugs to patients. Problems for all doctors are the appropriate usage and the understanding of the patient, whether or not he or she needs medication, and the usage reliability. Psychologically-oriented physicians see a greater need than do mechanistically-oriented physicians for use of mind-altering drugs. (*See* Appendix 23-1, Case 29.)

Narcotic medication is needed for pain relief. Its prescription is strictly controlled by federal and state law. The need for prescription of narcotics is part of the expertise of physicians. The physician has a duty to be prudent, diligent, honest, and scientific in prescribing narcotic medication. The same comments can be made about tranquilizer medication, sleeping medication, muscle relaxant medication, and psychotropic drugs. (*See* Appendix 23-1, Cases 30 to 34.)

In the management of benign pain patients using medication, there are a number of narcotic and non-narcotic analgesics available for oral and parenteral administration, but less than one-half of all pharmacies stock all of them on a routine basis. Despite the utility of oral morphine and methadone in severe cancer pain, less potent compounds are used for the "routine" pain complaints.

The choice of drugs should be based on assessment of the patient's medical status and a thorough assessment of pain. The medical status of the patient is important in the choice of drugs, in that the actions of certain analgesics are more confounded by disease than others. The side effect potential of certain drugs may be altered by renal dysfunction—the excitatory effect of meperidine on the central nervous system, for example.

Because the intensity of the pain (mild, moderate, and severe) is critical to the appropriate choice of drug, one should avoid unnecessarily potent drugs in situations where weaker analgesics are sufficient. (See Appendix 23-1, Case 35.) Non-opioids (e.g., acetaminophen) are used for mild pain; weak opioids (codeine or codeine derivatives) and their combination with non-opioids are used for moderate pain; strong opioids (morphine and related drugs) are used for more severe pain.

A thorough understanding of specific pain syndromes is of particular importance in identifying the situations in which the initial use of co-analgesics and/or analgesic adjuvants is warranted. These medications include nonsteroidal, anti-inflammatory agents, mild tranquilizer medication, and muscle relaxant chemicals. (*See* Appendix 23-1, Cases 36 and 37.)

§23.17 Long-Term Narcotic Therapy

Long-term narcotic therapy can be safely and effectively used to treat chronic pain in selected patients. The use of long-term narcotic medications in malignancy pain is well accepted by physicians; their use in chronic benign pain has been more controversial. Narcotics, along with adjuvant anti-depressant medications, should be used in select patients (patients in which all other therapies have been ineffective and patients who demonstrate no substance abuse tendencies). Close surveillance of patients, withdrawing of narcotics from those who are escalating dosages, and use of activity-directed therapies are effective and safe in a large group of difficult-to-treat patients.[9]

Physicians who prescribe neuroleptic drugs need to inform the patient of the at least 15 per cent risk of medication-causing tardive dyskinesia that may cause permanent neurological impairment. Neuroleptic drugs are used for a variety of mental states, generally related to agitation, hostility, and aggression. The physician uninformed of neuroleptic drug complications is well advised to seek expert consultation. (*See* Appendix 23-1, Cases 38 and 39.)

§23.18 Prescriptions by Different Physicians

The orthopedist is often involved in the care of a patient with several other doctors who are prescribing medication. More and more patients are uninformed or incapable of managing medications that may produce adverse reactions.

A typical scenario was recently seen by the author. A 78-year-old male was seen in the emergency room with acute agitation, confusion, and delerium. He had been fairly well until two days before, when a board-certified urologist saw him for urinary retention. Imiprimine, 75 mg, was prescribed and administered at bed time. The patient had been seeing an orthopedist for painful arthritis of the low back. The orthopedist, feeling part of his pain intensity was due to depression, prescribed amitriptyline, 100 mg, at bed time. These two medications were prescribed without the physicians communicating with each other, although the orthopedist had referred the patient to the urologist. The patient had additionally been taking Nytol (diphenhydramine HCL) for years to aid in sleep. The patient's mental alteration was due to the combined effect of the two anti-depressant medications—potentially fatal. The standard of care reasonably would ask the two physicians to communicate. The doctor has a duty not only to understand the medication he or she prescribes, but also to know the medications the patient is taking and their potential side effects and/or contraindications. The PDR and local pharmacist are excellent resources for the doctor to inform him- or herself of potential complications of mixing various drugs at various ages and various patient diagnostic states. Most pharmacists have computerized services that have this information available.

§23.19 Arthritis Medications

A relatively new group of medications are on the market to aid in pain control and the suppression of non-infectious inflammation; these are called

---

[9] Lu, *Study Suggests Long-Term Narcotic Therapy May Be Safe, Efficacious,* 3 Pain Topics 3 (1989).

nonsteroidal, anti-inflammatory drugs (NSAIDs). These drugs, like aspirin (acetylsalisylic acid) block certain physiological chemical cascades (prostaglandin) that mediate pain in inflamed joint or soft tissue systems. All NSAIDs work in a similar manner. Most have potentially severe adverse effect, generally affecting the gastrointestinal system, producing gastric erosion, ulcer, and potentially fatal bleeding. Kidney, liver, and blood-forming organ injuries have been reported with NSAIDs.

The physician's duty in the use of NSAIDs center around his or her being well-informed of the pharmacokinetics of the medication, of its potential complication, and of how that information fits the patient, and then to be assured that the patient is appropriately informed. (*See* Appendix 23-1, Cases 4 and 40.)

§23.20 Steroids

One class of drugs that the orthopedist uses often is corticosteroids to aid in control of inflammation. These chemicals are taken by mouth in larger doses for acute inflammatory states, and at times in small doses for prolonged periods for an inflammatory condition, including rheumatoid arthritis, post-traumatic synovitis, and vasculitis. They are believed to be somewhat helpful in acute brain injuries. Osteonecrosis (aseptic or avascular necrosis) of the head of the femur associated with corticosteroid therapy has been a renal (or other organ) transplant problem since its advent. The necessary use of corticosteroid to prevent organ implant rejection places the femoral head at high risk. Surgery to repair the disabling pain of osteonecrosis has been approached with trepidation in these high-risk patients; however, with current anesthesiology and follow-up skills, the risk is diminished.

§23.21 Corticosteroid Injections

Corticosteroid by injection is a second common therapeutic tool. It is useful in reducing pain in the area of tendonitis, tenosynovitis, enthetic and other myofascial trigger points, and intra-articularly in noninfected inflamed joints. Relative contraindications exist in repeated frequent use in weight bearing joints, as a small percentage will develop rapidly deteriorating articular surfaces, or will develop joints that behave like a Charcot or neurotropic joint. (*See* Appendix 23-1, Case 41.)

An absolute contraindication of corticosteroid injection is to inject the tendinous area attaching to bone, particularly weight bearing joints such as the tibial tendon of the Achilles tendon. These structures often rupture and heal poorly when so injected. The physiological effect of corticosteroids is to reduce inflammation (among other effects) and thereby block part of the healing process. Another absolute contraindication to corticosteroid injection is in areas of infection, as the steroids interfere with the immune process and thereby lessen tissue ability to cope with infection.

Corticosteroids are useful, even life-saving, in certain shock states, particularly anaphylaxis. It is routinely used in asthmatics and related chronic obstructive pulmonary states to reduce the inflammatory component of the disease, being administered orally, parenterally, or by lung atomization. Epidural injection of corticosteroids is a popular, effective (in most hands) method to reduce nerve root irritation pain in disc disease and perineural fibrosis. Not all orthopedists find this technique effective. Inadvertent or deliberate intrathecal injections of corticosteroid are prescribed by the manufacturer, there being reports of arachnoiditis developing, or worsening if present. (*See* Appendix 23-1, Case 42.)

The orthopedist needs to be well informed as to the pharmacokinetics of corticosteroid usage and contraindications. The patient is entitled to know of possible complications, such as hypercortisonism, aseptic necrosis, and other complications included in the "package insert" or the Physician's Desk Reference (PDR). (*See* Appendix 23-1, Cases 32, 33, and 43 to 45.)

Both intra-articular and extra-articular injection of hydrocortisone are frequently used by physicians for pain control. These steroids exert strong anti-inflammatory effects and represent great therapeutic benefit. These same steroids have adverse side effects. They can cause skin depigmentation if injected subcutaneously. They cause weakening and rupture when injected into tendon or ligament. These steroids can cause cartilage breakdown, particularly in weight bearing joints. These tissue breakdowns seem dose-related. It appears that hydrocortisone injection may be placed in para-ligament or tendon safely. It is the intra-ligament or inter-tendon injection that alters the collagen homeostasis, leading to tissue disruption.[10]

§23.22 Anabolic Steroids

Much has been written in the lay press regarding the use of anabolic steroids by athletes to improve their physical activities. Anabolic steroids, used regularly and combined with physical activity, will increase muscle mass, strength, and endurance, thereby improving physical capabilities. A continuing aerobic exercise training program is essential for maintenance of the effects.

The side effects of anabolic steroid use far outweigh the advantages in the eyes of most physicians. Premature aging, including premature growth arrest in adolescents with shortened stature, may occur. Cardiovascular problems leading to death are common. Sterility is reported. Gynecomastia

---

[10] Fitzgerald, Jr, *Intrasynovial Injection of Steroids—Uses and Abuses,* 51 Mayo Clin Proc 655 (1976); Gray & Gottlieb, *Intraarticular Corticosteroids—An Up-dated Assessment,* 177 Clin Orthop 235 (1983); Balch, *Repeated Corticosteroid Injection into Knee Joints,* 16 Rheum Rehabil 137 (1977); Bedi & Ellis, *Spontaneous Rupture of the Calcaneal Tendon in Rheumatoid Arthritis After Local Steroid Injection,* 29 Ann Rheum Dis 494 (1970); Ford & DeBender, *Tendon Rupture After Local Steroid Injection,* 72 South Med J 827 (1970); Kennedy Willis, *The Effects of Local Steroid Injections on Tendons: A Biochemical and Microscopic Correlative Study,* 4 Am J Sports Med 11 (1976).

with breast cancer has also recently been reported. Anabolic steroids have been outlawed in virtually all competitive sports, as they present an unfair and unethical competition advantage.[11]

§23.23 Antibiotics

Antibiotics may be the greatest single advance in medicine of the twentieth century, but their widespread usage entails risk. With the passing years, the attacking microorganisms have become increasingly resistant to existing antibiotics, leading pharmaceutical companies to develop even more potent drugs. There seems to be an upward spiraling war between microorganisms and antibiotics. The body's ability to cope with powerful chemicals is not unlimited. The more powerful the antibiotic becomes, the greater the threat to the body's natural symbiotic bacterial flora, hormonal functions, and immune system. The physician always has to weigh the prospective gains against possible body injury. It seems to be clear that use of antibiotics for casual illness, without bacterial culture with sensitivity testing, is not in favor by most physicians.

There is an ever-expanding list of antibiotics and medications used to treat infections. Antibiotics are most often used for bacterial infection. Specific antibiotics are indicated based on culture and sensitivity testing. Viral infections have few specific drugs. Some vaccines are useful in preventing or lessening the virulence of viral infection. Parasitic infections require still another type of medication. Each group of anti-infection medication has its own indications and risks. The field of usage of these drugs is becoming a subspecialty (infection medicine) in itself. Legal involvement most often derives from usage or failure of usage of drugs specified by sensitivity tests, or from complication alleging that the physician should have known the complication was probable. (*See* Appendix 23-1, Cases 46 to 55, and 57.)

§23.24 Alcoholism

Alcoholism leads to dysfunction in nearly all levels of the nervous system. The effects of alcohol are often difficult to differentiate from the effects of poor nutrition, trauma, and infection.

Acute alcohol intoxication is manifested by poor judgment, slowed reaction time, dysarthria, and/or ataxia. Twenty-four to 48 hours after consuming excessive alcohol, a person may have a grand mal seizure or a series of seizures known as "room fits" or "DTs" in the alcohol community. These seizures are generally self-limiting and occur only after alcohol withdrawal.

An electroencephalogram shows low voltage, fast activity, absent epileptic discharges, and photosensitive myoclonus; hypomagnesemia and alcolohsis frequent accompany these seizures. Standard anti-convulsants do not affect

---

[11] Friedl & Yesalis, *Self-Treatment of Gynecomastia in Body-builders Who Use Anabolic Steroids,* 17 Phys & SportsMed 67 (1989).

the course of these seizures, and thus have no place in the treatment of acute situations or prophylactically.

Three to five days after alcohol withdrawal, delerium, tremulousness characterized by tachycardia, dilated pupils, agitation, hyperactivity, fever, and auditory and visual hallucinations can occur. Adequate hydration and sedation, and search for endocrine disease, such as pancreatitis infection, must be instituted.

Computerized tomography has shown that alcoholism can lead to cerebral atrophy and dementia. In some persons, mentation and atrophic changes found in CT scans improve after prolonged absence. However, in some chronic alcoholics, the white matter in and near the corpus callosum degenerates, causing a permanent condition. Signs and symptoms refer ordinarily to a frontal lobe dysfunction, and include apathy, apraxia, incontinence, gait abnormalities, and forced reflex grasping.

The best known and most important severe brain infliction caused by alcoholism is the Wernicki-Korsakoff syndrome. This disorder is caused by thiamine deficiency and occurs in non-alcoholics with kidney disease and other uremia-producing diseases. It is occasionally seen in patients who are on forced diets of tea and toast only—a type of anorexia. Thiamine deprivation leads to (1) acute neuroma dysfunction, (2) breakdown of capillaries and blood vessels in selected regions of the brain, leading to clinical manifestations such as confusion and poor memory evidenced by confabulation and inability to remember recent events, (3) extra-articular movement abnormalities, nystagmus, sixth nerve congugated gaze and paresis, (4) ataxia and abnormal voice control caused by degeneration of anterior cerebellar vermis, and (5) peripheral neuropathy characterized by burning and numbness of the feet and absent ankle jerks with limb paralysis in the presence of severe nutritional deprivation. Tachycardia, postural hypotension, and sudden death are also common in patients with Wernicki syndrome. (Again, these are symptoms also commonly found in head injuries.)

Immediate treatment with thiamine is imperative. Although treatment quickly reverses ophthalmoplegia, mental changes and neuropathy do not improve after thiamine. In fact, neuropathy usually worsens gradually, despite the treatment, but improves if the patient remains abstinent and eats well.

The orthopedist will frequently see injured persons who are intoxicated from alcohol or drugs. He or she has an ethical and moral obligation to the patient to identify that problem and offer treatment. An active involvement by the physician in the alcoholism and/or drug abuse illness serves the patient and society in reducing deaths from disease and injury to others due to the addiction. With increasing frequency, persons who abet intoxication (such as bartenders) are being held liable for the tort behavior of the intoxicated person. It is a logical step to impune the physician who recognizes a patient with such a problem and fails to alert the patient or family. The patient's record should contain a notation of such advice.[12] (*See* Appendix 23-1, Case 57.)

§23.25 Bone Joint Infection

Pseudomonas aeruginosa bone and joint infections are rare. This bacteria is seen as a secondary invader in open wounds and burns. Pseudomonas does become an opportunistic infecting bacterium in chronically malnourished or immunosuppressed patients.

The other category of patient is the intravenous drug user, who often presents with a bone and joint Pseudomonas infection. Adequate debridement and appropriate antibiotic therapy based on culture and sensitivity, along with attention to drug withdrawal and nutrition and life-style improvement are all factors in treatment.[13]

---

[12] Waller, *The Physician's Role in Preventing Alcohol-Related Injuries,* 17 JAMA 2561 (1988); Berkelman, *Fatal Injuries and Alcohol,* 1 Am J Prev Med 21 (1985); Cullen, *Alcohol and Mortality in the Brusselton Report,* 11 Int J Epidemiol 67 (1982); Cyr & Wartman, *The Effectiveness Routine Screening Questions in the Detection of Alcoholism,* 259 JAMA 51 (1988); Chang & Astrachan, *The Emergency Department Surveillance of Alcohol Intoxication After Motor Vehicle Accident,* 260 JAMA 2533 (1988).

[13] Miskem, *Pseudomonas Aeruginosa Bone and Joint Infection in Drug Abusers,* 65A JBJ Surg 829 (1983).

Appendix 23-1 Cases

1 ***Hemingway v Ochsner Clinic,* 722 F2d 1220 (5th Cir 1984)** (hospital staff doctor gave plaintiff, a known diabetic, Cafergot, a potent vasoconstrictor, when he knew or should have known that plaintiff was being treated for acute arterial insufficiency because of injury to left leg and foot).

2 ***Witherell v Weimer,* 118 Ill 2d 321, 515 NE2d 68 (1987)** (it was alleged the defendant physician repeated prescriptions of oral contraceptives containing estrogen, resulting in plaintiff suffering from thrombophlebitis and causing her serious permanent injury. The plaintiff produced substantial expert evidence to the effect that defendant departed from the standard, supporting the jury finding that the defendant physician was negligent in continuing to prescribe birth control pills).

Comment: Physicians are often less than diligent in patient follow-up when prescribing medications which have side effects, unless the patient emphasizes a problem. The prudent physician will listen to the patient, understand the complaint (or complication), and stop or alter medication. The situation is more complicated when the patient is taking several medications concomitantly.

3 ***Kemp v Harper Grace Hospital,* No 101406 (Mo Ct App)** (plaintiff was hospitalized for catheterization procedure; medical history showed the plaintiff to be allergic to iodine. Defendant doctors failed to pretest or pretreat the patient, used Renograin (a soluble, iodine complex chemical) as a contrast medium. Patient sustained a major adverse reaction; gangrene of leg occurred and amputation was necessary. Verdict for defendant).

Comment: The medical behavior in *Kemp* was probably negligent and the plaintiff would have prevailed if the pleadings had been appropriately substantiated by expert opinion.

4 ***Incollingo v Ewing,* 444 Pa 263, 282 A2d 206 (1971)** (defendant physician was charged with malpractice for authorizing the refill of a drug originally prescribed by another physician without examining the patient for side effects. The drug eventually led to the patient's death. On appeal for judgment against him, defendant argued, inter alia, that it had not been proven that the doses prescribed by him, and not those prescribed by the other physicians, had caused the patient's death. The court affirmed the judgment against the defendant, holding, inter alia, that the evidence supported a verdict that both physicians were jointly liable).

5 ***Rivera v NYC Health & Hospitals Corp,* No 2753682 (NY Sup Ct 1988)** (patient developed tardive dyskinesia as a result of taking prescribed Thorazine as an outpatient for seven years. He started to develop a neck deformity, torticollis, and then other signs of tardive dyskinesia some three to four months prior to stopping the Thorazine. Plaintiff alleged the Thora-

zine should have been stopped at first sign of torticollis, although it was intermittent at first. Further, the plaintiff said he was not advised of long-term risks of raking Thorazine. Defendant did warn patient according to testimony, and torticollis was felt more probably related to stress than tardive dyskinesia. Court held that the physician did use reasonable judgment in using Thorazine in face of severity of patient's illness—schizophrenia).

Comment: Spastic torticollis is a poorly understood, stress-related entity. Reversible torticollis, though, is a described complication of Thorazine usage.

6 ***Feldman v Lederle Laboratories,* 561 A2d 288 (NJ Super Ct App Div 1989)** (manufacturer of a tetracycline-containing drug was not liable for a patient's tooth discoloration. Patient claimed that she was treated with Declomycin from her infancy into her fourth year. She was born in February 1960. Her physician father prescribed the medication for her 8 to 10 times during her infancy. In 1965, her father noticed that his daughter's teeth were stained a shade of gray. The family dentist informed him of the correlation between tetracycline and tooth staining. In a product liability action against the manufacturer, the patient claimed that it knew or should have known of the side effects before 1962, when it first asked the FDA for permission to place a warning on the drug. The FDA did not approve a warning until December 1963. The patient claimed that articles published in 1956 and 1958 observed that cystic fibrosis patients treated with tetracycline on a daily basis over a long period of time had staining of the teeth. None of the patients was treated with Declomycin, which was not marketed until 1959. The manufacturer argued that children receiving Declomycin in 1959 would not have their permanent teeth until about 1965, the earliest date that it was possible to identify it as a cause of tooth discoloration. After remand, a trial court entered judgment in favor of the patient. Reversing the decision, the appellate court said that the manufacturer was required to obtain FDA approval before it could place the tooth staining warning on the label of Declomycin. The court said that federal law requiring prior approval pre-empted any state law requirement for warning as soon as the defect was discovered and before FDA approval. The case was remanded for the entry of an order of judgment for the manufacturer).

7 ***Geston v Hunter,* 121 Ariz 33, 588 P2d 326 (1978)** (patient brought medical malpractice and product liability action against physician and drug manufacturer for physical illness suffered after physician treated patient's back by means of chemonuclelysis which involved use of investigational drug. The court, on appeal from judgment for defendant, was unpersuaded by the patient's argument from opposing absolute liability on the grounds that defendant had engaged in an abnormally dangerous activity. Court concluded the adoption of such position would extend boundaries of strict product liability. It was noted that the rules relating to "abnormally dangerous" activities are inapplicable to production of new drugs).

8 ***Ramon v Farr,* 770 P2d 131 (Utah 1989)** (package insert could not be used to establish the standard of care against a physician who prescribed a drug incorrectly. The court held that, although the information was in the package insert or the Physician's Desk Reference (PDR), which has the same information, package inserts are intended to serve such purposes as advertising and complying with governmental regulations, rather than establishing the applicable standard of care).

9 ***Paul v Boschenstein,* 105 AD2d 248, 482 NYS2d 870 (1984)** (physician admitted prescribing a dose of medicine exceeding manufacturer's package insert recommendation. Patient was injured. The court adopted rule set in *Mulder v Parke Davis & Co,* 288 Minn 332, 181 NW2d 882 (1970) in that the drug manufacturers make recommendations to medical profession concerning conditions under which their drug should be prescribed, the disorders it is designed to relieve, the precautionary methods which should be observed, and the dangers inherent in the drug's use. A physician's deviation from a drug manufacturer's recommendation would be prima facia evidence of physician's negligence if there is competent medical testimony that the patient's injury or death resulted from physician's failure to follow manufacturer's recommendations).

10 ***Mampe v Ayerst Laboratories,* 548 A2d 798 (DC 1988)** (physician prescribed Antabuse and warned his patient not to drink alcohol because she might die. The patient did drink, collapsed, and was hospitalized for three months. Plaintiff alleged manufacturer failed to warn of Antabuse risk, for failing to give adequate warning of severe complications that might result—in her case, severe neurologic sequelae. Court awarded summary judgment for manufacturer. Award was appealed, but was affirmed. It was shown that the doctor had not relied on package insert so the plaintiff could not rely on that information, but rather looked to the doctor who was absolved in that he had warned his patient that "she might die" if she used Antabuse and alcohol at the same time).

11 ***Young v Key Pharmaceuticals, Inc,* 770 P2d 182 (Wash 1989)** (court held that a pharmacist is not competent to testify as to physician's drug prescription being below the standard of care, and that a pharmacist is not competent to diagnose and/or treat illness).

12 ***Boyer v Smith,* 497 A2d 646 (Pa Super Ct 1985)** (orthopedic surgeon was sued by the wife of a patient. The wife had complained of back pain and wanted anti-inflammatory medication. Doctor prescribed one and warned her that stomach ulcers and gastroenteritis might develop. She took the medication and developed a severe adverse reaction, the exact nature not described. She had to be hospitalized for three weeks. She then filed suit against the doctor, claiming that obtaining informed consent to prescribed medication is just as necessary as it is with surgery. The issue was raised originally in *Malloy v Shanahan,* 280 Pa Super 440, 421 A2d 803 (1980), where an appellate judge denied the applicability of informed consent doctrine to medical prescriptions. A strongly worded dissent from the plurality opinion kept that case from setting precedent, however. The *Boyer* court refused to expand the doctrine of informed consent beyond surgery. When a plaintiff complains of misapplied drug therapy, he or she can charge negli-

gence, claimed the court, without claiming failure to obtain informed consent).

13 ***Smith v Weaver,* 407 NW2d 174 (Neb 1987)** (patient consulted physician because of fatigue, itching, hair loss, and soreness of facial bones, among other things. After a week of hospitalization, the physician diagnosed possible systemic lupus erythematosus. Approximately two years later, patient consulted physician because of increased swelling of hands, feet, stiffness of her whole body, and lightheadedness and dizziness. The physician again diagnosed possible lupus, prescribed Clinoril and allegedly advised the patient of primary or common side effects of the drug. The patient later denied he told her of any side effects. The next day the patient telephoned the physician reporting she had taken Clinoril tablets as instructed, that her hands were swollen, that she had vomited, and that her entire body was swollen and itched. The physician felt these were problems caused by the disease process and advised the patient to continue taking the drug. A day later, the patient again reported problems. Since there were no tests detecting allergy to the drug, the physician changed medication. The patient reported improvement but still had pain in her hands. The patient sued the physician alleging he was negligent in failing to warn her about possible side effects of Clinoril. Patient contended that after her experience with the drugs, she lacked energy, had pain and sores, and that her ability to speak and eat and sleep had been adversely affected by the medication. Physician said he had exercised reasonable and ordinary care and skill and knowledge of a member of the profession under the circumstances. A medical review panel confirmed this opinion and there was no counter expert evidence of record. The trial court then rendered a summary judgment for the physician. On appeal, patient contended that when it was claimed that a physician failed to warn of possible side effects of the drug, there is no requirement for specific technical and scientific knowledge. She contended since her circumstances surrounded an injury, a common experience and knowledge and observation, no expert was required. The supreme court said the state was committed by legislature to the "court of professional theory" under which expert evidence was necessary to establish what information would ordinarily be provided under prevailing circumstances by physicians in same or similar counties; therefore, in the present case, contradicted evidence that a physician followed the accepted standards rendered by factual issues of which physicians gave a patient a warning was immaterial, there being no confident evidence that he was required to give any warning).

14 ***Boyer v Smith,* 497 A2d 646 (Pa Super Ct 1985)** (court refused to extend doctrine of informed consent in case where doctor prescribed a pain medication without warning of any side effects. The patient had severe drug reaction. The court held that informed consent doctrine only applies to cases involving surgical or operative medical procedure and could not be extended to cases involving prescribed therapeutic medications. The court reasoned, in Pennsylvania, the informed consent doctrine is based on theory that performance of a medical procedure without patient's consent constitutes tech-

nical assault or battery, and to expand the doctrine to cases involving administration of drugs would constitute too radical a departure from legal foundation).

Comment: It remains negligent not to inform a patient of the known risks of a prescribed medication, aside from the informed consent doctrine.

15 ***Hayes v Hoffman,* 164 Ga App 236, 296 SE2d 216 (1982)** (verdict for physician was sustained when physician prescribed Butazoladin and patient sustained a severe allergic response. The drug was prescribed for arthritic complaints in patient's wrists. The plaintiff did not disclose all known information regarding her allergies and such nondisclosure might constitute contributory negligence on part of patient, although such evidence did not warrant jury charge on assumption of risk. The patient must exercise ordinary care for her or his own safety and give an accurate history to the physician).

16 ***Oukrop v Wasserburger,* 755 P2d 233 (Wyo 1988)** (doctor prescribed an overdose, despite being questioned by the pharmacist, and who failed to advise patient or his parents of the error, was assessed $750,000 damages. A dose 25 times usual dose of atropine was ordered to decrease saliva before oral surgery. The dentist realized an overdose had been ordered and called an internist friend, who advised the dentist to call poison control center for advice. The dentist went ahead with surgery, not advising the patient or his mother of overdose. After surgery, the patient began to hallucinate. His mother called dentist three times, was never told of overdose, and inferred the patient "probably" had been taking drugs. The patient ran away from home, slept in a haystack, and the operative site became infected. Months later, patient's personality changed, with forgetfulness and temper outbursts. Testimony of a pharmacist that atropine overdose left permanent brain damage in mice was allowed).

17 ***Rubin v Aaron,* No 1615-81 (NY Nassau County Sup Ct June 5, 1989)** (decedent, a 59-year-old salesman, was taking medication for high blood pressure and hanged himself. The drug, Reserpine, is known to cause depression in some patients. The doctor continued the Reserpine, the patient trying several times to commit suicide, losing his job and incidentally developing a perirectal abscess and fistula. Doctor said his records showed no mention of depression, although the doctor visits, particularly in the last of six years of treatment, were infrequent. Plaintiff alleged doctor prescribed wrong drug, causing depression, failed to see patient in his office regularly, and, toward the end, also prescribed Valium, another depressing drug. The doctor's records did not show that Valium was prescribed, but that was verified by pharmacist's records. Jury found doctor 80 per cent liable and patient 20 per cent liable and awarded $1,090,000, consisting of $240,000 for pain and suffering for Mr. Rubin, $200,000 for loss of services, $550,000 for Mrs. Rubin's pecuniary loss, and $100,000 for daughter's pecuniary loss).

18 ***Felix v Hoffman-LaRoche,* 540 So 2d 102 (Fla 1989)** (Supreme Court of Florida held that the adequacy of a manufacturer's drug warning can be a matter of law, and that the duty can shift to the prescribing physi-

cian. The court reasoned that summary judgment for the manufacturer was appropriate because the drug company's duty was to warn the physician, and no reasonable person could argue that the warning itself was inadequate. The implication of this decision is that the prescribing physician may become the target for more suits arising from harmful side effects of prescription drugs. Physicians can avoid this additional exposure by explaining possible dangers to their patients and ideally (although not practically) requiring patients to sign a consent form stating that the risks have been explained and are understood).

19 ***Wilschinsky v Medina,*** **108 NM 511, 775 P2d 713 (1989)** (plaintiff was injured by auto driven by patient of defendant doctor who had administered Demerol and later an anti-nausea medication. Patient was medically impaired by injection for driving. The patient had a medical procedure performed at a hospital requiring the pain relief medication. The plaintiff alleged the doctor was liable for not warning patient not to drive and to prevent her from driving while under the influence of the drug. The defendant pled that New Mexico malpractice laws did not require him to keep the patient "off the roads." The highest court pointed out that those laws were written before outpatient surgery was in vogue and those laws should be flexible, considering that outpatient surgery patients present a new risk to third parties. The suit was not dismissed on the defendant's objection, and was bound over. There was a firm objection by one justice).

20 ***Welde v Kuzulla,*** **140 Mich App 658, 365 NW2d 205 (1985)** (court applied the except to the general rule that a physician could be liable for injury or death to a nonpatient third party. The decedent died of injuries caused by vehicle operated by defendant's patient. The defendant had treated the driver with medication, and the theory of liability was that the medication was negligently administered. It was held that a special relationship exists when a physician determines or should have determined that a patient poses a serious threat to a third person. The court felt that insisting on compliance with the standard of care of the profession, did not impose an unreasonable burden on the physician. It was held that liability would properly be imposed when a doctor's negligence is the proximate cause of injuries and the doctor is in the best position to prevent harm).

21 ***Myers v Quesenberry,*** **Cal App 3d 888, 193 Cal Rptr 733 (1983)** (personal injury action arising out of accident in which automobile driver lost control of her car due to diabetic attack resulting in collision with plaintiff's automobile. Trial court erred in sustaining without leave to amend to doctor's demurrer to plaintiff's complaint, where plaintiff alleged that the doctors negligently failed to warn patient against driving in uncontrolled diabetic condition, proximally causing plaintiff's damages. The court held that a special relationship exists between a doctor and a patient which may support affirmative duties for benefit of third person; a doctor must warn patient if patient's condition or medication renders certain conduct, such as driving a car, dangerous to others, but liability will only be imposed for those injuries which are the foreseeable consequence of the doctor's negli-

gence. It could not be said that dangers presented to plaintiff and other persons by patient's driving was unforeseeable to doctors).

22 ***Duval v Goldin,* 139 Mich App 342, 362 NW2d 275 (1984)** (suit was brought alleging that a doctor's epileptic patient negligently caused injury to plaintiff. The theory of liability was that the doctor failed to prescribe or continue to prescribe anti-convulsant medication and failed to instruct his patient not to drive an automobile after the medication was discontinued. The court held the doctor did have a special relationship with his patient which was sufficient to use the exception to the rule that no one had a duty to protect an individual who is endangered by the behavior of another person).

23 ***Fowler v Forlaw,* 435 So 2d 839 (Fla Dist Ct App 1983)** (court held that a duty existed to a third party on an allegation of prescribing Quaalude pills to a known drug addict. While driving a car, under influence of the Quaaludes prescribed by defendant physician, an auto accident occurred at the fault of plaintiff and had resulted in death of person in other car).

24 ***Gooden v Tips,* 651 SW2d 364 (Tex Civ App 1983)** (in a similar fact situation, the court held that a duty by prescribing physician exists to warn a patient that driving may be impaired, and how. The court concluded that the doctor did not have a duty to control the actions of the patient, and that if the physician had appropriately warned the patient not to drive, there could be no liability on behalf of the physician).

25 ***Wilschimsky v Medina,* 775 P2d 713 (NM 1989)** (supreme court held that a physician who administers narcotic drugs in his or her office to a patient must take reasonable care to protect the general public against harm resulting from that patient's impaired ability to operate an automobile. This case involved a migraine headache patient who regularly took Percodan for a severe headache. When a headache did not subside, the patient would go to the doctor's office and receive an injection of Demerol (a stronger narcotic). After one particular time which led to the lawsuit, patient became nauseated and a second drug was given for that problem. Patient drove car toward home but was involved in auto accident in which another was injured. The injured party filed suit, alleging, in part, that the physician was negligent in giving drugs to this patient that impaired her judgment and caused drowsiness. Evidence was in dispute as to whether the doctor had warned the patient of the side effects. The court ruled that the physician owed a duty of care to the general public when he administered drugs to the patient. In recognizing a duty toward third parties, the court observed that the recent growth in outpatient treatment for conditions that once would have been treated as hospital inpatients has increased the risk of injury to the public from patient's driving under influence of therapeutic drugs. In the administration of drugs in the doctor's office, the burden is light in requiring the doctor to take preventative measures, given informed warning, require that another transport patient, etc. The court did hold that the doctor should be held by prevailing standards in the medical community and that ruling extend only to cases involving persons who are injured by patients driving

from a doctor's office after being given drugs that might affect driving competence. The court held that what fulfilled these fact situations was a jury question. A dissenting opinion argued that the majority ruling would exacerbate the medical liability crisis by significantly extending a physician's potential liability).

26 ***Breit v St Louis Memorial Hospital,*** **743 P2d 1254 (Wash Ct App 1987)** (back surgery patient sued hospital for injuries, and a pharmacologist affidavit describing a possible adverse reaction to morphine sulfate injection when the patient is in upright position was admissible in a malpractice action. The patient was ambulatory after a laminectomy and had full use of extremities, but was suffering considerable pain. On physician's orders, the nurse gave him an injection of morphine and assisted him from his bed to a chair. The patient was still in pain when the physician visited him. The physician ordered additional morphine. Shortly after the nurse administered the injection, the patient suffered loss of sensory and motor function, being paralyzed at that time. At the time of trial, he was residing in a convalescent center. The patient brought an action of damages against the hospital and others. The trial court considered affidavits by two nurses who offered an opinion that the patient's attending nurse breached the standard of care for nurses. One nurse stated administration of morphine while the patient was upright was poor nursing practice because of the risk of inducting hypotension. The treating physician stated that morphine might have caused pooling of blood in the lower extremities and sufficient hypotension to tender the patient unconscious or give him a stroke. His notes indicated that the patient was upright in the chair when the morphine was given. The nurse who gave him the injections stated that she was aware of the risks. A doctor in pharmacy testified that the likelihood of an adverse reaction to morphine injection was increased if the patient was in an upright position. He said the patient's paralysis could be attributed to a classic vascular insufficiency reaction to morphine. the trial court granted the hospital a motion for summary judgment. On appeal, the hospital contended the pharmacologist affidavit should not have been considered because he is not competent to testify. The court said that whether an expert was licensed to practice medicine was important but not dispositive as to whether he or she was qualified. The affidavit was introduced to show possible adverse reaction to morphine injection when a person was in an upright position and not to establish the standard of care for nurses. The pharmacologist's description of the use of the drug was appropriate and promptly considered, the court reversed the lower court's judgment and sent the case back for trial).

27 ***Los Alamos Medical Center v Coe,*** **58 NM 686, 275 P2d 175 (1954)** (patient's inquiry put the defendant doctor on notice when he told the patient she had no cause for alarm of becoming addicted to morphine. This doctor's reassurance was sufficient evidence of reckless indifference to take issue to jury on punitive damage claim. The court said that punitive damages may be awarded where negligence is wanton or gross, or where treatment was given or the operation performed with utter indifference as to the effect on the patient).

28 ***Anderson v Central General Hospital,*** **No 15113-83 (NY Nassau County Sup Ct May 19, 1988)** (66-year old-plaintiff sought treatment from her doctor for back pain. He prescribed Motrin and anti-inflammatory medication and Haproxin, a narcotic. During the four months she took medications, she reported to her doctor feeling sluggish, dizzy and had blood in her urine. She fell at home, was unconscious, fracturing ribs and humerus, was hospitalized where blood in urine indicated a kidney problem, but attempt to treat problem was made. The hospital released the patient after seven days, released her home to care of a student nurse who forgot to lock the patient's wheelchair, resulting in patient falling, fracturing her femur. Her condition worsened and acute renal failure ensued requiring dialysis for four years until she died of pneumonia. Action was brought against hospital and doctor who prescribed the drugs. Doctor was charged with prescribing drugs in excessive doses, ignoring symptoms of her kidney problems and failing to inform the patient of her condition. The hospital was allegedly liable for using a student nurse to supervise patient care, ignoring test results and failing to take urine measurements. The doctor argued that the drug treatment did not cause her falls or her death and the medical complications and death were caused by her excessive smoking, her diabetes or the pneumonia related to the rib fractures and nephritis. Hospital contended the use of student nurse was a judgment call and not medical malpractice. Jury found doctor liable for $182,000 for wrongful death and $95,000 for pain and suffering sustained in the first fall. Jury found hospital 66.6 per cent liable and doctor 33.3 per cent liable for second fall, and awarded $95,000, which was reduced to $70,000 by medical expenses. Net judgment was $345,680).

29 ***GNOC Corp v Aboud,*** **715 F Supp 644 (DNJ 1989)** (holding that two physicians may be negligent as well as liable in punitive damages when they allegedly encouraged a patron of the casino to gamble, knowing that alcohol was contraindicated on top of Percodan they had prescribed for him. Plaintiff contended that the doctors knew or should have known that alcohol would be served and should not have prescribed Percodan which they had prescribed for treatment of knee, back, and jaw pain complaints. Plaintiff further says the physicians were negligent in prescribing Percodan at the plaintiff's request without doing a physical examination, reviewing his medical records, taking a medical history, and consulting with prior treating doctors. The court denied summary judgment request of the physicians. According to the court, punitive damages can be awarded to "punish doctors for aggravated or outrageous conduct and deter similar conduct," and it is the jury's role, after hearing testimony, to determine if the physicians' conduct warranted an award of punitive damages).

Comment: *Aboud* does not answer questions of negligence, as it is a hearing on motions, which were denied because a question of fact existed for a jury. Physicians, of course, are held to a standard of practice that includes adequate history taking, review of available records, and consulting prior doctors if that is important to care at hand. Prescription of the mind-altering drug Percodan should not be made on request of a patient saying he forgot and left his prescription at home, with the history/physical mentioned above. The doctors do have a duty to warn patient of side effects and contraindications (use of alcohol) as they prescribed the drug. It is unlikely that doctors owe any duty to know that casinos serve alcohol to their patrons).

30 ***McCarroll v Reed,* 679 P2d 851 (Okla Ct App 1983), *rehg denied, cert dismissed,* (Okla 1984)** (patient claimed he became addicted to drugs prescribed by his physician treating him as an orthopedist and had a cause of action against him. The case was initially dismissed as there was no cause of action but it was then sent for retrial after being heard by superior courts. The patient consulted a physician and osteopath for insomnia secondary to neck and back pain. He sold the patient some 1,125 units of Placidyl, Valium, Tuinal, and Tenuate, all controlled drugs, over the next 13 months. The patient claimed as a result of this he had a severe addiction problem accompanied by an irresistible compulsion to commit crimes to finance his cravings for drugs. By the time he filed a suit against the physician for malpractice, he had been arrested seven times, lost two jobs, had four car accidents, and three motorcycle accidents. He had been divorced, lost custody of his child and faced a prison term of more than 20 years. In reversing the trial court's decision, the appellate court said the patient stated a claim for medical malpractice, and also suggested that punitive damages could be recovered if the patient could show oppression, fraud, or gross negligence).

Comment: It is incumbent on the prescribing physician to know a patient and his or her behavior with the use of controlled substances. In patients with addictive tendencies, adequate control of the symptoms, pain, anxiety, etc., is appropriate. But, recognize that addictive personality/addictive behavior is a separate illness in itself requiring treatment. As part of the informed consent for treating the patient, informing the patient of a potential addiction problem is a must.

31 ***Gregory v Bilsing,* 633 SW2d 356 (Tex Civ App 1982)** (patient claimed Demerol dependence due to the malpractice of a physician. Trial court should not have granted summary judgment. The patient sued her physician for damages because she said she became psychologically and physically dependent on Demerol which had been injected for back pain. She claimed the physician's treatment was contrary to proper and reasonably prudent medical practice as the proximate cause of her injury. She said she became dependent on Demerol in August 1977. In his motion to dismiss, the physician claimed it was barred because she failed to give him 60 days' notice before the suit was filed. On appeal, decision was reversed. There is no conclusive proof that the patient's cause of action accrued after August 29, 1977. Since there was an issue concerning the date the action accrued, summary judgment was improper. The case was remanded for re-hearing on the facts).

32 ***Mueller v Mueller,* 88 SD 446, 221 NW2d 39 (1974)** (jury found as a fact that the patient was addicted and the physician knew or should have known that she was addicted at the time, though he continued to administer medications (in this case, cortisone). Verdict for negligent treatment stood, in spite of the fact that the patient had inflammatory arthropathy for which cortisone relieved her pain, she was developing secondary effects of hypercortisonism to her detriment).

33 ***Scharf v Phillips,* 391 So 2d 223 (Fla Dist Ct App 1980)** (court affirmed judgment in favor of two physicians rejecting patient's contention that his drug addiction and attendant disruption of his personal life was the result of negligent prescription of Equanil and Nebutol. The finding was there was adequate reason to continue to treat the patient for his manic depressive psychoses and his alcohol condition).

34 **Controlled Substances Act (21 USCS §801)** (the Act states that it is unlawful for a physician to prescribe or dispense controlled substances or drug in violation of that Act which requires knowledge of the patient, examination of the patient and written prescription of a licensed physician who had appropriate narcotic licensure).

35 ***Harrington v Rush Presbyterian St Lukes Hospital,* No 79 L 15578 (Ill Cook County Cir Ct Oct 3, 1988)** (25-year-old homemaker, badly injured in an auto accident, became addicted to Darvocet pain medication. She was admitted to the psychiatric ward of a hospital and defendant doctor prescribed 42 tablets of Darvocet to be given twice the dose the patient had ever taken. The patient received medication from floor duty nurse, was found dead several hours later. It appeared no nurse checked in the interim, the patient being in rigor mortis when found. Plaintiff allegations included improper monitoring on the part of the nursing staff. Plaintiff verdict of $4 million, divided $2.4 million to the minor child for loss of society, $1 million to husband for loss of society and $500,000 to husband for loss of services. In settlement negotiation, $750,000 was demanded by plaintiff and $500,000 offered by defendant).

Comment: Implicit in this case is the duty of a nurse to recognize a probable error in physician orders (43 Darvocet tablets) and to contact the doctor or nursing supervisor to correct the error, or the appropriate refusal of a nurse to give the medication as prescribed.

36 ***Fleming v Baptist General Convention,* 742 P2d 1087 (Okla), *rehg denied* (1987)** (Oklahoma Supreme Court ruled that patient had a history of chronic severe pain for many years. In 1968, her personal physician prescribed a standing order for Talwin and Atarax to be given together on demand. From September 1968 through October 1971, she received at least 300 intramuscular injections at hospital emergency room. The injection sites were rotated between arms, thighs, and buttocks. On October 19, after receiving injections of the left thigh, the patient experienced immediate pain. Injection site began discoloring by the time she reached home. She went to the hospital and by the next day, skin and subcutaneous tissue down to the fascia deteriorated and gangrene set in. After tissue death ceased, the patient required a skin graft to close the wound. Injury remained open for more than two months because of the nature of the injury and the treatment given. The patient sued physician for prescribing the drugs and hospital for negligence. She contended injection given on October 19 was not given deep into the muscles, but into the fat between the skin and muscles. Jury returned

a verdict in favor of the physician but against the hospital in the amount of $60,000. On appeal, hospital contended there was total lack of evidence against the hospital saying the theory that the injury was caused by continuous injections came from the testimony of physician and was consistent with his conclusion drawn from reserve facts. The physician said there was no evidence of disruption of the deep muscle fascia and therefore whatever happened occurred in the subcutaneous tissue. He said again that such injections subcutaneously is not the accepted practice. The court said the causation of negligence was established through opinion testimony, that testimony established a breach of duty; therefore, the trial court did not err. The hospital also contended damages were excessive. The court pointed out that the patient lost skin and subcutaneous tissue in 2 × 7 inch area which were enclosed by skin grafting. The area was permanently numb and scar disfiguring. The court found that the trial court did not err).

37 ***Stewart v Bay Minette Infirmary,* 501 So 2d 331 (Ala 1986), *rehg denied* (1987)** (patient went to the emergency room because of back pain. He was given a pain killer, in spite of known history of taking six Valium tablets and three mixed drinks. The patient returned DOA from "probable" overdose, though autopsy was "undetermined." The appellate court held that there was sufficient expert testimony that "the doctor showed a disregard for the most basic standards of emergency care." The doctor testified that he "cautioned the patient about risks of mixing alcohol and Valium).

38 ***Carter v Metropolitan Dade County,* 253 So2d 920 (Fla App 1971), *cert denied,* 263 So2d 584 (Fla 1972)** (wrongful death action against hospital and its physician arising out of a death from Phenothiazine drug. The patient was responding fairly well to 100 mg per day dose and for no clear reason, her dose was gradually increased to 2,400 mg per day—three to four times the manufacturer's recommended dose. The court concurred with the manufacturer's recommendation that the smallest effective dose should be used. It is also noted that defendant doctors were aware of "sudden death phenomena" that is sometimes associated with this drug).

39 ***Stone v Smith, Kline & French Laboratories,* 447 So 2d 1301 (Ala), 731 F2d 1575 (11th Cir 1984)** (patient developed adverse reaction to Thorazine. Physician who prescribed it was said to have been adequately warned by manufacturer of certain hazards of Thorazine, that is, Thorazine-induced hepatitis. Patient did develop hepatitis and through she recovered, she had a period of increased impairment. In an action against the manufacturer of the drug, a federal court granted summary judgment for the manufacturer. On appeal, the court certified a question of law to the Alabama Supreme Court. The state court said that if warnings to the prescribing physician about an unavoidably unsafe prescription drug were adequate, even though the patient was not warned, then the warnings were sufficient as a matter of law. The patient conceded that her physician had adequately warned of adverse reaction including hepatitis problem. The supreme court affirmed summary judgment for the manufacturer).

40 ***Mulder v Parke-Davis & Co,*** **288 Minn 332, 181 NW2d 882 (1970)** (wrongful death action against physician and drug manufacturer alleging, among other things, the defendant physician had been negligent in failing to follow manufacturer's precautionary instruction for the use of the drug in question. Evidence by expert witness for plaintiff was that a careful physician not familiar with dangerous drug would follow manufacturer's instructions and this was refused by the court. Evidence was admitted that indicated the decedent's death was result of a condition that occasionally was caused by administration of the drug in question. Chloromycentin was the drug used for an infection. The patient developed a profound bone marrow depression and died, a complication that is described in the package insert. Hinged on the fact that the doctor used a larger dose than recommended by the manufacturer, because previous antibiotics had not effectively eradicated an infection, the doctor was held negligent absent expert testimony to the contrary for the excess dose and was additionally held negligent for not taking periodic blood tests for the possibility of aplastic anemia. This should have been evidence to the doctor. On petition of re-hearing, court expanded on decision as follows: Where a drug manufacturer recommends to the medical profession, (1) the condition under which this drug should be prescribed, (2) the disorder that it is designed to relieve, (3) precautionary measures which should be observed, and (4) warns of dangers which are inherent in its use, a doctor's deviation from such recommendations is prima facie evidence of negligence if there is constant medical testimony that the patient's injury or death resulted from the doctor's failure to adhere to the recommendation. Under such circumstances, it is incumbent on the doctor to disclose his reasons from departing from the procedures recommended by the manufacturer. Although it will ordinarily be a jury question whether the doctor has justified or excused his deviation, there may be situations where the matter exonerates him unless rebutted by competent medical testimony).

41 ***Lay v Orr,*** **No 400 209 (Cal Los Angeles County Super Ct 1988)** (patient had a long and complicated medical history of multiple illness including three cancers. Her present complaint was of multiple joint and muscle pain. She was seen and treated by an oncologist because of the history of three prior cancers. He felt diagnosis lay between lymphosarcoma and sarcoidosis, later proven by lung biopsy as sarcoid disease. For several years prior to that diagnosis, he had maintained patient on corticosteroids, the patient developing aseptic necrosis of the hip. The plaintiff claims that if diagnosis of sarcoidosis was made earlier corticosteroids would not be necessary, and aseptic necrosis hip would not have occurred. Expert testimony felt that oncologist's work-up was within standard of care even though CAT scans, pulmonary function tests and Gallium radioisotope scans were not ordered. Further expert testimony shows that aseptic necrosis concurs at least one-third of the time idiopathically, unrelated to steroid usage. Defendant verdict; demand for settlement by plaintiff was $250,000; defense offer—none).

42 ***Weil v Seltzer,*** **873 F2d 1453 (DC Cir 1989)** (physician had prescribed corticosteroid for an allergic condition, calling them antihistamine,

in spite of progressive deterioration and ultimate demise from steroid-related complication, including several pathological fractures, and pulmonary embolus containing bone marrow and bone spicules. The lower court held the patient contributorily negligent for not finding out the medication he was taking. The basis of the suit was negligent long-term medical care leading to known complicating fatal pulmonary embolus. Lower court awarded $4 million. On appeal, the defense pointed out the current treating physicians were equally, perhaps more, negligent for not ascertaining that the patient had been taking steroid or communication between doctors taking a medical history. The court held that the recent treating physicians could not be faulted as they asked the patient what medicines the patient was taking, and the real duty lay with the long-time, steroid-treating doctor for not informing patient of his medication and risks. Case was remanded for errors in allowing lay (patient) testimony regarding the defendant's prescribing habits).

43 ***Hutchinson v United States,* 838 F2d 390 (9th Cir 1988)** (federal court allowed a suit for lack of informed consent when patient developed aseptic necrosis head femur proximally related to prolonged prescriptive use of Prednisone. The court asked, but did not answer, "How safe must a procedure be before written consent is unnecessary?").

44 ***Gluckman v Halsey Drug Co,* 533 NYS2d 827 (1988)** (suit was brought against the manufacturer of Prednisone (corticosteroid) which was prescribed by physician for asthma for many years, and plaintiff developed steroid-related aseptic necrosis of femoral head. The defendant drug company was released, having adequately informed physician of that steroid risk through its advertisements and package inserts. The physician could be held liable for not informing the patient of the risk—following the intervening cause doctrine).

45 ***Hahn v Richter,* No 82-2895 (Pa D & C 3d)** (plaintiff alleged that Upjohn Drug failed to provide adequate warning regarding risk of injecting Depo-Medrol intrathecally. The defendant performed several intrathecal injections of Depo-Medrol from May 1977 to February 1980 after plaintiff had injured his low back. Soon after a January 1977 disc operation, the patient began having leg pain symptoms consistent with arachnoiditis, a scarring problem that occurs about nerve rootlet intrathecally. The arachnoiditis was verified by additional surgeries in October 1977 and March 1980. The plaintiff alleged that the Depo-Medrol, an anti-inflammatory chemical was the cause of this. Although some doctors feel that intrathecal Depo-Medrol lessens arachnoiditis and when used epidurally, reduces nerve root inflammatory irritation, the manufacturer does not, nor has not in its package insert, recommended Depo-Medrol use intrathecally. The jury found that Upjohn had provided adequate information for the physician to judge his therapy on).

Comment: At one time, the Upjohn Depo-Medrol package insert suggested that intrathecal injection might be contraindicated. When inquiring of the medical director, an answer was that no specific information in human beings was available to say that Depo-Medrol intrathecally would cause scarring, although some experimental work with monkeys was suggestive.

46 ***Rotan v Greenbaum,* 273 F2d 830 (DC Cir 1959)** (patient died within 15 minutes after receiving penicillin injection. The doctor had been told in the routine history that the patient was a hypersensitive patient; that is, had severe allergies but she had not experienced previous adverse reaction from penicillin. It was held that medical negligence would not stand in that the sensitivity to the drug was not known and could not have been known to the patient's absent prior history of sensitivity. A similar result was held in Smith v United States, 394 F2d 482 (5th Cir 1968), in which also the patient is a hypersensitive allergic person to other chemicals with no prior history to allergies to penicillin, that there is no skin testing that is either feasible or reliable).

47 ***Campos v Weeks,* 245 Cal App 2d 678, 53 Cal Rptr 915 (1966)** (malpractice action was filed against a physician who administered penicillin to a patient who subsequently suffered anti-phylactoid shock. The court held the doctrine of res ipsa loquitur inapplicable to the case. It stated that the rule of a particular injury suffered by a patient that rarely occurs does not in itself prove that the injury was probably caused by the negligence of those in charge. The court noted testimony that anti-phylactic shock can occur without negligence on the part of anyone and to permit the inference of negligence under the doctrine of res ipsa loquitur would be to place too great a burden on the medical profession. Further, on the issue of whether skin testing should have been done prior to administering penicillin, the tests are generally unreliable and are not ordinarily used in connection with penicillin. Expert testimony indicated in this type of case that doctors mainly rely on the history given by the patient whether there has been a particular allergy to any drug, particularly medications that are taken orally, and that is it not economically feasible to test all patients for possible adverse drug reactions, inasmuch as this would either require the physician to stock appropriate test solutions and would necessitate his spending a great amount of working time conducting tests rather than caring for patient, or would require that the patient be sent to an appropriate laboratory for such tests, which would result in an unnecessary financial burden).

48 ***Walstad v Univ Minn Hospital,* 442 F2d 634 (8th Cir 1971)** (patient received at least 12 injections of penicillin in spite of notation in the patient's hospital record that the patient was allergic to penicillin. Again, the defendant's verdict was affirmed as in *Tangora v Matanky, 231 Cal App 2d 468, 42 Cal Rptr 348 (1965),* in which the patient suffered anaphylactic shock and died after injection of penicillin. This was a patient who had no signs of allergy or hay fever or other allergic phenomena and the patient had told the physician she had penicillin several times previously).

Comment: In most cases of this sort, the culpability of the physician is based on the history taken from the patient, although it is known that hypersensitivity to many chemicals, including penicillin, can result when the patient is sensitized by any one of several injections and then receives an additional injection, the latter being the injection that precipitates an allergic response or even death—and, that this phenomena is not medically predictable at this time.

49 ***Garvey v O'Donoghue,* 530 A2d 1141 (DC 1987)** (three physicians were not liable for malpractice after a patient suffered tinnitus from the administration of Tobramycin. In early March 1980, the patient, who was a first-year nursing student, sought medical treatment for a sore throat. She was referred to an ear, nose, and throat specialist who diagnosed her condition as strep infection. On March 11, 1980, because her symptoms had not improved, she was admitted to the hospital complaining of sore throat, severe abdominal pain, and high fever. During the first full day's admission, the patient's temperature rose to 104.7°. While hospitalized, she was treated by several physicians who determined she was suffering from left tubal ovarian abscess about 7 cm in size. Diagnosis was confirmed by somography. Throat and vaginal cultures were taken at the time of admission which indicated several antibiotics, including tobramycin, would be effective against the offending organism, Beta Streptococcus. Both Tobramycin and Cefoxitin were administered IV for 14 days. Blood tests were conducted at least twice to monitor for side effects and antibiotics; however, the last monitoring was conducted eight days before the administration was concluded. At no time during the hospitalization did the patient complain of a hearing loss, hearing impairment of unusual sounds in ear. She was released from the hospital March 27, 1980. The patient testified she first noticed sounds in her ears a few weeks after being discharged from the hospital. She was examined and treated by two ENT specialists. The only evidence presented at trial that she suffered from tinnitus was her own testimony and her medical witnesses that she tried several methods of minimizing or covering the distracting sounds, including playing a radio at night, leaving the TV on and finally approaching a tinnitus massacre in the summer of 1984 with a malpractice action against three physicians. The patient claimed Tobramycin was a highly toxic drug and that more suitable and less dangerous drugs were available. In addition, she attempted to show both dosage level and duration of treatment of drugs exceeded recommended standards. The trial court returned a verdict in favor of the physician, and the patient appealed. Affirming the decision, the court said that the trial court did not err in allowing portions of the Physician's Desk Reference (PDR) and manufacturer's package insert to be admitted as evidence. The court said they were relevant and probative evidence on the medical standard of care for selecting, administering and monitoring the drugs. The court said that a pharmacologist was qualified to testify as expert witness as to the effects of Tobramycin on the patient and the proper dosage in respect to the patient's side).

50 ***United States v Kubrick,* 444 US 111 (1979)** (patient had an infected right femur that was treated with Neomycin and developed a hearing problem, as well as ringing in the ears. The United States Supreme Court held that the Neomycin administration, having a known history of producing ear injuries, was the probable cause of the plaintiff's ear damage, and that the treating physician knew or should have known of this).

51 ***Toner v Letterly Laboratories,* 828 F2d 510 (9th Cir 1987)** (drug manufacturer of Tri-Immunol was negligent in manufacturing the vaccine and liable for the patient's paralysis. The patient was paralyzed after vaccination. In a product liability action against the manufacturer of the vaccine, the patient contended it failed to develop an alternative vaccine that would have been safer than the one given to him in a special verdict. The jury found that the manufacturer was negligent in connection with the product and its negligence was the proximate cause of the patient's injury, and the patient was awarded damages in the amount of $1,131,200. On appeal, the manufacturer argued that the jury's instructions were inadequate for failure to state that certain drugs were unavoidably unsafe and that is was permissible to market such drugs despite their risk and inherent use. The court said the trial court instructions did adequately state, by Idaho law, by permitting jury to assess reasonableness of the manufacturer's conduct in light of all circumstances. The jury considered scientific knowledge and utility of the vaccine in the light of alternatives known by the manufacturer. The court said the jury could have found the manufacturer's failure to develop an alternative vaccine was unreasonable conduct, even though the danger imposed by the vaccine use was not greater than an ordinary consumer would reasonably expect. Expert testimony was that the injury would not have occurred had the manufacturer developed the alternative vaccine. The manufacturer argued that the patient failed to prove causation because he failed to show that the FDA would have approved the alternative vaccine. In absence of evidence that the FDA would not have approved the vaccine had the manufacturer submitted the product to it, the jury could infer that the patient's injury could have been avoided had the use of alternate vaccine, the court ruled).

52 ***Baker v United States,* 660 F Supp 204 (DDC 1986)** (patient demonstrated that Guillain-Barré syndrome was from a swine flu shot. This is another case in which reviewing the expert testimony both sides of court noted acute GBS was the most common form of the syndrome having existent GBS in connection with swine flu vaccination had not been definitely ruled out by experts. The court said that the patient established that the swine flu vaccine more likely than not had caused him to suffer GBS. There was evidence his first symptoms appeared within two weeks after the vaccination. Causation was established by the vaccination to the satisfaction of the court, and the case was remanded for damages).

53 ***Manko v United States,* 830 F2d 831 (8th Cir 1987)** (patient received swine flu vaccine on August 20, 1976 and began feeling ill about 10 days later. Condition worsened on January 25, 1977, and the diagnosis was Guillain-Barré syndrome. The court found that his GBS was caused by the vaccination—not by a viral illness, as the government contended. On appeal, the court affirmed the trial court's decision except for one small aspect of the damages. The court awarded the patient $14,000 to compensate the loss of money that his pension plan would have earned from 1977 through 1985, which would have increased the amount of his pension benefits,

although the court found the patient would have retired on his 70th birthday, July 21, 1982. Nevertheless, he was awarded loss of pension earnings from the time of his illness to the year 1985. However, there were no findings that the patient could have drawn on his pension plan until the year of 1985, and that the trustee would have been obligated to continue to manage the fund from the day of retirement through 1985. The court remanded the question of pension benefits to the trial court for recalculation. The trial court promptly refused to permit the patient's wife to join the lawsuit to recover for loss of consortium; she had not timely filed an administrative claim. The wife's injury was caused at the time of the husband's hospitalization, so was barred by the time she filed the claim).

54 ***Brown v United States,*** **715 F2d 463 (9th Cir 1983)** (serviceman was able to satisfy the trier of fact that there was a direct relationship between his receiving flu vaccine and the development of verifiable Guillain-Barré syndrome).

55 ***Lima v United States,*** **708 F2d 502 (10th Cir),** ***rehg denied*** **(1983)**

56 ***Peterson v United States,*** **567 F Supp 676 (D Idaho 1983)** (in each of these cases, expert testimony failed to prove that there was a direct link between receiving a flu shot and subsequent development of Guillain-Barré syndrome, a virus infection of the spinal cord and peripheral nerves. In Four, the expert proof was based on a medical expert reading a survey without weakness and that soreness in her arm at the side of the flu injection carried minimal, if any, real impairment. The third case pointed out that the neurologist for the government convinced the trier of fact that areflexia was required for the diagnosis of Guillain-Barré syndrome, that the patient had a brachioplexus neuropathy and pain but did not have areflexia).

57 ***Welch v Chandler,*** **No 103544 (Me Ct App)** (court held that the patient's refusal to return medical records to the defendant physician prior to trial would be fatal to the trial, as the defendant would be unstable to defend himself. In trial court, the plaintiff alleged the defendant improperly prescribed Percodan and other narcotics during a six-year period, causing the plaintiff to become addicted. The plaintiff had obtained the defendant doctor's medical records for review before trial. Only five pages of the chart were returned and two discovery orders were entered and ignored. The plaintiff admitted that some of the laboratory and x-ray files were missing, but denied retaining the remainder of the record. The court held that, when the plaintiff took the records, he had control over them and had a duty to return them on demand. The plaintiff's admitted failure to produce the file fatally compromised the defendant's ability to defend himself).

24

Anesthesia

§24.01 Generally

There are 2,000 anesthesia-related deaths each year in the United States, one per 10,000 surgeries. This is one of the reasons why anesthesiology has become a completely independent medical specialty and why many surgical procedures are considered improper except in hospital settings where fully-trained anesthesiologists are constantly on call. It is also the main reason why anesthesiology is the only specialty that prohibits residents from being on call for more than 24 consecutive hours. Sleeplessness may seem ominous in other specialties, but the slip of the knife is not deemed as dangerous as a slip of the anesthetic dial.

Despite preoperative planning and treatment, some patients' physical condition presents unacceptable anesthetic/surgical risks. These patients should have surgery cancelled, continue with nonoperative (medical) care, and be re-evaluated later. Often, family and patient counselling is helpful and therapeutic. Communication and hope have repeatedly been shown of great importance in treating the patient and dealing with family, and are the duty of competent physicians in all medical disciplines.

The orthopedic surgeon often has daily contact with the anesthesiologist. The "Captain of the Ship" doctrine is rarely followed by current jurisprudence, yet the orthopedist is involved with the anesthetic of his or her patient and may be legally vulnerable in several areas.

The surgeon is held to know the person giving anesthetic agents to his or her patient and if the surgeon is aware of the lack of competence of an anesthesiologist, or if the surgeon sees an error in progress and does not intervene and that error results in injury to the patient, the surgeon may incur liability. This responsibility follows to immediate postoperative care in the recovery room.

§24.02 Anesthesia Provider

The person providing the anesthesia must be either a physician (anesthesiologist) or a certified nurse anesthetist with formal anesthesia training. *Anesthetist* is often used as a generic designation for any person providing anesthesia, be it nurse or physician, whereas *anesthesiologist* refers to a physician only—one who has been trained in the specialty of administering anesthesia and its related endeavors. This person has no responsibility in the performance of surgery or assisting in surgery. His or her sole responsibility is the administering of anesthesia and anticipating complications that may occur, being ready to address those complications if and when they do occur. He or she must be assured that the equipment to give appropriate anesthesia is available, that anesthesia equipment is functioning properly, and that appropriate amounts and currently-dated medications are available, both for the giving of the anesthesia and the coping with complications, should they occur. It is the anesthesiologist's responsibility to check all these items prior to starting the anesthetic.

If a physician provides anesthesia, he or she is fully and independently responsible for his or her own activities and the consequences of them. A nurse anesthetist providing anesthesia may be directly supervised by the anesthesiologist or operating surgeon.

Depending on local statute, the nurse anesthetist may be an independent provider and be solely responsible (as the anesthesiologist), but more often he or she is under the supervision of an anesthesiologist and/or the surgeon, and those physicians become vicariously jointly liable for the anesthetist's behavior. Often, the anesthetist and the anesthesiologist are hospital employees; therefore, the hospital may become vicariously liable for negligent mishaps of the anesthetist/anesthesiologist.

The hospital incurs responsibility in the first instance as it credentials the anesthesiologist or anesthetist that it employs. A second level of responsibility exists when the hospital grants an exclusive privilege to practice anesthesia to an individual or a group. Under these circumstances, the hospital effectively controls its source of anesthesia services. Therefore, the hospital is responsible for ensuring the day-to-day quality of anesthesia care.

There are indicators of potential substandard practice that are easily available to the hospital, such as failure of an anesthesiologist to achieve specialty board-certification after a reasonable period of time or specified number of attempts, or allegations of anesthetic malpractice suits brought by patients, or evidence of substance abuse by the practitioner.

Major complications relating to anesthesia are rare with the properly preoperatively-evaluated patient. Complications will vary with the technique used, e.g., regional versus general, nitrous-narcotic versus balanced anesthesia. Problems may stem from inaccurate medication dosing (overdosing), electrolyte imbalance in the patient, unexpected blood loss during surgery, or progressive hypo- or hyperthermia. Most of these problems are under the control of the anesthesiologist.

In the immediate post-anesthetic period, maintenance of airway, reversal of narcosis, control of blood pressure and body temperature, and nausea with aspiration or possible aspiration pneumonia must be dealt with by the anesthesiologist and recovery room personnel. It is as important to have an adequately equipped recovery room managed by adequately trained recovery room personnel as in the operating room. Renal function must be protected and may be adversely affected by inadequate fluid. At the same time, cardiac function may be overloaded by too much fluid.

Maintenance of blood pressure (preventing shock) is of prime importance. It is essential to have at least one larger bore intravenous catheter in place at surgery and to keep open in the recovery room, as this intravenous route may be the life-saving conduit in case of an emergency requiring parenteral medication or blood.

§24.03 Anesthesia—The Medical Record

The orthopedist relies on the anesthesiologist to keep appropriate records documenting his or her anesthetic procedures. This record becomes of the greatest medical legal importance in litigation involving the anesthesiologist and/or orthopedist.

This record should record details of any procedures performed, the type and quantity of any medications administered, and the patient's vital signs as measured at frequent intervals. Most importantly, there must be a notation of the maneuvers that are specifically used. In obtaining anesthesia, such as endotracheal intubation or insertion of venous lines or other needling procedures, although they may be mundane and routine to the anesthesiologist, their notation is essential. A description of the position of the patient at the time of the administration of anesthesia, particularly if the patient is turned onto his or her side such as when administering spinal or epidural anesthesia, and which side the patient is lying on, is important.

The pre-anesthesia assessment should note important items, such as when the patient last ate, the nature of acute trauma if present, drug allergies, and important health problems, such as high blood pressure, diabetes, or seizure disorders.

Anesthesia records are typically placed on a form that is, in part, a graph, usually lined at five minute intervals. The patient's blood pressure and pulse need to be recorded this often at least. They should also be recorded immediately after instillation of medication or placement of needles or plastic tubes as part of an epidural or spinal block procedure.

Two major potential problems with the anesthesia record are unreliability, as information may be recorded either prospectively or retrospectively, and incompleteness, where information is either missing or illegible. Nursing records from the operating theatre and recovery room can be used in an attempt to confirm or verify the anesthesia record in regard to fluids given, blood loss, times, and, in some instances, vital signs.

§24.04 Hypotension

Hypotension is a physiological drop in the blood pressure to a level lower than the normal needed for adequate perfusion of blood to the vital structures. The anesthesiologist's and surgeon's greatest concerns lie in the effective management of their patient so that the brain receives adequate oxygen (adequate oxygen being a measure of the amount of blood flow), and blood flow being mediated in substantial part by blood perfused at normal blood pressures.

There are two components involved in hypotension. The anatomical component is occlusion of major vessels, ordinarily abdominal vessels, so that inadequate blood returns to the heart to be pumped. This is more obviously present in abdominal surgery and obstetrical cases, but occurs also in positioning of the orthopedic patient. For instance, a patient may be turned onto his or her face on special frames, pillows, or chest rolls during the preparation for spinal surgery, or placed in less than physiological position to manage pelvic, hip, or femoral fractures, utilizing a fracture table. This table has a peyineal post with traction applied to the legs, the legs in varying degrees of abduction and internal or external rotation. In the event of failure of compensation mechanisms to return blood to the heart, hypotension may occur due to inadequate cardiac output.

There are various pressure adjustments that are made by the vascular system to accomplish this. The precise mechanism is not known in great detail; however, the sympathetic nerve system (SNS) is the means used by the body to aid in these adjustments. When the SNS cannot function properly for whatever reason, then the uncompensated occlusion of abdominal vessels results in decreased blood flow, both to and from the heart, with hypotension resulting.

Hypotension may occur from the direct effect of medications on the heart musculature, allowing it to function inadequately as a pump, pumping blood at a decreased pressure. Hypotension may, and often does, occur when the peripheral vascular tree is dilated, be it for chemical, ischemic, or mechanical reasons. It is the anesthesiologist's responsibility to be attuned to each of these possibilities, to make an appropriate diagnosis, and to establish a remedy if hypotension occurs.

In the treatment of hypotension, it is often desirable to administer some medication that helps raise the blood pressure. Medication can accomplish this by constriction of the blood vessels to force what blood flow there is to push harder against the walls and increase the flow itself. Typical agents may have a specific effect on narrowing peripheral blood vessels, therefore, increasing peripheral resistance. Other groups of medications have their effect almost exclusively on the heart to increase its force of contraction. Ephedrine is the model of medications that are cardiac stimulants. Ephedrine works both by causing a release of catecholamines from sites within the body. Ephedrine or ephedrine-related chemicals are the agents of choice in decreasing hypotension secondary to spinal and epidural blocks. Ephedrine is one of many drugs, however, with many new ones being developed on a constant basis. The anesthesiologist (or the surgeon, if he or she is supervising anesthesia) should be keenly aware of the availability and effects of these drugs.

§24.05 Malignant Hyperthermia

Malignant hyperthermia is a genetically-determined disorder of muscle metabolism. The syndrome is precipitated by stress and has been associated with the administration of almost all anesthetic agents, although often with depolarizing muscle relaxant succinylcholine (Anectin) and the inhalation agent halothane (Fluothane). The syndrome manifests with a rapid rise in core temperature; however, the disease can occur without a major rise in temperature. If not detected, malignant hyperthermia may be fatal and requires continual diligence by the anesthesiologist. Regular monitoring of temperature, along with monitoring of the physiological parameters (blood pressure, pulse, blood oxygen, electrocardiograph) are standards of care.

Halothane and succinylcholine anesthetic are often implicated as triggers of the syndrome in susceptible persons. Early recognition of the problem is life-saving, requiring a high index of suspicion by a diligent, knowledgeable physician. Treatment requires immediate discontinuance of the anesthetic. Surgery must be aborted in a manner safe to the patient. The patient must be hyperventilated with oxygen and given, parenterally, sodium bicarbonate until blood gases revert to normal. Cooling the patient with ice, ice water submersion, and fan cooling is essential.

Physiological monitoring in the intensive care environment is important. Prophylactic use of Dantrolene is helpful in patients with known hyperthermia syndrome tendency. Its use permits repeated surgical anesthetic safety. Dantrolene is not effective as a therapy in the patient involved in active hyperthermia, but may lessen severity if given early.

§24.06 Hypoxia

The most feared of all anesthetic complications is anoxia with permanent brain damage. Inadequate airway, failure to maintain passive respiration associated with hypoxia, and inappropriate delivery of anesthetic agents may produce anoxia.

Primary hypoxia may be caused by inadvertent esophageal placement of intratracheal tube, failure of anesthetic equipment, disconnection of the breathing circuit from the gas machine, prolonged hypotension, inappropriate patient positioning, and anesthetic overdosing. There is no substitute for an alert, well-informed physician giving the anesthetic, who has a high index of suspicion and who provides continuous care for the patient. Long operations can be dull for the anesthesiologist, and alertness can easily be diluted by boredom, distraction, fatigue, or health problems in the anesthesiologist. The surgeon has a duty to be aware of these potential impediments.[1] (*See* Appendix 24-1, Cases 1 to 12.)

§24.07 Failed Intubation

When intubation of the trachea is attempted as part of anesthesia or as part of an emergency resuscitation procedure, placing the tube into the esophagus rather than the trachea can happen, resulting in anoxia with its adverse effects on the brain, heart, and other organs. This is a preventable error and is also the direct measure of the skill of the operator and an issue that is addressed regularly in in-service and training programs for emergency resuscitation personnel. Accurate placement of the endotracheal tube carries with it the need for knowledge of the anatomy of the throat, positioning favorable to placement of the tube, use of the equipment, the laryngoscope, and knowledge of appropriate tube sizes and of endotracheal tube air bag inflation—to make a tight seal, but not to instill so much pressure that it should cause a necrosis of the trachea. The length of time that the endotracheal tube is left in place is also critical for the same reason, for if the air bag that blocks air leak applies pressure long enough on the lining of the trachea, it may cause it to necrose—leading to dire consequences.

Body positioning of the patient by the anesthesiologist, surgeon, and operating room personnel is of utmost importance to the patient to prevent injury while the patient is anesthetized and unable to protect him- or herself. Many

---

[1] R.D. Miller, Anesthesia (2d ed 1986); Goldman, *Cardiac Risks and Complications of Noncardiac Surgery,* 98 Ann Int Med 504 (1983).

law suits are brought due to injury to peripheral nerves (arm and leg) from pressure in areas, when protection from pressure is the standard of care. Drastic manipulation of arms or legs may unduly stretch and damage nerves or vessels. Malposition of the neck in surgery may adversely affect circulation of the cervical spinal cord and lead to catastrophic paralysis. Malposition or change of position of the neck-shoulder when a patient is anesthetized with an endotracheal tube in place may lead to displacement of the tube, further leading to brain anoxia with permanent sequelae. This is a major preventable complication. (*See* Appendix 24-1, Cases 13 to 18.)

§24.08 Anesthetic and Intraoperative Deaths

It is estimated that the death rate in the first 48 hours after operation is 0.3 per cent. Of these deaths, about 10 per cent occur during induction of anesthesia, 35 per cent intraoperatively, and 55 per cent in the first 48 hours after operation completion. Inadequate ventilation and aspiration of gastric contents are preventable causes of anesthetic death. Sudden unexpected cardiac arrhythmias or asystole, drug-induced myocardial depression and progressive hypotension (often from surgical blood loss) are responsible for 10 to 15 per cent of deaths in the first 48 hours. Constant vigilance on the part of the anesthesiologist allows him or her to deal with these problems early, avoiding catastrophe in most cases.

Improvement in risk assessment for short-term morbidity has led to physician changes in clinical behavior. In reviewing five large studies in tertiary care facilities, the clinician appears to be sensitized to specific cardiac risk issues, many of which can be corrected before surgery, thus lessening operative risks.

These changes in clinical approach require a new set of weighted cardiac factors to predict operative events so that additional improvement is a goal. Objective forms of assessment and clinical judgment can function well in concert.

§24.09 Anesthesia and Patient Nutrition

Appearing frequently in the medical literature are articles relating to the nutritional status and immune state of the patient in respect to clinical care in general and surgical care with its effect on postsurgical complications. The operating surgeon is responsible to assess these factors, utilize available diagnostic and therapeutic information, and initiate this knowledge before surgery. The metabolically-compromised or poorly-nourished patient is a surgical risk. These problems continue into the postoperative period and, if not adequately dealt with, will predictably adversely affect the patient's convalescence. The same logic applies to the immunosuppressed patient, the patient with chronic infection, or the patient with other systemic states that adversely affect infection prevention or control. Postoperative wound infections occur in three to five per cent of "clean" cases in hospitals across

America. Urinary tract, pulmonary, and venipuncture site infections, however, add another substantial growth of hospital/surgery-related infection, many of which relate to the care and diligence of patient care offered by the care-givers.[2]

§24.10 Hypotensive Anesthesia

Hypotensive anesthesia during major hip or spinal surgeries is effective for decreased inter-operative and total blood loss in shortening the operative time. There is no significant difference in thromboembolism with hypo- and normo-tensive anesthesia. In spinal surgery, hypotensive anesthesia significantly reduces inter-operative blood loss. Blood requirement is decreased only in patients under 18, not adults.

To detect spinal cord dysfunction inter-operatively, somatosensory cortico-evoked potential monitoring or wake-up test, or the combination of the two, is generally used. A balanced anesthesia technique consisting of nitrous oxide narcotics and muscle relaxant is well suited for hypotensive anesthesia.

§24.11 Hypoxia versus Hypoxemia

Hypoxia refers to decreased concentration of oxygen; *hypoxemia* refers to decreased concentration of oxygen in the blood.

In a surgical patient, hypoxia is commonly seen in the intraoperative period, is estimated to be at least 15 per cent, and is responsible for many anesthetic disasters.

Hypoxia is caused by decreased arterial partial pressure of oxygen (PO_2) or lack of adequate tissue oxygenation (tissue hypoxia). The existence and location of the lack of oxygen must be defined. In investigating the cause of decreased arterial oxygen saturation (by testing blood levels), it should be determined whether the deficit is due to decreased alveolar oxygen (oxygen concentration in the air sacs of the lungs) or an impediment in the ability

---

[2] C.A. Moyer, The Assessment of Operative Risk. Surgery: Principles and Practice (4th ed 1970); Del Guercio & Cohn, *Monitoring Operative Risk in Elderly,* 243 JAMA 1350 (1980); Hooton, *The Joint Association of Multiple Risk Factors with Occurrence of Nosocomial Infection,* 70 Am J Med 960 (1981); Owens, *ASA Physical Status Classification: A Study of Consistency of Ratings,* 49 Anesthesiology 239 (1978); Knaus, *Relationship Between Acute Physiologic Derangement and Risk of Death,* 38 J Chronic Dis 295 (1985); A.K. Weiss, The Physiology of Aging. Surgery in the Aged. (L.J. Greenfield ed 1975); Pettigrew & Hill, *Indicators of Surgical Risk and Clinical Judgment,* 73 BJ Surg 47 (1986); Windsor & Hill, *Weight Loss with Physiologic Impairment: A Basic Indicator of Surgical Risk,* 207 Ann Surg NEJM 290 (1988); Christou, *Host Defense Mechanisms in Surgical Patients: A Correlative Study of the Delayed Hypersensitivity Skin-Test Response, Granulocyte Function and Sepsis,* 28 Can J Surg 39 (1985); Casey, *Correlation of Immune and Nutritional Status with Wound Complications in Patients Undergoing Vascular Operations,* 93 Surgery 882 (1983).

to oxygenate the blood as it passes through the lungs, with the result being an increase in the alveolar-arterial oxygen gradient.

Alveolar hypoxia may be caused by the inhalation of anesthetic gas mixed with insufficient oxygen concentration, a significant decrease in barometric pressure, or the development of severe hypercarbia (excess carbon dioxide levels). The anesthesiologist must have a plan for rapid assessment of the anesthetic machine and its attachments to insure adequate oxygen concentration in the inhalant mixture breathed by the patient, with attention to barometric pressure effects and the assessment of the adequacy of alveolar ventilation.

Increase in the alveolar-arterial oxygen gradient may be caused by anatomic shunting of deoxygenated venous blood from the systemic circulation to bypass the pulmonary capillaries where it would normally pick up oxygen. This deoxygenated venous blood is referred to as a *venous admixture,* and results in decreased arterial blood oxygen levels. Congenital heart disease may be a cause of shunting.

More common to the anesthesiologist is the development of hypoxia with shunting of alveolar-arterial oxygen gradient, due to a physiological shunting, not anatomical shunting, and the decreased pulmonary ventilation perfusion ratios. The principal cause of decreased ventilation perfusion ratio is a reduction in functional residual capacity caused by atelectasis, pneumonitis, lung water aspiration, or intrapulmonary hemorrhage.

Atelectasis (collapsed lung) is the most common cause of progressive hypoxemia under anesthesia and is routinely caused by the movement of the relaxed diaphragm toward the patient's head. Other causes of hypoxemia include insufficient title volume pneumothorax (area in the chest cavity), main-stem intubation, bronchial obstruction, plural effusion (swelling of the lining about the lungs), reduction in functional residual capacity, and retraction and compression of the lung during surgery.

Tissue hypoxia, in the absence of hypoxemia, may involve insufficient delivery of oxygen, poor oxygen utilization, or excessive oxygen demand. If the oxygen delivered to the tissues is not equal to, or greater than, the oxygen demand, tissue hypoxia occurs.

Various abnormalities may cause changes in arterial and mixed venous content leading to diminished arterial-mixed venous content difference and reduced oxygen delivery. They include decreased arterial partial pressure of oxygen, decreased hemoglobin and decreased hemoglobin saturation from hypoxemia, methemoglobinemia (an oxidized form of hemoglobin that cannot carry oxygen), or carboxyhemoglobin (a compound form by carbon monoxide poisoning).

Failure to meet the required oxygen demand, whether from insufficient oxygen content, inadequate perfusion, or inability to extract and utilize available oxygen, results in anaerobic metabolism and lactic acid retention.

Optimal resuscitation exists when there is no further increase in oxygen utilization with increased oxygen delivery.[3]

§24.12 Spinal and Epidural Anesthesia

It is necessary for the anesthesiologist to be appropriately aware of the anatomy of the spinal cord and the bony spinal support to effectively and safely administer spinal and/or epidural anesthesia.

One anesthesia colleague describes spine anatomy by using an analogy to a tree trunk—the spinal cord is like a vine growing up the back side of a tree. Unlike a vine, though, the cord does not sit out in the open; it is covered by small plates of bone, just as though someone had glued a vertical row of shingles over the vine on the back of the tree trunk. If you picture the skin lying over the shingles, then you have a rough understanding of the anatomical relationships involved in performing spinal or epidural anesthesia. It is possible to understand the passing of a needle through the skin and between the shingles of bone so that the space around the spinal cord is available to receive anesthetic medications.

Spinal anesthesia is the safest anesthesia for doing major abdominal torso or lower extremity surgery. By instilling appropriate drugs and properly positioning the patient, a select level of anesthesia can be achieved, lessening the respiratory risks of general anesthesia. Vasomotor instability, including shock and cardiac irregularity, or even death, can occur, so only medical persons skilled in spinal anesthesia are permitted to administer this form of anesthesia. Again, constant monitoring and being prepared for adverse reactions are the duty of the anesthesiologist. (*See* Appendix 24-1, Cases 19 and 20.)

Complications of spinal anesthesia include spinal headache (usually correctable with spinal blood patch). Spinal headache is due to leak of spinal fluid through the dural needle puncture site, that site most often sealing spontaneously. Multiple punctures to obtain a "satisfactory" needle position are more apt to leak. The *blood patch treatment* is done by placing, via a spinal needle, 20 cc of the patient's blood extradurally at the site of the spinal puncture. The problem of spinal headache is the same in spinal anesthesia as in spinal myelography and diagnostic spinal punctures. Spinal headache is lessened by the use of a small diameter needle (24-gauge or less).

Rarely is a nerve fiber impinged by the spinal needle, leading to local nerve scar and persistent distress. Far more often it is felt that a spinal nerve may be irritated, but not damaged, as the needle is passed. Intrathecal hemorrhage leading to arachnoiditis and infection are uncommon complications.

---

[3] R.K. Ausman & D.E. Snyder, Medical Library, Lawyers Edition 7-9 (Cumm Supp Sept 1989).

§24.13 Epidural Anesthesia

The term *epidural* takes it name from the covering around the spinal cord known as the dura. Around the outside of this covering and behind the bony shell making the spinal canal, there is a narrow space that is available to be filled with local anesthesic or other drugs that affect the transmission of nerve impulses up and down the spinal cord. There is no spinal fluid in this space, although there are a number of veins that have thin walls which enlarge easily and can easily be punctured.

The epidural procedure, be it for anesthesia or for doing medication instillation such as epidural corticosteroid, is performed by introducing a needle tip into this space and either injecting medication through the needle or passing a small plastic catheter through the needle to be left in place so that medication can be instilled minutes or hours later, so-called continuous anesthesia.

A special epidural needle usage is desirable; these needles have a short bevel and a relatively dull end so that perforation of the dura, producing a dural leak, is less apt to occur.

There are two advantages to the epidural block. When it is performed properly, there is no hole made in the dura. Since headaches result from spinal fluid leaking through such holes, the opportunity for this complication is avoided. Another advantage is the catheter in the epidural space. This provides a route for repeated injection of the drug or for changing concentrations or type of medication, this being more important in the case of administering anesthesia than for epidural steroid injection procedures.

The potential duration of an epidural anesthesia can be measured in hours—even days—and the same catheter can be used for prolonged procedures. An example is one used in obstetrics can also be used to manage postoperative pain in the first few days after an operation.

The disadvantages, however, are inherent in the advantages. Both the epidural needle and the catheter must be placed in the epidural space—not intradurally or outside the dura. Risk of bleeding is present when epidural veins are punctured. Risk of dural puncture with epidural leak occurs. This latter complication can be taken care of when recognized at the time by doing a blood patch procedure. The same blood patch procedure can be a secondary technique done in the days following an epidural procedure complicated by spinal headache by doing the blood patch as a second procedure. In this procedure, 20 cc of the patient's whole blood is drawn, the epidural space having been first entered with an epidural needle at the same level where the epidural procedure was previously carried out, and the 20 cc of blood is injected into the epidural space before it clots, but relying on that clotting to occlude the perforation, therefore blocking the epidural leak.

It takes considerable technical skill to find the epidural space. In the past, it was often recommended to go into the intradural space and obtain spinal fluid and come back out until spinal fluid could be withdrawn with inserting the needle syringe. However, with newer needles and more refined techniques, the delicate feel of the spinal needle passing through the ligamentum flavum but not yet passing through the dura has been perfected.

An alternate way of doing the epidural procedure is to go through the caudal area, through the caudal foramen at the tip of the sacrum. This requires a large bolus of fluid to carry the medication.

When leg pain is being dealt with with epidural steroid blocks or similar techniques, often only one leg is involved. The epidural then is performed with the patient on his or her side with the involved side down, allowing gravity to carry the material to the effected side. Great caution needs to be taken with these procedures to make sure intradural instillation of chemicals that will block nerve function do not migrate proximally to the point of interfering with respiration. As with all anesthetic procedures, ready availability of resuscitation equipment and resuscitation medication is an essential part of the preparedness.

When an epidural anesthesia is proposed, the physician administering it must know the pharmacology of the chemicals used. The more common chemicals are Lidocaine (Xylocaine) and Chloroprocaine (Nesacaine). Bupivacane was used some in the past, but is now completely unacceptable for the reasons discussed in the PDR. As of this writing, Chloroprocaine is in one sense the safest of the local anesthetics because it is least likely to cause systemic toxicity leading to seizures or cardiac arrest. It has, however, caused, on rare occasions, some permanent sensory loss to certain segments of the spinal cord that it comes into contact with during the procedure. Minimal dosage and constant monitoring seem to be the rules of appropriate spinal and/or epidural administration.

In additional to dural leaks that may occur during these procedures as complications, instillation of the medication into a vein—for the area is rich with epidural veins—can be catastrophic. Chemicals that will block nerve function, producing anesthesia, will also block conduction in the heart, producing asystole (cardiac arrest). No medication should ever be injected in the epidural area (or any other area of the body) without a gentle suction withdrawal to make sure you are not in a blood vessel.

Complications

In general, headache and backache are frequent complaints after any epidural or spinal anesthetic. It is often difficult to establish backache as a complication, for many people have backaches anyway and the position of surgery puts a strain on the backs of many people. This is more likely to cause a backache than the epidural instillation. Headache following epidural puncture has been discussed. It is perhaps the most frequent complication.

Direct trauma to a nerve rootlet can lead to loss of function or irritation of that nerve by virtue of localized arachnoiditis. When epidural catheters are used, occasionally one will break and remain within the epidural space, requiring surgical removal.

Complications leading to a nerve deficit following spinal anesthetic injections can be part of epidural techniques when the dura is inadvertently entered, and relate to direct mechanical trauma to the nerve root when contact of the nerve root is established by the occurrence of a paresthesia or an electric shock-like sensation that radiates down one leg. The paresthesia alone is not of great consequence. These sensations are extremely common in clinical practice and are not associated with nerve damage solely by virtue of their occurrence. Damage is thought to result from injections directly into the nerve tissue. This is marked by paresthesias that exist at the time of injection and escalate in intensity as injection is made. When a paresthesia is encountered while positioning the needle for spinal anesthetic, the needle should be repositioned to the point where no sensation is occurring before the injection has begun.

Epidural anesthesia is another nerve root blocking technique where an anesthetic drug is administered extradurally (does not penetrate the intrathecal space). Often, a small plastic catheter is used and left in place to continue additional doses of anesthesia. This is commonly done for obstetrical deliveries, but is also appropriate after lower extremity of low back surgery. Epidural catheter anesthesia is in vogue for chronic pain management, cancer pain management, and postoperative pain control.

Epidural narcotic pain control, with the drug usually given in the lumbar spine, must not be done on an outpatient basis, and is best done with a 24-hour monitor in a hospital intensive care unit (ICU) due to possible severe complications. These adverse results include respiratory arrest, cardiac arrest, and vomiting with risk of lung aspiration. Itching is often a problem. Some of the newer medications appear less risky, yet death occurs after or during epidural narcotic administrations. (*See* Appendix 24, Case 13.)

§24.14 Spinal Anesthesia with Anticoagulant Therapy

There is a controversy among anesthesiologists as to the appropriateness of giving spinal anesthesia to patients receiving anticoagulant therapy. The concern is the production of epidural or intrathecal bleeding. Most anesthesiologists believe the procedure is safe if appropriate laboratory studies, such as partial thromboplastin or activated clotting time, are done after the administration of heparin but before surgery. The surgeon who fails to do these tests may be negligent.[4]

§24.15 Intravenous Regional Anesthesia

In 1908, August Bier described the use of the intravenous route to obtaining regional anesthesia. The Bier Block (using two tourniquets) technique

---

[4] Eichhorn, *Spinal Anesthesia and Anticoagulant Therapy,* 262 JAMA 411 (1989); Tao & At-Etr, *Anticoagulation Following Placement of Epidural and Subarachnoid Catheters,* 55 Anesthesiol 618 (1981); Odom & Shi, *Epidural Anesthesiology and Anticoagulant Therapy,* 38 Anesthesiol 254 (1983); Stow & Burrows *Anticoagulants in Anesthesia,* 34 Can J Anesthes 632 (1987).

of intravenous administration of local anesthetic chemicals is popular throughout the country. Most complications relate to the toxic effect of local anesthetic agents and do not usually represent catastrophic problems.

In rare cases, unexplained thrombosis of the entire venous system may occur, often leading to amputation. Close attention to the dilutant mixed with lidocaine (usual anesthetic agent) is imperative. The chance for a misadventure is real, as the typical anesthesiologist has many vials and syringes of chemicals within reach.[5] (*See* Appendix 24-1, Case 21.)

Intravenous regional anesthesia is becoming more popular for extremity fractures. Bier block is superior using double tourniquet intravenous technique, giving satisfactory anesthesia for up to two hours. As the blood pressure cuff/tourniquets are reduced, a rapid release of anesthetic agents may result in cardiovascular arrest or shock due to depression of respiratory cardiovascular centers. (*See* Appendix 24-1, Case 22.)

§24.16 Regional Local Anesthesia

Local anesthetic injected into an affected part of the body or into an area of nerve supply proximal to a surgery site is a very common surgical anesthetic method. This procedure is most often done by the surgeon who must be knowledgeable as to nerve supply anatomy, as well as to the pharmacology of the anesthetic agents.

Injury due to local anesthetic allergy is an occasional preoperative complication. A variety of local anesthetic types (chemically) are available—some producing longer lasting anesthesia, some taking longer for onset of anesthesia response. Descriptive literature is available in the package insert provided with each local anesthetic vial.

The addition of vasoconstrictive agents (usually epinephrine) in very dilute doses will prolong the anesthetic effect.

Local anesthetic complications include:

1. Death from cardiac failure from giving too large of an amount or concentration of local anesthetic agent
2. Local ischemia and skin slough when too much vasoconstrictive agent is used
3. Gangrene of the digits when a local anesthetic containing vasoconstrictive agents is used, causing arteriolar vasospasm—a preventable error
4. Infection from poor skin preposition techniques
5. Injecting the wrong chemical in place of the local anesthetic agent

Regional blocks in lower extremities have limited use; sciatica femoral blocks for evaluation of knee injuries achieve satisfactory relaxation and analgesia in most patients. Obturator nerve blocks, however, carry an

---

[5] Thaller & Sharzer, *Extensive Necrosis of the Upper Extremity Secondary to Regional Intravenous Anesthesia,* 19 Contemp Orthop 132 (1989).

unacceptable high morbidity, running a risk of perforation of the obturator artery or interarterial infusion of the anesthetic agent.

Continuous brachioplexus blocks for long procedures and for treatment of reflex sympathetic dystrophy are used. In the lower extremity, continuing sciatic nerve block has been helpful in relieving pain in ischemic gangrene of the foot. (*See* Appendix 24-1, Case 21.)

§24.17 Patient-Controlled Pain Control

Patient-controlled analgesia (PCA) involves patient control of a mechanical device to self-administer analgesic drugs. There are many such devices and extensive literature discussion of devices, techniques, and benefits. These modern devices, without fail, function with less total narcotic use and more patient satisfaction. The devices are set so that narcotic overdoses will not occur. Malfunctioning of the device is a hazard, however, and requires skilled nursing attention.[6]

Since the introduction of curare into clinical practice, muscular paralysis has been mistakenly interpreted as a calm and painless state. Often, curare-like drugs are administered to ventilate patients to facilitate patient respiration and nursing care with the concomitant administration of analgesic and/or anti-anxiety agents. This unkindly allows the patient to suffer and may well reduce survival chances.

Benzodiazepines have no analgesic effects, so while patients are paralyzed and may be sedated, they may experience significant pain. Nursing surveillance and physician acumen must extend to patient comfort as well as diligence against mechanical failure.

In one large hospital, there were serious pharmacologic misconceptions regarding the effects of neuromuscular blockers and benzodiazepines among ICU staff. This is probably a nationwide problem.[7]

§24.18 "Wake Up" Anesthetic in Spinal Surgery

In operations that cause manipulation of the spinal cord, such as corrective operations for severe scoliosis or where spinal fractures are reduced by using traction, spinal cord function may be lost. This may result from loss of blood supply to the cord or stretching of nerve elements. Fracture reduction may cause bone fragments to impinge on the cord. The end result of any of these factors may be permanent paralysis that could be relieved by lessening traction or relieving compression.

The appropriate way to ascertain these problems in patients undergoing spinal reconstruction is to do a "wake up" test in which the anesthesiologist

---

[6] McGrath, *Comparison of One Technique of Patient-Controlled Post-operative Analgesia with Intramuscular Meperidine (Demerol),* 37 Pain 265 (1989).

[7] Loper, *Paralyzed with Pain: Need for Education,* 37 Pain 315 (1989).

awakens the patient before the surgical wound is closed, but after fixation devices that stabilize the correct spinal position have been inserted. If the patient is unable to fully move toes and feet, the distraction in the operative site must be revised until the patient can move toes.

Other testing using electromyogram methods—specifically "evoked potential monitoring"—measures the peripheral nerves in the legs and their ability to function. This is specific testing, but requires specialized equipment and a skilled technician to interpret.

To detect spinal cord dysfunction intraoperatively, a somatosensory cortico-evoked potential monitoring or wake-up test—or a combination of the two—is generally used. A balanced anesthesia technique consisting of nitrous oxide narcotics and muscle relaxant is well suited for hypotensive anesthesia.

If the failure to monitor patients operated in the above manner results in a postoperative patient who is paraplegic or paraparetic, it is negligence.

§24.19 Diabetes Mellitus

Diabetes mellitus (as distinguished from diabetes insipidus) notoriously complicates wound healing by decreasing microvascularity and adversely affecting the homeostatic sequence of tissue healing. Twenty per cent of persons are suspect diabetics, many with the diagnosis made at the time of surgery. Patients who are not known diabetics and who have preoperative hyperglycemia can generally be classified as having impaired glucose tolerance (secondary diabetes mellitus) or gestational diabetes, based on a history of past medical illness and a detailed description of current medications. However, if the patient's history does not suggest a diagnosis of impaired glucose tolerance or gestational diabetes and the patient is not stressed at the time of evaluation, the surgeon should suspect the presence of diabetes mellitus and treat the patient accordingly.

The classic sign of diabetes mellitus in an unstressed person includes excessive thirst (polydipsia), frequent urination (polyuria), and weight loss with a fasting blood sugar test over 140 mg%. The known or suspect diabetic should have insulin in doses to maintain blood sugar between 100 and 250 mg%.

There are two nongestational types of diabetes mellitus requiring the same treatment protocol in surgical patients: Type I (juvenile) and Type II (adult onset). Many diabetics can be treated with diet and oral hypoglycemic medications. Those with significant reduction of insulin output or insulin receptors may require parenteral insulin. Complications other than impaired wound healing include hyperglycemic crisis leading to coma and severe dehydration. Diabetic ketoacidosis may complicate hyperglycemia in susceptible patients and be life-threatening. Insulin shock from an overdose of insulin likewise may be lethal.

§24.20 Anesthesia in Obese Patients

Many surgeons hesitate to operate on the obese patient, due to the increased operative risk of morbidity and mortality. This is especially true of the morbidly obese—overweight by 100 pounds or more. Although the morbidity and mortality are greater, this risk can be reduced by attention to detail in pre- and postoperative care. The increased risks include (1) wound infection, wound dehiscence, or hernia, (2) thrombophlebitis or pulmonary embolus, (3) anesthetic calamities, (4) acute postoperative asphyxia in patients with obstructive sleep apnea syndrome, (5) acute respiratory failure, (6) cardiac failure, and (7) missed abdominal catastrophe, such as perforated viscus. Adult onset diabetes mellitus is common in the obese patient. A high degree of suspicion for peritonitis must be maintained after abdominal viscera surgery or after lumbar discectomy where inadvertent slipping of instruments anteriorly may have perforated a viscus. Awareness of the problems associated with respiratory insufficiency in obese patients should enable surgeons to avoid pitfalls when managing patients with obstructive pulmonary disease. The risk of deep vein thrombosis and pulmonary embolism is high, but use of intermittent pressure boots and early postoperative ambulation can minimize this risk.

Weight reduction by diet is associated with 95 per cent failure. Most studies show that morbidly obese patients can lose two-thirds of their excess weight within one year after gastric bypass or gastric stapling surgery. This weight loss is usually associated with correction of adult onset diabetes, and many other problems associated with obstructive pulmonary disease—hypertension, chronic venostasis, ulcers of legs, stress incontinence, gastric reflux and hiatal hernia, and a number of female hormone related problems. Weight loss is a beneficial prescription by the orthopedist, who should not hesitate to consider gastric bypass surgery as a good treatment in this situation, but the surgeon must be skilled in the procedure and current in the management of its physiologic complications.[8]

§24.21 Anesthesia in the Rheumatoid Patient

Rheumatoid arthritis is a systemic disorder capable of generating pathological changes in every organ system. The disease typically presents itself

---

[8] Mason, *Risk Reduction in Gastric Operations for Obesity,* 190 Ann Surg 158 (1979); Sugerman, P Baron, *Hemodynamic Dysfunction in Obesity Hypoventilation Syndrome and the Effects of Treatment with Surgically Induced Weight Loss,* 207 Ann Surg 604 (1988); Herbst, *Gastric Bariatric Operation in Insulin-Treated Adults,* 95 Surg 209 (1984); Drenick, *Excessive Mortality and Causes of Death in Morbidly Obese Patients,* 243 JAMA 443 (1980); Hoking, *Jejunoileal Bypass for Morbid Obesity: Late Follow-up in 100 Cases,* 308 NEJM 995 (1983); Sullivan, *Reversal of Obstructive Sleep Apnea by Continuous Positive Airway Pressure Applied Through the Nares,* 1 Lancet 862 (1981); DeDivitis, *Obesity and Cardiac Function,* 64 Circulation 447 (1981); Printen, *Venous Thromboembolism in the Morbidly Obese,* 147 Surg Gynecol Obstet 63 (1978);

as symmetric polyarthritis, although nonarticular structures of the eyes, lungs, and musculoskeletal, cardiovascular, and nervous systems may be affected.

Rheumatoid arthritis usually runs an indolent course, yet dramatic manifestations do occur. Among these emergencies are rupture of synovial cysts, sclera, or chordae tendineae, vasculitic phenomena, subluxation of the cervical spine, and arthritis of the cricarytenoid joints. Cricoarytenoid often remains unsuspected by clinicians until sudden airway obstruction occurs. This is a particular hazard if an anesthesiologist is uninformed or fails to use due care in giving endotracheal anesthesia. The ENT specialist, using a rigid laryngoscope, may induce tracheal obstruction. The simple physical examination by an orthopedic resident unrelated to rheumatoid arthritis, manipulating the neck, displacing the cricoarytenoid joint, and causing obstruction that would not permit intubation, requires emergency tracheostomy. It is important for the examining physician to recall how fragile patients with advanced rheumatoid arthritis may be.[9]

---

[9] Bamshad, *Acute Upper Airway Obstruction in Rheumatoid Arthritis of the Cricoarytenoid Joints,* 82 S Med J 507 (1989); Volk, *Medical Malpractice Handling of Obstetric & Neonatal Cases,* Sept 1989.

Appendix 24-1
Cases

1 ***Frick v Lee,* No 103054 (Mo Ct App)** (physician, an anesthesiologist, was having trouble inserting an endotracheal tube so he called a second anesthesiologist to assist. One expert testified that the delay in administering (via endotracheal tube) of adequate oxygen was cause of patient's worsened condition of brain damage and blindness in one eye. The court refused to allow evidence that the defendant had lost a law suit with similar facts in the recent past. The jury was instructed to presume an anesthesiologist, now deceased, exercises ordinary care and tendered adequate treatment in attempting to anesthetize a patient who now suffers brain damage and blind in one eye).

2 ***Gorham v Honeywell,* No 102386 (Mo Ct App)** (it was alleged the defendant anesthesiologist failed to observe manufacturer's warning in using intravenous Valium. A vein on dorsum of hand was cannulated with small plastic tube to introduce Valium. The manufacturer's package insert warned against use of small veins on back of hand, yet ample expert testimony was proffered saying that use of these veins was common practice, that most veins on back of hand are large. The court found that the package insert advice did not reflect a true situation and was not the standard of care).

3 ***Clickner v Shanley,* 533 NYS2d 832 (NY 1988)** ($1,125,000 verdict against hospital and physician was upheld. The damages were assessed as adverse malpractice result against orthopedist and hospital in care of patient involved in motorcycle accident sustaining compound fracture of leg. He developed severe postoperative brain problems with significant permanent damage. A $2,125,000 verdict against hospital and physician was upheld. A $2,500,000 verdict was split between auto driver causing accident and medical caretakers. The court failed to reduce amount by 10 per cent for contributory negligence saying the contributory negligence was unrelated to the malpractice but causation of accident).

4 ***Rogers v Meridian Park Hospital,* 772 P2d 929, 931 (Or 1989)** (plaintiff's theory was that an endotracheal tube was removed too soon after surgery, causing permanent anoxia related injury. Expert testimony said medical opinions differ as to how soon after surgery the endotracheal tube should be removed. Trial court gave the following instruction: "A physician is charged with applying without error those principles and learnings that are settled and agreed upon by all members of the medical profession. In some cases, there may be reasonable differences of opinion among members of the medical profession as to the nature of the patient's condition or the proper course of treatment. When there is such a difference of opinion, the physician must exercise reasonable judgment. A physician is liable for error in judgment if the physician fails to act with reasonable care and skill in

exercising that judgment. A physician is not liable for an error in judgment if the physician acts with reasonable care and skill in exercising such judgment." The jury returned a defense verdict; plaintiff appealed saying the instructions was confusing and did not set forth the applicable standard of care. The supreme court reversed, finding that the challenged jury instruction improperly focused on the physician's judgment rather than whether the physician exercised reasonable care. The court stated that "Medical malpractice actions are nothing more than negligence actions against medical professional, and the standard of care governing a physician's professional conduct is the degree of care, skill and diligence which is employed by other physicians under similar circumstances." In the court's view, instruction improperly suggested that a physician's duty to exercise reasonable judgment exists only where there are multiple acceptable methods of treating a given medical condition).

5 ***Bourass v LaFortune,* 711 F Supp 43 (D Mass 1989)** (anesthesiologist failed to disclose the cause of death following a surgery as being due to misplaced endotracheal tube and that death resulted from lack of oxygen to the brain. The family was told the death was due to cardiac arrest that resulted from the "cancer exploding." Defendant moved for summary judgment based on three year statute of limitation in wrongful death actions, to which the discovery rule does not apply. Plaintiff opposes the motion saying the statute of limitation was tolled under the fraudulent concealment doctrine. The court held that the surgeon and anesthesiologist and a judiciary duty in their physician-patient relationship imposing an affirmative duty to reveal the existence of facts which would support a malpractice action).

6 ***Barth v Rock,* 674 P2d 1265 (Wash Ct App 1984)** (five-year-old broke her arm while riding a bicycle. Physician performed a closed reduction but later the arm began to swell so the cast had to be split. That altered the alignment of the fracture and a second operation was performed seven days later. There was a problem with the general anesthetic used in the second procedure and the patient ultimately died, with an autopsy diagnosis of cerebral anoxia and edema. Her parents filed an action for wrongful death against the operating physician and the nurse anesthetist in the hospital. After a three-week trial, the jury returned a verdict in favor of the medical defendant. The trial court then granted a new trial on the basis that substantial justice was not done. In affirming the decision, the court noted that the testimony by the expert witness was clearly erroneous and misleading. He stated that a textbook he had relied on stated that there were 55 reported cases of allergic reaction to sodium pentothal. In fact, the textbook stated there were 55 reported cases of allergic reactions to barbiturates. In addition, both nurse anesthetist and operating room physician admitted they had not informed parents of the risks of general anesthetic, because each believed the other had done so. The trial court promptly granted a new trial on the grounds that it was a matter of law that there was no informed consent).

7 ***Mitzelfelt v Kamrin,* 549 A2d 935 (Pa 1988)** (expert testimony was required to verify allegation that during a neurosurgical procedure, the anesthesiologist, hired by hospital, allowed patient blood pressure to fall below 80/55 causing a permanent quadriparesis. The plaintiff proffered expert testimony from a physician that the blood pressure dropped and, in his opinion, caused the injury, but he would not state this with reasonable medical certainty. An award of $3,000,000 was given. On appeal, the defendants contended that verdict was improper as there was insufficient corroborating evidence with factual opinion of the one medical expert saying the drop in blood pressure "could" lead to the quadriparesis. Finding that the patient failed to provide the competent evidence necessary to establish that the anesthesiologist's conduct caused the quadriparesis, the court held that sufficient proof was lacking and reversed lower court's judgment).

8 ***Kerber v Sarles,* 542 NYS2d 94 (App Div 1989)** (fact that an expert submitted an affadavit, which stated that the injury to plaintiff's teeth resulted from excessive force administered by the anesthesiologist during foot surgery did not conclusively establish the cause of the injury and does not preclude application of res ipsa loquitur doctrine).

9 ***Baird v Sickler,* 69 Ohio St 2d 652, 433 NE2d 593 (1982)** (patient had an extensive decompressive laminectomy in neck carried out for spinal block caused by spondylosis superimposed upon a congenital (Klippel-Feil) deformity. A sitting position was elected as operative posture for patient. Endotracheal anesthesia done by a nurse anesthetist who was an independent contractor. The surgeon did not place endotracheal tube (the nurse anesthetist did) but he helped position the patient. Following surgery, the patient was permanently quadriplegic from C-6 distally. At trial, expert testimony was (1) faulty intubation and positioning of patient or (2) aggravation of a "minor injury" precipitated by intubation and position of patient resulting in hypotension. Verdict was for plaintiff. The case presented, the court said, unusual facts. The patient was a known high risk patient due to Klippel-Feil syndrome making the spinal cord vulnerable. The position of the patient on operating table is crucial and under control of surgeon. The nurse anesthetist, though employed by an independent anesthesiology group, was in this situation directly under control so the doctrine of "Captain of the Ship" and master-servant relationship play a part in the adjudication. The court handled this by holding the "loaned servant rule" made the surgeon liable under doctrine of respondeat superior).

10 ***Graddy v New York Medical College,* 19 AD2d 426, 243 NYS2d 940 (1963)** (patient suffered cardiac arrest due to the effects of improperly administered anesthesia. The anesthesiologist was a hospital employee. This was a prima facie case adjudged against the anesthesiologist; the hospital was held liable).

11 ***Perkins v Walker,* 406 NW2d 189 (Iowa 1987)** (orthopedist was not held liable for patient's stroke after back surgery. Patient was treated by an orthopedic surgeon for low back pain during the morning of September 5, 1979. He performed major surgery on her back. During postoperative care, the patient had a substantial drop in her blood pressure for a short period. Later that evening, she suffered a stroke. In an action against the orthopedic

surgeon, she claims her stroke was caused by an adrenal crisis, that she had been treated previously with topical steroid cream for treatment of psoriasis. Her experts claimed that the side effect of long term use of topical steroid was suppression of the adrenal gland. The adrenal gland then would not properly respond to stress, allowing the patient's blood pressure to drop which in turn could result in a stroke. Her experts claimed that the surgeon should have either delayed surgery and tested for adrenal suppression or covered the patient immediately prior to surgery with an injection of cortisol to compensate for the gland's inability to function properly. A trial court ruled in favor of the surgeon, but an appellate court reinstated the verdict in favor of the surgeon; the Iowa Supreme Court said the trial court did not err in instructing the jury that a surgeon cannot be found negligent merely because he made a mistake in diagnosis and treatment of the patient. The court said the instruction was proper because it questioned whether the surgeon should have covered by cortisol injection prior to surgery as a matter of judgment. There were clearly issues as to the surgeon's judgment in diagnosing whether the patient had suffered adrenal insufficiency or whether the cover with cortisol was appropriate).

12 ***Falcon v Memorial Hospital,*** **443 NW2d 431 (Mich Ct App 1989)** (court reinstated a malpractice action which alleged that a patient was deprived of 37.5 per cent of survival by the defendant's negligence in not providing the patient with a patent intravenous line to deal with emergencies. The patient died of amniotic embolus, the anesthesiologist did not start an IV prior to administrating the spinal block. Expert witness testified that this failure reduced the patient's chance of survival by 37.5 per cent. The appellate court had reversed using the contention that the plaintiff must show deprivation on a better than even chance, thus the plaintiff had not shown sufficient proximate cause. The court held that the claimant must establish "some probability" that a proper course of treatment would have been successful; the court concluded that the probability need not be greater than 50 per cent).

13 ***Fountain v Cobb General Hospital,*** **167 Ga App 36, 306 SE2d 37 (1983)** (action was brought against hospital and physician. Suit alleged negligence against physician in failure to discover and remove epidural catheter from epidural space of spine, which was allegedly proximate cause of subsequent surgery requiring removal of protruded intervertebral disc. Lay testimony given by plaintiff and her mother in law was insufficient to refute expert testimony of two physicians as to whether defendant exercised degree of skill and care exercised generally within the profession. Testimony by two nurses as to when to remove epidural catheter was held far less competent than testimony of specialist physicians).

Comment: It was not mentioned, but inferred that even medically uninformed laypersons and well-informed physicians could not advance a theory that would relate placement or tardy removal of an epidural catheter to those acts producing a protruded intervertebral disc.

14 ***Dziurlikowski v Morely,*** **143 Mich App 729, 372 NW2d 648 (1985)** (patient awoke from general anesthesia with brachial plexus palsy due to improper positioning of patient on operating table. The question at trial was whether such paralysis was a risk of surgery or due to negligence of the anesthesiologist. Plaintiff argued that hyperextension of the arm (causing paralysis) breached standard of care. The defendant argued that injury was a risk associated with anesthesia and could have occurred without negligence. The trial court instructed jury that "difficulties and uncertainties in practice of medicine are such that no one can be required to guarantee results." The court held that instruction improper and mandated defendant verdict).

15 ***Parks v Perry,*** **314 SE2d 287 (NC Ct App 1984)** (patient was given a general anesthetic, awoke and persisted with ulnar nerve damage that was severe enough that she lost function of her fourth and fifth fingers and because of this she could not continue her job at the telephone company. The case was filed against the surgeon, the anesthetist and the hospital. The anesthetist was a nurse anesthetist employee of the hospital. They were held liable, the surgeon was excused inasmuch as it was not his responsibility. The "Captain of the Ship" doctrine no longer is followed in most jurisdictions. It is the responsibility of the anesthetist to so position the patient so the ulnar nerve could not be damaged. The ulnar nerve, having been damaged, was negligence on the part of the anesthetist).

16 ***Jones v Harrisburg Poly Clinic Hospital,*** **410 A2d 403 (Pa Super Ct 1979)** (patient underwent GYN surgery including general anesthetic, with the left arm extended on an arm board out to the side to allow easy access for administration of IV fluids. When the patient awoke, she had severe pain in her neck, left shoulder and left arm and paralysis of the suprascapular nerve caused by improper positioning. The surgeon was joined in the suit but released. Res ipsa loquitur was pled, but the supreme court said it was improper. Expert testimony said the responsibility was that of the anesthesiologist to properly place the patient's arm).

17 ***Holmes v Gamble,*** **624 P2d 905 (Colo Ct App),** ***cert denied,*** **627 P2d 24 (Colo 1981)** (patient was installing sewer pipe when the ditch caved in. He required immediate surgery to his knee. The patient developed bilateral ulnar nerve neuropathies resulting from improper position on the operating table. The physicians contended that injury did not occur during the operation but probably occurred during the extrication of the patient from the ditch during transport to the clinic or in the postoperative period. At trial, the patient presented no expert testimony to show that either physician had been negligent. he relied on the doctrine of res ipsa loquitur to establish negligence against the physician. The court refused to submit the patient's claim to the jury on that basis and entered judgment for the physician on appeal. The court said the mere fact that the injury occurred was not evidence of negligence. The court said if it could not be inferred from the injury itself, it could not have occurred without negligence by the physician. Therefore, necessary testimony was necessary. The patient's expert stated that although bilateral ulnar neuropathy could develop after the patient was improperly positioned on the operating table, the facts present in the case did not warrant that conclusion).

Comment: As a defense to the adverse result to the plaintiff, the medical record did not include an examination of the patient, it made to mention of neurological examination of upper extremities or that examination had been carried out, a significant criticism on the post-injury, preoperative workup of the patient.

18 ***Kwasny v United States,*** **822 F2d 194 (7th Cir 1987)** (63-year-old man patient had virulent rheumatoid arthritis since the age of 30. His spine and knees were frozen in a bent position for the last 10 years and he had been unable to work. He had many operations, all of which had been performed with the use of general anesthetic. Before his last operation, the patient refused spinal anesthetic, though the physician thought it might be difficult to intubate him. The patient's neck was so bent that the physicians had to apply considerable force with a laryngoscope, lacerating his lip and loosening his tooth. When this was unsuccessful, physicians easily intubated through his nose. After the operation, neck tissue swelled, he suffered from breathing arrest requiring emergency tracheotomy two days later. He continued to complain about his breathing and six months later, the patient suffered an acute respiratory arrest and had a rapid downhill course and died. The death certificate listed acute respiratory failure, airway obstruction, kidney failure and rheumatoid arthritis among the many causes of death. The patient's widow brought an action for wrongful death under the Federal Tort Claims Act. She charged the patient's death was due to negligence by physicians employed by VA Hospital. The judge found negligent care with damages of $100,000 and loss of consortium of $350,000. On appeal, the court said the record contained adequate medical evidence that brutality, forcing a tube perforated the patient's wind pipe and the perforation caused the death. In the absence of perforation, he would not have died when he did. The court said it could not be presumed that the crippled patient derived no benefit from living or conferred unto others. The court said they had no basis for disturbing the award for loss of consortium. The court did find award for pain and suffering to be clearly excessive, and pointed out that the patient was unconscious throughout most of his last illness, finding that $175,000 was the highest reasonable estimate, though patient's pain and suffering was due to the government's negligence, the court ordered the judgment modified).

19 ***Dunlap v Marine,*** **242 Cal App 2d 162, 51 Cal Rptr 158 (1966)** (262-pound lady was given a spinal anesthesia anticipating C-section, although the baby was delivered vaginally prior to the surgery. The patient underwent cardiac arrest, open heart massage was carried out along with endotracheal anesthesias started by the anesthesiologist. Two other doctors were called in to assist the emergency and the woman's heartbeat was restored. There was some permanent damage that derived from the incident. The court rejected the plaintiff's contention that an inference of negligence arose under the doctrine of res ipsa loquitur which was neither met nor overcome, stating that whether the inference of negligence was overcome or not, was for resolution of trier of fact on conflicting testimony. The court also rejected the contention that as a matter of law in negligently administering spinal anesthetic was the proximate cause of the woman's injuries stating that on substantial evidence, the anesthesiologist established that cardiac arrest was not caused by anesthetic and that he, the anesthetist, was not required to show the exact cause from which the cardiac arrest occurred).

20 ***Herbert v Traveler's Indemnity Co,*** **239 So 2d 367 (La Ct App 1970)** (spinal anesthesiologist administered spinal anesthesia. When the point of the needle punctured the dura and entered the spinal canal, the patient gave a cry of intense pain and said his left leg felt as if it had been subjected to a severe electrical shock. Medical experts agreed that severe pain and a sensation of electric shock resulted from spinal needle coming in contact with a nerve root. One argument of the case was to justify what happened by a litany of excuses by the anesthesiologist. The court went on to state that facts were clearly evident from the testimony of the experts that there was an injury to the nerve root and it was not incumbent on the plaintiff to give a pathological explanation of the case. Whether the injection was made directly into the nerve roots was debatable, but the testimony left no doubt that injuries inflicted to the nerve roots would not have happened in normal routine spinal anesthetic procedure. A verdict against the physician stood).

21 ***Hove v McMaster,*** **621 P2d 694 (Utah 1980)** (doctor injected, intending local anesthetic, directly into nerve causing partial loss of nerve function. Negligence was inferred from facts; however, law suit failed by passage statute of limitation).

22 ***Warrick v Giron,*** **290 NW2d 166 (Minn 1980)** (25-year-old architecture student severed a tendon in his left index finger with scissors. He consulted an orthopedic surgeon at the university hospital and was scheduled for surgery. The patient had Reynaud's phenomena, polymyositis, asthma and arthritis. Because of the unpredictable result in anesthetizing only the patient's finger, the anesthesiologist administered an axillary block which anesthetized the entire arm. To provide a bloodless field, the physician used a tourniquet on the upper arm during the 45-minute surgery. The operation went as expected, but the effects of the anesthetic did not wear off. The arm and hand remained numb. Some sensory and motor function returned later but limited movement of wrist and hand continued. Inability to handle the architectural tools prevented him from pursuing his career. The patient delayed in filing malpractice so the Statute of Limitations had run in part and blocked the progress in the trial in part. Res ipsa loquitur was pled but was not appropriate. There is a report that the anesthesiologist filed with the complications conference of the hospital, but this was held to be privileged to the hospital. The report was inadmissible under statute, the court said. Therefore, there was insufficient evidence of negligent action by the anesthesiologist. A new trial was ordered).

Comment: It seems probable that there was an anesthesia misadventure. The patient probably would have been better served with a more effective discovery process.

23 ***Williams v St. Claire Medical Center* 657 SW2d 590 (Ky Ct App 1983)** (orthopedist was held liable for failure of supervision of a recently graduated nurse anesthetist. The surgery was to do an arthroscopy of the knee. Spinal anesthetic was to be carried out. The patient suffered cardiac arrest. Orthopedist was in the area, was called in to assist in resuscitation and participated in a closed-chest massage. Although the orthopedist was not in direct control of the situation (was in emergency services), he did have control over the nurse anesthetist inasmuch as he was chairman of the department of surgery, and the anesthesia section was a sub-unit of the department of surgery. There were no other physicians supervising the newly graduated nurse anesthetist. It was held vicariously the orthopedist was in control of the situation and participated in the negligence that occurred in the improper giving of a spinal anesthesia and some errors in the resuscitation. The appellate judges agreed that this fell under the doctrine of parent authority "though it was" indeed a radical departure from the established principles of malpractice liability).

24 ***Barth v Rock* 674 P2d 1265 (Wash App 1984)** (orthopedist was liable for an anesthetic complication. A five year old child was being operated for a closed reduction of a rather simple fracture. The pulse dropped to 15 beats per minute, and the question was whether the manipulation should be aborted and should he help attend to the anesthetic problem. He elected to quickly go ahead, set the fracture and immobilize it. The patient survived for 48 hours, never regained consciousness and then died. There was an informed consent issue that the parents were not informed of the risk of anesthesia. The orthopedist was criticized for negligence in not attending to the patient's anesthetic problem, for the fracture itself was not a life-threatening problem. A new trial was ordered on those two facts—the lack of informed consent and the question of negligence of the orthopedist in that they were not directly addressed in the trial and represented error as adjudged by the appellate court).

25 ***Vantrease v Haberstroh,* 540 So 2d 646 (Ala 1988)** (plaintiff had an epidural block for pain relief (obstetrical). A continuous epidural catheter technique was used. During the administration of the block, the patient felt and complained of electric shock which caused her arms and legs to "shoot out" and burning pain in her legs. Patient was left permanently paraplegic in lower extremities. The plaintiff claims that the injury to the spinal cord or its blood supply was caused by placement of the spinal needle or the catheter and that defendant failed to identify and attempt to correct problem for 24 hours, too late to prevent the catastrophe. They alleged res ipsa loquitur. The defendants argued that the plaintiff had a low lying spinal cord, that the spinal cord ischemia was unrelated to the placement of the needle to reach the spinal cord or for the catheter to sufficiently traumatize the cord and that the accident was due to an unpreventable vascular accident. The

jury awarded plaintiff $645,000 and awarded husband $175,000 for loss for consortium. The hospital had settled for an undisclosed sum prior to trial. The settlement demand by plaintiff was $1 million, with defendant offering $150,000).

Comment: An important point in the case as pointed out by counsel was that in a mock trial several months earlier the plaintiff had an epidural block two years earlier without problems and here the treating physician giving the block was not board-certified.

26 ***Diago v San Jose Medical Clinic,* No 524556 (Santa Clara County Super Ct, San Jose, Calif Oct 27, 1989)** (plaintiff, a post-polio, scoliotic-deformed youth had a spinal curvature of 115 degrees, still partially flexible so that surgical correction with spinal fusion was recommended. At surgery, Harrington rods were used to maintain corrected position of 70 degrees. The patient returned to recovery room where, when the patient was awakening from anesthesia, he could not move feet and toes. Realizing that too much tension had been placed on spinal cord by Harrington device, the patient was promptly returned to surgery and the tension problem corrected; there were 1½ hours between the two surgeries. Patient was permanently paraplegic. Plaintiff sued, alleging that "wake up testing" or use of evoked potential testing for spinal cord function before completing operation, but performed after distracting devices have been put in place, is the standard of care. Defendant stated he had to weigh the risk of paraplegia with risk of malignant hyperthermia (during minor operation, a close relative had died from malignant hyperthermia). Defense said the risk of malignant hyperthermia was over 50 per cent, but admitted that a drug to treat malignant hyperthermia was available in operating room. Plaintiff verdict for $250,000 to reimburse medical expenses; $5,393,191 for future medical expenses and rehabilitation and nothing for lost earning capacity. Settlement negotiation, plaintiff demand, $1 million, offer was $30,000).

27 ***Raise v Wood,* 540 So 2d 646 (Ala 1988)** (hospital was held liable for complication produced when the surgical nurse gave local anesthetic with adrenalin, when it should have been without adrenalin. Major surgical complication of bunion surgery occurred due to the wrong anesthetic according to two orthopedic experts. The operating surgeon, although sued, was not held vicariously liable as he did not know that nurse gave wrong local anesthetic agent. On appeal, the jury trial verdict was affirmed).

25

Physical Therapy Rehabilitation

§25.01 Generally

Virtually all injuries to the body, when soft tissues are healed enough to be stable, can be appropriately treated with physical therapy rehabilitation techniques. Many patients undergoing orthopedic surgery are good candidates to visit a physical therapist before surgery for instruction as to aftercare and rehabilitation of affected areas of the body.

Conservative treatment of an orthopedic problem generally includes physical-therapeutic methods. Chiropractic, and originally osteopathy, represent medical healing disciplines that use physical-therapeutic techniques exclusively.

The larger percentage of patients requiring physical therapy are those with injury or disease of the spine. Conservative care of the back, using multiple physical therapeutic methods, is discussed extensively in this chapter and can be used as a role model for other body systems needing similar treatment. The reader is referred to standard texts on physical therapy and rehabilitation for more specific discussions.

The *physiatrist* is a physician who has completed all medical school requirements, and who has been specially-trained in physical therapy and rehabilitation diagnostic and treatment methods. The physiatrist often supervises physical therapists and physical therapy aides.

The physical therapist is a college graduate, with an emphasis on physical therapy, who has completed state licensing requirements. The licensed physical therapy aide has completed the state board of medical examiners' requirements, usually attending a two-year college with basic physical therapy courses. Often, the registered (licensed) physical therapist can diagnose and prescribe treatment. Many states, though, require a physician prescription for application of physical therapy. The physical therapy aide can neither diagnose or prescribe treatment; he or she is required to follow instructions and to be supervised by a registered physical therapist.

Many doctors' offices have on-the-job trained therapists or nurses who follow the employer physician's orders under his or her supervision. Some legal issues center on unlicensed therapists or nurses administering treatments and charging fees as licensed therapists. Many physicians incur risks when placing sophisticated physical therapeutic or similar treatments in the hands of minimally-trained office personnel.

The orthopedic surgeon probably orders rehabilitation more frequently than most other medical disciplines. To accurately understand a patient, the rehabilitation expert must be aware of factors impinging on the case from its medical onset to presenting for consultation. Some of these subjects are learned in traditional medical training or continuing education, but others are not. In chronologic sequence, these include:

1. Pre-existing medical conditions, both physical and psychological

2. Pre-existing vocational status, employment, and training
3. Type of illness or injury and its natural history
4. First aid and emergency care
5. Personality and psychological reactions
6. Primary follow-up care (diagnosis and treatment)
7. Support treatments, e.g., physical therapy, work hardening, etc.
8. Clinical management consultant specialist opinions
9. Vocational rehabilitation (availability, personnel, and services)
10. Work availability within physical restrictions
11. Employer practices regarding rehiring or return to work
12. Administrative system incentives to return (or not return) to work
13. Insurer approach to claim (denial, obstruct, facilitate)
14. Attorney presence, orientation, etc.
15. Disability evaluation or similar assessment
16. Legal system—its efficiency, incentive, precedents, and complexity

Many different individuals are involved in these components of the disability determination process. The skills, attitudes, experience, talents, and personalities of each will impact the process.[1]

§25.02 Physical Therapist

The *physical therapist* is a highly trained paramedical person who specializes in the mechanical, and the chemical aspects to some extent, of rehabilitation of patients. His or her skills lie in excellent knowledge of the anatomy and pathology of the body, and should include a high degree of empathy for the patient and charismatic characteristics that motivate the patients to help themselves. This can be a difficult and frustrating job.

The therapist does very little laying-on-of-hands therapy that is curative. The therapist applies modalities that relax the patient, that stretch the patient, and, at times, that change the chemistry of underlying tissues.

Patient compliance is always the "bottom line" to physical therapeutic techniques. It is important that the patient understand what therapies are being administered and what the purposes are. The physical therapist also is in an excellent position to observe, understand, and treat any psychological ramifications of the pain syndrome.

On the issue of pain control, the physical therapist has a variety of tools that are helpful. Deep heat modalities, TENS units, alternative hot and cold packs, and ice massages are frequently helpful. If the patient describes an acute change in the pain pattern, suggesting disruption of soft tissue or bone,

---

[1] Nordin, *Orthopedics, Physical Rehabilitation and Ergonomics,* 18 Orthop Rev 67 (1989).

the physical therapist should report this immediately to the treating orthopedist.

Physical therapy rehabilitation of the elbow, as an example of a joint system, requires early mobilization as soon as soft tissues or bony structures heal enough to permit this, which is about three weeks for soft tissues (such as posterior dislocation of the elbow). Four to six weeks for internally-fixed supracondylar or epicondylar fractures or olecranon fractures are usually sufficient to allow active mobilization. Overstretching the elbow actively in extension, in particular, is contra-indicated because there is a tendency for a contracted brachialis muscle to overstretch too quickly and a complicating myositis ossificans frequently occurs.

The functional range of motion—20 to 30 degrees of extension, and 120 to 130 degrees of flexion—is a goal that physical therapy should achieve for the patient. Pronation and supination of 50 to 60 degrees are likewise important to achieve useful function. In patients who have persistent flexion and extension contractures after a sufficient period of physical therapy, usually four to six months, the orthopedic surgeon should be informed so the surgeon can consider open capsulotomy or other soft tissue releases.

§25.03 Therapy Techniques

Techniques that the physical therapist uses are generally divided into two categories—one to relieve pain, and the other to refer patients to other rehabilitative treatments. Treatment modalities include thermal therapy—specialized techniques in the use of cold (ice packs and ice massages) and heat (hot packs), ultrasound, short wave, microwave, infrared, and other similar techniques, including electrotherapy utilizing pain modulating stimulation devices such as transcutaneous nerve stimulation (TNS). The TNS unit is divided into conventional devices and acupuncture-like devices. Another technique is high voltage pulsed galvanic stimulation, and another is inferential electrotherapy. A second category of electrotherapy is electromyelographic biofeedback techniques. Alternate and static cervical and lumbar traction devices are another category. The above techniques are, for the most part, hands-on therapies by therapists to physicians.[2]

§25.04 Key to Rehabilitation

The key to rehabilitation is to understand the patient's physiological, physical, and mental capacities, and whether these capacities meet the demands of the work place. To achieve this, the physician must be acquainted with the demands at work and the complexity of the tasks—for example, the loads

---

[2] Nordin, *Orthopedics, Physical Rehabilitation and Ergonomics,* 18 Orthop Rev 67 (1989); Paris, *Physical Therapy Evaluation Principles,* presented at the Neuroskeletal Imaging and Surgery Spring Conference, Univ of Minnesota, Minneapolis, May 6, 1988.

imposed, the patient's strength and endurance, range and coordination of motions required, and environmental stresses. The reporting physician cannot render an accurate work ability or impairment without knowing these elements, and places him- or herself in an impeachable position when rendering opinions absent these considerations.

This approach has been highly developed in the area of sports medicine, where the aim is to match the player's ability to the demands of the playing field. In a similar manner, the abilities of the patient must be matched to the demands of the work place. More importantly, the work place should be matched to the worker, as the work place may be compared to a "chronically diseased" environment in many cases, but treatable. It is in this arena where the worker, the employer, and the physician must be ergonomically-oriented to best serve the patient worker.[3]

Most therapists recommend a *holistic* approach to rehabilitation. A total rehabilitation program dealing with musculoskeletally-impaired persons must include a full history and evaluation by the therapist in conjunction with the prescribing physician. (In some states, registered physical therapists may independently prescribe and treat patients with a physician's prescription). Typically, the therapist will use diagnostic therapeutic techniques, such as isokinetics, isotonics, sports psychology, nutrition, education, pain and stress management, substance abuse, and spirituality. This is described as holistic, leading to an integrated wellness program. Often, it has been shown that a lesser program, a program using "bits and pieces" or the common "shake and bake" therapies is incomplete, frequently ineffective, and often not cost-effective.[4] (*See* Appendix 25-1, Case 1.)

§25.05 Traction

Traction is a technique intended to stretch soft tissues and separate joint surfaces. Historically, it has been utilized since the time of Hippocrates. In the low back, traction is frequently used with the thought of distracting vertebral bodies, separating facets, putting stretch on the soft tissues, stabilizing the vertebral elements, enlarging the nerve root canal, and stretching tight musculature. In fact, none of these objectives are significantly achieved with the usual forms of traction. Bed traction with the patient in 20 to 25 pounds of pelvic traction does not put significant stretch on any of these structures. It has the advantage of holding the patient in a fixed position, if Fowler's position is used, tending to rotate the pelvis forward and thereby stretching some of the tissues mentioned above.

Current thinking is that minimal bed rest is appropriate for the acute low back pain condition. Pelvic traction during that short period therefore is a

---

[3] Nordin, *Orthopedics, Physical Rehabilitation and Ergonomics,* 18 Orthop Rev 67 (1989).

[4] Paris, *Physical Therapy Evaluation Principles,* presented at the Neuroskeletal Imaging and Surgery Spring Conference, Univ of Minnesota, Minneapolis, May 6, 1988.

device for holding the patient in position, not for actually distracting soft tissues. Mechanical devices and intermittent pelvic traction tables used by physical therapists can apply a greater amount of temporary traction to the low back to produce significant distraction of the low back; techniques where the patient is hung by the heels or has full body weight in a dependent posture are probably the most effective.

It has been shown that one-half to three-fourths of body weight must be applied to produce distraction. The body skin and soft tissues will not tolerate this amount of traction for any period of time. At this time, autotraction in the form of elevation of the lower extremities in a 90/90 position of flexion of hips and knees, allowing the buttocks to be dependent, or inverted body traction with the full body weight hanging dependent, are the most effective for any significant distraction of soft tissues. With autotraction or 90/90 traction or inverted traction, a degree of self-manipulation of the soft tissues of the facets of the intervertebral disc is possible.

There are distinct contraindications to traction, including malignancy, spinal cord compression, infection, and osteoporosis. Hypertension, cardiovascular disease, and eye pathology are contraindications to inverted traction. There are, additionally, some relative contraindications—old age, spinal joint instability, claustrophobia, and hiatal hernia are some.

The consensus of opinion is that, with one exception, no clear scientific evidence has been presented that traction therapy is of therapeutic value. The exception is the autotraction technique described by Lind.

§25.06 Back Rehabilitation

Using a mechanistic and behavioral approach to evaluating and treating the spine, a complete physical examination must be done before proceeding to any treatment. This examination can be extended to include those areas of the patient's body that may be contributing to dysfunction and pain. Keeping in mind that the dysfunction, and not the pain, will be treated, emphasis is placed on mechanistic and behavior.

There are 11 steps to the evaluation. These include:

1. Completing pain questionnaire and body chart
2. Initial observation
3. History
4. Structural examination
5. Active movements
6. Palpation: condition of soft tissues, position of vertebra, and mobility of segments
7. Neurological
8. Radiological
9. Summary of findings

10. Treatment plan
11. Prognosis

Dysfunction

Most back pain is caused not by a single traumatic incident, but by an accumulation of insults and faulty lifestyle. Many of us have such faulty lifestyles, and many of us have back pain. By treating the immediate cause of the pain and providing relief, but failing to educate the patient, we will eventually be embarrassed by our patient's repeated return and developing dependence on treatment. However, even the best management program is doomed to failure, and the patient to frustration, if the mechanical causes of the patient's dysfunction are not optimally treated. To treat them, they must be found with a careful and thorough examination of all aspects of the patient's condition.

Behavioral

While it is pain that brings the patient to us—the best long-term results are not achieved by relieving the pain, but by finding and treating dysfunctions that cause the pain. The patients are soon turned on to this concept, as the word "pain" is not used, and on subsequent reassessments, we concentrate on functional improvements.

The care the patient receives is tailored to fit clinical findings. In general, they will be directed at (1) correction of the dysfunctions, (2) correction of behavioral attitudes, and (3) correction of lifestyle.

To help achieve this, treatments are divided into three sections:

1. *Preparatory:* Heat, most forms of massage, relaxation, and inhibitory techniques, including acupressure, TENS
2. *Corrective:* Joint manipulation, distraction, and some forms of massage and perhaps some modalities such as ultrasound and exercises, including stabilization, for hypermobilities
3. *Supportive:* Therapeutic exercise, including instruction in functional utilization of neuromuscular system, back school, support, and taping

Joint manipulation is one of the principle tools for correcting dysfunction when that dysfunction demonstrates restricted motion. By improving joint motion, function and performance improve with increased tolerance to insult, there is decreased gait pain, and it aids in nutrition and repair.

In the management of back pain, the mechanistic approach, which seeks to improve function of the low back and the areas that relate to it, has definite advantages over concentrating on pain relief and seeing single (rather than multiple) dysfunctions to be the cause of the patient's complaint.

A typical patient may present with the following findings to which I have matched some appropriate treatments:

Finding	Appropriate Treatment
Short right leg, half inch	Lift in right heel
Restricted right hip motion	Manipulation
Restricted L3-4 facet motion	Manipulation
Loss of normal lordosis	Backward bending
Poor postural sense	Back school
Tight hip flexors, bilateral	Stretching, contract, relax

To help achieve these, I would no doubt use heat and massage. Manipulation is not a "stand alone" treatment.[5]

§25.07 Work Ability Testing Devices

Testing devices available today do not tell anything about work capacity. The patient must be taken to the work place for a valid work capacity evaluation.

There is no legally defensible scientific data available to physicians with which they could screen anybody in terms of strength and flexibility testing. A great deal of useful data is accumulating by use of isometric low back testing equipment, from which the knowledgeable physician can say that the data—the patient's work capacity—is "consistent with" but not "with reasonable medical certainty." That day may well be coming in the next few years.[6]

§25.08 Physiotherapy Diagnostic Scale Muscle Strength

It is important that the examining physician or therapist have standards to measure the strength of individual muscle groups. In this way, the status and response to treated muscle groups can be recorded and therapeutic plans made. A universally accepted scheme is presented by Csuka as follows:

Objective Gradation of Muscle Strength

5 (normal)	Motion against considerable manual force
4 (good)	Some motion possible against manual load
3 (fair)	Motion possible against gravity; not against applied load
2 (poor)	Motion possible with elimination of gravity as factor
1 (trace)	Palpable or visible contraction but no motion
0 (none)	No evidence of muscle contraction[7]

---

5 Paris, *Physical Therapy Evaluation Principles,* presented at the Neuroskeletal Imaging and Sergery Spring Conference, Univ of Minnesota, Minneapolis, May 6, 1988.

6 Nordin, *From Round Table Discussion,* Am Back Socy, Spring Symposium, Cambridge, Mass, 1989.

7 Csuka, *Objective Gradation of Muscle Strength,* 78 Am J Med 77 (1985).

§25.09 Results of Physical Therapy Treatment

Many methods are utilized for physical treatment of low back pain and each has its advocates. Most base their belief in that particular treatment on the fact that the patient improved. However, the majority of patients with acute low back pain who undergo no treatment at all eventually recover.

A general review of physical therapy treatment options reveals that most treatment methods have no scientific basis and are being passed on from one clinician to another by what Currier describes as "ecclesiastical succession."

Analyzing the literature carefully, as we must, we find that very few studies are properly designed and that there is, therefore, very little valid guidance in selecting the appropriate treatment regimen. Even studies frequently quoted fall short on important study criteria, leading to invalid conclusions.

A few properly designed research studies to help with decisionmaking in the treatment of low back pain are as follows:

1. Two days of bed rest were found to be as effective as seven, and two days reduced the time lost from work by 45 per cent compared to seven days
2. There appears to be short-term, but no long-term, benefits with immobilization/manipulation
3. Back school (purely lecture) is as effective as a form of physical therapy that included manipulation; both were found to be more effective than no treatment at all
4. The McKenzie regimen of individualized exercises was found more effective than back school or 90/90 traction in lumbar pain patients, acute and chronic
5. Posture correction is beneficial during the early treatment of low back pain

Since the anatomic cause of the majority of low back pain cannot be objectively evaluated or visualized, an individualized treatment program, based on each patient's self-report of pain, would seem to directly affect the underlying abnormality. There are many examples of this type of approach in solving other more familiar painful situations. This would appear to be a partial explanation for the apparent success of the McKenzie approach.

Most physical therapy options afford but one mode of treatment for all patients (traction, modalities, corsets, etc.) as though all low back pain has the same underlying cause. Only manipulation and an individualized exercise program allow customization of treatment to each patient's presentation. While the majority of low back pain episodes resolve with little or no treatment, at least 60 per cent of patients have recurrent symptoms within one year. Patient education as a part of treatment for the initial acute episode appears to be a helpful deterrent of recurrences.[8]

§25.10 Legal Aspects of Rehabilitation Centers

With the advent of aerobic types of rehabilitation centers, such as a sports medicine, cardiac rehabilitation, or work hardening type of facility, high-risk patients are frequently identified. The referring or treating physician is held to know a patient's capability and impairments that make him or her vulnerable to injury. Risk management of the rehabilitation center is helpful, but thoroughly knowledgeable therapists and obtaining fully informed consent are essential for the rehabilitation center and/or its personnel to be less vulnerable to litigation.

§25.11 Soft Tissue Treatment Modalities

There are many therapeutic modalities used in soft tissue injuries. In the acute injury, putting the area of injury at rest facilitates the healing process of a specific soft tissue system, such as muscle, skin, or tendons, and involves an orderly process that has been discussed. The healing time, if it is uninterrupted by other external or internal problems, goes through a cascade of stages and requires from three to eight weeks on the average.

It is desirable to keep the extremity, the joint systems of the extremity in particular, mobile during the healing phase. Mobilization of the injured area becomes a prime consideration after sufficient healing. At the same time, understanding and following the concept of treating the patient as a whole is helpful.

Although there are some truths in each of these formulations, it is believed that the whole person concept is the most attractive and useful in understanding and dealing with psychological aspects of physical disability. The basis of this concept is "we do not treat disease and injuries, but individuals who are suffering the effects of such disease and injuries, and these individuals often have socioeconomical, psychological, vocational, medical, and other problems, which may profoundly affect physical status."

According to this approach, successful rehabilitation may require evaluation using techniques of several disciplines and then manipulation of appropriate variables as needed to accomplish rehabilitation of the injured patient. An organic lesion, therefore, is but one of many factors, influencing a likelihood of re-employment. Failure to consider a single crucial variable may lead to failure of the entire treatment program. It is most important

---

[8] Puffer & Zachazewski, *Vigorous Physical Therapy Crucial for Overuse Injuries,* Orthop Produt News, Mar 1989, at 17.

to recognize the dynamic interaction of all the variables affecting the patient's basic personality organization.[9]

§25.12 Other Physical Modalities

I. Purpose
   A. To relieve pain
   B. To prepare patient for other treatments
II. Thermotherapy
   A. Cold
      1. Ice pack
      2. Ice massage
   B. Heat
      1. Hot packs
      2. Ultrasound
      3. Shortwave
      4. Microwave
      5. Infrared
      6. Other
III. Electrotherapy
   A. Pain modulating stimulation devices
      1. TENS
         (a) conventional
         (b) acupuncture
      2. HVPGS
      3. Inferential
   B. EMG Biofeedback

§25.13 Mobilizing Joints and Strengthening Muscles

The frozen shoulder syndrome, although not well-understood pathologically by the orthopedist, is one where there is frequently a sudden onset of painful limitation of motion. It tends to occur in certain personality types that are high on the anxiety scale—compulsive, obsessive individuals.

Manual manipulation for frozen shoulder under anesthesia is not universally accepted, although it has its advocates. Manipulation under anesthesia followed by intensive physical therapy probably does shorten the overall period of recovery of the frozen shoulder. There is, however, a natural tendency for the frozen shoulder to resolve itself in a period of time, albeit two or three years is not unusual.

Physical therapy therapeutic programs include guided passive and active range of motion, and gentle manipulations by the patient and by the thera-

---

[9] Puffer & Zachazewski, *Vigorous Physical Therapy Crucial for Overuse Injuries,* Orthop Produt News, Mar 1989, at 17.

pist. Techniques of improving extension and abduction by wall crawling on notched boards and/or using a shoulder wheel are helpful. These techniques are most often used after a period of heating the shoulder. In the most acute case, starting with pendulum exercises may be the first step.

In post-traumatic situations (fractures or dislocations with limitation of motion) where there has been sufficient time for soft tissues to heal, the physical therapist has an essential role in rehabilitation. In the usual situation, passive pendulum exercises to increase range of motion are first used. It is important to protect soft tissues or bony structures that are not healed well enough to tolerate active manipulation. Most soft tissue injuries are healed well enough in three weeks and fractures are stable enough in four to six weeks to start progressive active range of motion. It is important to obtain, as rapidly as possible, both active and passive ranges of motion. This may be a moderately painful experience for the patient. This is an area where the physical therapist, with his or her skills, charisma, and utilization of the concept of "no pain, no gain," is important.

Physical therapy rehabilitation of the elbow requires early mobilization as soon as soft tissues or bony structures heal enough to permit this. Again, three weeks for soft tissue healing, such as posterior dislocation of the elbow, and four to six weeks for internally-fixed supracondylar or epicondylar fractures or olecranon fractures are usually sufficient to allow active mobilization. Overstretching the elbow actively in extension, in particular, is contraindicated because there is a tendency for a contracted brachialis muscle to overstretch too quickly and complicating myositis ossificans frequently occurs.

The functional range of motion of 20 to 30 degrees of extension and 120 to 130 degrees of flexion is a goal that physical therapy should achieve for the patient. Pronation and supination of 50 to 60 degrees is the goal to achieve useful function. In patients who have persistent flexion and extension contractures after a sufficient period of physical therapy, usually four to six months, the orthopedic surgeon should be informed so the surgeon can consider open capsulotomy or other soft tissue releases. Other joint systems of the body follow this therapeutic paradigm.[10] (*See* Appendix 25-1, Case 2.)

§25.14 Overuse Syndromes

Many physical therapists and physiatrists feel that vigorous physical therapy is the cornerstone of the management of overuse syndromes that affect muscles and tendons. Early rest intervention to heal the inflamed tissues is necessary. Prevention of injury or recurrence is essential. Classification of overuse pain is important. The pain of tendonitis is usually classified as

---

[10] Puffer & Zachazewski, *Vigorous Physical Therapy Crucial for Overuse Injuries,* Orthop Produt News, Mar 1989, at 17; Rosomoff, *Physical Findings in Patients with Chronic Intractable Benign Pain of the Neck and/or Back,* 37 Pain 279 (1989); Hirschfield & Behan, *The Accident Process. Etiological Consideration in Industrial Injuries,* 186 JAMA 193 (1963).

(1) pain after activity only, (2) pain during activity that does not restrict activity, (3) pain during activity that does restrict performance, and (4) chronic unremitting pain.

The first type is treated with relative rest with 35 per cent reduction in workload—reducing the number of pitches or miles run. The second type is treated the same way, but with 50 per cent reduction and the addition of nonsteroidal medication. The third type by definition precludes competitive athletic performance. The patient should be encouraged to refrain from all activity loading the pain area. Physical therapy with heat stretch is used. Judicious use of corticosteroid injection may be considered, taking great care not to inject into musculotendinous juncture. The direct injection of corticosteroid into a muscle tendon interface has been shown to result in microstructure disarray and can lead to rupture. The fourth type should be treated with long-term physical therapy. Many of these patients have developed scarring about musculotendinous areas and degenerative changes within these units. Surgery may be necessary and prognosis may be guarded.[11]

§25.15 Why Exercise?

There is general acknowledgment that physically fit people are much better able to deal with life's physical and emotional demands. In addition, adequate levels of fitness are necessary to participate in many sports safely with optimal performance and enjoyment. The same situation exists for most work activities. It is important that patients understand that they should become physically fit before attempting a high level of sports participation or participation in some strenuous work activities.

Endurance exercise calls forth complex metabolic, cardiovascular, pulmonary, neurological, and hormonal adjustments that allow the body to respond to the demands of the working muscle.[12] (*See* Appendix 25-1, Case 3.)

§25.16 Aerobic Back Exercise

The most intensive of three exercise programs resulted in the greatest improvement for patients with chronic low back pain. No adverse effect was reported from the most intense exercise program. The benefits of intensive exercise were greater not only at the end of treatment, but at a three-month follow-up.[13]

---

[11] Puffer & Zachazewski, *Vigorous Physical Therapy Crucial for Overuse Injuries,* Orthop Produt News, Mar 1989, at 17.

[12] Dalsky, *Does Exercise Increase Bone Mass?,* Surg Rounds for Orthop, at 73.

[13] Manniche & Hesselsoe, *Clinical Trial of Intensive Muscle Training* for *Chronic Low Back Pain,* 24 Lancet 1472 (1988).

§25.17 Increase of Bone Mass by Exercise

The key to rebuilding bone mass and strength is achieving the proper training level and then continuing the exercise. The same philosophy is valid for increasing and maintaining muscle strength and endurance. Strict adherence to a program of simple exercise, such as walking, jogging, and stair climbing, increase bone mass and muscle strength. It is important to attend to diet and calcium intake. It has been further shown that the exercising patient will reach a plateau of bone mass and muscle strength after several months, but promptly lose both if he or she stops the exercises.[14]

§25.18 Diagnosis of Back Pain

Many schema are used to evaluate low back pain which facilitate diagnosis and treatment and tend to avoid errors or omission.

One back pain evaluation form includes:

1. Goals of evaluation
   (a) Psychological context
   (b) Diagnosis, rule out cauda equina impingement disease, non-mechanical disease, treatable diseases
2. Differential diagnosis
   (a) Spinal diseases, mechanical
   (b) Spinal diseases, non-mechanical
   (c) Visceral or vascular
3. Interview
   (a) Psychological issues
   (b) Medical review systems
   (c) Chief complaint
4. Physical examination
5. Testing
   (a) Decision analysis
   (b) X-rays
   (c) Blood and urine tests
   (d) Special studies

This, coupled with an allogram or information form, allows the orthopedist to have a fairly good idea prior to examination of what an appropriate diagnosis may be. Formats such as that published by Vert Mooney, M.D., including his pain drawing, are typical examples.[15]

---

[14] G. Dalsky, *Does Exercise Increase Bone Mass?,* Surg Rounds for Orthop, at 73; Hurme & Alaranta, *Factors Predicting the Results of Surgery for Lumbar Intervertebral Disk Surgery,* 9 Spine 933 (1987).

[15] Harsha, *What Does Pain Mean to the Patient in Treating His Back Pain?,* 3 J Neuro Orthop Surg 3 (1982).

§25.19 Conservative Treatment

"Conservative low back treatment" has evolved from passive to more active treatment in recent years. Some orthopedists continue to favor prolonged bed rest, although current concepts favor increased activity as soon as acute pain is under control (two to five days). This avoids the inescapable muscle-wasting of inactivity.

Pelvic traction has been a standby therapy for low back pain; however, it is well known that 20 to 30 pounds of traction on the pelvis in any posture does not distract low back tissue. Inverted (patient upside down) traction has some advocates, but not many patients can tolerate this, some get bleeding about the eyes, and cardiovascular diseases are contraindications.

"Laying on of hands" by a physical therapist, such as massage, use of deep heating devices, or ice techniques will facilitate patient self-help if the patient will participate in the exercises. Often, the patient stays passive and "laying on of hands" therapy is more like spa relaxation than restorative therapy. An aggressive treatment plan, including back school (formal patient education as to how the back works, heals, and is rehabilitated), exercise training to teach spinal stabilization (dynamic maintenance of posture control), trunk and general upper and lower body strengthening exercises and flexibility exercises, is the most successful therapy at this time. This aggressive plan is fashioned after the philosophy of a sports medicine clinic. The most rehabilitated patient is the patient who works hardest on him- or herself—physically, psychologically, and socially.[16]

§25.20 Chronic Intractable Low Back Pain

Chronic intractable benign pain is defined as non-neoplastic pain, greater than three months duration without objective physical findings and/or known noiciceptive peripheral input. A significant number of patients suffering from chronic low back pain or neck pain do not fit into known diagnostic (organic) categories. As many as 30 per cent of chronic low back pain patients have no organic findings on physical examination.

A careful, all-inclusive physical examination is a basic initial requirement in classification of chronic benign low back pain. It is particularly important for the orthopedist not to quickly diagnose chronic benign low back pain, or somatization disorder, or a more pejorative label, based on the fact that he or she has not exhausted all diagnostic resources. This area is a real test of the diagnostic (very nearly detective work) skill of the physician. Both visual analogue and verbal descriptors may provide sensitive tools for separating unpleasantness from intensity of pain. This is helpful and working with the patient's pain coping skills.[17]

---

[16] Rosomoff, *Physical Findings in Patients with Chronic Intractable Benign Pain of the Neck and/or Back,* 37 Pain 279 (1989); Yochelson, *Psychiatric Aspects of Backache,* 3 Curr Prac Orthop Surg 253 (1966).

[17] Yochelson, *Psychiatric Aspects of Backache,* 3 Curr Prac Orthop Surg 253 (1966).

§25.21 Workers' Compensation—Early Intervention

Vocational rehabilitation has attracted increasing attention in more and more states as advocates and detractors debate the appropriate use of this potentially beneficial, yet costly, workers' compensation benefit. The stated purpose of rehabilitation is to return the worker to a job as promptly as possible. In states with strong vocational rehabilitation programs, early intervention after injury and obtaining medical and vocational suggestions for planning a program of rehabilitation have been most productive. On the average, about 70 per cent of all injured workers, early-intervened and felt to be candidates for vocational rehabilitation, returned to work (not necessarily the same work) within two years of injury. Early intervention and management of workers by medical and rehabilitation personnel knowledgeable about this type of care has proven to be cost-effective. Intervention of probable case between 80 and 160 days of injury, seemed most effective timing in one state (Minnesota).[18]

One study found that those receiving compensation demonstrated 33 per cent less objective evidence of impairment, received nearly twice as many physical therapy treatments, and experienced 44 per cent less long-term improvement compared with patients not receiving compensation.

Several studies have shown that large numbers of patients operated on for protruded intervertebral discs found that private, non-compensable patients fared much better.

All explanations for less favorable results among patients receiving compensation have indicated a psychological factor. Multiple pathogenic mechanisms and behavioral syndromes have been suggested, including such concepts as "accident neurosis secondary gain," "the accident process," "acute traumatic neuroses" and other psychological explanations.

Although there is some truth in each of these formulations, it is believed that the whole person concept is the most attractive and useful in understanding and dealing with psychological aspects of physical disability. The basis of this concept is that "We do not treat disease and injuries, but individuals who are suffering the effects of such disease and injuries, and these individuals may often have socio-economical, psychological, vocational, ethical, and other problems which may profoundly affect physical status."

§25.22 Failed Back Syndrome

The *failed back syndrome* is not a specific entity, but several continuing back pain problems that impair the patient after treatment. Some patients who have had surgery and are still nonfunctional because of pain may be helped by additional invasive treatment. In others, further surgery may be

---

[18] *Rehabilitation in the Minnesota Worker's Compensation System,* 4 Workers' Comp Res Inst Brief 1 (1989).

inappropriate. A diagnostic therapeutic algorithm is an excellent tool in these cases.

Other failed back patients include any patient who has not responded after six months of adequate conservative or surgical care, or when the impairment returns soon after the treatment period. By use of a comprehensive algorithm, treatment of many chronic failed back patients can be effected.[19]

Conservative treatment modalities for pain reduction may include: nonsteroidal anti-inflammatory medication, low-dose antidepressant medication, transcutaneous electrical nerve stimulation, and "sports medicine" rehabilitative exercises. Evaluation of the degree of deconditioning to the area of the body using isokinetic equipment (such as Cybex or Lido) and concentration on muscle rebuilding at those areas are appropriate. Equally important is a tailored flexibility conditioning program. In most back pain patients, use of bed rest and spa-like therapies are not indicated and are often counterproductive.

Some doctors use such methods as manipulation, sclerotherapy, or acupuncture with reported success as ancillary treatment. Along with this, it is essential to treat the whole person starting from the first visit, understanding what the impairment (pain) means to the patient, what the patient's goals are, and how the patient's anger and/or disappointment relate to the pain.[20]

§25.23 Concurrent Lumbar Spinal Stenosis and Peripheral Vascular Disease

Intermittent claudication from peripheral vascular disease can be difficult to distinguish from neurogenic claudication secondary from lumbar spinal stenosis. The orthopedist must think of each entity when evaluating the patient presenting with low back pain, weakness, or limited endurance combined with leg discomfort produced by walking.

A surgical decision initially for either lumbar spinal stenosis or peripheral vascular disease is based on the pathology present. A lesion, such as an abdominal aneurysm, is certainly a treatment priority. In some patients, it is impossible to precisely determine the contribution of the vascular insufficiency in lumbar spinal stenosis to the patient's complaint until pathology

---

[19] Harsha, *Patient Participation in His Low Back Care,* 5 J Neuro Orthop Surg 17 (1984); Harsha, *Using Algorithm in Evaluation and Treatment of Low Back Pain,* presented at the 8th Annual Meeting of the American Academy of Neurological and Orthopedic Surgeons, Oct 23-26, 1984, Las Vegas, Nev; Hirschfield & Behan, *The Accident Process, #2. Toward More Rational Treatment of Industrial Injuries,* 186 JAMA 300 (1963).

[20] Rosomoff, *Physical Findings in Patients with Chronic Intractable Benign Pain of the Neck and/or Back,* 37 Pain 279 (1989); Yochelson, *Psychiatric Aspects of Backache,* 3 Curr Prac Orthop Surg 253 (1966).

is corrected. It is not uncommon for patients to require both vascular and spinal surgery for maximal improvement of their complaint.[21]

§25.24 Back Pain Rehabilitation Clinics

Many chronic back pain clinics offer one mode of treatment for all patients; that is, traction modalities, corsets, etc., as though all low back pain has the same underlying cause. Only manipulation and individualized exercise rehabilitation programs allow for customized treatment for each patient's presentation.

There is widespread recognition that chronic back pain disrupts many lives. An estimated 65,000 people in the United States suffer permanent back pain each year, and 1 per cent of our population is considered totally and permanently disabled due to chronic back pain.

In recent years, many chronic back pain patients are helped by directed multi-disciplinary chronic pain clinics. These programs include several interrelated methods, such as behavior modification, pain and stress coping skill improvement, physical therapy and patient directed therapies, nerve blocks, and TENS units. The results of these clinics in many reports have been excellent, but others have been less successful. A great deal depends on patient selection, with psychologically-motivated patients doing better than depressed, rigid-thinking patients.

§25.25 Manipulation

The orthopedist does not often use spinal manipulative therapy, although its utility is at times recognized. The osteopathic physician, as part of his or her training, may often use spinal manipulation as therapy. The chiropractor is trained to routinely use manipulative treatment of the spine, hoping to cure or improve many of the body's ailments.

It is essential for each disciple who does, in fact, manipulate a patient, to know that patient from an anatomical point of view, to have a verifiable diagnosis, and to know when spinal manipulation is appropriate and when it may injure a patient.

Throughout the world, the medical literature reports injuries, some devastating, following spinal manipulation. The patient with an incipient extruded nucleus pulposus (extruded disc) should not have vigorous spinal manipulation. A patient with a weakened annulus fibrosis with incipient protruded intervertebral disc may be converted into a frank protruded disc patient by spinal manipulation.[22]

---

[21] Harsha, *Patient Participation in His Low Back Care,* 5 J Neuro Orthop Surg 17 (1984).

[22] VanCamp, *Your Patient Asks: Why Exercise?,* 2 Your Patient & Fitness 13 (1989); Dalsky, *Does Exercise Increase Bone Mass?,* Surg Rounds for Orthop, at 73; Gallinaro & Cartesegna, *Three Cases of Lumbar Disc Rupture and One of Cauda Equinae Associated with Spinal Manipulation (Chiropraxis),* The Lancet Feb 19, 1983, at 411.

§25.26 Back School

Back school is an educational program that is very helpful to back injuries. It takes several forms, usually managed by a treating physician or one of his or her back treating personnel with a special skill. Anatomy, physiology, pharmaceutics, and physical therapy are common subjects, with the bottom line being that the patient understands him- or herself and the injury, what to expect, and, most important, what he or she can do to help.

Relaxation therapy can be important in allowing the patient to help a pain complaint. One such relaxation technique is an exercise with the patient lying supine, alternately tensing and relaxing each muscle group of the body, starting at the toes and ending in the scalp while breathing deeply using the abdominal muscles to their fullest. There is an element of self-hypnosis in the procedure, so some people are inherently more successful than others. When very relaxed, the patient can use the left brain with imagination to almost feel as if he or she can go inside the body to the spot that is causing the pain, and feel each muscle as it relaxes or apply the kind of heat deep inside that he or she wishes.

The idea of back school is appealing, but only in recent years has the value of the concept become established. The problem is that everyone recognizes the need, but it has been difficult to qualify the results.

To gauge the value of back school, we must take into account the natural recovery of back pain which, even in the most pessimistic reviews, approaches 85 per cent over a three-month period.

Back schools may be directed at a wide range of patients, and it is important to accept the difference between acute and chronic pain. We must also take into account the patient's age, sex, and occupation, as well as his or her workers' compensation status or the presence of pending litigation.

Back schools have a variety of main focuses. Some emphasize ergonomics, particularly in the work place. Others concentrate on fitness and exercise, while a third approach stresses the psychological aspect of pain control.

A combination of these approaches has been shown to be the most effective. Class size varies, as does the cost-effectiveness of the program. Specific interest in a treatment modality may dominate the program and destroy objectivity. There are questions as to how many hours of back school education are necessary before the program works, how often classes should be held, and how many classes there should be. There is a wide range of charges for back education/training/pain management programs. In the United States at this time, they range from $50 to $1,500.

In the evaluation of the deconditioned patient, which is commonly encountered in an orthopedic practice, there is a need for understanding the status of the patient—whether his or her condition is acute, sub-acute, or chronic. The principles of physical training for the deconditioned patient include an understanding by the physician and the patient of the ranges of motion of the affected body area, evaluation of isolated trunk strength, evaluation of aerobic capacity of the patient, and the ability of the patient to participate in functional task performances, such as lifting, carrying, climbing, kneeling, and crawling.

An integral part of the deconditioned patient, as is true of all pain patients, is identifying barriers to functional recovery, including the financial disincentive problems. The deconditioned patient who is about to have surgery will benefit with a conditioning program ahead of time to understand the surgery he or she is to have, the groups of muscles or parts of the body that are now deconditioned and which may be further deconditioned by the surgery, and what treatment modalities he or she can engage in to lessen those.

The value of a back education program can be measured in many ways. The patient acceptance and assessment value is non-scientific, but more than 90 per cent of participants consider back school useful. That number certainly says something about the lack of communication in the ordinary treatment of back pain by patient-physician visits only. The value of back education can be measured through reduction in pain. Most clinics report that 70 per cent of the attendees learn to control pain. Differentiation must be made between acute and chronic pain patients, and between clients dealing with primary physical problems and those treating chronic pain syndromes.

In the latter group, a success rate of 30 per cent is considered excellent. Return to work is an excellent measure of effectiveness. The more successful programs return from 50 to 90 per cent of their participants to gainful employment. Once again, the percentage varies between short-term and long-term problems. Perhaps the most interesting statistic is the recurrence rate following return to work. Contrary to popular belief, chronic back pain sufferers who complete an effective back education program generally retain adequate function. Fewer than 10 per cent develop chronic absenteeism.

Based on statistical analysis of patients completing a back education program, several factors appear to be important:

1. Patients who perform regular exercise show greater improvement
2. Patients who practice regular back care have greater pain relief
3. Patients who restrict their activities, avoid most activities, or use back braces on a regular basis do poorly
4. Patients who feel they understand their diagnosis do better

Back school should eliminate common misconceptions and make the patient aware that the severity of back pain does not reflect the nature of the physical problem. Most of all, an effective Back School must take the responsibility for the care of the painful back away from the doctor and return it to the patient where it rightfully belongs.[23]

---

[23] Manniche & Hesselsoe: *Clinical Trial of Intensive Muscle Training for Chronic Low Back Pain,* 24 Lancet 1472 (1988); VanCamp, *Your Patient Asks: Why Exercise?,* 2 Your Patient & Fitness 13 (1989); Dalsky, *Does Exercise Increase Bone Mass?,* Surg Rounds for Orthop, at 73; Hirschfield & Behan, *The Accident Process, #2. Toward More Rational Treatment of Industrial Injuries,* 186 JAMA 300 (1963); Hirschfield, *Some Thoughts on Disability,* 6 J Occupat Med 267 (1964).

§25.27 Back Support Mechanisms During Manual Lifting

Mechanisms thought to allow individuals to lift loads without injury to the vertebral elements appear to include the intra-abdominal pressure mechanisms, the thoraco-lumbar fascia mechanisms, and combinations of these mechanisms with the use of the erector spinae, multifidus, and psoas muscles.

There appears to be indications for various types of lifting positions with respect to the low back in flexion or extension. Lifting should be performed, in general, with the lumbar spine as straight as possible. Lifting in flexion should be performed quickly and lifting in extension safely and effectively may require muscle training. When lifting an object from the floor, some degree of lumbar flexion may be required. Using flexion for muscle injuries and extension for ligamentous injuries should be weighed against the patient's report of pain through the psychophysical testing.

Instruction in safe lifting techniques should include (1) planning the lift, (2) keeping the load close to the body, (3) avoiding twisting while lifting, and (4) bending at the knees. The thoraco-lumbar fascia provides a major support mechanism for lifting, regardless of the lumbar posture adopted. This structure has the best mechanical advantage of all lumbar tissues that provide an anti-flexion moment. It produces the least amount of intervertebral compression. Intra-abdominal pressure serves to increase tension along the thoraco-lumbar fascia, assisting in the anti-flexion moment. The author notes that whether or not a patient lifts in flexion or extension should depend on the type of injury and the response of the injury to mechanical stress.

Poor endurance of the back extensor muscles is a good predictor of future low back pain, and the lumbar multifidus was found to be generally deconditioned in a group of sedentary individuals. Instructions for lifting with a lordosis, which puts demands on the extensor muscles, must be augmented with strength and endurance training for these muscles. Failure to do so may result in future muscle injuries to the low back. It is not reasonable for a patient to expect to maintain a lordotic position when performing a floor lift. Some degree of flexion is required at the spine for most individuals to complete such a task. Intra-abdominal pressure, which assists in activating the thoraco-lumbar fascia, is greatest in the fully-flexed postures.

Preventive measures should be taken to avoid twisting while lifting, because such torsion combined with loading can damage the facet joints and intervertebral discs. Planning for a lift should include sizing up the load and determining whether help is needed and the pathways are clear. Lower lifts favor an extended lumbar spine to reduce creeping of the ligamentous tissue and lifting from the floor favors a flexed posture because it is necessary to flex somewhat during this task. Using a straight back position encompasses the combination of muscular control and support of the thoraco-lumbar fascia and intra-abdominal pressure mechanisms. The type of lift will produce the greatest support which will reduce the compressive forces of an extended spine and ligamentous stress of a flexed spine.

Lifting in the early stages of a low back injury is to be avoided because, as the individual starts to become more active when he or she returns to work, strategies for lifting should be applied. Lifting an object from the floor should be avoided when there has been an injury to the ligamentous system, as this can stress the injured tissues. Lifting should be avoided in the presence of a herniated intervertebral disc, as a lift in flexion stresses the posterior annulus and a lift in extension increases intradiscal pressure. Either posture could potentially worsen the injury. Studies reveal that the psoas major muscle is active in stabilization of the lumbar spine, depending on the particular position of the spine at the time. The psoas major adds stability to the spine by countering the pull of the deep posterior vertebral muscles. During lifting, the psoas major muscle acts as a stabilizer, which prevents excess lateral bending and rotation. (*See* Appendix 25-1, Case 4.)

§25.28 Braces

The use of back braces has been much more popular in orthopedics in the past than the present. The rationale for nonfracture, nondislocating traumas is to reduce the motion of the low back, believing that irritated ligaments and muscles can be placed at rest while they heal. The same is true with degenerating discs or protruding discs that have become centralized. Limiting flexion and extension facilitates the healing process.

It has been well shown that most braces, particularly rigid back braces, do not immobilize the low back significantly. Braces that have the abdominal corset which can be pulled tightly are most effective, whether it is a corset or a ridged brace, by virtue of increasing intra-abdominal pressure. This is an uncomfortable way of limiting motion of the low back and does not, as previously thought, facilitate abdominal muscular activity.

A back brace frequently is used to enhance muscle activity by giving appropriate proprioceptive feedback. Therefore, the most successful brace is one that has the greatest amount of tactile contact. Braces that offer gentle restriction but which are tissue compliant are the most acceptable clinically, but are not necessarily the most effective method of limiting low back motion.

Health selection, which transfers workers with health problems from occupations with heavy physical demands to occupations with light physical demands, may be a factor contributing to excessive morbidity in the latter group. For all disease and functional disorders that have been studied, an increased risk for future health problems was greatest in those who switched jobs for medical reasons. This relationship was most apparent in musculoskeletal disorders and impaired working capacities. The consensus indicates clearly that there is a negative health selection in physically light occupations.

According to this approach, successful rehabilitation may require evaluation using techniques of several disciplines and then manipulation of appropriate variables as needed to accomplish rehabilitation of the injured patient. An organic lesion, therefore, is but one of many factors influencing a likelihood of re-employment. Failure to consider a single crucial variable may lead to failure of the entire treatment program. It is most important to recognize the dynamic interaction of all the variables affecting the patient's basic personality organization.[24] (*See* Appendix 25-1, Case 5.)

[24] Hirschfield & Behan, *The Accident Process, #2. Toward More Rational Treatment of Industrial Injuries,* 186 JAMA 300 (1963); Foster, Jr, *Neuroses and Trauma,* 32 Clin Orthop 54 (1964); Miller, *Accident Neurosis,* 1 Brit Med J 919 992 (1961); Solomon, *Low Back Pain: The Psycho-Somatic Viewpoint,* 18 Indust Med 6 (1949); Stinchfeld & Sinton, *Criterian for Spine Fusion with Use of H Bone Graft During Disc Removal - 100 Cases,* 65 Arch Surg 542 (1952); Dodge, *Concurrent Lumbar Spinal Stenosis and Peripheral Vascular Disease,* 230 Clin Orthop & Rel Res 141 (1988); Gallion, *Perception of Disability in Chronic Back Pain Patients: A Long Term Follow-up,* 37 Pain 67 (1989); Sullivan, *Back Support Mechanism During Lifting,* 64 Phys Ther 38 (1989).

Appendix 25-1
Cases

1 ***Barnes v Schlein,* 473 A2d 122 (Conn 1984)** (malpractice action against an orthopedic surgeon was barred by the statute of limitation. The patient was injured in a slip and fall December 20, 1972, and was treated by surgery December 20, 1972, and again February 20, 1973. In April 1973, the surgeon advised her that she needed extensive physical therapy and further surgery to relieve the pain she was still experiencing. She obtained a second opinion from another physician on April 16, 1973. On December 16, 1975, she filed against the first surgeon for negligence in treating her and causing her to endure further surgery. The trial court granted the physician's motion on the ground that the action was filed more than two years after the patient discovered her injury. The case turned on the uncontradicted testimony of the patient that she was aware that something was wrong with her leg in April 1973, more than two years before the lawsuit was filed).

2 ***Farrell v St Vincent's Hospital,* 525 A2d 954 (Conn 1987)** (nurse and two orthopedic surgeons in a hospital were not negligent when treating a patient who suffered a re-fracture of a bone while the nurse was exercising his legs. The patient was hospitalized as a result of multiple injuries, including a fracture of the shaft of the left femur, dislocation of the right hip, and fracture of the left knee. The injury was suffered in an accident. Both legs were placed in traction, and the left leg remained in traction until December 1973. The traction was removed in favor of lifting and knee bending exercises. A part-time nurse employed by the hospital was assigned by one of the patient's orthopedic surgeons to perform exercises on the patient. The patient claimed that during the process of exercising his left leg, the nurse re-fractured the femur. On appeal from a verdict in favor of the nurse, the two surgeons, and the hospital, the patient argued that the trial court erred in excluding all evidence of acts of malpractice occurring after December 15, 1973. The court noted that the initial complaint stated that malpractice occurred on or about December 17, 1973, two days after trial had begun, and that the patient filed a complaint alleging that the nurse had actually re-fractured his leg on December 15, 1973. The trial court was correct in excluding any evidence or alleged negligence of malpractice beyond that date. The trial court did not err in excluding the deposition of one of the patient's expert witnesses, a radiologist, who received the x-rays after the radiologist had died at the beginning of the trial. The patient sought to introduce a deposition which had been taken prior to the trial, but the court ruled that the deposition was too confusing to be presented to the jury. Agreeing with that decision, the supreme court said that, during the deposition, the radiologist had made reference to a certain portion of the x-rays being analyzed using the words "here, here, and here" without any description as to where he was pointing. The jury, at best, would have to engage in speculation had that

deposition been used as evidence. Finally, the court said it would not rule on the patient's claim that the trial court erred in prohibiting the orthopedic surgeon from testifying as to the standard of care owed by a nurse in the hospital. The patient failed to object to the trial court's ruling that the orthopedic surgeon could not testify).

Comment: Nothing in this case states what the negligence might have been, but it does point out the hazards of dealing with patients in long-term immobilization in rehabilitation. Bones are soft and muscles are tight, contractured, and easily fractured or torn, yet it is essential to go ahead with the physical therapy as part of the rehabilitation.

3 ***Tart v McGann,* 697 F Supp 627 (ED Mo 1985)** (court reasoned that inadequate physician monitoring of exercise testing contributed to and led to a post-test myocardial infarction. The case was settled for $50,000).

4 ***Bilderback v Priestley,* 709 SW2d 736 (Tex Ct App 1986)** (malpractice action against an orthopedist who authorized a therapeutic course of weight lifting exercise for his patient, with adverse effects after it became clear that spinal stenosis was the problem. Weight lifting exercises, along with a loose body in the knee, aggravated the pain both in the knee and in the back. She saw another orthopedist who told her that the exercise aggravated her spinal stenosis. She filed a malpractice action. An expert was asked, "Would it be your professional opinion within community standards when a person is experiencing pain to increase the therapy and the poundage?" She replied it would not. In defense, the orthopedic surgeon claimed that the testifying physician was not of the same school as the defendant, and was therefore not familiar with the standard of orthopedic practice. The witness against the orthopedist had a Ph.D. in physics and biophysics. The defendant's witness, another orthopedist, testified that if his patient complained of continued pain, he would halt the physical therapy. A judgment against the orthopedist resulted).

Comment: This again is a case where different orthopedists would view the situation differently. In a case of lumbar spinal stenosis, once the diagnosis is made, it is unusual to have leg pain. Weakness, impaired ability to get around, and impaired ability to walk distances are part of the syndrome. Intermittent claudication type of discomfort is seen in the buttocks and hips with spinal stenosis. Most lumbar spinal stenosis patients are more comfortable in an extended position. Physical therapy to extend the low back, to strengthen the low back extensors, is common. It is hard for me to see that the knee extension exercise spoken of in this case would adversely affect a patient with lumbar spinal stenosis, unless the patient was forced to do the exercises in a forward flexed posture. Throughout the United States, I believe the judgment would have been different in most jurisdictions, under these facts.

5 ***Hughes v Webster Parish Police Jury,* 414 So 2d 1353 (La App 1982)** (45-year-old man was injured when he worked beneath a police vehicle. A clutch and pressure plate weighing 40 pounds fell on his chest. He said he experienced sharp pain on his lower back, went blind for a moment,

rested for about one-half hour after the accident, and then left the job to see his family physician. An orthopedist saw him on referral and noticed lumbosacral tenderness, prescribed a brace, and indicated he would be ready for duty in 12 days. However, he was treated for several years, unimproving, with a variety of treatments, including steroid injections, topical anesthesia, exercise, corset, and psychiatric evaluation, and was seen by two other orthopedists. He was seen at a pain center that noted only "mid-back spasms." Three possible diagnoses were suggested—malingering (considered to be unlikely), psychophysiological musculoskeletal disorder, or hysterical neurosis conversion. The psychiatrist said he could not sort out the orthopedic and emotional factors in the pelvic pain. The patient was somewhat socioeconomically deprived, had a seventh grade education, and limited experience at any job other than the type of work he was doing. He was still unable to be gainfully employed four years after the accident. The employer stopped disability payments. The Louisiana District Court rejected the injured man's plea for benefits on the basis of permanent and total disability. The Court of Appeals noted, however, that there had been no evidence that a rehabilitation program had been suggested to the employer 14 months after the accident. The case was remanded and a special pain clinic approach was ordered, designed to deal with the combination of orthopedic and emotional disabilities).

Comment: This is a common sort of case where a minimal injury will produce pain of an incapacitating nature. There are many headache problems that fall into this category. The vocabulary used to describe this situation is difficult in itself, with each specialist seeming to favor his or her terminology. It basically falls into the category of somatization disorder. Very rarely are there significant objective findings of injury, or if they were there, they are past the healing period. There is, however, a profound impairment that manifests itself by loss of endurance, ease of fatigue, and a pain complaint that is interpreted as overwhelming. Each case must be evaluated on its own merits, considering all factors of the case—physical, psychological, spiritual, socio-economical, ethnic, etc. It is certain that some of the patients are malingerers, but this is generally considered to be a minority. This is the sort of case in which third-party carriers and a number of orthopedists, as well as physicians in general, take the rather biased or arbitrary view that if there is not an objective finding, the odds are that the impairment is more related to the patient's lack of will power or willful misconduct, which very often works a disservice to the patient.

26

Blood Transfusions

§26.01 Whole Blood Transfusions

Whole blood transfusions are rarely used in surgical or traumatic situations, because packed red blood cell transfusions are more practical, safer, and more economical. Still, a certain percentage of transfused patients develop complications. Virtually all complications can be avoided by use of predeposit autologous blood transfusion programs, intraoperative blood salvage programs, selection of patients for intraoperative blood salvage programs, selection of patients for intraoperative isovolemic hemodilution, pharmacological approaches to blood loss, and directed donations. See the sources cited in this chapter for description of these techniques, which will probably replace the majority of multiple blood bank blood product transfusions in the coming years.

§26.02 Complications of Blood Transfusions

The risk of transmitting disease through blood transfusions continues even as additional blood donor screening and testing measures are implemented. Nevertheless, when a blood transfusion is necessary during the perioperative period, *autologous* (reinfusing the patient's own collected blood) is the safest option. Three methods for obtaining autologous blood to use during or after a planned surgical procedure are: (1) preoperative autologous blood donation, (2) peri-operative blood salvage, and (3) acute normovolemic hemodilution. These techniques can be used alone or in combination to decrease or eliminate the patient's exposure to homologous blood. However, because all transfusions carry some health risks and blood administration costs, autologous blood should not be collected or reinfused indiscriminately. Autologous blood services should be used only when absolutely necessary in patients who require transfusions and should not be employed for minor procedures where the need for transfusion is unlikely. The risk of transmitting such diseases as immunodeficiency virus or hepatitis A, B, or C (Delta) continues to fall as additional donor screening and testing measures are put in place.[1]

Despite public apprehension about contracting infectious diseases through blood transfusion, the nation's blood supply remains relatively safe. National estimates from the Federal Center of Disease Control indicate that only one patient received blood infected with the HIV virus for every 39,000 to 200,000 units transfused each year, and that 1 to 2 per cent of the three to four million people who receive a transfusion each year contract infectious hepatitis.[2] (*See* Appendix 26-1, Case 1.)

A few years ago, the odds of getting an HIV infection from a typical blood transfusion were 1 in 28,000. A recent study shows that the risk has dropped by as much as 30 per cent per year, since there are now fewer AIDS carriers donating blood, making the blood supply available safer than it has ever been.

The research showed that women are safer donors than men. The blood with more risk came from men making donations for the first time, and the study further revealed that some people donate blood simply to learn whether they are infected.

---

[1] The Expert Panel, *The Use of Autologous Blood,* 263 JAMA 414 (1990).

[2] Bailey, Jr & Mahoney, *The Use of Banked Autologous Blood in Patients Undergoing Surgery for Spinal Deformity,* 69A JBJ Surg 329 (1987); Kafer, *Automated Acute Normovolemic Hemodilution Reduces Blood Transfusion Requirements for Spinal Fusion,* 65 Anes & Analges 576 (1986); Kline, *A Method of Blood Conservation in Jehovah's Witnesses: Incirculation Diversion and Refusion,* 57 Anes & Analges 279 (1978); Mnhre, *Fatalities from Blood Transfusion,* 244 JAMA 1333 (1980); Office of Medical Applications of Research, National Institutes of Health: Consensus Development Conference Statement, US Dept of Health and Human Services, Bethesda, Md (June 27-29, 1988), *Perioperative Red Blood Cell Transfusion,* 260 JAMA 2700 (1988); Stevens, *Hepatitis B Virus Antibody in Blood Donors and the Occurrence of Non-A, Non-B Hepatitis in Transfusion Recipients. An Analysis of the Transfusion-Transmitted Virus Study,* 101 Ann Int Med 733 (1984).

Hemolytic transfusion reactions may be immediate or delayed. Acute hemolysis is a serious complication with recipient plasma antibodies reacting with donor red blood cell antigens to produce this problem. Delayed reactions also may be caused by antibodies to the transfused blood cells. These antibodies generally have come from prior transfusions, such as in pregnancy. The unpredictability of the hemolytic reactions is essentially life-threatening.

Symptoms of a hemolytic transfusion include pyrexia, rigors, chills, headache, chest pain, back pain, stomach pain, infusion site pain, respiratory distress, anxiety, and shock, although many of these may not be obvious in the anesthetized patient. The surgeon and anesthesiologist should be alert to any unexplained changes in hemodynamic variables combined with spontaneous bleeding, suggesting the possibility of a transfusion reaction. Hemoglobin will be present in the plasma; hemoglobinuria is seen and oliguria may follow. Embolization to the glomerulus of red blood cell membranes may result in acute renal impairment.

The moment a hemolytic transfusion reaction is recognized, infusion should be ceased. Treatment should include adequate hydration to achieve urine output of at least 60 ml/hr. Osmotic diuretic may be used to facilitate fluid offloading. Replacement of plasma volume with balanced salt solutions that include 30 to 40 mEq/L potassium chloride is necessary. Maintaining urinary pH above 7 with alkalinization is also helpful.

Most cases of transfusion reactions result from type mismatches caused by clerical error, administration of blood to the wrong patient, or incorrect identification of specimens. Other complications include allergic reactions and fever. Allergic reactions occur in about one per cent of all transfusions. Skin rash, urticaria, and pruritus are common, and bronchospasms, acute asthma, and anaphylaxis can also occur. The transfusion should be stopped when allergic reactions occur; the patient may require epinephrine, corticosteroids, and antihistamines. Fever is caused by the reaction between the recipient and donor white blood cells. Antipyretics are used to control the fever, and leukocyte-poor or washing red blood cells should be considered if the patient requires additional transfusions.

With older, stored blood there is a possible complication of impaired oxygen transport and concomitant increased oxyhemoglobin affinity. Partial pressure of oxygen producing 50 per cent saturation usually normalized within 24 hours of infusion; the contribution of the saturation is still not completely appreciated. The patient may appear hyperdynamic and tachycardiac with adequate blood gases; mixed venous PO_2, oxygen saturation, and arteriovenous oxygen content difference may be widened, indicating poor perfusion. These findings indicate sufficient oxygen delivery but inadequate utilization.

Hypokalemia, hyperkalemia, and hypothermia are additional complications to consider. The rapid infusion of blood into a central line can cause core cooling and lowering of myocardial temperature to the crucial 27.5 to 29.0° C. The heart is irritable at this temperature. Changes in calcium and potassium levels could trigger major arrhythmias. Use of blood warmers and careful monitoring help prevent these problems.

The most common causes of late death from transfusion are infectious complications, primarily those related to post-transfusion hepatitis, the most common being non-A, non-B hepatitis caused by a virus currently identified as the hepatitis C virus. An assay for detection of the antibody to the hepatitis C virus has been developed; it is both sensitive and specific, and should be routinely available in the near future. Hepatitis B, cytomegalo-virus infection, Epstein-Barr virus infection, and human immunodeficiency virus (HIV) infection are not uncommon in late death from transfusion. Testing of donor blood for hepatitis B virus and the antibody to HIV is now routine. The combination of testing for HIV and donor screening reduces the risk of acquired immunodeficiency syndrome (AIDS) developing as a result of a transfusion. Since early 1985, all donor blood has been screened for the antibody to the AIDS virus.

Chronic active hepatitis will develop in about one-third of transfused patients, representing a risk of one to two per cent per unit. The risk of AIDS developing from a transfusion is estimated variously to be between 0.015 and 0.050 per cent per unit transfused. Before screening for the AIDS virus was available, it was estimated that there was a slightly higher risk of 0.2 per cent per unit transfusion. The AIDS virus appears to lose its virulence as blood is stored beyond five days.

§26.03 Blood Banks

Blood banking is a unique industry. Purchasing power is concentrated in a few facilities, with the American Red Cross controlling 50 per cent of the blood banks (unit volume of blood). About 25 to 30 per cent of the balance is controlled by the Council of Community Blood Centers. Because of the hundreds of diverse products required, this concentrated marketplace comprises many smaller arenas, sharing the same customer, but divided by technology and need. New trends and technologies are developing. In surgical procedures, blood is being salvaged and reinfused. Health care is moving out of the hospital to dispensed sites and, to an extent, so are blood transfusions. Fear of AIDS has dramatically increased direct donations, and autologous blood donation/storing by the patient is becoming increasingly more commonplace.[3] (*See* Appendix 26-1, Cases 2 to 8.)

§26.04 Blood Cell Saver

The use of blood cell savers during major operations is desirable and is the modern trend. In one large series of hip arthroplasty operations, cell savers collected and re-transfused from 100 to 2,385 cc of blood and all non-

---

[3] Capozzi, *Techniques of Blood Conservation in Orthopedic Practice,* Surg Rounds for Orthop, Mar 1989, at 39.

patient donated blood transfusions were avoided, along with their potential complications.[4]

§26.05 Blood Bank's Duty to Inform

Blood banks and transfusion services should anticipate that patients contracting transfusion-transmitted diseases will claim that these facilities have a duty to warn or notify patients of potential transfusion risks. The physician treating the patient must obtain an informed consent from the patient by describing significant risks and possible alternatives. Precedent does not support extending informed consents to hospitals or blood banks, although there is a trend toward holding them liable for failure to obtain informed consent. Current legal cases, however, seem to be expanding the required informed consent to include all responsible parties to the transfusion and, in fact, include blood bank transfusing services as owing the patient a duty to at least inform of significant risk.[5] (*See* Appendix 26-1, Cases 9 to 11.)

§26.06 Informed Consent; Jehovah's Witnesses

The orthopedist often treats patients with religious beliefs that interfere with normal practice. This is particularly true of Jehovah's Witnesses, who will not consent to receiving whole blood or blood product infusions. Religious freedom is protected under the first amendment to the Constitution, which says that the United States Congress shall make no laws regarding the establishment or free exercise of religion. The fourteenth amendment tells the states that they also must abide by the first amendment.

The Jehovah's Witness affirms, under these Constitutional protections, that to accept blood transfusions would be against their religious beliefs. They rely on Old Testament scriptures: (1) "Only you shall not eat flesh with its life, that is, its blood. For your lifeblood I will surely require a reckoning . . . " (Genesis 9:4-5); (2) " . . . you shall eat neither fat nor blood." (Leviticus 3:17); (3) " . . . whoever eats any blood, that person shall be cut off from his people." (Leviticus 7:26-27); (4) "For the life of every creature is the blood of it . . . " (Leviticus 17:11); (5) " . . . only be sure that you do not eat the blood, for blood is the life . . . " (Deuteronomy 12:23). In the New Testament, Acts 15:29 and Acts 21:25 support the admonition to avoid blood. Refusal to "take blood" is an expression of the Jehovah's Witness religious belief. The courts are proscribed to examine the rationality or logic of the belief,

---

[4] Semkiw, *Post-operative Blood Salvage Using the Cell Saver After Total Joint Arthroplasty,* 71A JBJ Surg 823 (1989).

[5] Willett, *The Duty to Warn About Transfusion Risk,* 113 Arch Pathol Lab Med 307 (1989).

and may only affirm the constitutional guarantee. (*See* Appendix 26-1, Cases 12 to 14.)

In *Schoendorff v New York Hospital, 211 NY 125, 129 (1914),* Justice Cardozo stated that every competent adult has the right to determine what shall be done with his or her own body. Additionally, he said that when refusal to accept treatment is based on religious belief, interference with that belief may be a violation of his or her constitutional rights. In *In re, Directors of Georgetown College,* 331 F2d 1000 (DC Cir 1964), and *United States v George, 239 F Supp 752 (D Conn 1965)* the court went to the patient and was told by the patient that blood was refused, but that if ordered by the court, then the plaintiff and peers would be blameless in the sight of God. The justices therefore decided to "act on the side of life" and ordered blood transfusions. This inserted a variation in the consent rule relating to refusal of transfusion, when having been fully informed of the risks of the refusal. The consent should include a statement that if a court ordered a transfusion, that order would be resisted.

The consent must of necessity be flexible as the patient's condition worsens, or the thinking of the patient, family, or peers changes. In these cases, a continuing dialogue with the patient and careful recording on the patient's chart is essential.

In *In re Osborne, 294 A2d 372* (DC 1972), a patient who was severely injured refused blood transfusion, as did his wife, citing religious belief. They were fully informed of risk, the patient stating he would prefer "everlasting life" over accepting a blood transfusion. The court, hearing the hospital request for a court-ordered transfusion, concurred with constitutional rights and, further investigating the family situation, found that the immediate family members would be cared for adequately, should the patient die.

In *Prince v Massachusetts,* 321 NJ 463 (1962), the court reasoned that competent persons (parents) may be martyrs, but they cannot cause their children to become martyrs.

In *Muhlenberg Hospital v Patterson,* involving post-partum bleeding with deterioration of the mother's condition, the court held that allowing the mother's death impinged on the state's right and interest in protecting the child's nurturing, and allowed transfusion.

In *In re Sampson,* 317 NYS 2d 641 (1970), a child with severe facial deformity was denied access to blood transfusions necessary for elective corrective facial surgery. The patient was found to be a neglected child and the court ordered that blood be made available for corrective surgery. The court posited that the "state paramount duty is to insure his right to live and grow up without disfigurement, to grow up with sound mind and body."

In *Green v Sanderson, 286 A2d 681* (Pa 1971), similar logic was used in ordering a transfusion for corrective surgery on a severely scoliotic child. The court declared the child "neglected," and appointed a guardian who would authorize blood transfusion.

Physicians ask "Can I be held liable for seeking a court order for my patient in these circumstances?" In Harley v Oliver 404 F Supp 450 (WD Ark 1975) and Staelens v Yake, 432 F Supp 834 (ND Ill 1977) the court held that the physicians would be held free of liability in administering court-ordered transfusions.[6]

§26.07 Autologous Blood Transfusions

The preoperative autologous donation of whole blood or blood products is now a well established, safe, and efficient procedure for use in patients in whom it is anticipated that significant blood loss may occur with reduction of transfusion complications, both of allergic pyrogenic and risks of HIV virus transmission. The recent AMA Council report on "autologous blood transfusion" provides ample medical justification to initiate autologous blood programs where they are not already available.

An autologous transfusion is one in which the blood recipient serves as his or her own donor. This may occur in elective or planned surgery when the patient is able to have blood withdrawn by a blood bank and stored until the surgery. The average "well" person can donate four units of blood per four weeks.

In emergency situations, there is not enough time before transfusion to prepare autologous transfusion and still allow the patient to have sufficient blood reserves at the time of surgery.

There are several advantages to a patient donating his or her own blood: (1) there is no chance that the transfusion will infect the patient with any diseases, such as hepatitis, AIDS, or malaria, unless he or she already has them, (2) the patient will not suffer immune reactions against the transfused blood, (3) the patient, by prior donation of his or her blood, stimulates the body to make more blood at the time of the operation.

Autologous donation of blood requires the cooperation of the patient and the physician, and the medical direction of the hospital or independent blood bank. The surgeon must request the donation and specify how many units will probably be needed. In usual circumstances, the patient's hemoglobin level must be 11 gms/cc. The patient is placed on oral iron to stimulate patient's blood regeneration. The safest blood for transfusion is the patient's own blood.[7]

§26.08 Autotransfusion

It is acceptable to delay the procedure while awaiting the availability of autologous blood or a response to supplemental iron in elective operations. In elective or emergency procedures, the use of intraoperative autotransfusion should be considered. Autotransfusion is a safe and cost-effective method of sustaining red blood cell mass while decreasing demands on the

---

[6] V.V. Becker, Jr, *The Informed Consent for the Surgical Procedure: The Ramifications of Jehovah's Witnesses Beliefs.*

[7] *Autologous Blood Transfusions,* 256 JAMA 2378 (1986); McDonald, *Autologous Transfusions,* N Am Benefit Rev, Summer, 1989, at 12.

blood bank. It is particularly useful for cardiovascular and vascular procedures, for total joint replacements and spinal operations, as an adjunct to liver transplantation, and for the management of ruptured ectopic pregnancies. Autotransfusion is usually contraindicated in trauma and in the presence of bacterial or malignant cell contamination unless no other red blood cell source is available and the patient is in a life-threatening situation.

There are basically two types of autotransfusion devices: (1) collect, mix with anticoagulant, and return, and (2) collect, wash, process, and return. The use of processed, reclaimed red blood cells has not been shown to have significant advantages over the use of nonprocessed red blood cells. The simpler the system, the less likely it is that problems will occur. In elective situations, nurses, technicians, or anesthesia personnel can easily participate in the autotransfusion process. In emergency situations without additional personnel, such participation may not be possible. Systems that process reclaimed red blood cells may require trained technicians, particularly if the procedure is not done on a regular basis.

Predeposited autologous blood transfusion is probably the safest form of transfusion therapy, provided there are no clerical/laboratory errors. Predeposit of blood makes it possible for a patient to donate and have stored whole blood, red blood cells, plasma, and platelets for use during an elective procedure. This approach is possible because of advances in blood-banking technology that have extended the shelf life of blood products. In addition, intraoperative needs can be met more accurately because the volumes to be made available can be specified according to both the procedure and experience of the operating surgeon.

Transfusion of predeposited autologous blood is an acceptable technique for most areas of surgery. When combined with autotransfusion of blood lost during operation, predeposit of blood makes it possible to eliminate homologous blood transfusion in the majority of patients. Since the late 1970s, the shelf life of stored blood has increased from 21 days to approximately 45 days.

Red blood cell preservatives in large quantities may be toxic; however, some ingredients can have a positive effect. The concentration of adenine in preservative solutions varies from 0.03 to 0.09 mg/ml. Adenine in large quantities is an active vasodilator; in massive transfusions, it could induce hemodynamic changes, some of which are potentially beneficial, such as improved microcirculation. Similarly, the small amounts of mannitol in ADSOL could have a positive effect on the microcirculation.

§26.09 Blood Collection

A system to collect blood for subsequent reinfusion following major operations, such as total hip or knee replacements, is available and recently approved by FDA. It is available through Richards Medical Corporation, Memphis, Tennessee. The blood is collected as it is lost during surgery, and is filtered and reinfused at a substantial advantage to the patient. There are no allergic reactions, no virus disease transmissions, and it lessens the need for blood bank blood. Relatively little additional instruction of operating room personnel is needed. Reinfused blood has been shown to have better oxygen-carrying capacity than bank-stored blood.[8] (*See* Appendix 26-1, Cases 15 to 18.)

§26.10 Perioperative Autologous Transfusion

The decision to transfuse a specific patient should include consideration of the duration of anemia, intravascular volume, extent of the operation, probability of massive blood loss, and presence of coexisting conditions, such as impaired pulmonary function, inadequate cardiac output, myocardial ischemia, or cerebrovascular/peripheral circulatory disease. These factors represent the universe of considerations that comprise clinical judgment. No single measure can replace good clinical judgment as the basis for decisions regarding perioperative transfusion. However, current experience would suggest that otherwise healthy patients with hemoglobin values of 10 g/dl or greater rarely require perioperative transfusion, whereas those with acute anemia with resulting hemoglobin values of less than 7 g/dl will frequently require red cell transfusions. It appears that some patients with chronic renal failure tolerate hemoglobin values of less than 7 g/dl. The decision to transfuse red cells will depend on clinical assessment, aided by such laboratory data as arterial oxygenation, mixed venous oxygen tension, cardiac output, oxygen extraction ratio, and blood volume, when indicated.

It is essential to recognize that the combination of hypovolemia and anemia may lead to severe morbidity, mortality, or both, and that there is a minimum hemoglobin value for each individual below which severe morbidity, mortality, or both, due to inadequate oxygen delivery, is likely to occur.

Any adverse effect that occurs immediately before, during, or after the operation is considered to be perioperative morbidity. Morbid events include wound infection, delayed wound healing, bleeding, and impaired recovery. Many physicians and patients are concerned that anemia may increase perioperative morbidity.

In adults, anemia is considered if a hemoglobin value is less than 11.5 g/dl or a hematocrit level is less than 36 per cent in females, and a hemoglobin value is less than 12.5 g/dl or a hematocrit level is less than 40 per cent in males. The cause of anemia may be more important than its severity. Significant disease may be a determinant of morbidity. Mild anemia itself is not associated with perioperative morbidity. The principal concern is whether more severe anemia is related to morbid events. It is important to separate the effects of hypovolemia and decreased perfusion from the effects of anemia. If there is normal intravascular volume and normal tissue perfusion, there is no adverse effect on cardiovascular function until anemia is profound.

Healing of a surgical wound depends on angiogenesis, collagen deposition, and epithelialization. Oxygen tension and adequate perfusion are critically

---

[8] Interview by Sports Medicine News, Apr 1989, at 2.

important for wound healing. However, healing is not compromised by normovolemic anemia unless it is extreme. Animal experiments suggest that wound healing is impaired below a hematocrit value of 15 per cent. There is no support for transfusion to a certain level of hematocrit or hemoglobin to promote wound healing. Likewise, there is no clear evidence that anemia increases the frequency or severity of postoperative infections. There are also no data to suggest that transfusion of red cells has a salutary effect on infection.

In patients with renal failure, associated metabolic abnormalities, and anemia, there may be a prolonged bleeding time that appears to be corrected by increasing the hematocrit value. Some animal experiments also suggest that a decreased hematocrit value is associated with prolonged bleeding time. However, in nonuremic humans, no relation has been demonstrated between anemia and an increased bleeding time. Moreover, there is no clinical evidence that anemic patients have increased bleeding during or after surgery.

Phlebotomy has been demonstrated to decrease exercise tolerance in healthy individuals; however, there are no controlled studies of the relation between anemia and delayed recuperation or increased hospital stay.

In deciding whether to use red cell transfusion in the perioperative period, the need for possible improved oxygenation must be weighed against short-term and long-term risks. The disadvantages are of two general types: transmission of infection, and adverse effects attributable to immune mechanisms.

Any infectious agent present in the blood of a donor at the time of donation is potentially transmissible to a susceptible recipient. The consequence may be seen as clinical morbidity and mortality after an incubation period characteristic of the agent or recognized only by serologic or other types of laboratory testing. If the agent produces chronic infection, clinical morbidity and mortality may be be seen until years after the transfusion.

In modern blood-banking practice, bacterial contamination of red cell units is rare. For practical purposes, the transmissible agents of greatest concern are viruses:

1. Human hepatitis viruses are the most frequently transmitted infectious agents. The incidence of non-A, non-B infection after recent changes in criteria for donor acceptance and introduction of nonspecific laboratory tests (antibody to hepatitis B core antigen and alanine aminotransferase) is not precisely known, but it may be 1:100 or less per unit of blood. Hepatitis B virus infection, for which a specific screening procedure has been in use since 1971, still occurs, and the incidence was in the range of 1:200 to 1:300 per unit before recent changes in donor populations.
2. Human immunodeficiency virus (HIV), about which there is the greatest public concern, currently poses only a remote hazard because of donor selection and laboratory screening procedures. It is variously estimated that the risk of HIV transmission by transfusion is 1:40,000

to 1:100,000. That level of risk is unlikely to be appreciably decreased in the foreseeable future even if additional screening tests are added. The consequences of HIV infection are rarely seen until two or three years have elapsed, but ultimately morbidity and mortality are extremely high.

3. Cytomegalovirus infection occurs with moderate frequency among those recipients without prior infection. Most of these infections are asymptomatic except among immunocompromised persons.
4. Human T cell lymphotropic viruses (HTVL-I/II) occur with low but not negligible frequency, among donor populations in the United States. It is not known whether transfusion-transmitted infection with these viruses among adults results in T cell leukemia/lymphoma, neurologic disease, or both, several or many years later.
5. On rare occasions, other microbial agents, including parvoviruses, plasmodia, Epstein-Barr virus, and babesia, cause infection and disease.

It is known that with human hepatitis viruses the incidence of infection in recipients increases with the number of donor exposures. This relation is probably also true for other transfusion-transmitted infections. Therefore, if homologous transfusion is to be used, the number of units administered should be kept to a minimum.

Immunologic consequences also complicate homologous red cell transfusion. Hemolytic and nonhemolytic reactions are largely caused by alloimmunization to red cell and leukocyte antigens. Compatibility testing has virtually eliminated immediate hemolytic transfusion reactions; when they occur, they are largely caused by human error. Nonhemolytic febrile reactions occur in one to two per cent of recipients as a result of sensitization to leukocyte antigens. This may be minimized by the use of leukocyte-poor blood products.

Components of red cell transfusions, possibly leukocytes, may induce immunosuppression. The clinical significance of the phenomenon is unclear and is currently under investigation in a number of areas.

Although homologous red cell transfusion is continuously becoming safer and is a major therapy, it should not be considered a substitute for good surgical and anesthetic technique. Progress in anesthesia has allowed more time for the surgeon to be fastidious about hemostasis, and new surgical techniques have improved the surgeon's ability to control bleeding.

A variety of alternatives to homologous transfusions exist. The available literature does not permit a definitive recommendation concerning the cost-benefit or risk-benefit ratio of any of them. In most cases, the expected blood loss with the surgical procedure can be predicted from clinical evaluation. This prediction should be used in the selection of a strategy to minimize the use of homologous red cells.

Autologous transfusion programs eliminate the viral transmission and immunologic risks previously discussed. The practice appears useful for selected patients and is most valuable when major blood loss is anticipated. However, the risks of the procedure have not been fully evaluated. There are a number of complicated issues that deserve further investigation. These include the logistics of the process and concerns about unnecessary transfusions, errors in distribution, testing, and the disposition of unused units. Current experience with autologous transfusion is limited to about two per cent of transfusions in the United States.

Intraoperative autologous transfusion (cell saving) offers a surgical patient an adjunct to autologous blood or an alternative to homologous blood. The blood from the surgical field is suctioned into reservoirs via a sterile boule-lumen tube, allowing for anticoagulation of the blood after entering the suction line. The anticoagulant is usually heparin. The anticoagulated blood is drawn from the reservoirs into the centrifuge bowl (the intact red cells are kept in the centrifuge bowl due to the centrifugal action of the bowl), and the lysed cells, particulate matter, and supernatant fluid are spun off into a waste bag. When there are enough red cells saved to provide a unit of blood with a hematocrit of 50 to 70 per cent, the cells are washed with sterile saline. This step further washes out free hemoglobin, heparin, and other non-cellular debris. The end product of the process is approximately 240 ml of fresh washed red cells, which are placed in a transfer pack and reinfused to the patient by the anesthesiologist or perfusionist.

The advantages of intraoperative/postoperative salvaged red blood cells are as follows: autologous blood product does not require type and crossmatch, there is no risk of disease transmission, and there will be no transfusion reaction. There are some contraindications, however, including (1) cases involving contamination of the surgical field by bowel contents, (2) cases involving malignancy where an incision is made into the tumor, releasing malignant cells into the surgical wound, and (3) cases involving active infection at the surgical site (abscess, etc.).

Patient benefits are numerous with the use of intraoperative autotransfusion, including:

1. Eliminating the risk of transfusion-associated infections from homologous transfusions
2. Reducing the incidence and severity of hypothermia and coagulopathies associated with massive transfusion
3. Eliminating transfusion-associated incompatibility problems that might be found with banked homologous blood (febrile and allergic reactions)
4. Providing reassurance for undergoing operative procedure
5. Offering alternative type transfusion for patients undergoing operative procedures; reducing need for homologous donor transfusions by as much as 40 to 60 per cent
6. Eliminating risk of transfusion-associated allo-immunization

Additionally, advantages are apparent to the hospitals by offering intraoperative autotransfusion, such as:

1. Reduces blood processing costs, since no blood typing and crossmatching are required; lessens handling/storage problems associated with blood bank
2. Supports and supplements the hospital blood bank
3. Decreases liability in the event of litigation; potentially decreases malpractice insurance premium

The autologous platelet rich plasma program is a new concept aimed at reducing the amount of homologous blood products used in cardiac surgery. A nurse technician from a blood bank can sequester 500 to 800 ml of autologous platelet rich plasma (PRP) through a mobile plasma collection system. The end product is comparable to two units of plasma and to two to four units of platelets which are immediately hemostatically effective, not having been injured by perfusion through the pump oxygenator.

Future research should adhere to appropriate standards of research design, including adequate sample sizes, controls, multicenter sites, and randomization, where feasible. The panel identified the following research areas worthy of emphasis:

1. The effect of anemia on rate of recovery and length of hospital stay
2. Determination of risk of transfusion-transmitted infection with contemporary donor screening procedures and evaluation of new measures to identify infected donors
3. Determination of immune changes induced by transfusions and their clinical consequences, if any
4. Identification of organs that are specifically "at risk" for acute anemia and development of clinical monitors that measure directly or indirectly the state of perfusion and the presence of cellular hypoxia in those organs that are specifically sensitive to low hemoglobin values
5. Development of predictors that better define the need for perioperative transfusion
6. Development of appropriate blood substitutes
7. Performance of prospective controlled trials to evaluate the effects of increasing the hematocrit in anemic patients in the perioperative period
8. Evaluation and improvement of the safety and efficacy of autologous transfusion and intraoperative blood salvage procedures and definition of criteria for selection of patients
9. Development of measures for the improvement of the safety of homologous blood transfusion
10. Evaluation of the risks and benefits of directed donations; the existing data are inconclusive

Conclusions are as follows:

1. Available evidence does not support the use of a single criterion for transfusion, such as a hemoglobin concentration of less than 10 g/dl; no single measure can replace good clinical judgment as the basis for decisionmaking regarding perioperative transfusion
2. There is no evidence that mild to moderate anemia contributes to perioperative morbidity
3. Perioperative transfusion of homologous red cells carries documented risks of infection and immune changes; therefore, the number of homologous transfusions should be kept to a minimum
4. A variety of promising alternatives to homologous transfusion are being developed; these alternatives will reduce the use of homologous transfusion to some extent, and their development should be encouraged; however, in the foreseeable future, homologous blood will continue to be the therapeutic mainstay; therefore, primary attention should be devoted to the promotion of safe and effective transfusions from carefully selected volunteer donors
5. Future research is necessary to define the best indications for red cell transfusion and the safest methods of blood conservation and delivery

§26.11 Synthetic Blood

The Federal Food and Drug Administration have recognized synthetic blood products. One is a blood substitute consisting of hemoglobin, the oxygen-carrying molecule in red blood cells, encapsulated in bubbles that have the consistency of Jello. The bubbles are chemically similar to red blood cell membranes of the human. Several other blood synthetics are being developed and, when available, will help answer the problem of blood-induced infections, including AIDS.

§26.12 Patients "At Risk" for Complications

Recognition of patients with inadequate physiologic reserve and who are "at risk" for complications is important. The oxygen delivery system is complex because it involves cardiovascular responses and oxygen-carrying capacity. Most of the variables needed to define reserve parameters can only be determined through invasive monitoring with measurement of hemodynamic parameters and oxygen delivery and utilization. Without invasive monitoring, assessment of risk is an educated guess based on experience and clinical observation. ICU patients are often monitored with invasive devices, so it is relatively easy to measure hemodynamic and oxygen consumption parameters in this population. Positive changes in cardiac output and wedge pressure in response to volume loading are indicators of adequate reserve if no angina or excessive tachycardia is present.

§26.13 Transfusions and Abnormal Bleeding

It is important to note that any abnormal bleeding may be a manifestation of loss of vascular integrity. Failure to ligate a bleeding vessel or failure of a ligature or clip to hold can lead to bleeding that might be confused with coagulopathy. A high index of suspicion and early re-exploration usually resolve the problem and conserve blood product resources. Some patients who are bleeding are assumed to have a coagulopathy and are treated with large volumes of blood components before operative re-exploration. This induces a mild dilutional coagulopathy, in which clotting factors are present but diluted; this coagulopathy reverses spontaneously with control of the hemorrhage. Massive transfusion of red blood cells can be associated with abnormal bleeding arising from a dilutional thrombocytopenia. Once a dilutional thrombocytopenia is recognized, platelet transfusions can be provided.

Whole blood is rarely available, but if the concept of specific therapy for identified problems is used, it is rarely indicated. In certain transplant and trauma situations, total body exchange transfusion may be necessary to correct a major coagulopathy. However, a significant amount of time is required to process a unit of donated blood before it can be released for use, usually 18 to 24 hours.[9]

---

[9] W.C. Shoemaker, P.L. Appel & H.B. Kram, *The Role of Oxygen Transport Patterns in Pathophysiology, Prediction of Outcome and Therapy of Shock* Oxygen Transport and Utilization 65 (C.W. Bryan-Brown & S.M. Ayres eds 1987); Shah, Prichard & Newell, *Increased Cardiac Output and Oxygen Transport After Intraoperative Isovolemic Hemodilution: A Study in Patients with Peripheral Vascular Disease,* 115 Arch Surg 597 (1980); Kreuzer & Cain, *Regulation of the Peripheral Vasculature and Tissue Oxygenation in Health and Disease,* 1 Crit Care Clin 453 (1985); National Institutes of Health Consensus Development Conference Statement, Perioperative Red Cell Transfusion, 260 JAMA 2700 (1988) US Dept of Health and Human Services, Bethesda, Md (June 27-29, 1988), Allen & Allen, *The Minimum Acceptable Level of Hemoglobin,* 20 Int Anesthesiol Clin 1 (1982); Glover & Broadie, *Intraoperative Autotransfusion,* 11 World J Surg 60 (1987). Amberson, *Blood Substitutes,* 12 Biol Rev 48 (1987); G.P. Biro, Blood Substitutes and the Heart: A Critical View International Symposium on Artificial Blood Substitutes 233 (G. DeStasio ed 1987); Presidio, Osperaliero, "Divenere," USL BA/11—Bari/Carbonara, Italy.

Appendix 26-1
Cases

1 ***CW v Belle Bonfils Memorial Blood Center,* No 87 CV 4127 (Colo Denver County Dist Ct Mar 31, 1989)** (plaintiff incurred AIDS when she received a tainted blood transfusion on March 22, 1985. The blood bank had received AIDS testing kits on March 13, 1989. On that day, the bank drew blood from an infected donor. During the subsequent nine days, a training program was instituted, with April 1, 1985 being the target date for regular testing of all blood bank blood that was received after that date, but not of blood being stored and drawn before April 1, 1985. Although the blood bank could have tested all blood dispensed on March 22, it elected to send the one unit (unknown to be tainted) for plaintiff's reception. Besides alleging that the blood bank was negligent in failing to test for HIV antibody, plaintiffs alleged that the blood bank negligently failed to screen "at risk" donors. The result was $2.25 million awarded for pain and suffering, $1.4 million for economic loss, and $1.35 million for impairment. An additional $500,000 was awarded to the husband for loss of consortium).

2 ***Congelton v Baton Rouge General Hospital,* 444 So 2d 175 (La Ct App 1983), *rehg denied* (1984)** (doctrine of res ipsa loquitur could not be applied where there was direct evidence to explain the activities leading to an injury. A woman suffered injury when she was donating blood at a blood bank. During the phlebotomy, a technician drawing the blood positioned the needle and adjusted the tourniquet when the woman complained of pain, and again when she complained of tingling and numbness. When the technician offered to remove the needle, the woman decided to complete the procedure. After the phlebotomy, the woman complained that her arm was still numb, and the technician told her to call back the next day if her condition persisted. The woman did call back the next day, and the supervisor told her to return for examination by the head of the pathology department. She was then advised to see a neurologist, who found an injury to the left antebrachial cutaneous nerve. Another neurologist did an EMG and confirmed the diagnosis. The woman sued the hospital to recover for her injury, testifying that she had pain as soon as the technician started to draw the blood. The technician said the woman did not complain until the phlebotomy was almost completed. The trial court found that res ipsa loquitur was applicable in that the hospital failed to rebut the inference of negligence and awarded for the patient. On appeal, the court said that there was undisputed evidence that the injury was caused when the needle struck the nerve in the woman's arm, rendering the doctrine res ipsa loquitur inapplicable. All of the medical testimony at the trial indicated that the injury could have occurred in the absence of negligence. One physician testified that an injury of that type could happen even with the best medical technique, although testimony showed that the injury was highly unusual and extremely rare. The court

said that this did not alone justify res ipsa loquitur. A greater weight of testimony showed the hospital was negligent and was not the most plausible explanation of the injury. Finding that the woman failed to prove negligence in a preponderance of evidence, the court reversed the lower court's decision).

3 ***Zichichi v Middlesex Memorial Hospital,*** **528 A2d 805 (Conn 1987)** (hospital was not liable for serum hepatitis contracted after a blood transfusion. The patient contracted serum hepatitis after receiving several units of whole blood during the treatment for a ruptured spleen. He claimed that part of the normal business of the hospital was the sale of the original whole blood for the purpose of treating the patients, and the patient said the blood he received was defective and unreasonably dangerous. He sought recovery from the hospital for pain and suffering, loss of income and earning capacity, and increased medical expenses. On motion by the hospital, the court said that the state's blood shield statute barred the patient's product liability claim because the statute said blood was not a commodity subject to sale but was considered a medical service. To maintain his cause of action, the patient had to allege the sale of product. The trial court granted summary judgment in favor of the hospital. On appeal, the court said that once the transaction was labeled as service opposed to sale of product, it was outside of the purview of the product liability statute. The court said that the patient may have a claim against the hospital based on its negligence if he could show that the defective blood could have reasonably been detected and removed, and he may have been entitled to recovery from the suppliers for the failure to detect and remove).

4 ***Samson v Greenville Hospital System,*** **377 SE2d 311 (SC 1989)** (blood supplier may not be held strictly liable for the harm caused by a blood transfusion that was contaminated by the AIDS virus. The South Carolina blood shield statute, exempting blood supplies from liability for breach of implied warranty and stating that blood provision is a service, had been previously upheld. The court in this case reasoned that a similar rule should apply to strict liability claims).

5 ***Miles Laboratories v Doe,*** **11 Med Liab Rept 170 (1989)** (suit was filed by a plaintiff who received AIDS from contamination blood, on an implied warranty theory. The court reasoned that, in light of the strong public interest in maintaining an adequate blood supply and the fact that there was no scientific test to detect the presence of AIDS virus at the time of the patient's transfusions, the courts concluded as a matter of law that Restatement (Second) of Torts §402A comment K (which addresses blood products that are "unavoidably unsafe") was applicable. The fundamental purpose of the strict liability doctrine is to force hazardous products from the market, and that rationale is inapplicable to blood products which contain undetectable contaminants. For similar reasons, the defendants could not be subjected to liability for breach of the implied warranties of merchantability and fitness).

6 ***Cunningham v MacNeal Memorial Hospital,* 47 Ill 2d 443, 266 NE2d 897 (1970); *Reilly v Keen County Central Blood Bank, Inc,* 6 Wash App 172, 492 P2d 246 (1971), and *Hoffman v Misericordia Hospital Philadelphia,* 439 Pa 501, 276 A2d 867 (1970)** (these cases rejected the Perlmutter decision and held that strict liability applies. The real basis for these blood decisions appears to be that it is impossible to determine whether the hepatitis virus is present in whole blood, coupled with the fact that blood transfusions are often essential to medical treatment).

7 ***Brody v Overlook Hospital,* 127 NJ Super 331, 317 A2d 392 (1974)** (court rejected the sales service distinction as the basis for decision by reaching the same result on the theory that the inability to adequately test for hepatitis renders the blood an unavoidably safe product which, therefore, is not unreasonably dangerous).

8 ***Koenig v Milwaukee Blood Center,* 23 Wis 2d 324, 127 NW2d 50 (1964)** (this court relied on the leading case of *Perlmutter v Beth David Hospital,* 308 NW 100, 123 NE2d 792 (1954), which held that distribution of blood is a service rather than a sale of goods and that therefore no implied warranty exists. Perlmutter has been much criticized, not so much for its holding of strict liability being non-existent for contaminated blood as for reliance on its sales/service distinction, which was artificial enough when applied to hospitals but even more so when applied to a blood bank. Blood is a product which is furnished in connection for professional services and a narrow definition of what is a sale and a classification of the activity as a service is not helpful in analyzing the problem.

9 ***Krygier v Airweld, Inc,* 520 NY2d 476 (1987)** (identities of blood donors were protected by the Privacy Act, and a blood bank was entitled to a protective order precluding disclosure of the names and addresses of blood donors. The administrator for the estate of a patient who died from blood infected with the AIDS virus brought a wrongful death action against the blood bank. The administrator sought to discover the names and addresses of donors whose blood was supplied to the hospital for transfusion. The blood bank sought a protective order, contending that the information sought was privileged and that disclosure would violate the donor's right to privacy. The administrator contended that the physician-patient privilege did not apply to voluntary blood donations and that the donor's identity was not protected by any privacy rights. The court said that even if the physician-patient privilege was inapplicable, the blood bank's interest in maintaining the anonymity of donors, together with society's interest in maintaining a free flow of voluntary blood, far outweighed the reason to disclose all evidence necessary to prosecute a suit. The court found that the blood bank had persuasively argued that the disclosure of the donor's names would violate their right to privacy and that the blood bank was entitled to protect the donor).

10 ***Tarrant County Hospital District v Hughes,* 734 SW2d 675 (Tex Ct App), *rehg denied* (1987)** (court-ordered discovery of the identities and addresses of blood donors did not violate the donors' liberty interests. The

father of a patient who contracted AIDS and died after receiving blood transfusions sued the hospital for wrongful death. He accused the hospital of failing to exercise the degree of care and skill and treatment ordinarily expected, and failure to provide a wholesome blood product. In the record, the court said that it appeared that the hospital made no effort to determine whether any of its donors had been identified as having AIDS. The court said that the finding of injury to society's interest by limited discovery was no less speculative than determining an order would benefit—by discouraging blood donation by AIDS victim. The hospital did not provide evidence that showed the information sought would be used improperly. Since the trial court order showed proper concern for the protection of an individual's rights of privacy, the court denied the hospital's motion for demurer).

11 *Hoemke v New York Blood Center,* 720 F Supp 45 (SDNY 1989) (court held that physicians did not breach their fiduciary duty or inflict emotional distress on a patient who allegedly contracted AIDS from a blood transfusion that she received in 1981, when they finally learned that blood transfusions could spread the disease and warned her of that possibility. The court further pointed out that the doctors might rely on the statute of limitation bar and informed consent given by the patient at the time of receiving the blood transfusion).

12 *Public Health Trust v Wons,* 541 So 2d 96 (Fla 1989) (court held that an adult, whose life is in danger but who is competent to give informed consent, can refuse a blood transfusion based on his religion and its prohibition of blood transfusion. The patient was a Jehovah's Witness. The holding, as in many similar cases, reasoned that the patient's constitutional rights of privacy and free religious exercise outweighed the state's interest).

Comment: *Fosmire v Nicoleau,* 536 NYS2d 492 (App Div 1989) and *Young v Oakland General Hospital,* 437 NW2d 321 (Mich Ct App 1989) reached the same result.

13 *Fosmire v Nicoleau,* 536 NYS2d 492 (App Div 1989) (patient's constitutional rights were violated when a hospital went to court to request a blood transfusion specifically against a patient's wishes. The patient was a Jehovah's Witness and, for religious reasons, signed a permit for treatment but specifically excluded blood transfusions. Her medical problem was severe post-partem hemorrhage. The hospital said it was protection of the infant's right to have her mother for care. Court reasoned the father could do that duty or arrange care, thus the justices felt that an exception to the right of a patient's self-determination did not exist).

14 *In re Melideo,* 390 NYS2d 523 (1976) (plaintiff developed severe postoperative bleeding and needed blood transfusions. The patient and her husband specifically refused transfusion, and signed a document refusing and stating that they knew the risk. The hospital sought a court order to administer a blood transfusion. The court held that the right to refuse to accept treatment was a constitutional rights and that for the court to order otherwise would be unconstitutional).

15 ***Jackson v Muhlenberg Hospital,*** **96 NJ Super 314, 232 A2d 879 (1967)** (court held that, if it were established that a defendant blood bank and defendant hospital were negligent in the collection and handling of blood for transfusion, and that the negligence caused or contributed to the hepatitis virus present in the plaintiff, the negligent defendants could be liable to the plaintiff even though the virus might have been present without negligence).

16 ***Schmaltz v St Luke's Hospital,*** **521 P2d 787 (Colo Ct App 1974)** (absent a proven method of detecting the hepatitis virus in whole blood, no presumption that hospital or attending physician was negligent could be drawn solely from the fact that the patient developed hepatitis).

17 ***DiMarco v Hudson Valley Blood Services,*** **542 NYS2d 521 (App Div 1989)** (limitation period for an action by a patient who contracted AIDS from a blood transfusion began on the date of the patient's discovery of his illness, and his suit was therefore filed in time. The patient received numerous blood transfusions while undergoing open heart surgery in January 1985. He discovered in July 1986 that he had contracted AIDS when he was contacted by one of the blood banks from which he had received contaminated blood. In April 1988, he filed suit for negligence against the two blood banks that supplied the blood he received during the operation. A trial court granted summary judgment in favor of the blood banks on the ground that the action was barred by the statute of limitation. Applying the discovery rule, the court said that the statute of limitation began when the patient discovered he had AIDS, not when he received the blood transfusions. The statute of limitation provided that the three-year limitation period for personal injuries caused by latent effects of exposure to any substance should be computed from the date of discovery of the injury, the court said).

18 ***Kirkendall v Harbour Insurance Co,*** **No 88-2696 (8th Cir Oct 10, 1989)** (blood bank was not negligent in not testing one unit of blood for AIDS, as at the time in question only a limited number of test kits were available).

Comment: This was when test kits were first known, and the Health Department announced that a duty existed to test for AIDS. That fact is now moot, as all blood banks recognize this duty. However, an ever-expanding group of viral diseases are being identified, but without a blood-testing capability to demonstrate their presence.

27

Amputations

§27.01 Generally

Amputation remains the oldest, yet one of the most common, of all operations performed in modern times. There are over 400,000 amputees in the United States, with 85 per cent involving the lower extremity.

Common causes of amputation include (1) vascular disease, (2) trauma, (3) infection, (4) tumors, and (5) congenital problems. Complications of these amputations most often relate to ischemia. (*See* Appendix 27-1, Cases 1 to 10.)

Amputations are performed for a pathological condition, for whatever cause, and are done to eliminate pathology and restore function which otherwise would not be possible. Amputation itself introduces a new pathological state. It is essential that the new pathology be minimized as much as possible by skillful surgery, preserving as much function as possible. Amputation may be ablative, but it must be considered a reconstructive procedure restoring function through the use of a well-fitted prosthesis. Generally speaking, the lower the level of amputation, the more functional the stump. This is not always true when the mechanics of fitting the prosthesis may be hindered with an overlong stump.

Recent energy cost studies have confirmed that the lower the amputation level, if a satisfactory prosthesis can be fitted, the less the energy consumption by the body. This is especially true comparing above knee with below knee amputations. In upper extremity amputation, the superior function of low level amputation is self-evident. The greater the functional loss, the higher the complication rate.

A guiding principle for the surgeon doing an amputation is to perform it at the lowest level that viable tissue exists, which may be a problem to ascertain. This principle will help optimize functional recovery. Gentle tissue handling and anatomical repair, when possible, give a better stump. Preserving long skin flaps and minimal dissection between tissue planes, minimizing circulation disruption, is desirable. Meticulous hemostasis is of prime importance in preventing hematoma formation, infection, and delayed healing.

In amputations necessitated by trauma, prevention of infection is a major consideration. Wounds that are severe enough to require amputation are usually heavily contaminated and associated with extensive tissue devitalization. Most often, these amputations should not be primarily closed, but later revised when all dead tissue can be identified. This is a lesson learned from wartime injuries.

Late complications of amputations that primarily relate to the amputee's residual limb are best managed by a professional amputation team or clinic. These clinics are a combination of medical and paramedical personnel, each of whom has a special expertise in amputation management and whose combined evaluation and judgment is utilized in solving the amputee's complications. Typically, the amputation clinic team consists of an orthopedist, physical therapist, occupational therapist, and prosthetist. Social workers, industrial nurses, and vocational rehabilitation therapists may complete the team.

Complications of amputations can be divided into early and late categories. These are further divided into local (stump) and general (gait, ambulation) problems. Some problems are anticipated, such as with very short below knee amputations, but are accepted as a worthwhile trade-off considering the additional impairment of an above knee amputation. (*See* Appendix 27-1, Case 10.)

§27.02 Early Complications

Mortality following amputation varies according to the condition being treated and the patient's health and age. Rates of death from 10 to 40 per cent have been reported in lower extremity amputations done for peripheral vascular disease. Mortality for amputation below the knee is less than above knee amputation in a 2:1 ratio. Most deaths in the immediate postoperative period are related to vascular problems, such as pulmonary embolus, myocardial infarction, and cerebrovascular accident. Mortality is less with spinal anesthesia than inhalation anesthesia. Anticoagulant therapy is recommended by many surgeons and cardiologists.

Mortality and morbidity are lessened by early ambulation. Primary fitting at the time of surgery with weight-bearing dressings in below knee amputations facilitates ambulation and stump healing. This technique requires a well-trained, knowledgeable surgeon. Postoperative depressive mood disorder is frequent—not an abnormal reaction to "loss."

Wound hematomas occur when meticulous hemostasis is not effected during surgery, or for other physiological causes (bleeding diathesis, stump trauma) with a markedly increased chance of postoperative infection and skin necrosis. Aspiration or drainage of hematomas under strict sterile conditions is essential. If aspiration is not possible, surgical drainage may be done. In either case, culture and Gram stain and sensitivity studies of drainage and use of appropriate antibiotics complete the urgent postoperative hematoma care.

Wound disruption is fairly common in poorly-nourished patients, as well as in patients in whom the amputation skin and deep tissues were closed under too much tension. Delayed wound healing may occur for these same reasons.

Gangrene of the stump may occur if circulation is not adequate or is compromised by wound swelling, hematoma, or infection. Most often, gangrene indicates that too low a level of amputation was selected or that an adverse circulatory state has progressed.

Necrosis of the skin edge can occur for any of the above reasons, or because of pressure from the dressing or a poorly fitted, immediate postoperative prosthesis.

§27.03 Infection

Post-amputation infection can be a catastrophic complication, occurring in 15 per cent of amputations related to peripheral vascular disease. Treatment includes wound assessment and deciding to risk the status quo hoping antibiotics will permit healing, to open the wound with drainage and secondary closure, or to re-amputate at a higher level. All drainage must be cultured with Gram stain and intravenous antibiotics.

Anaerobic infection of the amputation stump can be extremely devastating as proximal extension may occur, requiring progressive proximal re-amputation and lessening the end functional result. These infections are best managed by wide-open debridement and packing the wound open, then later closing or revising.

Gas gangrene is not unusual and must be thought of and treated radically. Hyperbaric oxygen treatment may be life-saving. Every orthopedist should know the location of hospitals with hyperbaric units and how to refer this type of patient.

§27.04 Edema

Postoperative edema, due to venous back pressure, lymphatic obstruction, or postural positioning leads to dehiscence of skin incision and/or its breakdown. Use of pressure dressings or a rigid, well-fitted primary prosthesis generally corrects this problem. The orthopedist should be assured that those health care persons changing dressings and managing extremity positioning are trained and competent. Edema may result from heart failure or electrolyte imbalance.

§27.05 Pain

Post-amputation pain is expected, but must be attended. If it continues past the first few days, there is unusual fever, or pain is directly under finger pressure area, then hematoma, infection, or skin breakdown may be a concern. Phantom pain is a nerve deafferNation problem related to reflex sympathetic dystrophy and is a common and distressing problem. Neuromas at amputation sites may be triggers for phantom pains. Fitting with a prosthesis as early as possible lessens phantom pain for many. In most patients, phantom pain gradually wears out, although for some patients it may require years. Poor surgical techniques, poor treatment of the major nerves at amputation, and post-amputation infection have been suggested as phantom pain etiology, but this is difficult to verify.

§27.06 Contractures

Post below knee flexion contractures are easier to prevent than correct. Post-amputation dressing that places the knee nearly straight and active extension exercises to hold the knee straight are part of the post-amputation orders. A fixed contracture which always occurs in unattended patients, markedly impairs prosthesis use, and may completely frustrate functional prosthesis fitting.

On the day following amputation, and prior to surgery, if possible, the physical therapist should start working with the patient. For a fixed contracture, surgical soft tissue release in the popliteal space may help, but carries some risk to popliteal vessels. Wedging casts are not effective due to the geometrical design of the knee joint.

§27.07 Late Complications

Late complications, for the most part, result from poor skin care, progressive ischemia, or problems with prosthesis fitting. Pressure points in the prosthesis may cause skin breakdown. Sweat glands tend to overfunction in amputees and may cause maceration or superficial infection. Hair follicle infections are common. Ulcerations, once developed, may fail to heal owing to ischemia. Each of these problems requires specific treatment. These amputation problems require diligence by the patient, who must be educated by his or her surgeon or health care worker.

A poor amputation stump may result from surgical technique faults or complications with a need to revise. Redundant skin may be sufficient to require surgical revision. Neuromata may require resection; bone prominences may develop, requiring removal.

§27.08 Intractable Pain in the Amputee

The painful amputation stump is the single most common and disabling complication following amputation surgery. One series of 7,000 amputations reported that all patients suffered pain to some extent at some time in the first 15 years after amputation. Another study of 1,000 amputations found only 15 per cent free of pain or tenderness in the amputation stump.

§27.09 Chronic Amputation Pain

In evaluating post-amputation stump pain, those complications mentioned above should be ruled out. These include infection, abrasions, scarring, edema, skin disorders, and bone spurs. More obscure causes of amputation pain cannot be easily measured or accurately located, and it appears to affect different patients with different intensities; surgeons are often skeptical of the validity of the pain. However, pain is the very center of the patient's thoughts at home or work; he or she yearns for a pain-free stump, pain-free sleep, and the ability to work free of pain. The key to management of chronic stump pain is to determine the source of pain stimulus and eliminate it if possible.

There are two types of pain—in the stump, and phantom pain. They may coexist and either may occur any time. Stump pain may be locally caused by hypersensitivity of skin and deeper tissues during the period of adaptation to the prosthesis. This may be several months and is only lessened by weight bearing or use of the stump. Bursas over bony prominences, nerve compression by scar or fascial bands whose course was altered by surgery ischemia, causalgia (reflex sympathetic dystrophy), tumor, and neuromata may be present. Sympathectomy may help causalgia; testing first with lumbar sympathetic block with local anesthetic may be diagnostic. Discreet neuromata should be surgically excised, having a tendency to recur.

Severe and unremitting phantom pain felt in the amputated part is the most formidable and dreaded complication of major amputations. Phantom pain has been reported since 1551. Incapacitating phantom pain occurs in 2 to 15 per cent of lower extremity amputations. A classic description by Mitchell in Civil War amputees reads:

> A person in this condition is haunted, as it were, by constant or inconstant fracture phantom of so much of himself as has been lopped away—an unseen ghost of the lost part, and sometimes a presence made sorely inconvenient by the fact that while but faintly felt at times, it is at others acutely called to his attention by the pains or irritations which appears to suffer from a blow on the stump or a change in the weather.

In phantom pain, the amputated part—generally the more distant part (foot or hand)—is perceived to be present, moves with body activity, and responds to ambient temperature. The etiology of phantom pain has been the subject of years (centuries) of study. It represents a deafferenting phenomena and disassociation between peripheral efferent input and central afferent pain control.

Treatment of phantom pain is rarely improved by surgeries. Therapies directed at changing nerve function, as with drugs, ultrasound, and TENS may be helpful. Psychotherapy likewise may help. The best results seem to come from multifaceted pain clinic types of care.[1]

§27.10 Preserving Amputated Extremities—Reimplantation

When an extremity is accidentally severed, reimplantation may be possible. The cleaner the traumatic amputation cut, the more likely a satisfactory result. Very important to reimplantation of a severed extremity is the handling and preservation.

Wrapping the amputated part in a clean cloth and prompt cooling is best. Muscle deterioration in the amputated extremity is less by prompt immersion in an ice bath for 20 to 90 minutes (depending on the size of the part) and suspending the part over ice (the part must not touch ice). Placing the part in a styrofoam chest will fulfill this requirement.[2]

---

[1] N.C. McCollough III, *Complications of Amputation Surgery,* Complications in Orthopedic Surgery (C.H. Epps ed 1978); Aftana & Zubek, *Cutaneous Sensitivity of Unilateral Arm Amputees,* 18 Can J Psychol 101 (1974); Farley, *Painful Stump Neuromata Treatment,* 48 Minn Med 347 (1965); E.E. Harris, *Prosthetic Management of Lower Limb Amputation,* Modern Trends in Vascular Surgery (1970); Krainick, *Spinal Cord Stimulation in Post-Amputation Pain,* 4 Surg Neurol 167 (1975); Melzack, *Phantom Limb Pain: Amputation for Treatment of Pathological Pain,* 35 Anes 409 (1971); Weaver & Marshall, *A Functional and Social Review of Lower Limb Amputees,* 60 Brit J Surg 732 (1973).

[2] Bate-Smith & Bendall, *Factors Determining Time Course of Rigor Mortis,* 110 J Physiol 47 (1949); Eiken, *Limb Reimplantation. The Technique and Immediate Results. The Pathophysiological Effects,* 88 Arch Surg 48 (1964); Irving & Noakes, *The Protective Role of Hypothermia in Tourniquet-Induced Ischeania of Muscle,* 67B(2) J Bone Joint Surg 297 (1985); Jones, Smith & Douglas, *Reimplantation,* 286 Brit Med J:1 (1983); Kleinert, *An Overview of Reimplantation and Results of 347 Replants,* 20 J Trauma 390 (1980).

§27.11 Amputation in Diabetics

In gangrene about the foot and leg, especially in the diabetic person, there is always a problem as to what level to amputate. There are several methods to predict the viability of the extremity at the amputation site. The microcirculation in the skin is a primary determinant of wound healing after amputation.

The radioisotope washout method for determining skin perfusion is accurate, but expensive, time-consuming, and painful to the patient; therefore, it is not a popular technique. Skin perfusion can be measured non-invasively by the photoelectric technique, which is currently popular.[3]

§27.12 Level of Amputation

Various non-invasive vascular studies have been reported to provide valuable data for selection of the level of amputation. Transcutaneous PO_2 was found to be the most accurate measurement of successful healing of amputations, when combined with clinical judgment.[4] (*See* Appendix 27-1, Cases 11 to 15.)

§27.13 Amputation: Who Will Wear a Prosthesis?

Most patients (in one survey) under 45 years of age will wear a below knee prosthesis after below knee amputation. Many will have ongoing stump pain for which there is no satisfactory treatment. The stump pain precludes prosthesis wearing in 15 per cent of patients. The percentage for regularly wearing a prosthesis (13 hours per day or more) was much less in above knee amputees. Very few patients with hip disarticulation or hemipelvectomy amputations wear their prosthesis.[5]

---

[3] Dickhaut, *Nutritional Status: Importance in Predicting Wound Healing After Amputation,* 66A JJ Surg 71 (1984); Holstein, *Level Selection in Leg Amputation for Arterial Occlusive Disease: A Comparison of Clinical Evaluation and Shin Perfusion Pressure,* 53 Acata Orthop Scandinav 821 (1982); LoGerfo & Coffman, *Vascular and Microvascular Disease of the Foot in Diabetics. Implication for Foot Care,* 311 NEJM 1615 (1984); Christensen, *Results of Amputation for Gangrene in Diabetic and Non-Diabetic Patients,* 70A JBJ Surg 1514 (1988).

[4] Oishi, *The Role of Non-Invasive Studies in Determining Levels of Amputation,* 70A JBJ Surg 1520 (1988); Cederberg, *Doppler-Determined Segmental Pressures and Wound-Healing in Amputations for Vascular Disease,* 65A JBJ Surg 363 (1983); Dean, *Predictive Value of Ultrasonically Derived Arterial Pressure in Determination of Amputation Level,* 41 Am Surg 731 (1975).

[5] Purry & Hannon, *How Successful is Below Knee Amputation for Injury?,* 20 Injury 32 (1989).

§27.14 Limb Salvage

Extensive lower extremity tissue loss may preclude limb salvage despite successful arterial reconstruction. A variety of free musculocutaneous grafts have been shown to be viable coverage for large tissue losses, thereby preventing amputation. Typical transfer protocols include femorodistal, popliteal distal, or femoropopliteal bypass operations. Tibial angioplasty can be performed to provide sufficient inflow for free tissue transfer. Serratus anterior, scapular, latissimus dorsi, rectus abdominalis, gracilis ulnar, or temporalis free flaps can be used. Free tissue transfer grafting is a fairly new surgical technique with a wide range of uses and should be considered, particularly in trauma cases before amputation is represented (consent) to the patient as the only or preferable option of treatment. A second opinion from a trained microvascular surgeon is appropriate.[6]

§27.15 Foot Amputations

Ischemia and infections of the lower extremity are commonly encountered in associations with atherosclerosis and diabetes mellitus; these are common diseases, particularly in the elderly. These diagnoses may prompt consideration to amputate a portion of the foot distal to the proximal portion of the metatarsal in the foot. This amputation site has a favorable potential for weight bearing, but may not be suitable for removing all necrotic tissue back to viable tissue that will heal. Fatal infection may occur if all necrotic tissue is not excised.

Attempts to determine the most distal amputation site that can be safely selected have incorporated a variety of diagnostic methods. These include (1) transcutaneous oxygen monitoring, (2) local blood pressure measurements, (3) angiography, (4) Doppler vessel measurement, and (5) tissue pH measurement.

The goal of these measurements is to determine preoperatively the most distal amputation level that will allow removal of all infected, necrotic, painful tissue and then heal.

In most reports, no single clinical variable was a consistent contraindication. Radical local surgery, debridement, reconstructive vascular and soft tissue coverage operations, aggressive antibiotic therapy with frequent culture and sensitivity, and wounds that are healing slowly give the best chance of amputation healing at a lower functional level. There is a strong opinion among most amputation surgeons that risking a lower amputation, removing necrotic infected tissue, is "worth the risk," with little morbidity and lower mortality with good anesthetic control. Revision of a nonhealing or incompletely healing amputation is considered preferable to initially doing a "high" below knee or above knee amputation as the first procedure, because "you know" it will heal. (*See* Appendix 27-1, Case 12.)[7]

---

[6] Cronenwett, *Limb Salvage Despite Extensive Tissue Loss,* 124 Arch Surg 609 (1989).

[7] Hodge, *Amputation of the Distal Portion of the Foot,* 82 So Med J 1138 (1989).

Appendix 27-1
Cases

1 ***Carter v Carr,* 68 NC App 23, 314 SE2d 281 (1984)** (physician did not cause injury to patient whose leg had to be amputated after vascular surgery. The patient had a sudden severe cramp in the lower part of her left leg on June 26, 1974. She went to an emergency room, where a vascular surgeon examined her and determined that there was a blockage in the femoral artery and that surgery was necessary. He operated the next day. She continued to experience problems with her foot, which was amputated by the vascular surgeon July 10, 1974. Two days later, he amputated her leg above the knee; the site did not heal. An orthopedic specialist later did additional surgery. In a malpractice suit, the jury found that the patient was not negligently injured by the vascular surgeon and that she was not entitled to recover. The diseased blood vessels were present prior to the vascular surgeon's appearance. The surgeon further presented evidence that the husband delayed the operation because he insisted it not be done under local anesthetic, the normal procedure, but under general anesthesia. When it became clear that amputation was necessary, the patient and her husband insisted that they try to save the knee. The surgeon warned them that infection had spread to her upper leg and that amputation below the knee might not be sufficient and another operation might be necessary. The court reviewed the claims of error at trial in ruling on admission of evidence. One expert testified that the patient's husband refused to allow her to be treated at a medicaid clinic because it was beneath his dignity for her to be seen in a clinic where indigents were seen. That testimony supported the vascular surgeon's testimony that the husband often stood in the way of his wife and her receipt of proper medical care).

2 ***Valbert v Pass,* 866 F2d 237 (7th Cir 1989)** (plaintiff, an 82-year-old man, complained of pain above the right knee and inability to put weight on his leg. A surgeon made a diagnosis of obliterative arterial disease and started the patient on anticoagulant therapy. A consultant surgeon found decreased blood flow in leg using Doppler studies and recommended arteriograms to assess the location of decreased blood flow. The first surgeon did not feel the arteriogram was necessary. A second Doppler study was inconsistent with the first. The patient was admitted to a second hospital where diagnosis of arteriosclerosis with an occlusion was made; an arteriogram was done and a vascular dilator was used. An aneurysm of the popliteal artery was found, and an arterial bypass was carried out. Circulation was not improved and a below knee amputation was carried out. At trial against the first surgeon, a defense verdict resulted. On appeal, it was ruled that the verdict was against the weight of the evidence, which showed that the first surgeon should have done an arthrogram and that his negligence was the proximate cause of the amputation. The court noted that there was

conflicting expert testimony as to the first surgeon's negligence, but that no expert could say that the amputation would not have been necessary if bypass surgery had been performed earlier).

3 ***Hart v Browne,* 103 Cal App 3d 947, 163 Cal Rptr 356 (1980)** (plaintiff underwent a multiple orthopedic procedure to improve function in a paralytic problem. The result was poor and an amputation was recommended and carried out. The plaintiff hired counsel to ascertain if the care he received was up to "standard." The plaintiff first wanted only an expert opinion, and said that if the reviewing expert felt that there was no malpractice, he would not pursue the action. The examining orthopedist found no negligent treatment by the treating orthopedist. The case was dismissed and the statute of limitation subsequently ran. Several years later, the plaintiff's attorney learned that the examining orthopedist was being sued in several similar cases. The plaintiff then brought a malpractice action against the reviewing orthopedist, alleging fraud, deceit, and negligence. The trial court entered a nonsuit order. The court of appeals reversed. The appellate court held that the standard would be what a reasonable reviewing physician would do in the same or similar circumstances. Even though the physician in this case was not a treating physician, he was carrying out a medical function from which malpractice could result).

4 ***Overstreet v Nickelsen,* 170 Ga App 539, 317 SE2d 583 (1984)** (physician was medically negligent, but a patient also contributed substantially to a bad result. The patient cut her finger while slicing meat, and the superficial laceration was sutured. She was sent home by the emergency room physician. Pain continued, and the following day she went to a family physician who seconded the diagnosis that she received at the hospital—superficial lacerations. She last saw her general practitioners 16 days after injury. Pain persisted, so she consulted an orthopedist who discovered that the cut had damaged the flexor tendon sheath and radial digital nerve of one finger. Several additional operations failed to relieve the pain. Eventually, the finger had to be amputated).

5 ***Sherrill v McBride,* 603 SW2d 365 (Tex Civ App 1980)** (malignant melanoma was removed from a patient's foot. Due to complications from a catheter, a hemorrhage developed in his thigh, requiring amputation. This complication was not told the patient; he sued for lack of informed consent. There was expert testimony that the probability of the complication was remote. The jury properly determined that there was no deviation from the standard of care).

6 ***Mortensen v Memorial Hospital,* 105 AD2d 151, 483 NYS2d 264 (1984)** (plaintiff alleged that an orthopedist was negligent in not removing a mass in his leg. The plaintiff claimed that amputation was necessary as a result. The court instructed the jury that, in considering the question of proximate cause, the law does not require that the plaintiff show with certainty that his leg would have been saved if the surgeon had removed the tumor mass in early April. If it is concluded that there was a substantial possibility that amputation could have been avoided had that surgery been

performed in early April, and the defendant's negligence in failing to perform surgery deprived the plaintiff of the substantial possibility, the defendant was liable to the plaintiff. If, however, it is concluded that the substantial possibility did not exist, the plaintiff had not established that he suffered an injury at the hand of the defendant's negligence and was not entitled to recover. There is a question of defining substantial, and the court, when asked by the jury, said that a substantial possibility meant a "significant" or "realistic possibility." The jury returned that there was not a "substantial possibility, but that the doctor was negligent." The jury felt that there was the "slightest possibility of saving the leg," and that the plaintiff did not get that chance. The jury wished to award damages based on the negligence of the doctor (delay in surgery) and failure (by the surgeon) to get a second opinion, and not on the basis of the loss from amputation per se. The court said they must then find for the defendant. On appeal, the issue was the "degree of certainty required to causation in a medical malpractice action." The court again said it would require that a defendant's negligent act or omission be a "substantial" factor in bringing about the plaintiff's injury, and that the substantial factor need not be the only cause which produces the injury. The concept of a "substantial factor in bringing about an injury" and "substantial possibility of avoiding injury" are virtually indistinguishable. As such, the court seems to reject the concept of "any possibility" and the concept of specific percentages, and to adopt the concept of "but for" the defendant's negligence, the patient was deprived of a "significant" or "realistic" possibility of avoiding the alleged injury).

7 *Garfield Park Community Hospital v Vitacco,* 27 Ill App 3d 741, 327 NE2d 408 (1975) (infant had a fracture of the left femur treated by a Bryant's traction that was in place 11 days, but the bandages were never removed. Swelling and pain of the right foot developed, followed by decreasing temperature in the right foot. Deficiency in circulation developed, leading to gangrene requiring amputation. The question in this case was whether the physician or the hospital personnel were responsible for failure to detect the change in circulation. The physician was held liable, both for failure to recognize the diminished circulation and failure to promptly respond to the nurses' request for attention when they did in fact notice it).

8 *Crawford County State Bank v Grady,* 514 NE2d 532 (Ill App Ct 1987) (on February 26, 1979, a four-month-old child was taken to the hospital emergency room. A diagnosis of viral gastroenteritis, dehydration, and acidosis was made. The family pediatrician attempted to perform a duty down on the right saphenous vein of the right ankle to initiate parenteral therapy to reverse dehydration. When the effort was unsuccessfully started, IV therapy in the right femoral area was begun with the leg restrained and immobilized. On the evening of the day of admission, the child's chart indicated swelling and hardness of hip and leg. The leg was cold to the touch and there were ischemic changes. The IV therapy was ended on February 28; records indicated that heat was applied to the leg at various times. On March 1, the child's right foot showed gangrene; on March 7, the child was returned to the hospital where the foot was amputated. The guardian of the child's estate brought an action of malpractice against the pediatrician and hospital. The expert witness for the child said that if the pediatrician was not informed of the swelling of the child's buttock and thigh indicated in the nursing notes of February 27, 1988, it was a breach of the standard of care. He said that despite the documentation of the problem, nothing was done to treat it or to prevent further problems. The jury rendered a verdict against the physician and the hospital. On appeal, the hospital contended, among other things, that the verdict was excessive and that the record was devoid of any evidence of pain and suffering. The court found the amount of the verdict amply supported by the evidence presented. The child had lost her foot and would require additional surgery to correct the varus deformity of her right tibia. She would always walk with a limp and uneven gait, and would probably have degenerative arthritis changes in the good knee because of increased pressure on it. The injury had denied her a normal childhood. She also would continue to have severe pain and suffering. The court concluded that the jury's verdict constituted reasonable compensation and affirmed the lower court's judgment).

9 *McCleary v Wirtz,* 222 NW2d 409 (1974) (plaintiff sued a hospital and surgeon, charging that their negligence in care and treatment proximately caused the amputation of her leg. The hospital counterclaimed for the value of services and supplies furnished the plaintiff. The trial court directed verdicts in favor of the defendant, both in the plaintiff's suit and in the counterclaim. In affirming, the state's high court found, inter alia, a fatal lack of evidence of negligence on the part of the doctor in affixing a cast to the plaintiff's leg and the proximate cause between the need for amputation and the doctor's alleged failure to timely discover the circulatory problem in the patient's leg. The reasoning was that the circulatory problem pre-existed the injury and treatment, that the treatment the patient had did not adversely affect or worsen the circulation, and that the circulation was destined to become further impaired and to lead to amputation).

10 *In re* Harris, 477 A2d 727 (DC 1984) (patient was entitled to be examined by a physician and psychiatrist of her choice before a court-ordered amputation of her leg. The trial court authorized the hospital to schedule and perform the amputation of the patient's gangrenous right leg. The court said that there was a conflict of psychiatric opinion as to whether the patient was competent to make a treatment decision. There also was a conflict of medical testimony as to whether the gangrenous condition was so acute that amputation was necessary to save her life. In this situation, the appellate court found that there were insufficient findings of fact in the trial court record. It remanded the case to the trial court, with instructions that the patient be given an opportunity to undergo psychiatric examination and physician examinations by physicians of her choice. The trial court was then ordered to conduct a hearing and to report the findings to the appellate court within 10 days. It was not a life or death situation).

Comment: The competency of a patient is a difficult problem in many cases. The court itself rarely takes the posture of declaring competency or incompetency, but relies on competent medical opinion; yet, the court must often weight the opinions with the greatest probative value. This is the situation in this case.

11 ***Daniels v Weiss,* 385 So 2d 661 (Fla Dist Ct App 1980); (corrected on denial of rehearing July 21, 1980)** (diabetic patient injured his left foot December 5, 1974 while at work. Two days later when he had his foot treated, physicians suggested he be hospitalized immediately. The patient declined. Three days later he returned; the physician referred him to a hospital where he had staff privileges. The patient, however, insisted on being admitted to another hospital. The patient was treated by a second physician and his leg was later amputated. He filed a malpractice action against the physician who treated him, claiming that the amputation was a result of inadequate treatment. The trial court found the first physician 1 per cent negligent and the second physician 99 per cent negligent. The facts of the case state that the diabetes was not brought under control, that an attempt to preserve the foot by a lesser operation was appropriate, and that failure to do so was below the standard of care. The court further held that there was a known risk that a transmetatarsal amputation might not have worked, but that the patient was entitled to make that decision as part of his consent, rather than assenting to below knee amputation. There was a better than 50 per cent chance that the transmetatarsal amputation would have healed).

12 ***Hemingway v Ochsner Clinic,* 722 F2d 1220 (5th Cir 1984), *cert denied* 105 S Ct 114** (hospital staff doctor gave plaintiff, a known diabetic, Cafergot (a potent vasoconstrictor) when he knew or should have known that the plaintiff was being treated for acute arterial insufficiency. The patient sustained injury to the left leg and foot, leading to amputation).

13 ***Rees v Rodriques,* 701 P2d 1017 (Nev 1985)** (75-year-old woman presented to her physician with a swollen and painful right leg due to an arterial embolus. The practitioner first diagnosed varicose veins and prescribed elastic hose. The delay in diagnosis led to gangrene and amputation. The plaintiff's experts testified that the first treating doctor's treatment was below the standard of care. Experts concluded that elastic hose were contraindicated and that the leg could have been salvaged by embolectomy or arterial bypass surgery. This was sufficient to sustain the plaintiff's verdict).

Comment: Ordinarily, arterial occlusive disease in extremities is easily diagnosed or suspected, and is rarely confused with varicose veins. The pain can be confused with thrombophlebitis early. Diligence in physical examination and re-examination are the usual remedies.

14 ***Finn v Schannel,* 140 Wis 2d 763, 412 NW2d 147 (Ct App 1987)** (patient could not recover on a malpractice claim arising from the failure of a physician to reimplant four fingers lost in an industrial accident. On August 15, 1978, a machine press severed three fingers on the patient's right hand and partially severed the little finger. He was taken to the hospital; no attempt was made to retrieve the fingers from the press. They remained in the press overnight and became necrotic. The next morning, the physician removed tissue from the patient's hand and amputated the little finger and

remaining part of the others. The patient was left with a right hand with only an intact thumb and part of an index finger. The jury found with reasonable certainty that reimplantation would not have been successful. It awarded no damages for the patient's past or future lost earnings, but awarded $135,000 for his past and future mental and emotional distress. On appeal, the court said the jury's conclusions were inconsistent. The conclusion that reimplantation would have been unsuccessful required the court to strike the jury's finding that the two physicians in the hospital were negligent and to dismiss the claim).

15 ***Mortensen v Memorial Hospital,*** **105 AD2d 151, 483 NYS2d 264 (1984)** (surgeon removed a Baker's cyst in the back of a patient's knee. At the time of surgery, it was diagnosed as a tumor mass. It was first thought to be benign, but a pathologist later reported it to be malignant. The surgeon did not want to be the one to tell the patient he needed his leg amputated. In a second operation three months later, the mass was found to be expanded a great deal and involved bone. A mid-thigh amputation was carried out. The malpractice action was based on the failure of the surgeon to inform the patient and his family that there was a malignancy and that amputation was necessary. The surgeon was exonerated from negligence in performing the surgery. The surgery itself did not cause the need for amputation. The case was returned to the jury on the question of whether there was a "lost chance" and whether the delay in informing the patient made any difference as to the indication for amputation).

Comment: The patient is entitled to know from the onset the good as well as the bad aspects of his or her case, the prognosis, and what the treatment alternatives are after a surgical procedure demonstrates a change in the apparent diagnosis, as in the above case. There was an emotional trauma that the family experienced with this more than two-month delay; however, there was obviously no change in the operative procedure required for the initial lesion that the patient presented with to the first orthopedic surgeon.

28

Tumors

§28.01 Bone Tumors

The early recognition of malignant bone tumors is crucial to the survival of the patient and preservation of limbs. Early discovery is often made difficult by a vague presentation and presence of other conditions. With a thorough and systematic clinical and radiographic evaluation, though, many bone lesions can be diagnosed at an early stage. The possibility of bone tumor should be included in the differential diagnosis in patients presenting with progressive pain that increases at night and in patients with symptoms more severe than expected for a given injury or health problem. Referral to a regional cancer treatment center is appropriate for biopsy and definitive treatment when a lesion is suspected of being aggressive, unless the orthopedist is a cancer specialist knowledgeable in bone tumors.[1]

Bone tumors are a challenge to the physician, and only a thorough knowledge of clinical presentation, natural evolution, staging characteristics, histopathology, and response to treatment can lead to proper management. Some malignant bone tumors are life-threatening, but many tumors are benign and heal spontaneously or respond well to minimal surgical intervention.

With the increasing effectiveness of adjuvant chemotherapy, prognosis for many types of malignant bone tumors has improved. A combination of chemotherapy and limb-salvage procedures can now help survival rates, once possible only with radical amputation. Advances in reconstructive techniques allow many patients to retain or regain adequate function after the tumor is removed. Development of a staging system based on the biologic activity and extent of the lesion has enabled physicians to design more effective courses of treatment. (*See* Appendix 28-1, Cases 1-9.)

There is often disagreement between physician and attorney as to the cause of malignancy. These tumors are often first detected after injury, with the patient feeling the injury caused the malignancy or caused the tumor to spread and become life-threatening. (*See* Appendix 28-1, Case 8.)

§28.02 Classification

Bone tumors, whether benign or malignant, are classified by the cell or tissue type from which they originate: osseous, cartilaginous, fibrous, reticuloendothelial, and vascular. The histogenesis is usually determined by the tissue that the tumor cells produce. Tissue type can also be determined from histologic similarities between the tumor cells and normal cells. Tumors producing osteoid probably originate from osteoblasts. The origin of some lesions, however, such as giant cell tumor of bone, remains unknown.

Bone tumors can also be categorized by their biologic behavior—their ability to grow and extend beyond their natural barriers. The anatomic barriers include the capsule, a shell of bone or fibrous tissue around the lesion, and the reactive zone, formed by proliferation of mesenchymal, neovascular, and inflammatory tissue between the capsule and surrounding normal bone. Additionally, the compartmental boundaries are cortical bone, periosteum, and articular cartilage. Intracapsular lesions remain encased in an intact capsule, while those that breach the capsule are extra-capsular.

---

[1] O'Connor & Sim, *Early Recognition of Bone Tumors,* 6 J Musculoskel Med 124 (1989).

Intra-compartmental lesions remain in the compartment of origin and thus do not penetrate the bone cortex. Tumors that erode or destroy the bone cortex are extra-compartmental. Trauma or excision may also inadvertently spread tumor cells outside the compartment or origin.

§28.03 Benign Tumors

Benign tumors lack the capacity to metastasize. Their behavior ranges from completely inactive to wildly aggressive; these can often be predicted from a combination of clinical, radiographic, and histologic features. Benign tumors are classified as inactive, active, or aggressive. Both types can cause local destruction despite the inability to metastasize. Locally aggressive benign tumors are not uncommon in children.

Inactive benign tumors are also called static or latent. They are completely enclosed by a capsule of mature fibrous tissue or cortex-like bone. They remain localized and do not deform or expand the encasing bone. The reactive zone is minimal, and the histologic characteristics are benign (low cell-to-matrix ratio; mature, well-differentiated matrices; no hyperchromasia, anaplasia, or pleomorphism). Inactive benign tumors are usually asymptomatic.

Active benign tumors continue to grow and may deform the overlying cortical bone or articular cartilage. However, they remain encapsulated with a mature fibrous tissue or trabecular ring (rather than a cortical shell). The inner aspect of the capsule may be irregular, giving the tumor a septated or loculated appearance. A thin reactive zone develops around the tumor. Active benign tumors cause mild symptoms and occasionally lead to pathologic fractures and dysfunction.

Aggressive benign tumors have the invasive behavior of low-grade malignant tumors. As the tumor slowly penetrates normal tissue with fingerlike projections, the reactive zone forms a capsule or pseudo-capsule around the expanding lesion. Although this does not inhibit tumor growth, the pseudoencapsulation does prevent tumor nodules from extending directly into normal tissue. These lesions destroy or resorb the surrounding bone and permeate into adjacent bone or compartments. Aggressive benign tumors have a high cell-to-matrix ratio and clearly differentiated bone matrices of varying maturity. In contrast to the behavioral properties, the cytologic features are benign. Aggressive benign tumors are often symptomatic and are associated with pathologic fractures.

§28.04 Malignant Tumors

Malignant tumors have the ability to metastasize—that is, form new tumor foci at distant sites. The behavior of malignant tumors varies widely. Some are characterized by indolent local growth, low incidence of metastasis, and a protracted interval between recognition of the primary tumor and metastasis. Others exhibit aggressive destructive local growth, high incidence of metastasis, and the primary tumor and the metastasis are recognized simultaneously. Like benign tumors, malignant tumor behavior can often be predicted from a combination of clinical, radiographic, and histologic features. Aggressive behavior is usually demonstrated by the tumor's histologic mitotic activity, degree of cellular differentiation, and/or degree of tissue necrosis. This "histologic grade" best reflects the biologic activity of the tumor, the best option for treatment, and ultimate prognosis. Assessment of histologic type and grade is the key to successful treatment. Both surgical and nonsurgical treatments are used to alter the course of the disease. (*See* Appendix 28-1, Cases 9 and 10.)

§28.05 Low-Grade Sarcomas

Low-grade sarcomas are malignant tumors that grow slowly and invade local tissue, yet have a low risk of metastasis. The continuity of the capsule is interrupted in many places, and the generous reactive zone forms a pseudocapsule around the lesion. Isolated satellite nodules are usually found in the reactive zone. In contrast to the rapid destruction seen with high-grade sarcomas, low-grade sarcomas gradually erode the natural tumor barriers. With time, and especially with repeated cycles of unsuccessful excisions and recurrences, the risk of transforming into high-grade sarcomas or metastasizing to distant sites increases. Malignant cytologic features such as anaplasia, pleomorphism, hyperchromasia, and a modest number of mitoses are evident. Necrosis, hemorrhage, and vascular incursion of varying degrees are typical in malignant tumors; these features are rarely seen in benign tumors. Low-grade sarcomas are usually asymptomatic, appearing as slowly growing masses.

§28.06 High-Grade Sarcomas

High-grade sarcomas overgrow the wide reactive zone so fast that they appear to have very little or no pseudoencapsulation. Uninhibited by natural barriers, they extend to adjacent tissues by destroying cortical bone, articular cartilage, and joint capsules. The margin between the lesion and surrounding bone is poorly demarcated and has a diffuse permeative border. Satellite nodules occur in the reactive tissue, and "skip" metastases (tumor nodules in ostensibly uninvolved areas of the same bone) are found well outside the reactive zone, usually in the medullary canal. The histologic features include high cell-to-matrix ratio, poor differentiation of immature matrices, and all the cytologic characteristics of malignancy.

§28.07 Staging of Tumors

Staging studies, based on the progressive changes in the natural history of the lesion, are used to choose appropriate treatment and predict prognosis, response to treatment, and risk of local recurrence or metastasis. Bone tumors can be staged accurately only after careful clinical, radiologic, and histologic studies. Clinical and radiographic studies should be done prior to biopsy or other surgical procedures.

The stage of the lesion represents an inter-relationship among three factors: grade (G), an assessment of the biologic aggressiveness of the tumor; anatomic site or extent (T), intra-capsular, extra-capsular, or intra-compartmental/extra-compartmental; and presence or absence of metastases. Benign tumors are designated as Stage I (inactive, latent), Stage II (active), and Stage III (aggressive). Malignant tumors are designated as Stage I (low-grade invasive), Stage II (high-grade destructive), and Stage III (metastatic). Malignant tumors are further stratified as intra-compartmental or extra-compartmental. Tumors may undergo transition from one stage to another; benign tumors often become latent after skeletal growth has stopped. Certain benign tumors can become Stage I, II, or III sarcomas and malignant tumors can metastasize with time or after irradiation, inadequate excision, or repeated surgical intervention.[2]

§28.08 Treating Bone and Soft Tissue Tumors

Emphasis in treating bone and soft tissue neoplasms has shifted to limb salvage procedure. This requires accurate identification of the lesions and, even more important, the extent of the bone and/or soft tissue involvement. Imaging techniques play an important role in preoperative evaluation and staging; detecting local recurrence or metastasis after treatment is equally important. (*See* Appendix 28-1, Case 11.)

Diagnosis and characterization of bone lesions are often possible with routine x-rays and occasionally with the aid of tomography. However, the evaluation of soft tissue involvement or detection of primary soft tissue lesions is difficult.

Ultrasound examination is helpful in separating solid from cystic superficial lesions. CT scans and MRI studies are the standard techniques for outlining tumors and evaluating the extent of the tumors with essential information as to whether local resection or other limb salvaging procedures may be possible. MRI studies have superior soft tissue contrast compared to CT scanning. CT scan, on the other hand, can outline and show subtle calcifications that help characterize the histology of the lesion. Frequently, both CT scans and MRI studies are necessary for the best evaluation and staging of the tumor.

Evaluation of patients after surgery may be particularly difficult. Again, metal implants interfere with CT imaging, but there is little artifact produced in MRI studies. Differentiation of postoperative changes or scar tissue from tissue is difficult, and this seems to be best done by MRI studies.

Osteoid osteomas can often be identified on plain x-rays. If plain x-rays are negative or equivocal, bone scanning is performed. It is important to

---

[2] Enneking & Conrad III, *Common Bone Tumors,* 41 Clinical Symposia 3 (1983).

include views well above and below the lesion for the osteoid osteoma itself can be missed by virtue of the referred pain pattern that it frequently demonstrates. A small dose of Technetium-99 may be given preoperatively, and by using a small probe or gamma counter in the operating room the tumor can be localized so that complete resection can be carried out, preventing failure of the operative procedure.

Bone scans have been useful in detecting metastasis from soft tissue tumors and from primary bone tumors. Some patterns, such as multiple areas of increased uptake, are highly diagnostic of metastasis. Solid lesions must be correlated with x-rays to be certain that the increased uptake is not due to benign disease. MRI studies are frequently very helpful in separating benign from malignant lesions, using T1 and T2 weighted sequences. (*See* Appendix 28-1, Cases 6, 12, 13, 14 and 15.)

§28.09 Myeloma

Myeloma is the most common malignant bone tumor and accounts for nearly 50 per cent of malignant neoplasms involving the skeleton. It affects men twice as often as women, with its peak incidence in the seventh decade and rarely before the age of 40. Bone pain and pathological fracture involving the spine are frequent, although any bone may harbor the tumor.[3]

§28.10 Giant Cell Tumors

Giant cell tumors represent approximately 5 per cent of bone tumors, with more than one-half being located about the knee. Tumors show variable aggressiveness and a rare tendency to metastasize. Histological grading of tumors has not been particularly helpful in predicting recurrence. Recurrence may correlate with the method of tumor removal rather than with the initial grade of tumor. Treatment varies depending on the aggressiveness of the tumor, and includes curettage, chemical cauterization, thermal necrosis, and wide resection with reconstruction.[4] (*See* Appendix 28-1, Case 16.)

§28.11 Osteomyelitis versus Bone Tumors

The problem of the differential diagnosis between subacute osteomyelitis and primary bone tumors may be a difficult one. Presenting symptoms, duration of disease, laboratory data, and location of the pathological process are

---

[3] Mendez, *Myeloma,* Surg Rounds Orthop, Jan 1989, at 104; D.C. Dahlin & K.K. Unni, Bone Tumors (4th ed 1986); G.B. Greenfield, Radiology of Bone Disease (4th ed 1986).

[4] Schwartz & Shives, *Surgical Management of Giant Cell Tumor of Bone,* Complic in Orthop, Sept/Oct, 1989, at 155.

of little assistance. The final diagnosis and definitive treatment is usually made by open biopsy with pathological and bacteriologic studies. Failure to timely biopsy such lesions may delay or complicate the prognosis.[5]

§28.12 Enchondromatosis

Enchondromatosis is a non-hereditary skeletal disorder characterized by persistent cartilage in several bones. It has been recently recognized that there is a significant potential for malignant degeneration, particularly in people who have Maffucci syndrome, where the incidence of low-grade sarcoma is relatively high.[6]

§28.13 Bone Tumors versus Traumatic Injury

One of the great fears of a physician is missing an important diagnosis—for humane reasons, as well as for the medicolegal ramifications. The loss of time from treatment and the further progression of the illness can be catastrophic. Most traumatic sports injuries are strains, sprains, and contusions. A large number of these are overuse injuries, because the symptoms are nonspecific or similar to other conditions. Because soft tissue and bone tumors occur in the same areas as sport injuries, delay in treatment of a tumor often occurs, because it was thought to be a sports injury.

§28.14 Bone Tumors in Sports Injuries

Appearance of sports injuries can be deceiving. Often, the first examiner does not feel that the clinical picture is of sufficient severity to pursue an in-depth diagnosis or follow-up. Follow-up of these sport injuries is essential and should be the duty of the coach and/or trainer as well as the physician. The most commonly missed diagnoses are osteogenic sarcoma, myositis ossificans, osteoid osteoma, periosteal calcification, and fibrosarcoma. The following rules of thumb may be helpful:

1. If a patient does not respond to the initial treatment, assume the condition is more complicated than originally thought
2. If the original x-rays are of poor quality or were taken a long time ago, repeating them is indicated
3. If the patient has not responded to treatment despite apparently normal x-rays, other diagnostic tests and consultations should be sought[7]

---

[5] Amir, *Subacute Osteomyelitis Presenting as Bone Tumors,* 12 Orthop 245 (1989); Lindenbaum & Alexander, *Infections Simulating Bone Tumors,* 184 Clin Orthop 193 (1984).

[6] Schwartz, *The Malignant Potential of Enchondromatosis,* 69A JBJ Surg 269 (1987).

[7] McKirgan & Steingard, *Bone Tumors Masquerading as Traumatic Injury,* 17 Physician & SportsMed 121 (1989).

(*See* Appendix 28-1, Cases 8, 17 and 18.)

§28.15 Spine Tumors

Tumors invading the spine are usually classified as extra-dural or intra-dural and are further divided into extra-medullary or intra-medullary. An accurate diagnosis is made on histological data.

Extra-dural tumors are usually metastatic to the vertebra that subsequently invade the epidural space. Almost any neophyte can spread to the spine. Most common are lung, breast, and prostate. Primary bone tumors such as osteogenic sarcoma and giant cell tumor are occasionally seen. Spinal cord compression with associated symptoms usually develops late and may be slowly progressive, but a rapidly growing tumor can cause acute neurological deterioration secondary to infarction of the spinal cord. Areas of metastases in the spine are susceptible to trauma—to falls, etc.

The patient with known primary cancer who has spinal pain must be assumed to have metastasis. A radionucleotide bone scan reveals the lesion earlier than plain x-rays. If neurological symptoms are present, CT scans, MRI studies, or myelography are appropriate.

Epidural tumors must be treated before serious spinal cord dysfunction develops. Treatment, however, is controversial. High-dose corticosteroids should be administered, and the lesion should be irradiated if primary lesion is known. If there is no known primary tumor, if the tumor is known not to be radio-sensitive, or if the neurological status is rapidly deteriorating, surgical decompression should be done.

Radiation therapy is usually administered postoperatively. Intra-dural tumors include primary tumors, both benign and malignant, capable of producing rapid weakness in extremities, loss of urinary bladder and bowel control, and back pain. Evaluation of these is by the same tests mentioned above—CT scan, MRI, lumbar myelogram—and treatment of such tumors is by neurosurgical procedure.[8]

§28.16 Primary Tumors—Spine

Primary tumors of the spine are rare, accounting for about 10 per cent of all bone tumors and about 0.4 per cent of all tumors. Primary tumors are far less common than metastatic spine lesions, particularly in adults. Other non-neoplastic conditions producing spinal symptoms are much more common. Nevertheless, primary tumors of the spine represent a diagnostic and therapeutic challenge to the spinal surgeon. A high index of suspicion must be present if one is to accuratel˯ diagnose and successfully treat these lesions, since the most common early complaint is back pain. Although these lesions are often found in compromising locations—around the spinal cord,

[8] Weinstein, *Surgical Approach to Spine Tumors,* 12 Orthrop 897 (1989).

nerve roots, major organs, and blood vessels—results of treatment can positively affect survival and quality of life.

§28.17 Buttock Tumors

A patient's ability to describe and precisely locate pain may be quite poor or even misleading. When a patient complains of hip pain, he or she may be speaking of buttock or groin areas. In the low back, the pain may be felt in the buttocks and may be called hip pain by the patient. Because the physician accepts the patient's complaint at face value, he or she may not examine the buttock area and may miss the tumor mass. Common tumors found in the buttocks are lipomas, abscesses, and metastatic malignancy. These tumors are missed if palpation of the buttocks is not part of a routine physical examination of a patient complaining of "hip" or "back" pain. Palpation is best done with the patient in a prone position on the examining table.[9]

§28.18 Malignant Pelvic Tumors

A viable alternative to hemipelvectomy for the treatment of a malignant pelvic tumor is an operation in which the limb is salvaged. It is appropriate to salvage the limb when the procedure provides a satisfactory surgical margin or when an amputation cannot provide a better margin. Generally, function is better after a limb-sparing procedure than it is after hemipelvectomy and fitting of a prosthesis. Additionally, reconstructive procedures to increase function of the salvaged limb further improve the quality of life.

Tumor types appropriate for limb salvage typically include chondrosarcoma, osteosarcoma, fibrosarcoma, and Ewing sarcoma.[10]

§28.19 Soft Tissue Tumors of the Foot

While most soft tissue lesions about the foot or ankle are reactive or inflammatory, some are true neoplasms. Primary sarcomas arising distal to the knee comprise only eight per cent of approximately 4,500 sarcomas discovered each year; metastatic tumors at that location are rare. However, concern always exists as to whether or not a given lesion is a malignant process.

Many types of soft tissue lesions are encountered in the foot. There are 82 distinct benign and malignant soft tissue lesions and tumors of 10 major histogenic types that can arise in the distal part of the leg that are recognized by The World Health Organization classification system. Some of these are generally not considered to be true neoplasms, such as ganglion cysts and

---

[9] Hoffman, *Buttock Masses as a Cause of "Hip" Pain,* J Musculoskeletal Med, June 1989, at 111.

[10] O'Connor & Sim, *Salvage of the Limb in the Treatment of Malignant Pelvic Tumors,* 71A JBJ Surg 481 (1989).

xanthomas. Epidermal inclusion cysts or rheumatoid nodules may closely mimic true soft tissue tumors. The large number of different histogenic types, along with low incidence, makes it difficult for a physician to gain a lot of clinical experience with tumors and tumor-like lesions of the foot and ankle.

It is well known that initial treatment for a neoplasm, including management of biopsy, influences the final outcome of the patient. Therefore, the possibility that a tumor is malignant must always be considered.[11]

§28.20 Heterotropic Ossification

Hetertropic ossification about joints is a complication often seen following total joint replacements. Solid bony replacements in or about joint capsule and pericapsular tissue may lead to significant and/or painful limited joint motion. Causes are not known, but a great incidence is seen in surgeries (or injuries) in which residual bleeding and/or excessive soft tissue trauma has occurred (including surgical trauma). Prevention by good, clean, quick, skilled surgery lessens the chance of this complication. Use of prophylactic chemicals in patients "at risk" is recommended. Other high-risk patients include those with advanced hypertropic degenerative or post-traumatic joints.[12]

---

[11] Kirby, Shereff & Lewis, *Soft-Tissue Tumors and Tumor-Like Lesions of the Foot,* 71A JBJ Surg 621 (1989).

[12] Figgie, *Elbow Arthroplasty Includes Heterotropic Ossification Risk,* 12 Adv in Orthop Surg 1 (1988).

Appendix 28-1
Cases

1 ***Friedman v Radiology Group PC,* No 103033 (Mich Ct App)** (unanimous Michigan Court of Appeals affirmed summary judgment in favor of physician in a suit alleging failure to diagnose cancer, ruling that evidence of prior acts of alleged malpractice was properly excluded).

2 ***Schneider v Memorial Hospital for Cancer & Allied Disease,* 100 AD2d 583, 473 NYS2d 524 (1984)** (plaintiff's evidence justified jury's conclusion that (1) failure of defendant, on plaintiff's continued complaint of back pain, to take more vigorous measure to diagnose cause of pain, constituted departure from "standard" in view of expert testimony that plaintiff was at high risk of developing metastasis from her breast cancer, (2) the type of breast cancer she had typically spread to bone and often to the spine, and (3) delay in diagnosis of metastasis to her bones, and particularly her spine, was the cause of the collapse of two of her vertebral bodies and of consequent pain and loss of mobility).

3 ***Adams v Luros,* 406 NE2d 1199 (Ind Ct App 1980)** (physician allegedly negligently failed to diagnose a tumor in the mid-region of a patient's spinal cord. The patient consulted the physician in January 1973 for lower back pain, partial paralysis of the right leg, and toe drop. The physician admitted him to the hospital twice and did extensive tests, but could not diagnose the problem. The patient stated that the physician told him to live with it until it got better or worse. In 1976, the patient began to experience additional difficulty with his leg. Eventually, in 1977 he consulted another orthopedist who gave him a diagnosis of tumor in the mid-region of the spinal cord. The tumor was removed by surgery, but the patient was left without the use of his legs. The patient filed a suit against the physician on February 26, 1979 alleging that he was negligent in failing to order a myelogram. A default judgment was entered. Reversing the decision, the appellate court said that the trial court should not have granted summary judgment to the physician. The new statute of limitation in the Indiana Malpractice Act did not apply to the patient's claim. The case was retried, based on the fact that the patient did not have knowledge of the negligence until March 1977, and came within the statute of limitation).

Comment: In difficult diagnostic cases, rather than abandon and tell patients that they must live with their problem, it is prudent to continue to follow them and to continue to do appropriate diagnostic tests. It appears from the outset that myelography would have been appropriate in this case. Under current practice, MRI studies and CT scanning would have demonstrated the tumor quite readily. Criticism of the evaluation of the patient is appropriate.

4 ***Knopfer v Louisiana Patients' Compensation Fund,* 527 So 2d 326 (La Ct App 1988), *rehg denied* (July 29, 1988)** (patient was entitled

$500,000 in damages for misdiagnosis of a soft tissue tumor which was finally diagnosed as malignant melanoma. When a thigh tumor recurred and was re-excised, a definitive diagnosis was made. The first pathological slides were reviewed and the diagnosis of first surgery specimen was found to be wrong, being malignant melanoma then. Radical surgery on the thigh was carried out. The appellate court agreed that the patient's chance of survival was substantially reduced by the 18-month delay in making a correct diagnosis. The hospital and its pathologist tendered their $100,000 insurance limits, and the surgeon was released. The trial court awarded $500,000 plus future medical expenses).

5 ***Whitaker v Zirkle,*** **374 SE2d 106 (Ga Ct App 1988),** ***reh denied*** **(Oct 6, 1988),** ***cert denied*** **(Ga Nov 23, 1988)** (pathologist and hospital were not entitled to summary judgment, but an operating surgeon was absolved, in an action by a patient alleging misdiagnosis of malignancy. A mole removed 10 years before was interpreted by a pathologist as not cancerous. The tumor recurred and was reoperated, with a diagnosis of malignant melanoma. On re-review, the original tumor was interpreted as malignant. The statute of limitation was tolled by the fact that the patient did not know of the negligence until the second surgery).

6 ***Mortensen v Memorial Hospital,*** **105 AD2d 151, 483 NYS2d 264 (1984)** (plaintiff alleged that an orthopedist was negligent in not removing a mass in his leg and claimed that amputation was necessary as a result. The court instructed the jury that, in considering the question of proximate cause in the case, the law did not require that the plaintiff show with certainty that his leg would have been saved if the surgeon had removed the tumor mass in early April. If it were concluded there was a substantial possibility that amputation could have been avoided by surgery in early April, and defendant's negligence in failing to perform surgery deprived the plaintiff of the substantial possibility, the defendant was liable to the plaintiff. If, however, it were concluded that a substantial possibility did not exist, the plaintiff had not established that he had suffered an injury at the hand of the defendant's negligence, and was not entitled to recover. The court, when asked by the jury, said that "substantial possibility" meant a "significant" or "realistic possibility." The jury returned that there was not a substantial possibility, but that the doctor was negligent. The jury felt that there was the slightest possibility of saving the leg, and that the plaintiff did not get this chance. The jury wished to award damages based on the negligence of the doctor (delay in surgery) and the failure of the surgeon to get a second opinion, not based on loss from the amputation, per se. The court said that they must then find for the defendant. On appeal, the issue forwarded was the "degree of certainty required to causation in a medical malpractice action." The court again said it would require that a defendant's negligent act or omission be a "substantial" factor in bringing about the plaintiff's injury, but that the substantial factor need not be the only cause which produces the injury. The concept of a "substantial factor in bringing about an injury" and "substantial possibility of avoiding injury" are virtually indistinguishable. As such, the court seems to the reject the concept of "any possibility" and the concept of specific percentages, and to adopt the concept of "but for" the defendant's negligence, the patient was deprived of a "significant" or "realistic" possibility of avoiding the alleged injury).

7 ***Evers v Dollinger,* 95 NJ 399, 471 A2d 405 (1984)** (defendant negligently failed to diagnose a malignant tumor and affect prompt and proper treatment. The Supreme Court of New Jersey held that the increased risk that cancer would develop in the future, attributable to the delay in diagnosis and treatment, was a compensable injury. The court further held that the plaintiff could recover for mental suffering which resulted from the defendant's failure to diagnose and promptly treat the malignant tumor).

8 ***Hammond v Fidelity & Casualty Co,* 419 So 2d 829 (La)** (orthopedist, general surgeon, and an oncologist all offered prevailing medical views that cancer cannot be caused by orthopedic trauma. Nevertheless, the Louisiana Supreme Court held that physicians and jurists do not mean the same thing when they speak of "cause." The case at hand involved a truck driver who became painful while doing his regular work. He sprained his arm when his truck dropped into a hole, bruising it. It did not heal, and sarcoma was ultimately identified and appropriate surgery was carried out for the tumor, although from a physician's point of view, this was a difficult case to understand. The majority of a nine-justice tribunal acknowledged the weight of medical testimony, but noted that the lower court had "failed to distinguish the 'medical' meaning of cause from the 'legal' meaning of cause." A law review article was cited: "The doctor must realize that a determination of legal responsibility is not the same thing as a finding of a pathological cause or source for disease").

9 ***Kaplan v Berger,* 539 NE2d 1267 (Ill Ct App)(1989)** (neither defendant orthopedist communicated well with a patient who had a mass in right thigh. As a result, the patient was lulled into a state of false security and did not aggressively seek a diagnosis until metastatic schwannoma was later diagnosed. In 1981, the patient, who had a family and personal history of cancer (carcinoma of breast), consulted the first orthopedist regarding a mass in her right thigh; x-rays of the thigh were negative. The orthopedist made an appointment for the patient to have an ultrasound study, but did not discuss why or the possible diagnosis with patient, and did not make a return appointment with patient. The patient never obtained the ultrasound study. Several months later, the patient had a lump removed from her breast by another surgeon who found a mass in her thigh, but said he did not do "leg work," although he had removed a mass from her leg in the past. In February 1983, a neurosurgeon removed a mass from her right thigh with malignant diagnosis, and the tumor was noted to have spread to the groin in August 1983. The patient sued the two orthopedists in March 1985; they claimed that the statute of limitation had run and obtained summary judgment. The appellate court agreed that the patient could not know the nature of her problem until the time of biopsy. Further, the higher court found that the patient's failure to follow the first orthopedist's recommendations were

based on an understandable uncertainty caused by orthopedist inaction. Although aware that the patient had a mass in her thigh, the orthopedist did not take a family history (thought to be pertinent in this case) and did not tell the patient to return or make appropriate referral; this court felt that enough evidence existed for a jury to decide).

10 ***Stager v Schneider,* 494 A2d 1307 (DC 1985) (citing, Annotation)** (action against a radiologist and a surgeon for failing to inform a patient of a spot on a lung x-ray taken routinely before foot surgery. The patient later had a second surgery for removal of a malignant tumor of the lung. The patient was not contributorily negligent in not inquiring about the x-ray, but the treating physicians owed the patient a duty to inform her).

11 ***Ray v Wagner,* 286 Minn 354, 176 NW2d 101, 49 ALR3d 497 (1970)** (it was shown that a physician failed to inform a patient of a test that indicated the possibility of cancer, but that the communication of the information had been frustrated by the contributory negligence of the patient).

12 ***Schaecher v Reinwein,* 41 Ill App 3d 1055, 355 NE2d 351 (1976)** (orthopedic surgeon did a partial myelogram (lumbar) but did not carry the myelogram to the first cervical level or order a bone scan or electromyelogram, and performed a lumbar laminectomy without finding a cancerous tumor of the thoracic spine. The plaintiff's expert did not testify as to the standard of care in the defendant's community where there was no evidence that bone scans and electromyelograms were not available and where the plaintiff's expert offered no opinion as to the existence of a tumor at the time of diagnosis and treatment by the defendant).

Comment: This scenario happens often in orthopedic practice. Currently, most communities have or are close to sophisticated diagnostic facilities (CT scan, MRI studies, bone scanning, and electromyelograms). The bottom line is awareness of the possibility of a cervical or dorsal lesion explaining lumbar pathology.

13 ***Tams v Kolz,* 530 A2d 1217 (DC 1987)** (patient went to surgery for removal of a cancerous tumor located between her bladder and vaginal wall. In the five-hour operation, more than 400 items were used, including instruments, sutures, sponges, and lap pads. According to later testimony, the surgeon made a visual and manual examination of internal organs and ascertained that nurses' counts were correct before closing the incision. Four days following the operation, x-rays were taken of patient's abdomen and a copy was forwarded to the surgeon. One month after the patient's discharge from the hospital, x-rays were taken because of the patient's complaints of abdominal pain, which indicated a foreign object. At a second operation, the surgeon found a laparotomy pad that had adhered to an intestinal membrane. The damaged segment of the intestine was removed when the pad was extracted. The patient sued the surgeon for malpractice, alleging that he was negligent in failing to detect the pad before closing the first operation and failing to read the x-ray report which indicated presence of a foreign object. She contended that if she had been re-opened promptly, removal of the segment of the intestine would have been avoided. At trial, the physician

who testified for the patient indicated that the physician had a duty to read the x-ray report. He said that x-rays had indicated a drain was visible in the abdomen and that the concluding paragraph marked "Impressions" did not refer to that finding. He also said it was up to the radiologist to make it known to the physician that there was either a drain or a foreign body present. He pointed out that the key part of the report was the "Impressions" section, because anything significant would have been included in that. The court entered a jury verdict for the surgeon. On appeal, the court pointed out that the patient's expert had effectively limited the surgeon's duty in studying the x-ray reading to the "Impression" section. Therefore, even if the surgeon had read the section, he would have remained unaware that the x-ray had disclosed the possible foreign object. Because he failed to read the impression, this was not the cause of the aggravation of the patient's intestinal damage and the trial court ruling could not be considered erroneous).

14 ***Taylor v DiRico,*** **124 Ariz 513, 606 P2d 3 (1980)** (action against a surgeon alleging negligence in performing a biopsy (excision of "lump") in axilla, resulting in a fatal infection. The verdict for the plaintiff was supported by expert testimony as to the "standard" before and after surgery as to proper procedures to diagnose and treat lymphoma, which the surgeon contended killed the patient).

15 ***Leonhard v New Orleans East Orthopedic Clinic,*** **485 So 2d 1008 (La Ct App),** ***cert denied,*** **489 So 2d 919 (La 1986)** (malpractice action against an orthopedist for damages resulting from injury to a nerve root after the surgeon performed a vertebral needle biopsy on the plaintiff to diagnose a vertebral lesion and whether it was malignant. The failure of the surgeon to inform the patient that the malignancy would likely be incurable did not vitiate the patient's written consent to the procedure, since the biopsy was performed to rule out, rather than to diagnose, malignancy, and since informing the patient of the chances for recovery from cancer at the early stage of testing was unnecessary, inappropriate, and inadvisable).

Comment: The injury to the nerve root, where the risk of the procedure is usually avoidable by following correct technique, was probably negligent.

16 ***Aasheim v Humberger,*** **695 P2d 824 (1985)** (action against an orthopedic surgeon for diagnosing a plaintiff's knee condition as chondromalacia of the patella without taking x-rays which, when later taken, showed a giant cell tumor, requiring excision of the knee joint and implantation of a total knee prosthesis. The trial court erred in failing to give a "lost chance" instruction. Instead, the court instructed that the plaintiff was required to show only "that negligence on the part of the defendant deprived her of a reasonable medical probability of obtaining a better result," which meant that the plaintiff would have to establish there was better than a 50 per cent chance of obtaining a better result).

Comment: Giant cell tumors of bone embrace many tumor variations, with difficulty in prognosis. Some are benign, while others are malignant from the outset. Many benign tumors change in time to malignant.

17 ***Gray v Keiger,* 540 NE2d 1344 (1989)** (18-year-old had injuries in an automobile accident, including trauma to the left leg. The orthopedist x-rayed the leg, found no fracture, and observed a cystic lesion in lower tibia, but did no further investigation of the cyst. Two years later, the orthopedist saw the plaintiff for a ski injury and mentioned the cyst, but said that "it probably is benign." The patient sought a second opinion and, on biopsy, the diagnosis of adamantinoma was made—a tumor with the potential to metastasize and cause death. The orthopedist's negligence in failing to further investigate the lesion shown on x-rays during the first injury and treatment period, which lesions could have caused the patient's injuries and could have been prevented had the cancer been discovered and treated at the earliest date, led the Appeals Court of Massachusetts to affirm the plaintiff's verdict of $750,000).

18 ***LoDico v Caputi,* 517 NY2d 640 (App Div 1987)** (in May 1983, a patient noticed a sudden onset of numbness in his right thumb and first and second fingers. Several days later, he noticed that his entire right arm was weak and that his fingers were tingling. The arm/hand symptoms continued to persist for several days, and he noted pain in the posterior aspect of his neck. On May 9, 1983, he sought medical treatment from an osteopathic physician, who diagnosed the patient's condition as cervical-dorsal strain and treated him with oral medication as well as manipulation. Seven weeks later, the patient was seen by a neurologist who found no neurological abnormalities. Since the patient was not able to work after the onset of symptoms, he filed for workers' compensation benefits and directly reported to a physician for examination of disability. On September 9, 1983, a physician examined him and forwarded a report to the employer's workers' compensation company, which expressed the opinion that the patient had recovered from the alleged injury of May 1983, had no evidence of intervertebral disc injury, disease, or peripheral damage, and should be able to return to his usual work without restrictions and limitations. Subsequent to that examination, the patient was diagnosed as suffering from a brain stem tumor. The patient filed malpractice actions against several physicians, including the one who examined him for workers' compensation. The trial court denied his motion to dismiss the claim against him. He argued that there was never a physician-patient relationship between them. The court denied the physician's motion. The appellate court said the physician who had conducted the examination of the patient solely for the purpose of rating the injury for the insurance company for workers' compensation was not liable to him for failure to properly diagnose a latent brain tumor. The physician neither offered nor intended to treat or care for the patient, and he had no reason to believe the patient would rely on the report to the insurance company).

19 ***McGrady v Wright,* 151 Ariz App 534, 128 P2d 338 (1986)** (action against surgeon alleged failure to obtain informed consent and failure to discuss with the patient a possible brachial plexus injury or the consequences of not having a tumor about the shoulder removed. Expert evidence stated that a reasonable and prudent surgeon under such circumstances would

(1) biopsy the tumor and ascertain whether it was malignant, and then advise the patient of treatment options, and (2) having commenced the surgery and seen the extent of tumor, would have withdrawn to advise the patient of his options at that point. The evidence precluded a directed verdict for the defendant on the issue of informed consent. The duty of a physician to disclose risks is measured by the usual practices of the medical profession).

20 ***Sherrill v McBride,* 603 SW2d 365 (Tex Civ App 1980)** (malignant melanoma was removed from a patient's foot. Due to complications from a catheter, a hemorrhage developed in the thigh, requiring amputation. This remote complication was not explained to the patient and he sued for lack of informed consent. There was expert testimony that the complication was remote. The jury properly determined that there was no deviation from "standard," and the finding for the defendant was affirmed).

21 ***Bullock v Newman,* 368 SE2d 562 (1989)** (plaintiff was not informed of her cancerous condition until 87 days after her surgeon learned of the condition, and alleged a compensable injury by stating that, because her condition was allowed to persist throughout the delay in notification, she now suffered cancerphobia—the fear that cancer had spread throughout her body and would recur at a later date. The court held that a summary judgment for the defendant was not proper—that there was a genuine issue of fact as to whether the delay caused the patient to continue in pain which could have been eliminated or lessened if treatment had been started earlier. The case was set for trial on the facts).

22 ***Lohrmann v Pittsburgh Corning Co,* 782 F2d 1156 (4th Cir 1986)** (fear of getting cancer in potentially-related, cancer-causing situations must be more probable than not—at least a 51 per cent or greater chance for a jury to consider anxiety-type cancer fears).

23 ***Lopez v Sawyer,* 115 NJ Super 237, 279 A2d 116 (1971)** (this malpractice case deals with the allegation that physicians had fraudulently concealed their negligence in the treatment of a patient in failing to inform the patient of the diagnosis or test results showing cancer. The court observed that caution or empathy in telling the patient the diagnosis is appropriate, but jeopardizing treatment by doing so is negligent behavior).

24 ***Phipps v Kaiser Foundation Hospitals,* No 502400 (Cal App Div Super Ct, Los Angeles)** (pathologist who tested excised cancer specimen failed to inform a patient that all of the tumor may not have been excised. A second operation was necessary, with expert testimony that the patient had a 50 per cent chance of survival with recurrence at this time, less than before the first surgery, and that after radical surgery, he was now unable to return to work. Plaintiff was seeking $699,000 and had been offered $200,000. The final result was not reported).

29

Autogenous Bone Graft

§29.01 Generally

Bone grafts are classified according to (1) tissue composition, i.e., cortical and cancellous, (2) anatomical considerations, (3) site of origin (size and shape), (4) blood supply (non-vascularized, re-vascularized), (5) preservation method (fresh, frozen, freeze-dried), (6) additional chemical or physical manipulations, (7) demineralization, (8) irradiation, or (9) a combination of these variables. Each aspect mentioned can influence biological, immunological, and biomechanical properties of the graft, which in turn may affect its clinical efficiency.

The process of bone graft growth or incorporation represents an interaction of graft-derived and recipient site factors. The bone grafts are invaded by blood supply that starts from the host bed. There is an influx of bone-resorbing and bone-forming cells. These cells arise from the blood-forming origin stem cell. Osteoblasts are thought to come from stroma; precursor cells are found in bone marrow and osteoclasts are derived from monocytes, which in turn derive from stem cell origin.

The graft itself is passive. It is lattice work for the influx of granulation tissue and other cells that produce a chemical mediating influx of vascular and cellular activity (osteoconduction), and may provide signals to the host response capable of influencing, but not regulating the process, of incorporation. This is called *osteoinduction.*

Autogenous grafts and non-vasculized grafts are transplanted without an intact blood supply. Their vascularity starts with a hematoma that forms at the site of implantation of the graft with granulation tissue type of response bringing in fibrocytic cells first. These bring in the osteoclasts and osteoblastic precursors and there is an inflammatory response. Vascularization occurs by invasion of blood vessels that arise from the host bed.

Up to this point, cortical and cancellous bones behave in a similar fashion. The cortical grafts re-vascularize through pre-existing aversion canals as well as through the bone periphery. This process proceeds slowly throughout the graft following Phemister's description of "creeping substitution."

Cancellous bone re-vascularizes relatively quickly due to the increased porosity and loose distribution of the bony mass. Osteoblastic activity ensues, laying down new bone on pre-existing non-viable trabeculi. Osteoclastic activities increase to remove the dead bone which is gradually remodeled away. Cancellous bone is replaced more rapidly and more completely than corticografts.

It is important that the host bed be a vascular bed with healthy skin coverage and preferably free of infection, although sometimes grafts will take in an infected environment. Other factors will interfere with bone graft incorporation. These include ex-radiated tissue, tissue that is bathed either hemotogenously or locally with adverse chemicals, with adequate local oxygen saturation apparently being important.[1]

---

[1] Baron, Vignery & Horowitz, *Lymphocytes, Macrophages and the Regulation of Bone Remodeling,* 2 Bone Min Res 175 (1984); Canalis, *The Effects of Growth Factors on Bone Cell Replication and Differentiation,* 193 Clin Orthop 246 (1985); Raisz & Kream, *Regulation of Bone Formation, Part I,* 309 NEJM 29 (1983); Burwell, *The Function of Bone Marrow in the Incorporation of a Bone Graft,* 200 Clin Orthop 125 (1985); Nade, Armstrong, McCartney & Baggalay, *Osteogenesis After Bone and Bone Marrow Transplantation. The Ability of Ceramic Materials to Sustain Osteogenesis from Transplanted Bone Marrow Cells,* 181 Clin Orthop 255 (1983); Urist, *Purification of Bovine Bone Morphogenic Protein by Hydroxy Apatite Chromatography,* 81 Proceeding of the National Academy of Science United States 371 (1984).

§29.02 Pedicle

Vascularized grafts are transplanted with an intact circulation so bony necrosis is not a phase of the bone graft incorporation.[2]

§29.03 Allografts

The use of allografts avoids an operative removal of bone from the patient and its attendant morbidity. Use of allograft of bone in tumor replacement is an established and frequently used technique. In the last 15 years, the Massachusetts General Hospital has performed over 300 such operations. There were a variety of complications, but most were covered in the informed consents.[3] The possibility of transfer of disease from donor to recipient and the not unusual immunological response of rejection is a negative aspect that attaches to allografts. To avoid these problems, preservation techniques such as freezing and freeze-drying are currently in use. Preliminary results of each technique have been encouraging, but the ability of these grafts to withstand prolonged weight bearing and normal joint function has not been confirmed.

Bone grafting from one site on the patient to a recipient area is not devoid of problems. The same incision for graft harvesting and for the recipient surgery increases the risk of complications. Donor bone for spinal fusion is often taken from the posterior iliac crest, which means that the incision is close to the fusion site. As a result, infection in the donor site may easily spread to the fusion site. A remarkably high percentage of bone graft donor sites remain painful for years after the surgery and may increase the impairment to the low back. These are arguments for using bank or synthetic graft material. Autologous bone, however, is reliable graft material and is the preference of most orthopedic surgeons.[4]

Demineralized matrix preparation of bone has been used for several decades. Marshall Urist has shown that the matrix contains proteins, including what he terms bone morphogenic protein, that stimulate and favorably affect osteogenesis.

Synthetic bone substitutes such as hydroxy apatite and calcium phosphate crystalline preparations have been manufactured with the intent to duplicate the structure and chemical composition of bone mineral. These materials are biocompatible and, to varying degrees, biodegradable. They have a

---

[2] Prolo & Rodrigo, *Contemporary Bone Graft Physiology and Surgery,* 200 Clin Orthop 322 (1985).

[3] H.J. Mankin, Allograft Transplantation in Bone Tumor Management presented at the Israeli Orthopaedic Society, Herzlia, Israel (Dec 7-9, 1987), *reprint from* Department of Orthopedics, Massachusetts General Hospital, Boston.

[4] Prolo & Rodrigo, *Contemporary Bone Graft Physiology and Surgery,* 200 Clin Orthop 322 (1985).

lattice-work property, but in general tend to inhibit the in-growth of new bone.[5]

§29.04 Immunological

Like other transplanted tissues, genetic or histo-incompatibility may occur. Bone allografts evoke an immunological response of a nature and magnitude varying with the manner in which the graft is penetrated and planted. The potentially antigenic components of bone include collagen, matrix, and cells. Collagen is a weak sensitizer, matrix components are non-antigenic.

The diverse cells that appear in bone grafts, that is, osteogenic, chondrogenic, fibrous, fatty, neuromal, and hematopoietic, are potent sources of immunological reactions. For these reasons, fresh bone allografts do poorly as bone grafting material. In the field of immunology, immuno-suppressive drugs are being studied and hold promise to improve acceptability of the use of fresh allografts. It appears that the most successful use of allographic bone material is by the chemical alteration of the cellular components by freezing or freeze drying.

It is important that bone graft material, be it autogenous or allograft, be obtained in a strict sterile environment. Some of the avoidable sources of bone grafting complications occur through technical breaches of obtaining the graft or storing the graft or reconstituting the graft material. These complications are generally infectious.

Failure of autografts generally can be traced to inadequacies of the host bed that preclude or limit the necessary contributions or fail to protect the graft mechanically during the incorporation process. Preserved allografts have been used to successfully fill in bone defects such as cysts and in supplementing arthrodeses of joints and repair of non-unions. Osteochondral grafts that contain cartilage and are of a thin wafer subchondral bone have been used to resurface unicompartmental knee joints that have been destroyed by degenerative disease. Massive osseous and/or osteochondral allografts as part of limb-sparing tumor removal procedures are being done at several centers at this time. Failures such as non-union or resorbing or infection of massive allografts usually result from the inherent properties of the graft, as well as probably reflecting host bed or local systemic chemotherapy inhibition.

Demineralized bone grafts have been quite useful in inducing new bone

---

[5] Prolo & Rodrigo, *Contemporary Bone Graft Physiology and Surgery,* 200 Clin Orthop 322 (1985); Mankin, Allograft Transplantation in Bone Tumor Management presented at the Israeli Orthopaedic Society, Herzlia, Israel (Dec 7-9, 1987), *reprinted from* Department of Orthopedics, Massachusetts General Hospital, Boston; Holmes, Mooney, Bocholz & Tencer, *A Coralline Hydroxy Apatite Bone Graft Substitute. Preliminary Report,* 188 Clin Orthop 252 (1984); Goldberg, Powell, Schaffer, Zika & Bos, *Bone Grafting: Row of Histocompatibility in Transplantation,* 3 J Ortho Res 389 (1985).

formation in filling cystic defects and osseous gaps. This material is also useful in many dental situations.[6]

§29.05 Brain Death; Organ Donation

Human organ supply is the major factor limiting organ transplantation or bone allocating today. Although many of the issues related to organ supply are being addressed through education and legislation, medical management of the organ donor has received relatively little attention. Early organ donor recognition, a rapid diagnosis of brain death, and maintenance of physiological homeostasis before and after brain death are essential components of the intensive care management of the organ donor.

Uncertain donor-related factors and newer treatment modalities that might influence allograft function favorably require further investigation. As awareness concerning the problems encountered in the general management and life-support of the brain-dead organ donor increases and rational physiological therapy is applied, the organ supply can be protected and expanded.

There is widespread acceptance of the whole brain death criterion, but there is confusion about its legal and clinical applications. Health professionals have widely varying personal conceptions of death which are often confused and/or self-contradictory. Such confusion and differences in perception may prove troublesome in the following ways:

1. An increasing number of states are adopting new laws requiring health professionals to speak with families of all potential donors. Initial impressions indicate that these laws have not substantially increased the number of donations. If health care professionals lack clarity and consistency in their own understanding of death, how can they be effective in explaining it to others? Such confusion may be a contributing factor in health professionals' resentment toward required request laws as well as their discomfort about approaching families.
2. Confusion about the real status of potential donors (i.e., whether they are alive or dead) may contribute to the emotional discomfort of those who must manage them in intensive care units or in operating rooms, e.g., the discomfort often felt by operating room personnel when the ventilator is turned off following organ retrieval surgery.
3. As society contemplates the expansion of the potential donor pool to include other brain-damaged patients, who are clearly alive by today's legal and medical standards, the confusion may be compounded. Those who have accepted the whole brain criteria because they have a higher

---

[6] 33 G.E. Friedlaender, A.C. Powell & T.S. Thornhill, Immunology in Orthopedics Amer Acad Ortho Surg Ins Course: Lectures 531 (1984); Pelker, Friedlaender & Markham, *Biomechanical Properties of Bone Allografts,* 174 Clin Orthop 54 (1983); Mankan, Doppelt Tomford, *Clinical Experience with Allograft Implantation. The First 10 Years,* 174 Clin Orthop 69 (1983); Weiland, Moore & Daniel, *Vascularized Bone Autograft. Experience with 41 Cases,* 174 Clin Orthop 87 (1983).

> brain concept or merely think brain-dead patients are hopelessly dying may find it acceptable to take organs from certain patients currently defined as living, e.g., anencephalus or patients in persistent vegetative states, because such patients have clinical characteristics that are compatible with a less conservative concept of death. Some might seek to change the legal standards for death, thereby removing any obstacle to using other severely brain-damaged patients as donors. Without a greater consensus on a concept of death, such "conceptual gerrymandering" will only cause further confusion about, and perhaps greater resistance to, organ retrieval.

Health professionals should be learners in clarifying the issues in this important public debate before any policies or laws are changed, and to do so they must first clarify their own thinking.

Technology is no longer the rate-limiting factor in human organ transplantation. It is the ability to obtain organs from suitable donors, which depends largely on the attitude and commitment of health professionals.[7]

§29.06 Bone Grafting

The principal indications and techniques of bone graft procedures were well established before the internal fixation "metal" era of orthopedic surgery. Because of the necessity of using autogenous material such as bone pegs, or in some cases using wire loops, fixation of grafts was rather crude. Lane introduced internal fixation. Albee, Henderson, Campbell, Phemister, and others added osteogenesis to this principal to develop bone grafting for non-union into a practical procedure.

The two principals—fixation and osteogenesis—were not, however, efficiently and simply combined until Venable and Stuck initiated fixation by metal screws. Then came the bone bank with its obvious advantage of having bone available. There is now a variety of ways of harvesting, storing, and later using the bone bank material.

A bone bank is used for the following purposes: (1) to fill in cavities or defects from cysts, tumors, or other causes, (2) to bridge joints and thereby provide arthrodesis, (3) to bridge major defects or establish continuity of long bone, (4) to provide bone blocks to limit joint motion, (5) to establish union in a pseudarthrosis, and (6) to promote union or fill defects in delayed unions, mal-unions, fresh fractures, or osteotomies.

Cortical bone grafts are primarily used for fixation where structural strength is important. Cancellous bone grafts are used primarily to induce

---

[7] President's Commission for the Study of Ethical Problems in Medicine and Biomedical and Behavioral Research, *Defining Death: Medical, Legal and Ethical issues and the Determination of Death,* Government Printing Office, Washington DC (1981); Youngner, *Brain Death and Organ Retrieval,* 261 JAMA 2205 (1989); Broznick, *Organ Procurement: Many Causes, No Easy Solution,* 20 Transplant Proc 1010 (Supp 1988). JM Darby, et al Approach to Management of the Heartbeating 'Brain Dead' Organ Donor, 261 JAMA 2222 (1989).

osteogenesis. Bone grafting frequently will use both factors. Probably all or most of the cellular elements in bone graft, particularly in cortical graft, die and are slowly replaced by creeping substitution (Phemister), with the graft acting as a lattice-work where new bone invades. The harder, the more cortical the bone, the slower the replacement process. When selecting a graft or combination graft fitted to a specific case, the orthopedist must be aware of these two fundamental differences in bone structure. Once a graft has united with the host and is strong enough to permit unprotected use of the part, a metamorphosis of the bone structure takes place commensurate with functional demands. The application of Wolfe's Law applies here.

Bone grafts can be obtained, generally speaking, as autogenous grafts—that is, bone taken from the patient and reapplied to his or her body, or allografts where bone parts are taken from a donor and placed into a recipient. Grafts can also be taken, particularly in the case of autogenous grafts, and immediately applied to the patient; that is, from one incision to another, or autogenous grafts may be taken, preserved, stored, and later used on the patient.

Common sites for autogenous bone grafts are the fibula, tibia, and ileum. Methods of fixing the bone graft to the recipient site depend on the needs at hand. Little internal fixation is necessary when osteogenesis is the main purpose of the bone graft. Rigid fixation in the form of supplemental plates or screws may be indicated to hold cortical grafts placed for repair of delayed unions, non-unions, pseudarthrosis, or joint arthrodesis.

§29.07 Bone Growth

Bone formation is a process regulated by effects on bone cell replication and on differentiated function, which is primarily represented by change in bone collagen synthesis. The effects of hormones on bone formation have been researched extensively. Recent research describes important local growth factors. Systemic growth factors, such as epidermal growth factor and fibroblast growth factor, stimulate cell replication in skeletal and non-skeletal tissues, but inhibit differentiated function. Platelet-derived growth factor stimulates cell replication and generalized protein synthesis by differentiated cells. The only systemic factor that simultaneously stimulates bone cell replication and differentiation is insulin-like growth factors or somatomedin. The growth of skeletal and non-skeletal tissues also appears to be regulated by locally-synthesized factors. Bone contains an autogenous, bone-derived growth factor that stimulates bone collagen and DNA synthesis, while cartilage contains a somatomedin-like peptide that stimulates cartilage growth. Other non-collagenous bone protein, such as osteonectin and osteocalcin, might have a role in mineralization, but they have not as yet been reported to have a definite effect on bone formation. Bone also contains prostoglandins and local regulators of bone resorption, while the macrophage, an osteoclast-related cell, releases peptides that stimulate bone formation in vitro. In conclusion, bone formation is a complex process.[8]

§29.08 Bone Graft Physiology

In general, bone grafting operations are performed to stabilize painful joints, to promote healing of non-united fractures, and to restore structural and cosmetic conformity. Thus, bone grafts are used to fuse joints and growth plate cartilage, restore areas of major bone or joint loss in the appendicular skeleton (cysts, tumor, injury, failed arthroplasties, infection), and augment skeletal deficiency in the axial skeleton (cranium, nose, maxilla, mandible, peridondium).

Cancellous bone and/or cortical bone is most often used for filling cavities; cortical bone is optimal for reconstructing defects that require certain form and strength. Although cortical bone graft is strong when first implanted, the incorporation process may weaken it with fatigue fractures often occurring every six to eight months. For this reason, plates, screws, and intramedullary devices are frequently used to supplement strength.

In achieving function, an uninfected graft may follow one of three evolutionary paths: (1) it may become viable, in time acquiring the mechanical, cosmetic, and biologic characteristics of adjacent bone, (2) it may partially or completely resorb, leaving disfigurement and instability, or (3) it may become sequestered, encapsulated, and be treated by the body as a foreign body.

The most likely graft to achieve optimal function in man is the fresh autograph. In descending order, the frozen autograph, autolysed, antigen-extracted allograph (AAA bone) (vide infra), freeze-dried and frozen allographs variably accomplish goals of structural and cosmetic restoration.

Xenogenic grafts are no longer used in the United States. An xenoimplant evokes a hypersensitive response by the host and becomes encapsulated (sequestered) with obstruction of microanastamoses between vessels of the recipient and donor tissue.

Vascularized bone grafts (autographs) have increased in popularity concomitant with dramatically improved success rates in microvascular anastomses in the last few years. Vascular allografts have not been successfully developed to date.

§29.09 Biology of Bone Graft Incorporation

A bone graft transferred to a recipient orthopedic bed functions in several ways, leading ultimately to incorporation in the skeletal system of the host. Incorporation refers to the process of envelopment and interdigitation of donor bone tissue with new bone deposited by the recipient.

---

[8] Canalis, *Effect of Growth Factors on Bone Cell Replication and Differentiation*, 193 Clin Orthop Rel Res 246 (1985).

Osteogenesis (new bone formation) from surviving cells of the donor site is characteristic only of fresh autogenous bone. Whereas transplanted osteocytes die and leave empty lacunate in the transferred bone substrate, preosteoblasts, preosteoclasts, and osteoclasts can survive. Preosteoclast precursor cells may migrate into the graft, via the blood stream, from the marrow of host. Revascularization of the fresh graft occurs through microanastomoses with pre-existing microvessels in only a small percentage of grafts. Grafts share with biologic and non-biologic materials a three-dimension into which sprouting capillaries, perivascular tissue, and osteoprogenitor cells can grow. A fresh graft also provides the trellis-like structure for this ingrowth and additionally contains an inductive protein that stimulates osteogenesis.

Induction occurs when "two or more tissues of different natures of properties becomes intimately associated, defining Urist's osteoinduction as the process of recruitment of mesenchymal-type cells into cartilage and bone."

§29.10 Responsibilities of the Surgeon

Surgeons who use bone grafts and implants must understand the potentials and limitations of different materials. During the operation, sterility of the graft must be protected at all stages. Prolonged air and saline exposure and heat destroy cells and bone-inducting products. A tight (mortised) fit of the graft to the donor bed facilitates healing (fusion). Proper drainage of the operative site prevents a hematoma that might "float" the graft. Early ambulation and exercise stimulates blood flow and osteogenesis in the graft, following Wolff's law.

The growth hormone cascade stimulates bone growth starting with release in the brain of cerebral cortex neurotransmitter hormones. These stimulate the hypothalamus to release growth hormone releasing factor which in turn stimulates the anterior pituitary to release growth hormone. The growth hormone then stimulates the liver to make and release growth factors and somatodin. Somatodin hormone then stimulates bone and cartilage (and presumably bone graft) growth.[9]

Many surgeons have shown that fresh vascularized autografts offer the best "take" (bone incorporation into host bone). Fresh vascularized allografts in judiciously matched or immunosuppressed recipients offer attractive clinical possibilities.[10]

---

[9] Prolo & Rodrigo, Contemporary Bone Graft Physiology and Surgery, 200 Clin Orthop 322 (1985); Urist, *Bone Cell Differentiation and Growth Factors,* 220 Science (1983).

[10] Goldberg, *Bone Grafting: Role of Histocompatibility in Transplantation,* 3 J Orthop Res 389 (1985).

§29.11 Bone Banks

Opinions differ among orthopedic surgeons regarding the use of preserved homologous bone, although its practical advantages are many. Fresh autogenous bone must generally be obtained through a second incision, which adds to the size and length of the operation and to blood loss. After removal of a cortical graft from the tibia, the leg must be protected to prevent fracture at the donor site. At times, it may not be possible to obtain enough autogenous bone to meet the needs of the operation.

At this time, there are several techniques to preserve bone. The optimum methods have not been developed yet. The Campbell Clinic, one of the pioneers in bone grafting, is presently using deep freezing to −15°C and freeze-drying to residual moisture of two to five per cent. Temperatures down to −70° may be preferable.

Bone taken for a bone bank must be taken under sterile conditions. The bone material is cultured, both aerobically and anaerobically, and the bone is put through a preservative technique preferred by the surgeon or the laboratory facility harvesting the bone. In addition to freeze-drying, storage of bone in a solution of merthiolate has been used, but that is uncommon now. Other orthopedists have used sterilized homogenous bone preserved by gas sterilization. I believe most orthopedists agree with Hyatt that if osteogenesis is the prime concern, fresh autogenous bone is the best graft.

In the Annual Textbook of Orthopedics, (7th ed), it is pointed out that there are hazards of taking bone grafts. Disruption of continuity of bone and pathological fractures of the donor site are not unusual. Less common are infections. Nerve and blood vessel damage may occur. In the case of the ileum, a very common site of bone graft, bone taken close enough to the sacroiliac joint can result in instability of the joint itself, occasionally requiring surgical arthrodesis of that joint. If both tables in the mid-aspect of the ileum were violated, an iliac hernia can occur with incarceration of bowel (although this is uncommon) and secondary surgical repair of that may be necessary.

After removal of grafts, it is necessary to accurately oppose and suture the periosteum in the muscle origins with strong interrupted sutures. Bleeding from the ileum may be profuse. Avoiding Gel foam and bone wax are recommended, or to depend on wound packing and local pressure. Both Gel foam and bone wax are foreign materials. Bone wax is said to retard bone healing. Gel foam in large amounts has been associated with sterile serious drainage from wounds. Microcrystalline collagen has been reported to be more effective in reducing blood loss from cancellous bone and more effective than either thrombin powder or thrombin-soaked gelatin foam. Wound suction for 24 to 48 hours is the standard, at this time, to decompress donor site wounds if there is a risk of blood accumulation occurring in the operative site.[11]

---

[11] 2 L.C. Abbott, *The Use of Iliac Bone in the Treatment of Ununited Fractures,* AAOS Instructional Course Lectures (1944); Boyd, *Congenital Pseudarthrosis Treated*

§29.12 Biomechanical Properties of Bone Allografts

The biomechanical properties of allograft bone can be altered by the method chosen for its preservation and storage. These effects are minimal with deep freezing or low level radiation. Freeze drying markedly diminishes the torsional and bending strength of bone allografts but does not deleteriously affect compressive or tensile strength. Irradiation of bone with more than 3.0 mega-rad, or irradiation combined with freeze drying, appear to cause significant reduction in breaking strength. These factors should be considered when choosing freeze-dried or irradiated allogenic bone that will be subjected to significant loads following implantation. Again, it is emphasized that, when available, fresh autogenous bone is preferable for bone grafting.[12]

§29.13 Using Coral as Bone Graft Substitute

Although experimental at this time, a new bone grafting substitute made by conversion of the calcium carbonate skeletal structure of reef-building sea corals into pure hydroxypatite is being tested. Early results are promising, with complete incorporation of the material into the patient's bone, so that less (or none) of the patient's bone is necessary for the graft. The material is manufactured by Interpore International, Irving, California.

---

by Dual Bone Grafts, 23 JBJ Surg 497 (1941); H.B. Boyd, *The Bridging of Bone Defects,* AAOS Instructional Course Lectures (1944); 17 H.B. Boyd & S.W. Lipinski, *Causes and Treatments of Non-Unions of the Shafts of the Long Bone with a Review of 741 Patients,* AAOS Instructional Course Lectures (1960); Dineen & Gresham, *Rib Osteoperiosteografts. A Preliminary Report of Their Use and Treatment of Fresh and Ununited Fractures of Long Bones,* 44A JBJ Surg 1653 (1962); Doppelt, Tomford, Lucas & Mankin, *Operational and Financial Aspects of a Hospital Bone Bank,* 63A JBJ Surg 1471 (1981); Gresham, *The Freeze-Dried Cortical Bone Homograft. A Retinological and Histological Evaluation,* 37 Clin Orthop 194 (1964); Kreuz, Hyatt, Turner & Bassett, *The Preservations and Clinical Use of Freeze Dried Bone,* 33A JBJ Surg 863 (1951); 2 C.R. Murray, *The Principles Underlying All Bone Grafting Procedures,* AAOS Instructional Course Lecture (1944); Reynolds & Oliver, *Clinical Evaluation of the Merthiolate Bone Banks. A Preliminary Report,* 31A JBJ Surg 792 (1949); Swanson, Glessner, Jr Burdick & Mahaney, *Seven Years Experience with Irradiated Bone Graft Material,* 117 Surg, Gynecol Obstet 573 (1963); Tomford, Starkweather & Goldman, *A Study of the Clinical Incidence of Infection in the Use of Banked Allograft Bone,* 63A JBJ Surg 244 (1981); Bosworth, *Repair of Hernia Through Iliac Crest Defects,* 37A JBJ Surg 1069 (1955); Coventry & Tapper, *Pelvic Instability—a Consequence of Removing Iliac Bone for Grafting,* 54A JBJ Surg (1972); Froimson & Cumming, Jr, *Iliac Hernia Following Hip Arthodesis,* 80 Clin Orthop 89 (1971); Reid, Camp & Jacob,*Tourniquet Hemostasis: A Clinical Study,* 177 Clin Orthop 230 (1983); Wolfe & Kawamoto, *Taking the Iliac Bone Graft. A New Technique,* 60A JBJ Surg 411 (1978).

[12] Pelker, *Biomechanical Properties of Bone Allografts,* 174 Clin Orthop Rel Res 545 (1983).

§29.14 Vascularized Bone Grafts

In 1908, Carrel published Results of the Transplantation of Blood Vessels, Organs and Limbs, which heralded the birth of vascular surgery. The ability to now transplant a segment of live bone with its blood supply, either by pedicle transfer or by free transplant with anastamosis of the nutient vessel to local vessels, has assured the orthopedist's ability to fill and heal bone defects, thus bypassing the need for amputation and frequently preserving a functioning extremity. Using similar techniques, large soft tissue defects can be covered with skin and muscle as well as bone. These microvascular operations require surgeons trained and skilled in precision microscopic and plastic surgical methods. Many surgeons simply do not have the hand-eye coordination to do these procedures and should refer patients to the appropriate specialist.[13]

If neurovascular structures are intact or can be repaired, a large vascularized bone graft may be used for salvage of a seriously injured extremity, soon after injury or for reconstruction at a later date. The osteomuscular iliac graft is based on the deep circumflexed iliac vessel, and the osteomusculotanous flap is based on the deep and superficial iliac vessels. There are several osteomuscular grafts that are useful in filling bone defects and/or covering skin muscle bone defects. These procedures usually require the participation of a plastic and/or vascular surgeon.[14]

§29.15 AIDS from Donor Bone

In December 1988, the first case of AIDS virus was transferred to a patient from an unknown AIDS-infected bone graft donor. The details were released by the AIDS Program of the Center for Disease Control. The victim was at no known risk for HIV infection. The surgery performed was a bone graft stabilization procedure to correct or stabilize scoliosis. Fever, night sweats, and enlarged lymph nodes occurred 21 days after surgery. The symptoms remitted in about three and one-half days. AIDS was diagnosed.

The donor was a 52-year-old man who donated the head of a femur removed as part of a hip arthroplasty. The donated bone was stored at -80 degrees C for 24 hours without being sterilized, then placed into the spine to induce fusion. A 2×2 cm lymph node was found in the donor's neck on physical examination just prior to harvesting the bone graft. Two years later, he developed Pneumocystic Carni pneumonia and had positive testing for HIV antibodies. He died of AIDS nine months before AIDS was diagnosed in the patient who received the bone graft.

The United States Public Health Service indicated that, although HIV

---

[13] AJ Weiland, *Vascularized Bone Grafts,* 174 Clin Orthop Rel Res 87 (1983); Carrel, *Results of Transplantation of Blood Vessels, Organs and Limbs,* 51 JAMA 1662 (1908).

[14] Salibian, Anzel & Salyer, *Transfer of Vascularized Grafts of Iliac Bone to the Extremities,* 69A JBJ Surg 1319 (1987).

previously was transmitted through transplantation of heart, kidney, liver, pancreas, and skin, this was the first known bone graft transfer.[15]

§29.16 Electromagnetic Stimulation Bone Healing

The use of electromagnetic field stimulation in cases of fracture union failure was developed in Turkey in 1984. A two-coiled (one directional) magnetic field is used in the conventional system; a four-coiled field, using two perpendicular fields, has recently been developed which shows a higher success rate but has a mechanical bulk disadvantage.[16]

§29.17 Radiofrequency

At times, it is helpful to denervate an area of the body, generally facets in the spine to lessen pain originating from the facet. Two devices are commonly used. The more popular is radiofrequency, with electrical cauterizing current at the end of a probe, which is passed to the area to be denervated and a pulse of current is activated. The other method is cryotherapy, which uses a probe with liquid nitrogen to freeze when the probe has been put in place. These devices are occasionally used by neurosurgeons in brain surgery.

§29.18 References

Holmes & Mooney, *A Coralline Hydroxyapatite Bone Graft Substitute,* 188 Clin Orthop Rel Res 252 (1984)

---

[15] Edelman, Staff Writer, 8 Orthopedics Today 1 (1988).

[16] Cakirgil, *The Compared Effect of a Four-Coiled System in Pulsed Electromagnetic Field Stimulation,* 12 Orthopedica 1481 (1989).

30

Muscle Injuries

§30.01 Generally

Muscular complaints, including muscle contraction headache, represent 70 per cent of the complaints that patients give as a reason to consult their physician. Injury to muscle accounts for 50 to 60 per cent of those complaints.

Muscle tissue that has been lacerated or disrupted goes through a reparative process like other soft tissues. There is very little clinical research material available on the recovery of the muscle after such injury.

Muscle tissue can be sutured at the connective tissue or surrounding myotendinous tissue sufficient to hold sutures. The fate of the muscle might then depend on the nature of the recovery process. Muscle might regenerate across the laceration and restore muscle to its previous appearance. This has been shown for some thin muscles such as the platysma muscle. Muscle may heal with connective tissue scar with no regeneration of muscle across the injury gap. Recovery of muscle function then would depend on two separate situations. Has the muscle replaced itself with functional muscle at the site of injury, or is there a scar interface in between?

It is important to have strong and enduring muscle mass, but equally important to have strong, yet flexible ligaments supporting the underlying motion segment. Injury-preventing rehabilitation must address these two factors.[1]

---

[1] Davies & White, *Muscle Weakness Following Acentric Work in Man,* 392 Eur J Physiology 168 (1981); Roth & Davis, *Psychosomatic Complaints in Chronic Myofascial Pain,* presented at the First International Symposium on Myofascial Pain and Fibromyalgia (Minneapolis, Minn, May 8-10, 1989); Garrett, *Muscle Strains: Histology, Causes, and Treatment,* Surg Rounds Orthop, Jan 1989, at 43.

§30.02 Muscle-Skeletal Examination

This section outlines information that should be obtained on examination.

Patient History

1. Chief complaint
2. History of present illness

This should include a detailed longitudinal history of the disease process and a detailed description of the patient's current complaint. Current and past therapy for this disorder and response to treatment is beneficial. Hospitalizations, surgical procedures, and special diagnostic testing should be reported with dates and results.

A detailed description should be obtained of symptoms, including (1) the character, location, and radiation of any pain, (2) the mechanical factors which cause and relieve pain, (3) the currently prescribed medications and dosage, and (4) a description of the patient's usual activities. Symptoms of weakness or other motor loss or sensory abnormalities should be reported.

Physical Examination

1. General, including appearance, nutrition, structural abnormalities, blood pressure, pulse, height, and weight.
2. Gait and station should be described in detail, with examples of ability to tandem walk, walk on heels and toes, hop, bend, squat, arise, dress and undress, rise from a chair, get on examining table, and cooperate during examination.
3. Detailed description of orthopedic and pertinent neurological findings should include motion of spine in degrees from the vertical, motor and sensory abnormalities, and deep tendon reflexes. Motor function should be quantitated and the method of quantitation reported, including which number would represent paralysis and normal strength and how patient compares. When there is sensory deficit or pain, specific distribution of these must be described. Reflexes should be described as to intensity and symmetry.
4. Muscle bulk must be described and if asymmetrical, measurements should be given. Atrophy should be reported in terms of circumferential measurements of both thighs and lower legs (or appropriate areas of arms) at stated points above and below knee (or elbow) in inches or centimeters. Hand involvement should indicate grip strength.
5. Abnormalities involving joints should be described. Maximum passive range of motion should be reported of involved joints.
6. Gait and station should be reported. If an assistive device is used, we need an assessment of the necessity of this device. For example, how far can the patient ambulate unassisted?

7. If x-rays are requested, the report should be very detailed. The physician providing the formal interpretation should be identified.
8. All abnormalities should be explained or commented on if a definite explanation cannot be provided.

§30.03 Muscle Laceration

Direct injury—laceration of muscle tissue—heals in a predictable manner, depending on the degree of devitalization. The necrotic tissue is removed through the homeostatic reparative cascade typical in all areas of the body. Wound healing is a complex interaction of mechanical, physiologic, and biochemical events. An alteration in any facet of this intricate process leads to prolongation and/or abnormal wound healing, sometimes with devastating effects.

Lacerated muscle bellies, when healed, depending on the amount of muscle involved, recover about 60 per cent of their ability to produce tension and normal ability to shorten. After recovery, histologic and histochemical sections show that initially isolated nerve supply in the segment distal to laceration show varying degrees of denervation when healed, some returning function, but inevitably permanent scarring and functional loss. Overdevelopment of remaining muscle may compensate for the loss following laceration.[2]

In larger muscles, the rehabilitative process deals with muscle that has healed with a dense scar at the laceration site. In one study, the portion of the muscle containing the motor point remained physiologically active, whereas the portion of the muscle separated from the motor point and intramuscular enervation became fibrotic with features of denervated muscle. The portion isolated from the motor point healed and was able to transmit tension and shortening generated in the enervated portion.

Muscles so injured (lacerated) recover; however, the recovery is not complete. The muscle segment totally isolated from its motor point may not effectively contribute to the contractual function of enervated muscle. This is loss of endurance and strength of the injured muscle distal to the area of laceration. Muscles that are not sutured end to end undergo changes, with unstructurally sound scar filling the gap and limiting endurance and contractile strength.

The extent of physiological coverage is dependent on the architect of the muscle fibers. The ability of muscle to produce tension is proportionate to the cross-sectional area of the muscle fibers, and the ability to shorten is

---

[2] Davies & White, *Muscle Weakness Following Acentric Work in Man,* 392 Eur J Physiology 168 (1981); Roth & Davis, *Psychosomatic Complaints in Chronic Myofascial Pain,* presented at the First International Symposium on Myofascial Pain and Fibromyalgia (Minneapolis, Minn, May 8-10, 1989); Garrett, *Muscle Strains: Histology, Causes, and Treatment,* Surg Rounds Orthop, Jan 1989, at 43; Garrett, *Recovery of Skeletal Muscle After Laceration,* 9A J Hand Surg 683 (1984). Carrico, *Biology of Wound Healing,* 64 Surg Clin N Am 721 (1984).

relative to the length of the muscle fibers. A knowledge of what the muscle type is and the location of the injury in respect to the myoneural junction is helpful to the therapist involved in rehabilitating them.[3]

§30.04 Muscle Contusion

Bruising or a direct blow—blunt trauma—produces a different effect on muscle. The closer the muscle is to the bone, the greater the damage. In controlled blunt trauma, experimentally, disruption of muscle fibers does occur in a manner similar to lacerations. There is an intense inflammatory reaction with eventual clearing of necrotic material and formation of a dense connective tissue scar. Continuity of the muscle fibers is disrupted in the area of blunt trauma with the occurrence of myositis ossificans or metaplastic ossification. Such metaplasias have adverse effects on rehabilitation of that muscle group.

§30.05 Muscle Strain

Muscle trauma occurs more frequently as an indirect injury or strain in which there is no direct blow. Strains are among the most frequent injuries sustained in athletes. The high incidence of strain injuries of the back in occupation situations has been studied at length. These injuries are more prevalent in heavy manual labor and represent a large and costly problem for the national economy.

Studies of strain injuries in the extremities have stressed the frequency of these injuries in two joint muscles which are subjected to simultaneous stretch. Those frequently injured are the hamstring muscles, rectoris femoris and gastrocnemius. Muscles at risk for strain injuries often contain a high percentage of Type II fibers. These fibers are capable of faster speed of contraction with higher forces and poor endurance than Type I fibers. The type of fiber distribution present in muscle is related to what its normal physiological use and expectation is. It appears that muscles that require quick or powerful contraction are both higher in percentage of Type II fibers and more susceptible to injury.[4]

§30.06 Pathophysiology of Muscle Injury

When injured, overused, or overexerted, muscles produce increased fluid formation within the muscle fascicle, along with bleeding. If the bleeding

---

[3] Garrett, *Recovery of Skeletal Muscle After Laceration,* 9A J Hand Surg 683 (1984); Carrico, *Biology of Wound Healing,* 64 Surg Clin N Am 721 (1984); Bessinger, *Junior Doctoring,* 81 S Med J 1558 (1988); Knighton, *Role of Platelets and Fibrin in the Healing Sequence,* 196 Ann Surg 379 (1982).

[4] Safran, *The Role of Warmup in Muscle Injury Prevention,* 16 Am J Sports Med 123 (1988); Forest, *Current Concepts of Soft Connective Tissue, Wound Healing,* 70 Brit J of Surg 133 (1983).

is confined to one or two fascicles, those fibers may die, undergo necrosis, and become repaired by migration of myoblasts and fibroblasts from adjacent fascicles. These new muscles are functional muscle cells; however, the area of injury is also interspaced with an increased amount of connective tissue. The resulting repair of muscle fascicle will function normally, but has less endurance and greater ease of fatigue and takes a longer period of rehabilitation to return to normal function, if it ever does. How normal the function of any one injured muscle mass returns depends on the amount of muscle destruction. This discussion relates to muscle that has not been disrupted and that has not been severed from its neurological supply.

If muscles have been separated from neurological supply, the gap fills in with connective tissue; attenuated or abnormal muscle fibers may develop distally to the point of separation if the separation is also distal to the muscle fiber neuronal enervation. That muscle is basically scar tissue with little or no contractile ability with a varying degree of reenvervation but never approaching complete, and always with permanent functional impairment of that area of muscle injury.

As to time of muscle healing, muscle fascicular injury described above, whether it is stretching overuse, overexertion with fascicular necrosis to varying degrees, the healing process here from a microscopic point of view the muscle is restored in three to four weeks. The rehabilitation period to maximum improvement varies from weeks to months.[5]

There is a general agreement that strain injuries are very likely to recur. This may well be due to poor rehabilitation. There is also a general agreement that stronger muscle groups are less likely to be injured. This has been shown in workers who work at heavy manual labor or in hazardous situations. In one large study, San Francisco firemen were studied. Those who participated in an intense aerobic exercise plan to increase the flexibility of low back soft tissues and increase supportive musculature had substantially fewer on-the-job injuries than firemen who were on a home exercise plan taken from a booklet.[6]

Muscle imbalance and joint inflexibility are thought to predispose to indirect muscle injury. There is, however, a recent study to show that imbalance documented by isokinetic dynometers did not predispose to injury. Demonstrated ligamentous relaxation, including double-jointedness, is not necessarily a predictor of injury.

---

[5] Goldstein, *Clinical Applications for Exercise,* 17 Physician & SportsMed 83 (1989); Heathe, *Exercise Training Improves Lipoprotein Lipid Profiles in Patients with Coronary Artery Disease,* 105 Am Heart J 889 (1983).

[6] Stamford, *How Much Should I Exercise?,* 17 Physician & SportsMed 150 (1989); Duda, *Golfer's Use Exercise to Get Back in the Swing,* 17 Physician & SportsMed 109 (1989); Hagberg, *Effect of Exercise Training on the Blood Pressure and Hemodynamic Features of Hypertensive Adolescents,* 52 Am J Cardio 763 (1983); Brown & Myles, *The Relationship Between Aerobic Fitness and Certain Cardiovascular Risk Factors,* Aviation, Space & Envt Med, June 1983, at 543.

§30.07 Muscle Overload

Both trained and untrained persons are subject to post-exercise soreness. If severe enough, this can cause serious complications or mimic heart or liver damage through abnormal blood chemistry studies. Muscle spasms or cramps are perhaps the most common muscle symptoms after unusual exertion. The severe muscle spasms, commonly called "Charley horse," result from the sudden discharge of enough motor units to contract the whole muscle belly simultaneously. The pathophysiology of such dramatic contractions relates to fluid and electrolyte shifts involving intracellular and extracellular gradients of potassium, magnesium, and calcium. Dehydration is a significant risk factor for muscle cramps after prolonged exercise.

Muscle contraction involves release of calcium into the lateral spaces of the sarcoplasm, causing the actin and myosin contractile elements to slide together—the mechanics of muscle fiber contraction. Relaxation energy is used to release calcium back into the appropriate intracellular compartment. Insufficient stores of adenosine triphosphate (ATP) lead to contraction of muscle fiber without the capacity for relaxation.

Massage and gentle stretching may facilitate relaxation as chemical homeostasis is re-established. Prolonged cramping can lead to necrosis with fibrosis. Sustained contraction is seen in rigor mortis.

Exercise-related muscle injuries range from mild subclinical cases with abnormal CK (creatinine kinase) levels to severe rhabdomyolysis with multiple organ injury. Adequate training, controlled exercise intensity, and hydration are the best preventive strategies. Where electrolyte-containing fluids are superior to plain water is controversial. High salt (sodium) via salt pills appears contraindicated, as it is dehydrating to intracellular fluid spaces. Rest, nutrition, heat, and anti-inflammatory agents are treatment modalities. When serum enzymes in athletes are elevated, clinicians need to be wary of mistaking muscle injury for acute myocardial infarction or liver disease. Endocrine imbalance, metabolic, or inflammatory muscle conditions can mimic the above problems and should be ruled out.[7]

§30.08 Delayed Muscle Soreness and Injury

We have all experienced pain when we have used muscles that were not used to activity, such as over-exercising or some physical activity that was strange to those muscles. This pain ordinarily is felt from 24 to 72 hours after the activity. Exercise requiring high intensity and high force of production is more likely to cause soreness than low intensity, slower physical activity. This soreness has been shown to be associated with transient muscle weakness. The eccentric muscle contraction which refers to

---

[7] Safran, *The Role of Warmup in Muscle Injury Prevention,* 16 Am J Sports Med 123 (1988); Goldstein, *Clinical Applications for Exercise,* 17 Physician & SportsMed 83 (1989); Stamford, *How Much Should I Exercise?,* 17 Physician & SportsMed 150 (1989).

muscle activation associated with lengthening or strengthening of muscles rather than shortening them frequently are painful after overload type usage. The muscle soreness that does occur has been studied by electronic microscopy and other chemical techniques. These studies do demonstrate some changes. However, the soreness tends to recover spontaneously in a few days. The tendency for the soreness lessens with heavy activity as the exercising person gets into "better shape," and particularly with progressive isokinetic or isotonic exercise plans.

A controversy surrounds the musculoskeletal system regarding methods for improving and strengthening the muscle mass. The musculoskeletal system is a highly sophisticated vehicle by which individuals of all ages communicate not only with themselves but with those around them, although controversy surrounds methods used to improve and strengthen the system, especially in the elite—the athlete. Most agree that regular strengthening training exercises, regardless of the type, can be beneficial. Disorders are recognized and are felt to be most often brought on by overutilization, by deficient working habits, by lack of appropriate maintenance care and intercurrent stress and fatigue from repetitive daily tasks, as well as by poor sleeping patterns.[8]

§30.09 Measuring Muscle Injury

It is important that the examining physician or therapist have standards to measure the strength of individual muscle groups. In this way, the status and response to treated muscle groups can be recorded and therapeutic plans made. A universally accepted scheme is presented by Csuka in his Objective Gradation of Muscle Strength:

5 (normal): Motion against considerably applied manual force

4 (good): Some motion possible against manually applied load

3 (fair): Motion possible against gravity, but not against applied load

2 (poor): Motion possible with elimination of gravity as a factor

1 (trace): Palpable or visible contraction but no motion

0 (none): No evidence of muscle contraction

The physical therapist is frequently called on to improve function and reduce pain. The problems to be dealt with are limited motion due to the frozen shoulder syndrome or stiff painful elbow, wrist, or fingers.

Physical therapy programs are guided passive and active range of motion, gentle manipulations by the patie' t and by the therapist. These techniques

---

[8] Safran, *The Role of Warmup in Muscle Injury Prevention,* 16 Am J Sports Med 123 (1988); Goldstein, *Clinical Applications for Exercise,* 17 Physician & SportsMed 83 (1989); Stamford, *How Much Should I Exercise?,* 17 Physician & SportsMed 150 (1989).

are most often used after a period of heating the joint. In the most acute cases, starting with gentle exercises may be the first step.

§30.10 Treatment Methods

In post-traumatic situations—fractures or dislocations where there is limitation of motion, but sufficient time for soft tissues to heal—the physical therapist has an essential role in rehabilitation. In the usual situation, passive pendulum exercises to increase the range of motion are first used. It is important to protect soft tissues or bony structures that are not healed well enough to tolerate active manipulation.

Most soft tissue injuries are healed well enough in three weeks and fractures are stable enough in four to six weeks that progressive active range of motion can be started. It is important to obtain active and passive range of motion as rapidly as possible. This may be a moderately painful experience for the patient. This is an area where the physical therapist, with his or her skills and charisma, along with utilizing the concept of "no pain, no gain," is important.

On the issue of pain control, the physical therapist has a variety of tools that are helpful. Deep heat modalities, TENS units, alternate hot and cold packs, and ice massages are frequently helpful. If the patient describes an acute change in the pain pattern, suggesting disruption of soft tissue or bone, the physical therapist must immediately report this to the treating orthopedist.

§30.11 Contraindications to Exercise

Exercise has been shown an effective adjunct to good health and rehabilitation of deconditioned patients. Exercise should be prescribed for the patient in a specific manner, to avoid injury or other complications. Supervised exercises are effective and predictable. To tell the patient to "go exercise" is less than professional. Physicians must be cautious with sedentary patients who are "at risk" for the ravages of inactivity. When these people need an exercise plan, a pre-exercise physical examination is appropriate and medically necessary. A proper evaluation will identify (1) conditions in the patient which are contraindications to physical activity, (2) conditions which must be stabilized before beginning exercises or which should be monitored during an exercise program, and (3) the patient's overall health status and whether do other health problems need treatment to the patient's health benefit.

Absolute contraindications include (1) severe coronary heart disease and acute myocardial infarction, (2) unstable angina pectoris, (3) congestive heart failure, uncorrected, (4) uncontrolled high-grade ventricular or atrial arrhythmias, (5) severe valvular heart disease, including severe aortic or mitral stenosis, (6) uncontrolled hypertension with systolic over 200 or diastolic over 105 mm Hg, (7) pulmonary hypertension, and (8) recent pulmonary embolus or deep vein thrombosis.

Certain medical conditions must be treated or stabilized prior to beginning an exercise program. These are less severe than absolute contraindications to exercise, but must not be overlooked. Usually, the final decision regarding exercise will depend on the severity of the medical problem. Relative contraindications include (1) congenital heart disease, (2) congestive heart failure, (3) significant valvular heart disease, (4) cardio-arrhythmias, including heart block, (5) hypertension, (6) fixed-rate artificial pacemaker, (7) cardiomyopathy, (8) peripheral vascular disease, (9) possible digitalis or other drug toxicity, (10) electrolyte, particularly hypokalemia, abnormalities, (11) uncontrolled metabolic disease, (12) serious systemic disease, i.e., mononucleosis, hepatitis, (13) neuromuscular or musculoskeletal disease in which loading or overloading would directly cause injury or, in the compromised person, would increase the risk of inadvertent injury, (14) marked obesity, (15) anemia, and (16) psychosis.

The above restrictions can only be assessed by adequate history and physical examinations. Injudicious exercise prescription by an uninformed or careless physician places the patient "at risk" of preventable injury.

It has been shown in any exercise program that physiologic warming up and warming down protects the exercised muscle from injury.[9]

It is axiomatic among athletes that warming up before exercise helps prevent muscle strains and other injuries, yet it has never been proven scientifically. Experiments in rabbits compared tears in isometrically preconditioned muscles with tears in unstimulated muscle. The preconditioned muscle withstood significantly greater force and stretched farther before tearing than control muscles did. In addition, all pre-conditioned muscles stretched farther with any given force. Unanswered is whether the benefits are attributable to stretching or warming. Most athletes undergo warm-up as well as stretching before exercise.

The understanding of muscle physiology is a rapidly expanding field. It is well understood that underused muscles become weak and lack endurance, and that optimally-exercised muscles gain strength and endurance. The rehabilitation of muscle deconditioned patients is not a rapid process but is in proportion to the resistance the muscle works against as well as frequency. Equally important is the state of health of the person increasing muscle power. Age, nutrition, lack of toxic chemicals in system (alcohol, drugs, propranalol), as well as increased presence of some hormones (androgenic) have their positive or negative effects. Gender has some, but relative little, to do with muscle mass building.

Muscle soreness after use is less well understood, and may be a sign of overload. It has been shown that overloading of muscle masses that have

---

[9] Knighton, *Role of Platelets and Fibrin in the Healing Sequence,* 196 Ann Surg 379 (1982); Safran, *The Role of Warmup in Muscle Injury Prevention,* 16 Am J Sports Med 123 (1988); Forest, *Current Concepts of Soft Connective Tissue, Wound Healing,* Brit J of Surg 133 (1983); Goldstein, *Clinical Applications for Exercise,* 17 Physician & SportsMed 83 (1989).

little or no reserve or muscles with limited nerve input, i.e., post-stroke, post-polio, etc. can be permanently damaged by overload.[10]

§30.12 Work-Related Disorders

In a recent survey, musculoskeletal injuries accounted for 580,000 (18 per cent) of the estimated 3.2 million emergency room treated occupational injuries in the United States. Manual handling of materials, repetitive motions, and vibrations are especially important etiological factors.

Injuries associated with manual handling (unaided lifting and lowering) causes low back injury, the largest single subset of musculoskeletal injuries. Low back injuries account for one in five of all occupational injuries.

Repetitive motion associated trauma (cumulative trauma disorders) are common and include carpal tunnel syndrome, tendonitis, ganglionitis, tenosynovitis, bursitis, and epicondylitis. This injury may be caused or aggravated by repeated twisting or awkward positions of work. Vibration-associated injuries are seen in vehicle operations (truck, auto, taxi driving). The effects of vibration are poorly understood, but an increasing body of data suggest that low back pain, vertebrogenic pain, and degenerative disc disease may be vibration-associated and/or aggravated.

As estimated 1.2 million workers are exposed to segmental vibration, i.e., vibration principally of a part or parts of the body, such as hand-held power tools, chain saws, jack hammers, etc. Often, the extremities exposed to segmental vibration present with numbness and/or blanching of fingers with reduced sensitivity to heat, cold, or pain. Occasional increased sensitivity is noted.[11]

§30.13 Overuse Syndromes

Many physical therapists and physiatrists feel that vigorous physical therapy is the cornerstone in management of overuse syndromes that affect muscles and tendons preceded by early rest intervention to heal the inflamed tissues. Prevention of injury or recurrence is essential. Classification of overuse pain is important. The pain of tendonitis is usually classified as (1) pain after activity only, (2) pain during activity that does not restrict activity,

---

[10] Safran, *The Role of Warmup in Muscle Injury Prevention,* 16 Am J Sports Med 123 (1988); Forest, *Current Concepts of Soft Connective Tissue, Wound Healing,* Brit J of Surg 133 (1983); Goldstein, *Clinical Applications for Exercise,* 17 Physician & SportsMed 83 (1989); Stamford, *How Much Should I Exercise?,* 17 Physician & SportsMed 150 (1989).

[11] J.A. Tarantino & D.J. Oliveira, Litigating Neck and Back Injuries, (1988); Burnette & Ayoub, *Cumulative Trauma Disorders,* Pain Mgmt, July/Aug 1989, at 196; Klein, *Assessment of Workers Compensation Claims for Back Strains-Sprains,* 26 J Occup Med 443 (1984); Hadler, *Arm Pain and the Workplace,* Medicalegal Bull Fall, 1988, at 7.

(3) pain during activity that does restrict performance, and (4) chronic unremitting pain.

The first type is treated with relative rest, with 25 per cent reduction in work load or reducing the number of pitches or miles run.

The second type is treated the same way, but with 50 per cent reduction and addition of nonsteroidal medication.

The third type by definition precludes competitive athletic performance. The patient should be encouraged to refrain from all activity loading the pain area. Physical therapy with heat stretch is used. Judicious use of corticosteroid injection may be considered, taking great care not to inject into the musculotendinous juncture. The direct injection of corticosteroid into a muscle tendon interface has been shown to result in microstructure disarray and can lead to rupture.

The fourth type should be treated with long-term physical therapy. Many of these patients have developed scarring about musculotendinous areas and degenerative changes within these units. Surgery may be necessary. Prognosis may be guarded.

The repetitive small trauma overload syndromes, as seen in repetitive upper extremity work requirements on the job, probably do not permanently injure muscle fibers, but the muscle fibers often respond with reflex weakness—lost endurance and strength—producing ease of pain (often intolerable). Attempts to overdevelop these sore muscles occasionally lessen impairments, but are not routinely successful.

Conditioning exercise programs, under supervision, and prescribed by orthopedists or other physicians who understand exercise physiology and therapy, remain a major therapeutic tool. Pre-exercise stretching of muscles lessens muscle injury, but usually has no effect on post-exercise pain. That pain lessens as the muscle becomes stronger.

Exercise training improves lipoprotein lipid profiles in patients with coronary artery disease. Although the patient needs medical supervision, the "heart" patient ordinarily is benefited with supervised exercise. The same patient with deconditioned back and legs and shoulder girdle muscles (which is nearly always true of the "heart" patient) is likewise helped in his or her ambulation ability and pain control with a regular supervised, tailored exercise program.

Moderate endurance exercise training lowers blood pressure and can be an initial treatment for mild hypertension.[12]

---

[12] Heathe, *Exercise Training Improves Lipoprotein Lipid Profiles in Patients with Coronary Artery Disease,* 105 Am Heart J 889 (1983); Hagberg, *Effect of Exercise Training on the Blood Pressure and Hemodynamic Features of Hypertensive Adolescents,* 52 Am J Cardio 763 (1983); Brown & Myles, *The Relationship Between Aerobic Fitness and Certain Cardiovascular Risk Factors,* Aviation, Space & Envt Med, June 1983, at 543; Dalsky, *Does Exercise Increase Bone Mass,* Surg Rounds Orthop, p. 73.

§30.14 Why Muscles Hurt

Why muscles hurt in any situation is another enigma, although better physiological information is now available. Muscle that is anoxic or ischemic hurts; muscle that has an accumulation of waste products, such as lactic acid, is painful. Muscles with an imbalance in calcium ion concentration, as found in de-conditioning and overuse and overstretch phenomena, are painful. Microscopic evaluation of trigger points and of overused, weakened musculature show mitochrondrial changes in the nucleus of the muscle cells, although no one specific causative chemical variation can be attached to any one muscle pain at this date. Nevertheless, pain is real and impairing, but is self-limited if the metabolic defect is corrected and is lessened in its tendency for occurrence in the well-habilitated (rehabilitated de-conditioned) muscle masses. All this, then, is a rationale for an energetic, tailored, aerobic sports medicine type of flexibility and exercise rehabilitative program directed to the improvement of impairment of many injured and debilitated people.[13]

§30.15 Crushing Injuries

Crushing injuries to muscles cause an acute inflammatory response with a formation of granulation tissue and later extensive scarring. In many cases, periosteal bone formation (myositis ossificans) occurs. This occurs by intramembranous ossification within the scar. The ossification tends to resolve in time, but it may take a year or so. The bony mass, as well as the scar in the muscle, may remain tender to pressure. The muscle remains easy to fatigue and has limited endurance during the healing period and the period of rehabilitation that follows. Actual healing—that is, resolution of the inflammatory response and granulation tissue response—averages six weeks to three months. Surgical excision of the myositis ossificans bony mass, especially during the acute phase of the injury, frequently results in recurrence of the ossification and is not indicated. Removal of bony masses during the acute phase may lead to an inaccurate pathological diagnosis, as the pathological study frequently looks like a malignancy (osteogenic sarcoma). It has been well shown that myositis ossificans does not behave like a malignancy, does not metastasize, and in fact routinely reabsorbs.

Another mechanism of a crush injury occurs in wringer injuries, such as catching an extremity in the wringer of a washing machine. This was a fairly common type of injury in the past. Prompt and aggressive therapy is necessary in all such injuries to prevent tissue loss and to prevent impairment of normal function.

There are two disruptive forces in crush injuries—friction and compression. Friction injuries range in severity from mild abrasive burns to partial and full thickness skin losses. Avulsion of muscle attachment occurs if the patient forceably resists the pull of the rollers and cannot release the

---

[13] Stamford, *How Much Should I Exercise?*, 17 Physician & SportsMed 150 (1989).

wringer. Areas of subcutaneous hematoma and fat necrosis occurs and is significant enough that overlying skin may be separated from its nutrient blood supply.[14]

§30.16 Muscle Fatigability

There has been a question whether repetitive stretching of muscles will lead to muscle bellies' fatigability and injury. A classic experiment tends to support this. The separate effects of negative (acentric) and positive (concentric) work on stimulated and voluntary isometric contraction of the triceps surae were studied. Researchers reasoned that repetitive stretching of the triceps surae muscle during the acentric phase of the work in the "negative" leg affected the efficiency of the contractile machinery and caused actual muscle damage. Subjects engaged in this one-time experiment had muscle soreness for five to seven days afterward. It was suggested that repetitive stretching of the muscle actually damages the contractile myosin machinery directly and affects the cycling of cross bridges within the muscle fibers, resulting in loss efficiency of a normal contraction process. In fatigue testing, it was always the negative—the repetitively stretched leg—that showed a loss of force and ease of fatigue.

In a study of hamstring muscles from buttock to knee, realizing there are two joint muscles which are therefore subjected to increased stretch and force produced extrinsically by motion of the hip and knee joint, it has been shown that the high levels of tension in the hamstring muscles produced by intrinsic force reduction to resist those forces and extrinsic stretch make them prone to injury. These observations are important to people who have had previous hamstring stretch injuries, representing an element of potential permanent impairment to that muscle. Also in a preventive vein, this information is important to persons who do repetitive hip, knee, squat, bend, coming upright activities, etc.[15]

§30.17 Prevention of Injuries

Prevention of musculoskeletal injuries is by far more successful than treatment of injury. Prevention of injury or of reinjury is best effected by warm-up and warm-down of the parts of the body in use for the activity. Stretching of the part in use prior to vigorous use, taping or bandaging which substitutes for loss of proprioceptive sensation, as well as offer some protection against

---

[14] Allen, *Wringer Injuries in Children,* 97 Archives Surgery 194 (1968); Ritani & Siler, *Wringer Injuries of the Upper Extremity,* 113 SG&O 667 (Dec 1961) (with 11 references).

[15] Garrett, *Muscle Strains: Histology, Causes, and Treatment,* Surg Rounds Orthopedica, Jan 1989, at 43; Garrett, *Muscle Injuries and Inflammation,* 3 Ann Sports Med 71 (1987); Garrett, *Histochemical Correlates of Hamstring Injuries,* 12 Am J Sports Med 98 (1984); Poe, *CTD: A High-Profile Problem Without a Cure,* Occup Health & Safety News, Apr 1, 1989, at 7.

re-strain and supports circulation to a degree. Specific rehabilitation techniques for those areas that remain weak and to be effective, this practically always has to be an aerobic rehabilitation technique with the exception of proprioceptive retraining and done with a tilting board. Specific training guidance by an instructor into the activity engaged and in industry this would include specific instructions of employees of how to do their work activities safely, to optimize the equipment that is used for safety and does not lend to overload of musculature, avoiding static fixed positions or cumulative repetitive trauma.[16]

§30.18 Evaluation of Muscle Injuries

Muscle injuries may be difficult for the physician to evaluate and equally difficult for the attorney or other interested third party to evaluate and understand. Different from fractures, where objective evidence of injury is demonstrable, soft tissue muscle injuries regularly present with subjective symptoms and are void of objective findings. Muscle injuries often involve adjacent ligaments or terminal tendons; thus, the term "muscle soft tissue" is often used in discussion. That muscle injuries are painful and can lead to permanent impairment is accepted by informed persons dealing with them. Yet, they seem to have become associated with false or fraudulent claims which have been brought by malingerers or greatly exaggerating patients with their supportive medical persons. The "whiplash" injury, for instance, has taken on a negative connotation, in spite of good and repeated medical authority showing that the injury may result in substantial permanent disability. Because of this fact, and because the injury is basically subjective in presentation, the trier of fact must be convinced that the injury is real and worthy of compensation, as well as the insurance adjuster, defense counsel, physicians, and even the patient. Many patients are unnerved by lack of objective evidence of injury and begin believing that they imagine or exaggerate their pain, leading to an enhanced and guilt-based additional impairment.

Neck and low back muscle soft tissue injury patients may present as problem cases. The injured's personality or integrity may require understanding by the physician, attorney, and others as early in the case and care as possible. The initial history/interview is the time to determine whether the patient/client symptoms and behaviors are real or are more likely a factitious disorder characterized by simulation of physical or psychological impairment. The attorney or other interested third party has a duty not to introduce symptoms or behavior into a client's repertoire of "medical history." The patient/client may be a malingerer. While not a mental disorder,

---

[16] Garrett, *Muscle Strains: Histology, Causes, and Treatment,* Surg Rounds Orthop, Jan 1989, at 43; Safran, *The Role of Warmup in Muscle Injury Prevention,* 16 Am J Sports Med 123 (1988); C. Rose & D.K. Lawson, Introduction to the Musculoskeletal System, (1970).

it is a behavioral disorder that can be used to obtain money or other benefits and to avoid responsibility.

The chief distinction between the patient/client who is a malingerer and one who has a factitious disorder is that the malingerer has the goal of obtaining compensation without having a compensable injury, and the other has the goal of becoming a patient.[17]

§30.19 Muscle Pain Syndromes

There are three common, but poorly understood, pain conditions that are strongly identified with muscles. These are myofascial pain syndromes caused by trigger points, fibromyalgia (or fibrositis) that is characterized by tender points in muscle, and articular dysfunction (somatic dysfunction). These three entities have neither a diagnostic laboratory or imaging test nor an established etiology. Each depends on history and physical examination for diagnosis, and the three conditions strongly interact. Without established etiology or diagnostic tests against which to validate clinical diagnostic criteria, the boundaries of the three conditions are blurred.[18]

§30.20 Myofascial Pain Syndromes

This is a condition of muscles which causes pain which makes a patient think he or she has a pinched nerve. Pain tends to come and go, but usually presents most of the time. It is a condition for which there is no known cause or cure. Most of the patients with this problem describe pain in the neck, underneath the posterior aspect of the head—i.e., tension headache, shoulder blades, arms, chest muscles, and low back. The pain between the shoulder blade and low back is often described as a sensation of knots in the muscles—of a knife-like pain or a burning, searing pain.

Myofascial pain syndromes (MPS) may present with dull aches in the thigh or hip muscles. Most patients who have not had a distinct injury develop the first symptoms of MPS in their 20s, although children as young as 8 years of age have been reported to have some of these symptoms. It is rare for the symptoms to start spontaneously in individuals in their 50s or 60s.

Common characteristics of MPS include the coming and going and the increase and decrease of pain. The increased pain can be exquisite. There are certain precipitating factors that cause myofascial pain syndrome to flare up. These factors usually fall into three major groups: (1) environmental factors, including weather changes, cold drafts, dampness,

---

[17] W.N. Harsha, Using Algorithm in Evaluation and Treatment of Low Back Pain, (Oct 1984) (presented at 8th Annual Meeting of American Academy of Neurological and Orthopedic Surgeons, Las Vegas, Nevada); Holzman, *Back to School for Aching Backs,* Insight, Jan 9, 1989, at 54.

[18] See **ch 15** for discussion of patient behavior and various pain syndromes, particularly somatization.

or conditions at work—such as vibration exposures and sudden or prolonged intense noise, (2) emotional factors, which include all the daily stresses that we all experience, and (3) physical factors, including activities that often precipitate symptoms such as working with arms out in front of the body with the arms unsupported for a long period of time.

Most myofascial pain patients have certain types of personalities. They are basically neat, perfectionist, compulsive, organized, time oriented, tense, precise individuals. The men are persons who have a peg board in their garage so their tools fit in place; women often keep an immaculate, neat, organized house. They are the type of people who sweep up crumbs and cigarette butts as people drop them, and pick up the towels and clothing that others drop. They are usually compulsive, even obsessive about doing things correctly. They are often easily "bugged" by people who do not behave the way they do. It is rare, indeed, to find MPS in injured patients who are "laid back" and carefree, and who have little concern for what is going to happen tomorrow but live for what today offers.

Most MPS patients have a certain body build. They are slightly built in the shoulders, not very muscular, often round-shouldered, and their natural position of comfort is sloped forward. Many of them have been round shouldered since infancy. Perhaps the reason men have fewer symptoms is their larger muscle mass. A number of patients have a positive history of allergies. One study suggests that 50 per cent of the people with myofascial pain syndromes are either allergic to themselves or have a history of the immediate family of allergies. There is a suggestion that MPS runs in families and may be inherited on an autosomal dominant basis.

There is a relationship between MPS and bursitis. Although MPS starts with muscular symptoms, bursitis or a tendonitis syndrome often develops about 10 years later. The initial problems are usually in the shoulder or arm. When the shoulder is involved, it is called *rotator cuff tendonitis* or *bicipital tendonitis*. When the elbow is involved, it is called *tennis elbow*. When the thumb is involved, it is called *deQuervain's disease*. In the lower extremities, painful hip muscles are present, especially in a physically active person, developing bursitis over the greater trochanter at the attachment of the gluteus medius tendon.

Most patients who have had MPS for months or years develop a phenomenon called "jelling" or stiffening. Many middle-aged MPS patients state that they are more stiff and sore in the mornings than friends who engage in the same activities. The term "jelling" came about because the myofascial tissues involved in the syndrome "set" like jello. When one makes jello, it is liquid, but after it sets for a period of time, it gets very rubbery and solid; if it is warmed up, it becomes liquid again; after setting again, it becomes rubbery. A very similar situation occurs in the tissues involved in the MPS patient.

Most MPS patients experience common reactions to certain physical activities. They do not tolerate maintaining a sustained isometric position for prolonged periods of time, such as arms extended out in front of the body carrying out some repetitive activities. Good examples are typing, using a computer keyboard, playing the piano, or repetitive assembly jobs. These positions, when maintained for long periods of time, can be maddening for the patient with MPS. There are activities at home that seem to aggravate MPS—cooking with arms out in front of the body or cleaning house, or vacuuming and ironing, especially late in the day when arms are fatigued. When arms are used out in front of the body, pain in the backs of the shoulders gradually builds and radiates up into the neck and/or into the lower back.

Other factors that may aggravate MPS are illnesses, including flu-like symptoms. Women frequently experience a flare-up just before their menstrual period starts, especially those women who retain fluids. As menses start, they commence losing salt and MPS symptoms diminish. Environmental factors are important; cold drafts on muscles tend to aggravate myofascial pain. A cold draft from an office air conditioner, a movie theater, or a restaurant may precipitate an acute flare-up of MPS, even though the patient is completely relaxed and having a good time. Many patients develop an intolerance to swimming in cold water, which makes the joints stiff and sore very quickly. Therefore, in taking a history, it is found that most persons with MPS have given up swimming in cold water. MPS patients often feel weather changes coming—coldness, dampness, fog, rain, or snow. Many will flare up even in the summer when the temperature drops from the 80s to the 60s, particularly if associated with dampness. MPS patients will frequently hurt or feel uncomfortable if they camp out and try to sleep on the cold damp ground. Many of these patients have not done well on water beds unless they are warm; in fact a warm water bed can be therapeutic.

Although there are physical and environmental factors that aggravate MPS, the one factor that seems to aggravate symptoms more than anything else is emotional stress. Emotions play a significant role in keeping MPS active or making it worse. If the patient has something to do and feels he or she must finish it by the end of the day, and it is already late in the afternoon, the typical MPS patient will become tense. A housewife working at the sink while waiting for her children to come home from school may start to tense up as she attempts to start dinner while the children are screaming and fighting. Stress associated with working under time deadlines often brings on MPS flare-ups. Everybody's life is filled with some degree of stress that we all must learn to cope with; the hardest stresses to learn to live with for most MPS patients are stressful situations at home or work where the stresses of daily life are repetitive and unlikely to end.

It is helpful for the MPS patient to identify the stressors in his or her life. Dividing them into two groups may help—factors that "bug" the patient but do not change whether or not the patient worries about them (national politics, weather, inflation, etc.), and factors that may be modified by the patient (home, work, school, friends, enemies). Francis of Assisi's serenity prayer is an apt therapy in this situation. "God grant me the courage to accept things I cannot change, the power to change the things I can, and the wisdom to know the difference."[19]

§30.21 Trigger Points

Myofascial pain caused by trigger points is identified clinically by spot tenderness in a palpable band which exhibits a local twitch response. Trigger points characteristically refer pain and tenderness in predictable patterns. Digital pressure on an active trigger point can reproduce this pain. In time, a patient with multiple and/or severe perpetuating factors (mechanical and/or systemic) may develop multiple myofascial pain syndromes throughout the body, and present with chronic pain syndrome, which is perhaps the most common musculoskeletal pain syndrome the practitioner sees for diagnosis and treatment. Identifying perpetuating or aggravating job or postural habitus and correcting them are important treatment modalities.[20]

§30.22 Fibromyalgias

Fibromyalgia is identified by a minimal number of tender points in the muscles that present with obvious perpetuating causes, and pain in three or more regions for at least three months of duration. Many authors say these tender areas should appear in all of the four quadrants of the body—upper and lower, right and left. Fibromyalgia is strongly associated with non-REM sleep disorder. Current suggestions as to fibromyalgia's etiology range from an abnormality of muscle metabolism to a response to chronic psychological and/or physical stress. "True" fibromyalgia may be a systemic disease that affects many organs, including muscle.

As the diagnostic criteria are now defined, patients with chronic myofascial pain syndromes are not eliminated from the study of patients with fibromyalgia. Many studies include patients with tender points and trigger points

---

[19] Roth & Davis, *Psychosomatic Complaints in Chronic Myofascial Pain,* presented at the First International Symposium on Myofascial Pain and Fibromyalgia (Minneapolis, Minn, May 8-10, 1989); Garrett, *Muscle Strains: Histology, Causes, and Treatment,* Surg Rounds Orthop, Jan 1989, at 43; Forest, *Current Concepts of Soft Connective Tissue, Wound Healing,* 70 Brit J of Surg 133 (1983); Garrett, *Muscle Injuries and Inflammation,* 3 Ann Sports Med 71 (1987); Black & Martin, *Musculoskeletal Symptoms and Anxiety Disorders,* 5 J Musculoskel Med 67 (1988); Grusten, *The Mechanical Effects of Impact Acceleration on the Unconstrained Human Head and Neck Complex,* 18 Contemp Orthop 199 (1989); Ike, *Arthritis and Aerobic Exercise: A Review,* 17 Physician & SportsMed 128 (1989); W.N. Kelley, Textbook of Rheumatology (2d ed 1985); E.A. Awad, Pathological Changes in Fibromyalgia, (May 8-10, 1989) (presented at the First International Symposium on Myofascial Pain and Fibromyalgia, Minneapolis, Minnesota); Harsha, *What Does Pain Mean to the Patient in Treating His Back Pain,* 3 J Neuro Orthop Surg 3 (1982); Harsha, *Patient Participation in his Low Back Care,* 5 J Neurol Orthop Surg 17 (1984); Gallion, *Perception of Disability in Chronic Back Pain Patients: A Long Term Follow-up,* 37 Pain 67 (1989); Young, Stokes & Liles, *Effects of Joint Pathology on Muscle,* 219 Clin Orthop 21 (1987).

[20] Dalsky, *Does Exercise Increase Bone Mass,* Surg Rounds Orthop, at 73;

indiscriminately. Apparently, any condition or situation that disturbs non-REM sleep produces rheumatic pain modulation disorder that qualifies as fibromyalgia. The pain of myofascial trigger points can also regularly disrupt REM sleep or sleep in general, by virtue of compression of the trigger point producing pain and awakening the patient.

In the taking of a history relative to myofascial pain syndromes, Janet Travell (generally accepted as the first American physician to codify the several symptoms into diagnosed syndromes and to establish a treatment plan) recites the pain history and delineates three phases of this refractory myofascial pain syndrome: Phase 1—constant pain; Phase 2—pain only on motion or effort; Phase 3—no pain complaint, but referred tenderness, stiffness, and restricted range of motion.

In Phase 1, patients with continuous severe pain at rest due to hyperirritable active trigger points are unaware of activities that aggravate the pain. Pain is so intense that anything that makes it worse cannot be distinguished.

In Phase 2, pain with specific movements is due to less irritable active trigger points; relatively pain-free days occur. This phase is ideal for patient education. If such patients are encouraged to pay attention, they can recognize aggravating activities. The delayed onset of pain for up to 24 hours may obscure its cause.

In Phase 3, patients with only latent trigger points experience referred tenderness and are limited by restricted range of motion—"stiffness" but not pain. The shoulder or hip may be sore when weight bearing in recumbent position, which is not really painful but can disrupt sleep.

The orthopedist needs to be constantly aware of myofascial and fibromyalgia pain syndromes, for they in fact explain the most common cause of muscular pain complaints of patients who come to a doctor's office and represent 70 to 75 per cent of patients seen in chronic pain clinics. These entities account for the greatest number of patients who utilize chronic pain rehabilitative services. MPS patients with trigger points and fibromyalgia are regularly missed by treating physicians of all disciplines. It is not unusual for a patient with such a problem to see an orthopedist after having seen many physicians for a number of years, so that negligent failure to make the diagnosis becomes a potential legal problem.

In ruling out fibromyalgia and myofascial pain syndromes, the risk factors of the patients evaluated must be considered, including (1) rheumatoid arthritis or rheumatoid tendency, (2) chronic repetitive microtrauma, (3) female patients with chronic pain syndromes (75 per cent of myofascial pain syndromes and/or fibromyalgias are female), (4) hypothyroidism, (5) depressive mood disorder, (6) steroid withdrawal patients, and (7) a variety of poorly understood systemic viral infections, such as the Epstein-Barr syndromes. Although diagnosis of fibromyalgia and myofascial pain syndromes is not a process of exclusion for primary diagnostic criteria present for both, it is necessary to rule out a wide range of other potentially confusing entities.

§30.23 Treatment of Myofascial Pain Syndromes

As to treatment, myofascial pain syndromes are quite treatable by addressing the cause, be it postural, repetitive work trauma, residuals of a specific injury, and/or asymmetrical extremity muscle usage due to deformity or habit (posture). Myofascial pain syndromes that are untreated and that spread from more than one trigger point to several in time tend to meld into fibromyalgia-type of patients. In the fibromyalgia patients at this time, regardless of what treatment modality is used, one-third improve and two-thirds have no change. There is a plateau after which the fibromyalgia patient does not worsen.[21]

§30.24 Post-Polio Syndrome

The second most common condition in America that causes residual paralysis is poliomyelitis. The 400,000 polio survivors are "at risk" of developing a constellation of new medical problems called post-polio syndrome. After over 30 years of medical stability following recovery from polio, survivors are reporting a variety of new symptoms: (1) fatigue—a feeling of extreme exhaustion after minimal activity, with decreased endurance, (2) joint pain, often in the area previously not effected by "old" polio, (3) weakness, often progressive, in muscles previously affected and in new muscle groups, generally symmetrical, (4) new respiratory difficulties, at times requiring return to respiratory devices, and (5) cold intolerance, making muscle weakness more noticeable with bluish discoloration of extremities. Treatment of these problems presents a challenge to the physician and therapist. Overuse of muscles that operate at maximal capacity with minimal or no reserve can result in irreversible damage to muscle fibers, to terminal axonal sprouts, or even to anterior horn cells.

Use of exercise treatment in post-polio syndrome is different from treating deconditioned muscle groups that have reserve and recruitment ability. The physician and therapist must be aware of this and approach carefully. Supervised exercise does have an important place in treatment of the post-polio syndrome.[22]

---

[21] Harsha, *What Does Pain Mean to the Patient in Treating His Back Pain,* 3 J Neuro Orthop Surg 3 (1982); Harsha, *Patient Participation in his Low Back Care,* 5 J Neurol Orthop Surg 17 (1984); Gallion, *Perception of Disability in Chronic Back Pain Patients: A Long Term Follow-up,* 37 Pain 67 (1989); Young, Stokes & Liles, *Effects of Joint Pathology on Muscle,* 219 Clin Orthop 21 (1987).

[22] DR Jones, *Cardiorespiratory Responses to Aerobic Training by Patients with Post-poliomyelitis Sequelae,* 261 JAMA 3255 (1989); Cashman, *Late Denervation in Patients with Antecedent Paralytic Poliomyelitis,* 317 NEJM 7 (1987).

§30.25 Chronic Fatigue Syndrome

Another common complaint of orthopedists, as well as other physicians, in the differential diagnosis of muscle pain, whether or not related to trauma, is the chronic fatigue syndrome (CFS) or "Yuppie Flu."

The major criteria for diagnosis of CFS at this time is (1) new onset of persistent or relapsing, debilitating fatigue, lasting at least six months in a person with no prior history, (2) exclusion of numerous other clinical conditions that might give similar symptoms, including malignancy, autoimmune disease, bacterial, fungal, or parasitic diseases, (3) chronic psychiatric disease, (4) chronic inflammatory disease, (5) neuromuscular disease, (6) endocrine disease, (7) drug abuse, or (8) medication or toxic chemical side effects.

Patients with CFS often report chronic low-grade fever, sore throat, tender lymph nodes in the neck, axilla, or groin, unexplained generalized muscular weakness, myalgia, generalized fatigue, irritability, anxiousness, depression, and sleep disturbances. Physicians can often document the first three (fever, sore throat, tender lymph nodes) symptoms.

By nature, physicians are suspicious of illnesses they cannot see. One problem with diseases that are not fully understood is that a degree of arrogance among physicians exists. They feel that if they did not learn about it in medical school or training, then it does not exist. Physicians do not feel comfortable saying "I don't know," so they prefer not to deal with it. Treatment of CFS is symptomatic; it is unlikely that a direct link to trauma exists, but there is a strong argument that a vulnerable person with asymptomatic or minimally symptomatic CFS may be injured and activate into a symptomatic state.[23]

§30.26 Muscle Impairment Evaluation

Assessment of an individual's impairment requires the integration of clinical and laboratory observation with the patient's cognitive beliefs, psychological propensities, and behavior. In addition to the social support system and educational level, economic ramifications and litigation require consideration. The present legal system for disability determination tends to be based predominantly on the anatomical diagnosis or the physical or laboratory data, including numerical listing of joint range of motion. Often, physicians discount functional limitation not corroborated by "objective findings." The clinician depends heavily on the patient's symptoms and assessment of the patient's condition in the determination of treatment. Assessment instruments based solely on self-report have been shown to be both reliable and valid measures of functional status. This type of data is of particular importance in conditions where disability is secondary to muscular pain alone. Since there is often an absence of laboratory findings and lack of consensus

---

[23] Staver (AMN correspondent), *Meeting Shed Light on Chronic Fatigue (Yuppie Flu)*, Am Med News, May 26, 1989, at 9; A. McGehee-Harvey, J. Boardley III, & J.A. Barondess, Differential Diagnosis, Interpretation of Clinical Evidence, 3d ed (1979).

as to the evaluation of significant physical findings (trigger points, muscle tautness), dependence on reliable self-reporting, as well as on behavioral observations made by the clinician, are critical in discerning impairment, assessing the patient's clinical status, and developing appropriate treatment and rehabilitation goals. Several psychosocial assessment instruments are available, such as the pain body drawing, algorithm, pain-type descriptor, etc.

Articular dysfunction deals with pathological states around joints involving insertions of joint supportive ligaments as they attach to bone and in the fibers of the ligament itself. A dysfunctional ligament about a joint will regularly refer pain to adjacent muscles—muscles that attach in the area of the ligament or muscles that cross that joint.[24]

§30.27 Diagnosis of Muscle Pain

Several of the chemicals (medications) used to treat inflammatory aspects of arthritis, myofascial overload syndromes, and acute soft tissue injury may present risks or may be life-threatening. Aspirin, nonsteroidal anti-inflammatory chemicals, and corticosteroids may cause gastric ulceration, bleeding, and even death following excessive bleeding. These chemicals can cause significant renal damage. Corticosteroids may cause marked demineralization of bone with pathological fracture and frequently adversely affect the pituitary axis, producing a Cushing disease type syndrome. Physicians using these drugs must take a history of prior sensitivity or other side effects before prescribing and must closely monitor the patient. The patient is entitled to know and accept the risks of potential complication, or to reject the treatment.[25]

---

[24] J.A. Tarantino & D.J. Oliveira, Litigating Neck and Back Injuries. (1988); Holzman, *Back to School for Aching Backs,* Insight, Jan 9, 1989, at 54; Black & Martin, *Musculoskeletal Symptoms and Anxiety Disorders,* 5 J Musculoskel Med 67 (1988); W.N. Kelley, Textbook of Rheumatology, 2d ed (1985); E.A. Awad, Pathological Changes in Fibromyalgia, (May 8-10, 1989) (presented at the First International Symposium on Myofascial Pain and Fibromyalgia, Minneapolis, Minnesota); Gallion, *Perception of Disability in Chronic Back Pain Patients: A Long Term Follow-up,* 37 Pain 67 (1989); Young, Stokes & Liles, *Effects of Joint Pathology on Muscle,* 219 Clin Orthop 21 (1987); Spitzer, *The Arthritic Complaint in Primary Care: Prevalence Related Disability and Costs,* 3 J Rheum 88 (1976).

[25] Roth & Davis, *Psychosomatic Complaints in Chronic Myofascial Pain,* presented at the First International Symposium on Myofascial Pain and Fibromyalgia (Minneapolis, Minn, May 8-10, 1989); Garrett, *Muscle Strains: Histology, Causes, and Treatment,* Surg Rounds Orthop, Jan 1989, at 43; Garrett, *Muscle Injuries and Inflammation,* 3 Ann Sports Med 71 (1987); W.N. Harsha, Using Algorithm in Evaluation and Treatment of Low Back Pain, (Oct 1984) (presented at 8th Annual Meeting of American Academy of Neurological and Orthopedic Surgeons, Las Vegas, Nevada); A. McGehee-Harvey, J. Boardley III, & J.A. Barondess, Differential Diagnosis, Interpretation of Clinical Evidence, 3d ed (1979); V. Mooney, Diagnostic Injections, (May 6, 1988) (presented at Neurskeletal Imaging and Surgery Spring Conference, University of Minnesota, Minneapolis).

§30.28 Use of Strong Medications

There is a cadre of patients who function better and who are productive citizens with the regular use of closely-monitored pain or related medication. These patients must understand that the "strong" medications do have a substance abuse potential. Those patients, when under the regular attendance of their physician and closely monitored, are safely managed with these medications. This is a controversial point, with the ultraconservative physician being unwilling to take the risk of monitoring the patient and frequently having the opinion that prolonged use of any mind-altering drug is inappropriate. This is potentially a risky area of practice, for there are many critics of physicians who maintain patients on closely-monitored doses of mind-altering drugs, yet there is abundant pain management and psychiatric evidence that many patients can be kept independent without adverse effects of addiction when managed by competent, empathetic physicians, rather than the pain patient living a diminished quality of life. (See Chapter 21, on pain management.)

There is a wide, gray area in dealing with patients who fall into the above category, as compared to those who, for psychosocial reasons, are unable and unwilling to cope with the stresses of daily living and require the same medications for an element of comfort. This area is a source of controversy among physicians, and a source of frequent criticism by some physicians of the care that other physicians render. There appears to be a tendency for those physicians who criticize to be those in academic circles, those who are ultraconservative by nature, or those who have "been burned" by past patient experiences. These physicians may not have daily contact or total patient management of chronic pain patients. On the other hand, empathetic, caring, conscientious physicians who have daily contact with patients and those who are more psychologically oriented, treating the patient as a whole, see the utility and probable need for utilization of these medications for a select group of patients.[26]

§30.29 Other Causes of Muscle Pain

There have been a number of biochemical and histological studies of painful muscles. Up to 10 years or so ago, there was no objective laboratory or histological abnormality that could be demonstrated in myofascial pain syndrome patients, and particularly in the trigger points. In more recent years of more sophisticated testing equipment and more innovative studies of the metabolism of muscle, it has been well shown that there are several abnormalities that occur. As to electrophysiology of the muscle, it has been shown

---

[26] Black & Martin, *Musculoskeletal Symptoms and Anxiety Disorders,* 5 J Musculoskel Med 67 (1988); V. Mooney, Diagnostic Injections, (May 6, 1988) (presented at Neurskeletal Imaging and Surgery Spring Conference, University of Minnesota, Minneapolis); Gibson, *The Penetration of Antibiotics into the Normal Intervertebral Disc Space,* 69B J Bone Joint Surg 784 (1987); Deeb, *Intervertebral Disc space Infection After Chymopapain Injection,* 144 AJR 671 (1985).

that the trigger point of the banded fiber that responds to the "twitch" (which is the diagnostic phenomena of the myofascial trigger point) manifests increased EMG response. A series of high technological biochemical studies have shown that there are alterations in the oxydative enzyme production and utilization in both aerobic and anaerobic metabolism of muscle contraction and relaxation. In addition, there is a diminishing of ATP enzymes (the power source enzyme of all body processes). It is interesting also that the deconditioned musculature of the body has similar findings, except absent the trigger points. Deconditioned musculature is often tender, and that observation may parallel the tender spots found in fibromyalgia.[27]

§30.30 Tourniquet Paralysis Syndrome

A tourniquet may be applied as a first aid measure to stop bleeding in emergency situations, although it is usually less effective and more dangerous than direct pressure dressing. Tourniquets are often used in orthopedic surgery, plastic surgery, and nerve surgery when bloodless fields are necessary.

Paralysis after tourniquet application is not unusual and may be overlooked for several reasons. The tourniquet effect may result from inadvertent circumferential insult by surgical tourniquet. The paralysis and associated problem may be short-lived and the lesion may be mild and result in an incomplete paralysis, which may be interpreted as difficulty in moving because of recent surgery. The sensory examination is usually confined to testing of pain sensation with pin prick (ignoring other sensory modalities such as pressure, hot-cold, two-point discrimination, and position testing). When an adequate, complete, diligent examination, as in most diagnostic situations, is not carried out, few or no findings are made by the physician and a diagnosis of hysteria is often made.

In tourniquet paralysis, there is a disturbance in the function of the peripheral nerves which is due to the mechanical pressure of the tourniquet on the nerves and not the result of ischemia (primarily). A constellation of symptoms justifies the syndrome. This syndrome may present as:

1. Motor function: there is paralysis with hypotonia or atonia, but no appreciable atrophy.
2. Sensory examination shows a dissociation of the sensations. The fibers serving touch, pressure, vibration, and position sense occurs. Pain sensation is rarely lost. Heat and cold are incompletely altered and often are not altered at all.

---

[27] C. Rose & D.K. Lawson, Introduction to the Musculoskeletal System, (1970); Black & Martin, *Musculoskeletal Symptoms and Anxiety Disorders,* 5 J Musculoskel Med 67 (1988); Young, Stokes & Liles, *Effects of Joint Pathology on Muscle,* 219 Clin Orthop 21 (1987); Knighton, *Role of Platelets and Fibrin in the Healing Sequence,* 196 Annals of Surg 379 (1982).

3. There are no paresthesias or tingling after release of the tourniquet, which suggests impairment of touch fibers. There is not a Tinel's sign.
4. Sympathetic fibers are not affected. Pilomotor reflex is normal. Skin temperature is normal.
5. Electrical studies show that there is a block of conduction characterized by lack of response to stimulation of the motor nerve above the injury and a good response below injury. Electrical stimulation can localize the level of the lesion. Tourniquet paralysis or nerve damage is a preventable complication of treatment. If at high risk for some reason, the physician must so inform the patient. Several studies show that pneumatic tourniquet pressures used in surgery by many orthopedists are much higher than necessary for a bloodless operation field, and put nerves lying under the tourniquet at risk.[28]

§30.31 Compression Syndromes

Compressive forces produce edema in the muscle elements and connective tissue of the extremity. If the edema is massive and occurs in closed fascial compartments, vascular impairment of the distal extremity will occur. The most critical vessels to be affected are the small nutrient vessels to the nerves of the forearm and hand. The severity of the tissue damage depends on the duration of exposure to the traumatic forces, tightness of rollers, and method of release. (See Appendix 30-1, Case 1.)

Emergency surgical treatment may be necessary to lessen impairment. Perhaps the most important consideration is the recognition by a physician of the potential or in fact presence of a compartment compression syndrome and effect immediate fascial release. Treatment of open wounds by protection with sterile dressings and coverage with skin, if necessary by grafting, at an early date, is important. Compression dressing and elevation of the arm to lessen swelling are important. Resection of devitalized muscles as part of the surgical care is important; however, it may require several days to be identifiable.

The potential for significant permanent impairment for this type of injury is great. Impairment results from loss of muscle mass and muscle function,

---

[28] Moldaver, *Tourniquet Paralysis Syndrome,* 77 Tr Am Neurol A 189 (1952); Reid, *Tourniquet Hemostasis,* 177 Clin Orthop & Rel Res 230 (1983); Krackow, *A Maneuver for Improved Positioning of a Tourniquet in the Obese Patient,* 168 Clin Orthop & Rel Res 80 (1982); Saunders, *Effect of Tourniquet Time on Post-Operative Quadriceps Function,* 143 Clin Orthop & Clin Res 194 (1979); Shaw, *The Relationship Between Tourniquet Pressure and Underlying Soft Tissue Pressure in the Thigh,* 64A JBJ Surg 1148 (1982); Simon, *The Effect of a Thigh Tourniquet on the Incidence of Deep Venous Thrombosis After Operations on the Fore Part of the Foot,* 64A JBJ Surg 188 (1982); Tountas & Bergman, *Tourniquet Ischemia: Ultrastructural and Histochemical Observations of Ischemic Human Muscle and of Monkey Muscle Nerve,* 2 J Hand Surg 31 (1977) (with 23 references); Reid, *Tourniquet Hemostasis,* 177 Clin Orthop & Rel Res 230 (1983).

loss of nerve supply due to ischemia with weakness of grip and pinch and dexterity of the hand being the greater of the losses. Significant cosmetic damage frequently results. In areas where there has been substantial loss of muscle function, either by direct tissue loss or by loss of its motor nerve function, reconstructive surgeries with tendon transplants at a future date may be necessary.[29]

§30.32 Volkmann's Contracture

Volkmann's ischemic contracture was first described in 1881, and is generally considered to result from spasm of main arteries of the forearm and branches as a consequence of trauma to elbow or forearm. The sustained, but incomplete, interruption of arterial blood supply, together with venostasis, produces acute ischemic necrosis of forearm muscles, predominantly flexor muscles. Typically, muscle degeneration occurs in most vulnerable muscle bellies, in an oval configuration in mid flexor surface (Seddon's Infarct). Nerve fibers also are adversely affected by the ischemia with mechanical pressure caused by edema.

In some areas, muscle will regenerate, but most heal by fibrosis, which causes contractures. This contracture, due to scarring, may be superimposed on paralysis and a varying degree of deformity may result. Treatment of the contracture in its late stages includes reconstructive procedure to use

---

[29] Gallion, *Perception of Disability in Chronic Back Pain Patients: A Long Term Follow-up,* 37 Pain 67 (1989); Young, Stokes & Liles, *Effects of Joint Pathology on Muscle,* 219 Clin Orthop 21 (1987); DR Jones, *Cardiorespiratory Responses to Aerobic Training by Patients with Post-poliomyelitis Sequelae,* 261 JAMA 3255 (1989); Cashman, *Late Denervation in Patients with Antecedent Paralytic Poliomyelitis,* 317 NEJM 7 (1987); Staver (AMN correspondent), *Meeting Shed Light on Chronic Fatigue (Yuppie Flu),* Am Med News, May 26, 1989, at 9; A. McGehee-Harvey, J. Boardley III, & J.A. Barondess, Differential Diagnosis, Interpretation of Clinical Evidence, 3d ed (1979); Spitzer, *The Arthritic Complaint in Primary Care: Prevalence Related Disability and Costs,* 3 J Rheum 88 (1976); V. Mooney, Diagnostic Injections, (May 6, 1988) (presented at Neurskeletal Imaging and Surgery Spring Conference, University of Minnesota, Minneapolis); Gibson, *The Penetration of Antibiotics into the Normal Intervertebral Disc Space,* 69B J Bone Joint Surg 784 (1987); Deeb, *Intervertebral Disc space Infection After Chymopapain Injection,* 144 AJR 671 (1985); Knighton, *Role of Platelets and Fibrin in the Healing Sequence,* 196 Annals of Surg 379 (1982); Moldaver, *Tourniquet Paralysis Syndrome,* 77 Tr Am Neurol A 189 (1952); Reid, *Tourniquet Hemostasis,* 177 Clin Orthop & Rel Res 230 (1983); Krackow, *A Maneuver for Improved Positioning of a Tourniquet in the Obese Patient,* 168 Clin Orthop & Rel Res 80 (1982); Saunders, *Effect of Tourniquet Time on Post-Operative Quadriceps Function,* 143 Clin Orthop & Clin Res 194 (1979); Shaw, *The Relationship Between Tourniquet Pressure and Underlying Soft Tissue Pressure in the Thigh,* 64A JBJ Surg 1148 (1982); Simon, *The Effect of a Thigh Tourniquet on the Incidence of Deep Venous Thrombosis After Operations on the Fore Part of the Foot,* 64A JBJ Surg 188 (1982); Tountas & Bergman, *Tourniquet Ischemia: Ultrastructural and Histochemical Observations of Ischemic Human Muscle and of Monkey Muscle Nerve,* 2 J Hand Surg 31 (1977) (with 23 references); Reid, *Tourniquet Hemostasis,* 177 Clin Orthop & Rel Res 230 (1983).

residual muscle power and length by soft tissue release, tendon-lengthening, or bone-shortening procedures.

Prevention of Volkmann's contracture is of extreme importance. Compartment compression syndromes are part of the problem. Fasciotomy may be limb-saving, as may changing a flexed elbow into extension, even though loss of supracondylar fracture may result. It is better to reset a fracture than to lose 80 per cent function of the forearm and hand. This is an area demanding great diligence on the part of the treating surgeon, as most Volkmann's ischemic contractures are preventable.[30]

§30.33 High-Pressure Ischemia; Muscle versus Tourniquet

The concept that muscle ischemia is the same, regardless of cause, is faulty. Several recent experiments with tourniquets and with artificial compartments have been conducted, with the following results:

1. The metabolic and ultra-structural deterioration of skeletal muscle in high-pressure compartment syndrome is more severe than in muscle that has been rendered ischemic by tourniquet application.
2. The cause of the accelerated breakdown of high-energy phosphate and more extreme cellular acidosis seen in the compartment syndrome muscle is unknown, but it is possible that elevated tissue pressure may act synergestically with ischemia to produce a more severe degree of cellular deterioration than is produced by ischemia alone.
3. The marginal metabolic recovery after fasciotomy may be related to more severe mitachondrial changes, the extreme degree of cellular acidosis, incomplete re-perfusion of the tissue, or depletion of the total cellular-adenosine pool, which has been shown to limit re-synthesis of adenosine triphosphate.
4. The use of tourniquet ischemia studies as a pathophysiological frame of reference for discussing tolerance of skeletal muscle to ischemia in compartment syndromes may be misleading. Much of muscle physiology dogma as to muscle behavior and vulnerability is based on nonphysiological studies, except those observations aid the surgeon who must use a leg/arm tourniquet for the operation. A little pressure in tourniquet for the shortest safe operating time is the rule. As to compartment

---

[30] Tsuge, *Treatment of Established Volkmann's Contracture,* 57A JBJ Surg 925 (1975); Lapuk & Woodbury, *Volkmann's Ischemic Contracture,* 17 Orthop Rev 618 (1987).

syndromes, it seems that earlier fasciotomy will preserve more muscle function—the "wait and see" concept is inappropriate.[31]

§30.34 Muscle and Anxiety Symptoms

Musculoskeletal complaints such as sore muscles, back pain, fatigue, loss of strength, and limited endurance can result from anxiety-caused muscle tension, increased sensitivity to pain, or both. Somatic pains and anxiety have a complex interreaction. For example, muscular pain can become an excuse for avoiding fear-causing situations. A thorough physical examination after an equally-thorough history, with careful attention to psychiatric symptoms, will most often establish the diagnosis. Managing anxiety requires discussing the problem with patient in terms he or she understands, using anti-anxiety medicines familiar to the physician.[32]

§30.35 Compartment Syndrome

Compartment syndromes are most often seen in the forearm and leg; however, the thigh is often involved. Bleeding in the thigh following a direct blow injury, or at times following strenuous overuse, can threaten the viability of leg by occlusion of blood inflow, outflow, or both. Likewise, muscle and nerve necrosis may occur. The surgeon has to think of this problem and also separate it from other life-threatening problems, such as gas gangrene, which can start insidiously from a small puncture wound and become fulmonating in a matter of hours.[33]

---

[31] Moldaver, *Tourniquet Paralysis Syndrome,* 77 Tr Am Neurol A 189 (1952); Reid, *Tourniquet Hemostasis,* 177 Clin Orthop & Rel Res 230 (1983); Krackow, *A Maneuver for Improved Positioning of a Tourniquet in the Obese Patient,* 168 Clin Orthop & Rel Res 80 (1982); Saunders, *Effect of Tourniquet Time on Post-Operative Quadriceps Function,* 143 Clin Orthop & Clin Res 194 (1979); Shaw, *The Relationship Between Tourniquet Pressure and Underlying Soft Tissue Pressure in the Thigh,* 64A JBJ Surg 1148 (1982); Simon, *The Effect of a Thigh Tourniquet on the Incidence of Deep Venous Thrombosis After Operations on the Fore Part of the Foot,* 64A JBJ Surg 188 (1982).

[32] Black & Martin, *Musculoskeletal Symptoms and Anxiety Disorders,* 5 J Musculoskel Med 67 (1988); Komi & Buskirk, *Effect of Eccectric and Concentric Muscle Condition on Tension and Electrical Activity of Human Muscles,* 15 Ergonomics 417 (1972).

[33] Moldaver, *Tourniquet Paralysis Syndrome,* 77 Tr Am Neurol A 189 (1952); Reid, *Tourniquet Hemostasis,* 177 Clin Orthop & Rel Res 230 (1983); Krackow, *A Maneuver for Improved Positioning of a Tourniquet in the Obese Patient,* 168 Clin Orthop & Rel Res 80 (1982); Saunders, *Effect of Tourniquet Time on Post-Operative Quadriceps Function,* 143 Clin Orthop & Clin Res 194 (1979); Shaw, *The Relationship Between Tourniquet Pressure and Underlying Soft Tissue Pressure in the Thigh,* 64A JBJ Surg 1148 (1982); Simon, *The Effect of a Thigh Tourniquet on the Incidence of Deep Venous Thrombosis After Operations on the Fore Part of the Foot,* 64A JBJ Surg 188 (1982); Tountas & Bergman, *Tourniquet Ischemia: Ultrastructural and Histochemical Observations of Ischemic Human Muscle and of Monkey Muscle Nerve,* 2 J Hand Surg 31 (1977) (with 23 references); Reid, *Tourniquet Hemostasis,* 177 Clin Orthop & Rel Res 230 (1983).

To a distance runner who developed "shin splint," a posterior fascial compartment release was done using a 2 cm incision and blind severence of fascia with scissors. Pain persisted and worsened. Arteriovenous fistula was diagnosed by arteriogram. Repair of fistula was carried out several months later. The patient improved, but was unable to run at a pre-fasciotomy level—an unusual complication. To prevent this:

1. Assess bleeding and perform appropriate hemostasis with deflated tourniquet
2. Carefully place fasciotomy incisions away from high risk to local neurovascular structures
3. Make skin incisions that are adequate to visualize adjacent neurovascular structures
4. Monitor patient closely after surgery

§30.36 Cumulative Trauma Disorders (CTD)

Repetitive motion associated trauma (cumulative trauma disorders), are common and include carpal tunnel syndrome, tendonitis, ganglionitis, tenosynovitis, bursitis, and epicondylitis. These injuries may be caused or aggravated by repeated twisting or awkward positions of work. Vibration-associated injuries are seen in vehicle operations (truck, auto, taxi driving). The effects of vibration are poorly understood, but increasing data suggest that low back pain, vertebrogenic pain, and degenerative disc disease may be vibration-associated and/or aggravated.

An estimated 1.2 million workers are exposed to segmental vibration, i.e., vibration principally of a part or parts of the body, such as hand-held power tools, chain saws, jackhammers, etc. Often, the extremities exposed to segmental vibration present with numbness and/or blanching of fingers, with reduced sensitivity to heat, cold, or pain. Occasional increased sensitivity is noted.

In the survey mentioned above, nearly all the symptoms involved low back along with the neck/shoulder/arm pain complaints; 6 per cent of those lasted at least one month or more. Cumulative trauma disorders (CTD) were often felt to be a significant etiological factor in persons with neck/arm pain. The United States Surgeon General's Office and the National Institute of Occupational Safety and Health appear to accept CTD, stating "When job demands repeatedly exceed the biomechanical capacity of the worker, those activities become trauma producing. Hence, traumatogens are workplace sources of biomechanical strain that contribute to the onset of injuries affecting the musculoskeletal system."

In recent years, the fixed position of operating a computer or word processor, along with the fixed visual fatigue of looking at a video screen, have been shown to produce a variety of head, neck, and shoulder arm pains and carpal tunnel syndromes. Several states have laws requiring ergometric controls as well as industrial vocational changes, such as adjusting seat heights, angle of chair back, position of key board, and parabolic lighting to diffuse VDT light.

The above dictum is opposed by many physicians, responsible third-parties, or self-insured carriers. They point out that any upper extremity task poses a challenge to workers who experience any arm or neck discomfort. The challenge may prove insurmountable if there is no flexibility on the job. Under the banner of worker comfort and satisfaction, labor and management should seek job flexibility, task design, and proper renumeration.

The examining physician in evaluating CTD type cases must be informed of the work environment, as well as the psychosocial ramifications of his or her opinion, and that examiner may make him- or herself vulnerable to criticism. Honest doctors have honest differences of opinion, but opinion must be rationally based and non-biased.

There are a large number of work-related compensation cases representing the majority of job-related chronic neck and low back pain patients with myofascial pain syndromes melding toward fibromyalgia and which represent an astronomical cost to society. These deserve early diagnosis and adequate treatment.

The most effective treatment for each entity is change in the lifestyle of the patient, avoiding postures that are perpetuators of the pain complaint, added to an aerobic rehabilitation exercise type of program that (1) stretches all areas of the body in which there is limited motion, and (2) strengthens affected areas in a balanced manner to support each of the areas—the axial and appendicular skeleton. Medications include nonsteroidal anti-inflammatory and depressive mood chemicals.

Motivation in treatment of these muscle pain conditions is important. It has been shown that poorly motivated patients (those who are not willing to accept the pain of rehabilitation) rarely improve and become dependent indefinitely. The rehabilitation program itself produces pain in the areas of complaint as the patient works through the stretching and strengthening of muscle groups. Some patients find the discomfort so intense that they are not willing to accept the rigors of a treatment plan, and a substantial number of other patients become dependent on medication (often mind-altering medication) that is probably inappropriate for most patients. (See Chapter 25, on rehabilitation.)

The Occupational Safety and Health Administration (OSHA) attributed over 30 per cent of work-related illness in Michigan during the early 1980s to CTD. The National Institute of Occupational Safety and Health (NIOSH) placed musculoskeletal injuries, such as CTD, among the 10 most significant occupational health problems of the 1980s. Some estimates of cost of CTD, including back pain, reach $16 billion per year. OSHA cited two meat packing companies in 1987 for not correcting work patterns leading to CTDs.

Many physicians dealing with CTD recognize three stages:

1. Pain during work shift, with no change in work capacity or physical signs, and reversible in one month

2. Pain during sleep with reduced work capacity, and possible physical signs, persisting for months
3. Pain even with light work and nonrepetitive motion; leisure activities are affected, physical signs are present and symptoms persist for months or years

The cause of CTD is not fully understood. It appears that in susceptible persons, muscle (particularly the myotendinous juncture), becomes inflamed and swollen with changes of local anoxia, but also may impinge on nerves. In the upper extremity, any of the five tunnels of the arm (pronator, radial, and cubital at the elbow, and carpal and ulnar at the wrist) are vulnerable to minimal swelling with irritation of their contained nerves.

Classic research shows that ischemia on propagation velocity of the affected nerves results in increased metabolic byproduct concentrations rather than shortage of energy sources. There is local increased tissue acidity.

It is known that connective tissue is viscoelastic; it is differentially susceptible to rate and amplitude effects. A large, slow onset force applied to a tendon for a long period will cause mechanical damage to individual fibers and secondary inflammation. Large, sudden forces cause no damage if they are of short duration. Even very small forces can provoke damage if they elicit a damaging reflex response. Tendons are most vulnerable to quick tensions, oblique forces, traumas while under tension, new forces applied to a maximally enervated or already stretched muscles, and when the tendon is weaker compared to the attached muscle. Tendons in females are stiffer than males.

In industry, trauma to tendons can result from tensile, compressive, or shear stresses and associated deformation in the tendon. Muscles create tension in the tendon through contraction. Strain occurs in proportion to the cross section of the tendon. Bones and ligaments initiate compressive forces in the tendon corresponding to the applied force, the amount of bend required of the tendon, and the size of the contact area. Shear forces on the tendon result from the action of bones and ligaments on the tendon. The shear response of the tendon is relative to the force and velocity of this action, as well as to the contact surface characteristics.

Employers often fail to understand that a quick return to repetitive work, or denial of the CTD as an entity, with the patient placed back at the same job with the job unmodified and encouraged to "stay with it," and to "be tough" is detrimental to the patient. Often, the examining doctor is not well informed as to CTD or is biased against the concept and reports (unfairly) to the employer that the patient is ready for work, does not recommend change in job ergonomics, and tends to leave the patient with the thought and advice that there is nothing wrong, perhaps because the physician is unable to find objective pathology. This may be self-serving on the doctor's part, or playing the employer's game.

Carpal tunnel syndrome and other CTDs have been accepted as occupational disorders, with some practitioners not agreeing. Scaled-down job tasks in today's work place have increased productivity by limiting the movements of workers, yet the American Academy of Orthopedic Surgeons estimated the cost in workers' compensation and lost earnings to be $27 billion a year.

With workers performing a few work-related motions thousands of times per hour, cumulative trauma injuries are escalating. Work place preventive methods are in place, but not widely used by industry at this time. Surgery is an option in some CTD injuries, but ease of reinjury is common when returned to the same type of work.

§30.37 Common Upper Extremity CTD Injuries

1. Carpal tunnel syndrome: Compression and entrapment of the median nerve where it passes through the wrist into the hand
2. Tendonitis: Inflammation of the tendons in the wrist and forearm
3. Tenosynovitis: Inflammation of the tendons and their sheaths in wrist and forearm
4. White Finger: Damage to the circulation in fingers due to continuous contact with vibration
5. Trigger Finger: Tenosynovitis in fingers caused by contact pressure from a tool
6. deQuervain's disease: Fibrosis of the enveloping sheaths of the tendons abducting and extending thumb
7. Tennis elbow; epicondylitis: Inflammation origin flexor or extensor muscles of wrist and fingers, with tendonitis felt at elbow

Typical symptoms of CTD include (1) dropping small objects, (2) difficulty grasping large objects, (3) thumb weakness, radiation pain from neck at occiput, shoulder, forearm, elbow, wrist, and hand, (4) radiation of pain, numbness, tingling into shoulder, arm, elbow, forearm, and wrist, (5) swelling of volar aspect of forearm at and proximal to wrist, (6) limited motion in neck, and (7) sharp shooting pains that spread down the shoulder to the lateral aspect of the arm and the radial aspect of the forearm to the wrist. These symptoms often fit other pathologies, making accurate history and physical examination essential.[34]

---

[34] Burnette & Ayoub, *Cumulative Trauma Disorders,* Pain Mgmt, July/Aug 1989, at 196; Klein, *Assessment of Workers Compensation Claims for Back Strains-Sprains,* 26 J Occup Med 443 (1984); Pie, *CTD: A High-Profile Problem Without a Cure,* Occup Health & Safety News, Apr 1, 1989, at 7. Barker & Hines, *Arterial Occlusion in the Hands and Fingers Associated with Repeated Occupational Trauma,* June 28, 1944, at 345 (proc staff meeting, Mayo Clinic); Beals & Hickman, *Industrial Injuries of the Back and Extremities,* 54A JBJ Surg 1593 (1972); Omer, *Injuries to Nerves of the Upper Extremity,* 56A JBJ Surg 1615 (1974).

§30.38 Whiplash

Overall, the medical profession rejects the term *whiplash* except as a description of the mechanics of injury. Recent evidence shows that the soft tissue injury is due less to whipping of the neck back and forth than to injuries to the ligaments, muscles, and bones from elongation and angular acceleration. The neck does not whip back and forth, but decelerates as a response to protective muscular contraction.

The supportive ligaments will over-elongate, which describes "sprain." Chips of bone at the ligament attachment may elevate, but major bony disruptions are rare. The so-called whiplash injury is one of degree, from minimal muscle ligament strain to fracture dislocation.

It has been shown that a sudden, unexpected impact to the neck structures in vulnerable persons can produce incapacitating symptoms, while a violent impact in fortunate situations may produce no demonstrable injury or complaint. The healing time of soft tissue injuries (three weeks to three months) is not a measure of continuing symptoms. The whiplash patient is often the subject of much pejorative discussion, and is often unfairly convinced that he or she is less than adequate or perhaps less than honest, often to the disservice of the patient.[35]

§30.39 Barré Syndrome

The Barré syndrome, or posterior cervical syndrome, is a vital post-neck injury presented by M. Barré in 1926 at the Réunion-Neurologique De Strasbourg. The syndrome is largely subjective and is a complaint very frequently seen in the whiplash type injury. The Barré treatise is pin point accurate, based on exhaustive study, and fills the credibility gap which so many physicians find in the history of patients with cervical spine injury. The complaints are puzzling and confusing, and, to some, seem improbable. The patients habitually exhibit cranial symptoms on a subjective basis, but they are usually precise. Cervical complaints occur, but they are less frequent or definite. The Barré syndrome components are:

---

[35] Beals & Hickman, *supra* note 34; Gay & Abbott, *Common Whiplash Injuries of the Neck,* 152 JAMA 1689 (1953); LaRocca, *Acceleration Injuries of the Neck,* 25 Clin Neurosurg 209 (1978); McNab, *Acceleration Injuries of the Cervical Spine,* 446A JBJ Surg 1797 (1964); McKenzie & Williams, *The Dynamic Behavior of the Head and Cervical Spine During Whiplash,* 4 Biomech 477 (1971); H.E. Crowe, Injuries to the Cervical Spine, (1928) (presented at the Annual Meeting of the Western Orthopedic Association, San Francisco, Cal); Lowe, *Whiplash: Dynamic Injury of the Spine,* 2 Med J Aust 687 (1980) (letter); Braaf & Rosner, *Whiplash Injuries of the Neck: Symptoms, Diagnosis, Treatment and Prognosis,* 58 New York State Med J 1501 (1958); Saternus, *The Mechanics of Whiplash Injuries of Cervical Spine,* 88 Z Rechstsmed 1 (1982) (German, English abstract); Greaves, *Whiplash by Any Other Name,* 1 Med J. Aust 34 (1980) (letter).

Headache: Mainly suboccipital with reported tendency for radiation up over the parietal and frontal region and into the eyes

Vertigo: Mainly precipitated by turning the head

Tinnitus: Unusual

Eye Symptoms: Frequently described as eye fatigue of eyes, a blurring of vision; they ask if they should see an "eye doctor"

Hoarseness: Tends to come and go

Nuchal Crepitus: Common complaint, but often seen in cervical problems without injury

Severe Unremitting Fatigue: A feeling of being "all worn out," no pep, loss of enjoyment of life; very common

M. Barré and his pupil, M. Lieou, hypothesized that the vertebral artery goes into spasm by the irritated vertebral nerve. Noxious stimulation from the cervical sympathetic nervous systems at the site of injury appears to initiate the symptom complex. Barré syndrome impairments have a guarded prognosis, with impairments become permanent at times.[36]

§30.40 Temporomandibular Joint (TMJ) Pathology

Temporomandibular joint (TMJ) pathology is very nearly a fad at this time. Specialized clinics of dentists or physicians or paramedical personnel may relate all head pain, neck pain, and more extrinsic pain, such as shoulder girdle pain and upper extremity pain, to TMJ pathology.

This is unfortunate and does a disservice to the patient. TMJ pathology does represent, however, an entity capable of producing local temporomandibular pain (jaw pain) as well as referred pain to the ear, with earache and ear pain, and referred pain to the head as headache and head pain, as well as referred pain to the shoulder girdle soft tissue structures. A great deal is unknown in the pathophysiology of temporomandibular joint. The competent cause of pain appears to be, in most patients, pathology with the meniscus of the temporomandibular joint. The meniscus is an extension of the pterygoid muscular cutaneous juncture and is a myotendinous junction that extends then as a fibrocartilaginous disc curling over the flare of the mandibular condyle and attaching just anterior to the mastoid process in the cranium.

The meniscus can be damaged by normal wear and tear changes or by asymmetry of dental bite, but also is frequently damaged by mechanics that sprain the cervical spine—whiplash injury. In this instance, the mandible is thrown forward sharply, moving the meniscus and its attached pterygoid over the condyle, stretching and damaging the same, as well as damaging

---

[36] Gibson, *The Penetration of Antibiotics into the Normal Intervertebral Disc Space*, 69B J Bone Joint Surg 784 (1987).

the attachment to the cranium. Direct blows, "an upper cut injury," can place the stress on the pterygoid, on the meniscus, or can jam the condyle into the meniscus, traumatizing the same.

The bottom line of the temporomandibular joint pathology, for the most part, seems to be attrition or disruption of the fibers of the fibrocartilaginous meniscus, with elongation of the meniscus resulting in pathological lack of coverage of the condyle to the point where the meniscus may degenerate to a point of nothingness. Thus, the TM cartilage articulates without the interspacing meniscus. This situation then allows the cartilaginous surface of the condyle of the mandible to further degenerate, forming aseptic necrotic areas and/or degenerative arthritic areas. All these degenerative processes involving the meniscus or the articular surface of the temporomandibular joint are painful.

The TMJ is richly supplied with nerve endings; it is responsive to the same joint derangements as any other joint, such as knee or shoulder displacement, with referred pain into the stabilizing musculature and referred pain along the concurrent nerve supply if one follows back through the complex afferent and efferent nerve contributions.

For this reason, referred pain to the ear, to the occiput, to the side of the face, to the top of the head, to the upper cervical nerve roots, along the trapezius and levator scapulae and into the shoulder, are common. Autonomic nerve distributions are frequently involved, so that dizziness and balance can present as part of the TMJ.

It appears that temporomandibular pathology occurs for one of two reasons: (1) degenerative changes that are manifestations of postural or developmental abnormalities, and (2) trauma, probably the more common inciting cause.

Traumatic situations involving the autonomic nervous system are frequent. A neurovascular phenomena with irritation or with compromise of vertebral artery and its smaller definitive branches present with symptoms of dizziness, giddiness, tendency for black out—a syndrome not unlike (and very likely the same) the Barré syndrome seen in whiplash injuries of the neck.

There is a great deal of evidence that the temporomandibular joint syndrome and whiplash injuries of the neck may have a common pathological origin; however, each is a common post-traumatic entity in itself, absent symptoms in the other area.

The temporomandibular joint is a diarthroidial joint formed where the mandible articulated with the temporal bone of the cranium, located anteriorly to the ear bilaterally. The function of the TMJ is guided not only by the muscles of mastication, but also by complex action of all the muscles of the head and neck. Dysfuncti n of any of these muscles from trauma, disease, or manual positioning of the mandible may cause TMJ pain, injury, malposition or internal derangement of the joint itself or the joint support, injury to the internal pterygoid muscles with its fibrocartilaginous extension through the joint attaching to the cranium. This joint-contained muscle extension is often called the meniscus. The function of the TMJ is intertwined with the posture of the head as well as with the patient's dental occlusion.

Frustrating the diagnosis of TMJ syndrome is the fact that there usually is no one cause for the dysfunction, but several possibilities. Equally frustrating is that there is no consistent constellation of symptoms that can be categorized in the majority of patients. Many things are agreed among physicians dealing with this common and disabling problem. First proper diagnosis should be made before a therapy plan is started. Since there are multiple systems involved, most often the diagnosis involves more than one system, and treatment will often involve parts of several disciplines. Treatment is surgical and nonsurgical, with surgery very rarely being indicated.

Pain in TMJ syndrome most often involves the pain receptors within the TMJ, most often related to the fibrocartilaginous meniscus which is moved and kept in place by the internal pterygoid muscle. The positions of the mandible affect pressure and stretch on the meniscus, so that treatment often involves treatment of mandible position with dental splints and specific physiotherapies to strengthen support of the TMJ muscle. Surgical excision or repair of the meniscus has been advocated, but has a poor track record. Corticosteroid injection into the TMJ may be helpful, but clinically risky, as the meniscus, under tension from muscle pull, may disrupt or disrupt more, due to the deleterious effect of corticosteroids on the meniscus. In acute cervical muscle ligament sprains (whiplash), the mandible is sharply thrust forward by the same forces that sprain the neck, pulling on and injuring the TM meniscus.

Failure to recognize the TMJ syndrome reflects lack of diligence on the part of the examining physician, while denying its relationship to injury reflects defective information on the part of the physician.[37]

Temporomandibular joint pathology is very nearly a fad at this time. Specialized clinics of dentists or physicians or paramedical personnel relating all head pain, neck pain, and more extrinsic pain such as shoulder girdle pain and upper extremity pain to TM pathology.

§30.41 Length of Convalescence

Muscle ligament sprain injuries of the neck have a variable course of convalescence. The problem basically is one of healing muscle and ligaments to stabilize the joint, usually for 8 to 10 weeks. Problems of convalescence, though, deal with the neuromuscular and the discogenic injuries that frequent occur, and the peculiar propensity of the soft tissues of the neck and low back to behave differently than other areas of the body so far as standards of healing and standards of rehabilitation. These joint systems have a much greater range of motion, including flexion, extension, side bending, and twisting.

---

[37] Davies & White, *Muscle Weakness Following Eccentric Work in Man,* 392 Eur J Physiology 168 (1981).

The rich nerve supply to the soft tissues about the neck, mid-back, and low back, and their interface with vascular components and autonomic (sympathetic) nerve system, do make them structurally different from the appendicular skeleton. Nonetheless, it is well known that muscle ligament sprain injuries of the neck may heal promptly in just a few weeks, may require years to heal, or may never heal completely. A great deal of pejorative vocabulary is stated about the whiplash injury and the low back sprain injury because, in part, many physicians feel that soft tissue should heal in 8 to 10 weeks, and with a reasonable period of rehabilitation for a few weeks should see the patient back to full functional activity.

§30.42 Arthritis: A Description

Complaints related to arthritis are among the most common reasons patients consult their physicians. More than 100 disorders have been identified that may lead to arthritis, including psoriasis, hemophilia, and systemic lupus. Most patients with arthritis have either osteoarthritis (OA) or rheumatoid arthritis (RA).

Rheumatoid arthritis, a systemic disease, is characterized by inflammation in the synovial lining of the joints that results in cartilage and bone destruction.

Osteoarthritis, a more localized disease, is characterized by deterioration of the weight-bearing cartilage surfaces of the joint, hardening of subchondral bone, and bony overgrowth at joint margins.

Both conditions are associated with joint pain, loss of motion, muscular weakness, and reduced working capacity.[38]

§30.43 Honest Doctors' Honest Differences of Opinion

Neck, shoulder, and arm pain related to repetitive minor injuries at work or home frequently present a controversial problem in assessing proximate cause and the degree of injury-related impairment. A United States Health and Nutrition Examination Survey of 6,913 people over the country showed 80 per cent had musculoskeletal pain in the preceeding 12 months. All respondents who could recall at least one month of regional musculoskeletal pain were asked about its site, quality, and impact on function. Forty per cent had neck and shoulder pain, but only 6 per cent were disabled enough to take time off from work. These findings confirm the ubiquitous nature of memorable neck/arm pain and how we deal with it in our daily lives.

---

[38] Garrett, *Muscle Injuries and Inflammation,* 3 Ann Sports Med 71 (1987); Ike, *Arthritis and Aerobic Exercise: A Review,* 17 Physician & SportsMed 128 (1989); W.N. Kelley, Textbook of Rheumatology (2d ed 1985); Young, Stokes & Liles, *Effects of Joint Pathology on Muscle,* 219 Clin Orthop 21 (1987); Spitzer, *The Arthritic Complaint in Primary Care: Prevalence Related Disability and Costs,* 3 J Rheum 88 (1976).

Most people reported that on the days they recalled the neck/arm pain, they did not have other symptoms or impairments about their bodies. Men tended to ascribe arm pain complaints to injury; women felt it more often related to overload. Most reported symptoms as not very serious 42 per cent of the time, while 8 per cent said it was serious. Only 3 per cent sought medical advice; most others used no treatment or used home remedies, such as heat, limited motions, aspirin, or nonsteroidal anti-inflammatory drugs.

§30.44 References

Johnson, Cadambi & Seibert, *Incidence of Adult Respiratory Distress Syndrome in Patients with Multiple Musculoskeletal Injuries,* 25 J Trauma 375 (1985).

Cooney, *Complications of Colles' fracture,* 62A JBJ Surg 613 (1980).

Division of Surveillance, Hazard Evaluation and Field Studiese, Division Safety Research, National Institute for Occupational Safety and Health, *reported in* 249 JAMA 2301 (1983).

Eismant & Currier, *Surgical Management of Lumbar Intervertebral Disc Disease,* 71A JBJ Surg 1266 (1989).

Garrett, *Recovery of Skeletal Muscle After Laceration and Repair,* 9A J Hand Surg 683 (1984).

Demjen & Bakal, *Subjective Distress Accompanying Headache Attacks: Evidence for a Cognitive Shift,* 25 Pain 187 (1986).

Nunley, *Use of Anterior Branch of Anterior Branch of Medial Antebrachial Cutaneous Nerve as a Graft for the Repair of Defects of the Digital Nerve,* 71A JBJ Surg 563 (1989).

Walton & Rothwell, *Reactions of Thigh Tissues of Sheep to Blunt Trauma,* 176 Clin Orthop 273 (1983).

Mooney, Hopper, Davies & Tothill, *Blood Flow and Clearance in Tendons, Studies with Dogs,* 66B JBJ Surg 441 (1984).

Johnson, *Data on Distribution of Fiber Types in 36 Human Muscles,* 18 J Neurol Sci 111 (1973).

Calff, *Fiber Typing of the Quadriceps and Hamstrings Muscles in Man: Cause and Relationship to Injury,* 33 Surg Forum 534 (1982).

Gibson, *Quadriceps Muscle Wasting and Protein Synthesis,* JBJ Surg (1986) (British Proceedings and Report).

G.E. Omer & M. Spinner, *Peripheral Nerve Testing and Suture Techniques,* American Academy of Orthopedic Surgeons: Instructional Course (193 references).

Edmeads, *Migraine,* 138 Can Med Assn J 107 (1988).

Thornberry & Thomas, *Posture and Spinal Headache,* 60 Br J Anest 197 (1988).

Schlenker & Ringlestein, *Epidural Fibrin Clot for the Prevention of Post Spinal Headache,* 50 Psychiatry 1715 (1987).

Walton & Rothwell, *Reactions of Thigh Tissues to Blunt Trauma,* 176 Clin Orthop & Rel Res 273 (1983).

Mankin, *The Responsible Articular Cartilage to Mechanical Injury,* 64A JBJ Surg 460 (1982).

Carrico, Mehrhof & Cohen, *Biology of Wound Healing,* 64 Surg Clin N Amer 721 (1984).

J. Campbell, The Mythic Image (1975).

Masci, *Revention and Treatment of Infections Following Orthopedic Surgery,* Surg Rounds Orthop, April 1989, at 55.

Grace & Omer, *The Management of Upper Extremity Pit Viper Wounds,* 3 J Hand Surg 168 (1980) (with 35 references).

Caplin & Hoyt, *Infection Surveillence and Control in Severely Traumatized Patients,* 70 AJM 638 (1981).

Deitch, *Infection in the Compromised Host,* 68 Surg Clin N Am 181 (1988).

Strauss & Hart, *Hyperbaric Oxygen and the Skeletal Muscle-Compartment Syndrome,* 18 Contemporary Orthopedics 167 (1989).

Bassett & Bennett, *Introduction to the Physical and Physiological Bases of Hyperbaric Therapy,* Hypertrophic Oxygen Therapy 11 (H.K. Hunt & J.C. Davis eds 1977) (Undersea Medical Society, Inc., Bethesda, Md).

Nylander, *Reduction of Post-ischemic Edema with Hyperbaric Oxygen,* 76 Plast Reconstru Surg 596 (1985).

Strauss, *Reduction of Skeletal Muscle Necrosis Using Intermittent Hyperbaric Oxygen in a Model Compartment Syndrome,* 65A JBJ Surg 656 (1983).

Hagens & Akenson, *Pathophysiology of the Compartment Syndrome,* Compartment Syndromes and Volkmann's Contracture 47 (S.J. Mubarak & A.R. Hargens eds 1981).

Strauss, *Delayed Use of Hyperbaric Oxygen for Treatment of a Model Anterior Compartment Syndrome,* 4 J Orthop Res 108 (1986).

Strauss & Hart, *Cost Effective Issues in Hyperbaric Oxygen Therapy: Complicated Fractures,* J Hyperbaric Med (1989).

Rudolph, *Skin Grafting,* Surg Rounds Orthop, at 35, (Jan 1989).

R. Rudolph, Skin Grafting (1979).

Chronic Problem Wounds (R. Rudolph & J.M. Noe eds 1983).

Vecchione, *A Technique for Obtaining Uniform Split-Thickness Skin Grafts,* 109 Arch Surg 837 (1974).

Szabo, *Carpal Tunnel Pressure Readings May Determine Stages of Syndrome and Lead Patients to Solutions,* 3 Orthopedics Today 30 (1989).

Flowers III, *Efficiency of an Attachable Subcutaneous Cuff for the Prevention of Intravascular Catheter-Related Infection,* 261 JAMA 878 (1989).

J.E. Edwards, Jr, Candida Species: Principles and Practice of Infectious Disease 1435 (G.I. Mandell ed 2d ed 1985).

Thomas & Matsen III, *An Approach to the Repair of Avulsion of the Glenohumeral Ligaments in the Management of Traumatic Anterior Glenohumeral Instability,* 71A JBJ Surg 506 (Apr 1989).

Korkala, *Prospective Study in the Treatment of Severe Tears of the Lateral Ligaments of the Ankle,* 11 Ing Orthop 13 (1987).

Harringston, *Chronic Ankle Instability: What It Is and What Can Be Done For It,* 6 Musculoskel Med 35 (1989).

Leach, *Secondary Reconstruction of the Lateral Ligaments of the Ankle,* 160 Clin Orthop 201 (1981).

Matsen III, *A Practical Approach to Compartment Syndrome, Instructional Course Lectures, The American Academy of Orthopedic Surgeons,* Vol 32, at 88-92 (1983).

Green & Louis, *Compartment Syndrome of the Arm,* 65A JBJ Surg 270 (1983).

Langen & Ruggieri, *Acute Compartment Syndrome in the Thigh Complicated by Pseudoaneurysm,* 71A JBJ Surg 762 (1989).

Rooser, *Quadriceps Contusion with Compartment Syndrome: Evacuation of Hematoma,* 58 Act Orthop Scand 170 (1987).

Tarlow, *Acute Compartment Syndrome in Thigh Complicating Fracture of Femur,* 68A JBJ Surg 1439 (1986).

Amrotta & Richmond, *Arteriovenous Fistula After Posterior Compartment Fasciotomy to Tri Shin Splints,* 16 Physician & SportsMed 55 (1988).

Tsuge, *Treatment of Established Volkmann's Contracture,* 57A JBJ Surg 925 (1975).

Lapuk & Woodbury, *Volkmann's Ischemic Contracture,* 17 Orthop Rev 618 (1987).

Heppenstall, *A Comparative Study of the Tolerance of Skeletal Muscle to Ischemia,* 68A JBJ Surg 820 (1986).

S.P. Blau, *Emergencies in Rheumatoid Arthritis, reprinted in* T. Kanto, Therapy-Related Emergencies Ch II (1985).

Appendix 30-1
Cases

1 ***Jarvis v St Charles Medical Center,*** ***77*** **713 P 2d 216 (Or App 353, 1986)** (while patient was undergoing surgery for fracture of tibia, the orthopedist noticed symptoms suggesting compartment syndrome and performed a fasciotomy to relieve potentially damaging pressure. He ordered the nurses to check the patient every hour and call him if there was any sign of compartment syndrome. The following day, symptoms suggesting such syndrome occurred; they promptly called the surgeon who promptly relieved the pressure by spreading the cast. During the third post-operative night, the level of nursing alertness dropped dramatically. The nurses' log noted only sporadic checking of patient, not the hour-by-hour checks requested by the surgeon. Early the following morning, the physician found the patient's foot to be blanched with no pulse. In surgery an hour later, he noted some muscle necrosis already had occurred. The patient underwent a series of procedures, but was left with a leg that lost substantial function. Several experts appeared on both sides—one claiming that the orthopedist did not adequately spread the cast, although he had, in fact done the other procedures, anticipating the compartment syndrome, including the fasciotomy at the time of surgery. Other experts said that the hospital nurses were negligent in not monitoring and not fulfilling the orders of the surgeon. The ultimate result was that the hospital and its nurses were held responsible and the orthopedist was not).

Comment: Compression syndromes such as this can rapidly occur after significant trauma to an arm or leg, and requires hourly watching to prevent just the type of complication that occurred in this case. It did seem that the orthopedist was on the right track with his treatment plan, and when the marked decrease of circulation to the foot was discovered, further decompression was carried out.

2 ***Roger v Anderson*** **371 SE2d 619 (W Va 1988)** (13-year-old boy fell off a cliff and sustained a simple, nondisplaced fracture of the proximal tibia. He was admitted to the hospital where the nurses reported the toes were cold and white and numb. The next morning, the treating general surgeon casually, in the elevator, asked the orthopedist to check the x-rays. Two days later, the general surgeon asked the orthopedist to formally see the patient because he complained constantly of severe pain in his leg and foot. He did not examine the patient until the next day, diagnosed a compartment compression syndrome, and did a fasciotomy surgery, but did not debride necrotic tissue or order arteriograms of the popliteal artery. The next day, the nurse reported absent pedal pulses, but the orthopedist waited another three days before obtaining vascular consultation, during which time the general surgeon took no action. The boy's leg was eventually amputated above the knee. A pathologist reported a 1″ thrombus in the popliteal artery. The general

surgeon and vascular surgeon settled with the plaintiff before trial, and the orthopedist was liable for the balance of a $1,250,000 award).

Comment: A fracture of proximal tibial, like a knee dislocation, is at high risk of popliteal artery or vein damage, or both, and must be evaluated promptly to prevent the above problem. The symptoms, foot pain, coldness of foot, and absent pulses, are seen in arterial insufficiency as often as in compartment syndrome. The proper approach to this case would have been (1) to measure intracompartmental pressure, and (2) to assess the adequacy of circulation to the leg, probably best done by arteriography, although Doppler measurements would be helpful. These diagnostic tests are urgent—nearly emergency procedures to be carried out in hours, not days.

3 ***Killingsworth v Poon,* 307 SE2d 123 (67 Ga App 653, 1983)** (patient had a myofascial trigger point of pain at the back of her shoulder girdle. An injection of local anesthetic and steroid was used. The needle passed too deeply and caused a pneumothorax (collapsed lung). There was no medical expert testimony in this case, and although res ipsa loquitur was not invoked, the "common knowledge" doctrine was discussed. The example used by the court: "if a surgeon performs an appendectomy and unintentionally slits the patient's throat, the jury may not need the testimony of a medical expert to conclude the act was negligent." Moreover, said the court, "it is widely known and generally understood by laymen that subcutaneous injections ostensibly given for the relief of muscular pain should not, if administered correctly, result in a puncture of the internal organs." The court referred to a Georgia Law Review. "To put it more bluntly, medical defendants, as a class, are not deserving of any special dispensation from inferences of negligence that may be logically drawn from the circumstances. One suspects, but cannot prove, that the underlying judicial condemnation of res ipsa loquitur malpractice case is the instinct to provide justified protection").

31

Skin Injuries

§31.01 Generally

Skin is the largest organ of the body. It is an essential organ to life. Its principal use is regulating the temperature homeostasis of the body. Excessive heat in the body is expended through the skin via evaporation of sweat and radiant dissipation of heat. Injuries that block that function produce damage to the body as a whole and can produce death. Although uncommon, immersion injuries in which the skin is covered with impervious solutions such as paint, unless promptly removed, will cause the patient to die of heat exhaustion. Pranks have been reported in which the body is painted, as well as incidents of artist dancers who paint their body as part of their costume, with these results.[1]

Skin is richly supplied by nerve endings, many of them producing pain perception. Most notable of the severe pain conditions is the pain that follows debriding injuries, such as a ringer injury or road burn of injury in which layers of the skin have been denuded; this also includes electrical, chemical, and thermal burns. Skin pain is one of the major impairments following body traumas. (*See* Appendix 31-1, Case 1.)

Trauma to the skin manifests itself by the various ways in which injury will produce changes in the integrity of the skin itself. The skin is composed of two layers, the dermis and the epidermis, with each layer having several sublayers of its own. Injuries that debride the epidermis away from the dermis will heal without skin grafting. These are first- or second-degree injuries. Injuries that completely denude the subcutaneous fat of its overlying dermis require some type of surgical closure, either primary suture closure or skin or pedicle grafting. (*See* Appendix 31-1, Case 2.)

Trauma to the skin occurs from (1) laceration, (2) abrading, scraping, on friction, (3) bruising, (4) pressure for a prolonged period, (5) thermal burns, (6) freezing, (7) chemical destruction, (8) electrical burns, (9) primary and secondary infection, and (10) insect, snake, animal, and human bites. The severity of the injury parallels the amount of insult and the location of the skin (axilla versus between scapulae), the age of the patient, and the personal susceptibility of the injured person.

§31.02 Lacerations

Laceration of the skin may require suture repair, but often heals with minimal skin edge approximation with tapes or simple dressing. If the subcutaneous tissue is lacerated, the wound will gap, requiring sutures or staples for cosmetic closure.

Dirty, contaminated lacerations must be thoroughly debrided, excising nonviable skin edges, gavaging the wound of debris, freshening skin edges so skin edges are perpendicular, then effecting closure with sutures or staples.

Ragged lacerations are best treated by excising the skin edge, converting the wound to an oval lesion when possible, and effecting a fine hairline closure. In spite of the method of closure, some persons tend to heal skin with more visible scarring. Black persons are often keloid formers, healing with a thick, elevated, often itching scar that may present a cosmetic problem.

---

[1] Sitting & Deitch, *Effect of Bacteremia on Mortality after Thermal Injury,* 123 Arch Surg 1367 (1988).

§31.03 Abrasions

In skin trauma in which the outer layer of dermis is abraded, (blistered), a protective covering, often with topical antibiotic, is sufficient treatment. If the deeper layers of dermis are lost, but skin islands remain (often after road burns), a thorough cleansing and occlusive dressing with antibiotic coverage is adequate. Where substantial areas of full thickness skin are lost, skin grafting may be necessary. All skin losses tend to heal inward from new skin migrating toward the center of the wound. This is a slow process (covering one-quarter inch per week) and leaves new skin that will contract and "pucker."

Skin lesions of the face and neck heal well due to the excellent blood supply. Cosmetic closure is the goal, and is effected by meticulous skin edge approximation, using many fine sutures. As in all areas of the body, the more sutures and the finer the suture material, the more cosmetically pleasing the skin scar. For skin closure in the neck and face, 5-00000 or 6-000000 non-absorbable suture is preferable. For thicker skin suturing, 3-000 or 4-0000 is satisfactory. For thick skin, under tension 2-00 non-absorbable suture is occasionally necessary. In general, the less the skin edge tension, the better the scar.

Secondary excision of unsatisfactory skin scars is often done to improve cosmesis. Full-thickness skin graft, skin pedicle grafts, or free myocutaneous grafts with vascular anastamosis are often necessary to cover large skin, bone, or joint defects. These are technically difficult procedures best performed by a skilled plastic surgeon.

§31.04 Burns

In using burns as a model of skin injury, the amount of damage is in proportion to the amount of thermal input. Simple burns include damage to the superficial layers of the skin—first-degree burns—requiring no energetic treatment other than protection against invasion by bacteria (infection) and covering of the wound for comfort. These injuries heal promptly, requiring 7 to 10 days. The resultant new skin can be hypersensitive for many weeks and may produce discoloration of a cosmetic value for several months, but ultimately heals without impairment in most cases. (*See* Appendix 31-1, Cases 3 and 4.)

Second-degree burns are more severe, in which enough epidermis is lost that healing occurs by skin islands. Scars are left to varying degrees, rarely with contracture. The healed status of a second-degree burn ordinarily is a cosmetic problem, frequently with hypersensitive skin for several months, and carries the same risk as first-degree burns for ease of infection.

Third-degree burns are more severe burns in which both the epidermis and dermis are lost. The risk of infection is high, as is the risk of fluid imbalance from weeping of the burned area. These burns are frequently fatal if more than 60 per cent of the body is involved in the burn. These require a highly-specialized treatment field, and the significantly burned patient should be referred to a burn center, which now exist in most major cities in the United States. The healing period depends on how extensive the burn is and what complications develop. It is often necessary to do extensive skin grafting when a substantial amount of skin is lost; that is, over 50 per cent of the body. Often, that normal skin itself is not sufficient for harvesting skin grafting of the denuded areas. Ongoing research continues to develop other third-degree skin covering techniques, including plastic substances, cadaver skin, some types of animal skin, and skin cultures to generate new skin from the patient's own skin cells. In spite of this, a number of patients are lost due to extensive burn damage, and particularly if the burn is deeper than through the dermis and involves muscles, nerves, tendons, and bones. In these patients, major amputations are frequently necessary.

Infection is a common cause of death after burns or extensive soft tissue trauma. Many of these patients have a bacteremia not directly related to the injury, perhaps latent in the patient prior to injury but expressed and magnified by the injury. As the total body is involved in healing, great stress is placed on the immune system. Gram negative, Pseudomonas, and/or polymicrobial infections become life-threatening. The treating physician must be alert to this possibility, look for it early, and treat the infection vigorously. In burn patients, the larger the burn, the greater the septicemia risk and the greater the mortality.

§31.05 Treatment of Burns

Priority for treatment of severe third-degree burns requires:

1. Stabilization of the patient physiologically. This includes maintenance of adequate fluid intake by multiple intravenous instillation of appropriate fluids such as plasma and whole blood, requiring daily monitoring of electrolytes and replacing those electrolytes that are out of balance so that homeostasis of the body can approach normal.
2. Removal of necrotic tissue. It is essential to remove dead tissue so the healing process is facilitated and infection can be minimized. This requires daily dressing changes and frequent use of specialized physical therapy techniques. Dressing changes themselves produce fluid and blood loss that continues to require monitoring. At an early date, coverage of the areas of skin loss is necessary, frequently using various types of skin grafting. However, skin grafting cannot be successful on the patient who has a wound with necrotic tissue, a wound with infection, or inadequate nutrition.
3. Maintenance of patient's nutrition. Treatment is a very difficult problem when the patient is in constant pain, physiologically deprived, and taking pain medication—all tend to diminish appetite. Nutritional imbalance, therefore, becomes a vital problem.

4. Getting the patient ambulatory. Getting joint systems involved to move to prevent soft tissue contractures is important (a painful experience for the patient, but essential to ultimate convalescence).

In the typical severe burn patient, a burn surgeon, internal medicine specialist, an infectious disease specialist, and a physical therapist are in daily attendance with the patient, along with a skilled nursing staff. There are multiple socioeconomic problems attached to the severely burned patient. A social worker frequently is very helpful in this regard. Treatment (guidance) of the family is important so they understand the nature of the injury, the severity, what to expect, and how they should participate in the ongoing rehabilitation of the patient.

§31.06 Complications of Burns

Lifelong impairments often occur with severe burns, with skin contractures about joints, requiring surgical revision months or years after the burn. Severe psychological problems are common with chronic depression and/or chronic loss of self-image. It is difficult for a patient with a severely cosmetically burned face or extremities to present him- or herself to society. Family rejection ultimately is common. Suicide is not unusual. These are all factors in assessing impairment.

§31.07 Infections

Infection is defined as invasion of body tissues by bacteria that "set up housekeeping," become infective agents, and proceed to destroy significant parts of the body, requiring a healing phase. Often, the infected organism is a naturally occurring bacteria that resides on or in parts of the body, but with the patient's immune system diminished, becomes pathogenic. In burn patients, as in all patients with open wounds, the highest degree of sterile technique affords the best chance of minimizing infection from occurring and from worsening if it has occurred. This includes sterile techniques by all persons attending the patient—nurses and physicians. This involves the use of sterile gloves, sterile gowns, masks (at times), use of sterile techniques in changing dressings, and washing hands between patients so bacteria is not transferred from one patient to the other—something which is typically not done in hospitals at this time. In hospital areas suspect for infection, frequent culturing for bacteria and sensitivity tests are required so appropriate antibiotics can be administered. It is common for the patient initially to have a single infective organism such as Staphylococcus aureus. However, after the wound has been open for a few days, and particularly if there is necrotic tissue, a change in the bacterial flora ordinarily occurs in which saprophytic organisms (those frequently on our body change and invade the tissue). Common gram negative bacteria includes the Pseudomonas group. A wide range of antibiotics is available to help control infection, including tetanus antitoxin. Use of prophylactic antibiotics is appropriate in second- and third-degree burns. It is, however, essential to continue regular culturing and sensitivity testing, for often it is necessary to change antibiotics. It is not unusual to require antibiotics for a long period of time which have an adverse effect in themselves, some of them producing kidney, ear toxicity, or secondary infections in bowel, kidney, and lung. It is important to measure blood levels of antibiotics to assure that a therapeutic level is present. The bottom line with a severe burn, or with severe soft tissue loss of skin, for any reason, is a highly complex, significantly impairing, or lethal problem.[2] (*See* Appendix 31-1, Case 5.)

§31.08 Other Skin Injuries

Other injuries to the skin include allergic reactions to elements in the environment and also to medications that are prescribed. The allergic reaction ordinarily is a hive, but can be a premonitory sign of more a severe problem, including antiphylactic shock, which can lead to death. Skin lesions are ordinarily cared for by stopping the medication or removing the environmental source of the allergy. At times, however, the allergen is not known and requires skillful detective work on the part of the medical personnel.

§31.09 Crush Injuries

Another type of soft tissue trauma is the crush injury, including the wringer injury (less common in the past two decades), in which a person catches an arm or leg between rollers, sustaining a crushing injury to the soft tissues, but also a friction burn injury to the skin. Significant skin loss is frequent, depending on how long the pressure is applied and how long the friction is allowed to continue. These injuries are treated in a similar manner to burns so far as the skin is concerned; however, special attention to underlying soft tissues is essential. It is common for this injury to develop a compartment compression syndrome, that is, enough crushing of muscle leading to bleeding and edema in the muscles that pressure is placed on the nerves and vessels supplying the tissues distal to the injury. Loss of muscle function is common. If the extremity is not promptly decompressed, complications include permanent loss of function, contracture of fingers (it practically always happens in the forearms), and/or amputation from gangrene. Preventative therapy is prompt decompression of the extremity by fasciotomy. Compression syndrome is frequently overlooked or not diagnosed early, so complications can occur unexpectedly and quickly. Regular examination and re-examination of the areas of the injury, elevation of the injury with pressure dressings applied, antibiotics to protect against infections, and adequate

---

[2] Aplin & Hoyt, *Infection Surveillance and Control in Severely Traumatized Patients,* 70 Am J Med 638 (1981); Deitch, *Infection in the Compromised Host,* 68 Surg Clin N Am 181 (1988).

pain control are all elements of care. There is a high incidence of permanent complications with wringer or other crushing injuries of the extremities. Another example of crushing injury to the extremity occurs when a vehicle wheel runs over an arm or leg.

§31.10 Venomous Bites

Snake bites and insect bites can produce significant problems. Depending on the type of snake, various toxic complications may occur. The pit viper is the most common poisonous snake found in the United States and produces a toxin that causes soft tissue swelling and loss of skin, and may also lead to compression syndrome—not unlike a crushing injury. Prompt attention to possible complications is the treatment of choice. Coverage with antibiotics and tetanus antitoxin, along with close attention to compartment syndrome and maintenance of the patient's physiological state are the standard of care. It has been well shown that the old first aid techniques of putting stellate lacerations about the area of envenomation and trying to suck out the venom is not useful and, in fact, is inappropriate. Resting of the extremity, not using a tourniquet but not exercising the extremity, and prompt transfer to a definitive medical facility are essential parts of the treatment. Permanent complications that occur from this type of injury relate to the amount of soft tissue loss from the toxic material itself. (*See* Appendix 31-1, Case 6.)

Certain insect bites—bites from fiddle-back spiders or brown recluse spiders—may cause extensive skin loss for which secondary closure may be necessary. Complications from spider bites are rarely life-threatening, but can be very painful. The secondary complications are those related to skin coverage with scarring, potential infection, and certain pain syndromes, such as reflex sympathetic dystrophy.

§31.11 Toxic Shock Syndrome

Another category of infection that requires close attention by the treating physician is the possibility of toxic shock syndrome, initially thought to be limited to women who became secondarily infected with a toxin-producing streptococci from using absorbable tampons. In operative wounds or in lacerations that have been closed, the same situation may rapidly come on and take the patient's life. A typical situation is a relatively clean wound sutured, such as an operative wound that does well for a day or so. The wound itself is not particularly painful, but suddenly becomes painful. There is a high, spiking temperature; however, there is very little tissue reaction and no obvious local infection. The temperature continues to stay high; the patient becomes toxic and the wound then appears infected on the third or fourth day. Drainage of the wound, ideally before redness appears, and institution of appropriate antibiotics, is essential. The wound itself and blood cultures usually will not produce bacteria. Substantial doses of antibiotics that typically control streptococci are important. In the usual situation, once the acute phase of toxic shock syndrome is past, there is no permanent impairment.

§31.12 Hyperbaric Oxygen

In some areas where equipment is available, use of hyperbaric oxygen is helpful, such as in compartment syndrome gas gangrene. Use of this equipment depends on the experience and knowledge of the physician treating the patient and is not common; however, it can be life-saving. Muscle tissue that has been lacerated or disrupted goes through a reparative process like other soft tissues. There is very little clinical research material available on the recovery of the muscle after such injury.

§31.13 Cold Exposure

Nearly 7,000 deaths due to cold exposure have occurred in the United States in the last 10 years, many of these seen in emergency rooms and by orthopedists. Death due to hypothermia is common; more common are complications from cold tissue damage to the extremities—frostbite. It is important that cold tissue damage and hypothermia be promptly recognized and treated by the doctor. Gradual body warming with appropriate supportive care of the hypothermia may be life-saving. If the attending physician is not familiar with total hypothermia care, immediate consultation with an informed doctor is the standard of care.

Frostbite is freezing of the body's outer tissues (shell). Whereas superficial frostbite can be reversed with swift thawing, deep frostbite kills tissue and may produce gangrene. Gradual warming of deep tissues, aseptic protection, and "wait and see" are the treatment standards. This is a situation where appropriate care is delay in amputation or debridement until demarcation is clear. It is important not to do a mutilating surgery when a lesser procedure the next week might work. Attending to infection, nutrition, and general health are supplemental therapies.

§31.14 Skin Grafting

In situations where skin grafting is necessary, there are certain rules mentioned about burns that are essential for successful skin graft. A successful skin graft ordinarily will end up with a good, pliable skin coverage that does not contract significantly, particularly if it is protected with compressive hose or gloves for several months. There is, however, always a cosmetic defect that occurs with the graft of skin and the grafted skin frequently becomes hypersensitive to touch, or to cold or hot, for a protracted period (months to years). It is necessary to cover deep layers of skin when ligament is lost, when bone, metallic devices covering bone or healing fractures of bone are exposed. It is essential to have a graft host site that is well vascularized that includes at least subcutaneous tissue and often contains muscle. Successful skin grafting is most likely when a good wound bed is available, the proper kind of graft is selected, and the techniques of graft cutting and fixation are performed correctly. If the above criteria are followed, most skin grafts will take. Some surgeons have a fatalistic view that a certain percentage of all grafts must fail, and this prophecy is self-fulfilling. Most grafts are lost not because of technical errors, but because of poor preparation of the wound bed or inadequate immobilization. Technical errors, such as upside-down graft placement, graft placement over epithelized areas, skin graft that is too thick, or hematoma between the graft and the graft bed, account for failure. Close attention to nutrition and particularly to local or systemic infection is essential. These are highly-skilled plastic surgery techniques that have undergone rapid sophistication in the last 10 years. It is possible to cover a defect remote from the donor site of skin and muscle by taking the nutrient artery and vein and transplanting, doing an arterial and venous anastamosis to adjacent vessels at the recipient site. Pedicle grafts in situations like this give a much better definitive result than split-thickness grafts. Often, split-thickness skin grafts will not take, and when they do there is an indentation with sensitive skin, or easy breakdown of skin so that the area of graft continues to be vulnerable for the rest of the patient's life. Pedicle grafting is increasingly the treatment of choice to cover these defects with exposed deep tissues.[3] (*See* Appendix 31-1, Case 1.)

§31.15 Pressure Sores

Defects secondary to pressure (decubitus), tumor resection, or x-radiation can be large and very debilitating. These often lead to major complications, such as septicemia, renal failure, and death. Phases of healing of ulcerations, often seen in nursing homes, can be assessed by the color of the ulcer. Assessment is based on visually diagnosing the wound according to three color categories—red, yellow, and black.[4]

The red wound is uninfected and progresses promptly through the stages of healing, usually with good granulation of tissue. Tissue and vascular structures begin to regenerate. Red wounds may range in color from pale pink to ruby red.

Yellow wounds are contaminated. The presence of pus, debris, or exudate, or a combination, causes the area to appear creamy. These wounds may become stagnated in the inflammatory or proliferative phases.

The black wound contains necrotic tissue under an eschar and requires debridement before proliferation or remodeling can begin. The actual color

---

[3] Rudolph, *Skin Grafting,* Surg Rounds Orthop, Jan 1989, at 35; R. Rudolph, *Skin Grafting* (1979); *Chronic Problem Wounds* (R. Rudolph & J.M. Noe eds 1983); Vecchione, *A Technique for Obtaining Uniform Split-Thickness Skin Grafts,* 109 Arch Surg 837 (1974).

[4] Caceres, *Effective Wound Management and the New Color Concept,* 8 Geriatric Med 95 (1989).

ranges from brown to gray to deep black. There is no sensation in black wounds. (*See* Appendix 31-1, Cases 7 and 8.)

The goal is to convert all ulcers to red ones, using local methods of debridement, tissue-dissolving chemicals, and culture and sensitivity tests with consideration of systemic antibiotics. Close attention to adequate nutrition and avoidance of pressure on the skin ulcer are ongoing treatment factors. (*See* Appendix 31-1, Case 9.)

Soft tissue coverage is essential as part of a total patient care plan. Nutrition, removal of pressure, control of bowels and urine, along with adequate blood count and specific antibiotic coverage are all important parts of decubiti care. The use of large musculocutaneous pedicle or V-Y flaps is often helpful. It is essential to cover these ulcers with viable, durable soft tissues and to then protect them from pressure and moisture, including urine.

§31.16 Grease and Paint Gun Injuries

Another soft tissue injury involving skin is the high-compression injury. These represent a substantial, potentially impairing injury, usually to the hands. Injury to the hands themselves, of course, represents a potentially significant impairment.

Grease gun hand injuries require proper evaluation of the extent of damage and prompt surgical treatment of paint or grease. Pressure injection into the hand may well mark the difference between a well-functioning and a completely disabled hand. These chemicals may be accidentally expelled in a fine stream from a pressure gun at a pressure of 5,000 to 7,000 pounds per square inch, which is sufficient to cause instant ballooning of tissues through a minute wound of entrance, even though the hand may be several inches from the gun tip. This type of injury causes immediate, tense, painless swelling, and may be sufficient to cause ischemia in the entire finger. Within 24 hours, the patient develops severe throbbing, burning pain with signs of acute inflammation and often circulatory embarrassment in one or more digits. An x-ray reveals the presence of subcutaneous emphysema and is helpful in determining the extent of involvement. Early signs are associated with chemical irritation and with acute increase in tension, culminating in abscesses containing grease or paint, and frequently infarction of digital vessels with necrosis. Subsidence of the acute phase is usually followed by a longo period of disability characterized by recurrent infection, draining sinuses that exude paint or grease, and granulomatous foreign debris containing lesion. Later, phlemonous tumors, severe lymphedema, and erysipeloid lesions have required amputation. Squamous cell carcinoma may form in the scars and must be identified. (*See* Appendix 31-1, Case 10.)

Emergency treatment consists of evacuation of as much foreign material as possible. Any involved digit should be widely opened, treating the infection vigorously with debridement, drainage, and appropriate antibiotics. Frequent re-culture and sensitivity testing is also necessary. When all infection and chemical breakdown is controlled, staged reconstructive surgeries on tendons, nerves, and joints with skin coverage surgeries will be necessary.

§31.17 Chronic Repetitive Trauma

Chronic, repetitive, occupationally-related trauma to hands and fingers in susceptible patients may cause vasospasms or arterial occlusion. Use of vibrating tools seems to be another triggering mechanism. Treatment is symptomatic and changing hand-finger work activities.

Through the years, it has become increasingly evident that patients who are smokers heal much more poorly where there is skin loss, where there is skin grafting to be done, and particularly where there is pedicle grafting to be done. Also, smokers have a higher incidence of complications with infections and a higher incidence of reflex sympathetic dystrophy than nonsmokers.

Appendix 31-1
Cases

1 ***Tomei v Bloom, Inc,* 75 Mich App 661, 255 NW2d 727 (1977)** (patient sustained numbness about lower lip, with no disfiguring injury or loss of use of any part of her body. She was gainfully employed, maintained a home, and cared for two children. No pain was reported except for hypersensitivity to cold about her face. The award of $250,000 to the patient and $15,000 to her husband was reduced to $100,000 for the patient and $10,000 for the husband).

2 ***Baez v Dombroff,* 530 AD2d 847 (NY 1988)** (patient was left heavily scarred with a misshaped breast and chest wall. The patient claimed severe psychological damage, precluding her from wearing sport clothing or swimsuits in public. The surgeon admitted that the surgery was technically inferior and caused the misshaped chest wall. The jury awarded $2,625,000, which the court reduced to $1,500,000. On appeal, the appellate court held that $1,500,000 was excessive and disproportionate to the injury suffered, and that $750,000 was appropriate).

3 ***Aubert v Aubert,* 129 NH 422, 529 A2d 909 (1987)** (plaintiff was shot in the face by his wife with major permanently disfiguring wounds to the face and teeth loss. Multiple reconstructive surgeries were partially successful. Award of $343,000 was upheld).

4 ***Armellini Express Lines v Ansley,* 605 SW2d 297 (Tex Civ App 1980)** (substantial disfigurement of face and body due to automobile accident caused pain and suffering said to last remainder of life. A jury award of $624,000 was neither excessive nor required remittitur).

5 ***Woitalewicz v Wyatt,* 428 NW2d 216 (Neb 1988)** (court found numbness was a compensable disability after closure of traumatic wounds and postsurgical wounds from open surgery to repair a fractured jaw. Postoperative swelling and drainage occurred. The surgeon failed to obtain cultures, but prescribed antibiotics and osteomyelitis subsequently developed. A second surgery, removing dead bone and teeth, with a bone graft taken from the hip, was carried out. Expert testimony showed that the first surgeon was negligent, with substandard care leading to infection, numbness of skin, and the need for subsequent surgery. $185,000 was awarded the plaintiff. In rebuttal, the defendant argued that economic loss attributable to numbness was not a disability as a wage earner. The court held that disability alone was compensable totally separate from wage earning capacity, and that the jury could therefore find numbness (and the patient's tendency to bite the mouth, with infected ulcers resulting) compensable).

6 ***Buck v United States,* 433 F Supp 896) (MD Fla 1977)** (emergency room physician and his supervising surgeon were negligent in treating a rattlesnake bite victim. Neither had experience or knowledge of snake bites,

and neither attempted to recommend consultation (which was the main error) with a physician experienced in the knowledge of snake bite care. As a result, the patient's condition deteriorated and significant complications resulted).

7 ***Stogdill v Manor Convalescent Home, Inc,* 35 Ill App 3d 634, 343 NE2d 589 (1977)** (defendant testified that each time he saw a patient with a decubitus ulcer on left ankle, the patient had circulation in the foot adequate to cure the ulcer. A specialist testified that, under such facts, with proper care and treatment gangrene would not have developed and the leg would not have been lost. The evidence was sufficient to support the contention that the leg was lost due to the defendant doctor's negligence).

Comment: In a patient with this type of circulatory problem, sudden onset of gangrene is frequently explained by an acute occlusive event (arterial thrombosis) outside of the control of the physician.

8 ***Wise v Doctors Hospital,* 455 NE2d 1032 (Ohio Ct App 1982)** (trial court erred in refusing to admit the testimony of an expert witness in a malpractice case against a physician for the death of a patient from complications of a decubitus ulcer. The patient suffered a fall, used a considerable amount of drugs, was severely debilitated, and was placed in an intensive care unit where she was a difficult patient because of deterioration of her brain. She required frequent turning in her bed and frequent changing of bed sheets because of incontinence. A decubitus ulcer developed in the coccyx area and was treated routinely for two weeks when drainage and foul odor was noted. Antibiotics and chemical debriding agents were used. Later, it appeared that there was a rectal fistula and the patient was referred to a general surgeon. During surgery, septic shock developed and the patient died. The court ruled that this was an adverse result and not outside of expectations for the type of problem, and that the medical care was well within the standard of care).

9 ***Villetto v Weilbaecher,* 337 So 2d 132 (La Ct App 1979),** (patient slipped and fractured her left patella on October 12, 1973, and was admitted to a hospital where open reduction and internal fixation of the patella was performed. Posterior plaster splint and bandages were placed on the leg. After operation, the patient complained of a burning sensation in the back of her calf. The surgeon's associate saw her the day after surgery, noticed swelling and blisters on the back of her leg, and applied vaseline to them and re-wrapped the leg. The surgeon continued treatment by applying sterile dressings. On October 26, she was treated with soaks. On November 12, her treatment was changed to Elese to dissolve scars. This treatment was continued until December 27, when all open areas were closed. Physicians advised her to use baby oil at that time. In the malpractice suit, the court awarded her $7,000 for scarring and $3,000 for pain and suffering. The trial court found the surgeon negligent in not calling a consultant or referring her to a specialist. The skin problem was herpes zoster (shingles). Proper treatment was application with topical steroid, which would have left her with less scarring, according to the medical experts).

10 ***Sandone v Dallas Osteopathic Hospital,* 331 SW2d 476 (Tex Civ App 1960)** (patient received an injection of chemicals containing dextrose and potassium chloride. A local reaction with skin ulcer appeared. The allegation was that the hospital hired incompetent employees. The ruling was that, since there were several various other possible causes, such as an allergy which could not be anticipated, there is no way to specifically mark the glucose and potassium chloride injection as the cause. Therefore, there was no cause of action).

11 ***Sadnick v Doyle,* 157 Ill App 3d 279, 510 NE2d 603 (1987)** (surgeon was sued for alleged negligence in severing a nerve. A trial court wrongly prohibited a plastic surgeon from testifying about the standard of care for excising tattoos on the ground that he was not familiar with local standards in Illinois. The patient consulted a general surgeon for removal of a nickel-sized, aged tattoo from the side of her neck. The surgeon informed her that the procedure would produce a hairline scar that would blend in the crease of her neck. Two days after he excised the tattoo, the surgeon said the incision looked fine, but there was subsequently drainage. The patient's neck throbbed and swelled. The surgeon made two additional incisions, inserting drainage tubes, and told the patient that the incision would heal nicely and that her ear tingling and neck numbness would subside. The patient consulted a plastic surgeon because of loss of feeling in her neck and ear area, and the expanding swollen incision. Her neck stiffness subsided and the swollen, discolored scar healed, but it caused her embarrassment and affected her manner of dress. The patient brought an action for malpractice against the general surgeon. She alleged negligence in removing her tattoo and failing to warn her of complications of injuring her greater auricular nerve and causing excessive scarring. A plastic surgeon who practiced primarily in another country testified as to the standard of care in excising a tattoo in the area where he lived. He testified that while he was not familiar with local standards, he was familiar with state procedures. He said that certain minimal uniform standards were applicable to tattoo excision regardless of locality. He was of the opinion that all alternatives should have been offered the patient because no tattoo treatment is ideal. He said any physician who excised tattoos and did not warn the patient of complications deviated from the standard of care. He also said that the patient's nerve should not have been severed during the incision. The general surgeon testified that he had complied with the surgical standard of care by warning the patient of anticipated complications. After the court refused to allow the plastic surgeon's testimony because of unfamiliarity with local standards, a plastic surgeon who was an expert witness for the general surgeon was subpoenaed as an adverse witness to testify as the patient's expert. He said that a general surgeon in the area would be expected to mention scarring, but that not all possible risks and complications, such as nerve damage, would be mentioned. The court directed a verdict for the general surgeon. On appeal, the patient contended that the court inappropriately barred her expert testimony, and the appellate court said that a physician familiar with a nationally uniform minimum standard of medical practice is considered

knowledgeable about all localities. The court found that the trial court had wrongly prohibited the plastic surgeon's testimony about the relevant standard of care, its deviations, and the relationship to the cause of the patient's medication problems. Holding that the lower court had erred in granting the directed verdict, the court reversed and remanded for a new trial).

32

Tendon and Ligament Injuries

§32.01 Generally

Physicians dealing with injuries or pain complaints that may or may not reflect acute injury will find symptoms and complaints related to tendons or ligaments. The sites of injury and inflammatory complaints are usually at the origin or insertion. Disruptions of ligaments may occur in mid-substance with violent trauma but represents the stronger areas, as opposed to the site of bone attachment—the latter being avulsed by an insult before mid-substance is disrupted. Tendons rarely disrupt in mid-substance (unless fatigued by rubbing over bony prominences first, or involved and weakened by disease such as rheumatoid pathology). Typically, a tendon will pull off its bony attachment.

Treatment for tendon and ligament injuries is in many respects similar, yet many differences present as discussed in the following pages.

Current literature deals with some of the controversy about the cellular source of tendon healing. Previously, it was thought that most healing occurred in lacerated tendons due to new blood supply and fibroblasts brought by scar formation in adhesions formed between tendons and surrounding tissues. Recent studies have emphasized that there is an intrinsic ability of tendons to heal without adhesions. This is important knowledge and will have a large influence on initial treatment and postoperative management of tendon injuries. Scar tissue in the extrinsic blood supply is necessary for tendon healing and immobilization might be necessary to allow temporary adhesions. If healing is possible due to intrinsic nutrition of the synovial fluid, then motion might be begun early, decreasing adhesions and allowing more rapid return and a more full range of motion.

It appears that synovial effusion accounts for a large portion of nutrition of normal tendons. All tendons have a measurable blood flow, but differences in perfusion and diffusion suggest that most of the normal tendon nutrition comes from diffusion of surrounding tissues. Blood supply within the tendon comes primarily from the region of the muscle tissue and from the paratendon. Some blood supply also comes to the flexor tendons through the venicular, not present in extensor tendons.

It has been demonstrated that severed flexor tendons can repair without any extrinsic blood supply brought by scar tissue or adhesions. When flexor tendons are severed, repaired, and then transferred in the synovial cavity of the knee joint, superficial layers are able to heal and bridge suture gaps without adhesions to the surrounding synovium.

Presently, there is a great deal of evidence to show that tendon repair proceeds from intrinsic capabilities, either through cells within or covering the tendon, or from the synovial fluid. Likewise, it is probable that extrinsic fractures are active in tendon healing.

The intrinsic ability of tendons to heal has increased interest in the use of motion during the healing period. Motion might deprive the tendon of extrinsic blood supply through adhesions, but it might enhance ultimate recovery of range of motion. Controlled passive motion has a beneficial effect on healing flexor tendons. Mobilized tendons heal more quickly with early restoration of smooth tendon surfaces. More recent studies have shown that such healed tendons revascularize by two weeks with gaps healing by fibroblastic proliferation from the epitendon and endotendon.

Classic tendon healing studies show gradual return of strength of repaired tendons. However, collagen content does not appear to increase significantly after five or six weeks. The increased strength that occurs after five or six weeks is due to remodeling and reorganization of collagen rather than to absolute increase of collagen.

§32.02 Treatment of Tendon Injury

Despite the recent advent of understanding of the flexor tendon anatomy healing nutrition, full functional restoration is a challenge, particularly in the "no man's land" (that area between the metacarpophalangeal joint and the superficial tendon insertion of the PIP joint area).

Primary repair of both tendons with postoperative control motion is the treatment of choice for clean flexor tendon lacerations in this area. Suture techniques for repairing severed tendons vary. Repair should be effected with non-resorbable suture, leaving minimal roughness of edges of the coapted tendon surfaces. It is probably not necessary to suture the tendon sheath, and care should be taken to protect the pulley system from damage. Tendons that are early after repair may heal without adhesion in-growth, and they have a greater ultimate tension load strength and greater mobility than immobilized tendons.

The clinical techniques of postoperative immobilization involve the application of a dorsal splint to block the wrist and metacarpal joint extension and allow full interphalangeal extension. Immobilization without producing tension on the repair is accomplished by allowing either active digital extension or passive digital flexion.

When both flexor tendons of a finger are severed, the finger lies in an unnatural position—hyperextension. Active flexion is not possible. When the wound is distal to the wrist, the examiner may need to stabilize the finger to obtain specific finger motions. The profundus flexor tendon is severed when the distal interphalangeal cannot be flexed while the proximal interphalangeal joint is stabilized. When neither the proximal nor the distal phalangeal joint can be flexed while the metacarpal phalangeal joint is stabilized, both flexor tendons are severed.

The extensor tendon has been cut between the proximal and distal interphalangeal joint when active flexion of the latter joint is lost. Initially, a gross mallet finger may be present because the surrounding soft tissues have not been stretched by strong flexor digitorum profundus. Division of central slip of the extensor tendon between metacarpophalangeal and proximal interphalangeal results in loss of extension of the PIP joint. The long extensor tendon of the thumb stabilizes the metacarpophalangeal joint of the thumb. Division of the thumb is often overlooked as an intact short thumb extensor can actively extend the thumb as a unit but not the additional interphalangeal joint.

The purpose of tendon repair is to proximate the ends of a tendon or to fasten one in the tentatively joining tendon or bone and hold its position while healing. The suture attendant is a skillful technical procedure, the goal being to do it with as little reaction and scarring as possible. Ideally, there would be no blemish or roughness of the gliding surface of the tendon, having been previously removed. The healing tendon becomes increasingly fragile from the fifth to the tenth day. After this, tendon strength rapidly increases over the next two weeks. Using a technique that will allow some motion is desirable. Postoperative care, frequently including a type of splint that will allow motion but block that degree of motion that would put a stretch on the tendon—for instance, the use of a dorsal foot "knuckle" blocking splint.

When the wound laceration is caused by a sharp object and is reasonably clean, some tendons of the hand may be repaired at the time of wound closure. Some factors which determine which tendons may be so repaired are (1) elapsed time since injury, (2) area affected, (3) number of tendons involved, (4) severity of contamination, (5) presence or absence of an unstable fracture, and (6) general condition of surrounding tissues.

In the following incidents, divided tendons are usually not sutured primarily, but are left for secondary repair: (1) when injury is produced by a severe crush injury in which tendons will be more edematous and will heal with more adhesions than after a simple division, (2) when the site of the tendon division is near or at one or more displaced fractures, for the sutured tendon is more likely to adhere to the surrounding tissues, and (3) when the skin is avulsed or lost and skin grafting is necessary over the divided tendon.

When a lacerated flexor tendon is no longer considered a surgical emergency, definitive care can be delayed by several days, provided the wound is rendered clean, the hand is splinted, and prophylactic antibiotics are started. This is especially true when the patient must be transported to a center where a surgeon skilled in the techniques of tendon repair is available. However, prolonged delay may permit unacceptable retraction of tendons, and especially of nerves. Retraction of nerves is not easily overcome after two weeks. As a general rule, all flexor tendons should be repaired at whatever level they are severed. It is better to stabilize fractures and suture digital nerves and tendons at the time of initial repair than to delay and do a secondary procedure for tendon repair. Indeed, it may later be necessary to do a tendon graft.

In extensor tendons, the fingers can usually be repaired at almost any level that is clean. A traumatic suturing after excision of devitalized tissue usually sees a satisfactory extensor tendon repair result.

In the case of flexor tendon repair in the palm, certain anatomical differences in the flexor surface of the hands appear. They are typically divided into five zones because repair is different for each zone. Zone 1 extends just distal to the insertion of the sublimus tendon to the site of insertion of the profundus tendon. Zone 2 is a critical area of pulleys (the so-called Bunnell "no man's land") between the distal palmar crease and insertion of sublimus tendon. Zone 3 comprises the area of lumbrical origin between the distal margin and transverse carpal ligament and the beginning of the critical area. The pulleys are the first annulus. Zone 4 is the zone covered by the transverse carpal ligament. Zone 5 is the zone proximal to the transverse carpal ligament and includes the forearm.

Zone 1

Flexor digitorum profundus may be repaired primarily by direct suture to its distal stump or by advancement and direct insertion into the distal phalanx when the distance is less than 1 cm. The pull-out wire technique usually is used. When there is a delay in the diagnosis of the lacerated tendon and the tendon has retracted into the palm, the veniculum has been torn loose and repair should probably not be attempted; this would require threading the tendon through the bifurcation of the sublimus, which practically always scars down.

Zone 2

The critical area, or Bunnell's "no man's land," has been the subject of considerable discussion for decades as to which, if any, tendon divided here should be repaired primarily. Here, especially, the primary surgeon has the greatest influence on the final result. To be qualified to make the decision and perform primary repair, a surgeon should be sufficiently *skilled* to perform a tendon graft or tenolysis later should there be failure of primary repair. Primary repair frequently fails at this area as a result of adhesions. Most surgeons recommend that both sublimus and perfundus be repaired at this level. During the repair procedure, it is essential that the A2 and A4 pulleys be preserved. Ideally, the entire pulley system should be repaired. Pull-out sutures are not indicated and end sutures are appropriate with fine, non-resorbable material, and tenolysis is frequently necessary once the wound is stable. At best, tendon repair in this area is guarded.

Zone 3

The level of the muscle bellies of the lumbricus, as well as tendon, are frequently interrupted. Additional incisions are often needed to further expose this area. All tendons must be repaired primarily or delayed only a few days. Primary anastamosis of severed nerves is extremely important, since delayed repair—even a few weeks—results in the development of significant gaps between nerve endings. Lumbrical muscle bellies should not be sutured because this may increase the tension and produce a lumbrical plus finger.

Zone 4

All tendons and nerves in Zone 4 may be repaired primarily, although additional exposure may be necessary.

Zone 5

Lesions proximal to the transverse carpal ligament and all tendons and nerves lacerated in this area should be primarily repaired.

Delayed repair in any zone may be necessary in the face of severe wound contamination. Delayed repair of tendons is reasonable when other injuries are present and require immediate surgery. Repair should not be delayed, however, past two or three days, provided the wound has been cleaned. Prolonged delays permit unacceptable retraction of nerves and tendons. (*See* Appendix 3-1, Case 1.)

Other tendon disruptions are frequently missed at the time of injury or may occur slowly after injury, where the extensor tendon at the base of the distal phalanx is cut or avulsed. Ordinarily, holding the digit in hyperextension allows satisfactory results. Rarely is surgical repair necessary. If the PIP joint ruptures, the central extensor expansion allows a buttonhole deformity.[1]

§32.03 Tendon Repair Physiology

Modern observation in healing lacerated finger flexor tendons shows that tendons have an intrinsic ability to phagocytize old collagen and synthesize new collagen fibers. Consequently, clinical attempts to prevent or control the peripheral adhesions appear valid, since these adhesions are not essential for healing of tendon laceration.

These are important observations, as a change in postsurgical management of flexor tendon suture is evolving. Early (5 to 10 days) motion markedly lessens adhesions, which in turn impair finger motion. In the past, rigid immobilization of the repaired tendon for 4 to 6 weeks effected solid healing, but also restricted adhesion formation, requiring extensive postsurgery physiotherapy with limited expectations and possibility for second surgery to free adhesions. This, as in many areas, shows the necessity for the physician to keep abreast of the advances in medicine, particularly in the areas he or she operates.[2]

§32.04 Tendon Circulation

Anatomical arrangement of blood vessels in and around tendons has been extensively studied. It is thought that the blood supply is important in the

---

[1] Schuiner & Mass, *Operation for Collateral Ligament Ruptures of the Metacarpal-phalangeal Joint of the Fingers,* 71B JBJ Surg 388 (1989); Cooney, *Bursitis and Tendonitis in the Hand, Wrist & Elbow: An Approach to Treatment,* Minn Med 1983, at 491-94; Claes, *Biomechanical Properties of Human Ligaments,* 26 Aktuel Proble Peru Chir Orthop 10 (1983); Manske, *Intrinsic Flexor-Tendon Repair,* 66A JBJ Surg 385 (1984); Hooper, *Blood Flow and Clearance in Tendons,* 66B JBJ Surg 441 (1984); Fornage & Rifkin, *Ultrasound Examination of Tendons,* 26 Radiol Clin N Am 87 (1988); McGrath, *Local Steroid Therapy in the Hand,* 9 J Hand Surg 915 (1984); Dunn, *Gamekeeper's Thumb,* 11 Orthop Rev 52 (1973); Wepfer, *Calcific Tendonitis of Gluteus Maximum Tendon,* 9 Skeletol Radio 198 (1983).

[2] Fry, *Overuse Syndrome, Alias Tenosynovitis/Tendonitis: The Terminological Hoax,* 78 Plas Reconstru Surg 414 (1986).

maintenance of nutrition of the tendon; this role has recently been questioned. Tendons experimentally deprived of blood supply survive, apparently due to diffusion.

This is important in techniques of repair of lacerated tendons, for early motion will discourage adhesions that carry circulation to tendons but impair motion. Modern tendon laceration repairs favor early protected motion with much better results.[3]

Comment: These early motion, limited load after-care methods of tendon repairs are past the experimental surgery stage, but the competent surgeon will inform the patient of why this approach is used.

§32.05 Tendon Ruptures—Lower Extremity

Most tendon ruptures result from indirect trauma in tendons with preexisting degenerative changes, rather than from direct blows or lacerations. Quadriceps tendon ruptures usually occur in persons older than 40 years of age and who have chronic conditions, such as renal failure or rheumatoid arthritis, or who are taking corticosteroid medications on a long-term basis. The "telling sign" of patellar tendon rupture is the patient's inability to extend the knee. This is also true of ruptured patellar tendons.

When a posterior tibial tendon rupture remains undiagnosed, a secondary flat foot develops, causing decreased walking endurance, medial longitudinal arch pain, callous under the navicular tarsal, and abnormal shoe wear. The management of these tendon ruptures in the lower extremity is directed to restoring anatomical function, and they practically always require surgical repair.

§32.06 Tendonitis

Tendonitis describes an inflammatory reaction of tendons or tendon sheaths that manifests pain and tenderness with functional loss, involving a musculotendon unit. Most of these lesions are overuse problems, often related to work demands or avocational activities. Controversy exists as to whether pain in overuse syndromes is secondary to inflammation or results from stressing pain-sensitive tissues beyond their biologic tolerance. Whatever the cause, orthopedists and other physicians seeing these patients find the diagnosis of tendonitis difficult to make because the pain that results is not always localized or reproducible on palpation. Many other muscular, enthetic, and neurologic problems have a similar presentation.

Treatment is usually straightforward: avoidance of the precipitating activity, use of nonsteroidal anti-inflammatory agents (NSAIDs), and gentle stretching exercises, along with progressive strengthening of involved and antogonist muscle groups.

---

[3] Hooper, *Blood Flow and Clearance in Tendons,* 66B JBJ Surg 441 (1984).

§32.07 Pathophysiology

The pathophysiology of tendonitis generally involves inflammation of the synovial-lined fibro-osseous sheath that invests on tendon or a group of tendons. Nonspecific thickening of many tendon sheaths may occur in systemic diseases such as rheumatoid arthritis and amyloidosis, although the usual site is at a musculotendinous junction or in reaction to sheath. Where a true sheath is not present (as around the Achilles tendon), the peritendon tissue may be the primary site of involvement. Pain occurs when the trapped tendon attempts to glide within a tight sheath or retinacular restraint (as in deQuervain's disease or trigger fingers). Enthetic (where muscle or tendon originates or attaches) areas represent the second typical tendonitis locus.

Tendonitis may be difficult to distinguish from bursitis, and they often co-exist. One author has counted 156 discreet bursae. Those bursae close to joints are particularly susceptible to acute and chronic inflammation, responding to local microtrauma or systemic disease.

§32.08 Diagnosis

It may be necessary to rule out other soft tissue lesions before the diagnosis of tendonitis is made. The usual conditions that may confuse the diagnosis are polymyositis, myositis, compartment syndromes, fibromyalgia, and myofascial trigger points.[4]

§32.09 Polymyositis and Myositis

Polymyositis is an autoimmune disease manifested by non-suppurative muscle inflammation. This diagnosis embraces a group of pathologies, some of which have specific laboratory markers and others diagnosed by exclusion. Muscle biopsy may be necessary to make a diagnosis. EMG examination is of little value.

Myositis is a muscle disorder and may be metabolic in origin as a reflection of hyperparathyroidism, hypothyroidism, or result from infection (bacterial, viral, fungal, and parasitic). Biopsy and specific laboratory tests help here.

§32.10 Compartment Syndrome

Compartment syndromes of upper and lower extremities may mimic acute or chronic tendonitis. Increases in intracompartment pressure from trauma, inflammatory disease, acute injury, or overuse may compress contained muscle tendon units. If there is pressure for an extended time, tissue breakdown with potential muscle or tendon death may ensue. In addition to local pain,

---

[4] Cooney, *Bursitis and Tendonitis in the Hand, Wrist & Elbow: An Approach to Treatment,* Minn Med 1983, at 491-94; Fry, *Overuse Syndrome, Alias Tenosynovitis/Tendonitis: The Terminological Hoax,* 78 Plas Reconstru Surg 414 (1986).

the muscle tendon unit is painful and aids the diagnosis. Measurement of intracompartmental pressure with a Wick catheter or similar device is helpful. If intracompartmental pressure is greater than 25 to 30 mm Hg, surgical fasciotomy is indicated.

§32.11 Fibromyalgia

Fibromyalgia is a poorly understood system disease that has multiple tender muscle spots (a minimum of 11, to make diagnosis) in predictable areas combined with muscle fatigue, measurable weakness, and limited endurance involving most musculotendinous units in the body. These people are often depressed, anxious, and change from productive citizens to dependent, miserable people. At this time, there is no specific treatment for this disorder.

§32.12 Myofascial Pain Syndromes

Myofascial pain syndromes often start as an overload syndrome involving predictable areas of the body with development of painful trigger points. Pressure on these points usually elicits pain of varying degree, but typically refers pain to a remove (also predictable) area. The trigger points can be injected with local anesthetic, saline, massaged, stretched with skin cooling, and sustaining pain relief (and relief of referred pain). The entity usually starts with an overload situation, may spread to many areas (usually the neck and back), and may resemble fibromyalgia. Treatment is often dramatic as to trigger point pain relief and improvement of muscle strength and endurance and range of motion, only to promptly return when the adversive (repetitive) overload is resumed.

§32.13 Epicondylitis

Epicondylitis is an enthetic lesion at the origin of wrist/finger from lateral humeral epicondylar (most typically extensor carpi radial is brevis origin).

Medial epicondylitis occurs at the origin of wrist/finger flexor muscles, is usually less symptomatic and less disabling than lateral epicondylitis. Treatment for epicondylitis includes the avoiding the overload motions and activities that invariably trigger the pain syndrome. Limiting the motion of the elbow by sling or cast may help, avoiding pronation and supination elbow motions and fist-making and pinching with hand. NSAIDs may help. At times, local injection of respiratory hydrocortisone compounds may be used. Physiotherapy to "toughen" with "overloading" the elbow musculature may help. Often, lifestyle changes are necessary to avoid the overload which always triggers the pain syndrome.

Wrist tendons and their sheaths often react to overload with pain over the specific tendon, such as those abducting and extending the thumb (deQuervain's disease) or groups of flexor tendons under the transverse carpal ligament or the enthetic attachment of carpal flexors. Hand/wrist extensor tendons, except for the thumb, are rarely involved in tendonitis problems. Treatment is much like that for epicondylitis.

For surgical unroofing of deQuervain fibro-osseous tunnel, transverse carpal ligament release (also often necessary for accompanying medial nerve compression) is used. Resection or release of tendinous origins at elbow for intractable epicondylitis is an operation favored by some surgeons, but has a high degree of unsatisfactory results.

In most upper extremity tendonitis problems, persistent conservative care with avoiding overload will result in satisfied patients. The surgeon must always think of local nerve entrapment syndromes about the shoulder, elbow, and wrist, as they may imitate tendonitis.[5]

§32.14 Trigger Finger

Trigger finger or *stenosing tenosynovitis* can affect any digit, including the thumb. It is most common in the ring and middle fingers. In advanced cases, inflammation at the proximal (A-1) pulley of the flexor tendon sheath overlying the metacarpophalangeal joint may hold the digit in either a flexed or extended position. Generally, the tendon becomes thickened either proximally or distally to the pulley, causing a snapping or locking with an attempt at finger flexion or extension. Treatment includes surgically opening the thickened tendon sheath far enough to allow free motion of the tendon. Care is necessary to avoid opening pulleys that will allow a flexor tendon "bow string" deformity.[6]

§32.15 Lower Extremity Tendonitis

Greater trochanteric tendonitis occurs at the attachment of the gluteus medius tendon at the proximal tip and superior lateral aspect of the proximal femur, and gluteus maximus as it attaches to the proximal lateral greater trochanter. Often, an overload history is not given. There seems to be a relationship between femoral trochanteric tendonitis and postural low back habitus. Treatment is stretch maneuvers and hip abduction strengthening supervised by a physical therapist, local ice rubs, and steroid injection therapy.[7]

Comment: Trochanteric tendonitis pain is often missed in low back pain evaluation, prompting unnecessary tests and, occasionally, unnecessary surgery.

---

[5] Cooney, *Bursitis and Tendonitis i.. the Hand, Wrist & Elbow: An Approach to Treatment,* Minn Med 1983, at 491-94.

[6] Cooney, *Bursitis and Tendonitis in the Hand, Wrist & Elbow: An Approach to Treatment,* Minn Med 1983, at 491-94.

[7] Wepfer, *Calcific Tendonitis of Gluteus Maximum Tendon,* 9 Skeletol Radio 198 (1983).

§32.16 Patellar Tendonitis

Patellar tendonitis (jumper's knee) is usually a sport overload injury to the patellar tendon where it attaches to the patella or tibia. Repetitive kneeling and kicking activities seem to be the overload factor. Patellar hypermobility is frequently seen in this tendonitis. Local injection of steroids should be avoided in this entity, as the injection has been reported to cause tendon mucoid degeneration, leading to tendon rupture. Treatment is rest, avoiding knee bend/kick activities, and isometric resistive quadriceps exercises. Often, this is a very resistant tendonitis. Surgical excision of degenerative tendon has a part in treatment of resistant cases. The collateral ligament attachment, the tensor fascialata attachment, and the hamstring near or at the attachments are frequent sites of overload pain. These areas can be injected safely on a limited basis with steroid, and often respond to stretch/strengthening activities via a physical therapist. *Achilles tendonitis* is a frequent nagging problem seen in athletes, particularly joggers. Achilles tendonitis is also seen in foot problems, particularly over-pronation. Treatment is limiting overload, gentle heel cord stretching, and correcting foot posture. This tendonitis is an absolute contraindication for steroid injection. Achilles tendonitis may be a precursor to tendon rupture, the tendon having poor healing propensities at times, and much worse if pretreated with corticosteroids.

Tendonitis about the foot is unusual, with the posterior tibial tendon involvement in its fibro-osseous tunnel being most common. Rupture of this tendon may occur silently, leaving a severe progressive flat foot problem. It should be diagnosed early, as successful treatment is much better than in late cases. When marked deformity has occurred, foot fusion operations (triple arthrodesis) are often necessary.

Peroneal tendonitis occurs along the lateral ankle, and like the medial ankle painful posterior tendonitis, is often related to walking or jogging, due to foot posture imbalance.

Flexor hall is longus is vulnerable to tendonitis (at bunion joint this is called sesmoiditis) as a result of a tiptoe, pivot, or dancing-like repetitive posture.

The treatment for tendonitis about the ankle and foot includes avoiding or modifying the overload defect, anti-inflammatory medication, and *judicious* use of steroid injections, remembering that steroids injected into tendons may cause mucoid degeneration leading to rupture, which is particularly disabling when the posterior tibial tendon ruptures.[8]

---

[8] Ferretti, *Jumper's Knee,* 11 Am J SportsMed 58 (1983); Schepsis & Rullo, *Recognizing Lower Extremity Tendon Ruptures,* J Musculoskel Med, Oct, 1988, at 72; McMaster, *A Histological Assessment of Canine Anterior Cruciate Substitution with Bovine Xenograft,* 196 Clin Ortho 196 (1985); Andresh & Woods, *Dacron Augmentation in Anterior Cruciate Ligaments,* 183 Clin Ortho 298 (1984); McPherson, *Experimental Mechanical and Histological Evaluation of the Kennedy Ligament Augmentation Device,* Clin Orthop 196: 186 (1985); Aragona, Parsons, Alexander, & Weiss, *Medial Collateral Ligament Replacement with a Partially Absorbable Tissue*

§32.17 Rotator Cuff Tendon

The rotator cuff tendon of the shoulder is a common area of injury, frequently not caused by one mechanical insult but by repetitive micro-traumas aggravated by an extrinsic insult. The amount of impairment of this injury varies greatly with age, with the amount of disruption sometimes affecting the patient's ability to participate in physical therapy rehabilitation.

Subacromial impingement syndrome is one in which bursitis or tendonitis occurs, following repetitive usage at work or other situations. It allows the rotator cuff tendon at the shoulder to swell and to impinge on the subacromial bursa, the bursa becoming inflamed and scarred so that there is, in effect, less room for the rotator cuff to participate in the abduction, forward flexion, and external rotation motions of the glenohumeral joint without becoming impinged underneath the acromion. This situation, after an acute sprain or after repetitive usage of the arms (out in front or to the side, generally with the arm unsupported, doing work activities), may present a progressive permanent problem. On the other hand, it often resolves itself with limited activity, avoidance of placing the arm higher than shoulder level, and avoidance of repetitive elbow flexion, extension, forearm pronation, or supination and external rotation at the shoulder joint.

Standard physical therapies and rotator cuff muscular strengthening exercises additiionally tend to resolve the situation. At times, injections of steroid into the subacromial space are helpful. Great care needs to be taken in injecting corticosteroids into a tendinous tissue, for it has been well shown that the steroids may weaken and actually facilitate disruption of the tendon. This is more commonly observed in weight-bearing joints, but is an appropriate caution in the rotator cuff area. If the rotator cuff continues to impinge on the undersurface anterior lip of the acromion, a wear and tear phenomenon occurs in which disruption of the tendon, generally first at the supraspinatus tendon, occurs. Functional loss in abduction, external rotation, and forward flexion of the shoulder may develop; pain may limit motion and a situation may develop in which surgical repair of the rotator cuff tear may be necessary.

Prior to this, it is not unusual to require subacromial debridement to prevent the occurrence of rotator cuff. In the advanced case of rotator cuff tear, there may be a complete functional loss of abduction and external rotation ability of the shoulder, with or without pain, and marked impairment for use of the involved extremity. After an injury to the shoulder girdle, a prolonged period of impairment may result, requiring months or years to reach

---

Scaffold, 11 Amer J SportsMed 228 (1983); Leyshon, Channon, Jenkins & Ralis, *Flexible Carbon Fiber in Late Ligamentous Reconstruction for Instability of the Knee,* 66B JBJ Surg 196 (1984); Weiss, *Ligament Replacement with Absorbable Co-Polymer Carbon Fiber Scaffold,* 196 Clin Ortho 77 (1985); Witvoe & Christel, *Treatment of Chronic Anterior Knee Instability with Combined Intra- and Extra-Articular Transfer Augmented with Carbon PLA Fibers,* 196 Clin Orthop 194 (1985); Kennedy, *Application of Prosthetic to Anterior Cruciate Ligament Reconstruction and Repair,* 172 Clin Orthop 125 (1983).

the maximal level of healing. Often, a lifestyle change is necessary to avoid activities that place the shoulder girdle "at risk" for further subacromial trauma. In the usual sense, use of the arm (elbow, forearm, hand) is not adversely affected when work activities are done below the level of the shoulder, and particularly if the arm can be supported.

If, after a six to nine month period of conservative treatment, the patient has not improved, subacromial debridement surgery has a high degree of success in rehabilitating the patient to the point where he or she can do overhead work. This requires a skilled physical therapist and a well-motivated, cooperative patient. When the problem has proceeded to the point where there has been a rotator cuff tear, surgical repair of the small tear frequently is very helpful. Surgical repair of a larger or complete tear may be helpful, but frequently fails to produce a satisfactory result.[9]

§32.18 Tenodesis Long Head Biceps

Surgical tenodesis of the long head of the biceps tendon for "bicipital tendonitis" has been popular in the past. It is now considered part of the subacromial debridement syndrome, and if specific inflammation or strain of the long head biceps tendon is demonstrated at the time of acromioplasty (debride undersurface acromion), tenodesis or transplant of the long head biceps tendon can be carried out then.

§32.19 Calcaneal Tendons

There is considerable disagreement over the treatment of ruptured calcaneal tendons. Many authors advocate conservative treatment, using a plaster cast with the knee flexed and the ankle in full equinous position. This does allow the heel cord to heal in most situations, but it heals with weakening of calf plantar flexion power. Open operation of the calcaneal tendon is associated with frequent complication through a skin slough and tendon necrosis. Wound infection and nerve damage are not unusual. There is a persistent controversy in orthopedics which emphasizes the element of the time between the injury and the treatment of a ruptured Achilles tendon as critical in deciding whether surgical or nonsurgical treatment is best. The evidence suggests that the strength of plantar flexion in early conservative treatment is equal to that of operative treatment. At this time, there is a swing toward conservative treatment, with plaster immobilization and the foot in full equinous. For those orthopedists who prefer open surgery for this

---

[9] Neer, II, *Impingement Lesions,* 173 Clin Orthop 70 (1983); T.J. & R.J. Neviaser, Lesions of the Musculotendinous Cuff of the Shoulder (1981) (American Association of Orthopedic Surgeons instructional course lectures); Aldham, *Repair of Calcaneal Tendon Rupture: A Safe Repair,* 71B JBJ Surg 486 (1989).

problem, using a transverse incision and pull-out wire through the heel minimizes wound healing problems.[10]

§32.20 Tendoachilles Rupture

The typical person who ruptures his or her Achilles tendon is sedentary, is 30 to 40 years old, and is apt to participate in weekend sports only. Complete rupture of the tendon is a sign of degeneration. The consensus is that a sedentary lifestyle places less stress on the tendon, allowing decreased circulation and tendon strength. The initial rupture (partial) is often painless. Twenty-five per cent of heel cord ruptures are missed by the first examining physician.[11]

§32.21 Ligament Disease and Injury

The basic understanding of the biomechanics of ligament injury and biology of ligament healing has increased substantially in recent years. Much of this comes from interest in sports medicine. Ligaments sutured together do repair in a manner a bit different from tendons, in that generally there is not a smooth gliding surface that is essential to smooth function of the joint. Ligaments in apposition will heal and go through an increasing strength phase, not unlike tendon injuries. Ligaments that heal with gaps do not contract down and their function will be relaxed.

In major weight-bearing joints of the knees and ankles, there is rarely one ligament that contributes to the support of function, but a combination of perhaps a major ligament and external support which, if not disrupted, will take over the function of the disrupted ligament to a large degree.

Placing the acutely traumatized joint in a position of function and allowing sufficient time for ligaments to heal (five or six weeks) is customary at this time if the joint is not to be treated by open surgery. There continues to be a controversy over which ligament injuries should be treated by surgical repair and which should be treated by hinge casting, casting with continuous passive immobilization, etc.

The orthopedist must be well informed as to what the ligament support systems of a given joint are and must understand the secondary strengths that reinforce major supportive ligaments; utilization of those ligaments may avoid the necessity of surgery. At this time, the anterior cruciate ligament in the knee and the anterior tibiofibular ligament in the ankle, when disrupted, do not spontaneously degenerate and can produce, particularly in vigorously mobile people, stability and pain problems in the respective joints.

---

[10] Becker & Cofield, *Tendonitis of the Long Head of Biceps Brachii for Chronic Bicipital Tendonitis,* 71A JBJ Surg 376 (1989).

[11] Jozsa, *The Role of Recreational Sport Activity in Achilles Tendon Rupture: A Clinical and Pathoanatomic and Social Study,* 17 Am J SportsMed 338 (1989); Dutroit, *Long Term Results of Ankle Arthrodesis,* 73 Rev Chir Orthop 189 (1987); Hardaker, *Foot and Ankle Injuries in Theatrical Dangers,* 6 Foot & Ankle 59 (1985).

Muscle and ligament traumas occur more frequently as an indirect injury or strain in which there is no direct blow. Strains are among the most frequent injuries sustained in athletes. The high incidence of strain injuries of the back in occupational situations has been studied at length. These injuries are more prevalent in heavy manual labor and represent a large and costly problem for the national economy.

Studies of strain injuries in the extremities have stressed the frequency of these injuries in two joint muscles which are subjected to simultaneous stretch. Those frequently injured are the hamstring muscles, rectus femoris, and gastrocnemius. Muscles "at risk" for strain injuries often contain a high percentage of Type II fibers. These fibers are capable of faster speed of contraction with higher forces and poorer endurance than Type I fibers. The type of fiber distribution present in muscle is related to what its normal physiological use and expectation is. It appears muscles that require quick or powerful contraction are both higher in percentage of Type II fibers and more susceptible to injury.

There is a general agreement that strain injuries are very likely to recur. This may well be due to poor rehabilitation. There is also a general agreement that stronger muscles and larger ligaments are less likely to be injured. This has been shown in workers who work at heavy manual labor or in hazardous situations. One large series of San Francisco firemen studied, those who participated in an intense aerobic exercise plan to increase flexibility of low back soft tissues and increase supportive musculature had substantially fewer on-the-job injuries than firemen who were on a home exercise plan taken from a booklet.

Muscle imbalance and ligamentous inflexibility are thought to predispose to indirect muscle injury. There is, however, a recent study to show that imbalance (documented by isokinetic dynometers) did not predispose to injury and that demonstrated ligamentous relaxation, including double-jointedness, is not necessarily a predictor of injury.

We have all experienced pain when we have used muscles and joints unused to activity, such as over-exercising or some physical activity that was strange to those muscles. This pain is ordinarily felt from 24 to 72 hours after the activity. Exercise requiring high intensity and high force of production is more likely to cause soreness than the low intensity, slower type of physical activity. This soreness has been shown to be associated with transient muscle weakness. The eccentric muscle contraction which refers to muscle activation associated with lengthening or strengthening of muscles rather than shortening them, frequently are painful after overload-type usage. The muscle soreness that does occur has been studied by electronic microscopy and other chemical techniques; these studies do demonstrate changes. However, the soreness tends to recover spontaneously in a few days. The tendency for the soreness lessens with heavy activity as the exercising person gets into "better shape," and particularly with progressive isokinetic or isotonic exercise plans. Ligamentous pain follows a similar recovery phase.

Healing of ligaments, from a microscopic point of view, when fibers have been disrupted, torn, or overstretched, proceeds in an orderly manner if there is coaptation or near coaptation of the disrupted collagen fibers. This process becomes maximized in four to six weeks. However, strength, endurance, and resistance to ease of reinjury are not at their greatest for a minimum of six months.

In ligamentous injuries, in addition to the rehabilitation of the healed (but still not strong, not yet flexible) ligament, it is important in joint systems, particularly weight-bearing joint systems, to train the proprioceptive abilities of the ligament. This is done with a rocker board tilting in a variety of directions to reinstitute the proprioceptive ability of the ligaments. Failure to do this can lead to giving away of the ligaments with running, awkward positioning, and turning of ankles—such as stepping on a stone and being unable to right oneself quickly enough to prevent reinjury.

§32.22 Collateral Ligaments

Rupture of a collateral ligament of the metacarpal phalangeal joint is rare except in the thumb. In the thumb, rupture of the ulnar collateral ligament is common, a sports-type injury (called "gamekeeper's thumb"). When conservative treatment fails, i.e., immobilization, open repair is indicated. Often, in the thumb injury interposition adductor aponeurosis precludes coaptation of torn collateral ligaments, thus preventing sound ligament healing.[12]

§32.23 Gamekeeper's Thumb

The problem of instability of the metacarpophalangeal joint of the thumb due to rupture or laxity of the ulnar collateral ligament has frustrated many hand surgeons. The term "gamekeeper's thumb" originated in English, when, to kill a rabbit, the body was stabilized with one hand, and the head was sharply pulled with the other, straining the ulnar collateral ligament of the thumb (MCP joint). Some orthopedists prefer a cast or conservative treatment, but as in so many surgical indication controversies, many orthopedists believe that open surgical repair is best.

When ligament disruption is complete, surgical repair may be necessary; this is particularly true about the knee. However, many orthopedists feel that if the injured unstable joint (where the ligament disruption has been substantial) is placed into a plaster cast in a position of function, the patient can be returned to substantial activity without undue risk and without incapacitating symptoms after six weeks or so of healing and a significant period of rehabilitation. The exception, which often includes the knee, is in active, athletic individuals who want to go ahead and engage in contact sports. They, of course, are at higher risk for ease of reinjury, and the stresses of the sports

---

[12] Dutroit, *Long Term Results of Ankle Arthrodesis,* 73 Rev Chir Orthop 189 (1987).

activity are sufficient that the area of previous ligament injury is strained, often producing pain. There is no proven successful bracing that will protect joints, the knee included, although a variety are available and many have staunch advocates.

In the pathophysiology of ligament healing, soft tissues will reconstitute themselves back to essentially functioning normal tissues, as has been shown by healing stress testing. However, the unused muscles about the joint during the period of healing require a period of physical therapy rehabilitation. Most often, this does not present a problem for the patient.

There are some chronic instabilities that derive from ligament injuries, particularly if they occur in patients who also have degenerative joint disease. This is seen frequently in the base of the thumb (gamekeeper's thumb) and at the lateral ankle where recurrent sprains are frequent.[13]

Conservative treatment of ankle sprains has always been the preferred mode, particularly in closed sprain injuries. A number of studies show that even complete disruption of the lateral collateral ligaments, anterior tibial calcaneal, or tibial talo- and avulsion of the fibular calcaneal ligaments will render the ankle unstable, both with a positive anterior drawer sign and a positive inversion testing. However, a large number of these will heal satisfactorily with immobilization. One school of thought believes that better results are achieved by open repair of these ligaments. Diagnosis is generally not difficult. If evaluation and examination of the ankle joint with or without anesthesia does not lead to a conclusive diagnosis, then arthrographic study of the ankle joint may be helpful. Arthrographic study may also demonstrate tendon sheath tears that might not otherwise be appreciated. Open surgical repair of the torn ligaments is recommended by a small group of orthopedists. Some orthopedists feel that age is important and that complete tears in persons under 40 years of age should be subjected to open surgery.

Chronic instability in the ankle is caused by stretching or partial/complete disruption of the ankle ligaments (nearly always the anterior lateral ankle soft tissue supports) as a result of repeated ankle sprains of a severe acute injury. It may manifest as a sensation of the ankle feeling loose. Repeated inversion sprains, especially when walking on irregular ground, or recurrent lateral joint pain, follow vigorous activity. If left untreated, persistent lateral ankle instability may lead to progressive degenerative arthritis. Casting with specialized stirrup splints, followed by specific exercises in patients with acute sprains, will usually prevent chronic instability. Surgery for chronic instability gives good functional results and major improvement in the mild-to-moderate arthritic pain that develops secondarily to ankle instability.[14]

---

13 Dunn, *Gamekeeper's Thumb,* 11 Orthop Rev 52 (1973).

14 Hardaker, *Foot and Ankle Injuries in Theatrical Dangers,* 6 Foot & Ankle 59 (1985).

§32.24 Non-autogonous Ligamentous Reinforcements

Replacement of disrupted or weakened ligaments has become increasingly popular, particularly in sports medicine application, although there is frequently a controversy about whether open repair of disrupted ligaments by suture gives substantially improved results as opposed to closed repair effected by immobilization. There are situations where ligament repair and/or ligament replacement are clearly indicated. The indications for such open repair and/or replacement generally pretty much parallel the anticipated activity of the patient—what sports or work activities will be engaged in, tempered by age, amount of trauma present, and the possibility of repetitive surgeries. Absence of infection and adequate circulation are additional considerations.

Some statements are universal to all ligaments in the body. Three general types of studies of ligament function have been performed. The first is ligament stress under nearly physiological conditions in joints. The next is termination individual ligament rupture strength on isolated ligaments with bony attachments preserved. Finally, isolated ligaments are used to term specific ligament properties, such as modulus with elasticity extensibility and relaxation.

In reparative surgery, placement of transposed ligaments or the sutured disrupted ligaments is carried out, attempting to duplicate, as closely as possible, the normal functional parameters of the ligament. When this cannot be achieved, substitute ligaments can be introduced.

Transplantation of a ligament attached at one end to its normal bone such as patellar tendon to another part of the knee joint to replace cruciate ligament is an older and accepted technique. Advancement or movement or shortening or plicating collateral ligaments and capsule are likewise standard reparative or reconstructive techniques. Replacement of ligaments by transplantation of whole tendon or fascial tissues is an older technique but is currently less popular. Replacement with non-autogonous tendon or ligament transfer is used in select conditions. The proplast ligament consists of a high-strength core of polyaramid fiber. The Gore text prosthetic ligament, the xenotech ligament (which is a bio-prosthesis made of bovine tendon), and polyester bands are used as replacement ligaments.

Ligament augmentation devices, such as the Kennedy ligament (which is a structure of polypropylene yarn), and dacron tapes have been used with a degree of success. Finally, biodegradable tissue scaffolding synthetic fiber stints have been used within increasing frequency as have polylactic acid coated carbon fibers. Each of these devices mentioned is sutured in anatomical position and treated postoperatively as though it is autogonous material, that is protected against mobilization, or at least against stress, on the transplanted tissue for a period of healing of six to eight weeks, followed by progressive rehabilitation.

Appendix 32-1
Cases

1 ***Ramos v Pyati,* 534 NE2d 472 (Ill Ct App 1989)** (surgeon used a flexor tendon from the ring finger as a free graft to repair a defect in the patient's thumb flexor. The surgeon found the palmaris longis tendon unsuitable. After surgery, the patient had trouble using tools, had poor flexion of the ring finger, and could not return to work as a mechanic. The plaintiff alleged that no consent had been given to invade the palm for tendon graft harvesting, that the wrong type of tendon was harvested, and that no consent and no discussion was had before surgery about harvesting the ring finger tendon or of risk of weakening the hand and making mechanical work impossible. The plaintiff's expert confirmed these facts. The defendant appealed, stating that, according to medical literature, the flexor tendon is one of the acceptable tendon donors for tendon grafting (not necessarily the thumb, whose flexor tendon had less elastic material in it; thus, the ring finger flexor tendon was inappropriate, according to the plaintiff's expert). Therefore, the defendant maintained that his tendon donor was a matter of choice. The surgeon further asserted, on the consent issue, that the chance that the ring finger flexor tendon would be used was so remote that he was not obliged to mention it, and that even if the operation exceeded the scope of the patient's consent, no prudent patient would have refused it. The appellate court rejected the orthopedist's argument, pointing out that the literature, in fact, said that the flexor tendon could be used only if wrist, calf, toe extensor and small or index finger flexor tendons were unavailable. By choosing the tendon without exploring all other options, the surgeon failed to follow established protocol. According to the expert witness, the taking of the ring finger tendon would weaken that finger without fully restoring the thumb, so that a prudent patient would not accept such an arrangement. The trial court was affirmed).